Handbook of Chronic Fatigue Syndrome

Leonard A. Jason
Patricia A. Fennell
Renée R. Taylor

WILEY

John Wiley & Sons, Inc.

Copyright © 2003 by John Wiley & Sons. All rights reserved.

Published by John Wiley & Sons, Inc., Hoboken, New Jersey.
Published simultaneously in Canada.

Limit of Liability/Disclaimer of Warranty: While the publisher and author have used their best efforts in preparing this book, they make no representations or warranties with respect to the accuracy or completeness of the contents of this book and specifically disclaim any implied warranties of merchantability or fitness for a particular purpose. No warranty may be created or extended by sales representatives or written sales materials. The advice and strategies contained herein may not be suitable for your situation. You should consult with a professional where appropriate. Neither the publisher nor author shall be liable for any loss of profit or any other commercial damages, including but not limited to special, incidental, consequential, or other damages.

This publication is designed to provide accurate and authoritative information in regard to the subject matter covered. It is sold with the understanding that the publisher is not engaged in rendering professional services. If legal, accounting, medical, psychological or any other expert assistance is required, the services of a competent professional person should be sought.

Designations used by companies to distinguish their products are often claimed as trademarks. In all instances where John Wiley & Sons, Inc. is aware of a claim, the product names appear in initial capital or all capital letters. Readers, however, should contact the appropriate companies for more complete information regarding trademarks and registration.

For general information on our other products and services please contact our Customer Care Department within the United States at (800) 762-2974, outside the United States at (317) 572-3993 or fax (317) 572-4002.

Wiley also publishes its books in a variety of electronic formats. Some content that appears in print may not be available in electronic books. For more information about Wiley products, visit our Web site at www.wiley.com.

Library of Congress Cataloging-in-Publication Data:

Handbook of chronic fatigue syndrome / editors, Leonard A. Jason, Patricia A. Fennell, Renée R. Taylor
    p.   cm.
  Includes bibliographical references and index.
  ISBN 0-471-41512-X
  1. Chronic fatigue syndrome—Handbooks, manuals, etc. 2. Fatigue—Handbooks, manuals, etc. I. Jason, Leonard A. II. Fennell, Patricia III. Taylor, Renée R., 1970–
RB150.F37H36   2003
616'.0478—dc21

2002190915

Printed in the United States of America.
10 9 8 7 6 5 4 3 2 1

Contributors

Michael H. Antoni, PhD
Department of Psychology
University of Miami
Coral Gables, Florida

Ellen Bazelmans, PhD
Expert Center for Chronic Fatigue
University Medical Center Nijmegen
Nijmegen, Netherlands

Safedin H. Beqaj, PhD
Research Associate
Wayne State University School of
    Medicine
William Beaumont Hospital
Royal Oak, Michigan

Gijs Bleijenberg, PhD
Professor
Expert Center for Chronic Fatigue
University Medical Center Nijmegen
Nijmegen, Netherlands

Bryan D. Carter, PhD
Associate Professor
Department of Psychiatry and
    Behavioral Sciences
Department of Pediatrics
University of Louisville School of
    Medicine
Louisville, Kentucky

Trudie Chalder, PhD
Reader
Cognitive Behavioural Psychotherapy
Academic Department of
    Psychological Medicine and Health
    Services Research

Guy's, King's and St. Thomas' School
    of Medicine
London, United Kingdom

Chung-ho Chang, MD
Anatomic Pathology
Wayne State University School of
    Medicine
William Beaumont Hospital
Royal Oak, Michigan

**Anthony J. Cleare, BSc, MBBS,
MRCPsych, PhD**
Section of Neurobiology of Mood
    Disorders
Division of Psychological Medicine
The Institute of Psychiatry
London, United Kingdom

John DeLuca, PhD
Director of Neuroscience Research
Kessler Medical Rehabilitation
    Research and Education Corp.
Professor of Physical Medicine and
    Rehabilitation
University of Medicine and Dentistry
    of New Jersey
West Orange, New Jersey

Robert G. Deeter, PhD
Glaxo-Wellcome Co.
Research Triangle Park, North
    Carolina

W. Line Dempsey IV, MA
Workwell Physiology Services, Inc.
Ripon, California

Antonia Dittner, BA Hons (Oxon)
Research Worker
Department of Psychology
Institute of Psychiatry
London, United Kingdom

Ms. Kat Duff
El Prado, New Mexico

Howard J. Dworkin, MD
Clinical Assistant Professor
Department of Medicine
Wayne State University
Director, Nuclear Medicine
William Beaumont Hospital
Royal Oak, Michigan

Beatrice Ellis, PhD
Department of Anesthesiology
University of Washington School of
    Medicine
Seattle, Washington

Patricia A. Fennell, MSW, CSW-R
Albany Health Management
    Associates, Inc.
Latham, New York

James T. Fitzgerald, PhD
Department of Medical Education
University of Michigan School of
    Medicine
Ann Arbor, Michigan

Mary Ann Fletcher, PhD
E. M. Papper Laboratory of Clinical
    Immunology
University of Miami School of
    Medicine
Miami, Florida

Fred Friedberg, PhD
State University of New York at Stony
    Brook
Stony Brook, New York

Gloria Furst, MPH, OTR/L
National Institutes of Health
Bethesda, MD

Lynn M. Helder, PhD
University of Miami
Coral Gables, Florida

Byron Hyde, MD
Chairman
Nightingale Research Foundation
Ottawa, Ontario, Canada

Leonard A. Jason, PhD
Center for Community Research
DePaul University
Chicago, Illinois

Caroline King, PhD
Hines VA Hospital
Hines, Illinois

Nancy G. Klimas, MD
Department of Medicine
Veterans Administration Medical
    Center
Miami, Florida
Department of Medicine
Unversity of Miami School of Medicine
Miami, Florida

A. Martin Lerner, MD
Clinical Professor of Medicine
Wayne State University School of
    Medicine
Attending Physician
William Beaumont Hospital
Royal Oak, Michigan

Paul Levine, MD
George Washington University School
    of Public Health and Health Services
Washington, DC

Andrew Lloyd, AM, MBBS, MD, FRACP
Inflammation Research Unit
School of Medical Sciences
University of New South Wales
Sydney, NSW, Australia
Department of Infectious Diseases
Prince of Wales Hospital
Randwick, NSW, Australia

Kevin J. Maher, PhD
E. M. Papper Laboratory of Clinical
    Immunology
University of Miami School of Medicine
Miami, Florida

Kevin McCully, PhD
Associate Professor
Department of Exercise Science
University of Georgia
Athens, Georgia

Barbara G. Melamed, PhD
Division of Behavioral and Social
    Sciences
Mercy College
Dobbs Ferry, New York

William O'Neill, MD
Director
Cardiological Services
William Beaumont Hospital
Royal Oak, Michigan

Shawn G. Phippen, BA
Department of Sport Sciences
University of the Pacific
Stockton, California

**Audrius V. Plioplys, MD, FRCPC,
FAAP, CMD**
Chronic Fatigue Syndrome Research
    Center
Mercy Hospital and Medical Center
Chicago, Illinois

Judith Prins, MSc
Expert Center for Chronic Fatigue
Department of Medical Psychology
University Medical Center Nijmegen
Nijmegen, Netherlands

Judith A. Richman, PhD
Department of Psychiatry
University of Illinois at Chicago
Chicago, Illinois

Stanley Schwartz, MD
St. Francis Health System
Tulsa, Oklahoma

Joan L. Shaver, PhD, RN, FAAN
Professor and Dean
College of Nursing
University of Illinois at Chicago
Chicago, Illinois

Mark Scott Smith, MD
Department of Pediatrics
University of Washington School of
    Medicine
Children's Hospital and Regional
    Medical Center
Seattle, Washington

Christopher R. Snell, PhD
Department of Sport Sciences
University of the Pacific
Stockton, California

Sharon Song, PhD
Center for Community Research
DePaul University
Chicago, Illinois

Mr. Jon Sterling
NJCFSA, Inc.
Oradell, New Jersey

Staci R. Stevens, MA
Workwell Physiology Services, Inc.
Ripon, California

Julian M. Stewart, MD, PhD
Professor of Pediatrics
Research Professor of Physiology
Director
Center for Pediatric Hypotension
New York Medical College
Valhalla, New York

Tanya Stockhammer, PhD
Division of Child and Adolescent
    Psychiatry
Department of Psychiatry and
    Behavioral Sciences
University of Louisville School of
    Medicine
Louisville, Kentucky

Patrick F. Sullivan, MD, FRANZCP
Virginia Institute for Psychiatric and
  Behavioral Genetics
Virginia Commonwealth University
Richmond, Virginia

Renée R. Taylor, PhD
Department of Occupational Therapy
University of Illinois at Chicago
Chicago, Illinois

Lana Tiersky, PhD
School of Psychology
Fairleigh Dickinson University
Teaneck, New Jersey

Susan R. Torres-Harding, PhD
Center for Community Research
DePaul University
Chicago, Illinois

Dennis C. Turk, PhD
John and Emma Bonica Professor of
  Anesthesiology and Pain Research
Department of Anesthesiology
University of Washington School of
  Medicine
Seattle, Washington

Donald Uslan, MA, MBA, CRC
Northwest Counseling Associates
Seattle, Washington

Richard A. Van Konynenburg, PhD
Independent Researcher
Livermore, California

J. Mark VanNess, PhD
Department of Sport Sciences
University of the Pacific
Stockton, California

Donna E. Weiss, PsyD
Postdoctoral Associate
SMART-ENERGY/CFS Project
  Manager
Behavioral Medicine Research Center
Department of Psychology
University of Miami
Coral Gables, Florida

Marcus Zervos, MD
Clinical Professor of Medicine
Wayne State University School of
  Medicine
Director
Research Institute
William Beaumont Hospital
Royal Oak, Michigan

Foreword

I<small>N A</small> 1939 radio broadcast, Winston Churchill described the puzzling political actions of Russia as "a riddle wrapped in a mystery inside an enigma." This is also the case with Chronic Fatigue Syndrome (CFS), a novel illness that has only been described and studied closely since the mid-1980s. Despite almost twenty years of investigation, the underlying cause and pathophysiology of this puzzling disorder remain unknown. As a result, treatment remains "generic," symptom-based, and relatively ineffective. Worse, no diagnostic test—no gold standard—has ever been identified. Thus, the very existence of CFS remains controversial despite assurances from such venerable institutions as the Centers for Disease Control, the National Institutes of Health, and the World Health Organization that CFS is a true organic condition. Only the victims and those who have studied CFS intensively know incontrovertibly that this is "a real illness."

There are valid reasons for skepticism. First, the lack of a diagnostic test is unsettling to practitioners who rely on the laboratory to confirm their clinical impressions. Second, the major symptom, fatigue, is vague and nonmeasurable. There is no term in the English language that describes the malaise, lack of stamina, and bone-crushing exhaustion experienced by our patients. Third, physical examination and routine laboratory studies reveal no significant abnormalities. Thus, CFS does not fit the usual illness paradigm that disease is defined by injury, inflammation, or malfunction. In the past, if there was no visible sign of illness, then the problem was assumed to be psychiatric. But just because nothing appears to be wrong, is everything all right? CFS and related disorders have established a new paradigm: Illness can operate at a deeper level where only specialized probing of the immune, endocrine, and central nervous systems reveal evidence of malfunction and disease. Thus, the malfunction occurs on a molecular level rather than the traditional macroscopic or observable level. Many illnesses such as migraine, premenstrual disorder, attention disorders, functional bowel syndromes, and chemical sensitivity may follow this same new paradigm. Last, CFS is an invisible illness in the sense that victims do not appear ill and symptoms are "felt" rather than "seen." Who can sense in another individual such symptoms as pain, exhaustion, malaise, headache, or "foggy thinking"? It is not surprising that many uninformed health care providers glibly remark, "I'm not sure CFS is real," dismissing the illness as curtly as they would UFOs or the abominable snowman.

I have come to realize that CFS is most likely brought on by a variety of triggers including infection, inflammation, trauma, immunization, and surgery, acting in a unique fashion on susceptible individuals. What combination of factors is necessary for this illness to begin? Can we define what makes a person susceptible? My personal bias is that CFS is a modern illness, probably facilitated by stress and our environment. Lacking a specific treatment or cure, my personal approach to management has been to optimize health, search for treatable causes, palliate symptoms, and coach the victim to reach his or her personal best. I was once a strictly allopathic physician, but my experience has led me to a more wholistic and supportive approach.

Chronic illness is frequently associated with mood disorders and psychological stressors, and I have learned to accept that chronic fatigue will not improve until such issues are addressed aggressively. In this regard, Cognitive Behavioral Therapy (CBT) is highly acclaimed as a treatment for CFS. I posit, however, that it is the *attention* provided by CBT that is most effective because many approaches that encourage and support the patient—chiropractic, alternative medicine, exercise therapy, among them—have been shown more effective than the "benign neglect" of traditional medical therapy. The treatment of CFS is a lot like bariatric (weight loss) medicine in that the recidivism rate is extremely high and patients seem to do best when they are self-motivated and highly supported. Our goal as CFS specialists, then, should be to not only diagnose and treat our patients, but to coach and support them as well.

The *Handbook* addresses many of these areas. It is a delightful buffet line of information on CFS that contains a little something for everyone. It is a collection of essays, some scholarly, some leading edge, and others that are tantalizingly controversial. Each author has been given free reign to expound on his or her field of expertise. As a result, there is an incredible diversity in style and presentation, which makes the *Handbook* eminently readable and enjoyable. You can nibble on specific articles, or gorge yourself on whole sections!

Notably, the editors of the *Handbook* are not physicians. To their credit, they have included very inclusive sections on diagnosis, management, and specialized fields such as immunology, endocrinology, and autonomic disorders. In addition, there are controversial topics such as Lerner's cardiac hypothesis, and philosophical approaches from established practitioners like Byron Hyde. There are chapters on subjects that have not been broached before, such as nutrition, food intolerance, genetics, educational ramifications for children, and family influences on pain and fatigue.

This *Handbook* will appeal to a diverse group of readers including clinicians, researchers, allied health professionals, counselors, and even persons with CFS. It is a great resource for anyone who is interested in chronic fatigue, Chronic Fatigue Syndrome, or the many related conditions. I know that you will revel at this feast of information. Enjoy!

CHARLES W. LAPP, MD
Director, Hunter-Hopkins Center, Charlotte, North Carolina
Assistant Consulting Professor at
Duke University Medical Center, Durham North Carolina

Contents

Preface

CHRONIC FATIGUE SYNDROME (CFS) is a complex, sometimes controversial and often confusing condition characterized principally by persistent, unexplained physical and mental fatigue. The first case definition was made in 1988 (Holmes et al.). In 1994, an international panel of experts gathered to establish specific criteria that would identify individuals with CFS and distinguish CFS from other conditions with similar symptoms (Fukuda at al., 1994). As currently stated by the U.S. Centers for Disease Control (CDC): "In general, in order to receive a diagnosis of chronic fatigue syndrome, a person must satisfy two criteria:

1. Have severe chronic fatigue of six months or longer duration with other known medical conditions excluded by clinical diagnosis, and
2. Concurrently have four or more of the following symptoms: substantial impairment in short-term memory or concentration, sore throat, tender lymph nodes, muscle pain, multijoint pain without swelling or redness, headaches of a new type, pattern or severity, unrefreshing sleep, and postexertional malaise lasting more than 24 hours."

Researchers and clinicians continue to debate many aspects of CFS. Some have emphasized the role of psychological agents in the etiology and course of the disease and consider most patients presenting with CFS symptoms as having a form of somatic depression or a variant of hypochondriasis (Manu, Affleck, Tennen, Morse, & Escobar, 1996; Manu, Lane, & Matthews, 1988). Some have underscored the role of social-environmental factors, employing models that interpret somatic symptoms as emerging from painful or otherwise exploitative social interactions (Ware, 1998). Others have added to a growing body of evidence that individuals with CFS have distinctive physiological abnormalities, including abnormal SPECT scan findings (Schwartz et al., 1994), various forms of orthostatic intolerance, and autonomic nervous system dysfunction (Rowe & Calkins, 1998; Stewart, 2000), abnormal immune system functioning (Suhadolnik et al., 1997), associated reproductive abnormalities in women (Harlow, Signorello, Hall, Dailey, & Komaroff, 1998), and endocrinological abnormalities associated with hypothalamic-pituitary-adrenal axis functioning (Scott et al., 1999).

A number of studies have illustrated, however, that there are distinctions between CFS and psychiatric disorders such as depression (DeLuca, Johnson, Ellis, & Natelson, 1997; Demitrack, 1997), and a majority of researchers and practitioners now acknowledge a clear distinction between CFS and psychiatric disorder or support a biopsychosocial model for understanding the etiology and course of CFS (Jason et al., 1998; Jason, Taylor, Stepanek, & Plioplys, 2001).

What causes CFS remains unknown, and the clinical course varies greatly among individuals. Some recover, some get worse, but for many the condition is cyclical, alternating between periods of debilitating symptoms and periods of relative wellness. The CDC estimates that CFS affects approximately half a million individuals in the United States (CDC Web site, 2002). Others such as Jason and colleagues (Jason et al., 1999) indicate the rates might even be higher than 800,000. Although the illness was first diagnosed among well-educated, relatively affluent middle-aged women in the United States—leading to a stereotype of the disease as "yuppie flu"—researchers and clinicians have since identified the condition worldwide among individuals of both genders and all ages, races, social classes, and economic strata (Taylor, Friedberg, & Jason, 2001).

The editors of this *Handbook* have been working on issues related to CFS since the 1980s. We believe that it is vitally important for professionals in health care and related professions to fully understand any emerging illness that affects such a large number of individuals and that can persist for a significant portion of an affected individual's life, seriously impacting that person's ability to work or perform ordinary life functions. We have further come to believe that given the diversity of perspectives and the many systems affected by CFS—the physical, the psychological, and the social-economic—it is essential to have an authoritative, comprehensive, up-to-date, interdisciplinary volume that presents the broad spectrum of approaches to the understanding and investigation of CFS.

An additional impetus for this *Handbook* is our observation that there is a marked lack of community responsiveness to CFS. Individuals with CFS are severely impaired functionally, yet historically they have been underserved by medical and community-based programs. Individuals with CFS can be among the most disabled of those with chronic illness, and the condition can easily drain away most of their economic and social resources. Those with the fewest resources are often unable to provide for their own housing, and those unable to work have difficulty obtaining Social Security or other disability benefits despite the fact that the Social Security Administration recognizes CFS as a disability (Social Security Ruling 99-2p). Many individuals with CFS are misdiagnosed with psychiatric disorders and are misunderstood and sometimes disbelieved by coworkers, friends, and family. They are frequently turned down by community agencies for benefits received by other individuals with disabilities. When individuals with CFS do receive attention, they sometimes find that treatments do not work or are, at best, palliative for isolated symptoms. We hope that this *Handbook* will help lead to a greater understanding of the illness and to proper identification of and better treatment for individuals with CFS, both clinically and in the community at large.

The contributors to the *Handbook* are leaders in the field, whose insights are salient both to understanding CFS and for research and clinical practice. We believe this *Handbook* will provide health care and social services professionals, and community leaders with an essential overview of CFS that not only provides information, but also replicates the various approaches to CFS in such a way as to promote a more integrative understanding of the condition and maximize the likelihood of more effective future study.

The *Handbook* is organized into six parts: Part I, History, Diagnosis, and Classification, addresses a variety of issues surrounding the emergence of CFS as a recognized, defined condition. As becomes apparent throughout the book, however, controversy still surrounds the definition of CFS and indeed whether it constitutes a disease at all.

Renée Taylor, Leonard Jason, Judith Richman, Susan Torres-Harding, Caroline King, and Sharon Song provide a brief history of CFS-like conditions dating back 150 years and then present an overview of epidemiological research in Chapter 1, "Epidemiology." They critically examine prevalence studies that have emerged out of different settings, beginning with health-care and physician-identified samples and later encompassing randomized community-based populations. By turning to communities, the researchers found the condition to be far more prevalent among minorities, who had not appeared in earlier studies because of differences among different ethnic and socioeconomic groups in seeking health care help. The authors note regarding adolescent CFS that some evidence suggests a higher incidence of CFS than presently estimated. They posit that this discrepancy may be due to the fact that doctors have not thought to look for CFS in this age group.

Audrius Plioplys, in Chapter 2, "Differential Diagnosis in Medical Assessment" asserts that contrary to the thinking of some physicians, CFS is indeed a separate, specific illness, and one with medical history that he believes reaches back into the eighteenth century. He grants that the range of clinical manifestations in CFS fuels part of the doubt. After discussing the symptoms of CFS, the author surveys other kinds of conditions that clinicians must exclude before diagnosing CFS. He also urges caution in diagnosing CFS in children, partly for medical reasons and partly for financial ones. He concludes that CFS patients require a thorough history and physical examination as well as careful medical follow-up.

In Chapter 3, "The Complexities of Diagnosis," Byron Hyde delves into the difficulties involved in diagnosis and in coordinating clinical findings with the measurable categories needed for empirical research. In contradistinction to the CDC and many contributors to this volume, Hyde does not consider CFS to be a specific disease but rather a fatiguing state typified by a variety of signs and symptoms. He continues to regard CFS and ME as distinct conditions. His nuanced appreciation of the variety of symptoms patients may present has led him to conduct extensive, precise clinical assessments that he regards as prerequisite to appropriate treatment. No uniform treatment can be determined for CFS, he holds, because individual experience of the syndrome is too various to make a single approach meaningful. Whether clinicians agree with Hyde's conclusions about CFS as an illness or a syndrome, many will find his detailed presentation of methods and clinical views both enlightening and helpful.

In Chapter 4, "Sociocultural Context and Trauma," Patricia Fennell examines the how trauma arising from many different causes can impact the life of a patient with CFS.

Patrick Sullivan explores "Genetics" in Chapter 5. After a brief overview of the ways in which genetics interfaces with disease in general, Sullivan examines the very sparse literature on a possible genetic epidemiology for CFS. He believes that the data suggest that CFS-like illness is familial, with the familiarity being largely due to additive genetic factors. He also discusses potential research to further explore the connection between genetics and CFS.

In Chapter 6, "Postinfective Fatigue," Andrew Lloyd describes the historical evidence linking prolonged fatigue states to acute infectious diseases. He then provides a selective review of the more laboratory-intensive modern investigations based predominantly on cross-sectional case-control studies. Finally, he discusses the possible pathophysiology of postinfective fatigue states. He concludes that certain infections can trigger a protracted and disabling fatigue state consistent with the diagnosis of chronic fatigue syndrome, and that microbiological, immunological, and psychological factors are all likely to be relevant to the pathogenesis of postinfective fatigue states.

And finally, in Chapter 7, Kevin Maher, Nancy Klimas, and Mary Ann Fletcher consider "Immunology." Noting that CFS "often presents as an acute viral infection whose signs and symptoms fail to resolve," the authors consider that exploring the role of the immune system is logical. After a careful review of the literature investigating the role of a large array of immune factors (NK cell cytotoxity, lymphocyte proliferation, immune activation, cytokines, antinuclear antibodies, and so forth)—made exceptionally easy to review through the use of graphic presentations—the authors conclude that there is evidence of multiple immunologic abnormalities not only reported, but independently confirmed worldwide. Most discrepancies, they believe, result because of serious flaws in the studies. To correct this they suggest that future studies include multicenter longitudinal designs that address issues of symptom cycles, describe in detail the characteristics of the CFS population and control group characteristics, test common analytes, and use standardized methods and reputable laboratories.

The chapters in Part II, Phenomenology: Illness Course and Patient Perceptions, examine how the illness proceeds, how it is perceived and experienced by patients, and the multiple body and life systems that are affected by CFS.

In Chapter 8, "A Four-Phase Approach to Understanding Chronic Fatigue Syndrome," Patricia Fennell draws on years of clinical experience to present a phase approach to understanding CFS. This systems-based, longitudinal model describes the physical, psychological, and social-interactive experiences of individuals over the course of their experience with CFS. She provides a detailed account of CFS patient presentation as it fluctuates and as the effects of chronic illness produce additional issues. The author illuminates her general description by telling the story of one composite patient, a narration that takes into account the patient's physical, psychological, and social-economic experiences. The chapter also emphasizes the difficulties inherent in the experience of a disease that is hard to diagnose, fluctuating in its symptoms, and viewed with suspicion by much of the culture.

Chapter 9, "Social Effects of Chronic Disorders," by Kat Duff, utilizes individual interviews with CFS patients to dramatize the situation of all patients with CFS. She notes particularly the social stigmatization that they encounter. The chapter is rich in specific details. Duff draws attention to the disparity between the neutral language of medicine and the actual experience the patient, a disjunction that she believes tends to "erase" the patient and cause him or her to doubt their experience. Like Fennell, she calls attention to the special issues that arise for individuals suffering from a chronic illness.

Barbara Melamed examines the "Family Systems Perspective" in Chapter 10. As she points out, there is a wealth of data pointing to the importance of family and partners in CFS, but there have been very few studies. The author reviews the literature that exists and then describes briefly several instruments useful for evaluating family response to illness. Convinced that partners or family members need to be included in CFS therapy if it is to be successful, Melamed stresses the importance of conducting research on cost-effectiveness, as this is crucial to HMO acceptance.

In Chapter 11, "Clinical Perspectives and Patient Experiences," Jon Sterling takes up the vitally important subject of CFS patient support groups. These local organizations often provide patients with their first positive experience after becoming ill with CFS. Family, coworkers, and others in society at large—even health care professionals—can be disbelieving, stigmatizing, or dismissive. CFS support group members believe in a CFS patient's condition, understand how it feels to have CFS, recognize the strain that CFS can put on family, work, and social relationships, and trade useful information. The author acknowledges that some clinicians feel such groups can create difficulties by inadvertently providing misinformation, and he grants that support groups can vary greatly depending on their leadership. He further discusses the founding of the CFIDS Association of America, a national association begun in 1987 that is helping to provide reliable information about the illness to CFS patients, while at the same time advocating with clinicians, researchers, legislators, and the public for CFS.

Part III, Symptomatology, examines individual areas of physical symptom in patients with CFS. This part is of particular importance to understanding CFS, given the perception among many in health care that CFS is almost entirely a psychological condition requiring psychological rather than medical interventions.

In Chapter 12, "Pain and Fatigue," Dennis Turk and Beatrice Ellis examine one of the most common physical symptoms associated with CFS that also figures significantly in fibromyalgia. Since a large number of patients who have been diagnosed with fibromyalgia have also been diagnosed with CFS, the authors raise the possibility that the two conditions may eventually be found to be manifestations of one illness. Patients with either condition have many of the same symptoms, for determination of which clinicians must rely on patients' subjective description. Certain problems are inherent with self-reporting, so the authors discuss the pitfalls of self-reporting, call attention to methods that help produce the most accurate and comparable reporting, and describe measurement scales that help clinicians distinguish between perceived and actual physical disability. They delve into the connections between physical symptoms, depression, and disability and discuss various hypotheses about the association between fibromyalgia and CFS. With regard to treatment, the literature appears to demonstrate that an interdisciplinary approach is most effective with fibromyalgia patients, and the authors posit that the same is likely true for CFS patients.

Julian Stewart examines "Orthostatic Intolerance," in Chapter 13. Orthostatic intolerance (OI) is a confusing topic where the nomenclature is changing rapidly, but the author uses the phrase to encapsulate disorders of blood flow, heart rate, and blood pressure regulation that are most easily demonstrated during orthostatic stress. OI has several different acute and chronic variants unrelated to CFS, but certain symptoms of CFS resemble those of OI. These are particularly common in adolescents with CFS. Stewart reviews recent investigations into OI and CFS in great detail, closing with a brief discussion of medical and nonmedical treatments.

In Chapter 14, "Sleep Disorders," Joan Shaver provides a comprehensive overview of sleep as an issue in CFS. She first examines sleep as a behavior and then notes its connections with health issues in general. She particularly draws attention to the reciprocal nature of sleep, stress, and host defense. In a review of the literature about sleep disorders and CFS, she highlights the specific evidence that exists about perceived and measurable physiological sleep quality in CFS. As with many CFS symptoms, controversy arises over cause and effect. Does the CFS patient have impaired sleep because of CFS, or is impaired sleep producing the symptoms of CFS? In addition, she addresses the question of how clinicians can differentiate sleep impaired by CFS from sleep impaired by other conditions such as depression.

In Chapter 15, "Cardiac and Virologic Issues," Martin Lerner and his colleagues advance the controversial notion that CFS is primarily a cardiac disease. He explains that the defining studies have excluded cardiac issues because CFS patients at rest appear to have normal heart function. Heart difficulties occur only during exercise, and even then they are mild. But Lerner has observed increases of certain viruses linked to cardiac disease in patients with CFS, and he believes this to be significant. His chapter carefully details his research and the gradual emergence of his paradigm.

Anthony Cleare provides an exhaustive critical overview of the evidence of "Neuroendocrine Dysfunction" in Chapter 16. This examination investigates studies that address such subjects as the HPA axis, growth hormone, neurotransmitter dysfunction, and the serotonergic system, but also the problem of comorbidity and the changing definitions that have led to populations with different characteristics being studied as if they were homogeneous. He concludes that because CFS is multifactorial in origin, one factor is likely to include disturbances to the neuroendocrine system. In future studies, he suggests that researchers make an effort to separate risk, disposing, or trigger factors from factors that appear to prolong the condition.

Part IV, Assessment, focuses on what is an all-important aspect of responding to CFS. Because the condition involves an array of different symptoms that appear over time in different combinations and intensities in different patients, assessment is key to appropriate diagnosis and treatment.

In Chapter 17, "Measuring Symptoms and Fatigue Severity," Antonia Dittner and Trudie Chalder address the vexing problem of defining and measuring fatigue in CFS. After defining CFS, the authors discuss the general problem of measuring fatigue and locating its cause. They note behavioral measures of fatigue in terms of physical and mental impairment and/or disability. They then discuss a number of self-report scales that produce subjective measures of fatigue. Several physical, immunological, neurobiological, and psychological mechanisms have been proposed as underlying fatigue, including poor sleep quality, immunological or viral causes, and neuroendocrine changes. The authors point out that deconditioning leads to further fatigue, but that this is secondary to the initial condition. With regard to the psychological mechanisms for fatigue, the authors discuss methods of assessment of somatic symptoms and pain, coping behavior, illness attributions, negative automatic thoughts, illness perceptions, and psychological disorders. Context is also important in CFS, the authors assert, so that it is important to assess the context in which patients live and how this may impact the course of the patient's illness. Here again, it is necessary to distinguish between the perceived support that people with CFS receive and the actual support they receive. Because of the complex interrelationship between fatigue and other CFS symptoms, the authors recommend an integrative intervention approach such as cognitive behavioral therapy.

Kevin McCully, in Chapter 18, "Functional Capacity Evaluation," notes that functional capacity is the dominant symptom in CFS, but it is not always measurable. There has been a tendency to focus on cardio-physical and muscular-skeletal function—the ability to carry out particular tasks—rather than on the inability to sustain physical effort. McCully suggests that it may be better to concentrate on the patients' ability to maintain activity and what happens when they fail to tolerate a given exercise level. In reviewing the literature on exercise capacity, the author notes that the studies vary widely, with some finding a great deal of incapacity and others finding very little. In the area of exercise, there is also a question of cause and effect. Is lack of exercise producing the symptoms of CFS, or does CFS make exercise difficult to carry out?

In Chapter 19, "Structured Diagnostic Interviews and Self-Rating Scales," Fred Friedberg provides a comprehensive overview of psychiatric evaluation as it pertains to CFS. This is a vitally important issue, given the potential comorbidity of CFS with psychological illnesses and because CFS is defined by symptoms and behavior rather than by specific biomedical tests. The author examines and evaluates thoroughly all the principal forms of psychodiagnostic interview and the standard psychometric instruments. He calls attention to how they have been applied correctly and incorrectly, and he notes the inappropriate use of some tests.

John DeLuca and Lana Tiersky examine "Neurocognitive Assessment" in Chapter 20. Because cognitive dysfunction is one of the most frequent and debilitating symptoms of CFS, it is important for intervention and treatment to differentiate actual cognitive problems from patient perception of problems. It is also essential to distinguish CFS from other conditions that can produce cognitive difficulties. In addition, psychological and psychiatric comorbidities may affect cognitive function in patients with CFS. The authors find that CFS-related difficulties seem largely limited to attention and concentration, speed of processing, and verbal memory.

Part V, Treatment and Intervention, covers a wide range of approaches to treatment and intervention, including medical intervention and management, phase-based interventions, cognitive-behavioral therapies, nutritional interventions, and different exercise regimens.

Paul Levine, Stanley Schwartz, and Gloria Furst provide a broad overview of physical medicine and CFS in Chapter 21, "Medical Intervention and Management." They note that over the past decade CFS has become widely recognized as a specific but hetereogeneous disorder with multiple case definitions. They call attention to the fact that Fukuda's standard definition is a working one, in the process of revision. Their chapter focuses on the evaluation and management of those symptoms that are generally accepted by the medical community. They note that evaluation must be an ongoing process because over time symptoms change, wax and wane, and new symptoms can appear. The general management areas include pain, sleep disorders, important psychological symptoms such as depression, cognitive dysfunction, and physical and occupational rehabilitation. There are also management recommendations for particular symptoms that occur in some, but not all, individuals with CFS, such as fibromyalgia-like symptoms and the presence of various viral agents. They conclude by noting that appropriate management of CFS also requires clinicians to help patients adjust to living with a chronic illness that is socially impairing and financially draining.

In Chapter 22, "Phase-Based Interventions," Patricia Fennell provides a comprehensive, longitudinal presentation of assessment and treatment of CFS. In this systems-based, phase model, she examines not only the physical and psychological changes in patients, but also the changes that their illness produces in their social-interactive world. Because of the fluctuating nature of the illness and the changing ability of patients to cope as time passes, the author finds that a phase approach permits more effective assessment. This, in turn, permits more effective interventions because they can be targeted to times when patients will be capable of complying.

Gijs Bleijenberg, Judith Prins, and Ellen Bazelmans analyze an important variety of psychological treatment in Chapter 23, "Cognitive-Behavioral Therapies." The authors believe that cognitive behavioral therapy (CBT), combined with a graded exercise program, has been shown to produce the most consistent evidence of effectiveness in treatment. After a review of the studies, the authors describe a model of the perpetuating factors in CFS (as opposed to causative factors), and demonstrate how CBT works to overcome them. They note that CBT is contraindicated when a patient is involved in legal proceedings relating to his or her condition or when the patient is not motivated. Their clinical practice has also led them to differentiate between relatively active CFS patients and those who were "passive" or "low-active," and they have developed different specific goals and steps for each group. The goal of CBT is "recovery," which the authors define as the individual coming to regard him or herself as a healthy person. This is not, they emphasize, a return to the old self. The chapter describes CBT in detail, provides two case studies, and discusses pitfalls that therapists may face.

Michael Antoni and Donna Weiss connect stress and immunity to arrive at a treatment model in Chapter 24, "Stress and Immunity." The authors find that the physical symptoms of CFS are not inconsistent with chronic activation of the immune system and that many of the psychological manifestations can be considered as distress reactions that tend to exacerbate CFS symptoms. There are, they hold, multiple influences in the maintenance of CFS as well as in its etiology. They conclude that cognitive behavioral stress management is the most effective intervention to alter psychological responses. Cognitive behavioral stress management increases self-efficacy and control and decreases perceived pain and disability. The improved psychological attitude improves immune system functioning, and an improved immune system mounts a better defense against multiple viral attacks. Finally, the better defense improves physical symptoms and cytokine effects.

Donna Weiss, Lynn Helder, and Michael Antoni offer a detailed description of a multidimensional intervention program they developed for CFS in Chapter 25, "Development of the SMART-ENERGY Program." SMART, an acronym for Stress Management And Relaxation Training, addresses the interaction of CFS symptom severity, psychological factors, and immune system functioning in a cognitive-behavioral approach. The program seeks to provide participants with anxiety reduction skills, reduce mood changes, modify maladaptive beliefs and cognitive appraisals of stressful situations, enhance interpersonal conflict resolution skills and anger expression, enhance factors contributing to quality of life and self-esteem, and facilitate connectedness by providing a supportive group environment and increasing utilization of social support networks.

In Chapter 26, "Exercise Therapy" Christopher Snell and colleagues describe a typical vicious cycle in which CFS patients avoid exertion, become deconditioned, and therefore experience increased physical difficulties. He believes that most attempts at rehabilitation through conventional exercise programs are doomed to failure. His review of studies concerning exercise in CFS finds most to be inadequate and conflicting. Only three, he believes, meet standard validity criteria. Since diminished cardiac response is seen in some patients, the author believes that cardiac testing is important. He concludes that CFS patients can benefit from anarobic exercise programs and presents a very specific, three-phase program that involves patient education, exercise prescription and close monitoring, and finally a process for maintaining functional gains.

Richard Van Konynenburg addresses "Nutritional Approaches" in Chapter 27. He elicits several reasons why nutrition is important in the treatment of CFS even through there are only limited studies on the effects of different nutritional approaches. He notes that many CFS patients experience gastroenterological problems or food allergies or intolerances that interfere with adequate absorption of nutrients. The author also discusses the interactions between nutrients and between nutrients and medications, the question of balance among nutrients, and potential toxicity. Addressing a socioeconomic issue that concerns several authors, Van Konynenburg asserts that cost, convenience, simplicity, and variety are essential considerations when establishing diets for CFS patients because, to achieve compliance, patients must have food they can find easily, afford, and prepare. He agrees, with some modifications, with the nutritional recommendations of M. R. Werbach, and concludes by noting that any nutritional approaches should be monitored medically

Finally, in a very specific, hands-on contribution, Donald Uslan and his colleagues examine a broad range of rehabilitation interventions in Chapter 28, "Rehabilitation Counseling," As the authors of this chapter compellingly explain, patients with CFS can make good use of help in a wide range of areas, including coping with physical disabilities, pain, and stress; coping with daily living; dealing with issues of employment; and adjusting relationships with family members and significant others to meet the new living situation. The chapter discusses a range of workplace issues, including disability, and urges legal or professional guidance for most CFS patients in this arena. Uslan's colleagues each address rehabilitative areas of their specialty, including biofeedback, sleep, acupuncture, cognitive rehabilitation, physical therapy, and occupational therapy. Appropriate response to CFS, the authors believe, requires multidisciplinary, "managed" care, in which a variety of specialists contribute as a team to the patient's treatment.

Part VI, Pediatric and Community Issues, includes a discussion of pediatric CFS and issues involved in community-based service procurement.

Mark Scott Smith and Bryan Carter focus attention on "Chronic Fatigue Syndrome in Adolescence," in Chapter 29. After presenting the current definition of CFS, the authors suggest that CFS in adolescents may not be a homogeneous disorder and is unlikely to have a single cause. They examine viral infections, subtle immunological changes, the hypothalamic/pituitary/adrenal axis, sleep disorders, neuromuscular dysfunction, orthostatic intolerance, and atypical anxiety disorders and somatization. The authors believe mental health consultation to be appropriate in most pediatric cases, but find that neither patients nor parents want this because they do not see psychology as playing a role. As a consequence, physicians may need to carry this assessment out in their own offices, and the authors provide suggestions as to what is necessary. In terms of management, they recommend targeting individual symptoms for specific therapy, following an adaptive, rehabilitative model that encourages school attendance and association with peers. Follow-up is essential, as is obtaining input from both parents and patients separately. The authors stress the importance of clinicians remaining optimistic about outcomes.

Bryan Carter and Tanya Stockhammer close in on certain details of pediatric CFS in Chapter 30, "Psychological and Educational Issues in Children and Adolescents." After a literature review, the authors assert that differential diagnosis of CFS in young people is even more complex than it is in adults. The familiar problems of cause and effect in psyche and soma are magnified with this age group where "tiredness" often masks avoidant issues, just as do chronic headaches, abdominal pain, and other familiar somatizing conditions. CFS seriously impacts education because patients experience prolonged absenteeism and lengthy home schooling, even when compared with children sick with other illnesses. The authors make a number of recommendations, including developing strong working relationships with school personnel since even limited participation in school life provides all-important contact with peers as well as education. Carter and Stockhammer also examine the vital impact of parental response to childhood CFS. Research suggests that initially parents believe that the condition is physical or environmental rather than psychological, and that this attitude increases the time the child is sick. It is only over time that parents come to appreciate the psychological component. The authors recommend a variety of therapies, including family therapy, to help all parties develop active coping strategies and a more optimistic outlook. The authors conclude with recommendations for treatment by a multidisciplinary team in which the clinicians have reflected thoughtfully on their own attitudes to CFS and have integrated their concepts of the psychological and the medical.

Leonard Jason and Renée Taylor take an ecological approach to understanding CFS and hence to understanding "Community-Based Interventions," in Chapter 31. In this chapter, as in several others, attention focuses on how CFS impacts patients' social and economic life. Their condition usually reduces how much they can work, if at all, and how much they can continue to fulfill other social functions. Despite a growing body of evidence about CFS, many families and others still continue to think that patients are intentionally not trying to get better, and consequently withdraw support. The authors believe that understanding CFS requires understanding all the interpersonal, social, and larger issues involved. They also believe that participants must be involved in the design of both treatment of and research into CFS. Researchers must also examine patients' communities, the basic values of these communities, and the ways in which communities deal with problems. In assessing patients' identified needs, for example, the authors found advocacy services, volunteer caregiver services, and education of the medical profession, government, and the general public to have the highest priority. The authors draw on their extensive experience with the Chicago CFS Association to illustrate how communities can be engaged with CFS patients. They address essential problems such as employment and safe housing in considerable detail. They also discuss the value of community centers for providing information and referral, advocacy, civil rights information, housing and transportation assistance, and other needed help.

Given the broad perspective of this *Handbook*, it is our hope that the volume will engage the intellectual curiosity of a wide audience, including methodologists, clinical researchers, practitioners, social service personnel, and community leadership. Where readers encounter disjunction between the perspectives of various contributors, we encourage them to embrace these differences, rather than regarding them as contradictory, and utilize them to achieve a more balanced and sophisticated understanding of this baffling syndrome.

REFERENCES

Centers for Disease Control and Prevention. (2002). *Chronic fatigue syndrome: Demographics.* Available from http://www.cdc.gov/ncidod/diseases/cfs/demographics.htm#Common.

DeLuca, J., Johnson, S. K., Ellis, S. P., & Natelson, B. H. (1997). Sudden vs. gradual onset of chronic fatigue syndrome differentiates individuals on cognitive and psychiatric measures. *Journal of Psychiatric Research, 31,* 83–90.

Demitrack, M. A. (1997). Neuroendocrine correlates of chronic fatigue syndrome: A brief review. *Journal of Psychiatric Research, 31,* 69–82.

Fukuda, K., Strauss, S. E., Hickie, I., Sharpe, M. C., Dobbins, J. G., & Komaroff, A. (1994). The chronic fatigue syndrome: A comprehensive approach to its definition and study. *Annals of Internal Medicine, 121,* 953–959.

Harlow, B. L., Signorello, L. B., Hall, J. E., Dailey, C., & Komaroff, A. L. (1998). Reproductive correlates of chronic fatigue syndrome. *American Journal of Medicine, 105,* 94S–99S.

Holmes, G. P., Kaplan, J. E., Gantz, N. M., Komaroff, A. L., Schonberger, L. B., Strauss, S. E., et al. (1988). Chronic fatigue syndrome: A working case definition. *Annals of Internal Medicine, 108,* 387–389.

Jason, L. A., Richman, J. A., Friedberg, F., Wagner, L., Taylor, R., & Jordan, K. M. (1998). More on the biopsychosocial model of chronic fatigue syndrome. *American Psychologist, 53,* 1080–1081.

Jason, L. A., Richman, J. A., Rademaker, A. W., Jordan, K. M., Plioplys, A. V., Taylor, R., et al. (1999). A community-based study of chronic fatigue syndrome. *Archives of Internal Medicine, 159,* 2129–2137.

Jason, L. A., Taylor, R. R., Stepanek, Z., & Plioplys, S. (2001). Attitudes regarding chronic fatigue syndrome: The importance of a name. *Journal of Health Psychology, 6,* 61–71.

Manu, P., Affleck, G., Tennen, H., Morse, P. A., & Escobar, J. I. (1996). Hypochondriasis influences quality-of-life outcomes in patients with chronic fatigue. *Psychotherapy and Psychosomatics, 65,* 76–81.

Manu, P., Lane, T. J., & Matthews, D. A. (1988). The frequency of the chronic fatigue syndrome in patients with symptoms of persistent fatigue. *Annals of Internal Medicine, 109,* 554–556.

Rowe, P. C., & Calkins, H. (1998). Neurally mediated hypotension and chronic fatigue syndrome. *American Journal of Medicine, 105,* 15S–21S.

Schwartz, R. B., Komaroff, A. L., Garada, B. M., Gleit, M., Doolittle, T. H., Bates, D. W., et al. (1994). SPECT imaging of the brain: Comparisons of findings in patients with chronic fatigue syndrome, AIDS dementia complex, and major unipolar depression. *American Journal of Radiology, 162,* 943–951.

Scott, L. V., Teh, J., Reznek, R., Martin, A., Sohaib, A., & Dinan, T. G. (1999). Small adrenal glands in chronic fatigue syndrome: A preliminary computer tomography study. *Psychoneuroendocrinology, 24,* 759–768.

Social Security Ruling 99-2p. Available from www.ss.gov.

Stewart, J. M. (2000). Autonomic nervous system dysfunction in adolescents with postural orthostatic tachycardia syndrome and chronic fatigue syndrome is characterized by attenuated vagal baroflex and potentiated sympathetic vasomotion. *Pediatric Research, 48,* 218–226.

Suhadolnik, R. J., Peterson, D. L., O'Brien, K., Cheney, P. R., Herst, C. V., Reichenbach, N. L., et al. (1997). Biochemical evidence for a novel low molecular weight 2-5A-dependent Rnase L in chronic fatigue syndrome. *Journal of Interferon and Cytokine Research, 17,* 377–385.

Taylor, R. R., Friedberg, F., & Jason, L. A. (2001). A clinician's guide to controversial illnesses: Chronic fatigue syndrome, figromyalgia, and multiple chemical sensitivities. Sarasota, FL: Professional Resource Press.

Ware, N. C. (1998). Sociosomatics and illness course in chronic fatigue syndrome. *Psychosomatic Medicine, 60,* 394–401.

PART I

HISTORY, DIAGNOSIS, AND CLASSIFICATION

CHAPTER 1

Epidemiology

RENÉE R. TAYLOR, LEONARD A. JASON, JUDITH A. RICHMAN,
SUSAN R. TORRES-HARDING, CAROLINE KING, and SHARON SONG

VALID AND RELIABLE epidemiological data can be valuable tools in advancing scientific understanding of the etiology, natural history, diagnostic validity, and basic prevalence, incidence, and mortality of many poorly understood conditions. Chronic fatigue syndrome (CFS) and illnesses with similar symptoms have been described clinically for over 150 years (Wessely, Hotopf, & Sharpe, 1998). The term *neurasthenia* (fatigue as an illness in the absence of disease), which was coined in 1869 by George Beard, was one of the most prevalent diagnoses in the late 1800s (Wessely et al., 1998). But by the early part of the twentieth century, doctors seldom used the diagnosis of neurasthenia, and medical personnel sometimes may have diagnosed patients with severe fatigue as having either a depressive illness or another psychiatric condition.

In the past 45 years, unexplained fatigue-related illnesses with various labels (chronic fatigue syndrome, epidemic neuromyasthenia, and chronic encephalomyelitis) have been hypothesized to occur in well-documented clusters of outbreaks throughout the world (Levine, 1994). Although many of these outbreaks have been characterized by chronic fatigue, the patterning of associated physical and cognitive symptoms has varied across clusters, and clinical descriptions of these symptoms have not always conformed to the formal case definitions for chronic fatigue syndrome (Fukuda et al., 1997; Levine, 1997). Fukuda and associates (1997) investigated one such reported cluster and found no evidence for outbreak clustering. Symptoms and features of generic forms of fatigue that resembled CFS but did not meet the case definition were present in both the community in question and a control community. In another study of self-reported CFS-like illness, Shefer and colleagues (1997) surveyed 3,312 employees in two office buildings suspected to have housed an outbreak and in a comparable control building. Although the researchers identified a substantial number of employees with fatiguing illness in the two office buildings in question, the prevalence of CFS-like illness was not significantly different from that of the control building. By contrast, an investigation of a cluster outbreak of a CFS-like illness in 21 patients in West Otago, New Zealand (Levine, Snow, Ranum, Paul, & Holmes, 1997), found that 48% of the patients met the Fukuda et al. (1994) criteria for CFS. More common among documented outbreaks have been the associated characteristics of female gender and the coexistence of either physical or psychological stress (Levine, 1997). A nationwide survey conducted in Japan identified three distinct clusterings of two cases that met the Japanese version of the CDC criteria (Fukuda et al., 1994). The fatigue-related symptoms reported by different groups may have been influenced, in part, by differences in population characteristics involving social, economic, and cultural variables.

Prevalence estimates of CFS have varied from 3 to 2,800 cases per 100,000 (Jason et al., 1999; Wessely, 1995) depending on the population sampled. Moreover, there has been extraordinary variation in diagnostic practices within general medical settings (Wessely, 1995). Within the United States, findings from a retrospective chart review study indicated that physician workup for chronic fatigue is often incomplete (Ward, DeLisle, Shores, Slocum, & Foresman, 1996). Physicians under study were described as lax in ordering lab work and performing complete mental status and physical examinations, and they did not take an adequate history of patients' chief complaint of chronic fatigue, nor did they record patients' psychiatric and sleep histories adequately (Ward et al., 1996).

Only recently have CFS researchers noted that individuals within different sociocultural contexts vary greatly in their help-seeking behavior in response to illness, and in their economic access to the health care system (Mechanic, 1983). A growing number of investigations have challenged the early assumption that CFS is solely a disease of young to middle-aged White women (e.g., the "Yuppie Flu"). Reports by K. M. Bell, Cookfair, Bell, Reese, and Cooper (1991) and D. S. Bell, Bell, and Cheney (1994) have drawn increased attention to the occurrence of CFS in children, which will allow improved detection in this age group. Alisky, Iczkowski, and Foti (1991) found that more cases of CFS were reported in African Americans than would be expected from the percentage of African American patients in the physician's practice. Other researchers have found high rates of CFS among men, individuals of lower socioeconomic status, and people of color, including Latinos (Buchwald et al., 1995; Jason et al., 1999; Lloyd, Hickie, Boughton, Spencer, & Wakefield, 1990).

In a large-scale community-based study conducted by Jason and associates (1999), the prevalence of CFS was notably higher among Latinos and, to a lesser degree, African Americans, than among Caucasians. Similarly, Buchwald and colleagues (1995) found that women were not overrepresented in their study, Caucasians were underrepresented, and African Americans were overrepresented. With respect to gender, Lloyd and associates (1990) found a female-to-male ratio of 1.3 to 1.0. Studies in Australia (Lloyd et al., 1990) and in the United States (Jason et al., 1999) have emphasized the socioeconomic diversity of patients. Jason and associates found the highest CFS prevalence rates among skilled craftspersons, clerical, and salespersons; second highest rates occurred among unskilled laborers, machine operators, and semiskilled workers; and lowest rates were found among professionals.

Marked variability in prevalence rates across studies and within samples suggests that the prevalence of CFS may be significantly influenced by sociodemographic characteristics. Previous epidemiological studies of CFS have, for the most part, been conducted within medical settings (Buchwald et al., 1995), or by using rosters of those enrolled in health maintenance organizations (Richman, Flaherty, & Rospenda, 1994). More recent studies of randomly selected community-based samples more representative of the general population have revealed some of the underlying sociodemographic bases for the observed disparities in prevalence rates and heterogeneity in symptom presentations (Jason et al., 1999). The epidemiology of this syndrome has stimulated significant interest and controversy within the scientific community.

This chapter reviews the history of epidemiological research involving CFS, discusses the implications of current findings, and offers suggestions for future research. A history of prevalence research is provided and different methodological approaches to estimating the prevalence of CFS in adults, adolescents, and children are compared. In addition, the chapter reviews issues concerning the incidence and long-term prognosis of CFS as well as sociodemographic considerations.

CFS PREVALENCE

Studies of Patients in Medical Settings

In one of the earliest known studies of CFS prevalence, Ho-Yen (1988) surveyed general practitioners and reviewed data contained on viral serology requisitions to explore the prevalence of CFS. Ho-Yen used previously documented diagnoses such as "postviral fatigue" to count the number of individuals with probable CFS. Using this indirect method, this investigator suggested that the number of cases ranged from 51 to 131 per 100,000 residents of Great Britain. Sociodemographic variables were not examined in this investigation.

Two years later, David and associates (1990) examined self-reported CFS symptoms reported on a fatigue questionnaire from 611 general practice attendees in a London general practice. Of these patients, 10.5% reported substantial fatigue for one month or more. The profile of substantial fatigue did not differ from that of shorter duration, and participants attributed physical and nonphysical causes to their fatigue equally. The ratios of men and women reporting persistent fatigue were roughly equivalent (10.2% men and 10.6% women). However, these investigators found only one patient with a chronic fatigue syndrome-like illness who had at least 6 months of significant fatigue. This study was limited by nonrandom sampling methods, a small sample size, and the use of a single, self-report measure to roughly assess for the presence of CFS.

A third group of investigators from Great Britain screened 686 patients attending primary care physicians and identified 77 individuals with chronic fatigue (McDonald, David, Pelosi, & Mann, 1993). Of these, 65 patients underwent a comprehensive medical and psychological evaluation. Seventeen cases (26%) met the Sharpe et al. (1991) criteria for CFS. Patients were not excluded from a diagnosis of CFS if they met ICD-9 criteria for current neurotic depression or neurasthenia. Although this study used a more sophisticated, comprehensive evaluation to assess for CFS, its generalizability was nevertheless limited to those who could afford to seek primary medical care and were willing to do so.

In a smaller study, Conti and colleagues (1994) evaluated 63 patients attending a tertiary care fatigue clinic in the Lazio region of central Italy. Participants were selected on the basis of having recurrent or persistent fatigue lasting 6 months and fulfilling at least 4 minor U.S. 1988 CDC criteria for CFS. Individuals with a previously diagnosed illness associated with fatigue were excluded prior to evaluation.

Evaluation consisted of clinical examination, standard laboratory testing, and a self-administered questionnaire specifically designed to gain information about the length and severity of symptoms. A diagnosis of CFS based on CDC criteria was established in 6 (9.5%) of the 63 patients. Two participants were excluded because CFS occurred following infectious mononucleosis. Other alternative diagnoses were established in 37 (59%) of the 63 patients, and no definite diagnosis could be formulated for 18 patients (28.5%). Based on these findings, the researchers concluded that, in Italy, CFS seems to be an infrequent cause of severe and persistent fatigue in a selected population. However, the generalizability of findings from this study was limited to tertiary care patients, who tend to suffer more functional impairment, have a greater likelihood of psychiatric illness, and tend to have been ill for a longer period of time (Wessely, 1995). Its generalizability is further limited because not all individuals have independent access to tertiary medical care in Italy.

Minowa and Jiamo (1996) administered a nationwide survey to assess CFS prevalence according to the Japanese version of the CDC criteria (Fukuda et al., 1994) prepared by the CFS Research Group of Japan. The researchers surveyed the following clinical departments of a number of hospitals nationwide with 200 or more beds: internal medicine, pediatrics, psychiatry, and neurology. Adjusted for the response rate, the prevalence of CFS was estimated at 0.85 cases per 100,000. The proportion of postinfectious CFS was 14.8%, and three clusterings of two cases were reported. Similar to the other studies described in this section, these estimates may have been conservative due to differential participation in the survey among hospitals and their respective departments. Moreover, the generalizability of findings was limited to those using medical care.

PROSPECTIVE STUDIES IN MEDICAL SETTINGS

A group of U.S. researchers (Bates and associates, 1993) prospectively evaluated 1,000 consecutive patients in a primary care clinic to assess the prevalence of unusual, debilitating fatigue and the frequency with which it is associated with CFS. A general physical examination, a detailed medical history, standard laboratory testing, and a structured psychiatric interview and self-report inventory were used. Among the participants, 32.5% reported fatigue, and 27% complained of at least 6 months of unusual fatigue that interfered with their daily lives. Self-report or review of medical records revealed a medical or psychiatric condition that could explain the fatigue in 69% of the individuals with chronic fatigue. Thus, 8.5% of patients were assessed to have unusual, debilitating chronic fatigue with no apparent etiology. Three met the Holmes et al. (1988) CDC criteria for CFS, four met the Sharpe et al. (1991) criteria, and 10 met the Lloyd et al. (1990) definition. The respective point prevalence estimates were therefore 0.3%, 0.4%, and 1.0% using the CDC, British, and Australian case definitions. These estimates may only be representative of those who can afford and are motivated to attend a primary care clinic.

White and associates (1998) sought to determine CFS prevalence and the role of viruses in the etiology of CFS. They conducted a prospective cohort study of 250 primary care patients presenting with glandular fever or an upper respiratory tract infection. Six months after glandular fever, the most conservative estimate of CFS prevalence was 9%, compared with 0% as the most conservative estimate following an upper respiratory tract infection. Thus, these researchers concluded that glandular fever is a significant risk factor for CFS.

CASE IDENTIFICATION BY PHYSICIANS

Lloyd and coworkers (1990) conducted a study in a largely rural area of Australia. In this study, CFS cases were identified only if they sought medical care from sentinel physicians. Members of the community were not assessed directly. One hundred and four local medical practitioners were first asked to identify cases of CFS in their practice. From an overall population of 114,000, physicians were instructed to select those patients significantly disabled in their usual daily activities who had been suffering from chronic fatigue for at least 6 months. None of the patients had an alternative diagnosis. Twenty-six medical practitioners identified 49 patients. Forty-eight of those patients were screened further with a 50-item questionnaire forwarded by mail. To be retained in the study, patients had to report moderate to severe symptoms during the previous month on at least one of the two questions related to fatigue ("Excessive muscle fatigue with minor activity" and "Prolonged feeling of fatigue after physical activity lasting hours or days") and on at least one of the two questions related to neuropsychiatric functioning (e.g., "loss of concentrating ability or memory loss"). Following this stage, 42 cases were then retained for further medical and psychiatric evaluation. A physician and a psychiatrist were able to diagnose 28 of these 42 cases through mutual consensus. Because none of the 42 cases showed any abnormality on a full blood workup nor did any of them have an alternative diagnosis, all were classified as meeting the Lloyd et al. definition of CFS. With age-standardization, the CFS prevalence rate was 39.6 cases per 100,000. These individuals were found to be of predominantly lower to middle socioeconomic status, with occupations such as unskilled laborers, truck drivers, and dressmakers. Of the 42 individuals with CFS, 57% were females and 43% were males, a female-to-male ratio of 1.3:1.0.

A serious problem with this study occurred in the initial phase of patient identification (Jason, Wagner, et al., 1995). Only 25% of the original 104 physicians approached agreed to participate in notifying cases. Moreover, only 10.6% of the 50 physicians recontacted had actually notified cases. The remaining practitioners reported that they either failed to notify cases or that there were no cases in their practice. As Jason and coworkers noted, some of the medical practitioners may not have adequately surveyed their patients for CFS. Interestingly, the authors reported that some of the physicians who agreed to participate were skeptical of the validity of CFS.

Ho-Yen and McNamara (1991) conducted an extensive postal survey of 195 general practitioners on 10 local government lists in two health boards and were more successful in recruiting physicians (they obtained a 91% response rate). However, the central methodology used to estimate prevalence in this study was not rigorous. In this survey, practitioners were asked to document their attitudes about the validity of CFS and their experience in terms of workload and the characteristics of the patients affected. A majority of general practitioners (71%) accepted the existence of CFS, but 22% were undecided. Among the doctors who supported the validity of CFS, a prevalence of 1.3 per 1,000 patients was found. The incidence for this area was 1.7 cases per 1,000 patients. Within their sample, these researchers found that CFS tends to peak between the ages of 30 and 44 years. Of the patients who agreed to provide more detailed information, 22% were teachers or students, 16% were retired, 13% were homemakers, 11% worked in service industries (e.g., shops, hotels, banks), 9% were secretarial or clerical staff, 9% were skilled workers (e.g., painters, joiners, fitters, electricians), 8% were unskilled workers, 7% were hospital workers, and 5% were professionals (e.g., lawyers, ministers, civil servants).

In a more rigorous investigation with a similar sampling strategy, the United States Centers for Disease Control and Prevention (CDC) initiated an ongoing epidemiological study in four cities: Atlanta, Reno, Grand Rapids, and Wichita (Gunn, Connell, & Randall, 1993). From among 900 eligible physicians, 408 sentinel physicians were asked to identify patients who had unexplained, severe fatigue for 6 months or more after a normal workup, or patients with chronic illnesses characterized by two or more of a group of specified symptoms lasting for 6 months or more. Less than half (44%) of the eligible physician population agreed to refer patients to the study, leaving an unknown number of eligible patients of nonparticipating physicians unidentified (Gunn et al., 1993). The patients were subsequently referred for a standardized, intensive medical and psychological evaluation that included a full medical history and structured psychiatric interview taken by a site nurse, a review of previous medical records, and a basic panel of standardized laboratory diagnostic tests. The profiles were examined independently by four members of a Physician Review Committee. Prevalence rates of CFS were found to range from 4.0 to 8.7 individuals per 100,000 cases (Reyes et al., 1997). The majority of cases were White women who were well educated and potentially high-income earners.

Like the Australian study (Lloyd et al., 1990), the CDC study is limited by nonrandom sampling methods. Gunn and colleagues (1993) acknowledged that it was unclear whether the aforementioned demographic findings reflected actual differences in prevalence or were the result of referral bias or differences in utilization patterns of the health care system. In addition, the study excluded all patients with preexisting affective anxiety, and somatization disorders in the overall tally of individuals with CFS. For these reasons, the estimates provided by Gunn and coworkers are probably conservative (Buchwald et al., 1995).

Bazelmans and associates (1999) sought to determine the prevalence of CFS as recognized by general practitioners in the Netherlands using a postal questionnaire. These researchers experienced more success in obtaining responses from the physicians sampled—60% of the physicians returned the questionnaire. Of that group, 73% identified one or more patients with CFS in their practice for an estimated prevalence of 112 per 100,000.

Many of these studies suggest that chronic fatigue and CFS are common in primary care, and both phenomena represent a considerable public health burden (Wessely, Chalder, Hirsch, Wallace, & Wright, 1997). However, prevalence estimates from these studies are only representative of those who can afford and are motivated to attend a health care facility. Population-based studies may offer a broader perspective on the epidemiology of CFS that is not based on medical care access and utilization patterns.

POPULATION-BASED SURVEYS USING HEALTH CARE ROSTERS

Pawlikowska and coworkers (1994) obtained responses to a postal questionnaire on fatigue from 15,283 individuals registered within 6 general practices in the

South of England. The individuals were recorded in the general practice register as having mild fatigue. The response rate was 48.3%. Among those who responded, 18.3% reported excessive fatigue, with 4.7% reporting fatigue lasting at least 6 months and for 50% of the time. The cause of the fatigue was attributed to myalgic encephalomyelitis (a roughly equivalent name for CFS in Great Britain) in 0.2% of the respondents. The general prevalence estimate for CFS in Great Britain was therefore 6 cases per 100,000 seen in general practice. These investigators found that chronic fatigue is more common in lower social classes and that the apparent overrepresentation of CFS in higher social classes might be due to the effects of selection bias. However, their diagnosis of CFS relied solely on self-report, and participants who reported having CFS did not undergo systematic medical and psychological evaluations (Buchwald et al., 1995).

Using the Pawlikowska et al. (1994) sample, Wessely et al. (1995) conducted a prospective study to determine the presence of CFS in 1,199 people who presented to primary care with symptoms of common infection and 1,167 who were seen for other reasons. At postinfection of 6 months, 84% of participants underwent successful evaluation. Within the infectious case group, 9.9% reported chronic fatigue. Within the noninfectious control group, 11.7% reported chronic fatigue. There were no differences in the proportions of case groups who met criteria for chronic fatigue syndrome, and there was no effect of sex or social class. The authors therefore concluded there was no evidence that common infective episodes in primary care are related to the onset of chronic fatigue and chronic fatigue syndrome.

In a second study that employed the Pawlikowska et al. (1994) sample, Wessely et al. (1997) examined the prevalence of chronic fatigue and CFS in 2,376 primary care attendees aged 18 through 45 years. The researchers identified 214 participants who fulfilled criteria for chronic fatigue lasting 6 months or longer. Of these individuals, 185 (86%) with chronic fatigue and a group of matched nonfatigued controls agreed to be interviewed for a case control study using health and fatigue questionnaires. Measures of fatigue included self-report questionnaires assessing for the presence of CFS (Fukuda et al., 1994), other forms of fatigue, functional impairment, somatic symptoms, and psychological morbidity (including depression and anxiety). In addition, nurses used a structured psychiatric interview to assess for the presence of psychiatric disorder. Results suggested that the point prevalence of chronic fatigue was 11.3%, falling to 4.1% if all comorbid psychological disorders were excluded. The point prevalence of CFS (Fukuda et al., 1994) was 2.6%, falling to 0.5% if all comorbid psychological disorders were excluded. Functional impairment in both chronic fatigue and CFS was profound and was associated with psychological disorder. Wessely and associates found that there was no excess of upper social class in chronic fatigue or CFS, and they suggested that selection bias might account for previous suggestions of an association with higher socioeconomic status. After adjustment for psychological disorder, being female was modestly associated with chronic fatigue and CFS. The racial composition of the sample was not presented, and this study did not utilize complete medical examination to rule out exclusionary conditions in diagnosing CFS.

In a subsequent study by Euga, Chalder, Deale, and Wessely (1996), those individuals with a CFS diagnosis in the community sample described previously were compared with people diagnosed in a hospital unit specializing in CFS. Whereas 74% of the community sample had a psychiatric diagnosis before the onset of their fatigue, only 21% of the hospital sample had a previous diagnosis. The community sample had significantly worse mental health scores and were more likely to be impaired in their work. Fifty-nine percent believed that their illness might be due to psychological or psychosocial causes (compared with 7% for the hospital sample). Wessely et al. (1997) indicated that, of the 2.6% with CFS in the community sample, only 0.5% had no psychological disorder. In another study of CFS and psychiatric symptoms done by the Wessely group (Wessely, Chalder, Hirsch, Wallace, & Wright, 1996), 36 individuals were diagnosed as having CFS from a cohort of 1,985 primary care patients. Among the CFS subgroup, only 64% had sleep disturbances and 63% had postexertional malaise. These percentages are low, given that both symptoms are critical features of CFS. Wessely and colleagues' finding of an increased prevalence of CFS reflects the use of the new Fukuda et al. (1994) case definition, and possibly indicates the inclusion of pure psychiatric cases in the category of CFS disorders. Thus, using a broad or narrow definition of CFS has an important influence on CFS prevalence estimates and the related issue of psychiatric comorbidity.

Similar to the sampling strategy used by the previously referenced researchers, Lawrie and Pelosi (1995) obtained responses to a postal survey eliciting information about fatigue, psychiatric symptoms, and sociodemographic data from 1,000 randomly selected patients registered at a local health center in a semirural town in Great Britain. Problematic fatigue was reported by 38% ($n = 262$) of respondents—32% of men and 43% of women. Twenty-five percent of the sample ($n = 176$) complained of some degree of fatigue for 6 months or longer. Chronic fatigue, defined as problematic fatigue of at least 6 months' duration, was found in 14% ($n = 96$) of responders—12.5% of men and 15% of women. Thirteen percent of responders ($n = 93$) reported fatigue at least half of the time, with women (17%) being more likely than men (10%) to suffer from frequent fatigue. Problematic, chronic, and frequent fatigue, as required by the Sharpe et al. (1991) criteria for CFS, was found in 5% ($n = 15$) of men and 7% ($n = 25$) of women. After excluding those with a documented physical illness, 1.1% ($n = 8$) possible CFS patients were identified (4 men and 4 women). For these 8 individuals, medical records from the health center were examined to verify that possible cases had consulted their general practitioners and that potential physical or psychiatric illnesses excluding chronic fatigue had been ruled out. As a result, CFS (Sharpe et al., 1991) was identified as definite in 0.56% ($n = 4$) of 695 eligible cases, a point prevalence of 560 per 100,000 cases. Two were men and two were women, and their average age was 40 years. All individuals with CFS were working and in upper- or middle-class occupations. None of them were in the health care professions. The duration of fatigue ranged between 6 months and 5 years, with an average of 23 months. One man with a positive monospect test attributed fatigue to glandular fever, one woman attributed it to long-standing myalgic encephalomyelitis, and the other two individuals attributed it to overwork.

These investigators concluded that previously reported sociodemographic associations of CFS may reflect medical referral patterns and that conclusions from their study must be interpreted with caution due to the small sample size and the response bias away from lower social classes. In general, these findings were limited by nonrandom sampling methods.

Buchwald and associates (1995) conducted a study involving a random sample of 4,000 individuals on an HMO roster in the Seattle area. Seventy-seven percent ($n = 3,066$) of the individuals surveyed responded. The initial screening survey included the following two queries, which were intended to assess for the presence of the two major criteria of the 1988 CDC case definition of CFS: "Have you felt unusual fatigue or loss of energy, either constantly or repeatedly, for at least the past 6 months?" and "Does this state of fatigue interfere with your work or responsibilities at home such that you have had to reduce your level of activity by at least one-half?" Those answering yes to both questions then reviewed a list of exclusionary medical and psychiatric diagnoses, and if any of these conditions were present, respondents were considered to be ineligible for further study.

Participants selected with unexplained chronic fatigue were evaluated using a questionnaire that requested information about medical history and fatigue and related symptoms, validated measures of functional status and psychological distress, medical record review, a physical examination, and standardized blood tests. In addition, a structured psychiatric interview, the Diagnostic Interview Schedule, was completed to rule out exclusionary psychiatric illnesses in individuals who appeared to meet the 1988 CDC criteria for CFS. A history of preexisting psychiatric illness (other than somatoform pain disorder) for more than 1 year before the onset of CFS or any previous substance abuse precluded the diagnosis of CFS. The diagnosis was not excluded if the onset of a nonpsychotic psychiatric disorder occurred at the same time as or after the onset of CFS.

On the basis of history, physical examination, and laboratory tests alone, 6 of the 74 cases of chronic fatigue appeared to meet the CDC criteria for CFS. Following administration of the psychiatric interview, 3 individuals were excluded on the basis of preexisting psychiatric illness. One had a history of alcohol and substance abuse and major depression, and 2 others had premorbid dysthymia. Thus, three individuals were determined to have CFS, for a prevalence rate of 75 to 267 cases per 100,000. The prevalence estimates put forth by Buchwald and associates (1995) are likely to be conservative for several reasons including that they represented only those individuals with access to health insurance.

HIGH-RISK SAMPLES

A growing body of research has suggested that occupational circumstances may play a role in CFS. In particular, Jason and associates (1993) directly sampled a group of 3,400 nurses through a mailed questionnaire. In this group, 202 nurses (6%) indicated that they experienced significant, debilitating fatigue for at least 6 months. These 202 nurses received a follow-up telephone interview, and 82 who either self-reported having CFS or reported most of the symptoms of CFS were selected for further study. This subgroup received a structured psychiatric interview and their medical records were requested. A physician review team then reviewed all collected information. Thirty-seven of the nurses met the criteria for current CFS, and five additional nurses met the criteria for past CFS (Jason & Wagner, 1998). Thus, a CFS point prevalence rate of 1,088 per 100,000 was determined. This estimate was higher than those found by many other epidemiological studies and likely reflected that nurses may be at higher risk for developing CFS due to occupational stress, exposure to viruses and other pathogens in the work setting, and shift work that is disruptive to biological rhythms. Thus, it was not possible to generalize these findings to the entire population.

If CFS affects members of various professions at different rates or in different ways, this may reveal new information regarding the etiology and characteristics of the illness. In a recent epidemiological study of CFS in a community sample (Jason et al., 2000a), health care workers composed over 15% of the group of individuals with CFS, which is significantly higher than the composition of health care workers in the general U.S. population. Similarly, Coulter (1988) found that 40% of the members of a large U.S. patients' organization for individuals with CFS were associated with the health care professions, and Ramsay (1986) has identified an overrepresentation of doctors among individuals with CFS. The most recent community-based survey of CFS-like illness conducted by the CDC in San Francisco (Steele et al., 1998) also found that CFS prevalence was elevated among clerical workers and those engaged in health care occupations.

Findings such as these suggest that certain occupational stressors, such as exposure to viruses, stressful shift work that is disruptive to circadian rhythms, and excessive workload may compromise the immune system and put health care workers at greater risk of infection or illness (Akerstedt, Torsvall, & Gillberg, 1985; Jason & Wagner, 1998; Leese et al., 1996). Hypothetical explanations highlighting the role of disrupted circadian rhythms are, in part, supported by biological findings among a sample of nurses working five consecutive night shifts (Leese et al., 1996). Disruptions in pituitary-adrenal responses to CRH in that sample were highly consistent with the neuroendocrine abnormalities typically found in individuals with CFS (Leese et al., 1996). However, these findings must be interpreted in light of other studies that have not found an overrepresentation of professionals among individuals with CFS (Euga et al., 1996).

COMMUNITY-BASED INTERVIEW STUDY

Kawakami, Iwata, Fujihara, and Kitamura (1998) invited all adults (230 men and 278 women) living in Kofu, Japan, to participate in a baseline interview survey to assess the prevalence of CFS according to the Fukuda et al. (1994) criteria. The 207 town residents who agreed to participate were interviewed using a structured psychiatric diagnostic interview. Approximately one year later, 137 respondents to the baseline interview completed a follow-up interview. The point prevalence rate of CFS based on interview findings was 1.5%. This rate was higher than those found in studies of CFS in Western countries and may indicate a need for future research on cross-cultural differences in the prevalence of CFS.

RANDOM COMMUNITY-BASED SAMPLES

Price and associates (Price, North, Wessely, & Fraser, 1992) used the Diagnostic Interview Schedule (DIS) to assess the lifetime prevalence of medical and psychological symptoms in a large, stratified, random sample of a general population known as the Epidemiologic Catchment Area Program. These investigators used questions from the psychiatric interview to assess for the presence of CFS according to the Holmes et al. (1988) definition. Results from the DIS suggested that chronic fatigue in the general population is common. A total of 23% of the participants reported having experienced persistent fatigue sometime during their lives. However, with the exclusion of comorbid physical illness, psychiatric illness, substance abuse, and weight loss, and with the inclusion of 5 of the 7 minor criteria, the authors concluded that CFS appeared to be quite rare in the general population. Only 1 of 13,538 people examined with the DIS was found to meet an approximated diagnosis of CFS. The prevalence estimate was therefore 7.4 cases per 100,000. Those individuals who only met some of the approximated CDC criteria ("Fatigue Symptom Complex Group") were otherwise diagnosed to have exclusionary medical or psychiatric illness or substance abuse problems.

The researchers noted several limitations within their study. The first limitation was that not all of the symptoms in the 1988 CDC criteria for CFS were available for analysis, and the definition therefore represented a significant departure from all standard definitions of CFS (Jason, Wagner, et al., 1995), including the CDC criteria. For example, the DIS question used to assess the presence of 6 or more months of fatigue was the following question from the depressive disorders section: "Has there ever been a period lasting 2 weeks or more when you felt tired out all the time?" The reduction in usual activities item was, "Giving up usual activities for several weeks or more." In addition, three of the minor criteria and physical criteria were not represented by questions on the DIS: mild fever, sore throat, and painful lymph nodes. A second limitation was that all symptoms were assessed on a lifetime basis. It was therefore impossible to assess the timing of the fatigue syndrome in relation to the conditions of the four CDC exclusion criteria.

Price and coworkers (1992) contend that they may have wrongly excluded some participants with coexisting medical and psychiatric disorders that could have occurred at a different time from their exclusion criteria. At the same time, lifetime assessment may have overestimated the number of individuals with CFS by introducing people whose various symptoms were spread out over a long period instead of occurring within a short period of CFS onset. Furthermore, these researchers criticized the CDC criteria for its restrictive exclusion criteria. As defined by CDC in their study, the exclusions eliminated 90% of those who would otherwise meet the minor criteria in their particular community sample. In addition to limitations acknowledged by the authors, this study was also limited by its lack of methodological rigor. Selected participants did not receive medical workup, laboratory testing, medical record review, or an account of medical history beyond what was gathered in the psychiatric interview.

Beginning in January 1993, Jason and colleagues conducted a pilot study (Jason, Taylor, et al., 1995) in preparation for a larger community-based investigation (Jason et al., 1999). A randomly generated, Chicago area community sample of 1,031 residents of diverse ethnicity and socioeconomic status were contacted by telephone and administered a 3-page screening questionnaire to assess for the presence of chronic fatigue and related symptoms. Excluding commercial listings and numbers that the telephone company reported as disconnected, 93% of the sample was ultimately contacted. Respondents were selected for further evaluation on the basis of having at least one of the following criteria: (1) A participant self-reported having CFS, had no exclusionary medical illnesses, and met minimum fatigue severity criteria; or (2) a participant had most of the symptoms of CFS according to the 1988 CDC definition. Those individuals identified as having a profile suggestive of CFS were recontacted by telephone and were offered fifty dollars for completing a psychiatric and physical evaluation. For the psychiatric evaluation, a lay interviewer administered the Diagnostic Interview Schedule, and a licensed psychiatrist familiar with the diagnosis of CFS conducted a standardized, independent psychiatric evaluation. For the medical examination, medical records were gathered, a full medical history was taken, and one of two physicians gave participants a standardized physical examination. Standard laboratory tests of blood and urine samples were conducted, and participants completed additional, self-administered questionnaires measuring functional status, fatigue severity, coping styles, and social support. A physician review committee consisting of the examining psychiatrist and physicians reviewed all completed cases and ultimately made the final diagnosis of CFS.

Only 11% of the entire sample of 1,031 participants refused to be interviewed. Five percent of the sample indicated that they had unexplained, severe fatigue for 6 months or more. Of those 5% with chronic fatigue, 32% were male, 46% minority, and 34% had a high school education or less. With respect to attribution for fatigue, 11% indicated psychosocial causes (i.e., work, family, lifestyle), 17% psychological distress (i.e., anxiety, depression), 21% physical causes (i.e., cancer, heart disease), 15% were not sure why they were fatigued, 11% indicated that they had CFS in the past, and 25% felt that they currently had CFS. Of the fatigued group, 64% indicated that they had no current medical doctor overseeing their illness. Two individuals were judged to have current CFS, and one individual was judged as having had it in the past. The point prevalence rate was therefore 0.2%, suggesting a prevalence rate of 200 per 100,000 (Jason, Taylor, et al., 1995). These results were limited by the small size of the initial sample.

The CDC also conducted a community-based survey in San Francisco (Steele et al., 1998). Using telephone interviewing between June 1 and December 1, 1994, these investigators surveyed 8,004 households, providing data on 16,970 adult and minor residents. Of the 14,627 adults in the screened population, 6.3% reported they had been fatigued for 1 month or longer; and 4.3% reported severe fatigue lasting 6 months or longer. In this group with chronic fatigue, 51.5% reported a medical or psychiatric diagnosis that could plausibly explain their fatigue. The investigators classified 33 adults (0.2% of the study population) as having CFS-like illness, and 259 (1.8%) as having idiopathic chronic fatigue. Relative to Whites, CFS-like illness was significantly elevated among African Americans and Native Americans, and CFS-like illness was more prevalent among people with annual household incomes below $40,000. CFS-like illness was also elevated among clerical workers and those engaged in health care occupations. These findings suggest that unexplained chronic fatigue does not primarily affect White, affluent professionals. Based on this population-based telephone survey, the authors estimated that the prevalence of CFS-like illness is between 0.076% and 0.233% (76 and 233 per 100,000). Conclusions about CFS from this study were limited by self-report methodology. In the absence of medical and psychiatric examinations, it was not possible to estimate the true prevalence of CFS.

From 1995 until 1998, Jason and colleagues (1999) initiated a large-scale epidemiological study of CFS prevalence funded by NIAID utilizing methodology that was modeled, in large part, after that used in the Jason, Taylor, et al. (1995) pilot study. Jason and associates (1999) attempted to contact a stratified sample of 28,673 households in Chicago by telephone. The sample was stratified to ensure a representative sample of the diverse ethnic and socioeconomic groups comprising the Chicago general population. Of that sample, 18,675 individuals were screened for CFS symptomatology. Based on the initial screening, participants with significant fatigue and CFS symptoms (CFS-like) and a control group were selected to receive a semistructured psychological evaluation and a complete physical examination. Previous medical records were gathered and questionnaires assessing fatigue and symptom severity, functional capacity, and other psychosocial variables were administered. An independent physician review team blind to initial classification (CFS-like vs. control) reviewed all cases to ascertain a CFS diagnosis. Approximately 0.4% of the sample was determined to have CFS, and rates of CFS were higher among Latino and African American respondents when compared with White respondents (Jason et al., 1999). These rates translate to as many as 800,000 adults in the United States with this syndrome, suggesting that CFS is one of the more common chronic health conditions.

Reyes, Nisenbaum, Stewart, and Reeves (1998) conducted a study using a similar methodology and reported on the first phase of the second CDC population-based prevalence study of fatigue-related disorders. Nearly 25% of the population of Sedgewick County (Wichita), Kansas was surveyed. Within a random sample of greater than 90,319 persons (derived from 34,018 households), and 56,154 adults aged 18 to 69, they further interviewed 4,215 adults who reported one or more months of fatigue and 4,149 adults who reported no fatigue. From this sample, 3,534 were identified with prolonged fatigue, 2,766 with chronic fatigue, and 556 with a CFS-like disorder. With respect to ethnicity, 87.8% of the overall sample was White. At a conference of the American Association for Chronic Fatigue Syndrome (AACFS) in Boston, Dr. Reyes stated that of 556 who appeared to have the syndrome, 300 (54%) agreed to undergo physical examination and laboratory testing, and 39 individuals were diagnosed with CFS, translating to a rate of 69 cases per 100,000. Only six of these individuals had been diagnosed with CFS prior to the study. Controlling for the fact that 4% of households had no phone, Reyes and associates then conducted a weighted analysis (probability of being selected adjusting for nonresponders) comparing the sample to the overall population. The rate of CFS was estimated to be about 240 per 100,000. The CDC has now recommended that all future epidemiological research involve randomly selected, community-based samples.

From the studies reviewed herein, a great deal can be learned about the relationship between methodological approaches to epidemiology and resulting descriptions of the nature and prevalence of this syndrome. Most apparent from this review is that prevalence estimates of fatigue in the population and the sociodemographic profiles of those affected vary according to geographic region and according to whether participants are recruited from specialized tertiary care settings, primary care settings, patient registries/insurance rosters, or community-based settings. Estimates may differ, in part, due to biases introduced by more homogeneous samples, such as medically derived samples consisting only of individuals able to access and/or utilize health care. This is a particularly salient issue within the United States, where medical care is not equally accessible to all citizens and physicians are not equally educated in the diagnosis and treatment of CFS (Richman et al., 1994). This review emphasizes the unique contribution to be made by random community sampling to evaluate the prevalence of CFS, particularly within communities characterized by ethnic and socioeconomic diversity.

Pediatric CFS

Few studies of the epidemiology of CFS have been conducted with children and adolescents. As a result, relatively little is known about the etiology, natural history, diagnostic validity, prevalence, incidence, and prognosis of CFS within the pediatric population. Of the few that have been conducted, estimates of CFS or

CFS-like illness in early and middle childhood suggest no occurrence of CFS or CFS-like illness under the age of 12 (Dobbins et al., 1997), or predict that CFS is as rare as 5.5 cases per 100,000 children (Lloyd et al., 1990). In adolescent children above the age of 12, CFS has been estimated at a rate of 8.7 per 100,000 (Gunn et al., 1993), 24 per 100,000 (Dobbins et al., 1997), and 47.9 per 100,000 (Lloyd et al., 1990). This section describes the methodological details of pediatric prevalence studies and cites some potential reasons for discrepant findings.

Lloyd and associates (1990) were the first to include prevalence estimates of CFS for children of all ages in an Australian community population study. They used a structured case-finding technique according to which medical practitioners referred patients. Using a questionnaire, participants were screened for fatigue symptomatology and then were physically examined and interviewed to rule out other diagnoses. A multidisciplinary team of professionals reached diagnostic consensus regarding CFS on all cases. CFS was estimated to occur in 5.5 per 100,000 cases for children aged 0 to 9, and in 47.9 per 100,000 cases for children and adolescents aged 10 to 19. CFS was estimated at 37.1 per 100,000 for the entire population of adults and children. Thus, findings suggested that adolescents might have a higher risk for developing CFS than some adult age groups. A difficulty with the study that limits the validity of prevalence estimates was the low number of medical practitioners who participated and identified cases of CFS in their practices (11 out of 50 doctors participated). This may have been due to lack of education about CFS or doubts about the validity or existence of CFS. Given that the population in this study was obtained through physician referral, members of the community who do not or cannot access medical care for their symptoms were not included in the study.

Within the United States, the CDC conducted a surveillance study in Atlanta, Reno, Grand Rapids, and Wichita to investigate the prevalence of CFS in adolescents living in different geographic areas (Gunn et al., 1993). Local physicians identified and referred patients who fulfilled CDC diagnostic criteria for CFS. Only 44% of eligible physicians agreed to participate in the study. Based on the Holmes et al. (1988) criteria, the researchers identified chronic fatigue symptomatology in approximately 8.7 cases per 100,000 and estimated CFS as occurring in 2.7 cases per 100,000 among adolescents aged 12 to 17. No inquiries about fatigue or CFS symptoms were made for children under the age of 12. The limitations identified in the adult sample also apply to the adolescent sample. Nonrandom sampling methods were employed, and referral for case ascertainment was not consistent among participating physicians. As a result, estimates derived from this study were probably conservative.

Among a second generation of CDC studies, a community-based investigation including children and adolescents was conducted in San Francisco (Dobbins et al., 1997). This study employed random digit dialing to households as a means of identifying children and adolescents with chronic fatigue and CFS-like illness. Estimates were made for children aged 2 to 11, indicating that 71.9 per 100,000 were identified as having symptoms of chronic fatigue, and 0 per 100,000 presented with CFS-like symptoms. In adolescents aged 12 to 17, 465.7 per 100,000 were found to have chronic fatigue symptoms, and 116.4 per 100,000 were diagnosed with CFS-like conditions. However, because the study did not include a medical evaluation, the actual number of CFS cases in that population could not be determined, and thus, only "CFS-like" illness could be diagnosed.

The CDC conducted another study involving referrals from school nurses from junior and senior high schools in Wichita, Kansas, and Reno, Nevada. A prevalence of 24.0 per 100,000 CFS was found for the 12- to 17-year-old age group (Dobbins et al., 1997). As in other medical referral studies, dependence on CFS expertise of the referring nurse, as well as reliance on previous diagnoses by physicians (rather than current evaluations), limited the reliability and generalizability of these findings.

The only existing rigorous community-based study of CFS prevalence (Jordan et al., 2001) was recently conducted in conjunction with a Chicago study using a similar methodology (Jason et al., 1999). A brief questionnaire aimed to screen for pediatric CFS in children between the ages of 5 and 17 was administered with the adult screening questionnaire, and 12,938 households were interviewed. Of the target group of 3,895 children aged 5 to 17 years, 172 (4.4%) were reported to experience fatigue and 175 (4.5%) were reported to experience school or memory problems. Seventy-five (1.9%) were reported to have problems with both fatigue and with school or memory.

Follow-up interviews were designed to obtain further information about the child's health condition and symptoms, symptom severity, medical history, school attendance, and activity level. These interviews were conducted with children and adolescents identified through the initial telephone screening process as having fatigue or school problems and at least four or more CFS symptoms listed on the initial questionnaire.

In the third stage of the project, psychiatric and medical evaluations were conducted on the pediatric sample. The Structured Clinical Interview for the *DSM-IV*—Child version (Hien et al., 1997) was administered to children and their caretakers to assess for the presence of Axis I psychiatric diagnoses that would exclude a participant from a CFS diagnosis (Fukuda et al., 1994), or explain fatigue-related symptomatology. Participants also received a complete physical examination with laboratory testing to diagnose CFS and rule out exclusionary medical conditions (Fukuda et al., 1994). In addition, self-report information about the participants' medical history and current health status was gathered. An independent panel of physicians then reviewed all information in each case to determine a final CFS diagnosis. Physician reviews were completed on 34 screened positive cases and 23 screened negative cases. Results of physician review revealed a CFS prevalence of 0.06%, or 60 cases per 100,000 (Jordan et al., 2001).

With the exception of the Jordan et al. (2001) study, minimal attention has been paid to critical features of CFS in children and adolescents. Existing studies have either been based on physician referrals or have not included the medical examinations necessary to diagnose CFS. Because of limitations imposed by selection bias, investigators cannot use these studies to estimate the magnitude of the disorder among children and adolescents. In addition, they do not accurately describe the relative distribution of CFS across gender, ethnicity, and socioeconomic status.

STUDIES OF THE INCIDENCE AND PROGNOSIS OF CHRONIC FATIGUE SYNDROME

Most epidemiological studies have lacked the ability to accurately estimate the overall incidence of CFS in the general population and determine its relative distribution across important sociodemographic groups (such as low socioeconomic status groups with inadequate access to health care treatment). There is a clear need for incidence and follow-up studies of CFS to address important issues involving the actual magnitude of this syndrome, its relative distribution across sociodemographic groups (racial-ethnic, socioeconomic, age, and gender), and its long-term prognosis. Since the functional disability associated with CFS may interrupt work and family life, obtaining accurate epidemiological data is essential to assessing the public health and policy ramifications of this disorder. This section reviews existing incidence and follow-up studies of CFS.

In a follow-up investigation based on a prior prevalence study that used postal survey methodology (Lawrie & Pelosi, 1995), Lawrie, Manders, Geddes, and Pelosi (1997) resurveyed respondents one year after the initial survey and interviewed them again 18 to 22 months later. After controlling for confounding variables, premorbid fatigue score was the only significant predictor for developing chronic fatigue (psychiatric morbidity and physical attribution for fatigue were not risk factors). Of the new chronic fatigue cases, 75% of those who had consulted their general practitioner for fatigue were probable psychiatric cases, whereas only 17% of those who had not consulted their general practitioner were psychiatric cases. Two incident cases of CFS were identified among the new chronic fatigue cases, and two additional long-standing cases of CFS were found among the group that was ill at the time of the first prevalence study (all cases were equally divided between the genders). At an 18-month follow-up interview, the two incident cases of CFS described themselves as having recovered within a year (only one had a psychiatric diagnosis), whereas the two more long-standing prevalence cases both had psychiatric diagnoses and neither had recovered from CFS. Based on that follow-up, Lawrie and associates (1997) estimated the annual incidence of CFS as 370 per 100,000, and the prevalence as 740 per 100,000. This is the only published study of CFS incidence, and the findings suggest that prevalence and incidence data might differ in important ways. Nevertheless, the Lawrie et al. sample was relatively small, and it involved a relatively homogeneous, nonrandom sample in Great Britain. In addition, pediatric cases were not included.

Follow-up studies generally suggest that illness attribution and coping styles are important predictors of long-term outcome in CFS. Wilson and associates (Wilson, Hickie, Lloyd, & Wakefield, 1994) conducted a 3-year follow-up study of patients previously enrolled in a placebo-controlled treatment study. These researchers found that many remained functionally impaired over time. Psychological factors were found to be important determinants of outcome such that participants who cope with distress by somatization (presenting physical rather than psychological symptoms) and discount the possible modulating role of psychosocial factors, are more likely to have an unfavorable outcome.

Russo and colleagues (1998) followed tertiary care clinic patients with chronic fatigue for 2½ years and found that patients whose psychiatric disorders and physical examination signs were still present at follow-up were more likely to have persistent fatigue and work disability. Clark and associates (1995) also followed tertiary care clinic patients and found that the factors that predicted persistent illness in chronic fatigue patients included having more than eight medically unexplained physical symptoms, a lifetime history of dysthymia, a duration of chronic fatigue that was more than 1½ years, less than 16 years of formal education, and age over 38 years. Sharpe and colleagues (Sharpe, Hawton, Seagroatt, & Pasvol, 1992) conducted a follow-up of tertiary care patients 6 weeks to

4 years after an initial clinic visit and similarly found that longer illness duration, belief in a viral cause of the illness, limiting exercise, changing or leaving employment, belonging to a self-help organization, and current emotional disorder predicted greater functional impairment.

Bombardier and Buchwald (1995) compared functional outcomes in patients with chronic fatigue and CFS and found that individuals who met the Holmes et al. (1988) definition of CFS had poorer prognosis than individuals who did not meet CFS criteria. As in the Clark et al. (1995) study, the coexistence of dysthymia predicted poorer outcome across groups. Kroenke, Wood, Mangelsdorff, Meier, and Powell (1988) conducted a one-year follow-up and found that a minority (28%) of CFS patients improved. Consistent with findings of other studies, older patients and individuals with higher scores on a measure of functional impairment had a poorer prognosis at follow-up. Vercoulen and associates (1996) found that improvement in CFS was related to a sense of control over symptoms and to not attributing the illness to physical causes. Reyes et al. (1999) found that those who recovered from CFS were similar demographically to those who remained ill.

Taylor, Jason, and Curie (2002) examined predictors of increased fatigue severity and predictors of continued chronic fatigue status at a follow-up within a random community-based sample of individuals previously evaluated in a prevalence study of chronic fatigue and CFS. Findings revealed that baseline fatigue severity was the only variable that predicted increased fatigue severity at the follow-up in the overall sample of individuals with and without chronic fatigue. In the smaller sample of individuals with chronic fatigue, baseline fatigue severity, worsening of fatigue with physical exertion, and feeling worse for 24 hours or more after exercise significantly predicted continued chronic fatigue status (vs. improvement) at follow-up.

Camacho and Jason (1998) compared individuals who had recovered from CFS with those who had not. Analyses showed no significant differences between groups on measures of optimism, stress, and social support, although a few significant differences were noted on measures of fatigue and coping. Not surprisingly, those who had recovered from CFS had less fatigue and spent less time focusing on symptoms than those who had not recovered. Compared with healthy controls, those who recovered more often used positive reinterpretation and growth strategies of coping. The findings are consistent with what would be expected for persons dealing with a chronic illness.

Despite growing knowledge about long-term predictors of CFS outcome, uncertainty remains regarding the course of CFS and how the syndrome impacts quality of life over time. A review of prospective outcome studies in CFS patients (Joyce, Hotopf, & Wessely, 1997) revealed that a majority of patients report some improvement 1½ to 4 years after initial medical evaluation, although substantial recovery occurs in less than 10% of cases. Also, one-fourth to one-third of CFS patients report worsening illness over time. The summary article by Joyce et al. concluded that psychiatric disorder and patient belief in a physical cause for their symptoms were predictors of poor outcome in every study. However, as Hedrick (1997) noted: "Some studies found no prospective relationships; others found relationships on only one or a few of numerous factors; and different factors were found to be significant in different studies. More importantly, the strength of such relationships is often so low to be of little significance in either understanding the etiology of CFS or guiding its treatment" (p. 724). Thus, several questions remain unanswered regarding the incidence of CFS in a randomly selected, ethnically and socioeconomically diverse urban community population. Significant need for such information highlights the importance of continued study in this area.

SOCIODEMOGRAPHIC CONSIDERATIONS

Several epidemiological studies have highlighted commonalities among individuals with CFS, including greater likelihood of being female, Caucasian, and of higher socioeconomic status (Gunn et al., 1993; Reyes et al., 1997). However, community-based studies involving representative samples of ethnically and socioeconomically diverse populations indicate that the prevalence of CFS is actually higher for Latinos and African Americans than for Caucasians (Jason et al., 1999), and higher for individuals of lower socioeconomic status than for those of higher socioeconomic status (Wessely et al., 1997). Ethnic group differences found in a community sample of patients with CFS indicate that individuals classified as minorities experience significantly more severe symptomatology including sore throats, postexertional malaise, headaches, and unrefreshing sleep than Caucasians, and they additionally report poorer general health status (Jason et al., 2000b). In addition, Latinos who are female, older, and have higher SES report the highest relative severity of fatigue (Song, Jason, & Taylor, 1999). Higher rates of CFS among low-income groups and ethnic minorities may be attributed to psychosocial stress, behavioral risk factors, poor nutrition, inadequate health care, more hazardous occupations, or environmental exposures (Jason et al., 1999).

CFS continues to be more prevalent among women than men (Jason et al., 1999), and there is some evidence to indicate that there are gender-related differences in the impact of CFS as well as in its prevalence. Among a sample of individuals with CFS, women were found to have a higher frequency of fibromyalgia, tender/enlarged lymph nodes, and lower scores on physical functioning. Men had higher frequency of pharyngeal inflammation and a higher lifetime prevalence of alcoholism (Buchwald, Pearlman, Kith, & Schmaling, 1994). Jason and associates (2000b) found that women with CFS had significantly poorer physical functioning, more bodily pain, and poorer emotional role functioning, significantly more severe muscle pain, and significantly more impairment of work activities than men with CFS in a community-based sample. Findings for increased symptom severity and poorer functional outcomes among women may involve certain predisposing vulnerabilities that may be more likely to occur in women than in men. These could include biological factors such as reproductive correlates (Harlow, Signorello, Hall, Dailey, & Komaroff, 1998) and biopsychosocial factors such as stress-associated immune modulation (Glaser & Kiecolt-Glaser, 1998).

SUMMARY AND FUTURE DIRECTIONS

Epidemiological studies of CFS have been conducted in health care samples, physician-identified populations, health care roster populations, and in randomly selected community-based populations (Friedberg & Jason, 1998). The first generation of CFS epidemiological studies relied on referrals from physicians or health facilities. Ethnic minorities living in underserved regions and individuals of lower socioeconomic status, who not only tend to manifest higher levels of chronic illness but also are less likely to receive adequate medical care, were not commonly represented in these earlier studies. This may have led to an underestimation of CFS among minority groups (Richman et al., 1994) and misconceptions about the phenomenology of this syndrome. Studies of the prevalence of CFS in diverse community-based random samples have demonstrated higher prevalence in individuals of Latino and African American identification, and more specific study of the reasons for such differences is recommended.

In addition, there is an imminent need for studies of the incidence and long-term prognosis of CFS in multiethnic, socioeconomically diverse random community-based samples. Moreover, researchers should continue to examine sociodemographic and cross-cultural subgroups of individuals with CFS so that sociocultural correlates of this condition can be examined and understood using rigorous methodologies. Examination of such differences is essential for the proper conceptualization of many illnesses, and failure to examine sociodemographic subtypes with respect to CFS can lead to inappropriate conclusions about the degree to which CFS affects different segments of the population. Ethnicity is a fundamental source of diversity and potential misunderstanding in the biomedical arena (Brown, Ballard, & Gregg, 1994). Ethnic diversity provides important contextual information about CFS that no investigation has yet pursued comprehensively.

REFERENCES

Akerstedt, T., Torsvall, L., & Gillberg, M. (1985). Sleepiness and shift work: Field studies. *Sleep, 5,* S95–S106.

Alisky, J. M., Iczkowski, K. A., & Foti, A. A. (1991). Chronic fatigue syndrome [Letter to the editor]. *American Family Physician, 44,* 56, 61.

Bates, D. W., Schmitt, W., Buchwald, D., Ware, N. C., Lee, J., Thoyer, E., et al. (1993). Prevalence of fatigue and chronic fatigue syndrome in a primary care practice. *Archives of Internal Medicine, 153,* 2759–2765.

Bazelmans, E., Vercoulen, J. H., Swanink, C. M., Fennis, J. F., Galama, J. M., van Weel, C., et al. (1999). Chronic fatigue syndrome and primary fibromyalgia syndrome as recognized by GPs. *Family Practice, 16,* 602–604.

Bell, K. M., Cookfair, D., Bell, D. S., Reese, P., & Cooper, L. (1991). Risk factors associated with chronic fatigue syndrome in a cluster of pediatric cases. *Reviews of Infectious Diseases, 13,* S32–S38.

Bell, D. S., Bell, K. M., & Cheney, P. R. (1994). Primary juvenile fibromyalgia syndrome and chronic fatigue syndrome in adolescents. *Clinical Infectious Diseases, 18,* S21–S23.

Bombardier, C. H., & Buchwald, D. (1995). Outcome and prognosis of patients with chronic fatigue and chronic fatigue syndrome. *Archives of Internal Medicine, 155,* 2105–2110.

Brown, P. J., Ballard, B., & Gregg, J. (1994). Culture, ethnicity, and the practice of medicine. In A. Stoudemire (Ed.), *Human behavior: An introduction for medical students* (2nd ed., pp. 84–104). Philadelphia: Lippincott.

Buchwald, D., Pearlman, T., Kith, P., & Schmaling, K. (1994). Gender differences in patients with chronic fatigue syndrome. *Journal of General Internal Medicine, 9,* 387–401.

Buchwald, D., Umali, P., Umali, J., Kith, P., Pearlman, T., & Komaroff, A. L. (1995). Chronic fatigue and chronic fatigue syndrome: Prevalence in a Pacific Northwest health care system. *Annals of Internal Medicine, 123,* 81–88.

Camacho, J., & Jason, L. A. (1998). Psychosocial factors show little relationship to chronic fatigue syndrome recovery. *Journal of Psychology and the Behavioral Sciences, 12,* 60–70.

Clark, M. R., Katon, W., Russo, J., Kith, P., Sintay, M., & Buchwald, D. (1995). Chronic fatigue: Risk factors for symptom persistence in a two and one-half year follow-up study. *American Journal of Medicine, 98,* 187–195.

Conti, F., Priori, R., DePetrillo, G., Rusconi, A. C., Arpino, C., & Valesini, G. (1994). Prevalence of chronic fatigue syndrome in Italian patients with persistent fatigue. *Annals of Italian Medicine International, 9,* 219–222.

Coulter, P. (1988). Chronic fatigue syndrome; an old virus with a new diagnosis. *Journal of Community Health Nursing, 5,* 87–95.

David, A. S., Pelosi, A., McDonald, E., Stephens, D., Ledger, D., Rathbone, R., et al. (1990). Tired, weak, or in need of rest: Fatigue among general practice attenders. *British Medical Journal, 301,* 1199–1202.

Dobbins, J. G., Randall, B., Reyes, M., Steele, L., Livens, E. A., & Reeves, W. C. (1997). The prevalence of chronic fatiguing illnesses among adolescents in the United States. *Journal of Chronic Fatigue Syndrome, 3,* 15–27.

Euga, R., Chalder, T., Deale, A., & Wessely, S. (1996). A comparison of the characteristics of chronic fatigue syndrome in primary and tertiary care. *British Journal of Psychiatry, 168,* 121–126.

Friedberg, F., & Jason, L. A. (1998). *Understanding chronic fatigue syndrome: An empirical guide to assessment and treatment.* Washington, DC: American Psychological Association.

Fukuda, K., Straus, S. E., Hickie, I., Sharpe, M. C., Dobbins, J. G., & Komaroff, A. (1994). The chronic fatigue syndrome: A comprehensive approach to its definition and study. *Annals of Internal Medicine, 121,* 953–959.

Fukuda, K., Dobbins, J. G., Wilson, L. J., Dunn, R. A., Wilcox, K., & Smallwood, D. (1997). An epidemiologic study of fatigue with relevance for the chronic fatigue syndrome. *Journal of Psychiatric Research, 31,* 19–29.

Glaser, R., & Kiecolt-Glaser, J. K. (1998). Stress-associated immune modulation: Relevance to viral infections and chronic fatigue syndrome. *American Journal of Medicine, 105,* 35–42.

Gunn, W. J., Connell, D. B., & Randall, B. (1993). Epidemiology of chronic fatigue syndrome: The Centers-for-Disease-Control study. In B. R. Bock & J. Whelan (Eds.), *Chronic fatigue syndrome* (pp. 83–101). New York: Wiley.

Harlow, B. L., Signorello, L. B., Hall, J. E., Dailey, C., & Komaroff, A. L. (1998). Reproductive correlates of chronic fatigue syndrome. *American Journal of Medicine, 105,* 94S–99S.

Hedrick, T. E. (1997). Summary of risk factors for chronic fatigue syndrome is misleading [Letter to the editor]. *Quarterly Journal of Medicine, 90,* 723–725.

Hien, D., Matzner, F., First, M., Spitzer, R., Williams, J., & Gibbon, M. (1997). The Structured Clinical Interview for *DSM-IV,* Childhood version (KID-SCID). Washington, DC: American Psychiatric Press.

Holmes, G. P., Kaplan, J. E., Gantz, N. M., Komaroff, A. L., Schonberger, L. B., Straus, S. E., et al. (1988). Chronic fatigue syndrome: A working case definition. *Annals of Internal Medicine, 108,* 387–389.

Ho-Yen, D. O. (1988). The epidemiology of postviral fatigue syndrome. *Scottish Medical Journal, 33,* 368–369.

Ho-Yen, D. O., & McNamara, I. (1991). General practitioners' experience of the chronic fatigue syndrome. *British Journal of General Practice, 41,* 324–326.

Jason, L. A., Richman, J. A., Rademaker, A. W., Jordan, K. M., Plioplys, A. V., Taylor, R., et al. (1999). A community-based study of chronic fatigue syndrome. *Archives of Internal Medicine, 159,* 2129–2137.

Jason, L. A., Taylor, S. L., Johnson, S., Goldston, S. E., Salina, D., Bishop, P., et al. (1993). Prevalence of chronic fatigue syndrome-related symptoms among nurses. *Evaluation and the Health Professions, 16,* 385–399.

Jason, L. A., Taylor, R., Wagner, L., Holden, J., Ferrari, J. R., Plioplys, A. V., et al. (1995). Estimating rates of chronic fatigue syndrome from a community based sample: A pilot study. *American Journal of Community Psychology, 23,* 557–568.

Jason, L. A., Taylor, R. R., Kennedy, C. L., Jordan, K., Song, S., Johnson, D., et al. (2000a). Chronic fatigue syndrome: Occupation, medical utilization, and subtypes in a community based sample. *Journal of Nervous and Mental Diseases, 188,* 568–576.

Jason, L. A., Taylor, R. R., Kennedy, C. L., Jordan, K., Song, S., Johnson, D., et al. (2000b). Chronic fatigue syndrome: Sociodemographic subtypes in a community-based sample. *Evaluation and the Health Professions, 23,* 243–263.

Jason, L. A., & Wagner, L. I. (1998). Estimating the prevalence of chronic fatigue syndrome among nurses. *American Journal of Nursing, 105,* 91S–93S.

Jason, L. A., Wagner, L., Taylor, R., Ropacki, M. T., Shlaes, J., Ferrari, J. R., et al. (1995). Chronic fatigue syndrome: A new challenge for health care professionals. *Journal of Community Psychology, 23,* 143–164.

Jordan, K. M., Mears, C. J., Katz, B. Z., Jason, L. A., Rademaker, A., Huang, C., et al. (2001). *Prevalence of pediatric chronic fatigue syndrome in a community-based sample.* Manuscript submitted for publication.

Joyce, J., Hotopf, M., & Wessely, S. (1997). The prognosis of chronic fatigue and chronic fatigue syndrome: A systematic review. *Quarterly Journal of Medicine, 90,* 223–233.

Kawakami, N., Iwata, N., Fujihara, S., & Kitamura, T. (1998). Prevalence of chronic fatigue syndrome in a community population in Japan. *Tohoku Journal of Experimental Medicine, 186,* 33–41.

Kroenke, K., Wood, D., Mangelsdorff, D., Meier, N., & Powell, J. (1988). Chronic fatigue in primary care: Prevalence, patient characteristics and outcome. *Journal of the American Medical Association, 260,* 929–934.

Lawrie, S. M., Manders, D. N., Geddes, J. R., & Pelosi, A. J. (1997). A population-based incidence study of chronic fatigue. *Psychological Medicine, 27,* 343–353.

Lawrie, S. M., & Pelosi, A. J. (1995). Chronic fatigue syndrome in the community: Prevalence and associations. *British Journal of Psychiatry, 166,* 793–797.

Leese, G., Chattington, P., Fraser, W., Vora, J., Edwards, R., & Williams, G. (1996). Short-term night-shift working mimics the pituitary-adrenocortical dysfunction in chronic fatigue syndrome. *Journal of Clinical Endocrinological Metabolisim, 81*(5), 1867–1870.

Levine, P. H. (1994). Epidemic neuromyasthenia and chronic fatigue syndrome: Epidemiological importance of a cluster definition. *Clinical Infectious Diseases, 18,* S16–S20.

Levine, P. H. (1997). Epidemiologic advances in chronic fatigue syndrome. *Journal of Psychiatric Research, 31,* 7–18.

Levine, P. H., Snow, P. G., Ranum, B. A., Paul, C., & Holmes, M. J. (1997). Epidemic neuromyasthenia and chronic fatigue syndrome in West Otago, New Zealand: A 10-year follow-up. *Archives of Internal Medicine, 14,* 750–754.

Lloyd, A. R., Hickie, I., Boughton, C. R., Spencer, O., & Wakefield, D. (1990). Prevalence of chronic fatigue syndrome in an Australian population. *Medical Journal of Australia, 153,* 522–528.

McDonald, E., David, A. S., Pelosi, A. J., & Mann, A. H. (1993). Chronic fatigue in primary care attenders. *Psychological Medicine, 23,* 987–998.

Mechanic, D. (1983). The experience and expression of distress: The study of illness behavior and medical utilization. In D. Mechanic (Ed.), *Handbook of health care and the health professions* (pp. 591–607). New York: Free Press.

Minowa, M., & Jiamo, M. (1996). Descriptive epidemiology of chronic fatigue syndrome based on a nationwide survey in Japan. *Journal of Epidemiology, 6,* 75–80.

Pawlikowska, T., Chalder, T., Wessely, S., Wright, D., Hirsch, S., & Wallace, P. (1994). A population based study of fatigue and psychological distress. *British Medical Journal, 308,* 763–766.

Price, R. K., North, C. S., Wessely, S., & Fraser, V. J. (1992). Estimating the prevalence of chronic fatigue syndrome and associated symptoms in the community. *Public Health Reports, 107*(5), S14–S21.

Ramsay, M. (1986). *Postviral fatigue syndrome: The saga of royal free disease.* London: Gower Medical.

Reyes, M., Gary, H. E., Jr., Dobbins, J. G., Randall, B., Steele, L., Fukuda, K., et al. (1997, February 21). Descriptive epidemiology of chronic fatigue syndrome: CDC surveillance in four cities. *Morbidity and Mortality Weekly Report Surveillance Summaries, 46*(No. SS-2), 1–13.

Reyes, M., Nisenbaum, R., Stewart, G., & Reeves, W. C. (1998, October) Update: Wichita population-based study of fatiguing illness. In L. A. Jason & W. Reeves (Chairpersons), *New insights into the epidemiology of CFS.* Symposium presented at the American Association for Chronic Fatigue Syndrome Conference, Cambridge, MA.

Reyes, M., Dobbins, J. G., Nisenbaum, R., Subedar, N., Randall, B., & Reeves, W. C. (1999). Chronic fatigue syndrome progression and self-defined recovery: Evidence from the CDC surveillance system. *Journal of Chronic Fatigue Syndrome, 5,* 17–27.

Richman, J. A., Flaherty, J. A., & Rospenda, K. M. (1994). Risk factors for chronic fatigue syndrome: Flawed assumptions derived from treatment-based studies? *American Journal of Public Health, 84,* 282–284.

Russo, J., Katon, W., Clark, M., Kith, P., Sintay, M., & Buchwald, D. (1998). Longitudinal changes associated with improvement in chronic fatigue patients. *Journal of Psychosomatic Research, 45,* 67–76.

Sharpe, M. C., Archard, L. C., Banatvala, J. E., Borysiewicz, L. K., Clare, A. W., David, A., et al. (1991). A report-chronic fatigue syndrome: Guidelines for research. *Journal of the Royal Society of Medicine, 84,* 118–121.

Sharpe, M., Hawton, K., Seagroatt, V., & Pasvol, G. (1992). Follow up of patients presenting with fatigue to an infectious diseases clinic. *British Medical Journal, 305,* 147–152.

Shefer, A., Dobbins, J. G., Fukuda, K., Steele, L., Koo, D., Nisenbaum, R., et al. (1997). Fatiguing illness among employees in three large state office buildings, California, 1993, was there an outbreak? *Journal of Psychiatric Research, 31,* 31–43.

Song, S., Jason, L. A., & Taylor, R. R. (1999). The relationship between ethnicity and fatigue in a community-based sample. *Journal of Gender, Culture, and Health, 4,* 255–268.

Steele, L., Dobbins, J. G., Fukuda, K., Reyes, M., Randall, B., Koppelman, M., et al. (1998). The epidemiology of chronic fatigue in San Francisco. *American Journal of Medicine, 105,* 83S–90S.

Taylor, R. R., Jason, L. A., & Curie, C. J. (2002). A follow-up study of a community-based sample with chronic fatigue. *Psychosomatic Medicine, 64,* 319–327.

Vercoulen, J. H., Swanink, C. M., Fennis, J. F., Galama, J. M., van der Meer, J. W., & Bleijenberg, G. (1996). Prognosis in chronic fatigue syndrome: A prospective study on the natural course. *Journal of Neurology, Neurosurgery, and Psychiatry, 60,* 489–494.

Ward, M. H., DeLisle, H., Shores, J. H., Slocum, P. C., & Foresman, B. H. (1996). Chronic fatigue complaints in primary care: Incidence and diagnostic patterns. *Journal of the American Osteopathic Association, 96*, 34–46.

Wessely, S. (1995). The epidemiology of chronic fatigue syndrome. *Epidemiologic Reviews, 17*, 139–151.

Wessely, S., Chalder, T., Hirsch, S., Wallace, P., & Wright, D. (1996). Psychological symptoms, somatic symptoms, and psychiatric disorder in chronic fatigue and chronic fatigue syndrome: A prospective study in the primary care setting. *American Journal of Psychiatry, 153*, 1050–1059.

Wessely, S., Chalder, T., Hirsch, S., Wallace, P., & Wright, D. (1997). The prevalence and morbidity of chronic fatigue and chronic fatigue syndrome: A prospective primary care study. *American Journal of Public Health, 87*, 1449–1455.

Wessely, S., Chalder, T., Hirsch, S., Pawlikowska, T., Wallace, P., & Wright, D. J.M. (1995). Postinfectious fatigue: Prospective cohort study in primary care. *Lancet, 345*, 1333–1338.

Wessely, S., Hotopf, M., & Sharpe, M. (1998). The nature and extent of fatigue. In *Chronic fatigue and its syndromes* (pp. 1–92). Oxford, England: Oxford University Press.

White, P. D., Thomas, J. M., Amess, J., Crawford, D. H., Grover, S. A., Kangro, H. O., et al. (1998). Incidence, risk, and prognosis of acute chronic fatigue syndromes and psychiatric disorders after glandular fever. *British Journal of Psychiatry, 173*, 475–481.

Wilson, A., Hickie, I., Lloyd, A., & Wakefield, D. (1994). The treatment of chronic fatigue syndrome: Science and speculation. *American Journal of Medicine, 96*, 544–550.

CHAPTER 2

Differential Diagnosis in Medical Assessment

AUDRIUS V. PLIOPLYS

C HRONIC FATIGUE SYNDROME (CFS) is often misunderstood. Indeed, many physicians doubt its existence. It does exist, however; and it can have a devastating impact, as patients who were formerly active and fully employed may become virtually bedridden and unable to work.

The syndrome has a long medical history. Over the years, it has had numerous other names including chronic Epstein-Barr virus syndrome, chronic mononucleosis syndrome, postviral fatigue syndrome, and epidemic myalgic encephalomyelitis. Sir Richard Manningham, in 1750, reported patients who had symptoms of "listlessness with great lassitude and weariness all over the body." In 1869, Dr. George Miller Beard proposed the term *neurasthenia*. Every century has contributed new symptoms, names, and diagnostic criteria for this debilitating illness, but its etiology and pathogenesis are still unknown. In 1988, the case definition of CFS was first introduced by the Centers for Disease Control ([CDC]; Holmes et al., 1988). Since then, investigators all over the world, but especially in Australia and Great Britain, have made numerous attempts to better define CFS (Lloyd, Hickie, Boughton, Spencer, & Wakefield, 1990; Sharpe et al., 1991). More recently, the CDC, the National Institutes of Health (NIH), and the International Chronic Fatigue Syndrome Study Group proposed new diagnostic criteria (Fukuda et al., 1994). The 1994 revised criteria for the diagnosis of CFS are presented in Table 2.1.

CFS is characterized by the sudden onset of debilitating fatigue together with symptoms such as fever, sore throat, painful lymph nodes, weakness, muscle aches, headaches, depression, sleep disturbance, memory difficulties, and confusion. These symptoms can persist from 6 months to many years and can dramatically reduce the patient's quality of life. Since the primary symptoms are muscular fatigue and pain, along with symptoms of encephalopathy (lethargy and cognitive difficulties), it has been proposed that CFS be renamed myalgic encephalopathy (S. Plioplys & Plioplys, 1995).

Table 2.1
Revised Criteria for the Diagnosis of Chronic Fatigue Syndrome by the
Centers for Disease Control, the National Institutes of Health, and
the International Chronic Fatigue Syndrome Study Group

Major Criteria

1. Unexplained, persistent, or relapsing chronic fatigue that is of new or definite onset (not lifelong).
2. Fatigue is not due to ongoing exertion.
3. Fatigue is not substantially alleviated by rest.
4. Fatigue results in substantial reduction in previous levels of occupational, educational, social, or personal activities.

Additional Symptoms

1. Self-reported impairment in short-term memory or concentration severe enough to cause substantial reduction in previous levels of occupational, educational, social, or personal activities.
2. Sore throat.
3. Tender cervical or axillary lymph nodes.
4. Muscle pain.
5. Multijoint pain without joint swelling or redness.
6. Headaches of a new type, pattern, or severity.
7. Unrefreshing sleep.
8. Postexertional malaise lasting more than 24 hours.

Source: "The Chronic Fatigue Syndrome: A Comprehensive Approach to Its Definition and Study," by K. Fukuda et al., 1994, *Annals of Internal Medicine, 121,* pp. 953–959.

Note: A case of CFS must fulfill all the major criteria, plus 4 or more of the additional symptoms. Each additional symptom must have persisted or recurred during 6 or more consecutive months of illness and must not have predated the fatigue. A patient who does not fully meet the CFS criteria may be diagnosed as having Idiopathic Chronic Fatigue.

CFS affects mainly young and middle-aged adults. The most common age for onset is between 20 and 40 years. The female-to-male ratio is 2 or 3:1. The mean time to recovery, when it occurs, is about 2 years, but a review of follow-up studies showed full recovery for less than 10% of CFS patients (Joyce, Hotopf, & Wessely, 1997). All socioeconomic groups are represented, and the majority of patients are women, minority groups, and persons with lower levels of education and occupational status (Jason et al., 1999). Based on our epidemiological study results, the prevalence of CFS in the United States is 422 per 100,000 (Jason et al., 1999).

CLINICAL MANIFESTATIONS

Doubt and misunderstanding about CFS are fueled in part by the range of its clinical manifestations. One must remember that CFS is not a disease but a syndrome. A disease is a discrete pathogenic process, usually with clearly defined diagnostic procedures and treatments. In contrast, a syndrome may have multiple etiologies producing a similar, but variable, symptom complex.

Variability in CFS begins with its onset. In our clinical experience, CFS develops acutely in about 75% of cases. In the other 25%, the onset is gradual, or the patient may have intermittent episodes that eventually become chronic (A. V. Plioplys & Plioplys, 1997). Typically, a previously healthy patient experiences an acute flu-like illness; the fever subsides, but the fatigue and muscle and joint symptoms continue. Cases typically occur in isolation, but there are reports of clusters in which several patients have developed chronic fatigue after the same viral illness (Holmes et al., 1987). However, CFS is not virus-specific and may follow infection with any number of viruses that cause a flu-like illness.

Abnormal immune system activation appears to be the central event in CFS. Although we do not have specific markers for CFS, subtle abnormalities in cell-mediated and humoral immunity have been detected in affected patients (S. Plioplys & Plioplys, 1995). The abnormalities often vary from study to study, but taken together, they support the notion of immune dysregulation. If the mechanism of CFS involves a continuing immune response to an initial viral infection, the production of cytokines, including interferons and interleukins, may cause some of the symptoms. These immune mediators can cause muscle and central nervous system (CNS) symptoms, including fatigue.

Fatigue is, of course, a daily occurrence in almost everyone's life. It has normal variations; some people experience more fatigue than others or react to fatigue more negatively. In addition, fatigue is a prominent feature in many medical conditions. The major diagnostic criteria shown in Table 2.1 are intended to differentiate the fatigue of CFS from that of other conditions.

The first major criterion is that the fatigue cannot have been a lifelong condition. The second is that it is not caused by overwork. We have seen patients who had two or three jobs, got very little sleep at night, and were chronically tired. That is not CFS; it is sleep deprivation.

The third major criterion is that rest does not significantly alleviate the fatigue. Patients with chronic fatigue can sleep undisturbed through the night, yet wake up feeling just as tired as when they went to bed. During the day, they can nap for two to three hours at a stretch, but feel no better on awakening.

The fourth major criterion is that the fatigue must have resulted in a substantial reduction in previous levels of occupational, educational, social, or personal activities.

The additional symptom criteria (Fukuda et al., 1994) focus on characteristic clinical features of CFS that the physician should specifically ask about when taking the history. For example, the fatigue may affect mental as well as physical functioning. In our clinical experience, over 90% of CFS patients have cognitive deficits, most often affecting memory and concentration. Another characteristic feature is postexertional fatigue. When patients with CFS overexert themselves, they often experience two to three days of such extreme fatigue that they are bedridden.

ADDITIONAL SYMPTOM CRITERIA

Besides having to meet all of the four major criteria, the patient must meet four of the eight additional symptom criteria listed in Table 2.1 for the diagnosis of CFS (Fukuda et al., 1994). In our clinical CFS practice, the most common additional symptoms have been memory and concentration difficulties, unrefreshing sleep, and postexertional malaise.

DIFFERENTIAL DIAGNOSIS

Table 2.2 lists medical illnesses for the differential diagnosis of CFS (Komaroff, 1994). These illnesses must be considered by the physician during the initial and subsequent medical evaluations of the CFS patient. Although each of these diseases may produce chronic fatigue, this is not a list of exclusionary criteria. Also, this list is not exhaustive. Many other, albeit rare, medical conditions may also produce chronic fatigue.

CLINICAL HISTORY

In evaluating someone with fatigue symptoms, besides reviewing the diagnostic criteria for CFS (Table 2.1), the physician must obtain a thorough medical history. It is essential to try to identify a medical, psychological, or environmental cause for the fatigue, which then can be appropriately addressed. Alcohol or other substance

Table 2.2
Differential Diagnosis of Chronic Fatigue Syndrome

Endocrine	**Hematologic**
Hypothyroidism	Anemia
Diabetes	Lymphoma
Addison's disease	
Cushing's disease	**Metabolic**
	Hypokalemia
Rheumatological	Hypomagnesemia
Systemic lupus erythematosus	Hyponatremia
Rheumatoid arthritis	Hypercalcemia
Fibromyalgia	
Sjogren's syndrome	**Psychiatric**
Polymyalgia rheumatica	Depression
Polymyositis	Psychosis
Neurological	**Other**
Sleep disorders	Chronic illness (cardiac, hepatic,
Multiple sclerosis	pulmonary, renal)
Myasthenia gravis	Chronic pain
	Medication side effects (e.g., beta-
Infectious	blockers)
Lyme disease	Alcohol or other substance abuse
Human immunodeficiency virus infection	Heavy-metal toxicity
Chronic hepatitis B and C infection	Occult malignancy
Fungal disease	Sarcoidosis
Tuberculosis	
Subacute bacterial endocarditis	

Modified from "Clinical Presentation of Chronic Fatigue Syndrome," by A. L. Komaroff, 1994, in S. E. Straus (Ed.), *Chronic Fatigue Syndrome*, pp. 61–84, New York: Marcel Dekker.

Note: This is a list of illnesses that must be considered by the physician during the initial and subsequent medical evaluations of the CFS patient. This is not a list of exclusionary criteria. Please note that this list is not exhaustive.

abuse, prescription and over-the-counter medication intake, and food supplements used must be carefully reviewed. Questioning about past medical and psychiatric history is necessary, as is a review of the medical and psychiatric histories of relatives. This section includes a discussion of several clinical topics that have frequently come up in clinical practice at the CFS Research Center.

Depression

Many physicians think that CFS is a psychiatric disorder—in particular, a depression. It is true that most depressed patients are tired, some significantly so, and fatigue is one of the diagnostic criteria for major depression. Depression is also common in CFS, but it is a consequence of the disorder rather than intrinsic to it. Patients with CFS become depressed because of the limitations the illness imposes on their lives. On the other hand, 25% to 40% of patients with CFS do not have depression or another psychiatric disorder (Kruesi, Dale, & Straus, 1989).

Often direct questioning can enable distinguishing between the two conditions. We simply ask the patient, "What is the primary problem? Is the fatigue making you depressed or is the depression making you tired?" Most patients—perhaps 85%—will easily choose one or the other. For patients who are unsure, other aspects of the history can provide the answer.

In the history, the chronology of events can often provide the distinction. A typical history of CFS shows this pattern: "This illness came on, I became unable to work and I lost my job, and now I'm depressed about my situation in life." In a depressed patient, the events often follow a different order: A stressful event occurred—often a major loss, such as a divorce, death of a relative, or loss of a job—followed by the onset of fatigue and other depressive symptoms.

Further, the CFS patient and the depressed patient describe their conditions in different terms. Depressed patients explain their lack of physical activity in terms of motivation: "I'm not interested" or "I don't care." Patients with CFS speak in terms of physical impediment: "I want to, but I can't."

Tolerance of physical activity is another diagnostic clue. In CFS, too much physical activity exacerbates the condition. In depression, physical activity improves the sense of well-being.

Sleep patterns in the two disorders also are different. In our CFS clinical experience, once asleep, patients with CFS generally sleep through the night. Depressed patients typically wake up early in the morning and cannot fall asleep again.

The final distinction is the response to antidepressant medication. In patients with endogenous depression, the agents can produce significant improvement, whereas patients with CFS show minimal improvement. We would stress, however, that antidepressants should not be used to differentiate the two conditions. Antidepressant therapy may be appropriate in CFS, but only to provide symptomatic relief of secondary depression.

Sleep Disorders

Specific questions should be directed toward uncovering sleep disorders—especially obstructive sleep apnea and narcolepsy, which may be confused with CFS. The physician should consider disorders that can disrupt sleep and lead to sleep deprivation, such as restless legs syndrome. Environmental factors may also be involved: A crying infant, traffic, or other noises can interfere with sleep, or the patient may be working nights and find it difficult to sleep during the day. Patients with urinary or gastrointestinal tract illnesses may wake up repeatedly during the night to use the bathroom. Their sleep would be fragmented and ineffective, thus producing daytime fatigue.

Inquiries should be made about snoring, which is a characteristic of obstructive sleep apnea syndrome. Narcolepsy is classically accompanied by sleep paralysis, hypnagogic or hypnopompic hallucinations, and cataplexy. When patients have restless legs syndrome, the bed partner often can attest to how much kicking occurs during sleep (and may in turn suffer fragmented sleep and fatigue). Each of these fully treatable, specific sleep disorders can lead to chronic fatigue and would thus exclude the diagnosis of CFS.

A sleep inventory, which should be taken in every patient with possible CFS, can include these questions. Other items in the inventory are the hours of sleep patients get each night, the naps taken during the day, and sleep quality (do they sleep deeply; is the sleep restorative). If aspects of the history suggest a sleep disorder, the patient should be referred to a polysomnography laboratory for a formal sleep study.

MEDICATIONS

The history should include a review of all medications the patient is taking, since fatigue is a recognized side effect of various agents. Patients who are taken off beta-blockers, for example, may suddenly become much more energetic.

PHYSICAL EXAMINATION

Because CFS is largely a diagnosis of exclusion, the physician must consider the possibility of other medical conditions. Therefore, the physical examination must be very thorough. In general terms, almost all CFS patients that we have seen have had normal physical examination findings. Thus, any abnormalities detected during this step of the evaluation must be carefully and thoroughly evaluated. An exclusionary criterion that is readily detected at the start of the physical examination is that the body mass index must be less than 45 (Fukuda et al., 1994). The reason is that severe obesity itself can be a cause of chronic fatigue, and we agree with this exclusionary criterion. In actual clinical practice, we have never seen a case for evaluation of CFS who fit into this exclusionary category.

Particular attention must be placed on the physical examination when an aspect of the patient's history is not typical for CFS. For example, we have seen patients who are older than usual for CFS—in their late 50s or early 60s—who complained of progressive fatigue, both with mental and physical activity becoming increasingly difficult. On physical examination, they had increased muscle tone and a blank facial expression. Their diagnosis was Parkinson's disease. We have also seen a patient in her early 20s, which is somewhat young for CFS. Physical examination disclosed ataxia and lower extremity hyperreflexia. An MRI (magnetic resonance image) of the brain showed plaques compatible with multiple sclerosis. Fatigue can be the presenting complaint in multiple sclerosis and may become more debilitating than the neurological impairment.

Neurally Mediated Hypotension

There have been reports that patients with CFS may have neurally mediated hypotension, a condition in which blood pressure may drop with standing. Treatments include mineralocorticoids, beta-blockers, and increased dietary sodium. Using identical tilt-table protocols (Bou-Holaigah, Rowe, Kan, & Calkins, 1995), we have not been able to reproduce these results in 10 investigated CFS patients.

Some autonomic nervous system disorders, such as idiopathic orthostatic hypotension and the Shy-Drager syndrome, involve abnormal blood pressure regulation and often produce severe fatigue. These disorders respond to the pharmacological treatments used for neurally mediated hypotension. Although patients with autonomic nervous system disorders might present first at a CFS center, that would be an extremely rare phenomenon. In our clinical experience with over 300 referred CFS cases, we have not identified a single patient who had an autonomic nervous system disorder. Thus, this disease process most likely will account for less than 1% of CFS cases.

It is likely that most of the patients described as having neurally mediated hypotension actually have chronic intravascular volume depletion. It is most probable that the individuals studied have been involved in long-standing food faddism (e.g., sodium restriction because "salt is bad for you"), and the resulting volume contraction is exacerbated by a warm climate. Evidence to support this hypothesis is an epidemiological study of CFS in England, in which in adjoining areas, there was a 10-fold greater incidence of CFS in an affluent community, as opposed to a lower income community. It is likely that in the lower income community, food high in salt content was not restricted (A. V. Plioplys, 1999).

In many cases, there is the compounding difficulty of antidepressant use, which can directly affect autonomic nervous system functioning. The treatments proposed, mineralocorticoids, have long-term complications including osteoporosis, diabetes, increased susceptibility to infections, and cataracts. The other commonly used category of medicine, beta-blockers, likewise can have significant side effects including depression and fatigue. One of our young CFS patients who started taking beta-blockers for neurally mediated hypotension, against our medical advice, lapsed into severe depression and tried to commit suicide. These proposed pharmacological treatments can be dangerous.

A recent report by the authors who first reported neurally mediated hypotension is of considerable concern (Rowe et al., 2001). In this study of 100 CFS patients with neurally mediated hypotension, fludrocortisone acetate improved function in only 14% of cases, whereas placebo improved function in 10% of cases—a result that was not statistically significant. This result of a treatment failure in the hands of the primary authors who described this condition strongly argues against the role of neurally mediated hypotension as causing CFS symptoms.

Laboratory Studies

The standard laboratory workup that we have used in all cases seen for CFS includes a complete blood count, a comprehensive serum metabolic panel (including glucose, electrolytes, calcium, liver function tests, renal function tests), magnesium, thyroid function tests, erythrocyte sedimentation rate, rheumatoid factor, antinuclear antibody titer, urinalysis, and an intermediate-strength purified protein derivative. We have also performed serum carnitine levels (total, free, and acyl) because carnitine deficiency conditions may produce chronic fatigue (A. V. Plioplys & Plioplys, 1995; A. V. Plioplys & Plioplys, 1997). Although this screening panel is slightly broader than that currently recommended (Fukuda et al., 1994; Schluederberg et al., 1992), these tests are all essential. If any of the screening tests are abnormal, then additional investigations should be done as necessary.

The performance of more than just the basic laboratory studies depends on the history and physical examination. We have routinely tested for HIV and hepatitis B infections (with an assay for hepatitis B surface antigen). However, in over 300 evaluations, we have yet to have a positive result. One can reasonably argue that these two tests should only be ordered for those patients who have risk factors for these infections. We measure antibody titers for Lyme disease in patients who have a history of possible exposure to ticks, since chronic fatigue can be a symptom of this disease. Sleep studies are appropriate if a primary sleep disorder is suspected; an MRI head scan may be necessary in selected cases. We performed a tilt-table test looking for neurally mediated hypotension in 10 CFS cases and obtained normal results in all. We had used an identical protocol to that previously described (Bou-Holaigah et al., 1995). Instead of doing an expensive tilt-table test, an excellent, and totally free, screening procedure is to check orthostatic blood pressures during the initial physical examination. The blood pressure and pulse are checked with the patient lying down, then while sitting up, and finally while standing. If there is a significant drop in blood pressure, further cardiovascular investigations may be warranted.

REVIEW OF EXCLUSIONARY CRITERIA

In the revised criteria for the diagnosis of CFS (Fukuda et al., 1994), in the section dealing with conditions that would exclude the diagnosis of CFS, the first exclusionary condition is "any active medical condition that may explain the presence of chronic fatigue, such as untreated hypothyroidism, sleep apnea, and narcolepsy, and iatrogenic conditions such as side effects of medication." We fully agree with this statement.

In clinical practice, it is important to use good clinical judgment, based on clinical experience, in deciding whether an illness is the cause of the fatigue, or whether it is simply an incidental illness that is not contributing to fatigue. In the revised criteria for the diagnosis of CFS (Fukuda et al., 1994), the second exclusionary condition is "any previously diagnosed medical condition whose resolution has not been documented beyond reasonable clinical doubt and whose continued activity may explain the chronic fatiguing illness. Such conditions may include previously treated malignancies and unresolved cases of hepatitis B or C virus infection." Furthermore, Fukuda et al. clarified the issue of previous medical illnesses; once adequately treated and documented as such with laboratory tests (such as hypothyroidism and asthma), they should not exclude the diagnosis of CFS. Furthermore, illnesses such as Lyme disease or syphilis that have been fully treated should not exclude the subsequent development and diagnosis of CFS. We fully agree with all of these statements.

The difficulty with the exclusionary criteria as presented by Fukuda et al. (1994) occurs in the sections dealing with psychiatric diagnosis and substance abuse.

PSYCHIATRIC DIAGNOSES

Active serious psychiatric illnesses, including major depressive disorder with psychotic or melancholic features, bipolar disorder, schizophrenia, delusional disorders, anorexia nervosa, or bulimia nervosa can be associated with significant fatigue and should exclude the diagnosis of CFS. However, the exclusionary requirement that "any past" significant psychiatric condition should exclude the diagnosis of CFS is extreme. We have seen many patients who had an episode of significant depression, years or decades previously, who then came down with a classic history and picture of CFS. In these cases, the psychiatric historical illness should be considered in the same way as a medical illness. Once a medical illness is fully resolved, it then cannot account for fatigue and should not exclude the diagnosis of CFS. Similarly, once psychiatric illnesses are fully resolved, according to the clinician's best clinical judgment, they should not exclude the diagnosis of CFS.

For research purposes, psychiatric past histories and current comorbid psychiatric conditions should be closely documented and tracked to enable analyzing subsets of CFS patients separately in doing data analysis. For example, in CFS patients without comorbid psychiatric histories, there is a significant association with abnormal brain MRI scan findings, but not in CFS patients with psychiatric histories (Lange et al., 1999).

SUBSTANCE ABUSE

Active alcohol or substance abuse can produce fatigue and should exclude the diagnosis of CFS.

Obtaining accurate information from the patient can be a major problem for the clinician. Chronic alcoholics will uniformly significantly underestimate and underreport the amount of alcohol they consume. Individuals who abuse illegal substances may not report this activity for fear that the medical record may be used for criminal prosecution against them. If the clinician has not received information about the substance abuse taking place, then naturally the diagnosis of CFS is not going to be excluded on this basis.

However, the way this exclusionary criterion is worded is of concern (Fukuda et al., 1994). The stated substance abuse issue would exclude the diagnosis of CFS if it occurred 2 years before the onset of CFS symptoms, or at any time after the onset. We have seen patients who reported various degrees of substance abuse that had occurred and had been fully resolved well before the onset of CFS symptoms, but not outside the 2-year window. In these cases, we used the diagnosis of CFS since the issue of substance abuse appeared to have been medically fully resolved. Furthermore, we have seen cases of classic CFS where the patients, during their CFS illness, would occasionally abuse substances. In these cases, our own best clinical judgment was that they indeed had CFS, and the substance abuse was not causing fatigue.

Incidentally, the exclusionary criteria (Fukuda et al., 1994) do not include a definition of what constitutes substance abuse. Although criteria for alcohol and other substance abuse have been defined within the psychiatry community (American Psychiatric Association [APA], 1994), in actual medical practice, these criteria are seldom, if ever, used. I have frequently seen patients diagnosed with alcoholism who would drink only one or two glasses of wine a day. If alcohol or other substance use (not abuse) takes place in low dosages or infrequently, then this should not exclude the diagnosis of CFS.

Thus, substance abuse should be equivalent to a medical illness—once the problem has been resolved, it cannot further produce fatigue and should not exclude the diagnosis of CFS. However, the clinician should be ever vigilant for significant underreporting and active denying of this problem.

CFS IN CHILDREN

The issue of diagnosing CFS in children has been raised (Bell, 1995). If CFS were a distinct disease process, there is no a priori reason why it should not occur in younger individuals. Diagnosing CFS in adolescents may not be difficult. The same criteria used in adults may be applied, or simply modified. Defining CFS in children less than 13 years of age is an entirely different problem (A. V. Plioplys, 1997).

The clinical manifestations of fatigue in younger individuals are extremely different from those seen in adults. In young children, fatigue-producing diseases most commonly manifest paradoxical symptoms. Sleep deprivation and the sedative effect of phenobarbital, when used for epilepsy, do not produce the fatigue that is seen in adults. Instead, they produce inattention, hyperactivity, and behavioral disorders.

Fatigue is a nonspecific symptom that can arise from varied medical conditions. There are many more diseases with the potential to produce fatigue in young children than in adults. Categories of additional illnesses that need to be considered include central nervous system (CNS) infections (acute or chronic), degenerative CNS disorders, genetic-metabolic disorders, CNS space-occupying lesions, convulsive disorders, myopathies, neuropathies, and mitochondrial disorders. It would be impossible to arrive at an exclusionary list of possibilities. It would also be impossible to define a recommended minimal list of diagnostic procedures that should be performed to rule out fatigue-causing diseases, as has been done in adults (Fukuda et al., 1994). In addition, psychiatric processes may produce chronic fatigue. Besides depression, anxiety disorders, and somatization disorder—which occur in adults—school phobia, parental pressure, and dysfunctional family dynamics are among the possibilities in children.

It is paramount not to miss diagnoses of childhood neurological diseases because there are many treatable conditions. Also, among those that are incurable, many inherited diseases may recur in subsequent pregnancies or in other family members. In these cases, knowledge of the disease is important for family genetic counseling.

For the past 10 years, the author has provided all of the child neurology consultation services to a managed care program serving approximately 200,000 members in the Chicago area. Although many children and adolescents were referred with fatigue symptomatology, in all cases a medical or psychological explanation for the fatigue was found.

In the CFS Research Center, we have seen and evaluated over 300 referred patients. There were no referred children and only six adolescents. In each of the adolescent cases, the patient showed tremendous belligerence to the medical history and physical examination and did not comply with recommended diagnostic tests or with suggested treatment programs. The impression of these adolescents was that their basic problem lay in a psychological disturbance, probably in relation to familial dynamics.

There is no urgency to label a younger individual with CFS, since there is no specific treatment for this condition. However, diagnosing CFS in children may lead to (1) a delay in the diagnosis of a treatable medical disease; (2) termination of investigations for rare or novel conditions that may respond to novel therapies (such as the treatment of lethargy in children with chronic neurological handicaps and Rett's syndrome [A. V. Plioplys, Bagherpour, & Kasnicka, 1994; A. V. Plioplys & Kasnicka, 1993]); (3) failure to detect psychological or familial difficulties that may lead to fatigue; (4) the development of a lifelong disability lifestyle in the patient and family.

Financial pressures should be a serious consideration in making medical choices. Managed care organizations are trying to decrease the amount spent on medical evaluations and medicines. Once a label of CFS is applied, these organizations may refuse to pay for even the most basic laboratory investigations. This problem is particularly acute in childhood where more extensive, and expensive, initial evaluation procedures may be clinically necessary.

Caution is necessary when diagnosing CFS in adolescents. A condition that has received much publicity is neurally mediated hypotension (discussed earlier). Claims have been made that up to 95% of CFS patients suffer from it. The treatment of neurally mediated hypotension includes the use of fludrocortisone and beta-blockers (Bou-Holaigah et al., 1995). The most likely explanation for postural hypotension in adolescents is that they are simply fluid and electrolyte depleted and develop fatigue as a secondary symptom. This is not an inconsequential problem since these adolescents are being subjected to all of the potential complications of long-term mineralocorticoid use. Furthermore, a recent study (Rowe et al., 2001) reported no significant benefit from using fludrocortisone in the treatment of this condition.

Despite all of the arguments cautioning against the use of the diagnostic term CFS in childhood, the number of reported cases seems to escalate and the number of published articles on the subject expands. In certain pediatric circles, the diagnosis of CFS has become epidemic (not the illness—but the overuse of the term). The entire subject has become surrounded by a degree of fanaticism. This emotional commitment to the diagnosis of childhood CFS has led to the publication of poor clinical and research reports in prestigious medical journals. One example will suffice (Krilov, Fisher, Friedman, Reitman, & Mandel, 1998). In this report of 58 children and adolescents, 50% had symptoms for less than 6 months. Many acute medical and psychological illnesses may take up to 6 months to fully resolve. Thus it is not surprising that at the time of follow-up, 43% were cured and 52% had significantly improved. Furthermore, 24% of the cases had laboratory test abnormalities that would have explained their fatigue. Finally, 60% of the studied group had "significant allergies, often including asthma" (allergic symptoms are frequently accompanied by fatigue). Thus, the majority of the cases in this report had other readily identifiable medical conditions—all of which were confused with the diagnosis of CFS.

Given all of the uncertainties and difficulties associated with trying to diagnose CFS in children and adolescents, it is preferable to simply not use this diagnosis at all.

MEDICAL THERAPY

For the most part, treatment of CFS is symptomatic. Before prescribing medications, however, the physician should offer the patient advice on common issues that face patients with CFS.

Numerous dietary therapies have been proposed, including megadoses of vitamins and very restricted and specialized diets. These can be expensive, and there is no evidence that they have any beneficial effect. Certainly it is sensible for patients to adhere to sound nutritional practices, and taking a multivitamin supplement is a reasonable recommendation, as it would be for anyone.

Scheduled physical activity is also important. CFS patients must balance two opposing needs. On the one hand, they must engage in some physical activity or they will suffer worsening fatigue from muscle atrophy and cardiovascular deconditioning. On the other hand, a sudden burst of physical activity can precipitate a relapse. Hence, patients must learn to pace themselves. Each patient will have a different capacity for physical activity. Each must determine what that is, then continue to test his or her limits, planning to do just a little bit more every day.

We recommend that patients record their exercise in a daily diary to document progress and provide psychological support. Patients may see, for example, that six months ago all they could do was walk around the house, and now they can go out and walk around the block; while they are not yet completely well, they are at least on the road toward recovery. Each person's recovery will be different: One will improve quickly; another will make slow progress, and a few may not improve at all.

Whereas patients need to have a positive long-term mind-set, for the short term they must respect that they have a physical disability. They cannot force themselves out of their condition by sheer willpower alone. Patients who try to do so end up triggering relapses and in some cases progressive deterioration.

PHARMACOLOGICAL THERAPY

Medical therapy for CFS is symptomatic. Antidepressants can be of benefit for the secondary depression often seen in these patients. As in primary depression, the usual first-line agents are the selective serotonin reuptake inhibitors—fluoxetine, paroxetine, bupropion, and sertraline.

Because patients with CFS often are sensitive to medicines, treatment should be started at a very low dose. A standard dose—for example, 20 mg a day of fluoxetine—is usually too strong. We tend to be extremely cautious and start fluoxetine at 5 or 10 mg a day, using pediatric formulations. After several weeks, the dose can be increased slowly. While these agents may help with mood and depression-related sleep problems, they will not relieve the fatigue.

Ironically, CFS patients frequently have difficulty falling asleep because they are so tired. Clonazepam works very well for that. Often 0.5 mg is sufficient, but one can titrate upward if necessary. Clonazepam or alprazolam can be useful for relief of anxiety, another major concomitant of CFS.

A nonsteroidal anti-inflammatory agent may be of benefit for the myalgias and arthralgias of CFS. Patients must take care not to overuse such an agent to avoid gastric problems.

We enrolled 30 CFS patients into a crossover medication trial comparing the effectiveness of amantadine and L-carnitine. Our previous investigations have shown L-carnitine to be a very effective medicine in treating the lethargy seen in different neurological conditions (A. V. Plioplys et al., 1994; A. V. Plioplys & Kasnicka, 1993). Our results showed that L-carnitine is of significant benefit in CFS patients and is tolerated without side effects (A. V. Plioplys & Plioplys, 1997).

Many other medications have been used to treat CFS. We have tried other medicines in our patients, but have been unable to duplicate the success reported by other groups. For example, isolated reports have suggested that amantadine—which is one of the most effective agents for relieving fatigue in patients with multiple sclerosis—might also work in patients with CFS. We found this medicine to be ineffective and actually poorly tolerated by our patients (A. V. Plioplys & Plioplys, 1997).

Cognitive-behavioral techniques have also been used with success in CFS patients. Counseling and support groups may help patients cope with their symptoms and socioeconomic problems that often occur as a result of this illness. A major problem facing many CFS patients is not medical but financial. Most of them have been very productive, holding full-time jobs and perhaps following a profession. When their illness strikes, suddenly they cannot work—and loss of job often leads to loss of medical insurance. Eventually, most of these patients apply for disability benefits.

CLINICAL EXPERIENCE

During the first year of the operation of the CFS Research Center, the number of patients referred for evaluation of CFS was 75. The final diagnoses in this group of patients are presented in Table 2.3. All of the patients had undergone extensive medical evaluations before seeing us, and all carried the diagnosis of CFS as

Table 2.3
List of Final Diagnoses

CFS:	50	Idiopathic hypersomnia	1
		Obstructive sleep apnea	1
Neurological Disorders	6		
Multiple sclerosis	2	**Other Diseases**	5
Tension headaches	2	Medication side effects	2
Brain stem stroke	1	Chronic allergic rhinitis	2
Early Parkinson's disease	1	Carnitine deficiency	1
Psychiatric Disorders	6	**Incomplete Evaluation**	4
Depression	5		
Anorexia nervosa	1	**Other Diagnoses Total**	21
Sleep Disorders	4		
Narcolepsy	1		
Restless legs syndrome	1		

Note: In the first year of operation of the CFS Center, a total of 75 patients were seen and evaluated for this condition. The final diagnoses are listed. Of all the patients, 21 (28%) had diseases other than CFS.

made by the referring physicians. Yet, 28% of these presumed CFS patients had entirely different diseases that required different management. For comparison, the misdiagnosis rate in referred CFS patients to the CDC was 18% (Fukuda et al., 1994).

During follow-up of our CFS patients, five of them developed a significant medical disease that required a change in medical management. Two developed diabetes mellitus, one hypothyroidism, one hyperthyroidism, and one Cushing's disease from an adrenal tumor. These clinical developments underscore the need for reevaluations of patients with CFS on a regular basis. These patients are not immune to medical illnesses and may become ill from another chronic condition. Furthermore, in these cases, it is possible that the original medical cause of their fatigue only become apparent years after the onset of fatigue, and years after the diagnosis of CFS.

COMPARISON WITH PREVIOUS CLINICAL REPORTS

Our results differ from a previous report in which 405 fatigued patients were evaluated in a chronic fatigue medical clinic (Manu, Lane, & Matthews, 1993). There was no prescreening of patients—anyone who had fatigue for more than one month in duration could make an appointment and be seen. Of these 405 patients, 74% had a psychiatric diagnosis explaining their fatigue (depression being the primary one) and only 7% had other medical diseases. Our patient population, in contrast, was a highly referred population that had undergone extensive previous medical testing. Only 6 out of 75 patients seen (8%) had a psychiatric explanation for their fatigue. None of our patients were seen for the first time for fatigue-related symptoms. Thus, our results cannot be compared with this report (Manu et al., 1993).

It is interesting to compare our results with reports from yet other outpatient medical clinics. Kroenke, Wood, Mangelsdorff, Meier, and Powell (1988) reported that of 102 fatigued patients seen in a medical clinic, 80% had a psychiatric diagnosis. In another study of 1,000 patients seen in a general medical clinic, 271 had significant fatigue of more than 6 months' duration (Bates et al., 1993). Of these 271 patients, 171 (63%) had an identifiable medical cause for their fatigue, 9 (3%) had a psychiatric diagnostic explanation, and 6 (2%) had substance abuse. Thus, in different medical clinics, a psychiatric explanation of chronic fatigue can range from 3% to 80%. This again emphasizes that our clinical results cannot be directly compared with previously published ones.

CONCLUSION

CFS is a frustrating condition both for the patients and for the physicians attempting to elucidate the cause of this process and to provide their patients with effective treatments. The important first step in the medical evaluation process is a thorough history and physical examination. Once this first step has been accomplished, the clinician can sort the majority of fatigued patients into potential diagnostic categories. Even though the initial screening laboratory tests are most commonly entirely normal, on occasion they indicate other treatable conditions and, therefore, should be done in all cases seen. Careful and thorough medical follow-up is necessary because the underlying cause of CFS may eventually manifest itself, and patients with CFS are not immune to the development of other medical diseases.

The diagnostic criteria in use today (Fukuda et al., 1994) are an excellent starting point. We agree with the great majority of differential diagnostic recommendations that have been made, but not with all of them. For research purposes in particular, stratification of subsets of CFS patients on the basis of medical and psychiatric historical details, comorbid conditions, and laboratory test findings may be of value in elucidating the cause of CFS in well-defined subsets of patients.

REFERENCES

American Psychiatric Association. (1994). *Diagnostic and statistical manual of mental disorders* (4th ed.). Washington, DC: Author.

Bates, D. W., Schmitt, W., Buchwald, D., Ware, N. C., Lee, J., Thoyer, E., et al. (1993). Prevalence of fatigue and chronic fatigue syndrome in a primary care practice. *Archives of Internal Medicine, 153,* 2759–2765.

Beard, G. (1869). Neurasthenia or nervous exhaustion. *Boston Medical and Surgical Journal, 3,* 217–220.

Bell, D. S. (1995). Diagnosis of chronic fatigue syndrome in children and adolescents: Special considerations. *Journal of Chronic Fatigue Syndrome, 1,* 29–36.

Bou-Holaigah, I., Rowe, P. C., Kan, J. S., & Calkins, H. (1995). *Journal of the American Medical Association, 274,* 961–967.

Fukuda, K., Straus, S. E., Hickie, I., Sharpe, M. C., Dobbins, J. G., & Komaroff, A. (1994). The chronic fatigue syndrome: A comprehensive approach to its definition and study. *Annals of Internal Medicine, 121,* 953–959.

Holmes, G. P., Kaplan, J. E., Gantz, N. M., Komaroff, A. L., Schonberger, L. B., Straus, S. E., et al. (1988). Chronic fatigue syndrome: A working case definition. *Annals of Internal Medicine, 108,* 387–389.

Holmes, G. P., Kaplan, J. E., Stewart, J. A., Hunt, B., Pinsky, P. F., & Schonberger, L. B. (1987). A cluster of patients with a chronic mononucleosis-like syndrome. Is Epstein-Barr virus the cause? *Journal of the American Medical Association, 257,* 2297–2302.

Jason, L. A., Richman, J. A., Rademaker, A. W., Jordan, K. M., Plioplys, A. V., Taylor, R. R., et al. (1999). A community-based study of chronic fatigue syndrome. *Archives of Internal Medicine, 159,* 2129–2137.

Joyce, J., Hotopf, M., & Wessely, S. (1997). Prognosis of chronic fatigue and chronic fatigue syndrome: A systematic review. *Quarterly Journal of Medicine, 90,* 223–233.

Komaroff, A. L. (1994). Clinical presentation of chronic fatigue syndrome. In S. E. Straus (Ed.), *Chronic fatigue syndrome* (pp. 61–84). New York: Marcel Dekker.

Krilov, L. R., Fisher, M., Friedman, S. B., Reitman, D., & Mandel, F. S. (1998). Course and outcome of chronic fatigue in children and adolescents. *Pediatrics, 102,* 360–366.

Kroenke, K., Wood, D. R., Mangelsdorff, D., Meier, N. J., & Powell, J. B. (1988). Chronic fatigue in primary care. *Journal of the American Medical Association, 260,* 929–934.

Kruesi, M. J. P., Dale, J., & Straus, S. E. (1989). Psychiatric diagnoses in patients who have chronic fatigue syndrome. *Journal of Clinical Psychiatry, 50,* 53–56.

Lange, G., DeLuca, J., Maldjian, J. A., Lee, H. J., Tiersky, L. A., & Natelson, B. H. (1999). Brain MRI abnormalities exist in a subset of patients with chronic fatigue syndrome. *Journal of the Neurological Sciences, 177,* 3–7.

Lloyd, A. R., Hickie, I., Boughton, C. R., Spencer, O., & Wakefield, D. (1990). Prevalence of chronic fatigue syndrome in an Australian population. *Medical Journal of Australia, 153,* 522–528.

Manningham, R. (1750). *The symptoms, nature, and causes of the febricula or little fever: Commonly called nervous or hysteric fever; the fever on the spirits; vapors, hypo or spleen* (2nd ed.). London: J. Robinson.

Manu, P., Lane, T. J., & Matthews, D. A. (1993). Chronic fatigue syndrome: Clinical epidemiology and aetiological classification. *Chronic fatigue syndrome* (pp. 23–42). Chichester, England: Wiley (Ciba Foundation Symposium 173).

Plioplys, A. V. (1997). Chronic fatigue syndrome should not be diagnosed in children. *Pediatrics, 100,* 270–271.

Plioplys, A. V. (1999). Different rates of chronic fatigue syndrome amongst high school students in two British boroughs. *Journal of Chronic Fatigue Syndrome, 5,* 97–98.

Plioplys, A. V., Bagherpour, S., & Kasnicka, I. (1994). L-carnitine as a treatment of lethargy in children with chronic neurologic handicaps. *Brain and Development, 16,* 146–149.

Plioplys, A. V., & Kasnicka, I. (1993). L-carnitine as a treatment for Rett syndrome. *Southern Medical Journal, 86,* 1411–1413.

Plioplys, A. V., & Plioplys, S. (1995). Serum levels of carnitine in chronic fatigue syndrome: Clinical correlates. *Neuropsychobiology, 32,* 132–138.

Plioplys, A. V., & Plioplys, S. (1997). Amantadine and L-carnitine treatment of chronic fatigue syndrome. *Neuropsychobiology, 35,* 16–23.

Plioplys, S., & Plioplys, A. V. (1995). Chronic fatigue syndrome (Myalgic Encephalopathy): A review. *Southern Medical Journal, 88,* 993–1000.

Rowe, P. C., Calkins, H., DeBusk, K., McKenzie, R., Anand, R., Sharma, G., et al. (2001). Fludrocortisone acetate to treat neurally mediated hypotension in chronic fatigue syndrome. *Journal of the American Medical Association, 285,* 52–59.

Schluederberg, A., Straus, S. E., Peterson, P., Blumenthal, S., Komaroff, A. L., Spring, S. B., et al. (1992). Chronic Fatigue Syndrome research: Definition and medical outcome assessment. *Annals of Internal Medicine, 117,* 325–331.

Sharpe, M. C., Archard, L. C., Banatvala, J. E., Borysiewicz, L. K., Clare, A. W., David, A., et al. (1991). A report-chronic fatigue syndrome: Guidelines for research. *Journal of the Royal Society of Medicine, 84,* 118–121.

CHAPTER 3

The Complexities of Diagnosis

BYRON HYDE

T HE VIEWS IN this chapter are those of the author and do not necessarily reflect those of the editors of this book. Since 1985, I have restricted my practice to the investigation of patients with myalgic encephalomyelitis/chronic
fatigue syndrome (ME/CFS) and the underlying causes of their illnesses. Whenever possible, I spend an entire day and part of the next examining the patient,
and this has allowed me to observe anomalies that might elude other physicians.
I then embark on a systematic mapping of the patient's structures, systems, and
organs. Only then do I reach a conclusion about the disease process that I am trying to understand and uncover. Few physicians have such a luxury of time. Because this protocol is costly for the medical system under which physicians
generally practice, I do not suggest that the readers of this chapter must follow it.
It might lead to financial difficulties if the physician is a fee-for-service physician
or practices within a medical group that dictates the amount of time to be spent
on consultations.

My methodology has produced certain views and findings that may be inconsistent with many in this field. The opinions expressed here are, in large part,
a result of my own clinical experience and are not derived from empirical findings from controlled research studies. At the Nightingale Research Foundation,
Bonnie Cameron, Lydia Neilson, and I did a survey of 2,000 patients in 1990–1994
that has informed many of my opinions, but the study was not published.

INVESTIGATION OF ME/CFS

In our text, *The Clinical and Scientific Basis of Myalgic Encephalomyelitis/Chronic Fatigue Syndrome* (Hyde, Goldstein, & Levine, 1992), I distinguished between ME
and CFS. More recently, and specifically at the biennial CFS Symposium held in
Seattle in 2001, some individuals, dissatisfied with the name chronic fatigue syndrome, suggested changing it to myalgic encephalomyelitis or some variation of
that name. This would be unwise. Although ME and CFS share many characteristics, the titles often represent two distinct groups of illnesses.

MYALGIC ENCEPHALOMYELITIS (ME)

The term *myalgic encephalomyelitis* was based on clinical descriptions of an illness that has occurred both sporadically among the general population and in clusters or epidemics, usually in hospitals or schools. Over 60 such epidemics have been described in the medical literature (Acheson, 1992; Henderson & Shelokov, 1992; Hyde, 1992) since Sandy Gilliam, Assistant Surgeon General of the United States and later Dean of Medicine at Johns Hopkins, first described the 1934 epidemic in the Los Angeles County General Hospital (1938). B. Sigurdsson et al. (1950) in Iceland, D. A. Henderson, and A. Shelokov, in the United States (1959a, 1959b); A. Wallis, in 1955, and A. M. Ramsay, in 1988, and John Richardson, in England (1992); and P. Behan, in Scotland (Behan & Behan, 1988; Behan, Behan, & Bell, 1985), have all added to this growing literature. This group of illnesses has been given many names, but these have distilled down to myalgic encephalomyelitis (ME), a term used primarily in the United Kingdom, Canada, and Australia.

These various clinical descriptions include these characteristics:

- A sporadic and epidemic postinfectious illness most frequently occurring in the late summer or early autumn, with an incubation period from 4 to 7 days. The epidemic illness is most commonly acquired in hospitals, schools, or domiciliary institutions at a time when an increase of similar sporadic illness occurs among the general population. Although the illness is seen in diverse occupations, health care workers, teachers, and students are the most commonly affected.

- The epidemic illnesses have been associated with infrequent deaths involving CNS (central nervous system) changes. Many of these changes have been subcortical brain changes. Deaths in sporadic cases have been rare but have been associated with acute cardiac arrest, with no signs of coronary disease, and frequently suicide. Deaths other than suicide are uncommon.

- Onset of the primary ME illness usually follows abruptly during the recovery phase of an often banal infection (if an infection is noted at all) or within 4 to 20 days of an immunization. Frequently one observes the onset of an ME-like illness after multiple infectious episodes. The primary infectious illness and the ME illness do not resemble each other. Most infectious illnesses are described as upper respiratory tract, flu-like, gastrointestinal and, less commonly, hepatic illness or pneumonia. Traumatic incidents associated with minor infectious illness or travel to foreign countries. These associations often follow within 30 days of a series of immunizations.

- ME illness in adults is associated with measurable changes in the CNS and autonomic function and at times injury to the cardiovascular, endocrine, and other organs and systems. It is described as (1) a systemic illness often of subnormal temperatures; (2) marked muscle fatigability; (3) an acute onset of CNS changes of memory impairment, mood changes, sleep disorders, irritability, and reactive depression; (4) involvement of the autonomic nervous system resulting in tachycardia, coldness of the extremities, urinary frequency, bowel changes, pallor, and sweats; (5) diffuse and variable involvement of the CNS leading to severe headaches, visual problems, ataxia, weakness, cramps, and sensory changes; (6) muscular and neck pain, acute fleeting spasmodic pain and tenderness, and myalgia.

- In children in the acute phase, there is depression with weeping, significant loss of energy, retardation and impairment of thought and memory process, disorders of sleep, behavioral disorders, acute onset of school problems, often of a serious nature, with a reluctance to attend school, and with a significant weight loss. Children are usually diagnosed as hysterical or school phobic.
- The initial period of illness lasts from weeks to up to two years and tends to be more severe. During this period, the patient either recovers, remains, or relapses in a chronic phase of variable severity. The chronic phase is often sufficient to prevent return to school or work for either long periods or permanently.
- Dr. Michael Goldberg, of Tarzana, California, believes that this illness often results in children being rejected, abused, and abandoned to the street or to juvenile criminal activity. Dr. John Richardson (1992), of Newcastle, and others have documented significant associated cardiac and cardiovascular injury as well as other organ injuries associated with the usual CNS and autonomic changes in this group of patients. Dr. Seymour Grufferman (1992), of Pittsburgh, has described an increased incidence of malignancies, often lymphomatous, associated with individuals in clusters of ME/CFS. A similar finding was initially described in some of the patients in the Lake Tahoe epidemic (Daugherty et al., 1991; Peterson et al., 1992).

All ME descriptions were concerned with chronic or recurrent acute onset illnesses. The ME descriptions deal with primarily CNS and autonomic changes and, at times, with easy fatigability and with poor or delayed recovery of CNS or muscular abilities. Although ME clinical descriptions noted the infectious onset and infrequently the postimmunization history of ME illness, neither pharyngitis nor involvement of lymph nodes was ever mentioned in any of the clinical descriptions of the actual chronic illness manifestations.

Host factors are important in ME. At the time of the initial illness, the patient often appears to be either temporarily or chronically immune-compromised by one or more of the following:

- Exhaustion from overwork or night shifts
- Repetitive infectious disease
- Recent immunization
- Significant illness or trauma
- Toxic chemical exposure

As in all diseases, there is a significant variation in the degree and range of injury. Those who are least injured often simply return to school or work and operate at a lower productivity and escape diagnosis. Those who are most injured or die are easily recognized at disease onset or shortly after as CNS, cardiovascular, or organ injury. Because of their overwhelming illness and the specificity of the end-organ injury, they are never diagnosed as ME except in epidemic or cluster situations. Overwhelming fatigue is often a feature of the chronic illness phase (Fukuda et al., 1994). After a few months, however, this profound fatigue often changes and some patients begin to feel normal until they are challenged by any physical, intellectual, emotional, or sensory stress. In this new phase, the patient has rapid fatigability and poor recovery after any stressor. These patients begin to feel they inhabit a body and mind significantly different from usual, and sometimes they panic. The adult patient with moderate to major illness rarely recovers totally, but usually does improve (Joyce, Hotopf, & Wessely, 1997). It is an unacceptable improvement. Those adults who are still significantly ill at two years can still improve but only a few ever return to any degree of normal function. Unlike adults, the majority of children and adolescents, even those seriously injured, who have proper care and are in a positive economic environment, tend to recover substantially or at least improve significantly over time (Marshall, 1999).

CHRONIC FATIGUE SYNDROME (CFS)

The physician and patient alike should remember that CFS is *not* a disease. It is a chronic fatigue state as described in four definitions starting with that published by Dr. Gary Holmes of the CDC and others in 1988 (Holmes, Kaplan, Gantz, et al., 1988; Holmes, Kaplan, Schonberger, et al., 1988). The definition created by Lloyd, Hickie, Boughton, Spencer, and Wakefield (1990) is also widely used in Australia. There are two subsequent definitions. The Oxford definition of 1991 (Sharpe et al., 1991) and the 1994 NIH/CDC definitions (Fukuda et al., 1994) are basically, with a few modifications, copies of the first definition. Where the one essential characteristic of ME is acquired CNS dysfunction, that of CFS is primarily chronic fatigue. By assumption, this CFS fatigue can be acquired abruptly or gradually. Secondary symptoms and signs were then added to this primary fatigue anomaly. None of these secondary symptoms is individually essential for the definition and few are scientifically testable. Despite the list of signs and symptoms and test exclusions in these definitions, patients who conform to any of these four CFS definitions may still have an undiagnosed major illness, certain of which are potentially treatable. Although the authors of these definitions have repeatedly stated that they are defining a syndrome and not a specific disease, patient, physician, and insurer alike have tended to treat this syndrome as a specific disease or illness, with at times a potentially specific treatment and a specific outcome. This has resulted in much confusion, and many physicians are now diagnosing CFS as though it were a specific illness. They either refer the patient to pharmaceutical, psychiatric, psychological, or social treatment or simply say, "You have CFS and nothing can be done about it."

The CFS definitions have another curiosity. If in any CFS patient, any major organ or system injury or disease is discovered, the patient is removed from the definition. The CFS definitions were written in such a manner that CFS becomes like a desert mirage: The closer you approach, the faster it disappears and the more problematic it becomes.

SIGNIFICANT DIFFERENCES BETWEEN ME AND CFS

Though the symptoms of CFS resemble those of ME, the differences are so significant that they would exclude ME patients from the 1988 and 1994 CDC diagnoses of CFS. The following features of ME separate it from CFS:

- The epidemic characteristics
- The known incubation period
- The acute onset

- The associated organ pathology, particularly cardiac.
- Infrequent deaths with pathological CNS changes.
- Neurological signs in the acute and sometimes chronic phases.
- The specific involvement of the autonomic nervous system.
- The frequent subnormal patient temperature.
- The fact that chronic fatigue is not an essential characteristic of the chronic phase of ME.

However, there are four essential differences between ME and CFS that are perhaps more important than any of the preceding differences:

1. No one in composing the two CDC definitions told anyone not to investigate the CFS patients during the first 6 months of illness; they simply stated that the CFS is characterized by an illness of 6 or more months of chronic fatigue. Undoubtedly, it was unintentional. Yet obviously CFS following infectious disease begins in day one of the first 6 months or even in the days before this initial period. Researchers into CFS have simply avoided that essential area. The inception of an illness is always the most fertile area of research into cause and pathology.
2. Organ disease in CFS has been avoided. By definition, it does not occur. If significant primary or secondary organ disease occurs, then this would be a cause of the fatigue and the illness would not be CFS (Fukuda et al., 1994).
3. The inventors of the second CDC CFS definition laid out certain guideline examinations (Fukuda et al., 1994). They never stated that no other testing should be done, but for all purposes, these very preliminary tests have been used for inclusion guidelines in CFS research papers. Research physicians have apparently forgotten that we do not know what CFS is from a pathophysiological basis. For this reason, not only have most physicians avoided exhaustive testing but many have decried exhaustive testing as foolish.
4. This is the most important essential difference. Nowhere in any of the four definitions of CFS is there a discussion of acute versus gradual onset illness. This has allowed physicians to include any patient who fits the 1988 or 1994 or U.K. definitional characteristics into the CFS illness spectrum. Because none of these definitions mentions gradual onset CFS disease, gradual onset patients, as a group, not only fit the four definitions but also totally obstruct CFS as a disease category. The reason for this statement is simple. Gradual onset CFS frequently represents nondiagnosed major disease or pathophysiological anomaly. Many patients with a diagnosis of CFS today have nondiagnosed major diseases. These patients warp any statistical or scientific examination of the CFS patient. Most of the patients I have seen from Canada, the United States, or from the United Kingdom with gradual onset CFS illness have nondiagnosed major medical illness or anomaly. This fourth essential difference defines the cornerstone of investigation of much CFS.

PREMISES CONCERNING THE PATIENT AND THE DISEASE ENTITY

The patient with the diagnosis of ME/CFS is chronically and potentially seriously ill with (1) a poorly understood illness of a pathophysiological nature or

(2) a missed classical disease entity. The typical patient has seen many excellent physicians, who have failed to discover the cause of the patient's illness other than to variously call it ME or CFS, psychiatric illness, somatization, or more charitably, "I simply do not know." These physicians have repeatedly performed many tests but have generally failed to find any significant or substantial indication of cause or nature of the patient's disease.

At least some of the patients with an initial diagnosis of *gradual onset* ME or CFS have another and potentially treatable classical disease or anomaly. These ME/CFS patients require a total investigation and essentially a total body mapping to understand the pathophysiology of their illness and to discover what other physicians may have missed. In many instances, patients appear to know more about ME/CFS than their physician and in fact have directed their own investigation under the directional guidance of a kind and supportive clinician.

These patient-directed investigations usually jump from one trendy test of little value to another consuming vast amounts of funds and time. Rarely, however, do the physician and patient end up with any substantial scientifically supportable disease entity or diagnosis other than that with which they started—ME/CFS. One can assume that many of the patient's physicians have spent the proverbial 8 minutes that an average North American or British physician spends with the average patient. Likewise, most internists will have spent 40 minutes doing a classical history and physical that can generally detect obvious acute disease or advanced disease of a progressive nature, but is usually irrelevant in understanding a chronic pathophysiological illness.

I assume that none of the patient's illnesses is due to a psychiatric cause until I have completed my investigation. In the end, although these patients may have significant anxiety and problems caused by loss of income, social status, and meaning, less than 5% have any significant psychiatric illness. Initially in 1985 to 1990, I was able to unravel the causative disease or illness in the ME/CFS group in no more than 10% to 20% of the patients I examined. By 2000, I was able to discover the major elements of the underlying disease pathophysiology in 70% to 80% of the patients I examined. Each year, my success ratio has improved. Because of this, I believe that the 20% to 30% failure rate in defining the pathophysiology of this group is due to my own deficiencies as a physician and/or the deficiencies of the available technologies. One should not blame patients for their illness or jump too casually to a psychiatric or sociological diagnosis.

For me, a patient with an initial diagnosis of ME/CFS can be a gold mine of disease, missed injuries, physical and physiological anomalies, and genetic curiosities.

PHILOSOPHY AND ECONOMIC ETHICS OF INVESTIGATION

I base my philosophy of examination and testing of ME/CFS patients on the following considerations:

- The majority of ME/CFS patients who seek medical assistance in my practice tend to be middle-income individuals or professionals. Many have been unable to work for years. The patient's loss of income for one year usually represents more than $30,000, and I have seen patients who have lost an income in excess of $500,000 per year. These individuals tend to range in age between 20 and 40 and are in the prime of their work life when they first fall ill. If they cannot return to work, the gross income loss to themselves, an insurer, or the state—or simply the loss of their productive life—can often reach $1 million to $15 million.

- The technological component of a reasonably complete investigation and body mapping rarely should cost more than $10,000. The term *body mapping* is an idiom I adapted from another profession. Prior to becoming a physician, I worked as a geophysicist, and to evaluate an anomaly, it was necessary to first map the terrain in detail with surveying and geophysical tools to measure the size, depth, and nature of the anomaly. Diamond drilling and core analysis often followed the initial measurements. I helped discover several mines that people had often walked over without even realizing what they had missed. The investigation of an ME/CFS patient is similar to the research leading to the discovery of a gold or nickel mine or an oil deposit. Before you can know and understand what anomaly you are dealing with, it is sometimes necessary to do a total body mapping. This may cost approximately $10,000. At this point, many physicians and insurers will throw up their hands in exasperation. They cannot justify spending such a considerable sum to investigate a patient who, in their judgment, has an obviously psychiatric/somatic illness or is simply too lazy to return to work and has been properly investigated by several reputable physicians.

- The majority of ME/CFS patients cost themselves, or the medical system in which they operate, far more than $10,000 over the course of their illness in a totally nonstructured series of haphazard investigations. Even compared with a year's income, $10,000 represents a fraction of the patient's or employer's loss. When compared with a lifetime loss of $1 million to $15 million, such an investigation cost is paltry.

- Although individual patients may know a great deal more than I do about some particular aspect of some particular disease or pathology, they are not physicians. Nor is the patient usually trained as a physician, and rarely does the patient understand the rigors of scientific medicine. Some physicians, in attempting to earn a reasonable living in these economically challenging times, have also relinquished their investigational skills. It is not for nothing that medical training is so prolonged. Medicine is a difficult profession; medical investigation is a difficult pursuit; the investigational physician can never know enough or have enough tools or instruments to measure everything that needs to be measured. Faced with the challenge of ME/CFS illness, no physician can presume to understand the pathophysiology of this group of illnesses; particularly after only an hour with the patient and a few standard tests.

- The chronic ME/CFS patient deserves, at least once, a complete investigation that includes mapping of (1) body structures, (2) organs, and (3) systems. Where little or nothing is initially discovered, the same physician should repeat this investigation after a few years. Over time, even chronic disease tends to be progressive and more visible to investigation. Also, physician skills and professional knowledge continue to improve. Patients routinely arrive in my office telling me they have had a complete workup, but few of these patients have had what I consider to be even basic investigation.

- The investigation of a known illness such as heart valve disease or a brain tumor is relatively simple and can be completed with an economy of tests and examinations. A chronic disease process that is poorly defined or is of unknown origin requires a different approach.

THE PHILOSOPHY OF TREATING ME/CFS DISEASE

Though ME/CFS usually represents significant disease processes, the underlying pathophysiologies or physical anomalies causing these processes are so varied that it is unreasonable and perhaps even dangerous to suggest or embark on any uniform treatment.

Although CFS has been defined as a syndrome, patient, physician, and even government agencies have increasingly tended to speak about CFS as a specific disease entity with a potentially specific treatment or treatments. Whether this suggested treatment protocol employs pharmaceuticals, cognitive or physical retraining, or alternative medications and treatments, these treatment modalities and philosophies are not medically justifiable and are often potentially dangerous to the patient.

In the past two centuries, the development of Western medicine was based on autopsy, physiology, pathology, and reproducible tests. The goals were to define and, where possible, treat the causes and/or the pathophysiology of the disease process. This philosophy of modern Western medicine has been the basis for almost all of the great medical cures and treatments for specific diseases during the nineteenth and twentieth centuries. To date, however, this approach has largely been missing in the investigation and understanding of ME/CFS disease.

There has been an immoral intervention by the insurance industry into the philosophy of physicians and health workers treating this group of disease entities. This corporate insurance company intervention has used the mechanism of sponsoring medical symposiums to produce a uniform, insurance-friendly policy. Insurance companies have reputedly placed large numbers of rheumatologists and specific subspecialists in a given area under a significant annual retainer, injuring not only patient access but also negatively influencing other physicians who may not be aware of this economic relationship.

INFLUENTIAL FACTORS IN TREATMENT

The definitions of myalgic encephalomyelitis (ME), chronic fatigue syndrome (CFS), and fibromyalgia have colored all investigations of this illness group. The definitions of myalgic encephalomelitis and chronic fatigue syndrome describe what may originally have been the same disease, but the differing definitions have caused confusion.

Fibromyalgia and Vascular Pain

Both ME and CFS patients may have associated pain that includes fibromyalgia (Taylor, Friedberg, & Jason, 2001). Some have no associated pain dysfunction. The pain syndromes, and there are many, vary in intensity and tend to be worse in the first years of illness and after the patient has encountered physical, intellectual, sensory, or emotional stressors. Although some researchers have found specific chemical changes in the spinal fluid of these patients, and others have demonstrated subcortical SPECT (single photon emission computed tomography) anomalies (Goldstein, 1992), it is likely that in the future measurable findings may be found in the posterior columns and posterior root ganglia. If physiological spinal cord changes occur, they have not been subjected to scientific scrutiny because specific noninvasive testing modalities are not yet available.

Instead of following neurological pathways, some of these pain mechanisms are probably vascular. If this is true, this may suggest injury to the autonomic system. Any physician subjecting this category of patient to a thallium chemical cardiac stress test will know that many of these patients experience severe incapacitating pain that sometimes lasts for days, even several weeks. Although I do not know if there is a CNS or spinal basis to these pain phenomena, the paradoxical thallium test would suggest a vascular basis to the pain dysfunction in this group of patients.

Raynaud's phenomenon is a common secondary occurrence in both ME/CFS and fibromyalgia. When significant fibromyalgia occurs in conjunction with ME or CFS, the chronic disability tends to be additive.

ACUTE AND GRADUAL ONSET ILLNESS

I tend to arbitrarily place acute onset patients in the ME category and the gradual onset in the CFS category. This arbitrary categorization is not entirely satisfactory. Some patients have no idea if their illness started abruptly or gradually. Even so, overlap in these two groups makes it an imperfect analysis. Remember, a patient with ME is a patient whose primary disease is CNS change, and this is measurable. The primary disease of a patient with CFS is fatigue, and fatigue is neither definable nor measurable.

The gradual onset CFS group is of particular concern to me. It is in this group that occult disease, whether malignant, space occupying, organ pathology, or vascular injury of the CNS or cardiac system, is most frequently observed. A typical ME-like history can often be due to a malignancy (Richardson, 1992) or other pathology that should be located as soon as possible. Whether a patient fell ill abruptly or gradually, or has been ill for many years, is no excuse not to search for a potentially treatable malignancy or a cardiac, vascular, or other organ illness. Patients with ME/CFS are not immune from developing other illnesses that may be potentially terminal.

THE RATIONALE FOR INVESTIGATION

Scientific Medicine   The tradition of Western scientific medicine is to isolate the cause of the illness, measure it, and specifically treat that cause if possible. Without being able to understand and measure the nature and degree of the underlying injury or disease, it is impossible to measure the effectiveness of any treatment. Some causes of ME/CFS-like illness are eminently treatable, and effective treatment may allow the patient to go back to work or school.

Understanding   Patients want to know and have the right to know what has happened to them.

Insurance Indemnity   Some, if not most, insurance companies do not accept the diagnosis of ME or CFS as a basis for disability even if the patient is permanently bedridden or confined to a wheelchair. The physician must be able to demonstrate the underlying injury to a court, if need be, to assist the truly disabled patient in claiming a disability pension. Although this does not treat the disease, at times it can materially restore the disabled individual to acceptable financial stability, without which life often becomes intolerable.

Financial and Social Loss   The majority of patients with ME/CFS-type illness tend to be professionals or individuals with an above-average education and a successful career, who may forfeit significant income because of work loss in their lifetime (Anderson & Ferrans, 1997). Each of these patients requires a complete clinical, laboratory, and scientific investigation at least once. Although I have seen some patients who were charged $20,000 to $100,000 for $3,000 worth of tests, a complete technical investigation should cost less than $10,000. Many physicians and corporate organizations think that the state or their company cannot afford to investigate a patient in such depth, even though the state or insurance company has no difficulty in paying that patient $10,000 to $20,000 a year or more in social benefits if the disability is accepted. A thorough evaluation of the patient could help eliminate this problem of rational accountability.

THE IN-DEPTH EVALUATION

PATIENT HISTORY

In addition to the regular history, prior to the first visit, I have the patient provide a full extended family genealogical health history going back three or even four generations and including siblings of each generation, all of their known illnesses, and cause of death. Patients who know their birth parents usually can obtain this history. Frequently, mapping this genetic history suggests or even reveals the source of the CFS patient's real illness. Patients with ME sometimes have a curious history. I often find an excess of recurring and major neurological illnesses in previous generations. Even though paralytic poliomyelitis was relatively rare, it is common to find one or more polio victims in the family tree. I have often wondered if these patients do not suffer from a specific immunological dysfunction to neuropathic viruses.

GEOGRAPHIC HISTORY: A POTENTIAL INVESTIGATIONAL BLIND SPOT

Patients, as they should be, are very concerned about toxic chemical exposure as a cause of their illness. Physicians and governments pay lip service to this concern, but perhaps because of lack of technology, I have found little supportive evidence to substantiate toxic chemical exposure as a cause for chronic ME/CFS (Crowley, Nelson, & Stovin, 1957; Shelokov, Habel, Verder, & Welch, 1957). However, patients who have a history of being raised on an active twentieth-century farm or a village with no central water supply are potentially victims of well water toxic chemical exposure.

Well water is normally only routinely examined for bacteria, and in my experience, farm and village well water is almost never examined for pesticides or herbicides. In villages and towns that rely on local or central well water, whose source is near a major farm area, chemical factory, or dry cleaner, the users of this water may have been subjected to toxic chemical exposure in their water for decades. This type of exposure can lead to a gradual immune breakdown. Hair or serum analysis may not demonstrate these old exposures. Many of these toxins are lipophilic and a fat biopsy (liposuction) should be considered in this group. Since pesticides, herbicides, and all organophosphates accumulate in fat and the brain is essentially fat, the brain should be considered to be a natural reservoir of these chemicals. The brain, of course, is also the major immune-regulating organ of the body. Since we cannot routinely do brain biopsies, analysis of samples of liposuction fat may help to identify toxic levels of these chemicals.

Psychiatric History

Patients frequently hide their family psychiatric history. Often I am assured that there is no psychiatric history, and then after an exhaustive examination, I find no physical causes for the patient's illness. Patients with ME/CFS with no observable pathology are very infrequent. I then go back and ask specific questions of each family member. Infrequently, I find a severe psychiatric history. Having said this, I doubt if more than 2% to 5% of ME/CFS patients have a primary psychiatric history. Why should there be fewer psychiatric patients in this group? The patients that I see, particularly in the acute onset group, are primarily professional middle-class individuals. They have worked hard for years to further their careers, and most persons with major initial psychiatric illness would have simply failed to achieve this success.

Physical Examination

The severity of ME/CFS illness is not usually accompanied by significant observable physical changes in the regular physical examination. This causes some physicians to assume that there is no major disease present in patients with ME/CFS. Yet most male patients I have seen have never had a rectal or women a vaginal exam, and almost none have ever had anyone look into their nasal passages.

The physical examination does not start on the examining table. My physical examination often starts with the moment the patient gets out of a car to come into my office. Severely ill patients seldom come since they cannot get out of bed or handle the nine steps to my office. These patients I see only in their homes. The mild cases, who keep working or going to school, are rarely if ever seen by a physician. I have an advantage in often being able to see the patient from my window. Typical moderate to moderately severe ME patients often cannot get out of a car normally. Patients who have driven any distance often physically lift their legs out, first one leg then the other, hold onto the car door frame, and struggle out. Their upper leg flexors are unusually weak. Sometimes they have short-term foot drop and cannot raise their foot. I have a simple gate catch that a child can open instantly. I have seen patients work for several minutes without being able to open the latch. A sign on my outside door says "ring and enter," and often the patient simply rings and stands there. Once inside, the patient often goes down the steps one at a time, one foot leading while holding firmly on to the banister.

During the daylong examination, I often accompany patients for tests in the hospital simply to observe them. They frequently do not walk normally; they get lost in their purses or wallets attempting to find their identification. Walking with these patients is often like walking with a tortoise. They can be slow, clumsy, sometimes walking with a wide leg stance. Some have a movement disorder that does not conform to the classical Parkinson or upper motor neuron disorders. These patients have obvious CNS injury but simply do not fit into neat categories.

Initially, patients are often excited about seeing me, their adrenaline pumping, and a physician who saw some of these patients for only up to an hour would reasonably conclude that they were high-energy patients with nothing wrong. This is misleading. During the course of a day's examination, the patient may change from a brighter than normal person to one who resembles a blank-faced zombie, a patient who can talk and walk only with difficulty or not at all. Sometimes their voices become scanning, and they begin verbally to stumble. Normally, I take the patient to lunch. This helps me diagnose the infrequent bulimics. Sometimes patients are fine all day, but when I see them on the second day, they have often, in physical and intellectual terms, gone to pieces. A one-hour physical examination will rarely pick up ME/CFS pathology.

Oral Temperature   Prior to the office visit, I have patients take a temperature reading at specific times, 4 times a day for three days, and also ask them to have a healthy friend of the same age and sex provide a similar temperature series for comparison. This is not a good test due to the variation of procedures and menstrual cycles, but the patient with acute onset ME/CFS frequently has a substantially subnormal temperature. In 15 years of examining chronic ME or CFS patients in Canada, the United Kingdom, and Australia, and in CFS clinics in the United States, I have found an elevated temperature on only two or three occasions. The significance of elevated temperature in the CFS definition eludes me. Patients have subnormal or normal temperatures.

Cervical and Axillary Glands   The initial CDC case definition for CFS suggested as a physical criterion, "Palpable or tender cervical and axillary lymph nodes" (Holmes et al., 1988). Few of the signatories of that definitional paper were actually clinicians who had ever seen any ME/CFS patients on a regular basis. The Oxford Group corrected that and simply stated, "There are no clinical signs characteristic of the condition" (Sharpe et al., 1991, p. 119).

ME/CFS patients frequently have surface hypersensibility or pain syndromes, but since 1985, I have rarely found significant cervical or axillary glands in an ME/CFS patient. Sometimes they do have painful elliptical swellings. When they occur, they can be quite large but are fleeting. One is located above and to the right of the left mammary gland. Often if you ask, the patient will go to that point but say it "isn't there today." Over the years, several ME/CFS patients have told me that they have had their left breast biopsied at this exact site for possible malignancy and nothing was found.

Another location is a row of these elliptical swellings in the left axilla at the chest wall muscle edge. These may come out during the first few years of illness at any time and later when the patient is tired. They are subcutaneous and tender and in severe cases cause a bruise or discoloration over the spot. You can roll them under the ball of the finger. They are exquisitely painful. They are never constant.

In the past, I have had two patients biopsied and found that there were no abnormal lymph nodes but a bundle of histiocytes. Dr. J. Gordon Parish demonstrated to me that often the subcutaneous anterior upper legs are also "lumpy" in these patients. If you find enlarged lymph glands in the cervical or axillary areas, look for other causes than ME/CFS.

OTHER PHYSICAL FINDINGS

Of the following 20 abnormal findings in these patients, none is strong enough to excite most internists or neurologists. The findings are not usual in a healthy patient, however, and many are not specific to ME/CFS. There tend to be more findings in the early illness, but some persist and appear to increase during the course of the day:

1. Ghastly pallor of face with frequent lupus-like submaxillary mask
2. Parkinsonian rigidity of facial expression and altered walk
3. Scanning, disjointed speech, or reversals
4. Nasal passage obstruction and inflamed areas around tonsillar pillars
5. Sicca syndrome of conjunctiva and mucous membranes
6. Drenching sweats often reported, but seen most frequently later in day
7. Raynaud's phenomenon with infrequent loss of normal fingerprint
8. Unequal pupils and contrary pupil reaction to light
9. Tongue tremor
10. Rare Adie's pupil with absent patella reflex
11. Positive modified Romberg
12. Frequent equivocal Babinski/plantar reflex on one side
13. Cogwheel leg raising and lowering motion that increases during the day
14. Frequently reported muscle twitching; infrequently seen in office after exercise
15. Sometimes marked falling pulse pressure in arterial pressures taken first when prone, then sitting, then standing
16. Rapid heart rate on minor activity such as standing
17. Associated fibromyalgia
18. Unusual sensitivity of cervical vertebrae area
19. Laryngeal stridor when fatigued
20. Nodular thyroid

EXAMINING TEST RESULTS

The patient may have had a large number of tests and physician reports. These should be examined in detail. Sometimes these tests disclose the clues to diagnosis that have been missed. Never simply accept an MRI, PET (positron emission tomography), SPECT, or X-ray report that states it is normal. When possible, review the film or printout yourself. If you feel uncomfortable doing that, find a specialist who can assist you. Recently, I saw a patient who had been seen at a major U.S. neurological clinic in Boston for three days at a cost of $12,000. Part of this examination included an MRI that was read as normal. When I asked a neuroradiologist to check this for me, he stated there was a significant lateral shift of the ventricles and to look for a malignancy or atrophic condition.

Some ME/CFS patients (e.g., patients with spherocytosis and sickle cell anemia), tend to have an unusually low erythrocyte sedimentation rate (ESR). Elevation of ESR may suggest an active inflammatory disease. Persistent elevation may indicate an acute infection, a malignancy, or a missed rheumatoid disease. ESR is an inexpensive nonspecific test, and some medical organizations impugn it. All high ESR patients should be rechecked for chronic infectious, malignant, and rheumatoid disease. Physicians should always repeat all abnormal tests before coming to any conclusions since it may be a false abnormal.

ORDERING TESTS

Routine Blood and Chemical Tests   I ask patients to have their own physician do locally any tests that have not already been done. It saves patients both time and money. Most physicians are happy to assist, but a few simply refuse, perhaps because they believe that the patient has no measurable physical illness. For example, glucose tolerance tests are increasingly frowned on by significant members of the medical community as being expensive and unnecessary in the evaluation of diabetes mellitus. These physicians are correct; however, a glucose tolerance test does more than simply define diabetes—it can demonstrate *hypoglycemia,* that much maligned illness that has passed out of vogue. I always do insulin levels with my glucose tolerance tests and frequently discover derangement of insulin response in some ME/CFS patients.

The following tests should be considered for all ME/CFS patients:

1. Routine CBC with sedimentation, blood smear, ferritin, and IBC. Many patients have a significant ferritin and IBC anomaly with normal Hb and Ht.
2. Eosinophil count.
3. Before ordering B12, check with the patient, who often is consuming vast amounts of B12 in vitamin combinations that will give abnormal highs.
4. Urinalysis and culture.
5. Immune and protein electrophoresis.
6. Immune panel only if it can be done in the immediate vicinity.
7. TSH, FT3, FT4, and thyroid antibody tests.
8. Thyroid ultrasound must be done on all patients. In the past two years, I have diagnosed six cases of thyroid malignancy with ultrasound. Often, these patients have normal serum thyroid tests.
9. Parathyroid Ab, Ca, and Ph.
10. Complete lipid profile.
11. HIV 1 and 2, treponema antibodies, hepatitis B (surface and core ab) and C, toxoplasmosis, histoplasmosis, Lyme disease.
12. Tuberculin skin test for all patients who have not received immunization.
13. Stools for parasites, ova, and blood × 3.
14. SGOT (AST), SGPT (ALT), bilirubin, BUN, uric acid.
15. ANA and rheumatoid battery if suggested.
16. PA and lateral X-ray of chest and X-ray of sella tursica and sinuses.
17. Fasting and 3-hour glucose and glucose tolerance if indicated.
18. Smooth and striated muscle ab and mitochondria ab.
19. Street drug profile to include cannabis, cocaine, LSD, and so on.
20. Prostate specific antigen (PSA) on all males over 25.

Thyroid Disease   It is well known that the thyroid is one of the essential glands that regulate energy and temperature, and it is equally well known that ME/CFS patients tend to have both energy and temperature disregulation. For this reason, I not only do free T4 and TSH on all patients but also do thyroid antibody tests. Even with major thyroid disease, the TSH may be normal. TSH appears to have a diurnal rhythm as do cortisol levels; TSH may vary from week to week. Even with all of these tests returning as normal, I do a thyroid ultrasound on all ME/CFS patients. I then do a needle biopsy on all hypervascular nodules found or solitary nodules over 1 cm in diameter. Thyroid ultrasound is noninvasive and inexpensive. I examined one patient who had been seen by over 20 physicians in the United States and found a malignant thyroid. In the past 18 months, I have discovered 5 ME/CFS patients with a malignant thyroid requiring thyroidectomy and three with missed Hashimoto's thyroiditis. Curiously, each of these patients with a malignant thyroid also had a history of spending much of the day before a computer terminal at work. I do not know if the computer terminal association is more than a simple fortuitous association. These patients with significant thyroid pathology as found on ultrasound and biopsy often have relatively normal TSH, free T4 and, less frequently, relatively normal thyroid antibody tests. Their thyroid pathology, however, is only part of a general autoimmune dysfunction, certainly involving the CNS but undoubtedly other areas as well. NeuroSPECT scans in these patients, as well as their immune tests also tend to be grossly abnormal. Once the thyroid problem is successfully treated, the patient occasionally gets better, but more often does not. The SPECT immune anomalies tend to persist.

Discussion   For some, this list of tests would already appear to be excessive. However, I cannot count the times that I have found abnormal thyroid and parathyroid function in this group of patients. HIV does not normally cause a fatigue syndrome except in its final stages and I rarely find HIV or positive treponema tests in this group. I may find one HIV every two years, but every year I discover several unexpected cases of either hepatitis B or C in ME/CFS patients. Some of these patients are sexually active and have seen 20 physicians who have not ordered these tests or discovered these illnesses.

Low levels of elevated ANA are almost to be expected in many ME/CFS patients, particularly early in their illness. Over time, the ANA levels tend to fall in those who do not go on to develop clinical rheumatoid disease. I occasionally find scleroderma antibodies in patients with clearly defined Sicca syndrome. At least 50% of my patients have either significantly abnormal immune or, much less frequently, abnormal protein electrophoresis that sometimes leads to the diagnosis of specific diseases.

If immune tests are not done on the same day the blood sample is taken, the levels will not be correct. These tests are very expensive and serve little purpose for either patient or physician unless they are part of a total investigation and are performed in an expert laboratory. Immune abnormalities should be repeated with a suitable hiatus to make sure they do not reflect an acute infectious anomaly.

I almost never find evidence of street drugs in these patients. However, it is amazing how few patients have had a chest X-ray in the previous decade, and at times I find major lung, mediastinum, and cardiac pathology. Although gross observable pituitary anomalies on routine X-ray occur with increased frequency in this group, they tend to be few and far between. One should be aware in doing pituitary or adrenal tests that birth control medication can cause variables in this group of tests that at first would appear pathological. I recently examined a beautiful teenage girl with a moon-shaped face, hair changes, and marked striae who had been treated with corticosteroids by her physician for adrenal dysfunction. She had all the usual corticosteroid side effects and all that was behind it was that she was on birth control pills. There was no adrenal dysfunction.

I have now seen several children previously diagnosed with CFS who proved simply to have intestinal parasites. Once treated, these patients immediately bounced back to health. A positive eosinophil count is a good indication to look for parasites.

I do a PSA on every male above 25. I had a very good friend, a wonderful cardiologist, who in a jovial manner told me one day he had CFS. I asked if I could examine him and he declined saying it would get better. His CFS was discovered, too late, to be a prostatic carcinoma. If there is a family history of prostate disease, I do a transrectal ultrasound as well as a PSA, which may pick up prostate malignancy later than one would want to.

Most physicians would not find the preceding series of tests all that alarming unless they believe that the ME/CFS group of illnesses is an invented phenomenon. This simple set of tests may lead to other tests that define the disease of at least 25% of the group who are mistakenly diagnosed with ME/CFS. Without this baseline, it is pointless to do more expensive tests since the tests already mentioned may suggest the illness. Even physicians who agree that this set of tests is reasonable may balk at additional tests.

Two Cautions

Testing for Legal Purposes   Although I have seen patients win disability claims with one good proof, it is better to be prepared to give at least three significant pieces of evidence demonstrating proof of disability. Then if one proof is discounted, your multiple evidence may be sufficient to win over the judge. Some investigations may take up to two years. If your patient's disability case will possibly go to court before then, you should urge the patient to first obtain a lawyer experienced in insurance law to advise both the patient and yourself. A lawyer will make sure that the insurance company does not invalidate the claim by creating delays. Some states in the United States and all insurance companies have widely different approaches to disability claimants. Your patient requires necessary legal protection from the onset. Do not delay this essential step of making sure your patient has a lawyer before you spend significant time on investigation. It does patients no good to find that they are chronically ill with little chance of recovery if they then also lose the right to claim on their disability insurance. An expert lawyer may be as essential to the welfare of these patients as an expert investigation.

Lumbar Puncture   There are two important points to be aware of in doing a lumbar puncture. The most important is that during the early days or weeks of the disease, the patient may have a significant increase in intracranial pressure. *Always use a small-bore needle.* Do not forget to take the spinal fluid pressure reading as well as the fluid. Since 1985, I have seen two patients where the physician's use of a large-bore needle for the puncture resulted in the brain stem being herniated into the upper spinal canal causing a permanent iatrogenic partial paralysis. The second point to remember is that many patients with acute onset ME/CFS may demonstrate IgG oligoclonal bands in their spinal fluid. These do not usually go on to develop multiple sclerosis (MS). Do not frighten or advise patients prematurely that they have MS without meeting the full obligatory MS criteria.

Viral Causes of Acute Onset ME or CFS

Thousands of physicians in North America, Europe, and Austral-Asia have expended considerable funds to study the possible viral causes of ME/CFS. Some physicians have their pet theories, but none has been proven to be correct. Viral antibody tests are a particular waste of time and money since all humans are a virtual bank of hundreds if not thousands of viruses, some of whose antibodies are reactivated with a wide range of viral challenges. Only in epidemic situations where a rising viral antibody titer can be captured is it worthwhile to do antibody tests. Since acute onset disease has an incubation period of 4 to 7 days, usually at the lower limit, it makes little sense to ruminate about herpes virus 6 with an incubation of approximately 10 to 12 days or EBV with an incubation period of around 40 days. Even with a positive SPECT as a marker, we have not found a consistent viral cause. But having said this, I should add that we have never found any chronic viral infection by PCR on any patient with definite gradual onset CFS.

In acute onset ME patients with clear SPECT changes, however, we have had positive enterovirus PCR in about 10% of these patients for up to 3 years post-illness onset. The enterovirus that we have found has often been a new, nonlisted enterovirus similar to ECHO 25. This positive finding begins to drop at 2 years, and we have not found an elevation after 3 years. We have not found this virus in normal healthy controls with the exception of two normal patients who had received massive blood transfusions. Another curious feature is that many acute onset ME patients have incredibly high polio 1, 2, or 3 antibody levels. They obviously do not have polio, but perhaps some of the viruses that cause acute onset ME are similar in nature to poliovirus. Even so, 10% of acute onset illness represents about 5% of the total number of ME/CFS cases. If it is an answer, it is only a partial answer at best. Enterovirus PCR is also very difficult to perform and many North American labs do not have the experience to perform this test accurately. I noticed that a physician for the National Institutes of Health (NIH) was doing their enterovirus analysis in Scotland, where I was doing mine. The difference is that the NIH physician was not screening patients for acute and gradual onset illness or investigating them in any detail to remove patients with major missed disease.

Doppler Ultrasound and Echocardiograms

The most important tests that I do are Doppler scans and echocardiograms. They are more productive than MRIs or almost any other group of tests in uncovering pathology in ME/CFS patients. The following tests, which I do on all patients, pick up another 25% of the underlying cause of disease:

- Visual carotid Doppler from aortic arch
- Visual transcranial Doppler to include vertebral and basilar arteries

- Thyroid ultrasound
- Echocardiogram and Doppler

Discussion   Dr. John Richardson from Newcastle upon Tyne has followed ME patients in Durham and Northumberland counties of the United Kingdom for three to four generations. I am aware of no other physician in the world with such a historic view of ME patients. He has repeatedly demonstrated that many ME patients go on to develop structural heart injury. The injury is usually valvular or related to pericardial effusion, and although most settle down, some do not and may develop myopathy. So I started to look at the hearts of these patients.

I have found that during the first year of acute onset ME/CFS disability, the incidence of pericardial effusion is unusually high. This seems to settle down with no apparent short-term problem, and after a year, the cases of pericardial fluid decrease considerably. However, the incidence of valvular disease in people in their 30s and 40s appears to be higher than in the normal population. When I find a significant valvular injury, I then repeat the echocardiogram yearly, and more frequently if the patient develops shortness of breath. I have observed several cases of elevated right heart pressure, significant septal defects, and increased myocardial wall thickening. Some who have had the injured valve replaced have miraculously returned to normal health. Are these incidental findings? I do not know, but Dr. Richardson has identified more than several hundred cardiopathies in his ME practice. I had two heart valve replacements in this group in the past year out of a total of 50 new patients.

Carotid and Transcranial Doppler   Few physicians investigating ME/CFS employ the visual carotid and transcranial Doppler. This is a major error. It is a relatively inexpensive and totally safe procedure that does things no other type of test can do. On rare occasions, you will find aneurysms and subclavian steal anomaly with this test. Carotid atherosclerosis—sometimes substantial—is often found in patients with lipid dysfunction. This is a treatable condition and can be part of the cause of a CNS fatigue syndrome. You may say that any internist or cardiologist can pick up carotid pathology with a stethoscope, but few do who do not have an office Doppler. The carotid scan is also essential if you wish to do a transcranial Doppler.

I examined a patient from the United States who had been diagnosed as having CFS in two major U.S. CFS clinics. She was given alternative medications and told to return in one year. She had complete obstruction of the vertebral basilar arteries and approximately 80% and 90% obstruction in either carotid. I was amazed that she was still alive. She was successfully operated on in Boston and her CFS has significantly improved.

The transcranial Doppler is not a perfect test. Patients with small foramen magnum space are difficult to visualize. But it will demonstrate high level internal carotid and other arterial obstruction that is beyond the normal range of a stethoscope. Only rarely do I get the chance to investigate posttraumatic mitral valve area (MVA) patients who develop an acute fatigue syndrome where personality or intellectual change has given rise to the diagnosis of CFS. In two of the past four such patients, I have demonstrated small subcortical arterial blowouts that had been missed by neurologists and that were possibly the cause of their pathophysiology.

In patients with ME/CFS, it is possible to demonstrate spasmodic disease of both major and smaller arteries with no typical evidence of migraine. This arterial pathology may be the end organ underlying cause of some ME patients' illness. Often MRIs and MRAs miss such arterial physiological pathology. Why? The technology of the MRA consists of a receiving computer revolving around the brain that may only give a picture of the maximum arterial diameter. In other words, what you see on the MRA is not reality but one view of reality. With the transcranial Doppler, the operator actually watches and films the kinetic movement of the arteries within the brain and can measure the velocity of the blood flow. Not only can you see these arteries move; if they are in spasm, you can observe this as well. Like ME/CFS muscles, ME brains are sometimes in significant pathological spasm. This knowledge may lead to more effective treatments of ME/CFS disease. Arterial spasm may account for some, but not all, of the SPECT changes that are routinely seen in ME patients.

I often find partial or complete vertebral or basilar artery obstruction. Frequently, I find left middle cerebral artery spasm or obstruction and, less frequently, frontal artery spasm in ME/CFS patients who do not report a migraine history. Left middle cerebral arterial field hypoperfusion is typical of ME.

ULTRASOUND

Consider using the following ultrasound scans:

1. Abdominal and pelvic organs and aorta
2. Prostatic ultrasound
3. Femoral and popliteal arteries in patients with leg pain

Discussion Like many physicians, I have never been able to palpate a spleen except in the most extreme cases, such as you find in malaria. (We don't have much malaria in Canada.) Like most physicians, however, I can pick up an enlarged spleen with ultrasound. Early on in the ME/CFS disease, you will find a small number of enlarged spleens, but this becomes infrequent as the disease progresses past one year. Fatty infiltration of the liver is regularly seen and is usually dietary. I infrequently discover metastatic cancer (CA) in the liver. It is rare to uncover other major organ pathology to account for CFS. Organ pathology is more common in women, where too frequently we have found ovarian and pelvic tumors—some malignant (Billy Wilder's wife was diagnosed with CFS in 1989 and nothing was done for her condition; she subsequently died of ovarian cancer). Ultrasound is a fairly inexpensive noninvasive type of testing, and I do it on every patient. I routinely find pelvic pathology in as many as 30% of females. In the past three years, I have found only three pelvic malignancies—fortunately, the discoveries saved two patients' lives.

FURTHER EXAMINATION OF THE HEART AND CARDIOVASCULAR SYSTEM

The following tests are recommended:

1. 24-hour Holter monitor
2. Stress ECG or chemical stress test

3. Cardiac PET scan
4. Circulating red blood cell and serum volume

Discussion   I routinely use a Holter monitor on all patients. The cardiologist often reports these as normal. *Do not trust this report.* What the cardiologist or computer is basing the report on is the number of ischemic events. However, read the lowest heart rate at night, and note that it sometimes falls to the low 40s. Though this may be normal in an athlete, it is not in a sedentary ME/CFS patient. For a patient who is not active all day long and has an average heart rate that flirts with 100 beats per minute or more, you know that this is not normal. These abnormal tests, however, are often reported as normal. We routinely pick up significant abnormal ischemic events. Similarly, as high as 10% of our patients have coronary artery disease. This is verified on stress test. So often do I find significant ischemic hearts in this group despite their young age that I now do stress tests only in the cardiology department.

Patients with ME/CFS frequently cannot do exercise tests, and so I then do chemical testing as a second best. Several of our patients have reacted severely to the chemical test with excruciating pain. This is not true angina, and although the pain sometimes ceases as soon as the chemical is stopped and the antidote given, sometimes it persists for weeks after the procedure with no sign of coronary artery disease. I do not understand this phenomenon, but it is obviously vascular. The cardiologists state that this pain does not occur with the same frequency in non-ME/CFS patients and now recognize it as a sign of pain or fibromyalgia associated with ME/CFS.

The cardiologists routinely do cardiac PET scans on my patients with positive Holters and to date have only very rarely found ischemic muscle pathology. Dr. Peter Behan from Glasgow has demonstrated routine abnormal myocardial PET scans on his ME patients (Behan & Behan, 1988; Behan et al., 1985). Once again, I have not figured out why he can get these and our cardiac unit cannot.

I do circulating blood volume on all patients. Dr. David Bell, a pediatrician in New York, was the first to demonstrate this useful test. It serves little purpose for most physicians, however, unless they test all patients with the same protocol and the nuclear medicine department has experience with this test. In our hospital, we find a wide variety of circulatory changes in relation to surface volume. I have some ME patients with a circulating red blood cell volume less than 50% of expected and a very large number with the range of 60% to 70%. What this test means is that blood is pooling somewhere in the body and that this blood is probably not available for the brain. In effect, there may be a reduced perfusion of oxygen and a reduced perfusion of insulin, growth factor, and other essential nutrients and chemical triggers in these patients.

When blood flow to the heart decreases sufficiently, the organism has an increased risk of death. Accordingly, the human body operates in part with pressoreceptors that protect and maintain heart blood supply. When blood flow decreases, pressoreceptors decrease blood flow to noncardiac organs and shunt blood to the heart to maintain life. This, of course, robs those areas of the body that are not essential for maintaining life and means the brain, muscles, and peripheral circulation are placed in physiological difficulty. This may cause much of the symptoms in ME/CFS patients. It probably suggests an intrinsic autonomic failure in these patients. We see SPECT changes in the subcortical brain responsible in part for maintaining reasonable autonomic function. *I repeat*, this test—circulating blood volume—is not useful except in labs with technicians who can do it correctly, in patients who follow a precise protocol, and in relationship to the complete assessment. Many patients want to run off and obtain one and then say, "This proves I have ME or CFS." Neither this test nor any single test proves the presence of disease.

DIAGNOSTIC TESTS OF MYALGIC ENCEPHALOMYELITIS

Consider the following tests:

1. SPECT
2. Xenon SPECT
3. PET
4. Neuropsychological Testing

Discussion   The primary diagnostic criterion for ME is acquired CNS change. We have excellent tools for measuring these physiological and neuropsychological CNS changes: SPECT, xenon SPECT, PET, and neuropsychological testing. CFS patients may not have any of these findings, particularly if their illness is due to some of the problems previously discussed.

Ever since Dr. Jay Goldstein asked Dr. Ishmael Mena, Nuclear Radiologist then at Harbor-UCLA Medical Center, to measure brain dysfunction in an ME/CFS patient's brain with his SPECT scan (Goldstein, 1992; Mena, 1991), it has been one of the most important tests for me in the evaluation of ME.

I do not describe a patient as having ME unless there is an abnormal SPECT. If the SPECT is normal, I often repeat it along with xenon SPECT. If the brain scans remain normal, I conclude that it is unlikely to be ME. I then refer to the patient as a CFS patient and search for other causes of the fatigue syndrome. Few people listened to Drs. Goldstein and Mena at the time. The problem was not with the physicians but that the CFS definition did not fit their discovery. Their discovery did precisely fit ME.

What is a SPECT? This is a computer-driven technology that demonstrates the microcirculation of the terminal arterioles in the brain and/or the function of areas of the individual brain cells. An ME patient has an abnormal brain SPECT. In this technology, there is a microcirculatory phase and a cellular phase. To my knowledge, the technology cannot distinguish whether the problem is in the brain cell or in the microcirculation, or both, unless a two-phase test is performed.

In some cases of MRI spectography of arm muscle of ME patients, it has been shown that because of an abnormal buildup of normal metabolites, the muscle cell actually shuts down to prevent cell death. This cell field shutdown is probably what is happening to the true ME patient's cell physiology in the brain. It probably explains in part the so-called brain fog and the dysfunction after the brain is stressed. It probably also explains muscle dysfunction. In legal cases, I also attempt to send the patient for xenon scan, which demonstrates the significant shutdown of the brain after exercise. I also send the patient for PET scans to obtain confirmatory changes in this completely different technology. Neither xenon SPECT nor PET is necessary except for research or legal cases, but both give a great deal of information about the pathophysiology of this disease to the knowledgeable physician. Xenon SPECT scans are almost impossible to find.

In visual terms, SPECT changes come down to two basic types of radical changes to brain physiology. The typical SPECT change in an ME patient is a decreased perfusion in the cortex in the area of the left middle cerebral artery and the branches leading to the posterior parietal lobes. This can also affect the anterior cerebral artery on the same side. Less commonly, this pathophysiology occurs on both sides involving both left and right middle cerebral arteries and anterior frontal arteries. Still less frequently, the findings are noted primarily on the right. To my knowledge, no one has published on whether there is an increased right brain abnormality in left-handed patients. Among other functions, the left middle cerebral artery covers the areas of the brain for visual and auditory recognition and interpretation. Decreased function of this CNS area creates a significant memory problem in that the patient has difficulty laying down new information and retrieving old information in the presence of added information (any external sensory stimuli/stress).

Often there are also significant changes in the subcortical regions, specifically in the brain stem, cerebellum, and basal ganglia area. Some authorities have identified fibromyalgia changes in the immediate subcortical areas; however, I have not verified this. Another finding that we frequently discover is sometimes referred to as a vascul*itis* pattern (the "itis" part of myalgic encephalomyelitis). This change is identical to what one finds in a patient with HIV dementia. The pattern is irregular and basic SPECT structures appear distorted. Patients with this vasculitis pattern are some of our most severely affected. Once again, the referring physician needs to actually see the scan and be able to read it since the neuroradiologist often only does a partial report. The brain is a big area and you have to be able to ask the neuroradiologist to check specific areas for anomalies. This is where your ability to read these scans is important. There are also problems with the SPECT equipment. Unless the neuroradiologist has a reasonably up-to-date SPECT scanner and appropriate columneter and associated software, the results may simply not be as good as they could be. SPECT scans are only helpful in physicians who understand them; then they can be essential in the diagnosis. They should always be done in conjunction with a carotid and transcranial Doppler to rule out obstructive arterial disease, which is not uncommon in these patients.

NEUROPSYCHOLOGICAL TESTING

This is a complex type of testing, and a physician should attempt to locate an experienced neuropsychologist without ties to the insurance industry. Most neuropsychologists today are employed by the insurance industry, and if they find too much pathology, I suspect that they are no longer engaged. Do not be fooled by a negative insurance-paid neuropsychological report; psychologists whose primary training is not neuropsychology prepare many of these reports. Discussion of this area would require an expert such as Sheila Bastien.

EXPENSIVE TESTS

The following tests require sophisticated, costly equipment:

1. Magnetic resonance imaging
2. Magnetic resonance angiography
3. MRI pectography

4. Tilt table
5. Sleep function

Magnetic Resonance Imaging (MRI)   An MRI is what every patient wants, but which few patients need. But the physician may require the added certainty of the information it can provide. The MRI does not necessarily demonstrate the disease pathophysiology of an ME patient, but it may demonstrate the cause of a CFS patient's illness (Hyde, Biddle, & McNamara, 1992). Many physicians simply do an MRI of a patient and almost nothing else. When it comes back as normal, the physician or the insurance company then tells such patients that nothing is wrong with their CNS and so they can go back to work or school. It is a mistaken belief that a brain dysfunction can be seen in an MRI evaluation. Generally an MRI is useful for one purpose, to demonstrate abnormal anatomy. Some neuroradiologists do not read MRIs very well, particularly if they read the scans and not the computer module. On the computer, you can blow up areas in doubt and also obtain different images. Nevertheless, MRI is changing. It would be useful if all MRIs had the computer software to print out the volume of the entire brain and its subdivisions individually—the ventricles and certain brain organs such as the cerebellum. This capability is technically possible and exists in some centers. The brain areas could be measured for later comparison to facilitate observing rate of atrophy or increase of ventricular volume. There are changes on some ME/CFS brains but what I use the MRI for is simply to rule out malignancy, ventricular or pituitary changes, and brain atrophy not seen clearly on a CT scan or routine radiography. This is important since I infrequently discover both MS and non-MS demyelinating and calcified areas suggestive of a previous focal infection.

I have a patient who had a profound sleep and memory disturbance diagnosed as ME/CFS after returning from Africa. The instant I stopped talking to her to answer the telephone, she would fall asleep in my office. One day, I let her sleep from 9 in the morning until 5 in the evening simply to see when she would wake up. She didn't. So I woke her up at 5 o'clock to tell her it was time to go home. I sat there all day doing paperwork and she didn't once awaken. She was negative for all of the usual sleep-inducing illnesses common in Africa and had a totally normal MRI. The diagnostic clue in her history was that the African town in which she had stayed was overrun by millions of rats and she had been bitten. I made a presumptive diagnosis of Weil's disease with a CNS infection involving the sleep centers.

She gradually recovered over a period of 2 to 3 years only to fall ill again with a stroke and renewed sleep dysfunction. The repeat MRI at that time demonstrated calcification of the substantia nigra area of the basal ganglia and this Von Economo-like disease affecting the basal ganglia probably contributed to her profound sleep problem. Just because an MRI or any test is normal does not mean that it will stay normal. The patient's visible symptoms are sometimes a better barometer that something is wrong than the best tests that a scientist can devise.

Magnetic Resonance Angiography (MRA)   An MRA is simply an MRI scan that highlights the arterial blood supply. An MRA demonstrates arterial obstruction but does not show the arterial activity that can sometimes be seen on transcranial Doppler. I have not done many of these, but they have been useful in posttraumatic cases of ME/CFS (Hyde, Biddle, et al., 1992). I have found more pathology in the less expensive transcranial Dopplers than in MRAs.

MRI Spectography   Because these capabilities are few and far between, I have not used them except in the United Kingdom, in Oxford. MRI spectography has demonstrated the abnormal buildup of metabolic by-products during normal activity of ME patients muscle cells (Hyde, Biddle, et al., 1992). When this occurs, the cell effectively shuts down to prevent cell destruction. This is seen graphically when Olympic runners' muscles seize, often just before the finishing line. This may be what is happening in the brain cells that tend to shut down when stressed by normal activity.

Tilt Table Examination   I frequently find gross abnormalities in ME/CFS patients with this test. A circulating blood volume and a complete cardiac investigation should be done first. This is not a test to undertake lightly since the patient's heart sometimes stops and may have to be restarted. This test should only be done in major hospital centers in the presence of an appropriate physician where such emergency capabilities can be instituted. With this test, I have found significant pathology in about 10% of ME/CFS patients suggesting significant autonomic disease. There is, however, a wide discrepancy in the protocols of this type of testing, and so it is difficult to compare results. Some physicians strap the patient onto the table preventing movement that would induce circulation and others leave the patient relatively free allowing some movement-induced circulation.

Sleep Function Testing   This is a useful and important test for all patients. Many ME/CFS patients have sleep dysfunction that tends to be worse in the first year or two of illness. Often involuntary movements and pain spasms provoke this dysfunction, and the patient simply cannot obtain the necessary sleep. The chronicity of the disease poses a possible danger in placing these patients on long-term analgesics or hypnotics because the patient rapidly becomes accustomed to them while the overall pain and movement-induced sleep dysfunction persists. However, it is sometimes possible to correct obstructive sleep apnea when it is found.

Pros and Cons of Electroencephalograms (EEGs) and Quantitative Electroencephalograms (QEEGs)

In court, I am sometimes asked why I did not do an EEG. There are major problems with EEGs. Although they are sometimes positive during the first few weeks of illness, they are rarely performed at this time unless the patients complain of severe headache during epidemics. An EEG only records activity on the outer millimeter of the brain. Almost all ME patients tend to have involuntary movement disorders that are worse when the patient first falls ill and tend to decrease with time. Yet the neurologist reading an EEG almost never states an EEG is abnormal unless the patient has an active seizure disorder or is brain dead. An average neurologist will spend 10 minutes or much less reading an EEG, whereas it would take a PhD student weeks to measure any abnormalities in a scientific manner. Nevertheless, there is much to measure in an EEG, and what would take the PhD student weeks to read will take a computer microseconds.

A QEEG is simply an EEG attached to a computer that contains appropriate software. A QEEG will immediately demonstrate tumors and brain activity or lack of it related to specific stimuli that are simply not possible to detect on a non-computer-driven EEG. Using QEEG technology operated by an expert physician, we have been able to demonstrate not only lack of normal activity in ME patients but migration of the normal activity centers from injured areas to different parts of the brain. We have also been able to demonstrate that there is considerable interference between the damaged center and the new center. The patient can dampen this interference when not fatigued, but as the stress continues, the interference-dampening capability of the brain fails and the patient goes into a memory and CNS dysfunction situation. Research would be beneficial in this area.

FUNDAMENTAL ADVICE

The following guidelines are useful for all clinicians:

1. When a patient presents with fatigue with no obvious cause, the physician is obliged to search for an occult malignancy, cardiac disease, other organ disease, or chronic infection.
2. When a patient presents with changes in mentation, the physician should think in terms of atherosclerotic disease, other arterial injuries, or changes involving the brain. Some of these are easily and inexpensively measured with a Doppler exam.
3. Common things are common. First check out common illnesses that can cause brain dysfunction and fatigue.
4. Never trust your instincts in making a diagnosis. Bizarre behavior does not necessarily mean the patient needs psychiatric treatment, nor does totally normal behavior mean the patient is free from significant injury or illness.
5. If you cannot measure and confirm the dysfunction with scientific or physical tests, you cannot be certain that your diagnosis is correct.
6. Listen to and watch the patient carefully, and take a detailed history. Trust a patient's complaints, but do not trust a patient's self-diagnosis; patients are often wrong or caught up in the latest fad diagnosis. You spent years studying medicine to learn how to make the correct diagnosis, and on the basis of that diagnosis, you may be able to help the patient.
7. Once you have made a diagnosis or have found an anomaly to explain an illness, remember to complete your investigation—several illnesses or medical anomalies may be contributing to the ill health of a single patient. The injury that you find may be part of a larger spectrum of illnesses, some of it treatable.
8. Patients who arrive at the office of a new physician and who have been completely investigated by many excellent physicians are sometimes dismissed as psychiatric or faking. It is in these patients that I find all of the pathology, and some of it is obvious. Rarely do physicians do more than a routine series of tests. The belief that CFS is a psychological illness is the error of our time.
9. If you discover any significant but modest cardiac valve or other cardiac disease on first examination, repeat the Doppler or any essential test in 6 months if the patient develops shortness of breath, otherwise yearly, as this may represent a progressive injury.

If you fail to find any cause of disease, do not assume that the patient has a psychiatric disease or a school or work avoidance. Sometimes either your knowledge or the necessary technology has not been in place to make the diagnosis. Sometimes the patient's symptoms preclude easy recognition of the illness at that date.

CASE STUDIES

Case 1

A new patient, a teacher, came in carrying reams of computer-driven notes. He was 52 years old and had been ill for 18 months. I started by simply asking him his name; a two-hour tirade followed. I did not attempt to stop him although his words were quite irrational. He berated the more than 10 physicians and 4 hospitals he had attended during the previous 18 months. He stated that they had sometimes asked him to leave after a few minutes without so much as examining him. He told me, "They had the nerve to infer that I was a psychiatric patient." He had lost his job as a teacher due to his illness, and these physicians were not willing to help him obtain his disability payments. He said he slept all the time. He said he was still tired after sleeping. He said that he had lost his memory and couldn't teach. He said that he had not received a disability insurance check for over a year. Yet it was apparent to me, and probably to his other physicians, that this patient had a mental illness. His physicians had referred him to psychiatrists who diagnosed a psychosis and placed him on antipsychotic medication. He reacted badly to these medications. He insisted they were wrong; he had diagnosed himself as having chronic fatigue syndrome. He conformed to the CFS definition. He did not complain of his severe obesity. He did not complain of his strong odor, but possibly the smell and the unstoppable irrational babble explained why some of his physicians had asked him to leave their office. The patient was obviously psychotic.

Yet his presumptive and actual diagnosis that was later confirmed was fairly easy to make. During the 2 hours in my office in which I simply sat back and let him talk, hoping he would slow down, he excused himself to urinate 4 or 5 times. Although I did nothing other than to listen to him, he was very happy when he left because I had not only listened but also asked him to come back. As he left, I gave him a requisition for a fasting and 3-hour blood sugar and a few other simple tests.

In four days when he returned, I was able to tell him that he was severely diabetic and that he had an extreme hyperlipidemia. I referred him to the diabetic clinic the next day, where treatment was started immediately. In the two weeks that followed, I was able to demonstrate that he had had a recent myocardial infarct. Within two weeks of the start of his treatment for diabetes, his psychosis had totally disappeared; he talked rationally in a perfectly normal manner; and I was able to take a reasonable history. He was placed in the hands of cardiologists, dieticians, and exercise physiologists. A letter of the findings was sent to his insurer and within 30 days he had received his back disability benefits from the previous year.

The physicians who had seen this patient were undoubtedly competent professionals. They had trusted their instincts and they had made a correct diagnosis. He did have a psychosis, but they did not go far enough to diagnose a relatively easily treatable diabetic encephalopathy. Yet had I been satisfied with the diagnosis of diabetes and diabetic encephalopathy, I would have missed the hypertension, the severe hyperlipidemia, and the myocardial infarct. This example shows why all patients who present with a self-diagnosis of ME or CFS, or a physician referral of ME/CFS, should be given a complete and structured history, as well as a physical and technological examination. Unusual behavior does not always indicate primary psychiatric disease. Often patients have multiple disease problems to explain their illness.

Case 2

This patient phoned me from the United States to ask for an appointment. The young man had visited two major U.S. clinics and had been seen by over 20 physicians in the United States and Great Britain. They had diagnosed him as either having CFS or psychiatric problems. He was a brilliant professional with an extremely high salary who simply wished to get back to the work and life he loved. His story is typical of many patients I have seen. He had been ill with a significant upper respiratory tract infection (URTI) including a severe sore throat. For some unknown reason, his physician decided to give him a combined hepatitis B and A immunization at this time. Within a week after the injection, he was severely ill with intellectual and fatigue dysfunction. He soldiered on for several months mainly through the courtesy of his associates and then finally had to stop. One of his insurance companies refused to pay him. Despite seeing many physicians and going to two of the most important medical clinics in the United States, he was no further along. He brought all of the tests performed on him over the previous two years. It proved to have been a very incomplete investigation, but there were clues. There was a minor TSH discrepancy on one of his tests. On physical exam, there was not much in his thyroid but it was a bit irregular. I ordered antithyroid antibodies that came back incredibly elevated, and the initial ultrasound came back as a nodular thyroid. A thyroid uptake scan came back with a diagnosis of Graves' disease, but this did not fit what appeared to be a Hashimoto's thyroiditis. I referred him to an endocrinologist in his hometown and asked for a biopsy. It came back as malignant plus Hashimoto's thyroiditis. The thyroid was removed, and he was placed on treatment for metastasis as a precaution.

However, his neuro-SPECT demonstrated a significant vasculitis pattern. What probably happened is that the hepatitis B portion of the immunization paralyzed his normal immune response to the ongoing infection. The existing presumed viral infection then became chronic. I have seen this scenario in many cases of post-hepatitis B immunization injury. The companies producing hepatitis B immunization serum now clearly state in their brochures not to immunize when the patient is ill. When these immunizations first came out, however, they were touted as being the safest immunization ever invented and the suggestion was that they could be given without any negative consequence. Immunizations are powerful tools and should not be used in a patient with an acute ongoing infectious illness. This patient has other injuries that I will not go into, but he has classical ME with the abnormal vasculitis pattern scan. His ME illness is still active, but hopefully will settle down.

Case 3

This patient also called me from the United States. She had been seen and diagnosed as CFS by several clinics and ME/CFS physicians. It seemed foolish for her to waste her time and money. She had significant brain dysfunction and overwhelming fatigue. She had CFS. Her initial investigation took the morning, and I was able to obtain a carotid and transcranial Doppler that afternoon. The exam revealed severe hyperlipidemia and an 80% obstruction of both internal carotids and a complete obstruction of the basilar artery feeding the brain. Her cause of CFS was obvious, but experienced physicians investigating ME/CFS and other neurologists and internists in the United States had missed it. The obstruction in one of the arteries was removed and she improved.

Case 4 Group

This Canadian government employee fell ill at a party, along with several other family members. She had typical acute onset ME including significant CNS dysfunction and rapid exhaustion with physical or intellectual stressors. Her twin daughters also fell ill and had to stop school. A teenage neighbor across the street who was not at the party fell ill the same week; all had the same symptom picture. The next-door neighbor developed leukemia and the neighbor three doors down was diagnosed with Crohn's disease all in the same two weeks. Was it coincidence? Possibly. The girl across the street was ill for 6 months with severe ME/CFS and then recovered totally and not only went back to her university but got top marks in her class.

One of the identical twins recovered and returned to university classes with minor ongoing problems. The other identical twin attempted to return to school but failed miserably. Five years later, the mother and the one twin are still ill. The SPECT brain scans are typical of ME. Why did one twin recover? With PCR (polymerase chain reaction), we were able to find that the mother and the one twin still ill had had a persisting and consistent novel enterovirus for over three years. The twin who recovered had no enterovirus and her immune system had gotten rid of this infection. The ill mother and daughter both have persisting antibodies to their mitochondria.

Another group also in Ottawa fell ill the same week, again at a party; all were family members. One had the same persisting enterovirus that we had followed for three years; the others we were not able to test because government cutbacks had closed our facility. The one woman with the persisting virus was a physical education instructor and government employee and was now suffering from chronic severe CNS problems and rapid exhaustion. A vasculitis SPECT brain pattern has persisted since she was first ill. She had severe dysautanomia and peripheral nerve injuries.

Interesting enough, her uncle, who fell ill at the same party, had CNS problems and profound exhaustion only after playing hockey, a very active sport. He developed rapidly advancing coronary valve injury and this valve had to be replaced. He has been advised to cease playing hockey and has done so; he is now active in golf without any further problems.

Another family member at the same party developed acute psychotic disease and recovered. The enterovirus finding is interesting. We have never recovered this virus in a gradual onset CFS patient. We have never found it in any normal controls except for two individuals who had both received massive blood transfusions and had heart disease. We have found this virus in only about 10% of acute onset patients and have not been able to recover it in patients after 3 years of illness. It is hard not to believe that some ME is not viral related.

CONCLUSION

Thirty years ago when a patient presented to a hospital clinic with unexplained fatigue, any medical school physician would have told the students to search for an occult malignancy, cardiac or other organ disease, or chronic infection. The concept that there is an entity called chronic fatigue syndrome has totally altered that essential medical guideline. Patients are now being diagnosed with CFS as though it were a disease. It is not. It is a patchwork of symptoms that could mean anything. The original concepts of searching for occult disease are relevant to patients presenting today with CFS, ME, and other fatiguing illnesses. Furthermore, because you do not find pathology does not mean there is none. From 1985 until 1988, I investigated ME/CFS patients in a manner that I thought was exhaustive. I found disease then in only about 10% to 20% of patients. Were the remaining 80% to 90% suffering from somatization, psychiatric disease, or simply faking? No, the error of analysis was in my ability. After I met and received training from specialists including Dr. Charles Poser, a neurologist at Harvard, Dr. John Richardson in the United Kingdom, Dr. Jay Goldstein in Beverly Hills, and Dr. Ishmael Mena, at the University of California-Los Angeles , my ability to diagnose a ME/CFS patient's disability rose 50% to 80%. Today, I usually find the underlying measurable cause of disease in 70% to 80% of the patients that I investigate. Are the remaining 20% suffering from somatization or psychiatric disease? I don't think so. I think I am simply missing the underlying diagnosis.

REFERENCES

Acheson, E. D. (1992). The clinical syndrome variously called benign myalgic encephalomyelitis, Iceland disease and epidemic neuromyasthenia. In B. M. Hyde, J. Goldstein, & P. Levine (Eds.), *The clinical and scientific basis of myalgic encephalomyelitis/chronic fatigue syndrome* (pp. 129–158). Ottawa, Ontario, Canada: Nightingale Research Foundation Press.

Anderson, J. S., & Ferrans, C. E. (1997). The quality of life of persons with chronic fatigue syndrome. *Journal of Nervous and Mental Diseases, 185,* 359–367.

Behan, P., & Behan, W. (1988). Postviral fatigue syndrome. *CRC, Critical Reviews in Neurobiology, 4*(2), 157–178.

Behan, P., Behan, W. M., & Bell, E. (1985). The postviral fatigue syndrome, an analysis of the findings in 50 cases. *Journal of Infection, 10,* 211–222.

Crowley, N., Nelson, M., & Stovin, S. (1957). Epidemiological aspects of an outbreak of encephalomyelitis at the Royal Free Hospital, London, in the summer of 1955. *Journal of Hygiene, 55,* 102.

Daugherty, S. A., Henry, B. E., Peterson, D. L., Swarts, R. L., Bastien, S., Thomas, R. S., et al. (1991, January). Chronic fatigue syndrome in northern Nevada. *Reviews of Infectious Diseases, 13*(Suppl. 1), S39–S44.

Fukuda, K., Straus, S. E., Hickie, I., Sharpe, M. C., Dobbins, J. G., & Komaroff, A. (1994). The chronic fatigue syndrome: A comprehensive approach to its definition and study. *Annals of Internal Medicine, 121,* 953–959.

Gilliam, A. G. (1938). Epidemiological study of an epidemic, diagnosed as poliomyelitis, occurring among the personnel of the Los Angeles County General Hospital during the summer of 1934. *Public Health Bulletin, 240.*

Goldstein, J. A. (1992). Chronic fatigue syndrome: Limbic encephalopathy in a dysfunctional neuroimmune network. In B. M. Hyde, J. Goldstein, & P. Levine (Eds.), *The clinical and scientific basis of myalgic encephalomyelitis/chronic fatigue syndrome* (pp. 400–406). Ottawa, Ontario, Canada: Nightingale Research Foundation Press.

Grufferman, S. (1992). Epidemiologic and immunologic findings in clusters of chronic fatigue syndrome. In B. M. Hyde, J. Goldstein, & P. Levine (Eds.), *The clinical and scientific basis of myalgic encephalomyelitis/chronic fatigue syndrome* (pp. 189–195). Ottawa, Ontario, Canada: Nightingale Research Foundation Press.

Henderson, D. A., & Shelokov, A. (1959a). Epidemic neuromyasthenia—clinical syndrome? *New England Journal of Medicine, 260*(15), 757–764.

Henderson, D. A., & Shelokov, A. (1959b). Epidemic neuromyasthenia—clinical syndrome? (concluded). *New England Journal of Medicine, 260*(16), 814–818.

Henderson, D. A., & Shelokov, A. (1992). Epidemic neuromyasthenia—clinical syndrome. In B. M. Hyde, J. Goldstein, & P. Levine (Eds.), *The clinical and scientific basis of myalgic encephalomyelitis/chronic fatigue syndrome* (pp. 159–175). Ottawa, Ontario, Canada: Nightingale Research Foundation Press.

Holmes, G. P., Kaplan, J. E., Gantz, N. M., Komaroff, A. L., Schonberger, L. B., Straus, S. E., et al. (1988). Chronic fatigue syndrome: A working case definition. *Annals of Internal Medicine, 108,* 387–389.

Holmes, G. P., Kaplan, J. E., Schonberger, L. B., Straus, S. E., Zegans, L. S., Gantz, N. M., et al. (1988). Definition of chronic fatigue syndrome [Letter to the editor]. *Annals of Internal Medicine, 109,* 512.

Hyde, B. M. (1992). A bibliography of ME/CFS epidemics. In B. M. Hyde, J. Goldstein, & P. Levine (Eds.), *The clinical and scientific basis of myalgic encephalomyelitis/chronic fatigue syndrome* (pp. 176–186). Ottawa, Ontario, Canada: Nightingale Research Foundation Press.

Hyde, B. M., Biddle, R., & McNamara, T. (1992). Magnetic resonance in the diagnosis of ME/CFS, a review. In B. M. Hyde, J. Goldstein, & P. Levine (Eds.), *The clinical and scientific basis of myalgic encephalomyelitis/chronic fatigue syndrome* (pp. 425–431). Ottawa, Ontario, Canada: Nightingale Research Foundation Press.

Hyde, B. M., Goldstein, J., & Levine, P. (Eds.). (1992). *The clinical and scientific basis of myalgic encephalomyelitis/chronic fatigue syndrome.* Ottawa, Ontario, Canada: Nightingale Research Foundation Press.

Joyce, J., Hotopf, M., & Wessely, S. (1997). The relationship of chronic fatigue and chronic fatigue syndrome: A systematic review. *Quarterly Journal of Medicine, 90,* 223–233.

Lloyd, A. R., Hickie, I., Boughton, C. R., Spencer, O., & Wakefield, D. (1990). Prevalence of chronic fatigue syndrome in an Australian population. *Medical Journal of Australia, 153,* 522–528.

Marshall, G. S. (1999). Report of a workshop on the epidemiology, natural history, and pathogenesis of chronic fatigue syndrome in adolescents. *Journal of Pediatrics, 134*(4), 395–405.

Mena, I. (1991, May 18). *Study of cerebral perfusion by neuro-SPECT in patients with chronic fatigue syndrome.* Presented at Chronic Fatigue Syndrome: Current Theory and Treatment conference, Bel Air, CA.

Peterson, D. L., Strayer, D. R., Bastien, S., Henry, B., Ablashi, D. V., Breaux, E. J., et al. (1992). Clinical improvements obtained with ampligen in patients with severe chronic fatigue syndrome and associated encephalopathy. In B. M. Hyde, J. Goldstein, & P. Levine (Eds.), *The clinical and scientific basis of myalgic encephalomyelitis/chronic fatigue syndrome* (pp. 634–638). Ottawa, Ontario, Canada: Nightingale Research Foundation Press.

Ramsay, A. M. (1988). *Myalgic encephalomyelitis and postviral fatigue states* (2nd ed.). London: Gower Medical.

Richardson, J. (1992). ME, the epidemiological and clinical observations of a rural practitioner. In B. M. Hyde, J. Goldstein, & P. Levine (Eds.), *The clinical and scientific basis of myalgic encephalomyelitis/chronic fatigue syndrome* (pp. 85–92). Ottawa, Ontario, Canada: Nightingale Research Foundation Press.

Sharpe, M. C., Archard, L. C., Banatvala, J. E., Borysiewicz, L. K., Clare, A. W., David, A., et al. (1991). A report-chronic fatigue syndrome: Guidelines for research. *Journal of the Royal Society of Medicine, 84,* 118–121.

Shelokov, A., Habel, K., Verder, E., & Welch, W. (1957). Epidemic neuromyasthenia: An outbreak of poliomyelitis-like illness in student nurses. *New England Journal of Medicine, 257,* 345.

Sigurdsson, B., Sigurjonsson, J., & Sigurdsson, J. (1950). Disease epidemic in Iceland simulating poliomyelitis. *American Journal of Hygiene, 52,* 222.

Taylor, R. R., Friedberg, F., & Jason, L. A. (2001). *A clinician's guide to controversial illnesses: Chronic fatigue syndrome, fibromyalgia, and multiple chemical sensitivities.* Sarasota, FL: Professional Resource Press.

Wallis, A. L. (1955). *An investigation into an unusual disease seen in epidemic and sporadic form in a general practice in Cumberland in 1955 and subsequent years.* Unpublished doctoral thesis, University of Edinburgh, Scotland.

CHAPTER 4

Sociocultural Context and Trauma

PATRICIA A. FENNELL

THE CONTINUING EXPERIENCE of multiple traumas may be one of the most salient aspects of chronic fatigue syndrome (CFS). Recent research has drawn attention to the effects of cumulative trauma or adversity, which may result in a spectrum of trauma-related disorders, ranging from the somewhat benign (e.g., anxiety) to the severe (e.g., posttraumatic stress disorder (PTSD; Alonzo, 2000; Dohrenwend, 2000; Fullilove, Lown, & Fullilove, 1992; Turner & Lloyd, 1995). Cumulative adversity can affect the patient's ability to cope with the illness experience, the health care system, and other life domains (Alonzo, 2000). As a result, patients may develop impeded responses to their own symptoms and the use of health care as a result of an accumulated burden of adversity. The intent of this chapter is to identify and elucidate the types of traumas associated with CFS. It addresses the possible causes of such traumas, the potential effects on individuals, and heightens clinicians awareness.

THE EVOLVING DEFINITION OF TRAUMA

Increasingly, the formal clinical definitions of trauma found in the *Diagnostic and Statistical Manual of Mental Disorders* (*DSM-IV*) are coming under critical scrutiny (Alonzo, 2000; Asmundson et al., 2000; Blank, 1993; Fullilove et al., 1992; Scott & Stradling, 1994; Turner & Lloyd, 1995). Although there is legitimacy in current definitions, concerns remain, especially in situations involving, for example, lifelong trauma (Herman, 1992; Mezey & Robbins, 2001). Further, Herman, in a paper about survivors of prolonged and repeated trauma, provides strong evidence that current definitions must be expanded to account for a variety of stress-related disorders. These include, but are not limited to, the stressful response to a traumatic event (World Trade Center disaster), prolonged and repeated trauma (prisoner of war, Holocaust survivor), and continual trauma (chronic illness). In summary, Yehuda and McFarlane (1995) state:

After a review of the relevant research findings that have emerged in the last decade regarding the prevalence, longitudinal course, and neurobiology of PTSD, [it is suggested] that although current data have supported PTSD as a distinct diagnostic entity, some of the specific features of the disorder are different from those originally developed. (p. 42)

Results of a community-based sample study suggest that, in medical practice, when evaluating and treating individuals with chronic fatigue and unexplained somatic symptoms, it is essential to consider coexisting psychosocial and psychiatric issues (Taylor & Jason, 2000). In addition, some biological abnormalities occurring in PTSD individuals have also occurred in individuals with CFS and fibromyalgia syndrome (FMS; Taylor, Friedberg, & Jason, 2001). An argument can be made that there is an underlying biopsychosocial relationship between PTSD and chronic fatigue.

Accordingly, these definitions may not be inclusive enough to capture what many clinicians and researchers believe to be genuine trauma experiences associated with CFS and other chronic illnesses or conditions. The traumas can vary widely, and individuals suffer the effects differently. The individual's history and their circumstances at the time of any trauma can further affect their perception of it. Additionally, the degree to which patients can be traumatized by the reactions of others to their illness depends a great deal on what others think, feel, and believe about CFS.

FAILURE TO DIAGNOSE TRAUMA

Research indicates that PTSD is routinely undiagnosed in clinical settings. Clinicians on the primary care level tend not to consider this disorder, and they often do not recognize it or differentiate it from other symptomological aspects of illness (Zimmerman & Mattia, 1999). As a consequence, trauma is underreported and not integrated into treatment plans. This situation is changing somewhat for particular medical conditions, but much work remains to be done, especially when dealing with chronic illnesses such as CFS.

TRAUMAS ASSOCIATED WITH CFS

TRAUMAS CAUSED BY CFS ONSET

The recognition that something is very wrong—the moment when the individual actually experiences the onset of CFS—may be as traumatizing as the actual effects of the illness itself. The symptoms, much like the symptoms of other chronic illnesses, can result in physical, emotional, cognitive, social, and lifestyle changes that cause additional pain and difficulty for patients and their families. Thus, it is hardly surprising that the individual's realization of the onset of the illness is frightening, sad, and inevitably accompanied by loss (Alonzo, 2000; Baldwin, 1978; Botha, 1996; Lindy, Green, & Grace, 1987).

TRAUMAS CAUSED BY FAMILY RESPONSE

Even though patients may gradually come to terms with their CFS and learn productive ways to live with it, their families may have less success. The individual's changed life, which the illness produces, may be more than a spouse has bargained for. Parents may simply not want to believe that a son or daughter with CFS is not going to get appreciably better, and the children of patients very often find it difficult to acknowledge, or relate, to this changed parent in their lives. None of these reactions is lost on the patient, and each can cause trauma apart from the actual disease symptoms (Cannon & Cavanaugh, 1998; Fisher & Weihs, 2000; Hayes, 1997; Heinzer, 1998; Pless & Nolan, 1991; Scambler & Hopkins, 1990; Ware, 1998). Some families attempt to shield patients from anything that reminds them of their condition, or the situation the illness forces onto the individual. One researcher refers to this as the "trauma membrane" (Lindy, Grace, & Green, 1981). As part of this shielding, families may discourage patients from seeking treatment or from carrying out treatment protocols because these would remind the patient of the [unhappy] condition.

Those who live, love, and work with CFS patients can also be traumatized (Hayes, 1997; Rolland, 1994; Scott & Stradling, 1994). These people also may experience trauma as a result of the illness onset, their witnessing of the patient's suffering, or their own difficulties as a result of their changed life. They, too, can suffer from society's judgments and responses to their loved ones. Family members as well as patients have premorbid and comorbid issues. They may be divorcing the newly ill patient, or they may find that their spouse cannot have children because of the chronic illness. Dependent children may be involved, who are going through their own developmental crises. Those associated with the patient also may experience iatrogenic traumatization.

TRAUMAS CAUSED BY SOCIETAL RESPONSE

The culture is constructed around an idealized work ethic in which healthy, productive individuals are considered the most socially useful and are valued accordingly. Given this, those who are very young, very old, differently-abled, or infirm may be loved, indulged, or even admired, but are not seen as contributing to the good of society and thus can be actively devalued. People with CFS are often unable to engage in economically productive work at their former pace. Because they frequently have no outward signs of illness or disability, they may seem to be simply trying to escape from doing their fair share, or engaging in self-serving victimization (Bartley & Owen, 1996; Bates, Rankin-Hill, & Sanchez-Ayendez, 1997; Henderson, 1997; Plehn, Peterson, & Williams, 1998; Pless & Nolan, 1991; Scambler & Hopkins, 1990; Stuart & Noyes, 1999; Tait, Chibnall, & Richardson, 1990; Ware 1998, 1999).

Accordingly, society's response to those with CFS can be extremely hurtful, and these potentially traumatizing events tend to repeat over and over again. Such responses can occur in the workplace, at home between family members, or in any environment or situation where the patient's CFS may become an issue (Bartley & Owen, 1996; Cannon & Cavanaugh, 1998; Fisher & Weihs, 2000; Heinzer, 1998; Ware, 1999; Ware & Kleinman, 1992).

The medical community, the media, and the public have at times stigmatized, belittled, or sensationalized chronic illnesses such as CFS (Ax, Gregg, & Jones, 1998; Ballweg, 1997; Brody, 2000; Lewis, 1999; Marbach, Lennon, Link, & Dohrenwend, 1990; Scambler & Hopkins, 1990; Schiller, Crystal, & Lewellen, 1994; Stuart & Noyes, 1999; Ware, 1998). It was only a few years ago that the term "yuppie flu" was used to stereotype individuals suffering from CFS (Barshay, 1993). If people look healthy, it is difficult to believe that they are actually suffering from an illness. In our culture, we expect to see a scar, a crutch, a wheelchair, or some other obvious physical sign of illness or disability.

PREMORBID AND COMORBID TRAUMAS

It is also important to consider traumatic events that are independent of the patient's CFS, but that may be confused with it or influence how the patient processes it. Premorbid traumas occurred prior to the onset of the chronic illness (Blum, Potthoff, & Resnick, 1997; Ware & Kleinman, 1992). They include such things as childhood incest, assault as an adult, active duty in the armed services, time spent in a war zone, torture, natural disasters, and car accidents. Recent examples addressing research specific to trauma, stress, and CFS have included sexual abuse (Taylor et al., 2001) and natural disasters (Lutgendorf et al., 1995).

Comorbid traumas can include developmental transitions and upheavals, such as the birth of a child, the decision to return to work, or the death of a loved one (Alonzo, 2000; Gatchel & Gardea, 1999; Van Mens-Verhulst & Bensing, 1998). Comorbid traumas may also consist of the illness of family members, caregiving responsibilities, divorce, assault, robbery, or any other unusual life event. It is important to recognize that trauma can result from the stress of even a positive situation, such as a new marriage, a longed-for pregnancy, or a new job.

Clinicians also need to recognize and help their patients see that CFS may lengthen the processing of any and all life changes. The illness often impairs decision making and causes chaotic thinking, short-term memory loss, and many other cognitive or physical impairments. Avoiding or ignoring issues that arise out of CFS may confuse both patients and clinicians regarding, for example, the grief the patient feels when a child leaves home or the misery caused by perpetual pain and/or exhaustion. Those who provide treatment need to help patients define their experiences on all levels. By separating current external events from emotional and physiological responses to CFS, clinicians can help mitigate the disruption surrounding transitional upheavals and the mental or cognitive disorientation associated with the changes wrought by the illness.

Finally, clinicians must keep in mind that although these other traumas are unrelated to the chronic illness, they are part of the cumulative trauma package.

VICARIOUS TRAUMAS

Vicarious traumatization affects clinicians as well (Clark & Gioro, 1998; Rosenberg & Molho, 1998). Any clinician can be upset by witnessing the onset of CFS or distressed by its chronic nature. The inability to provide a treatment, a prescription, a procedure, or cure can produce frustration and despair or even anger. All clinicians have their own premorbid and comorbid issues, and all experience countertransference.

Clinicians can also suffer guilt by association and clinical marginalization because of the patients they choose to treat (Engel, 1977). Clinicians who treat the poor, the disenfranchised, and the chronically ill often report that they experience stigmatization or discrimination from their peers. One primary care physician reported being warned by her HMO not to take on any more of "those chronically ill patients" (communication to the author). Another physician who was very effective in treating a particular chronic illness group let it be known that she did not want the larger patient community to learn of her effectiveness with these patients. Her HMO had already hinted that she was "misplacing" her efforts and had told the office staff to consider her caseload for such patients closed. Another physician practicing in a popular tourist area was strongly encouraged by local politicians to move his practice elsewhere because he championed the care of a particular group of patients (communication to the author).

IATROGENIC OR CLINICALLY INDUCED TRAUMAS

Iatrogenic trauma is usually associated with a medical response or intervention to a physiological illness (Cuijpers, 1998; Epstein, Quill, & McWhinney, 1999; Kirmayer, Robbins, & Paris, 1994; McCahill, 1995; Stuart & Noyes, 1999). In addition to mistakes or unexpected adverse events, such as a new illness contracted because of a hospital stay, iatrogenic trauma can also arise out of appropriate medical care. This second kind of traumatization may involve the actual treatment, and could also involve frustrating or frightening experiences with the health care system over time (Alonzo, 2000; Alonzo & Reynolds, 1996). These kinds of trauma can affect how patients respond to treatment, and whether they even continue with their medical care.

In the context of CFS, it is necessary to extend the concept of iatrogenic illness into two other areas. The first is the domain of medical intervention that is not considered procedure-specific, such as informal contact with the patient and the patient interview and assessment (Hampton & Frombach, 2000). The second area where iatrogenic response is possible is psychological care (van der Kolk, McFarlane, & Weisaeth, 1996). As in all chronic illness, opportunities multiply for iatrogenic traumatization.

All of these traumas interface with each other. Over time, they can accumulate into a significant clinical concern (Alonzo, 2000).

POTENTIALLY TRAUMAGENIC SOCIOCULTURAL FACTORS

Six sociocultural factors can seriously exacerbate patients' experience of trauma. These factors influence how clinicians think about illness in general, and CFS in particular. If clinicians do not consciously consider these factors and process their own reactions to them, then their patients, the patients' families, and sometimes even the clinicians themselves may suffer trauma (Fennell, 1995, 2001, 2004).

1. Intolerance of Suffering   Early and medieval Christianity enfolded the concept of suffering into a religious schema where it served negatively as a punishment for sin but positively as God's method of testing and strengthening faith and bringing believers closer to Christ and salvation. When Descartes split the body from the mind/spirit, he also separated the physical aspects of pain and suffering from the spiritual and emotional ones. As far as science was concerned, humans became genderless bodies that responded to stimuli, whether of pain or pleasure. These feelings had no intrinsic meaning, and pain and suffering had no purpose. Medical practitioners following a scientific approach sought to relieve or end suffering by aggressively attacking its somatic manifestations, the only ones which were demonstrably physical and material (Ballweg, 1997; Bendelow & Williams, 1995; Gamsa, 1994; Stuart & Noyes, 1999).

Mental and spiritual suffering, which is nebulous and subjective from the scientific point of view, remained the province of religion or philosophy. Increasingly, as science became the privileged new approach to knowledge and understanding, religion was relegated to a peripheral cultural role in Western society. In addition, the containment that religion had provided for suffering—whatever meaning could be ascribed to it—was sidelined also. But religious attitudes did not die out altogether, even among convinced materialists. They were simply pushed to the margins of cultural influence, where they continued to nurture now often-unconscious attitudes among the population at large (Bendelow & Williams, 1995).

Despite Descartes, however, suffering inextricably involves both body and mind/spirit. It is impossible to separate physical suffering from mental and emotional suffering. Moreover, scientists quickly discovered that they could not measure physical suffering objectively. Inevitably, they had to rely on an individual's self-reporting, which not only was subjective, but also varied enormously according to the individual's background and circumstances. Although flawed data on pain had to be used in day-to-day medical practice, it was sufficiently subjective to discourage researchers, until recently, from investigating pain and suffering in general (Armstrong, 1990; Ballweg, 1997; Stuart & Noyes, 1999; Turk & Rudy, 1991).

Suffering is a ubiquitous human condition, with certain identifying characteristics. It increases in relation to how uncontrollable it is or how uncontrollable the sufferer believes it will be and how long it will continue. When suffering persists, people experience a profound sense of helplessness and also of hopelessness. They feel that their bodies are running out of the physical resources that combated the pain. They perceive their suffering as intolerable and at the same time as interminable. Ambiguity about their prospects produces anxiety about the future, which further exacerbates their suffering. Moreover, with suffering comes a loss of physical, cognitive, and emotional viability and hence a greatly diminished sense of self. This loss produces debilitating grief at the same time that the sufferers need to engage in the difficult readjustment to their new condition (Bendelow & Williams, 1995; Do Rozario, 1997).

Chronicity and ambiguity deeply affect the sense of suffering. People can often endure more severe pain if it is acute—that is, if it is pain that lasts, or they believe will last, only a short duration. In a sense, suffering comes into existence when pain, even mild pain, persists and shows no indication of ever ending.

By and large, contemporary Americans ascribe no positive value to suffering. It is mysterious, enigmatic, frightening, and many times, meaningless. They expect and demand aggressive action by medical practitioners to end suffering immediately. Americans do not want to suffer themselves, and they do not like to be around others who are suffering. It makes them unhappy to see others suffer, and they fear suffering. It reminds them that all life is fragile, and people are easily hurt or disabled. Witnesses to suffering cannot help but think about their own death, or their possible future suffering (Barshay, 1993).

When the person suffering is someone an individual loves, the witness is often compassionately engaged, especially if the suffering does not persist for a long time. But long-term suffering strains even the most loving relationships. People who are suffering and those witnessing their suffering feel grief and often suffer as well. Yet contemporary society frowns on any public expression of such feelings, especially among men. Both sufferers and witnesses are prevented from relieving themselves and finding recognition and acceptance of their powerful emotions. Instead, they are forced to push the feelings inward, where they fester and often reemerge in behavior that is destructive to self or others. It is important to remember that trauma can occur to witnesses as well as sufferers when appropriate expressions of grief are closed off (Ballweg, 1997; Barshay, 1993; Stuart & Noyes, 1999).

Clinicians, whose profession puts them in constant proximity to people who are suffering, protect themselves against reactions of avoidance, anger, and despair by doing precisely what science advocates and the public desires. They locate a cause for the suffering as quickly as possible and provide appropriate treatment to end it. If, however, they cannot find the cause, or if the suffering persists even with treatment, some clinicians can become frustrated and even angry. Their personal fears can begin to emerge. In self-protection, some may conclude that the suffering cannot have a physical genesis, but must proceed instead from psychological causes. Psychological causes carry an implicit judgment of characterological failure, causing the sufferer to experience iatrogenic health care in the form of blame (Cameron & Gregor, 1987; Kontz, 1989; Stuart & Noyes, 1999).

When clinicians are frustrated because they cannot perform "competently," this can be quickly communicated to patients. The health care professional's preference for clear physical symptoms is also obvious. Patients receive negative reinforcement for accurate reporting, and thus, subsequently limit the information they provide clinicians to acceptably physical or "real" events. In addition, because some clinicians also subtly encourage only good news or reports of progress and improvements, patients adapt, and thus censor how they describe their illness experience.

The diagnostic controversy that surrounds CFS can become a traumatic issue when encountered in a health care provider's office. Some members of the medical community tend to be skeptical of CFS. They may convey to patients the notion that they are not really ill and that their condition indicates characterological inferiority or defect, or even deliberate malingering (Cameron & Gregor, 1987; Kontz, 1989; Stuart & Noyes, 1999). Patients develop a fairly predictable set of responses to such attitudes. They think and worry more about their disease after a visit to the doctor. They feel confused about their identify and what is real. As a result, many patients experience more anger and sadness and decide to avoid health care providers entirely (Ballweg, 1997; McCahill, 1995; Stuart & Noyes, 1999).

CFS patients who formerly participated successfully in mainstream culture may find that the illness has exposed them to social abandonment and rejection for the first time in their lives. To make matters worse, it has occurred for reasons beyond their control. Ironically, racial minorities and the economically deprived are less likely to suffer this particular effect because they have already experienced it time and time again. For them, chronic illness is just one more instance of unfairness in an unfair world.

The greatest trauma caused by the culture's intolerance of suffering is the violation of the social contract. People who have diligently performed as worthy partners, parents, workers, and friends suddenly find that something beyond their control has turned them into second-class citizens who are easily dismissed and barely tolerated. A partner's vow to be loyal "for better or for worse" frequently becomes meaningless. The health care professionals, who supposedly cure illness, not only fail to help them, but may even imply that their suffering is their own fault (Alonzo, 2000).

2. Intolerance of Ambiguity   Most people in Western culture are intolerant of ambiguity. They dislike the not-yet-known or the unknowable, and therefore they avoid—even fear—complexity or chaos. They want issues to be clear and straightforward, and solutions preferably clear-cut. The prevalence of science and technology in today's society has contributed to this cultural intolerance by elevating quantitative systems of thinking and, whether intended or not, simultaneously devaluating qualitative and subjective systems of knowing. In today's cultural milieu, all that is true or real should be observable, measurable, and ultimately knowable. Anything that does not yield to these criteria is suspect. People continue to have doubts about situations or problems as long as the situations remain ambiguous.

In terms of the soma-psyche dichotomy, it is the physical body that is knowable, whereas the psyche is unknowable, and hence, suspect. The cultural elevation of the quantitative and allegedly objective, above the qualitative and subjective, has contributed to the view that ambiguous situations or problems are potentially dangerous and possibly immoral, and therefore should be avoided. Ambiguity generates a sense of powerlessness and impotence. A person who does not comprehend what something is cannot take action, which heightens this sense of helplessness. With ambiguity, one is often rendered impotent. No matter how horrible a disease may be, if it has a comprehensible cause, known symptomatology, and an acknowledged, even if deadly, prognosis, it is often more bearable for the sufferer, family, friends, and clinicians, than a condition of unknown origin with an unclear prognosis (Armstrong, 1990; Ballweg, 1997; Bendelow & Williams, 1995; Stuart & Noyes, 1999).

In today's society, individuals experiencing chronic illnesses and suffering must endure the ambiguity of their condition, without the aid of spiritual and psychological devices, which used to be part of Western culture and are commonplace in other traditions such as Buddhism. Whereas Western society's aggressive determination to eradicate physical suffering keeps it from falling into the kind of quietism or indifference to suffering that can characterize some cultures, it has also lost familiarity with philosophical and spiritual conceptions of suffering and the meaning and solace they may offer.

People in contact with CFS patients are sometimes frightened, simply because the condition is ambiguous. They fear potential contagion or contamination. This may be an atavistic survival instinct on the part of humans as a species, but even when science has clearly identified modes of disease transmission, people still fear contamination, as AIDS has shown over and over again. If the etiology of an illness is unclear, perhaps it is easy to catch. If the prognosis is unclear, who knows what might be in store if one caught the disease? People are adrift along a continuum of the unknown, from the origin of the illness to its outcome (Armstrong, 1987; Barshay, 1993; Scambler & Hopkins, 1990).

Flooding in to alleviate the anxiety caused by ambiguity comes the notion of a "just" world and deserved punishment. People automatically begin to distance themselves from those who are suffering, especially if the cause is ambiguous. By specifying to themselves how they would have avoided the situation, solved it differently, or responded differently, people create a comforting belief that they can avoid personal tragedy by using farsighted protective action. This creates a false sense of calm and control over the uncertainty of living. As a defense mechanism, it supports the illusion that the people are invulnerable to illness, disability, and mortality. It also facilitates the ugly, yet somehow comforting, blaming of the victim. Perhaps individuals with CFS have actually brought it on themselves, or perhaps they are lazy or faking, trying to get out of work or other responsibilities. Perhaps they are immoral or flawed in some other way, which makes the disease an appropriate retribution.

The intolerance of ambiguity may produce a sense of powerlessness and then guilt, depression, and grief. As ordinary participants in the culture at large, some CFS patients internalize the message that they have probably caused their problem by some personal action and therefore deserve their condition. They suffer in addition because they feel, sometimes quite correctly, that they are a burden to those they love. Rejection and abandonment are not false fears, but realities that are all too often a part of the lives of the chronically ill.

Clinicians can also experience profound powerlessness when they treat CFS patients. It is frustrating when the knowledge accumulated from years of study, hard work, and experience can produce no measurable or meaningful effect in a patient. Human nature, unfortunately, often makes it preferable to blame the patient rather than continue to experience a sense of incompetence and failure.

The most serious harmful effect arising out of society's intolerance of ambiguity is that CFS patients are openly or subtly held to be responsible for their condition, an attitude that the chronically ill usually share. As a consequence, they suffer strong feelings of guilt, depression, and grief.

3. Intolerance of Chronicity   Americans do not like chronicity; it upsets the society's action- and achievement-oriented culture. The society prefers illnesses that are acute because although they disturb personal and organizational output, they do so in a predictable manner. Heart disease, appendectomies, and medicated depressions return individuals to the workplace in a fairly timely manner. But problems or illnesses that do not have a distinct beginning, middle, and end, and are not easily treatable, run contrary to a perceived notion that health problems will respond to powerful drugs or advanced technological intervention. CFS, with its unclear etiology, course, and outcome, is frustrating, potentially expensive, and consequently devalued.

The medical profession focuses on achieving cures; that is, returning patients to essentially the same status they had before the disease. The public has come to expect cures, especially in the past 50 years, with the amazing progress of science in pharmaceuticals and the technological tools of diagnosis and treatment (Armstrong, 1987; Stuart & Noyes, 1999). When medicines or other treatments do not return the patient to normal, both clinician and patient can experience a sense of failure and both can feel varying degrees of responsibility for it. Since CFS is not amenable to cure, and the patient does not return to "normal," both clinician and patient may repeatedly suffer powerful feelings of failure (Ax, Gregg, & Jones, 1997; Banks & Prior, 2001).

Many people do not understand chronic illnesses at all, particularly the fact that these illnesses are chronic, that is, that they do not go away. When people see improvement in a chronically ill friend, family member, or even in themselves, they believe this change is the start of a long, slow climb back to total health, or normalcy. A single relapse may cause only disappointment or sorrow, but several relapses, or even prolonged failure to return to "normal," can generate annoyance and anger in those who are not ill, as well as varying degrees of self-loathing in those who are chronically ill, or rather, not "normal."

Family resources are often insufficient to support patients with CFS properly, and society provides little help. CFS patients may find it difficult to continue to earn money at the same rate as they did before, or sometimes to earn any money at all. They may need help—sometimes only periodically, but other times constantly—to carry out the basic activities of feeding, clothing, and sheltering themselves. Many partners of CFS patients simply cannot adjust to the new situation and divorce the ill spouse, leaving that individual with even fewer resources to manage the illness (Joung, van de Mheen, Stronks, van Poppel, & Mackenbach, 1998).

Moreover, CFS patients are again punished because people tend to be annoyed with them, avoid their company, or desert them if they take proper care of themselves. This includes the patients' acknowledging how they really feel and what they actually can do. Instead, they are rewarded for unhealthy self-care—for behaving as though they were feeling well. When the strain of operating so counter-to-reality becomes too much, some react by withdrawing altogether. Sufficient social isolation and depression eventually lead some to commit suicide.

The failure of CFS patients to return to normal health can cause them to experience identity confusion. Are they a person attached to an illness, or an illness attached to a person? In their experience, clinicians and others in their social world regard them almost wholly in terms of their illness, as though they no longer had any other attributes. At the same time, and often in consequence of the multiple traumas they have suffered, CFS patients can themselves become totally absorbed by their illnesses. They attend obsessively to the disease to the exclusion of all other interests. This obsession is, perhaps, the most harmful effect from society's intolerance of chronicity. It is also the most insidious, because even when patients are finally ready to branch out from their preoccupation, society—and sadly sometimes clinicians as well—keep viewing them solely in terms of their illness.

4. *Immediate Cultural Climate toward Disease*   Every illness—whether tuberculosis or atherosclerosis, lupus, or AIDS—is born into a specific cultural climate about disease that comprises all of that society's currently existing illness tolerances and intolerances. An illness that emerges for the first time today, for example, is born into a society which has experienced and formed attitudes about AIDS and multiple sclerosis. The new economic environment of medicine also influences social attitudes because people fear that costly new diseases may prevent HMOs from covering their own medical needs adequately. Society's attitudes toward disease are continuously evolving (Cooksey & Brown, 1998; Cullen, 1998). This is not the same environment as the one that existed in 1950 (Armstrong, 1990; Wilson, 2000).

How society looks at illness in general and an individual's specific illness in particular makes a significant difference to that person's experience. But no matter how socially acceptable an illness has become, the individual, simply by having it, is marked as being outside society's primary defining group—the healthy (Bendelow & Williams, 1995; Thornton, 1998).

The public also tends to perceive the chronically ill as damaged goods. They become social examples of what the public does not want to have happen to them. The experiences of the chronically ill can mark them permanently as separate, different.

5. *Illness Enculturation Process*   Every disease has a history, a chronology during which it is recognized, assessed, researched, and treated. Concomitantly with discussion in professional discourse, new illnesses become part of general social discourse as well, but social understanding of an illness usually lags well behind medical understanding, especially in popular media presentations. Nonetheless, it is through this process that disease is culturally constructed and becomes a social reality (Armstrong, 1990; Clarke, 1994).

When an illness first appears in a culture, it is viewed with skepticism and fear until the society has investigated the phenomenon and decided how to respond to it. Initially, patients are often shunned or treated as immoral as well as sick, as happened with AIDS. Acquiring multiple sclerosis in 1950 was entirely different from contracting it today. Over time, the patterns or effects of a disease come to be recognized, and social fears are put into perspective. Eventually, the disease becomes integrated into the cultural consciousness, or enculturated.

The enculturation of any chronic illness usually works to the benefit of those who suffer from it. When a syndrome first attracts attention, those exhibiting its symptoms and the people they approach for help are puzzled by the problem at best and disbelieving at worst. Neither the sufferers nor clinicians have adequate language to describe the condition. They are forced to rely on terms appropriate to other conditions, which almost inevitably misrepresent the situation. If one lacks the language to describe something, its reality is a constant matter of question.

Besides lacking language or even metaphors to describe the new experience, both patients and clinicians lack models for assessment and treatment. Again they rely on approaches that have been useful with other illnesses, but for chronic illnesses, old approaches are almost always unsatisfactory. Assessments do not adequately capture the nature of the symptoms or the way they are expressed over time, and treatments fail not only to produce cures, but even to improve the quality of life.

After an illness first appears, there usually follows a period during which the health care profession struggles to determine its authenticity and describe its etiology and symptoms. This is never a matter of "pure" science. Political and economic issues always cloud the investigation, sometimes by outright denial of funds or social support, and sometimes more subtly through pervasive cultural attitudes that affect researchers just as they do all other members of the society.

During the enculturation period, the media are free to say anything about a new condition and make any evaluation of people who claim to be sick with it. Given the predispositions of the culture, the responses are often disbelief in the condition as an actual physical illness, ridicule, annoyance, and condemnation, with the obvious attendant effects on those suffering with it. Only "bleeding hearts" or the professionally compassionate are sympathetic. The ill are stigmatized and distrusted.

As the disease achieves description and acceptance in the medical world, it gradually becomes more acceptable in the larger society. Patients who develop a chronic condition now have vocabulary to describe their symptoms—to themselves, to family, to employers, and to medical professionals. Clinicians have either become familiar with the condition or can readily find professional literature discussing it. The public comes to believe that those suffering with the condition have a genuine illness.

6. *Media*   The media function as a forum for public opinion and judgment. They are the vehicles in which professional and social discourse converge and are thoughtfully repackaged for purchase. In the repackaging process, the media exert their own particular influence on the development of social discourse. They can create or enlarge stereotypes that appeal to and reinforce cultural prejudices. The media make public judgments, they publicly determine roles and worth in society, and they organize public ridicule or support (Kirkwood & Brown, 1995).

When the media reinforce cultural prejudices, targeted groups are publicly judged, and scapegoating (which can be a manifestation of the "just" world notion) occurs. Public assignments of social role and subsequent worth can be clearly spelled out in black and white for the chronically ill and their families as they read the latest popular description of their illness on the pages of supermarket tabloids. Patients may be supported or ridiculed, but whatever the case, their personal problem has been identified, evaluated, and socially scripted for all the world to see. The effect of having a personal tragedy so publicly exhibited, even if no one ever mentions it to the sufferer, can be harmful.

Media presentations can invade privacy directly as well. People who hear about irritable bowel syndrome or fibromyalgia on TV remember that a fellow employee has missed work because of this sickness. Suddenly that person loses all health privacy, and fellow workers become instant experts on the condition. If the media has construed the condition as ridiculous or self-generated, the employee can suffer negative public judgment and may find life at work much more difficult.

But even if the condition has been treated with sympathy, the article has transgressed the privacy of persons with the sickness. Since TV discussions rarely convey the nuances of living with a chronic condition, these patients must deal with misinformed sympathy, which is difficult to address successfully. In addition, individuals with CFS know that what is sympathy now may quickly turn to scorn, ridicule, or anger if some other TV show or tabloid article presents a negative or derogatory story.

The reality that a chronic illness makes sufferers liable to public judgment about their character and their morals increases their social isolation. It is nearly impossible to ignore broadly held public judgments about oneself, so the chronically ill may withdraw from social contact. Although they may have had strong social support prior to the onset of their illness, chronicity frequently erodes these connections. When the chronically ill come from deprived or disrupted backgrounds, especially those that involve poverty or race, the situation can be worse, and the individuals will have fewer resources to help cope with the situation. With the attendant loss of privacy, the chronically ill report increased fear and anxiety, magnified feelings of grief, and a lowered sense of worth.

REFERENCES

Alonzo, A. A. (2000). The experience of chronic illness and posttraumatic stress disorder: The consequences of cumulative adversity. *Social Science and Medicine, 50,* 1475–1484.

Alonzo, A. A., & Reynolds, V. R. (1996). Emotions and care-seeking during acute myocardial infarction: A model for intervention. *International Journal of Sociology and Social Policy, 16*(9/10), 97–122.

Armstrong, D. (1987). Theoretical tensions in biopsychosocial medicine. *Social Sciences and Medicine, 30*(11), 1225–1227.

Armstrong, D. (1990). Use of the genealogical method in the exploration of chronic illness: A research note. *Social Science and Medicine, 30*(11), 1225–1227.

Asmundson, G. J., Frombach, I., McQuaid, J., Pedrelli, P., Lenox, R., & Stein, M. B. (2000). Dimensionality of posttraumatic stress symptoms: A confirmatory factor analysis of *DSM-IV* symptom clusters and other symptom models. *Behavioral Research and Therapy, 38*(2), 203–214.

Ax, S., Gregg, V. H., & Jones, D. (1997). Chronic fatigue syndrome: Sufferers' evaluation of medical support. *Journal of the Royal Society of Medicine, 90*, 250–254.

Ax, S., Gregg, V. H., & Jones, D. (1998). Chronic fatigue syndrome: Illness attributions and perceptions of control. *Homeostatis, 39*(1/2), 44–51.

Baldwin, B. A. (1978). A paradigm for the classification of emotional crises: Implications for crisis intervention. *American Journal of Orthopsychiatry, 48*(3), 538–551.

Ballweg, M. (1997). Blaming the victim: The psychologizing of endometriosis. *Obstetrics and Gynecology Clinics of North America, 24*(2), 441–453.

Banks, J., & Prior, L. (2001). Doing things with illness: The micro politics of the CFS clinic. *Social Science and Medicine, 52*, 11–23.

Barshay, J. (1993). Another strand of our diversity: Some thoughts from a feminist therapist with severe chronic illness. In M. E. Millmuth & L. Holcomb (Eds.), *Women with disabilities: Found voices* (pp. 159–169). Binghamton, NY: Hayworth Press.

Bartley, M., & Owen, C. (1996). Relation between socioeconomic status, employment, and health during economic change, 1973–1993. *British Medical Journal, 313*, 445–449.

Bates, M. S., Rankin-Hill, L., & Sanchez-Ayendez, M. (1997). The effects of the cultural context of health care on treatment of and response to chronic pain and illness. *Social Science and Medicine, 45*(9), 1433–1447.

Bendelow, G. A., & Williams, S. J. (1995). Transcending the dualism: Toward a sociology of pain. *Sociology of Health and Illness, 17*(2), 139–165.

Blank, A. S. (1993). The longitudinal course of posttraumatic stress disorders. In J. R. Davidson & E. B. Foa (Eds.), *Posttraumatic stress disorder: DSM-IV and beyond* (pp. 3–22). Washington, DC: American Psychiatric Press.

Blum, R. W. M., Potthoff, S. F., & Resnick, M. D. (1997). The impact of chronic conditions on Native American adolescents. *Families, Systems and Health, 15*(3), 275–282.

Botha, L. F. H. (1996). Posttraumatic stress disorder and illness behavior in HIV+ patients. *Psychological Reports, 79*, 843–845.

Brody, J. E. (2000, August 1). Fibromyalgia: Real illness, real answers. *New York Times*, Health & Fitness section, p. 8.

Cameron, K., & Gregor, F. (1987). Chronic illness and compliance. *Journal of Advanced Nursing, 12*, 671–676.

Cannon, C. A., & Cavanaugh, J. C. (1998). Chronic illness in the context of marriage: A systems perspective of stress and coping in chronic obstructive pulmonary disease. *Families, Systems and Health, 16*(4), 401–418.

Clark, M. L., & Gioro, S. (1998). Nurses, in direct trauma, and prevention. *Image: Journal of Nursing Scholarship, 31*(1), 85–87.

Clarke, A. (1994). What is a chronic disease? The effects of a re-definition in HIV and AIDS. *Social Science and Medicine, 39*(4), 591–597.

Cooksey, E., & Brown, P. (1998). Spinning on its axes: *DSM* and the social construction of psychiatric diagnosis. *International Journal of Health Services, 28*(3), 525–554.

Cuijpers, P. (1998). Prevention of depression in chronic general medical disorders: A pilot study. *Psychological Reports, 82,* 735–738.

Cullen, J. (1998). The needle and the damage done: Research, action research, and the organizational and social construction of health in the "information society." *Human-Relations, 51*(12), 1543–1564.

Dohrenwend, B. P. (2000, March). The role of adversity and stress in psychopathology: Some evidence and its implications for theory and research. *Journal of Health and Social Behavior, 41,* 1–19.

Do Rozario, L. (1997). Spirituality in the lives of people with disability and chronic illness: A creative paradigm of wholeness and reconstitution. *Disability and Rehabilitation, 19*(10), 427–434.

Engel, G. L. (1977). The need for a new medical model: A challenge for biomedicine. *Science, 196,* 129–136.

Epstein, R., Quill, T. E., & McWhinney, I. R. (1999). Somatization reconsidered: Incorporating the patient's experience of illness. *Archives of Internal Medicine, 159,* 215–222.

Fennell, P. A. (1995). CFS sociocultural influences and trauma: Clinical considerations. *Journal of Chronic Fatigue Syndrome, 1*(3/4), 159–173.

Fennell, P. A. (2001). *The chronic illness workbook: Strategies and solutions for taking back your life.* San Francisco: New Harbinger.

Fennell, P. A. (2004). *Managing chronic illness using the Four-Phase treatment approach: A mental health professionl's guide to helping chronically ill people.* Hoboken, NJ: Wiley.

Fisher, L., & Weihs, K. L. (2000). Can addressing family relationships improve outcomes in chronic disease? *Journal of Family Practice, 49*(6), 561–567.

Fullilove, M. T., Lown, E. A., & Fullilove, R. E. (1992). Crack 'hos and skeezers: Traumatic experiences of women crack users. *Journal of Sex Research, 29*(2), 275–287.

Gamsa, A. (1994). The role of psychological factors in chronic pain. II: A critical appraisal. *Pain, 57,* 17–29.

Gatchel, R. J., & Gardea, M. A. (1999). Their importance in predicting disability, response to treatment, and search for compensation. *Neurological Clinics of North America, 17*(1), 149–167.

Hampton, M. R., & Frombach, J. (2000). Women's experience of traumatic stress in cancer treatment. *Health Care for Women International, 21,* 67–76.

Hayes, V. E. (1997). Families and children's conditions: Knowledge development and methodological considerations. *Scholarly Inquiry for Nursing Practice: An International Journal, 11*(4), 259–291.

Heinzer, M. M. (1998). Health promotion during childhood chronic illness: A paradox facing society. *Holistic Nursing Practice, 12*(2), 8–16.

Henderson, P. A. (1997). Psychosocial adjustment of adult cancer survivors: Their needs and counselor's interventions. *Journal of Counseling and Development, 75,* 188–194.

Herman, J. L. (1992). Complex PTSD: A syndrome in survivors of prolonged and repeated trauma. In M. J. Horowitz (Ed.), *Essential papers on post traumatic stress disorder* (pp. 82–98). New York: New York University Press.

Joung, I. M. A., van de Mheen, H. D., Stronks, K., van Poppel, F. W. A., & Mackenbach, J. P. (1998). A longitudinal study of health selection in marital transitions. *Social Science and Medicine, 46*(3), 425–435.

Kirkwood, W. G., & Brown, D. (1995). Public communication about the causes of disease: The rhetoric of responsibility. *Journal of Communication, 45,* 55–76.

Kirmayer, L. J., Robbins, J. M., & Paris, J. (1994). Somatoform disorders: Personality and the social matrix of somatic disease. *Journal of Abnormal Psychology, 103*(1), 125–136.

Kontz, M. M. (1989). Compliance redefined and implications for home care. *Holistic Nurse Practice, 3*(2), 54–64.

Lewis, J. (1999). Status passages: The experience of HIV-positive gay men. *Journal of Homosexuality, 37*(3), 87–115.

Lindy, J. D., Grace, M. C., & Green, B. L. (1981). Survivors: Outreach to a reluctant population. *American Journal of Orthopsychiatry, 51*(3), 468–478.

Lindy, J. D., Green, B. L., & Grace, M. C. (1987). The stressor criterion and posttraumatic stress disorder. *Journal of Mental and Nervous Diseases, 175*, 269–272.

Lutgendorf, S. K., Antoni, M. H., Ironson, G., Fletcher, M. A., Penedo, F., Baum, A., et al. (1995). Physical symptoms of chronic fatigue syndrome are exacerbated by the stress of Hurricane Andrew. *Psychosomatic Medicine, 57*, 310–323.

Marbach, J. J., Lennon, M. C., Link, B. G., & Dohrenwend, B. P. (1990). Losing face: Sources of stigma as perceived by chronic facial pain patients. *Journal of Behavioral Medicine, 13*(6), 583–604.

McCahill, M. E. (1995). Somatoform and related disorders: Delivery of diagnosis as first step. *American Family Physician, 52*(1), 193–203.

Mezey, G., & Robbins, I. (2001, September 8). Usefulness and validity of posttraumatic stress disorder as a psychiatric category. *British Medical Journal, 323*, 561–563.

Plehn, K., Peterson, R., & Williams, D. (1998). Anxiety sensitivity: Its relationship to functional status in patients with chronic pain. *Journal of Occupational Rehabilitation, 8*(3), 213–222.

Pless, B., & Nolan, T. (1991). Revision, replication and neglect: Research on maladjustment in chronic illness. *Journal of Child Psychology, 32*(2), 347–365.

Rolland, J. S. (1994). *Families, illness, and disability: An interactive treatment model.* New York: Basic Books.

Rosenberg, M., & Molho, P. (1998). Nonviolent (empathic) communication for health care providers. *Haemmophilia, 4*, 335–340.

Scambler, G., & Hopkins, A. (1990). Generating a model of epileptic stigma: The role of qualitative analysis. *Social Science and Medicine, 30*(11), 1187–1194.

Schiller, N. G., Crystal, S., & Lewellen, D. (1994). Risky business: The cultural construction of AIDS risk groups. *Social Science and Medicine, 38*(10), 1337–1346.

Scott, M. J., & Stradling, S. G. (1994). Posttraumatic stress disorder without the trauma. *British Journal of Clinical Psychology, 33*, 71–74.

Stuart, S., & Noyes, R., Jr. (1999). Attachment and interpersonal communication in somatization. *Psychosomatics, 40*(1), 34–43.

Tait, R. C., Chibnall, J. T., & Richardson, W. D. (1990). Litigation and employment status: Effects on patients with chronic pain. *Pain, 43*, 37–46.

Taylor, R. R., Friedberg, F., & Jason, L. A. (2001). *A clinician's guide to understanding controversial illnesses: Chronic fatigue syndrome, fibromyalgia, and multiple chemical sensitivities.* Sarasota, FL: Professional Resource Press.

Taylor, R. R., & Jason, L. A. (2000). *Chronic fatigue, abuse-related traumatization, and psychiatric disorders in a community-based sample.* Manuscript submitted for publication.

Thornton, J. (1998). We're all wackos: A new model of health. *International Journal of Sociology and Social Policy, 18*(9/10), 119–125.

Turk, D. C., & Rudy, T. E. (1991). Neglected topics in the treatment of chronic pain patients: Relapse, noncompliance, and adherence enhancement. *Pain, 44*, 5–28.

Turner, R. J., & Lloyd, D. A. (1995, December). Lifetime traumas and mental health: The significance of cumulative adversity. *Journal of Health and Social Behavior, 36,* 360–376.

van der Kolk, B. A., McFarlane, A. C., & Weisaeth, L. (Eds.). (1996). *Traumatic stress: The effects of overwhelming stress on mind, body and society.* New York: Guilford Press.

Van Mens-Verhulst, J., & Bensing, J. (1998). Distinguishing between chronic and nonchronic fatigue: The role of gender and age. *Social Science and Medicine, 47*(5), 621–634.

Ware, N. C. (1998). Sociosomatics and illness course in chronic fatigue syndrome. *Psychosomatic Medicine, 60,* 394–401.

Ware, N. C. (1999). Toward a model of social course in chronic illness: The example of chronic fatigue syndrome. *Culture, Medicine and Psychiatry, 23,* 303–331.

Ware, N. C., & Kleinman, A. (1992). Culture and somatic experience: The social course of illness in neurasthenia and chronic fatigue syndrome. *Psychosomatic Medicine, 54,* 546–560.

Wilson, A. (2000). On the history of disease-concepts: The case of pleurisy. *History of Science, 38*(3), 271–319.

Yehuda, R., & McFarlane, A. C. (1995). Conflict between current knowledge about posttraumatic stress disorder and its original conceptual basis. In M. J. Horowitz (Ed.), *Essential papers on post traumatic stress disorder* (pp. 41–60). New York: New York University Press.

Zimmerman, M., & Mattia, J. I. (1999). Is posttraumatic stress disorder underdiagnosed in routine clinical settings? *Journal of Nervous and Mental Disorders, 187*(7), 420–428.

CHAPTER 5

Genetics

PATRICK F. SULLIVAN

THE TITLE OF this chapter carries an implicit question: Does chronic fatigue syndrome (CFS), in fact, have a genetic component? The answer to this question is—without equivocation—yes. Although that claim might strike some as controversial and excessively dogmatic, the intent in this chapter is to show the ways in which genetic factors may contribute to CFS.

First, CFS might result from deterministic variation in one or more genes in which this genetic variation is both necessary and sufficient. Many classical Mendelian disorders (e.g., cystic fibrosis, Huntington disease) are caused this way. In such instances, having the wrong number of copies of a disease gene carries a very high probability of disease.

Second, CFS might result from genetic variation in a probabilistic, necessary-but-not-sufficient manner: Inheritance increases the risk of CFS but actually developing it requires an additional event. Examples of these additional events include bad luck (e.g., a random event like injury in a terrorist attack), a highly traumatic or stressful life event, or exposure to an infectious agent. In this more complex causal model, genes are important but cannot of themselves cause a disease.

Third, CFS could result from entirely nongenetic mechanisms. In this instance, how are genes relevant? The answer is partly semantic but, more substantively, requires consideration of the central role of inheritance. The genes we inherit play central roles in the structure and function of our bodies in both health and disease. Consider an insult that happens entirely by chance (e.g., an injury in a freak accident). Even if an individual's genes are not causally involved, any such insult will trigger a set of responses mediated by changes in gene expression as the body works to repair damage. Many of these changes will be localized and transient (e.g., the body's response in healing a cut). Some changes that result from a chance injury could be longer lasting and more systemic (e.g., a severe accident with significant brain injury and substantial orthopedic trauma).

Preparation of this chapter was supported by AI38429 and NS41483. I thank Dr. Cynthia Bulik and Ms. Fran Davis for critical comments.

To complicate matters further, some diseases are caused by both deterministic and probabilistic genetic alterations and result in substantial changes in gene expression. Genetic variation in at least three genes (presenilin-1, presenilin-2, or amyloid precursor protein) can cause Alzheimer's disease deterministically (Levy-Lahad & Bird, 2000), and a variant of the apolipoprotein E gene is consistently but more probabilistically associated with the illness (Farrer et al., 1997). Finally, whatever its cause, Alzheimer's disease is associated with changes in gene expression in many brain regions (Hata et al., 2001; Ho et al., 2001).

It is difficult to imagine a human illness—including CFS—that does not involve genes in some way. Thus, the chief focus of this chapter is to review the evidence for the hypothesis that genetic variation is causal to CFS. The data are incomplete, and this is an active area of research. As the limited data available provide support for this hypothesis and as researchers have already begun searching for genes associated with CFS, the chapter concludes with a discussion of gene-finding approaches relevant to CFS.

GENETIC EPIDEMIOLOGY

Definition

Of the many definitions of genetic epidemiology (Khoury, Beaty, & Cohen, 1993; Morton & Chung, 1978; Thomas, 2000), the common intention is to understand the etiology of an idiopathic disorder. The approach is integrative—instead of focusing on the environment and treating inheritance as noise (as might a classical epidemiologist) or focusing on inheritance and treating environmental influences as noise (as might a classical geneticist), the genetic epidemiological approach attempts to understand the joint effects of genes and environment (Thomas, 2000).

This approach has been widely used in medicine for disorders whose etiology resists elucidation (Crumpacker et al., 1979; Kaprio et al., 1982). Given that so little is known for certain about the etiology of CFS and given the persistent controversies as to its existence as a discrete entity or whether it is more parsimoniously classified as something else, application of the methods of genetic epidemiology to CFS is warranted.

The impact of genetic epidemiology may be particularly profound for disorders that do not have laboratory features, discriminating objective signs, or pathognomonic physical examination. Before a seminal twin study (Folstein & Rutter, 1977) and subsequent replications (Cook, 1998) demonstrated an overwhelming genetic influence, autism was generally believed to result from adverse early rearing. A few decades ago, it was commonly held that schizophrenia resulted from social factors or rearing environment. Twin, adoption, and family studies played pivotal roles in reconceptualizing it as a neuropsychiatric disorder with a substantial genetic etiologic component (Kendler & Diehl, 1995). Although the stigma associated with these conditions has not faded entirely, it can no longer be seriously doubted that these represent valid disorders with a physical basis.

The First Step

There are two basic steps or components to the genetic epidemiological approach. The first step generally deals with latent underlying constructs, and the second attempts to make latent constructs manifest.

The first or "broad" step is descriptive and attempts to uncover the mix of genetic and environmental components of causation. The broad step seeks to answer a few basic questions: Is the trait in question familial; does it run in families? If so, can the reasons for the observed familiality be determined? To what extent does the observed familiality of a trait result from genetic effects and to what extent from environmental effects?

Three quasi-experimental designs are available in humans to address these questions. Each design focuses on clusters of individuals with known genetic and/or social relationships.

Familiality   Family studies are the obvious approach to the elucidation of familiality. Family studies can be conceptualized as a type of case-control study as described in detail elsewhere (Khoury et al., 1993; Weissman et al., 1986). Cases are probands with the disorder of interest; controls have no history of the disorder and are usually matched for confounding variables such as age and gender. The outcome of interest contrasts the prevalence of the disorder in the biological relatives (usually first-degree relatives) of cases versus controls. In such studies, however, genetic and environmental determinants are confounded.

Estimating the Impact of Genes and Environment   Adoption and twin studies are the two principal approaches to delineating genetic and environmental effects in humans. Adoption studies are a social quasi-experiment in which the offspring of one set of parents are reared from early in life by unrelated strangers. In contrast, twin studies are a biological quasi-experiment that contrasts pairs of genetically identical monozygotic (one ovum) with dizygotic (two ova) twins who share half their genes on average. Both types of twins share many relevant environmental exposures. These designs can be combined in the study of twins reared apart. In theory, adoption studies are an elegant way to separate the relative contributions of genetic and environmental influences; however, practical and ethical difficulties make them difficult to conduct and probably explain their relative dearth. In contrast, twins are fairly numerous, are often cooperative with research, and are thus the subject of many investigations.

The Types of Causes   Since family, adoption, and twin studies essentially analyze the resemblance of relatives, their analysis reveals broad descriptions of the causes of the trait under study. They cannot of themselves pinpoint specific genetic or environmental risk factors.

A common analytic approach to these genetically informative study designs focuses on variation in liability to a disorder. If the continuous traits of height, cholesterol level, or a measure of fatigue were measured in a large number of individuals, we would certainly find considerable variation across individuals.

In an analogous, but somewhat more complex manner, individuals vary in liability to discrete traits (e.g., the presence or absence of a disorder like CFS). A liability-threshold model is often used that assumes the existence of an unmeasured, continuously distributed latent liability to illness. An individual's place on this latent liability is determined additively by numerous genetic and/or environmental risk factors. Individuals with liability scores above a certain threshold develop the trait, and individuals below the threshold do not develop it (Falconer, 1965; Falconer & Mackay, 1996).

If we scale the total variation to 100%, analyses of family, adoption, and twin data attempt to determine the proportions of the total variance attributable to genetic and environmental sources. Table 5.1 depicts the three types of causes commonly estimated in genetic epidemiological studies. The approach is described succinctly (Kendler, 1993) and in detail elsewhere (Neale & Cardon, 1992; Plomin, DeFries, McClearn, & Rutter, 1997).

Briefly, a^2 is the proportion of variance in a trait due to additive genetic effects. Environmental effects are of two types, those shared (c^2) and unshared (e^2) by members of a family. To some extent, referring to c^2 and e^2 as "environmental" is misleading because they can be biological effects. Classically, c^2 would include environmental risk factors such as neighborhood of residence, peers, school quality, and general parental attitudes, but it can include infectious agents and toxic exposures provided siblings share these factors. Similar considerations apply to e^2, but by definition, siblings must not share the risk factors. By the same token, under certain circumstances, unequivocally environmental influences can profoundly affect estimates of a^2

Note that a^2, c^2, and e^2 sum to 100%. In a family study, the variance can be decomposed into familial ($a^2 + c^2$) and nonfamilial components (e^2), whereas a^2, c^2, and e^2 can be separately estimated in adoption and twin studies. In an adoption study, the greater similarity of adoptees to biological parents reveals genetic effects, and greater similarity to adoptive parents reveals shared environmental effects. In a twin study, genetic effects are revealed by greater similarity of monozygotic twins in comparison to dizygotic twins.

THE SECOND STEP

The second or "narrow" step is much more reductionistic and attempts to develop a precise model of the etiology of the trait that tackles the complexities of causation (Hill, 1965; Rothman, 1986). Can the precise genetic and environmental risk factors be identified? How do these risk factors act and interact to produce the trait?

A great many study designs can address this question. In fact, what is termed here as the narrow step usually is conducted without reference to genetic epidemiology (e.g., investigations of immune dysfunction or infectious exposures in

Table 5.1
Types of Causes

Effect	Abbreviation	Definition
Additive genetic	a^2	Cumulative effect of numerous genes acting additively
Common environmental	c^2	Environmental effects shared or common to a sibling pair
Specific environmental	e^2	Environmental effects specific to an individual and not shared

CFS). Within the genetic epidemiological context, several study designs are typically employed and are described toward the end of this chapter.

THE GENETIC EPIDEMIOLOGY OF CFS

FAMILY STUDIES

Four family studies have been published in the literature as of August 2002. First, Swanson et al. (Swanson, Moore, & Nobrega, 1978) compared two groups of patients referred for psychiatric evaluation of idiopathic severe fatigue with groups of medical and psychiatric controls without fatigue. Family history was assessed by self-report. This study had numerous methodological limitations (Khoury et al., 1993; Weissman et al., 1986). Most critically, the prevalence of "severe fatigue" in the first-degree relatives of fatigued probands was neither assessed nor reported so that familiality could not be determined.

Second, Endicott (1999) conducted a family history study using individuals ascertained from his outpatient private practice over an 11-year period. Forty-five patients met the 1988 CDC case definition for CFS (Holmes et al., 1988); the comparison groups consisted of patients with good health ($N = 90$) and patients selected without regard to physical health ($N = 45$). Family history was assessed in an unblinded fashion using semistructured instruments. Few relatives were personally interviewed. Significantly more patients with CFS had a first-degree relative with CFS-like illness (16%) compared with either control group. The odds ratio for the presence of CFS in the relatives of CFS cases versus controls was 52.8 (95% CI: 2.9–945).

Third, Woodman and colleagues (Woodman, Stout, Hardardottir, & Hartz, 2001) have published an abstract describing a family interview study of CFS that compared the family histories of clinically ascertained probands with CFS and rheumatoid arthritis. The brevity of the report precludes full analysis, but the study appears to have been rigorously conducted in that structured diagnostic interviews were used in personal interviews with all available first-degree relatives. These are critical methodological components of modern family studies as they minimize the impact of biases that generally inflate estimates of familiality. CFS was significantly familial with 32% of the first-degree relatives of CFS probands and only 6% of the relative of probands with rheumatoid arthritis meeting criteria for CFS. The odds ratio for the presence of CFS in the relatives of CFS cases versus controls was 7.2 (95% CI: 3.9–13.3).

Fourth, Torres-Harding and Jason (Torres & Jason, 2003) described the family histories of subjects with CFS and a control. These subjects were all ascertained from the general population (as opposed to clinical sources) which is important if treatment seeking for an illness is related to having a family history of that illness (Sullivan et al., 1996). The occurrence of fatigue or chronic fatigue was nonsignificantly more common in the relatives of subjects with CFS (25% vs. 9.3%) with an odds ratio of 3.3 (95% CI: 0.9–12.0). This study had several methodological difficulties. In particular, family history was not systematically or blindly assessed, and the analyses did not take into account the number and types of relatives across groups.

Searches of the CRISP database at the U.S. National Institutes of Health (www.commons.cit.nih.gov/crisp) revealed no funded family studies of CFS or fatiguing illness.

ADOPTION STUDIES

To my knowledge, there are no published or planned adoption studies of CFS or of fatiguing illness.

TWIN STUDIES

As of August 2002, there were no published twin studies of CFS.

Swedish Twin Registry   The Swedish Twin Registry (www.mep.ki.se/twins) is a birth record-based registry encompassing all of Sweden. It is the largest twin registry in the world, and the comprehensive birth, health, and death data in Sweden make it one of the best. It was established in the late 1950s to study the risk factors for cancer and cardiovascular diseases while controlling for genetic propensity to disease. A bibliography listing publications from the Swedish Twin Registry contains more than 300 entries and is available on the Web site.

An ongoing data collection effort will inform the genetic epidemiology of CFS. With my colleagues Drs. Nancy Pedersen and Birgitta Evengård in Sweden and Drs. Cynthia Bulik and Mike Neale in the United States, we have obtained funding to analyze these twin data. A state-of-the-art tracking and computerized interviewing system was used to assess CFS and its key physical and psychiatric co-morbidities—fibromyalgia, irritable bowel syndrome, tension headache, allergy/eczema, generalized anxiety disorder, and major depression. Data collection has been completed for 31,405 twins aged 42 to 64 years. Medical records and physical examinations will be requested for all twins with presumptive CFS.

We hope the Swedish study will allow a clear look at the genetic epidemiology of rigorously defined CFS. As this study is based on a very large sample ascertained from the general population, the risk of referral bias will be minimized.

Additional Twin Studies   Three twin studies of phenotypes relevant to CFS have been published. First, Hickie and colleagues (Hickie, Kirk, & Martin, 1999) studied 1,004 adult twin pairs from the volunteer Australian twin registry who completed the Schedule of Fatigue and Anergia and found the following components of variation: a^2 42%, c^2 0%, and e^2 58%.

Second, Farmer and colleagues (Farmer, Scourfield, Martin, Cardno, & McGuffin, 1999) studied 656 twin pairs aged 5 to 17 years. For disabling fatigue lasting at least one month (per the report of the parent or guardian), they reported the following components of variation: a^2 54%, c^2 19%, and e^2 26%.

Finally, the study with the most relevant data to date is by Buchwald et al. (Buchwald et al., 1999; Buchwald et al., 2001). These researchers studied a volunteer sample of female twins where one or both members of a twin pair reported CFS-like illness (the symptoms of CFS excluding certain medical and psychiatric conditions but without physical examination and laboratory studies). They reported the following components of variation: a^2 51%, c^2 42%, and e^2 8%. Volunteer registries of this sort are vulnerable to ascertainment bias; for example, if concordant twin pairs are more likely to volunteer, then this could bias the results. Similar variance component estimates were obtained even when an ascertainment ratio as large as four was assumed.

SUMMARY

Taken together, the extant data on the genetic epidemiology of CFS provide tantalizing hints. The data suggest that CFS-like illness is familial with the familiality largely due to additive genetic factors.

The dearth of data on CFS stands in marked contrast to the extensive published family, adoption, and twin data for other disorders in medicine. There are considerably more extensive genetic epidemiological data on cardiovascular disease (Austin, 1996; Boomsma & Gabrielli, 1985; Nance, 1984; Vogler et al., 1997), peptic ulcer disease (Raiha, Kemppainen, Kaprio, Koskenvuo, & Sourander, 1998), alcoholism (Heath, 1995), smoking behaviors (Sullivan & Kendler, 1999), major depression (Sullivan, Neale, & Kendler, 2000), eating disorders (Bulik, Sullivan, Wade, & Kendler, 2000), schizophrenia (Kendler & Diehl, 1995), and other psychiatric disorders (Sullivan & Kendler, 1998). In fact, for the purposes of a formal meta-analysis (Glass, McGaw, & Smith, 1981; Petitti, 1994; Sullivan et al., 2000), no studies would be included as none meet a basic set of inclusion criteria. At this point, it would be inappropriate to further interpret the data on CFS given the lack of rigorously conducted primary studies.

The lack of data on CFS is puzzling, but the situation may improve in the next few years. High-quality family studies paired with twin studies are particularly important as these two designs are predicated on different assumptions; convergent or divergent results across the two study types provide an important check on the conclusions. For major depression, for example, five of five family studies, two of three adoption studies, and five of five twin studies all provide strikingly consistent results (Sullivan et al., 2000). For disorders like major depression or CFS where we understand so little about their basic validity and pathophysiology, such consistency augments considerably the confidence with which we can draw conclusions from the findings.

THE POSSIBILITIES OF TWIN STUDIES

Arriving at consistent estimates of a^2, c^2, and e^2 provides broad-step data about a disorder. In practice, these are derived from twin studies; adoption studies can accomplish the same ends, but are much more rarely conducted. Data about the basic architecture of a trait are important of themselves and have led to marked shifts in research agendas for several disorders (e.g., autism, schizophrenia, and obesity). However, there are other ways that twin data can provide further insight into the etiology of a trait.

GENDER

If a study contains all five types of twin pairs (monozygotic male and female pairs, dizygotic male and female pairs, plus dizygotic male-female pairs), it is possible to investigate the impact of gender on the genetic and environmental architecture of a trait (Kendler & Prescott, 1999; Neale & Cardon, 1992). This is particularly important for disorders with strong gender effects (e.g., CFS). The patterns of a^2, c^2, and e^2 may differ in men and women, and these analyses could provide insight into gender-specific dissimilarities.

Comorbidity

Perhaps the greatest utility of twin studies is in the analysis of comorbidity. CFS is highly comorbid with other idiopathic medical syndromes (e.g., fibromyalgia and irritable bowel syndrome) and psychiatric disorders (e.g., major depression and generalized anxiety disorder), especially in clinical samples. Comorbidity is so prevalent that it is almost a defining feature of CFS. The high prevalence of comorbidity has led to widespread skepticism about whether CFS is a discrete illness, along with suggestions that CFS is more parsimoniously considered a *forme fruste* of some other disorder(Kendell, 1991; Manu, Lane, & Matthews, 1988, 1993; Manu, Matthews, & Lane, 1988). A persistent suggestion about CFS is that it is more parsimoniously classified as major depression. Inadequate explanations of the comorbidities of CFS have contributed in no small measure to arguments favoring its invalidation.

Wessely, Nimnuan, and Sharpe (1999) reviewed functional somatic syndromes in 10 medical specialties (e.g., CFS in infectious disease, fibromyalgia in rheumatology, irritable bowel syndrome in gastroenterology, tension headache in neurology). The authors began with the following thesis: "We postulate that the existence of specific somatic syndromes is largely an artifact of medical specialisation . . . the differentiation of specific functional syndromes reflects the tendency of specialists to focus on only those symptoms pertinent to their specialty, rather than any real differences between patients"(p. 936). This hypothesis is not novel but the authors backed their contention with a semisystematic literature review. In reviewing the literature, the core diagnostic symptoms of the predominant case definitions for these 10 conditions overlapped considerably.

Twin studies of multiple disorders can assist in understanding the causes of comorbidity. It is important that the sample be population-based. Having comorbid disorders multiplicatively increases the chance of membership in a clinical sample (Berkson, 1946). Therefore, significant but artifactual associations between two disorders might emerge in clinical samples that do not exist in the population. As selection bias is likely in many clinical samples of CFS (e.g., for education and occupation), any conclusions about the comorbidities of CFS must be qualified. Thus, although clinical patients with CFS commonly meet criteria for other disorders, we do not know whether the observed associations are the result of bias. In addition, twin studies of comorbidity require very large sample sizes to detect plausible effects.

Multivariate twin models can elucidate the basis of comorbidity. Three aspects are of particular interest. First, two disorders can co-occur because the genes that influence vulnerability to one disorder influence vulnerability to the other (pleiotropy). The degree to which the same genes influence both disorders can be expressed as their genetic correlation. Whereas a genetic correlation of zero means that genes for one disorder have no influence on the liability to a second disorder, a correlation of unity means that the genetic factors underlying the disorders are identical. Second, shared-environmental factors that predispose to both disorders could lead to the observed comorbidity. For example, being raised by parents with a particular rearing style or in a family of a certain socioeconomic class could influence the vulnerability. Third, individual-specific environmental factors—such as stressful life events, trauma, or exposure to a viral illness—could increase the risk for several disorders. Just as a genetic correlation summarizes the degree of resemblance of the genetic factors influencing two disorders, environmental correlations express the degree of similarity of the environmental risk factors for two disorders.

Family studies cannot discriminate between genetic and shared-environmental sources of comorbidity. Twin studies can resolve all three sources. Moreover, multivariate twin analyses (Neale & Cardon, 1992) may be used to posit (Klein & Riso, 1994) and to evaluate formally (Neale & Kendler, 1995) models of the relationship among several disorders. These hypotheses include that the disorders co-occur because of chance, bias, population stratification, and overlapping symptoms. Additional possibilities include that the disorders are manifestations of one basic disorder, that they have correlated genetic and/or environmental liabilities, and that one disorder causes the other (causal models).

Understanding the causes of comorbidity can lead to insight about the nature, validity, and definition of CFS. In fact, the speculations of Wessely et al. (1999) can be directly tested: multivariate twin models can posit and test a set of hypotheses that represent fundamentally similar conditions.

CONDITIONAL ANALYSES

Some traits are conditional in that developing the trait requires a prior event (Neale, Harvey, & Kendler, 2001). The clearest examples are in connection with drug addiction—an individual must necessarily begin to smoke and then smoke regularly prior to being eligible to develop nicotine dependence (Kendler, Neale, Sullivan, Gardner, & Prescott, 1999). Twin analyses of these multistage processes can reveal whether the components of variation (i.e., a^2, c^2, and e^2) are similar or disparate at different points in the process.

Certain events must occur before an individual can develop CFS. An individual must first experience prolonged fatigue (at least 1 month in duration) and then chronic fatigue (at least 6 months in duration) prior to developing the full syndrome of CFS. Some individuals will never experience prolonged fatigue, some will develop prolonged fatigue but never chronic fatigue, and so on. Moreover, the presence of four of eight signs and symptoms as specified by the CDC criteria (Fukuda et al., 1994) may or may not co-occur with fatigue of varying duration.

Twin models have been developed that investigate the components of variation that impact at different stages in a conditional process (Neale et al., 2001). For CFS, a three-stage model (prolonged fatigue → chronic fatigue → CFS) is potentially interesting. From the results of Buchwald et al. (Buchwald et al., 2001), the expectation is that environmental effects will be important for the development of prolonged fatigue, whereas genetic effects are increasingly prominent for chronic fatigue and CFS.

LIMITATIONS OF TWIN STUDIES

ASSUMPTIONS

There are several potential threats to the interpretation of data from twin studies. First, the critical equal environment assumption (EEA) posits that monozygotic and dizygotic twins are equally correlated in their exposure to environmental events that are etiologically relevant to the disorder under study. If this were not true, the greater similarity of monozygotic versus dizygotic twins for a disorder could result from environmental and not genetic factors. In this situation, conclusions that a trait has genetic etiologic components could be wrong. The EEA has been examined repeatedly, and there is considerable evidence supporting its validity (Kendler & Gardener, 1998; Kendler, Neale, Kessler, Heath, & Eaves, 1994). Second, conclusions about a disorder from twins may not generalize to singletons if there are protective or risk factors specific to twins. Moreover, twins are distinctive from singletons in potentially important ways, particularly in obstetric complications and perinatal events (Bryan, 1992).

Finally, some unknown or poorly measured bias may be responsible for the results from twin studies. Heritability in liability estimates from family studies provides an important cross-check of this possibility. Convergent results from family and twin studies suggest either that the assumptions of both methods are problematic or—more parsimoniously—that the results reflect the fundamental nature of the disorder.

Without recourse to a more formal experimental design, it is not possible to prove that the results from twin studies are uncontaminated by all conceivable biases and violations of critical assumptions. However, convergent data across and within genetic epidemiological study designs would be reassuring.

RESOLUTION

The power of a twin study varies with many factors (Martin, Eaves, Kearsey, & Davies, 1978; Neale, Eaves, & Kendler, 1994). The prevalence of a discrete trait is one of the most critical determinants of statistical power. Realistic power calculations suggest that even with very large sample sizes (on the order of those available in the Mid-Atlantic and Swedish Twin Registries), statistical power may not be optimal for the detection of small effects (e.g., common environmental effects on the order of 5%–10%). A solution to this problem is to focus not on the estimates of a^2, c^2, and e^2 alone but instead on the 95% confidence intervals bounding the estimate. Considerable confusion has arisen (Fairburn, Cowen, & Harrison, 1999) when investigators focus on the point estimates instead of on the confidence intervals (Bulik et al., 2000).

The nature of the effect is also important. For complex reasons (Neale et al., 1994), the power of a twin study is best at estimating a^2, c^2, and e^2. Other effects can, in theory, be included in twin models. Gene-environment (GxE) interactions have been hypothesized to be important in the etiology of many complex traits. For example, a genetic vulnerability to CFS might be expressed if and only if an individual is exposed to an infection, marked stress, or an important environmental trauma. Twin studies generally have poor power to resolve GxE interactions, and their presence will lead to an increase in the estimate of individual-specific environmental effects.

MEASUREMENT ERROR

Measurement error inflates estimates of individual-specific environmental effects (e^2) at the expense of additive genetic (a^2) and/or shared environmental influences (c^2) (Neale & Cardon, 1992). Substantial measurement error can distort conclusions about the architecture of a trait (Kendler, Neale, Kessler, Heath, & Eaves, 1993).

CAVEATS ABOUT THE MEANING OF A^2

There are several critical caveats when interpreting the results from twin studies. This section describes some common errors of interpretation.

Many readers misunderstand twin studies (especially when covered by the lay press), particularly the meaning of estimates of a^2. The heritability in liability to a trait (or a^2) is the proportion of total trait variance accounted for by additive genetic influences. Estimates of a^2 (and its confidence interval) are subject to the assumptions noted earlier. This parameter is a property of a large sample of individuals and not any one person. Furthermore, it is specific to a sample in place and time and may or may not generalize to other samples. It may help to consider a^2 as akin to a population parameter such as prevalence: The prevalence of CFS is estimated with greater or lesser precision in groups that differ in place and time.

So, the following statements are incorrect: "*The* heritability of CFS is 50%" (a^2 is sample-specific, and therefore there is no single estimate); "twin studies show that the *chance* of developing CFS is 50%" (a^2 is not a probability); "50% of *my* CFS is due to genes" (a^2 applies to groups and not individuals).

In addition, it is important to avoid common errors in the substantive interpretation of results of twin studies—particularly for a^2 (Rutter & Plomin, 1997). The major error is the imposition of a sort of genetic determinism. If estimates of a^2 for a trait are perceived as being high, many readers assume that the trait is predestined and the actions, choices, and responsibilities of individuals are negligibly or minimally important. Some even assume that high estimates of a^2 mean that a disorder is less amenable to treatment.

This "genes rule" perspective may be relevant to rare Mendelian disorders, but it is not terribly relevant to complex traits such as CFS. It is highly likely that CFS is a "complex trait" (Lander & Schork, 1994) that is characterized by heterogeneity (multiple causal pathways to the same outcome, some more environmental, some more genetic, and others somewhat equally environmental and genetic). Moreover, the genetic influences are likely to be subtle and probabilistic instead of strong and deterministic so that the life experiences and the intentions, choices, and efforts that people make are critically important.

Also, estimates of a^2 in the broad step do not prove the existence of a gene or genes that confer predisposition or protection to a trait—violations of the assumptions or ascertainment bias can lead to erroneous conclusions. Furthermore, estimating a^2 obviously does not identify where in the human genome such genes are located.

DETERMINING CAUSALITY

Finding an association between a risk factor and a disorder is a fairly common occurrence in biomedical research. Causality is easy to hypothesize but very difficult to prove (Hill, 1965; Rothman, 1986).

Assume that CFS is found to have a significant familial component that appears (from twin data) to be mostly or entirely genetic in origin and, further, that this is not a mere artifact nor due to an assumptional violation. (We use a^2 in this example, but we could just as easily consider c^2 or e^2.) How do we know that this is causal?

The answer is that we do not. In essence, the data are consistent with a causal genetic influence but do not—and cannot—of themselves prove causality. The genetic variation detected might not be for CFS per se, but for a more fundamental trait (e.g., propensity for certain infections or marked proneness to the adverse effects of stress). In addition, the case definitions of CFS (e.g., Fukuda et al., 1994) were created by expert committees—it is unlikely that these case definitions will map directly onto the manner in which some putative genetic variation for CFS exerts its influence. Proving causality requires alternative scientific approaches.

FINDING GENES FOR CFS

Given the dearth of data on the genetic epidemiology of CFS, it is remarkable that some investigators have begun to evaluate candidate genes for CFS (Harmon, McMaster, McCluskey, Shields, & Whitehead, 1997; Underhill, Mahalingam, Peakman, & Wessely, 2001). This may not be rational if CFS has minimal or no genetic etiologic components. However, this area of inquiry likely will lead to numerous papers in the next five years no matter whether data are present or absent from twin studies. These studies are inexpensive and deceptively easy to conduct; but unless investigators conduct them with care and thoughtfulness, the results from the most common study design are more likely to confuse than to clarify (Sullivan, Eaves, Kendler, & Neale, 2001).

The Magnitude of the Problem

Excellent introductions to molecular genetics are available in print (Strachen & Read, 1999) and on the Internet (Online Mendelian Inheritance in Man [OMIM™]; Primer on Molecular Genetics). Assume that a search for genetic variation predisposing to CFS is rational; what is the magnitude of the problem? The human genome contains an estimated 30,000 to 40,000 genes (Lander et al., 2001); this estimate remains a matter of debate and even wager among geneticists (www.ensembl.org/Genesweep). These genes are nonrandomly scattered across the genome, which consists of some 3,300,000,000 base pairs on 22 pairs of autosomal and one pair of sex chromosomes.

A key problem is the large search domain—the prior probability of any one gene being causal for a complex trait like CFS is so low that any association at conventional Type I error probabilities has an overwhelming chance of being a false positive (Crowe, 1993; Kidd, 1993).

Traditional Study Designs

Two designs are commonly used in the search for genes for complex traits. In an *association study* (Gambaro, Anglani, & D'Angelo, 2000; Risch, 2000; Sullivan et al., 2001), the frequency of a specific genetic marker is compared across groups of affected and unaffected individuals. *Linkage studies* (Craddock & Owen, 1996; Lander & Schork, 1994; Ott, 1991; Sham, 1998; Terwilliger & Goring, 2000) study the correlation between a disease and inheritance of specific chromosomal regions through families. The units of analysis are family pedigrees that are often selected so as to increase the chance of a gene segregating in the family. Typical selection strategies include the presence of multiple affected relatives (especially affected sibling pairs) or families with early-onset cases of illness. A popular approach is the *genome scan* in which individuals in a large number of pedigrees are genotyped for 300 to 500 genetic markers spaced approximately evenly throughout the genome. With statistical analysis, regions of the genome that tend to be correlated with the disease under study can be identified. With further—and often highly intensive—follow-up work, predisposing genetic variation can be identified.

The studies have different advantages and disadvantages. Association studies are more powerful but require specification of candidate genes for the disorder. One reason for conducting an association study is to attempt to learn more about the trait. There is little prior knowledge about the pathophysiology of the trait making the selection of candidate genes far less than reasonably confident. Because the pool of candidate genes is usually very large, the vast majority of positive statistical results are likely to be false positives. Linkage studies using the genome scan approach can identify regions of the genome containing causal genetic variations that were previously unsuspected. Linkage studies have been very successful for classical Mendelian disorders and much less successful for complex traits.

MOLECULAR GENETICS OF COMPLEX TRAITS

Linkage and association studies have been used for dozens of complex traits in the past 10 to 15 years (e.g., Type I and Type II diabetes mellitus, obesity, cardiovascular disease, schizophrenia, alcoholism, autism, hypertension). A simple PubMed search for the phrase "genome scan" yielded nearly 500 hits, and a search for "genetic association study" yielded 10 times as many hits. CFS researchers contemplating the use of one of these genetic designs would be wise to learn from the accumulated experience with these designs.

Even advocates of these methods would have to acknowledge that clear success in identifying genetic variation for complex traits has been infrequently encountered. Genome scans often narrow the genomic search region considerably (e.g., from over 3 billion base pairs to 10 to 20 million base pairs), but generally have had a hard slog finding the precise source of genetic variation within such a region. Notable successes in complex disorders have certainly influenced the use of case-control association studies (e.g., Alzheimer's disease [Farrer et al., 1997] and Type I diabetes mellitus [Cudworth & Wolf, 1982]). More often, however, there is a confusing mix of positive and negative findings for the same candidate gene and disorder.

ALTERNATIVE APPROACHES

Given the difficulties with complex traits, might other approaches be potentially more fruitful? It is becoming increasingly evident that the path from DNA to the function of a protein is often extremely complicated. There is a hierarchy of macromolecules (from DNA to RNA to messenger RNA to protein) with multiple levels and types of controls at each step (Table 5.2) (Banks et al., 2000). A multitude of generally poorly understood factors exert positive and negative control over transcription; similar concerns hold for RNA processing, translation or messenger RNA to protein, and for posttranslational protein modifications.

For complex traits, the classic approaches have included linkage and association studies to detect genetic variation at the DNA level. Gene expression arrays have allowed the quantification of expression of thousands of genes simultaneously. More

Table 5.2
From Gene to Expressed Protein

Macromolecule	Transition	Modifications	Detection
DNA			Linkage/association
↓	Transcription	Gene expression controls	
RNA			
↓	Processing	Alternative splicing RNA editing	
Messenger RNA			Expression array
↓	Translation	Translation control Degradation control	
Protein			Proteomics
↓	Post-translation	Multiple modifications (e.g., phosphorylation, glycosylation)	
Effects			

recently, similarly highly parallel proteomic approaches have been developed to investigate the presence and to characterize thousands of proteins simultaneously.

RNA expression and proteomic approaches capture a snapshot of activity within a tissue. For example, it is possible to compare the expression of genes or the presence of proteins between cancerous and normal prostate tissue. Moreover, the highly parallel approach may be a more realistic model for biological systems that typically operate in highly interlinked webs and networks.

With such studies, it may be possible to develop novel approaches to gene discovery that bypass the historical difficulties of gene finding with complex traits. There are many conceptual and technical difficulties for a complex trait like CFS. Unlike the situation with cancer, the anatomical site of the pathology of CFS is unknown, meaning that identification of abnormal and normal tissue is difficult or speculative. Moreover, some anatomic sites are difficult to access (e.g., brain). False negative results are a concern: Both gene expression and proteomic approaches usually require robust differences between abnormal and normal tissues, and the detectable differences may be much greater than that causing the differences between tissues. Finally, the statistical analyses of these data carry a considerable risk of false positive results due to the thousands of statistical comparisons that must be undertaken (Tusher, Tibshirani, & Chu, 2001).

CONCLUSION

Despite considerable research, the etiology of CFS remains elusive. Investigators have suggested many theories on the pathophysiology of CFS based, at first, on the prominence of symptoms suggesting an acute-viral illness or a psychiatric disorder. Subsequent investigations have documented abnormalities in disparate domains including sleep architecture, neuroendocrine responses, virological studies, immune function, brain structure and function, and divergent psychological profiles (Komaroff & Buchwald, 1998; Sharpe, 1996). Despite the demonstration of abnormalities across these and other domains, such findings remain largely isolated observations; the interactions and relationships among them are unexplored. The diversity and apparent unrelatedness of findings have led to major theoretical problems in our understanding of CFS.

Many investigators have postulated that CFS is a heterogeneous condition of complex and multifactorial etiology. Based on the accumulated data, Levine concluded: "It is now increasingly likely that the risk factors for CFS lie more prominently in the host than the environment" (Levine, 1997,p. 16) (with host factors referring to "genetic predisposition" or the individual's manner of coping with stress; Lewis, Cooper, & Bennett, 1994).

The literature on the genetic epidemiology of CFS is sparse. It is conceivable that the situation will improve within the next five years. Some investigators are anticipating that genetic effects will be shown to be important in advance of empirical demonstration. It is unlikely that CFS will readily yield to any single experimental approach. Disentangling the roles of genes and environment in the etiology of CFS is likely to be an interesting if highly effortful undertaking.

REFERENCES

Austin, M. A. (1996). Genetic epidemiology of dyslipidaemia and atherosclerosis. *Annals of Internal Medicine, 28*, 459–463.

Banks, R. E., Dunn, M. J., Hochstrasser, D. F., Sanchez, J. C., Blackstock, W., Pappin, D. J., et al. (2000). Proteomics: New perspectives, new biomedical opportunities. *Lancet, 356*, 1749–1756.

Berkson, J. (1946). Limitations of the application of fourfold table analysis to hospital data. *Biometics Bulletin, 2*, 47–53.

Boomsma, D. I., & Gabrielli, W. F., Jr. (1985). Behavioral genetic approaches to psychophysiological data. *Psychophysiology, 22*, 249–260.

Bryan, E. (1992). *Twins and higher multiple births: A guide to their nature and nurture.* London: Edward Arnold.

Buchwald, D., Herrell, R., Ashton, S., Belcourt, M., Schmaling, K., & Goldberg, J. (1999). The chronic fatigue twin registry: Method of construction, composition, and zygosity assignment. *Twin Research, 2*(3), 203–211.

Buchwald, D., Herrell, R., Ashton, S., Belcourt, M., Schmaling, K., Sullivan, P., et al., (2001). A twin study of chronic fatigue. *Psychosomatic Medicine, 63* (6), 936–943.

Bulik, C. M., Sullivan, P. F., Wade, T. D., & Kendler, K. S. (2000). Twin studies of eating disorders: A review. *International Journal of Eating Disorders, 27*, 1–20.

Cook, E. H. (1998). Genetics of autism. *Mental Retardation and Developmental Disabilities Research Reviews, 4*, 113–120.

Craddock, N., & Owen, M. J. (1996). Modern molecular genetic approaches to psychiatric disease. *British Medical Bulletin, 52*, 434–452.

Crowe, R. R. (1993). Candidate genes in psychiatry: An epidemiological perspective. *American Journal of Medical Genetics, 48*, 74–77.

Crumpacker, D. W., Cederlöf, R., Friberg, L., Kimberling, W. J., Sörensen, S., Vandenberg, S. G., et al. (1979). A twin methodology for the study of genetic and environmental control of variation in human smoking behavior. *Acta Genetica Medica et Gemellologica, 28*, 173–195.

Cudworth, A. G., & Wolf, E. (1982). The genetic susceptibility to type I (insulin-dependent) diabetes mellitus. *Clinical Endocrinology and Metabolism, 11*, 389–396.

Endicott, N. A. (1999). Chronic fatigue syndrome in private practice psychiatry: Family history of physical and mental health. *Journal of Psychosomatic Research, 47,* 343–354.

Fairburn, C. G., Cowen, P. J., & Harrison, P. J. (1999). Twin studies and the etiology of eating disorders. *International Journal of Eating Disorders, 26,* 349–358.

Falconer, D. S. (1965). The inheritance of liability to certain diseases, estimated from the incidence among relatives. *Annals of Human Genetics (London), 29,* 51–76.

Falconer, D. S., & Mackay, T. F. C. (1996). *Introduction to quantitative genetics* (4th ed.). London: Longman Group.

Farmer, A., Scourfield, J., Martin, N., Cardno, A., & McGuffin, P. (1999). Is disabling fatigue in childhood influenced by genes? *Psychological Medicine, 29*(2), 279–282.

Farrer, L. A., Cupples, L. A., Haines, J. L., Hyman, B., Kukull, W. A., Mayeux, R., et al. (1997). Effects of age, sex, and ethnicity on the association between apolipoprotein E genotype and Alzheimer disease. A meta-analysis. APOE and Alzheimer Disease Meta Analysis Consortium. *Journal of the American Medical Association, 278,* 1349–1356.

Folstein, S., & Rutter, M. (1977). Infantile autism: A genetic study of 21 twin pairs. *Journal of Child Psychology and Psychiatry, 18,* 297–321.

Fukuda, K., Straus, S. E., Hickie, I., Sharpe, M. C., Dobbins, J. G., & Komaroff, A. (1994). The chronic fatigue syndrome: A comprehensive approach to its definition and study. *Annals of Internal Medicine, 121,* 953–959.

Gambaro, G., Anglani, F., & D'Angelo, A. (2000). Association studies of genetic polymorphisms and complex disease. *Lancet, 355,* 308–311.

Glass, G. V., McGaw, B., & Smith, M. L. (1981). *Meta-analysis in social research.* Beverly Hills, CA: Sage.

Harmon, D. L., McMaster, D., McCluskey, D. R., Shields, D., & Whitehead, A. S. (1997). A common genetic variant affecting folate metabolism is not over-represented in chronic fatigue syndrome. *Annals of Clinical Biochemistry, 34*(Pt. 4), 427–429.

Hata, R., Masumura, M., Akatsu, H., Li, F., Fujita, H., Nagai, Y., et al. (2001). Up-regulation of calcineurin Abeta mRNA in the Alzheimer's disease brain: Assessment by cDNA microarray. *Biochemical and Biophysical Research Communications, 284,* 310–316.

Heath, A. C. (1995). Genetic influences on drinking behavior in humans. In H. Begleiter & B. Kissin (Eds.), *Genetics of alcoholism* (pp. 82–121). New York: Oxford University Press.

Hickie, I., Kirk, K., & Martin, N. (1999). Unique genetic and environmental determinants of prolonged fatigue: A twin study. *Psychological Medicine, 29,* 259–268.

Hill, A. B. (1965). The environment and disease: Association or causation. *Proceedings of the Royal Society of Medicine, 58,* 295–300.

Ho, L., Guo, Y., Spielman, L., Petrescu, O., Haroutunian, V., Purohit, D., et al. (2001). Altered expression of a-type but not b-type synapsin isoform in the brain of patients at high risk for Alzheimer's disease assessed by DNA microarray technique. *Neuroscience Letters, 298,* 191–194.

Holmes, G. P., Kaplan, J. E., Gantz, N. M., Komaroff, A. L., Schonberger, L. B., Straus, S. E., et al. (1988). Chronic fatigue syndrome: A working case definition. *Annals of Internal Medicine, 108*(3), 387–389.

Kaprio, J., Hammar, N., Koskenvuo, M., Floderus-Myrhed, B., Langinvainio, H., & Sarna, S. (1982). Cigarette smoking and alcohol use in Finland and Sweden: A cross-national twin study. *International Journal of Epidemiology, 11,* 378–386.

Kendell, R. E. (1991). Chronic fatigue, viruses, and depression. *Lancet, 337,* 160–161.

Kendler, K. S. (1993). Twin studies of psychiatric illness: Current status and future directions. *Archives of General Psychiatry, 50,* 905–915.

Kendler, K. S., & Diehl, S. R. (1995). Schizophrenia: Genetics. In H. I. Kaplan & B. J. Sadock (Eds.), *Comprehensive textbook of psychiatry* (6th ed., pp. 942–957). Baltimore: Williams & Wilkins.

Kendler, K. S., & Gardener, C. O. (1998). Twin studies of adult psychiatric and substance dependence disorders: Are they biased by differences in the environmental experiences of mono- and dizygotic twins in childhood and adolescence? *Psychological Medicine, 28,* 625–633.

Kendler, K. S., Neale, M. C., Kessler, R. C., Heath, A. C., & Eaves, L. J. (1993). The lifetime history of major depression in women: Reliability of diagnosis and heritability. *Archives of General Psychiatry, 50,* 863–870.

Kendler, K. S., Neale, M. C., Kessler, R. C., Heath, A. C., & Eaves, L. J. (1994). Parental treatment and the equal environment assumption in twin studies of psychiatric illness. *Psychological Medicine, 24,* 579–590.

Kendler, K. S., Neale, M. C., Sullivan, P. F., Gardner, C. O., & Prescott, C. A. (1999). A population-based twin study in women of smoking initiation and nicotine dependence. *Psychological Medicine, 29,* 299–308.

Kendler, K. S., & Prescott, C. A. (1999). A population-based twin study of lifetime major depression in men and women. *Archives of General Psychiatry, 56,* 39–44.

Khoury, M. J., Beaty, T. H., & Cohen, B. H. (1993). *Fundamentals of genetic epidemiology.* New York: Oxford University Press.

Kidd, K. K. (1993). Associations of disease with genetic markers: Déjà vu all over again. *American Journal of Medical Genetics (Neuropsychiatric Genetics), 48,* 71–73.

Klein, D. N., & Riso, L. P. (1994). Psychiatric disorders: Problems of boundaries and comorbidity. In C. G. Costello (Ed.), *Basic issues in psychopathology* (pp. 19–66). New York: Guilford Press.

Komaroff, A. L., & Buchwald, D. S. (1998). Chronic fatigue syndrome: An update. *Annual Review of Medicine, 49,* 1–13.

Lander, E. S., Linton, L. M., Birren, B., Nusbaum, C., Zody, M. C., Baldwin, J., et al. (2001). Initial sequencing and analysis of the human genome. *Nature, 409,* 860–921.

Lander, E. S., & Schork, N. J. (1994). Genetic dissection of complex traits. *Science, 265,* 2037–2048.

Levine, P. H. (1997). Epidemiologic advances in chronic fatigue syndrome. *Journal of Psychiatric Research, 31,* 7–18.

Levy-Lahad, E., & Bird, T. D. (2000). Alzheimer's disease: Genetic factors. In S.-M. Pulst (Ed.), *Neurogenetics* (pp. 317–333). New York: Oxford University Press.

Lewis, S., Cooper, C. L., & Bennett, D. (1994). Psychosocial factors and chronic fatigue syndrome. *Psychological Medicine, 24,* 661–671.

Manu, P., Lane, T. J., & Matthews, D. A. (1988). The frequency of the chronic fatigue syndrome in patients with symptoms of persistent fatigue. *Annals of Internal Medicine, 109,* 554–556.

Manu, P., Lane, T. J., & Matthews, D. A. (1993). Chronic fatigue and chronic fatigue syndrome: Clinical epidemiology and aetiological classification. In G. R. Bock & J. Whelan (Eds.), *Chronic fatigue syndrome* (pp. 23–31). New York: Wiley.

Manu, P., Matthews, D. A., & Lane, T. J. (1988). The mental health of patients with a chief complaint of chronic fatigue. *Archives of Internal Medicine, 148,* 2213–2217.

Martin, N. G., Eaves, L. J., Kearsey, M. H., & Davies, P. (1978). The power of the classical twin study. *Heredity, 40,* 97–116.

Morton, N. E., & Chung, C. S. (1978). Preface. In N. E. Morton & C. S. Chung (Eds.), *Genetic epidemiology.* New York: Academic Press.

Nance, W. E. (1984). The relevance of twin studies to cardiovascular research. *Progress in Clinical and Biological Research, 147,* 325–348.

Neale, M. C., & Cardon, L. R. (1992). *Methodology for the study of twins and families.* Dordrecht, The Netherlands: Kluwer Academic.

Neale, M. C., Eaves, L. J., & Kendler, K. S. (1994). The power of the classical twin study to resolve variation in threshold traits. *Behavior Genetics, 24,* 239–258.

Neale, M. C., Harvey, E., & Kendler, K. S. (2001). *Multivariate extensions to the modelling of initiation and progression.* Manuscript submitted for publication.

Neale, M. C., & Kendler, K. S. (1995). Models of comorbidity for multifactorial disorders. *American Journal of Human Genetics, 57,* 935–953.

Online Mendelian Inheritance in Man (OMIM™). World wide web URL: http//www3 .ncbi.nlm.nih.gov/omim/: Johns Hopkins University, Baltimore.

Ott, J. (1991). *Analysis of human genetic linkage.* Baltimore: Johns Hopkins University Press.

Petitti, D. B. (1994). *Meta-analysis, decision analysis, and cost-effectiveness analysis.* New York: Oxford University Press.

Plomin, R., DeFries, J. C., McClearn, G. E., & Rutter, M. (1997). *Behavioral genetics* (3rd ed.). New York: Freeman.

Primer on Molecular Genetics. World wide web URL: http://www.ornl.gov /TechResources/Human_Genome/publicat/primer/intro.html: U.S. Department of Energy.

Raiha, I., Kemppainen, H., Kaprio, J., Koskenvuo, M., & Sourander, L. (1998). Lifestyle, stress, and genes in peptic ulcer disease: A nationwide twin cohort study. *Archives of Internal Medicine , 158,* 698–704.

Risch, N. J. (2000). Searching for genetic determinants in the new millennium. *Nature, 405,* 847–856.

Rothman, K. J. (1986). *Modern epidemiology.* Boston: Little, Brown.

Rutter, M., & Plomin, R. (1997). Opportunities for psychiatry from genetic findings. *British Journal of Psychiatry, 171,* 209–219.

Sham, P. C. (1998). *Statistics in human genetics.* New York: Wiley.

Sharpe, M. (1996). Chronic fatigue syndrome. *Psychiatric Clinics of North America, 19,* 549–573.

Strachen, T., & Read, A. P. (1999). *Human molecular genetics* (2nd ed.). New York: Wiley.

Sullivan, P. F., Eaves, L. J., Kendler, K. S., & Neale, M. C. (2001). Genetic case-control association studies in neuropsychiatry. *Archives of General Psychiatry, 58* (11), 1015–1024.

Sullivan, P. F., & Kendler, K. S. (1998). The genetic epidemiology of "neurotic" disorders. *Current Opinion in Psychiatry, 11,* 143–147.

Sullivan, P. F., & Kendler, K. S. (1999). The genetic epidemiology of smoking. *Nicotine and Tobacco Research, 1*(Suppl. 2), 549–555.

Sullivan, P. F., Neale, M. C., & Kendler, K. S. (2000). The genetic epidemiology of major depression: Review and meta-analysis. *American Journal of Psychiatry, 157,* 1552–1562.

Sullivan, P. F., Wells, J. E., Joyce, P. R., Bushnell, J. A., Mulder, R. T., & Oakley-Browne, M. A. (1996). Family history of depression in clinic and community samples. *Journal of Affective Disorders, 40,* 159–168.

Swanson, D. W., Moore, G. L., & Nobrega, F. T. (1978). Family history of alcoholism in patients with chronic fatigue. *Journal of Clinical Psychiatry, 39,* 754–755.

Terwilliger, J. D., & Goring, H. H. (2000). Gene mapping in the 20th and 21st centuries: Statistical methods, data analysis, and experimental design. *Human Biology, 72,* 63–132.

Thomas, D. C. (2000). Genetic epidemiology with a capital "E." *Genetic Epidemiology, 19,* 289–300.

Torres, S. H., & Jason, L. A. (2003, Jan.). *Family medical history of persons with CFS.* Poster presented at the American Association of Chronic Fatigue Syndrome Conference. Chantilly, Virginia.

Tusher, V. G., Tibshirani, R., & Chu, G. (2001). Significance analysis of microarrays applied to the ionizing radiation response. *Proceedings of the National Academy of Sciences, USA, 98,* 5116–5121.

Underhill, J. A., Mahalingam, M., Peakman, M., & Wessely, S. (2001). Lack of association between HLA genotype and chronic fatigue syndrome. *European Journal of Immunogenetics, 28*(3), 425–428.

Vogler, G. P., McClearn, G. E., Snieder, H., Boomsma, D. I., Palmer, R., de Knijff, P., et al. (1997). Genetics and behavioral medicine: Risk factors for cardiovascular disease. *Behavioral Medicine, 22,* 141–149.

Weissman, M. M., Merikangas, K. R., John, K., Wickramaratne, P., Prusoff, B. A., & Kidd, K. K. (1986). Family-genetic studies of psychiatric disorders: Developing technologies. *Archives of General Psychiatry, 43,* 1104–1116.

Wessely, S., Nimnuan, C., & Sharpe, M. (1999). Functional somatic syndromes: One or many? *Lancet, 354*(9182), 936–939.

Woodman, C. L., Stout, L., Hardardottir, H., & Hartz, A. (2001). Chronic fatigue syndrome and psychiatric illness: A family study. *Psychosomatic Medicine, 63,* 94–95.

CHAPTER 6

Postinfective Fatigue

ANDREW LLOYD

INDIVIDUALS SUFFERING FROM acute infective illnesses typically develop a constellation of systemic symptoms including fever and musculoskeletal pain, as well as fatigue. In both humans and animals, increased slow wave sleep and stereotyped behavioral responses, including reduced motor activity, social withdrawal, and anorexia also accompany infections (Hart, 1988). These characteristic physical and behavioral correlates of infection result primarily from the host immune response to the pathogen, as they are reproduced in infections resulting from a wide range of microbiological agents (Vollmer-Conna, 2001). Many, but not all, of the features of acute sickness behavior are evident in the prolonged illness marked by fatigue, which is commonly reported to follow acute infection.

This chapter reviews the evidence linking prolonged fatigue states to acute infectious diseases. There is a discussion of the historical data, which arose primarily from observations of subjects in retrospective case series. This is followed by a selective review of laboratory-intensive investigations of the modern era, which are predominantly based on cross-sectional case-control studies. The insights gleaned from the limited number of prospective cohort studies now underway are then highlighted. Finally, there is a discussion of the possible pathophysiology of postinfective fatigue states. The insights gleaned from studies conducted in the 1950s of patients with brucellosis, which have recently been reaffirmed in the context of infectious mononucleosis and Q fever, are highlighted. The conclusion of the chapter is that postinfective fatigue states are prevalent and predominantly short-lived, but that in a small subset of individuals certain infections can trigger a protected and disabling fatigue state consistent with the diagnosis of chronic fatigue syndrome (CFS; Fukuda et al., 1994). Microbiological, immunologic, and psychological factors are all likely to be relevant to the pathogenesis of postinfective fatigue states.

HISTORICAL PERSPECTIVE

The most widely known predecessor to CFS is the disorder termed *neurasthenia*, which was first delineated by George Beard, an American neurologist (1869). This popular clinical diagnosis at that time featured profound physical and mental fatigue as well as depression. Although even the first descriptions of neurasthenia included a link with febrile illness, the observation that specific infectious diseases precipitated a subsequent fatigue state came with the microbiological revolution of the late nineteenth and early twentieth centuries. Notable among the infections linked to postinfective fatigue states were brucellosis, which is caused by infection with intracellular bacteria of the *Brucella sp.* (Evans, 1934), and infection with Epstein-Barr virus (EBV), the causative agent of infectious mononucleosis (Isaacs, 1948).

Brucellosis is a bacterial infection acquired from exposure to livestock (i.e., a zoonosis), which manifests with abrupt onset of fever, headaches, fatigue, and drenching sweats (Marston, 1861). In a small percentage of cases, the acute illness may be followed by relapses or by chronic, localized infection in which the organism is cultured from blood or tissue months or even years after the original infection. This propensity to chronic infection is attributed to the fact that the organism survives within tissue macrophages, relatively hidden from host immunity (Spink, 1952). The same author reviewed the outcomes of 65 patients who had been diagnosed with acute brucellosis, most of whom were abattoir workers or farmers who had been exposed to *Brucella abortus* in this setting but who had not received antibiotic treatment (Spink, 1951). Ten patients (16%) recovered uneventfully within 3 months of onset of symptoms. Twenty-five patients (39%) remained symptomatic for 3 to 12 months, and during this period persistence of the organism was evident in blood or tissue cultures. Thirty patients (46%) had persisting illness for more than one year, of whom 17 had ongoing evidence of active infection. The remaining group of 13 patients (20% of the original 65 patients) complained of ongoing ill health marked by fatigue, musculoskeletal pain, and depression, but without objective evidence of ongoing infection. A similar rate of unexplained, ongoing illness lasting 12 months or more was evident in a separate group of 61 cases who had received antibiotic treatment in the acute phase. Based on these data, Spink suggested three possible explanations for the ongoing, unexplained illness: (1) occult, active infection; (2) a neurological complication triggered by the original infection; or (3) an emotional reaction to the original infection.

This association of a largely subjective syndrome of chronic fatigue with discrete infections, such as brucellosis, sparked considerable controversy and led to further studies by Cluff and colleagues (Cluff, Trever, Imboden, & Canter, 1959; Imboden, Cluff, Canter, & Trever, 1959; Trever, Cluff, Peeler, & Bennett, 1959). Sixty patients who had accidentally acquired acute *Brucella melitensis* or *Brucella suis* infection while working in a microbiological research laboratory were studied in a retrospective case analysis. Forty-eight patients (80%) had received antibiotic therapy, but their outcomes were indistinguishable from those who did not receive treatment. Chronic, unexplained illness lasting 12 months or more developed in 24 (40%), of whom 16 could be followed up in the reported analysis 4 to 8 years later. Ten of these 16 patients remained unwell (labeled as the *chronic-symptomatic* cases), whereas 6 had recovered (labeled as the *chronic-recovered* cases). In addition, eight patients who had recovered uneventfully in the acute illness were identified for follow-up (labeled as *acute recovered* cases). The clinical and laboratory characteristics of the acute phase of the illness, such as maximum temperature or peak antibody titer, did not predict outcome status. A series of clinical and laboratory studies on these three groups at follow-up did not reveal significant objective differences between them.

By contrast, psychological disorder, notably depression, was significantly more common in both chronic-recovered and chronic-symptomatic individuals when compared with the acute-recovered cases. Thus, so-called chronic brucellosis was tentatively linked to psychological disorder either as a risk factor for the condition, or arising as a consequence of the long-standing illness. It should be noted that sensitive detection techniques, such as polymerase chain reaction (PCR) to identify persistent nucleic acids of the microorganisms, or immunoassays to identify microbial antigens in tissues, were not available at the time of these studies. Thus, low-level persistence of the pathogen was not definitively resolved.

The critical issue of whether the chronic fatiguing illness led to psychological disorder or conversely whether depression and other mental illness resulted from chronic ill health was studied, again by Imboden (Imboden, Cantor, & Cluff, 1961), in a prospective evaluation of civil servants before the Asian influenza epidemic of 1957. In this study, 600 employees of the same research facility associated with the brucellosis cases described earlier were screened using a psychological and personality inventory, the Minnesota Multiphasic Personality Inventory (MMPI) and other instruments. Subsequently, 26 individuals became infected and symptomatic during the influenza outbreak. Imboden subsequently conducted a post hoc analysis on the preillness data of the 600 individuals to classify them as "psychologically vulnerable" based on scores above the median split in three or more of the four scores on the instruments; "nonvulnerable" (three or more scores below median); or "intermediate." The ratio of subclinical influenza episodes to clinically symptomatic illnesses was approximately 6:1 in the group as a whole and did not differ in the study groups. By contrast, the incidence of documented, symptomatic influenza illness was 11 of 96 (11.4%) in the vulnerable group, 11 of 306 (3.5%) in the nonvulnerable group (3.5%; $p < .02$), and 4 of 78 (5.0%) in the intermediate group. The severity of the acute illness in the two major groups was comparable. However, the duration of symptoms was also increased in the vulnerable group, with a mean duration of 7.9 days in the nonvulnerable cases and longer than 3 weeks in the vulnerable cases. Thus, this study pointed to premorbid psychological vulnerability as an important determinant of protracted recovery after infection, although that time point for this analysis was very early in the postinfective period (i.e., weeks). Several subsequent studies have reaffirmed this notion, including a study of early postinfective outcomes after tularemia in volunteers (Canter, 1972) and one of upper respiratory infection (Barsky, Goodson, Lane, & Cleary, 1988). In addition, psychological vulnerability has been associated with increased susceptibility to infection in elegant volunteer studies with common cold viruses (Cohen, Tyrrell, & Smith, 1991). In a subsequent report on the original influenza cohort, Cluff (1991) suggested that the psychologically vulnerable group may have had a heightened awareness of the manifestations of disease (i.e., they may have been prone to somatization). In combination, these data provide strong evidence implicating premorbid (i.e., preinfection) psychological distress as a risk factor for greater symptomatic infection and for protracted recovery in the early postinfective period. Again, sensitive immunologic and molecular microbial detection techniques were not used in these studies to definitively resolve whether low-level persistence of the pathogens was underpinning the severe and prolonged symptoms (potentially via an immunologic disturbance induced by psychological distress).

More recently, Lyme disease has been linked to fibromyalgia and CFS in a fashion analogous to brucellosis. Lyme disease is a tick-borne infection, caused by the spirochete *Borrelia bugdorferi* (Bugdorfer et al., 1982). The illness manifests with an insidious rash (erythema migrans) accompanied by malaise, fatigue, and musculoskeletal pain. Weeks later, neurological and cardiac manifestations of chronic infection may occur; and months to years later, chronic arthritis and neurological complications such as encephalitis may follow (Steere, 1989). This organism is also recognized to persist intracellularly within the macrophage lysosomal compartment (Montgomery, Nathanson, & Malawista, 1993). Initial reports from tertiary referral clinic series suggested that up to half of the patients with prior treated Lyme disease who were presenting with late sequelae, had no evidence of active infection, but had musculoskeletal pain and fatigue syndromes consistent with either fibromyalgia or CFS (Dinerman & Steere, 1992; Sigal, 1990). Subsequently, a population-based retrospective case-control study was undertaken in a U.S region endemic for Lyme to verify this potential association (Shaddick et al., 1994). The subjects with prior treated Lyme disease ($n = 38$) had a mean duration from disease onset to study evaluation of 6.2 years. Compared with the control group ($n = 43$), they had more arthralgia, fatigue, concentration difficulties, distal paresthesia, and worse global health status scores. Thirteen patients in the Lyme disease group had residual symptoms apparently attributable to the infection, of whom 3 (8%) had no objective findings on examination or investigation and are likely to have met diagnostic criteria for fibromyalgia (Wolfe et al., 1990) or CFS (Fukuda et al., 1994). It should be noted again that sensitive detection techniques such as polymerase chain reaction (PCR) to identify persistent nucleic acids of the borrelia, or immunoassays to identify microbial antigens in tissues, were not conducted in these studies. Thus, low-level persistence of the pathogen was not definitively resolved. Nevertheless, based on an assumption of persistence of the pathogen, investigators have conducted a randomized, placebo-controlled treatment trial (Klempner et al., 2001). This study included patients with well-documented, previously treated Lyme disease who had persistent musculoskeletal pain, neurocognitive symptoms, and fatigue. The treatment was appropriately prolonged, consisting of one month of intravenous ceftriaxone followed by oral doxycycline for two months—or matching placebos. No significant difference in symptomatic status or functional outcome was detected between active drug and placebo treatment groups.

CASE-CONTROL STUDIES

Over the past two decades, numerous case-control studies with a laboratory emphasis have been conducted examining the potential association markers of infection with specific viruses and CFS. This selective review includes studies of EBV, enteroviruses, human herpes virus-6 (HHV-6), and a novel human T lymphotropic virus (HTLV)-II-like retrovirus. These studies tend to generate hypotheses, but the numerous confounding variables (such as the adequacy of matching of cases and controls, and the sensitivity and specificity of the laboratory assays) limit their interpretation.

EPSTEIN-BARR VIRUS

In addition to the early reports providing circumstantial links between persistent fatigue states and EBV infection, laboratory studies reported in the 1970s and 1980s raised the possibility of abnormally persistent EBV antibody responses and perhaps ongoing viral activity in patients with chronic symptoms. The initial report was of an altered pattern of immunoglobulin G (IgG) antibodies directed against the restricted (R) component of the early antigen (EA) complex, instead of the usual diffuse (D) component, as well as high titers of IgG antibodies against the viral capsid antigen (VCA; Henle, Henle, & Horwitz, 1974; Horwitz, Henle, Henle, & Schmitz, 1975). Early case-control studies (Jones et al., 1985; Straus et al., 1985) compared patients with chronic fatigue (predominantly following mononucleosis illnesses) with a group of asymptomatic, but EBV-seropositive, subjects. IgM anti-VCA antibodies were detected up to 3 years after the initial acute infection in a minority of patients (22% and 7% respectively), and significantly elevated titers of IgG anti-VCA and anti-EA antibodies were observed in the chronically fatigued patients. These findings were interpreted to support the concept of chronic, active infection with EBV as the likely pathogenesis of CFS, and of the utility of high titer anti-EBV IgG antibody levels as a useful laboratory marker for its diagnosis. However, the patients included were likely to have been highly selected cases, referred to centers with an interest in EBV because of the predetermined findings of high titer antibodies and a persistent clinical syndrome. Follow-up studies of healthy subjects 2 to 9 years after infectious mononucleosis have commonly shown high antibody titers to both VCA and EA (Horwitz, Henle, Henle, Rudnick, & Latts, 1985). Several subsequent studies have failed to find evidence for abnormal continued replication of EBV or for an altered serological response in patients with CFS (Gold et al., 1990; Sumaya, 1990). Thus, it appears very unlikely that EBV infection or reactivation is the underlying cause of CFS in the majority of patients. However, prospective cohort studies have implicated EBV infection as the trigger for CFS in some patients (Bennett et al., 1998; Buchwald, Rea, Katon, Russo, & Ashley, 2000; White, Thomas, et al., 1995). These studies are reviewed in detail on the following pages.

Enteroviruses

The association between enteroviral infection and CFS was first considered in relation to several apparent epidemics of the disorder. Cases in these *myalgic encephalomyelitis* (ME) outbreaks were similar in presentation to poliomyelitis, and the clusters occurred concurrently with polio epidemics (Gilliam, 1938; Pellew, 1951; Sigurdsson, Sigurjonsson, Sigurdsson, Thorkelsson, & Gudmundsson, 1950). However, virological or serological evidence for enteroviruses was not found.

Serological studies of enteroviruses analogous to those pursuing EBV infection were performed. Early reports of elevated titers of neutralizing antibodies against Coxsackie B (Behan, Behan, & Bell, 1985; Calder, Warnock, McCartney, & Bell, 1987; Keighley & Bell, 1983) were refuted by a definitive case-control study using standard enteroviral serology (Miller et al., 1991) and a failure to replicate in other populations (Lindh et al., 1996). A more sophisticated virological and serological case-control study attempted enterovirus isolation from fecal samples after an acid-dissociation procedure designed to separate the virus from IgG antibodies, as well as a detection technique for the enteroviral antigen, VP1, in serum, again after acid-dissociation (Yousef et al., 1988). A significantly greater number of patients with CFS than control subjects had the virus isolated (22% vs. 7%) and VP1 antigen detected (51% of patients had levels three standard deviations above control subjects). However, the significance of the VP1 detection component of this study was cast into doubt by subsequent reports of frequently positive results in the serum of patients with other neurological and psychiatric disorders (Halpin & Wessely, 1989; Lynch & Seth, 1989). Subsequent studies have also been unable to replicate identification of enterovirus in the stools (Mawle et al., 1995; Swanink et al., 1994).

Further evidence potentially in support of an etiological role for enteroviruses in chronic fatigue syndrome came from the demonstration of enteroviral RNA in muscle biopsies of a subset of patients (20 of 96 patients in one study and 32 of 60 in another study). The enteroviral sequences were detected by slot-blot RNA hybridization (Archard, Bowles, Behan, Bell, & Doyle, 1988), or by reverse transcriptase polymerase chain reaction (RT-PCR; Gow et al., 1991). However, one of these groups subsequently failed to replicate their own, earlier findings (Gow et al., 1994), and several other researchers have similarly failed to demonstrate an association between persistent enteroviral genomes and chronic fatigue syndrome (Lindh et al., 1996; McArdle et al., 1996).

HUMAN HERPES VIRUS 6

During efforts to resolve the significance of EBV serology in the diagnosis of CFS, antibody titers against several other viruses were noted to be elevated in this patient group (Holmes et al., 1988). Reactivity to the herpes viruses, including Cytomegalovirus and HHV-6, was prominent. Others reproduced this serological evidence for altered HHV-6 activity in patients with chronic fatigue syndrome (Levine et al., 1992). In the largest systematic examination of HHV-6, investigators studied 259 patients with a viral-like illness of abrupt onset followed by chronic fatigue, who were part of an apparent epidemic of this syndrome in Lake Tahoe, Nevada, in 1985 (Buchwald et al., 1992). Viral cultures augmented by immunofluorescence and PCR detection systems were used to demonstrate the presence of HHV-6 in peripheral blood mononuclear cells in 70% of 113 patients, but only 20% of 40 control subjects. The apparently active replication of HHV-6 in these patients was thought to represent reactivation of latent infection because abundant evidence indicates that the great majority of individuals acquire HHV-6 infection early in life. Other case-control studies using both serological and PCR techniques have yielded generally negative evidence for HHV-6 reactivation (including specific examination of HHV-6A and B) in patients with CFS (Di Luca et al., 1995; Hay & Jenkins, 1994; Patnaik, Komaroff, Conley, Ojo-Amaize, & Peter, 1995; Secchiero et al., 1995; Swanink et al., 1995; Yalcin, Kuratsune, Yamaguchi, Kitani, & Yamanishi, 1994). The significance of HHV-6 reactivation to the pathophysiology of CFS therefore remains unclear. Resolution of the relationship awaits longitudinal studies in patients and control subjects followed from primary HHV-6 infection or from onset of the syndrome (Wessely, Hotopf, & Sharpe, 1998).

RETROVIRUSES

In 1991, a highly publicized study raised the possibility of retroviral infection in patients with CFS (Defreitas et al., 1991). Primers based on the sequence of the human T lymphotropic virus (HTLV)-II gag gene were used in PCR to amplify DNA prepared from lymphocytes of patients with CFS and control subjects. Amplified products were obtained from 10 of 12 adults with CFS, 13 of 18 children with the disorder, 7 of 20 healthy family contacts of these children, and none of 20 control subjects. Sequences of several other retroviral genes including HTLV-I *gag* and HTLV-II *tax* were not detectable in patients or control subjects. This paper also reported the detection of antibodies to HTLV-I in 6 of 12 adults and 11 of 18 children with CFS.

Several subsequent case-control studies have failed to confirm this finding, or to obtain molecular or serological evidence for any known retrovirus (Flugel, Mahnke, Geiger, & Komaroff, 1992; Gow et al., 1992; Heneine et al., 1994; Khan et al., 1993). Two of these studies in particular, used combinations of PCR, Western blotting, and immunofluoresence for several known retroviruses on samples obtained from well-characterized cases of CFS (Gow et al., 1992; Khan et al., 1993). In addition to the failure to identify reverse transcriptase activity in patient samples, these data provide strong evidence against any role for retroviruses, including endogenous retroviruses, in the etiology of CFS (Gelman, Unger, Mawle, Nisenbaum, & Reeves, 2000).

OTHER INFECTIONS

Several other viral and intracellular pathogens have been tentatively linked to a subsequent postinfective fatigue syndrome in limited case reports or case series, including parvovirus B19, Borna disease virus, Inoue-Melnick virus, the Australian arbovirus, Ross River virus (RRV); and the rickettsial pathogen, *Coxiella burnetii*, which causes Q fever, among others (reviewed in Fekety, 1994; Wessely et al., 1998).

PROSPECTIVE COHORT STUDIES

The powerful insights into epidemiology and pathogenesis gleaned from prospective cohort studies are exemplified by the four longitudinal studies described in this section. In contrast with the often ambiguous outcomes of case-control studies, and the possible biases in retrospective series, these studies offer the best potential to elucidate the incidence and risk factors for postinfective fatigue and to determine the underlying basis of the illness.

The comprehensive, prospective primary care study of symptomatic minor viral infections conducted by Wessely and colleagues (1995) argues strongly against an etiologic role for such infections in CFS. In this study, a large-scale community screen of psychological health and fatigue states was conducted ($n = 15,283$) prior to a subsequent nested case-control cohort analysis of subjects with acute viral illnesses (predominantly upper respiratory tract infections or gastroenteritis; $n = 1,199$) and subjects presenting without apparent infection ($n = 1,177$). Follow-up of these cohorts 6 months later revealed that subjects in the viral infection cohort were not more likely to have a chronic fatigue syndrome than those in the control cohort. Importantly, those who had rated themselves as significantly fatigued or psychologically distressed prior to presenting to the doctor were significantly more likely to go on to develop CFS. Both a prior fatigue state and psychological disorder independently predicted chronic fatigue, whereas the viral infection itself did not. There was an association between prior psychological distress and the generalized postviral symptoms (malaise, fatigue, etc.), but not local symptoms (sore throat, tender glands, etc.).

By contrast, the tentative link between EBV infection and a postviral fatigue syndrome has been firmly endorsed by three cohort studies. The first of these studies was conducted by White and colleagues and has been reported in three separate analyses (White et al., 2001; White, Grover, et al., 1995; White, Thomas, et al., 1995). The study enrolled 245 patients with either infectious mononucleosis diagnosed by Monospot test ($n = 118$; 77%) or suspected upper respiratory tract infection ($n = 127$; 23%). In the infectious mononucleosis group, 108 (92%) had confirmed primary EBV infections, three had HHV-6 infection, three had cytomegalovirus infection, and six had no agent identified for the clinical illness. The comparison group had a range of infections implicated including hepatitis A, adenovirus, influenza A, toxoplasmosis, rubella, and 75 (68%) with no cause identified. Of the combined group, 101 (41%) had a fatigue syndrome (empirically defined) associated with significant functional impairment at the time of enrollment. The fatigue state persisted for 1 month or more in 71 individuals from this group (73%), for 2 months or more in 43 (43%), and for 6 months or more in 9 (9%). Of the combined group, 69 (28%) had a depressive disorder diagnosed by standardized interview at enrollment. This psychological disturbance persisted for 1 month or more in 28 individuals from this group (49%), for 2 months or more in 21 (32%), and 6 months or more in 10 cases (15%). Importantly, the fatigue syndrome was most prevalent in those with mononucleosis documented to be due to EBV infection, and was shown to be essentially independent of psychological disorder. Further analysis by logistic regression of the baseline data for premorbid health status revealed that psychiatric disorders, emotional personality traits, and social adversity in the 12 months prior to enrollment predicted the likelihood of psychological disorder in the cohort, but not the postinfective fatigue syndrome. By contrast, a positive Monospot test and cervical lymphadenopathy at baseline predicted the fatigue syndrome. In addition, a surrogate measure of reduced aerobic fitness derived from recording the pulse rate before and after a simple standardized exercise at 1 month after enrollment, was predictive of the fatigue syndrome at 2 months and 6 months.

A more simple observational cohort study of 150 subjects with infectious mononucleosis due to EBV infection (Buchwald et al., 2000) confirmed the incidence estimates previously described. In this study, self-assessed failure to recover was reported by 55 cases (37%) at 2 months and 17 (11%) at 6 months. The predominant symptoms in those who reported nonrecovery were fatigue, sore throat, and malaise. The baseline predictors of nonrecovery at 6 months included female sex (odds ratio [OR] = 3.3; 95% confidence interval [CI] 1.0–12.0), and a greater number of life events more than 6 months before the illness (OR = 1.7; 95% CI 1.1–2.5). Although this study is limited by its predominantly self-reported data set, and the lack of defined fatigue syndrome or ongoing systematic assessment of psychological distress, the data confirm the expectation that approximately 10% of adults who develop symptomatic infectious mononucleosis will develop a postinfective fatigue syndrome lasting 6 months or more. In addition, the role of premorbid adverse life events as a risk factor for postinfective fatigue appears well established.

The fourth cohort study, which remains largely unpublished to date, has chosen the ambitious goal of defining the incidence of postinfective fatigue syndromes in three infection groups studied in parallel. The Dubbo Infection Outcomes Study has been enrolling subjects in rural Australia with serologically confirmed infection due to EBV, Ross River virus, or Q fever (Bennett et al., 1998). A detailed medical and psychological evaluation of all enrolled subjects is conducted at baseline. This is repeated at 6 months in all symptomatic cases and matched (recovered) comparison subjects, to designate cases for chronic fatigue syndrome (Fukuda et al., 1994), as well as to identify medical and psychiatric co-morbid conditions. Preliminary data from the first 169 subjects enrolled into this cohort has also confirmed that the incidence of postinfective fatigue syndrome at 6 months after the onset of illness is approximately 10% in all three infective groups. The pattern of symptoms in the EBV cohort is illustrated in Figure 6.1. Thus, strong corroborated evidence is now available to implicate specific infections, notably EBV, in causing a postinfective syndrome.

The Dubbo Infection Outcomes Study is also examining the microbiological and immunologic predictors of delayed recovery. These investigations have been driven by three separate prior investigations, which raise the hypothesis that abnormal persistence of the pathogen and impaired host responses may underlie postinfective fatigue states. The first of these observations was made in relation to Q fever infection, which has been previously implicated as causing a postinfective fatigue syndrome in retrospective case series (Ayres et al., 1998; Marmion et al., 1996). Similar to *Brucella sp.* and *B. Bugdorferi, C. burnetii* is an intracellular pathogen superbly adapted to reside and persist within the acidic environment of the macrophage phagolysosome (Williams & Thompson, 1991). Thus, the notion of persistence of the microorganism as a key component of the pathogenesis of postinfective fatigue resurfaced with the report of persistent microbial nucleic acids in 30 patients with postinfective fatigue following serologically documented and appropriately treated Q fever (Harris, Storm, Lloyd, Arens, & Marmion, 2000). The study included five subjects who previously had Q fever but without persistent sequelae, seven Q fever vaccines, and six healthy seronegative subjects. Tissue samples from patients with documented chronic, localized Q fever infection (endocarditis or chorioamnionitis) were included as positive controls. Cell culture and guinea pig

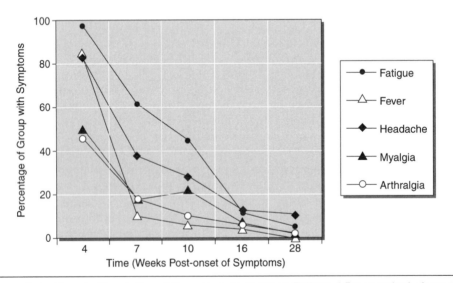

Figure 6.1 Time to Resolution of Symptoms in Patients Followed Prospectively from the Time of Diagnosis of Serologically Documented Acute EBV Infection (*n* = 50). *Source:* "The Relationship between Fatigue, Psychological and Immunological Variables in Acute Infectious Illness," by B. K. Bennett, I. B. Hickie, U. S. Vollmer-Conna, et al., 1998, *Australia and New Zealand Journal of Psychiatry 32*, pp. 180–186; A. Lloyd et al., unpublished data.

inoculation of peripheral blood mononuclear cells, liver biopsy, or bone marrow in the postinfective fatigue cases did not result in isolation of *C. burnetii*. However, using PCR for DNA amplification of two coxiella DNA sequences resulted in the detection of coxiella DNA in 4 of 30 samples from the postinfective fatigue patients, and none of the 18 control samples. PCR amplification from 11 of 20 bone marrow aspirate samples and 2 of 14 liver biopsy samples obtained from patients with post-Q fever fatigue were also positive. The amplicons were sequenced in four of the positive results, which confirmed complete identity with *C. burnetii* genome sequence in all cases.

The second prior observation relates to Ross River virus, the Australian mosquito-borne viral infection, which typically manifests with arthritis and rash. Retrospective case series have implicated this infection as a common cause of a postinfective fatigue syndrome (Selden & Cameron, 1996; Westley-Wise, Beard, Sladden, Dunn, & Simpson, 1996). Preliminary evidence for the proof-of-principle of the association of persistent viral RNA and ongoing symptoms was reported by studies of synovial biopsies taken from subjects with 5 weeks of ongoing symptoms following acute RRV infection. In 2 of 12 synovial biopsies, RRV RNA was found by detection of specific amplicons from the E2 region in an RT-PCR assay. In addition, all biopsies revealed histological evidence of hyperplasia of the synovial lining, vascular proliferation, and mononuclear cell infiltration (Soden et al., 2000). Interestingly, persistent noncytolytic infection with RRV has also been demonstrated in monocyte-derived macrophages, fibroblasts, and muscle cells (Linn, Aaskov, & Suhrbier, 1996).

The third prior observation relates to the adequacy of the host immune response to EBV infection and its ability to control viral replication and terminate clinical illness in infectious mononucleosis. Bharadwaj et al. (2001) described a pilot study of two individuals with divergent clinical outcomes from primary EBV infection. In one subject, a broadly directed cytotoxic T lymphocyte (CTL) response to EBV epitopes was detected by tetramer staining of antigen-specific cells and enzyme-linked immunospot (ELISPOT) detection of gamma interferon-producing cells, in association with rapid clearance of EBV DNA from peripheral blood mononuclear cells and resolution of clinical illness. By contrast, the second case featured a narrowly focused CTL response, higher EBV viral load, and a protracted clinical course marked by fatigue over 4 months duration.

In combination, these prior data support the hypothesis that microbial persistence and an ongoing host response to the organism may drive ongoing symptoms in postinfective fatigue states. Experiments to examine this hypothesis are underway based on samples and data collected in the Dubbo Infection Outcomes Study.

PATHOGENESIS

The clinical course of most acute infections ranges from asymptomatic to severe, disabling symptomatology. This spectrum of disease is at least partially due to the magnitude of the immune response induced to control the invading organism, rather than a direct effect of microbial replication or tissue injury. Cytokines, such as the interleukins (IL)-1, IL-2, and IL-6, tumor necrosis factor (TNF), and the interferons are released in a cascade of cellular activation induced by microbial antigens. Fever, somnolence, and loss of appetite—symptoms characteristic of the host response in acute inflammation (often termed *sickness behavior*) have been shown in animal studies to be induced in a dose-dependent fashion by systemic or intrac-erebral injections of the proinflammatory cytokines, IL-1, TNF-a, and IL-6, which play a pivotal role in the orchestration of the acute phase response (Dantzer, 2001; Dantzer et al., 1996). Conversely, administration of specific antagonists such as the IL-1 receptor antagonist (IL-1Ra) inhibits many of these central cytokine effects (Rothwell & Hopkins, 1995). Only limited human data regarding the effects of these cytokines are available, but administration of these and other cytokines produces prominent constitutional symptoms, including fever, anorexia, and fatigue (Dinarello, 1984; Tracey, Vlassara, & Cerami, 1989; Van Snick, 1990).

As the onset and resolution of the fatigue associated with acute infection usually parallel these manifestations of cytokine activity, such as fever, cytokines may also mediate fatigue in this setting, potentially via an effect on the central nervous system. Tissue macrophages, which are a focus for persistence of many pathogens implicated in postinfective fatigue, are a major source of pro inflammatory cytokines. Accordingly, the immunologic hypothesis for postinfective fatigue syndrome has proposed that an abnormal cellular immune response to precipitating infectious agents results in chronic and excessive cytokine production, which may directly mediate protracted symptoms by acting on the central nervous system (Wakefield & Lloyd, 1987). Numerous case-control studies of cellular immunity in patients with chronic fatigue syndrome seeking to validate this hypothesis have produced varied and often conflicting results and will not be discussed in this chapter (reviewed in Lloyd, Wakefield, & Hickie, 1993; Strober, 1994). However, the ambiguities in the results of these studies are likely to relate in part to the heterogeneity within the label of chronic fatigue syndrome (Hickie et al., 1995; Wilson et al., 2001). Accordingly, prospective cohort studies evaluating microbiological factors and immunologic alterations in subjects followed from the time of onset of defined infections are likely to provide the best opportunity to clarify the pathogenesis of postinfective fatigue syndrome. Even in this setting, the clues from the cohort studies conducted to date suggest that the outcomes will be complex with both psychological as well as host immune and pathogen factors likely to be important.

REFERENCES

Archard, L. C., Bowles, N. E., Behan, P. O., Bell, E. J., & Doyle, D. (1988). Postviral fatigue syndrome: Persistence of enterovirus RNA in muscle and elevated creatine kinase. *Journal of the Royal Society of Medicine, 81,* 326–329.

Ayres, J. G., Flint, N., Smith, E. G., Tunnicliffe, W. S. Fletcher, T. J. Hammond, K., et al. (1998). Post-infection fatigue syndrome following Q fever. *Quarterly Journal of Medicine, 91,* 105–123.

Barsky, A. J., Goodson, J. D., Lane, R. S., & Cleary, P. D. (1988). The amplification of somatic symptoms. *Psychosomatic Medicine, 50,* 510–519.

Beard, G. (1869). Neurasthenia, or nervous exhaustion. *Boston Medical and Surgical Journal, 3,* 217–221.

Behan, P., Behan, W. M. H., & Bell, E. (1985). The postviral fatigue syndrome: An analysis of findings in 50 cases. *Journal of Infection, 10,* 211–222.

Bennett, B. K., Hickie, I. B., Vollmer-Conna, U. S., et al. (1998). The relationship between fatigue, psychological and immunological variables in acute infectious illness. *Australia and New Zealand Journal of Psychiatry, 32,* 180–186.

Bharadwaj, M., Burrows, S., Burrows, J. M., Moss, D. J., Catalina, M., & Khanna, R. (2001). Longitudinal dynamics of antigen-specific CD8+ cytotoxic T lymphocytes following primary Epstein-Barr virus infection. *Blood, 98,* 2588–2589.

Buchwald, D. S., Cheney, P. R., Peterson, D. L., Henry, B., Wormsley, S. B., Geiger, A., et al. (1992). A chronic illness characterized by fatigue, neurologic and immunologic disorders, and active human herpes type 6 infection. *Annals of Internal Medicine, 116,* 103–113.

Buchwald, D. S., Rea, T., Katon, W., Russo, J., & Ashley, R. L. (2000). Acute infectious mononucleosis: Characteristics of patients who report failure to recover. *American Journal of Medicine, 109,* 531–537.

Bugdorfer, W., Barbour, A. G., Hayes, S. F., Benach, J. L., Grunwaldt, E., & Davis, J. P. (1982). Lyme disease—a tick-borne spirochetosis? *Science, 216,* 1318–1319.

Calder, B., Warnock, P., McCartney, R., & Bell, E. (1987). Coxsackie B viruses and the postviral syndrome: A prospective study in general practice. *Journal of the Royal College of General Practitioners, 37,* 11–14.

Canter, A. (1972). Changes in mood during incubation of acute febrile illness and the effects of pre-exposure psychological status. *Psychosomatic Medicine, 34,* 424–430.

Cluff, L. E. (1991). Medical aspects of delayed convalescence. *Reviews in Infectious Diseases, 13*(Suppl. 1), S138–S140.

Cluff, L. E., Trever, R. N., Imboden, J. B., & Canter, A. (1959). Brucellosis. II. Medical aspects of delayed convalescence. *Archives of Internal Medicine, 103,* 398–405.

Cohen, S., Tyrrell, D., & Smith, A. (1991). Psychological stress and susceptibility to the common cold. *New England Journal of Medicine, 325,* 606–612.

Dantzer, R. (2001). Cytokine-induced sickness behaviour: Where do we stand? *Brain, Behaviour, and Immunity, 15,* 7–24.

Dantzer, R., Bluthe, R.-M., Aubert, A., et al. (1996). Cytokine actions on behavior. In N. J. Rothwell (Ed.), *Cytokines in the nervous system.* RG Landes Co.

Defreitas, E., Hilliard, B., Cheney, P. R., Bell, D. S., Kiggundu, E., Sankey, D., et al. (1991). Retroviral sequences related to human T-lymphotropic virus type II in patients with chronic fatigue immune dysfunction syndrome. *Proceedings of the National Academy of Science, USA, 88,* 2922–2926.

Di Luca, D., Zorzenon, M., Mirandola, P., Colle, R., Botta, G. A., & Cassai, E. (1995). Human herpesvirus 6 and human herpesvirus 7 in chronic fatigue syndrome. *Journal of Clinical Microbiology, 33,* 1660–1661.

Dinarello, C. A. (1984). Interleukin-1. *Reviews in Infectious Diseases, 6,* 51–95.

Dinerman, H., & Steere, A. C. (1992). Lyme disease associated with fibromyalgia. *Annals of Internal Medicine, 117,* 281–285.

Evans, A. C. (1934). Chronic brucellosis. *Journal of the American Medical Association, 103,* 665.

Fekety, R. (1994). Infection and chronic fatigue syndrome. In S. E. Straus (Ed.), *Chronic fatigue syndrome* (pp. 101–179). New York: Marcel Dekker.

Flugel, R. M., Mahnke, C., Geiger, A., & Komaroff, A. L. (1992). Absence of antibody to human spumaretrovirus in patients with chronic fatigue syndrome. *Clinical Infectious Diseases, 14,* 623–624.

Fukuda, K., Straus, S. E., Hickie, I., Sharpe, M. C., Dobbins, J. G., & Komaroff, A. (1994). The chronic fatigue syndrome: A comprehensive approach to its definition and study. *Annals of Internal Medicine, 121*(12), 953–959.

Gelman, I. H., Unger, E. R., Mawle, A. C., Nisenbaum, R., & Reeves, W. C. (2000). Chronic fatigue syndrome is not associated with expression of endogenous retroviral p15E. *Molecular Diagnostics, 5,* 1555–1556.

Gilliam, A. (1938). *Epidemiological study of an epidemic diagnosed as poliomyelitis occurring among the personnel of the Los Angeles County General Hospital during the summer of 1934.* Washington, DC: Government Printing Office, U.S. Public Health Service, Public Health Bulletin No. 240.

Gold, D., Bowden, R., Sixbey, J., Riggs, R., Katon, W. J. Ashley, R., et al. (1990). Chronic fatigue: A prospective clinical and virologic study. *Journal of the American Medical Association, 264,* 48–53.

Gow, J. W., Behan, W. M. H., Clements, G. B., Woodall, C., Riding, M., & Behan, P. O. (1991). Enteroviral RNA sequences detected by polymerase chain reaction in muscle of patients with postviral fatigue syndrome. *British Medical Journal, 302,* 692–696.

Gow, J. W., Behan, W. M. H., Simpson, K., McGarry, F., Keir, S., & Behan, P. (1994). Studies of enteroviruses in patients with chronic fatigue syndrome. *Clinical Infectious Diseases, 18*(Suppl. 1), S126–S129.

Gow, J. W., Simpson, K., Schliephake, A., et al. (1992). Search for a retrovirus in the chronic fatigue syndrome. *Journal of Clinical Pathology, 45,* 1058–1061.

Halpin, D., & Wessely, S. (1989). VP-1 antigen in chronic fatigue syndrome. *Lancet, 1,* 1028–1029.

Harris, R. J., Storm, P. A., Lloyd, A., Arens, M., & Marmion, B. P. (2000). Long term persistence of Coxiella burnetii in the host after primary Q fever. *Epidemiology Infection, 124,* 543–549.

Hart, B. (1988). Biological basis of the behaviour of sick animals. *Neuroscience and Biobehavioural Reviews, 12,* 123–137.

Hay, J., & Jenkins, F. J. (1994). Human herpesviruses and chronic fatigue syndrome. In S. E. Straus (Ed.), *Chronic fatigue syndrome* (pp. 181–198). New York: Marcel Dekker.

Heneine, W., Woods, T. C., Sinha, S. D., Khan, A. S., Chapman, L. E., Schonberger, L. B., et al. (1994). Lack of evidence for infection with known human and animal retroviruses in patients with chronic fatigue syndrome. *Clinical Infectious Diseases, 18*(Suppl. 1), S121–S125.

Henle, W., Henle, G. E., & Horwitz, C. A. (1974). Epstein-Barr virus specific diagnostic tests in infectious mononucleosis. *Human Pathology, 5,* 551–565.

Hickie, I., Lloyd, A., Hadzi-Pavlovic, D., Parker, G., Bird, K., & Wakefield, D. (1995). Can the chronic fatigue syndrome be defined by distinct clinical features? *Psychological Medicine, 25,* 925–935.

Holmes, G. P., Kaplan, J. E., Stewart, J. A., Hunt, B., Pinsky, P. F., & Schonberger, L. B. (1988). A cluster of patients with a chronic mononucleosis-like syndrome. *Journal of the American Medical Association, 257,* 2297–2302.

Horwitz, C. A., Henle, W., Henle, G., & Schmitz, H. (1975). Clinical evaluation of patients with infectious mononucleosis and development of antibodies to the R component of the Epstein-Barr virus-induced early antigen complex. *American Journal of Medicine, 58,* 330–338.

Horwitz, C. A., Henle, W., Henle, G., Rudnick, H., & Latts, E. (1985). Long-term serological follow-up of patients for Epstein-Barr virus after recovery from infectious mononucleosis. *Journal of Infectious Diseases, 151,* 1150–1153.

Imboden, J. B., Cantor, A., & Cluff, L. E. (1961). Convalescence from influenza. A study of the psychological and clinical determinants. *Archives of Internal Medicine, 108,* 393–398.

Imboden, J. B., Cluff, L. E., Canter, A., & Trever, R. N. (1959). Brucellosis. III: Psychological aspects of delayed convalescence. *Archives of Internal Medicine, 103,* 398–405.

Isaacs, R. (1948). Chronic infectious mononucleosis. *Blood, 3,* 858–861.

Jones, J. F., Ray, C. G., Minnich, L. L., Hicks, M. J., Kibler, R., & Lucas, D. O. (1985). Evidence for active Epstein-Barr virus infection in patients with persistent, unexplained illnesses: Elevated early antigen antibodies. *Annals of Internal Medicine, 102,* 1–7.

Keighley, B. D., & Bell, E. J. (1983). Sporadic myalgic encephalomyelitis in a rural practice. *Journal of the Royal College of General Practitioners, 33,* 339–341.

Khan, A. S., Heneine, W. M., Chapman, L. E., Gary, H. E., Jr., Woods, T. C., Folks, T. M., et al. (1993). Assessment of a retrovirus sequence and other possible risk factors for the chronic fatigue syndrome in adults. *Annals of Internal Medicine, 118,* 241–245.

Klempner, M. S., Hu, L. T., Evans, J., Schmid, C. H., Johnson, G. M., Trevino, R. P., et al. (2001). Two controlled trials of antibiotic treatment in patients with persistent symptoms and a history of Lyme disease. *New England Journal of Medicine, 345,* 85–92.

Levine, P. H., Jacobsen, S., Pocinki, A. G., et al. (1992). Viral, epidemiologic and virologic studies in four clusters of the chronic fatigue syndrome. *Archives of Internal Medicine, 152,* 1611–1616.

Lindh, G., Samuelson, A., Hedlund, I., Evengard, B., Lindquist, L., & Ehrnst, A. (1996). No findings of enterovirus in Swedish patients with chronic fatigue syndrome. *Scandinavian Journal of Infectious Diseases, 28,* 305–308.

Linn, M. L., Aaskov, J. G., & Suhrbier, A. (1996). Antibody-dependent enhancement and persistence in macrophages of an arbovirus associated with arthritis. *Journal of General Virology, 77,* 407–411.

Lloyd, A. R., Wakefield, D., & Hickie, I. (1993). Immunity and the pathophysiology of chronic fatigue syndrome. *Ciba Foundation Symposium, 173,* 176–187.

Lynch, S., & Seth, R. (1989). Postviral fatigue syndrome and the VP-1 antigen. *Lancet, 2,* 1160–1161.

Marmion, B. P., Shannon, M., Maddocks, I., et al. (1996). Protracted debility and fatigue after acute Q fever. *Lancet, 347,* 977–978.

Marston, J. A. (1861). Report on fever (Malta). *Great Britain Army Medical Department Reports, 3,* 486–488.

Mawle, A., Nisenbaum, R., Dobbins, J., Gary, H. E., Jr., Stewart, J. A., Reyes, M., et al. (1995). Seroepidemiology of chronic fatigue syndrome: A case control study. *Clinical Infectious Diseases, 21,* 1386–1389.

McArdle, A., McArdle, F., Jackson, M., Page, S., Fahal, I., & Edwards, R. (1996). Investigation by polymerase chain reaction of enteroviral infection in patients with chronic fatigue syndrome. *Clinical Science, 90,* 295–300.

Miller, N. A., Carmichael, H. A., Calder, B. D., et al. (1991). Antibody to Coxsackie B virus in diagnosing postviral fatigue syndrome. *British Medical Journal, 302,* 140–143.

Montgomery, R. R., Nathanson, M. H., & Malawista, S. E. (1993). The fate of Borrelia bugdorferi, the agent for Lyme disease, in mouse macrophages. Destruction, survival, recovery. *Journal of Immunology, 15,* 909–915.

Patnaik, M., Komaroff, A. L., Conley, E., Ojo-Amaize, E. A., & Peter, J. B. (1995). Prevalence of IgM antibodies to human herpesvirus 6 (HHV-6) early antigen (P41/38) in patients with chronic fatigue syndrome. *Journal of Infectious Diseases, 172,* 1364–1367.

Pellew, R. (1951). A clinical description of a disease resembling poliomyelitis seen in Adelaide 1949–1951. *Medical Journal of Australia 1,* 944–946.

Rothwell, N. J., & Hopkins, S. J. (1995). Cytokines and the nervous system. II: Actions and mechanisms of action. *Trends in Neuroscience, 18,* 130–136.

Secchiero, P., Carrigan, D. R., Asano, Y., Benedetti, L., Crowley, R. W., & Komaroff, A. L. (1995). Detection of human herpesvirus 6 in plasma of children with primary infection and immunosuppressed patients by polymerase chain reaction. *Journal of Infectious Diseases, 171*, 273–280.

Selden, S. M., & Cameron, A. S. (1996). Changing epidemiology of Ross River virus disease in South Australia. *Medical Journal of Australia, 165*, 313–317.

Shaddick, N. A., Phillips, C. B., Logigian, E. L., Steere, A. C., Kaplan, R. F., Berardi, V. P., et al. (1994). The long-term clinical outcomes of Lyme disease: A population-based retrospective cohort study. *Annals of Internal Medicine, 121*, 560–567.

Sigal, L. R. (1990). Summary of the first 100 patients seen at a Lyme disease referral center. *American Journal of Medicine, 88*, 577–581.

Sigurdsson, B., Sigurjonsson, J., Sigurdsson, J. H. J., Thorkelsson, J., & Gudmundsson, K. G. (1950). A disease epidemic in Iceland simulating poliomyelitis. *American Journal of Hygiene, 52*, 222–238.

Soden, M., Vasudevan, H., Roberts, B., Coelen, R., Hamlin, G., & La Brooy, J. (2000). Detection of viral ribonucleic acid and histologic analysis of inflamed synovium in Ross River virus infection. *Arthritis and Rheumatism, 43*, 365–369.

Spink, W. W. (1951). What is chronic brucellosis? *Annals of Internal Medicine, 35*, 358–374.

Spink, W. W. (1952). Some biologic and clinical problems related to intracellular parasitism in brucellosis. *New England Journal of Medicine, 247*, 603–605.

Steere, A. C. (1989). Lyme disease. *New England Journal of Medicine, 321*, 586–596.

Straus, S. E., Tosato, G., Armstrong, G., Lawley, T., Preble, O. T., Henle, W., et al. (1985). Persisting illness and fatigue in adults with evidence of Epstein-Barr virus infection. *Annals of Internal Medicine, 102*, 7–16.

Strober, W. (1994). Immunological function in chronic fatigue syndrome. In S. E. Straus (Ed.), *Chronic fatigue syndrome* (pp. 207–240). New York: Marcel Dekker.

Sumaya, C. (1990). Serologic and virologic epidemiology of Epstein-Barr virus: Relevance to chronic fatigue syndrome. *Reviews in Infectious Diseases, 13*(Suppl. 1), S19–S25.

Swanink, C., Melchers, W., van der Meer, J., Vercoulen, J. H., Bleijenberg, G., Fennis, J. F., et al. (1994). Enteroviruses and the chronic fatigue syndrome. *Clinical Infectious Diseases, 19*, 860–864.

Swanink, C., Vercoulen, J., Bleijenberg, G., Fennis, J., Galama, J., & van der Meer, J. (1995). Chronic fatigue syndrome: A clinical and laboratory study with a well-matched control group. *Journal of Internal Medicine, 237*, 499–506.

Tracey, K. J., Vlassara, H., & Cerami, A. (1989). Cachectin/tumor necrosis factor. *Lancet, 1*, 1122–1125.

Trever, R. W., Cluff, L. E., Peeler, R. N., & Bennett, I. L. (1959). Brucellosis, I. Laboratory-acquired acute infection. *Archives of Internal Medicine, 103*, 381–397.

Van Snick, J. (1990). Interleukin-6: An overview. *Annual Reviews of Immunology, 8*, 253–289.

Vollmer-Conna, U. S. (2001). Acute sickness behaviour: An immune system-to-brain communication? *Psychological Medicine, 31*, 761–767.

Wakefield, D., & Lloyd, A. R. (1987). The pathophysiology of myalgic encephalomyelitis. *Lancet, 2*, 918-919.

Wessely, S., Chalder, T., Hirsch, S., Pawlikowska, T., Wallace, P., & Wright, D. (1995). Postinfectious fatigue: Prospective cohort study in primary care. *Lancet, 345*, 1333–1338.

Wessely, S., Hotopf, M., & Sharpe, M. (1998). CFS: Viruses and immunity. In *Chronic fatigue and its syndromes* (pp. 165–197). Oxford, England: Oxford University Press.

Westley-Wise, V. J., Beard, J. R., Sladden, T. J., Dunn, T. M., & Simpson, J. (1996). Ross River virus infection on the North Coast of New South Wales. *Australia and New Zealand Journal of Public Health, 20*, 87–92.

White, P. D., Grover, S. A., Kangro, H. O., Thomas, J. M., Amess, J., & Clare, A. W. (1995). The validity and reliability of the fatigue syndrome that follows glandular fever. *Psychological Medicine, 25,* 917–924.

White, P. D., Thomas, J. M., Amess, J., Grover, S. A., Kangro, H. O., & Clare, A. W. (1995). The existence of a fatigue syndrome after glandular fever. *Psychological Medicine, 25,* 907–916.

White, P. D., Thomas, J. M., Kangro, H. O., Bruce-Jones, W. D., Amess, J., Crawford, D. H., et al. (2001). Predictions and associations of fatigue syndromes and mood disorders that occur after infectious mononucleosis. *Lancet, 358,* 1946–1954.

Williams, J. C., & Thompson, H. A. (1991). *Q fever: The biology of coxiella burnetii.* Boca Raton, FL: CRC Press.

Wilson, A., Hickie, I., Hadzi-Pavlovic, D., Wakefield, D., Parker, G., Straus, S. E., et al. (2001). What is chronic fatigue syndrome? Heterogeneity within an international multicentre study. *Australia and New Zealand Journal of Psychiatry, 35,* 520–527.

Wolfe, F., Smythe, H. A., Yunus, M. B., Bennett, R. M., Bombardier, C., Goldenberg, D. L., et al. (1990). The American College of Rheumatology 1990 criteria for the classification of fibromyalgia: Report of the multicenter criteria committee. *Arthritis and Rheumatism, 33,* 160–172.

Yalcin, S., Kuratsune, H., Yamaguchi, K., Kitani, T., & Yamanishi, K. (1994). Prevalence of human herpesvirus 6 variants A and B in patients with chronic fatigue syndrome. *Microbiology and Immunology, 38,* 587–590.

Yousef, G. E., Bell, E. J., Mann, G. F., Murugesan, V., Smith, D. G., McCartney, R. A., et al. (1988). Chronic enterovirus infection in patients with postviral fatigue syndrome. *Lancet, 1,* 146–150.

CHAPTER 7

Immunology

KEVIN J. MAHER, NANCY G. KLIMAS, and MARY ANN FLETCHER

C HRONIC FATIGUE SYNDROME (CFS) has been estimated to affect up to a half million people in the United States (Gunn, Connell, & Randall, 1993; Jason et al., 1999; Reyes et al., 1997; Steele et al., 1998). The etiology of this illness is uncertain, and hypothetical mechanisms have included infections, psychiatric trauma, and exposure to toxins (Bell, Baldwin, & Schwartz, 1998; Pall & Satterle, 2001; Straus et al., 1985). Because no physical or laboratory diagnostic criteria are pathognomonic for CFS, its diagnosis is made on the basis of clinical signs and symptoms (Holmes et al., 1988; Lloyd, Hickie, Boughton, Spencer, & Wakefield, 1990; Sharpe et al., 1991). CFS often presents as an acute viral infection whose signs and symptoms fail to resolve. This similarity to the presentation of viral infections has led to hypotheses that suggest a microbial pathogenesis, and many studies have examined the immune system for signs of such infection. The immune system is known to play a role in controlling infection and orchestrating multisystem responses (acute phase response, fever, altered metabolism, myalgia, somnolence, and sickness behavior). Many aspects of humoral and cellular immunity, including functional activity, protein expression, and molecular transcription have been considered (see Figure 7.1).

Through these studies, defects have been reported for nearly every aspect of immune function, and in many instances, these reports have been confirmed by independent studies. Although studies to determine the presence of an infectious process have not been definitive, an emerging body of evidence has demonstrated alterations in the immune system. However, the literature on immune dysfunction in CFS is not fully concordant; a significant number of reports describe findings that are in opposition. In this review, we summarize this literature, attempt to define concordance among studies and, where possible, suggest reasons for the disparities.

METHODS

This review comprises reports that have been published from 1988 to 2002 and that used the definitions of CFS described by either the CDC (Holmes et al., 1988), or

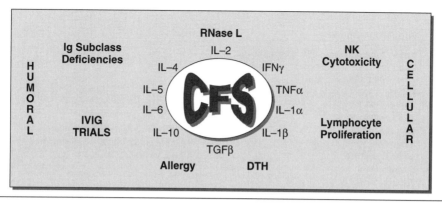

Figure 7.1 Laboratory Assessment of Chronic Fatigue Syndrome Has Included Multiple Tests for a Variety of Immunologic Markers

by the British (Sharpe et al., 1991), or Australian (Lloyd, Hickie, Boughton, et al., 1990) working groups. Papers referring to conditions such as neurasthenia and chronic EBV infection, while describing similar perhaps overlapping conditions, are not included here. Instead, we use the case definitions as they were intended, to delineate a more homogeneous population for study. We reviewed more than 100 primary reports in the literature that described some aspect of immune function and included 87 that used one of the case definitions previously mentioned. Authorship and host institutions were noted, and 44 research groups were identified. Papers that did not use a case definition to select their subjects were excluded. Each unique finding from the reports was tabulated and summarized for each research group. Because it was presumed that regional coauthors often study overlapping, if not identical, populations, multiple reports of a unique finding from a single group were counted as a single event. The number of nonexcluded research groups reporting a specific finding was summed and presented along with the total number of CFS subjects studied across the groups.

RESULTS

NATURAL KILLER CELL CYTOTOXICITY

In assessing immune dysfunction in the pathogenesis of CFS, a number of groups have reported on the activity of natural killer (NK) cells (recently reviewed in Fletcher, Maher, & Klimas, 2002). Fifteen articles are discussed here (Aoki, Miyakoshi, Usuda, & Herberman, 1993; Barker, Fujimura, Fadem, Landay, & Levy, 1994; Caligiuri et al., 1987; Gold et al., 1990; Kibler, Lucas, Hicks, Poulos, & Jones, 1985; Klimas, Salvato, Morgan, & Fletcher, 1990; Levine et al., 1998; Masuda, Nozoe, Matsuyama, & Tanaka, 1994; Mawle et al., 1997; Ogawa et al., 1998; Ojo-Amaize, Conley, & Peter, 1994; Rasmussen et al., 1994; See, Broumand, Sahl, & Tilles, 1997; Wemm & Trestman, 1991; Whiteside & Friberg, 1998). Of these, 11 reported decreased NK activity in CFS subjects compared with healthy controls, whereas four groups found no difference (see Figure 7.2). Although each set of conclusions has been confirmed multiple times, the obvious discrepancy between the findings demands that the studies be considered more closely. Three groups

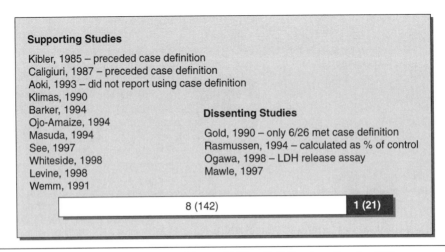

Figure 7.2   Decreased Natural Killer Cell Dysfunction in CFS

reported on decreased NK cytotoxicity among fatigued patients with symptoms similar to or perhaps overlapping with CFS, but they did not use one of the case definitions described earlier (Aoki et al., 1993; Caligiuri et al., 1987; Kibler et al., 1985). Because these populations cannot be determined to conform to the case definitions, they will not be considered further. In the article by Gold (Gold et al., 1990), the authors noted no significant difference in NK cytotoxicity between 26 patients with fatigue and the controls, but also stated that of the 26 subjects studied, only 6 met the CDC case definition. Because the authors made no attempt to describe these subjects in a separate analysis, this population was not considered comparable to those of the case-defined studies and was therefore excluded from further analysis.

The next consideration on these reports is given to methodology. Of the remaining 11 reports, 10 measured the release of radioisotopes from labeled target cells (e.g., ^{51}Cr) as the end point of cytotoxicity. One study (Ogawa et al., 1998) measured the release of lactate dehydrogenase from target cells. This method is sufficiently different from the other method to invalidate it for direct comparison and was excluded. In the paper by Rasmussen (Rasmussen et al., 1994), a ^{51}Cr-release assay was used, but the CFS subjects' cytotoxicity values were reported as a percentage of the control subjects' cytotoxicity values that was run the same day. The problem with this approach can be demonstrated by considering the data presented in Figure 7.3.

These data, which were generated in our laboratory, are similar to that presented previously. They demonstrate that although the average NK cytotoxicity of the CFS group is reduced relative to the control population, there is considerable variation in the activities of the healthy controls (CTS) and considerable overlap between the two populations. The method of presenting the results as a ratio to a control is therefore highly dependent on which CFS subjects and which control subjects are paired for analysis on any particular day. Because the remaining 9 studies reported their results as percentage of cytotoxicity and in lytic units, this nonconventional method of data analysis was considered sufficiently different from the rest as to be noncomparable. The data from this study were therefore excluded, leaving 9 groups (Barker et al., 1994; Broumand et al., 1997; Klimas

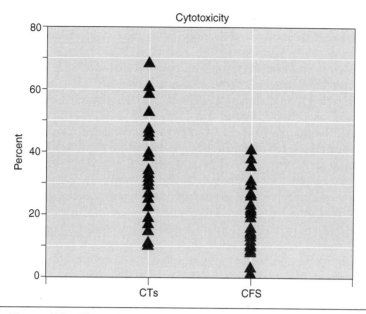

Figure 7.3 Natural Killer Cell Dysfunction in CFS Cytotoxicity

et al., 1990; Levine et al., 1998; Masuda et al., 1994; Mawle et al., 1997; Ojo-Amaize et al., 1994; Wemm & Trestman, 1991; Whiteside & Friberg, 1998) who reported on NK function using similar methods to study similar populations. Eight of these groups, studying a combined population of 142 subjects, reported significantly decreased NK cytotoxicity among case-defined CFS subjects relative to controls, while one group, Mawle et al., studying 21 subjects found no significant difference. Mawle et al. suggested that the limited population size may have prevented their finding significant differences from controls. However, the decreased NK activity in CFS was found in 8 studies with a range of CFS subjects from 8 to 30. Another more likely possibility for the discordant result may lie in the population characteristics that were reported in a subsequent article (Reeves et al., 2000), and suggested that the majority of subjects in this study were HHV-6 negative and experienced slow onset of illness. Others have reported a high prevalence of HHV-6 infection and acute mode of onset, suggesting that variability exists even among case-defined populations (Ablashi et al., 2000; Buchwald et al., 1992).

From the preceding, we conclude that the clear majority of reports independently confirm a significant decrease in NK activity of CFS subjects relative to the controls. This body of research represents one of the most consistent findings on an immune deficit in individuals with CFS. Furthermore, this example demonstrates the need to consider methodological differences when comparing studies.

LYMPHOCYTE PROLIFERATION

Another common assessment of cellular immunity is the measurement of the ability of lymphocytes to be stimulated by various agents. This stimulation process, which culminates in cell division, is measured typically by the incorporation of the radiolabeled nucleotides into nascent DNA, as a measure of the induced replication. Eight groups conducted studies to consider the mitogen-induced proliferative responses of lymphocytes from CFS (Gupta & Vayuvegula, 1991; Keller et al., 1994; Klimas et al., 1990; Lloyd, Hickie, Hickie, Dwyer, & Wakefield, 1992; Lloyd, Wakefield, Boughton, & Dwyer et al., 1989; Mawle et al., 1997; Milton, Clements, & Edwards, 1991; Rasmussen et al., 1994; Straus, Fritz, Dale, Gould, & Strober, 1993; Visser et al., 1998). Three research groups (Keller et al., 1994; Klimas et al., 1990; Lloyd et al., 1989, 1992; Straus et al., 1993) studying a total of 179 CFS subjects found a significant decrease in proliferation, whereas five groups studying a total of 141 subjects found no significant differences from controls (Gupta & Vayuvegula, 1991; Mawle et al., 1997; Milton et al., 1991; Rasmussen et al., 1994; Visser et al., 1998) as shown in Figure 7.4. Laboratory methods were comparable and therefore could not account for the discrepant findings. As mentioned, the population for the Mawle study consisted predominantly of individuals with slow onset illness. When subanalyses were conducted in this study, individuals with acute onset had decreased proliferative responses to *Candida* relative to controls, suggesting again that population differences may account for some of the variability in findings.

DELAYED TYPE HYPERSENSITIVITY

Two groups assessed in vivo cellular function through the testing of delayed type hypersensitivity on case-defined populations using similar materials and methods (Lloyd et al., 1989; Mawle et al., 1997; Wilson, Hickie, Lloyd, Hadzi-Pavlovic, & Wakefield, 1995). This test measures the delayed T cell response to a series of allergens by the skin prick/puncture method (see Figure 7.5). One group studied two cohorts of 57 and 103 subjects, with case-defined CFS and reported a prevalence of impaired delayed hypersensitivity in 88% and 45% of their subjects, respectively (Hickie et al., 2000; Lloyd et al., 1989; Wilson et al., 1995). The second group studied 26 case-defined CFS subjects and found no significant differences in DTH relative to the control group. No methodological discrepancies, other than population size or composition, could be identified between the reports that suggested a reason for the different findings.

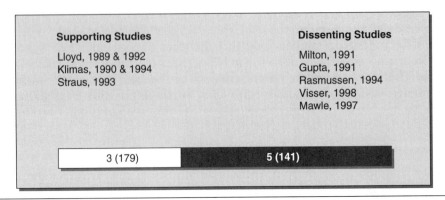

Figure 7.4 Laboratory Evidence of Alterred Cellular Function: Decreased Mitogen Stimulated Lymphocyte Proliferation

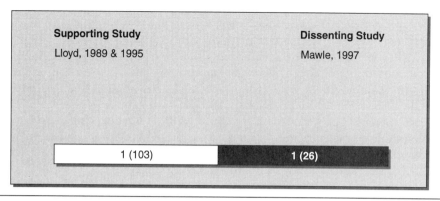

Figure 7.5 Laboratory Evidence of Altered Cellular Function: Decreased Delayed Type Hypersensitivity

IMMUNE ACTIVATION

One of the findings that appears throughout the CFS literature is that of increased immune activation among those with CFS (see Figure 7.6). Immune activation is broadly defined, and a variety of immunologic tests may provide evidence of it. When the concept is considered in a general way, 18 groups reported findings that could be interpreted as supporting the association of immune activation with CFS (Bates et al., 1995; Bennett et al., 1997; Borish et al., 1998; Buchwald, Wener, Pearlman, & Kith, 1997; Chao, Gallagher, Phair, & Peterson, 1990; Cheney, Dorman, & Bell, 1989; Conti, Magrini, Priori, Valesini, & Bonini, 1996; Gupta, Aggarwal, See, & Starr, 1997; Gupta & Vayuvegula, 1991;

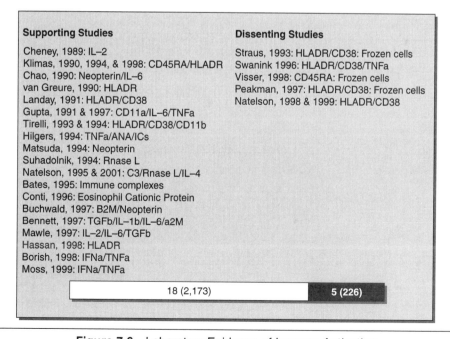

Figure 7.6 Laboratory Evidence of Immune Activation

Hanson, Gause, & Natelson, 2001; I. S. Hassan, Bannister, Akbar, Weir, & Bofill, 1998; Hilgers & Frank, 1994; Klimas, 1998; Klimas et al., 1990, 1994; Landay, Jessop, Lennette, & Levy, 1991; Matsuda, Gohchi, & Gotoh, 1994; Mawle et al., 1997; Moss, Mercandetti, & Vojdani, 1999; Natelson, Ellis, Braonain, Deluca, & Tapp, 1995; Suhadolnik et al., 1994; Tirelli, Marotta, Improta, & Pinto, 1994; Tirelli et al., 1993; van Greure & Bouic, 1990). Five groups reported no evidence of activation (Natelson et al., 1998, 1999; Peakman, Deale, Field, Mahalingam, & Wessely, 1997; Straus et al., 1993; Swanink et al., 1996; Visser et al., 1998). The reports included here used varied methods to measure gene expression, protein expression, and cellular function as evidence of immune activation. Therefore, we have considered each analytic variable as a separate category in the following sections.

INCREASED T MEMORY CELLS

When the receptors of lymphocytes are engaged, a series of events ensues as part of the activation process. This process includes the modulation of cell surface proteins that both increase (i.e., CD69, CD45RO, CD25, HLA-DR) and decrease (i.e., CD45RA) their cell surface antigenic epitopes (see Figure 7.7). Various combinations of cell surface markers have been used to distinguish virgin (antigen naive) lymphocytes from antigen experienced (memory) cells. Of seven groups reporting on the measurement of naive and memory cells, three groups collectively studying 197 subjects found evidence of decreased naive/increased memory cells (Hanson et al., 2001; Klimas et al., 1990; Tirelli et al., 1994), whereas one group studying 49 subjects found no difference compared with controls CFS (Natelson et al., 1998; Peakman et al., 1997; Visser et al., 1998; Zhang et al., 1999). The conclusions of the group reporting no evidence of decreased naive cell numbers (Natelson et al., 1998; Zhang et al., 1999) were recanted in a subsequent paper in which statistical methodologies were cited as the cause for change (Hanson et al., 2001).

Although CD45RA is a cell surface marker that has been shown to be relatively stable during cryopreservation, the cells need to be frozen under tightly controlled conditions that ensure proper antigenic preservation. Furthermore, investigators have reported the variable loss of certain subsets as a result of manipulations such as density sedimentation for the preparation of peripheral blood mononuclear

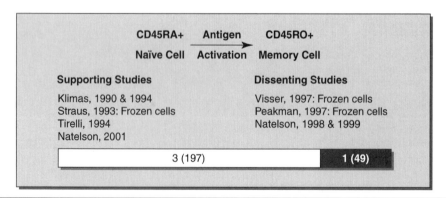

Figure 7.7   Laboratory Evidence of Immune Activation: Decreased CD45RA/Increased CD45RO

cells and cryopreservation. As a result, procedures using fresh whole blood have become the preferred methods for phenotyping (Centers for Disease Control and Prevention, 1997). The remaining two groups that found no evidence of altered naive/memory distributions in CFS (Peakman et al., 1997; Visser et al., 1998) and one group that found decreased CD45RA (Straus et al., 1993) studied cryopreserved cells, which may reflect variability in outcomes as a function of methodology. The remaining three groups reporting decreased naive/increased memory cells in CFS all used fresh preparations. No other methodological issues were described that might account for the discrepancies.

CD38

Activated T lymphocytes, as well as some NK cells, monocytes, and terminally differentiated B cells, express the transmembrane glycoprotein CD38 (Barclay, Birkeland, & Brown, 1993; McMihael, Beverley, & Gilks, 1987). Eight groups reported on the expression of CD38 on lymphocytes from CFS subjects. Elevation of this activation marker has been noted in HIV infection and found to be associated with a poor prognosis (Giorgi et al., 1993). Three groups collectively studied 297 subjects with CFS (Barker et al., 1994; Hanson et al., 2001; Landay et al., 1991) and found increased CD38 expression in CFS, while five groups collectively studying 139 subjects found no difference from controls (Natelson et al., 1998; Peakman et al., 1997; Straus et al., 1993; Swanink et al., 1996; Vedhara et al., 1997; Zhang et al., 1999) as shown in Figure 7.8. One group that reported no significant differences between controls and CFS subjects (Zhang et al., 1999) provided data suggesting an elevation (CFS: 58 ±1.9 vs. Controls: 51 ±1.7; mean% CD38 ±s.e.). In a subsequent article, this group reported a significant elevation in CD38 among CFS subjects and stated that the earlier discrepant conclusions (Hanson et al., 2001; Zhang et al., 1999) may have been based on improper statistical methods (Natelson et al., 1998). Of the other dissenting studies, two used frozen cells (Peakman et al., 1997; Straus et al., 1993). The accurate assessment of CD38 was precluded in these studies because it is a marker that is variably sensitive to cryopreservation and its antigenicity is destroyed to varying degrees in the process (Patarca, Maher, Goodkin, & Fletcher, 1997). Furthermore, as mentioned, the manipulation during cryopreservation can result in alterations in the proportions

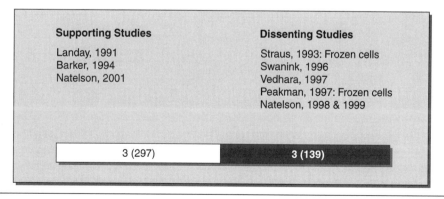

Figure 7.8 Laboratory Evidence of Immune Activation: Increased CD38

of lymphocyte populations. As noted in one study (Straus et al., 1993), viability following freezing is variable. The authors note that this may be due to the loss of specific cryosensitive populations such as NK cells. The proportions of other phenotypic subsets, which are commonly reported would all be affected by such losses. Due to these difficulties, the studies using cryopreserved samples were not considered comparable to those studying nonfrozen samples and were therefore not considered. This left three groups collectively studying 309 CFS subjects reporting elevations of CD38 and three groups studying 161 subjects reporting no difference. Other than the statistical methods noted, methodology was not an apparent source of confound in these remaining studies.

CD28

An important pathway of T-cell activation involves the CD28 transmembrane glycoprotein (June, Ledbetter, Linsley, & Thompson, 1990). Four groups described the expression of this activation marker in CFS (Barker et al., 1994; Hanson et al., 2001; I. S. Hassan et al., 1998; Natelson et al., 1998; Swanink et al., 1996). Three groups reported significant elevations in lymphocyte populations expressing CD28 among a combined population of 227 CFS subjects (Barker et al., 1994; Hanson et al., 2001; I. S. Hassan et al., 1998) as shown in Figure 7.9. Two groups reported no significant differences in expression of CD28 relative to controls (Natelson et al., 1998; Swanink et al., 1996). As mentioned, the conclusions of Natelson et al. in 1998 may have been due to inadequate statistical methods as a later report by the same group demonstrated significant elevations of this subset (Hanson et al., 2001). Swanink reported that the expression of CD8+CD28+ was not elevated to a significant level but reported a marginally significant p value of .054 (Swanink et al., 1996). Such a finding might be an indication of increased expression. The conclusions drawn from data are highly dependent on selection and interpretations of statistical methods.

CD26

CD26 is an ectoenzyme in the membrane of activated T lymphocytes and is involved in proliferation (Kameoka, Tanaka, Nojima, Schlossman, & Morimoto,

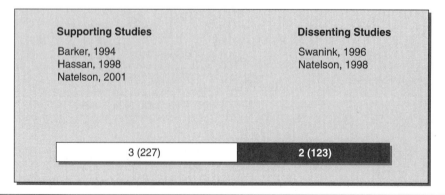

Figure 7.9 Laboratory Evidence of Immune Activation: Increased CD8+CD28+

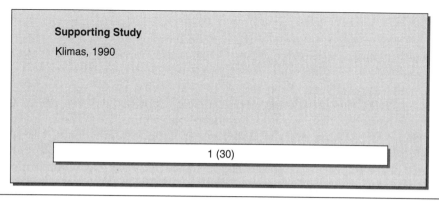

Figure 7.10   Laboratory Evidence of Immune Activation: Increased CD26+

1993). Klimas et al. (1990), was the only group to report on elevated CD26 in CFS among a group of 30 CFS subjects and this finding awaits independent confirmation (see Figure 7.10).

HLA/DR

Several investigators have reported elevated major histocompatibility class II HLA/DR antigen expression on lymphocytes of CFS patients (see Figure 7.11). Klimas et al. (1990; 30 CFS patients) and Barker et al. (1994; 35 patients) reported elevated proportions of CD8+ T cells expressing this activation marker. I. S. Hassan et al. (1998) found elevations of mean fluorescence intensity of HLA-DR on both CD4+ and CD8+ T cells in their study of 44 subjects. Tirelli et al. (1993; 30 CFS subjects) reported elevated proportions of CD8+ T lymphocytes expressing HLA-DR. In contrast, Landay et al. (1991; 147 CFS subjects), Swanink et al. (1996; 76 CFS subjects), and Natelson et al. (1998; 48 CFS subjects) found no elevation in proportion of CD8 cells expressing HLA/DR. Differences in methodology that would account for the discrepant findings were not apparent.

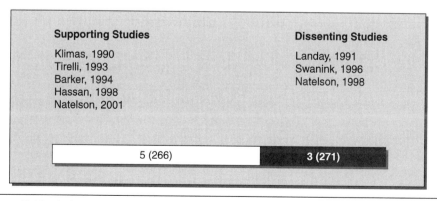

Figure 7.11   Laboratory Evidence of Immune Activation: Increased HLA/DR Expression

CD5+CD19+

Another phenotype of interest is that of the lymphocytes that coexpress T cell and B cell surface antigens (e.g., CD5+CD19+) as shown in Figure 7.12. Although this phenotype is not generally considered a marker of activation, these lymphocytes, which typically reside in the peritoneal cavity, have been reported to be associated with the production of autoreactive antibodies (Burastero, Casali, Wilder, & Notkins, 1988; Casali, Burastero, Nakamura, Inghirami, & Notkins, 1987; Dauphinee, Tovar, & Talal, 1988; Plater-Zyberk, Maini, Lam, Kennedy, & Janossy, 1985). Three independent groups collectively tested 86 subjects for the presence of lymphocytes coexpressing CD5 and CD19 (or CD20) and found evidence for elevation of this subset in CFS subjects (Klimas et al., 1990; Mawle et al., 1997; Tirelli et al., 1994). Because this subset has also been shown to be elevated in infectious mononucleosis (IM; Hassan, Feighery, Bresnihan, & Whelan, 1990), it is of interest that one study had selected CFS subjects who showed evidence of increased serological reactivity to EBV, the etiologic agent of IM (Klimas et al., 1990). The second study found similar elevations of CD5+CD19+ lymphocytes in CFS but among a group of 26 subjects with no evidence of EBV reactivity, indicating that elevations of the CD5+CD19+ subset can occur in CFS in the apparent absence of EBV infection or reactivation (Tirelli et al., 1994). Although the third group found no evidence of elevated CD5+CD19+ lymphocytes on their initial analyses, a subanalysis demonstrated that this subset was elevated among those subjects who were sick for longer than 63 months (Mawle et al., 1997).

Neopterin

Neopterin, a molecule produced and secreted by activated macrophages, is often measured in serum as a marker of cellular activation (Fuchs et al., 1988; Patarca & Fletcher, 1997; Wachter, Fuchs, Hausen, Reibnegger, & Werner, 1989) as shown in Figure 7.13. Six groups reported its production in subjects with CFS. Three groups collectively studying 191 CFS subjects reported significant elevations in mean serum neopterin levels relative to controls (Buchwald et al., 1997; Chao et al., 1990; Matsuda et al., 1994), while three groups studying 85 CFS subjects found no differences relative to controls (Linde et al., 1992; Lloyd, Hickie, Brockman, Dwyer, & Wakefield, 1991; Patarca, Klimas, Lutgendorf, Antoni, & Fletcher,

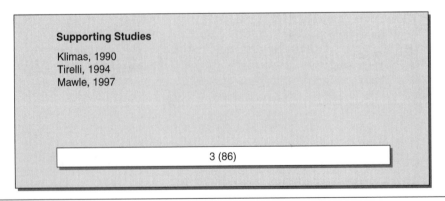

Supporting Studies

Klimas, 1990
Tirelli, 1994
Mawle, 1997

3 (86)

Figure 7.12 Laboratory Evidence of Immune Activation: Increased CD5+CD19+

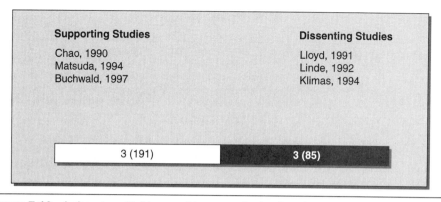

Figure 7.13 Laboratory Evidence of Immune Activation: Increased Serum Neopterin

1994). In the report by Chao, the elevated mean concentrations were apparently due to elevations among 30% of the subjects with CFS (relative to 0% of controls). In a similar fashion, two of the reports indicating no significant mean increase relative to controls reported that 12% (Patarca et al., 1994) and 20% (Linde et al., 1992) of CFS subjects had increased serum concentrations of neopterin (relative to 0% and 10% of controls, respectively). Lutgendorf et al. reported that higher perception of cognitive difficulties is associated with higher neopterin levels and with lower lymphoproliferative response to phytohemagglutinin (Lutgendorf et al., 1995). This suggests that among CFS subjects, a subset with elevated serum neopterin exists, and population size and compositions may limit the determination of statistical significance.

CYTOKINES

Numerous cytokines have been measured in serum, plasma, cell lysates, and culture supernatants by enzyme-linked immunosorbent assay (ELISA), radioimmunoassay (RIA), bioassay, and molecular methods (Borish et al., 1998; Gupta et al., 1997; Klimas et al., 1990; LaManca et al., 1999; Lloyd, Gandevia, Brockman, Hales, & Wakefield, 1994; MacDonald et al., 1996; Mawle et al., 1997; Moss et al., 1999; Patarca et al., 1994; Patarca-Montero, Antoni, Fletcher, & Klimas, 2001; Straus, Dale, Peter, Dinarello, 1989; Swanink et al., 1996). One of these, TNFα, is known to be an endogenous pyrogen (Arnason, 1991) and to produce slow-wave sleep (Shoham, Davenne, Cady, Dinarello, & Krueger, 1987). Because of its potential to mediate some of the symptoms of CFS, it has received considerable attention and 10 different groups have reported their findings (see Figure 7.14). These are discussed here as being representative of the cytokine group and to illustrate the challenges facing the interpretation of this field of research.

The range of testing methods used to study cytokines can be appreciated in this example where methods included measurement by ELISA of serum (Lloyd et al., 1994; MacDonald et al., 1996; Mawle et al., 1997; Patarca et al., 1995; Straus et al., 1989), ELISA of cell lysates (Borish et al., 1998), reverse transcriptase/polymerase chain reaction (RT/PCR) of cell-associated mRNA (Borish et al., 1998; LaManca et al., 1999), ELISA of unstimulated and mitogen-stimulated cultures (Gupta et al., 1997; Klimas et al., 2001; Mawle et al., 1997; Patarca-Montero et al., 2001), and

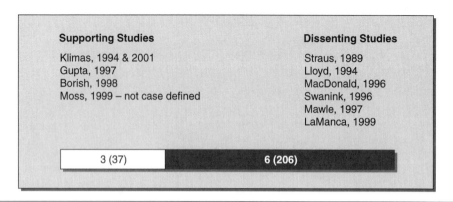

Figure 7.14   Laboratory Evidence of Immune Activation: Increased TNF-α

RIA of stimulated monocyte culture supernatants (Swanink et al., 1996). As each method has differing sensitivities and specificities, direct comparisons across differing analytical platforms become problematic. An initial glance at the data for TNFα reveals 4 studies that found elevated production in CFS (Borish et al., 1998; Gupta et al., 1997; Moss et al., 1999; Patarca et al., 1994) and 6 that found no difference (LaManca et al., 1999; Lloyd et al., 1994; MacDonald et al., 1996; Mawle et al., 1997; Straus et al., 1989). Six groups measured TNFα protein in serum, one in cellular lysates, two in unstimulated and PHA-stimulated PBMC cultures, and one in LPS-stimulated cultures of monocytes. Three groups also studied cell-associated TNFα mRNA transcripts. Two groups (Moss et al., 1999; Patarca et al., 1994) collectively studying 279 CFS subjects found significantly elevated mean concentrations of TNFα in the serum of subjects with CFS relative to controls. Four groups collectively studying 112 CFS subjects found no difference in serum TNFα relative to controls (Lloyd et al., 1994; MacDonald et al., 1996; Mawle et al., 1997; Straus et al., 1989).

Multiple reasons can be suggested for this discrepancy. First, among those studies finding elevated mean serum concentrations, both pointed out that the elevated mean was due to a subset of subjects who demonstrated quantifiable TNFα in serum. Moss et al., reported that 32% of the 240 CFS subjects studied had elevated TNFα concentrations that drove the mean. In addition, they noted that females with CFS had a mean concentration of TNFα that was three times higher than that in the male subset (98.2 ±17.6 vs. 31 ±4.5 pg/ml), which appeared not to differ from the controls (27.7 ±4.5 pg/ml). Thus variations in the population gender and size might account for some of the discrepancy. In this light, the findings of Moss are not discordant with Lloyd et al., who reported no significant difference in serum TNFα in a group of 12 male subjects with CFS relative to controls. Another potential source of discrepancy among the remaining reports is that TNFα is a labile molecule and accurate measurement requires punctilious adherence to protocols designed to retain its activity during handling. Klimas and colleagues have published that TNFα (and its receptors TNFRI and TNFRII) appears to cycle over the course of the illness and to correlate with health measures (Patarca et al., 1994). This suggests a confound that further impedes our ability to identify significant relationships from studies that used cross-sectional designs such as those reviewed here. Furthermore, one study reported elevated serum TNFα relative to the control group, but noted a similar elevation of TNFα in subjects with allergy (non-CFS; Borish et al., 1998). As the majority of the CFS subjects in this study were atopic (15 of 18), history of allergy is a variable that should be noted and considered as a potential source of immune dysfunction and compounding morbidity.

CIRCULATING IMMUNE COMPLEXES

When antigen and its corresponding antibody are present together at near molar equivalent concentrations, they bind and form a lattice of cross-linked proteins. These immune complexes are produced in response to infectious, neoplastic, autoimmune, and iatrogenic processes. Depending on their physical character, they may be deposited in tissues and precipitate an inflammatory process that damages tissues and organs. This process occurs in poststreptococcal glomerulonephritis, in which bacterial antigens complexed with antibody are trapped in the glomerular basement membrane, where they activate the complement system and incite an inflammatory process that destroys kidney structure and function.

Four reports assessed the presence of circulating immune complexes in subjects with CFS (see Figure 7.15). Two studies found evidence of increased frequency of immune complex formation in CFS (Bates et al., 1995; Natelson et al., 1995), and two studies found no evidence (Mawle et al., 1997; Milton et al., 1991). One group assayed for complexes using three methods on a cohort of 64 subjects (Natelson et al., 1995). The first assay measured the amount of Ig bound to staphylococcal protein A (SPA) which has a specific affinity for the Fc portion of IgG. Here the authors reported an elevated incidence of increased immune complexes among individuals with CFS (42%) relative to their control population (10%). In the second assay, they found an elevated incidence of increased immune complex binding to a lymphoblastoid (Raji) cell line of 29%, relative to an incidence of 18% among the controls. The third assay, which measures the binding of immune complexes via the complement product C1q, found a decreased immune complex binding capacity of 22% relative to the control incidence of 9%. The second report also measured immune complexes using the C1q binding assay but found increased frequency of elevated concentrations among their cohort of 181

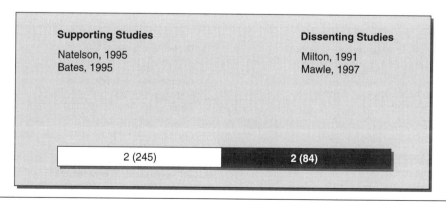

Figure 7.15 Laboratory Evidence of Immune Activation: Increased Circulating Immune Complexes

subjects (35% of CFS vs. 2% of controls; Milton et al., 1991). The third report used both the C1q binding assay and the SPA assay and found no significant differences from the controls (Mawle et al., 1997). The final report measured the immunoglobulin concentration, by radial immunodiffusion, of a polyethylene glycol precipitate of serum (Milton et al., 1991). These investigators reported no significant difference in the relative concentrations between subject groups. The differences in the assay methods (which differ in their sensitivities and specificities) as well as the data presentation (i.e., frequency of elevated values vs. concentrations) compromise our ability to determine the relevance of immune complex formation in association with CFS.

ANTINUCLEAR ANTIBODIES

The presence of antinuclear antibodies (ANAs) is associated with rheumatologic disorders such as systemic lupus erythematosus and rheumatoid arthritis. Seven groups undertook investigation into a possible autoimmune process underlying CFS by measuring ANAs in the sera of CFS subjects (see Figure 7.16). Three groups (Bates et al., 1995; Konstantinov et al., 1996; Nishikai & Kosaka, 1997; von Mikecz, Konstantinov, Buchwald, Gerace, & Tan, 1997) reported on a combined total of 678 subjects and presented data showing elevated titers of ANAs. In contrast, three groups (Gold et al., 1990; Lloyd, Hickie, Wakefield, Boughton, & Dwyer, 1990; Rasmussen et al., 1994) studying a total of 167 subjects reported against the presence of elevated titers of antinuclear antibodies in the serum of CFS subjects. Testing methodologies were not apparent sources of discrepancy. However, the larger numbers of subjects tested among those studies finding elevations may suggest inadequate statistical power among the dissenting studies.

ALLERGY

Ten studies considered the incidence of coexisting allergies as a potential component in the pathogenesis of CFS (Baraniuk, Clauw, & Gaumond, 1998; Bell, Cookfair, Bell, Reese, & Cooper, 1991; Borish et al., 1998; Conti et al., 1996; Friedberg, Dechene, McKenzie, & Fontanetta, 2000; Khan et al., 1993; MacDonald et al., 1996; Manian, 1994; Mawle et al., 1997; Steinberg et al., 1996) as shown in Figure 7.17. These

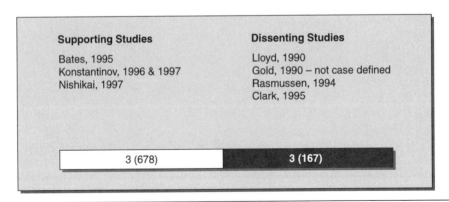

Figure 7.16   Laboratory Evidence of Immune Activation: Increased Anitnuclear Antibodies

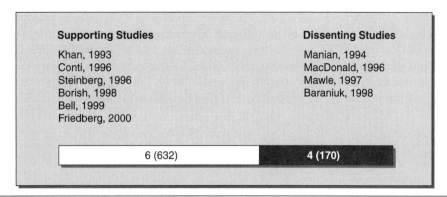

Figure 7.17 Laboratory Evidence of Immune Activation: Allergy

studies document evidence of allergic signs or symptoms in 30% to 89% of the subjects with case-defined CFS. The methods used to determine these incidences included patient self-report, standardized questionnaires, skin testing for in vivo sensitization to specific allergens and RAST (radioallergosorbent) testing for the determination of allergen-specific IgE. RAST testing was used to demonstrate elevations of allergen-specific IgE among 77% of the CFS population compared with 0% of the control population (Conti et al., 1996). Four other groups performed skin testing. One of these reported no difference in the incidence of positive skin tests in 35% of CFS subjects relative to 44% of the control population (Baraniuk et al., 1998). The other three groups (Borish et al., 1998; Steinberg et al., 1996; Straus, Dale, Wright, & Metcalfe, 1988) reported incidences of positivity in 50% to 83% of CFS subjects, which they concluded is elevated relative to reported incidences of 20% among unselected Caucasian populations (Chan-Yeung, Vedal, Lam, & Enarson, 1985; Gergen, Turkeltaub, & Kovar, 1987). Baraniuk et al. suggest that this apparent elevation is due to prevalence studies that cite rates of allergy well below those of other studies and that community-based controls would be a more appropriate comparison (Baraniuk et al., 1998). Other reports suggest that the incidence of positive skin tests in industrialized countries has increased to near 50% (Aberg, Hesselmar, Aberg, & Eriksson, 1995; Barbee, Kaltenborn, Lebowitz, & Burrows, 1987; Peat, Haby, Spijker, Berry, & Woodcock, 1992; Sibbald, Rink, & D'Souza, 1990). Also, the study by Borish et al. reported a prevalence of 83% positive skin tests among CFS subjects and among 70% of the non-CFS depressed control group. Self-reports of allergic symptoms ranged from 60% to 89% of the CFS groups relative to 23% to 60% of the controls. Baraniuk et al. noted that although 76% of CFS subjects had rhinitis (vs. 23% of controls), 46% had nonallergic rhinitis suggesting that causes other than atopy may promote the symptoms (Baraniuk et al., 1998). These studies highlight the need for population-controlled studies that use objective tests to demonstrate clinical allergy. It needs to be noted that skin tests for immediate cutaneous hypersensitivity and RAST testing for allergen-specific IgE have limited ability to predict symptomatic allergy. The presence of such IgE is necessary for the development of Type I hypersensitivity reactions. However, other factors are also important in the establishment of the allergic state and explain the absence of clinical allergy among some individuals with elevated RAST values or positive skin tests.

These difficulties in defining studies to determine the role of allergy in the genesis of CFS should not obviate the consideration that coexisting allergy among individuals with CFS contributes significantly to the morbidity and immune profiles of those with CFS as it does in non-CFS subjects. The determination of allergy, and its symptomatic associations, should be noted in all studies as a possible confound in the determination of illness burden and laboratory findings.

IMMUNOGLOBULIN LEVELS

A number of groups have studied the serum levels of immunoglobulin classes and subclasses (see Figure 7.18). Bates et al. studied a group of 497 CFS subjects and found significant elevations of IgG relative to the control group (Bates et al., 1995). Four other groups collectively studied 130 subjects and found no significant difference from controls (Gupta & Vayuvegula, 1991; Mawle et al., 1997; Natelson et al., 1998; Rasmussen et al., 1994). Rasmussen et al. found significant decreases in IgA among 21 CFS subjects relative to controls, whereas four groups studying 605 subjects found no difference (Bates et al., 1995; Gupta & Vayuvegula, 1991; Mawle et al., 1997; Natelson et al., 1998). Four groups collectively studying 130 subjects found no significant differences in IgM concentrations compared with controls (Gupta & Vayuvegula, 1991; Mawle et al., 1997; Natelson et al., 1998; Rasmussen et al., 1994), while one group studying 496 subjects reported marginally significant elevations of IgM (Bates et al., 1995). Two groups reported decreased IgG1 or IgG3 (Lloyd et al., 1989; Natelson et al., 1998) in case-defined CFS; three others reported no difference from controls (Bennett, Fagioli, Schur, Schacterle, & Komaroff, 1996; Gupta & Vayuvegula, 1991; Rasmussen et al., 1994). Methodological discrepancies were not apparent. One group reported intravenous IgG efficacious (Lloyd, Hickie, Wakefield, et al., 1990) but failed to replicate that original finding in a later study (Vollmer-Conna et al., 1997). A second group also found no therapeutic benefit from intravenous Ig administration, suggesting that if deficiencies in IgG subclasses did exist in a significant number of CFS subjects, correcting this deficit did not alter the course of the illness significantly (Peterson et al., 1990).

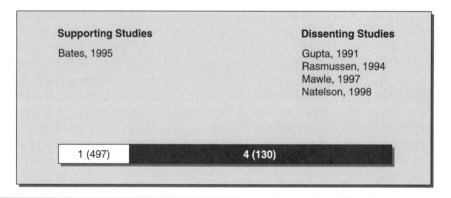

Figure 7.18   Laboratory Evidence of Immune Activation: Increased Serum IgG

RNASE L

The final immune measure we present here (see Figure 7.19) is the interferon inducible antiviral RNase L pathway, which three groups studying 135 subjects with CFS have independently verified as being activated in CFS (De Meirleir et al., 2000; Matsuda et al., 1994; Suhadolnik et al., 1994). It is hypothesized that the distinct production of low molecular weight forms of RNase L may serve as a diagnostic marker for CFS. One group (Gow, 2001) reported no significant elevation of the antiviral pathway in 22 subjects with CFS, but noted elevation among a group of patients with acute infection.

Methodological differences may have contributed the apparently discrepant conclusions of the reports reviewed here as Gow et al. measured gene expression by rtPCR, whereas De Meirleir et al. and Suhadolnik et al. measured enzymatic activity.

SUMMARY

Although we have not presented data on every aspect of immunology that has been studied in relation to CFS, nor have we included every published study in this review, we have presented evidence of multiple immunologic abnormalities. Furthermore, these abnormalities not only have been reported, but also have been independently confirmed by multiple research groups around the world. In many cases, there were three to four independent confirmations and in the case of NK cytotoxicity, eight different groups using similar methods on similar populations confirmed the defect. So it would be fair to conclude that within at least a subset of CFS, there is strong evidence of immune dysfunction. Among the most consistently reported findings are elevations in the CD5+CD19+ subset and decreased natural killer cell cytotoxicity and decreased naive cells.

There are multiple reports of contrary findings for many of these analytes. We have tried to include the published evidence that would explain the discrepancies.

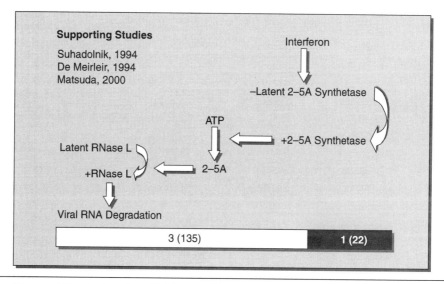

Figure 7.19   Laboratory Evidence of Immune Activation: Increased RNase L

For some analytes, however, the reasons are not apparent. With this realization comes the need to consider the limitations of the literature on CFS.

A simple observation can be made from Figure 7.20, which demonstrates that population size varies between studies. The studies finding significant relationships between an immunologic marker and CFS appear to have larger study populations than those reporting negative results. This suggests that some of these studies may have failed from inadequate statistical power.

Another limitation to the literature is that the majority of reports provide little more than a reference and a statement that the subjects met the criteria for the case definition. Frequently, there is no mention of the mode of onset, duration of illness, associated inflammatory symptoms, presence of allergy, or temporal relationship to ovulation in women.

CFS is an illness punctuated by periods of remission and relapse. Klimas and colleagues noted that cytokine expression within individuals was not static but cycled with symptoms and correlated with health measures (Patarca et al., 1994). In addition, the majority of CFS patients are women who experience cyclical hormonal variations. Cannon reported that the secretion of IL-1Ra was elevated in CFS but only during the follicular phase of the menstrual cycle (Cannon et al., 1997). These findings show that the biology of CFS is dynamic and that even a single subject may not yield consistent findings over time.

The literature about this aspect of CFS is deficient because the majority of studies were cross-sectional in design and have not accounted for the cyclical nature of the illness (see Figure 7.21). This deficiency may easily account for some of the variability in the findings between groups. Along these lines, important questions remain as to whether these immune dysfunctions cycle; whether they

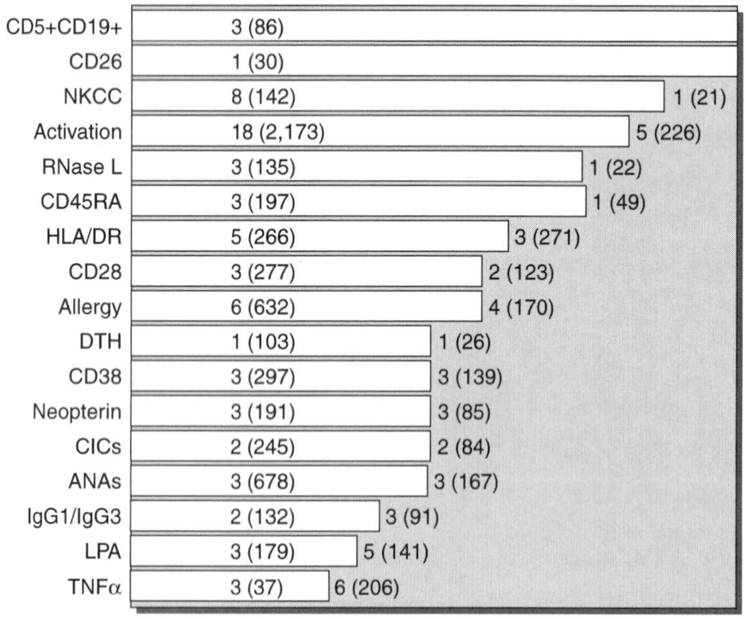

CD5+CD19+	3 (86)	
CD26	1 (30)	
NKCC	8 (142)	1 (21)
Activation	18 (2,173)	5 (226)
RNase L	3 (135)	1 (22)
CD45RA	3 (197)	1 (49)
HLA/DR	5 (266)	3 (271)
CD28	3 (277)	2 (123)
Allergy	6 (632)	4 (170)
DTH	1 (103)	1 (26)
CD38	3 (297)	3 (139)
Neopterin	3 (191)	3 (85)
CICs	2 (245)	2 (84)
ANAs	3 (678)	3 (167)
IgG1/IgG3	2 (132)	3 (91)
LPA	3 (179)	5 (141)
TNFα	3 (37)	6 (206)

Figure 7.20 Literature on CFS Contains Many Reports on Immune Function Utilizing Multiple Methods. The overlap of testing methods between these studies is limited.

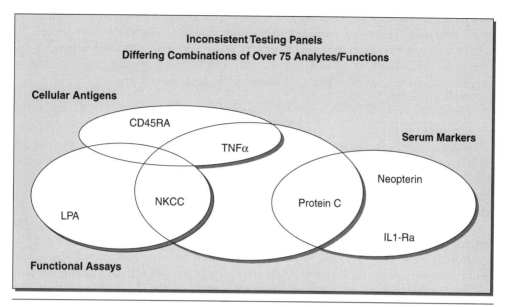

Figure 7.21 Limitations of the Literature

precede, coincide, or follow periods of exacerbation; or whether they are unrelated to symptomatic illness. Also unknown is the proportion of CFS subjects who experienced temporal dysregulation of the immune system.

The literature on CFS also illustrates deficiencies in laboratory methodologies. We have highlighted some that were apparent from the literature, but others likely exist that were not noted on report. Preanalytic variables represent those variables that affect the final analysis but occur prior to the testing phase. These include issues on sampling time, shipping conditions, transit time, and processing methods. Studies that send their samples to commercial laboratories relinquish control of this aspect of their study to outside parties. It is known that many analytes such as cytokines and NK activity can be exquisitely sensitive to temperature and time.

The breadth of analytic variables reported in the literature also confounds our ability to make firm conclusions from many of the studies. In this review, more than 75 immunologic analytes and functions were measured across the 105 studies. Yet each measure was conducted in only a handful of studies because each report chose a different panel of tests. The groups used various methods with differing sensitivities and specificities to study a single analyte (e.g., cytokine determinations measured mRNA expression and protein concentrations in serum, cells, or stimulated culture supernatants). Even within a single method, variations were common such as differing mitogens in proliferation assays, and the use of fresh versus cryopreserved lymphocytes for immunophentyping.

All studies referenced here presented their findings relative to a control population that may have been a group of fatigued subjects not fitting the case definition or that may have been a group of healthy controls. Rarely is this population defined in any detail. Physical conditioning, substance use, past illness, medication use, and levels of stress and coping are all important variables that should commonly be, but rarely are, reported.

The last set of variables relates to those postanalytical steps that follow data acquisition. Examples were provided in the papers of Rasmussen, who reported NK activity as a percentage of control, and Natelson, who attributed his lack of evidence for activation to insensitive statistical methods. In addition, inadequate statistical power may have plagued some of the smaller studies.

CONCLUSION

Substantial evidence exists in the literature to support the concept of immune dysfunction in chronic fatigue syndrome, but there are sufficient flawed and contradictory studies to make drawing this conclusion difficult. To effectively move the field of chronic fatigue syndrome forward, future studies must circumvent the limitations that have been outlined here. To this end, future studies should include multicenter longitudinal designs that will address cyclic variation. Detailed characterization of both the CFS and control groups will be necessary to permit clinical subgrouping. And finally, common analytes should be tested using common, standardized methods by laboratories that demonstrate successful participation in proficiency testing programs.

REFERENCES

Aberg, N., Hesselmar, B., Aberg, B., & Eriksson, B. (1995). Increase of asthma, allergic rhinitis and eczema in Swedish schoolchildren between 1979 and 1991. *Clinical and Experimental Allergy, 25*(9), 815–819.

Ablashi, D. V., Eastman, H. B., Owen, C. B., Roman, M. M., Friedman, J., Zabriskie, J. B., et al. (2000). Frequent HHV-6 reactivation in multiple sclerosis (MS) and chronic fatigue syndrome (CFS) patients. *Journal of Clinical Virology, 16*(3), 179–191.

Aoki, T., Miyakoshi, H., Usuda, Y., & Herberman, R. B. (1993). Low NK syndrome and its relationship to chronic fatigue syndrome. *Clinical Immunology and Immunopathology, 69*(3), 253–265.

Arnason, B. G. (1991). Nervous system-immune system communication. *Reviews of Infectious Diseases, 13*(Suppl. 1), S134–S137.

Baraniuk, J. N., Clauw, D. J., & Gaumond, E. (1998). Rhinitis symptoms in chronic fatigue syndrome. *Annals of Allergy, Asthma, and Immunology, 81*(4), 359–365.

Barbee, R. A., Kaltenborn, W., Lebowitz, M. D., & Burrows, B. (1987). Longitudinal changes in allergen skin test reactivity in a community population sample. *Journal of Allergy and Clinical Immunology, 79*(1), 16–24.

Barclay, N. A., Birkeland, M. L., & Brown, M. L. (1993). *The leukocyte antigen factsbook.* San Diego, CA: Academic Press.

Barker, E., Fujimura, S. F., Fadem, M. B., Landay, A. L., & Levy, J. A. (1994). Immunologic abnormalities associated with chronic fatigue syndrome. *Clinical Infectious Diseases, 18*(Suppl. 1), S136–S141.

Bates, D. W., Buchwald, D. S., Lee, J., Kith, P., Doolittle, T., Rutherford, C., et al. (1995). Clinical laboratory test findings in patients with chronic fatigue syndrome. *Archives of Internal Medicine, 155*(1), 97–103.

Bell, I. R., Baldwin, C. M., & Schwartz, G. E. (1998). Illness from low levels of environmental chemicals: Relevance to chronic fatigue syndrome and fibromyalgia. *American Journal of Medicine, 105*(3A), 74S–82S.

Bell, K. M., Cookfair, D., Bell, D. S., Reese, P., & Cooper, L. (1991). Risk factors associated with chronic fatigue syndrome in a cluster of pediatric cases. *Reviews of Infectious Diseases, 13*(Suppl. 1), S32–S38.

Bennett, A. L., Chao, C. C., Hu, S., Buchwald, D., Fagioli, L. R., Schur, P. H., et al. (1997). Elevation of bioactive transforming growth factor-beta in serum from patients with chronic fatigue syndrome. *Journal of Clinical Immunology, 17*(2), 160–166.

Bennett, A. L., Fagioli, L. R., Schur, P. H., Schacterle, R. S., & Komaroff, A. L. (1996). Immunoglobulin subclass levels in chronic fatigue syndrome. *Journal of Clinical Immunology, 16*(6), 315–320.

Borish, L., Schmaling, K., DiClementi, J. D., Streib, J., Negri, J., & Jones, J. F. (1998). Chronic fatigue syndrome: Identification of distinct subgroups on the basis of allergy and psychologic variables. *Journal of Allergy and Clinical Immunology, 102*(2), 222–230.

Buchwald, D. S., Cheney, P. R., Peterson, D. L., Henry, B., Wormsley, S. B., Geiger, A., et al. (1992). A chronic illness characterized by fatigue, neurologic and immunologic disorders, and active human herpesvirus type 6 infection. *Annals of Internal Medicine, 116*(2), 103–113.

Buchwald, D. S., Wener, M. H., Pearlman, T., & Kith, P. (1997). Markers of inflammation and immune activation in chronic fatigue and chronic fatigue syndrome. *Journal of Rheumatology, 24*(2), 372–376.

Burastero, S. E., Casali, P., Wilder, R. L., & Notkins, A. L. (1988). Monoreactive high affinity and polyreactive low affinity rheumatoid factors are produced by CD5+ B cells from patients with rheumatoid arthritis. *Journal of Experimental Medicine, 168*(6), 1979–1992.

Caligiuri, M., Murray, C., Buchwald, D., Levine, H., Cheney, P., Peterson, D., et al. (1987). Phenotypic and functional deficiency of natural killer cells in patients with chronic fatigue syndrome. *Journal of Immunology, 139*(10), 3306–3313.

Cannon, J. G., Angel, J. B., Abad, L. W., Vannier, E., Mileno, M. D., Fagioli, L., et al. (1997). Interleukin-1 beta, interleukin-1 receptor antagonist, and soluble interleukin-1 receptor type II secretion in chronic fatigue syndrome. *Journal of Clinical Immunology, 17*(3), 253–261.

Casali, P., Burastero, S. E., Nakamura, M., Inghirami, G., & Notkins, A. L. (1987). Human lymphocytes making rheumatoid factor and antibody to ssDNA belong to Leu-1+ B-cell subset. *Science, 236*(4797), 77–81.

Centers for Disease Control and Prevention. (1997). 1997 revised guidelines for performing CD4+ T-cell determinations in persons infected with human immunodeficiency virus (HIV). Centers for Disease Control and Prevention. *MMWR. Morbidity and Mortality Weekly Report, 46*(RR-2), 1–29.

Chan-Yeung, M., Vedal, S., Lam, S., & Enarson, D. (1985). Immediate skin reactivity and its relationship to age, sex, smoking, and occupational exposure. *Archives of Environmental Health, 40*(1), 53–57.

Chao, C. C., Gallagher, M., Phair, J., & Peterson, P. K. (1990). Serum neopterin and interleukin-6 levels in chronic fatigue syndrome [letter]. *Journal of Infectious Diseases, 162*(6), 1412–1413.

Cheney, P. R., Dorman, S. E., & Bell, D. S. (1989). Interleukin-2 and the chronic fatigue syndrome. *Annals of Internal Medicine, 110*(4), 321.

Conti, F., Magrini, L., Priori, R., Valesini, G., & Bonini, S. (1996). Eosinophil cationic protein serum levels and allergy in chronic fatigue syndrome. *Allergy, 51*(2), 124–127.

Dauphinee, M., Tovar, Z., & Talal, N. (1988). B cells expressing CD5 are increased in Sjogren's syndrome. *Arthritis and Rheumatism, 31*(5), 642–647.

De Meirleir, K., Bisbal, C., Campine, I., De Becker, P., Salehzada, T., Demettre, E., et al. (2000). A 37 kDa 2–5A binding protein as a potential biochemical marker for chronic fatigue syndrome. *American Journal of Medicine, 108*(2), 99–105.

Fletcher, M. A., Maher, K., & Klimas, N. G. (2002). Natural killer cell function in chronic fatigue syndrome. *Clinical and Applied Immunology Reviews, 2,* 129–139.

Friedberg, F., Dechene, L., McKenzie, M. J., II, & Fontanetta, R. (2000). Symptom patterns in long-duration chronic fatigue syndrome. *Journal of Psychosomatic Research, 48*(1), 59–68.

Fuchs, D., Hausen, A., Reibnegger, G., Werner, E. R., Dierich, M. P., & Wachter, H. (1988). Neopterin as a marker for activated cell-mediated immunity: Application in HIV infection. *Immunology Today, 9*(5), 150–155.

Gergen, P. J., Turkeltaub, P. C., & Kovar, M. G. (1987). The prevalence of allergic skin test reactivity to eight common aeroallergens in the U.S. population: Results from the second National Health and Nutrition Examination Survey. *Journal of Allergy and Clinical Immunology, 80*(5), 669–679.

Giorgi, J. V., Liu, Z., Hultin, L. E., Cumberland, W. G., Hennessey, K., & Detels, R. (1993). Elevated levels of CD38+ CD8+ T cells in HIV infection add to the prognostic value of low CD4+ T cell levels: Results of 6 years of follow-up. The Los Angeles Center, Multicenter AIDS Cohort Study. *Journal of Acquired Immune Deficiency Syndrome, 6*(8), 904–912.

Gold, D., Bowden, R., Sixbey, J., Riggs, R., Katon, W. J., Ashley, R., et al. (1990). Chronic fatigue: A prospective clinical and virologic study. *Journal of the American Medical Association, 264*(1), 48–53.

Gow, J. W., Simpson, K., Behan, P. O., Chaudhuri, A., McKay, I. C., & Behan, W. M. (2001). Antiviral pathway activation in patients with chronic fatigue syndrome and acute infection. *Clinical Infectious Diseases, 33,* 2080–2081.

Gunn, W. J., Connell, D. B., & Randall, B. (1993). Epidemiology of chronic fatigue syndrome: The Centers for Disease Control Study. *Ciba Foundation Symposium, 173,* 83–92, 93–101.

Gupta, S., Aggarwal, S., See, D., & Starr, A. (1997). Cytokine production by adherent and nonadherent mononuclear cells in chronic fatigue syndrome. *Journal of Psychiatric Research, 31*(1), 149–156.

Gupta, S., & Vayuvegula, B. (1991). A comprehensive immunological analysis in chronic fatigue syndrome. *Scandinavian Journal of Immunology, 33*(3), 319–327.

Hanson, S. J., Gause, W., & Natelson, B. (2001). Detection of immunologically significant factors for chronic fatigue syndrome using neural-network classifiers. *Clinical and Diagnostic Laboratory Immunology, 8*(3), 658–662.

Hassan, I. S., Bannister, B. A., Akbar, A., Weir, W., & Bofill, M. (1998). A study of the immunology of the chronic fatigue syndrome: Correlation of immunologic parameters to health dysfunction. *Clinical Immunology and Immunopathology, 87*(1), 60–67.

Hassan, J., Feighery, C., Bresnihan, B., & Whelan, A. (1990). Increased CD5+ B cells in infectious mononucleosis. *British Journal of Immunology, 74*(3), 375–376.

Hickie, I. B., Wilson, A. J., Wright, J. M., Bennett, B. K., Wakefield, D., & Lloyd, A. R. (2000). A randomized, double-blind placebo-controlled trial of moclobemide in patients with chronic fatigue syndrome. *Journal of Clinical Psychiatry, 61*(9), 643–648.

Hilgers, A., & Frank, J. (1994). Chronic fatigue syndrome: Immune dysfunction, role of pathogens and toxic agents and neurological and cardial changes. *Wiener Medizinische Wochenschrift, 144*(16), 399–406.

Holmes, G. P., Kaplan, J. E., Gantz, N. M., Komaroff, A. L., Schonberger, L. B., Straus, S. E., et al. (1988). Chronic fatigue syndrome: A working case definition. *Annals of Internal Medicine, 108*(3), 387–389.

Jason, L. A., Richman, J. A., Rademaker, A. W., Jordan, K. M., Plioplys, A. V., Taylor, R. R., et al. (1999). A community-based study of chronic fatigue syndrome. *Archives of Internal Medicine, 159*, 2129–2137.

June, C. H., Ledbetter, J. A., Linsley, P. S., & Thompson, C. B. (1990). Role of the CD28 receptor in T-cell activation. *Immunology Today, 11*(6), 211–216.

Kameoka, J., Tanaka, T., Nojima, Y., Schlossman, S. F., & Morimoto, C. (1993). Direct association of adenosine deaminase with a T cell activation antigen, CD26. *Science, 261*(5120), 466–469.

Keller, R. H., Lane, J. L., Klimas, N., Reiter, W. M., Fletcher, M. A., van Riel, F., et al. (1994). Association between HLA class II antigens and the chronic fatigue immune dysfunction syndrome. *Clinical Infectious Diseases, 18*(Suppl. 1), S154–S156.

Khan, A. S., Heneine, W. M., Chapman, L. E., Gary, H. E., Jr., Woods, T. C., Folks, T. M., et al. (1993). Assessment of a retrovirus sequence and other possible risk factors for the chronic fatigue syndrome in adults. *Annals of Internal Medicine, 118*(4), 241–245.

Kibler, R., Lucas, D. O., Hicks, M. J., Poulos, B. T., & Jones, J. F. (1985). Immune function in chronic active Epstein-Barr virus infection. *Journal of Clinical Immunology, 5*(1), 46–54.

Klimas, N. (1998). Pathogenesis of chronic fatigue syndrome and fibromyalgia. *Growth Hormone and IGF Research, 8*(Suppl. B), 123–126.

Klimas, N., Patarca, R., Walling, J., Garcia, R., Mayer, V., Moody, D., et al. (1994). Clinical and immunological changes in AIDS patients following adoptive therapy with activated autologous CD8 T cells and interleukin-2 infusion. *AIDS, 8*(8), 1073–1081.

Klimas, N., Patarca-Montero, R., Maher, K., Smith, M., Bathe, O., & Fletcher, M. A. (2001). Clinical and immunological effects of autologous lymph node cell transplant in chronic fatigue syndrome. *Journal of Chronic Fatigue Syndrome, 8*(1), 39–55.

Klimas, N. G., Salvato, F. R., Morgan, R., & Fletcher, M. A. (1990). Immunologic abnormalities in chronic fatigue syndrome. *Journal of Clinical Microbiology, 28*(6), 1403–1410.

Konstantinov, K., von Mikecz, A., Buchwald, D., Jones, J., Gerace, L., & Tan, E. M. (1996). Autoantibodies to nuclear envelope antigens in chronic fatigue syndrome. *Journal of Clinical Investigation, 98*(8), 1888–1896.

LaManca, J. J., Sisto, S. A., Zhou, X. D., Ottenweller, J. E., Cook, S., Peckerman, A., et al. (1999). Immunological response in chronic fatigue syndrome following a graded exercise test to exhaustion. *Journal of Clinical Immunology, 19*(2), 135–142.

Landay, A. L., Jessop, C., Lennette, E. T., & Levy, J. A. (1991). Chronic fatigue syndrome: Clinical condition associated with immune activation. *Lancet, 338*(8769), 707–712.

Levine, P. H., Whiteside, T. L., Friberg, D., Bryant, J., Colclough, G., & Herberman, R. B. (1998). Dysfunction of natural killer activity in a family with chronic fatigue syndrome. *Clinical Immunology and Immunopathology, 88*(1), 96–104.

Linde, A., Andersson, B., Svenson, S. B., Ahrne, H., Carlsson, M., Forsberg, P., et al. (1992). Serum levels of lymphokines and soluble cellular receptors in primary Epstein-Barr virus infection and in patients with chronic fatigue syndrome. *Journal of Infectious Diseases, 165*(6), 994–1000.

Lloyd, A., Gandevia, S., Brockman, A., Hales, J., & Wakefield, D. (1994). Cytokine production and fatigue in patients with chronic fatigue syndrome and healthy control subjects in response to exercise. *Clinical Infectious Diseases, 18*(Suppl. 1), S142–S146.

Lloyd, A., Hickie, I., Brockman, A., Dwyer, J., & Wakefield, D. (1991). Cytokine levels in serum and cerebrospinal fluid in patients with chronic fatigue syndrome and control subjects [letter]. *Journal of Infectious Diseases, 164*(5), 1023–1024.

Lloyd, A., Hickie, I., Hickie, C., Dwyer, J., & Wakefield, D. (1992). Cell-mediated immunity in patients with chronic fatigue syndrome, healthy control subjects and patients with major depression. *Clinical and Experimental Immunology, 87*(1), 76–79.

Lloyd, A., Hickie, I., Wakefield, D., Boughton, C., & Dwyer, J. (1990). A double-blind, placebo-controlled trial of intravenous immunoglobulin therapy in patients with chronic fatigue syndrome. *American Journal of Medicine, 89*(5), 561–568.

Lloyd, A. R., Hickie, I., Boughton, C. R., Spencer, O., & Wakefield, D. (1990). Prevalence of chronic fatigue syndrome in an Australian population. *Medical Journal of Australia, 153*(9), 522–528.

Lloyd, A. R., Wakefield, D., Boughton, C. R., & Dwyer, J. M. (1989). Immunological abnormalities in the chronic fatigue syndrome. *Medical Journal of Australia, 151*(3), 122–124.

Lutgendorf, S., Klimas, N. G., Antoni, M., Brickman, A., Patarca, R., & Fletcher, M. A. (1995). Relationships of cognitive difficulties to immune markers: Depression and illness burden in chronic fatigue syndrome. *Journal of Chronic Fatigue Syndrome, 1,* 23–42.

MacDonald, K. L., Osterholm, M. T., LeDell, K. H., White, K. E., Schenck, C. H., Chao, C. C., et al. (1996). A case-control study to assess possible triggers and cofactors in chronic fatigue syndrome. *American Journal of Medicine, 100*(5), 548–554.

Manian, F. A. (1994). Simultaneous measurement of antibodies to Epstein-Barr virus, human herpesvirus 6, herpes simplex virus types 1 and 2, and 14 enteroviruses in chronic fatigue syndrome: Is there evidence of activation of a nonspecific polyclonal immune response? *Clinical Infectious Diseases, 19*(3), 448–453.

Masuda, A., Nozoe, S. I., Matsuyama, T., & Tanaka, H. (1994). Psychobehavioral and immunological characteristics of adult people with chronic fatigue and patients with chronic fatigue syndrome. *Psychosomatic Medicine, 56*(6), 512–518.

Matsuda, J., Gohchi, K., & Gotoh, N. (1994). Serum concentrations of 2′, 5′-oligoadenylate synthetase, neopterin, and beta-glucan in patients with chronic fatigue syndrome and in patients with major depression [letter]. *Journal of Neurology, Neurosurgery, and Psychiatry, 57*(8), 1015–1016.

Mawle, A. C., Nisenbaum, R., Dobbins, J. G., Gary, H. E., Jr., Stewart, J. A., Reyes, M., et al. (1997). Immune responses associated with chronic fatigue syndrome: A case-control study. *Journal of Infectious Diseases, 175*(1), 136–141.

McMihael, A. J., Beverly, P. C. L., & Gilks, W. (1987). *Leukocyte typing III: White cell differentiation antigens.* New York: Oxford University Press.

Milton, J. D., Clements, G. B., & Edwards, R. H. (1991). Immune responsiveness in chronic fatigue syndrome. *Postgraduate Medical Journal, 67*(788), 532–537.

Moss, R. B., Mercandetti, A., & Vojdani, A. (1999). TNF-alpha and chronic fatigue syndrome. *Journal of Clinical Immunology, 19*(5), 314–316.

Natelson, B. H., Denny, T., Zhou, X. D., LaManca, J. J., Ottenweller, J. E., Tiersky, L., et al. (1999). Is depression associated with immune activation? *Journal of Affective Disorders, 53*(2), 179–184.

Natelson, B. H., Ellis, S. P., Braonain, P. J., DeLuca, J., & Tapp, W. N. (1995). Frequency of deviant immunological test values in chronic fatigue syndrome patients. *Clinical and Diagnostic Laboratory Immunology, 2*(2), 238–240.

Natelson, B. H., LaManca, J. J., Denny, T. N., Vladutiu, A., Oleske, J., Hill, N., et al. (1998). Immunologic parameters in chronic fatigue syndrome, major depression, and multiple sclerosis. *American Journal of Medicine, 105*(3A), 43S–49S.

Nishikai, M., & Kosaka, S. (1997). Incidence of antinuclear antibodies in Japanese patients with chronic fatigue syndrome. *Arthritis and Rheumatism, 40*(11), 2095–2097.

Ogawa, M., Nishiura, T., Yoshimura, M., Horikawa, Y., Yoshida, H., Okajima, Y., et al. (1998). Decreased nitric oxide-mediated natural killer cell activation in chronic fatigue syndrome. *European Journal of Clinical Investigation, 28*(11), 937–943.

Ojo-Amaize, E. A., Conley, E. J., & Peter, J. B. (1994). Decreased natural killer cell activity is associated with severity of chronic fatigue immune dysfunction syndrome. *Clinical Infectious Diseases, 18*(Suppl. 1), S157–S159.

Pall, M. L., & Satterle, J. D. (2001). Elevated nitric oxide/peroxynitrite mechanism for the common etiology of multiple chemical sensitivity, chronic fatigue syndrome, and posttraumatic stress disorder. *Annals of the New York Academy of Sciences, 933,* 323–329.

Patarca, R., & Fletcher, M. A. (1997). Pteridines and neuroimmune function and pathology. *Journal of Chronic Fatigue Syndrome, 3,* 69–86.

Patarca, R., Klimas, N. G., Garcia, M. N., Walters, M. J., Dombroski, D., Pons, H., et al. (1995). Dysregulated expression of soluble immune mediator receptors in a subset of patients with chronic fatigue syndrome: Cross-sectional categorization of patients by immune status. *Journal of Chronic Fatigue Syndrome, 1,* 81–96.

Patarca, R., Klimas, N. G., Lutgendorf, S., Antoni, M., & Fletcher, M. A. (1994). Dysregulated expression of tumor necrosis factor in chronic fatigue syndrome: Interrelations with cellular sources and patterns of soluble immune mediator expression. *Clinical Infectious Diseases, 18*(Suppl. 1), S147–S153.

Patarca, R., Maher, K., Goodkin, K., & Fletcher, M. A. (1997). Cryopreservation of peripheral blood mononuclear cells. In N. Rose, E. Conway de Macario, J. D. Folds, C. Lane, & R. M. Nakamura (Eds.), *Manual of clinical laboratory immunology* (pp. 281–286). Washington, DC: ASM Press.

Patarca-Montero, R., Antoni, M., Fletcher, M. A., & Klimas, N. (2001). Cytokine and other immunologic markers in chronic fatigue syndrome and their relation to neuropsychological factors. *Applied Neuropsychology, 8*(1), 51–64.

Peakman, M., Deale, A., Field, R., Mahalingam, M., & Wessely, S. (1997). Clinical improvement in chronic fatigue syndrome is not associated with lymphocyte subsets of function or activation. *Clinical Immunology and Immunopathology, 82*(1), 83–91.

Peat, J. K., Haby, M., Spijker, J., Berry, G., & Woolcock, A. J. (1992). Prevalence of asthma in adults in Busselton, Western Australia. *British Medical Journal, 305*(6865), 1326–1329.

Peterson, P. K., Shepard, J., Macres, M., Schenck, C., Crosson, J., Rechtman, D., et al. (1990). A controlled trial of intravenous immunoglobulin G in chronic fatigue syndrome. *American Journal of Medicine, 89*(5), 554–560.

Plater-Zyberk, C., Maini, R. N., Lam, K., Kennedy, T. D., & Janossy, G. (1985). A rheumatoid arthritis B cell subset expresses a phenotype similar to that in chronic lymphocytic leukemia. *Arthritis and Rheumatism, 28*(9), 971–976.

Rasmussen, A. K., Nielsen, H., Andersen, V., Barington, T., Bendtzen, K., Hansen, M. B., et al. (1994). Chronic fatigue syndrome: A controlled cross-sectional study. *Ugeskrift for Laeger, 156*(46), 6836–6840.

Reeves, W. C., Stamey, F. R., Black, J. B., Mawle, A. C., Stewart, J. A., & Pellett, P. E. (2000). Human herpesviruses 6 and 7 in chronic fatigue syndrome: A case-control study. *Clinical Infectious Diseases, 31*(1), 48–52.

Reyes, M., Gary, H. E., Dobbins, J. G., Randall, B., Steele, L., Fukuda, K., et al. (1997). Surveillance for chronic fatigue syndrome: Four U.S. cities, September 1989 through August 1993. *Morbidity and Mortality Weekly Report, 46*(SS02), 1.

See, D. M., Broumand, N., Sahl, L., & Tilles, J. G. (1997). In vitro effects of echinacea and ginseng on natural killer and antibody dependent cell cytotoxicity in healthy subjects and chronic fatigue syndrome or acquired immuno deficiency syndrome patients. *Immuno Pharmacology, 35*(3), 229–235.

Sharpe, M. C., Archard, L. C., Banatvala, J. E., Borysiewicz, L. K., Clare, A. W., David, A., et al. (1991). A report—chronic fatigue syndrome: Guidelines for research. *Journal of the Royal Society of Medicine, 84*(2), 118–121.

Shoham, S., Davenne, D., Cady, A. B., Dinarello, C. A., & Krueger, J. M. (1987). Recombinant tumor necrosis factor and interleukin 1 enhance slow-wave sleep. *American Journal of Physiology, 253*(1, Pt 2), R142–R149.

Sibbald, B., Rink, E., & D'Souza, M. (1990). Is the prevalence of atopy increasing? *British Journal of General Practice, 40*(337), 338–340.

Steele, L., Dobbins, J. G., Fukuda, K., Reyes, M., Randall, B., Koppelman, M., et al. (1998). The epidemiology of chronic fatigue in San Francisco. *American Journal of Medicine, 105*(3A), 83S–90S.

Steinberg, P., McNutt, B. E., Marshall, P., Schenck, C., Lurie, N., Pheley, A., et al. (1996). Double-blind placebo-controlled study of the efficacy of oral terfenadine in the treatment of chronic fatigue syndrome. *Journal of Allergy and Clinical Immunology, 97*(1, Pt 1), 119–126.

Straus, S. E., Dale, J. K., Peter, J. B., & Dinarello, C. A. (1989). Circulating lymphokine levels in the chronic fatigue syndrome [letter]. *Journal of Infectious Diseases, 160*(6), 1085–1086.

Straus, S. E., Dale, J. K., Wright, R., & Metcalfe, D. D. (1988). Allergy and the chronic fatigue syndrome [Review]. *Journal of Allergy and Clinical Immunology, 81*(5, Pt 1), 791–795.

Straus, S. E., Fritz, S., Dale, J. K., Gould, B., & Strober, W. (1993). Lymphocyte phenotype and function in the chronic fatigue syndrome. *Journal of Clinical Immunology, 13*(1), 30–40.

Straus, S. E., Tosato, G., Armstrong, G., Lawley, T., Preble, O. T., Henle, W., et al. (1985). Persisting illness and fatigue in adults with evidence of Epstein-Barr virus infection. *Annals of Internal Medicine, 102*(1), 7–16.

Suhadolnik, R. J., Reichenbach, N. L., Hitzges, P., Sobol, R. W., Peterson, D. L., Henry, B., et al. (1994). Upregulation of the 2–5A synthetase/RNase L antiviral pathway associated with chronic fatigue syndrome. *Clinical Infectious Diseases, 18*(Suppl. 1), S96–S104.

Swanink, C. M., Vercoulen, J. H., Galama, J. M., Roos, M. T., Meyaard, L., Van der Ven-Jongekrijg, J., et al. (1996). Lymphocyte subsets, apoptosis, and cytokines in patients with chronic fatigue syndrome. *Journal of Infectious Diseases, 173*(2), 460–463.

Tirelli, U., Marotta, G., Improta, S., & Pinto, A. (1994). Immunological abnormalities in patients with chronic fatigue syndrome. *Scandinavian Journal of Immunology, 40*(6), 601–608.

Tirelli, U., Pinto, A., Marotta, G., Crovato, M., Quaia, M., De Paoli, P., et al. (1993). Clinical and immunologic study of 205 patients with chronic fatigue syndrome: A case series from Italy [letter]. *Archives of Internal Medicine, 153*(1), 116–117, 120.

van Greure, C. H., & Bouic, P. J. (1990). Aberrant in vitro HLA-DR expression in patients with chronic fatigue [letter]. *South African Medical Journal, 78*(4), 219–220.

Vedhara, K., Llewelyn, M. B., Fox, J. D., Jones, M., Jones, R., Clements, G. B., et al. (1997). Consequences of live poliovirus vaccine administration in chronic fatigue syndrome. *Journal of Neuroimmunology, 75*(1/2), 183–195.

Visser, J., Blauw, B., Hinloopen, B., Brommer, E., de Kloet, E. R., Kluft, C., et al. (1998). CD4 T lymphocytes from patients with chronic fatigue syndrome have decreased interferon-gamma production and increased sensitivity to dexamethasone. *Journal of Infectious Diseases, 177*(2), 451–454.

Vollmer-Conna, U., Hickie, I., Hadzi-Pavlovic, D., Tymms, K., Wakefield, D., Dwyer, J., et al. (1997). Intravenous immunoglobulin is ineffective in the treatment of patients with chronic fatigue syndrome. *American Journal of Medicine, 103*(1), 38–43.

von Mikecz, A., Konstantinov, K., Buchwald, D. S., Gerace, L., & Tan, E. M. (1997). High frequency of autoantibodies to insoluble cellular antigens in patients with chronic fatigue syndrome. *Arthritis and Rheumatism, 40*(2), 295–305.

Wachter, H., Fuchs, D., Hausen, A., Reibnegger, G., & Werner, E. R. (1989). Neopterin as marker for activation of cellular immunity: Immunologic basis and clinical application. *Advances in Clinical Chemistry, 27*, 81–141.

Wemm, K. M., Jr., & Trestman, R. L. (1991). The effects of a laboratory stressor on natural killer cell function in chronic fatigue syndrome patients [letter]. *Psychosomatics, 32*(4), 470–471.

Whiteside, T. L., & Friberg, D. (1998). Natural killer cells and natural killer cell activity in chronic fatigue syndrome. *American Journal of Medicine, 105*(3A), 27S–34S.

Wilson, A., Hickie, I., Lloyd, A., Hadzi-Pavlovic, D., & Wakefield, D. (1995). Cell-mediated immune function and the outcome of chronic fatigue syndrome. *International Journal of Immunopharmacology, 17*(8), 691–694.

Zhang, Q., Zhou, X. D., Denny, T., Ottenweller, J. E., Lange, G., LaManca, J. J., et al. (1999). Changes in immune parameters seen in Gulf War veterans but not in civilians with chronic fatigue syndrome. *Clinical and Diagnostic Laboratory Immunology, 6*(1), 6–13.

PART II

PHENOMENOLOGY: ILLNESS COURSE AND PATIENT PERCEPTIONS

CHAPTER 8

A Four-Phase Approach to Understanding Chronic Fatigue Syndrome

PATRICIA A. FENNELL

HETEROGENEITY AND PHASE DESCRIPTION

C HRONIC FATIGUE SYNDROME (CFS) exhibits heterogeneous symptoms in multiple body systems, and these symptoms fluctuate over the lifetime of those afflicted (Fennell, 1993, 1995a, 1995b, 1998, 2001, 2004; Friedberg & Jason, 1998; Jason, Fennell, Taylor, Fricano, & Halpert, 2000). Moreover, CFS involves multiple domains in the lives of patients—the physical, the psychological, and the social-interactive (Engel, 1977; Fennell, 2001, 2004; Nicassio & Smith, 1995). Because of this heterogeneity, a phase description of the course of illness in CFS may better elucidate the nature of the condition. Patients present differing symptomatology during each phase and thus respond differently during specific instances of data collection and clinical interviews over time. In collapsing these responses, important distinctions about experience of the illness can be lost, which in turn may distort or obscure understanding of the illness (Jason, Fennell, Taylor, Fricano, & Halpert, 2000).

Several decades ago, stage theories became a useful method of organizing information in different fields into typologies, categories, or hierarchical constructs (Erikson, 1959; Kohlberg, 1959; Kubler-Ross, 1969; Piaget, 1952). Such frameworks have had a variety of applications (Weinstein, Rothman, & Sutton, 1998). They help researchers understand how individuals use medical services (Rakowski et al., 1992); they aid in the adoption of preventive behavior (Blalock et al., 1996); and they suggest how to stop unhealthy behaviors (Brownell, Marlatt, Lichtenstein, & Wilson, 1986; DiClemente, 1991; Prochaska & Velicer, 1997; Prochaska, DiClemente, & Norcross, 1992; Prochaska, Norcross, & DiClemente, 1994). By helping to organize research that might seem unrelated or contradictory when not conceptualized from a stage framework, the application of such models offers important heuristic contributions to scientific and social disciplines. In addition, these models often suggest new areas and domains of inquiry, as theorists and investigators use the templates to make more precise, targeted predictions (Berger & Thompson, 1995).

The phase model used in this chapter takes the increasingly popular construct of stage theory and revises and expands it to define four phases of adaptation that occur in CFS, and potentially many other chronic illnesses. It is important to recognize that for patients with any chronic condition, the situation in their lives is *imposed*. The Four-Phase Model, developed by the author (Fennell, 1993, 1995b), maps a process that most individuals do not enter into willingly. This fact distinguishes the model significantly from stage theories that focus solely on intentional change within the psychological domain (Prochaska et al., 1992).

The Four-Phase description of CFS attempts to capture the changing experience of patients over time in their physical, psychological, and social-interactive worlds. Because patients in later phases have recognized and accepted the chronic and ambiguous nature of CFS and are working to create a complete life in the present, their interpretations of pain, fatigue, cognitive dysfunction, and so forth change. Sometimes, the patient's more integrated life and improved coping skills make the symptoms less problematic even when they are more pronounced than they were at an earlier phase of the illness.

By serving as a narrative or cognitive map, the phase description helps to lessen fear and anxiety for CFS patients and their families. They now have a method of validating their experiences and making them known to others. The narrative helps them develop a sense of what is happening to them and provides a degree of order and coherency about their illness experience. In addition, the mapping aspect of the phase process helps promote understanding and adjustment to the cognitive impairments in concentration, memory, and decision making that often afflict those with CFS.

Like other stage theories, which have argued that matching intervention to stage provides the best outcomes (DiClemente, 1991; Prochaska & Velicer, 1997; Prochaska et al., 1992, 1994), the Four-Phase Model presents what may be expected over time and indicates appropriate times and ways to intervene to improve the patient's quality of life. Conversely, attempting interventions at the wrong time may prove less effective and may undermine the possibility of the same interventions being effective at a later phase when the patient would ordinarily be receptive to such interventions. The Four-Phase Model may also suggest more comprehensive interventions that take into account interaction among the multiple domains in which patients experience CFS.

THE FOUR-PHASE MODEL

The Four-Phase Model can be used in describing the course of CFS and in assigning patients to the appropriate phases. The 20-item Fennell Phase Inventory is available (Fennell, 1998), and applications of the instrument have been conducted with CFS populations (Jason et al., 1999; Jason, Fennell, et al., 2000; Jason, Fricano, et al., 2000). Phase 1 is a period of chaos and crisis. It lasts from the onset of the disease through an emergency state when patients typically seek medical help. The phase usually concludes when patients receive a diagnosis or when their symptoms become stable and recognizable to them. Phase 2 is a period of stabilization. Initially, patients attain a plateau of symptoms. They become familiar with the symptoms and achieve some success in coping with them. Patients begin to feel a degree of control returning to their lives. In Phase 3, characterized by resolution, patients acknowledge that they have a chronic illness, and that their lives have thus been changed forever. With this recognition, however, can come existential despair. If patients are able to develop meaning in their lives, they begin to construct a new self that deals with the practical aspects of their illness; yet, they are not overwhelmed or totally preoccupied with it. Phase 4 is one of integration. Patients solidify their newly constructed self and reach out into the world again to participate as fully as they can in as complete a life as their physical condition permits.

Patients ordinarily proceed through the phases in sequence, but as in other nonhierarchical stage models, they can slip back into a prior phase or recycle, sometimes several times (Prochaska et al., 1994; Sutton, 1997). Attainment of integration (Phase 4) is not a permanent condition. Crises, especially those brought about by non-CFS illnesses, accidents, or personal tragedies can throw patients back into the chaos of Phase 1. Even when such crises arise out of issues unrelated to CFS, however, patients who have progressed through the phase process have gained knowledge that makes it possible for them to process subsequent crises more swiftly and efficiently (DiClemente, 1991). Patients more quickly understand what is happening to them, know techniques to help improve their situation, and have the skills to seek and use necessary clinical help.

DEVELOPMENTAL LIFE PROCESSES

It is also important to note that patients with CFS experience ordinary developmental and life processes simultaneously with the phases of CFS. The dips and surges of adolescent adjustment, for example, may synchronize with phases of CFS in ways that exacerbate both developmental and illness effects. The sequence of physical and psychological reactions attendant on the death of a loved one or a decision to return to work can have profound interactions with the experience of CFS. The issues related to the event and to CFS have to be teased apart from each other for patients to develop and refine successful illness-coping skills.

GENERAL DESCRIPTION AND COMPOSITE CASE HISTORY

The following section describes the course of CFS using the Four-Phase Model to help illustrate how patients present in the physical-behavioral, the psychological, and the social-interactive domains during each phase of the model. The general description of the three domains in each phase includes a table outlining its characteristics. A composite case history illustrates how these generalizations manifest in actual patients.

CFS THROUGH THE LENS OF THE FOUR-PHASE MODEL

PHASE 1: CRISIS

Physical-Behavioral Domain The physical functioning of a person with CFS in Phase 1 occurs in three stages (see Table 8.1). First is coping. Patients experience

Table 8.1
Phase 1: Trauma/Crisis

Physical–Behavioral

- Coping stage
- Onset stage
- Acute emergency stage

Psychological

- Loss of psychological control; ego loss
- Intrusive shame, self-hatred, despair
- Shock, disorientation, dissociation
- Fear of others, isolation, mood swings

Social–Interactive

- Shock experienced by others, disbelief, revulsion
- Vicarious traumatization
- Family and organizational maturation
- Suspicion/Support continuum

varying combinations of fatigue, sore throat, increasing cognitive confusion, muscle and/or joint pain, and nonrestorative sleep, etc. CFS can have a gradual or a sudden onset. Since the onset of CFS can frequently occur following an illness like flu or a respiratory infection, patients may attribute their CFS symptoms to a very slow recovery. They sometimes try to ignore them.

Next, they enter onset, where their symptoms more insistently demand their attention. It becomes more and more difficult for the patients to believe that the symptoms are related to the prior illness. After a period of time that varies between long and short depending on the severity of symptoms, patients enter an acute emergency state and almost always seek medical help, even if they have not done so previously.

Generally, with chronic illnesses, patients receive a reasonably firm diagnosis at the end of Phase 1. CFS can be more problematic. It is less familiar to many primary care physicians than illnesses like rheumatoid arthritis or multiple sclerosis. The diagnostic process requires the presence of several symptoms occurring simultaneously as well as the exclusion of other illnesses that share some of the same symptoms. One of the defining symptoms—profound fatigue—needs to be ongoing for at least 6 months. This particular diagnostic parameter in itself can mean that patients may live for a considerable time in crisis with debilitating symptoms before they receive a diagnosis.

Psychological Domain   Patients who have a lengthy onset—and CFS patients often wait a long time for diagnosis—may use denial as a coping mechanism. Since they frequently receive little recognition and support from either the health care community or society at large, CFS patients often collude with others in their life to deny their symptoms. They try to maintain their daily lives.

If their condition continues to deteriorate, denial can give way to intrusive feelings of fear, self-hatred, despair, and disorientation. Some patients report that they feel they are somehow responsible for what is happening to them, but they do not believe they can do anything about it.

Typically in Phase 1, CFS patients regularly report receiving conflicting advice and some disbelief from health care professionals. The patients do not know how to describe their condition to themselves or others. They may feel shame, emotional isolation, fear of others, mood swings, and intense confusion.

By the time they contact their doctor, many CFS patients present with urgency. They usually hold the locus of treatment and cure to be totally outside themselves. They can be highly self-pathologizing; they suffer from fear and shame, experience intrusive ideations about dying, and exhibit a high degree of denial. They typically have little or no tolerance for the ambiguity of their condition.

Social-Interactive Domain   When CFS patients can no longer hide their symptoms from others, they find that some of their friends, family members, acquaintances, coworkers, and health care providers regard them as malingering or mentally ill. These others may think the CFS patients are trying to get out of work, which increases the burden on everyone around them. When the patients are women, health care professionals sometimes attribute their suffering to "depression." The disbelief and suspicion that CFS patients sometimes encounter can make them very cautious. These patients may be afraid to express how they actually feel or may misrepresent how they feel. Simultaneously, they may withdraw emotionally from others to avoid further rejection and negative stereotyping.

Some CFS patients continue to try to work during Phase 1, which often creates difficulties with coworkers and supervisors. Increasingly, they may be late to work and unable to complete tasks in a timely matter. Eventually they are usually absent a great deal. Initial concern on the part of fellow workers can, therefore, give way to irritation and resentment as others have to take up the patients' workload. Some patients run through their sick leave so quickly that they have to take unpaid leave or attempt to get disability. Disability may be difficult to obtain at this stage of the illness.

Three critical issues become evident during Phase 1. First, CFS patients can be traumatized by the physical, psychological, and social impact of the acute emergency stage (Alonzo, 2000; Baldwin, 1978; Botha, 1996; Lindy, Greene, & Grace, 1987). Second, their friends, family, coworkers, and clinicians can be vicariously traumatized by what is happening (Clark & Gioro, 1998; Engel, 1977; Hayes, 1997; Rolland, 1994; Rosenberg & Molho, 1998; Scott & Stradling, 1994). And third, these significant others begin to queue up on a continuum that extends from suspicion to support in response to the CFS patients. These social responses are often negative, if not stigmatizing, and can cause CFS patients further secondary traumatization. It is possible to propagate or mitigate ongoing traumatization depending on the level of supervision and support in the health care organizations employing the clinicians and the maturation, premorbidity, and comorbidity of the patients' social network (Alonzo, 2000; Fennell, Levine, & Uslan, 2001; Fullilove, Lown, & Fullilove, 1992; Turner & Lloyd, 1995). A supportive social network can permit the disruption of work and social exchange that the emergency stage brings while containing and buffering it for the patients. An effective health care organization provides support and supervision to providers who experience the daily grind of chronic suffering so they can avoid vicarious traumatization, subsequent burnout, and inflicting unintentional iatrogenic traumatization.

BETTY'S STORY: PHASE 1

Physical-Behavioral Domain   Betty is a married white woman in her late 30s. She has two children, Lisa, age 13, and Michael, age 11. Bob, her husband, is a computer hardware troubleshooter, which often requires him to work out of town for one or two weeks at a time. Betty works part-time at a bank in the suburb where the family lives.

Over the past several months, Betty has been increasingly distracted by a number of physical symptoms that are beginning to frighten her because they are interfering with her life and her work. She is exhausted most of the time and is not sleeping well. She thinks at first that she is just not completely recovered from a recent respiratory infection, but months are passing, and she still feels completely drained. Betty has never been sick with more than occasional colds, so she rarely goes to the doctor. She does not think her situation is very different from that of a lot of her friends, because all the working mothers she knows are always tired, too. She just keeps trying to carry on with her regular activities, snatching whatever moments she can to nap or at least rest.

Betty is just entering Phase 1. Physically and behaviorally, Betty is in a coping stage. Even though she does not feel well, she tries to ignore her symptoms, to push them out of her consciousness, and to continue her regular activities.

Eventually, however, Betty's exhaustion, and now muscle pain, and headaches make it impossible for her to ignore her symptoms, and she enters the onset stage. Betty finally goes to see her doctor.

The doctor listens to Betty describe her symptoms and gives her a cursory physical examination. They talk a bit about her situation at work and at home. The doctor tells Betty that she does not appear to have anything physically wrong with her. He thinks her exhaustion may be due to her poor sleep. And what with the many demands of her job and family life, it sounds as though stress may be causing her difficulties. He also thinks that she is mildly depressed, but not enough to require medication. The doctor recommends that Betty relax, try to get to bed earlier, cut back at work, and perhaps join an exercise class to help relieve her stress.

Betty wants to follow the doctor's suggestions, but she does not dare cut back on work because the family needs the income from her job. And she cannot see how to fit an exercise class into her already tight schedule. Also, it is not so much that she gets to bed late as that she wakes frequently at night and cannot get back to sleep again because her body aches and her mind races. Her symptoms get worse. Not only is she extremely fatigued, she is having increasingly frequent trouble thinking.

Betty is now entering the acute emergency stage. She goes back to her primary care physician who orders some blood tests and refers her to a psychiatrist to deal with her stress level and rule out clinical depression. The psychiatrist reports that Betty appears to be suffering from reactive depression in response to her physical condition. The blood work results raise questions that cause the primary care doctor to refer Betty to a rheumatologist. For months, she is examined, tested, and generally shuttled about in a diagnostic limbo. It is not until almost a year later that the rheumatologist gives Betty a tentative diagnosis of chronic fatigue syndrome. Even now, none of the doctors are really sure it is CFS.

But having a diagnosis, even a tentative one, makes an enormous difference to Betty, for it finally gives her a way to understand and describe her experiences to herself and others.

Psychological Domain   During Betty's lengthy coping and subsequent onset stage, she uses denial as a coping mechanism. Denial, particularly, comes into play after her initial visit to her primary care physician, who tells her that she is mildly depressed and suffering from the stress of a woman's life today. She colludes with her doctor, her husband, and people at work because it makes it possible for her to live her daily life.

But as Betty's symptoms worsen, other feelings begin to intrude. Like all people, Betty has constructed two selves while growing up—a private persona and a public persona. And like everyone, Betty reveals more or less of her private persona to individuals in her life depending on how intimate she is with them and what particular situation she is in. As Betty's condition continues to deteriorate, she finds that her private persona is beginning to impinge on her public persona in ways that she cannot control. One day at a staff meeting at the bank, Betty suddenly bursts into tears, embarrassing herself, her superior, and her coworkers. This behavior is not the self that Betty recognizes. She is not the sort of person who cries in public. She is greatly ashamed of herself and begins to wonder what could possibly be wrong with her. She cannot bear her loss of self-control.

Betty's shame and self-hatred occur at the same time that she is feeling increased fear and despair. Could she actually be dying or perhaps losing her mind? She knows she feels terrible physically and is getting worse, but maybe something is also wrong with her mind. She feels shock, even dissociation. It is important to remember that at this point no one has yet given Betty's situation a label. No one knows what is going on.

Betty has no way to express how she is feeling and when she tries, the people she talks to can only make up explanations and suggestions for improvement based on their own personal experiences, not on an understanding of what is happening to her. Betty feels increasingly isolated because she fears what is happening to her and what other people will think of her. She is particularly afraid to talk to the person who used to be closest to her—her husband, Bob. Betty and Bob have already been having marital difficulties due to conflicts over money and the amount of time Bob is forced to be away from home. Betty feels that Bob, by default, gets out of his fair share of home and child-care duties. She cannot quit her job to stay home full time because the family cannot make ends meet without her salary. In any case, she likes her job, which she does very well. She has received a lot of praise at work, especially from her superior, and she and Bob have both been hoping that she will get a promotion. The new position would bring in more money, but Betty would have to work full time.

In part as a consequence of her pain, her fears, her lack of useful information about her condition, and her growing isolation, Betty now begins to suffer mood swings. Half the time she is in tears, she says, and the other half she is furious. Bob has tried to be sympathetic, but now he is getting annoyed. The children act scared of her and disappear whenever possible. Even Betty's coworkers find her snappish and distracted, whereas she used to be pleasant and cooperative.

Social-Interactive Domain   Many of Betty's psychological mechanisms and reactions result directly from what is happening in her social-interactive life. During the coping and onset stages, Betty's family, friends, and coworkers respond in various ways to what they see of her experiences. When she is in denial, they notice only that she is tired a lot of the time and sometimes missing work. For a while they are sympathetic. She is a hard worker, and her female coworkers, particularly, have strong personal understanding of how hard it is to juggle a job, home, and children. As Betty accomplishes less and misses more work, however, they become critical. They have difficult lives too, but they manage to come to work, and they accomplish their assigned tasks.

Betty's children think that she is acting strange. She does not behave like the mother they are used to. Bob finds her unpredictable and emotionally extreme. He is used to hearing Betty say she is tired, but her complaints seem so serious that Bob is genuinely worried and urges her to go to the doctor. The doctor's diagnosis of stress seems reasonable to Bob, and he makes an effort to help more by staying in town or taking only short jobs away from home. But that cannot go on forever, and Betty does not seem to change. He thinks she could do a lot more if she tried, but she seems just to complain or sleep.

During the acute emergency stage, while Betty is being examined and tested extensively, Bob sometimes wonders whether anything is actually wrong with Betty. Maybe it is all in her head. Some of her coworkers feel that way, too. Maybe Betty is having a kind of nervous breakdown.

Finally, Betty gets her diagnosis, however tentative, of CFS. Although this gives her the relief of a name and an explanation, she now finds that the illness has put her squarely on the forefront of a cultural debate. Caught in a mesh of divergent popular beliefs regarding her partially understood disease, Betty finds that some of her friends and coworkers—even some of the medical personnel she sees—view her negatively. For the first time in her life, Betty begins to experience rejection by the society at large. She becomes very cautious about expressing her fears or revealing her pain because she does not want others to withdraw from her. Not only is she afraid of other people now, but her physical condition itself interferes with her reaching out socially to other people.

Betty's home life was already stressed prior to the onset of her illness, and her illness has exacerbated the situation. At the bank, Betty's immediate supervisor is sympathetic because the supervisor's sister, with whom she is very close, has fibromyalgia. The supervisor has a good grasp of Betty's problems and wants to help. Upper levels of management, however, think that Betty should probably be replaced, and it is unclear how effective the supervisor's advocacy will be. On the medical front, Betty's primary physician has become very involved with her case and would like to spend more time on it, but the HMO only permits 15 minutes per patient visit. The doctor cannot spend as much time as he would like talking with Betty, but must focus on assessment and treatment of her acute physical symptoms, which are the only chargeable ones as far as the HMO is concerned. The doctor cannot discover in depth how Betty is feeling or how she is coping with the whole illness experience.

PHASE 2: STABILIZATION

Physical-Behavioral Domain   As CFS patients enter Phase 2, they usually proceed physiologically to a plateau. Their fatigue follows predictable patterns, their muscle-joint pain remains stable or diminishes, they begin to recognize when they will have greater or lesser cognitive function, and so forth. During this period, symptoms stabilize and assume a somewhat familiar pattern. This in turn helps orient patients cognitively and psychologically. Table 8.2 lists the stages and characteristics of Phase 2.

Table 8.2
Phase 2: Stabilization/Normalization Failure

Physical–Behavioral

- Plateau
- Stabilization

Psychological

- Increased caution/Secondary wounding
- Social withdrawals/Social searching
- Service confusion/Searching
- Boundary confusion

Social–Interactive

- Interactive conflict/Cooperation
- Vicarious secondary wounding
- Vicarious traumatic manifestation
- Normalization failure

Psychological Domain   When CFS patients finally get a diagnosis, they almost always feel an initial sense of profound relief. Getting a name for their experience demystifies some of the disturbing uncertainties about their symptoms. Even when CFS patients do not get a diagnosis, they can begin to feel some increasing control when they discern a pattern in their symptoms and discover relationships between actions and symptoms. At the same time, their self-pathologizing and intrusive ideations usually decrease.

During both Phase 1 and Phase 2, CFS patients can experience stigmatization, rejection, and iatrogenic traumatization (Alonzo, 2000; Alonzo & Reynolds, 1996; Hampton & Frombach, 2000; Kwoh et al., 1992; Salmon, Peters, & Stanley, 1999; Starfield et al., 1981). As a result, they and their families may censor what they say and to whom. Patients often pretend to be well; they may attempt to "pass" for normal. At the same time, they frequently withdraw from hurtful social contacts; and when possible, they turn to others with CFS and to nontraumatizing clinicians.

The initial relief occasioned by diagnosis usually fades quickly. As CFS patients discover that their condition is not widely understood and that no treatment options promise a cure, they often begin searching for clinicians who can help them. This seeking behavior is natural to Phase 2 and, in many ways, is a sign of health. The patients are attempting to exert control over their losses and to reject the disempowerment they experienced in Phase 1. But confusion, urgency, and desperation can intensify as they make the rounds of medical providers and encounter conflicting opinions. Some CFS patients report a general lack of support and guidance from health care providers when they try to find out more about their illness.

CFS patients are also caught up in limit rejection and boundary confusion in Phase 2. They can no longer perform as they used to, but familial and community pressures, to say nothing of their own internal desires, make them attempt to maintain their former roles and schedules. Many people repeatedly fail. Their feelings of guilt and shame heighten an increasing sense of failure, worthlessness, and anomie.

CFS patients gradually learn that they can no longer do easy tasks like shopping or cleaning or even walking upstairs. They sometimes cannot perform simple tasks like balancing the checkbook. Like children, they are not completely confident about how their body, brain, or emotions will behave in any given situation.

As CFS patients progress through Phase 2, they start to understand the relationship between their activities and their symptoms. With appropriate guidance, they also develop insight into their own attitudes and those of the people around them. Maintaining insight is notoriously difficult. For CFS patients without strong clinical and social support, it can be easy to turn to destructive anodynes such as alcohol or drugs, which will usually spiral the patient back into a Phase 1 crisis. This can also happen when patients work beyond their capacity in an attempt to behave as they did before they became ill. Some patients never really leave Phase 1, while others endlessly cycle between Phase 1 and Phase 2 (Prochaska et al., 1994). They are not able to achieve Phase 3 acknowledgment of chronicity because they cannot tolerate the implications of permanent illness.

Social-Interactive Domain   In Phase 2, CFS patients encounter increased conflict as friends, family members, coworkers, and some care providers lose patience. By and large, society's model for illness is that of an acute condition. People are usually tolerant of CFS patients when they first become sick, but this is with the expectation that they will eventually be cured and return to their normal functioning. The persistence of symptoms can frustrate the patients' support networks. Part of their irritation stems from their own experience of vicarious secondary wounding. The response to CFS can dramatically alter the lifestyles and work habits of spouses and parents. These people witness the patients' suffering, but also their own and that of other family members. They can suffer "guilt by association," that is, the family is stigmatized for the patient's illness. Even clinicians can find themselves stigmatized when they treat the CFS population. It is not at all uncommon for significant others to depart sometime during Phase 2.

At the same time that CFS patients face increasing difficulties with their traditional support network, they begin to actively seek out a new network of friends and more information about their illness (Gilden, Hendryx, Clar, Casia, & Singh, 1992; Hinrichsen, Revenson, & Shinn, 1985; Humphreys, 1997; Nash & Kramer, 1993). It is often among these others of "like kind" that patients begin to establish a nucleus for a new community of supporters who will accept them as they are, with CFS.

Patients who are still working in Phase 2 usually find their functioning at work stabilizes at the same time as their physical symptoms. But they frequently cannot maintain the full work schedule that they had before the illness. In some cases, they ask for a leave of absence or take sick leave because they believe that a cure will allow them to return to full-time employment. Others ask for part-time work, quit their jobs, or are asked to resign. This adds a serious financial worry to all the other problems of CFS.

Betty's Story: Phase 2

Physical-Behavioral Domain   During Phase 2, Betty attempts to create order out of chaos. Her physical situation seems to have stabilized. No new symptoms have suddenly surprised her. None of her present symptoms seem to be getting worse. Her symptoms do not disappear, but they rarely exceed patterns that she is beginning to decipher. If she has a bad night sleeping, she knows that she will probably have a bad day. She will have more pain and more cognitive confusion. If she does two hours of steady work, she knows that her body aches are likely to increase and her glands will probably swell. Life is still very difficult, but Betty has identified a set of parameters around which she can function. Her health care professionals discuss a few of these parameters with her, but for the most part Betty discovers them on her own. To some extent, her newfound knowledge also orients the people around her.

While in Phase 2, Betty suffers two physical relapses. Each time, she suddenly becomes far more exhausted than usual. She cannot even lift herself out of bed without physical assistance, but feels as though she is being pulled down through her bed toward the center of the earth. Her head aches, her glands are very swollen, she has nausea, and she becomes intolerant of light and sound. She cannot organize her thinking at all. But both times she relapses, she eventually returns to a plateau of stabilized symptoms that she recognizes and can negotiate.

Psychological Domain   Unlike many people with a chronic illness, Betty actually receives a diagnosis. Initially, she feels enormous relief. Finally, she has an explanation for why she is so exhausted, why she cannot sleep, why she has muscle pain and headaches, and why she sometimes becomes mentally confused. Her uncertainties also lessen as she begins to recognize her symptom pattern. Furthermore, diagnosis gives her a way to learn about her condition so that she can exert a semblance of control over her life again. She reads everything she can about CFS and seeks out others with CFS so that she can discuss her situation in a supportive setting.

But Betty quickly learns that the diagnosis does not explain how her illness started or what is going to happen in the future, so ambiguity returns. No one seems to know what to do to cure her. No one can make her symptoms stop, and no one seems willing or able to tell her how she is supposed to live her life under these conditions.

Like most people in this country, Betty grew up believing that if she worked hard and told the truth, everything would come out all right in her life. But here she is, working hard to get better, telling the truth when she talks to family members and friends and clinicians, and yet a significant percentage of the time she finds, not acceptance, but rejection from many people. In fact, she is sometimes being blamed. So Betty has become extremely cautious. She carefully censors what she says and to whom. Whenever she possibly can, Betty acts as though she is well and nothing is wrong with her.

Betty decides to avoid such secondary wounding by withdrawing from any social contacts that may evoke negative judgments. Instead, she tries to get in touch with other CFS patients and CFS advocates because they are likely to be helpful and will understand her situation. She continues to read and research her condition and seeks sources of emotional sustenance to make up for the losses she has suffered.

Because her medical outcome is uncertain, and Betty still believes that cure must be a possibility, she suspects that her health care professionals are not adequate to deal with her problem. She collects the names of other doctors from friends and new CFS acquaintances and attempts to find a professional who will offer her better treatment and, she hopes, a cure. This behavior erodes the relationship she established with her primary care physician, who regards her actions as dysfunctional.

Because Betty finds little guidance and meets with confusing responses and even outright hostility as she tries other doctors, she attempts alternative treatment. A practitioner of shiatsu massage listens to her with enormous empathetic patience. Betty's cousin urges her to try acupuncture. A coworker swears that a complicated vitamin and supplement regime returned her bedridden niece to full functioning and could do the same for Betty.

Betty has lost a sense of her boundaries. To others, she seems to have returned to "normal"—a false appearance that she helps to create by her "passing" behavior. Betty's family and employer are encouraging, even urging, her to return to her former roles and schedules. But Betty cannot do this without serious repercussions. She has trouble getting up in the morning. Her husband has to make the children's school lunches. She can no longer serve on committees at work because she can just barely keep up with her regular obligations. Nothing about her body or her emotions or her mind acts the way it did in the past, and yet Betty keeps trying to behave as though she were the person she used to be. Despite her efforts, Betty fails daily at what she attempts, and daily she feels guilty and ashamed. Increasingly, she feels worthless.

Social-Interactive Domain   Betty experiences growing conflicts with family, friends, and some of her medical care providers as they lose patience with her failure to become symptom-free or to adjust to her illness in a way that allows her to return to her former functioning. Although she has a diagnosis, such treatment as she receives does not produce rapid, let alone complete, improvement. At one point when she was barely sleeping, Betty's doctor put her on a course of medication. She improved, but she still has consistent difficulties.

Bob has told Betty that she is no longer the person he married and this is not the life he signed up for. She has got to change if their marriage is to continue. Betty can tell that her coworkers are annoyed and believe that she could function a lot better if she just pulled herself together and put her mind on the job. One of them knows a CFS patient of higher functioning and tells others at work that she cannot understand why Betty does not manage as well as her friend does. Betty is not imperceptive. She knows that people think she is not trying hard enough. To make matters worse, a close friend with deep religious convictions has urged Betty to pray, saying that if Betty has a sincere desire to get better and asks for God's help, God will cure her. Betty does not share her friend's convictions, but deep inside she fears that maybe she is sick because she is somehow unsatisfactory in God's eyes.

As Betty goes through cycles of relapse and remission, all the people in her life experience them as well. They become as exhausted by the process as Betty does, and they are traumatized just as she is. Bob has lost the wife he married and the life he had, and his new life is not at all what he wants. Their son, Michael, has always liked school and has done well, but now his grades are beginning to suffer. Lisa is behaving badly at home, and she has taken up with a troubled crowd at school. Betty does not know whether this is just a part of adolescence, or whether Lisa and Michael are reacting to her health problems and her squabbles with Bob over money, the division of labor at home, and her condition.

Betty's husband and children are not mean-spirited. They are sad and scared to see this person who is very important to them suffer pain, confusion, and unhappiness. Outside the house, they suffer a kind of guilt by association. Lisa's friends sometimes treat her as though she is as weird as her mother, and Lisa overheard one of them say that Lisa's mom was an alcoholic who was always sleeping it off. Bob's boss is clearly concerned about whether Bob will be able to fulfill his job obligations, given the demands of Betty's illness. Some secretly wonder whether CFS might be catching and just for safety's sake, many keep their distance.

Even Betty's doctor is affected. Some clinicians who treat CFS patients report that colleagues are skeptical when making referrals. Specialists in CFS sometimes even meet skepticism in social settings. A neurologist to whom Betty's doctor was going to refer her said that he did not think CFS was a valid diagnosis and that he believed Betty was suffering from a psychological condition. In addition, few health insurance organizations encourage doctors to engage in the extensive, prolonged dialogue that chronically ill patients require.

Because normalization failure is so common in Phase 2, it is not unusual for either the chronically ill or those around them to turn to such anodynes as alcohol or drugs, and for people in the social network to avoid or abuse the chronically ill individual. Any of these factors or even a totally new factor can produce another crisis in the chronically ill, returning them to Phase 1. Bob's mother dies and the entire family must deal with that loss. Later, Betty has a high fever during a bout with flu that triggers a severe relapse.

Without informed clinical guidance, many chronically ill people become caught in a repeating cycle of Phase 1 and Phase 2 (Prochaska et al., 1992, 1994). Each new crisis produces new wounding and secondary wounding (Alonzo, 2000; Fullilove et al., 1992; Turner & Lloyd, 1995). With luck, following each crisis the patient manages to arrive at a plateau of manageable symptoms, until the next crisis sends the whole system into chaos again. Some people, particularly those on the margins of society who have almost no sources of support, never escape Phase 1, but are buffeted from crisis to crisis, relieved only by alcohol and drugs.

Betty is not in that position. She has some warm and loyal friends. Her supervisor persuades the bank management to let Betty take a position with fewer hours. And a social worker newly affiliated with Betty's doctor's office becomes involved in helping Betty cope with CFS.

PHASE 3: RESOLUTION

Physical-Behavioral Domain   Many Phase 3 CFS patients maintain a continued plateau, but relapses occur. Sometimes old symptoms worsen or new symptoms appear. Some CFS patients experience improvement. If a relapse takes place, it is sometimes in response to the typical cycling of CFS symptoms, but it may also be triggered by persistent attempts to engage in precrisis tasks, roles, and pursuits. True entry into Phase 3 comes, however, when CFS patients recognize that they cannot perform as they used to in the past. Table 8.3 lists the stages and characteristics of Phase 3.

Psychological Domain   CFS patients in Phase 3 suffer a secondary emotional crisis or grief reaction when they acknowledge the chronic nature of their condition. They finally realize that their lives have changed forever, and they begin

Table 8.3
Phase 3: Resolution

Physical–Behavioral

- Emergency stage/Diminishment; improvement
- Continued plateau/Stabilization
- Relapse

Psychological

- Grief reaction/Compassion response
- Identification of precrisis self
- Role and identity experimentation
- Returning locus of control
- Awareness of societal effects
- Spiritual development

Social–Interactive

- Breaking silence/Engulfment in stigma
- Confrontation
- Role experimentation: social, vocational
- Integration/Separation/Loss of supporters

the process of mourning their precrisis self. They typically feel demoralized and devalued, for they see that they can no longer carry out their roles in life—as parent, worker, lover, friend—in the way they had always thought they would. They may question what good they are, who they are, and why they should continue to exist at all. This appropriate, necessary grief reaction—their "dark night of the soul"—is a tenuous time. Individuals can be lost in their own understandable withdrawal, fall victim to predatory providers, or succumb to despair and thoughts of suicide.

If, however, they can work through this existential angst and establish meaning in their lives, CFS patients can then take marked steps toward constructing an authentic new self and a new life. Meaning is established over the phase process through three transformational steps: (1) The allowance of suffering as opposed to its rejection and the subsequent rejection of the suffering self; (2) the development of a compassionate response to the suffering of the rejected, sick, stigmatized self; and (3) the development of respect for their suffering and their ability to live with it and despite it. Creative activity is one of the most successful paths leading to the discovery of meaning. So, too, is a sustaining faith on the part of the care provider that the CFS patient can construct an authentic new self and develop a complete, three-dimensional life.

As CFS patients move through Phase 3, they develop a strongly internalized locus of control and increased tolerance for the ambiguity and chronicity of CFS. They openly express compassion for themselves, and they begin to reconstruct an illness narrative that eliminates the harmful social messages they have endured until now. Their work to achieve meaning involves them in philosophical or spiritual development that offers an ongoing framework for adapting to new experiences, whether good or bad.

Social-Interactive Domain   In Phase 3, CFS patients may undergo even greater losses than they did in Phase 2 as significant others depart, clinicians give up, and friends disappear. They may continue to experience abandonment, isolation, and stigmatization. At the same time, they continue to pursue new friendships and the support of others with CFS. Some Phase 3 patients can still feel engulfed in stigma and some do not, but in either case they now refuse to remain silent. They speak up against stigmatization and confront it instead of avoiding persons who behave inappropriately toward them. As they work through their existential issues and begin constructing a new authentic self, they begin experimenting with new social roles and sometimes with new jobs or vocations. They may engage in social or political activism related to CFS.

BETTY'S STORY: PHASE 3

Physical-Behavioral Domain   In Phase 3, Betty enjoys long periods of stabilized symptoms, sometimes even improvement, but she still has relapses. Most of these are simply in the nature of the illness. As Betty comes to comprehend the chronicity and the ambiguity inherent in her condition, she lets go of her search for an elusive cure and works instead to integrate her illness into a new life.

Psychological Domain   Twice in Phase 2, Betty suffered severe relapses brought about in part by her repeated attempts to do all the things that her precrisis self did. Throughout that time, she wanted to be her former self, and everyone around her wanted her to be that person, too. But repeated relapses have taught her that she cannot sustain the roles that she had always thought she would fulfill as spouse, parent, worker, or friend, or at least not in the way she used to imagine. Betty comes to understand that her life has changed entirely and forever.

With the help and encouragement of her new CFS friends and the social worker, she explores and expresses the grief she feels for the loss of her old self and she mourns the end of that life.

At this point, all the major existential questions come into play. Betty wonders, "Who am I?" "What good am I?" "Why did this happen to me?" "Why should I live?" "Is there any value to my life?" During this painful period, she struggles to locate a meaning for her existence and her suffering. Betty is very vulnerable. She could be lost because of her considerable social withdrawal. She could fall victim to cynical and predatory providers. She could give way to despair and attempt to kill herself.

But Betty is fortunate. Her new friends and the social worker help Betty navigate the difficult course between necessary grieving for her past self and foundering in clinical depression. She learns not to reject but to allow her new suffering self and to have compassion for herself and her suffering as well. This is not an easy task because Betty is constantly receiving messages from people she knows telling her that if she stays the way she is, if she remains ill, then they no longer want her among them.

To move forward from grief and mourning, Betty tries to discover meaning for what has happened to her and locate a way to live in the future. She begins to engage in philosophical or spiritual thinking in order to come to a new place. Betty starts by learning to respect the person she is now—not the person she might become, but who she is right now.

As is typically the case, Betty does this through a creative act that becomes an act of meaning development. She decides to write a journal describing her experiences. Other people she knows have done things as various as taking up painting, becoming CFS advocates, even becoming gourmet cooks. One friend of hers actually made a movie. In composing her journal, Betty re-creates herself—she integrates herself and begins to discover meaning in her experience.

Betty draws heavily on her social worker's clinical skills, personal support, and encouragement and on a variety of wisdom traditions that seem to speak to her. Betty is not religious in the traditional sense. In fact, she regards herself as an atheist. But since she has consciously begun thinking about the basic issues of life and meaning, she has discovered aspects of Buddhism and Celtic philosophy that resonates strongly with her personal vision of what is significant in life.

Social-Interactive Domain   The strides Betty makes in her psychological evolution during Phase 3 do not occur in a benignly static social environment. She endures a considerable blow when she and Bob agree that they must divorce. At first, Betty worries terribly about how she will manage. She still has a job at the bank, but she has always been on Bob's health plan. As part of the divorce settlement, he agrees to keep her and the children covered. As time passes, Bob demonstrates that he will continue to meet his financial obligations to her and the children. He is also good about having the children visit regularly, which gives Betty needed quiet time and reduces her anxiety that the divorce will cause harmful distance between the children and their father. Betty knows that in this divorce experience she is much more fortunate than one of her friends with CFS who kept custody of her children, but lost her home when she subsequently lost her job.

Encouraged by a CFS friend, Betty explicitly asks Lisa and Michael for help at home. To her surprise, Lisa responds enthusiastically, especially to cooking. Michael is good about drying dishes and starting a load of dirty clothes in the washer if reminded, but recently he has gotten restive about living with "a bunch of women." Betty, who could not have endured letting him go two years ago, now feels confident about his basic attachment to her and is planning to let him spend his next school year with his father.

At the bank, Betty feels competent to deal with her present job requirements, and her coworkers have gotten so used to her condition that they have more or less forgotten it. Her confidence was further bolstered when the social worker offered to conduct a workplace consultation on her behalf. Betty decided that it was not necessary at the present time, but she felt she had someone on her side if she should need it.

Betty knows, however, that her job security depends almost entirely on her supervisor, and she has begun investigating other part-time work she might do, perhaps at home. The social worker has also reminded Betty that she is eligible for disability if she is unable to work, and she has been inquiring among her CFS friends about this as well.

In any social arena now, Betty refuses to pretend or to keep silent about her illness. When people react badly or seek to label or stigmatize her, she may confront them about their bias. She has been surprised at how empowered such behavior makes her feel, and she is even thinking about becoming formally involved in advocacy work. The end of her marriage and the inevitable loss of some old friends and acquaintances have forced Betty to consider new roles and to seek new friends. Although this experience has been intensely painful, Betty has survived it. She is surprised to find how positive the process has turned out to be and how much she likes her new self.

As Betty freely acknowledges, it would have been very hard for her to navigate this passage without the devoted and informed help of her care provider—the social worker. Not only did this woman affirm the realities of Betty's trauma and illness, but she listened and counseled sympathetically as Betty traversed the process of finding her new self. She suggested a number of books that she thought might help Betty think about the philosophical questions involved, and put her in touch with a clinical expert in issues of major loss who helped Betty discover what problems had bedrock significance for her.

PHASE 4: INTEGRATION

Physical-Behavioral Domain CFS patients in Phase 4 may experience physiological plateau, improvement, or relapse. By this time, CFS patients recognize the cyclic nature of their illness and no longer regard relapse as failure. Relapse is simply the beginning of another cycle that they must integrate. This understanding manifests the true nature of recovery for CFS patients, which is the integration of their CFS into an ongoing, full life. When patients experience new symptoms or familiar ones worsen, they contact their health care providers immediately. Otherwise, they maintain a sensible monitoring of their condition and see clinicians on whatever schedules their clinicians have advised. Table 8.4 lists the stages and characteristics of Phase 4.

Psychological Domain Phase 4 CFS patients have achieved a true integration of the precrisis self with the newly claimed respected self who has suffered and endured. They maintain this achievement through a daily commitment to allowing their suffering, meeting it with compassion, and treating it with respect. Life for them will necessarily include small daily acts of bravery in the presence of stigmatization, rejection, or the pains of CFS itself. Patients do this in an exercise of free will, not because they are forced to. They formulate and then live up to a

Table 8.4
Phase 4: Integration

Physical–Behavioral
- Recovery stage
- Continued plateau/Improvement/Relapse

Psychological
- Role/Identity integration
- New personal best
- Continued spiritual and emotional development

Social–Interactive
- New and reintegrated supporters
- Alternative vocation/Activities

new "personal best." They continue to work on meaning development in conjunction with their continuing pursuit of philosophical or spiritual development.

Social-Interactive Domain   In Phase 4, CFS patients continue to be involved in creative and social action. They expand their circle of supporters, but their increased self-assurance and self-confidence also permits them to attempt reintegrating old supporters who fell away in the past. They are often willing and able to help these people learn, if these old friends wish to be reintegrated. Although many CFS patients have difficulty maintaining a full-time work schedule, many of them, especially in Phase 4, find vocational activities that allow them to participate to the limit of their abilities in activities that they value.

BETTY'S STORY: PHASE 4

Physical-Behavioral Domain   For the most part, Betty experiences continuous plateau, and occasionally she enjoys periods of distinct improvement. But she has also had three relapses, one severe and two lesser ones. Betty now realizes that relapses happen, and she no longer regards them as some failure on her part. But short of death, which will happen to everyone eventually, she intends to try to reintegrate herself after each relapse experience. Betty comprehends that integration is the "recovery" she should strive to maintain.

Psychological Domain   Betty maintains her new self by consciously recognizing who she is now and by standing with herself. This does not mean that life has become easy. Sometimes Betty cannot climb stairs at all. Sometimes she is so debilitated she must use a wheelchair, which she hates. She can still become mentally confused, especially if she overextends. She still experiences some difficult moments of stigmatization and rejection, and even her own pain. But she speaks out against bias and has learned to endure the symptoms of her illness. She has created a new ideal self and takes pleasure in seeing how well she can live up to it.

Betty finds that a constant, active, conscious consideration of meaning and purpose enriches her life and places her experiences, both positive and negative, in a context larger than herself. She still finds great solace in Buddhist conceptions of suffering, but she has also discovered a new trove of wisdom in the material discussed in an online Great Books group that she has joined.

Social-Interactive Domain   Betty continues to nurture the new friendships that she began establishing in Phase 3. She also sought out her younger sister, from whom she had been estranged as an adult, and the two have found they enjoy the openness and honesty of their new relationship as much as they like reminiscing about their childhood. Betty's frankness about her condition and her refusal to accept derogatory estimations make it perfectly clear to people who she is now, and some admire her for it and see the truth of her self-assessment.

Betty is about to change her job. While she worked at the bank, and when she was at home sick, she became adept with computers, so she has decided to take a position running a Web site and chat room. Although Bob has remarried—an event that threw Betty into an emotional crisis—he is intrigued with her new job and enjoys discussing it with her. Relations between the two are better than they have been for many years.

Betty even dares to contemplate entering a meaningful sexual relationship again. One of her CFS friends remarried recently, which gives her hope, and she has met a man she likes very much in a monthly writing class. Because of his encouragement, she sent part of her journal to a CFS newsletter.

Betty knows that crises and disasters happen all the time in life. She worries a lot about her children. One of Michael's friends was just arrested for stealing a car, and she thinks that Lisa may have had a pregnancy scare. One of her CFS friends took a terrible turn for the worse and has been bedridden for 3 months. This scares Betty terribly, for she knows the same could happen to her. But Betty is learning to separate those things she can control from those she cannot. Although it is a continuous effort, she endeavors to exert herself for the things she can affect and to endure with grace those she cannot.

REFERENCES

Alonzo, A. A. (2000). The experience of chronic illness and posttraumatic stress disorder: The consequences of cumulative adversity. *Social Science and Medicine, 50,* 1475–1484.

Alonzo, A. A., & Reynolds, V. R. (1996). Emotions and care-seeking during acute myocardial infarction: A model for intervention. *International Journal of Sociology and Social Policy, 16*(9/10), 97–122.

Baldwin, B. A. (1978). A paradigm for the classification of emotional crises: Implications for crisis intervention. *American Journal of Orthopsychiatry, 48*(3), 538–551.

Berger, K. S., & Thompson, R. A. (1995). *The developing person through childhood and adolescence.* New York: Worth Publications.

Blalock, S. J., DeVellis, R. F., Giorgino, K. B., DeVillis, B. M., Gold, D. T., Dooley, M. A., et al. (1996). Osteoporosis prevention in premenopausal women: Using a stage model approach to examine the predictors of behavior. *Health Psychology, 15,* 84–93.

Botha, L. F. H. (1996). Posttraumatic stress disorder and illness behavior in HIV+ patients. *Psychological Reports, 79,* 843–845.

Brownell, K. D., Marlatt, G. A., Lichtenstein, E., & Wilson, G. T. (1986). Understanding and preventing relapse. *American Psychologist, 41*(7), 765–782.

Clark, M. L., & Gioro, S. (1998). Nurses, indirect trauma, and prevention. *Image: Journal of Nursing Scholarship, 31*(1), 85–87.

DiClemente, C. C. (1991). Motivational interviewing and the stages of change. In W. R. Miller & S. Rollnick (Eds.), *Motivational interviewing: Preparing people for change* (pp. 191–202). New York: Guilford Press.

Engel, G. L. (1977). The need for a new medical model: A challenge for biomedicine. *Science, 196,* 129–136.

Erikson, E. H. (1959). Identity and the life cycle: Selected papers. *Psychological Issues, 1,* 50–100.

Fennell, P. A. (1993). A systematic, four-stage progressive model for mapping the CFIDS experience. *CFIDS Chronicle, 1*(3/4), 40–46.

Fennell, P. A. (1995a). CFS sociocultural influences and trauma: Clinical considerations. *Journal of Chronic Fatigue Syndrome, 1*(3/4), 159–173.

Fennell, P. A. (1995b). The four progressive stages of the CFS experience: A coping tool for patients. *Journal of Chronic Fatigue Syndrome, 1*(3/4), 69–79.

Fennell, P. A. (1998). Capturing the different phases of the CFS illness. *CFIDS Chronicle, 11*(3), 3–16.

Fennell, P. A. (2001). *The chronic illness workbook: Strategies and solutions for taking back your life.* San Francisco: New Harbinger.

Fennell, P. A. (2004). *Managing chronic illness using the Four-Phase treatment approach: A mental health professionl's guide to helping chronically ill people.* Hoboken, NJ: Wiley.

Fennell, P. A., Levine, P., Uslan, D., & Furst, G. (2001). *Applications for the practicing physician: A multidisciplinary approach.* AACFS Conference, Seattle, WA.

Friedberg, F., & Jason, L. A. (1998). *Understanding chronic fatigue syndrome: An empirical guide to assessment and treatment.* Washington, DC: American Psychological Association.

Fullilove, M. T., Lown, E. A., & Fullilove, R. E. (1992). Crack 'hos and skeezers: Traumatic experiences of women crack users. *Journal of Sex Research, 29*(2), 275–287.

Gilden, J. L., Hendryx, M. S., Clar, S., Casia, C., & Singh, S. P. (1992). Diabetes support groups improve health care of older diabetic patients. *Journal of the American Geriatrics Society, 40,* 147–150.

Hampton, M. R., & Frombach, J. (2000). Women's experience of traumatic stress in cancer treatment. *Health Care for Women International, 21,* 67–76.

Hayes, V. E. (1997). Families and children's chronic conditions: Knowledge development and methodological considerations. *Scholarly Inquiry for Nursing Practice: An International Journal, 11*(4), 259–291.

Hinrichsen, G. A., Revenson, T. A., & Shinn, M. (1985). Does self-help help? An empirical investigation of scoliosis peer support groups. *Journal of Social Issues, 41*(1), 65–87.

Humphreys, K. (1997, Spring). Individual and social benefits of mutual aid self-help groups. *Social Policy,* 12–19.

Jason, L. A., Fennell, P. A., Klein, S., Fricano, G., Halpert, J. A., & Taylor, R. R. (1999). An investigation of the different phases of the CFS illness. *Journal of Chronic Fatigue Syndrome, 5*(3/4), 35–54.

Jason, L. A., Fennell, P. A., Taylor, R. R., Fricano, G., & Halpert, J. A. (2000). An empirical verification of the Fennell Phases of the CFS illness. *Journal of Chronic Fatigue Syndrome, 6*(1), 47–56.

Jason, L. A., Fricano, G., Taylor, R. R., Halpert, J., Fennell, P. A., Klein, S., et al. (2000). Chronic fatigue syndrome: An examination of the phases. *Journal of Clinical Psychology,* December, 1497–1508.

Kohlberg, L. (1959). *Stages in the development of moral thought and action.* New York: Holt.

Kubler-Ross, E. (1969). *On death and dying.* New York: Macmillan.

Kwoh, C. K., O'Connor, G. T., Regan-Smith, M. G., Olmstead, E. M., Brown, L. A., Burnett, J. B., et al. (1992). Concordance between clinician and patient assessment of physical and mental health status. *Journal of Rheumatology, 19*(7), 1031–1037.

Lindy, J. D., Greene, B. L., & Grace, M. C. (1987). The stressor criterion and posttraumatic stress disorder. *Journal of Nervous and Mental Diseases, 175,* 269–272.

Nash, K., & Kramer, K. D. (1993). Self-help for sickle cell disease in African American communities. *Journal of Applied Behavioral Science, 29,* 202–215.

Nicassio, P. M., & Smith, T. W. (1995). *Managing chronic illness: A biopsychosocial perspective.* Washington, DC: American Psychological Association.

Piaget, J. (1952). *The origins of intelligence in children.* New York: International Universities Press.

Prochaska, J. O., DiClemente, C. C., & Norcross, J. C. (1992). In search of how people change: Applications to addictive behavior. *American Psychologist, 47*(9), 1102–1114.

Prochaska, J. O., Norcross, J. C., & DiClemente, C. C. (1994). The transtheoretical model of change and HIV prevention: A review. *Health Educational Quarterly, 21*(4), 471–486.

Prochaska, J. O., & Velicer, W. F. (1997). The transtheoretical model of health behavior change. *American Journal of Health Promotion, 12*(1), 38–48.

Rakowski, W., Dube, C., Marcus, B. H., Prochaska, J. O., Velicer, W. F., & Abrams, D. B. (1992). Assessing elements of women's decisions about mammography. *Health Psychology, 11*, 111–118.

Rolland, J. S. (1994). *Families, illness, and disability: An interactive treatment model.* New York: Basic Books.

Rosenberg, M., & Molho, P. (1998). Nonviolent (emphatic) communication for health care providers. *Haemmophilia, 4*, 335–340.

Salmon, P., Peters, S., & Stanley, I. M. (1999). Patients' perceptions of medical explanations for somatization disorders: Qualitative analysis. *British Medical Journal, 318*, 371–376.

Scott, M. J., & Stradling, S. G. (1994). Posttraumatic stress disorder without the trauma. *British Journal of Clinical Psychology, 33*, 71–74.

Starfield, B., Wray, C., Hess, K., Gross, R., Birk, P., & D'Lugoff, B. (1981). The influence of patient-practitioner agreement on outcome of care. *American Journal of Public Health, 71*(2), 127–130.

Sutton, S. R. (1997). Transtheoretical model of behavior change. In A. Baum, S. Newman, J. Weinman, R. West, & C. McManus (Eds.), *Cambridge handbook of psychology, health and medicine* (pp. 180–183). Cambridge, MA: Cambridge University Press.

Turner, R. J., & Lloyd, D. A. (1995, December). Lifetime traumas and mental health: The significance of cumulative adversity. *Journal of Health and Social Behavior, 36*, 360–376.

Weinstein, N. D., Rothman, A. J., & Sutton, S. R. (1998). Stage theories of health behavior: Conceptual and methodological issues. *Health Psychology, 17*, 290–299.

CHAPTER 9

Social Effects of Chronic Disorders

KAT DUFF

J ULIA, A STRIKING, soft-spoken young woman of mixed heritage with a keen mind and passionate convictions, is a political activist. She came down with chronic fatigue syndrome (CFS) while in college and within months developed several serious infections. She became so tired that she lost much of her ability to think or function. There were days she was unable to cook a meal or converse with a neighbor. At first, the doctors could not find anything wrong. One recommended antidepressants, as if she were not really sick. "I wanted to shout at him: 'Wake up! Listen!'" she told me in a flash of fury. We were sitting across the table in a small coffee shop, and I had asked her to describe her experience of living with CFS, so that I could draw from several personal histories—not just my own—in writing this chapter. After telling me that her health was much better some four years after the onset of her illness, Julia leaned back, paused, and reflected: "It was one of Dante's circles of Hell. I lay in bed, caught in this horrible internal reality with no connection to anyone outside, because no one knew what was going on inside."

At the end of our conversation, Julia told me a dream she had the worst year of her illness in which she had sores all over her body that were bleeding and full of pus. In the dream, she kept asking people to call an ambulance, but no one would listen to her (J. Roll, personal communication, December 2000).

THE PHANTOM DISEASE

The social and psychological effects of living with CFS derive from several sources: the physical symptoms of the disease, the cultural response to fatiguing illnesses, and the efforts the sick make to stretch lives worth living between these circumstances. For those who want a schematic map of CFS experience, I recommend Patricia A. Fennell's four-stage model that delineates what most people with CFS undergo during the course of their illness, from the initial onset to the eventual integration (Fennell, 1993, 1995). This chapter takes a less linear approach in an effort to stay true to the confounding ambiguity, unpredictability, and changeability of the CFS experience.

Fatiguing illnesses like CFS are commonly hard to diagnose and even harder to treat within the confines of contemporary medical knowledge. The best of doctors shake their heads, baffled and frustrated. As a result, our society typically views fatiguing illnesses, and the people beset by them, with suspicion and neglect.

The erasure begins with language. Look at the words used to describe the symptoms of CFS in the Centers for Disease Control and Prevention (CDC) definition: (incapacitating) chronic fatigue, impaired memory or concentration, sore throat, tender lymph nodes, muscle pain, headaches, unrefreshing sleep, postexertion malaise, and multijoint pain (Fukuda et al., 1994). These words and phrases may be proper medical terms, but to those who embody them, they are cruel euphemisms that do not begin to describe the experience of living with CFS.

"Tender lymph nodes" can feel like long thin knives twisting into the neck, groin, or underarms, and may become so painful that patients cannot move their arms or legs without crying aloud. "Impaired memory" can make it impossible to complete a thought, remember what one was just told, dial a phone number, recall a friend's name, follow directions, find the car, or operate an ATM machine. Fatigue is so overwhelming that many people with CFS do not have the energy to brush their teeth in the morning or take their clothes off at night. Some are unable to stand long enough to heat up a can of soup; others are too weak to open a door or sit up in a chair. A trip to the post office may take all of the person's energy for the day.

On a good day, someone with CFS might be able to go to the grocery store or wash the bedroom windows, but always with the danger of triggering postexertion malaise. The term *malaise* is defined as "an indefinite feeling of uneasiness, or lack of health" in medical usage. It does not even hint at the extremity of the experience—the burning muscles, splitting headaches, leaden exhaustion, fevers, and despair that develop within hours of physical activity and last for weeks, if not months. At best, symptom descriptors of CFS are inadequate to the lived reality; at worst, they minimize and deny the full horror of it and betray a medical bias against unexplained illnesses.

To some extent, this discrepancy between words and experience is a problem of language, and of the English language in particular. Some observers argue that pain shatters language, or that it is a language of its own apart from the everyday one we use to relate with others in the world (Scarry, 1985). There are many varieties of suffering for which English has no words, just as there are worlds of pleasure and ecstasy that it cannot articulate. As many a frustrated writer can attest, stories of spiritual revelation have a way of falling flat and sounding stupid, while descriptions of sexual experience often come across as laughable or pornographic. In the Western world, written language was originally developed to record the commercial transactions of goods, and it has never lost this utilitarian purpose and focus on observable things. As the dominant language for scientific inquiry and economic enterprise throughout the world, English has become an extraordinarily apt tool for detecting, naming, and describing the interactions of observable physical entities; but it is clumsy, if not inept, at giving expression to inwardly felt experience.

People with CFS and other fatiguing disorders find themselves in the curious position of having to endure a devastating disease without a consistent, identifiable physical marker or pathogen. As Julia's story makes clear, one can be so sick as to be unable to work or attend school, and yet look "fine" and have "normal" lab test results. There are no skin lesions, swollen joints, palpable growths, or elevated white blood cell counts; the symptoms and impairments of these disorders are largely invisible to the naked eye and microscopic lens. Moreover, they fluctuate unpredictably, migrate around the body, and involve almost every organ system that enables us to live, breathe, and function fully. Although research has begun to verify situational cardiac disturbances, enzyme pathway disruptions, neurological abnormalities, and malfunctions of the hypothalamus-pituitary-adrenal axis that could account for many of CFS patients' complaints, the etiology of this syndrome remains unknown. Its very existence is still questioned in many quarters (Lapp, 2000). We are quick to ignore and reject what we cannot see and do not understand.

I have a friend whose mother developed pain in her abdomen several years ago. She went to her doctor, who ran a few tests, assured her nothing was wrong, and sent her home with suggestions for diet changes. The pain increased, making it difficult to eat. She consulted another doctor, who ran more tests and dismissed her with the advice to take aspirin if needed. My friend was told that "complaints like these" are common among elderly people, and she had the impression the doctor was suggesting her mother was undergoing something psychological, such as a growing fear of death or the early stages of dementia. Her mother stopped eating solid foods, lost 20 pounds, and refused to go to another doctor. "They have already told me nothing's wrong," she insisted. "I'm just getting old."

My friend began to wonder whether her mother was manufacturing or exaggerating complaints to get attention. The weight loss confused and angered her, as she vacillated between worrying that her mother was seriously ill, and fuming that her mother could not be more direct in asking for what she needed. This went on for several months, until her mother called in the middle of the night with excruciating pain. My friend arranged for an ambulance to take her to the hospital and flew down to see her again. The hospital doctors ran more tests, including a CT scan, and found cancer that had metastasized throughout her mother's abdomen.

My point in telling this story is not to complain about inadequate or incompetent medical care; frankly, I am amazed that physicians can identify disease at all these days, given the complexity of our physical existence, the massive body of available knowledge, and the limits of time and testing imposed by managed care. More interesting to me is the assumption embedded in this not-so-unusual story that experience is not real until it can be detected on a biological level. My friend's mother had "nothing wrong," despite her voiced pain and visible weight loss, until cancerous growths were found inside her body; only then did her illness assume a legitimate existence. Until that point, aspersions were cast not on the medical personnel unable to detect the disease, but on the patient for voicing complaints that could not be scientifically verified.

Many initially undetectable and incomprehensible diseases—and the individuals beset by them—have followed this torturous path from repudiation to legitimacy. Asthma, lupus, multiple sclerosis, Lyme disease, and Agent Orange disease were all initially dismissed as psychiatric in origin until adequate tests could be found or developed to verify their reality. Now CFS is making that journey.

The CDC first published a "working definition" of chronic fatigue syndrome in 1988 and revised it in 1994. Diagnosis is made by confirming the existence of four or more of eight debilitating symptoms with relatively sudden onset and lasting more than 6 months, ruling out other diseases that could account for the symptoms, such as mononucleosis, multiple sclerosis, Lyme disease, postpolio syndrome, thyroid deficiency, cancer, and lupus. There is still no definitive diagnostic test. Public denial of the reality of CFS in the United States is well documented (Johnson, 1996). Trivializing media portrayals, medical bias, and the refusal of the CDC to study the disease or educate the public about it have fueled this disbelief. The vast majority of sufferers (approximately 80%) have been women, in a culture that has historically dismissed "female complaints," which may contribute to this communal denial.

People with CFS commonly report that they have had to consult several—sometimes 20 or 30, even 50—physicians before they find one who can give them a diagnosis. Only those patients with money, time, and confidence to spare can continue such a frustrating and demoralizing search, which explains in part why CFS originally got its reputation as "yuppie flu." The implication was that it was a fad among young urban professionals trying to pursue careers, raise families, and play extravagantly. In fact, research indicates that CFS is most prevalent among African Americans and Latinos who work skilled, semiskilled, and unskilled jobs, and that less than 10% get a diagnosis (Jason, Richman, et al. 1999). The CDC has also found that CFS is more common than lung cancer, breast cancer, and HIV infection in women; yet it receives little serious attention in the press or medical community (Kenny, 1998).

This public denial has devastating consequences for those afflicted. The economic relief our society offers the seriously ill—sick pay, insurance coverage, disability benefits, and Social Security—is difficult, if not impossible, to access without a medical diagnosis. Unable to work, many people with CFS run through their savings and slide into poverty within months unless they are supported by another, are independently wealthy, or are well enough to work part-time. Some have lost their homes and have had to borrow from friends, live in cars, or move in with reluctant relatives because they have had no other options. Treatment, be it symptom-relieving medication or simple rest, is too often out of reach.

When authority figures like doctors and Social Security officials shake their heads in disbelief, family, friends, and associates are apt to lose faith and question whether the sick person might just be lazy, depressed, hysterical, or manipulative. Familial and societal support structures can easily crumble in the wake of CFS and other debilitating, hard-to-diagnose illnesses. Almost everyone I interviewed for this chapter told me only a few people in their lives believed they were truly sick and understood the full extent of their debility. Some friends and family remain in touch and continue to care without necessarily believing or understanding; the rest fall away. Unable to face the patient's suffering, feeling helpless to stop it, and fearing that reaching out would endanger them, they turn away and disappear.

A parallel crumbling occurs inside people with CFS, as they begin to doubt their own body-based knowledge and experience, a process that writer Dorothy Wall called "self-erasure" (Wall, 2000). When I was at my sickest, I remember thinking things like: "I can't believe this is happening. It can't be this bad. I must be exaggerating. Maybe it's menopause, stress, nerves, age, or a bad flu bug. It will pass like everything else. In a month I'll be laughing about my hysteria. Forget about it and go on." The moment I felt better, I would resume my previous activities, ignoring my increasing tiredness, muscle aches, forgetfulness, dizziness, sore lymph nodes, fever sweats, and chills. As a result, my illness progressed until I collapsed and literally could not get off the floor.

While denial may lower the mortality rate among heart attack survivors, it is dangerous to those living with fatiguing disorders because it feeds a vicious cycle of overactivity, exhaustion, and exacerbation of symptoms. Every time people with CFS go beyond their limits (which may simply entail washing their hair, standing in line in the cold for a movie, or attending Thanksgiving dinner), they pay a dear price. It might mean a bad headache, terrible joint pain, days of mental fog and depression, or weeks—even months—of recovery. CFS seems uniquely fashioned to undo our cultural habits of ignoring physically felt experience to remain active and productive. Survival requires the sick to honor their inward experience, even if the world will not acknowledge its validity.

With a vigilant self-awareness, sick people learn to notice the tiniest shifts in their bodies—the skin crawling on the back of the neck, the inability to remember a name or finish a sentence, a scratchiness at the top of the throat—and take heed. They monitor how they feel every hour of the day to determine what they can and cannot do next. In so doing, they begin to manage their symptoms and stabilize a modicum of health. Many people with CFS will tell you that when they learned to recognize their limits and live within them, their health began to turn around. For some, it has put them on the road to recovery and kept them there. For others, it put the brake on a downward slide and stabilized a frightening situation. It does not control or relieve all symptoms, but it lessens fatigue over time and replenishes reserves of energy.

When people with CFS use the information they gather from monitoring their symptoms and energy levels to make decisions, they also restore a trust in their own authority under the siege of cultural pressures. They simply cannot afford to obey those unspoken social rules that take valuable energy—to stand listening until someone has finished talking, wait in line for their turn, return phone calls, or stay until the end of the performance—when their health is at stake. The social shame and embarrassment that enforce these conventions are small prices to pay for immediate relief and long-term restoration. Sawnie, who has lived with CFS for 5 years, explained: "I've lost all pride. I'm shameless about lying down. I'll lie down in the middle of a busy airport if I have to—and I have" (S. Morris, personal communication, January 2001).

THE ENDLESS LETTING GO

Jorna's mother had CFS for 8 years. Each year, her condition worsened, and there was no indication that it would ever improve. Her husband could not believe the extent of her pain and disability, and grew increasingly frustrated and annoyed. She stopped asking for help or support from anyone. Her despair grew to mammoth proportions, and finally she killed herself. A year later, Jorna was diagnosed with CFS.

Since her diagnosis, Jorna's health has gone up and down, in what many describe as the "roller coaster" of living with this disease. When I spoke with Jorna, she was closing her small therapy practice to get the rest she needed, hoping she could get disability to support herself. Her dog Shadow lay on a couch nearby, a silent guardian presence. Jorna spoke slowly and softly, occasionally losing her train of thought, but persisting in the desire to describe her experience with honesty and precision. At one point, frustrated with the effort to find apt words, Jorna leaned forward and said, "I feel like a stone in a river, just being worn away, worn away" (J. White, personal communication, November 2000).

The losses that attend CFS are legion. People routinely become unable to work full-time, engage in physical activity, take vacations, socialize with friends, attend cultural events, and care for themselves or their loved ones. Marriages and partnerships founder and sometimes fall apart. In turn, these conditions erode the individual's sense of identity, independence, and community. The societal context of denial around this illness strips more away: financial and social support, confidence and trust in oneself and others, and faith in a just world. The absence of public concern, the paucity of research, and the lack of effective treatments or cures take away the last thing human beings have to hold onto in catastrophic times: hope.

Studies that compare the quality of life of people living with various illnesses indicate that individuals with CFS experience greater "functional severity" than individuals studied with heart disease, virtually all cancers, HIV, and all other chronic illnesses (Anderson & Ferrans, 1997). No wonder CFS patients sometimes envy people with terminal illnesses. As a friend of mine once said: "People with cancer fight to live, and people with CFS wish they could die."

The disease itself undoubtedly accounts for much of this debility, but an unresponsive and stigmatizing environment can only make things worse, as people struggle with unnecessary fear, anger, and shame, and those with limited support are forced to work or do chores that worsen their condition. In addition, for those 9 out of 10 patients unable to get a diagnosis, there is no way to bridge their agonizing inner reality with the outer world of shared meanings that we call culture. This compounds isolation, and pain continues unmediated by social context, trapping the person in a private hurricane. Psychosocial clinician and researcher Patricia Fennell has found that many CFS patients display the signs and symptoms of posttraumatic stress, a combination of psychic numbing and intrusive pain first identified in veterans of war, but also found in survivors of abuse and disaster (Carpman, 1995). Jorna's image of feeling like a stone in the river speaks to the sense of being relentlessly and unendingly beaten, worn down, and reduced to the earlier, elemental state of an inanimate rock. In the words of musician Keith Jarrett, CFS "should be called the forever dead syndrome" (Oulette, 1999).

One of the trickiest things about CFS and other vacillating immune disorders is that each loss does not happen just once; it happens many times over, as symptoms come and go, hopes rise and fall, and denial takes hold and breaks down. Jeanne, who first developed CFS in 1987, mostly recovered five years later, and then relapsed in 1997, speaks of cycling through Elizabeth Kubler-Ross's stages of grief over and over again. "There's the anger, the denial, the bargaining, the acceptance and—bang—you're back in the rage." Hope is naturally buoyant; it springs from the tiniest of cracks, and denial is quick to take advantage. Jeanne explained: "As soon as I start to feel better, I really think it (the CFS) is gone. I think I'm well . . . Then I am so surprised when I get sick again" (Winer, personal interview). These cycles can occur in the course of a day or stretch out over months, but each one hits as hard as the others, just as a second or third death is no easier than the first.

Repetition does not dull disappointment; it just whittles away at expectation. Everyone I interviewed spoke of hoping to recover, but not one is counting on it. They have all been through so many unexplained reversals in the course of their illnesses and have tried so many promising treatments that could not cure. Well-meaning friends are often confused and frustrated by people with CFS who do not want to hear about yet another expensive untested promised cure. The friends fail to realize that sick people have already spent precious money, energy, and hope in search of a cure, only to end up poorer, more depleted, and further discouraged. For many, it is safer and wiser not to expect full recovery; it is better to be pleasantly surprised than tearfully disappointed.

It is also more realistic. In 1999, a national study of patients with severe cases of CFS found that only 4% fully recovered, while 39% partially recovered (Hill, Tiersky, Scavalla, Lavietes, & Natelson, 1999). A recent CDC study concluded that the "recovery probability" for CFS is 48% over a 10-year period. However, the study's definition of recovery included the presence of ongoing symptoms at a lesser degree (Reyes et al., 1999). In fact, all of the subjects studied by the CDC continued to experience some CFS symptoms. Dr. Dan Peterson, one of the first doctors to identify a CFS outbreak (in Nevada, more than 15 years ago) stated on CNN that none of his patients have fully recovered (CNN, 1999, as cited in Munson, 2000). Although it is still too early to use figures like these for prognosis, it is probably fair to say that many improve with time and careful living—and some do not.

My interviewees expressed gratitude for feeling better; two even knocked on wood in hopes that their improved health would continue. They also discussed the daily accommodations they make to avoid the perilous swings of denial, overactivity, and defeat that can sabotage a fragile recovery. Jeanne, who was an advanced karate student and trial attorney when she fell ill with CFS, spoke of having to make "huge changes in her lifestyle, longings and expectations . . . in an unending struggle between what I want to accomplish and do and the reality of it hitting me over and over and over again that I can't do it." Later, she added: "I have this sinking feeling that the only way to get better is to give up my life for a few years, but I don't want to and besides, there's no guarantee."

One of the ironies of this illness is that striving for anything—even recovery—usually makes the condition worse. Our American habits of reaching beyond our means and seeking to improve our condition meet with immediate negative reinforcement in CFS, usually in the form of aggravated symptoms. Like Pavlov's dogs, we learn to avoid the activity that brought the painful shock until we have replenished our energy and enthusiasm to try again. In short, we accommodate. When I first asked Jorna about getting CFS, she responded, "It knocked the wind out of me. It really humbled me. I used to think I could do anything." At the end of the interview, she stated simply, "I can't count on creating anything anymore. I feel stripped."

People with CFS often use images of being worn down, stripped naked, and reduced to next to nothing to describe their experience of the illness and what it requires of them. "It's an endless letting go," Jeanne explained, "and when you think you've let go of enough, then you get to let go of some more." The person can fight it savagely and—like the snakebite victim—hasten collapse, or can give in to what is happening, let go, and be still. As Jorna pointed out: "If I can sink into the stillness of the stone [in the river], I'm OK." For people living with CFS and similar disorders, the remedy for a bad day is consistently the same: Stop whatever you are doing, lie down, and rest. Some read if they can, or call a friend, but everyone lets go in some way. "Sometimes I pray," confided Jeanne, "but if I'm smart, I just give up. Whenever I do give up, it's always better."

This place of letting go stretches like a razor-thin ridge between the chasms of panic and depression so familiar to people with debilitating and untreatable chronic disorders. At the point—or even thought—of giving up one more thing after all the others, panic sometimes flares, activating all the systems of the body that participate in fight-or-flight instincts, and showing itself in visible physical expressions, from sweating to shaking to striking out. It is no fun, takes a toll on what is left of the person's health and, as Jeanne remarked, it "puts a real crimp in your personality." Panic, however, is something others can sometimes understand, and when they do, it builds a bridge into the social and cultural world from which the sick are exiled.

Sawnie described an episode when the combination of exhaustion and a flu so recalled her initial descent with CFS that she became terrified she might be entering a major relapse. Her partner, who has become accustomed to her occasional bouts of panic, put his arm around her and said, "Ah, the hundred and tenth way to die," and they laughed together, dispelling the fear. Sawnie still laughs when she tells the story. Panic is one of the ways pain comes out of its cage in our bodies and enters into communication, albeit in a preliterate and metaphoric language. Like seismic aftershocks, posttraumatic frights help us articulate and integrate the big loss by practicing with smaller ones. I try to remind myself that when I am terrified of what may happen, I am actually trying to digest what has already happened.

Depression is also a natural consequence of loss, and the repeated and continuing losses that attend chronic, debilitating, hard-to-diagnose illnesses leave many despondent. This "secondary depression," as it is called in the literature, is often worse for those with CFS, due to the functional severity of the illness and the social stigmatization that surrounds it. I have yet to meet a person with CFS who has not experienced periods of abject despair. For some, assisted suicide is a serious option. Three individuals have sought and received Jack Kevorkian's help in recent years.

It is particularly difficult for people with CFS to speak of their despair, because physicians and government researchers dismissed the illness as a form of depression for many years, abandoning patients without diagnosis, treatment, access to assistance, or hope for a cure. People with CFS sought each other out, formed support groups, created national organizations, and fought for responsible research into the disease. Since then, clinicians and researchers have delineated clear differences between CFS and depression in psychological, immunologic, and neurological tests, and in responses to exercise (Jorge & Goodnick, 1997). The myth that CFS is "only in the head" has been refuted in the literature, if not always in public opinion.

However, research has also shown that there is no clear line between physical and mental disorders; in fact, the body/psyche split that is a basic tenet of modern medicine is viewed by many as a false distinction inherited from seventeenth-century European thinking. No state of disease or health is purely mental, emotional, or physical. To avoid the old "chicken or the egg" dilemma in considering causation, it is probably best to think of mental, emotional, and physical correlates of a given syndrome that operate simultaneously.

Jorna commented that the first sign she notices when she is heading into an episode of aggravated symptoms is that her thinking begins to get more negative. Then she experiences an emotional shift, a growing irritability. Finally, within two hours, a fever arrives. This repeated experience has convinced Jorna that there is a physiological basis to her mental and emotional symptoms, including depression. Her observation is confirmed by studies that reveal changes in blood flow and neurotransmitter activity, both of which affect thought and mood, in the brains of people with CFS (DeLuca, 2000). It is also reinforced by the experience of many individuals who report that mental and emotional stresses have as much impact on their symptoms as physical exertion.

I have twice had the experience of symptoms "switching gears" from one mode to another. The first time occurred during the second year of my illness, when I was still feeling unwell, worn down, and exhausted on all levels. I had been experiencing bouts of nausea that kept me up much of the night, running between bed and bathroom. On this particular night, I was lying down, trying to hold still to keep myself from vomiting, when I suddenly burst out crying in deep soulful sobs. I had no idea what I was crying about, but at some point, I realized I was no longer sick to my stomach. I could sit up and reach over for tissues without repercussions. A few minutes later, my symptoms reversed themselves; in a split second, the crying was over and my stomach was roiling again. These switches occurred two or three more times that night, but never in response to my wish or intent.

The second time that I watched my symptoms slip gears into a different mode occurred over the course of a weekend meditation retreat, at the end of my third year of illness. I had mostly accommodated to the restraints of living with CFS and had started to see the first signs of improvement. If I overexerted myself, it now took only weeks instead of months to recover my previous level of functioning. I returned from the second day of the workshop feeling relatively good physically, much to my surprise. That physical improvement maintained in the weeks that followed, but all hell broke out emotionally, without any incidents to provoke it. I found myself dealing with an intense rage that seemed to swing like the barrel of a gun, first aimed at myself, then at the person in front of me, and back to me. The anger was familiar to me, but I had never experienced it with this magnitude, and I could not identify any precipitating triggers. It was as if some powerful energy within me had migrated to another place and erupted in a new form.

To cope with depression, people with chronic diseases, including CFS, take antidepressants, address negative thought patterns (reminding themselves that it won't always be this bad, that other people suffer too, that they are loved no matter what, etc.), reach out to others, and practice meditation. These are all good tools for lessening and managing despair, but they do not always work and rarely, if ever, eradicate it.

Depression, like many symptoms, can actually require and bring about its own antidote. By eroding optimism, banishing denial, and dissolving meaning, it prompts a major reassessment of goals and strategies. As the person scales down ambitions and expectations to the limitations of the illness, it becomes easier to live with CFS and even find some value in its circumscribed world. It is a process of surrender and accommodation, not to social convention, but to the demands of the person's own being.

I think of surrender as the daily practice of acceptance, something we do because it is the only thing that helps, even if we do not believe in it—like agnostics who pray in emergencies. Even though accepting the grim realities of chronic illness can call forth fresh grief, rage, and despair in the ongoing process of mourning required of the sick, it also offers a reprieve that many experience as true grace. The problem is that most people—including those who meditate regularly—say they do not know how to get there and stay there. In a culture that encourages heroic battles (especially in "battling" life-threatening diseases), acceptance appears lame, weak, and shameful, and few have learned the art of it. People with CFS find it particularly difficult to approach acceptance because they are always defending themselves against accusations of malingering and having to insist on how debilitating and intolerable their symptoms are to prove they are real. However, despite all the forces that allay themselves against depression's steady flow toward the place of acceptance, the body requires the surrender that catches the current. As Julia succinctly declared: "Rest is productive!"

LIVING INSIDE THE ENVELOPE

When Sawnie came down with CFS 5 years before our talk, she had to leave her full-time job with an environmental organization she had raised from infancy. She also quit running and swimming, stopped going out and, as her money ran out, gave up her independence to allow her boyfriend to move in and take care of her. Once they had survived the adjustment period, Sawnie joked with friends that she had to "come down with a deathly illness" to be willing to live with someone. When I asked her how CFS had changed her life, Sawnie replied: "I know where the edge of the world is for me now. . . . There's a limit, so I have to prioritize."

CFS, like many debilitating chronic illnesses, imposes strict and uniquely individual limits within which the sick must live. Many activities are simply out of the question, and those are sacrificed first. Others are not out of the question, but require so much energy, preparation, and recovery time that they are rarely, if ever, worth the expense. For example, Jeanne remarked that "the thought of driving twenty-five miles to Denver in order to eat out and go to a movie with friends seems like such a safari. I have to rest for days ahead of time, and if I go, I'm so scared that I'm going to get sick I don't have any fun."

Then there are the tasks necessary to care and provide for oneself: washing, dressing, cooking, cleaning, making money, and so on. These chores typically consume most—if not all or more—of the available supply of energy for those who are sick with CFS. If there is any life force remaining for pleasurable or meaningful activity, it must be carefully parceled out. Sawnie likened living with CFS to having a gun held to your head. Prioritization becomes a ruthless necessity.

Since the illnesses under discussion vacillate mysteriously, prioritization occurs on a daily—even hourly—basis, which explains why sick people often have to cancel plans at the last minute. This unreliability inevitably affects relationships with family, friends, and coworkers, who experience their own losses and disappointments, and often question, or feel hurt by, the choices that are made. When sick people are too exhausted to do something, they are usually too tired to explain why or to hear about the impact their decisions have had on others. At those moments, they are often brusque, aloof, tearful, or muddled, rarely clear and caring. They simply do not have the resources to take care of anyone else.

People with CFS seek the nourishment they need to replenish their reserves in different ways, but they typically use the same measure to decide how effective it is: how they feel afterward. Sawnie goes to bed, reads if she can, and picks up the phone. From the onset of her illness, Sawnie resisted isolation. She also refused to spare others the harsh details of her situation. "If people were going to be my friends," she told me, "they were going to have to be able to bear hearing about my reality . . . to some extent, I still have that attitude." Jorna, on the other hand, relies on the love of friends and family, but rarely reaches out to them when she is at her worst. On those days, she looks out the window by her bed and "breathes in the spaciousness of the sky," while her dog and cat sleep nestled against her body. Julia, whose friends were too "young to understand illness because they hadn't experienced it," just cried on her bad days. While each woman chose a different form of solace, I suspect all would say that it was the only thing within the limitations of their illnesses that worked for them.

Rarely do people request the physical company of others when they are sickest. People with CFS are often surprised to learn how fatiguing face-to-face contact can be; it takes valuable energy to follow a conversation, obey common courtesies, and expose oneself to the tangled emotions that characterize relations between the sick and the well. People with CFS and other immune disorders commonly develop sensitivities to everyday things, like sunlight, noise, mold, perfume, and foods. There is a psychological equivalent that Sawnie termed a "psychic permeability," the tendency to absorb whatever is within one's personal field, be it the discouragement of a loved one, the devotion of a pet, or the dismissive attitude in a newspaper article about CFS. For this reason, people with CFS often find themselves in the paradoxical position of feeling isolated and crowded at the same time, as if they were living without a layer of skin.

Emotional and physical defenses require energy that people with CFS do not have until they are well into recovery. In the meantime, the sick have little choice but to avoid toxic influences to the best of their abilities—staying away from foods that provoke allergic reactions, people who are draining, chemicals that worsen symptoms, and activities that exhaust them—even if they love them. Moreover, they are the only ones who can judge which foods, people, and jobs have to go, because they alone have suffered the consequences of partaking. In this way, CFS requires its victims to claim their freedom—and responsibility—to wield the knife that severs attachments and just say no. In psychological jargon, it is the task of establishing boundaries for one's own well-being.

Many in the medical field and in popular culture question using avoidance as a strategy for dealing with CFS and other immune-related illnesses, suggesting that inactivity can become its own vicious cycle by excluding the beneficial physiological and neurological effects of exercise and exposure (Butler, Chalder, & Wessely, 1991). Everyone has heard a friend, neighbor, or colleague say something like: "You've just been in bed too long. You've got to get up and go out. Go shopping or skiing, whatever." Most sick people have told themselves the same things.

In the mid-1990s, however, research began to be published supporting conservation of energy and moderation of activity as the most viable strategies to manage symptoms and begin recovery for people with CFS (King, Jason, Frankberry, Jordan, & Tyron, 1997). This research has developed into what is now called the *envelope theory*, which holds that people can avoid relapses and increase energy by keeping their activity within the envelope of their perceived energy levels day by day. I find it to be an elegant approach to health because it relies on the individual's own perceptions, instead of on outside "objective" tests that cost time, money, and energy. Tests cannot follow daily fluctuations and rarely offer useful information about CFS. The envelope theory also affirms what people with CFS instinctively understand: Rehabilitation is an individual process. No two people, "cases," or recoveries are the same.

There is a parallel between the strict limits imposed by the illness itself and the boundaries the sick must declare to live as well as possible. The sicker a person is, the smaller the world necessarily becomes. Dorothy Wall, who came down with CFS in 1980, described her situation as ". . . a late-twentieth-century Emily Dickenson imitator, my life enclosed, the world viewed through a bedroom window."

Affliction enforces this constriction, and yet with time, many experience a kind of freedom in stepping out of the race. Dorothy continues: "The edges of pine tree and maple framed my world. Hummingbirds darted past, a breeze, a sling of vaporous clouds, bringing life to this still etching I observed day after day" (Wall, 2000).

There is usually a period in the course of this illness when the sick remove themselves from the world and withdraw into some place deep inside for nourishment. My memory of this place is that I was miserable there much of the time, but I also experienced stretches of peace, moments of revelation, and times when I sensed important shifts occurring inside me like continental plates sliding along some fault line under the ocean. There is something holy about this experience of inner depth that is akin to the mysteries of death and dying. I remember dreaming of crawling back down into the dark den I had come from, floating out through a hole in the clouds, or pouring myself through a sieve, as my psyche attempted to translate what was happening to me. Sawnie was unequivocal in naming her experience: "I was dying. It was the very early stages, but I now have an idea of what it may be to begin crossing that river. It's not going to be a strange place when I get there."

In that innermost place, where we connect with who we are when we stop doing and just be, the sick sometimes remember their soul's desires. However, these yearnings rarely announce their arrival with blaring trumpets. More often, they slip silently into consciousness and emerge much later as a great pleasure in communing with animals, for example, or a longing to paint images of one's dreams, an obsessive need to finish old business, a fascination with the intricacies of children's minds, or gratitude for the ability to love without strings. Remembering brings satisfaction, but it can also be painful, as people struggle past the wreckage of previous ideals, beliefs, and identities to find a sense of worth that is not dependent on what they can give or accomplish. I suspect it was this awareness that prompted Jorna to reflect: "On a soul level I am grateful (to have CFS), but on an ego level it's scary and awful."

After a year of illness, Sawnie decided to go back to school for a master's degree in fine arts. As a poet and writer, she had wanted to get her MFA for years, but her job was consuming and there were no graduate schools in her area, so she put the dream aside. Then, with the gun of CFS to her head, Sawnie decided to go back to school no matter what it took. She found a nonresidency writing program and wrote in bed on a laptop computer for the entire first year, and by the second year, she was well enough to work at her dining table. For Sawnie, like so many with CFS and related disorders, the slow climb toward recovery involved the twin efforts of avoiding what drains and seeking what replenishes.

Relations between the sick and their loved ones undergo parallel processes of reorganization. If the relationship has been based on something the person with CFS can no longer do, such as physical recreation, travel, intellectual discussion, or socializing with large numbers of people, then both individuals experience loss, and must find another basis for relating. Sometimes partners cannot find a new connection; those that do may simply enjoy discussing family, watching movies, telling dreams, or sharing intimacies of touch and whispered confidences.

The roles and responsibilities negotiated by every couple and family also require major revision. For many, it is the first time they have openly discussed what has previously been assumed. The sick person who has to delegate tasks may feel guilty about not doing more and depending on others, while family members who pick up the slack often feel burdened and restricted by added responsibilities. Both parties need to voice their feelings, and friends and fellow sufferers do best to hear them out, to spare significant others. Each family member cycles through Kubler-Ross's stages of grief at his or her own pace, but they all have to come to terms with the new roles sickness has foisted on them, and look for ways to lessen the load.

Studies indicate that if somebody can help a person with CFS by doing household chores for just one hour per week, health improves (Shlaes & Jason, 1996). That is not much, and the simple deeds of asking, giving, and receiving are surprisingly rejuvenating for all involved. The desperation spawned by chronic illness can call forth, in the best of circumstances, an honesty and interdependency that feeds souls and strengthens relationships. That has been Sawnie's experience and enabled her to state, ". . . being ill played a part in what needed to happen anyway."

MEANING AMID ACCOMMODATION

Jeanne was a public defender with a black belt in karate. She had just returned from a month in Nicaragua on a work brigade when she developed CFS. For the first year, she was too ill to work at all. After that, she was able to open a small private practice with flexible hours to accommodate her illness and pay the bills. Five years later, the illness went into remission. At the time, she thought she had cured herself, and began to speak of the gifts of illness. Then, 6 years later, she had a relapse, and she has been sick ever since. Now, 3 years into her second bout of CFS, Jeanne is too sick to work out in karate, but manages to stretch and swim at the spa. She finished our conversation over tea with a soliloquy on living with CFS:

> The good things that come of CFIDS [chronic fatigue and immune disfunction syndrome] pale in comparison to the inconvenience and horror of having to deal with this weird ambiguous illness . . .
>
> > Can I find enough other things to make my life meaningful? Probably.
> > I don't care if it's made me a better person or not.
> > Has it made me better able to empathize with other people? Probably.
> > Has it softened me as a person? Probably. I like that.
> > But I hate the illness. I really hate it.

I have yet to meet a person with CFS who did not wrestle with the question of meaning. To some extent, it is human nature to search for an explanation when life takes a turn we neither expected nor desired. Suddenly we find ourselves outside the bounds of what we believed likely or possible, struggling to stretch our minds and hearts to encompass what has happened, so the world will make sense again, and we will know what to do next. It is also easier to endure hardship if we can make it meaningful, even if the experience itself has no intrinsic purpose. When I asked Jorna how she keeps going, she responded with carefully chosen words: "I assume some meaning, something for me to learn in the process, if only to keep opening my heart."

The issue of meaning in illness has become painfully controversial in contemporary American culture, as factions in our society from the religious right to the alternative left are challenging scientific interpretations of disease. In this context of ideological flux, people are asking a wide range of questions: Is illness genetic? Is it caused by a physical pathogen? Is it psychological? Is it real? Is it stress-related? Is it environmentally induced? Is it the sick person's fault? Does it relate to childhood experiences? Is it a function of personality style? Is it chance? Is it the wrath of God? Is it the soul's calling?

The answers to these questions have enormous consequences for social policy—and for the sick who stand at any of these crossroads. Friends, family, neighbors, coworkers, even relative strangers, are often quick to offer interpretations and advice based on their beliefs, without realizing how confusing, burdensome, and invasive they are being. This is especially true when the illness is hard to diagnose and treat because it provokes people's fears of the unknown and uncontrollable. Finding fault with the victims is a way to feel immune from the danger. Debilitating illnesses for which there are no cures challenge beliefs held both by patients and everyone around them, including medical professionals. For some, it is their first experience of major defeat. Those who once thought, as Jorna did, that they can do anything they want if they put their minds to it, are shocked, disbelieving, and furious when they cannot conquer the illness, cure the disease, or protect a loved one from pain. Eventually, their beliefs about themselves and the world have to change, so that what seemed at first glance to be failure can become a lesson in humility, a serving of wisdom, and a nudge toward reverence for that which is beyond our powers to control.

Illness, like so many undeserved hardships, also sabotages notions of a just world. For those who have already known injustice firsthand, this may not be big blow; but for the rest of us, the unfairness of illness is one of the toughest parts to swallow. The sick ask: "Why me?" Everyone around asks: "Why her? Why him?" These ubiquitous questions reveal an underlying assumption shared by most Americans raised on the "bootstrap" ethic of self-improvement: that we get what we deserve.

Unmitigated suffering shatters expectations of justice, and in so doing, it paves the way for compassion. If we can be overcome and defeated by this vague and ambiguous disease, we can certainly empathize with others who are beaten down by circumstances beyond their control. Everyone I interviewed spoke of becoming more compassionate toward others as a result of their illness. Sawnie remarked that she goes "to a lot of trouble to be gracious and meet people in good faith" now, realizing that she has no idea "what somebody else is bringing to the table." Jorna observed that living with CFS made her a better therapist, as she was "more able to be with suffering with no judgment."

Along with compassion comes patience, something that is learned in the slowed-down time of those interminable afternoons or midnight hours, and in the repeated motions of waking every day without the promise of a better future. This is not to say that these "gifts" are worth the price the sick pay for them, or that illness does not also make people cross and ugly at times; it is to remind us all that good can be gleaned from the meanest of harvests.

When Julia reflected, from her sickbed, on her years as an ecological activist, she realized that she had been operating under the influence of a "false dichotomy": that her needs as a person were opposed to those of the earth. "I could be fearless for the earth," she added, "but not for myself." Now she understands that the two are not separate and that both meet in a respect for her body. As beliefs change to include new experience, values shift. People with CFS with several years under their belt occasionally say they are glad that the illness has forced them to relinquish their ambition and perfectionism, to notice and appreciate small things, and to stop living in the future and focus on the present. I agree with that when I am doing well, as I am now; but when I am at my worst, gratitude dissolves as quickly as snowballs on a hot stove, and all that is left is the determination to keep putting one foot in front of the other.

As for larger questions of meaning, people with CFS spend so much energy fending off everyone else's interpretations of what is significant that they often have neither the heart nor will to find their own definition of meanin—or even trust that there is one that could help instead of hurt. Most prefer to look for what they are learning from living with the illness in an effort to get what they can from a difficult situation, allowing existential questions of purpose to remain a mystery. As Willie Wilkinson, a writer and public health consultant with CFS put it: "We learn how to make tools out of what we've got, and to live with what we're missing" (Wilkinson, 2000). In research lingo, this attitude is termed "optimistic cognitive appraisal," and it has been consistently shown to improve immune functioning and overall health.

There comes a point in living with any major chronic illness, when people make their sickness their own in some way and integrate it into the patchwork quilts of their lives and identities. This point comes long after the initial onset and crisis when illness so consumes those it has chosen, they can hardly think or talk of anything else. It follows innumerable rounds of denial, during which people think they have recovered or cured themselves, only to be shocked and shattered by the next outbreak of symptoms. It arrives when the sick decide to stop fighting the illness and learn to live with it. Nadine Goranson described her point of reckoning:

> About a year into my illness, I remember resting on my living room sofa one afternoon as the sun filtered in through the sheer curtains and hanging plants, splotches of sunlight dancing across the tapestry rug. It was my favorite time of day in that room. As I noticed the warmth of the sun and the shadows it cast, I realized for the first time that I wasn't doing anything. I wasn't worrying about money. I wasn't questioning the meaning of life. I wasn't foggily planning an herbal attack against my latest symptoms. I certainly wasn't moving around. I wasn't sad or happy or frustrated or angry. I just was.
>
> With that realization, I then quickly reminded myself that I had a terrible illness and that I wasn't doing anything about it. No stoic affirmations churned in my head. No mustering-up of energy. No medication review. And I realized, surprisingly, that life went on. Life went on and so did I—but suddenly without the fear, without the anxiety, without the guilt. It was just life—not a contest, not a race, not an accomplishment. It was just my life—and CFIDS was a part of it. I realized that CFIDS and I were going to have to get along together (Goranson, 2000).

Most people with CFS get better, some recover, and some never improve, and no one knows why. Sawnie, who is partially recovered, says that living with CFS is "like having a handicap." She continued: "I am aware of the limitations on my life and I want to take advantage. I want to be in that big run of fish as long as I can to the fullest of my ability." Jorna, whose health has worsened in recent months, has made her own kind of truce with her illness: "I don't know if I will ever get well. I have to trust a deeper healing is going on even if I have this illness the rest of my life."

REFERENCES

Anderson, J. S., & Ferrans, C. E. (1997). The quality of life of person with chronic fatigue syndrome. *Journal of Mental and Nervous Disorders, 185*(6), 359-367.

Butler, S., Chalder, T., & Wessely, S. (1991). Cognitive behavior therapy in chronic fatigue syndrome. *Journal of Neurology, Neurosurgery and Psychiatry, 54*, 153-158.

Carpman, V. L. (1995). Keynote address: Patricia A. Fennell, CSW.-R. *CFIDS Chronicle, 8*(4), 24.

DeLuca, J. (2000). Neuro-cognitive impairment in CFS. *CFS Research Review 1*(3), 1-3.

Fennell, P. A. (1993). A systematic, four-stage progressive model for mapping the CFIDS experience. *CFIDS Chronicle, 6*(3), 40-46.

Fennell, P. A. (1995). The four-progressive stages of the CFS experience: A coping tool for patients. *Journal of Chronic Fatigue Syndrome, 1*, 69-79.

Fukuda, K., Straus, S. E., Hickie, I., Sharpe, M. C., Dobbins, J. G., & Komaroff, A. (1994). The chronic fatigue syndrome: A comprehensive approach to its definition and study. *Annals of Internal Medicine, 121*(12), 953-959.

Goranson, N. (2000). Silent trespass. In P. Munson *Stricken: Voices from the hidden epidemic of chronic fatigue syndrome* (pp. 59-60). New York: Haworth Press.

Hill, N. F., Tiersky, L. A., Scavalla, V. R., Lavietes, M., & Natelson, B. H. (1999). National history of severe chronic fatigue syndrome. *Archives of Physical Medicine and Rehabilitation, 80*, 1090-1094.

Jason, L. A., Richman, J. A., Rademaker, A. W., Jordan, K. M., Plioplys, A. V., Taylor, R. R., et al. (1999). A community-based study of chronic fatigue syndrome. *Archives of Internal Medicine 159*(18), 2129-2137.

Johnson, H. (1996). *Osler's web.* New York: Crown.

Jorge, C. M., & Goodnick, P. J. (1997). Chronic fatigue syndrome and depression: Biological distinction and treatment. *Psychiatric Annals, 27*(5), 365-371.

Kenny, K. (1998). Wichita study reveals much about who has CFIDS. *CFIDS Chronicle, 11*(6), 25.

King, C. P., Jason, L. A., Frankberry, E. L., Jordan, K. M., & Tyron, W. (1997). Think inside the envelope. *CFIDS Chronicle, 10*(4), 10-14.

Lapp, C. W. (2000). The role of laboratory tests in diagnosis of chronic fatigue syndrome. *CFS Research Review, 1*(1), 6-8.

Munson, P. (2000). *Stricken: Voices from the hidden epidemic of chronic fatigue syndrome.* New York: Haworth Press.

Oulette, D. (1999, February 28). A piano genius battles back: Keith Jarrett emerges from long bout with chronic fatigue syndrome to perform tonight. *San Francisco Chronicle, Sunday Datebook,* p. 37.

Reyes, M., Dobbins, J. G., Nisenbaum, R., Subedar, N. S., Randall, B., & Reeves, W. C. (1999). Chronic fatigue progression and self-reported recovery: Evidence from CDC surveillance system. *Journal of Chronic Fatigue Syndrome, 5*(1), 17-27.

Scarry, E. (1985). *The body in pain.* Oxford, England: Oxford University Press.

Shlaes, J. L., & Jason, L. A. (1996). A buddy/mentor program for PWC's. *CFIDS Chronicle, 9*(1), 21-25.

Wall, D. (2000). Encounters with the invisible. In P. Munson *Stricken: Voices from the hidden epidemic of chronic fatigue syndrome* (p. 30). New York: Haworth Press.

Wilkinson, W. (2000). Stealth. In P. Munson *Stricken: Voices from the hidden epidemic of chronic fatigue syndrome* (p. 83). New York: Haworth Press.

CHAPTER 10

Family Systems Perspective

BARBARA G. MELAMED

D ESPITE A WEALTH of data pointing to family influences in the expression of chronic pain and chronic disease, few articles on chronic fatigue syndrome (CFS) discuss this topic (Deale & David, 1994). This chapter reviews the studies that exist and presents data from a study that looked at the patient-spouse independent reporting.

Why is there such a research neglect of family interactive behavior in these couples? There are likely to be multiple answers to this question. Until the development of the Family Resources Inventory (Cordingley, Wearden, Appleby, & Fisher, 2000), there were no specific CFS inventories of the contextual family in which the disease presented itself. Many of the patients sought medical solutions to their problems and primarily used family members to support and transport them for health care. Another reason for slowness in this front is the devastation of victimization. Many physicians did not accept the authenticity of the illness and equated the depression, which is comorbid in at least 50% of the cases, as psychiatric in nature. Research from funding agencies still has not come up with biological markers of the disease, so it remains a diagnosis by exclusion. Partners feel a certain level of guilt, helplessness, and fear of contagion that clinicians should deal with at confirmation of diagnosis, before maladaptive habits can set in. A new scale devised by Shlaes, Jason, and Ferrari (1999) may be useful in measuring and altering negative attitudes of family members toward CFS.

This chapter reviews the literature on social support, with a focus on chronic illness literature involving adults. There are few research findings and current studies for support of family counseling and/or conjoint therapy in the CFS literature that bear on this topic.

DEFINITION AND PREVALENCE

Chronic fatigue syndrome is an illness with unknown etiology and a high degree of uncertainty. It is primarily characterized by feelings of exhaustion, musculoskeletal pain, weakness, cognitive disturbances, and reduction in ability to function for at least 6 months. It cannot be explained by other medical conditions. The majority of afflicted patients also present with depression, somatic preoccupation, and sleep disturbances (Ware, 1993). Patients often complain of a loss of valued social roles, the stress of frequent medical intervention, and the uncertainty, stigmatization, and intrusiveness of the illness.

Despite the poor understanding of CFS, the illness is far more common than previously thought. One community study cites the prevalence as 0.4% (Jason et al., 1999). Twenty-four percent of patients in primary care clinics report having experienced fatigue lasting one month or longer, though extended fatigue is not equivalent to a diagnosis of chronic fatigue syndrome (Bates et al., 1993). Nonetheless, physicians are sometimes reluctant to diagnosis CFS, and the illness may be more common than believed.

The combination of physical and psychological manifestations of this disorder has led various investigators to consider the effects of psychosocial factors on the severity of symptoms and adjustment of patients to their chronic illness. Chronic medical conditions often result in upheaval and disruption in a patient's personal relationships, leisure activities, and occupation. Frequently, individuals with CFS must shift their role functions, as they no longer can provide financially for the family, engage in social activities, or attend to household responsibilities. The spouse often must deal with the added burdens of paying bills, taking care of patient and family, fulfilling household chores, and adapting to the life changes and uncertainties that accompany chronic illness. Furthermore, patients rely on their spouses to provide them with emotional, instrumental, and informational support in their daily struggle with CFS (Melamed & Brenner, 1990). Thus, when assessing the effects of psychosocial factors on patient adjustment, it is essential to consider the spouse-patient interaction as the core unit of the study. It was found that the greater the disruption in the spouse's life due to the condition of lupus, the more maladaptive was the patient's behavior. In addition, women with osteoporosis who felt that it was important to be functionally independent had more negative reactions to spousal support, particularly if they had concurrent depressive symptomatology and fewer self-care behaviors (Martire, Stephens, Druley, & Wojno, 2002).

CAREGIVER BURDEN

Most support networks and Internet sites are directed at the patient although the spouse and children often suffer the consequences of having a sick family member.

Q: Why do you think so many marriages/relationships fail when one partner has a chronic illness?

GREGG: I'm sure there are many reasons. I think many couples put almost all their focus on healing the body. Meanwhile, they leave the emotional and relational fronts undefined against "The Intruder." Society doesn't help. It tells the healthy partner to put on a happy-face mask, to be the ultimate positive thinker. Taken to the extreme, this approach prevents a couple from connecting at a deeper level. In fact, it can form a wedge that drives people apart. It can be uncomfortable or downright scary to take off the mask, but real growth in any relationship occurs when true thoughts and feelings are expressed during tough times (www.chronicfatigue.about.com/library/weekly/aa071200a.htm).

Caregiver burden is an understudied area in the CFS literature. Wallender, Schmitt, and Koot (2001) found that mothers of children with disabilities experience depression and health disorders. Toseland and associates undertook an interesting study of frail older adults in an HMO setting (2001). It revealed that caregivers who went to a 2-hour session once a week for 8 weeks and 10 monthly follow-up group sessions (compared with a usual care model) showed significantly reduced depression by maintaining social integration, increasing effectiveness in solving pressing problems, and increasing knowledge of community services. There was a change in caregivers' feelings of competence and the way they responded to the care. The therapy, however, did not have any measurable impact on care recipients. The Impact of Burden Scale used (Montgomery & Borgatta, as cited in Wallender et al., 2001), which measures both the objective and subjective burden for caregivers, could easily be adapted to studying the difficulties of living with spouses who have CFS. One study (Antoni et al., 1994) did look at illness burden, but only the Sickness Impact Scale was used to measure the patient's level of burden. They found that the largest proportion of the variance that accounted for illness burden came from social interaction, home management, and communications. This again supports the need to make an effort to work with caregivers, spouses, and other family members.

SOCIAL SUPPORT

Social support, optimism, coping mechanisms, illness uncertainty, level of adjustment, and stress have all been reported as significant factors in patients' psychological well-being and physical outcome. Social support helps patients understand the issues they face, motivates them to take instrumental actions, and enables them to cope more effectively by reducing emotional distress (Cohen, 1988; Thoits, 1986; Wortman, 1985). Social support also reinforces positive health behaviors, thus preventing or minimizing illness and symptom reporting and increasing treatment compliance (Umberson, 1992). Studies have suggested that negative or avoidant cognitive strategies, such as catastrophizing and wishful thinking, are maladaptive and are associated with poorer outcomes. Attempts to restructure thoughts to be more positive are considered adaptive coping mechanisms and are associated with positive outcomes (Brenner, Melamed, & Panush, 1994; Zautra & Manne, 1992).

Patients who share adaptive coping behaviors with their spouses in response to the illness are more likely to react positively to provisional support. However, when a couple fails to concur on acceptance of diagnosis and adaptation responses, the patient's own coping abilities will better predict the best health outcome. In examining the role of social support in 41 adults with CFS, of whom 25 had a primary support giver, the results indicated that there were no differences among patients with and without support on measures of mood and perceived stress. There was no relationship between beliefs concerning etiology of CFS in couples and whether the patient and his or her support provider agreed on the amount of support offered and the extent of support given. An exploratory analysis (Kelly, Soderlund, Albert, & McGarrahan, 1999) revealed that verbal, emotional-cognitive support generally was more predictive of mental health than was tangible, less communicative support. Thus, agreement between partners about illness adjustments and other psychosocial factors is an important factor in the physical and emotional functioning of the patient (Heijmans, de Ridder, & Bensing, 1999; Melamed, Brackis, & Faccenda, 1997; Schmaling, Smith, & Buchwald, 2000). In fact, the degree of disagreement as to the seriousness of the illness influenced their ratings of fatigue and dysfunction. The spouse whom a patient sees as most solicitous actually leads to the most fatigue dysfunction. Few studies ask family members how they react to patients. It may be that by taking over the chores of the patient they limit activity, which may lead to deconditioning of muscle tone.

Romano and her colleagues (1991, 1992) observed patterns of behavior in couples in pain and healthy controls. They found that solicitous behavior was more likely to precede and follow pain behavior among couples where one partner had chronic pain than among healthy control couples. Solicitous responses to pain behavior predicted more physical disability among patients with chronic pain who were also depressed, as well as among patients with greater subjective pain. In fact, the general assumption that social support from relatives is invariably a positive event has proved misguided. We need a better definition of *solicitous* than the literature currently provides. Dependency, overprotectiveness, and resentment between partners may weaken the benefits of helping behavior (Manne & Zautra, 1989, 1990). There is often less than 50% agreement between the husband and wife in terms of daily marital satisfaction (Arias & O'Leary, 1985; Melamed & Brenner, 1990). In an observational study of husbands and wives where the wife suffered rheumatoid arthritis, the patient's perception of spouse supportiveness was more important than the spouse's own report of what he or she was doing to help (Williamson, Robinson, & Melamed, 1997). Perceived family criticism even affects glucose control in insulin-dependent diabetics (Klausner, Koenigsberg, Skolnick, & Chung, 1995). Therefore, it appears that the perception of being criticized or belittled exacerbates disease symptoms. This may occur because anger is likely to increase cortisol secretion. It may also be that when the patient is criticized, there is then a lack of compliance with the regimen.

Patients with CFS have varying degrees of functional ability in their personal and occupational lives. A few studies have suggested significantly higher prevalence rates (as high as 64%) of emotional neglect and abuse and physical abuse usually between family members of individuals with CFS compared with families with patients from other chronic illness groups (rheumatoid arthritis and multiple sclerosis) or a healthy control (Van Houdenhove et al., 2001). Regardless of the patients' clinical criteria, some report severe psychological and physical impediments in their lifestyles, whereas others do not complain of any emotional stressors and are only mildly affected in their physical levels of daily functioning.

GENETIC PRECURSORS

Family characteristics were evaluated in terms of frequency of mental and physical problems in three groups of patients: one with CFS and a psychiatric diagnosis, a control group with relatively good health, and a second control group selected without regard to reported family history. Research suggests that patients with CFS report a greater number of family members with other health problems including increased prevalence of cancer, autoimmune disorders, and CFS sensations. Although this increase in parent problems among patients with CFS is notable, there is little to suggest that it is causally related to the onset of

CFS (Endicott, 1999). A study (Levine et al., 1998) examined blood samples from 20 family members (8 affected, 2 unaffected) and 8 healthy controls and found natural killer cells (NK) were significantly lower in the affected immediate family members than concurrently tested normal controls. After observing that some offspring had pediatric malignancies, they concluded that low NK activity may be a result of a genetically determined immunologic abnormality predisposing them to CFS and cancer.

In another study (Walsh, Zainal, Middleton, & Paykel, 2001) that examined the first-degree relatives of individuals with CFS, cases reflected greater familial loading for affective disorder. Results showed that there was a higher rate of CFS in the relatives of cases of CFS compared with the relatives of medical control patients. This may implicate an etiologic cause of CFS. On the other hand, people may model the symptoms of those they interact with on a daily basis.

A study (Feinstein, Weissman, Fraiden, Melamed, & Natelson, 1999) on relationships of couples during the early diagnosis phase (6 months) of CFS found that couples (partners residing in the same household for at least 7 years) who were most in agreement about the adjustment to illness had a more optimistic attitude. They did better on outcome variables than those who reported an unsatisfactory marriage with patients who exhibited more inhibition of aggression. There was no direct relationship between reported marital satisfaction and outcome. If network support outside of the marriage is considered, then there is a significant negative relationship with the impact of illness. Patients' positive perceptions and negative perceptions of their spouses' helping behaviors were not significantly related with sickness impact. Particularly interesting was that those patients who had difficulty expressing anger (they endorsed turning anger inward) were not functioning as well as those who were high in anger control. On the Arthritis Impact Scale, which measures social relationships, suppressing anger had a detrimental effect. It may be that the patients are reluctant to endorse negative perceptions of their spouse because of their dependency.

In evaluating the outcomes, two scales widely used in the literature were adopted:

1. The *Sickness Impact Profile-Relationship Scale* (SIP) (Gilson et al., 1975) is a valid and reliable test measure, with a 20-item checklist, that is sensitive to patients' adjustment to their chronic illness. The subscale assesses patient irritability, social isolation, insensitivity to others, and decreased interests as a result of the chronic illness. Patients check only items that are true on the day they complete the questionnaire.
2. The *Arthritis Impact Measurement Scale (AIMS)* is a self-report questionnaire divided into categories to measure abilities in physical and mental functioning including mobility, physical activity, pain, depression, anxiety, dexterity, social activity, and activities of daily living.

Anger styles were examined with paired *t* tests and the following results occurred. Anger In and Anger Control and Anger Expression were all significantly related with the SIP. Only Anger Out was unrelated. The AIMS revealed that only Anger In related to problems associated with social relationships. Thus, it appears that suppressing anger has a detrimental effect possibly mediated by changes in cortisol secretion. Thirty-three percent of the patients met the criteria for moderate depression. Depression had a direct effect on symptomatology. Instead of being a mood disorder similar to dysthymia or major depression, CFS may act by limiting the patients' social network, thereby reducing the number of individuals who could provide emotional and instrumental support.

The Mishel Illness Uncertainty Scale (MUIS I; Mishel, 1981) is a 30-item questionnaire with two factors: ambiguity of disease and patients' ability to predict symptomatology and illness outcome. The first subscale ranges from 48.00 to 94.00 ($M = 61.57$, $SD = 10.75$), where higher scores indicate less degree of uncertainty. It was found that the patients' illness uncertainty, measured by the MUIS I, had a significant relationship to positive functioning ($z = -2.077$, $p = .43$). The more uncertainty patients have about their illness, the more it impacts negatively on their functioning.

T tests using a Mann-Whitney *U* were conducted on nonparametric data to evaluate the relationship between social support, illness uncertainty, depression, and dyadic adjustment with sickness impact. A comparison of two groups of variables was made on one variable in which the independent variable under consideration was transformed into a dichotomous variable and the dependent variable was sickness impact profile. The independent variables that were considered in the equation were depression, dyadic satisfaction, patients' positive perception of spouse, patients' negative perception of spouse, and anger control. Patient marital satisfaction, as measured by the Dyadic Adjustment Scale, and patient depression, indicated by the CES-D (Radloff, 1977), both related to the sickness impact of patients with CFS ($z = -1.807$, $p = .071$ and $Z = 1.689$, $p = .093$ respectively).

Patient depression had a significant positive correlation with the SIP ($p < .001$). As patients manifest more depressive symptoms, the sickness tends to impact their lives to a much greater extent. Patient marital satisfaction did not indicate a significant relationship with sickness impact, yet it was highly correlated with patient perception of spouse. Thus, dyadic adjustment tends to act as a moderating variable of sickness impact and may only show significant relationships with the outcome variable when support from the social network is considered. Support from the social network other than a spouse, illness uncertainty, patient marital satisfaction and depression, and Anger In all yield strong associations with the SIP. Contrary to expectations, patients' positive perceptions of their spouse and patients' negative perceptions of their spouse did not yield a significant relationship with sickness impact. It may be the discrepancy of support needed and support provided that determines outcome. Also, as mentioned, patients may be reluctant to endorse negative perceptions of their spouse because of their dependency.

Couples should consider assertiveness training. The fact that perception of support from spouse did not directly affect the outcome measures reflects the multidimensional quality of the support measure. Further research should be performed to specify and disentangle the different aspects of support provision, as well as to consider whether the patient believes the support is helpful, harmful, or neutral (Melamed et al., 1997). Also, it may be important to consider the perception of social support the patient has outside the couple relationship. When the patient with CFS has adequate social support network members, it is likely to reduce the couple's tension.

There is evidence to support that being in a close relationship such as marriage predicts better adjustment to stressors (Burman & Margolin, 1992; Cohen & Wills, 1985; Ross, Mirowsky, & Goldstein, 1990; Wills, 1990). Significant others are thought to reduce the effects of the stressor by providing effective emotional and instrumental support (Barrera, 1986).

Individuals with CFS may be more likely to include others with CFS in their social support network (i.e., as a result of attending illness-related support groups). The Ray social support scale (1992) illustrated that positive support provision from the social network other than the spouse had a significant relationship with sickness impact ($z = -2.286$, $p = .023$). The more others were available to the patient, the better their functioning. This may indicate that patients who rely heavily on a social network outside the spouse do not depend as much on their spouse for emotional and instrumental support. If the patient can rely on other people, a social network can act as a healthy buffer for a marriage. Thus, marital satisfaction may improve with a better social network. Revenson and Majerovitz (1991) evaluated direct versus buffering effects of the same variables on spouses of patients with rheumatoid arthritis. They found that marital adjustment was related to lower depression through a direct pathway. In contrast, support from the social network outside the spouse reduced the spouses' depression by buffering the effect of severity of the patient's illness. The sicker the patient, the more the spouse benefited from having support from the broader network.

Patients' ratings of adjustment/acceptance were also significantly related to scores on the MUIS I ($p < .001$). Thus, as patients' ambiguity about illness becomes more pronounced, it greatly reduces their level of psychosocial adjustment. Because chronic fatigue syndrome has a relapsing-remitting course, planning for the future provokes much uncertainty between partners (Melamed et al., 1997). The unpredictable course of CFS leaves both members of the couple with a feeling of uncontrollability and often a sense of learned helplessness. They need to learn to be flexible in their plans and share with others their alternate plan should they be unable to fully accomplish a goal at any particular point in time.

Although these findings are based on a small cross-sectional population, they emphasize the importance of considering psychosocial factors when determining the degree to which illness affects a person's life. Greater efforts should be made toward eliminating these stressors by providing therapeutic interventions that educate couples about beneficial support methods, helpful coping mechanisms, stress-alleviating techniques, and better ways to communicate needs to each other. Chronic fatigue support groups and individual psychotherapy can assist patients in coping with the daily stressors that tend to heighten frustration with their illness and ultimately increase its impact. They provide alternative ways of dealing with problems in mobility and anger. A professional should monitor these groups, as a hostile group may interfere with interaction with health care providers who are not always sympathetic to their problems. Many patients prefer the diagnosis of fibromyalgia to CFS because they then can go to rheumatologists who are somewhat more accepting of rehabilitation and the use of mild antidepressants.

IMPLICATIONS FOR FUTURE RESEARCH

Despite a lack of biological or other etiologic markers for CFS, the prognosis and the maintenance of this chronicity may reflect patients' beliefs about the condition. Close supportive relations may also affect patients' adaptation to restricted lifestyles and to participation in treatment regimens. The victimization that patients encounter in dealing with health care professionals and the disruption of their wider social networks make them much more reliant on close family members. Thus, it is critical to examine family relationships. The Family Questionnaire leads to four response scales: sympathetic-empathic; active engagement, rejecting-hostile, and concern with self. Although family members were least likely to report rejecting-hostile attitudes, the reliability of the scales and their correlation with negative attitudes on the Positive and Negative Affect Scale (PANAS; Watson, Clark, & Telleen, 1988) make the questionnaire a useful contribution to the literature. It is likely that family approaches would have a better result if couples were included in part of the therapy.

From the perspective of how health management organizations might receive this treatment, we cited a study that demonstrated advantages and reduction in needed services when both spouse caregivers and care recipients were assessed. If it is the bottom line that runs health care, we need to generate data on couples therapy that demonstrates fewer doctors' visits, limited drugs, diminished hospital visits, improved mobilization, and more positive affect among patients.

This review identifies a critical but often neglected aspect of treatment of patients with chronic fatigue syndrome. Although we know that the illness effects both the husband and the wife, few studies have looked at the dyad as the focus of concern. There exist measures as indicated to measure not only deficits in the patient's abilities, but resources in the couple. Thus, assertiveness skills and problem-solving which includes flexibility to deal with the uncertainty of the course of the illness are taught. There is still much research to be done to convince managed care organizations that covering the caregiver's medical and emotional needs would ultimately reduce the tax that these couples cause on the system.

REFERENCES

Antoni, M., Brickman, A., Lutgendorf, S., Klimas, N., Imia-Fins, A., Ironson, G., et al. (1994). *Clinical Infectious Diseases, 18*(Suppl. 1), S73–S78.

Arias, L., & O'Leary, K. D. (1985). Semantic and perceptual discrepancies in discordant and nondiscordant marriages. *Cognitive Therapy Research, 9,* 51–60.

Barrera, M., Jr. (1986). Distinctions between social support concepts, measures, and models. *American Journal of Community Psychology, 14,* 413–445.

Bates, D. W., Schmitt, W., Buchwald, D., Warfe, N. C., Lee, J., Thoyer, E., et al. (1993). Prevalence of fatigue and chronic fatigue syndrome in primary care practice. *Archives of Internal Medicine, 153,* 2759–2765.

Brenner, G. F., Melamed, B. G., & Panush, R. S. (1994). Optimism and coping as determinants of psychosocial adjustment to rheumatoid arthritis. *Journal of Clinical Psychology in Medical Settings, 1*(2), 115–134.

Burman, B., & Margolin, G. (1992). Analysis of the association between marital relationships and health problems: An interactional perspective. *Psychological Bulletin, 112,* 39–63.

Cohen, S. (1988). Psychosocial models of the role of social support in the etiology of physical disease. *Health Psychology, 7,* 262–297.

Cohen, S., & Wills, T. A. (1985). Stress, social support, and the buffering hypothesis. *Psychological Bulletin, 98,* 310–357.

Cordingley, L., Wearden, A., Appleby, L., & Fisher, L. (2000). The Family Response Questionnaire: A new scale to assess the responses of family members to people with chronic fatigue syndrome. *Journal of Psychosomatic Research, 51,* 417–424.

Deale, A., & David, A. (1994). Chronic fatigue evaluation and management. *Journal of Neuropsychiatry, 6,* 189–194.

Endicott, N. A. (1999). Chronic fatigue syndrome in private practice psychiatry: Family history of physical and mental health. *Journal of Psychosomatic Research, 47,* 343–354.

Feinstein, S., Weissman, H., Fraidin, L., Melamed, B. G., & Natelson, B. (1999). *Social support on sickness impact in chronic fatigue syndrome.* Unpublished manuscript, Ferkauf Graduate School of Psychology, Bronx, NY.

Gilson, B. S., Gilson, J. S., Bergner, M., Bobbit, R. A., Kressel, S., Pollard, W. E., et al. (1975). The Sickness Impact Profile: Development of an outcome measure of health care. *American Journal of Public Health, 65,* 1304–1310.

Heijmans, M., de Ridder, D., & Bensing, H. (1999). Dissimilarity in patients' and spouse representations of chronic illness: Exploration of relations to patient adaptation. Coping and adaptive outcome in chronic fatigue syndrome: Importance of illness cognitions. *Journal of Psychosomatic Research, 45,* 39–51.

Jason, L. A., Richman, J. A., Rademaker, A. W., Jordan, K. M., Plioplys, A. V., Taylor, R., et al. (1999). A community based study of chronic fatigue syndrome. *Archives of Internal Medicine, 159*(R), 2129–2137.

Kelly, K., Soderlund, K., Albert, C., & McGarrahan, A. G. (1999). Social support and chronic fatigue syndrome. *Health Communication, 11,* 21–34.

Klausner, E., Koenigsberg, H., Skolnick, N., & Chung, H. (1995). Perceived familial criticism and glucose control in insulin-dependent diabetes mellitus. *International Journal of Mental Health, 24,* 64–75.

Levine, P. H., Whiteside, T. L., Frieberg, D., Bryant, J., Colclough, G., & Herberman, R. B. (1998). Dysfunction of natural killer activity in a family with chronic fatigue syndrome. *Clinical Immunology and Immunopathology, 88,* 96–104.

Manne, S., & Zautra, A. (1989). Spouse criticism and support: Their association with coping and psychological adjustment among women with rheumatoid arthritis. *Journal of Personality and Social Psychology, 56,* 608–617.

Manne, S., & Zautra, A. (1990). Couples coping with chronic illness: Women with rheumatoid arthritis and their healthy husbands. *Journal of Behavioral Medicine, 13,* 327–342.

Martire, L. M., Stephens, M. A., Druley, J. A., & Wojno, W. C. (2002). Negative reactions to received spousal care: Predictors and consequence: Miscarried support. *Health Psychology, 21,* 167–176.

Melamed, B. G., Brackis, E., & Faccenda, K. (1997). Revisiting social support and chronic illness: A dyadic approach. *Mind/Body Medicine, 2*(1), 1–6.

Melamed, B. G., & Brenner, G. (1990). Social support and chronic medical stress an interaction-based approach. *Journal of Social and Clinical Psychology, 9,* 104–117.

Mishel, M. H. (1981). The measurement of uncertainty in illness. *Nursing Research, 30,* 258–263.

Radloff, L. S. (1977). The CES-D scale: A self-report depression scale for research in general populations. *Applied Psychological Measurement, 1,* 385–401.

Ray, C. (1992). Positive and negative social support in a chronic illness. *Psychological Reports, 71,* 977–978.

Revenson, T. A., & Majerovitz, D. (1991). The effects of chronic illness on the spouse: Social resources as stress buffers. *Arthritis Care and Research, 4,* 63–72.

Romano, J., Turner, H., Friedman, L., Bulcroft, R. A., Jensen, M. P., Hops, H., et al. (1991). Observational assessment of chronic pain patient-spouse behavioral interactions. *Behavior Therapy, 22,* 549–567.

Romano, J., Turner, H., Friedman, L., Bulcroft, R. A., Jensen, M. P., Hops, H., et al. (1992). Sequential analysis of chronic pain and spouse responses. *Journal of Consulting and Clinical Psychology, 60,* 777–782.

Ross, C. E., Mirowsky, J., & Goldstein, K. (1990). The impact of the family on health: The decade in review. *Journal of Marriage and the Family, 52,* 1059–1078.

Schmaling, K., Smith, W., & Buchwald, D. S. (2000). Significant other responses are associated with fatigue and functional status among patients with chronic fatigue syndrome. *Psychosomatic Medicine, 62,* 444–450.

Shlaes, J. L., Jason, L. A., & Ferrari, J. R. (1999). The development of the Chronic Fatigue Syndrome Attitudes Test: A psychometric analysis. *Evaluation and the Health Professions, 22,* 442–465.

Thoits, P. A. (1986). Social support as coping assistance. *Journal of Consulting and Clinical Psychology, 54,* 416–423.

Toseland, R. W., McCallion, P., Smith, T., Huck, S., Bourgeios, P., & Gartska, T. A. (2001). Health education groups for caregivers in an HMO. *Journal of Clinical Psychology, 57,* 551–570.

Umberson, D. (1992). Gender, marital status, and the social control of health behavior. *Social Science and Medicine, 34,* 907–917.

Van Houdenhove, B., Neerinckx, E., Lysens, R. R., Vertommen, H., Van Houdenhove, L., Onghena, P., et al. (2001). Victimization in chronic fatigue syndrome and fibromyalgia in tertiary care. *Psychosomatics, 42,* 21–28.

Wallender, J., Schmitt, H., & Koot, H. M. (2001). Quality of life measurement in children and adolescents: Issues, instruments, and applications. *Journal of Clinical Psychology, 57,* 571–585.

Walsh, C. M., Zainal, N. Z., Middleton, S. J., & Paykel, E. S. (2001). A family history of study of chronic fatigue syndrome. *Psychiatric Genetics, 11,* 123–128.

Ware, N. C. (1993). Society, mind, and body in chronic fatigue syndrome: An anthropological view. *Journal of Chronic Fatigue Syndrome, 173,* 62–82.

Watson, D., Clark, L., & Telleen, A. (1988). Development and validation of brief measures of positive and negative affect: The PANAS scales. *Journal of Personality and Social Psychology, 54,* 1963–1970.

Williamson, D., Robinson, M., & Melamed, B. (1997). Pain behavior, spouse responsiveness, and marital satisfaction in rheumatoid arthritis. *Behavior Modification, 21,* 97–118.

Wills, T. A. (1990). Social support and interpersonal relationships. *Review of Personality and Social Psychology, 12,* 265–289.

Wortman, C. B. (1985). The role of social support in adaptation and recovery from physical illness. *Social Support and Health,* 281–302.

Zautra, A. J., & Manne, S. L. (1992). Coping with rheumatoid arthritis: A review of a decade of research. *Annals of Behavioral Medicine, 14*(1), 31–39.

CHAPTER 11

Clinical Perspectives and Patient Experiences

JON STERLING

SUPPORT GROUPS FOR CHRONIC FATIGUE SYNDROME: AN AVENUE FOR LEGITIMACY AND THE RECOVERY OF SELF-ESTEEM

WHEN I WAS a school principal, there was a parable I was fond of telling students who had a problem but were reluctant to open up. A little girl is late walking home from school. Her worried mother inquires what happened, and the little girl explains that her best friend Sara's doll fell and broke and that she sat down on the sidewalk to help fix it. "Is your friend's doll okay now?" the mother asks. "No," the little girl responds, "but I helped Sara cry."

Nonprofit, member-run support groups are now widely recognized for their positive contribution in helping people cope with stressful life and health predicaments. Surgeon General C. Everett Koop stated, "The benefits of mutual aid are experienced by millions of people who turn to others with a similar problem to attempt to deal with their isolation, powerlessness, alienation, and the awful feeling that nobody understands" (Koop, 1992, p. xviii). Studies show the doubling of support organizations nationally from 1986 through 1998 (Madara, 1999). A Harvard study shows a high rate of participation in such groups. At some time in their lives, 18.1% of the U.S population has attended a self-help group. In 1997, 7.1% of U.S adults attended a support group (Kessler, Mickelson, & Zhao, 1997). Other studies attest to the efficacy of support groups, large and small, in helping people cope with specific situations such as addiction, bereavement, physical disability, and mental health problems.

In disorders like chronic fatigue syndrome (CFS), in which societal and medical delegitimization is common, support groups offer appropriate and vital avenues for exchange of resources, medical information, and mutual aid. Many patients with CFS report that they received the first validation of their condition from peers. Sharing with fellow patients the symptoms and the losses associated with CFS is, for many, the incipient step that facilitates acceptance of and adjustment to the illness. And like many who attend support groups of all kinds, patients with CFS claim that, beyond the social support and collective wisdom gained from participation, they received their first educational materials on their disorder from support groups. Yet, remarkably, there is a strong undercurrent of public and professional opinion against CFS support groups. The allegation is that such groups reinforce negativity in patients, becoming, in effect, repetitive gripe sessions with little positive outcome. A judge in a disability hearing contradicted a patient's testimony about her positive CFS support group experience with, "What's clear to me about your condition is that they [the support group] helped you construct a belief system in mysterious illness." A pediatrician who was reported by the parents of a teenager with CFS to be "medically knowledgeable of and sensitive to CFS and very supportive of our fight for special education needs with the school district," ended an otherwise positive consult with, "Whatever you do, don't join that CFS support group. They'll just bring you down." For fear of offending him and losing his support, the parents did not inform the pediatrician that they were uplifted by attending that maligned support group and had even been referred to him by that group. At the U.S. Department of Health & Human Services/Chronic Fatigue Syndrome Coordinating Committee State of Science Conference sponsored by the National Institutes of Health (NIH) on October 23/24, 2000 in Arlington, Virginia, an NIH-funded CFS investigator reported that her research showed that one of the characteristics of CFS patients who do not recover is support group attendance. That particular piece of her study sounds a bit like the old chicken-and-egg saw. It could just as easily have been postulated and proven that a characteristic of illness is that the sick visit the doctor more often than the chronically well.

One might conclude from the preceding sample of opinion that there is something fundamentally wrong with patient-led support organizations for CFS. There is still some professional resistance to Alcoholics Anonymous (AA) and Gamblers Anonymous (GA) support groups for long-term resolution of addiction disorders. But are support groups for addiction problems, worthy as they are, the models to equate with CFS support groups?

Support groups exist for practically every disease and condition, but rare would be the cancer researcher or oncologist who would mock cancer survivor support groups. Rarer still would be the therapist or family physician who would advise patients who have lost a loved one to shun a grief support group. And though doctors seldom acknowledge the existence of support groups for medical professionals, they maintain many such groups. They focus on professional issues ranging from doctors impaired by alcohol and drug abuse to doctors and nurses disabled by latex intolerance to doctors dealing with the stress of malpractice litigation.

Misery does indeed love company, and going through hard times alone is an experience that humanity historically has avoided whenever possible. But why do many professionals who ought to know better reject this social axiom for CFS? Is this the ultimate paradigm for the delegitimization of CFS? Do the preceding opinions imply that since CFS is not real, the need for support is imaginary? Or parenthetically, is the argument that since CFS is really depression, sufferers will only depress themselves further by meeting together without the guidance of a professional facilitator? My guess is that member-run support groups for depression suffer less delegitimization from this opinion than similarly organized support groups for CFS.

Answers to these questions may indeed be directly related to the attitudes the general public and medical community have about CFS as an illness and, concomitantly, toward individuals who claim to suffer from it. Shlaes, Jason, and Ferrari (1999) concluded, "It is possible that negative attitudes toward people with CFS are a function of past government and media portrayals of CFS as either nonexistent or a function of a neurotic, overworked, stressed way of life." It certainly was not helpful to public perception of CFS as a serious disorder that the media in the mid-1990s turned flawed Centers for Disease Control research on the prevalence and demographics of CFS into sound bites about yuppie flu. Other examples of the media's careless treatment of CFS abound, even when reporting on the publication of peer-reviewed research studies funded by the National Institutes of Health (NIH). Dr. Peter Rowe's research at Johns Hopkins Hospital on pediatric orthostatic intolerance in adolescents with CFS was spun by one network into a segment on how "pickles may be the cure for a mysterious illness."

Such coverage has contributed greatly to a public perception of CFS as a self-induced, self-indulgent, primarily somatic condition. Such ill-founded beliefs about CFS have had an adverse effect on all aspects of the disorder, from the kinds of research conducted on the syndrome to the way physicians treat persons with CFS to the way family and friends view them to the way disability and health insurers review them. These perceptions have even shaped the way people with CFS view themselves (Jason et al., 1998). For persons with CFS, isolated by misunderstanding as well as by illness, the past decade has been medically, economically, socially, and psychologically devastating. With nowhere to turn for sympathy or help, it is not surprising that persons with CFS seek support from each other. One could postulate that the negative view of the value of CFS support groups merely follows the belief structure already in place for other aspects of the condition. But that might be too simplistic to explain why researchers familiar with CFS or doctors and judges who recommend support groups for other maladies seemingly go out of their way to put down support groups for CFS.

Significantly, Shlaes, Jason, and Ferrari's (1999) research also found that people do not have negative attitudes toward CFS based on interaction with individuals with CFS. Thus, one might assume that knowledge gained from interaction with persons who have CFS would result in more positive attributions toward the disease. Over the past few years, increasing numbers of physicians and lawyers have become familiar with CFS and have treated these patients with increased sensitivity and knowledge.

In the same vein, the prejudice against CFS support groups, rooted in ignorance about their accomplishments, should decrease as the general public and professionals become aware of the groups' amazing success in offering their members a varied and positive program of empowerment. The average life of volunteer-led support groups of all kinds is under two years. Groups collapse for many reasons, and often the reasons are not pejorative, but CFS patient-led support groups must survive the additional challenge of having many potential members who are unaware that they suffer from the condition. The most recent prevalence work (Wichita Study) conducted by the Federal Centers for Disease Control (Atlanta) found that 85% of persons with CFS were either misdiagnosed or undiagnosed (Reyes et al., 2002). Another major challenge for CFS support groups is that many of those who are diagnosed are too physically ill to attend. Many CFS support group leaders voice their concern about declining attendance and the difficulty of finding patients willing or able to assume even minimal leadership roles. Beyond luck, what separates well-functioning groups with expanding membership rolls and activities from those that remain small or die out is often the residual functional capacity of those who run the group's activities. It is also sometimes a matter of structure and leadership, key elements in all organizational activities.

Groups that are blessed with leaders and members who bring administrative and personnel skills to the table are obviously better able to facilitate growth and accomplishment than those not as fortunate. Groups, however, are not confined to the happenstance of who shows up. Many resources are available on how to start support groups and facilitate them to accentuate the members' strengths and give all members an important role to play within their capacities (CFIDS [Chronic Fatigue and Immune Dysfunction Syndrome] Association of America, 1996).

I have been involved in CFS support organizations for a dozen years now, and I am still in awe of how local support groups get started. Usually one or two patients or the parent or spouse of a PWC (person with CFIDS) will, while bearing the burden of acute illness or being the caregiver, find a meeting place, advertise the advent of the group, and seek resources from organizations like the Self Help Clearinghouse or sister CFS associations. Even more inspiring is the growth and metamorphosis of many of these groups.

Limited by lack of financial support and energy, some CFS groups remain local and simply provide a forum to validate symptoms and share the tribulations of a chronic illness. Yet, as 1 out of 20 Americans endure a chronic illness of some kind and have support groups, the existence of hundreds of local CFS groups nationally is, in of itself, not exceptional. What is exceptional is that many of the local CFS groups have grown to be much more than this, both organizationally and in terms of expanded activities.

In some states, notably Connecticut, Massachusetts, and New Jersey, the many city and county CFS support groups combined in the early 1990s to form statewide CFS organizations. Although other local groups also have expanded their agendas, these state organizations have, without paid staff, managed to incorporate, apply for, and receive nonprofit status. Consequently, they have been able to raise funds.

The corporate charters of these state groups usually focus on three areas. They remain loyal to their original purpose of encouraging and supporting patients and their families by operating support groups throughout their states, but they have added two key areas of indirect support to their members. They are encouraging medical education by disseminating reliable information about CFS, and they are promoting research into the cause, cure, and treatment of CFS. To achieve their primary goal, these organizations regularly publish newsletters, offer phone support systems and free lending libraries (especially useful for homebound patients), provide materials and training for their support group leaders, and offer physician and attorney referrals. To achieve their medical and public education goals, they set up exhibition booths at health fairs and medical conferences and hold their own annual patient conferences with expert speakers on CFS, usually centering on research, clinical management, and coping skills. They have even begun to specialize. The CFIDS/FM Association of Connecticut has developed an excellent program and materials on CFS and adolescents. In the same vein, the New Jersey CFS Association offers two $1,000 scholarships each year to high school seniors with CFS who are continuing their education in college or vocational school.

They have also developed a political agenda to actualize their education programs. Realizing that CFS with its 800,000 sufferers nationwide (Jason et al., 1999) is a major public health concern and thus a public policy issue, these larger patient support organizations have turned to their governors and legislators for help. Urging their members to become advocates as well as patients, they have initiated CFS bills that have passed or are pending in all three states. The New Jersey bill appropriates $95,000 to the New Jersey Department of Health and Senior Services to construct a manual for primary care physicians on diagnosing and managing the care of CFS patients (John & Oleske, 2002). The consensus manual attracted a panel of distinguished physicians for its authorship and was promulgated to 14,000 physicians in the state. The authors believe that the manual will become the standard of care for CFS. Also, the New Jersey Association has, with university teaching hospitals, sponsored medical conferences for continuing medical education credits on CFS. These larger support organizations have established research grant programs with scientific review committees, which have funded pilot research projects around the United States ranging from studies on fatigue management to investigating the role that viruses might play in CFS.

Agendas and accomplishments among these very active CFS support groups vary widely and usually relate to local conditions and/or what is perceived as a priority by the particular patient community. The Chicago CFS Association in conjunction with DePaul CFS researchers is pursuing group housing for patients in financial distress because of disability from CFS. They are also collaborating with DePaul on a research study that is evaluating the efficacy of structured, peer-facilitated CFS management groups and one-to-one peer counseling. The goal of the Chicago CFS Association is to develop and disseminate a national resource directory for persons with CFS.

Other groups, sensing the need to raise awareness of the general public, have supported the efforts of Kim Snyder, a documentary filmmaker and PWC, whose project, *I Remember Me,* recently won top awards at the Denver International, Sarasota, and Hamptons film festivals. The film was released to art house cinemas in 2001 and nationally broadcast on the Sundance cable network in 2002. Every year, scores of support groups from Miami to Seattle conduct CFS Awareness Day activities in bookstores, malls, and hospitals. Many support groups, including several online, have dedicated themselves to changing the name of the illness, believing that the word fatigue, more than anything else, has prevented the illness from gaining wider acceptance among the medical and scientific community and the public. In response to their advocacy, the Department of Health and Human Services (DHHS) committed itself in 1999 to changing the name. It formed a work group composed of CFS researchers, physicians, and advocates to study the complex problems involved and to come up with a new name. This work group reports to the DHHS Chronic Fatigue Syndrome Coordinating Committee (CFSCC), which advises the U.S. Secretary of Health on CFS issues. Many in the CFS community feel that the CFSCC itself was formed in response to the advocacy of CFS support organizations throughout the United States in the mid-1990s.

It is remarkable. What started with small groups of individual patients seeking validation of their illness from each other has grown into larger organizations seeking an adequate and fair response to their illness from the government, the medical community, and the general public. Perhaps the most striking story of all is that of the CFIDS Association of America (CAA), the nation's and the world's largest nonprofit, charitable CFS education and advocacy group.

Since its founding in 1987, the CAA has raised and invested over $3.7 million in CFS research. It has conducted symposia on CFS research topics with NIH and CDC sponsorship and has developed a medical curriculum on CFS in conjunction with the Health Resource Services Administration. The CAA conducts lobby days in Washington to accelerate the government's response to CFS and provides patients and support group leaders with a vast array of educational materials. Volunteers make up the CAA's board of directors, but it has paid staff and is a highly professional organization. Yet, lest we forget, it started with a few CFS patients in Charlotte, North Carolina, in search of a place to meet to share their suffering.

The accomplishments of volunteer-led CFS support groups throughout the United States should give pause to even those most dismissive of the disease. At the least, it should ameliorate some of the more egregious myths about CFS sufferers held by skeptical physicians, disability insurers, and the general public. If CFS patients are slackers, they certainly toil industriously when they are up to it. If they are depressives, they certainly get out of their funks long enough to develop agendas to resolve some aspects of their condition. If they are indeed yuppies—products of the self-indulgent, stressed-out 1980s and 1990s—they look outside themselves long enough to develop programs that help their peers.

Over the years, the many activities of support groups have benefited all persons with CFS. More and more doctors recognize CFS as a serious, debilitating illness. More researchers are getting interested. The government has responded with better prevalence studies and program announcements. Even the press has come a long way from the yuppie flu reporting of the early 1990s. There is somewhat more acceptance among the general public. Yet the benefits to those who participate in CFS support group activities go beyond these accomplishments. Many CFS patients are disabled, have lost livelihoods, are isolated by illness, and have lost family and friends. Stigmatization by the medical community and public has attacked their self-esteem, and the lack of efficacious treatment has caused them to lose hope. Participation in support group activities can empower these patients and help them rekindle their lives. Their participation, no matter how limited in terms of the hours spent, gives them a road back to accomplishment. By helping themselves and others, they rebuild their self-esteem. Because of the natural history of the illness (according to the CDC's Wichita Study, only 12% of CFS patients recover fully), few CFS patients achieve medical recovery. Yet CFS support groups provide a way for patients to recover their spirit from the havoc a chronic illness has wreaked on their lives.

Looking forward, CFS support groups may play a more prominent role in legitimizing both the needs of CFS patients and the perception of CFS. They may develop priorities for the special needs of persons with CFS in terms of housing, jobs, and social services (Jason & Taylor, 2003). Community-based volunteer groups and government agencies should serve disabled, homebound CFS patients in the same ways that these agencies provide daily assistance to those suffering from other debilitating illnesses. Persons with CFS who are still able to work should also be able to obtain from their employers reasonable accommodations so that they can stay on the job.

CFS support groups may also focus on the creation of Centers for Excellence in the treatment of CFS at teaching hospitals. Such centers for other diseases, especially syndromes such as AIDS, have improved clinical practice and helped in the development of customized treatment plans. Support groups may also ask for patient representatives to sit on the research committees of the cooperative research centers for CFS that the NIH has already established. Many studies on CFS might have been significantly improved with patient input at the design and implementation level, a practice that is not uncommon for other diseases.

In general, CFS support groups are striving to mainstream their illness—to make CFS and its public health implications a household name. This is not an easy task. But five years ago, the United States Surgeon General starring in a public service announcement about CFS would have seemed a daydream. Support groups and CFS advocates made that happen in 2002. Knowing the hardships they have already endured and prevailed against, I am certain that CFS support groups will achieve even greater success in the future.

REFERENCES

CFIDS Association of America. (1996). *Starting & running a CFIDS support group: A manual for group leaders.* Charlotte, NC: Author.

Jason, L. A., Richman, J. A., Friedberg, F., Wagner, L., Taylor, R. R., & Jordan, K. M. (1998). More on the biopsychosocial model of chronic fatigue syndrome. *American Psychologist, 53,* 1080–1081.

Jason, L. A., Richman, J. A., Rademaker, A. W., Jordan, K. M., Plioplys, A. V., Taylor, R., et al. (1999). A community-based study of chronic fatigue syndrome. *Archives of Internal Medicine, 159*(18), 2129–2137.

Jason, L. A., & Taylor, R. R. (2003). Service needs, service procurement, and community-based interventions. *Handbook of chronic fatigue syndrome.* New York: Wiley.

John, J. F., Jr., & Oleske, J. M. (2002, April). *A consensus manual for the primary care and management of chronic fatigue syndrome.* Lawrenceville, NJ, The Academy of Medicine of New Jersey, The University of Medicine and Dentistry of New Jersey, The New Jersey Department of Health and Senior Services.

Koop, C. E. (1992). Foreword. In A. H. Katz, H. L. Hendrick, D. H. Senberg, L. M. Thompson, T. Goodrich, & A. H. Kutscher (Eds.), *Self-help: Concepts and applications* (p. xviii). Philadelphia: Charles Press.

Kessler, R. C., Mickelson, K. D., & Zhao, S. (1997). Patterns and correlates of self help group membership in the United States. *Social Policy, 27,* 27–46.

Madara, E. J. (1999). Self help groups: Options for support, education and advocacy. In P. G. O'Brien, W. L. Kennedy, & K. A. Ballard (Eds.), *Psychiatric nursing: An integration of theory and practice* (p. 172). New York: McGraw-Hill.

Reyes, M., Nisenbaum, R., Hoaglin, D., Stewart, J., Randall, D., Unger, B., et al. (2002). *Prevalence and incidence of chronic fatigue syndrome in Wichita, Kansas.* Manuscript submitted for publication.

Shlaes, J. L., Jason, L. A., & Ferrari, J. R. (1999). The development of the Chronic Fatigue Syndrome Attitudes Test. *Evaluation and the Health Professions, 22*(4), 442–465.

PART III

SYMPTOMATOLOGY

CHAPTER 12

Pain and Fatigue

DENNIS C. TURK and BEATRICE ELLIS

A PERVASIVE SET of unexplained physical symptoms significantly interfere with the physical and emotional functioning of patients who have fibromyalgia syndrome (FMS) and chronic fatigue syndrome (CFS). Although the cardinal symptoms are pain and fatigue for FMS and CFS, respectively, there is considerable overlap in the signs and symptoms of these two diagnoses. Fatigue is acknowledged as a problem by over 78% of FMS patients (Wolfe et al., 1990), and pain is a prevalent symptom reported in patients with CFS (Buchwald, 1996; Buchwald & Garrity, 1994).

Since patients in both diagnostic categories share prominent symptoms of pain and fatigue, along with sleep problems and cognitive difficulties, some have suggested that there is actually one syndrome whose symptom constellation varies between patients (e.g., Wessely & Hotopf, 1999). Jason, Taylor, and Kennedy (2000) estimated that 20% to 70% of FM patients meet criteria for CFS, and 35% to 75% of CFS patients meet criteria for FMS.

The samples used in the different studies are likely to have contributed to these wide ranges in comorbidity. Most samples have comprised patients being evaluated at tertiary care facilities specializing in the disorders. These patients are likely to be more disabled by their symptoms. In a community sample, Jason, Taylor, and Kennedy (2000) found a lower rate of comorbidity between CFS and FMS. Following such community samples longitudinally would allow us to address the converging of symptoms and extent of overlap.

Some clinical investigators who have observed the similarity and overlap of symptoms in CFS and FMS have suggested that CFS and FM may be examples of "functional somatic syndromes," along with irritable bowel syndrome and multiple chemical sensitivities (Barsky & Borus, 1999; Morriss et al., 1999). There

Preparation of this chapter was supported by grants from National Institute of Arthritis Musculoskeletal and Skin Diseases (AR 44724 and AR 47298) and the National Institute of Child Health and Human Development, National Center for Rehabilitation Research (HD33989) awarded to the first author.

is also considerable controversy about the extent to which these disorders may overlap with psychiatric diagnoses of somatization and depression (see, e.g., Johnson, DeLuca, & Natelson, 1999).

Whether FMS and CFS are independent or have a common underlying (as yet unknown) causal mechanism, and whether that mechanism is physical or psychiatric, these two debilitating syndromes greatly affect the quality of life for many people (Burckhardt, Clark, & Bennett, 1993). At this point, it is best to conceptualize these conditions in the same way as other chronic disorders—as having both physical and emotional components.

The majority of the chapters in this book focus on CFS. Thus, before considering some of the difficulties in assessing patients and treating FMS and CFS, it is necessary to describe the features and classification methods used to diagnose FMS. In this chapter, we discuss symptom measurement problems that are common to both syndromes, as well as the roles of depression, disability, symptom perception, and patient heterogeneity in the diagnoses of CFS and FMS. We also provide an overview of treatment issues and make recommendations for the treatment of patients with CFS and FMS. Finally, we highlight some of the questions that continue to plague CFS and FMS individually and as potentially overlapping disorders.

FIBROMYALGIA SYNDROME

Fibromyalgia syndrome is a chronic musculoskeletal pain disorder, often classified as a nonarticular rheumatologic condition. The cardinal features of FMS are generalized pain and hypersensitivity to palpation at specific body locations, or *tender points* (TPs; see Figure 12.1 on p. 213 and Table 12.1 on pp. 214–215). In addition, patients with FMS typically report functional limitations and psychological dysfunction, including chronic fatigue (78.2%), sleep disturbance (75.6%), feelings of stiffness (76.2%), headaches (54.3%), irritable bowel disorders (35.7%), and depression and anxiety (44.9%) (Wolfe et al., 1990). As part of an ongoing study on FMS, we asked 97 patients to specify what factors were associated with improvement and exacerbation of their symptoms (see Table 12.2 on p. 216). Fifty-nine percent reported increases in physical activity as an aggravating factor, whereas resting and relaxing were associated with improvement of symptoms in 51% to 62% of the patients.

The natural course of FMS symptoms seems to be chronic and nonprogressive, with fluctuations in symptom severity. Radiographic and laboratory findings tend to be negative. Despite the absence of any definitive neurophysiological pathology, FMS patients report substantially compromised quality of life compared with patients who have other rheumatologic and chronic diseases (Burckhardt et al., 1993). There is currently no known cure for this syndrome.

Since the early nineteenth century, medical professionals have reported the constellation of symptoms for the syndrome under different names (e.g., tension myalgia, psychogenic rheumatism, fibromyositis). FMS is a prevalent condition, estimated to affect 3 to 6 million people in the United States (Goldenberg, 1987). In general populations, the prevalence of FMS is estimated to range from 0.66% to 10.50% (Schochat, Croft, & Raspe, 1994). The variability may have resulted from differences in classification criteria since these studies used different diagnostic criteria. FMS is one of the most common disorders evaluated in outpatient rheumatologic clinics (White, Speechley, Harth, & Østbye, 1995).

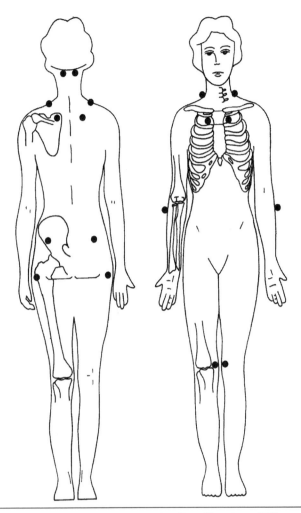

Figure 12.1 Location of Tender Points Used for Classification of Fibromyalgia Syndrome

Fibromyalgia syndrome is more commonly observed in women, with the female-to-male ratio of people seeking treatment approximately 8 to 1. In community samples, however, the ratio of females to males is closer to 3 to 1. The number of people diagnosed with FMS tends to increase from the second through the sixth decade of life. Although FMS seems to be relatively common in the general population, symptoms in the population-based FMS tend to be less severe and disabling compared with FMS in patients who seek treatment (Prescott et al., 1993).

The proposed classification criteria for FMS is based on the American College of Rheumatology (ACR) multicenter study published in 1990 (Wolfe et al., 1990). The results of this study suggest that the only factors that are sensitive and specific for FMS are (1) history of widespread pain of at least 3 months' duration and (2) report of pain on palpation of at least 11 of 18 specific TPs (see Table 12.1 and Figure 12.1).

The procedures proposed to evaluate the ACR criteria are relatively broad and imprecise. Several groups of investigators have attempted to increase the precision

Table 12.1
Manual Tender Point Survey (MTPS)

General Procedures

1. The MTPS is performed at the *beginning* of the physical examination with the gowned patient seated on the front end of the examining table.
2. Read the explanation of the standard patient instructions to the patient.
3. Examine the survey sites in numerical order.
4. Survey sites are first located *visually and with light palpation.*
5. The examiner uses the thumb pad of his/her *dominant* hand throughout the exam. Thumb pad pressure is applied perpendicularly at the site.
6. The examiner presses each survey site for 4 seconds *only once,* increasing the force by 1 kg per second.
7. Immediately record each response after the site is tested.

Procedure for Each Tender Point

1. Forehead [Control Site]
Patient position: Seated; head in neutral position.
Examiner position: Front.
Procedure: 1. Support the back of the head with the *non*dominant hand.
  2. Press perpendicularly to the geographic center of the forehead.

2. and 3. Occiput
Patient position: Seated; head loosely flexed forward approximately 30 degrees.
Examiner position: Beside and behind.
Procedure: 1. Support the head with the nondominant hand on the forehead.
  2. Move the examining thumb up midline of the neck to the nuchal ridge, then laterally one thumb width to the insertion of the suboccipital muscles on the occiput.
  3. Press at this point just below the nuchal ridge.

4. and 5. Trapezius
Patient position: Seated, head in neutral position.
Examiner position: Beside and behind.
Procedure: 1. Identify the midpoint of the upper border of trapezius.
  2. Press down.

6. and 7. Supraspinatus
Patient position: Seated.
Examiner position: Beside and behind.
Procedure: Press immediately above scapular spine, near the medial border of the scapula.

8. and 9. Gluteal
Patient position: Seated.
Examiner position: Beside and behind.
Procedure: Position the one hand (right for R side, left for L side) loosely on the iliac crest and place the space between the thumb and index finger on the mid axillary line; the thumb falls naturally on the survey site on gluteus medius, just anterior to gluteus maximus. Press perpendicularly with the examining thumb.

Table 12.1 *Continued*

10. and 11. Low Cervical

Patient position: Seated; head in neutral position.

Examiner position: Beside.

Procedure: 1. Identify the tip of the mastoid process and cricoid cartilage (C6) below the thyroid cartilage.
2. Go straight down from the mastoid process to C5–C7 range (cricoid level).
3. Support the other side of the neck.
4. Press toward the opposite shoulder.

12. and 13. Second Rib

Patient position: Seated.

Examiner position: Beside.

Procedure: 1. Find the sternal notch, move down to angle of Louis.
2. Move to the first palpable rib (second rib), one thumb width lateral to manubrium sterni.
3. Support the patient's back.
4. Press the upper border.

14. and 15. Lateral Epicondyle

Patient position: Seated; hands on lap.

Examiner position: Beside.

Procedure: 1. Support the forearm with the examiner's nondominant hand.
2. Press the point 2-cm distal to the epicondyle.

16. Right Forearm [Control Site]

Patient position: Seated.

Examiner position: Beside.

Procedure: 1. Support the forearm with the examiner's nondominant hand.
2. Press at junction of distal and middle one-third of forearm.

17. Left Thumb [Control Site]

Patient position: Seated.

Examiner position: Beside.

Procedure: 1. Support the thumb with the examiner's nondominant hand.
2. Press the entire nail area of the left thumb.
3. Do not squeeze the thumb between the examiner's thumb and forefinger.

18. and 19. Greater Trochanter

Patient position: Lying on opposite side; leg loosely fixed at the hip and knee.

Examiner position: Beside.

Procedure: Press perpendicularly one thumb width posterior to the trochanteric prominence.

20. and 21. Knee

Patient position: Lying on back; feet slightly apart.

Examiner position: Beside.

Procedure: Press just above the joint line at the medial fat pad.

Table 12.2
Modulating Factors Associated with FMS Symptoms

Worse with	%	Better with	%
Poor sleep	67	Rest	62
Stress	65	Warm bath	61
Exercise	59	Heat	57
Cold	57	Relaxation	51
Depression	51		

for assessing the ACR criteria. MacFarlane and colleagues (MacFarlane, Croft, Schollum, & Silman, 1996) have proposed a specific coding system to refine the definition of "widespread pain" (i.e., three of four body quadrants and along midline). To provide a reliable and standardized method to evaluate TPs, Starz, Sinclair, Okifuji, and Turk (1997) developed a protocol adapted from the ACR multicenter study (Wolfe et al., 1990). It is called the "Manual Tender Point Survey" (MTPS) and includes detailed, step-by-step procedures (Table 12.1).

The MTPS protocol specifies (1) the order of palpation, (2) patient response instructions, (3) pressure application technique, (4) precise locations of palpation sites, and (5) patient and examiner position. The MTPS yields a pain rating score for each site, from 0 (no pain at all) to 10 (worst pain ever experienced). This 11-point scale permits greater sensitivity for detecting changes in TP severity than simply the number of positive TPs and can be used to evaluate changes over time or outcome of treatments. A videotape and a printed guide were developed to increase the consistency of performing the MTPS (Starz et al., 1997).

Several studies have been performed to establish the reliability, validity, sensitivity, and specificity of the MTPS. In one study (Okifuji, Turk, Sinclair, Starz, & Marcus, 1997), 65 FMS patients were examined twice using the MTPS. A physician and physical therapist performed the MTPS, 1 to 2 hours apart. For the ACR TP criterion (Wolfe et al., 1990), the two examiners agreed that 57 patients met the criterion and 2 did not (91% agreement). The mean TP counts were 16.18 ($SD = 2.47$) for the physician examiner and 15.26 ($SD = 3.20$) for the physical therapist examiner. The difference was not statistically significant. The agreement rate for positive findings of each TP ranged from 77% to 90%, with the average of 84%. The examiners reached overall agreement rates of 79%. The results support the interrater reliability of the MTPS.

The validity of the MTPS was demonstrated in a study comparing FMS sufferers with chronic headache patients (Okifuji, Turk, & Marcus, 1999). Seventy FMS and 70 headache patients were examined using the MTPS. The mean TP pain severity rating of FMS patients ($M = 5.33$, $SD = 1.98$) was significantly higher than the mean TP severity rating of headache patients ($M = 1.80$, $SD = 1.80$). A series of t tests to evaluate whether the two groups differed on the TP pain severity rating for each TP revealed that the FMS patients consistently reported significantly greater pain severity than did the headache patients.

To determine pressure pain sensitivity of tender points and control points in FMS and patients with other types of chronic pain disorders, we evaluated 178 patients with pain problems. Fifty-three FMS subjects, 46 chronic pain, 41 chronic headache, 38 rheumatoid arthritis, and 20 pain-free subjects were examined.

Group comparisons revealed that pressure pain severity was significantly different across groups for tender points and control points. As can be seen in Figure 12.2, FMS patients reported significantly higher levels of pain than other groups for both tender points and control points. Patients with non-FMS pain disorders reported significantly higher levels of pain compared with healthy controls in both tender points and control points. Moreover, whereas the majority of non-FMS patients reported fewer than 18 positive tender points, the distribution of FMS patients seems to be located to the right, more severe end of the total tender point severity. The distributions are significantly different across groups.

As noted, the MTPS permits an examiner to obtain the number of positive tender points as well as a pain severity score for each TP. Although the ACR criterion requires only that positive TP counts be 11 or greater, severity of TP pain may be an important parameter in understanding the experience of FMS. In an ongoing study of 76 FMS patients who were evaluated using the MTPS, the distribution of the TP counts is negatively skewed, with over 50% of patients reporting 18 positive TPs. However, the distribution of total TP severity scores more closely approximated a normal distribution. When we examined the TP severity scores of the 39 patients who had all 18 TPs positive, the distribution of the TP severity scores was also close to normal. This suggested the wide range of severity within a group of patients with an identical number of positive TPs. Additional analyses revealed that high TP severity was associated with other FMS somatic symptoms such as high levels of fatigue, pain, and quality of sleep; whereas cognitive, behavioral, and affective factors did not differentiate patients

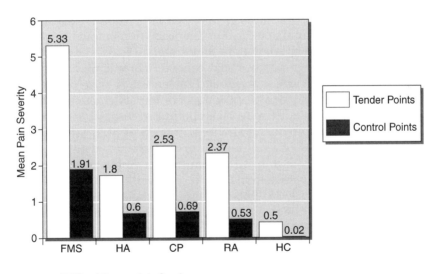

Figure 12.2   Mean Tender Point and Control Points Pain Severity Scores for Fibromyalgia Syndrome, Other Chronic Pain Syndromes, and Healthy Controls

with high TP severity from patients with low TP severity. These results suggest that physical symptoms and psychosocial symptoms are both present in FMS but are at least partially independent of each other. TP severity may be a useful parameter with which to study FMS, especially since the severe skew in the distribution of the number of TPs likely restricts analytical methods.

We can compare the features of CFS with those of FMS. This permits us to identify some of the similarities as well as differences between these two syndromes.

CHRONIC FATIGUE SYNDROME

CFS is characterized by severe and debilitating fatigue of unknown etiology that persists for 6 months or longer and significantly interferes with daily activities. As was the case in FMS, the cardinal symptom relies on self-report data. Additional symptoms include pain, cognitive problems such as memory or concentration decrements that interfere with functioning, nonrefreshing sleep, and postexertional malaise of 24 hours or longer.

As was the case for FMS, the diagnosis of CFS can be difficult because there are no pathognomonic diagnostic criteria, and symptoms such as fatigue and pain accompany many disorders and syndromes. The diagnosis of CFS is made after comprehensive study of neurological, endocrine, and other factors eliminates other causes for these symptoms. Thus, it is primarily a diagnosis by exclusion.

Both CFS and FMS patients report a panoply of somatic and psychological symptoms. Although no organic pathology has been identified, patients' quality of life is substantially compromised. Friedberg and Jason (1998) concluded that, in addition to refining the assessment of fatigue, pain, and other symptoms, clinicians must take into account the ways in which these symptoms affect individuals' lives. People with chronic medical problems do not simply have a "broken" body part that needs to be fixed, nor are they simply a set of symptoms; they are humans who exist within a psychosocial context. Chronic disorders affect not only body parts, but the entire individual. Problems may arise when symptoms make it difficult or impossible to work at a job, or to participate in other desired activities. Most people do not live in isolation but in a social context. Interpersonal problems can develop when patients with CFS or FMS avoid activities or responsibilities out of fear of overexertion or uncertainty about whether their health status will allow them to fulfill commitments. Spouses, family members, and significant others may have to take on responsibilities formerly carried out by the person with CFS or FMS. This can lead to resentment and distress. The condition affects not only the identified person with CFS or FMS but the entire family and significant others as well. The interpersonal problems are compounded because other people may not believe that these people are suffering or impaired since they typically do not look ill.

In the remainder of this chapter, we consider conceptual and methodological issues associated with reliance on self-reports, look at the relationship between self-reports and actual performance of activities, and discuss developments in research investigating pain mechanisms and treatment efficacy. We examine the recent debate over the importance of addressing patient heterogeneity in treating FMS patients and suggest that the same issues are pertinent to CFS. We highlight the implications of the available information for treating people diagnosed with FMS and CFS. Finally, we suggest topics for future research.

PROBLEMS CREATED BY DEPENDENCE
ON SUBJECTIVE SYMPTOMS

Perhaps the greatest impediment to answering questions about causality and developing effective treatment is that there are no objective measures of pain and few objective measures of fatigue (e.g., actigraphy) symptoms. Since no identifiable objective pathology is associated with either FMS or CFS, the severity of symptoms is determined primarily by patients' subjective reports, either during interviews or in response to standardized questionnaires. Assessment tools such as actigraphy can provide some objective data; however, we do not know how well these measures correspond to subjects' pain or fatigue experiences. When comparing people's self-reports of their symptom levels, there is no way of measuring their actual experience. It would be like asking them how hungry they are.

Hunger, like pain and fatigue, is a subjective experience that can only be assessed by a person's self-report or by observation of behavior. An observer can ask a person to rate his current degree of hunger, his usual level of hunger, or his average rate of hunger over the past month on some self-report scale. Alternatively, an interviewer might observe a person's behavior—say, her caloric intake—and make an inference about her state of hunger. We can perform assays of blood glucose levels to obtain an objective indication of the levels of nutrients, and we can determine the number of calories consumed by careful monitoring of the person's food intake. However, the correlation between hunger and calories consumed or glucose levels is far from perfect. Thus, knowing caloric intake may not provide an accurate indication of the hunger, which remains a subjective experience. Like pain and fatigue, it is impossible to experience someone else's hunger and it is equally difficult to describe the experience of hunger to someone else.

The subjectivity of the defining symptoms and the lack of objective physical signs invite skepticism that contributes to the distress of people diagnosed with FMS and CFS. The plight of the patient with unverifiable symptoms is captured by Ivan Illich (1976, pp. 147–148):

> Just as "my pain" belongs in a unique way only to me, so am I utterly alone with it. I cannot share it. I have no doubt about the reality of the pain experience, but I cannot tell anybody what I experience. I surmise that others have "their" pain, even though I cannot perceive what they mean when they tell me about them. I am certain about the existence of their pain only in the sense that I am certain of my compassion for them. And yet, the deeper my compassion, the deeper is my certitude about the other person's utter loneliness in relation to his experience.

This can be compared with a remark made by Ellen Scarry (1985): "To have great pain is to have certainty, to hear that another person has pain is to have doubt."

PROBLEMS OF ASSESSMENT OF SYMPTOMS

Pain assessment in FMS involves two areas: (1) patients' reports of their typical pain and (2) evaluation of hypersensitivity to palpation of specific tender points. Research investigating pain assessment techniques has shown that how clinicians conduct the evaluation will influence patients' reports. Many of the issues discussed for assessing pain are equally relevant for assessing fatigue.

SELF-REPORTS

One person's internal rating scheme may be entirely different from another's, and there is no way to compare them. To go back to the example of assessing hunger, we can ask someone to rate her hunger "right now" on an 11-point scale, where 0 is equal to "not at all hungry" and 10 is equal to "famished." If the respondent rates her current hunger as "5," we have no way of knowing how that rating of 5 compares to anyone else's rating of 5. We can try to base our interpretation on some normative sample, but as noted by Illich when he describes pain, we cannot really know the person's subjective experience. We make an inference based on our own experience. In addition, self-reports will likely fluctuate over time, not only because of changes in symptoms but also based on a respondent's mood state, attentional focus, and other factors that can influence the report.

These measurement problems pose difficulties for clinicians and researchers alike. Even after establishing a diagnosis, some kind of consistent assessment scheme is necessary to evaluate the course of symptoms over time, on their own as well as in response to treatment. In a clinical context, subjective reports of decline, improvement, and functional status may be sufficient for concerns that are most relevant to a patient. Is she feeling better or worse? Is he able to do more or fewer activities? Is she able to return to work? However, more reliable and valid measurements are needed to develop meaningful guidelines for research and practice.

WORDING

The phrasing of questions will influence patients' responses. In particular, the clinician must consider quality, location, and interval. For example, the question "Do you *currently* have pain?" or "What is your *current* level of fatigue?" might receive a different response by replacing the word currently with *usually* or *often*. Similarly, adding the modifier *severe* might elicit different responses. Patients have many ways to estimate their subjective states. If they are asked to rate pain in each body area, or to respond to an open-ended question such as "tell me about your pain in general," different processes are involved.

TIMING OF ASSESSMENT

Clark, Burgos-Vargas, Medina-Palma, Lavielle, and Marina (1998) examined the prevalence of FMS in children. They collected self-reported pain responses and then conducted TP examinations in those who indicated the presence of widespread pain. Only 24 of 548 children who completed the questionnaire reported pain, and 7 met the two criteria for FMS (1.2% prevalence). This prevalence rate can be compared with previous studies showing 3.2% to 6.2% prevalence. The authors speculate that methodological variance, such as conducting a TP examination before the questionnaire may sensitize and bias how children report pain, and noted the importance of such procedural differences in epidemiological studies.

ANCHORING AND RECALL BIAS

Any time people are asked to report a symptom during a period of time, their current state (level of symptom) will serve as an anchor for their judgments. A current level of pain that is severe will have a different impact on reports of average level of pain than will a current level of pain judged to be mild. Similarly, the level of fatigue patients are experiencing at the time of assessment will influence their retrospective estimate of their usual fatigue or average fatigue over the past week. Think of the process that patients must go through to respond to the question about their average level of fatigue. Patients may consider their current level of fatigue, make a judgment of whether this is typical, consider the most and least level of fatigue during the past week, average these together, and then adjust the rating depending on whether they decide they are more or less fatigued now than usual.

Daily diaries may reduce the anchoring biases in symptom reporting. Regular recording of symptoms on some fixed schedule will permit more valid assessment of fluctuations in symptoms. The daily recording method provides advantages since it reduces time for recollection compared with retrospective reports over lengthier time intervals. Its validity, however, depends on patients' compliance. If patients do not complete the ratings daily but do so retrospectively, such as at the end of a recording period, then the diary method loses its advantage over the retrospective recall.

Some investigators have developed a protocol using computer technology to facilitate real-time assessment of symptoms. In these studies, patients have used programmed hand-held computers to prompt them to rate their symptoms at predetermined intervals (Affleck et al., 1998). Patients are given a window of time in which to respond and do not have access to previous ratings. Thus, they are unable to modify earlier ratings or use them as anchors for the current rating. There are also some disadvantages, not the least of which are cost and inconvenience.

PAIN AND FATIGUE BEHAVIORS

As noted, the only way to determine how much of a subjective symptom, such as pain and fatigue, patients are experiencing is to ask them for a verbal report or to observe their behavior. The latter method requires making inferences about the patient's behavior and how it relates to their subjective experience. A specific set of behaviors has been labeled *pain behaviors* (Fordyce, 1976). Pain behaviors consist of overt expressions of pain, distress, and suffering; self-report of pain is also a pain behavior. That these behaviors are observable means that they have the potential to elicit a response from others. It would be equally feasible to establish a set of *fatigue behaviors* from which an observer would infer the extent of a patient's fatigue (e.g., lying down during the day, facial expression indicating a lack of energy).

The responses of significant others can serve as reinforcers of these behaviors. The consequences of these response behaviors may lead to increased expression of the initial behaviors even in the absence of physical causation. Several studies have supported the important role of the contingencies of reinforcement on the maintenance of pain behaviors (e.g., Romano et al., 1995; Turk, Kerns, & Rosenberg, 1992).

Health care professionals may also reinforce patient behavior by their responses. The physician who prescribes medication in response to the patient's report may be reinforcing the report of pain (Turk & Okifuji, 1997). Patients learn that their behavior elicits a response from the physician, and if the response provides relief of pain, they may learn to report pain to obtain the desired outcome. This is the case when pain medication is prescribed on a *take as needed (prn)* basis.

To take the medication, the patient must indicate that the pain has increased. If the medication provides some relief, then the anticipated outcome may maintain the attention to and self-rating of pain.

How might this affect a CFS patient? Assume that a patient is being encouraged to exercise to build up his physical conditioning. If the patient engages in the exercise and as a result feels increased fatigue, he may avoid exercise in the future. Increased avoidance of exercise has a reinforcing effect—the patient may avoid increased fatigue—but there is a consequence, increased physical deconditioning. If a family member observes from the patient's behavior that the patient is having a "bad day," the family member may express concern and provide attention. What does a patient learn from this response? Displaying a particular set of behaviors—fatigue behaviors—results in attention, sympathy, and support. Patients are not intentionally being manipulative, but through learning, anticipated consequences come to control their behavior. Family members who react with skepticism or criticism to a patient's fatigue behaviors may condition a patient to deny or minimize her fatigue. The patient then may ignore her symptoms and overdo activities, experiencing increased symptomatology, as well as conflict, withdrawal, or other additional distress.

Pain behaviors are generally regarded as maladaptive since they interfere with functional states. This assumption has rarely been questioned although there is some evidence that factors other than environmental contingencies, such as physical, cognitive, and affective ones are important determinants in overt expression of pain (Turk & Okifuji, 1997).

Turk and Okifuji (1997) evaluated the relative contributions of physical, operant, cognitive, and affective components to pain behavior (Turk, Wack, & Kerns, 1985). They observed 63 FMS patients during an hour-long interview and recorded pain behaviors. In a regression analysis, demographic, physical, and pain severity variables and positive reinforcements were entered hierarchically, followed by the cognitive or affective factors, which were entered independently. The results indicated that the physical examination and diagnostic test results and reports of performance of functional activities were significantly associated with pain behaviors, accounting for 22% of the variance. Pain severity and responses by significant others, however, were not significant contributors, adding only 3% and 0% to the total variance, respectively. Cognitive and affective factors added significant amounts of variance, 21% and 17%, respectively. The total model accounted for 53% of the variance in observed pain behaviors. These results suggest that behavioral expressions of pain are likely to be associated with a complex interaction of physical, cognitive, and affective factors.

PHYSICAL SYMPTOMS, DEPRESSION, AND DISABILITY

There is wide variability in work disability and other activity limitations in CFS and FMS populations (Bombardier & Buchwald, 1996; Christodoulou et al., 1998; Deale, Chalder, Marks, & Wessely, 1997). There are multiple views on how pain, fatigue, cognitive problems, or other symptoms are related to disability, both directly on routine activities and in terms of possible secondary gain arising from disability compensation. We are far from certain about how other factors, including personality characteristics and depression and anxiety symptoms, contribute to observed disability, either in conjunction with or independent of symptoms.

DEPRESSION

Depressive disorders are a prevalent co-occurring problem in a substantial proportion of FMS patients. Studies suggest that from 14% to 71% of FMS patients have a concurrent diagnosis of depression with a substantial minority reporting premorbid histories of depression (Burckhardt et al., 1994; Hudson, Hudson, Pliner, Goldenberg, & Pope, 1985). The wide range of depression reported in these studies may be attributed to variability in sample selection and differences in criteria and methods used to diagnose depression. However, even if one takes the lowest estimate, the prevalence of depression in FMS patients far exceeds that of healthy community populations whose prevalence is estimated as 2.7% to 4.6% for men and 4.6% to 6.5% for women (Myers, Weissman, & Tischler, 1984).

It is unclear whether the prevalence of depression in FMS is higher than for other chronic pain syndromes. Rates of depression among heterogeneous samples of chronic pain patients range from 10% to 90% and average around 40% (Romano & Turner, 1985). Some studies have found higher rates of depression in FMS patients than in rheumatoid arthritis (RA) patients (Alfici, Sigal, & Landau, 1989), although others report comparable rates (Ahles, Khan, Yunus, Spiegel, & Masi, 1991; Kirmayer, Robbins, & Kapusta, 1988). Examinations of the severity of depressive symptoms using self-report instruments suggest that, in general, FMS patients report significantly higher levels of depressive symptomatology compared to persons with RA and healthy persons (e.g., Krag, Norregaard, Larsen, & Danneskiold-Samsoe, 1994). Fibromyalgia syndrome is associated not only with high degrees of concurrent depression but also with high prevalence of lifetime depressive disorders and family histories of depression (Aaron et al., 1996).

Similarly for CFS, prevalence estimates for concurrent, premorbid, and lifetime diagnoses of depression vary widely, depending on sampling, assessment instruments, and scoring criteria. Rates of depression are lower in community CFS samples compared with those seeking treatment (Jason et al., 1999). In addition, as CFS diagnostic criteria have evolved over the years, different people are classified with CFS (e.g., 8 vs. 4 "minor" symptoms; including vs. excluding concurrent psychiatric diagnoses), making direct comparisons across CFS samples difficult. Standardized interviews provide different prevalence rates of depression, depending on what instruments are used, and on whether interviewers rate certain symptoms as somatically or psychiatrically based (e.g., Johnson, DeLuca, & Natelson, 1996a; Taylor & Jason, 1998). Finally, when questionnaire measures of depression score somatic, cognitive, and affective items separately, the response patterns suggest that CFS patients as a group endorse somatic symptoms but endorse fewer symptoms such as guilt, self-reproach, and anhedonia than do depressed patients (Johnson, DeLuca, & Natelson, 1996b; Powell, Dolan, & Wessely, 1990; see Friedberg & Jason, 1998; Johnson et al., 1999, for reviews of these findings).

There has been much discussion and debate about the direction of causality for distressing physical symptoms and emotional distress. For example, does premorbid depression cause the symptoms characteristic of CFS and FMS? Does living with chronic disabling symptoms cause the prevalent emotional distress in people diagnosed with CFS and FMS, or does some third variable mediate the symptom-depression (e.g., perceived impact on life, perceived lack of control over life, neuro-hormonal factors) relationship? Some studies suggest that the symptoms of FMS and CFS result from premorbid depression (e.g., Hudson & Pope, 1996). However, there is growing evidence that emotional distress may be secondary to the onset of symptoms, and it may be mediated by the impact of symptoms on ability to engage in usual physical functioning (e.g., Okifuji, Turk, & Sherman, 2000).

In the absence of definitive pathophysiology in FMS and CFS, the psychogenic hypothesis may seem reasonable. However, several empirical findings challenge this hypothesis. First, not all FMS or CFS patients are depressed. If FMS and CFS were variants of depressive disorder, a concordance rate of near 100% would be expected. Research also suggests that depression is more prevalent in treatment-seeking patients with FMS. Among those FMS patients who are not seeking treatment, the prevalence of depression is comparable to that of healthy individuals (Aaron et al., 1996). These discrepancies tend to dispute the hypothesis that FMS is primarily a manifestation of a psychiatric disorder.

A second hypothesis regarding the association between FMS and CFS and depression suggests that depression may be reactive to the problems and challenges associated with these chronic syndromes. FMS and CFS are not terminal, nor are they always progressive; however, significant disability and decline in quality of life have been noted. Although depression in FMS patients is correlated with a number of painful tender points (TPs) and pressure force on TPs to elicit pain (Wolfe et al., 1997), depressed mood does not seem to be associated with other parameters of pain, such as pain duration, self-reported pain severity, and sensitivity to non-TP sites (Celiker, Borman, Oktem, Gokce-Kutsal, & Basgoze, 1997; Wolfe, 1998). These results do not present strong support for the hypothesis that depression is solely a reaction to the severity and chronicity of FMS. Indeed, living with constant, widespread pain and disability, with no known pathology and no universally effective treatment, may trigger depressive moods.

The third hypothesis regarding the association between FMS and CFS and depression is that they share a common pathophysiology such as neurohormonal imbalance or deficit (Pillemer, Bradley, Crofford, Moldofsky, & Chrousos, 1997). Again, that not all FMS and CFS patients are depressed argues against this hypothesis. Moreover, factors known as markers of depression are not always present in FMS and CFS. Thus, neither the depressive spectrum nor the shared pathophysiology models seem adequate to explain the prevalence of depression observed in FMS and CFS patients. The relationship between severity of FMS and CFS symptoms and severity of depressive mood has yet to be satisfactorily explained. Prospective studies are needed to clarify this relationship. Some as yet unknown factors likely mediate depression in these patients and may explain why some patients diagnosed with FMS and CFS become depressed and others do not. The high prevalence of depression makes it important to identify the factors that contribute to it as well as the ones that prevent or buffer against it in FMS and CFS patients. None of the aforementioned hypotheses appear sufficient to explain the FMS-depression and CFS-depression relationship. Thus, a neglected question is why, given the chronicity and significant impact of FMS and CFS on all domains of patients' lives, all FMS and CFS patients do not become depressed (Okifuji et al., 2000). Delineation of the discriminating factors would help clarify the relationship between these syndromes and depression.

As noted, the defining characteristics of CFS and FMS are subjective. People diagnosed with these conditions report that they experience high degrees of pain, fatigue, and sleep disturbance; have difficulty with cognitive tasks such as memory, concentration, and attention; and that their performance on routine activities is greatly affected. An important consideration is the relationship between the *perception* of the impact of symptoms compared with the actual effects on performance of activities.

FUNCTIONAL DISABILITY

Exercise intolerance, reports of weakness, and functional disabilities are significant problems in FMS and CFS (Bengtsson, Henriksson, & Jorfeldt, 1986; Bennett, 1981). Previous research has demonstrated that painful TPs are more prevalent in physically deconditioned people (Granges & Littlejohn, 1993) and that exercise programs often reduce pain sensitivity (Martin et al., 1996; Wigers, Stiles, & Vogel, 1996). Thus, reduced physical conditioning may be an important contributing factor in FMS. Research on physical conditioning and activity performance of FMS patients, however, has provided inconsistent results. FMS patients exhibit significantly lower levels of muscle strength and endurance than do healthy people (Lindh, Johansson, Hedberg, & Grimby, 1994; Norregaard, Bulow, & Danneskiold-Samsoe, 1994) and other chronic myofascial pain patients (Jacobsen & Danneskiold-Samsoe, 1992).

Daily physical exertions, based on patients' recall, have been reported to be significantly lower in FMS patients compared with healthy people (Norregaard, Bulow, & Danneskiold-Samsoe, 1994). Moreover, despite comparable levels of cardiovascular reactivity, FMS patients tend to terminate exercise at lower workloads than healthy individuals due to perceived exhaustion (van Denderen, Boersma, Zeinstra, Hollander, & van Neerbos, 1992). Several studies report below-average levels of aerobic conditioning in the majority of FMS patients (Bennett, Clark, Campbell, & Burckhardt, 1992; Mannerkorpi, Burckhardt, & Bjelle, 1994). Other studies, however, report that FMS patients' aerobic capacity does not differ significantly from age-matched healthy people although FMS patients consistently rate the exercise as more fatiguing (Mengshoel, Forre, & Komnaes, 1990; Norregaard, Bulow, Mehlsen, & Danneskiold-Samsoe, 1994).

Studies investigating muscle physiology blood flow, and bioenergetics also have not consistently identified specific abnormalities in FMS (Joos, De Meirleir, & Vandenborne, 1993; Simms, Roy, & Hrovat, 1994). Surface electromyographic activity during isokinetic tasks reveals no specific abnormality in the fatigue mechanisms in the local muscles of FMS patients (Elert, Rantapaa-Dahlqvist, Henriksson-Larsen, & Gerdle, 1992). Thus, these studies do not explain the decreased level of muscle conditioning observed in FMS. FMS patients may be as aerobically fit as others but perceive the exercise as more demanding, show reduced endurance and strength, and report reduced activity levels. Some investigators have suggested that people with CFS perceive their exertion as requiring unusually rigorous effort, thereby feeling more fatigued than would be expected on the basis of physiological exertion alone (e.g., Lawrie, MacHale, Power, & Goodwin, 1997; Rosen, King, Wilkinson, & Nixon, 1990). Their avoidance of activity may reflect their anticipation of postexertional malaise, whereas activity avoidance in FMS patients may be more closely tied to their anticipation of increased pain.

EFFECTS OF EXPECTANCY IN PHYSICAL FUNCTIONING

Physical performance on exercise tasks relies on subjects' voluntary effort. Research shows that motivation based on people's expectations about their own physical ability can influence reports of physical exertion (Blalock, DeVellis, & DeVellis, 1992). Thus, it is necessary to consider cognitive and affective factors when evaluating physical functioning in people with chronic pain and rheumatic disorders. Expectations typically develop as a result of prior experiences. Thus, a deficit in the central processing of physical sensations may initiate a dynamic process, resulting in (1) underestimation of physical functioning, (2) lowered expectations for performing physical activity, (3) inhibition of activity, and (4) gradual physical deconditioning. The increased deconditioning may lead to even greater fatigue and reduced activity—a vicious circle is established and perpetuated.

Patients' expectations about their physical ability play an important role in coping and adaptation since their assessment of the adequacy of their resources to match situational demands—self-efficacy belief—influences their degree of disability (Bandura, 1977). FMS patients' self-efficacy beliefs about performance of activities have been shown to be related to impaired performance on physical tasks (Buckelew, Murray, Hewett, Johnson, & Huyser, 1995). Several studies have demonstrated the importance of FMS patients' self-efficacy beliefs by showing that pretreatment self-efficacy beliefs predict posttreatment activity. Moreover, improvements in self-efficacy have been shown to be associated with FMS patients' performance of physical activities following completion of a rehabilitation program (Buckelew et al., 1995, 1996).

Reports of mild cognitive dysfunction are prevalent in CFS and FMS. The majority of patients report significant problems in concentration and memory. FMS patients have been compared to patients with post-Lyme syndrome (PLS), depressed people, and healthy people. PLS patients exhibited significantly greater levels of memory impairment than did FMS or depressed patients (Buchwald, Pearlman, Umali, Schmaling, & Katon, 1996) even though FMS patients scored higher on self-report scales indicating somatic concerns, including concerns about memory. When objectively assessed, the adverse effects of FMS on cognitive functions seem to be marginal at best. Several investigators have reported mild levels of difficulty in effortful processing for long-term memory associated with depressed FMS patients (Landro, Stiles, & Sletvold, 1997; Sletvold, Stiles, & Landro, 1995).

Results of neurocognitive testing are frequently incongruent with patients' subjective assessment of their neurocognitive functioning. Research shows that patients with CFS and depression tend to underestimate their ability to perform cognitive tasks (Schmaling, Diclemente, Cullum, & Jones, 1994), just as they underestimate their physical abilities. In their review, Tiersky, Johnson, Lange, Natelson, and DeLuca (1997) noted reports of difficulties in complex problem solving and cognitive efficiency. They also pointed out that, while affective factors influenced subjects' self-reported cognitive impairment, this degree of impairment was not always found on objective measures. Furthermore, a study (Christodoulou et al., 1998) demonstrated a relationship between cognitive and functional disability in CFS patients even after statistically controlling for depressive symptoms and other psychiatric conditions. These studies suggest that cognitive impairment and perceived cognitive disability need to be further examined in both FMS and CFS.

Pain and functional limitations are substantially elevated in both FMS and CFS patients. In a preliminary clinical study, Turk and colleagues (Turk, Okifuji, Sinclair, & Starz, 1996) found that the relationships between pain and disability and between pain and physical functioning were significant, whereas there was no significant association between observed physical functioning and disability in FMS patients (Figure 12.3). These results suggest that FMS is associated with patients' inaccuracy in perceiving their physical capabilities. However, this study was based on patients' retrospective reports and may be biased by memory, self-report, and other factors. Some patients may have wanted to demonstrate how well they could function despite their pain. High rates of functional disability in terms of unemployment and disability compensation have been reported in the CFS literature as well (Buchwald et al., 1996; Deale et al., 1997). Prospective studies are definitely needed to increase understanding of the discrepancy between actual and perceived performance.

PERCEPTIONS OF CAUSE OF SYMPTOMS

THE EFFECT OF TRAUMATIC ILLNESS OR INJURY

Beliefs of having been injured or infected may affect cognitive mechanisms of symptom perception in chronic pain. These beliefs may be associated with the traumatic onset of an illness, and the thought that activity will lead to additional harm and symptom exacerbation. Thus, the acknowledgment that symptoms followed a specific pathological cause appears to greatly increase fear. Preoccupation with bodily symptoms is commonly observed among those who have been involved in motor vehicle accidents (MVA; Hodge, 1971). Such hypervigilance may predispose patients to attend selectively to all somatic perturbations that might otherwise be ignored and to avoid activities that they believe will contribute to further problems (i.e., fear avoidance). Moreover, exposure to noxious agents (events, pathogens) may alter the interpretation of physical sensations.

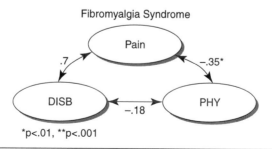

Figure 12.3 Relationships among Pain, Disability (DISB), and Physical Functioning (PHY) in Fibromyalgia Syndrome

Patients may have a tendency to identify any physical sensation as abnormal, harmful, and noxious, thereby increasing anxiety. These changes may, consequently, lower pain threshold and tolerance, increase activity avoidance, and exacerbate general deconditioning and fatigue.

Experiencing a traumatic injury or viral illness may also alter how people evaluate sensory information. Pain perception and sensitivity may be altered by involvement in an accident. Lee, Giles, and Drummond (1993) observed that post-MVA victims reported lower pain tolerance compared with healthy subjects. It is not known whether decreased pain tolerance among posttrauma patients is due to subtle, if not gross, changes in physiology that could result in pain hypersensitivity. This could also be due to the result of changes in psychological processes involving selective attention and fear appraisals. Elevated body awareness and anticipation of pain may result in a pain-sensitive perceptual system, in which the individual may focus more on physical sensations and interpret relatively benign sensory input as pain. Some people may be predisposed to hypervigilance and fear avoidance based on high or chronic levels of negative affectivity.

Several studies have examined differences in mode of onset of CFS. The results suggest that those with a sudden onset differ in severity of symptoms, emotional distress, and premorbid psychiatric history. The results, however, are contradictory. Jason, Taylor, Kennedy, Song, et al. (2000) found that people with sudden onset were more likely to have more severe physical symptoms and lifetime histories of psychiatric diagnoses. In contrast, DeLuca, Johnson, Ellis, and Natelson (1997) found that those with gradual onset of CFS had more concurrent psychiatric diagnoses than those with sudden onset of symptoms. There are several possible explanations for these apparently contradictory findings. One is that the Jason study used a large community sample, whereas the DeLuca sample was substantially smaller and consisted of people seeking treatment. Future research will need to examine these differences; however, there appear to be differences among people with CFS depending on the onset of their symptoms.

A substantial number of patients with diverse chronic pain syndromes attribute the onset of their pain to some type of trauma such as a motor vehicle accident (MVA) or a work-related injury. Turk and Okifuji (1996) examined a heterogeneous sample of chronic pain patients and determined that 75% attributed the onset of their symptoms to a physical trauma, most commonly an MVA or work-related injury. Using a standardized system for evaluating physical pathology (Rudy, Turk, & Brena, 1988), we found no significant differences in the physical findings between the groups who reported a traumatic onset compared with those who reported an insidious onset. To eliminate the possible confound of compensation status, we performed analyses of the relationships between the two types of onset and chronic pain for the subset of patients who were not receiving or actively seeking compensation. The patients who attributed their pain to a specific sudden trauma reported significantly higher levels of emotional distress, life interference, and pain severity than did the patients who indicated that their pain had a gradual, insidious onset although no differences in physical pathology were identified between these groups.

Turk and Okifuji (1996) replicated the results on perceptions of the causes of symptoms with a sample of patients with FMS. In this study, 50% of the patients attributed the onset of their symptoms to a physical trauma. Once again, we found no significant difference in physical pathology between those with a sudden traumatic versus gradual insidious onset of symptoms. Again, controlling for compensation status, we found that the patients with traumatic onset of symptoms reported more pain, greater life interference, physical disability, and affective distress.

SYMPTOM ATTRIBUTION AND TREATMENT

Interestingly, Turk and Okifuji (1996) also found that patients who attribute symptoms to a physical trauma were significantly more likely to receive physical treatments for symptoms including nerve blocks, physical therapy, and transcutaneous electrical nerve stimulation. These traumatic-onset patients were five times more likely to be prescribed opioid medication even though they did not reveal greater physical pathology. Thus, physicians provide different treatment for patients who report sudden, traumatic onset to their symptoms, independent of objective indications of physical pathology.

In a second study, Turk and Okifuji (1997) observed that physicians were more likely to prescribe opioid medication based on patients' reports of disturbed mood, greater impact on their lives, and behavioral presentation but, once again, not physical pathology or even reported pain severity. The role of the physician's behaviors in the maintenance of symptoms and disability of pain sufferers has been frequently noted (Hadler, 1997; Reilly, 1999).

The attribution of pain and related symptoms to a physical trauma seems to add an additional emotional burden and to exacerbate the problems of chronic pain patients. These results are consistent with studies of a heterogeneous sample of patients with chronic pain (Geisser, Roth, Bachman, & Eckert, 1996) and FMS (Greenfield, Fitzcharles, & Esdaile, 1992). In addition, patients whose painful symptoms follow an accident have been shown to be more refractory to treatment than patients with nontraumatic onset (DeGood & Kiernan, 1996; Tsushima & Stoddard, 1990). In the CFS literature as well, attribution of symptoms to somatic causes is associated with poorer outcomes (e.g., Joyce, Hotopf, & Wessely, 1997; DeLuca et al., 1997; Deale, Chalder, & Wessely, 1998; Jason, Taylor, Kennedy, Song, et al., 2000).

HETEROGENEITY WITHIN FMS AND CFS POPULATIONS

FMS and CFS patients report a plethora of somatic and psychological symptoms. In the past few decades, several approaches have been tested for the treatment of CFS and FMS (e.g., corticosteroids, benzodiazepines, tricyclic antidepressants, growth hormone, aerobic exercises, cognitive-behavior therapy, multidisciplinary rehabilitation). Despite the extensive research efforts, however, no treatment has proven to be universally effective. Research has suggested that some treatments are effective for some symptoms for some patients. However, we do not yet understand why these treatments may be effective, nor can we reliably predict what works best for whom.

Results from the studies investigating pathophysiological mechanisms and efficacy of treatments for FMS and CFS have been equivocal. Some problems with the current literature may be related to the heterogeneity of the population and subtypes of patients on many factors (e.g., demographics, precipitating events,

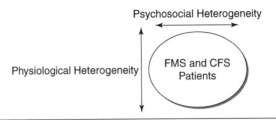

Figure 12.4   Dual Classification Model of FMS

duration of symptoms, occupation, emotional distress, stressful life events, coping, and adjustment) (DeLuca et al., 1997; Jason, Taylor, Kennedy, Song, et al., 2000; Turk & Flor, 1989).

Several investigators (e.g., Dworkin & LeResche, 1992; Scharff, Turk, & Marcus, 1995; Turk, 1990) recommend a dual-diagnostic system for chronic pain disorders, allowing for both biomedical and psychosocial diagnoses (see Figure 12.4). Our research has focused on the psychosocial aspects and has been the first step toward the comprehensive, dual-diagnostic classification of FMS that may be equally appropriate for CFS. This emphasis on psychosocial and behavioral factors, however, does not mean that we view FMS or CFS as primarily psychological disorders. Future research should lead to a more refined taxonomy in the classification of FMS and CFS that can complement the psychosocial-behavioral diagnosis.

To clarify the heterogeneity, Turk and colleagues (1996) examined whether FMS patients could be classified into subgroups based on their psychological adaptation to pain. The Multidimensional Pain Inventory (MPI; Kerns, Turk, & Rudy, 1985) has been used in several chronic pain populations to classify patients into one of the three MPI profiles (Turk & Rudy, 1990). These profiles are Dysfunctional (DYS: high levels of pain, functional limitation, and affective distress), Interpersonally Distressed (ID: similar to DYS but further characterized by low levels of support from their significant other), and Adaptive Coper (AC: low levels of pain, distress, and disability). Using the MPI, approximately 87% of FMS patients could be classified into one of the three MPI profiles. Table 12.3 shows distributions of the MPI profiles in FMS patients and in other chronic pain patients who had been identified in previous research (Turk et al., 1996).

Table 12.3
Distributions of the MPI Profiles in
Various Pain Disorders (*n*)

MPI Profiles	FMS (141) (%)	LB (200) (%)	HA (245) (%)	TMD (200) (%)
DYS	28	62	44	46
ID	37	18	26	22
AC	35	20	30	32

AC = Adaptive coper; DYS = Dysfunctional; FMS = Fibromyalgia; HA = Headache; ID = Interpersonally distressed; LB = Low back pain; MPI = Multidimensional pain inventory; TMD = Temporomandibular disorders

ROBUSTNESS OF THE MPI PROFILING

Comparing the taxonometric structure and profiles of several major but distinct chronic pain groups who, despite the presence of pain, differ in important ways can test the generalizability of the MPI taxonomy. Figure 12.5 shows the mean MPI scale scores for three groups of pain patients: FMS, cancer, and non-FMS, noncancer chronic pain patients (CP) (Turk et al., 1996; Turk & Rudy, 1990; Turk, Sist, et al., 1998). A multivariate analysis of variance (MANOVA) with the MPI

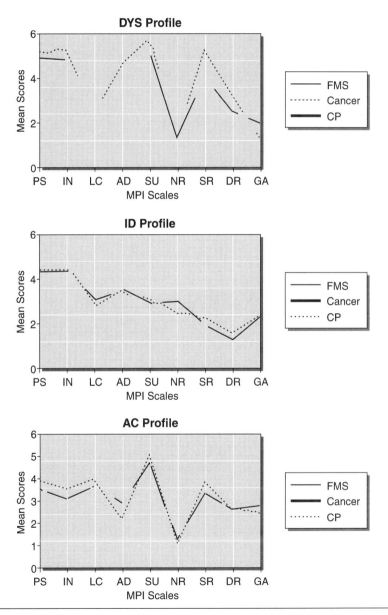

Figure 12.5 Mean MPI Scale Scores in Three Groups of Chronic Pain Patients by MPI Profile

scale scores as the dependent variables and pain diagnosis as the independent variable was computed.

The MANOVA produced significant results, with the exception of the Life Control scale, which was marginal. Thus, the three groups of pain patients report different mean scores on the scales of the MPI. However, the covariance structure among the MPI scales (profile patterns) seems remarkably consistent among the three MPI profiles despite the differences in physical diagnoses and mean scale scores. The results suggest that, although there may be variability in the mean scale scores of the MPI, all three profiles are present in each biomedical diagnostic group. From Figure 12.5, one could hypothesize that FMS, cancer, and CP patients who are classified within the same MPI profile may be more similar to each other in subjective experience and response to symptoms than are patients with the same pain diagnosis but who are classified to a different MPI profile. These results suggest that although different physical diagnostic groups may require common biomedical treatment targeting the pathophysiological mechanisms underlying each disorder, they may also benefit from specific psychosocial interventions tailored to their psychosocial-behavioral characteristics (MPI-based profiles).

VALIDITY OF THE MPI CLASSIFICATION

To ascertain whether the three MPI profile groups differ only in the areas in which they are supposed to differ (discriminant validity), we conducted a series of univariate comparisons, followed by post hoc analysis. The areas of interest included observed physical functioning, pain, depressive moods, perceived functional limitation, and quality of interpersonal relationships. These variables were measured using standardized self-report instruments or protocols (physical functioning). As expected, the three groups did not differ in observed physical functioning such as lumbar flexion, "fingertips to floor," straight leg raise, and cervical range of motion. However, the analyses revealed that (1) the DYS patients reported significantly higher levels of pain than AC patients, (2) the DYS and ID groups reported significantly higher levels of depressed mood and perceived disability, and (3) the ID patients rated their interpersonal relationships with significant others to be significantly lower in quality compared with the DYS and AC patients. These results replicate the original MPI development research (Kerns et al., 1985) and support the convergent and discriminant validity of the MPI (Turk et al., 1996). Post hoc analysis of the co-occurring symptoms demonstrates that the three groups did not differ in the prevalence of symptoms. The results reinforce the suggestion that psychosocial dimensions of FMS may be independent of biomedical-physical dimensions.

DIFFERENTIAL RELATIONSHIP BETWEEN ACTUAL AND PERCEIVED PHYSICAL FUNCTIONING BY MPI PROFILE

Current conceptualizations of chronic pain emphasize the interactions among multiple factors associated with the disorder. Interestingly, objective and subjective aspects of chronic pain disorders do not always correlate highly. In FMS, we replicated this result using structural equation modeling. As a group, there was a substantial association between pain and subjective report of disability, a modest relationship between pain and observed physical ability, and no relationship between subjective disability and observed physical ability. However, when the MPI profiles were taken into consideration, correlational analyses revealed group differences in the relationship between actual (observed) and subjective ratings of physical functioning. These findings provide further support for the hypotheses that FMS patients are not a homogeneous group and that MPI classification, based on psychological adaptation to pain, may be helpful in developing patient-specific treatment programs.

TREATMENT EFFICACY OF AN
INTERDISCIPLIARY FMS PROGRAM

Given the multiple symptoms of FMS, many have advocated employing a multi-component rehabilitation approach. In a preliminary study, Turk, Okifuji, Sinclair, and Starz (1998b) examined the efficacy of an interdisciplinary treatment program for 67 FMS patients, including 6-month follow-up. The treatment program consisted of 6 half-day sessions, spaced over 4 weeks. Each session included medical (education, medication management), physical (aerobic and stretching exercises), occupational (pacing, body mechanics), and psychological (pain and stress management) components.

The comparisons between the pretreatment and posttreatment scores revealed significant improvement in the targeted areas of pain severity, sense of control, depression, and fatigue, but remained at the pretreatment levels for nontargeted variables such as support from significant others. Results at follow-up revealed that the majority of treatment gains were sustained for 6 months following completion of treatment, although there was a statistically significant relapse in reported fatigue.

Turk et al. (1998b) analyzed the clinical significance of the improvement in pain severity, using the Reliable Change (RC) Index (Jacobson, Follette, & Revenstorf, 1984). Forty-two percent of treated patients were identified as successful responders. To delineate factors that would predict improvement in FMS pain, Turk et al. conducted a discriminant analysis with six pretreatment variables that were considered to be particularly relevant in pain reports: pretreatment levels of pain, depression, activity, perceived disability, solicitous responses from others, and whether FMS onset was attributed to a known cause (idiopathic). All variables except the pretreatment level of pain yielded meaningful associations. Thus, patients who reported an idiopathic onset, who were relatively active and coping well, and who have solicitous partners tended to report significant improvement in pain. With these six variables, 77% of the patients could be accurately classified as responders or nonresponders. The results suggest that patients' responses to a standard treatment vary and that different treatment approaches may be needed to meet clinical characteristics of FMS sufferers (Turk et al., 1998b).

DIFFERENTIAL TREATMENT RESPONSES AS A FUNCTION OF THE MPI PROFILES

Based on the significant differences in adaptation to the chronic pain condition across psychosocial subgroups of FMS patients, Turk et al. (1998a) hypothesized that the MPI subgroups would respond differently to a standard rehabilitation treatment protocol. Patients who completed the FMS program were classified into one of the three MPI profiles on the basis of their pretreatment MPI scores.

Planned comparisons were conducted to evaluate whether the changes between pretreatment and posttreatment were significant. Overall, the patients in the DYS group improved in most areas, whereas the ID patients, who reported levels of pain and disability comparable to those of the DYS group, failed to respond to the treatment. There was little change in the AC patients, possibly due to a ceiling effect. The results further support the need for different treatments targeting characteristics of subgroups and suggest that psychosocial characteristics of FMS patients are important predictors of treatment responses and may be used to customize treatment. Whereas the ID patients may require additional treatment components addressing clinical needs specific to this group (e.g., interpersonal skills), some components of the standard interdisciplinary treatment may be unnecessary for the AC patients (Turk et al., 1998b).

The modest results in the past studies may be related to the failure to consider that FMS patients are not a homogeneous group. This may be the case for CFS as well. Combining patients with diverse features may have contributed to the conflicting results that characterize the FMS and CFS literatures. Turk et al. (1996) have suggested that the diagnostic classification of FMS is probably a generic label for several associated conditions, each with some distinct characteristics. We have cited several studies to support this hypothesis for FMS. For CFS, Johnson et al. (1999), have identified two groups: one with a sudden illness onset that appears to have less psychiatric comorbidity but greater cognitive difficulty; the other with gradual onset, psychiatric symptomatology, and less cognitive difficulty. Studies reporting on psychiatric status typically find that psychiatric symtomatology is associated with poorer outcomes (e.g., Joyce et al., 1997; Russo et al., 1998).

Several authors have also recommended taking into account exercise and activity levels before illness. They note that athletes and nonathletes have significant differences in their thresholds for training, deconditioning, and average and expected activity levels (e.g., Jain & DeLisa, 1998; Shephard, 2001). Heterogeneity of FMS can be assessed on the two independent dimensions: physiological and psychosocial (Turk et al., 1996). As seen in Figure 12.4, patients in the same level of psychosocial factors may be very different from each other on the physiological dimension, and vice versa.

TREATMENT RECOMMENDATIONS

A comprehensive discussion of treatment for CFS and FMS is beyond the scope of this chapter. Thus, we simply highlight some key points.

Research has suggested that some treatments are effective for some symptoms for some patients. However, we do not yet understand why these treatments may be effective, nor can we reliably predict what works best for whom. Since both CFS and FMS involve physical symptoms that interfere with well-being and functioning, a biopsychosocial model of treatment is recommended that considers psychosocial and behavioral characteristics of patients as well as their physical symptoms.

Information and reassurance are essential for treating FMS and CFS. The lack of a definitive explanation for the symptoms often produces fear. Patients may be afraid that something serious but as yet unidentified is causing the symptoms, that the symptoms will become progressively worse, that there is nothing that can be done, that psychological (imaginary) factors are causing all the problems, or that they will be simply told to learn to live with symptoms without being told *how*.

People with CFS and FMS need to have realistic goals. Health care providers should address the patients' concerns, provide reassurance, and clarify what can reasonably be expected. It can be very demoralizing to be told you have a chronic illness, because the term *chronic* has the connotation of forever. Consider how you would feel if you were told, "You have disabling symptoms that, although not progressive, will persist 24 hours a day, 365 days a year, for the rest of your life." The patient and provider must have congruent goals, and the provider must avoid attitudes and behaviors that may delegitimize patients' experience (e.g., Ware, 1992). Clinicians must ensure that treatment goals are mutually understood and agreed on. People may be willing to tolerate some degree of pain if they can have more energy for work or other activities. Health care providers must also take into account which areas of functioning are most important for their patients' quality of life (e.g., Gorbatenko-Roth, Levin, Altmaier, & Doebbling, 2001).

Many FMS and CFS patients fear that being active will make their symptoms worse and thus they avoid activity to prevent more pain, fatigue, and injury. In a sense, they have learned that if something causes distress, they should avoid it—hurt and harm become equivalent.

A common feature of both CFS and FMS is physical deconditioning. Thus, exercise to improve endurance and flexibility is appropriate for both pain and fatigue. There may be both direct and indirect benefits of exercise. Direct benefits might include increased production of endorphins with a concomitant reduction in pain. There may also be indirect benefits from an increased perception of control that counteracts the sense of helplessness commonly observed in patients and thereby restores their morale (e.g., Fulcher & White, 1997; McCain, Bell, Mai, & Halliday, 1998; McCully, Sisto, & Natelson, 1996). To combat the passivity and the downward spiral of deconditioning and disability, it is important to teach patients proper body mechanics, sleep hygiene, and pacing of activities. Cognitive-behavior therapy focuses on the person's thoughts, feelings, and behaviors. It also addresses the role of environmental factors in maintaining and exacerbating symptoms while facilitating disability. Although cognitive-behavioral therapy is not a cure, it can help people control their symptoms and regain control of their lives.

Several behavioral approaches may be helpful. Time management, pacing, and relaxation training focus specifically on behavior. People learn to make choices about which activities they can realistically accomplish on a given day. A pacing exercise calls for them to set up a daily time quota for a particular activity and to spend only the preset time on that activity—no more and no less. The quota is based on a portion of each individual's known capacity for that activity. They are asked to perform the activity for several days, up to the point where they are beginning to feel pain or fatigue or other sign that they have reached their limit. Using this as a baseline, they then set up a manageable activity plan, with gradually increasing activity levels that they are likely to be able to maintain.

Activity schedules should be established in advance and should not be based on pain, fatigue, or other symptoms. This assignment often requires a significant psychological adjustment. Patients have typically adjusted their activity based on their pain and fatigue levels, trying to maximize their activity on good days. Conscientious or high-achieving patients also may have difficulty with the notion of starting a project or task and not necessarily completing it.

Examination of dysfunctional thoughts can influence attitudinal components of coping responses. Health care professionals should raise patients' awareness of their negative thought patterns, such as catastrophic, black-white, or unrealistically global or negative thinking; filtering, or biased awareness of negative information; and unrealistic appraisals of control and self-efficacy. Efforts should be made to enable these people to develop adaptive cognitions that permit more hope, or a belief that they may be able to do something to improve their situation. Taking action or trying new behaviors in turn may encourage them to make further efforts, all of which can alter their self-concept in a positive direction and away from passive suffering. Assertiveness training, in particular, can help people develop attitudes and behaviors that work in their interpersonal contexts. As patients shift from feeling responsible for everything for everyone, to acknowledging limits and asking for help, they may need to learn communication skills to facilitate cooperation from family, friends, and coworkers. This may be of particular importance for those patients who fit the characteristics of being "interpersonally distressed" within the MPI classification described earlier. As patients become less preoccupied or burdened by their illness experience, they may need to practice teaching others how much, or how little, they want to discuss or focus on their symptoms, and help others to see them in their new, more active, light.

Even though psychological factors did not cause the initial symptoms, living with debilitating symptoms can create emotional distress and interpersonal problems. Thus, people may benefit from the cognitive and behavioral skills included in treatment, but this should not be taken as an indication that their symptoms are all psychosomatic. The psychosocial components of treatment interventions can be beneficial in several ways. Learning useful strategies reduces patients' dependence on their health care providers or on significant others to help them keep going. Specific training around setbacks or flare-ups of symptoms is particularly important in coping with a chronic condition. Developing a specific plan to address problems during these episodes can prepare patients psychologically so that they are less discouraged or overwhelmed by such episodes.

Psychosocial interventions addressing interpersonal issues can strengthen people's use of other techniques. Significant others (e.g., spouses, other family members, partners) can learn how they can be most helpful to the affected person, whether through instrumental, direct problem-solving support, or through emotional support and validation of the person's experience and efforts. Attention to family interactions is also crucial in addressing problems of FMS, CFS, and other chronic illnesses (e.g., Schmaling & Sher, 2000; Turk & Kerns, 1985).

Psychosocial interventions provided in groups allow for sharing of concerns and advice, and for validation of individual experiences. Less disabled participants can gain a greater awareness of their progress, and they can provide advice and hope to more disabled patients, often more plausibly than can a nonpatient health care provider. More disabled participants can learn from others who have managed to make progress and enjoy good outcomes despite their symptoms.

Preliminary studies using a cognitive-behavioral approach have been generally positive in reducing symptoms and related distress, but not in eliminating all symptoms of CFS or FMS (e.g., Kroenke & Swindle, 2000; Nielson, Walker, & McCain, 1992). Large-scale studies with appropriate control groups and adequate follow-up periods are required to confirm the effectiveness of the cognitive-behavioral approach. To date, only one study (Turk et al., 1998a) has addressed the characteristics of FMS treatment responders. Research is needed to determine what set of CFS and FMS patients, with what characteristics, can benefit from generic cognitive-behavioral treatments combined with activity therapy. The failure of many patients to achieve and maintain positive outcomes indicates, most assuredly, that *one size does not fit all.*

Medication that targets key symptoms (i.e., fatigue, sleep, depression) should also be considered as an adjunct to exercise and cognitive-behavioral therapy (Goldenberg, Felson, & Dinerman, 1986; Goodnick & Sandoval, 1993; O'Malley et al., 2000). Providing some symptomatic relief may enable patients to sleep better and to engage in paced physical activities. In particular, antidepressant medication may work because it addresses actual depression symptoms, but may also improve sleep quality or somehow reduce pain severity, even at doses that are typically lower than those used for depression. To our knowledge, there have been no blinded, randomized controlled trials with long-term follow-ups evaluating the effectiveness of such combined treatments.

UNANSWERED QUESTIONS ABOUT CFS AND FMS

Are CFS and FMS two distinct disorders, or one disorder with differing presentations? If these are different disorders, this would imply the need for different treatments or at least the customization of some components to fit the unique features of each one.

What symptoms are most problematic for which patients? As we refine our understanding of each patient's experience with CFS and FMS, we can begin to target interventions more effectively. To use an analogy, we need to move from the current all-you-can-eat approach to the greater precision of an à la carte plan. Patients with similar experiences might receive group interventions most appropriate for those symptoms—an example of the treatment matching described earlier. In addition to matching treatment to patients' characteristics, treatment might be focused on addressing the problems that patients perceive as most important. Alternatively, at least in some instances within a treatment program, it may be important to help patients identify problems. Patients may identify pain as their only problem and assume that every aspect of their lives would be ideal if only they could eliminate their pain. If this is not possible, then these patients may need to give more attention to the problems created by the pain, since some of these difficulties (e.g., family stress, inactivity) may be addressable even when pain persists.

What treatment(s) is (are) most effective for which symptoms? Exercise may improve pain, energy, and morale but have little impact on interpersonal problems. Cognitive restructuring to alter emotional distress may have little impact on physical functioning. Cognitive-behavioral strategies may be related to improved coping in terms of time and activity management as well as a more positive outlook. Relaxation training may improve pain. Affected people will benefit from any treatment component that allows them to believe that change is possible and that strengthens their feelings of mastery or control. We can sum this up with the general question, "What treatment components, with what characteristics, are best for which set of patients, and what manner of delivery will have the best outcomes?"

What treatment or combination of treatments is associated with best long-term outcomes? Intervention strategies can be extremely effective during the course of treatment and shortly thereafter. Many treatment outcome studies have immediate beneficial effects, but problems of nonadherence to recommendations and relapse are common and can be particularly discouraging. The challenge is to develop treatments that have positive outcomes and are maintained on important measures that generalize beyond the treatment context. This includes activities that can be sustained in the long term, such as regular exercise and activity pacing, as well as a self-efficacy perspective that enables people to recognize what they can do and encourages them to continue doing it. Maintenance and generalization are particularly important factors, since there is no cure, and people must continue to engage in self-management activities, including regular exercise, for the foreseeable future.

Rates of a complete cure of CFS and FMS are virtually nonexistent (e.g., Joyce et al., 1997). They are, therefore, *chronic* diseases. We need to approach these syndromes with a broad, biopsychosocial model of treatment that provides patients with tools to regain control, where they can, of their functioning and quality of life. These strategies must also be realistic within the contexts of their daily lives. A mindful approach must take into account what these people can address physically (e.g., with exercise and relaxation training), psychologically (e.g., with cognitive approaches to adaptive thinking and self-efficacy), and socially (e.g., by reconciling their necessary and desired activities in their home and work lives).

Pain and fatigue are phenomenological experiences that integrate past (predisposition, learning history), current (present neuroendocrinologic processing), and future (expectation, beliefs). The subjectivity of these symptoms makes the assessment challenging. We have touched on some methodological issues in this review. Every researcher and clinician must be aware that when we assess pain and fatigue, we are assessing a subjective experience and thus reliable techniques with strong discriminant and convergent validity become critical.

FMS and CFS are perplexing and challenging syndromes for researchers, clinicians, patients, and their significant others alike. Factors contributing to pain and fatigue have been evaluated, including sensitization processes, hormonal factors, neuropeptides, sleep disruption, dysautonomia, and peripheral influences. In each area, there are promising findings that need to be studied further and integrated into our current understanding of how pain and fatigue are processed and experienced. We need to move forward to examine what treatment works best for whom. By matching treatment to specific patients' characteristics, we should be able to optimize treatment efficacy; reduce many patients' symptoms, vastly improving their functioning and quality of life; and accomplish all of this in a cost-effective manner.

REFERENCES

Aaron, L. A., Bradley, L. A., Alarcon, G. S., Alexander, R. W., Triana-Alexander, M., Martin, M. Y., et al. (1996). Psychiatric diagnoses in patients with fibromyalgia are related to health care-seeking behavior rather than to illness. *Arthritis and Rheumatism, 39,* 436–445.

Affleck, G., Tennen, H., Urrows, S., Higgins, P., Abeles, M., Hall, C., et al. (1998). Fibromyalgia and women's pursuit of personal goals: A daily process analysis. *Health Psychology, 17,* 40–47.

Ahles, T. A., Khan, S. A., Yunus, M. B., Spiegel, D. A., & Masi, A. T. (1991). Psychiatric status of patients with primary fibromyalgia, patients with rheumatoid arthritis, and subjects without pain: A blind comparison of *DSM-III* diagnoses. *American Journal of Psychiatry, 148,* 1721–1726.

Alfici, S., Sigal, M., & Landau, M. (1989). Primary fibromyalgia syndrome: A variant of depressive disorder? *Psychotherapy and Psychosomatics, 51,* 156–161.

Bandura, A. (1977). Self-efficacy: Toward a unifying theory of behavioral change. *Psychological Review, 84,* 191–215.

Barsky, A. J., & Borus, J. F. (1999). Functional somatic syndromes. *Annals of Internal Medicine, 130,* 910–921.

Bengtsson, A., Henriksson, K. G., & Jorfeldt, L. (1986). Primary fibromyalgia: A clinical and laboratory study of 55 patients. *Scandinavian Journal of Rheumatology, 15,* 340–347.

Bennett, R. M. (1981). Fibrositis: Misnomer for a common rheumatic disorder. *Western Journal of Medicine, 134,* 405–413.

Bennett, R. M., Clark, S. R., Campbell, S. M., & Burckhardt, C. S. (1992). Low levels of somatomedin C in patients with the fibromyalgia syndrome: A possible link between sleep and muscle pain. *Arthritis and Rheumatism, 35,* 1113–1116.

Blalock, S., DeVellis, B., & DeVellis, R. (1992). Psychological well-being among people with recently diagnosed rheumatoid arthritis: Do self-perceptions of abilities make a difference? *Arthritis and Rheumatism, 35,* 1267–1272.

Bombardier, C. H., & Buchwald, D. (1996). Chronic fatigue, chronic fatigue syndrome, and fibromyalgia: Disability and health care use. *Medical Care, 34,* 924–930.

Buchwald, D. (1996). Fibromyalgia and chronic fatigue syndrome: Similarities and differences. *Rheumatic Disease Clinics of North America, 22,* 219–243.

Buchwald, D., & Garrity, D. (1994). Comparison of patients with chronic fatigue syndrome, fibromyalgia, and multiple chemical sensitivities. *Archives of Internal Medicine, 154,* 2049–2053.

Buchwald, D., Pearlman, T., Umali, J., Schmaling, K., & Katon, W. (1996). Functional status in patients with chronic fatigue syndrome, other fatiguing illnesses, and healthy individuals. *American Journal of Medicine, 101,* 364–370.

Buckelew, S. P., Huyser, B., Hewett, J. E., Parker, J. C., Johnson, J. C., Conway, R., et al. (1996). Self-efficacy predicting outcome among fibromyalgia subjects. *Arthritis Care and Research, 9,* 97–104.

Buckelew, S. P., Murray, S. E., Hewett, J. E., Johnson, J., & Huyser, B. (1995). Self-efficacy, pain, and physical activity among fibromyalgia subjects. *Arthritis Care and Research, 8,* 43–50.

Burckhardt, C. S., Clark, S. R., & Bennett, R. M. (1993). Fibromyalgia and quality of life: A comparative analysis. *Journal of Rheumatology, 20,* 475–479.

Burckhardt, C. S., O'Reilly, C. A., Wiens, A. N., Clark, S. R., Campbell, S. M., & Bennett, R. M. (1994). Assessing depression in fibromyalgia patients. *Arthritis Care and Research, 7,* 35–39.

Celiker, R., Borman, P., Oktem, F., Gokce-Kutsal, Y., & Basgoze, O. (1997). Psychological disturbance in fibromyalgia: Relation to pain severity. *Clinical Rheumatology, 16,* 179–184.

Christodoulou, C., DeLuca, J., Lange, G., Johnson, S. K., Sisto, S. A., Korn, L., et al. (1998). Relation between neuropsychological impairment and functional disability in patients with chronic fatigue syndrome. *Journal of Neurology, Neurosurgery and Psychiatry, 64,* 431–434.

Clark, P., Burgos-Vargas, R., Medina-Palma, C., Lavielle, P., & Marina, F. F. (1998). Prevalence of fibromyalgia in children: A clinical study of Mexican children. *Journal of Rheumatology, 25,* 2009–2014.

Deale, A., Chalder, T., Marks, I., & Wessely, S. (1997). Cognitive behavior therapy for chronic fatigue syndrome: A randomized controlled trial. *American Journal of Psychiatry, 154,* 408–414.

Deale, A., Chalder, T., & Wessely, S. (1998). Illness beliefs and treatment outcome in chronic fatigue syndrome. *Journal of Psychosomatic Research, 45,* 77–83.

DeGood, D. E., & Kiernan, B. (1996). Perception of fault in patients with chronic pain. *Pain, 64,* 153–159.

DeLuca, J., Johnson, S. K., Ellis, S. P., & Natelson, B. H. (1997). Sudden versus gradual onset of chronic fatigue syndrome differentiates individuals on cognitive and psychiatric measures. *Journal of Psychiatric Research, 31,* 83–90.

Dworkin, S., & LeResche, L. (1992). Research diagnostic criteria for temporomandibular disorders: Review, criteria, examinations and specifications, critique. *Journal of Craniomandibular Disorders, 6,* 301–355.

Elert, J. E., Rantapaa-Dahlqvist, S. B., Henriksson-Larsen, K., & Gerdle, B. (1992). Muscle performance, electromyography and fibre type composition in fibromyalgia and work-related myalgia. *Scandinavian Journal of Rheumatology, 21,* 28–34.

Fordyce, W. E. (1976). *Behavioral methods for chronic pain and illness.* St. Louis, MO: Mosby.

Friedberg, F., & Jason, L. A. (1998). *Understanding chronic fatigue syndrome: An empirical guide to assessment and treatment.* Washington, DC: American Psychological Association.

Fulcher, K. Y., & White, P. D. (1997). Randomised controlled trial of graded exercise in patients with the chronic fatigue syndrome. *British Medical Journal, 314,* 1647–1652.

Geisser, M. E., Roth, R. S., Bachman, J. E., & Eckert, T. A. (1996). The relationship between symptoms of posttraumatic stress disorder and pain, affective disturbance and disability among patients with accident and nonaccident related pain. *Pain, 66,* 207–214.

Goldenberg, D. L. (1987). Fibromyalgia syndrome: An emerging but controversial condition. *Journal of the American Medical Association, 257,* 2782–2787.

Goldenberg, D. L., Felson, D. T., & Dinerman, H. (1986). A randomized, controlled trial of amitriptyline and naproxen in the treatment of patients with fibromyalgia. *Arthritis and Rheumatism, 29,* 1371–1377.

Goodnick, P. J., & Sandoval, R. (1993). Psychotropic treatment of chronic fatigue syndrome and related disorders. *Journal of Clinical Psychiatry, 54,* 13–20.

Gorbatenko-Roth, K. G., Levin, I. P., Altmaier, E. M., & Doebbling, B. N. (2001). Accuracy of health-related quality of life assessment: What is the benefit of incorporating patients' preferences for domain functioning? *Health Psychology, 20,* 136–140.

Granges, G., & Littlejohn, G. O. (1993). A comparative study of clinical signs in fibromyalgia/fibrositis syndrome, healthy and exercising subjects. *Journal of Rheumatology, 20,* 344–351.

Greenfield, S., Fitzcharles, M. A., & Esdaile, J. M. (1992). Reactive fibromyalgia syndrome. *Arthritis and Rheumatism, 35,* 678–681.

Hadler, N. M. (1997). Fibromyalgia, chronic fatigue, and other iatrogenic diagnostic algorithms: Do some labels escalate illness in vulnerable patients? *Postgraduate Medicine, 102,* 161–172.

Hodge, J. R. (1971). The whiplash neurosis. *Psychosomatics, 12,* 245–249.

Hudson, J. I., Hudson, M. S., Pliner, L. F., Goldenberg, D. L., & Pope, H. G., Jr. (1985). Fibromyalgia and major affective disorder: A controlled phenomenology and family history study. *American Journal of Psychiatry, 142,* 441–446.

Hudson, J. I., & Pope, H. G., Jr. (1996). The relationship between fibromyalgia and major depressive disorder. *Rheumatic Disease Clinics of North America, 22,* 285–303.

Illich, I. (1976). *Medical nemesis: The exploration of health.* Hammondsworth, England: Penguin Books.

Jacobsen S., & Danneskiold-Samsoe, B. (1992). Dynamic muscular endurance in primary fibromyalgia compared with chronic myofascial pain syndrome. *Archives of Physical Medicine & Rehabilitation, 73,* 170–173.

Jacobson, N. S., Follette, W. C., & Revenstorf, D. (1984). Psychotherapy outcome research: Methods for reporting variability and evaluating clinical significance. *Behavior Therapy, 15,* 336–352.

Jain, S. S., & DeLisa, J. A. (1998). Chronic fatigue syndrome: A literature from a psychiatric perspective. *American Journal of Physical Medicine and Rehabilitation, 77,* 160–167.

Jason, L. A., Richman, J. A., Rademaker, A. W., Jordan, K. M., Plioplys, A. V., Taylor, R. R., et al. (1999). A community-based study of chronic fatigue syndrome. *Archives of Internal Medicine, 159,* 2129–2137.

Jason, L. A., Taylor, R. R., & Kennedy, C. L. (2000). Chronic fatigue syndrome, fibromyalgia, and multiple chemical sensitivities in a community-based sample of persons with chronic fatigue syndrome-like symptoms. *Psychosomatic Medicine, 62,* 655–663.

Jason, L. A., Taylor, R. R., Kennedy, C. L., Song, S., Johnson, D., & Torres, M. A. (2000). Chronic fatigue syndrome: Occupation, medical utilization, and subtypes in a community-based sample. *Journal of Nervous and Mental Diseases, 188,* 568–576.

Johnson, S. K., DeLuca, J., & Natelson, B. H. (1996a). Assessing somatization disorder in chronic fatigue syndrome. *Psychosomatic Medicine, 58,* 50–57.

Johnson, S. K., DeLuca, J., & Natelson, B. H. (1996b). Depression in fatiguing illness: Comparing patients with chronic fatigue syndrome, multiple sclerosis, and depression. *Journal of Affective Disorders, 39,* 21–30.

Johnson, S. K., DeLuca, J., & Natelson, B. H. (1999). Chronic fatigue syndrome: Reviewing the research findings. *Annals of Behavioral Medicine, 21,* 258–271.

Joos, E., De Meirleir, K., & Vandenborne, K. (1993). 31P magnetic resonance muscle spectroscopy in fibromyalgia. *Journal of Rheumatology, 20,* 1985–1986.

Joyce, J., Hotopf, M., & Wessely, S. (1997). The prognosis of chronic fatigue and chronic fatigue syndrome: A systematic review. *Quarterly Journal of Medicine, 90,* 223–233.

Kerns, R. D., Turk, D. C., & Rudy, T. E. (1985). The West Haven-Yale Multidimensional Pain Inventory (WHYMPI). *Pain, 23,* 345–356.

Kirmayer, L. J., Robbins, J. M., & Kapusta, M. A. (1988). Somatization and depression in fibromyalgia syndrome. *American Journal of Psychiatry, 145,* 950–954.

Krag, N. J., Norregaard, J., Larsen, J. K., & Danneskiold-Samsoe, B. (1994). A blinded, controlled evaluation of anxiety and depressive symptoms in patients with fibromyalgia, as measured by standardized psychometric interview scales. *Acta Psychiatrica Scandinavica, 89,* 370–375.

Kroenke, K., & Swindle, R. (2000). Cognitive-behavioral therapy for somatization and symptom syndromes: A critical review of controlled clinical trials. *Psychotherapy and Psychosomatics, 69,* 205–215.

Landro, N. I., Stiles, T. C., & Sletvold, H. (1997). Memory functioning in patients with primary fibromyalgia and major depression and healthy controls. *Journal of Psychosomatic Research, 42,* 297–306.

Lawrie, S. M., MacHale, S. M., Power, M. J., & Goodwin, G. M. (1997). Is chronic fatigue syndrome best understood as a primary disturbance of the sense of effort? *Psychological Medicine, 27,* 995–999.

Lee, J., Giles, K., & Drummond, P. D. (1993). Psychological disturbance and exaggerated response to pain in patients with whiplash injury. *Journal of Psychosomatic Research, 37,* 105–110.

Lindh, M. H., Johansson, L. G., Hedberg, M., & Grimby, G. L. (1994). Studies on maximal voluntary muscle contraction in patients with fibromyalgia. *Archives of Physical Medicine and Rehabilitation, 5,* 1217–1222.

MacFarlane, G. J., Croft, P. R., Schollum, J., & Silman, A. J. (1996). Widespread pain: Is an improved classification possible? *Journal of Rheumatology, 23,* 1628–1632.

Mannerkorpi, K., Burckhardt, C. S., & Bjelle, A. (1994). Physical performance characteristics of women with fibromyalgia. *Arthritis Care and Research, 7,* 123–129.

Martin, L., Nutting, A., MacIntosh, B. R., Edworthy, S. M., Butterwick, D., & Cook, J. (1996). An exercise program in the treatment of fibromyalgia. *Journal of Rheumatology, 23,* 1050–1053.

McCain, G. A., Bell, D. A., Mai, F. M., & Halliday, P. D. (1988). A controlled study of the effects of a supervised cardiovascular fitness training program on the manifestations of primary fibromyalgia. *Arthritis and Rheumatism, 3,* 1135–1141.

McCully, K. K., Sisto, S. A., & Natelson, B. H. (1996). Use of exercise for treatment of chronic fatigue syndrome. *Sports Medicine, 21,* 35–48.

Mengshoel, A. M., Forre, O., & Komnaes, H. B. (1990). Muscle strength and aerobic capacity in primary fibromyalgia. *Clinical and Experimental Rheumatology, 8,* 475–479.

Morriss, R. K., Ahmed, M., Wearden, A. J., Mullis, R., Strickland, P., Appleby, L., et al. (1999). The role of depression in pain, psychophysiological syndromes and medically unexplained symptoms associated with chronic fatigue syndrome. *Journal of Affective Disorders, 55,* 143–148.

Myers, J. K., Weissman, M. M., & Tischler, G. L. (1984). Six-month prevalence of psychiatric disorders in three communities 1980 to 1982. *Archives of General Psychiatry, 41,* 959–967.

Nielson, W. R., Walker, C., & McCain, G. A. (1992). Cognitive-behavioral treatment of fibromyalgia: Preliminary findings. *Journal of Rheumatology, 19,* 98–103.

Norregaard, J., Bulow, P. M., & Danneskiold-Samsoe, B. (1994). Muscle strength, voluntary activation, twitch properties, and endurance in patients with fibromyalgia. *Journal of Neurology, Neurosurgery, and Psychiatry, 57,* 1106–1111.

Norregaard, J., Bulow, P. M., Mehlsen, J., & Danneskiold-Samsoe, B. (1994). Biochemical changes in relation to a maximal exercise test in patients with fibromyalgia. *Clinical Physiology, 14,* 159–167.

Okifuji, A., Turk, D. C., & Marcus, D. A. (1999). Comparison of generalized and localized hyperalgesia in recurrent headache and fibromyalgia patients. *Psychosomatic Medicine, 61,* 771–778.

Okifuji, A., Turk, D. C., & Sherman, J. J. (2000). Evaluation of the relationship between depression and fibromyalgia syndrome: Why aren't all patients depressed? *Journal of Rheumatology, 27,* 212–219.

Okifuji, A., Turk, D. C., Sinclair, J. D., Starz, T. W., & Marcus, D. A. (1997). A standardized Manual Tender Point Survey. I: Development and determination of a threshold point for the identification of positive tender points in fibromyalgia syndrome. *Journal of Rheumatology, 24,* 377–383.

O'Malley, P. G., Balden, E., Tomkins, G., Santoro, J., Kroenke, K., & Jackson, J. L. (2000). Treatment of fibromyalgia with antidepressants: A meta-analysis. *Journal of General Internal Medicine, 15,* 659–666.

Pillemer, S., Bradley, L. A., Crofford, L. J., Moldofsky, H., & Chrousos, G. P. (1997). The neuroscience and endocrinology of fibromyalgia. *Arthritis and Rheumatism, 40,* 1928–1939.

Powell, R., Dolan, R., & Wessely, S. (1990). Attributions and self-esteem in depression and chronic fatigue syndrome. *Journal of Psychosomatic Research, 21,* 665–673.

Prescott, E., Jacobsen, S., Kjoller, M., Bulow, P. M., Danneskiold-Samsoe, B., & Kamper-Jorgesen, J. (1993). Fibromyalgia in the adult Danish population. I: Prevalent study. *Scandinavian Journal of Rheumatology, 22,* 238–242.

Reilly, P. A. (1999). How should we manage fibromyalgia? *Annals of Rheumatic Diseases, 58,* 325–326.

Romano, J. M., & Turner, J. A. (1985). Chronic pain and depression: Does the evidence support a relationship? *Psychological Bulletin, 97,* 18–34.

Romano, J. M., Turner, J. A., Jensen, M. P., Friedman, L. S., Bulcroft, R. A., Hops, H., et al. (1995). Chronic pain patient: Spouse behavioral interaction predict disability. *Pain, 63,* 353–360.

Rosen, S. D., King, J. C., Wilkinson, J. B., & Nixon, P. G. (1990). Is chronic fatigue syndrome synonomous with effort syndrome? *Journal of the Royal Society of Medicine, 83,* 761–764.

Rudy, T. E., Turk, D. C., & Brena, S. F. (1988). Differential utility of medical procedures in the assessment of chronic pain patients. *Pain, 34,* 53–60.

Russo, J., Katon, W., Clark, M., Kith, P., Sintay, M., & Buchwald, D. (1998). Longitudinal changes associated with improvement in chronic fatigue patients. *Journal of Psychosomatic Research, 45,* 67–76.

Scarry, E. (1985). *The body in pain.* New York: Oxford University Press.

Scharff, L., Turk, D. C., & Marcus, D. A. (1995). Psychosocial and behavioral characteristics in chronic headache patients: Support for a continuum and dual-diagnostic approach. *Cephalalgia, 15,* 216–223.

Schmaling, K., Diclemente, J., Cullum, C., & Jones, J. F. (1994). Cognitive functioning in chronic fatigue syndrome and depression: A preliminary comparison. *Psychosomatic Medicine, 56,* 383–388.

Schmaling, K. B., & Sher, T. G. (Eds.). (2000). *The psychology of couples and illness: Theory, research, and practice.* Washington, DC: American Psychological Association.

Schochat, T., Croft, P., & Raspe, H. (1994). The epidemiology of fibromyalgia. *British Journal of Rheumatology, 33,* 783–786.

Shephard, R. J. (2001). Chronic fatigue syndrome: An update. *Sports Medicine, 31,* 167–194.

Simms, R. W., Roy, S. H., & Hrovat, M. (1994). Lack of association between fibromyalgia syndrome and abnormalities in muscle energy metabolism. *Arthritis and Rheumatism, 37,* 794–800.

Sletvold, H., Stiles, T. C., & Landro, N. I. (1995). Information processing in primary fibromyalgia, major depression and healthy controls. *Journal of Rheumatology, 22,* 137–142.

Starz, T. W., Sinclair, J. D., Okifuji, A., & Turk, D. C. (1997). Putting the finger on fibromyalgia: The manual tender point survey. *Journal of Musculoskeletal Medicine, 14,* 61–67.

Taylor, R. R., & Jason, L. A. (1998). Comparing the DIS with the SCID: Chronic fatigue syndrome and psychiatric comorbidity. *Psychology and Health: International Review of Health Psychology, 13,* 1087–1104.

Tiersky, L. A., Johnson, S. K., Lange, G., Natelson, B. H., & DeLuca, J. (1997). Neuropsychology of chronic fatigue syndrome: A critical review. *Journal of Clinical and Experimental Neuropsychology, 19,* 560–586.

Tsushima, W., & Stoddard, V. (1990). Ethnic group similarities in the biofeedback treatment of pain. *Medical Psychotherapy, 3,* 69–75.

Turk, D. (1990). Customizing treatment for chronic pain patients: Who, what, and why. *Clinical Journal of Pain, 6,* 255–270.

Turk, D. C., & Flor, H. (1989). Primary fibromyalgia is > than tender points: Toward a multiaxial taxonomy. *Journal of Rheumatology, 16,* 80–86.

Turk, D. C., & Kerns, R. D. (Eds.). (1985). *Health, illness, and families: A life-span perspective.* New York: Wiley-Interscience.

Turk, D. C., Kerns, R. D., & Rosenberg, R. (1992). Effects of marital interaction on chronic pain and disability: Examining the downside of social support. *Rehabilitation Psychology, 37,* 259–274.

Turk, D. C., & Okifuji, A. (1996). Perception of traumatic onset, compensation status, and physical findings: Impact on pain severity, emotional distress, and disability in chronic pain patients. *Journal of Behavioral Medicine, 19,* 435–453.

Turk, D. C., & Okifuji, A. (1997). What factors affect physicians' decisions to prescribe opioids for chronic noncancer pain patients? *Clinical Journal of Pain, 13,* 330–336.

Turk, D. C., Okifuji, A., Sinclair, J. D., & Starz, T. W. (1996). Pain, disability, and physical functioning in subgroups of patients with fibromyalgia. *Journal of Rheumatology, 23,* 1255–1262.

Turk, D. C., Okifuji, A., Sinclair, J. D., & Starz, T. W. (1998a). Differential responses by psychosocial subgroups of fibromyalgia syndrome patients to an interdisciplinary treatment. *Arthritis Care and Research, 11,* 397–404.

Turk, D. C., Okifuji, A., Sinclair, J. D., & Starz, T. W. (1998b). Interdisciplinary treatment for fibromyalgia syndrome: Clinical and statistical significance. *Arthritis Care and Research, 11,* 186–195.

Turk, D. C., & Rudy, T. E. (1990). The robustness of an empirically derived taxonomy of chronic pain patients. *Pain, 43,* 27–35.

Turk, D. C., Sist, T. C., Okifuji, A., Miner, M. F., Florio, G., Harrison, P., et al. (1998). Adaptation to metastatic cancer pain, regional/local cancer pain, and noncancer pain: Role of psychological and behavioral factors. *Pain, 74,* 247–256.

Turk, D. C., Wack, J. T., & Kerns, R. D. (1985). An empirical examination of the "pain-behavior" construct. *Journal of Behavioral Medicine, 8,* 119–130.

van Denderen, J. C., Boersma, J. W., Zeinstra, P., Hollander, A. P., & van Neerbos, B. R. (1992). Physiological effects of exhaustive physical exercise in primary fibromyalgia syndrome (PFS): Is PFS a disorder of neuroendocrine reactivity? *Scandinavian Journal of Rheumatology, 21,* 35–37.

Ware, N. C. (1992). Suffering and the social construction of illness: The delegitimization of illness experience in chronic fatigue syndrome. *Medical Anthropology Quarterly, 6,* 347–361.

Wessely, S., & Hotopf, M. (1999). Is fibromyalgia a distinct clinical entity? Historical and epidemiological evidence. *Best Practice and Research in Clinical Rheumatology, 13,* 427–436.

White, K. P., Speechley, M., Harth, M., & Østbye, T. (1995). Fibromyalgia in rheumatology practice: A survey of Canadian rheumatologists. *Journal of Rheumatology, 22,* 722–726.

Wigers, S. H., Stiles, T. C., & Vogel, P. A. (1996). Effects of aerobic exercise versus stress management treatment in fibromyalgia: A 4.5 year prospective study. *Scandinavian Journal of Rheumatology, 25,* 77–86.

Wolfe, F. (1998). What use are fibromyalgia control points? *Journal of Rheumatology, 25,* 546–550.

Wolfe, F., Anderson, J., Harkness, D., Bennett, R. M., Caro, X. J., Goldenberg, D. L., et al. (1997). Health status and disease severity in fibromyalgia: Results of a six-center longitudinal study. *Arthritis and Rheumatism, 40,* 1571–1579.

Wolfe, F., Smythe, J. A., Yunus, M. B., Bennett, R. M., Bombardier, C., Goldenberg, D. J., et al. (1990). The American College of Rheumatology 1990 criteria for the classification of fibromyalgia: Report of the multicenter criteria committee. *Arthritis and Rheumatism, 36,* 160–172.

CHAPTER 13

Orthostatic Intolerance

JULIAN M. STEWART

T HE TERM *ORTHOSTASIS* literally means standing upright. Orthostatic intolerance therefore can be defined as "the *development of symptoms* during upright standing relieved by recumbence" (Low et al., 1995). Current thought
about the role of orthostatic intolerance (OI) in chronic fatigue syndrome (CFS)
represents a convergence of viewpoints from two areas:

1. Research by clinicians who initially studied chronic fatigue syndrome.
2. Research by clinical pharmacologists and physiologists studying neurovascular, orthostatic, and gravitational (i.e., space) phenomena.

As time has passed, these group distinctions have blurred such that investigators now almost ubiquitously study both areas regardless of point of origin. Many
are trained neurologists involved in studies of the autonomic nervous system. Some
are students of endocrinology. Still others are cardiovascular or integrative physiologists. The first group of clinician investigators is epitomized by Peter Rowe and
his group at Johns Hopkins, who noted clinical findings in CFS patients that were
similar to findings in patients with simple faint. They conceived using the well-
known orthostatic stress test, upright tilt, to probe for potential orthostatic abnormalcy in CFS patients. The second group of investigators, epitomized by the late,
esteemed, David Streeten, and represented by David Robertson (Vanderbilt University) and Phillip Low (Mayo Clinic) come from scientific domains outside CFS.
They are students of orthostatic intolerance, of the autonomic nervous system, and
of integrative neurovascular physiology in a widespread patient base. Some of their
patients have well-described illnesses such as primary autonomic failure or multiple
system atrophy. In increasing numbers, patients have a form of chronic orthostatic
intolerance characterized by upright tachycardia and severe debilitating orthostatic
symptoms. Among other names, this illness has been variably designated the hyperadrenergic tachycardia syndrome (Streeten, 1990), the idiopathic postural orthostatic tachycardia syndrome (POTS) (Schondorf & Low, 1993), the postural tachycardia
syndrome (again POTS) (Sandroni, Opfer-Gehrking, Benarroch, Shen, & Low, 1996),

or neuropathic postural tachycardia syndrome (Hill, 1951; Jacob et al., 2000). Apart from rare patients with autonomic failure, chronic orthostatic intolerance with day-to-day disability appears almost always to be POTS (Robertson, 1999). Both groups have since read, reinterpreted, and cross-pollinated each other's work spawning hybrid investigators drawn to CFS by the weight of patient observations and by the striking similarity between the symptomatic definitions of CFS and chronic orthostatic intolerance. Based on data collected from all these researchers, it is fair to say on the one hand that orthostatic intolerance in chronic fatigue syndrome is POTS, and on the other hand, that POTS contributes importantly to CFS as an etiologic factor in many patients. At least in female adolescents, CFS seems to be POTS.

This chapter begins with a brief general review of orthostatic intolerance, moves on to a review of the emergence of orthostatic intolerance as an important pathophysiological factor in CFS, and proceeds to investigations into the mechanisms of chronic orthostatic intolerance in POTS.

ORTHOSTATIC INTOLERANCE

Orthostatic intolerance (OI) is a confusing topic. Much that has been written about OI as it applies to the chronic fatigue syndrome has also been puzzling. Some of the confusion emanates from recent appreciation of clinical variants in orthostatic intolerance, some from our emerging understanding that diverse pathophysiologies underlie OI and some from nomenclature that seems to change rapidly. For example, the term *orthostatic intolerance* would logically imply the presence of illness or abnormalities when upright. This may not be strictly true: Blood flow and blood pressure regulation are often abnormal while supine or sitting, but may not be as apparently abnormal as when upright. Orthostasis is a physiological stressor. Successful standing requires interplay of physical, neurological, humoral, and vascular factors. An example where such interactions often prove inadequate is pure autonomic failure whose sufferers demonstrate orthostatic hypotension as a primary finding but who have autonomic abnormalcy in all physical positions. Thus, orthostatic intolerance encapsulates disorders of blood flow, heart rate, and blood pressure regulation, which are most easily demonstrable during orthostatic stress, but are often present in all positions. Although orthostatic intolerance may be the most outstanding finding in these disorders, it is only the most obvious manifestation of more widespread impairment in integrative neurovascular physiology.

Orthostatic intolerance may be roughly divided on the basis of patient history into acute or chronic variants.

ACUTE ORTHOSTATIC INTOLERANCE

Cardiac and Noncardiac   Acute orthostatic intolerance usually manifests as presyncope or syncope, defined as a transient loss of consciousness (present in syncope) and postural tone (present in both syncope and presyncope), with rapid recovery. It is caused by cerebral malperfusion (low brain blood flow) usually resulting from a large and abrupt fall in blood pressure. Not all syncope is orthostatic. Some patients, particularly adults with antecedent heart disease, have cardiac abnormalities. Arrhythmia often directly causes sudden loss of consciousness with cardiac abnormalities. Structural bases frequently underlie these rhythm problems including muscle disease, coronary artery disease, and aortic stenosis, but these need not be present. Cardiac syncope should be regarded as life threatening. Although cardiac syncope is not often closely associated with orthostasis, it may be, thus making it hard to distinguish cardiac from noncardiac syncope. The lack of classic history for simple faint including known precipitants (standing, environmental heat, emotion) and prodromal symptoms (nausea, blurred vision, headache) help distinguish cardiac syncope from simple faint, but this may be difficult at times. Causes of cardiac syncope include the Wolfe-Parkinson-White syndrome (abnormal electrical tracts within the heart), long QT syndrome (a not uncommon rhythm problem placing patients at risk for dangerous fast heart rates), arrhythmogenic right ventricular dysplasia (an abnormal part of the right heart which may develop abnormal heart rhythms), cardiomyopathies (heart muscle disease), left ventricular outflow obstruction (obstruction of flow from the heart to the body), myocardial infarction (heart attack), primary pulmonary hypertension (lung vessel disease), and, most commonly, ventricular tachycardia, bradyarrhythmias, and related arrhythmic events (Kapoor, 1992). In distinguishing syncope, the first job is to evaluate the patient for possible cardiac syncope. Therefore, cardiologists are often involved early in the evaluation. When cardiac disease is found, it is treated specifically. Cardiac syncope may first manifest during exercise, which is the most physiological stressor of the coronary, systemic, and pulmonary circulations and of overall cardiac function. Exercise-related syncope or syncope with cardiac symptoms such as tachycardia or chest pain should raise a red flag for underlying heart disease (Reisdorff & Prodinger, 1998). Cardiogenic syncope has been well described in numerous texts (Grubb & Kosinski, 1998) and is not a central topic for discussion because it bears little relation to orthostatic intolerance in CFS.

Simple Faint   Patients may, however, have simple faints, known variably as neurocardiogenic syncope, neurally mediated syncope, and vasovagal syncope going back to the original descriptive designation given by Sir Thomas Lewis (Hill, 1951; Lewis, 1932). Many syncopal patients have no intercurrent illness; between faints they are well. We will return to fainting a bit later.

Chronic Orthostatic Intolerance

Chronic orthostatic intolerance is by definition chronic. Patients are ill on a longstanding basis. Chronic OI may be confused with syncope because chronic illness can sometimes be punctuated by acute syncopal episodes. Therefore, we must rely heavily on the history to determine whether there is chronic illness. Symptoms of chronic orthostatic intolerance are shown in Table 13.1 and include day-to-day dizziness in all patients, with a high incidence of altered vision (blurred, whiteouts, blackouts), fatigue, nausea, neurocognitive deficits, sleep problems, sensation of feeling hot, and palpitations (Jacob & Biaggioni, 1999; Narkiewicz & Somers, 1998; Robertson & Robertson, 1994).

A large fraction of patients also experience headache, tremulousness, difficulty breathing or swallowing, sweating, pallor, and other vasomotor symptoms. Most forms of orthostatic intolerance are not life threatening, although circumstances can conspire to create considerable risk: Fainting while driving can prove lethal.

There is common overlap with mitral valve prolapse, fatigue states, and fibromyalgia as indicated in Table 13.1.

PHYSIOLOGY OF ORTHOSTASIS

FLUID SHIFTS WITH UPRIGHT POSTURE

Physiologically relevant investigations of orthostasis are most appropriately performed in humans because the cardiovascular system of quadrupeds (four-legged) mammals is adapted to a quadrupedal stance. Studies must be performed unrestrained and conscious which rules out related bipedal primates as suitable subjects. Some experimentation has been successfully performed in quadrupedal mammals, but all have had to be justified through their relation to human physiology. Quadrupeds have a distinct orthostatic advantage over humans: While at rest, blood reservoirs (mostly veins) are at a similar level as the brain and heart in all animals. When humans assume a standing position, on the order of 750 ml of thoracic blood is abruptly translocated downward filling venous blood reservoirs below the heart and removing venous return (blood returning via veins from the body to the heart) from the heart while reducing cerebral perfusion (blood flow to the brain) due to the hydrostatic change in blood pressure (Blomqvist & Stone, 1983).

On the other hand, more than 70% of vascular capacitance (ability of blood vessels to hold blood) in dogs is situated at or even above cardiac level with the brain at a similar level. Arterial blood pressure and venous pressures while standing are illustrated in Figure 13.1. In humans, upright posture is a fundamental stressor requiring rapid and effective circulatory and neurological compensations to

Table 13.1
Symptoms of Orthostatic Intolerance

- Lightheadedness
- Tremulousness
- Nausea/Abdominal pain
- Sweating, pallor
- Weakness
- Headache
- Fatigue
- Exercise intolerance
- Chest pain
- Shortness of breath
- Neurocognitive/Sleep disorders
- Anxiety/Palpitations
- Vasomotor symptoms
- Other features:
  - Mitral valve prolapse
  - Irritable bowel
  - Fibromyalgia
  - Chronic fatigue

Adapted from "Effects of Volume Loading and Pressor Agents in Idiopathic Orthostatic Tachycardia," by G. Jacob, J. R. Shannon, et al., 1997, *Circulation, 96*, pp. 575–580.

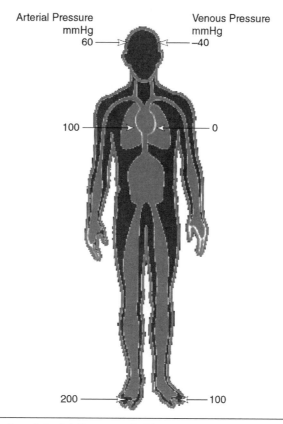

Arterial Pressure
mmHg
60 →

Venous Pressure
mmHg
← −40

100 → ← 0

200 → ← 100

Figure 13.1 Standing Arterial Pressure (left) and Venous Pressure (right) Are Superimposed

maintain blood pressure, cerebral blood flow, and consciousness. If it were not for these compensatory mechanisms, the precarious positioning of the brain well above the neutral cardiac point (roughly at the right atrium) and the large venous reservoirs below the neutral point would cause blood pressure to decrease rapidly due to gravitational pooling of blood within the dependent veins. Cerebral ischemia (lack of blood) and loss of consciousness would rapidly follow. Once consciousness and postural tone is lost, the resultant fall would render a person recumbent causing blood remobilization and restored consciousness (Rowell, 1986). It would seem that evolution dictated a trade-off between manual dexterity and orthostatic competence.

NORMAL COMPENSATORY MECHANISMS THAT PREVENT
ORTHOSTATIC INTOLERANCE

These are summarized in Table 13.2 and explained in the following sections. Humans have multiple somewhat redundant mechanisms to prevent orthostatic dysfunction. Thus, the failure of one compensatory mechanism may be partly compensated by others.

Table 13.2
Response to Orthostasis

The Muscle Pump

Neurovascular = Autonomic nervous system and autoregulation

Neurohumoral – Adrenal-Renal: Epinephrine, renin, AVP, aldosterone, ANP, histamine, bradykinin, adenosine

THE MUSCLE PUMP

Our primary defense against pooling is the "muscle pump," shown in Figure 13.2, in which contractions of leg and gluteal muscles propel sequestered venous blood back to the heart (Blomqvist, 1986; J. P. McCarthy et al., 1997; P. McCarthy & Snyder, 1992; Ten Harkel, van Lieshout, & Wieling, 1994). This action is often likened to a "second heart." Muscle may also be involved in neurogenic compensation through chemoreceptors. Muscle contraction encourages blood flow through the capillaries and venous systems by reducing venous pressure, thereby increasing the pressure difference between leg arteries and leg veins. Defective muscle pump is an important reason that astronauts are vulnerable to orthostatic stress after exposure to low gravity; they rapidly develop leg muscle atrophy and refractory lower limb pooling. The muscle pump is

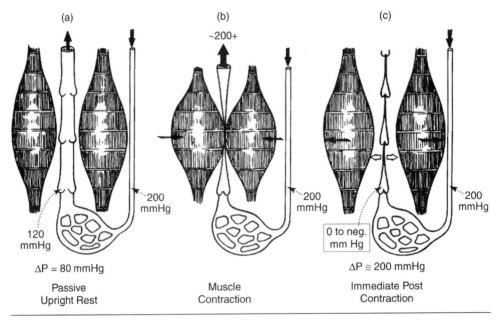

Figure 13.2 Effects of the Muscle Pump. While standing quietly, venous pressure can reach 120 mmHg resulting in venous congestion and edema. Muscular contraction empties the veins and encourages forward flow. *Source:* Figure 1-14. In *Human Cardiovascular Control*, by L. B. Rowell, 1993, NY: Oxford University Press.

also partly defeated during quiet standing and is nearly completely defeated while standing without motion.

Neurovascular Compensation

The second line of defense against orthostatic intolerance is neurovascular adjustment. This includes rapid increases in arterial resistance to blood flow (vasoconstriction—the ability of arteries to narrow) limiting flow to the extremities and to the splanchnic vascular bed (the vascular system of the viscera, liver, and spleen) while promoting passive emptying (Bondar et al., 1997; Brown & Hainsworth, 2000; Jacobsen et al., 1993). Figure 13.3 illustrates that vasoconstriction increases arterial resistance at a relatively low angle of tilt corresponding roughly to a seated position. This is normally associated with release of norepinephrine from nerve endings in the lower extremities, as illustrated by the work of Jacob and associates. Figure 13.4 shows norepinephrine spillover (release) at rest and with orthostasis (Jacob et al., 2000). This indicates that even a mild degree of orthostasis results in norepinephrine release that acts to contract peripheral blood vessels, thus restricting pooling and maintaining blood pressure.

Splanchnic venoconstriction occurs, further enhancing venous emptying (Blomqvist et al., 1983; Folkow, 1989; Hill, 1951). However, there is little evidence for active venoconstriction (contraction of veins) in other vascular beds such as the

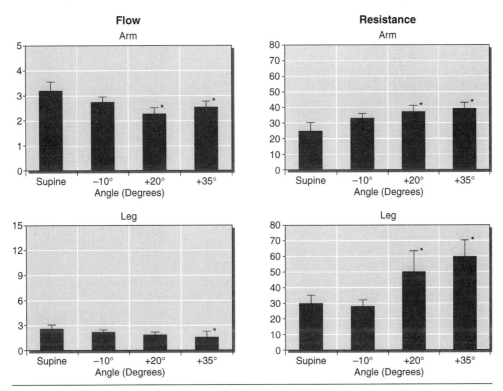

Figure 13.3 Blood Flow and Arterial Resistance in the Arms and Legs during Low Angle Incremental Tilt. Flow decreases and the resistance to flow increases with relatively small upright tilt.

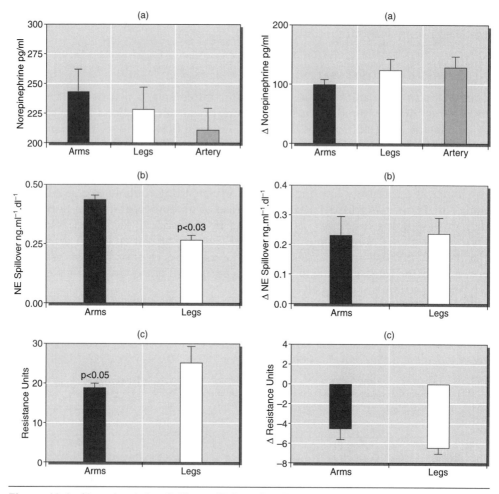

Figure 13.4 Norepinephrine Spillover (Release) at Rest and with Orthostasis. *Source:* "The Neuropathic Postural Tachycardia Syndrome," by G. Jacob et al., 2000, *New England Journal of Medicine, 343,* pp. 1008–1014.

skin and skeletal muscle in response to orthostasis. Work from our laboratory and others indicates that the capacitance vessel volume-pressure relations (which define the ability of veins to enlarge with pressure) in the forearm and calf are independent of upright position (Schlegel et al., 2001; Stewart, 2002; Stewart, Lavin, & Weldon, 2001). This indicates that limb venoconstriction is not an important aspect of the acute orthostatic response. It remains possible that peripheral venoconstriction occurs in response to nonorthostatic stimuli. Under these circumstances, venoconstriction could influence venous pooling without necessarily responding directly to orthostasis.

However, veins and venules contribute to the orthostatic regulation of venous return to the heart by passive elastic properties. Elastic recoil of the veins returns blood to the heart. If arterial vasoconstriction curtails inflow, the main venous reservoirs can empty. This is at least true while supine (e.g., during hemorrhage) (Donegan, 1921; Rothe, 1983). Precisely what happens during orthostasis in humans is not clear because gravity may result in persistent venous filling despite reflex vasoconstriction. Reflex compensatory mechanisms during orthostatic challenge are primarily controlled by the high-pressure arterial baroreceptors (pressure receptors) located in the carotid sinus, aortic arch, and perhaps the proximal coronary arteries. These receptors cause vasoconstriction and heart rate changes. Low pressure cardiopulmonary receptors within the left atrium and pulmonary vein ostia can alter renal resistance to blood flow and peripheral resistance. Recent evidence seems to show that the low pressure receptors, and also the ventricular receptors, make no important contribution to orthostatic adjustment (Mancia & Mark, 1983; Mark & Mancia, 1983). Work by Biaggioni and associates (Biaggioni, Costa, & Kaufmann, 1998) has also implicated the vestibular-otolith (inner ear) system as containing afferent neurogenic postural signaling sensors. Less well appreciated are local myogenic (arterial smooth muscle), metabolic (low oxygen, high carbon dioxide, adenosine), and venoarteriolar (axon reflexes detecting increased venous pressure and causing reflex arterial vasoconstriction) mechanisms for vascular control that may be equally important in the legs during orthostasis (Blomqvist & Stone et al., 1983; Bondar et al., 1997; Henriksen, Skagen, Haxholdt, & Dyrberg, 1983).

HUMORAL EFFECTS

Later during orthostasis, humoral (hormonal) effects may enhance the defense against cerebral hypoperfusion (low blood flow) through the activation of the renin-angiotensin-aldosterone system and the release of epinephrine (adrenaline) and vasopressin (ADH), as well as through central nervous system effects (Vargas et al., 1986). These mechanisms have delayed onset on the order of minutes following orthostasis (Rundgren, Jonasson, Appelgren, Eriksson, & Leksell, 1984; Starc & Stalcup, 1987) and, therefore, are less important for the immediate response to postural change and more important for chronic responses. Over longer time courses, humoral mechanisms can be a highly effective means for altering blood volume and sympathetic tone. Epinephrine may even have an instrumental role in mechanisms of vasovagal syncope since an epinephrine surge invariably accompanies the onset of syncope (see later in this chapter). It is as yet impossible, however, to separate cause from effect; that is, to determine whether epinephrine causes fainting through vasodilation or whether increased epinephrine is a compensatory response to the fall in blood pressure preceding an overt faint.

INTEGRATIVE RESPONSE

During quiet standing, compensatory mechanisms are incomplete (Figure 13.5). While blood pressure is more or less maintained, blood flow is not. Thus, systolic blood pressure is relatively unchanged, and diastolic blood pressure increases due to decreased stroke volume (the amount of blood pumped by each heartbeat) thereby ensuring coronary artery perfusion. However, overall cardiac output decreases by an estimated 25% due to impaired heart filling only partially offset by an increase in heart rate (Wang, Marsgall, & Shepherd, 1960). There is even a normal decrease in cerebral blood flow (on the order of 6%). Cerebral arterial pressure is decreased due to the hydrostatic column between heart and brain, and thus cerebrovascular autoregulation is functioning near its

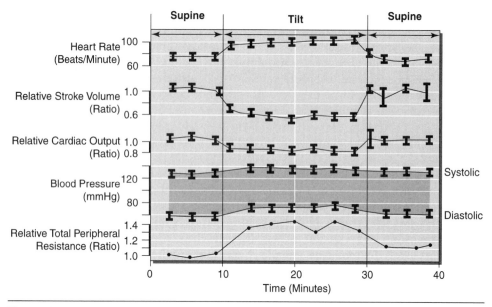

Figure 13.5 The Integrative Response to Upright Tilt or Standing—A Decrease in Stroke Volume, Cardiac Output and an Increase in Diastolic BP, Heart Rate, and Total Peripheral Resistance. *Source:* J. J. Smith , J. E. Bush, V. T. Wiedmeier, F. E. Tristani, 1970, *Journal of Applied Physiology, 29*, p. 133.

limit when an individual is standing upright (Rowell, 1986). Standing is a perilous venture.

CLASSIFICATION OF ORTHOSTATIC INTOLERANCE

THE ORTHOSTATIC STRESS TEST

Patterns of exercise intolerance are best illustrated through exercise stress testing. Similarly, patterns of orthostatic intolerance are best illustrated through orthostatic stress testing, by which upright stress can be imposed in a controlled fashion and the physiological response monitored in detail. There are three standard forms of such testing: standing, passive upright tilt using a tilt table, and lower body negative pressure. To negate the muscle pump, these techniques are typically used with the patient motionless. Most investigators study the neurovascular and neurohumoral responses. Lower body negative pressure (Baisch et al., 2000), developed by NASA scientists and others as a research tool, simulates many features of orthostasis using external negative pressure on the legs, buttocks, and lower abdomen under well-controlled conditions. In this technique, the patient remains supine and is encased from the waist down in a chamber capable of sustaining a vacuum up to −100 mmHg. However, it is a pure research tool and is beyond the scope of the present discussion. Of the two remaining stress tests, standing is the most physiological. However, difficulties with patient movement and standardization may make standing difficult to apply and to compare. Standing motionless can be particularly difficult for some patients with chronic orthostatic intolerance and for some children. Movement invokes the muscle pump and makes measurements harder to perform and to interpret.

While there are some fundamental differences in the response to tilt compared with standing, especially during the first few minutes (Hyatt, Jacobson, & Schneider, 1975; Spodick & Lance, 1977), upright tilt and standing are substantially equivalent after that early period elapses (Bloomfield et al., 1997). Therefore, the most commonly used standard orthostatic stress test device is the head-up tilt (HUT) table typically employing angles varying from 60° to 90° from the horizontal for 10 to 45 minutes as the orthostatic stimulus. As a reference, 0° is supine, 90° is completely upright, and −10° would be a slight head-down tilt. Some investigators add medications to passive tilt to potentiate orthostatic stress. This produces more true positive tests (and more false positives) although the physiological underpinnings of pharmacological potentiation are often flimsy. Obviously, even this supposed "standard"' test is not altogether standardized. Upright testing is, therefore, best thought of as a physiological stressor (i.e., an orthostatic stress) instead of as a strictly objective test yielding clear-cut unassailable objective results. In a physiological context, "positive" and "negative" tests are less important than normal versus abnormal physiological responses during testing. The entire notion of positive or negative is easily refuted. Everyone has a response to orthostasis that may or may not be a normal physiological response. Often, fainting is regarded as the "positive" endpoint, which by exclusion ignores much interesting and important pathophysiology. Provocative drugs provoke more fainting and include isoproterenol, nitroglycerin, and adenosine (Mittal et al., 1999; Raviele et al., 2000). These are all vasoactive agents (agents that affect blood vessel size or function) and disturb the underlying physiology. However, a school of thought believes that epinephrine may play a key role in the onset of simple faint, and therefore, the use of isoproterenol as a provocative stimulus in the context of syncope investigation becomes more reasonable. Use of isoproterenol in patients with chronic orthostatic intolerance is more problematic since it disturbs physiological vasodilation and related vascular changes under these circumstances. Still other investigators have used substances intended to improve orthostatic tolerance while performing orthostatic stress tests. These include esmolol and other beta-blockers (Ovadia & Thoele, 1994). While tending to reduce syncope during testing in those with acute orthostatic intolerance (i.e., fainters), preliminary data from our lab indicate worsened orthostatic tolerance in patients with chronic orthostatic intolerance acutely administered esmolol.

UPRIGHT (HEAD-UP) TILT TABLE TESTING

Although head-up tilt was used to evoke autonomic reflexes and vascular responses in early NASA experiments, it was first used as a clinical testing agent for the evaluation of syncope in 1986 (Kenny, Ingram, Bayliss, & Sutton, 1986). The device comprises a table driven by an electrical motor with a supportive footboard enabling positioning of a patient at varying angles of upright tilt as in Figure 13.6. Although it would seem that an angle of 90° (straight up) is most physiological, this usually induces excessive false positives (patients with no history of orthostatic intolerance who have orthostatic intolerance induced during testing). Lesser angles such as 60° or 70° are customarily used (Benditt et al., 1996). It is not a particularly accurate clinical test. Even without excessive angles of tilt and without pharmacological potentiation, about 25% of adolescents with no prior fainting history will faint during testing. Moreover, among habitual

Figure 13.6 Upright Tilt to 70°

fainters, approximately 25% to 30% will not faint during the test on a given day. Also, results are not ideally repeatable: A positive or negative test on one day will not ensure a positive or negative test on another day, although some patients consistently faint. As tests go, it is fraught with error. As stresses go, it is excellent and controllable. Following a resting period, the patients are placed upright and their response over a period of tilt assessed—this is usually anywhere up to 30 to 45 minutes as tolerated. At a minimum, blood pressure and continuous electrocardiography are assessed. Typically, continuous blood pressure assessment such as finger plethysmography or arterial tonometry is used, and respirations are also assessed. Researchers have also used techniques to assess peripheral, thoracic, and central nervous system blood flow. The central clinical purpose of tilt table testing is to reproduce symptoms of orthostatic intolerance in a setting in which hemodynamic variables can be assessed. This is not the only purpose of orthostatic stress testing. Most often there is correlation between symptoms and changing physiological signs, but the definition of orthostatic intolerance *requires* symptoms. If the patient's defining symptoms are not reproduced but the patient has a simple faint, the test must be regarded as false-positive and not a sign of real-life orthostatic intolerance. As noted, healthy control subjects with no prior history of fainting may faint during testing. Recent data suggest that the physiology of false positives is itself interesting (Leonelli et al., 2000). Therefore strict application of the term *negative* to these patients may be incorrect. Other patterns of hemodynamic disturbance, such as postural tachycardia and the dysautonomic response, seem invariably associated with symptoms and are more reliable indicators of chronic impairment.

Upright tilt (or standing or lower body negative pressure [LBNP]) has a related function as a research tool to evoke the orthostatic response—a complex interplay between arterial baroreflex, vasculature, local factors, and the central nervous system. It is therefore not a "black box" apparatus with positive or negative responses. Everyone has a physiological response to orthostatic challenge. The black box approach has been popular among cardiologists using a descriptive paradigm to categorize patients who faint. They were seeking to compare patterns of syncope during upright tilt with cardiogenic syncope due to electrical or mechanical events. Thus, as shown in Figure 13.7, a positive response associated with primary bradycardia (slowing of the heart) was designated "cardioinhibitory." A positive response associated with primary hypotension but not bradycardia was denoted "vasodepressor," and a vasovagal response in which both heart rate and blood pressure fell in concert was denoted "mixed" (Guzman, Sanchez, Marquez, Hermosillo, & Cardenas, 1999; Petersen, Williams, Gordon, Chamberlain-Webber, & Sutton, 2000). Through the efforts of neurologists and integrative physiologists studying a wide range of orthostatic intolerance, this paradigm has been largely

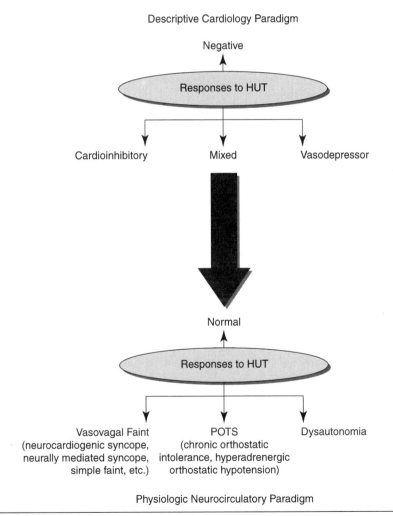

Figure 13.7   A Comparison of the Paradigms for Tilt Table Results

superseded by a physiological approach emphasizing the responses of neurovascular and neurohumoral circulatory control mechanisms to orthostatic stress.

Patterns of Orthostatic Stress

Figure 13.8 depicts the main variants of heart rate and blood pressure responses to 70° upright tilt. The normal heart rate and blood pressure response to upright tilt is a modest tachycardia with a 10 to 20 beats/min increase in heart rate. There is no significant fall in systolic blood pressure, although diastolic pressure and mean arterial pressure rise somewhat. As explained, these occur as a result of the rapid translocation of blood to the lower body. This translocation is a normal response. Everyone pools to greater or lesser extent and at varying rates (the time it takes blood to reach the lower body). The term *pooling*, however, will be reserved for visual signs of excess blood and fluid collections in the lower body. Modest tachycardia, as well as vasoconstriction, occur as part of the normal response to orthostasis.

Three common abnormal upright tilt responses are also shown. The three are vasovagal syncope, dysautonomia, and postural tachycardia syndrome or POTS. Vasovagal syncope can be produced in many patients with CFS but is often not spontaneously present: In real life, CFS patients do not often faint, but they can be made to during an upright tilt test. True dysautonomia is rarely present in CFS. POTS is the rule in adolescents with CFS and may also be common in adults with CFS. These abnormal responses are presented as a rough guide to help organize observed heart rate and blood pressure changes into recognizable patterns in patients with known orthostatic intolerance. The overall assessment emphasizing patient history and severity of impairment must be combined with physiological data to reach any useful conclusion concerning the nature and treatment of orthostatic intolerance in a particular patient.

Vasovagal Syncope (Classic Simple Faint) Typically, patients easily tolerate the early stages of tilt with little change in systolic blood pressure and have no symptoms. Following the passage of time, from as little as a few minutes to as long as 7 to 20 minutes, patients develop orthostatic symptoms often associated with deep inspirations and an initial slow fall in blood pressure (which can be seen by inspecting the figure closely). This earlier slow fall in blood pressure is not always observed (Furlan et al., 1998) but is coincident with a decrease in vasoconstriction of the peripheral arteries resulting in vasodilation. Active dilation may also play a complementary role to release of vasoconstriction. Shortly thereafter, there is an abrupt and simultaneous fall in blood pressure and heart rate. Vasoconstriction occurs as part of the normal neurovascular response to orthostasis and is necessary to maintain blood pressure with orthostasis. Blood pressure and heart rate may plummet precipitously, and asystole (heart stopping) may occur and continue while the patient remains upright. When this happens, there is a rapid loss of central nervous system activity and often a release of peripheral neurological responses resulting in muscular movements that mimic a tonic-clonic seizure (epilepsy). This is denoted *convulsive syncope*. No true seizure activity is present, as confirmed in the 1950s by Gastaut (Gastaut, 1957) and reconfirmed using HUT methods by Grubb and coworkers in the 1990s (Grubb et al., 1991). Such episodes, while relatively uncommon, are dramatic, and beginning practitioners of the HUT art periodically rediscover these phenomena. Fainting may occur in chronic fatigue

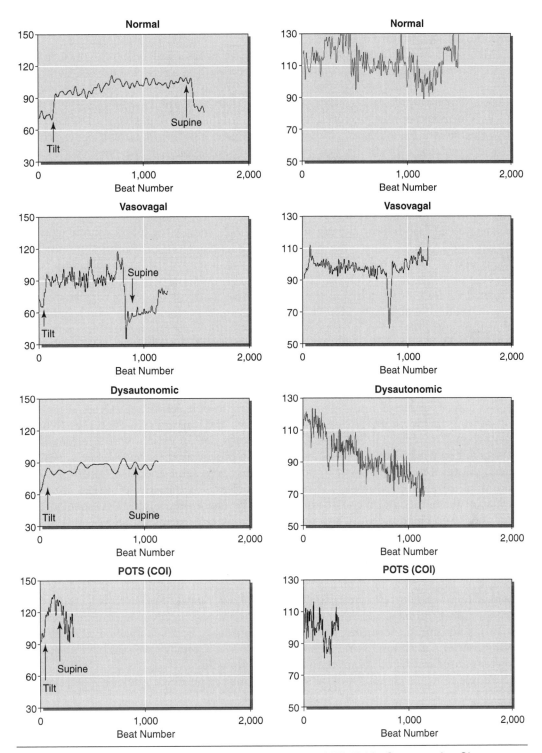

Figure 13.8   Four Basic Characteristic Patterns of Tilt Table Outcome Are Shown

syndrome but, as explained, it is most likely an acute punctuation of a more chronic orthostatic intolerant state.

MECHANISMS FOR VASOVAGAL FAINT   Until recently, most research concerning orthostatic intolerance was primarily concerned with syncope. Even here, there is no consensus about mechanism. Mosqueda-Garcia and associates (Mosqueda-Garcia, Furlan, Tank, & Fernandez-Violante, 2000) have published an excellent review. The most popular proposed mechanism, discussed and perhaps dismissed as the mechanism for syncope, holds that fainting results from a stretch reflex from the left ventricle. This is akin to the classic Bezold-Jarisch cardiac chemoreflex. A left ventricle that is underfilled because of reduced venous return presumably activates the reflex. This produces sympathetic activation, enhanced contractility, and a resultant "paradoxical reflex" mediated by unmyelinated C-fibers coursing from the ventricle to the central nervous system and causing vagally mediated bradycardia as well as vasodilation (Oberg & Thoren, 1972). Increasing blood volume would be expected to help relieve underfilling while negative inotropic agents should help to reduce cardiac contractility. However, just because a reflex is possible, does not make it probable. Research has called into question both hypercontractility and decreased ventricular stretch (Liu et al., 2000). Also, patients receiving cardiac transplants retain the ability to faint (Lightfoot, Rowe, & Fortney, 1993), which implies that the ventricular receptor theory cannot explain all simple faints. Most significantly, animal research performed by Hainsworth and associates (Hainsworth, 1995; Vallbona, Lipscomb, & Carter, 1966; Wright, Drinkhill, & Hainsworth, 2000) has convincingly demonstrated that once coronary afferents of the baroreflex are separated from ventricular receptor action, little in the way of Bezold-Jarisch like reflex activity remains under physiologically achievable conditions. Other theories of fainting include epinephrine or renin surges and vasopressin decreases (Klingenheben, Kalusche, Li, Schopperl, & Hohnloser, 1996), which would rationalize the common use of isoproterenol as adjunctive provocation (Rowell & Seals, 1990). Such surges have been shown to occur in those who faint and, like fainting, take minutes to develop. However, it remains unclear whether these surges are the cause of the hemodynamic abnormalities or the result of attempted compensation for decreased blood pressure and peripheral resistance during incipient fainting. A decrease in cerebral blood flow has also been shown to occur in syncopal patients and may precede a large fall in blood pressure (Rodriguez, Snider, Cornel, & Teixeira, 1999). Cerebral syncope is thought to exist independent of blood pressure changes. Blood flow is similarly impaired in chronic orthostatic intolerance in which hypotension does not usually occur (Low, Novak, Spies, Novak, & Petty, 1999). Other proposed mechanisms include changes in CNS neurotransmitters such as serotonin, norepinephrine, neuropeptide Y, and substance P (Grubb & Karas, 1998). Causation has not been established. In summary, we still have no complete understanding of the mechanism of simple faint.

People with the chronic fatigue syndrome may experience syncope. With sufficient provocation, anyone can experience a simple faint. This will occur with increased frequency in persons with chronic orthostatic intolerance and POTS (discussed later in this chapter) but often only under conditions such as upright tilt table testing.

Dysautonomic Orthostatic Intolerance   Included in this group are patients with true "orthostatic hypotension" defined by the American Autonomic Society as a persistent fall in systolic/diastolic blood pressure of > 20 / 10 mmHg within 3 minutes of assuming the upright position (Anonymous; 1996). Such criteria may be overly lenient but are reasonable starting points for comparison. The dysautonomic group harbors patients with autonomic failure. Autonomic failure includes primary forms such as primary (pure) autonomic failure, in which the peripheral nerves fail to function, and multiple system atrophy, in which there is a progressive failure of central and peripheral neurological systems. Secondary forms of autonomic failure occur with Parkinson's disease and diabetes. Dysautonomia may also be drug induced. Acute forms may occur during infectious and inflammatory diseases or be related to peripheral neuropathies, for example, Guillian-Barre syndrome. Standard tests of circulatory autonomic function such as timed breathing and the quantitative Valsalva maneuver demonstrate signs of circulatory autonomic dysfunction. Other manifestations of dysautonomia are often present including pupillary, gastrointestinal, and sweating abnormalities. Neurological damage such as occurs in cerebral palsy and trauma may result in autonomic dysfunction in addition to other neurological disability. Responses to orthostasis in such patients differ from those in truly dysautonomic patients in that compensatory mechanisms may adapt the patient to orthostasis (e.g., increased blood volume), which occurs less often in the true dysautonomic. There is little support for an important role for true dysautonomia in chronic fatigue syndrome in the sense given here. Since there is evidence that some aspects of autonomic vascular control are impaired in CFS, it may be more likely that a partial dysautonomia occurs. However, bona fide dysautonomia can produce fatigue and should be included in the differential diagnosis of the CFS patient.

Dysautonomic orthostatic intolerance is depicted in Figure 13.8. Blood pressure falls, while there is little change in heart rate throughout the course of the tilt (Bondar et al., 1997). The appropriate cardiac response of the baroreflex to hypotension is tachycardia, which fails to occur or is blunted in these illnesses. Patients may be so brittle that they are hypertensive supine (Shannon et al., 2000), hypotensive upright, and may lose consciousness because of overzealous splanchnic vasodilation (possibly due to vasoactive intestinal polypeptide) after a heavy meal (Mathias, 1991).

Treatments favor volume loading and midodrine which, as noted, often results in recumbent hypertension. Specific therapy for chronic disease is largely experimental, and acute therapy for acute illness remains specific for the specific disease and patient.

Chronic Orthostatic Intolerance and the Postural Tachycardia Syndrome (POTS) POTS was defined and described by Drs. Schondorf and Low at the Mayo Clinic (Schondorf & Low, 1993), but has been with us under different aliases at least since 1940 (MacLean & Allen, 1940) and probably for hundreds of years. Synonyms abound, and Table 13.3 lists recently used nomenclature. It is characterized by an upright rapid heart rate (tachycardia) and sometimes a resting tachycardia. Evidence suggests that the syndrome is heterogeneous, but the common physiological feature is a thoracic hypovolemia in which too little blood is filling the heart. This produces the tachycardia as a normal reflex response. The physiology is similar to dehydration.

POTS is the most common reason for referral for orthostatic intolerance in adults (Low et al., 1995; Robertson, 1999; Schondorf & Low, 1993; Stewart, 2000). It is an emerging form of orthostatic intolerance in children (Karas, Grubb, Boehm, & Kip,

Table 13.3
Terms Used for Chronic Orthostatic Intolerance

Idiopathic orthostatic intolerance
Idiopathic orthostatic tachycardia
Postural orthostatic tachycardia syndrome
Orthostatic tachycardia syndrome
Hyperadrenergic postural hypotension
Sympathotonic orthostatic hypotension
Hyperdynamic beta-adrenergic state
Idiopathic hypovolemia
Mitral valve prolapse syndrome
Soldier's heart
Vasoregulatory asthenia
Irritable heart
Orthostatic anemia
Chronic fatigue syndrome

Adapted from Jacob et al., 1999, *Circulation 99*, pp. 1706–1712.

2000; Stewart, Gewitz, Weldon, & Munoz, 1999) and was first reported in the pediatric population by our laboratory. Patients often have day-to-day disability—a feature not shared with those with simple faint. The chronic disease often waxes and wanes but is always present to some extent. Traditional tests of autonomic function are often normal in these patients although there are reports of some degree of dysautonomia. Patients are often unable to hold a job or attend school. It is probably the most common form of chronic orthostatic disability, affecting on the order of one million Americans. It is present in virtually every patient with day-to-day orthostatic intolerance (Robertson, 1999). Understanding of its pathophysiology remains incomplete. The central finding in POTS is upright tachycardia with symptoms of orthostatic intolerance, although hypotension and resting tachycardia may also be present. Many adults may even experience hypertension; it is also not rare to have both high and low blood pressure in the same individual. An operational definition of the syndrome includes symptoms of orthostatic intolerance associated with an increase in heart rate from the supine to upright position of more than 30 beats per minute or to a heart rate greater than 120 beats per minute within 10 minutes of head-up tilt (Low et al., 1995). Such a response is depicted in Figure 13.8. In the case shown, the POTS patient became immediately symptomatic following the start of HUT and required the tilt table to be put down within a few minutes. Although the patient was not hypotensive, hypotension may follow or occur with tachycardia if protracted. Often, if hypotension occurs, it is delayed beyond the onset of the symptoms and of the tachycardia, and therefore, only manifests during the artificially sustained orthostasis enforced during HUT. The form taken by hypotension may be vasovagal fainting. At least in our experience, however, fainting is mainly confined to the contrived circumstances of tilt testing. As shown in Figure 13.9, symptoms during testing are temporally related to a decrease in cerebral blood flow, an increase in cerebrovascular resistance, and (as yet

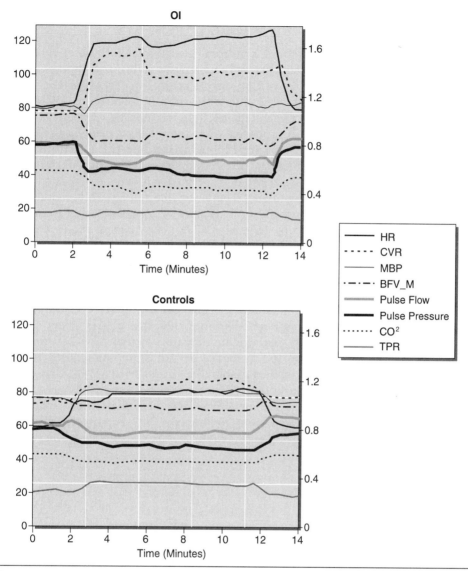

Figure 13.9   Changes in Heart Rate (HR), Cerebral Vascular Resistance (CVR), Mean Blood Pressure (MBP), Blood Flow Velocity (BFV), Carbon Dioxide (CO2), and Total Peripheral Resistance during Upright Tilt in an Orthostatic Intolerant [POTS] Patient and a Healthy Control. *Source:* "Hypocapnia and Cerebral Hypoperfusion in Orthostatic Intolerance," by V. Novak et al., 1998, *Stroke, 29,* pp. 1876–1881.

unexplained) hyperventilation with attendant hypocapnia (low carbon dioxide), which may account in part for cerebral vasoconstriction (Novak et al., 1998). Cerebral malperfusion (low blood flow) is well correlated with neurocognitive defects in POTS (Jacob et al., 1999; Low et al., 1999).

Onset of symptoms in POTS often follows an infectious disease and may be related to inflammatory mediators. Further data and hypotheses concerning POTS appear later in this chapter.

ORTHOSTATIC INTOLERANCE IN THE
CHRONIC FATIGUE SYNDROME

The symptoms of the chronic fatigue syndrome closely match those of chronic orthostatic intolerance. Research suggesting that orthostatic intolerance plays a significant role in the symptomatology of CFS has its origins in the important work of Peter Rowe and associates at Johns Hopkins University. In their initial observations, Rowe and coworkers (Bou-Holaigah, Rowe, Kan, & Calkins, 1995; Rowe, Bou-Holaigah, Kan, & Calkins, 1995) produced what they termed *neurally mediated hypotension* in 21 of 22 adult patients with CFS using head-up tilt. Figure 13.10 provides an example of heart rate and blood pressure changes during upright tilt in neurally mediated syncope. Comparison of this figure with Figure 13.8 shows a pattern of orthostatic intolerance similar to patients who faint with a sudden rapid fall of heart rate and blood pressure. Thus in this context, neurally mediated hypotension refers to simple faint. In earlier work performed in adolescents with CFS, Rowe reported somewhat different findings. Those patients had tachycardia often associated with hypotension during orthostasis (Rowe et al., 1995). Indeed, a high incidence of POTS-like orthostatic intolerance has been confirmed in adolescents (Stewart, Gewitz, Weldon, Arlievsky, et al., 1999; Stewart, Gewitz, Weldon, & Munoz, 1999) approaching 90% in some series. It is likely that POTS occurs with much greater frequency in adolescents than in adults. It is equally likely that the very high incidence reported by pediatric investigators represents an overestimate based on referral bias. The reported incidence of orthostatic intolerance in adults with CFS from other laboratories is variable (De Becker et al., 1998; De Lorenzo, Hargreaves, & Kakkar, 1996; De Lorenzo, Hargreaves, & Kakkar, 1997; Freeman & Komaroff, 1997; LaManca et al., 1999; Low, 1998; Poole, Herrell, Ashton, Goldberg, & Buchwald, 2000; Schondorf, Benoit, Wein, & Phaneuf, 1999; Schondorf & Freeman, 1999; Smit, Bolweg, Lenders, & Wieling, 1998; Soetekouw, Lenders, Bleijenberg,

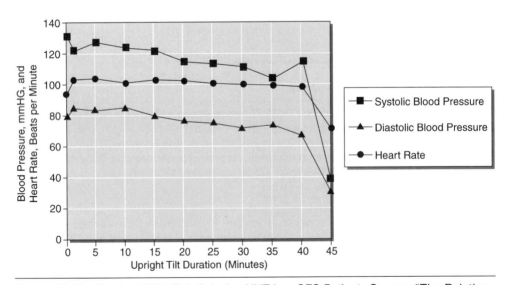

Figure 13.10 Sudden NMH (Faint) during HUT in a CFS Patient. *Source:* "The Relationship between Neurally Mediated Hypotension and the Chronic Fatigue Syndrome," by I. Bou-Holaigah et al., 1995, *Journal of American Medical Association, 274*, pp. 961–967.

Thien, & van der Meer, 1999; Streeten & Anderson, 1998). A meta-analysis implies significantly increased incidence of orthostatic intolerance in CFS patients compared with healthy control subjects. Factors contributing to this variability include the use of different criteria to diagnose orthostatic intolerance, variability in the natural history of CFS, lack of delineation of selection criteria for subjects and controls, including age and gender, and varying methods of orthostatic stress testing. This last is critical. Rowe, for example, required hypotension in his definition of orthostatic intolerance in CFS: neurally mediated hypotension. This definition may be too restrictive excluding many patients who otherwise would meet the more generalized criteria for orthostatic intolerance presented earlier. It is, therefore, interesting how frequently hypotension was observed in Rowe's initial group of adult patients. This may reflect the conditions under which orthostatic testing was performed. These included the use of pharmacological potentiators (e.g., isoproterenol), the type of orthostatic stress employed (tilt vs. standing), restriction of movement, the duration of testing, environmental conditions (e.g., temperature), time of day, fasting or nonfasting, and on or off prescription medications. Nevertheless, the metaconsensus of these studies suggests that orthostatic intolerance is an important aspect of CFS pathophysiology.

Since the autonomic nervous system is integral to the orthostatic response, investigators have proposed that there are autonomic defects in CFS (Appenzeller, 1987; De Becker et al., 1998; Freeman & Komaroff, 1997; Pagani & Lucini, 1999). In an important work, Freeman and Komaroff reported an incidence of 25% positive tilt among their patients using a 5-minute screening tilt and active standing without stringent movement restriction. Sustained tilt testing was only performed in a minority of patients. More extensive autonomic tests were performed. Resting tachycardia and a pronounced upright tachycardia were often found in symptomatic patients thereby fulfilling criteria for POTS. Overt findings of autonomic dysfunction were relatively sparse although some patients had abnormal Valsalva and periodic breathing assessments. Similar findings had been previously found by Sisto et al. (1995) during paced breathing, while Soetekouw et al. (1999) and De Becker and colleagues (1998) demonstrated a modest degree of autonomic dysfunction in patients. Other groups looking at small numbers of patients have not found orthostatic intolerance in a group of CFS patients despite using the Johns Hopkins protocol. However, their criteria for OI may vary from current neurovascular physiology concepts (Poole et al., 2000). A more extensive study made on unselected patients demonstrated a likely figure for OI prevalence in CFS on the order of 40% in adults (Schondorf et al., 1999).

Investigations by De Lorenzo and associates (1997) demonstrated a connection with delayed orthostatic hypotension described by David Streeten (Streeten & Anderson, 1992) as a variant of "hyperadrenergic orthostatic hypotension" (hypotensive POTS). Later work by Streeten and Anderson (Streeten, 1998; Streeten & Anderson, 1998) and by De Lorenzo and associates (1997), demonstrated a potential connection with POTS and in particular with delayed orthostatic hypotension in those maintained in a prolonged upright position. This was also demonstrable in Stewart's work as a later finding in POTS and CFS (Stewart, Gewitz, Weldon, & Munoz, 1999). Similar findings were described in a wide variety of CFS patients by Streeten and Bell (Streeten, Thomas, & Bell, 2000), who also showed decreased blood volume amenable to erythrocyte (erythropoietin) and plasma (florinef) expansion. That work contained the interesting observation that an aviation pressure suit could reverse orthostatic intolerance in CFS patients. Streeten proposed that the chronic fatigue in the syndrome depended closely on the regulation of heart rate and blood pressure (Streeten, 1998).

Further clues concerning the role of orthostatic intolerance in CFS came from studies of teenagers performed by Rowe and associates (Rowe & Calkins, 1998; Rowe et al., 1999; Stewart, 2000; Stewart, Gewitz, Weldon, Arlievsky, et al., 1999; Stewart, Gewitz, Weldon, & Munoz, 1999; Stewart, Weldon, Arlievsky, Li, & Munoz, 1998) and by Stewart. The data suggest an extremely high incidence of orthostatic intolerance in teenagers. Studies of the case incidence of CFS in the pediatric age groups remain incomplete. In his earliest pediatric series, Rowe found POTS. Stewart found a preponderance of POTS in his early patients who often had obvious acrocyanosis (blue or purple extremities) and dependent edema (swelling—see Figure 13.11).

A loss of heart rate variability and instability of blood pressure have been demonstrated (Figure 13.12 on p. 267). Increased heart rate and altered baroreflex (the controller for blood pressure and heart rate) gain suggested withdrawal of vagal tone (Figure 13.13 on p. 268). Similar baroreflex alterations have been demonstrated in POTS by Stewart in adolescents (Stewart, 2000).

Using a more elegant analysis, Farquhar and Freeman (Farquhar, Taylor, Darling, Chase, & Freeman, 2000) showed similar findings in adults (Figure 13.14 on p. 269). They also found a decrease in plasma volume in some patients, which may have contributed to orthostatic intolerance and has been an inconstant finding in POTS and CFS patients alike. An indirect connection to POTS was also established through later work by Rowe, who noted a disproportionate representation of findings of the Ehlers-Danlos syndrome (Rowe et al., 1999) in a large fraction of patients he followed with CFS.

Tanaka, Matsushima, Tamai, and Kajimoto (2002) have demonstrated cerebral malperfusion in association with forms of chronic orthostatic intolerance in CFS. As in POTS (Low et al., 1999), symptoms such as neurocognitive deficits correlate well with cerebral malperfusion.

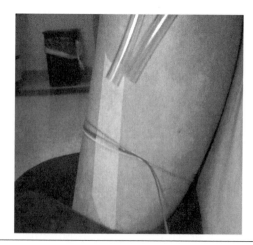

Figure 13.11   Pooling in a Lower Extremity

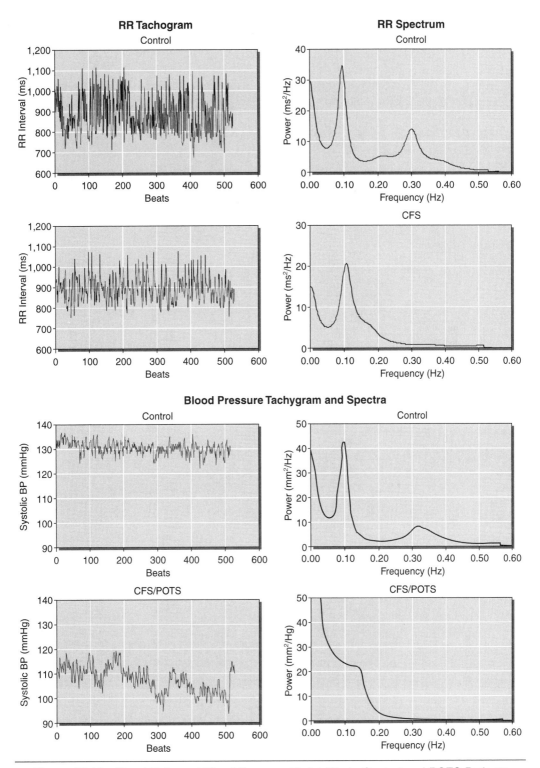

Figure 13.12   Heart Rate and Blood Pressure Variability in Control and POTS Patients

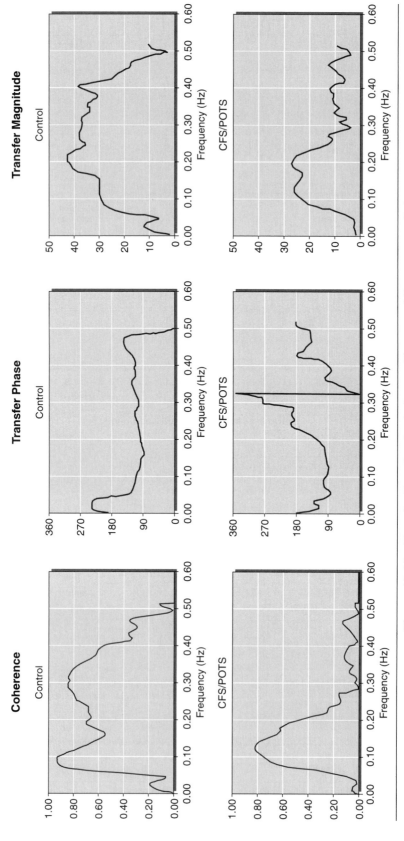

Figure 13.13 Transfer Function Analysis as a Measure of Baroreceptor Gain

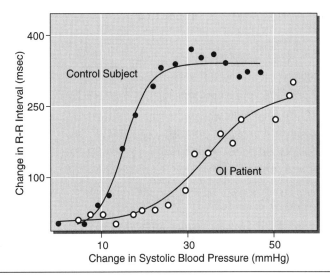

Figure 13.14 The Complete Baroreflex Curve in POTS (OI) and Control. *Source:* "Abnormal Baroreflex Responses in Patients with Idiopathic Orthostatic Intolerance," by Farquhar et al., 2000, *Circulation, 102,* pp. 3086–3091.

In summary, orthostatic intolerance in most adolescents (and many adults) with CFS appears to be POTS. The symptoms and complaints of patients with chronic orthostatic intolerance and POTS are similar to symptoms of CFS. Forms of medical therapy exist for orthostatic intolerance (to be discussed). Thus, investigations into POTS may illuminate pathophysiology and treatment of at least a subset of patients with CFS.

IMPORTANCE OF CHRONIC FATIGUE SYNDROME AS ORTHOSTATIC INTOLERANCE (POTS)

The defining heart rate abnormalities in POTS suggested a partial dysautonomia (Schondorf & Low, 1993). Freeman and Komaroff (1997) found similar abnormalities in CFS (Tables 13.4 and 13.5). Schondorf and Low's original data are strikingly similar to data from the Freeman and Komaroff article. Since that paper, plasma epinephrine and norepinephrine have been shown to be normal to increased in resting patients with CFS and increased when upright compared with control subjects, fulfilling Streeten's hyperadrenergic criteria. Streeten hypothesized that vascular abnormalities related to decreased alpha adrenergic function (Streeten, 1990, 1999) with intact cardiomotor innervation explained the tachycardia. This means that blood vessels or their control are defective but that heart function and in particular heart rate are under appropriate control although responding to abnormal circulatory conditions. This has led some investigators to postulate idiopathic hypovolemia (low blood volume) (Fouad, Tadena-Thome, Bravo, & Tarazi, 1986) that almost certainly forms a subset of patients with CFS. However, as shown in Figure 13.15 on page 271 taken from Farquhar et al., the relationship of CFS to low intravascular volume is not clear (Farquhar, Hunt, Taylor, Darling, & Freeman, 2002). As in earlier work by Streeten (on pheochromocytoma; Streeten & Anderson, 1996) and others, a chronic state of adrenergic activation (i.e., activation of the

Table 13.4
Test of Baseline Autonomic Function

	CFS	Controls
Supine systolic blood pressure (mmHg)	112.0 ± 3.6	104.4 ± 1.75[a]
Supine diastolic blood pressure (mmHg)	67.8 ± 2.4	65.0 ± 1.6
Supine heart rate (beats/min)	72.5 ± 2.0	65.0 ± 2.8
Sitting systolic blood pressure (mmHg)	116.4 ± 4.5	108.6 ± 1.9
Sitting diastolic blood pressure (mmHg)	69.3 ± 2.1	70.4 ± 2.1
Sitting heart rate (beats/min)	83.5 ± 2.8	70.7 ± 1.7[b]

Test results expressed as mean ± SEM. [a]$p < .005$, [b]$p < .001$.

CFS = Chronic fatigue syndrome.

Adapted from "Does the Chronic Fatigue Syndrome Involve the Autonomic Nervous System?" by R. Freeman and A. L. Komaroff, 1997, *American Journal of Medicine, 102*, pp. 357–364.

sympathetic nervous system) can produce reduced intravascular volume. Conversely, reduced intravascular volume can activate the autonomic nervous system. Thus, the finding of hypovolemia may be either cause or effect. Similar heart rate, blood pressure, catecholamine (epinephrine and norepinephrine) changes, and blood volume differences have been described in a subset of POTS patients but not in others with relative hyporeninism (Jacob, Biaggioni,

Table 13.5
Tests of Sympathetic and Parasympathetic Autonomic Function

	CFS	Controls
Expiratory:inspiratory ratio	1.24 ± .03	1.39 ± 0.03[b]
Maximum-minimum heart rate (beats/min)	22.1 ± 1.8	28.4 ± 2.2[a]
Valsalva ratio	2.01 ± 0.1	1.78 ± 0.1[a]
Isometric exercise (mmHg)	7.7 ± 1.4	8.5 ± 1.7
Valsalva phase II systolic blood pressure fall (mmHg)	−28.1 ± 5.8	−5.8 ± 5.7[a]
Standing systolic blood pressure fall (mmHg)	−2.8 ± 2.3	−0.4 ± 1.4
Standing diastolic blood pressure fall (mmHg)	6.3 ± 2.5	4.2 ± 1.6
Standing maximum heart rate (beats/min)	97.9 ± 3.0	79.8 ± 2.1[b]
Standing heart rate increase(beats/min)	22.6 ± 2.6	14.5 ± 1.8[a]
Tilt table systolic blood pressure fall (mmHg)	−14.7 ± 2.2	−7.1 ± 1.6[c]
Tilt table diastolic blood pressure fall (mmHg)	−2.0 ± 2.4	2.4 ± 1.6[a]
Tilt table maximum heart rate (beats/min)	100.2 ± 3.5	80.4 ± 2.3[b]
Tilt table heart rate increase(beats/min)	31.8 ± 3.4	18.6 ± 2.1[a]

Test results expressed as mean ± SEM. [a]$p < 0.05$, [b]$p < .01$, [c]$p < .001$.

CFS = Chronic fatigue syndrome.

Adapted from "Does the Chronic Fatigue Syndrome Involve the Autonomic Nervous System?" by R. Freeman and A. L. Komaroff, 1997, *American Journal of Medicine, 102*, pp. 357–364.

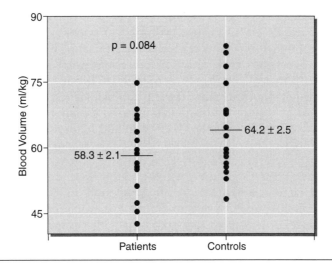

Figure 13.15 Individual and Means ±SE Data for Blood Volume Expressed Relative to Body Weight in Those with Chronic Fatique Syndrome (CFS) (*n* = 17 and Controls *n* = 17). There is a trend for blood volume to be lower in the patients (*p* = .089). *Source:* "Blood Volume and Its Relation to Peak O(2) Consumption and Physical Activity in Patients with Chronic Fatigue," by Farquhar et al., 2002, *American Journal of Physiology and Heart Cir-circulation Physiology, 282*, pp. H66–H71.

Mosqueda-Garcia, Robertson, & Robertson, 1998; Jacob, Robertson, et al., 1997). Supportive evidence from volume loading with intravenous saline infusions and vasoconstrictor experiments using midodrine showed transient success in remediating POTS (Jacob, Shannon, et al., 1997). Similar interesting findings in the CFS literature (De Lorenzo et al., 1997) have largely been interpreted within a framework of the hypothalamus-pituitary-adrenal axis (Clauw & Chrousos, 1997), but they also make sense within the POTS paradigm.

Patients with POTS or CFS frequently display acrocyanosis and swelling ("pooling") in the lower extremities. The literature contains potential explanations for abnormal venous pooling and fluid collection in POTS including impaired innervation of the veins or in their response to sympathetic stimulation (Jacob, Robertson, et al., 1997; Streeten & Scullard, 1996). One such explanation favors an autonomic neuropathy that predominantly affects the lower extremities (Jacob, Robertson, et al., 1997). $\forall_1$-adrenergic denervation hypersensitivity results—the number of receptors for norepinephrine and epinephrine increases. A second explanation invokes decreased $\exists_1$-receptor sensitivity (Andersen et al., 1985; Mares, Davies, & Taylor, 1990); a third, $\forall_1$-receptor supersensitivity (Grubb & Kosinski, 1998); a fourth altered venoconstriction (Streeten, 1990); while a fifth (Brown & Hainsworth, 1999) suggests increased capillary filtration and thus increased leak of fluid from the blood into the surrounding tissues as an explanation. However, $\forall_1$-adrenergic control of venous filling in response to baroreflex stimulation during orthostasis is important only in the splanchnic circulation in humans (Donegan, 1921; Rothe, 1983), whereas involvement of skeletal muscle $\exists_1$-receptors remains controversial (Donegan, 1921; Osadchii, Pugovkin, Sergeev, & Maliavko, 1980; Rowell, 1986; Vargas et al., 1986). $\forall_1$-adrenergic effects may also alter venous filling, but only indirectly through arterial vasoactivity (Rowell, 1986). In this regard, Stewart has shown that blood pooling in POTS and CFS results from a defect in arterial vasoconstriction that may be baroreflex sensitive in some cases and baroreflex insensitive in others (Stewart & Weldon, 2001). Increased venous filling and enhanced microvascular filtration (fluid leaking from the blood into the peripheral tissues) during orthostasis results in pooling. Blood is redistributed peripherally, and redistribution is enhanced during orthostasis producing increased microvascular filtration and dependent edema. Central hypovolemia (decreased blood volume to fill the heart) causes reflex tachycardia. POTS produces a circulation at high risk for simple fainting or neurally mediated hypotension (NMH) due to an underfilled thoracic vascular bed. In many ways, the physiology resembles hemorrhage or hypovolemia (low blood volume) in that tachycardia and malperfusion are noted first but can proceed to hypotension (low blood pressure) or loss of consciousness or both. Strong support for a defect in adrenergic vasoconstriction comes from Jacob and coworkers who have recently demonstrated reduced norepinephrine spillover in patients with POTS consistent with defective innervation of the periphery. Findings were accentuated in the lower extremities (Jacob et al., 2000).

It is likely, however, that many etiologies for POTS exist. An example is the recent discovery by Robertson and associates of an aberrant gene for the norepinephrine reuptake transporter protein. This produces alternating hypertension and hypotension in the same patient (and her twin sister) dependent on the state of norepinephrine stores (Shannon et al., 2000). The gene seems confined to a single family, but such results indicate neurovascular abnormalities that can potentially result in postural tachycardia and associated symptoms of orthostatic intolerance.

It is uncertain how important active venoconstriction is to the orthostatic response. Venous capacitance properties in POTS could be abnormal because of altered vascular structure, altered muscle tone, or both. One such example may occur in the Ehlers-Danlos syndrome (EDS) (Rowe et al., 1999). However, perhaps paradoxically, excess lower extremity pooling seems to be uncommon in common variants of EDS (e.g., type 3, preliminary data). Also, preliminary data indicate no change or even a decrease in lower limb venous distensibility compared with normal.

A potential link between altered vasoreactivity and antecedent inflammatory disease is the chronic elaboration of cytokines with potent vasoactive consequences such as IL-1, IL-6, and tumor necrosis factor alpha. Such a link seems established in the chronic fatigue syndrome in which POTS and orthostatic intolerance occur with high frequency (Patarca, Klimas, Lutgendorf, Antoni, & Fletcher, 1994; Press, Teukolsky, Vetterling, & Flannery 1992; Swanink et al., 1996; Visser et al., 1998).

Medical and nonmedical treatments for POTS exist but are rarely curative and often incompletely palliative. Treatment must be individualized and highly integrated with findings based on a thorough assessment. Agents that expand blood volume such as fludrocortisone and erythropoietin are sometimes useful by increasing thoracic blood volume. However, a double-blind placebo control study of unselected adults with CFS failed to demonstrate efficacy of fludrocortisone in relieving orthostatic intolerance (Rowe et al., 2001). These data do not indicate that fludrocortisone is ineffective in all cases of CFS with orthostatic intolerance, but suggest a need for individualized patient treatment of carefully selected patients.

Other actions and maneuvers that can help increase thoracic blood volume include elevating the head of the bed (a low angle upright tilt that causes blood volume to increase), ingesting salt and water, avoiding dehydration, and providing intravenous fluids (Jacob, Shannon, et al., 1997). Intravenous fluid loading is of short-term benefit only. Large meals can provoke all forms of orthostatic intolerance through splanchnic (gut, liver, and spleen) vasodilation, which may be mediated through the vasoactive intestinal polypeptide (Mathias et al., 1989); small, frequent meals are best. Vasoconstrictive agents such as midodrine or phenylpropanolamine are sometimes useful but not always. These contract the blood vessels of skeletal muscle and other tissues. Selective serotonin reuptake inhibitors have met with some success in the treatment of CFS and orthostatic intolerance alike (Grubb & Karas, 1998; Montastruc et al., 1998). Mechanisms of action in orthostatic intolerance remain as yet unclear. Rapid ingestion of water has been advocated as a benign and temporarily effective means to raise blood pressure (Jordan et al., 2000). Support hose and physical maneuvers can reduce pooling for whatever reason (van Lieshout, Ten Harkel, & Wieling, 1992). Bulking leg muscles has a similar effect. Physical therapy and physical rehabilitation are generally thought to be beneficial for most forms of orthostatic intolerance and have gained support from the literature (Bouvette, McPhee, Opfer-Gehrking, & Low, 1996; Brilla, Stephens, Knutzen, & Caine, 1998; Mtinangi & Hainsworth, 1999). This approach has also been suggested in CFS (Fulcher & White, 1997). I certainly advocate enhanced activity. Orthostatic training in which patients stand for progressively greater lengths of time has also been advocated (Di Girolamo, Di Iorio, Leonzio, Sabatini, & Barsotti, 1999; Ector, Reybrouck, Heidbuchel, Gewillig, & van de Werf, 1998). Treatment success is sporadic because we are not directly addressing the pathophysiology. Further research is needed to clarify these issues.

CONCLUSION

Orthostatic intolerance is common but often misunderstood. It is an evolving field of integrative physiological study. There are many similarities between symptoms of chronic orthostatic intolerance and chronic fatigue syndrome. Orthostatic intolerance has been demonstrated in CFS and is most common in adolescents with CFS, where it is characterized by the postural tachycardia syndrome (POTS). POTS appears to be a disease state characterized by redistribution of blood away from the central circulation to the periphery due to impaired vasoconstriction. It is likely that POTS plays an important role in generating some or many symptoms of CFS. However, like CFS, POTS remains a heterogeneous entity of varied etiologies. Until investigators achieve better understanding, treatment remains guesswork and not science.

REFERENCES

Andersen, E. B., Lindskov, H. O., Marving, J., Boesen, F., Beck-Nielsen, H., & Hesse, B. (1985). Decrease in beta-receptor density explaining the development of pind. *Danish Medical Bulletin, 32*(3), 194–196.

Anonymous. (1996). Consensus statement on the definition of orthostatic hypotension, pure autonomic failure, and multiple system atrophy. *Neurology, 46,* 1470.

Appenzeller, O. (1987). The autonomic nervous system and fatigue. *Functional Neurology, 2*(4), 473–485.

Baisch, F., Beck, L., Blomqvist, G., Wolfram, G., Drescher, J., Rome, J. L., et al. (2000). Cardiovascular response to lower body negative pressure stimulation before, during, and after space flight. *European Journal of Clinical Investigation, 30*(12), 1055–1065.

Benditt, D. G., Ferguson, D. W., Grubb, B. P., Kapoor, W. N., Kugler, J., Lerman, B. B., et al. (1996). Tilt table testing for assessing syncope: American College of Cardiology. *Journal of American College of Cardiologists, 28*(1), 263–275.

Biaggioni, I., Costa, F., & Kaufmann, H. (1998). Vestibular influences on autonomic cardiovascular control in humans. *Journal of Vestibular Research, 8*(1), 35–41.

Blomqvist, C. G. (1986). Orthostatic hypotension [clinical conference]. *Hypertension, 8*(8), 722–731.

Blomqvist, C. G. & Stone, H. L. (1983). Cardiovascular adjustments to gravitational stress. In J. T. Shepherd, F. M. Abboud, & S. R. Geiger (Eds.). *Handbook of Physiology* (Vol. 3, pp. 1025–1063). Bethesda, MD: American Physiological Society.

Bloomfield, D. M., Kaufman, E. S., Bigger, J. T., Jr., Fleiss, J., Rolnitzky, L., & Steinman, R. (1997). Passive head-up tilt and actively standing up produce similar overall changes in autonomic balance. *American Heart Journal, 134*(2, Pt. 1), 316–320.

Bondar, R. L., Dunphy, P. T., Moradshahi, P., Kassam, M. S., Blaber, A. P., Stein, F., et al. (1997). Cerebrovascular and cardiovascular responses to graded tilt in patients with autonomic failure. *Stroke, 28*(9), 1677–1685.

Bou-Holaigah, I., Rowe, P. C., Kan, J., & Calkins, H. (1995). The relationship between neurally mediated hypotension and the chronic fatigue syndrome. *Journal of American Medical Association, 274*(12), 961–967.

Bouvette, C. M., McPhee, B. R., Opfer-Gehrking, T. L., & Low, P. A. (1996). Role of physical countermaneuvers in the management of orthostatic hypotension: Efficacy and biofeedback augmentation. *Mayo Clinic Proceedings, 71*(9), 847–853.

Brilla, L. R., Stephens, A. B., Knutzen, K. M., & Caine, D. (1998). Effect of strength training on orthostatic hypotension in older adults. *Journal of Cardiopulmonary Rehabilitation, 18*(4), 295–300.

Brown, C. M., & Hainsworth, R. (1999). Assessment of capillary fluid shifts during orthostatic stress in normal subjects and subjects with orthostatic intolerance. *Clinical Autonomic Research, 9*(2), 69–73.

Brown, C. M., & Hainsworth, R. (2000). Forearm vascular responses during orthostatic stress in control subjects and patients with posturally related syncope [see comments]. *Clinical Autonomic Research, 10*(2), 57–61.

Clauw, D. J., & Chrousos, G. P. (1997). Chronic pain and fatigue syndromes: Overlapping clinical and neuroendocrine features and potential pathogenic mechanisms. *Neuroimmunomodulation, 4*(3), 134–153.

De Becker, P., Dendale, P., De Meirleir, K., Campine, I., Vandenborne, K., & Hagers, Y. (1998). Autonomic testing in patients with chronic fatigue syndrome. *American Journal of Medicine, 105*(3A), 22S–26S.

De Lorenzo, F., Hargreaves, J., & Kakkar, V. V. (1996). Possible relationship between chronic fatigue and postural tachycardia syndromes. *Clinical Autonomic Research, 6*(5), 263–264.

De Lorenzo, F., Hargreaves, J., & Kakkar, V. V. (1997). Pathogenesis and management of delayed orthostatic hypotension in patients with chronic fatigue syndrome. *Clinical Autonomic Research, 7*(4), 185–190.

Di Girolamo, E., Di Iorio, C., Leonzio, L., Sabatini, P., & Barsotti, A. (1999). Usefulness of a tilt training program for the prevention of refractory neurocardiogenic syncope in adolescents: A controlled study. *Circulation, 100*(17), 1798–1801.

Donegan, J. F. (1921). The physiology of veins. *Journal of Physiology (London), 55,* 226–245.

Ector, H., Reybrouck, T., Heidbuchel, H., Gewillig, M., & van de Werf, W. F. (1998). Tilt training: A new treatment for recurrent neurocardiogenic syncope and severe orthostatic intolerance. *Pacing and Clinical Electrophysiology, 21*(1, Pt. 2), 193–196.

Farquhar, W. B., Hunt, B. E., Taylor, J. A., Darling, S. E., & Freeman, R. (2002). Blood volume and its relation to peak O(2) consumption and physical activity in patients with chronic fatigue. *American Journal of Physiology and Heart Circulation Physiology, 282*(1), H66–H71.

Farquhar, W. B., Taylor, J. A., Darling, S. E., Chase, K. P., & Freeman, R. (2000). Abnormal baroreflex responses in patients with idiopathic orthostatic intolerance. *Circulation, 102*(25), 3086–3091.

Folkow, B. (1989). Myogenic mechanisms in the control of systemic resistance. Introduction and historical background. *Journal of Hypertension Supplement, 7*(4), S1–S4.

Fouad, F. M., Tadena-Thome, L., Bravo, E. L., & Tarazi, R. C. (1986). Idiopathic hypovolemia. *Annals of Internal Medicine, 104*(3), 298–303.

Freeman, R., & Komaroff, A. L. (1997). Does the chronic fatigue syndrome involve the autonomic nervous system? *American Journal of Medicine, 102*(4), 357–364.

Fulcher, K. Y., & White, P. D. (1997). Randomised controlled trial of graded exercise in patients with the chronic fatigue syndrome [see comments]. *British Medical Journal, 314*(7095), 1647–1652.

Furlan, R., Piazza, S., Dell'Orto, S., Barbic, F., Bianchi, A., Mainardi, L., et al. (1998). Cardiac autonomic patterns preceding occasional vasovagal reactions in healthy humans. *Circulation, 98*(17), 1756–1761.

Gastaut, H. F. W. M. (1957). Electroencephalographic study of syncope, its differentiation from epilepsy. *Lancet, 2,* 1018–1025.

Grubb, B. P., Gerard, G., Roush, K., Temesy-Armos, P., Elliott, L., Hahn, H., et al. (1991). Differentiation of convulsive syncope and epilepsy with head-up tilt testing [see comments]. *Annals of Internal Medicine, 115*(11), 871–876.

Grubb, B. P., & Karas, B. J. (1998). The potential role of serotonin in the pathogenesis of neurocardiogenic syncope and related autonomic disturbances. *Journal of Interventional Cardiac Electrophysiology, 2*(4), 325–332.

Grubb, B. P., & Kosinski, C. M. (1998). *Syncope: Mechanisms and management.* Armonk, NY: Futura.

Guzman, C. E., Sanchez, G. M., Marquez, M. F., Hermosillo, A. G., & Cardenas, M. (1999). Differences in heart rate variability between cardioinhibitory and vasodepressor responses to head-up tilt table testing. *Archives of Medical Research, 30*(3), 203–211.

Hainsworth, R. (1995). Cardiovascular reflexes from ventricular and coronary receptors. *Advances in Experimental Medicine and Biology, 381,* 157–174.

Henriksen, O., Skagen, K., Haxholdt, O., & Dyrberg, V. (1983). Contribution of local blood flow regulation mechanisms to the maintenance of arterial pressure in upright position during epidural blockade. *Acta Physiologica Scandinavica, 118*(3), 271–280.

Hill, L. (1951). The influences of the force of gravity on the circulation of the blood. *Journal of Physiology (London), 18,* 15–53.

Hyatt, K. H., Jacobson, L. B., & Schneider, V. S. (1975). Comparison of 70 degrees tilt, LBNP, and passive standing as measures of orthostatic tolerance. *Aviation and Space Environmental Medicine, 46*(6), 801–808.

Jacob, G., Atkinson, D., Jordan, J., Shannon, J. R., Furlan, R., Black, B. K., et al. (1999). Effects of standing on cerebrovascular resistance in patients with idiopathic orthostatic intolerance. *American Journal of Medicine, 106*(1), 59–64.

Jacob, G., & Biaggioni, I. (1999). Idiopathic orthostatic intolerance and postural tachycardia syndromes. *American Journal of Medical Sciences, 317*(2), 88–101.

Jacob, G., Biaggioni, I., Mosqueda-Garcia, R., Robertson, R. M., & Robertson, D. (1998). Relation of blood volume and blood pressure in orthostatic intolerance. *American Journal of Medical Sciences, 315*(2), 95–100.

Jacob, G., Costa, F., Shannon, J. R., Robertson, R. M., Wathen, M., Stein, M., et al. (2000). The neuropathic postural tachycardia syndrome. *New England Journal of Medicine, 343*(14), 1008–1014.

Jacob, G., Robertson, D., Mosqueda-Garcia, R., Ertl, A. C., Robertson, R. M., & Biaggioni, I. (1997). Hypovolemia in syncope and orthostatic intolerance role of the renin-angiotensin system. *American Journal of Medicine, 103*(2), 128–133.

Jacob, G., Shannon, J. R., Black, B., Biaggioni, I., Mosqueda-Garcia, R., Robertson, R. M., et al. (1997). Effects of volume loading and pressor agents in idiopathic orthostatic tachycardia. *Circulation, 96*(2), 575–580.

Jacobsen, T. N., Morgan, B. J., Scherrer, U., Vissing, S. F., Lange, R. A., Johnson, N., et al. (1993). Relative contributions of cardiopulmonary and sinoaortic baroreflexes in causing sympathetic activation in the human skeletal muscle circulation during orthostatic stress. *Circulation Research, 73*(2), 367–378.

Jordan, J., Shannon, J. R., Black, B. K., Ali, Y., Farley, M., Costa, F., et al. (2000). The pressor response to water drinking in humans: A sympathetic reflex? *Circulation, 101*(5), 504–509.

Kapoor, W. N. (1992). Hypotension and syncope. In Eugene Braunwald (Ed.), *Heart disease* (pp. 875–886). Philadelphia: Saunders.

Karas, B., Grubb, B. P., Boehm, K., & Kip, K. (2000). The postural orthostatic tachycardia syndrome: A potentially treatable cause of chronic fatigue, exercise intolerance, and cognitive impairment in adolescents. *Pacing and Clinical Electrophysiology, 23*(3), 344–351.

Kenny, R. A., Ingram, A., Bayliss, J., & Sutton, R. (1986). Head-up tilt: A useful test for investigating unexplained syncope. *Lancet, 1*(8494), 1352–1355.

Klingenheben, T., Kalusche, D., Li, Y. G., Schopperl, M., & Hohnloser, S. H. (1996). Changes in plasma epinephrine concentration and in heart rate during head-up tilt testing in patients with neurocardiogenic syncope: Correlation with successful therapy with beta-receptor antagonists. *Journal of Cardiovascular Electrophysiology, 7*(9), 802–808.

LaManca, J. J., Peckerman, A., Walker, J., Kesil, W., Cook, S., Taylor, A., et al. (1999). Cardiovascular response during head-up tilt in chronic fatigue syndrome. *Clinical Physiology, 19*(2), 111–120.

Leonelli, F. M., Wang, K., Evans, J. M., Patwardhan, A. R., Ziegler, M. G., Natale, A., et al. (2000). False positive head-up tilt: Hemodynamic and neurohumoral profile. *Journal of American College of Cardiologists, 35*(1), 188–193.

Lewis, T. (1932). A lecture on vasovagal syncope and the carotid sinus mechanism: With comments on Gower's and Nothnagel's syndrome. *British Medical Journal, 1,* 873–876.

Lightfoot, J. T., Rowe, S. A., & Fortney, S. M. (1993). Occurrence of presyncope in subjects without ventricular innervation. *Clinical Science, 85*(6), 695–700.

Liu, J. E., Hahn, R. T., Stein, K. M., Markowitz, S. M., Okin, P. M., Devereux, R. B., et al. (2000). Left ventricular geometry and function preceding neurally mediated syncope. *Circulation, 101*(7), 777–783.

Low, P. A. (1998). Autonomic neuropathies. *Current Opinion in Neurology, 11*(5), 531–537.

Low, P. A., Novak, V., Spies, J. M., Novak, P., & Petty, G. W. (1999). Cerebrovascular regulation in the postural orthostatic tachycardia syndrome (POTS). *American Journal of Medical Sciences, 317*(2), 124–133.

Low, P. A., Opfer-Gehrking, T. L., Textor, S. C., Benarroch, E. E., Shen, W. K., Schondorf, R., et al. (1995). Postural tachycardia syndrome (POTS). *Neurology, 45*(4, Suppl. 5), S19–S25.

MacLean, A. R., & Allen, E. V. (1940). Orthostatic hypotension and orthostatic tachycardia: Treatment with the "head-up" bed. *Journal of American Medical Association, 115,* 2162–2167.

Mancia, G., & Mark, A. L. (1983). Arterial baroreflexes in humans. In J. T. Shepherd, F. M. Abboud, & S. R. Geiger (Eds.), *The cardiovascular system: Peripheral circulation and organ blood flow* (pp. 755–793). Bethesda, MD: American Physiological Society.

Mares, A., Jr., Davies, A. O., & Taylor, A. A. (1990). Diversity in supercoupling of beta 2-adrenergic receptors in orthostatic hypotension. *Clinical Pharmacology and Therapeutics, 47*(3), 371–381.

Mark, A. L., & Mancia, G. (1983). Cardiopulmonary baroreflexes in humans. In J. T. Shepherd, F. M. Abboud, & S. R. Geiger (Eds.), *The cardiovascular system: Peripheral circulation and organ blood flow* (pp. 795–813). Bethesda, MD: American Physiological Society.

Mathias, C. J. (1991). Postprandial hypotension. Pathophysiological mechanisms and clinical implications in different disorders [clinical conference]. *Hypertension, 18*(5), 694–704.

Mathias, C. J., da Costa, D. F., Fosbraey, P., Bannister, R., Wood, S. M., Bloom, S. R., et al. (1989). Cardiovascular, biochemical and hormonal changes during food-induced hypotension in chronic autonomic failure. *Journal of Neurological Sciences, 94*(1/3), 255–269.

McCarthy, J. P., Bamman, M. M., Yelle, J. M., LeBlanc, A. D., Rowe, R. M., Greenisen, M. C., et al. (1997). Resistance exercise training and the orthostatic response. *European Journal of Applied Physiology, 76*(1), 32–40.

McCarthy, P., & Snyder, J. C. (1992). Orthostatic hypotension: A potential side effect of psychiatric medications. *Journal of Psychosocial Nursing and Mental Health Services, 30*(8), 3–5.

Mittal, S., Stein, K. M., Markowitz, S. M., Slotwiner, D. J., Rohatgi, S., & Lerman, B. B. (1999). Induction of neurally mediated syncope with adenosine. *Circulation, 99*(10), 1318–1324.

Montastruc, J. L., Pelat, M., Verwaerde, P., Brefel-Courbon, C., Tran, M. A., Blin, O., et al. (1998). Fluoxetine in orthostatic hypotension of Parkinson's disease: A clinical and experimental pilot study. *Fundamentals of Clinical Pharmacology, 12*(4), 398–402.

Mosqueda-Garcia, R., Furlan, R., Tank, J., & Fernandez-Violante, R. (2000). The elusive pathophysiology of neurally mediated syncope. *Circulation, 102*(23), 2898–2906.

Mtinangi, B. L., & Hainsworth, R. (1999). Effects of moderate exercise training on plasma volume, baroreceptor sensitivity and orthostatic tolerance in healthy subjects. *Experimental Physiology, 84*(1), 121–130.

Narkiewicz, K., & Somers, V. K. (1998). Chronic orthostatic intolerance: Part of a spectrum of dysfunction in orthostatic cardiovascular homeostasis? *Circulation, 98*(20), 2105–2107.

Novak, V., Spies, J. M., Novak, P., McPhee, B. R., Rummans, T. A., & Low, P. A. (1998). Hypocapnia and cerebral hypoperfusion in orthostatic intolerance. *Stroke, 29*(9), 1876–1881.

Oberg, B., & Thoren, P. (1972). Increased activity in left ventricular receptors during hemorrhage or occlusion of caval veins in the cat: A possible cause of the vaso-vagal reaction. *Acta Physiologica Scandinavica, 85*(2), 164–173.

Osadchii, L. I., Pugovkin, A. P., Sergeev, I. V., & Maliavko, R. P. (1980). Systemic vascular reactions to increases in total blood flow. *Fiziol.Zh.SSSR Im I. M.Sechenova, 66*(10), 1481–1487.

Ovadia, M., & Thoele, D. (1994). Esmolol tilt testing with esmolol withdrawal for the evaluation of syncope in the young. *Circulation, 89*(1), 228–235.

Pagani, M., & Lucini, D. (1999). Chronic fatigue syndrome: A hypothesis focusing on the autonomic nervous system [see comments]. *Clinical Sciences, 96*(1), 117–125.

Patarca, R., Klimas, N. G., Lutgendorf, S., Antoni, M., & Fletcher, M. A. (1994). Dysregulated expression of tumor necrosis factor in chronic fatigue syndrome: Interrelations with cellular sources and patterns of soluble immune mediator expression. *Clinical Infectious Diseases, 18*(Suppl. 1), S147–S153.

Petersen, M. E., Williams, T. R., Gordon, C., Chamberlain-Webber, R., & Sutton, R. (2000). The normal response to prolonged passive head up tilt testing. *Heart, 84*(5), 509–514.

Poole, J., Herrell, R., Ashton, S., Goldberg, J., & Buchwald, D. (2000). Results of isoproterenol tilt table testing in monozygotic twins discordant for chronic fatigue syndrome [in process citation]. *Archives of Internal Medicine, 160*(22), 3461–3468.

Press, W. H., Teukolsky, S. A., Vetterling, W. T., & Flannery, B. P. (1992). *Numerical recipes in C.* (pp. 59–70). Cambridge, England: Cambridge University Press.

Raviele, A., Giada, F., Brignole, M., Menozzi, C., Marangoni, E., Manzillo, G. F., et al. (2000). Comparison of diagnostic accuracy of sublingual nitroglycerin test and low-dose isoproterenol test in patients with unexplained syncope. *American Journal of Cardiology, 85*(10), 1194–1198.

Reisdorff, E. J., & Prodinger, R. J. (1998). Sudden cardiac death in the athlete. *Emergency Medicine Clinics of North America, 16*, 281–294.

Robertson, D. (1999). The epidemic of orthostatic tachycardia and orthostatic intolerance. *American Journal of Medical Sciences, 317*(2), 75–77.

Robertson, D., & Robertson, R. M. (1994). Causes of chronic orthostatic hypotension. *Archives of Internal Medicine., 154*(14), 1620–1624.

Rodriguez, R. A., Snider, K., Cornel, G., & Teixeira, O. H. (1999). Cerebral blood flow velocity during tilt table test for pediatric syncope. *Pediatrics, 104*(2, Pt. 1), 237–242.

Rothe, C. F. (1983). Reflex control of veins and vascular capacitance. *Physiological Reviews, 63*(4), 1281–1342.

Rowe, P. C., Barron, D. F., Calkins, H., Maumenee, I. H., Tong, P. Y., & Geraghty, M. T. (1999). Orthostatic intolerance and chronic fatigue syndrome associated with Ehlers-Danlos syndrome. *Journal of Pediatrics, 135*(4), 494–499.

Rowe, P. C., Bou-Holaigah, I., Kan, J. S., & Calkins, H. (1995). Is neurally mediated hypotension an unrecognised cause of chronic fatigue? [see comments]. *Lancet, 345*(8950), 623–624.

Rowe, P. C., & Calkins, H. (1998). Neurally mediated hypotension and chronic fatigue syndrome. *American Journal of Medicine, 105*(3A), 15S–21S.

Rowe, P. C., Calkins, H., DeBusk, K., McKenzie, R., Anand, R., Sharma, G., et al. (2001). Fludrocortisone acetate to treat neurally mediated hypotension in chronic fatigue syndrome: A randomized controlled trial. *Journal of American Medical Association, 285*(1), 52–59.

Rowell, L. B. (1986). *Human circulation: Regulation during physical stress.* New York: Oxford University Press.

Rowell, L. B., & Seals, D. R. (1990). Sympathetic activity during graded central hypovolemia in hypoxemic humans. *American Journal of Physiology, 239*(H1197), H1197-1206.

Rundgren, M., Jonasson, H., Appelgren, B., Eriksson, S., & Leksell, L. G. (1984). Vasopressin release in response to acute hypotension induced at different time intervals in the conscious sheep. *Acta Physiologica Scandinavica, 121*(4), 393–399.

Sandroni, P., Opfer-Gehrking, T. L., Benarroch, E. E., Shen, W. K., & Low, P. A. (1996). Certain cardiovascular indices predict syncope in the postural tachycardia syndrome. *Clinical Autonomic Research, 6*(4), 225–231.

Schlegel, T. T., Brown, T. E., Wood, S. J., Benavides, E. W., Bondar, R. L., Stein, F., et al. (2001). Orthostatic intolerance and motion sickness after parabolic flight. *Journal of Applied Physiology, 90*(1), 67–82.

Schondorf, R., Benoit, J., Wein, T., & Phaneuf, D. (1999). Orthostatic intolerance in the chronic fatigue syndrome. *Journal of Autonomic Nervous System, 75*(2/3), 192–201.

Schondorf, R., & Freeman, R. (1999). The importance of orthostatic intolerance in the chronic fatigue syndrome. *American Journal of Medical Sciences, 317*(2), 117–123.

Schondorf, R., & Low, P. A. (1993). Idiopathic postural orthostatic tachycardia syndrome: An attenuated form of acute pandysautonomia? *Neurology, 43*(1), 132–137.

Shannon, J. R., Flattem, N. L., Jordan, J., Jacob, G., Black, B. K., Biaggioni, I., et al. (2000). Orthostatic intolerance and tachycardia associated with norepinephrine-transporter deficiency. *New England Journal of Medicine, 342*(8), 541–549.

Sisto, S. A., Tapp, W., Drastal, S., Bergen, M., DeMasi, I., Cordero, D., et al. (1995). Vagal tone is reduced during paced breathing in patients with the chronic fatigue syndrome. *Clinical Autonomic Research, 5*(3), 139–143.

Smit, A. A., Bolweg, N. M., Lenders, J. W., & Wieling, W. (1998). No strong evidence of disturbed regulation of blood pressure in chronic fatigue syndrome. *Ned.Tijdschr Geneeskd., 142*(12), 625–628.

Soetekouw, P. M., Lenders, J. W., Bleijenberg, G., Thien, T., & van der Meer, J. W. (1999). Autonomic function in patients with chronic fatigue syndrome. *Clinical Autonomic Research, 9*(6), 334–340.

Spodick, D. H., & Lance, V. Q. (1977). Comparative orthostatic responses: Standing vs. head-up tilt. *Aviation and Space Environmental Medicine, 48*(5), 432–433.

Starc, T. J., & Stalcup, S. A. (1987). Time course of changes of plasma renin activity and catecholamines during hemorrhage in conscious sheep. *Circulatory Shock, 21*(2), 129–140.

Stewart, J. M. (2000). Autonomic nervous system dysfunction in adolescents with postural orthostatic tachycardia syndrome and chronic fatigue syndrome is characterized by attenuated vagal baroreflex and potentiated sympathetic vasomotion. *Pediatrics Research, 48*(2), 218–226.

Stewart, J. M. (2002). Pooling in chronic orthostatic intolerance: Arterial vasoconstrictive but not venous compliance defects. *Circulation, 105*(19), 2274–2281.

Stewart, J. M., Gewitz, M. H., Weldon, A., Arlievsky, N., Li, K., & Munoz, J. (1999). Orthostatic intolerance in adolescent chronic fatigue syndrome. *Pediatrics, 103*(1), 116–121.

Stewart, J. M., Gewitz, M. H., Weldon, A., & Munoz, J. (1999). Patterns of orthostatic intolerance: The orthostatic tachycardia syndrome and adolescent chronic fatigue. *Journal of Pediatrics, 135*(2, Pt. 1), 218–225.

Stewart, J. M., Lavin, J., & Weldon, A. (2001). Orthostasis fails to produce active limb venoconstriction in adolescents. *Journal of Applied Physiology, 91*(4), 1723–1729.

Stewart, J. M., & Weldon, A. (2001). Reflex vascular defects in the orthostatic tachycardia syndrome of adolescents. *Journal of Applied Physiology, 90*, 2025–2031.

Stewart, J. M., Weldon, A., Arlievsky, N., Li, K., & Munoz, J. (1998). Neurally mediated hypotension and autonomic dysfunction measured by heart rate variability during head-up tilt testing in children with chronic fatigue syndrome. *Clinical Autonomic Research, 8*(4), 221–230.

Streeten, D. H. (1990). Pathogenesis of hyperadrenergic orthostatic hypotension. Evidence of disordered venous innervation exclusively in the lower limbs. *Journal of Clinical Investigation, 86*(5), 1582–1588.

Streeten, D. H. (1998). The nature of chronic fatigue [editorial]. *Journal of American Medical Association, 280*(12), 1094–1095.

Streeten, D. H. (1999). Orthostatic intolerance. A historical introduction to the pathophysiological mechanisms. *American Journal of Medical Sciences, 317*(2), 78–87.

Streeten, D. H., & Anderson, G. H., Jr. (1992). Delayed orthostatic intolerance [see comments]. *Archives of Internal Medicine, 152*(5), 1066–1072.

Streeten, D. H., & Anderson, G. H., Jr. (1996). Mechanisms of orthostatic hypotension and tachycardia in patients with pheochromocytoma. *American Journal of Hypertension, 9*(8), 760–769.

Streeten, D. H., & Anderson, G. H., Jr. (1998). The role of delayed orthostatic hypotension in the pathogenesis of chronic fatigue. *Clinical Autonomic Research, 8*(2), 119–124.

Streeten, D. H., & Scullard, T. F. (1996). Excessive gravitational blood pooling caused by impaired venous tone is the predominant noncardiac mechanism of orthostatic intolerance. *Clinical Sciences, 90*(4), 277–285.

Streeten, D. H., Thomas, D., & Bell, D. S. (2000). The roles of orthostatic hypotension, orthostatic tachycardia, and subnormal erythrocyte volume in the pathogenesis of the chronic fatigue syndrome. *American Journal of Medical Sciences, 320*(1), 1–8.

Swanink, C. M., Vercoulen, J. H., Galama, J. M., Roos, M. T., Meyaard, L., Van der Ven-Jongekrijg, J., et al. (1996). Lymphocyte subsets, apoptosis, and cytokines in patients with chronic fatigue syndrome. *Journal of Infectious Diseases, 173*(2), 460–463.

Tanaka, H., Matsushima, R., Tamai, H., & Kajimoto, Y. (2002). Impaired postural cerebral hemodynamics in young patients with chronic fatigue with and without orthostatic intolerance. *Journal of Pediatrics, 140*(4), 412–417.

Ten Harkel, A. D., van Lieshout, J. J., & Wieling, W. (1994). Effects of leg muscle pumping and tensing on orthostatic arterial pressure: A study in normal subjects and patients with autonomic failure. *Clinical Sciences, 87*(5), 553–558.

Vallbona, C., Lipscomb, H. S., & Carter, R. E. (1966). Endocrine responses to orthostatic hypotension in quadriplegia. *Archives of Physical Medicine and Rehabilitation, 47*(7), 412–421.

van Lieshout, J. J., Ten Harkel, A. D., & Wieling, W. (1992). Physical manoeuvres for combating orthostatic dizziness in autonomic failure. *Lancet, 339*(8798), 897–898.

Vargas, E., Lye, M., Faragher, E. B., Goddard, C., Moser, B., & Davies, I. (1986). Cardiovascular haemodynamics and the response of vasopressin, aldosterone, plasma renin activity and plasma catecholamines to head-up tilt in young and old healthy subjects. *Age Ageing, 15*(1), 17–28.

Visser, J., Blauw, B., Hinloopen, B., Brommer, E., de Kloet, E. R., Kluft, C., et al. (1998). CD4 T lymphocytes from patients with chronic fatigue syndrome have decreased interferon-gamma production and increased sensitivity to dexamethasone. *Journal of Infectious Diseases, 177*(2), 451–454.

Wang, Y., Marsgall, R. J., & Shepherd, J. T. (1960). The effect of changes in posture and graded exercise on stroke volume in man. *Journal of Clinical Investigations, 39*, 1051–1061.

Wright, C., Drinkhill, M. J., & Hainsworth, R. (2000). Reflex effects of independent stimulation of coronary and left ventricular mechanoreceptors in anaesthetised dogs [in process citation]. *Journal of Physiology, 528*(Pt. 2), 349–358.

CHAPTER 14

Sleep Disorders

U NREFRESHING SLEEP (STARTING at the onset of chronic fatigue and persisting for at least 6 months) is one of the concurrent symptoms in the case definition of chronic fatigue syndrome (CFS), generated through the Centers for Disease Control and Prevention (Fukuda et al., 1994). Many people with CFS also report other sleep difficulties. However, it remains speculative whether sleep disturbances or physiology during sleep predispose to or precipitate CFS as part of underlying altered physiology or whether sleep disturbances result from uncomfortable symptoms associated with CFS, thereby perpetuating or worsening its manifestations, or perhaps both. Scientific studies of sleep specifically associated with CFS are sparse, but in this chapter, broader as well as specific observations are reviewed to provide insight into the potential roles of sleep disturbances in CFS. This chapter begins with observations about insomnia as related to health, sleep as a behavior and the challenges to its measurement, and specific evidence to date about perceived and physiological sleep quality in CFS. The chapter concludes with brief discussions of the reciprocal nature of sleep, stress and host defense, other controversial issues related to sleep and recuperation, and treatments for sleep improvement as related to CFS and chronically fatiguing conditions.

SLEEP AND SLEEP LOSS AS RELATED TO HEALTH

Scientists are now only beginning to understand the ways in which sleep is basic to health and survival. Poor sleep results in impaired performance, is a precursor to many injury accidents, impairs tissue healing, alters the immune system, and in some cases may herald early onset of psychiatric impairment, particularly major depression. Chronic sleep loss has such profound daytime personal, social, and economic consequences that it deserves consideration within most paradigms of the study of human health. Comparisons of subjects with and without insomnia show that those with insomnia exhibit the following effects:

Excessive daytime sleepiness.	Poor attention, memory, problem-solving abilities.
Slower physical reaction times.	Reduced social stability.
Fewer job promotions.	10 times more absence days from work.
More likelihood of incurring traffic/ occupational accidental injuries.	Higher numbers of medical problems.
At least 2 times more health care provider visits.	Higher hospitalization rates (Leger, 2000).

Insomnia, defined as perceived insufficient or inadequate (poor quality) sleep, is the most commonly reported symptom or sleep problem in industrialized countries. According to epidemiological surveys, about one third of the population report sleep problems and 10% to 15% report moderate to severe insomnia that is chronic or persistent (Roth, Roehrs, Costa e Silva, & Chase, 1999). Individuals reporting insomnia describe difficulties with falling and/or remaining asleep for a desired period of time, restless or troubled sleep, or sleep that is unrefreshing—they wake up tired. *Tiredness* or *sleepiness* as a consequence of sleep disruption or loss (one definition of *fatigue*) affects large numbers of people in their everyday lives. Fatigue in this context is related to the tendency to fall asleep and the effort needed to resist it. Of note is that the hallmark fatigue symptom in CFS refers to a profound lack of energy or exhaustion and fatigability on exertion, not sleepiness. Thus, sleepiness and fatigue are presumably separable phenomena. Most people with primary or secondary insomnia do not seek medical treatment for it directly, and clinicians still underrecognize its importance to health, diagnosis, and treatment. Sleep disturbances in people not previously experiencing insomnia consistently accompany profound physical and emotional/mental distress and environmental duress (e.g., major catastrophes, divorce, or bereavement). Furthermore, sleep difficulties have long been recognized in emotional disorders such as depression and anxiety disorders (Lustberg & Reynolds, 2000; Thase, 2000) as well as with somatoform, personality, obsessive-compulsive, and posttraumatic stress disorders (Mellman, 1997; Pillar, Malhotra, & Lavie, 2000). Although lesser acknowledged, insomnia is highly associated with major physical diseases/illnesses. Insomnia is concurrent with musculoskeletal pain disorders such as rheumatoid arthritis and fibromyalgia (Drewes, 1999b; Drewes et al., 2000). It has also been associated with cardiovascular (Conte, Rigon, Perrone, & Lauro, 1999; Schwartz et al., 1999), pulmonary (George, 2000; Lewis, 1999; McNicholas, 2000), and renal (Parker, 1997) conditions. Although the pathologies involved in major disease processes might affect physiological sleep regulation mechanisms, this aspect is not easily separated from effects of the psychological distress component of having disease or illness. Moreover, it is difficult to determine if the sleep disturbances are a function of other symptoms, most particularly pain.

Even though insomnia can be attributed to particular circumstances and conditions, it can evolve into a persistent symptom not clearly associated with particular events. From long-standing observations of individuals with chronic insomnia, a derived line of thought is that insomnia in otherwise healthy adults is predisposed, precipitated, and perpetuated by a propensity to have high levels of *internalized anxiety* or *anxiety-tension,* and therefore, it is deemed *stress-related.* Although insomnia (perceived inadequate or insufficient sleep) is a symptom and is measured using self-report, sleep as a behavior can be measured physiologically. Comparisons of experiential and physiological dimensions of sleep enrich the potential for understanding sleep and its relationship to wellness and illness.

UNDERSTANDING SLEEP AND ITS ASSESSMENT

THE BEHAVIORS OF SLEEP

Although the details of its necessity for health and well-being are unknown, sleep represents a set of behaviors alternating on a regular basis every 24 hours with waking behaviors (i.e., has a circadian rhythm). Compared with waking, sleep manifests as a series of brain, somatic, and behavioral state changes, not the least of which is the loss of conscious awareness. Sleep is a dynamic and complex state of being with special challenges of assessment, measurement, and interpretation because motivated behaviors and the ability to self-report in real time are absent. Although hypotheses to explain the regulation of sleep and wake have been advanced, investigators have not yet reached consensus for any one explanation (Beersma, 1998; Cai, 1991; Horne, 2000; Rechtschaffen, 1998; Taylor, Vana, & Givon, 2000). It has been suggested that sleep has an environmental safety function because it immobilizes humans during hours of darkness, a feature not particularly necessary with the advent of artificial lighting. More importantly, sleep has a restorative or recuperative function, especially through sleep-related somatic and brain cell metabolic features and through enforced rest. Heart rate, blood pressure, and overall cellular metabolism are reduced although replication in certain cell types is accelerated during sleep. The necessity of sleep is inferred from sleep disruption or loss studies. Sleep disruption or loss has negative consequences in the form of energy, somatic, and mental performance deficits and increased negative affective and somatic symptoms.

The study of sleep is a highly transdisciplinary enterprise. Biological scientists seek to understand the biological basis for regulation of sleep/wake states. Behavioral scientists seek to understand the function of sleep for preserving daytime behaviors and health, determine normative patterns across age groups or species, and learn why some affective and physical disorders are closely associated with altered sleep patterns. Abnormal behaviors during sleep such as apneas (breathing cessation episodes) and large muscle movements (periodic limb movements) interest clinical scientists. Moreover, clinical scientists seek to understand how sleep, or more precisely *sleep loss or discontinuity,* is related to health and illness, what can be done to promote sleep, and how environments and life contexts affect sleep. Environments include critical care units, hospitals, long-term care centers, nursing homes, private homes, and outer space. Sleep patterns with enduring pain, injury, major transitions, and illness conditions such as CFS, among others, also intrigue clinical scientists. The measurement of sleep and sleep problems can include experiential (self-report), behavioral (observations), and physiological (polysomnography) modalities.

SLEEP ASSESSMENT

Self-Reported Sleep   The recognition of sleep difficulties generally is initiated through self-report. Anecdotally, people can describe multiple dimensions of their sleep patterns, such as taking too long to fall asleep, sleeping only short durations, too many and/or lengthy awakenings or arousals, premature awakenings, or excessively light or nonrestful sleep. Daytime consequences of poor sleep also can be described. Self-reported sleep patterns and quality can be systematically assessed by retrospective recall or global impressions using sleep history instruments or by concurrent reports on sleep diaries or logs that are maintained for a specified period. Commonly assessed features include bed and wake times, time to fall asleep, number and duration of awakenings. Further common items include:

How would you rate the quality of your sleep?	(very good to very poor)
How satisfied are you with your sleep?	(very to not at all satisfied)
How rested do you feel (on awakening)?	(very to not at all rested)
How clearheaded do you feel (on awakening)?	(very to not at all clearheaded)

Several standardized sleep questionnaires for research have been developed, a commonly used one being the Pittsburgh Sleep Quality Index (PSQI). It is used to assess overall sleep quality, latency, duration, and habitual efficiency, as well as attributions for difficulties, use of sleeping medication, and daytime dysfunction (Buysse, Reynolds, Monk, Berman, & Kupfer, 1989).

Physiologically Recorded Sleep   Sleep quality also can be assessed by polysomnography (PSG) involving polygraph recording of surface brainwave activity (electroencephalogram, EEG), facial muscle tension (electromyogram, EMG), and eye movements (electrooculogram, EOG). The EEG during sleep reflects the summation of neuronal synaptic events that can be recorded by surface electrodes positioned on the scalp generally according to standard placements. Sleep also can be measured using activity monitors, such as a wristwatch-type device that can distinguish whether the wearer is asleep or awake but does not allow sleep stage determination.

Early in sleep-related research, standardized sleep stage criteria were adopted for scoring PSG data from each of the somnographic channels, usually in 30-second epochs. Sleep scoring using these criteria became the gold standard for describing physiological sleep (Rechtschaffen & Kales, 1968). Using brain-wave analysis of the PSG records, sleep is recognized by signs of *transitional* sleep (Stage 1), which transcends into *light* sleep (Stage 2), and progressively descends into *deep* (delta) sleep (Stages 3 and 4), also called slow wave sleep (SWS). During this movement from light to deep sleep, brain waves progressively change from mixed frequency and low amplitude waves to increasingly slower frequency and higher amplitude waves. These stages are referred to as nonrapid eye movement (NREM) sleep stages to distinguish them from the next recognized stage of sleep called rapid eye movement (REM) sleep. Figure 14.1 shows representative EEG brain waves for each stage of sleep.

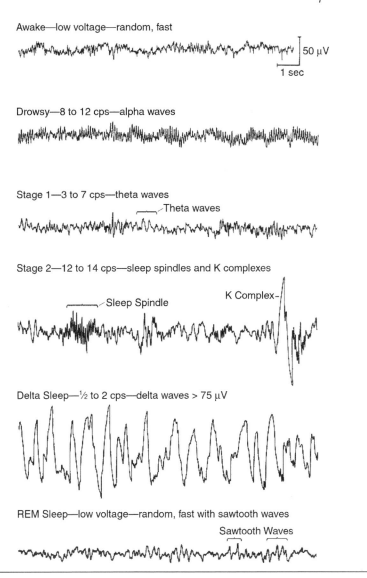

Figure 14.1 Human Sleep Stages

The movement from light to deep to REM sleep lasts 1 to 2 hours and constitutes one complete sleep cycle. Consequently, a night of sleep consists of 4 to 6 cycles of sleep, depending on the duration of the cycles and total sleep period duration. Figure 14.2 shows a histogram of the sleep stages and repeating cycles for a young adult. As people age, sleep becomes more fragmented (more stage changes and waking), and less deep sleep (as scored by conventional parameters) is evident. Physiological status indicators (e.g., heart rate, blood pressure, breathing rate) vary across the sleep stages. During NREM sleep stages, the breathing and heart rate become regular and slow and blood pressure is lower; whereas during REM sleep, these indicators become more erratic. Sleep-related disorders

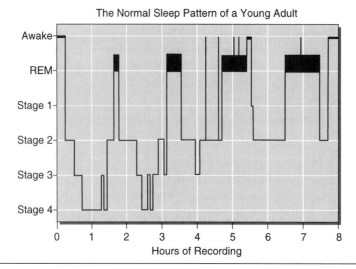

Figure 14.2 Sleep Histogram of Young Adult over Nighttime Recording

such as apneas (breathing cessation) and periodic leg movements (large muscle motor movements) can intrude on sleep and can be frequent or severe enough to seriously disturb sleep. Therefore, PSG monitoring often includes heart rate, breathing, and leg movement measurement.

Variables to describe sleep quality can be derived from PSG scoring. These include time to fall asleep (sleep onset latency), time to enter a sleep stage (e.g., REM latency), percentage of time or number of minutes spent over the night in each stage, number or duration of awakenings after sleep onset, number of sleep stage changes, or number of arousals (EEG arousals or movement arousals). The total time in bed and the amount of physical sleep occurring as a proportion of the time spent trying to sleep (sleep efficiency) can be calculated.

Comparing Self-Reported and Recorded Sleep Variables Using answers to selected questions on a sleep log or diary, it is possible to calculate variables for use in parallel comparisons to PSG variables:

What time did you go to bed last night? What time did you wake/get up?	(time in bed)
How long did it take to fall asleep?	(sleep onset latency)
How many times did you wake up? How long were you awake?	(wake after sleep onset)
Time in bed minus sleep onset latency minus wake after sleep onset.	(sleep efficiency)

To reiterate, sleep can be assessed using self-reported perceptions and physical means, and can also be judged by direct behavioral observations. Each method has its advantages and drawbacks. PSG measurement reveals the details of the stages of sleep but is time-consuming and expensive, and the instrumentation can interfere with natural sleep. Self-report methods are important for symptom assessment, but they are subject to preferred or biased answers and the propensity to report negative impressions indiscriminately. In fact, people's impressions of their sleep quality or patterns do not always match those dimensions determined through polysomnography. Behavioral observations create less direct interference with sleep but are tedious, time-consuming, and subject to inaccurate documentation.

SLEEP QUALITY IN CHRONIC FATIGUE SYNDROME

PERCEIVED SLEEP QUALITY

In CFS, accurate prevalence of insufficient or inadequate sleep (i.e., insomnia), including unrefreshing sleep is elusive from the few published studies available. However, a majority of people with CFS appear to have sleep difficulties (Vercoulen et al., 1994). Investigators have assessed sleep with a variety of questions, making comparisons across studies difficult. Unrefreshing sleep can only be inferred from certain questions. Using a standardized clinical neuropsychiatric assessment instrument, Sharpley, Clements, Hawton, and Sharpe (1997) reported that nearly all (95%) of 20 subjects (10 men and 10 women) with CFS reported sleep difficulties. The features of reported difficulties are summarized in Table 14.1 along with perceptions reported on a sleep questionnaire for 68 people with CFS, reported by Krupp, Jandorf, Coyle, and Mendelson (1993).

In the Krupp study, subjects with CFS were more likely to report *sleeping lightly* ($p < .01$) and *feeling drowsy on awakening* than either people with multiple sclerosis ($p < .05$) or healthy controls ($p < .01$) (Krupp et al., 1993). In two other studies, significantly more subjects with CFS compared to healthy controls described unrefreshing sleep ($n = 14$, $p > .0001$; and $n = 12$, $p < .01$) (Morriss, Wearden, & Battersby, 1997; Whelton, Salit, & Moldofsky, 1992). Of 258 subjects, 53% reported insomnia in a study of symptom patterns in CFS of long duration (≥ 10 yrs) (Friedberg, Dechene, McKenzie, & Fontanetta, 2000). These data show that perceived disrupted or poor quality sleep affects many people with CFS and often persistently over time.

Perceptions of unrefreshing sleep are evident in several conditions, especially those involving pain and fatigue, and have been documented most particularly in fibromyalgia. Unrefreshing sleep was considered a diagnostic feature of fibrositis (prior label for fibromyalgia) by some early investigators although sleep

Table 14.1
Perceived Sleep Quality in Chronic Fatigue Syndrome

Sleep Variable	Sharpley et al. (1997) (%) ($n = 20$)	Krupp et al. (1993) (%) ($n = 68$)
Poor quality	70	15
Delayed sleep	20	N/R
Difficulty staying asleep	30	N/R
Early awakenings	5	27
Sleeping lightly		37
Awaken drowsy		76

difficulties are not part of the currently accepted standard diagnostic criteria for fibromyalgia. Yet, 76% of people with fibromyalgia in a large multicenter study reported feeling tired or unrefreshed from sleep on awakening (Wolfe et al., 1990). Individuals with fibromyalgia report difficulty falling asleep, have fewer hours of sleep, encounter more trouble maintaining sleep, awaken early in the morning, and take more sleep medications than subjects with arthritis or controls of similar age (Harding, 1998; Jennum, Drewes, Andreasen, & Nielsen, 1993; Moldofsky, 1989; Uveges et al., 1990). We found that a small group of midlife women with fibromyalgia, compared to those without, reported significantly poorer quality on almost all sleep variables (Shaver et al., 1997). Moreover, in a follow-up laboratory sleep study of women *with* ($n = 18$) and *without* ($n = 15$) fibromyalgia (no differences in body mass index or activity levels), we found that women with fibromyalgia rated their overall sleep quality more negatively ($p < 0.01$) and estimated longer sleep latencies (31.5 ±35.9 min; 11.6 ±8.1 min, $p < .04$) (unpublished data) than those women without fibromyalgia.

PHYSIOLOGICAL (PSG) SLEEP QUALITY IN CFS

To date, PSG data have failed to substantiate highly profound or consistent changes in physical sleep variables in people with CFS. Seven reports of PSG variables in people with CFS (one with adolescents) were found in the literature and five of these incorporated healthy comparison groups for control, as summarized in Table 14.2.

Although data from the controlled studies are mixed, some evidence suggests that individuals with CFS have fragmented and less efficient sleep. They spent more time in bed trying to sleep, took longer to fall asleep, had more awake time after sleep onset and therefore, had lower sleep efficiencies than healthy control subjects. Whether their sleep is lighter according to stages or changed in structure is not yet well substantiated.

The PSG sleep features of CFS show some similarities to those found in fibromyalgia. Individuals with fibromyalgia show PSG evidence of less consolidated and efficient sleep. When compared with age-matched controls, people with fibromyalgia generally showed more wakefulness and NREM Stage 1 (transitional sleep) with reduced sleep efficiency (time asleep/time in bed) but minimal differences in other aspects of sleep (Anch, Lue, MacLean, & Moldofsky, 1991; Jennum, Drewes, Andreasen, & Nielsen, 2001; Jennum et al., 1993). In a pilot study of sleep in age-matched women with and without fibromyalgia symptoms, we found more wakefulness and NREM Stage 1 along with more fragmentation of sleep (Shaver et al., 1997). In this very small group, the disrupted sleep pattern was mainly evident in the first half of the night compared with the entire night. In a larger study of fibromyalgia women with severe symptoms, half of whom met CFS criteria, we confirmed by PSG that they took longer to fall asleep, spent more time awake after sleep onset, and had lower sleep efficiencies than women without the conditions. Women with fibromyalgia also displayed lighter sleep with more transitional (Stage 1) and less Stages 2 and 3 (deep) sleep, compared with control women (unpublished data). These data support the idea that sleep is disrupted in fibromyalgia, but the factors related to these changes have yet to be explained.

Table 14.2

Summary of Polysomnographic (PSG) Variables in Studies of Subjects with Chronic Fatigue Syndrome

PSG Features	Whelton et al. (1992) (n=14) (12 HC)	Morriss et al. (1993) (n=12) (12 HC)	Fischler et al. (1997) (n=49) (20 HC)	Sharpley et al. (1997) (n=20) (20 HC)	Stores et al. (1998) (n=18) (12–17 yo) (18 HC)	Krupp et al. (1993) (N=16) 0 controls	Manu (1992) (N=30) (15=CFS) 0 controls
TIB	NR	561:491 min $p < .001$	NS	520:470 min $p < .001$	NR	NR	NR
TST	NS	NS	339:382 min $p < .001$	NS	NS	NR	NS
SOL	26:12 min $p < .006$	NS	40:22 min $p < .001$	NR	NS	NR	30–37 min
Latency to REM sleep	NS	NS	NS	NS	NS	NR	116–106 min
WASO	NR	$p < .05$	NR	$p < .05$	$p < .001$	NR	NR
Sleep efficiency	86%:95% $p < .001$	90%:96% $p < .05$	77%:88% $p < .001$	80%:87% $p < .05$	90%:98% $p < .001$	80%	NR
% Stage 1 (transitional)	NS	NS	14%:9% $p < .001$	NS	NS	NR	NS
% light sleep (Stage 2)	NS	NS	38%:46% $p < .001$	NS	21%:36% $p < .01$	NR	NS
% deep sleep (Stage 4)	NS	NS	9%:6% $p = .06$	NS	NS	NR	18%–19%
Fragmentation or stage shifts	NR	NR	29:22/hr $p < .001$	NR	NR	NR	NR
Alpha-delta wave intrusion	$p < .001$	NS (2 CFS and 2 control)	NR	NR	NR	NR	8/30—no other sleep differences

NR = Not reported; NS = Not significant; SOL = Sleep onset latency; TIB = Time in bed; TST = Total sleep time; WASO = Wake after sleep onset

IS POOR SLEEP PRIMARY OR SECONDARY?

A dilemma is whether to frame poor sleep in either CFS or fibromyalgia as part of the, as yet, mysterious primary physiological changes underlying the conditions or as secondary to discomfort or functional changes in the conditions. In relation to discomfort, muscle and multijoint pain also are on the concurrent symptom list for CFS. The interactive features of pain and sleep have long been known. Careful analysis of prospective 30-day diary reports of sleep quality and pain intensity in women with fibromyalgia has revealed that poor sleep was associated with higher daytime and concurrent pain, and a night of poor sleep was followed by a more painful day (Affleck, Urrows, Tennen, Higgins, & Abeles, 1996). Careful determination as to whether disrupted sleep (self-reported or PSG recorded) is associated more strongly in individuals meeting criteria for CFS with a strong pain component compared with those who have no or little pain is not evident in the literature.

THE RECIPROCAL NATURE OF STRESS, SLEEP, AND IMMUNE FUNCTION

Chronic fatigue syndrome has been conceptualized on a spectrum of stress-related, functional disorders characterized by profound fatigue, and frequently pain, that also includes fibromyalgia, temporomandibular disorders, irritable bowel syndrome (functional bowel disorder), and irritable bladder, among others. Overlapping manifestations of these conditions in many people have been observed, particularly with fibromyalgia (Buchwald, 1996). As such, emerging evidence of the interactive features of the hypothalamic-pituitary-adrenal (HPA) stress axis, autonomic nervous system, sleep, and the immune system could be enlightening for all of these conditions.

STRESS EMOTIONAL AROUSAL AND PHYSIOLOGICAL ACTIVATION

Stress is defined in multiple ways scientifically but represents the interface of mental/mind and somatic/body function. Related viewpoints include that *stressors* are those environmental elements that provoke emotional arousal and physiological activation adjustments to defend against or be protected from harm or adapt to novel circumstances within one's environment. While minor stressors occur daily, the more intense ones generally represent perceived or real threats to one's integrity or status within one's environment, for example, impending injury, job loss. The dominant physiological activation pattern associated with exposure to stressful circumstances largely involves the HPA axis and the sympathetic nervous system (SNS). The neuroendocrine components most often assessed include corticotropin-releasing hormone (CRH), adrencorticotropic hormone (ACTH), cortisol (humans) or corticosterone (rats), vasopressin, and the sympatho-adrenomedullary catecholamines (norepinephrine and epinephrine). *Turn on* of these stress hormones and others skews metabolism to be predominantly catabolic (breakdown or energy use). This activation pattern is adaptive when it occurs in a widely periodic manner and dissipates within a short time. However, intense, frequent, or continuous activation can lead to chronic up-regulation of the stress emotional arousal and physiological activation mechanisms with negative health consequences.

Sleep patterns normally are synchronized with stress-related neuroendocrine function. For example, the early phase of nighttime sleep (proportionately more SWS than in later phase) normatively coincides with suppressed HPA axis activity. This is observed as nadirs in ACTH and cortisol hormones but peaks in growth hormone (GH). During late phase sleep (proportionately more REM sleep), adrenocortical activity escalates to reach maximal cortisol output shortly after awakening.

STRESS EXPOSURE, SLEEP, AND STRESS ACTIVATION

Both acute and chronic stress exposure have an effect on sleep patterns and the normal circadian rhythms of various stress activation indicators as reviewed by van Reeth and colleagues (2000). Acute and chronic stress exposure in rats has slow wave and REM sleep architectural effects that disappear with removal of the stimuli. However, rats subjected to stress *in utero* display profound and lasting endocrine (i.e., prolonged stress-induced corticosterone patterns) and sleep (i.e., less SWS, and more REM sleep and sleep fragmentation) changes. Patients with posttraumatic stress disorder (PTSD) uniformly report sleep problems and have high stress hormone metabolites coinciding with low PSG total sleep time (Mellman, Kumar, Kulick-Bell, Kumar, & Nolan, 1995). Given the difficulties of controlling variables within human subjects, Wistar Kyoto rats are a strain that displays sleep abnormalities, depressive and anxiety-like behaviors, abnormal rhythms of corticosterone, and thyroid-stimulating hormones as well as a hyper-response to stress. This represents a promising animal model for studying sleep and stress.

Sleep manipulations affect stress hormone plasma levels, and stress hormone manipulations affect sleep patterns. For example, sleep deprivation leads to sustained elevated cortisol, including at times when it is normally inhibited. An implication is that sustained hypercortisol accompanying sleep loss might impair the recovery time of the HPA axis, which is most adaptive if the recovery is rapid. Indeed, it has been speculated that chronic stress exposure and sleep loss together increase vulnerability to nerve cell impairment, particularly in the hypothalamus (van Reeth et al., 2000). Thus, chronic sleep loss could augment certain outcomes of glucorticoid excess, such as cognitive deficits and decreased carbohydrate tolerance. A naturalistic circumstance of partial sleep loss is people doing shift work, and all indications point to it as stressful. Sleep/wake adaptations in the rhythms of stress neuroendocrine indicators (e.g., cortisol), in permanent, let alone rotational shift work, are incomplete for most workers, and many report chronic sleep difficulties. Shift work has been associated with higher risks of health problems such as ischemic heart disease, gastrointestinal disorders, substance abuse, poor immune function, and infertility problems (van Reeth et al., 2000). Further evidence of the stress/sleep relationships emanates from observations that PSG sleep patterns are affected by administration of CRH (less SWS and REM sleep), ACTH (delayed sleep onset, fragmented sleep, and less SWS), and cortisol (increased SWS and reduced REM sleep). These features reveal that the interaction between sleep and stress physiology is inextricably intertwined but in ways that remain incompletely understood (van Reeth et al., 2000).

STRESS AND INSOMNIA

Insomnia as a symptom often emerges or is evident in highly stressful circumstances. In its primary form, that is, not associated with any obvious mental or physical illness and disease, insomnia can be considered not as a symptom but as a sleep problem/diagnosis. According to the International Classification of Sleep Disorders (ICSD), *acute* insomnia is defined < *subacute* as 1 to 6 months and *chronic insomnia* as > 6 months. Often stressful situational conditions are associated with transient insomnia (e.g., death of a spouse, major catastrophes), usually in a temporary fashion, and are ICSD classed as *an adjustment sleep disorder*. The propensity to experience chronic primary insomnia is thought to be related to people's personality styles being skewed toward stress-related hyperarousal (emotional) and hyperactivation (physiological), which in turn likely are shaped by genetic makeup and environmental exposure. Family history tends to be a risk factor (Bastien & Morin, 2000). Numerous behavioral factors can contribute to persistent insomnia. These include substance abuse, taking medications that disturb sleep (e.g., corticosteroids, thyroid hormones, long-term hypnotic use, among others), inability to sleep in synchrony with circadian rhythms, and sleep-disruptive lifestyles (Hajak, 2000).

Primary Persistent Insomnia and Stress Activation/Arousal   People with primary persistent insomnia display excess emotional arousal and HPA axis and SNS activation. For example, they score higher than people with good sleep on instruments that measure psychological distress such as the Minnesota Multiphasic Personality Inventory, the Profile of Mood States, or Symptom Checklist 90R instruments. Elevated norepinephrine and cortisol levels and a high metabolic rate are evident in subjects with as compared to without chronic primary insomnia (Adam, Tomeny, & Oswald, 1986; Bonnet & Arand, 1995). Furthermore, heart rates during sleep and during performance tasks were found to be higher in people with compared to people without insomnia (adults, mean age 34 years) (Stepanski, Glinn, Zorick, Roehrs, & Roth, 1994). Using heart rate variability as an indicator of the relative dominance of SNS to parasympathetic nervous system activity, people with chronic insomnia have been found to have SNS accentuation, compared with control subjects who have no sleep problems (Bonnet & Arand, 1998). However, it remains unclear whether sleep disturbances drive a stress response in primary chronic insomnia or whether the propensity to be stress aroused and activated drives sleep disruptions, or perhaps both. No matter which or whether one predominates, these features reinforce one another.

Daytime Consequences of Insomnia   In general, sleep disruption and loss in healthy individuals lead to reduced mental and physical performance and perceived daytime tiredness or sleepiness. Despite sleep loss, individuals with chronic insomnia do not display excessive daytime sleepiness as measured by the commonly used Multiple Sleep Latency test. This test consists of providing 4 or 5 opportunities to nap in a darkened sleep room for 20-minute episodes that are spaced at 2-hour intervals during the day. The faster people fall asleep, the more sleepiness is inferred to exist. Typically, latencies of < 5 min and > 10 min are considered to indicate pathological sleepiness and normality, respectively. Like subjects with chronic insomnia, people with CFS have not tested excessively sleepy in the day-time, using the Multiple Sleep Latency test (Fischler, 1999). These data are sparse but imply that high stress arousal and activation is overriding the factors that drive sleepiness. Or perhaps the nighttime sleep loss or disruption is not profound enough to affect daytime sleepiness.

SLEEP, THE HYPOTHALAMIC PITUITARY ADRENAL STRESS AXIS, AND IMMUNE FUNCTION

As described in previous sections, sleep and the HPA axis stress elements are linked. In general, hypoactivity of HPA axis with hypocortisolemia has been observed in CFS and fibromyalgia (Demitrack & Crofford, 1998). It has also been noted that enduring SNS overactivity is part of the picture of chronic insomnia, CFS, and related conditions. Autonomic function tests in people with CFS have produced suggestive data for reduced vagal modulation and sympathetic responsiveness to stimuli (Sisto et al., 2001). It has been postulated that enduring sympathetic hyperactivity (i.e., at rest) might represent a neural functional correlate of fatigue (Pagani & Lucini, 1999). Stress neuroendocrine hormones, the SNS, and sleep also are highly interactive with the immune system and together make up a host defense system that is complex and represents multiple points of potential dysregulation.

Sleep and Immune Function   Infectious signs and symptoms in CFS have spawned much study into the immune function arm of host defense. Systemic coordination of host defense involves cytokines that link the immune and nervous systems. The relative balance of type 1/proinflammatory cytokines (e.g., interleukin 12 [IL-12], tumor necrosis factor-alpha, and interferon-gamma) and type 2/anti-inflammatory cytokines (e.g., IL-transforming growth factor-beta) can be skewed in either direction by many factors, including stress emotional arousal and physiological activation, sleep loss or disruption (see next), and environmental challenges, including pathogens. It has been posited that the interaction of psychological factors (distress associated with either CFS-related symptoms or other stressful life events) and immune changes contribute to the chronicity of symptoms and altered immune surveillance function in CFS. Chronic lymphocyte overactivation with cytokine abnormalities that include perturbations in plasma levels of proinflammatory relative to anti-inflammatory cytokines have been found, although details of the picture are far from clear (Patarca-Montero, Antoni, Fletcher, & Klimas, 2001). Some provocation of changes in lymphocyte function occurs through the SNS as reviewed by Elenkov and colleagues (Elenkov, Wilder, Chrousos, & Vizi, 2000). While as yet rudimentarily understood, norepinephrine is released from sympathetic nerve terminals in primary and secondary lymphoid organs on activation of the SNS system, and the target immune cells express adrenoreceptors. Thus, locally released NE or circulating catecholamines, such as epinephrine, affect lymphocyte traffic, circulation, and proliferation, and modulate cytokine production and the functional activity of lymphoid cells (Elenkov et al., 2000).

Also relevant is to consider sleep as an element of host defense, as reviewed by Benca and Quintas (1997). Sleep is changed in the early phases of infections, and its disturbance, regardless of infection, could establish or reinforce immune vulnerabilities. It is argued that sleep be considered part of the acute-phase response to infection, mediated by cytokines (especially interleukin-1, tumor necrosis factor-alpha, and interleukin-6). Increases in sleep accompany infectious illness, and the amount of deep sleep during infection has been related to mortality rates in animals. Studies of sleep loss have shown conflicting immune function effects in humans due to the variety of outcome indicators and methods for depriving sleep that have been used. However, in general, sleep loss is believed to be detrimental to host defense. This idea is supported in the prolonged sleep deprivation studies in animals, with consequential observations of bacteremia, increased metabolism, hyperphagia, weight loss, hypothermia, and eventual death (Rechtschaffen, Bergmann, Everson, Kushida, & Gilliland, 1989).

Chronic Fatigue Syndrome, Stress, and Sleep

Much more research is needed to reveal the interactions between the sleep, stress, and immune subsystems as explanatory factors for the manifestations of CFS. The interconnectedness of these subsystems means that the unraveling of a cogent explanatory framework for CFS and related conditions will require extensive research, approached from all angles. It is plausible that persistent stress arousal/activation, with its negative effects on sleep, alters the immune elements of the host defense system thereby priming the system for vulnerability. This may drive an inability to adequately adjust to an extraordinary challenge or set of challenges, provoking the classical manifestations of CFS.

CONTROVERSIES RELATED TO SLEEP, RECUPERATION, AND CHRONICALLY FATIGUING CONDITIONS

Sleep Continuity and Duration

A controversy among investigators is whether sleep disruption, sleep loss, or both lead to performance and mood state deterioration and symptom generation. Alternatively stated, the question remains whether sleep continuity and/or duration are most important to recuperation and feeling good. It is well known that sleep deprivation, complete, partial, or selective by sleep stage, produces performance and mood degradation. Investigations to mimic the sleep patterns of lighter and more fragmented sleep as seen in CFS or fibromyalgia have generated some evidence that sleep patterns are related to symptom generation or perpetuation. Studies of selective slow-wave (deep) sleep deprivation, using noise stimuli in healthy subjects, have produced increased tiredness or fatigue (Lentz, Landis, Rothermel, & Shaver, 1999; Older et al., 1998) and reduced pain thresholds (Lentz et al., 1999). In our study of sedentary women, slow wave sleep deprivation led to self-reported musculoskeletal discomfort and low arousal (a subscale with tiredness/alertness items) (Lentz et al., 1999) as well as an increased sensitivity to pressure at points known to be painful in fibromyalgia. That lighter and/or more fragmented sleep has a negative effect on symptoms of pain and fatigue is supported by these observations, but it remains unclear what aspects of disturbed sleep physiology contribute to or result from pain or fatigue in fibromyalgia or other painful and fatiguing conditions.

Although reduced sleep duration is detrimental to daytime alertness, mood, and function, it has been argued that sleep fragmentation rather than sleep duration is important to the recuperative function of sleep. This remains controversial, as reviewed by Wesensten and colleagues (Wesensten, Balkin, & Belenky, 1999). Studies of varied sleep fragmentation rates while preserving total sleep time have shown that higher fragmentation rates lead to more daytime sleepiness. This suggests that fragmentation affects recuperation independent of sleep duration (total sleep time). However, Wesensten has pointed out that Stage 1 (transitional) sleep almost invariably increases with any means of imposing sleep stage disruptions. She argues that this stage of transitional sleep might not have the recuperative properties of light (Stage 2) and deep NREM (Stages 3 and 4) sleep. Although typically included as a sleep stage, if Stage 1 sleep is subtracted from the calculation of total sleep time, a deficit in sleep duration then emerges in protocols using applied sleep fragmentation. The difficulty (or impossibility) of disconnecting sleep fragmentation from sleep lightening makes this issue an unresolved scientific challenge. Moreover, whether lighter, more fragmented sleep is specific to conditions such as CFS or fibromyalgia or perhaps to chronic pain or fatigue remains unclear. Regardless, if more transitional sleep (Stage 1) and less stable sleep with more fragmentation occur in CFS, this circumstance can represent sleep loss and diminished recuperation with sleep.

ALPHA WAVE INTRUSION INTO NREM SLEEP

More than 25 years ago, based on observations in patients with fibromyalgia, it was postulated that alpha brain wave (7.5–11 Hz) intrusion into stages of NREM sleep (called alpha-delta sleep) was characteristic of and a marker for nonrestorative or unrefreshing sleep (Moldofsky, Scarisbrick, England, & Smythe, 1975). From Table 14.2, it can be seen that this variable was reported in two of the CFS sleep studies with mixed results. The idea of alpha-delta sleep being a marker of nonrestorative sleep was perpetuated in the fibromyalgia clinical literature prior to much corroboration of its validity. Other investigators, primarily using visual scoring methods or in a few cases spectral analysis of the brain wave recordings, have confirmed increased alpha activity in NREM sleep in some individuals with fibromyalgia (Branco, Atalaia, & Paiva, 1994; Carette, Oakson, Guimont, & Steriade, 1995; Drewes, 1999a). Others have not confirmed this observation (Shaver et al., 1997) or only reported a trend for increased alpha activity in fibromyalgia (Manu, Lane, & Matthews, 1994). In one study, there were no differences in pain, fatigue, or sleep quality scores between patients with and without increased alpha activity (Carette et al., 1995). Moreover, an alpha-delta sleep pattern has been described in psychiatric patients (Sadeh, Hauri, Kripke, & Lavie, 1995), in patients with chronic pain disorders (Wittig, Zorick, Blumer, Heilbronn, & Roth, 1982), and in some patients with insomnia (Schneider-Helmert & Kumar, 1995). In one paper, people with chronic primary insomnia were compared to people with nonorganic pain. Both groups displayed severe sleep maintenance disturbances but did not differ on any other sleep variables. The occurrence of alpha sleep was high in both groups and not specially related to pain (Schneider-Helmert & Kumar, 1995). The marker of alpha-delta sleep is unlikely to be specific to CFS, and its relationship to people perceiving nonrestorative sleep has yet to be definitively substantiated. Furthermore, it is subject to variability by methods of recording.

Sleep-Related Disorders

Another controversy related to sleep is whether people with CFS are at higher risk to manifest sleep-related disorders such as sleep apnea and hypopnea syndrome, periodic limb movements, and narcolepsy or whether these are comorbid conditions that worsen the manifestations of CFS and motivate individuals to seek help. There appears to be a high prevalence of sleep-related disorders (apnea/hypopnea, periodic leg movements, and narcolepsy) in some of the CFS sleep studies summarized in Table 14.2 and one other (Buchwald, Pascualy, Bombardier, & Kith, 1994), as summarized in Table 14.3. The answer is obscured, however, because of small sample sizes, clinic-based subject recruitment, and subject selection based on suspected sleep disorders. Clinic-based samples increase the likelihood that subjects exhibit comorbid conditions or are experiencing a higher degree of emotional suffering related to their condition compared with community-based samples. Individuals seeking help for functional disorders are postulated to have more psychosocial factors at play than those who do not seek medical help (Drossman, Hu, & Jia, 2000). In one study of 46 unselected clinic patients meeting the Oxford criteria for CFS, 54% of patients had no primary sleep disorder (Le Bon et al., 2000). More studies are needed that involve community-based populations. In addition, twin studies and studies incorporating careful assessment of sleep-related disorders and comparisons with other persistent fatiguing conditions or the absence of persistent fatiguing conditions would be illuminating.

TREATING INSOMNIA (POOR SLEEP) IN THE CONTEXT OF CHRONIC FATIGUE SYNDROME

Chronically fatiguing conditions, including CFS, negatively affect perceptions of sleep quality. Common descriptions include that sleep does not bestow its usual recuperative and energizing properties; it seems unrefreshing and perhaps lighter than desired. Evidence from studies of sleep stage disruption or restriction indicates that sleep fragmentation (less ability to sustain sleep stages for blocks of time, especially deeper stages) and sleep loss lead to negative mood. Cognitive and physical performance decrements are also noted, as well as increased muscle discomfort and pain sensitivity. Therefore, sleep pattern changes at the very least reinforce many symptoms common to CFS, and improving sleep is likely to reduce symptoms. However, published sleep improvement studies in CFS are sparse.

Effective treating of the concurrent symptoms often improves sleep that is disrupted by symptoms such as pain. However, sleep (insomnia) also should be considered as a primary target symptom for improvement in CFS. Behavioral treatments, often adjunctive to drugs, provide a foundation for sustained improvement. Treatments for primary insomnia can include judicious use of drugs, such as short-term sleeping pills; for example, zolpidem tartrate (Ambien®), zaleplon (Sonata®), or short-acting benzodiazepines to break into a cycle of nighttime sleeplessness. Generally, prescription sleep medications should be limited

Table 14.3

Summary of Sleep-Related Disorders in Studies of Sleep and Chronic Fatigue Syndrome

	Whelton et al. (1992) (n = 14) (12 HC)	Morriss et al. (1993) (n = 12) (12 HC)	Fischler et al. (1997) (n = 49) (20 HC)	Sharpley et al. (1997) (n = 20) (20 HC)	Krupp et al. (1993) (n = 16) (0 HC)	Buchwald et al. (1996) (n = 59) (38 = CFS) (0 HC)	Manu (1992) (n = 30) (15 = CFS) (0 HC)	Le Bon et al. (2000) (n = 46) (0 HC)
Sleep disorders (SD)	2 = SAHS 1 = PLM 1 control = PLM	6 = Insomnia 1 = hyper-somnia	21/46 = SAHS ≥ 5 1 = PLM	Screened out	2 = SAHS 8 = PLM 3 = EDS	26 = SAHS 7 = Hyper-somnia	3 = SAHS 5 = PLM 1 = SAHS and PLM 1 = Narcolepsy	21 = AHI > 5 3 = AHI > 20 2 = PLM + AHI > 5
Notes	Community Sample	Outpatient clinic 0 = MD	CFS clinic 7 = MD	Infectious Disease clinic 0 = MD	Referrals, support group 6 = MD	Clinic—suspected SD 24 = psych. disorder	CFS clinic 20 = MD	CFS clinic 29 = Current or past psych. disorder

AHI = Apnea/hypopnea index; EDS = Excessive daytime sleepiness; HC = Healthy control subjects; MD = Major depression; PLM = Periodic leg movements; SAHS = Sleep apnea/hypopnea syndrome; SD = Sleep disorder to short-term (7 to 10 days) and episodic use and are not recommended as main-stay treatment for insomnia.

It has been argued that manifestations of CFS are suggestive of a disorder of the sleep-wake cycle, and a main goal of treatment is to "reset" the biological clock (Hickie & Davenport, 1999). Many of the behavioral treatments for persistent insomnia encompass behavioral strategies that facilitate greater synchrony of sleeping and waking with the light-dark cycle in which one lives, associate bedtime with drowsiness, promote relaxation, and avoid behaviors that interfere with sleep. Behavioral treatments for insomnia include counseling people to engage in good sleep hygiene and to ritualize the bedtime routine and, in severe cases of insomnia, to practice stimulus control or sleep restriction. In general, it is recommended not to spend lengthy periods in bed struggling to fall asleep but instead to leave the bedroom, engage in relaxing activities, and return to bed when feeling drowsy. Additionally, sleep should be restricted to a consistent nighttime period, and the individual should arise at a consistent time regardless of when he or she fell asleep. On arising in early morning, exposure to bright light (can be done with artificial light but better with natural light) helps turn off melatonin (a hormone that regulates circadian and seasonal rhythms), which peaks during the night (Hickie & Davenport, 1999). Recommendations include curtailing daytime sleep and avoiding strenuous exercise or ingestion of substances known to have activating effects, particularly caffeine, especially within a few hours of bedtime. Features of these main behavioral sleep improvement treatments are summarized in Table 14.4. Cognitive-behavioral therapies to induce a state of deep relaxation have been shown to be effective for primary insomnia, as well as other symptoms in chronically fatiguing conditions. Referral to an accredited sleep disorders center for specialized assessment and treatment is warranted for individuals who have persistent severe insomnia, sleep-related breathing disorders, narcolepsy, severe restless leg syndrome, or periodic limb movements in sleep.

CONCLUSION

As discussed, sleep and stress are inextricably linked but in ways that remain unclear. It has been postulated that high stress acts as a precursor or perpetuator of CFS manifestations and those of potentially related conditions. Stress is known to interfere with sleep and the opposite; sleep disruption or loss is known to be stressful (emotionally arousing and physiologically activating). One line of thought about primary persistent insomnia is that it is likely to be manifested when individuals have a propensity toward a sustained hyperaroused (psychological/emotional) and activated (physiological) stress status. This style propensity may make certain individuals vulnerable to host defense system breakdowns manifested as CFS. Certain individuals might exhibit insomnia prior to or along with the breakthrough of symptoms indicative of CFS or related chronically fatiguing conditions. In addition to interfering with adequate sleep and disturbing the sleep and waking rhythms, excess stress arousal/activation also affects immune functions. Moreover, superimposing poor sleep on stress arousal and activation may alter the capacity of the stress system to drive adjustments that protect or defend against harm and challenges in the environment, thereby generating or worsening symptoms. For these reasons, sleep improvement should be a cardinal goal in managing CFS. The circular or spiral relationships of stress and sleep present two

Table 14.4
Behavioral Treatments for Insomnia

Resist Behaviors That Interfere with Sleep	Ritualize Cues for Sleep	Relax to Control Tension	Regularize Sleep and Wake Patterns
Avoid heavy meals. Have a light snack before bed (mainly starch, some protein, warm drink). Avoid strenuous exercise close to sleep (within 2–3 hours). Regular daily exercise helps sleep. Avoid tobacco, alcohol, and caffeine (coffee, tea, colas, and chocolate). Alcohol can assist with falling asleep, but overall disrupts sleep patterns. (Sleep hygiene)	Use the bedroom only for sleep (sexual activity an exception). Make environment quiet, dark, and comfortable in temperature. Lie down only when sleepy. If not asleep in 10 minutes, get up, go elsewhere, read or do something boring, lie down when drowsy—no longer than 10 minutes—repeat as necessary. (Stimulus control)	Assume a comfortable posture. Clear mind by stopping disturbing thoughts. Tune out distractions by concentrating on breathing, sensations, a sound, or scene. Practice, practice, practice (15 minutes, 2 times/day). Use biofeedback, deep relaxation with verbal training (e.g., tapes), pleasant visual images with relaxing bodily sensations such as warmth or heaviness or meditation. (Relaxation techniques)	Do not nap during day if nighttime sleep is disturbed. Define optimal sleep length (feel good in the daytime). Set alarm and get up same time A.M.—no matter amount of previous night's sleep. (Important behavior) Go to bed at a time based on current sleep duration (even if short); get up at consistent time. When able to sleep 95% of that duration, lengthen sleep time by 30 minutes; go to bed 30 minutes earlier—when sleep 95% of lengthened time—repeat until reach optimal length. (Sleep restriction therapy)

intriguing investigative challenges: (1) a search for evidence to clarify postulated connections within the context of CFS, and (2) the testing of interventions to alter sleep and stress arousal/activation.

REFERENCES

Adam, K., Tomeny, M., & Oswald, I. (1986). Physiological and psychological differences between good and poor sleepers. *Journal of Psychiatric Research, 20,* 301–316.

Affleck, G., Urrows, S., Tennen, H., Higgins, P., & Abeles, M. (1996). Sequential daily relations of sleep, pain intensity, and attention to pain among women with fibromyalgia. *Pain, 68,* 363–368.

Anch, T. A., Lue, F., MacLean, A. W., & Moldofsky, H. (1991). Sleep physiology and psychological aspects of the fibrositis (fibromyalgia) syndrome. *Canadian Journal of Psychology, 45,* 179–184.

Bastien, C. H., & Morin, C. M. (2000). Familial incidence of insomnia. *Journal of Sleep Research, 9,* 49–54.

Beersma, D. G. (1998). Models of human sleep regulation. *Sleep Medicine Reviews, 2,* 31–43.

Benca, R. M., & Quintas, J. (1997). Sleep and host defenses: A review. *Sleep, 20,* 1027–1037.

Bonnet, M. H., & Arand, D. L. (1995). 24-hour metabolic rate in insomniacs and matched normal sleepers. *Sleep, 18,* 581–588.

Bonnet, M. H., & Arand, D. L. (1998). Heart rate variability in insomniacs and matched normal sleepers. *Psychosomatic Medicine, 60,* 610–615.

Branco, J., Atalaia, A., & Paiva, T. (1994). Sleep cycles and alpha-delta sleep in fibromyalgia syndrome. *Journal of Rheumatology, 21,* 1113–1117.

Buchwald, D. (1996). Fibromyalgia and chronic fatigue syndrome: Similarities and differences. *Rheumatic Diseases Clinics of North America, 22,* 219–243.

Buchwald, D., Pascualy, R., Bombardier, C., & Kith, P. (1994). Sleep disorders in patients with chronic fatigue. *Clinical Infectious Diseases, 18*(Suppl. 1), S68–S72.

Buysse, D. J., Reynolds, C. F., Monk, T. H., Berman, S., & Kupfer, D. J. (1989). The Pittsburgh Sleep Quality Index: A new instrument for psychiatric practice and research. *Psychiatry Research, 28,* 193–213.

Cai, Z. J. (1991). The functions of sleep: Further analysis. *Physiology and Behavior, 50,* 53–60.

Carette, S., Oakson, G., Guimont, C., & Steriade, M. (1995). Sleep electroencephalography and the clinical response to amitriptyline in patients with fibromyalgia. *Arthritis and Rheumatism, 38,* 1211–1217.

Conte, G., Rigon, N., Perrone, A., & Lauro, S. (1999). Acute cardiovascular diseases and respiratory sleep disorders. *Minerva Cardioangiology, 47,* 195–202.

Demitrack, M. A., & Crofford, L. J. (1998). Evidence for and pathophysiologic implications of hypothalamic-pituitary-adrenal axis dysregulation in fibromyalgia and chronic fatigue syndrome. *Annals of the New York Academy of Sciences, 840,* 684–697.

Drewes, A. M. (1999a). *Pain and sleep disturbances.* Aalborg, Denmark: Aalborg University.

Drewes, A. M. (1999b). Pain and sleep disturbances with special reference to fibromyalgia and rheumatoid arthritis [Editorial]. *Rheumatology, 38,* 1035–1038.

Drewes, A. M., Nielsen, K. D., Hansen, B., Taagholt, S. J., Bjerregard, K., & Svendsen, L. (2000). A longitudinal study of clinical symptoms and sleep parameters in rheumatoid arthritis. *Rheumatology, 39,* 1287–1289.

Drossman, D. A., Hu, Y., & Jia, H. (2000). The influence of psychosocial factors on health care utilization in patients with functional bowel disorders (FBD). *Gastroenterology, 118,* A842.

Elenkov, I. J., Wilder, R. L., Chrousos, G. P., & Vizi, E. S. (2000). The sympathetic nerve— an integrative interface between two supersystems: The brain and the immune system. *Pharmacological Reviews, 52,* 595–638.

Fischler, B. (1999). Review of clinical and psychobiological dimensions of the chronic fatigue syndrome: Differentiation from depression and contribution of sleep dysfunctions. *Sleep Medicine Reviews, 3,* 131–146.

Fischler, B., Le Bon, O., Hoffmann, G., Cluydts, R., Kaufman, L., & De Meirleir, K. (1997). Sleep anomalies in the chronic fatigue syndrome. A co-morbidity study. *Neuropsychobiology, 35,* 115–122. Flanigan, M. J., Morehouse, R. L., & Shapiro, C. M. (1995). Determination of observer-rated alpha activity during sleep. *Sleep, 18,* 702–706.

Friedberg, F., Dechene, L., McKenzie, M., & Fontanetta, R. (2000). Symptom patterns in long-duration chronic fatigue syndrome. *Journal of Psychosomatic Research, 48,* 59–68.

Fukuda, K., Straus, S. E., Hickie, I., Sharpe, M. C., Dobbins, J. G., & Komaroff, A. (1994). The chronic fatigue syndrome: A comprehensive approach to its definition and study. *Annals of Internal Medicine, 121,* 953–959.

George, C. F. (2000). Perspectives on the management of insomnia in patients with chronic respiratory disorders. *Sleep, 23*(Suppl. 1), S31–S35.

Hajak, G. (2000). Insomnia in primary care. *Sleep, 23,* S54–S63.

Harding, S. M. (1998). Sleep in fibromyalgia patients: Subjective and objective findings. *American Journal of the Medical Sciences, 315, 367–376.*

Hickie, I., & Davenport, T. (1999). A behavioral approach based on reconstructing the sleep-wake cycle. *Cognitive and Behavioral Practice, 6, 442–450.*

Horne, J. A. (2000). REM sleep—by default? *Neuroscience and Biobehavioral Reviews, 24, 777–797.*

Jennum, P., Drewes, A. M., Andreasen, A., & Nielsen, K. D. (1993). Sleep and other symptoms in primary fibromyalgia and in healthy controls. *Journal of Rheumatology, 20, 1756–1759.*

Jennum, P., Drewes, A. M., Andreasen, A., & Nielsen, K. D. (2001). Sleep and other symptoms in primary fibromyalgia and in healthy controls. *Journal of Rheumatology, 20, 1756–1759.*

Krupp, L. B., Jandorf, L., Coyle, P. K., & Mendelson, W. B. (1993). Sleep disturbance in chronic fatigue syndrome. *Journal of Psychosomatic Research, 37, 325–331.*

Le Bon, O., Hoffmann, G., Murphy, J., De Meirleir, K., Cluydts, R., & Pelc, I. (2000). How significant are primary sleep disorders and sleepiness in the chronic fatigue syndrome? *Sleep Research Online, 3, 43–48.*

Lentz, M. J., Landis, C. A., Rothermel, J., & Shaver, J. L. (1999). Effects of selective slow wave sleep disruption on musculoskeletal pain and fatigue in middle aged women. *Journal of Rheumatology, 26, 1586–1592.*

Lewis, D. A. (1999). Sleep in patients with respiratory disease. *Respiratory Care Clinics of North America, 5, 447–460.*

Lustberg, L., & Reynolds, C. F. (2000). Depression and insomnia: Questions of cause and effect. *Sleep Medicine Reviews, 4, 253–262.*

Manu, P. (1992). The pathophysiology of chronic fatigue syndrome: Confirmations, contradictions, and conjectures. *International Journal of Psychiatry Medicine, 22, 397–408.*

Manu, P., Lane, T. J., & Matthews, D. A. (1994). Chronic fatigue and chronic fatigue syndrome: Clinical epidemiology and aetiological classification. *Ciba Foundation Symposium, 173, 23–31.*

McNicholas, W. T. (2000). Impact of sleep in COPD. *Chest, 117, 48S–53S.*

Mellman, T. A. (1997). Psychobiology of sleep disturbances in posttraumatic stress disorder. *Annals of the New York Academy of Science, 821, 142–149.*

Mellman, T. A., Kumar, A., Kulick-Bell, R., Kumar, M., & Nolan, B. (1995). Nocturnal/daytime urine noradrenergic measures and sleep in combat-related PTSD. *Biological Psychiatry, 38, 174–179.*

Moldofsky, H. (1989). Sleep and fibrositis syndrome. *Rheumatology Diseases Clinics of North America, 15, 91–103.*

Moldofsky, H., Scarisbrick, P., England, R., & Smythe, H. (1975). Musculoskeletal symptoms and NREM sleep disturbance in patients with fibrositis syndrome and healthy subjects. *Psychosomatic Medicine, 37, 341–351.*

Morriss, R., Sharpe, M., Sharpley, A. L., Cowen, P. J., Hawton, K., & Morris, J. (1993). Abnormalities of sleep in patients with the chronic fatigue syndrome. *British Medical Journal, 306, 1161–1164.*

Morriss, R. K., Wearden, A. J., & Battersby, L. (1997). The relation of sleep difficulties to fatigue, mood and disability in chronic fatigue syndrome. *Journal of Psychosomatic Research, 42, 597–605.*

Older, S. A., Battafarano, D. F., Danning, C. L., Ward, J. A., Grady, E. P., Derman, S., et al. (1998). The effects of delta wave sleep interruption on pain thresholds and fibromyalgia-like symptoms in healthy subjects: Correlations with insulin-like growth factor I. *Journal of Rheumatology, 25, 1180–1186.*

Pagani, M., & Lucini, D. (1999). Chronic fatigue syndrome: A hypothesis focusing on the autonomic nervous system. *Clinical Science, 96,* 117–125.

Parker, K. P. (1997). Sleep and dialysis: A research-based review of the literature. *American Nephrology Nurses' Association Journal, 24,* 626–639.

Patarca-Montero, R., Antoni, M., Fletcher, M. A., & Klimas, N. G. (2001). Cytokine and other immunologic markers in chronic fatigue syndrome and their relation to neuropsychological factors. *Applied Neuropsychology, 8,* 51–64.

Pillar, G., Malhotra, A., & Lavie, P. (2000). Posttraumatic stress disorder and sleep—what a nightmare! *Sleep Medicine Reviews, 4,* 183–200.

Rechtschaffen, A. (1998). Current perspectives on the function of sleep. *Perspectives in Biology and Medicine, 41,* 359–390.

Rechtschaffen, A., Bergmann, B. M., Everson, C. A., Kushida, C. A., & Gilliland, M. A. (1989). Sleep deprivation in the rat. X: Integration and discussion of the findings. *Sleep, 12,* 68–87.

Rechtschaffen, A., & Kales, A. (1968). *A manual of standardized terminology, techniques, and scoring systems for sleep stages of human subjects.* Los Angeles: UCLA, Brain Information/ Brain Research Institute.

Roth, T., Roehrs, T., Costa e Silva, J., & Chase, M. (1999). Public health and insomnia; consensus statement regarding its status and needs for future action. *Sleep, 22,* S417–S420.

Sadeh, A., Hauri, P., Kripke, D. F., & Lavie, P. (1995). The role of actigraphy in the evaluation of sleep disorders. *Sleep, 18,* 288–302.

Schneider-Helmert, D., & Kumar, A. (1995). Sleep, its subjective perception, and daytime performance in insomniacs with a pattern of alpha sleep. *Biological Psychiatry, 37,* 99–105.

Schwartz, S., McDowell, A. W., Cole, S. R., Cornoni-Huntley, J., Hays, J. C., & Blazer, D. (1999). Insomnia and heart disease: A review of epidemiologic studies. *Journal of Psychosomatic Research, 47,* 313–333.

Sharpley, A., Clements, A., Hawton, K., & Sharpe, M. (1997). Do patients with "pure" chronic fatigue syndrome (neurasthenia) have abnormal sleep? *Psychosomatic Medicine, 59,* 592–596.

Shaver, J. L., Lentz, M., Landis, C. A., Heitkemper, M. M., Buchwald, D. S., & Woods, N. F. (1997). Sleep, psychological distress, and stress arousal in women with fibromyalgia. *Research in Nursing and Health, 20,* 247–257.

Sisto, S. A., Tapp, W., Drastal, S., Bergen, M., DeMasi, I., Cordero, D., et al. (2001). Vagal tone is reduced during paced breathing in patients with the chronic fatigue syndrome. *Clinical Autonomic Research, 5,* 139–143.

Stepanski, E., Glinn, M., Zorick, F. J., Roehrs, T., & Roth, T. (1994). Heart rate changes in chronic insomnia. *Stress Medicine, 10,* 261–266.

Stores, G., Fry, A., & Crawford, C. (1998). Sleep abnormalities demonstrated by home polysomnography in teenagers with chronic fatigue syndrome. *Journal of Psychosomatic Research, 45,* 85–91.

Taylor, L., Vana, A., & Givon, L. (2000). The evolution of sleep: A reconsideration of the development of the quiet sleep/active sleep cycle. *Medical Hypotheses, 54,* 761–766.

Thase, M. E. (2000). Treatment issues related to sleep and depression. *Journal of Clinical Psychiatry, 61*(Suppl. 11), 46–50.

Uveges, J. M., Parker, J. C., Smarr, K. L., McGowan, J. F., Lyon, M. G., Irvin, W. S., et al. (1990). Psychological symptoms in primary fibromyalgia syndrome: Relationship to pain, life stress, and sleep disturbance. *Arthritis and Rheumatism, 33,* 1279–1283.

van Reeth, O., Weibel, L., Spiegel, K., Leproult, R., Dugovic, C., & Maccari, S. (2000). Interactions between stress and sleep: From basic research to clinical situations. *Sleep Medicine Reviews, 4,* 201–219.

Vercoulen, J. H., Swanink, C. M., Fennis, J. F., Galama, J. M., van der Meer, J. W., & Bleijenberg, G. (1994). Dimensional assessment of chronic fatigue syndrome. *Journal of Psychosomatic Research, 38,* 383–392.

Wesensten, N. J., Balkin, T. J., & Belenky, G. (1999). Does sleep fragmentation impact recuperation? A review and reanalysis. *Journal of Sleep Research, 8,* 237–245.

Whelton, C. L., Salit, I., & Moldofsky, H. (1992). Sleep, Epstein-Barr virus infection, musculoskeletal pain, and depressive symptoms in chronic fatigue syndrome. *Journal of Rheumatology, 19,* 939–943.

Wittig, R. M., Zorick, F. J., Blumer, D., Heilbronn, M., & Roth, T. (1982). Disturbed sleep in patients complaining of chronic pain. *Journal of Nervous and Mental Diseases, 170,* 429–431.

Wolfe, F., Smythe, H. A., Yunus, M. B., Bennett, R. M., Bombardier, C., Goldenberg, D. L., et al. (1990). The American College of Rheumatology 1990 criteria for the classification of fibromyalgia. Report of the multicenter criteria committee. *Arthritis and Rheumatism, 33,* 160–172.

CHAPTER 15

Cardiac and Virologic Issues

A. MARTIN LERNER, ROBERT G. DEETER, WILLIAM O'NEILL,
HOWARD J. DWORKIN, MARCUS ZERVOS, SAFEDIN H. BEQAJ,
CHUNG-HO CHANG, and JAMES T. FITZGERALD

BEGINNING SUDDENLY IN 1988, a 51-year-old male patient of mine became light-headed and fatigued, and experienced a deep ongoing mid-chest ache. The fatigue would worsen through the day, and he often felt an irregular heartbeat punctuated by many ventricular premature contractions. Playing tennis (his usual avocation) was out of the question. As the months passed without improvement, this patient met criteria for diagnosis of a malady previously unfamiliar, the chronic fatigue syndrome (CFS; Fukuda et al., 1994; Holmes et al., 1988). Over a 13-year search with the help of enduring colleagues, I conducted a series of studies focusing on the cause and the prospectives for therapy of this life-altering malady. A paradigm has slowly developed, and this chapter traces that evolution. In September 2000 at the 40th International Conference on Antimicrobial Agents and Chemotherapy in Toronto, Canada, I presented some of this work (Lerner, 2000).

Clinical study of this patient's illness (1988–1996) ultimately showed that he had a dilated cardiomyopathy. Therefore, further study of other patients and their cardiac involvement followed easily. I discovered that he had a persisting positive IgM antibody titer to Epstein-Barr virus, virus capsid antigen. Other early patients demonstrated intermittent high titer IgG (or occasionally IgM) antibodies to titers cytomegalovirus (HCMV), reminiscent of the very high HCMV IgG serum titers of some patients with human immunodeficiency virus infections. The present paradigm was then in incubation phase (Lerner, Zervos, Dworkin, Chang, & O'Neill, 1997).

Dr. Lerner owns U.S. patents to (1) diagnose chronic fatigue syndrome (CFS) and (2) cardiomyopathy by Holter monitoring and (3) treat CFS with antiviral medicines. A further patent (4) describes serologic methods to diagnose CFS.

The authors wish to enthusiastically and gratefully thank Ms. Deanna Byrd, Mrs. Maureen Miller, and Mrs. Deborah McNeilance for suggestions and editorial assistance in the compilation of this manuscript.

Defining studies of CFS had excluded cardiac disease on the basis of a normal (or almost normal) standard resting 12-lead electrocardiograms and normal resting 2-D echocardiograms (Fukuda et al., 1994; Holmes et al., 1988; Lerner, 2000; Lerner, Zervos, Dworkin, Chang, & O'Neill, 1997). The cardinal symptom of CFS is exercise intolerance, and initial CFS studies demonstrated electrical repolarization abnormality and left ventricular dysfunction in CFS patients only at exercise (Lerner, Lawrie-Hoppen, & Dworkin, 1993). Cursory review of the literature revealed that EBV and HCMV mononucleosis resemble the illness CFS and that cardiac complications of EBV/HCMV are well known. The paradigm that CFS may be a primary cardiac disease was enhanced (Ando, Shiramizu, & Hisanou, 1992; Arbustini et al., 1992; Hebert, Yu, Towbin, & Rogers, 1995; Kief & Liebowitz, 1993; LeBlanc et al., 1998; Maisch et al., 1993; Millett, Tomita, Marshall, Cohen, & Hannah, 1991; Schonian, Crombach, & Maisch, 1993; Tiula & Leinikki, 1972; Tyson, Hackshaw, & Kutcher, 1989; Webster, 1957). The concepts, then, of herpesvirus latency (Roizman, 1993); "recurrent infection" (Roizman, 1993); "incomplete virus multiplication" (Lerner, 2000); "dense bodies," "noninfectious enveloped virus particles" (Gibson & Imiere, 1984); "virus gene products," "nonstructural and structural virus epitopes (proteins)" (Lerner, Beqaj, & Deeter, 2002) were added, and a thesis was a working model. This work does not contradict the large array of data, some of it referenced here, documenting chronic immune activation in CFS (Buchwald et al., 1992; Caligiuri et al., 1987; Klimas, Salvato, Morgan, & Fletcher, 1993; Komaroff, 2000; Landay, Jessop, Lennette, & Levy, 1991; Suhadolnik et al., 1994) in CFS. We provide a thesis as to why this multiply documented abnormality occurs.

First, we present a new paradigm (theory of etiology) for the chronic fatigue syndrome based on incomplete EBV/HCMV multiplication, particularly in the heart. Second, the specific virus serologic basis for the diagnosis of complete versus incomplete virus multiplication is outlined. Third, virus serologic findings in the infectious mononucleosis syndrome caused by either EBV or HCMV are contrasted with the persisting incomplete, variably complete virus multiplication of CFS. Fourth, subsets and subgroups of EBV and HCMV CFS as single virus or coinfection are outlined. Definitions for subset subgroup diagnosis of CFS follow. Fifth, case studies of CFS patients with long-term incomplete virus multiplication are given, illustrating a failure to induce herpesvirus (EBV/HCMV) latency, which is necessary for patient recovery. Subsequently, this immunological failure leads to the development of the long-term, life-altering fatigue of CFS. Sixth, the physiology of the symptoms of CFS is deduced from its cardiac pathophysiology. Finally, research findings are presented, namely abnormal 24-hour Holter monitoring, left ventricular dysfunctions, cardiac biopsies of cardiomyopathy, and preliminary results of antiviral therapy (based on the specific serum antibody virus directed subset/subgroup EBV/HCMV diagnosis).

THE CARDIAC EPSTEIN-BARR VIRUS (EBV)/CYTOMEGALOVIRUS (HCMV) PARADIGM OF CHRONIC FATIGUE SYNDROME (CFS)

The chronic fatigue syndrome is caused by incomplete, variably complete herpesvirus multiplication in the heart usually with EBV and/or HCMV and, at

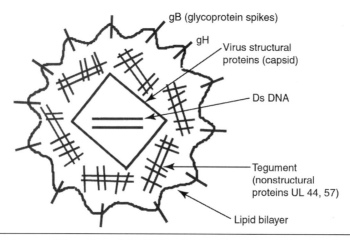

gB (glycoprotein spikes)

gH

Virus structural proteins (capsid)

Ds DNA

Tegument (nonstructural proteins UL 44, 57)

Lipid bilayer

Figure 15.1 Herpes Virus Complete Virion Assembled Intact Showing Biophysical Component Parts, Double Stranded DNA Genome, Virus Structural Proteins (Capsid) Tegument (Nonstructural Proteins, Including UL 44 and UL 57 of HCMV) and Lipid Bilayer Containing Antigenic Structural Glycoprotein Spikes Such as g B and g H of HCMV. The DS DNA codes for over 200 gene products, (proteins) structural and nonstructural processing.

times, by herpesvirus 6[1] in immunocompetent persons (Lerner, 2000; Lerner, Beqaj, & Deeter, 2002; Lerner, Zervos, Dworkin, Chang, & O'Neill, 1997). Although noninfectious-enveloped virus particles and dense bodies, both incomplete forms of herpesvirus formation and assembly are readily evident in electron microscope studies in tissue cultures (Gibson & Imiere, 1984; Koszinowski, Reddehase, & del Val, 1992; Morgan, Rose, Holden, & Jones, 1959; Reddehase & Koszinowski, 1984; Roizman, 1993), these incomplete virus forms have not been previously related to clinical disease.

Herpesvirus multiplication in a susceptible human cell such as the human cardiac myocyte produces complete virions (Figure 15.1) and virus structures lacking essential components (incomplete virions). By complete virus multiplication, we infer that the whole virus is completely replicated and assembled. Virus multiplication may be inhibited at either the replication or the assembly. We name such inhibition incomplete virus multiplication (Lerner, 2000; Lerner, Beqaj, & Deeter, 2002). Complete virions contain an inner central double-stranded linear DNA (DS DNA) surrounded by capsid (virus internal structural proteins) and a lipid-covering bilayer punctuated by glycoprotein spikes (such as g B, g H in Figure 15.1); g B and g H are external structural virus proteins of HCMV. Between the capsid and the enclosing lipid bilayer is the viral tegument containing the processing viral gene products necessary for virus synthesis. The herpes virus genome codes for over 200 proteins, but only 20 to 30 of the gene products are structural epitopes of the glycoprotein spikes or capsid (Koszinowski et al., 1992; Reddehase & Koszinowski, 1984; Roizman, 1993).

---

[1] Our own studies with HV6 have been few.

The gene products (virus-specific processing proteins) of the tegument are not ordinarily expressed immunologically (e.g., produce specific serum antibodies) when complete intact new virus is present. If virus multiplication is not completely successful, complete virus is not formed (incomplete virus multiplication). When incomplete virus multiplication occurs, nonstructural viral epitopes are *then* exposed to the extracellular space, and, subsequently, to the immune system of the host. When these processing virus proteins of the tegument are hidden, protected within the lipid bilayer of the herpesvirus (Figure 15.1), they do *not* induce serum antibodies in the host (Lerner, 2000; Lerner, Beqaj, & Deeter, 2002). Nonstructural epitopes are immunologically silent when complete virus multiplication occurs (Koszinowski et al., 1992; Lerner, 2000; Lerner, Beqaj, & Deeter, 2002; Reddehase & Koszinowski, 1984). This paradigm, to our knowledge, has not been previously explicitly stated.

The CFS cardiac paradigm continues: Incomplete, variably complete herpesvirus multiplication in the cardiac myofiber leads to cardiac dysfunction, first appearing clinically as sinus tachycardias at rest with or without ventricular premature contractions. Sinus tachycardia at rest is accompanied by abnormal electrical repolarizations of the heart recorded at Holter monitoring as oscillating repetitive abnormal T-wave flattening and T-wave inversions (Lerner et al., 1993; Lerner, Goldstein, et al., 1997). Ultimately, cardiac left ventricular power dysfunction and left ventricular dilatation result (Dworkin, Lawrie, & Lerner, 1997). The cardiac symptoms of CFS follow (e.g., exercise intolerance, palpitations, fatigue, dull chest ache, syncope, orthostatic hypotension; Dworkin et al., 1997; Lerner, Goldstein, et al., 1997; Lerner, Zervos, Dworkin, Chang, & O'Neill, 1997). The paradigm continues. In CFS patients, the putative causative herpes viruses multiply in many other bodily sites, but it is the cardiac involvement that determines CFS. CFS may be caused by a single herpesvirus virus infection, or by simultaneous coinfections with several herpesviruses (Lerner, Zervos, Dworkin, Chang, & O'Neill, 1997). A virus etiology for CFS has been extensively investigated. No virus cause has been found (Ablashi, 1994; Buchwald, Ashley, Pearlman, Kith, & Komaroff, 1996; Buchwald & Komaroff, 1991; Gold et al., 1990; Gow, Behan, & Simpson, 1994; Heneine et al., 1994; Levy, 1994). The reasons for our prior failure lie in: (1) recognition of persisting coinfection(s), (2) recognition of the clinical importance of incomplete herpesvirus multiplication and the dynamics of herpesvirus latency, and (3) the centrality of cardiac involvement in CFS.

SOME SERUM ANTIBODY STUDIES IN PRIMARY EBV AND HCMV INFECTIOUS MONONUCLEOSIS

Case Report 1

EBV Mononucleosis (Niederman, McCollum, Henle, & Henle, 1968).[2] On September 13, 1998, I saw an acutely ill 18-year-old young woman with high fevers (4 days, 101–102° F), dysphagia (5 days), and enlarged tonsils. She had an intense

[2] Epstein-Barr virus, HCMV, and HV6 are members of the Family Herpesviridae. EBV is Human herpesvirus 4 (a, gamma subfamily virus); HCMV is designated Human herpesvirus 5 (a beta subfamily virus; and HV6 is Human herpesvirus 6 (also a beta subfamily virus).

exudative pharyngitis with bilateral submandibular adenopathy. A throat culture revealed no *Streptococcus pyogenes*. AST and ALT were mildly elevated (91 and 129, respectively, negative < 50), and the white blood cell count was normal. Serum EBV viral capsid antigen IgM (VCA, IgM) was 112 (negative, ELISA test < 20), and the EBV antibody titer to diffuse early antigen (EA) was 167 (negative, ELISA test < 20). The diagnosis of EBV infectious mononucleosis was apparent (Thorley-Lawson, 1989).

The EBV EA antibody is a polymeric antibody response to as many as 12 nonstructural early EBV polypeptides that are transactivators for the EBV lytic cycle (Thorley-Lawson, 1989). *The EA antibody is, therefore, by definition, a response to nonstructural EBV epitopes representing incomplete EBV virus multiplication.*[3] EBV, VCA is a late viral gene product. The EBV, VCA IgM antibody, represents a response to EBV structural epitope(s), and often indicates complete virus multiplication. In EBV primary infectious mononucleosis, both complete and incomplete virus multiplication are present in explosive infection. No specific cellular or humeral host immune response has yet developed. Infectious mononucleosis is a primary exposure infection. Explosive virus multiplication occurs, first in the throat; viremia follows, and type B-lymphocytes become a primary site for latent infection. By latent infection, we imply that the EBV viral DS DNA is inactive (not producing complete virus or virus proteins). The EBV virus DS DNA during latent infection is present as a nonintegrated circular closed episome in the nucleus of infected cells (Kief & Liebowitz, 1993; Roizman, 1993). Recovery from EBV-mononucleosis follows successful induction of EBV latency.

At Holter (24-hr electrocardiographic monitoring) study in this young woman with EBV mononucleosis, there were *no* abnormal T-wave inversions, and only a rare abnormal oscillating T-wave flattening. Two-D echocardiogram was also normal. With rest, fever resolved within two weeks, clinical symptoms improved, and after several months this young woman returned to full health. AST and ALT returned to normal. On October 11, 1998, her serum EBV, VCA IgM decreased to 53, but her EBV EA antibody titer was still 175. On July 12, 1999, VCA IgM and EA titers were once again completely normal, 21 and 28, respectively.

SUMMARY

This is an example of primary EBV infection with, initially, both complete and incomplete virus multiplication followed by complete recovery. There was no cardiac involvement. Holter monitoring was normal. Recovery was complete, and EBV latency was induced successfully. (I, of course, refer to the developing EBV CFS cardiac paradigm where successful latency is *not* achieved.)

Case Report 2

HCMV Mononucleosis (Klemola, Von Essen, Henle, & Henle, 1970). A 19-year-old young woman was seen November 7, 2000, with sudden onset of syncope, malaise, and chest ache, necessitating bedrest. Initially, fever was present, but

---

[3] To our knowledge, this interpretation of the meaning of the EBV EA antibody response has not been previously stated.

when seen approximately two weeks after becoming ill, she was afebrile. At physical examination, she was unremarkable, except for a grade 2 to 3 holosystolic murmur of a preexisting mitral valve prolapse. Her spleen, however, was enlarged at percussion of the left upper quadrant. The 24-hour Holter monitoring showed abnormal oscillating T-wave flattening and T-wave inversions. Two-D echocardiogram confirmed mitral valve prolapse, but was otherwise negative. A stress MUGA study showed normal left ventricular function with normal cardiac wall motion (Dworkin et al., 1997). She is being followed and continues to improve. She returned to school January 2001.

On September 30, 1999, when seen prior to her current illness, HCMV (V), IgG(V)[4] and IgM(V) ELISA antibody titers were negative. Initially (November 7, 2000), HCMV (V), IgM(V) titer (ELISA) was now positive at 112 (negative, < 18) and HCMV (V) IgG was 56 (negative, < 18). HCMV, viral protein (VP)[5] was also positive, titer, 3 (negative, < 1). HCMV VP is a viral capsid antigen (see Figure 15.1). Antibody to VP also likely indicates incomplete HCMV multiplication. HCMV IgM antibodies to the nonstructural HCMV epitopes p52 (value, 11.52, negative < 1) and CM2 (value, 6.33, negative < 1) were positive. HCMV p52 antigen is a recombinant protein produced in *E. coli* containing the full HCMV UL44 gene product. UL44 is an HCMV polymerase processivity factor. HCMV CM2 is a recombinant protein chimeric antigen fused to N and C termini containing part UL44 and part UL57 gene products. UL57 is an SS DNA binding protein. Both CM2 and p52 elicit only IgM antibodies. UL44 and UL57 are HCMV nonstructural epitopes indicating (when specific antibody is present) incomplete HCMV virus multiplication (Geysen, Meolen, & Barteling, 1984; Landini, 1993; Landini, Lazzarotto, Maine, Ripalti, & Flanders, 1995; Landini et al., 1990; Vornhagen et al., 1996).

Therefore, in this primary HCMV infection, like EBV primary infections, antibodies to *both* structural and nonstructural virus epitopes are produced during early explosive infection. The virologic dynamics of primary HCMV mononucleosis, thus, resemble those of primary EBV mononucleosis. This patient with HCMV mononucleosis was seen improving December 27, 2000. The HCMV (V) IgG titer was now 103 (negative < 18), HCMV (V) IgM was 21 (negative < 18), HCMV IgG (VP) was 3.08 (negative < 1), and CM2 and p52 IgM HCMV antibodies remained positive at 6.88 (negative < 1) and 3.70 (negative < 1), respectively. HCMV, VP, CM2 and p52 assays were performed using Copalis (Coupled Light Scattering) Multiplex Antibody Assays.[6]

Paradigm

In both primary HCMV and primary EBV infections, explosive virus multiplication in an immunocompetent, previously susceptible host leads to antibody responses to both structural and nonstructural virus epitopes. With recovery, IgG

---

[4] The antigen we denote as HCMV (V) antigen is a lysate of HCMV grown in human fibroblast tissue culture.

[5] HCMV VP is a sucrose density purified HCMV human fibroblast tissue culture lysate (Diasorin, Stillwater, Minnesota).

[6] Tests were performed by Safedin Beqaj, PhD, VP p52 and CM2 antigens were obtained from Diasorin, 1990 Industrial Blvd., PO Box 285, Stillwater, Minnesota 55082.

antibodies to structural epitopes persist, but IgM antibodies to nonstructural (and structural) epitopes EBV EA and HCMV, IgM (V), p52 and CM2 antibodies disappear (Lerner, 2000; Lerner, Beqaj, & Deeter, 2002).[7]

SOME SERUM ANTIBODY STUDIES IN CFS (INCOMPLETE EBV/HCMV MULTIPLICATION)

Case Report 3

Incomplete herpesvirus multiplication and CFS. The clinical histories and essentially negative physical examinations of CFS patients are well known (Fukuda et al., 1994; Holmes et al., 1988; Lerner et al., 1993). The typical patient in our clinic is a 37-year-old woman who suddenly has a nondescript flu-like illness, leading imperceptibly to an ongoing exhaustive fatigue and ultimately to an inability to carry on life's ordinary activities. The patient requires a prone resting interval (or actual naps) in bed at midday or later day. Recurring sore throats are frequent, and no pathological bacteria are isolated from the affected pharynx. Sometimes, small hard-white plaques (associated with chronic pharyngeal EBV multiplication) can be seen in the throat.[8] Ongoing light-headedness (wooziness), palpitations at rest, and vague dull left chest aches unrelated to activity ensue, but come on at the end of the day as fatigue worsens. Diffuse muscle aches continue. Fluctuating cervical adenopathy is present. Any physical exertion is followed by worsening symptoms for days—sometimes putting the patient to bed for several days. With passage of time, symptoms continue and may worsen. An accompanying illness-induced depression is common (Fukuda et al., 1994; Holmes et al., 1988; Lerner et al., 1993).

When confusing diagnostic possibilities such as rheumatic fever (American Heart Association, 1965) and Lyme arthritis are excluded, our data suggest this syndrome may be associated with chronic herpesvirus incomplete, variably complete single EBV, or single HCMV multiplication in the heart. A more severe subset of CFS may be associated with incomplete, variably complete coinfections with EBV, together with HCMV. In each case, CFS involves the appropriate herpesvirus (in incomplete, variably complete) cardiac multiplication. Rheumatic fever is diagnosed using Jones criteria (revised; American Heart Association, 1965). An antistreptolysin O titer greater than 400 is required. Acute rheumatic fever may be mistaken for CFS. For purposes of this work, positive serum antibody titers (ELISA IgM or IgG, or Western Blot IgM or IgG) to *Borrelia burgdorferi* make the diagnosis of *Lyme Borreliosis* and exclude a diagnosis of CFS. Chronic Lyme disease may mimic or accompany CFS. The Laboratory Corporation of America, Livonia, Michigan, performs Lyme serologic tests. The two most common CFS-confounding diagnoses at our clinic are Lyme disease and rheumatic fever.

Therefore, according to the cardiac paradigm, this hypothetical patient with CFS (Fukuda et al., 1994; Holmes et al., 1988) exhibits (1) evidence of cardiac involvement with abnormal Holter monitoring and (2) serologic evidence of incomplete EBV (e.g., EA positive antibody titers in serum; Luka, Chase, & Pearson, 1984; Thorley-Lawson, 1989; Tsai, Williams, & Glaser, 1999) and/or HCMV incomplete

---

[7] EBV, VCA, and HCMV (V) and HCMV (VP) are structured epitopes.
EBV EA and HCMV p52 and CM2 are nonstructural epitopes.
[8] A. M. Lerner (clinical observations).

multiplication (e.g., positive HCMV, p52 and/or CM_2 IgM antibody titers in serum; Griffiths & Grundy, 1987; Klemola et al., 1970; Lerner, Beqaj, & Deeter, 2002). There may be occasional IgM EBV or IgM HCMV (V) serum antibodies, but usually there are none. IgG HCMV (V) and IgG EBV antibodies to several structural epitopes are constant. The absence of rising serum IgG titers over ensuing weeks to months and the absence of IgM serum antibody titers to classical structural herpesvirus epitopes is by convention interpreted as an absence of active EBV and/or HCMV infection. Serologic parameters for herpesvirus structural epitopes do not detect incomplete HCMV or EBV multiplication, which appears to be critical to CFS (Figure 15.2).

EBV/HCMV SUBSETS AND SUBGROUPS IN CFS

Using the variables outlined, EBV/HCMV chronic fatigue syndrome may be represented by chronic incomplete, variably complete EBV and/or HCMV multiplication. The appropriate method of serologic diagnosis (diagnosis by specific epitope detection in serum) is outlined (see following section in this chapter). This specific temporal diagnosis (*not* evidence of past, but of ongoing present infection) is used to guide specific antiviral therapy. As shown in Table 15.1, in a single patient there are potentially nine categories of complete/incomplete EBV/HCMV infection. Antiviral therapy is directed toward inducing this complete, incomplete herpesvirus multiplication into a latent state in which there is little or no virus intracellular gene product production. Antiviral therapy is directed toward EBV or HCMV (or both) according to the subset, subgroup analysis. Specific serologic testing defines the subgroup classification.

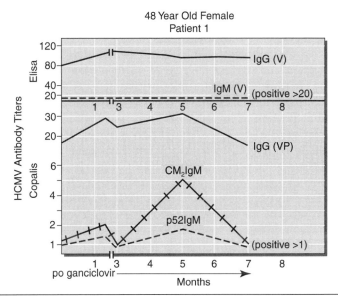

Figure 15.2 Serologic Findings Demonstrating Incomplete Herpes Virus Multiplication in CFS. HCMV IgG (V) and HCMV IgM (V) are stable, unchanging. The presence of IgM p52 and CM_2 antibodies indicate incomplete HCMV multiplication.

Table 15.1

Subset, Subgroup Classification of EBV/HCMV Chronic Fatigue Syndrome

Subset A	EBV-CFS	Subgroup I	Single-virus EBV incomplete virus multiplication
		Subgroup II	Single-virus EBV incomplete variably complete virus multiplication
		Subgroup III	Single-virus EBV complete virus multiplication
Subset B	HCMV-CFS	Subgroup I	Single-virus HCMV incomplete virus multiplication
		Subgroup II	Single-virus HCMV incomplete variably complete virus multiplication
		Subgroup III	Single-virus HCMV complete virus multiplication
Subset C	EBV-HCMV Coinfection		Thus, any combination of Subset A, Subgroups I, II, and III plus B, I, II, III in combination are possible. There are, therefore, nine possible subset subgroups of EBV, HCMV-CFS.

SEROLOGIC DIAGNOSIS OF COMPLETE AND INCOMPLETE EBV AND HCMV MULTIPLICATION IN CFS

A. *EBV complete virus multiplication* is diagnosed by assaying: viral capsid antigen EBV (VCA); VCA is a structural epitope (Luka et al., 1984).
   1. A significant rise in serum antibody to EBV, VCA taken at intervals of 2 to 4 weeks makes a diagnosis of *EBV complete virus multiplication*. The two sera are preferably tested at the same time with the same control.
   2. The diagnosis of *EBV complete virus multiplication* is also made by demonstrating the single presence of a positive EBV, VCA, IgM antibody titer.
B. *EBV incomplete virus multiplication* (Niederman et al., 1968; Thorley-Lawson, 1989; Tsai et al., 1999).

   Incomplete EBV virus multiplication is recognized by a positive antibody titer, IgM or IgG, to total diffuse EBV early antigen polypeptides (nonstructural gene products). The EBV EA (early antigen) is a polymeric antibody to as many as 12 nonstructural early EBV polypeptides. These are EBV EA polypeptides, 17 to 85 KD BML F1, BMRF1, BAM[a] H1–0 and BMRF1 which are transactivators for the lytic cycle, both restricted and diffuse components.
C. *HCMV complete virus multiplication* is diagnosed by assaying HCMV (V) structural epitope. HCMV(V) antigen is a human fibroblast tissue culture lysate of HCMV strain AD69 (Griffiths & Grundy, 1987; Pednealt, Robillard, & Harvy, 1993).

   HCMV complete virus multiplication is diagnosed by demonstrating a significant rise in HCMV ELISA IgG structural antibodies in paired sera taken at intervals of 14 to 28 days. The two sera are preferably tested at the same time with the same controls. The diagnosis of HCMV *complete virus multiplication* is also made by demonstrating the presence in a single serum of a positive IgM ELISA HCMV (V) antibody titer (Luka et al., 1984).

D. *HCMV incomplete virus multiplication* (Geysen et al., 1984; Landini, 1993; Landini et al., 1990, 1995; Vornhagen et al., 1996).

The diagnosis of incomplete HCMV multiplication is made by the single presence of specific Copalis IgM Multiplex antibody assays.

OBSERVATIONAL AND CONTROLLED DATA SUPPORTING THE EBV/HCMV INCOMPLETE VIRUS CARDIAC PARADIGM IN CFS

HOLTER MONITORING

A single 58-year-old male patient suddenly became ill in 1988 with CFS. I found repetitively oscillating negative to flat T-waves, alternating with normal upright T-waves at 24-hour electrocardiographic recordings. The coronary arteries at angiogram were patent, but global left ventricular dilatation and a decreased left ventricular ejection fraction of 44% (normal, < 50%) was present. Repetitive Holter monitoring and MUGAs showed no improvement over the course of eight years, until 1996. I confirmed EBV complete virus multiplication with a positive serum antibody titer to EBV, VCA, IgM. HCMV IgG (V) serum titers were completely negative.

From 1982 to 1990, 300 patients from an internal medicine-infectious diseases specialty practice underwent 24-hour Holter monitoring. The group included 24 individuals with CFS (Lerner et al., 1993). The population was restricted to individuals 50 years old or younger. Ischemic heart disease was excluded in each case by coronary angiogram and/or myocardial perfusion rest/stress (thallium 201 or TC-99 sestamibi). Resting *standard* electrocardiograms were negative (Table 15.2). These same procedures were done in 116 control patients without CFS. Of the CFS patients, 75% were women; non-CFS patients were equally divided between the sexes ($p = .03$; see Figure 15.3a and b on p. 315). The mean ages of the groups were 36 years (CFS) and 38 years (non-CFS). Both groups were essentially free of chronic diseases, including diabetes mellitus, hypertensive vascular disease, and coronary artery disease. Standard electrocardiograms in the CFS and non-CFS groups were similar ($p > .05$; Table 15.3 on p. 315). Approximately 60% of the ECG records were normal, but there were isolated T-wave flattenings or inversions in two leads, usually standard leads I and III in the CFS patients (45.8%; $p > .05$). At 2-D echocardiogram, mitral valve prolapse was seen in 22.7% of the CFS patients and 24.5% of the non-CFS patients ($p > .05$).

Holter monitoring, however, was abnormal in 100% (all) of CFS patients, but was abnormal in 22.4% of the non-CFS controls ($p < .01$). Ischemic heart disease, cardiomyopathy, hypertensive vascular disease, and electrolyte abnormalities can produce similar abnormal oscillating T-wave changes (Lerner et al., 1993). Abnormal T-waves at Holter monitoring do *not* make a diagnosis of CFS, but a *normal* 24-hour Holter monitoring in a fatigued patient makes the diagnosis of CFS unlikely ($p < .05$; Lerner, Goldstein, et al., 1997). Left ventricular dysfunction (decreased ejection fraction and/or abnormal cardiac wall motion) by radionuclide ventriculography stress multiple gated acquisition (MUGA) study was seen in eight of these original CFS patients (Lerner et al., 1993).

Table 15.2
Demographics and Chronic Diseases: Comparison of
Patients with and without CFS

Demographics	24 Patients with CFS	116 Patients without CFS	p Value
Sex, %			
Female	75	50	.03
Male	24	50	
Race, white, %	95.8	89.7	NS
Age, year, mean	36	38	NS
Marital status: married, %	54.2	62.1	NS
Education, %			
College graduate or higher	58.3	53.4	NS
Income, %			
$25,000 to $50,000	45.8	32.5	NS
$50,000	25	28.1	NS
Chronic diseases, %			
Diabetes mellitus	0	0.7	NS
Hypertensive vascular disease	0	16.4	.03
Coronary artery disease	0	8.6	NS

NS = Not significant

Source: "Repetitively Negative Changing T-Waves at 24-h Electrocardiographic Monitors in Patients with Chronic Fatigue Syndrome (Left Ventricular Dysfunction in a Cohort)," by A. M. Lerner, C. Lawrie-Hoppen, and H. J. Dworkin, 1993, *Chest, 104,* pp. 1417–1421. Reprinted with permission.

The first Holter monitoring study (Lerner et al., 1993) was repeated in a randomized double-blinded study with two uninvolved cardiologists as readers of the Holter monitors (Lerner, Goldstein, et al., 1997). Sixty-seven CFS patients were compared with 78 non-CFS patients matched for age (CFS, mean age 40 years; non-CFS, 36 years), place, time, and absence of known other confounding medical diseases. Patients in both groups had normal resting 12-lead ECGs, rest/stress myocardial perfusion studies (thallium 201 or TC-99 sestamibi studies), and 2-dimensional echocardiograms (except for incidental findings of mitral valve prolapse without significant regurgitation or an incidental nonsignificant aortic stenosis). Among CFS patients, oscillating T-wave inversion (61%) occurred, while similar T-wave inversion occurred in 34% of non-CFS patients, $p < .01$. Oscillating abnormal T-wave flattening occurred in 96% of CFS patients, but it occurred in 71% of non-CFS patients, $p < .01$. The *statistical sensitivity of these abnormal T-wave flattenings at Holter monitoring was 0.96 (49/51),* and for T-wave inversions the statistical sensitivity was 0.61 (31 / 51; Table 15.4 on p. 316). The statistical specificities of these data are 0.29 (22 / 77) for T-wave flattenings and 0.66 (51 / 77) for T-wave inversions. *Therefore, the absence of these T-wave changes may be used to exclude CFS in a patient with fatigue of unknown cause* (Lerner, Goldstein, et al., 1997).[9]

---

[9] Patients with EBV or HCMV infections without cardiac involvement (by this definition) do not have CFS. Holter monitoring used was Applied Cardiac Systems, Laguna Hills, California. The original definitions (Fukuda et al., 1994; Holmes et al., 1988) of CFS do not include Holter monitoring. Our studies, to date, to our knowledge, have not been tested by other investigators.

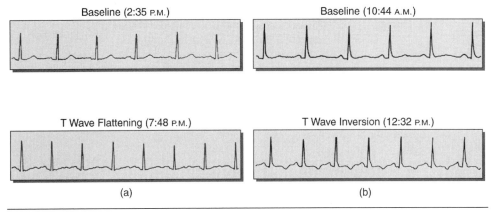

Baseline (2:35 P.M.) Baseline (10:44 A.M.)

T Wave Flattening (7:48 P.M.) T Wave Inversion (12:32 P.M.)

(a) (b)

Figure 15.3a, b Left, This Holter Strip Shows a Normal Sinus Rhythm at 90/Min. (Standard Lead I) at 2:35 P.M., October 4, 1993 from This 30-Year-Old Woman with CFS). At 7:48 P.M., there is a sinus tachycardia of 122/min. At this time, repetitive flattening T-waves are apparent. Her right ventricular biopsy showed cardiomyopathic changes. Right at 10:44 A.M., September 20, 1993, this 51-year-old man with CFS shows a normal sinus rhythm at 80/min. with upright T-waves. At 12:32 P.M., there is a sinus tachycardia at 115/min. Seven inverted T-waves from a larger series are shown with the tachycardia. The right ventricular endomyocardial biopsy in this patient showed cardiomyopathic changes.

These Holter monitoring findings relate well to the studies of Rowe, Bou-Holaigah, Kan, and Calkins, 1995.

PROGRESSIVE CARDIOMYOPATHY

Abnormal left ventricular dynamics were again reported at rest and stress MUGA studies in 11 CFS patients (Dworkin et al., 1997; Lerner et al., 1993). Our nuclear medicine colleagues and collaborators were startled by the unique repeated dyscoordination of the left ventricle at MUGA study in affected CFS patients

Table 15.3
Electrocardiographic Findings for Patients with and without CFS

	Patients with CFS	Patients without CFS	p Value
Standard electrocardiogram, initial, abnormal, %	45.8	33.9	NS
Mitral valve prolapse, at echocardiogram, %	22.7	24.5	NS
Holter monitor, initial, changing T-wave inversions, or flat T-waves, %	100	22.4	<.01

NS = Not significant

Source: "Repetitively Negative Changing T-Waves at 24-h Electrocardiographic Monitors in Patients with Chronic Fatigue Syndrome (Left Ventricular Dysfunction in a Cohort)," by A. M. Lerner, C. Lawrie-Hoppen, and H. J. Dworkin, 1993, *Chest, 104,* pp. 1417–1421. Reprinted with permission.

Table 15.4

Incidence of T-Wave Inversions and T-Wave Flattenings in
CFS and Non-CFS Patients at Holter Monitoring

T-Wave Findings	($n = 51$)	CFS ($n = 77$)	non-CFS p Value
Inversion	61%	34%	<.01
Flattening	96%	71%	<.01
Sensitivity of flattening	0.96 (49/51)		
Sensitivity of inversion	0.61 (31/51)		
Specificity of flattening	0.29 (22/77)		
Specificity of inversion	0.66 (51/77)		

Source: "Cardiac Involvement in Patients with Chronic Fatigue Syndrome as Documented with Holter and Biopsy Data in Birmingham, Michigan, 1991–1993," by A. M. Lerner, J. Goldstein, et al., 1997, *Infectious Diseases in Clinical Practice, 6,* pp. 327–333. Reprinted with permission.

(Dworkin et al., 1997). Among the cardiac abnormalities were abnormal wall motion at rest and stress, dilatation of the left ventricle, and segmental wall motion abnormalities. The left ventricular ejection fraction was found to be below normal (< 50%) in 3 of 11 patients in this report (Table 15.5 on p. 317; Dworkin et al., 1997). Five (of 11) patients had left ventricular blood pool area enlargement (left ventricular dilatation). Left ventricular wall motion abnormalities were seen in 7 of the 11 CFS patients. One CFS patient had repeatedly elevated creatine phosphokinase levels (increased MB band) and further, a flat response to exercise.

In an effort to determine the prevalence of abnormal cardiac wall motion in CFS, a prospective consecutive case series of 98 CFS patients (87% women) seen during the years 1987–1994 was analyzed. Control patients were 450 prechemotherapy cancer patients (72.1% women) with no chronic diseases other than their cancers, no known cardiac disease, *and* no cardiac symptoms (dyspnea, syncope, chest pain, or ankle edema). Resting MUGA studies (cancer patients) and rest/stress MUGA studies were done for CFS patients. Prechemotherapy cancer patients were on the average 12 years older than CFS patients ($p < .0001$), but abnormal cardiac wall motion at rest was seen in 10 of 87 (11.6%) CFS patients and in 8 of 450 (1.8%) prechemotherapy cancer control patients ($p = .0001$). Abnormal cardiac wall motion at stress exercise was seen in 24% of the CFS patients. MUGA studies were done in the same nuclear medicine laboratory (cases and controls). Nuclear medicine readers were unaware of an ongoing study. These data suggest that CFS is a primary myocardial disease (Lerner, Sayyed, et al., 2002).

CARDIAC BIOPSIES

Right ventricular endomyocardial biopsies were performed in 15 CFS patients suspected to have HCMV-CFS on the basis of high IgG HCMV (V) serum antibody titers, and low or no evidence of EBV multiplication by serologic tests described here. Cardiac tissues were cultured in human fibroblast tissue cultures for infectious HCMV. Cardiac tissues were examined by light and electron microscopy. All cardiac biopsies were negative for HCMV virus isolation in human fibroblast

Table 15.5
Myocardial Dynamics in 11 Patients with the Chronic Fatigue Syndrome

Patient No.	Age (Years)	Sex	Date	Ejection Fraction (%)		Heart Enlargement	Wall Motion Abnormalities	
				Rest[a]	Maximum Stress		Rest	Stress
1	38	M	10/88	49	60	−	+	+
2	46	F	10/91	73	77	+	−	−
3	44	F	08/91	63	53	−	−	+ Apical
			03/92	51	36	−	+ Infero/apical	+ Infero/apical
			07/92	49	54	+	−	+ Infero/apical
			09/92	57	63	+	+ Infero/apical	+ Infero/apical
4	31	F	11/90	65	61	−	−	−
			07/91	67	69	+	−	−
5	34	F	07/92	46	55	−	+ Apex	+ Apex
6[b]	46	F	09/92	59	57	−	−	−
			10/92	58	63			
			12/92	57	56			
7	29	F	10/92	61	73	+	−	−
8	48	F	04/91	66	57	−	−	+ Infero/apical
9	42	F	09/91	65	72	−	+ Apex	+ Apex
10	30	M	04/92	58	81	+	−	−
			07/92	56	79	+		
			09/92	60	72	+	+ Septal	−
11	30	F	03/93	54	60	−	+ Tardekinesis apex −	

+ = Present; − = Negative

[a] Normal resting ejection fraction—50%, normal response to maximum stress—5% above resting ejection fraction.

[b] This patient had a flat ejection fraction response to exercise and repeatedly positive creatine phosphokinase MB band. Cardiac catherization was normal.

Source: "Abnormal Left Ventricular Myocardial Dynamics in Eleven Patients with Chronic Fatigue Syndrome," by H. J. Dworkin, C. Lawrie, and A. M. Lerner, 1997, *Clinical Nuclear Medicine, 19*, pp. 675–677. Reprinted with permission.

tissue cultures (indicating no complete virus multiplication). Through the kind courtesies of Drs. Richard Buller and Gregory Storch (Washington University School of Medicine, St. Louis, Missouri), cardiac tissues from 8 CFS patients and 21 controls who had ischemic heart disease were examined by polymerase chain reactions for HCMV and EBV nucleic acids. Two CFS patients and four control patients yielded HCMV DNA.

The failure to demonstrate HCMV DNA in the hearts of more CFS patients is perplexing. Sampling error, low viral loads, or incomplete HCMV DNA expression in the hearts of CFS patients are possible explanations. Varying degrees of cardiomyopathic changes (Figure 15.4a on pp. 318–319 and b on pp. 319–320) characterized by myofiber disarray, myofiber dissolution, myofiber dropout with fibrous replacement and occasional myofiber hypertrophy were seen. All CFS and control patients were negative for EBV DNA by polymerase chain reactions. (These CFS patients were selected to have no EBV disease.)

After endomyocardial biopsies, two CFS patients suffered severe pericardial bleedings. Both CFS patients recovered from their bleeds, but *this procedure was stopped;* we suspect that the hearts of CFS patients are fragile and friable. *We do not recommend further myocardial biopsies.*

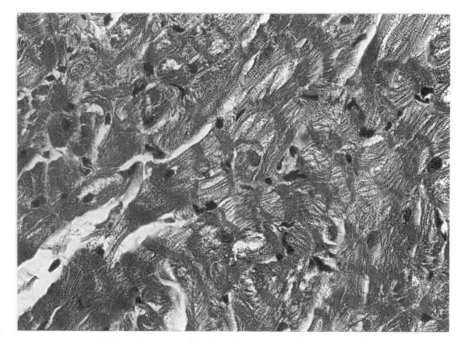

a. Light micrograph: Myofiber disarray in 27-year-old male.

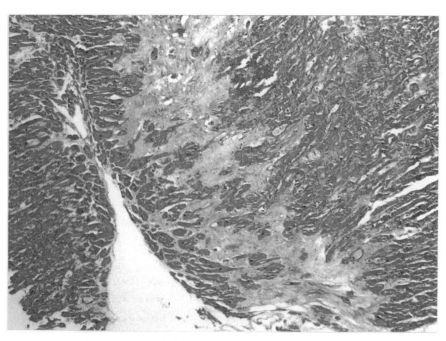

a. Light micrograph: Interstitial fibrosis in 45-year-old female.

Figure 15.4 Light Micrograph and Electron Micrographs of CFS Patients, Right Ventricular Endomyocardial Biopsies

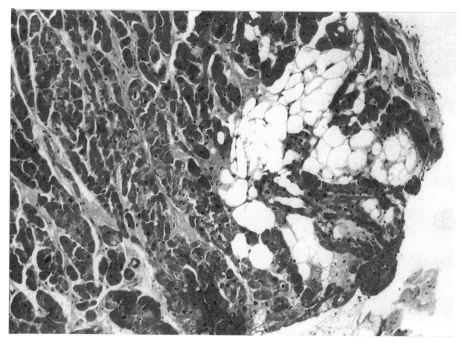

a. Light micrograph: Fatty deposition plus
smaller areas of interstitial fibrosis in 45-year-old female.

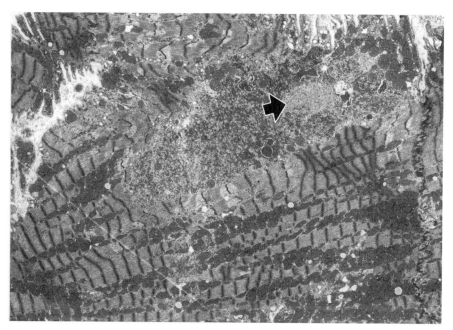

b. Electron micrograph from 51-year-old male
(× 3,500): Showing myofiber disarray and necrosis.

Figure 15.4   *Continued*

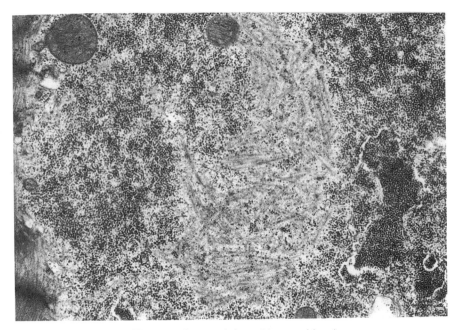

b. Electron micrograph from 51-year-old male
(× 3,500): Further detail of myofiber disarray.

Figure 15.4 *Continued*

EBV/HCMV SEROLOGIC STUDIES IN CFS PATIENTS

A viral etiology of CFS is suspected by many investigators, but none has been established (Ablashi, 1994; Buchwald et al., 1996; Buchwald & Komaroff, 1991; Gold et al., 1990; Gow et al., 1994; Heneine et al., 1994; Komaroff, 2000; Levy, 1994). Patients with CFS suffer a state of chronic immune activation (Buchwald et al., 1992; Klimas et al., 1993). There are increased numbers of CD8 + cytotoxic T lymphocytes with antigenic markers of activation and depressed function of natural killer cells (Caligiuri et al., 1987; Komaroff, 2000; Landay et al., 1991). Biochemical evidence of chronic immune activation consistent with persisting virus infection is supported further by an enzymatic cascade with increased levels of two polypeptides, 2–5A synthetase and 2–5A-dependent ribonuclease I in the circulating lymphocytes of many CFS patients (Suhadolnik et al., 1994). Some patients with CFS, however, do not have these markers, and another undiagnosed illness is likely (Komaroff, 2000). A systemic lymphocyte/macrophage virus infection(s) is suspected. However, multiple studies using classical methods to diagnose virus infection consistently do not reveal a single virus cause of CFS (Ablashi, 1994; Buchwald et al., 1996; Buchwald & Komaroff, 1991; Gold et al., 1990; Gow et al., 1994; Heneine et al., 1994; Lerner, Sayyed, et al., 2002; Levy, 1994; Straus et al., 1985).

The diagnosis of virus infection in humans may utilize virus isolation from appropriate specimens, recognition of viral DNA or viral RNA by polymerase chain reaction or hybridization techniques, and recognition of viral antigens in body fluids or tissues to viral structural conformational epitopes (Landini, 1993). A single positive serum IgM antibody titer in a given patient may also make a diagnosis of current viral infection (primary or reactivation) if the latter test is sufficiently sensitive and specific (Vornhagen et al., 1996). None of these methods, to date, has confirmed a specific viral etiology for CFS.

In the case of CFS and the EBV/HCMV paradigm of incomplete persistent (long-term) virus infection, active infection in this subset is present. Randomized double-blinded, placebo-controlled trials of antiviral therapy seem appropriate. An initial randomized double-blinded, placebo-controlled trial of valacyclovir in single-virus EBV CFS is underway, approved by the U.S. FDA and WBH Human Investigation Committee, and supported by Glaxo-Wellcome Company. Our studies suggest a major 2-virus (EBV, HCMV) etiology of CFS with incomplete virus multiplication as the pathogenetic mechanism of CFS in immunocompetent CFS patients. Classical methods searching for a single virus etiology of CFS have been unsuccessful (Ablashi, 1994; Buchwald et al., 1996; Buchwald & Komaroff, 1991; Gold et al., 1990; Gow et al., 1994; Heneine et al., 1994; Levy, 1994).

Eleven CFS patients with high HCMV (V) serum titers of ELISA IgG structural antibodies (e.g., g B, g H), but no ELISA HCMV IgM structural antibodies, were studied (Griffiths & Grundy, 1987; Lerner, Zervos, Dworkin, Chang, Fitzgerald, et al., 1997; Lerner et al., 2001; Pednealt et al., 1993). Epstein-Barr VCA, IgM, and total antibody to EBV diffuse early antigen were also assayed by ELISA methodology (Luka et al., 1984; Tsai et al., 1999). The trial was abruptly stopped because of pericardial bleedings following two endomyocardial biopsies.

Figure 15.5 shows the courses of 11 CFS patients as described by tests for serum HCMV and EBV antibodies to structural epitopes over 54 to 72 consecutive

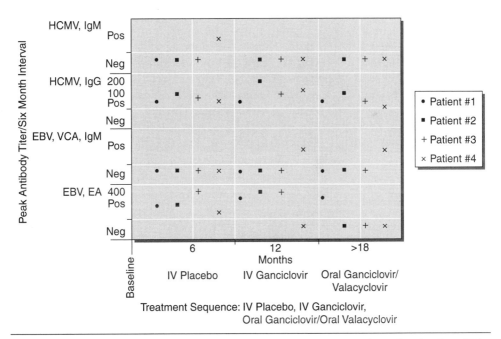

Figure 15.5 Serologic Findings in Four CFS Patients with EBV/HCMV Coinfections Followed for >18 Consecutive Months. During the first 6 months of placebo, EBV, EA serum antibody titers remain positive, while EBV, VCA IgM are consistently negative. Structural epitopes to HCMV (V) IgG remain unchanged. A single isolated HCMV, IgM (V) is present in patient 4 at the completion of IV placebo. In three CFS patients, EBV EA serum titers are negative after valacyclovir. These serologic data using structural conformational HCMV and EBV epitopes do not suggest persistent active infection with either virus.

months. These results show that HCMV IgM (V) and EBV VCA IgM antibodies are only intermittently present and are usually absent. This two-part sequence describes a variable intermittent presence of complete EBV/and/or HCMV multiplication in CFS patients:

1. HCMV IgG (V) antibodies are constant through the observation period of 54 to 72 consecutive months. There are no fourfold or greater rises or falls in serum antibody titers. (Classically, this means there is no present active infection, only *past* virus multiplication.)
2. EBV EA antibodies are often present. (Interpretations of the clinical meaning of EBV EA antibodies have previously been uncertain.) We have suggested that the presence of EA EBV serum antibodies indicates a presence of EBV incomplete virus multiplication.[10]

CLINICAL EVALUATIONS BY THE ENERGY INDEX POINT SCORE

A series of questions was used to calculate the Energy Index Point Score (EI; Lerner, Begaj, Deeter, Dworkin, et al., 2002). At each patient visit (at 4- to 6-week intervals), the symptoms of wooziness including cognitive dysfunction, palpitations at rest, muscle aches, and dull aching chest pains are recorded (Table 15.6). The EI measures the CFS patient's functional capacity in activities of daily living. By definition, an EI of £5 is present in CFS patients. At random, 22 healthy, non-CFS persons were compared with 20 earlier CFS patients seen at this clinic. The non-CFS sample included 17 women and 5 men whose mean age was 35 years (median age, 38 years; range 19–62 years). The mean EI of the non-CFS group was 9.9 (median EI 10; range 7.5–10). The CFS patients included 16 women and 3 men whose mean age was 41 years (median age 42 years; range 16–53 years). The mean EI point score of the CFS group was 3.6 (median EI 4; range 1–5). The gender and ages of the CFS and non-CFS groups were similar (Fisher's exact test and t test). The EIs (CFS, 3.6, and non-CFS, 9.9) of the groups were different ($p < .0001$). The power of this t test is 10. The effect size of these data is 0.25. A small effect size is 0.5 and a large effect size is 0.8 (Lerner, Zervos, Dworkin, Chang, Fitzgerald, et al., 1997). The EI point score correlates well and is converted easily to Kcal/day (Sallis, Haskell, & Wood, 1985).

OBSERVATIONAL AND PRELIMINARY CONTROLLED THERAPEUTIC STUDIES: THESIS

The cardiac EBV/HCMV paradigm for causation of CFS requires the following four conditions:

1. Exclusion of confounding illnesses, including chronic *Lyme borreliosis* and rheumatic fever.

---

[10] Please see Figure 15.2, in which IgM HCMV p52 and CM2 antibodies describe active HCMV incomplete virus multiplication; while studies for HCMV structural epitopes indicate no active infection (past experience only).

Table 15.6
CFS Energy Index Point Score

Grade 0:	Patients are confined to bed by number and severity of symptoms listed below.
	• Bedridden, up to bathroom only.
Grades 1–2:	Any activity leads to overwhelming, incapacitating fatigue. Patients are light-headed, unable to think clearly, concentrate, or read for any extended period (over 60 minutes). Left-sided chest aches, palpitations, sore throats, and feverishness are frequent. Muscle aches are common. Patient can be out of bed only for intermittent, brief parts of each day.
	• Grade 1: Out of bed (sitting in chair) 30 minutes to 1 hour daily.
	• Grade 2: Out of bed, more than 30 minutes at a time, up to 2 hours per day.
Grades 3–5:	With great effort, patients can be out of bed and perform nonphysical activities for several hours each day. Any exertion markedly worsens fatigue. Patients variably express light-headedness and inability to think clearly or read normally. Left-sided chest aches, palpitations, sore throats, and feverishness are frequent. At Energy Indices grade 3 or 4, patients cannot perform a 40-hour per week sedentary job or maintain the duties of a homemaker (e.g., cooking, cleaning, doing laundry, shopping, driving, etc.).
	• Grade 3: Out of bed 2 to 4 hours per day.
	• Grade 4: Out of bed 4 to 6 hours per day.
	• Grade 5: Can work at sedentary job; working 40 hours per week is difficult.
Grades 6–9:	Patients can assume normal activities, maintain a 40-hour workweek, and, with pacing, maintain a household. Overwhelming fatigue is lessened. Rare-to-no light-headedness, foggy thinking, chest aches, palpitations, feverishness, and sore throat are present. Patients can perform light physical work (or exercise) in moderation without fatigue.
	• Grade 6: Daily naps in bed, may maintain a 40-hour sedentary job plus light, limited housekeeping and/or social activities.
	• Grade 7: No naps in bed and out of bed at 7:00 A.M. until 9:00 P.M. Able to work a sedentary job plus light housekeeping and/or social activities.
	• Grade 8: No naps and is able to manage full work (sedentary job) plus manage the household.
	• Grade 9: May exercise at approximately ½ to ⅔ normal without excessive fatigue.
Grade 10:	Patients are well, with normal energy level, stamina, and sense of well-being. Exercise in moderation leads to an increased sense of well-being. Light-headedness, difficulties in concentrating and reading ability, chest aches, palpitations, sore throats, and feverishness are absent.
	• Grade 10: Normal.

Source: A series of questions was used to calculate the Energy Index Point Score (EI). A. M. Lerner and R.G. Deeter, copyright 1999.

2. Specific recognition of intermittent variably complete and incomplete HCMV and/or EBV virus multiplication.
3. Cardiological studies using Holter monitoring, 2-D echocardiogram, and rest/stress MUGA studies. If Holter monitoring shows deep ischemic-appearing inverted T-waves, myocardial perfusion imaging to exclude ischemic heart disease is necessary.
4. If confounding illnesses are excluded, properly directed randomized double-blinded placebo-controlled trials of antiviral therapy in CFS patients may establish or refute the paradigm.

BRIEF OUTLINE OF PHARMACOKINETICS AND DOSING OF ANTIVIRAL DRUGS IN PROPOSED STUDIES DIRECTED BY SEROLOGIC EBV/HCMV SUBSET CLASSIFICATION

Toxicities of valacyclovir and ganciclovir in CFS patients who are immunocompetent are often mild, in contrast to severe toxicities that are common in immunocompromised patients (Lerner, Beqaj, Deeter, Dworkin, et al., 2002; Lerner, Zervos, Dworkin, Chang, Fitzgerald, et al., 1997). In several patients, cidofovir has been used in HCMV CFS when ganciclovir was not clinically appropriate (studies of ocular complications of AIDS Clinical Trials Group, 1997). We have found that valacyclovir is safe, provided hydration is adequate. We ask CFS patients to drink six to eight 8-ounce glasses of water daily. Renal insufficiency is a contraindication to valacyclovir, ganciclovir, and cidofovir. With valacyclovir, patients may develop red blood cell macrocytosis and diarrheas. We have seen serious platelet abnormalities with valacyclovir, and thrombocytopenia resulted once with ganciclovir.

Treatment of EBV-infected cells with acyclovir eliminates linear forms of EBV DNA necessary for complete virus multiplication (Kief & Liebowitz, 1993). The inhibitory concentration of acyclovir in Raji cell tissue cultures (ID_{50}) to EBV is 7µm. The ID_{50} is 0.1µm (Vero cells) and 0.7µm (HeLa cells). Acyclovir does not affect covalently closed circular DNA associated with latent paranuclear episomes in infected circulating B-lymphocytes. Although acyclovir is not absorbed well enough by the gastrointestinal tract to achieve the required blood levels to inhibit EBV multiplication, its valyl derivative (valacyclovir) is better absorbed, completely converted to acyclovir and reaches concentrations in serum in excess of the ID_{50} of EBV (Kief & Liebowitz, 1993; Laskin, 1984; Pagano, Sixbey, & Lin, 1983; Purifoy et al., 1993; Straus et al., 1988; Weller et al., 1993; Yao, Ogan, Rowe, Wood, & Rickinson, 1989).

After informed consent, appropriate CFS patients may be given valacyclovir at a dosage of 1.0–1.5 gm every 6 hours for 6 months. If the patient's weight is > 80 kg, 1.5 gm valacyclovir is given q6h. Serum acyclovir blood levels may be followed. Valacyclovir is not effective in the therapy of HCMV infection. The EI score and serological parameters outlined here guide the duration of therapy. When serologic parameters are negative (e.g., EBV, VCA IgM, EBV EA), valacyclovir dosing is tapered, and the serologic parameter followed in continued visits of the CFS patient. The therapy may be necessary for > 6 months or longer, depending on the clinical and laboratory findings. Serial serum incomplete HCMV IgM antibody titers (p52, CM_2) may also guide duration of anti-HCMV therapy.

Despite its in vitro activity against EBV, we have not found ganciclovir useful in EBV CFS. We have repeatedly observed rises in EBV serologic parameters *during* administration of ganciclovir. Ganciclovir inhibits HCMV multiplication in vitro at 0.02 to 3.5 µg/ml. When ganciclovir is given at 5 mg/kg IV q12h, effective systemic concentrations are achieved (Spector et al., 1993). In preliminary trials, 4 to 6 weeks of intravenous ganciclovir (cytovene) followed by oral suppression with oral ganciclovir 1.0 to 1.5 gm every 8 hours was given. Valgancyclovir with significantly greater oral absorption may be as effective as intravenous ganciclovir (Brown, Banken, Saywell, & Arum, 1999). More recently, cidofovir (Vistide) at a dosage of 5 mg/kg intravenously given on Day 1, Day 7, and then every 10 days has been used in early preliminary open trials of HCMV CFS (Studies of Ocular complications of AIDS Research Group in Collaboration with the AIDS Clinical Trials Group, 1997). With cidofovir, pretherapy intravenous hydration in a short-stay unit of the hospital and constant nursing supervision with the opportunity for overnight stays are necessary. Oral probenecid is given to facilitate renal safety of cidofovir by slowing renal tubular secretion of this nucleoside. Cidofovir is *not* given in an outpatient setting.

A SMALL PRELIMINARY TRIAL OF ANTIVIRAL THERAPY

In January 1995, a double-blinded placebo-controlled Phase III crossover study of CFS patients was begun (Lerner et al., 2001). Eleven CFS patients (10 women) were each followed for 18 consecutive months. Their mean age was 42.7 years. They had had CFS for a mean of 21.8 months. Before administration of antiviral nucleosides, endomyocardial biopsies were done. Cardiac tissues and bloods were negative in human fibroblast tissue cultures for HCMV by virus isolation. Cardiomyopathic findings were seen in cardiac biopsies of CFS patients. The study was stopped prematurely when two CFS patients undergoing right ventricular endomyocardial biopsies suffered serious pericardial bleedings.

At entry, patients had positive HCMV (V) IgG serum antibody titers, with or without HCMV (V) IgM antibody titers, both tested by ELISA methods (Griffiths & Grundy, 1987; Pednealt et al., 1993). Serum antibody titers to EBV, VCA-IgM and EBV-EA were also tested (Luka et al., 1984; Tsai et al., 1999). The treatment group received intravenous ganciclovir, 5 mg/Kg q12h for 30 days. Intravenous ganciclovir was followed by oral ganciclovir, 1 gm po q8h. At the completion of the 6-month postganciclovir observation period, if there was no improvement and if elevated EBV antibody titers suggested coinfections, oral valacyclovir, 1 gm q6h was added to continuing oral ganciclovir. Antiviral nucleosides by mouth then continued through the 18 months of the study (Lerner et al., 2001).

Antibody titers to structural epitopes (HCMV, V and HCMV, V, IgM) and EBV, VCA, IgM and EBV, EA were repeated at 3-month and 6-month intervals. Unchanging high-positive HCMV (V) IgG antibody titers were present through the 18-month trial. At baseline, one of 11 CFS patients had a positive HCMV (V) IgM antibody titer. This HCMV (V), IgM titer was absent after 30 days of IV ganciclovir. Four of the 11 CFS patients had coinfections with EBV as indicated by positive EA antibody titers. After valacyclovir, EBV EA antibody titers fell or became negative in three of these CFS patients. These serologic titers are consistent with HCMV and, when present, EBV incomplete herpesvirus multiplication in CFS (Figure 15.5).

Symptom scores (e.g., chest pain, wooziness, palpitations, muscle aches) were assessed at 30-day intervals. (A symptom score is zero if none of these four symptoms are present.) At baseline, the mean symptom score for the CFS patients *was* 0.81. After 6 months, four CFS patients receiving intravenous placebo had a mean symptom score of 0.5. When assessed 6 months after intravenous ganciclovir, the symptom mean occurrence score for the entire cohort of 11 CFS patients was 0.38. Six months later, the mean cumulative symptom score was 0.28; and at 18 months, the mean symptom score was 0.19.

At baseline, the mean Energy Index Point Score (EI) for the entire group was 3.5. After 6 months, four CFS patients receiving intravenous placebo had a mean EI of 3.9. When assessed 6 months after intravenous ganciclovir, the mean EI was 4.4. At this point, as indicated by the presence of positive EBV, VCA-IgM and/or EA antibody titers, valacyclovir was added, and oral ganciclovir was continued. Six months later, the mean EI for the 11 patients was 5.8; and at 18 months, the mean EI was 6.1 (Lerner, Zervos, Dworkin, Chang, Fitzgerald, et al., 1997). This protocol, or its modification, may be useful in a suitably sized, randomized, double-blinded CFS placebo-controlled trial of antiviral therapy in CFS.

CONCLUSION

The unique pathological physiology of CFS appears to be (1) involvement of the heart and (2) the preponderance of herpesvirus incomplete virus sequential multiplication with little-to-no evidence of complete virus multiplication. In contrast to complete virus multiplication, which leads to immediate lysis of the infected cell, these studies show that incomplete virus multiplication produces a noninflammatory cardiac pathology, inducing a slowly progressive apoptosis. Abnormal oscillating flattened and/or ischemic T-waves at 24-hr Holter monitoring of a patient with life-altering fatigue raises the probability of a diagnosis of CFS cardiomyopathy, or excludes this diagnosis in other fatigue states. Standard electrocardiogram, 2-D echocardiogram, stress MUGA, and myocardial perfusion studies further define the cardiac status in CFS patients. A major subset of CFS patients suffers persistent incomplete, variably complete herpesvirus multiplication in the heart *with single* EBV or single HCMV, or *coinfection* HCMV/EBV. The EBV/HCMV subset, subgroup in CFS patients can be defined by specific serologic test. We propose protocols for double-blinded, placebo-controlled trials of antiviral therapy for CFS.

REFERENCES

Ablashi, D. V. (1994). Viral studies of chronic fatigue syndrome [Review]. *Clinical Infectious Disease, 94*(18, Suppl. 1), S130–S133.

American Heart Association. (1965). Jones criteria (Revised) for guidance in the diagnosis of rheumatic fever. *Circulation, 32,* 664.

Ando, H., Shiramizu, T., & Hisanou, R. (1992). Dilated cardiomyopathy caused by cytomegalovirus infection in a renal transplant recipient. *Japan Heart Journal, 33,* 409–412.

Arbustini, E., Grasso, M., Diegoli, M., Percivalle, E., Grossi, P., Bramerio, M., et al. (1992). Histopathologic and molecular profile of human cytomegalovirus infection in patients with heart transplants. *American Journal of Clinical Pathology, 98,* 205–213.

Brown, F., Banken, L., Saywell, K., & Arum, I. (1999). Pharmacokinetics of valganciclovir and ganciclovir following multiple oral dosages at valganciclovir in HIV- and CMV-seropositive volunteers. *Clinical Pharmacokinetics, 37,* 167–176.

Buchwald, D., Ashley, R. L., Pearlman, T., Kith, P., & Komaroff, A. L. (1996). Virol serologies in patients with chronic fatigue and chronic fatigue syndrome. *Journal of Medical Virology, 50,* 25–30.

Buchwald, D., Cheney, P. R., Peterson, D. L., Henry, B., Wormsley, S. B., Geiger A., et al. (1992). A chronic illness characterized by fatigue neurologic and immunologic disorders and active herpes virus type 6 infection. *Annals of Internal Medicine, 116,* 103–113.

Buchwald, D., & Komaroff, A. L. (1991). Review of laboratory findings for patients with chronic fatigue syndrome. *Reviews in Infectious Diseases, 13,* S12–S18.

Caligiuri, M., Murray, C., Buchwald, D., Levine, H., Cheney, P., Peterson, D., et al. (1987). Phenotypic and functional deficiency of natural killer cells in patients with chronic fatigue syndrome. *Journal of Immunology, 139,* 3306–3313.

Dworkin, H. J., Lawrie, C., & Lerner, A. M. (1997). Abnormal left ventricular myocardial dynamics in eleven patients with chronic fatigue syndrome. *Clinical Nuclear Medicine, 19,* 675–677.

Fukuda, K., Straus, S. E., Hickie, I., Sharpe, M. C., Dobbins, J. G., & Komaroff, A. (1994). The chronic fatigue syndrome: A comprehensive approach to its definition and study. *Annals of Internal Medicine, 121,* 953–959.

Geysen, H. M., Meolen, R. H., & Barteling, S. J. (1984). Use of peptide synthesis to probe viral antigens for epitopes to a resolution of a single amino acid. *Proceedings of the National Academy of Sciences, USA, 81,* 3998–4002.

Gibson, W., & Imiere, A. (1984). Selection of particles and proteins for use as human cytomegalovirus subunit vaccines. *Birth Defects Original Article Series, 20,* 305–324.

Gold, D. R., Bowden, R., Sixbey R., Riggs, R., Katon, W. J., Ashley, R., et al. (1990). Chronic fatigue: A perspective clinical and virologic study. *Journal of the American Medical Association, 264,* 48–53.

Gow, J. W., Behan, W. M., & Simpson, K. (1994). Studies on entero viruses in patients with chronic fatigue syndrome. *Clinical Infectious Diseases, 18,* S126–S129.

Griffiths, P. D., & Grundy, J. E. (1987). Molecular biology and immunology of cytomegalovirus. *Biochemical Journal, 241,* 313–324.

Hebert, M. M., Yu, C., Towbin, J. A., & Rogers, B. B. (1995). Fatal Epstein-Barr virus myocarditis in a child with repetitive myocarditis. *Pediatric Pathology Laboratory Medicine, 15*(5), 805–812.

Heneine, W., Woods, T. C., Sinha, S. D., Khan, A. S., Chapman, L. E., Schonberger, L. B., et al. (1994). Lack of evidence for infection with human and animal retroviruses in patients with chronic fatigue syndrome. *Clinical Infectious Diseases, 18*(Suppl. 1), S121–S125.

Holmes, G. P., Kaplan, J. E., Gantz, N. M., Komaroff, A. L., Schonberger, L. B., Straus, S. E., et al. (1988). Chronic fatigue syndrome: A working case definition. *Annals of Internal Medicine, 108,* 387–389.

Kief, E., & Liebowitz, D. (1993). Epstein-Barr virus. In B. Roizman, R. J. Whitley, & C. Lopez. *The human herpes viruses* (pp. 107–172). New York: Raven Press.

Klemola, E., Von Essen, R., Henle, G., & Henle, W. (1970). Infectious mononucleosis-like disease with negative heterophile agglutination test. Clinical features in relation to Epstein-Barr virus and cytomegalovirus antibodies. *Journal of Infectious Diseases, 121,* 608–614.

Klimas, N. G., Salvato, F. R., Morgan, R., & Fletcher, M. A. (1993). Immunological abnormalities in chronic fatigue syndrome. *Journal of Clinical Microbiology, 68,* 229–233.

Komaroff, A. L. (2000). The biology of chronic fatigue syndrome. *American Journal of Medicine, 108*(2), 169–171.

Koszinowski, U. H., Reddehase, M. J., & del Val, M. (1992). Principles of cytomegalovirus antigen presentation in vitro and in vivo. *Seminars in Immunology, 4,* 771–779.

Landay, A. L., Jessop, C., Lennette, E. T., & Levy, J. A. (1991). Chronic fatigue syndrome: Clinical condition associated with immune activation. *Lancet, 338,* 707–712.

Landini, M. P. (1993). New approaches and perspectives in cytomegalovirus diagnosis. *Progress in Medical Virology, 40,* 157–177.

Landini, M. P., Guan, M. X., Jahn, G., Lindenmaier, W., Mach, M., Ripalti, A., et al. (1990). Large-scale screening of human sera with cytomegalovirus recombinant antigens. *Journal of Clinical Microbiology, 28,* 1375–1379.

Landini, M. P., Lazzarotto, T., Maine, G. T., Ripalti, A., & Flanders, R. (1995). Recombinant mono and poly antigens to detect cytomegalovirus-specific immuno-globulin M in human sera by enzyme immunoassay. *Journal of Clinical Microbiology, 33*(10), 2535–2542.

Laskin, O. L. (1984). Acyclovir pharmacology and clinical experience. *Archives of Internal Medicine, 144,* 1241–1246.

LeBlanc, M. H., Boudriau, S., Doyle, D., Gagnon, A., Beaudoin, D., Coulombe, D., et al. (1998). Epstein-Barr virus mediated graft rejection in heart transplant patients implication of the cardiac cytoskeleton. *Transplantation Proceedings, 30*(3), 918–924.

Lerner, A. M. (2000). New and emerging infections: Myocarditis and idiopathic cardiomyopathy. *Programs and abstracts of the 40th Interscience Conference on Antimicrobial Agents and Chemotherapy (Toronto)* 530–31. Abstract No. b49.

Lerner, A. M., Beqaj, S. H., & Deeter, R. G. (2002). IgM antibodies to human cytomegalovirus polymerase processivity factor (UL44) and a SS DNA binding protein (UL57) tegument proteins in a subset of patients with chronic fatigue syndrome. *In Vivo, 16,* 153–160.

Lerner, A. M., Beqaj, S. H., Deeter, R. G., Dworkin, H. J., Zervos, M., Chang, C. H., et al. (2002). A six-month trial of valacyclovir in the Epstein-Bar virus subset of chronic fatigue syndrome: Improvement in left ventricular function. *Drugs of Today, 38,* 549–568.

Lerner, A. M., Goldstein, J., Chang, C. H., Zervos, M., Fitzgerald, J. P., Dworkin, H. J., et al. (1997). Cardiac involvement in patients with chronic fatigue syndrome as documented with Holter and biopsy data in Birmingham, Michigan, 1991–1993. *Infectious Diseases in Clinical Practice, 6,* 327–333.

Lerner, A. M., Lawrie-Hoppen, C., & Dworkin, H. J. (1993). Repetitively negative changing T-waves at 24-h electrocardiographic monitors in patients with chronic fatigue syndrome (left ventricular dysfunction in a cohort). *Chest, 104,* 1417–1421.

Lerner, A. M., Sayyed, T., Dworkin, H. J., Gottipolu, P., Zervos, M., Goldstein, J., et al. (2002). *Abnormal cardiac wall motion in a subset of chronic fatigue syndrome.* Unpublished data.

Lerner, A. M., Zervos, M., Chang, C. H., Beqaj, S., Goldstein, J., O'Neill, W., et al. (2001). A small randomized, placebo-controlled trial of antiviral therapy for patients with chronic fatigue syndrome. *Clinical Infectious Diseases, 32,* 1657–1658.

Lerner, A. M., Zervos, M., Dworkin, H. J., Chang, C. H., Fitzgerald, J. P., Goldstein, J., et al. (1997). A new cardiomyopathy: A pilot study of intravenous ganciclovir in a subset of the chronic fatigue syndrome. *Infectious Diseases in Clinical Practice, 6,* 110–117.

Lerner, A. M., Zervos, M., Dworkin, H. J., Chang, C. H., & O'Neill, W. (1997). A unified theory of the cause of the chronic fatigue syndrome. *Infectious Diseases in Clinical Practice, 6,* 239–243.

Levy, J. A. (1994). Viral studies of chronic fatigue syndrome. Part III. *Clinical Infectious Diseases, 18,* S117–S120.

Luka, J., Chase, R. C., & Pearson, G. R. (1984). A sensitive enzyme-linked immunosorbent assay (ELISA) against the major EBV-associated antigens, I., Correlation between ELISA and immunofluorescence titers using purified antigens. *Journal of Immunological Methods, 67,* 145–156.

Maisch, B., Schonian, U., Crombach, M., Wendl, I., Bethge, C., Herzum, M., et al. (1993). Cytomegalovirus associated inflammatory heart muscle disease. *Scandinavian Journal of Infectious Diseases, 88,* 135–148.

Millett, R., Tomita, T., Marshall, H. E., Cohen, L., & Hannah, H. (1991). Cytomegalovirus endomyocarditis in a transplanted heart: A case report with in situ hybridization. *Archives of Pathology and Laboratory Medicine, 115,* 511–515.

Morgan, C., Rose, H. M., Holden, M., & Jones, E. P. (1959). Electron microscopic observations on the development of herpes simplex virus. *Journal of Experimental Medicine, 110,* 643–651.

Niederman, J. C., McCollum, R. W., Henle, G., & Henle, W. (1968). Infectious mononucleosis. Clinical manifestations in relation to EB virus antibodies. *Journal of the American Medical Association, 203*(3), 205–209.

Pagano, J. S., Sixbey, J. W., & Lin, J. C. (1983). Acyclovir and Epstein-Barr virus infection. *Journal of Antimicrobial Chemotherapym, 12*(Suppl. B), 113–121.

Pednealt, L., Robillard, L., & Harvy, P. (1993). Comparison of four enzyme immunoassays for the detection of cytomegalovirus IgG antibodies. *Clinical Diagnostics Virology, 1,* 215–223.

Purifoy, D. J., Beauchamp, L. M., de Miranda, P., Ertl, P., Lacey, S., Roberts, G., et al. (1993). Review of research leading to new anti-herpesvirus agents in clinical development: Valacyclovir hydrochloride, a specific agent for Varicella zoster virus. *Journal of Medical Virology, 41*(Suppl. 1), 139–145.

Reddehase, M. J., & Koszinowski, U. H. (1984). Significance of herpesvirus immediate early gene expression in cellular immunity to cytomegalovirus. *Nature, 312,* 369–371.

Roizman, B. (1993). The family herpes virus: A brief introduction. In B. Roizman, R. J. Whitley, & C. Lopez (Eds.), *The human herpes viruses* (pp. 3, 443). New York: Raven Press.

Rowe, P. C., Bou-Holaigah, I., Kan, J. S., & Calkins, H. (1995). Is neurally mediated hypotension an unrecognized cause of chronic fatigue? *Lancet, 345,* 623–624.

Sallis, J. F., Haskell, W. L., & Wood, P. D. (1985). Physical activity assessment methodology in the Five-City Project. *American Journal of Epidemiology, 121,* 91–106.

Schonian, U., Crombach, M., & Maisch, B. (1993). Assessment of cytomegalovirus DNA and protein expression in patients with myocarditis. *Clinical Immunology and Immunopathology, 68,* 229–233.

Spector, S. A., Weingeist, T., Pollard, R. B., Dieterich, D. T., Samo, T., Benson, C. A., et al. (1993). A randomized controlled study of intravenous ganciclovir therapy for cytomegalovirus peripheral retinitis in patients with AIDS. *Journal of Infectious Diseases, 168*(3), 557–563.

Straus, S. E., Dale, J. K., Tobi, M., Lawley, T., Preble, O., Blaese, R. M., et al. (1988). Acyclovir treatment of the chronic fatigue syndrome. Lack of efficacy in a placebo-controlled trial. *New England Journal of Medicine, 319,* 1692–1698.

Straus, S. E., Tosato, G., Armstrong, G., Lawley, T., Preble, O. T., Henle, W., et al. (1985). Persisting illness and fatigue in adults with evidence of Epstein-Barr virus infection. *Annals of Internal Medicine, 102*(1), 7–16.

Studies of Ocular Complications of AIDS Research Group in Collaboration with the AIDS Clinical Trials Group. (1997). Parental cidofovir for cytomegalovirus retinitis in patients with AIDS: The HPMPC peripheral cytomegalovirus retinitis trial. A randomized, controlled trial. *Annals of Internal Medicine 126*(4), 264–274.

Suhadolnik, R. J., Reichenbach, N. L., Hitzges, P., Sobol, R. W., Peterson, D. L., Henry, B., et al. (1994). Up regulation of the 2–5A synthetase/RNase I pathway associated with chronic fatigue syndrome. *Clinical Infectious Diseases, 18*(Suppl. 1), S96–S104.

Thorley-Lawson, D. A. (1989). Immunological responses in Epstein-Barr virus and the pathogenesis of EBV-induced diseases. *Biochimica et Biophysica Acta, 948,* 263–288.

Tiula, E., & Leinikki, P. (1972). Fatal cytomegalovirus infection in a previously healthy boy with myocarditis and consumption coaguloapthy as presenting signs. *Scandinavian Journal of Infectious Diseases, 4*(1), 57–60.

Tsai, C. H., Williams, M. V., & Glaser, R. (1999). Characterization of two monoclonal antibodies to Epstein-Barr virus early antigen which react to two different epitopes and have different biologic function. *Journal of Virological Methods, 33,* 47–52.

Tyson, A. A., Hackshaw, B. T., & Kutcher, M. A. (1989). Acute Epstein-Barr virus myocarditis simulating myocardial infarction with cardiogenic shock. *South Medical Journal, 82*(9), 1184–1187.

Vornhagen, R., Hinderer, W., Sonneborn, H. H., Bein, G., Matter, L., Enders, G., et al. (1996). IgM-specific serodiagnosis of acute human cytomegalovirus infection using recombinant autologous fusion proteins. *Journal of Virological Methods, 60*(1), 73–80.

Webster, B. H. (1957). Cardiac complications of infectious mononucleosis: A review of the literature and report of five cases. *American Journal of the Medical Sciences, 234,* 62–70.

Weller, S., Blum, M. R., Doucette, M., Burnette, T., Cederberg, D. M., de Miranda, P., et al. (1993). Pharmacokinetics of the acyclovir pro-drug valacyclovir after escalating single and multiple dose administration to normal volunteers. *Clinical Pharmacology and Therapeutics, 54*(6), 595–605.

Yao, Q. Y., Ogan, P., Rowe, M., Wood, M., & Rickinson, A. B. (1989). The Epstein-Barr virus: Host balance in acute infectious mononucleosis patients receiving acyclovir anti-viral therapy. *International Journal of Cancer, 43*(1), 67–71.

CHAPTER 16

Neuroendocrine Dysfunction

ANTHONY J. CLEARE

O VER THE PAST decade, numerous studies have attempted to link CFS or similar states to neuroendocrine dysfunction. This chapter provides an overview of the accumulated evidence. It includes not only studies looking directly at endocrine function, but also those using endocrine tests to assess other etiologic factors, such as monoamine dysfunction.

Although often thought of as a new illness, CFS has striking parallels with the Victorian concept of neurasthenia (Wessely, Hotopf, & Sharpe, 1998). Furthermore, although the suggestion that CFS might be related to hypothalamic pituitary adrenal (HPA) axis dysfunction first appeared in the scientific literature in the 1980s, earlier generations of physicians had already visited this ground. Thus, the term hypoadrenia or "a bit of Addison's disease" was often used from 1902 to 1925—though without firm scientific grounding (Tattersall, 1999). We turn first, then, to this issue, and whether these physicians were in fact ahead of their time.

HPA AXIS DISTURBANCE IN CFS

The interest in the role of the HPA axis in CFS developed from the observations that conditions in which there is low circulating cortisol, such as Addison's disease (Brosnan & Cowing, 1996), glucocorticoid withdrawal (Avgerinos, Chrousos, Nieman, Oldfield, Loriaux, & Cutler, 1987), and bilateral adrenalectomy (Riordain, Farley, Young, Grant, & van Heerden, 1994) are characterized by debilitating fatigue along with other symptoms often seen in CFS, such as arthralgia, myalgia, sleep disturbance, and mood disorder (Baxter & Tyrel, 1981). Thus, the first hypothesis to be tested was that fatigue (or other symptoms) in CFS is mediated by low circulating levels of cortisol.

STUDIES OF BASAL HPA AXIS FUNCTION

There have been many studies of unstimulated cortisol levels. These have used three basic methods: blood sampling, 24-hour urinary free cortisol (UFC) excretion measurement, and saliva. The largest group of studies to date used plasma samples, usually a single sample (Altemus et al., 2001; Bearn et al., 1995; Cleare et al., 1995; Cleare, Miell, et al., 2001; Demitrack et al., 1991; Dinan et al., 1997; Gaab et al., 2002a; Hamilos et al., 1998; Kavelaars, Kuis, Knook, Sinnema, & Heijnen, 2000; Kuratsune et al., 1998; MacHale et al., 1998; Moorkens, Berwaerts, Wynants, & Abs, 2000; Ottenweller, Sisto, McCarty, & Natelson, 2001; Poteliakhoff, 1981; Scott, Burnett, Medbak, & Dinan, 1998; Scott, Medbak, & Dinan, 1998a, 1998b; Scott, Salahuddin, Cooney, Svec, & Dinan, 1999; van Rensburg et al., 2001; Yatham et al., 1995). As noted in Table 16.1, most of the studies failed to show any differences between patients and controls, although around one quarter showed lowered levels. Taking only those studies in which serial rather than single blood specimens were obtained, that proportion increases to around one half. Nevertheless, these studies have several problems. First, many were not looking specifically at this question, the data having been extracted by

Table 16.1
Sites of Possible HPA Axis Abnormalities in CFS

Level (Figure 16.1)	Finding	Investigating Groups (Number)	Papers Published (Number)	Replication (Positive: Negative Studies)
1	Hippocampal atrophy	1	1	—
1	Impaired rate-sensitive negative feedback	1	1A	—
1	Reduced suprahypothalamic drive to HPA axis	1	H	—
2–3	Enhanced negative feedback			
	In vivo (dexamethasone suppression)	3	2 + 1A	2:1
	In vitro	2	3	2:1
2	Impaired CRH and/or AVP release from hypothalamus	2	2	2:0
3	Impaired pituitary response to CRH	4	4 + 1U	4:1
4	Blunted adrenal cortex response to ACTH			
	Direct (ACTH test)	3	3	2:1
	Indirect (CRH test)	4	4 + 1U	2:3
4	Adrenal gland atrophy (CT scan)	1	1	—
1–4	Impaired HPA response to stressor			
	Response to awakening	2	1 + 1U	1:1
	Response to exercise	2	2	2:0
	Response to social stress	1	1	—
5	Low basal cortisol			
	In blood: all studies	13	22	5:17
	In blood: studies with serial specimens	5	6	3:3
	In urine	5	6	4:2
	In saliva	4	5	1:4

A = Abstract
U = Unpublished data

this author for the purposes of this chapter; thus, they were probably underpowered. Furthermore, plasma samples involve intravenous cannulation and hospital attendance, which are both likely to induce a stress response on top of any baseline changes. Finally, they also measure both the biologically active free cortisol and bound cortisol (Kirschbaum & Hellhammer, 1994). Thus, only limited information can be drawn from these studies.

A more naturalistic method of assessing basal HPA axis function is through measuring free cortisol in 24-hour samples of urine. These studies have generally been larger and were specifically designed to investigate whether basal HPA axis function is reduced in CFS. Six studies to date have used this method (Cleare, Blair, Chambers, & Wessely, 2001; Cleare, Miell, et al., 2001; Demitrack et al., 1991; Hamilos et al., 1998; Scott & Dinan, 1998; Young et al., 1998). Of these, four have found reduced cortisol output in CFS. This includes the largest study of the HPA axis to date. Cleare, Blair, et al. (2001) recruited 121 patients and found the mean cortisol output to be 66.6 ±36.8 nmol/day in CFS compared with 97.0 ±52.9 nmol/day in healthy controls. Importantly, this finding held whether or not subjects had comorbid psychiatric illness or were taking any medication (Figure 16.1). There was no apparent effect of disability or illness duration on cortisol output. Despite these relatively consistent findings, it has been argued that 24-hour UFC is an unreliable indicator of HPA activity, particularly at the lower end of the spectrum (Thompson, Rubin, & McCracken, 1992). Also, only 2% to 3% of circulating cortisol is excreted as free cortisol, the rest entering metabolic pathways (Raven & Taylor, 1996); shifts in these pathways could theoretically alter free cortisol output independently of circulating cortisol levels.

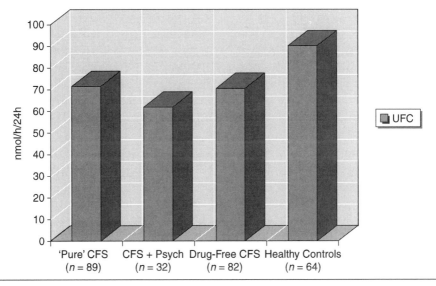

Figure 16.1   Twenty-Four Hour Urinary Free Cortisol (UFC) Values in CFS Patients without (Pure CFS) or with (CFS + Psych) Psychiatric Comorbidity, in CFS Patients Medication Free for 2 Months or More (Drug-Free CFS) and in Healthy Controls. Data taken from "Plasma Leptin in Chronic Fatigue Syndrome, and a Placebo-Controlled Study of the Effects of Low-Dose Hydrocortisone on Leptin Secretion," by A. J. Cleare, S. S. Sookdeo, J. Jones, V. O'Keane, and J. P. Miell, 2001, *Clinical Endocrinology.*

Salivary cortisol has advantages over blood in that it is noninvasive and can be undertaken in naturalistic settings, and is therefore less likely to be affected by stress responses if carried out carefully. Also, it arguably measures a more relevant parameter—the biologically active free cortisol. Table 16.1 summarizes the results of studies to date using this method (Gaab et al., 2002b; Strickland, Morriss, Wearden, & Deakin, 1998; Wood, Wessely, Papadopoulos, Poon, & Checkley, 1998; Young et al., 1998). A clear pattern has yet to emerge from these studies, though they provide less support for lowered basal levels of cortisol.

Some of the previously listed studies have also measured basal ACTH levels in CFS. Results from these have not suggested consistent changes. Although there is no evidence of hypopituitarism in CFS, some studies have reported elevated levels of ACTH (Demitrack et al., 1991; MacHale et al., 1998).

Just one study has attempted to measure CRH itself. Demitrack et al. (1991) measured CSF levels of CRH and ACTH in 19 CFS patients (again with high psychiatric comorbidity) and 26 controls at 0900 h after strict bed rest. No differences were apparent.

DYNAMIC STUDIES OF THE HPA AXIS

There are several reasons for undertaking dynamic studies of the HPA axis. First, if one accepts that there is a mild hypocortisolism, at least in some patients, it is necessary to attempt to detect where there may be abnormalities in the control of the HPA axis. Second, challenge tests may detect more subtle disturbances of the axis than simply measuring basal levels of cortisol. They may also be more reliable indicators of disturbance, less susceptible to extraneous influences. Third, such investigations may allow hypotheses of etiology to be refined, such as how various stresses may exert effects on the disorder or be implicated in the etiology. This has parallels in the investigation of the HPA axis in other stress-related disorders, such as major depression.

Figure 16.2 shows an outline of the HPA axis, and Table 16.1 summarizes the evidence for and against dysfunction at various levels of the axis.

CRH Test   The CRH challenge test has been the most widely used challenge test in CFS. The first study using this test was published in 1991 by Demitrack and colleagues; blunted ACTH but normal cortisol responses were found in a sample of patients who were chronically ill (mean illness duration 7.2 years) and with high rates of psychiatric comorbidity. Three groups have since attempted to replicate these original findings (Cleare, Miell, et al., 2001; Kavelaars et al., 2000; Scott, Medbak, & Dinan, 1998a). Two of the four subsequent studies have found blunted ACTH responses, although the largest study, by our group, found normal ACTH response but blunted cortisol responses in 37 CFS patients who were medication free and without comorbid depression (Cleare, Miell, et al., 2001). Some of the inconsistencies in the results of CRH challenges may result from the challenges being carried out at different times of the day, or by the use of both ovine and human CRH in differing doses. However, there are many confounds within and between studies that could affect the results; these are discussed later in the chapter.

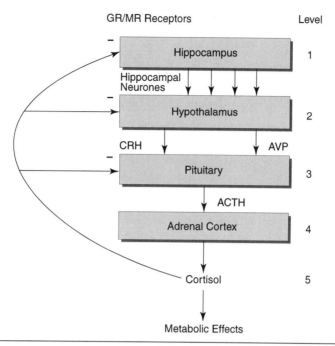

Figure 16.2 Schematic Representation of the HPA Axis. Level of abnormality in CFS relates to Table 16.1. GR = Glucocorticoid receptor; MR = Mineralcorticoid receptor; CRH = Corticotropin releasing hormone; AVP = Arginine vasopressin; ACTH = Corticotropin.

AVP Argenine vasopressin (AVP) acts synergistically with CRH to promote ACTH release (Antoni, 1993; Lamberts, Verleun, Oosteron, DeJong, & Hackeng, 1984). The ACTH response to AVP is critically dependent on central levels of CRH, since this response is potentiated by CRH coadministration in a dose-dependent manner and covaries with the circadian changes in hypothalamic CRH (DeBold et al., 1984; Salata, Jarrett, Verbalis, & Robinson, 1988). Thus, Altemus et al. (2001) argued that the ACTH response to AVP acts as an indirect index of ambient hypothalamic CRH levels, especially in the morning when CRH levels are relatively high. In 19 medication-free CFS patients, they found a reduced ACTH response, which they attributed to a lower level ambient level of hypothalamic CRH. However, as the authors admit, several other explanations for the findings are possible. One theory is that there may be abnormalities of AVP release or receptors. Supporting this, Bakheit et al. (Bakheit, Behan, Watson, & Morton, 1993) found basal levels of AVP to be significantly reduced in response to water deprivation challenge in CFS patients. Further support came from Scott et al. (Scott, Medbak, & Dinan, 1999) who used desmopressin (DDAVP), an AVP analogue, both alone and in coadministration with CRH. They found that, as in their original CRH test study (Scott et al., 1998a), there were blunted ACTH and cortisol responses in CFS subjects. DDAVP alone had a negligible effect in patients or controls. However, the coadministration of DDAVP was able to normalize responses in CFS, such that both CFS and healthy controls had the same ACTH and cortisol responses. They hypothesized that this was due to upregulated AVP receptors on the pituitary in CFS, consistent with a hypothesized hypothalamic AVP deficiency.

ACTH Test   Demitrack et al. (1991) undertook a careful dose-response study of 12 CFS and 10 healthy controls in which 4 doses of ACTH (Cortrosyn 0.003, 0.01, 0.1, and 1.0 mg/kg) or placebo were administered on 5 separate days at 1800 h. Once again, there was a high rate of comorbid depression in this sample. Dose-response curves were significantly different in patients and controls: At low doses of ACTH, only CFS subjects showed cortisol rises above placebo, suggesting a hypersensitivity of the adrenal cortex to ACTH. However, at higher doses of ACTH, cortisol responses were significantly lower than controls, suggesting an overall reduced maximal secretory capacity of the adrenal cortex. Two further studies have administered an ACTH test in CFS. Both used only one dose of ACTH (Synacthen), the standard low dose 1-mg challenge (Grinspoon & Biller, 1994; Rasmuson, Olsson, & Hagg, 1996). The first (Scott, Medbak, & Dinan, 1998b) reported findings in keeping with those of Demitrack and colleagues (1991), including significantly attenuated cortisol responses overall. However, our group (Hudson & Cleare, 1999) could detect no difference in cortisol responses between CFS and controls groups, though there was a trend toward a blunted response in males only.

Insulin Stress Test (IST)   Although a preliminary study of 9 patients had suggested some abnormal responses during this test (Bearn et al., 1995), a more thorough study administered this test to 16 medication-free CFS subjects with no comorbid depression and 16 matched healthy controls (Cleare, Miell, et al., 2001). There was no difference in ACTH or cortisol responses. This was confirmed in another center in a large sample (Moorkens et al., 2000). However, a recent study found a blunted ACTH response but normal cortisol response to the IST (Gaab et al., 2002a). Since the IST remains the gold standard test for adrenal insufficiency, this suggests that CFS is not associated with frank hypocortisolism. However, such an approach is probably too blunt to be useful in detecting more subtle endocrine changes that might be present in CFS.

Other Challenges to the HPA Axis   Because of the exercise intolerance reported by CFS subjects, two studies have used a maximal exercise challenge to the HPA. In the first study, 17 CFS subjects and 14 controls were compared, with measures before, 4 minutes after, and 1 day after a period of exercise to exhaustion (Ottenweller et al., 2001). CFS subjects showed reduced ACTH response immediately after this stressor, although cortisol responses did not differ. Interestingly, the time to exhaustion on the test was related to basal cortisol levels: Lower plasma cortisol was associated with a shorter duration of exercise. There were no differences the following day, suggesting that endocrine disturbance is not related to the prolonged fatigue noted by CFS subjects after exercise. Gaab and colleagues (Gaab et al., 2002b) used two naturalistic, nonpharmacological challenges (exercise to exhaustion on a cycle ergometer and social stress using the Trier Social Stress Test) in 21 CFS subjects and 20 controls. They found lower ACTH, but normal cortisol responses to both challenges, similar to the pattern of response to the IST that they also found in this group of subjects. However, the differences in ACTH response disappeared when the lower baseline levels of ACTH in CFS subjects were controlled.

Feedback Tests   One of the theories about the underlying cause of hypocortisolism in CFS is that of enhanced negative feedback of corticosteroid receptors on the hypothalamus or pituitary. Feedback to the HPA axis is provided via Type 1 and Type 2 glucocorticoid receptors in the hippocampus, hypothalamus, and pituitary. Methods to investigate this included in vivo and in vitro experiments.

One of the first studies did not specifically investigate CFS, but it was an ambitious epidemiological study, administering questionnaire measures and a standard 1 mg overnight dexamethasone suppression test to 266 community dwelling subjects (Hyyppa, Lindholm, Lehtinen, & Puukka, 1993). From these, the authors identified 41 subjects who scored positive on simple measures of fatigue. They found no relation between postdexamethasone cortisol levels and fatigue, though there was a positive correlation between depression level and postdexamethasone cortisol levels.

However, preliminary reports of studies in patients with CFS suggested abnormal feedback. Dexamethasone, acting on hypothalamus and pituitary, induced super suppression of cortisol in one preliminary study, providing evidence for increased negative feedback (Poland, Lin, Lutchmansingh, & McCracken, 1996). Hydrocortisone infusion, acting on fast-feedback mechanisms in the hippocampus, provided similar results (Lavelle & Dinan, 1996). The most convincing evidence to date of an enhanced feedback sensitivity of glucocorticoid receptors comes from a carefully conducted study by Gaab et al. (2002b). They used salivary cortisol measures before and after low-dose dexamethasone (0.5 mg), a regime more sensitive to hypersuppression than the standard 1-mg test used in depression, in 21 CFS patients and 21 healthy controls. There was again evidence of heightened negative feedback in CFS patients compared to controls, with reduced postdexamethasone salivary cortisol output. The authors note the similarity of this finding with other conditions related to stress, such as burnout syndrome (Pruessner, Hellhammer, & Kirschbaum, 1999), posttraumatic stress disorder (Yehuda, Boisoneau, Lowy, & Giller, 1995), adolescents exposed to earthquake-related trauma (Goenjian et al., 1996), women with histories of childhood sexual abuse (Stein, Yehuda, Koverola, & Hanna, 1997), and chronic pelvic pain (Heim, Ehlert, Hanker, & Hellhammer, 1998). They hypothesize that precipitating or chronic stress in CFS patients may underlie the finding.

Further support for the presence of increased glucocorticoid receptor function and increased negative feedback comes from studies that have used in vitro models. Visser et al. (1998) looked at CD4 positive T-cells from subjects with CFS and found that a lower concentration of dexamethasone was needed to inhibit CD4 function, indicating increased sensitivity to dexamethasone. A follow-up study measured GR receptor function directly on the blood mononuclear cells of 10 CFS and 14 control subjects (Visser et al., 2001). There was no difference in GR affinity or number, or of GR m-RNA expression. However, the peripheral white blood cells from patients with CFS were again more sensitive to dexamethasone. They concluded that the abnormality in the GR was likely to be in postreceptor binding signal transduction.

Not all studies have found increased glucocorticoid receptor function (Kavelaars et al., 2000; Taerk, Toner, Salit, Garfinkel, & Ozersky, 1987). However, there are problems with these studies. One specifically studied adolescents, and the results may not apply more generally (Kavelaars et al., 2000). Another used CFS subjects also suffering from depression (Taerk et al., 1987). Finally, one study used the GH response to dexamethasone challenge, an unusual and unreplicated methodology that may have been susceptible to GH function changes (see discussion later in this chapter), and used a polysymptomatic group suffering from fibromyalgia and IBS as well as CFS (Majeed, Dinan, Thakore, Gray, & Behan, 1995).

In summary, at present it appears that heightened negative feedback, mediated through increased sensitivity of glucocorticoid receptors, may be part of the explanation for the hypocortisolism in CFS.

Sample Confounds

Many difficulties are inherent in undertaking studies of the HPA axis, and other endocrine systems, in CFS. In particular, comorbid depressive or other psychiatric illness is present in approximately half to two thirds of CFS patients in most samples where it is looked for (Wessely et al., 1998). Since high circulating cortisol or other endocrine disturbances frequently occur in major depression (Dinan, 1994), this may affect the results of studies of CFS. Similarly, several studies have shown hypocortisolism and HPA axis disturbances in atypical major depression, a subtype of depression in which fatigue is a prominent complaint along with hypersomnia, hyperphagia, and rejection sensitivity (Gold, Licinio, Wong, & Chrousos, 1995). Although some studies have carried out thorough psychiatric assessment using gold standard structured psychiatric assessments, many have not. Even those that do so may not fully exclude effects of depression. For example, the subjects studied by Wood et al. (1998) were said to have had a diagnosis of major depression excluded, but 5 out of 10 subjects had Beck Depression Inventory scores within the mild-moderate depression range. Another confounding factor is length of illness. The study by Demitrack and colleagues (Demitrack et al., 1991) used subjects with a particularly long illness duration (mean 7.2 yrs). Other studies that failed to find reduced basal cortisol levels used subjects who had been ill for much less time (Wood et al., 1998; Young et al., 1998). Not all studies have adequately controlled for past or current use of medication that might affect the HPA axis. Matching of patients and controls has not always been sufficiently close. It is also noteworthy that changes to the CDC case definition in between studies have made it less dependent on the number of physical symptoms present (Fukuda et al., 1994; Holmes et al., 1988; Schluederberg et al., 1992). Thus, the populations studied may have differed because of this, too. Finally, few studies report detail of fatigue severity, sleep disturbance, or functional capacity. Given the independent effects of such factors on the HPA axis (Spath-Schwalbe, Scholler, Kern, Fehm, & Born, 1992; Stupnicki & Obminski, 1992), it is important to exclude the possibility that any HPA axis changes are epiphenomena.

Summary

It is not altogether surprising that a clear, consistent pattern has failed to emerge, given the sample confounds described. Weighing up the observed evidence suggests that there may be heterogeneity within and between samples, but that the best designed studies support a mild hypocortisolism in at least some subjects with CFS. Indeed, a recent meta-analysis of all studies of 24-hour UFC and morning and afternoon plasma cortisol levels confirmed this suggestion. It found moderate overall effect sizes for reduced 24-hour UFC (-0.73) and morning cortisol (-0.35) but with substantial heterogeneity between studies, and larger effects sizes in samples recruited from tertiary compared with primary care (Harvey, Purdie, Bushnell, & Ellis, 2001). There were no differences in afternoon plasma cortisol levels.

There are numerous theories why some patients with CFS show hypocortisolism or abnormal responses to dynamic challenges, though many findings and theories are not compatible. We (Parker, Wessely, & Cleare, 2001) have noted that the initial study by Demitrack and colleagues (1991) from the National Institutes of Health (NIH) raised three related theories for the mediation of symptoms in CFS: (1) Symptoms are due directly to low circulating cortisol; (2) symptoms are due to abnormalities of central neurotransmitters involved in HPA axis function, such as CRH; and (3) symptoms are a result of a more complex disturbance of the relationship between the two. We concluded that, although there is evidence in support of all three hypotheses, some form of (3) is most likely.

What might this disturbance be? Demitrack et al. (1991) hypothesize a deficient suprahypothalamic drive, and reduced hypothalamic output of CRH. However, this would be expected to result in an upregulation of pituitary CRH receptors, and consequently enhanced ACTH responses to exogenously administered CRH. This has not been a finding in any study. In contrast, Scott et al. (1998a; Scott & Dinan, 1999) have suggested that CFS is a stress-related disorder. They hypothesize that initial stress may cause an elevation in CRH with consequent downregulation of CRH receptors on the pituitary corticotrophs. Second, they hypothesize that this downregulation fails to normalize following the alleviation of stress, or the subsequent reduction in CRH levels, an example of abnormal plasticity in the CRH receptor. Primary pathology located in the adrenal glands has been suggested as an explanation for some findings, though why this may occur is unclear (Cleare, Miell, et al., 2001). Cleare and Wessely (1996) and Gaab et al. (2002a) have hypothesized that chronic stress, whether from external or internal factors, may be present in CFS, which could explain the findings. Finally, there is a parallel between the endocrine findings in CFS and in some other disorders, including posttraumatic stress disorder, seasonal affective disorder, and atypical depression. The findings may be a nonspecific marker of vulnerability to suffer from these conditions (Heim, Ehlert, & Hellhammer, 2000).

FUTURE STUDIES

It will be important to know how any endocrine changes evolve as CFS develops, since most studies are done on patients who have been ill for many years. Studies of high-risk cohorts could help in this aim, and several such studies are ongoing. Preliminary results from a study recently completed by our group, which measured salivary cortisol profiles in subjects with EBV infection (who have a rate of chronic fatigue of around 15% six months afterward; White et al., 1998), suggested no link between the development of chronic fatigue and low cortisol in this time frame (Candy et al., in press). It will also be important to assess whether factors that could lead to trait HPA axis changes were present prior to the illness onset. One example might be childhood abuse; this has strong effects on the HPA axis (De Bellis et al., 1994; Heim et al., 2000), and has also been linked to the etiology of patients with unexplained physical symptoms like fatigue.

It is also not yet known what happens to CFS patients after recovery from the illness. It might be hypothesized that clinical recovery would be paralleled by alterations in endocrine status. Studies using hydrocortisone replacement are described later in this chapter, but the most effective treatments so far discovered for CFS are nonpharmacological, namely graded exercise and cognitive-behavioral therapies (Whiting et al., 2001). In a recently completed study, we found that cognitive-behavioral therapy not only improved symptoms and reduced disability in CFS, but also led to heightened ACTH and cortisol responses to CRH and increases in the output of salivary cortisol throughout the day. It thus reversed the abnormalities present when those tests were performed in the same patients prior to treatment (Cleare et al., unpublished data).

In the final analysis, it seems unlikely that there is a single change to the HPA axis in CFS. The etiology of HPA axis changes in CFS is probably, like that of CFS itself, multifactorial. Many factors could potentially affect the HPA axis making it likely that different alterations to the HPA axis may occur. The heterogeneity of these features in CFS in the different studies may be a factor underlying the divergent findings seen to date. An approach more likely to bear fruit in unraveling the etiology of HPA axis dysfunction in CFS would involve measuring more precisely the confounding variables to allow a multidimensional understanding of HPA axis changes in CFS. Future studies in CFS might include diurnal measures of sleep, physical activity, and neuroendocrine parameters; comprehensive dimensional psychiatric assessment; patients tested at different time points of the illness (i.e., during acute, subacute, and chronic fatigue of varying durations); prospective cohort study designs; assessment of possible early life effects on the HPA such as childhood abuse; and careful assessment of other factors, such as drugs (including the frequent use of herbal and other complementary medicines), diet and psychosocial stresses, that might affect the HPA axis (see Table 16.2).

DHEA AND DHEA-S ABNORMALITIES IN CFS

Dehydroepiandrostenedione and its sulfate (DHEA-S) are derived from the zona reticularis of the adrenal, as opposed to glucocorticoids, which are produced in the zona fasciculate. DHEA-S circulates at levels of about one order of magnitude

Table 16.2
Methods for Assessing Multidimensional Model of HPA Axis Dysfunction in CFS

Factor to Be Measured	Possible Methods
Illness phase	Prospective studies, high-risk cohorts, assessment on recovery of CFS
Sleep	Questionnaire, actigraphy, polysomnography
Psychiatric illness	Structured interview, self-report questionnaires
Early life abuse	Questionnaire, Interview
Medication use	Self-report, doctor report
Psychosocial stress	Structured interviews, self-report questionnaires
Physical activity	Actigraphy, self-report
Diet	Self-report, prospective diaries, weight charting

greater than those of cortisol. Reductions in circulating DHEA and DHEA-S have been associated with age-related conditions including coronary artery disease, memory impairment, and type 2 diabetes (Baulieu, 1996). The exact role of DHEA and DHEA-S remains unclear, though there are some theoretical links between these hormones and mood and energy (Barrett-Connor, von Muhlen, Laughlin, & Kripke, 1999; Baulieu, 1996; Wolkowitz et al., 1999). The role of dynamic challenge tests in assessing DHEA function is also unclear, though Scott et al. (Scott, Svec, & Dinan, 2000) note that DHEA represents one of the stress hormones released by the adrenal cortex.

The results of studies investigating DHEA and DHEA-S function are summarized in Table 16.3 (De Becker et al., 1999; Kuratsune et al., 1998; Ottenweller et al., 2001; Scott, Salahuddin, et al., 1999; Scott et al., 2000; van Rensburg et al., 2001). Once again, an inconsistency between studies is notable, though some impairment is apparent in the majority. How any DHEA abnormalities relate to changes in cortisol function has not been adequately addressed. The finding of low DHEA in some studies has led to tests of DHEA as a therapy.

GROWTH HORMONE AXIS DISTURBANCE IN CFS

The rationale for studying growth hormone in CFS has come from several sources. First, there are parallel findings in the fibromyalgia literature, where low GH function has been linked to sleep disturbances and muscle pain (Parker et al., 2001). Also, GH deficiency in adults may be associated with symptoms such as fatigue and myalgia (Wallymahmed, Foy, & MacFarlane, 1999). There are also suggestions that other fatigue states such as those occurring postoperatively may be associated with GH changes (Vara-Thorbeck, Guerrero, Ruiz-Requena, & Garcia-Carriaz, 1996).

In CFS, small preliminary studies suggested low basal GH levels and low levels of GH peripheral mediators such as insulin-like growth factor-1 (IGF-1) and IGF-2 (Allain et al., 1997; Berwaerts, Moorkens, & Abs, 1998), although this was not replicated in other studies (A. L. Bennett, Mayes, Fagioli, Guerriero, & Komaroff, 1997; Buchwald, Umali, & Stene, 1996; Ottenweller et al., 2001). The study by Allain et al. (1997) also demonstrated a reduced GH response to insulin-induced hypoglycemia, though Berwaerts et al. (1998) failed to repeat this.

Two large and comprehensive studies have now been published investigating all aspects of the GH-IGF system. Our own study enrolled 37 CFS subjects and closely matched healthy controls (Cleare, Sookdeo, Jones, O'Keane, & Miell, 2000). We failed to find any significant differences in either baseline (IGF-1 & 2 and IGFBP-1, 2, & 3) or dynamic tests (GHRH test and IST) of GH function. We concluded that there is no evidence for GH deficiency in CFS patients free from comorbid psychiatric illness. The second study also used basal measures of GH and the IST in 73 CFS patients and 23 healthy controls, and additionally measured GH responses to clonidine (33 CFS and 6 controls) and argenine hydrochloride (39 CFS and 19 controls) in some subjects (Moorkens et al., 2000). In contrast to the first study, there was reduced nocturnal GH release and a reduced GH response to the IST in CFS. As in the first study, however, there were no changes in insulin-like growth factors, and the GH response to the other challenges was not blunted. Although some results seem conflicting between these two large studies, the latter study seemed to have less close age and sex matching of patients and control groups. It is not clear

Table 16.3
Studies of DHEA/DHEA-S in CFS

Study	Subjects	Illness Duration	Comorbid Psychiatric Illness (Method of Assessment Stated, If Any)	Method	Cortisol Findings in CFS Patients
Kuratsane et al. (16)	17 CFS (CDC) 35 Healthy	Not given	No data	1 blood sample at 0900h	Basal DHEA: no difference Basal DHEAS: Low
	49 CFS (CDC) 35 Healthy	Not given	No data	Overnight urine collection	17-ketosteroids sulfate: Low
De Becker et al. (80)	22 CFS (CDC) 14 Healthy	Not given	Primary psychiatric disorders excluded	1 blood sample at 0900 h 250 µg ACTH (Synacthen) challenge test	Basal DHEA: no difference DHEA response: Low in CFS
Scott et al. 1999 (22)	15 CFS (CDC) 15 Major Depression 11 Healthy	Not given	Free from comorbid psychiatric illness (SCID)	1 blood sample at 1200–1400 h	Basal DHEA: Low in CFS (c.f. both healthy and depressed controls) Basal DHEAS: Low in CFS (compared with healthy controls)
Scott et al. 2000 (79)	19 CFS (CDC) 10 Healthy	Not given	Free from comorbid psychiatric illness (SCID)	1 blood sample at 1200 h 1 µg ACTH (Synacthen) challenge test	Basal DHEA: no difference DHEA response: no difference DHEA/Cortisol ratio: no difference at baseline, but trend for differential change over time

Study	Sample	Duration	Psychiatric assessment	Blood sampling	Results
Ottenweller et al. (26)	17 CFS (CDC) 14 Healthy	All < 6 years (mean not given)	No major psychiatric diagnosis in 5 years prior to illness onset. 9/17 CFS had current major depression (Q-DIS)	1 blood sample: time not stated Exercise to exhaustion	Basal DHEA-S: no difference DHEA-S response: no difference
Van Rensburg et al. (24)	15 CFS (CDC) 15 Healthy	Not given	No data	1 blood sample at 0830 h	Basal DHEA-S: Low (in CFS females [$n = 10$] vs. control females [$n = 10$])
Cleare et al. (unpublished data)	16 CFS (CDC) 16 Healthy	Not given	Free from comorbid psychiatric illness (assessment by 2 psychiatrists using SSI-CFS)	1 blood sample at 0900 h 1μ/kg CRH challenge test	Basal DHEA: High Basal DHEA-S: no difference DHEA response: no difference

SCID = Structured Clinical Interview for *DSM-IIIR*; Q-DIS = Quick Diagnostic Interview Schedule; SSI-CFS: Semistructured Interview for CFS (Sharpe et al., 1997); CDC = Centers for Disease Control.

how rigorously subjects with fibromyalgia—in whom there is also evidence of GH abnormalities, and who frequently also fill criteria for CFS—were excluded. Similarly, the lack of a rigorous exclusion of depression may skew findings, given the finding in some studies of impaired GH function in depression (Dinan, 1998).

OTHER ENDOCRINE DISTURBANCES IN CFS

A few studies have investigated possible alterations in other endocrine axes.

Leptin

Leptin is a recently discovered hormone closely linked to appetite and weight regulation in humans.

Comparison of basal leptin levels in 32 CFS subjects, medication free and with no psychiatric comorbidity, and matched controls found no differences (Cleare, Sookdeo, Jones, O'Keane, & Miell, 2001). Thus, there is no evidence that disturbances in leptin secretion underlie the appetite and weight symptoms in CFS.

Melatonin

It has been suggested that melatonin supplementation might be beneficial for reported sleep disturbance or circadian rhythm changes (see following discussion) in CFS. However, in a careful study, Knook, Kavelaars, Sinnema, Kuis, and Heijnen (2000) measured nocturnal (1700 h–0200 h) saliva melatonin in 13 medication-free adolescents with CDC-defined CFS and 15 matched controls. They found increased levels in the patients, rather than the decreased levels they had expected to be associated with impaired sleep quality. In combination with findings of no different (Korszun et al., 1999) or increased (Cleare et al., unpublished data) melatonin levels in adult CFS, there appears to be no rationale for melatonin treatment in CFS. One interpretation of the increased levels of melatonin is that it represents a marker of increased susceptibility to stress-induced hypothalamic disruption (Korszun et al., 1999).

DISTURBANCES IN CIRCADIAN RHYTHMICITY

An interesting hypothesis regarding endocrine influences on symptoms in CFS relates to circadian rhythms. It is hypothesized that a broken circadian cycle (as in jet lag) may be responsible for some symptoms in CFS. Symptoms of jet lag include fatigue, myalgia, sleep rhythm disruption, appetite change, and other somatic symptoms, again paralleling symptoms in CFS (Hamilos et al., 2001).

Relatively few studies have attempted to measure circadian rhythms of hormones or other parameters in CFS. MacHale et al. (1998) demonstrated a significantly attenuated diurnal variation of serum cortisol in CFS, though the absolute concentrations at each time point were not significantly different compared with controls. There was also a significant relationship between the degree of diurnal variation in cortisol and measures of functional capacity. A similar finding of reduced diurnal variation seemed apparent in the study by Hamilos et al. (1998), mainly due to a reduced peak cortisol level. Further support for this comes from the demonstration of a significant decrease in the early morning surge of cortisol in a small group of CFS patients (Demitrack & Crofford, 1998; Papadopoulos et al.,

1997). However, several other studies have not found significant changes in diurnal variation in the circadian rhythm of cortisol (Wood et al., 1998; Young et al., 1998). Once again, any abnormalities found need to be evaluated in the context of similar changes being detectable in fibromyalgia, pain syndromes, and depressive illness (Carroll, Curtis, & Mendels, 1976; Lascelles, Evans, Mersky, & Sabur, 1974; McCain & Tilbe, 1989).

Although most studies show the timing of the circadian cycle of pituitary hormone release or temperature to be essentially normal in CFS (Hamilos et al., 1998, 2001), one study did suggest a desynchronization of the temperature and melatonin rhythms (Williams et al., 1996).

If circadian changes are present in CFS, it is not clear whether they are a primary abnormality or are secondary to disrupted sleep patterns or other behavioral changes. In either case, such circadian changes may well be contributing to some symptoms in CFS; as such, treatments aimed at resynchronizing rhythms may be helpful. Modifying unhelpful sleep patterns is an important component of cognitive behavioral therapy for CFS (Wessely et al., 1998).

IMAGING STUDIES OF ENDOCRINE STRUCTURES

Advances in imaging technology have allowed direct visualization of previously inaccessible small structures such as adrenal glands and brain areas responsible for control of endocrine function.

The results from the ACTH challenge studies suggestion impaired adrenal function led to a study assessing adrenal gland size using computerized tomography (Scott, Teh, Reznek, Martin, Sohaib, & Dinan, 1999). This found significant adrenal gland atrophy, with reductions in right and left limbs of >50%, in 8 CFS subjects compared with a bank of 55 controls. However, since subjects were chosen specifically to have a blunted cortisol response to ACTH, the authors admit that this may not generalize to all CFS subjects; indeed, it is possible that normals selected for low cortisol responses would also show smaller adrenal glands. The finding contrasts with studies showing hypertrophied adrenal glands in depression (Nemeroff et al., 1992).

Only one study has imaged the hippocampus in CFS. It found no evidence of frank atrophy on MRI, but magnetic resonance spectroscopy did find a reduced N-acetylaspartate in the right hippocampus, suggesting some degree of neuronal loss (Brooks, Roberts, Whitehouse, & Majeed, 2000). The finding of hippocampal atrophy is interesting, since it has been linked to the presence of depression and to high cortisol states (McEwen & Magarinos, 1997). Given the high incidence of a history of depression in CFS, hippocampal atrophy may be the result of this history. Whether any hippocampal changes are reversible, or linked to endocrine dysfunction, has not been investigated.

NEUROTRANSMITTER DYSFUNCTION AND NEUROENDOCRINOLOGY IN CFS

SEROTONERGIC SYSTEM

There is a complex interaction between the HPA axis and serotonin systems in the brain. Many studies have demonstrated that glucocorticoids can have an inhibitory effect on central serotonin (5-HT) neurotransmitter function (De Kloet, Sybesma, & Reul, 1986; McAllister-Williams, Ferrier, & Young, 1998), whereas

5-HT is implicated in stress-induced CRH secretion (Delbende et al., 1992; Dinan, 1994). Numerous studies have attempted to determine the functional status of serotonergic systems in CFS by measuring the neuroendocrine responses to challenge with serotonergic drugs. These drugs are thought to act on 5-HT pathways that project from the raphe nuclei to the paraventricular nucleus of the hypothalamus. These in turn stimulate the release of hypothalamic peptides involved in prolactin and ACTH secretion from the anterior pituitary (Checkley, 1980). Measuring the serial prolactin and ACTH or cortisol responses to 5-HT agonist drugs gives a putative index of hypothalamic-5-HT neurotransmitter function.

Several serotonergic drugs have been used in CFS. The first set of studies has used drugs that activate the whole serotonin system rather than specific receptor types. Two studies have used d-fenfluramine, a drug that selectively causes the release of 5-HT from presynaptic neurones, as a challenge (Cleare et al., 1995; Sharpe, Hawton, Clements, & Cowen, 1997). Measuring prolactin and/or cortisol responses to stimulation, both found evidence of enhanced serotonergic responses in CFS subjects selected to be free of comorbid major depression, in contrast to the finding of impaired responses in major depression (Cleare et al., 1995). Furthermore, there was also evidence that the heightened serotonergic responses were inversely related to the lowered basal cortisol levels in one of the studies (Cleare et al., 1995). We suggested that HPA and 5-HT function may be pathologically altered in opposite directions in CFS and depression, and that such alterations may be related to the characteristic symptom profiles, such as insomnia, anorexia, and agitation in depression and the reverse of these in CFS. Two other studies have not found increased responses to fenfluramine (Bearn et al., 1995; Yatham et al., 1995), though methodological factors may explain this. Thus, in one study, there was poor age and gender matching (Bearn et al., 1995), and in another there was significant psychiatric comorbidity (Yatham et al., 1995). The latter study used racemic d,l-fenfluramine, a preparation that is less neurochemically specific than d-fenfluramine, in that it has additional catecholaminergic effects.

Other studies have looked at individual 5-HT receptor function. The first study was by Bakheit, Behan, Dinan, Gray, and O'Keane (1992), who measured the prolactin response to buspirone, a 5-HT_{1A} receptor partial agonist. They found a significantly raised prolactin response in CFS subjects compared with controls, suggesting upregulation of postsynaptic 5-HT_{1A} receptors in the hypothalamus. However, the specificity of buspirone has been questioned, as it is also a D_2 antagonist, an effect likely also to mediate prolactin release (Maskall, Zis, Lam, Clark, & Kuan, 1995; Meltzer, Lowy, Nash, & Koenig, 1991). Sharpe et al. (1996) repeated the challenge test in CFS, but also measured the GH response, since GH release is more likely to be mediated solely by 5-HT_{1A} receptors (Cowen, 1993). Although they confirmed an enhanced prolactin response, GH responses were normal, consistent with the interpretation that abnormalities in dopamine rather than serotonin neurotransmission may underlie the enhanced prolactin response. This latter interpretation also relies on the integrity of the GH axis, a finding confirmed in some but not all studies (see elsewhere in this chapter). Another study used ipsapirone, a more specific 5-HT_{1A} partial agonist than buspirone (Dinan et al., 1997). In healthy controls, there was a dose-dependent rise in ACTH and cortisol, but in CFS the ACTH (but not cortisol) response was significantly attenuated. There are several possible explanations for the finding, including decreased responsivity of 5-HT_{1A} receptors responsible for controlling the HPA axis at the hypothalamic level. However, because this group found decreased responsivity of pituitary CRH receptors (Scott et al., 1998a), the reduced pituitary responsiveness is perhaps a more likely possibility. What is evident from this study is that there is a disturbance of the 5-HT-HPA axis interaction. Further support for there being an abnormality in 5-HT$_{1A}$ receptors comes from a PET study showing reduced binding of the specific 5-HT$_{1A}$ radioligand WAY100635 (Cleare et al., unpublished data).

OPIOIDERGIC SYSTEM

The opioidergic system exerts a predominantly inhibitory influence on the HPA axis in humans (Taylor, Dluhy, & Williams, 1983). Scott, Burnett, Medbak, and Dinan (1998), hypothesized that downregulation of the HPA axis in CFS might be secondary to increased opioidergic tone. They tested this by administering naloxone, an opiate receptor antagonist, to 13 CFS patients and 13 healthy controls. Naloxone reduces the inhibitory opioidergic tone, leading to an acute rise in ACTH levels. CFS subjects showed an attenuation of the ACTH response to naloxone, contrary to the authors' prediction that the hypothesized increased opioidergic tone would heighten the ACTH response. Although there are difficulties in interpreting the results of antagonist challenges such as the naloxone test, they hypothesized that there might be reduced opioidergic tone in CFS. A study that found decreased levels of the opioid b-endorphin (Conti et al., 1998) provided some support for this hypothesis. If true, then decreased opioidergic tone is a potentially interesting finding, since it has also been shown in pain-prone individuals (Terenius & Wahlstrom, 1978) and could theoretically contribute to the symptoms of myalgia, arthralgia, and headaches that are part of the CFS symptomatology (Fukuda et al., 1994).

OTHER NEUROTRANSMITTERS

The study of cerebral spinal fluid (CSF) and plasma by Demitrack et al. (1992) revealed a reduction in the main metabolite of noradrenaline, MHPG. Of interest, therefore, is a study suggesting that fatigued athletes differed from nonfatigued athletes by having lower plasma noradrenaline (Odagiri, Shimomitsu, Iwane, & Katsumura, 1996). However, no studies of noradrenergic function in CFS have been published. There has been one study investigating cholinergic function in CFS, which used the growth hormone response to pyridostigmine, an anticholinesterase inhibitor. CFS patients showed enhanced responsivity, suggesting upregulated cholinergic receptors (Chaudhuri, Majeed, Dinan, & Behan, 1997). However, the results need to be interpreted with the possible GH system dysfunction in mind.

GENETICS AND NEUROENDOCRINE DYSFUNCTION IN CFS

An exciting development in the area was described in a paper by Torpy and colleagues (Torpy et al., 2001). The results open up speculation that in a small number of subjects with CFS, there may be a genetic basis for the observed HPA axis abnormalities. Torpy and colleagues described a pedigree in which they were able to identify a novel mutation in the gene controlling the production of corticosteroid-binding globulin (CBG). Among the 32 family members tested, 3 were homozygous for the mutation and had no detectable CBG, while 19 were heterozygotes, with levels reduced by approximately 50% from the normal reference range. Total cortisol levels were very low in the homozygotes and positively correlated with CBG levels in the heterozygotes, but free cortisol levels were similar in all members. Of interest was the finding that 86% of the heterozygotes and two thirds of the homozygotes had troublesome chronic fatigue that met the CDC criteria for idiopathic chronic fatigue. Five of these cases met full criteria for CFS, and other pain syndromes and fibromyalgia were also commonly present. Based on these results, the authors suggest that the CBG abnormalities may be directly related to the pathophysiology of fatigue in this pedigree. They suggest that further pedigrees be sought to confirm these findings, and also that mutations for CBG should be sought in cases of CFS or idiopathic chronic fatigue. A further suggestion is that those with identifiable CBG abnormalities may be the most likely to respond to hydrocortisone therapy, as described in this chapter.

The accumulating evidence of a genetic predisposition for chronic fatigue in general (Roy-Byrne et al., 2002), indicates that searches for specific genes that mediate this predisposition may prove fruitful. However, in CFS in general, there is not an evident reduction in CBG. Studies to date that have measured CBG in unselected samples have found raised levels (Demitrack et al., 1991).

ENDOCRINE TREATMENTS FOR CFS

Effective treatments for CFS remain a goal for future development. The most successful treatments to date have been rehabilitation strategies based on cognitive-behavioral or graded exercise principles, while few drug therapies have been found helpful in well-conducted randomized controlled trials (RCTs) to date (Whiting et al., 2001). Do the possible endocrine disturbances present in CFS open up a new avenue for treatment? This section reviews the studies performed to answer this question.

HYDROCORTISONE

If low circulating cortisol may mediate some or all of the symptoms in CFS, replacement of the hypothesized deficiency should lead to improvements in those symptoms. Two randomized controlled trials have tested this hypothesis. The first, by McKenzie et al. (Mckenzie et al., 1998) prescribed hydrocortisone in a dose regimen attempting to approximate the normal diurnal variation in cortisol (13 mg/m^2 [about 20–30 mg] at 8 A.M., and 3 mg/m^2 [about 5 mg] at 2 P.M., daily). Seventy patients with CDC-defined CFS (many with comorbid psychiatric diagnoses) were randomized to receive active or placebo treatment for 3 months. There was a moderate but significant benefit detectable on a global health scale completed daily by patients, though not on other more specific measures of fatigue or disability. However, endocrine assessment revealed significant adrenal suppression in 12 out of 33 patients on hydrocortisone; as the authors noted, such a high rate of a potentially serious side effect precludes the use of this dose of hydrocortisone. We carried out a second study (Cleare et al., 1999) using much lower doses: 5 mg to 10 mg hydrocortisone given at 9 A.M. This dose was chosen to represent the amount of hydrocortisone likely to replace the observed reduction of approximately 30% in 24-hour UFC seen in the previous studies. Thirty-two subjects entered a randomized, crossover study, taking each treatment for 28 days. There was a clinically significant fall in fatigue scores in 34% on active treatment (most of whom (28%) reported levels of fatigue at or below the population median score), compared with 13% (9%) on placebo. There were accompanying reductions in self-rated disability scores in those whose fatigue improved. Importantly, on this dose of hydrocortisone, there was no significant adrenal suppression, and no other serious adverse effects.

Although the pretreatment endocrine status did not predict who would respond to treatment, those patients who responded to treatment showed a normalization of their pretreatment blunted cortisol response to CRH (Cleare, Miell, et al., 2001). Similarly, there were other measurable physiological effects of hydrocortisone (such as increased leptin levels) that differentiated responders from nonresponders (Cleare et al., 2000), suggesting that those who responded may have had upregulated glucocorticoid receptors. This ties in with the results of studies showing enhanced glucocorticoid receptors in CFS. Overall, these findings support the contention that low cortisol levels (or correlates of low cortisol levels) may contribute to symptoms and disability in CFS. However, our study was short term only, and the positive effects wore off rapidly on the switch to placebo. Routine use of this strategy as a treatment is not recommended without further evaluation.

DHEA

A similar approach has been suggested for DHEA, to replace a hypothesized deficit. As discussed, there is also conflicting evidence for the assumption that DHEA is reduced in CFS. Nevertheless, there has been one pilot study of the administration of DHEA (Himmel & Seligman, 1999); this investigated 23 female subjects with CFS who had been specifically chosen to have suboptimal levels of DHEA at baseline (defined as <2.0 mg/ml). Subjects received a mean dose of 58 mg/day DHEA for 6 months in an open study. The mean DHEA level rose from 0.88 to 4.12 mg/ml in this period. Modest improvements were seen in fatigue, pain, and mood, but the open nature of the study, the selected nature of the subjects and the lack of a placebo control group limit any conclusions that can be drawn from this.

FLUDROCORTISONE

The use of fludrocortisone is based on a different set of observations: the putative presence of autonomic disturbances in CFS. Fludrocortisone is used, with or without a high salt diet, as a treatment for these, rather than as a replacement for any hypothesized mineralocorticoid deficit. Nevertheless, there have been claims that a combined glucocorticoid and mineralocorticoid treatment is likely to be most effective, despite the lack of any supporting evidence (Baschetti, 1999). An initial uncontrolled trial of fludrocortisone was positive (Bou-Holaigah, Rowe, Kan, & Calkins, 1995). However, subsequent well-powered randomized trials have shown no effect of fludrocortisone over placebo, and researchers have concluded that this is an ineffective strategy (Peterson et al., 1998; Rowe et al., 2001).

GROWTH HORMONE

Based on their findings of impaired GH function in CFS (a situation not present in other large studies of GH function, as noted) Moorkens et al. (Moorkens, Wynants, & Abs, 1998) carried out a small randomized controlled trial of GH hormone replacement in CFS. They selected 20 patients with a demonstrated deficiency of GH, defined as a peak nocturnal level <10 mg/l. Patients entered a double-blind phase of 3 months on GH or placebo followed by a 9-month open phase. After 12 months of therapy, there was no overall improvement in questionnaire measures of quality of life, despite improvements in measures of GH function. Thus, despite some abnormal findings in some samples, there seems little compelling evidence that GH dysfunction plays a major role in the symptomatology of CFS.

ENDOCRINE CHANGES IN FIBROMYALGIA, A RELATED DISORDER

Fibromyalgia is a condition defined by widespread muscle pain and the presence of tender points, but it is also characterized by fatigue and sleep disturbances. Most authors agree that the symptomatology of fibromyalgia overlaps with CFS, and some now believe that the two are essentially the same condition (Wessely, Nimuan, & Sharpe, 1999). Of particular interest to this chapter are the findings from neuroendocrine studies. On many, but not all endocrine parameters, there are marked similarities between fibromyalgia and CFS. Several studies have now demonstrated reduced 24-hour urinary free cortisol in patients with fibromyalgia (Crofford et al., 1994; McCain, Cameron, & Kennedy, 1989). Also, fibromyalgia patients show a blunted HPA axis response to exhaustive physical exercise (van Denderen, Boersma, Zeinstra, Hollander, & van Neerbos, 1992) and to exogenous CRH (Griep, Boersma, & de Kloet, 1993). In contrast to CFS, however, studies have also found *enhanced* ACTH responses to CRH stimulation (Crofford et al., 1994; Griep et al., 1993). The reason for this divergence is not clear, though one explanation suggests differential changes in AVP between the conditions (Demitrack, 1997). Whereas in CFS, AVP levels have been found to be low (Bakheit et al., 1993), the AVP response to postural challenge seems to be high in fibromyalgia. Since AVP acts synergistically with CRH to release ACTH, these alterations in AVP are consistent with the differences demonstrated in ACTH responses for the two syndromes.

One of the earlier observations in fibromyalgia was that there was a distinct disturbance of Stage 4, non-REM sleep, characterized by alpha-wave intrusion into the delta rhythm (Moldofsky, Scarisbrick, England, & Smythe, 1975). Furthermore, depriving healthy subjects of this stage of sleep leads to symptoms similar to those seen in fibromyalgia. Since approximately 80% of the total daily production of GH is secreted during this stage of sleep, R. Bennett, Clark, Campbell, and Burckhardt (1992) hypothesized, and found, low levels of IGF-1 in fibromyalgia. Whether these low levels are etiologically related to muscle pain is not yet clear, and the findings have not been replicated by others (Buchwald et al., 1996). Nevertheless, Bennett and colleagues followed up their earlier finding of low IGF-1 levels in 30% of patients by conducting a randomized, double-blind, controlled trial of growth hormone replacement (R. Bennett, Clark, & Walczyk, 1998). However, they only included those who had low levels of the IGF-1. Daily subcutaneous growth hormone injections resulted in a sustained increase in IGF-1 levels, and at 9 months, a significant overall improvement in symptomatology and number of tender points. The authors conclude that although the high cost-benefit ratio precludes its therapeutic use in fibromyalgia patients as a whole, the study provides further support for the theory that a secondary growth hormone deficiency may be responsible for some of their symptoms.

Thus, comparison of CFS with fibromyalgia highlights both similarities and differences in neuroendocrinology. It may be that the differences reflect distinct pathophysiologies for the two syndromes. However, the similarities, in both reduced HPA activation, symptomatology, and abrupt stress-related onset, suggest some common etiology for some patients. It may also be that some of the hormonal differences arise from differences in behavioral adaptation to chronic fatigue and chronic pain. Further studies are needed that make direct comparisons between fibromyalgia and CFS on biological, behavioral, psychological, and symptom variables.

CONCLUSION

Chronic fatigue syndrome is most likely a heterogeneous condition with a multifactorial origin. One of these factors is likely to include disturbances to neuroendocrine systems. Most studied to date has been the HPA axis, and on balance, there appears to be reduced HPA axis function in at least some patients. Evidence from the trials of replacement therapy have linked this to symptom production or persistence. However, the site and etiology of the disturbance in the axis remains unclear, and several interpretations of the data are available. It remains possible that central correlates of low circulating cortisol, such as CRH or serotonin abnormalities, mediate the link with fatigue and other symptoms. Furthermore, because many factors may impinge on the HPA axis in CFS, such as inactivity, sleep disturbance, psychiatric comorbidity, medication, and ongoing stress, HPA axis disturbance is likely to be heterogeneous and of multifactorial etiology.

Some models of CFS attempt to separate those factors that act as risk factors, or predisposing factors, those that act as triggers, or precipitating factors, and those that act to prolong the condition, or perpetuating factors (Wessely et al., 1998). This approach has not yet been adequately applied to endocrine disturbances because most studies have been undertaken on patients ill for several years.

To obtain a clearer assessment of the etiologic and pathophysiological relevance of endocrine changes in CFS, several future directions are likely to be useful. First, to study the importance of endocrine disturbances at the onset of the illness, prospective cohort studies in groups at high risk of CFS are needed. These might include EBV infection (Candy et al., in press), major surgery (Salmon & Hall, 1997), and those previously treated for cancer (Loge, Abrahamsen, Ekeberg, & Kaasa, 1999). It may also be useful to test patients before and after recovery from CFS, to identify those abnormalities that may relate to symptoms, those that may be epiphenomena, and those that may be trait markers. Finally, it is vital to undertake full multidimensional assessments in these studies. Without detailed measurement of the confounding features outlined in this review, there is little likelihood of unraveling the influence of those factors on the observed endocrine changes in CFS.

REFERENCES

Allain, T. J., Bearn, J. A., Coskeran, P., Jones, J., Checkley, A., Butler, J., et al. (1997). Changes in growth hormone, insulin, insulin like growth factors (IGFs), and IGF-binding protein-1 in chronic fatigue syndrome. *Biological Psychiatry, 41*(5), 567–573.

Altemus, M., Dale, J. K., Michelson, D., Demitrack, M. A., Gold, P. W., & Straus, S. E. (2001). Abnormalities in response to vasopressin infusion in chronic fatigue syndrome. *Psychoneuroendocrinology, 26,* 175–188.

Antoni, F. (1993). Vasopressinergic control of pituitary adenocorticotrophin secretion comes of age. *Frontiers in Neuroendocrinology, 14,* 76–122.

Avgerinos, P. C., Chrousos, G. P., Nieman, L. K., Oldfield, E. H., Loriaux, D. L., & Cutler, B. G. (1987). The CRH test in the postoperative evaluation of patients with Cushing's syndrome. *Journal of Clinical Endocrinology and Metabolism, 65,* 906–913.

Bakheit, A., Behan, P., Dinan, T., Gray, C., & O'Keane, V. (1992). Possible upregulation of hypothalamic 5-hydroxytryptamine receptors in patients with postviral fatigue syndrome. *British Medical Journal, 304,* 1010–1012.

Bakheit, A. M., Behan, P. O., Watson, W. S., & Morton, J. J. (1993). Abnormal arginine-vasopressin secretion and water metabolism in patients with postviral fatigue syndrome. *Acta Neurologica Scandinavica, 87,* 234–238.

Barrett-Connor, E., von Muhlen, D., Laughlin, G. A., & Kripke, A. (1999). Endogenous levels of dehydroepiandrosterone sulfate, but not other sex hormones, are associated with depressed mood in older women: The Rancho Bernardo Study. *Journal of the American Geriatrics Society, 47,* 685–691.

Baschetti, R. (1999). Investigations of hydrocortisone and fludrocortisone in the treatment of chronic fatigue syndrome. *Journal of Clinical Endocrinology and Metabolism, 84*(6), 2263–2264.

Baulieu, E.-E. (1996). Dehydroepiandrosterone (DHEA): A fountain of youth? *Journal of Clinical Endocrinology and Metabolism, 81,* 3147–3151.

Baxter, J. D., & Tyrel, J. B. (1981). The adrenal cortex. In P. Felig, J. D. Baxter, A. E. Broadus, & L. A. Frohman (Eds.), *Endocrinology and metabolism* (pp. 385–510). New York: McGraw-Hill.

Bearn, J., Allain, T., Coskeran, P., Munro, N., Butler, J., McGregor, A., et al. (1995). Neuroendocrine responses to d-fenfluramine and insulin-induced hypoglycemia in chronic fatigue syndrome. *Biological Psychiatry, 37*(4), 245–252.

Bennett, A. L., Mayes, D. M., Fagioli, L. R., Guerriero, R., & Komaroff, A. L. (1997). Somatomedin C (insulin-like growth factor I) levels in patients with chronic fatigue syndrome. *Journal of Psychiatric Research, 31,* 91–96.

Bennett, R., Clark, S., Campbell, S., & Burckhardt, C. (1992). Low levels of somatomedin C in patients with fibromyalgia. *Arthritis and Rheumatology, 35,* 1113–1116.

Bennett, R., Clark, S., & Walczyk, J. (1998). A randomised, double-blind, placebo-controlled study of growth hormone in the treatment of fibromyalgia. *American Journal of Medicine, 104,* 227–231.

Berwaerts, J., Moorkens, G., & Abs, R. (1998). Secretion of growth hormone in patients with chronic fatigue syndrome. *Growth Hormone and IGF Research, 8,* 127–129.

Bou-Holaigah, I., Rowe, P., Kan, J., & Calkins, H. (1995). The relationship between neurally mediated hypotension and the chronic fatigue syndrome. *Journal of the American Medical Association, 274,* 961–967.

Brooks, J., Roberts, N., Whitehouse, G., & Majeed, T. (2000). Proton magnetic resonance spectroscopy and morphometry of the hippocampus in chronic fatigue syndrome. *British Journal of Radiology, 73,* 1206–1208.

Brosnan, C. M., & Cowing, N. F. C. (1996). Addison's disease. *British Medical Journal, 312,* 1085–1087.

Buchwald, D., Umali, J., & Stene, M. (1996). Insulin-like growth factor-I (somatomedin C) levels in chronic fatigue syndrome and fibromyalgia. *Journal of Rheumatology, 23,* 739–742.

Candy, B., Chalder, T., Cleare, A. J., Wessely, S., Peakman, M., Zuckerman, M., et al. (in press). Predictors of fatigue following the onset of infectious mononucleosis. *Psychological Medicine.*

Carroll, B., Curtis, G., & Mendels, J. (1976). Neuroendocrine regulation in depression. I: Limbc system-adrenocortical dysfunction. *Archives of General Psychiatry, 33*(9), 1039–1044.

Chaudhuri, A., Majeed, T., Dinan, T., & Behan, P. O. (1997). Chronic fatigue syndrome: A disorder of central cholinergic neurotransmission. *Journal of Chronic Fatigue Syndrome, 3,* 3–16.

Checkley, S. A. (1980). Neuroendocrine tests of monoamine function in man: A review of basic theory and its application to the study of depressive illness. *Psychological Medicine, 10,* 35–53.

Cleare, A. J. (2002). Hydrocortisone treatment in CFS, *International Journal of Neuropsychopharmacology, 5*(Suppl. 1), S37.

Cleare, A. J., Bearn, J., Allain, T., McGregor, A., Wessely, S., Murray, R. M., et al. (1995). Contrasting neuroendocrine responses in depression and chronic fatigue syndrome. *Journal of Affective Disorders, 35*(4), 239–283.

Cleare, A. J., Blair, D., Chambers, S., & Wessely, S. (2001). Urinary free cortisol in chronic fatigue syndrome. *American Journal of Psychiatry, 158,* 641–643.

Cleare, A. J., Heap, E., Malhi, G. S., Wessely, S., O'Keane, V., & Miell, J. (1999). Low-dose hydrocortisone in chronic fatigue syndrome: A randomised crossover trial. *Lancet, 353,* 455–458.

Cleare, A. J., Miell, J., Heap, E., Sookdeo, S., Young, L., Malhi, G. S., et al. (2001). Hypothalamo-pituitary-adrenal axis function in chronic fatigue syndrome, and the effects of low-dose hydrocortisone therapy. *Journal of Clinical Endocrinology and Metabolism, 86*(8), 3545–3554.

Cleare, A. J., Sookdeo, S. S., Jones, J., O'Keane, V., & Miell, J. P. (2000). Integrity of the growth hormone/insulin-like growth factor system is maintained in patients with chronic fatigue syndrome. *Journal of Clinical Endocrinology and Metabolism, 85,* 1433–1439.

Cleare, A. J., Sookdeo, S. S., Jones, J., O'Keane, V., & Miell, J. P. (2001). Plasma leptin in chronic fatigue syndrome, and a placebo-controlled study of the effects of low-dose hydrocortisone on leptin secretion. *Clinical Endocrinology, 55,* 113-119.

Cleare, A. J., & Wessely, S. C. (1996). Chronic fatigue syndrome: A stress disorder? *British Journal of Hospital Medicine, 55,* 571–574.

Cleare, A. J., et al. (unpublished data). (Preliminary data presented at British Association for Psychopharmacology Summer Meeting 2000, Cambridge, UK).

Conti, F., Pittoni, V., Sacerdote, P., Priori, R., Meroni, P. L., & Valesini, G. (1998). Decreased immunoreactive beta-endorphin in mononuclear leucocytes from patients with chronic fatigue syndrome. *Clinical and Experimental Rheumatology, 16,* 729–732.

Cowen, P. J. (1993). Serotonin receptor subtypes in depression: Evidence from studies in neuroendocrine regulation. *Clinical Neuropharmacol, 16,* 0362–5664.

Crofford, L., Pillemer, S., Kalogeras, K., Cash, J. M., Michelson, D., Kling, M. A., et al. (1994). Hypothalamic-pituitary-adrenal axis perturbations in patients with fibromyalgia. *Arthritis and Rheumatism, 37*(11), 1583–1592.

De Becker, P., De Meirleir, K., Joos, E., Campine, I., Van Steenberge, E., Smitz, J., et al. (1999). Dehydroepiandrosterone (DHEA) response to i.v. ACTH in patients with chronic fatigue syndrome. *Hormone and Metabolic Research, 31*, 18–21.

De Bellis, M., Chrousos, G., Dorn, L., Burke, L., Helmers, K., Kling, M. A., et al. (1994). Hypothalamic-pituitary-adrenal axis dysregulation in sexually abused girls. *Journal of Clinical Endocrinology and Metabolism, 78*(72), 249–255.

DeBold, C. R., Sheldon, W. R., DeCherney, G. S., Jackson, R. V., Alexander, A. N., Vale, W., et al. (1984). Argenine vasopressin potentiates adrenocorticotrophin release induced by corticotropin releasing factor. *Journal of Clinical Investigation, 73*, 533–538.

De Kloet, E., Sybesma, H., & Reul, J. (1986). Selective control by corticosterone of serotonin-1 receptors capacity in raphe-hippocampal system. *Neuroendocrinology, 42*, 513–521.

Delbende, C., Delarue, C., Lefebvre, H., Bunel, D. T., Szafarczyk, A., Mocaer, E., et al. (1992). Glucocorticoids, transmitters, and stress. *British Journal of Psychiatry* (Suppl. 15), 24–35.

Demitrack, M. (1997). Neuroendocrine correlates of chronic fatigue syndrome: A brief review. *Journal of Psychiatric Research, 31*, 69–82.

Demitrack, M., & Crofford, L. (1998). Evidence for and pathophysiologic implications of hypothalamic-pituitary-adrenal axis dysregulation in fibromyalgia and chronic fatigue syndrome. *Annals of the New York Academy of Sciences, 840*, 684–697.

Demitrack, M. A., Dale, J. K., Straus, S. E., Laue, L., Listwak, S. J., Kruesi, M. J., et al. (1991). Evidence for impaired activation of the hypothalamic-pituitary-adrenal axis in patients with chronic fatigue syndrome. *Journal of Clinical Endocrinology and Metabolism, 73*(6), 1224–1234.

Demitrack, M., Gold, P., Dale, J., Krahan, D., Kling, M., & Straus, S. (1992). Plasma and cerebrospinal fluid monoamine metabolism in patients with chronic fatigue syndrome: Preliminary findings. *Biological Psychiatry, 32*, 1065–1077.

Dinan, T. G. (1994). Glucocorticoids and the genesis of depressive illness: A psychobiological model. *British Journal of Psychiatry, 164*, 365–371.

Dinan, T. G. (1998). Psychoneuroendocrinology of depression: Growth hormone. *Psychological Clinics of North America, 21*, 325–339.

Dinan, T. G., Majeed, T., Lavelle, E., Scott, L. V., Berti, C., & Behan, P. (1997). Blunted serotonin-mediated activation of the hypothalamic-pituitary-adrenal axis in chronic fatigue syndrome. *Psychoneuroendocrinology, 22*, 261–267.

Fukuda, K., Straus, S., Hickie, I., Sharpe, M., Dobbins, J., & Komaroff, A. (1994). The chronic fatigue syndrome: A comprehensive approach to its definition and study. *Annals of Internal Medicine, 121*, 953–959.

Gaab, J., Huster, D., Peisen, R., et al. (2002a). Hypothalamus-pituitary-adrenal axis reactivity in chronic fatigue syndrome and health under psychological, physiological, and pharmacological stimulation. *Psychosomatic Medicine, 64* 951–962.

Gaab, J., Huster, D., Peisen, R., et al. (2002b). The low dose dexamethasone suppression test in chronic fatigue syndrome and health. *Psychosomatic Medicine, 64*, 311–318.

Goenjian, A. K., Yehuda, R., Pynoos, R. S., Steinberg, A. M., Tashjian, M., Yang, R. K., et al. (1996). Basal cortisol, dexamethasone suppression of cortisol, and MHPG in adolescents after the 1988 earthquake in Armenia. *American Journal of Psychiatry, 153*, 929–934.

Gold, P. W., Licinio, J., Wong, M. L., & Chrousos, G. P. (1995). Corticotropin releasing hormone in the pathophysiology of melancholic and atypical depression and in the mechanism of action of antidepressant drugs. *Annals of the New York Academy of Sciences, 771*, 716–729.

Griep, E., Boersma, J., & de Kloet, R. (1993). Altered reactivity of the hypothalamic-pituitary adrenal axis in the primary fibromyalgia syndrome. *Journal of Rheumatology, 20,* 469–474.

Grinspoon, S. K., & Biller, B. M. (1994). Clinical review 62: Laboratory assessment of adrenal insufficiency. *Journal of Clinical Endocrinology and Metabolism, 79,* 923–931.

Hamilos, D. L., Nutter, D., Gershtenson, J., Ikle, D. I., Hamilos, S. S., Redmond, D. P., et al. (2001). Circadian rhythm of core body temperature in subjects with chronic fatigue syndrome. *Clinical Physiology, 21*(2), 184–195.

Hamilos, D. L., Nutter, D., Gershtenson, J., Redmond, D. P., Clementi, J. D., Schmaling, K. B., et al. (1998). Core body temperature is normal in chronic fatigue syndrome. *Biological Psychiatry, 43*(4), 293–302.

Harvey, A., Purdie, G., Bushnell, J., & Ellis, P. (2001). Are cortisol levels low in chronic fatigue syndrome? A meta-analysis. *AHMF conference.* Third International Clinical and Scientific Meeting on ME/CFS. Sydney, Australia, www.ahmf.org/01harvey.html.

Heim, C., Ehlert, U., Hanker, J. P., & Hellhammer, D. H. (1998). Abuse-related posttraumatic stress disorder and alterations of the hypothalamic-pituitary-adrenal axis in women with chronic pelvic pain. *Psychosomatic Medicine, 60,* 309–618.

Heim, C., Ehlert, U., & Hellhammer, D. H. (2000). The potential role of hypocortisolism in the pathophysiology of stress-related bodily disorders. *Psychoneuroendocrinology, 25,* 1–35.

Heim, C., Newport, D. J., Heit, S., Graham, Y. P., Wilcox, M., Bonsall, R., et al. (2000). Pituitary-adrenal and autonomic responses to stress in women after sexual and physical abuse in childhood. *Journal of the American Medical Association, 284*(5), 592–597.

Himmel, P., & Seligman, T. (1999). A pilot study employing dehydroepiandrosterone (DHEA) in the treatment of chronic fatigue syndrome. *Journal of Clinical Rheumatology, 5,* 56–59.

Holmes, G., Kaplan, J., Gantz, N. M., Komaroff, A. L., Schonberger, L. B., Straus, S. E., et al. (1988). Chronic fatigue syndrome: A working case definition. *Annals of International Medicine, 108*(3), 387–389.

Hudson, M., & Cleare, A. J. (1999). The 1microg short synacthen test in chronic fatigue syndrome. *Clinical Endocrinology, 51,* 625–630.

Hyyppa, M., Lindholm, T., Lehtinen, V., & Puukka, P. (1993). Self-perceived fatigue and cortisol secretion in a community sample. *Journal of Psychosomatic Research, 37,* 589–594.

Kavelaars, A., Kuis, W., Knook, L., Sinnema, G., & Heijnen, C. J. (2000). Disturbed neuroendocrine-immune interactions in chronic fatigue syndrome. *Journal of Clinical Endocrinology and Metabolism, 85,* 692–696.

Kirschbaum, C., & Hellhammer, D. H. (1994). Salivary cortisol in psychoneuroendocrine research: Recent developments and applications. *Psychoneuroendocrinology, 19,* 313–333.

Knook, L., Kavelaars, A., Sinnema, G., Kuis, W., & Heijnen, C. J. (2000). High nocturnal melatonin in adolescents with chronic fatigue syndrome. *Journal of Clinical Endocrinology and Metabolism, 85,* 3690–3692.

Korszun, A., Sackett-Lundeen, L., Papadopoulos, E., Brucksch, C., Masterson, L., Engelberg, N. C., et al. (1999). Melatonin levels in women with fibromyalgia and chronic fatigue syndrome. *Journal of Rheumatology, 26*(12), 2675–2680.

Kuratsune, H., Yamaguti, K., Sawada, M., Kodate, S., Machii, T., Kanakura Y., et al. (1998). Dehydroepiandrosterone sulfate deficiency in chronic fatigue syndrome. *International Journal of Molecular Medicine, 1*(1), 143–146.

Lamberts, S., Verleun, S., Oosteron, R., DeJong, F., & Hackeng, W. (1984). Corticotrophin-releasing factor (ovine) and vasopressin exert a synergistic effect on adrenocorticotropin release in man. *Journal of Clinical Endocrinology and Metabolism, 58,* 298–303.

Lascelles, P., Evans, P., Mersky, H., & Sabur, M. (1974). Plasma cortisol in psychiatric and neurological patients with pain. *Brain, 97,* 533–538.

Lavelle, E., & Dinan, T. G. (1996). *Hypothalamo-pituitary-adrenal axis function in chronic fatigue syndrome: A study of fast feedback mechanisms.* Royal College of Surgeons of Ireland research meeting, Dublin.

Loge, J., Abrahamsen, A., Ekeberg, O., & Kaasa, S. (1999). Hodgkin's disease survivors more fatigued than the general population. *Journal of Clinical Oncology, 17,* 253–261.

MacHale, S. M., Cavanagh, J. T., Bennie, J., Carroll, S., Goodwin, G. M., & Lawrie, S. M. (1998). Diurnal variation of adrenocortical activity in chronic fatigue syndrome. *Neuropsychobiology, 38,* 213–217.

Majeed, T., Dinan, T., Thakore, J., Gray, C., & Behan, P. (1995). Defective dexamethasone induced growth hormone release in chronic fatigue syndrome; evidence for glucocorticoid receptor resistance and lack of plasticity? *Irish Colleges of Physicians and Surgeons, 24,* 20–24.

Maskall, D. D., Zis, A. P., Lam, R. W., Clark, C. M., & Kuan, A. J. (1995). Prolactin response to buspirone challenge in the presence of dopaminergic blockade. *Biological Psychiatry, 38,* 235–239.

McAllister-Williams, R. H., Ferrier, I. N., & Young, A. H. (1998). Mood and neuropsychological function in depression: The role of corticosteroids and serotonin. *Psychological Medicine, 28,* 573–584.

McCain, G., Cameron, R., & Kennedy, J. (1989). The problem of long-term disability payments and litigation in primary fibromyalgia. *Journal of Rheumatology, 16*(Suppl. 19), 174–176.

McCain, G., & Tilbe, K. (1989). Diurnal hormone variation in fibromyalgia syndrome: A comparison with rheumatoid arthritis. *Journal of Rheumatology, 16*(Suppl. 19), 154–157.

McEwen, B. S., & Magarinos, A. M. (1997). Stress effects on morphology and function of the hippocampus. *Annals of the New York Academy of Sciences, 821,* 271–284.

McKenzie, R., O'Fallon, A., Dale, J., Demitrack, M., Sharma, G., Deloria, M., et al. (1998). Low-dose hydrocortisone treatment of chronic fatigue syndrome: Results of a placebo-controlled study of its efficacy and safety. *Journal of the American Medical Association, 280,* 1061–1066.

Meltzer, H. G. G., Lowy, M., Nash, J., & Koenig, J. (1991). Effects of buspirone: Mediation by dopaminergic and serotonergic mechanisms. In G. Tunnicliff, A. S. Eison, & O. P. Taylor (Eds.), *Buspirone: Mechanisms and clinical aspects* (pp. 177–192). San Diego, CA: Academic Press.

Moldofsky, H., Scarisbrick, P., England, R., & Smythe, H. (1975). Musculoskeletal symptoms and non-REM sleep disturbances in patients with fibrositis syndrome and healthy subjects. *Psychosomatic Medicine, 37,* 341–351.

Moorkens, G., Berwaerts, J., Wynants, H., & Abs, R. (2000). Characterization of pituitary function with emphasis on GH secretion in the chronic fatigue syndrome. *Clinical Endocrinology, 53,* 99–106.

Moorkens, G., Wynants, H., & Abs, R. (1998). Effect of growth hormone treatment in patients with chronic fatigue syndrome: A preliminary study. *Growth Hormone and IGF Research, 8,* 131–133.

Nemeroff, C. B., Krishnan, K. R., Reed, D., Leder, R., Beam, C., & Dunnick, N. R. (1992). Adrenal gland enlargement in major depression: A computed tomographic study. *Archives of General Psychiatry, 49,* 384–387.

Odagiri, Y., Shimomitsu, T., Iwane, H., & Katsumura, T. (1996). Relationships between exhaustive mood state and changes in stress hormones following an ultraendurance race. *International Journal of Sports Medicine, 17,* 325–331.

Ottenweller, J. E., Sisto, S. A., McCarty, R. C., & Natelson, B. H. (2001). Hormonal responses to exercise in chronic fatigue syndrome. *Neuropsychobiology, 43,* 34–41.

Papadopoulos, E., Crofford, L. J., Engleberg, N. C., Korszun, A., Brucksch, C., Eisner, S., et al. (1997). Impaired HPA axis activity in chronic fatigue syndrome and fibromyalgia. *Society of Biological Psychiatry, 41*(7) (Supp. 11), S29.

Parker, A. J. R., Wessely, S., & Cleare, A. J. (2001). The neuroendocrinology of chronic fatigue syndrome and fibromyalgia. *Psychological Medicine, 31,* 1331–1345.

Peterson, P. K., Pheley, A., Schroeppel, J., Schenck, C., Marshall, P., Kind, A., et al. (1998). A preliminary placebo-controlled crossover trial of fludrocortisone for chronic fatigue syndrome. *Archives of Internal Medicine, 158*(8), 908–914.

Poland, R. E., Lin, K.-M., Lutchmansingh, P., & McCracken, J. P. (1996). *Biological markers in CFS and neurasthenia.* X World Congress of Psychiatry, Madrid, Spain.

Poteliakhoff, A. (1981). Adrenocortical activity and some clinical findings in chronic fatigue. *Journal of Psychosomatic Research, 25,* 91–95.

Pruessner, J. C., Hellhammer, D. H., & Kirschbaum, C. (1999). Burnout, perceived stress, and cortisol responses to awakening. *Psychosomatic Medicine, 61,* 197–204.

Rasmuson, S., Olsson, T., & Hagg, E. (1996). A low dose ACTH test to assess the function of the hypothalamic-pituitary-adrenal axis. *Clinical Endocrinology, 44,* 151–156.

Raven, P., & Taylor, N. F. (1996). Sex differences in the human metabolism of cortisol. *Endocrine Research, 22,* 751–755.

Riordain, D., Farley, D., Young, W., Grant, C., & van Heerden, J. (1994). Long term outcome of bilateral adrenalectomy in patients with Cushing's syndrome. *Surgery, 116,* 1088–1093.

Rowe, P. C., Calkins, H., DeBusk, K., McKenzie, R., Anand, R., Sharma, G., et al. (2001). Fludrocortisone acetate to treat neurally mediated hypotension in chronic fatigue syndrome: A randomised controlled trial. *Journal of the American Medical Association, 285,* 52–59.

Roy-Byrne, P., Afari, N., Ashton, S., Fischer, M., Goldberg, J., & Buchwald, D. (2002). Chronic fatigue and anxiety/depression: A twin study. *British Journal of Psychiatry, 180,* 29–34.

Salata, R. A., Jarrett, D. B., Verbalis, J. G., & Robinson, A. G. (1988). Vasopressin stimulation of adrenocorticotropin hormone (ACTH) in humans: In vivo bioassay of corticotropin-releasing factor (CRF), which provides evidence for CRF mediation of the diurnal rhythm of ACTH. *Journal of Clinical Investigation, 81,* 766–774.

Salmon, P., & Hall, G. M. (1997). A theory of postoperative fatigue: An interaction of biological, psychological, and social processes. *Pharmacology, Biochemistry, and Behavior, 56,* 623–628.

Schluederberg, A., Straus, S. E., Peterson, P., Blumenthal, S., Komaroff, A. L., Spring, S. B., et al. (1992). Chronic fatigue syndrome research: Definition and medical outcome assessment [NIH conference]. *Annals of Internal Medicine, 117,* 325–331.

Scott, L., Burnett, F., Medbak, S., & Dinan, T. (1998). Naloxone-mediated activation of the hypothalamic-pituitary-adrenal axis in chronic fatigue syndrome. *Psychological Medicine, 28,* 285–293.

Scott, L., & Dinan, T. (1998). Urinary free cortisol excretion in chronic fatigue syndrome, major depression and in healthy volunteers. *Journal of Affective Disorders, 47,* 49–54.

Scott, L., & Dinan, T. (1999). Neuro-endocrine abnormalities in chronic fatigue syndrome: Focus on the stress axis. *Balliere's Clinical Psychiatry, 3,* 419–432.

Scott, L. V., Medbak, S., & Dinan, T. G. (1998a). Blunted adrenocorticotropin and cortisol responses to corticotropin-releasing hormone stimulation in chronic fatigue syndrome. *Acta Psychiatrica Scandinavica, 97,* 450–457.

Scott, L. V., Medbak, S., & Dinan, T. G. (1998b). The low dose adrenocorticotropin test in chronic fatigue syndrome and in health. *Clinical Endocrinology, 48,* 733–737.

Scott, L. V., Medbak, S., & Dinan, T. G. (1999). Desmopressin augments pituitary-adrenal responsivity to corticotropin-releasing hormone in subjects with chronic fatigue syndrome and in healthy volunteers. *Biological Psychiatry, 45*(11), 1447–1454.

Scott, L. V., Salahuddin, F., Cooney, J., Svec, F., & Dinan, T. G. (1999). Differences in adrenal steroid profile in chronic fatigue syndrome, in depression and in health. *Journal of Affective Disorders, 54,* 129–137.

Scott, L. V., Svec, F., & Dinan, T. (2000). A preliminary study of dehydroepiandrosterone response to low-dose ACTH in chronic fatigue syndrome and in healthy subjects. *Psychiatry Research, 97*(1), 21–28.

Scott, L. V., Teh, J., Reznek, R., Martin, A., Sohaib, A., & Dinan, T. G. (1999). Small adrenal glands in chronic fatigue syndrome: A preliminary computer tomography study. *Psychoneuroendocrinology, 24,* 759–768.

Sharpe, M., Clements, A., Hawton, K., Young, A., Sargent, P., & Cowen, P. (1996). Increased prolactin response to buspirone in chronic fatigue syndrome. *Journal of Affective Disorders, 41,* 71–76.

Sharpe, M., Hawton, K., Clements, A., & Cowen, P. J. (1997). Increased brain serotonin function in men with chronic fatigue syndrome. *British Medical Journal, 315,* 164–165.

Spath-Schwalbe, E., Scholler, T., Kern, W., Fehm, H. L., & Born, J. (1992). Nocturnal adrenocorticotropin and cortisol secretion depends on sleep duration and decreases in association with spontaneous awakening in the morning. *Journal of Clinical Endocrinology and Metabolism, 75,* 1431–1435.

Stein, M. B., Yehuda, R., Koverola, C., & Hanna, C. (1997). Enhanced dexamethasone suppression of plasma cortisol in adult women traumatized by childhood sexual abuse. *Biological Psychiatry, 42,* 680–686.

Strickland, P., Morriss, R., Wearden, A., & Deakin, W. (1998). A comparison of salivary cortisol in chronic fatigue syndrome, community depression and healthy controls. *Journal of Affective Disorder, 47,* 191–194.

Stupnicki, R., & Obminski, Z. (1992). Glucocorticoid response to exercise as measured by serum and salivary cortisol. *European Journal of Applied Physiology and Occupational Physiology, 65,* 546–549.

Taerk, G., Toner, B., Salit, I., Garfinkel, P., & Ozersky, S. (1987). Depression in patients with neuromyasthenia (benign myalgic encephalomyelitis). *International Journal of Psychiatry in Medicine, 17,* 49–56.

Tattersall, R. (1999). Hypoadrenia, or "a bit of Addison's disease." *Medical History, 43,* 450–457.

Taylor, T., Dluhy, R., & Williams, G. (1983). Beta-endorphin suppresses adrenocorticotrophin and cortisol levels in normal human subjects. *Journal of Clinical Endocrinology and Metabolism, 57,* 592–596.

Terenius, L., & Wahlstrom, A. (1978). Physiological and clinical relevance or endorphins. In J. Hughes (Ed.), *Centrally acting peptides* (pp. 161–178). Baltimore: University Park Press.

Thompson, L. M., Rubin, R. T., & McCracken, J. T. (1992). Neuroendocrine aspects of primary endogenous depression: XII Receiver operating characteristics and kappa analyses of serum and urine cortisol measure in patients and matched controls. *Psychoneuroendocrinology, 17,* 507–515.

Torpy, D. J., Bachmann, A. W., Grice, J. E., Fitzgerald, S. P., Phillips, P. J., Whitworth, J. A., et al. (2001). Familial corticosteroid-binding globulin deficiency due to a novel null mutation: Association with fatigue and relative hypotension. *Journal of Clinical Endocrinology and Metabolism, 86*(8), 3692–3700.

van Denderen, J., Boersma, J., Zeinstra, P., Hollander, A., & van Neerbos, B. (1992). Physiological effects of exhaustive physical exercise in primary fibromyalgia syndrome (PFS): Is PFS a disorder of neuroendocrine reactivity? *Scandinavian Journal of Rheumatism, 21,* 35–37.

van Rensburg, S. J., Potocnik, F. C., Kiss, T., Hugo, F., van Zijl, P., Mansvelt, E., et al. (2001). Serum concentrations of some metals and steroids in patients with chronic fatigue syndrome with reference to neurological and cognitive abnormalities. *Brain Research Bulletin, 55*(2), 319–325.

Vara-Thorbeck, R., Guerrero, J. A., Ruiz-Requena, E., & Garcia-Carriaz, M. (1996). Can the use of growth hormone reduce the postoperative fatigue syndrome? *World Journal of Surgery, 20,* 81–86.

Visser, J., Blauw, B., Hinloopen, B., Brommer, E., de Kloet, E. R., Kluft, C., et al. (1998). CD4 T lymphocytes from patients with chronic fatigue syndrome have decreased interferon-gamma production and increased sensitivity to dexamethasone. *Journal of Infectious Diseases, 177*(2), 451–454.

Visser, J., Lentjes, E., Haspels, I., Graffelman, W., Blauw, B., de Kloet, R., et al. (2001). Increased sensitivity to glucocorticoids in peripheral blood mononuclear cells of chronic fatigue syndrome patients, without evidence for altered density or affinity of glucocorticoid receptors. *Journal of Investigative Medicine, 49*(2), 195–204.

Wallymahmed, M. E., Foy, P., & MacFarlane, I. A. (1999). The quality of life of adults with growth hormone deficiency: Comparison with diabetic patients and control subjects. *Clinical Endocrinology, 51,* 333–338.

Wessely, S., Hotopf, M., & Sharpe, M. (1998). *Chronic fatigue and its syndromes,* Oxford, England: Oxford University Press.

Wessely, S., Nimnuan, C., & Sharpe, M. (1999). Functional somatic syndromes: One or many? *Lancet, 354,* 936–939.

White, P. D., Thomas, J. M., Amess, J., Crawford, D. H., Grover, S. A., Kangro, H. O., et al. (1998). Incidence, risk and prognosis of acute and chronic fatigue syndromes and psychiatric disorders after glandular fever. *British Journal of Psychiatry, 173,* 475–481.

Whiting, P., Bagnall, A. M., Sowden, A. J., Cornell, J. E., Mulrow, C. D., & Ramirez, G. (2001). Interventions for the treatment and management of chronic fatigue syndrome: A systematic review. *Journal of the American Medical Association, 286,* 1360–1368.

Williams, G., Pirohamed, J., Minors, D., Waterhouse, J., Buchan, I., Arendt, J., et al. (1996). Dissociation of body-temperature and melatonin secretion circadian rhythms in patients with chronic fatigue syndrome. *Clinical Physiology, 16*(4), 327–337.

Wolkowitz, O. M., Reus, V. I., Keebler, A., Nelson, N., Friedland, M., Brizendine, L., et al. (1999). Double-blind treatment of major depression with dehydroepiandrosterone. *American Journal of Psychiatry, 156*(4), 646–649.

Wood, B., Wessely, S., Papadopoulos, A., Poon, L., & Checkley, S. (1998). Salivary cortisol profiles in chronic fatigue syndrome. *Neuropsychobiology, 37,* 1–4.

Yatham, L., Morehouse, R., Chisholm, B., Haase, D., MacDonald, D., & Marrie, T. (1995). Neuroendocrine assessment of serotonin (5-HT) function in chronic fatigue syndrome. *Canadian Journal of Psychiatry, 40,* 93–96.

Yehuda, R., Boisoneau, D., Lowy, M. T., & Giller, E. L., Jr. (1995). Dose-response changes in plasma cortisol and lymphocyte glucocorticoid receptors following dexamethasone administration in combat veterans with and without posttraumatic stress disorder. *Archive of General Psychiatry, 52,* 583–593.

Young, A. H., Sharpe, M., Clements, A., Dowling, B., Hawton, K. E., & Cowen, P. J. (1998). Basal activity of the hypothalamic-pituitary-adrenal axis in patients with the chronic fatigue syndrome (neurasthenia). *Biological Psychiatry, 43,* 236–237.

PART IV

ASSESSMENT

CHAPTER 17

Measuring Symptoms and Fatigue Severity

ANTONIA DITTNER and TRUDIE CHALDER

Problems of definition and measurement have dogged research on fatigue and chronic fatigue; indeed, much of the controversy surrounding chronic fatigue syndrome arises because the condition has no known etiology or single underlying process. This chapter first focuses on definitions of fatigue, chronic fatigue, and chronic fatigue syndrome and then outlines approaches to assessment, available instruments, and associated theoretical frameworks. We do not seek to provide detailed psychometric information, to offer advice on specific assessment tools, or to directly compare them.

FATIGUE, CHRONIC FATIGUE, AND THE CHRONIC FATIGUE SYNDROME

Apart from being one of the defining characteristics of CFS, fatigue is a feature of physical conditions such as cancer, neurological conditions such as multiple sclerosis and Parkinson's disease, and psychiatric conditions such as depression and anxiety. In these conditions, fatigue can be chronic and disabling; many describe it as their worst symptom (Fisk, Pontefract, et al., 1994; Pepper, Krupp, Friedberg, Doscher, & Coyle, 1993; Shulman, Taback, Bean, & Weiner, 2001; Winningham et al., 1994). It is hard to find a condition where fatigue is not present to some degree, and the management of illness-related fatigue is now recognized as an important factor in improving quality of life.

Not only is fatigue an important feature of medical conditions, it is a common experience in everyday life. In a study of general practice attenders, 10.2% of men and 10.6% of women were found to have "substantial fatigue for one month or more" (David et al., 1990). Another study (Pawlikowska et al., 1994), also in general practice patients, found that 18.3% of respondents reported "substantial fatigue lasting six months or longer."

The ubiquity of fatigue presents problems of definition and hence measurement. Everyone has some concept of fatigue, even without experiencing the chronic symptoms that are the subject of this chapter. In defining the "normal" experience of fatigue, again we encounter problems. Many people distinguish between tiredness and the more extreme fatigue or exhaustion. Most would agree on a difference between aching muscles after vigorous exercise, headaches and lack of concentration after a mental challenge, weakness and exhaustion after a bout of the flu, and sleepiness after having stayed up all night (Wessely, Hotopf, & Sharpe, 1998).

Fatigue is not a discrete concept, either in its common form or in its presentation in health settings. There are many aspects of fatigue and the relationship between normal fatigue in the general population, chronic fatigue in known medical conditions, and medically unexplained chronic fatigue is uncertain.

Chronic fatigue syndrome (CFS) is the name given to a heterogeneous condition characterized by profound fatigue that is exacerbated by minor physical and mental effort. Other somatic symptoms of uncertain origin include muscle pain, unrefreshing sleep, and mood disturbance. The Centers for Disease Control (CDC) revised criteria for CFS (Fukuda et al., 1994) require the following: presence of persistent or relapsing fatigue, which is new or definite but unexplained, and that lasts for 6 or more months; and at least four out of a range of symptoms including cognitive impairments, sore throat, muscle pain, or tender lymph nodes, which have been present for at least 6 months but which do not predate the fatigue. The U.K. criteria (Sharpe et al., 1991) are somewhat less restrictive, requiring the patient to have severe, disabling fatigue of definite onset affecting physical and mental functioning, with a minimum duration of 6 months, leading to substantial impairment of premorbid activity levels.

Although labels such as myalgic encephalomyelitis (ME), chronic Epstein-Barr virus syndrome, and postviral fatigue syndrome (PVFS) have sometimes been used in place of CFS, there is neither a unique set of symptoms associated with the condition nor a pathological marker. Clinicians generally prefer the operational label CFS because it describes the end result instead of a disease process (Sharpe et al., 1991).

The relation of chronic fatigue to chronic fatigue syndrome has been debated at length (Wessely, 2001). Particularly problematic are the heterogeneity of the symptoms associated with CFS and their overlap with symptoms of other conditions such as fibromyalgia, irritable bowel syndrome, and psychiatric disorder (Wessely, 2001). Although CFS would seem to defy simple definition and measurement, there has been progress in the form of deconstructing it into components that allow the assessment of dimensions of fatigue and other symptoms and investigations into possible relationships between them. These measures and some of the studies in which they have been used are the subject of this chapter and are discussed with emphasis on the central feature of chronic fatigue syndrome—fatigue. However, we favor a mechanistic approach, whereby all symptoms are considered in the context of each other and of the individual.

THE MEASUREMENT OF FATIGUE

The many ways in which investigators have measured fatigue reflect the difficulty in defining it as a symptom. Early attempts were in terms of capacity for work. The Italian physiologist Mosso (1904) measured performance in subjects during repetitive movement over time. He drew four conclusions. First, performance deteriorates over time; that is, there is a *behavioral* result. Second, the correlation between the feeling of fatigue and behavior, as measured by the decrement in output, was poor, so there is a *subjective* element. Third, there must be a *mechanism* or process that mediates fatigue subject to the amount of work performed. Fourth, *contextual* processes, such as other demands placed on the subject at the same time should be considered. This analysis resulted in the separation of fatigue into measurable components.

After World War I, the British Industrial Fatigue Research Board was set up to produce a definitive measure of fatigue and reported, memorably, "that the term fatigue be banished from scientific discussion and consequently that attempts to obtain a fatigue test be abandoned" (Muscio, 1921). This pessimism resulted from the impossibility of identifying any single process or mechanism as being responsible for fatigue.

The same is true today. However, there is a wide range of ways to assess fatigue and other symptoms associated with CFS. These are discussed in the following sections according to the components of fatigue identified by Mosso at the beginning of the twentieth century.

BEHAVIORAL MEASURES OF FATIGUE

In practical terms, behavior can be a useful measure of the degree to which fatigue and other symptoms, such as pain, have a functional impact on a person's life. Functional impact has been categorized (World Health Organization, 1980) into *impairment*, relating to a reduction in physical or mental capacities, *disability*, relating to the inability to perform a human function such as walking, and *handicap*, relating to the social disadvantage that results from the disability.

IMPAIRMENT

Physical Impairment   As already mentioned, early work such as that of Mosso focused on fatigue as the result of physical work. The obvious problem with experiments of this kind using normal subjects is that they investigate acute rather than chronic fatigue, which may well be mediated by different processes. Impairment in physical function in patients who are already reporting fatigue, though, can be measured in a similar way. Whole body output can be measured using a cycle ergometer or a treadmill (Jones & Mellersh, 1946; Riley, Ahern, & Follick, 1988), while defatigability can be measured by physiological variables such as maximal heart rate levels, oxygen consumption, and blood lactate levels during exercise (Fischler et al., 1997).

Results from studies measuring differences between these variables in people with and without CFS have been inconsistent. Fatigability of individual muscles or motor units has been measured neurophysiologically (Thomas, 1987); however evidence of peripheral fatigue in CFS has not been found. Objective measures of fatigue do not correlate with subjective reports of fatigue severity, which is borne out by the fact that there is no clear relationship between subjective fatigue and disease severity in conditions such as cancer (Smets et al., 1998) and Parkinson's disease (Shulman et al., 2001).

Mental Impairment   People with CFS typically report problems with concentration and memory (Wessely & Powell, 1989). Here, too, there are discrepancies between objective and subjective measures. Self-report measures include the Everyday Attention Questionnaire (Martin & Jones, 1986) and the Cognitive Failures Questionnaire (Broadbent, Cooper, Fitzgerald, & Parkes, 1982). Alternatively, cognitive performance can be measured by objective tests of cognitive function such as the computerized CANTAB test (Sahakian & Owen, 1992) or tests of attention (e.g., Stroop test), memory, and reasoning. Studies of objective impairment in patients with CFS have been inconclusive (Ray, Phillips, & Weir, 1993; Schmaling, DiClementi, Cullum, & Jones, 1994; Smith, 1991). This may be because the tests are not tapping the relevant cognitive domain, are not sufficiently sensitive, or CFS patients interpret or focus on their cognitive performance differently from controls.

DISABILITY

Disability caused by mental or physical functional impairment can be assessed using generic quality-of-life measures. These include self-rated measures such as the Quality of Life Index (Ferrans & Powers, 1985, 1992), the self- or observer-rated World Health Organization Quality of Life instrument, short version (WHOQOL-BREF; World Health Organization, 1997) and observer-rated measures such as Karnofsky's 100-point scale (Karnofsky, Abelmann, Craver, & Burchenal, 1948). One of the most widely used measures of disability and one that has also been found to be useful in CFS patients (Buchwald, Pearlman, Umali, Schmaling, & Katon, 1996) is the Medical Outcomes Survey Short Form-36 (Stewart, Hays, & Ware, 1988; Ware & Sherbourne, 1992). This is a 36-item scale containing eight subscales—*physical, social, emotional* and *role functioning, body pain, mental health, vitality,* and *general health.* Also found to be useful measures of disability in CFS are the Sickness Impact Profile (SIP; Bergner, Bobbitt, Carter, & Gilson, 1981), which comprises eight subscales (*home management, mobility, alertness behavior, sleep/rest, ambulation, social interactions, work,* and *recreation and pastimes*) and the Work and Social Adjustment Scale (Marks, 1986). Finally, there is a fatigue-specific disability scale—the Fatigue Impact Scale (Fisk, Ritvo, Ross, Haase, & Marrie, 1994)—which assesses functional impairment as well as the social and emotional impact of fatigue.

HANDICAP

Handicap refers to the social consequences of disability, which is included to a degree in some of the measures previously mentioned. The London Handicap Scale specifically addresses these issues (Harwood, Jitapunkul, Dickinson, & Ebrahim, 1994; Harwood, Rogers, Dickinson, & Ebrahim, 1994). This scale assesses dimensions of handicap mobility, occupation, physical independence, social integration, orientation, and economic self-sufficiency.

SUBJECTIVE MEASURES OF FATIGUE

Given the subjectivity of fatigue, self-report measures are the most appropriate form of assessment. With the growing recognition of fatigue as a feeling state that can be assessed, such instruments have proliferated. They differ in terms of the populations for which they have been designed and validated, the kinds of items they contain (and in turn the information that can be derived from them), their length, and their scoring methods. Some of the scales available for use in CFS patients are discussed here. Many fatigue scales have not been validated for use in CFS patients and, until they are, must be considered unsuitable for this population.

UNIDIMENSIONAL SCALES

The simplest and quickest scales available are single-item scales such as the Rhoten Fatigue Scale (Rhoten, 1982) and single items from other measures such as the Zung Depression Scale (SDS; Zung, Richards, & Short, 1965)—*get tired for no reason*—the Beck Depression Inventory (BDI; Beck, Ward, Mendelson, Mock, & Erbaugh, 1961)—*get tired*—and the Centre for Epidemiological Studies Depression Scale (CES-D; Radloff, 1977)—*everything is an effort.* Although quick to administer, these items do not provide any information about the quality of the patient's fatigue and there is limited evidence as to their validity in CFS.

Multi-item unidimensional scales can capture heterogeneous symptoms and behaviors in a single score. Many are relatively brief and therefore quick to administer and score.

Probably the best known and the most used fatigue scale is the Fatigue Severity Scale (Krupp, LaRocca, Muir-Nash, & Steinberg, 1989). It consists of nine items and is scored on a 7-point Likert scale. The FSS has been found to be reliable and valid in a range of populations including CFS. The name of the scale, however, is misleading. The scale assesses the impact of fatigue on specific types of functioning rather than the severity of fatigue-related symptoms.

The Schedule of Fatigue and Anergia (SOFA; Hickie et al., 1996) was developed specifically for assessing chronic fatigue. The SOFA is a measure of phenomenology and severity and comprises items that are specifically related to CFS symptoms. It is available in two forms—the SOFA/CFS for the identification of CFS cases in specialist clinics and the SOFA/GP for the identification of prolonged fatigue syndromes in community and primary care settings. The SOFA contains 10 items and is scored on 5-point Likert scales with differing anchor points for severity and chronicity for the two forms. Both scales have been demonstrated to have good diagnostic validity and to be useful screening instruments for patients with CFS (sensitivity = 93%; specificity = 95%) and PFS (sensitivity = 81%; specificity = 100%).

MULTIDIMENSIONAL SCALES

Multidimensional scales can be used for a more detailed qualitative and quantitative assessment. Typically they include subscales providing information separately on different aspects of fatigue (e.g., sensory, affective/motivational, cognitive/evaluative dimensions). They are generally longer and the validities of the individual subscales vary.

The Fatigue Questionnaire (also referred to as the Fatigue Rating Scale, the Chalder Fatigue Scale, and the Fatigue Scale) was developed for hospital and community studies of CFS and consists of 11 items loading onto two dimensions—mental and physical. This factorial structure has been confirmed in several studies (Loge, Ekeberg, & Kaasa, 1998; Morriss, Wearden, & Mullis, 1998). The score can be calculated using either the General Health Questionnaire

(Goldberg, 1972) bimodal response system or a 4-point Likert scale. The Fatigue Questionnaire was validated against a fatigue item in the revised Clinical Interview Schedule (Lewis, Pelosi, Araya, & Dunn, 1992) and, using a cutoff score of 3/4, it was found to have sensitivity of 75.5% and specificity of 74.5%. The measure is a valid tool for assessing fatigue severity, although it is recommended to use it in conjunction with other measures. So far it would appear to have good clinical validity. A Norwegian study of fatigue in the general population (Loge et al., 1998) showed a continuous distribution, with those receiving disability allowances and reporting disease and current health problems scoring the highest.

Also designed for CFS patients, the Checklist Individual Strength (CIS; Vercoulen et al., 1994) is a longer scale (20 items) loading onto four dimensions and scored on a 7-point Likert scale. The dimensions are *subjective experience of fatigue, concentration, motivation,* and *physical activity.* The CIS has been found to have excellent psychometric properties in CFS patients and has been widely used in this population (Servaes, van der Werf, Prins, Verhagen, & Bleijenberg, 2001; Vercoulen et al., 1994).

The Profile of Fatigue-Related Symptoms (PFRS; Ray, Weir, Phillips, & Cullen, 1992) was developed as a multidimensional measure of a range of symptoms in CFS, not just fatigue. Its subscales are *emotional distress, cognitive difficulty, fatigue,* and *somatic symptoms* and are designed to be directly relevant to the condition. It was intended for use in patients to assess the severity and pattern of their CFS, to compare the symptomatology within CFS and across conditions and for studies investigating the relation of subjective symptoms to physiological, immunological, and other findings.

It has been found to have good concurrent validity with other measures of symptoms in CFS, such as the Modified Somatic Perception Questionnaire and measures of mood such as the Zung Depression scale, which are discussed in the next section.

Whether to use a measure that assesses a variety of symptoms (e.g., the PFRS) or a scale that measures only fatigue is a matter of choice. There is no gold standard for fatigue and no "pure" fatigue measure, and this should be borne in mind when selecting a scale. The variety of self-report scales illustrates the many dimensions of fatigue, its subjectivity, and its relation to factors such as emotion, cognition, and physical activity. In the following section, we consider the relationship between these factors and other instruments with which they can be assessed.

MEASURING FATIGUE AS A MECHANISM

Many internal mechanisms have been proposed to underlie fatigue including physical, immunological, neurobiological, and psychological.

Physical Mechanisms

It has been suggested that neuromuscular disease underlies the problems seen in CFS. Whereas this would explain some symptoms such as fatigue and muscle pain, it fails to explain symptoms such as poor concentration and short-term memory difficulties and the fact that physical *and* mental effort can make CFS worse. Muscle strength, endurance, and fatigability are normal in most people with CFS, and there is no evidence of changes in muscle structure that cannot be explained by the consequence of illness (Wessely, 1996). There is certainly no single measurable mechanism underlying neuromuscular fatigue in all cases.

Fatigue and tiredness can often be a result of disturbed or missed sleep. Components of sleep quality can be assessed using a polysomnograph—the name given to a composite record of electroencephalogram (EEG) recordings of the electrical activity of the brain, and measures of muscle tone and eye movement. There is evidence of various types of sleep disorder (e.g., insomnia, hypersomnia) in people with CFS (Wessely et al., 1998). Sleep patterns can also be assessed with self-report measures such as the Sleep Timing Questionnaire (Monk, Buysse, Welsh, Kennedy, & Rose, 2001) or a sleep diary such as the Pittsburgh Sleep Diary (Monk et al., 1994).

IMMUNOLOGICAL MECHANISMS

The most common attribution by people with CFS for both the etiology and continuation of their condition is a virus (Clements, Sharpe, Simkin, Borrill, & Hawton, 1997). The evidence for this is, however, inconclusive. No common virus has been found to cause CFS (Wessely et al., 1995), and although some infections (glandular fever, hepatitis) are known to lead to persistent fatigue, this outcome is relatively rare (Hotopf, Noah, & Wessely, 1996). Whereas viral infection can explain the onset of chronic fatigue in many cases (White et al., 1998), it is not sufficient explanation for its chronicity (Buchwald, Sullivan, & Komaroff, 1987).

NEUROENDOCRINOLOGY

There has been much interest in the neuroendocrinology of chronic fatigue syndrome, and recent evidence suggests that neuroendocrine changes might relate to the subjective experience of symptoms in CFS. The hypothalamic-pituitary-adrenal axis (HPA) has received interest due to its role as an interface between the endocrine systems in the body and the neurotransmitter systems in the central nervous system. There is evidence that conditions of low circulating cortisol such as Addison's disease and bilateral adrenalectomy are accompanied by debilitating fatigue. Interestingly, in conditions such as these, other symptoms overlap with those of CFS including myalgias, and sleep and mood disorders (Parker, Wessely, & Cleare, 2001).

The HPA plays a primary role in the body's response to stress, both physical and psychological. It is regulated by long and short feedback loops that respond to fluctuations in plasma cortisol and by hypothalamic secretions of corticotrophin-releasing hormone (CRH), which also acts as a neurotransmitter in cortex and limbic regions. At a highly simplistic level, CRH stimulates the pituitary, which in turn leads to the systemic release of ACTH. Control of the HPA is also achieved through reciprocal interaction with the 5-HT (serotonin) system.

Disruption of these systems has been implicated in neuroendocrine theories of depression (Checkley, 1996; Michelson, Licinio, & Gold, 1995) in which there are high levels of plasma cortisol and abnormal 5-HT transmission. It has also been found that in CFS patients there is a similar disruption, marked by *low* levels of plasma cortisol and the *reverse* of vegetative behaviors such as insomnia, anorexia, and agitation that are seen in depression (Parker et al., 2001). Low circulating cortisol may also explain the nonspecific immune responses in CFS (Wessely et al.,

1998). These findings provide interesting information about the mechanisms underlying CFS, but it is not known whether these changes are primary or secondary to behavioral changes.

INACTIVITY AND THE EFFECTS OF DECONDITIONING

For a mechanism to explain fatigue, it has to be shown that the changes involved are primary to the condition. Without proof of this for any of the mechanisms previously outlined, or indeed for any others, the possibility remains that these changes could be secondary instead of causal. Physiological, immunological, neuroendocrine, and sleep and mood changes can all result from inactivity (Wessely et al., 1998). In fact, physical changes can be seen in normal volunteers after only a week of inactivity (Lamb, Stevens, & Johnson, 1965). There is also evidence that mental inactivity can lead to symptoms such as the mental deficits seen in CFS (Zuber & Wilgosh, 1963). Other consequences of inactivity include reduced visual acuity and heat and cold intolerance (White, 2000). Again, inactivity is itself a consequence of many illnesses, but its role in perpetuating the condition should also be considered (Wessely et al., 1998).

PSYCHOLOGICAL MECHANISMS

In the absence of specific factors to explain the cause of CFS or objective markers of the condition, either mental or physical, the assessment of subjective factors provides the most useful information. In any condition, subjectivity is important. Patients' beliefs about their illness and their coping behavior can greatly affect illness outcome, and CFS is no different in this respect. Self-report measures may provide the best indication of severity of symptoms, illness impact, and patient distress. An objective assessment of physical impairment has little meaning in isolation. Of greater significance are variables such as patients' expectation of the level of exercise that they should be able to achieve based on their past capability compared with their present level of performance and the degree of satisfaction they get from achieving it.

In considering psychological mechanisms for fatigue, relevant areas for assessment include symptoms, coping behavior, illness attributions, negative automatic thoughts, illness perceptions, and psychiatric/psychological disorder.

SYMPTOMS

Somatic Symptoms   An example of a self-report symptom questionnaire is the Physical Symptom Checklist, also called the Somatic Symptom Checklist. This checklist (Wittenborn & Buhler, 1979) is a 32-item list of symptoms, and patients indicate whether they have experienced the problem in the past week by circling "yes" or "no." This simply assesses which symptoms are present but gives no indication of severity.

Pain   Self-report measures of pain include the West Haven-Yale Multidimensional Pain Inventory (MPI) and the McGill Pain Questionnaire (MPQ). The MPI (Kerns, Turk, & Rudy, 1985) consists of 52 items, and has 13 subscales. It was designed to assess the subjective experience and personal impact of pain and has been found to be both reliable and valid in patients with chronic pain but has not been validated in CFS patients.

The McGill Pain Questionnaire (Melzack, 1983) has been widely used in chronic pain patients and in other conditions to describe the quality of the patient's pain. It has four components: (1) a drawing of a human figure on which patients indicate the location of their pain, (2) a list of 78 adjectives from which patients circle words that describe their individual experience, (3) questions about prior pain experience, and (4) a present pain intensity index. By definition, it is a subjective measure, and it has received criticism for its lack of validity and reliability (Tollison & Hinnant, 1996).

Symptom Perception According to some authors, the perception of symptoms is key in the perpetuation of CFS. (Barsky, Goodson, Lane, & Cleary, 1988) developed the five-item Amplification Scale to assess a patient's tendency to experience symptoms more intensely. It was found to have reasonable psychometric properties. A high score on the Amplification Scale was related to dysphoria and general discomfort while controlling for medical morbidity, demonstrating the importance of perceptual style and emotion in the experience of pain.

The Modified Somatic Perception Questionnaire (MSPQ) is a 13-item scale, developed in the context of backache and designed to measure somatic and autonomic symptoms that might indicate anxiety and increased somatic vigilance. The scale has been found to be reliable and valid in patients with chronic low back pain; it has not been validated in CFS patients although it has been used in psychological studies of CFS (Ray et al., 1992).

It has been found (Hickie et al., 1995) that patients who report more somatic symptoms are more likely to experience severe anxiety and depression. Scores on somatic perception questionnaires may indicate that patients are in need of psychological intervention. Ray et al. (Ray, Jefferies, & Weir, 1995a) found that people who were fearful of symptoms were more likely to focus on them, which in turn was associated with increased fatigue, "giving up," and withdrawal of effort from the illness. Increased attention also intensifies awareness, perception, and experience of symptoms (Salkovskis, 1992).

COPING BEHAVIOR

Coping in the context of illness can be defined as:

> . . . cognitive and motor activities which a sick person employs to preserve his bodily and psychic integrity, to recover reversibly impaired function and compensate to the limit for any irreversible impairment. (Lipowski, 1970)

To investigate behavioral and emotional coping strategies and the ways in which these factors possibly mediate CFS symptoms, Ray et al. (Ray, Weir, Stewart, Miller, & Hyde, 1993) developed the Illness Management Questionnaire (IMQ) and validated it in this population. The questionnaire assesses patients' approaches to their illness over the past 6 months. There are four subscales (derived from factor analysis): maintaining activity (17 items), accommodating to the illness (13 items), focusing on symptoms (9 items), and information-seeking (6 items).

The Ways of Coping Scale (Blakely et al., 1991) is an empirically derived measure that assesses problem-focused coping (coping directed toward problem solving or actively changing the source of stress) and emotion-focused coping (where the patient seeks to lessen or manage stress associated with the condition). In a comparison of people with CFS and irritable bowel syndrome, it was found that CFS patients were more likely to use problem-focused rather than emotion-focused coping.

The COPE (Coping Orientations to Problems Experienced; Carver, Scheier, & Weintraub, 1989) consists of theoretically derived scales that assess the ways in which people respond to stress. It comprises scales assessing problem-focused coping—*active coping, planning, suppression of competing activities, restraint coping,* and *seeking social support;* emotion-focused coping—*seeking emotional support, positive reinterpretation,* and *growth, acceptance, denial,* and *turning to religion;* and dysfunctional coping—*behavioral disengagement* and *venting of emotions.*

Similarly the Utrecht Coping Scale has been used in assessing responses to illness (Shreurs, van der Willige, Tellegen, & Brosschot, 1993). This is a Dutch measure consisting of 49 items and seven scales including *problem-focused coping, behavioral-avoidant coping,* and *cognitive-avoidant coping.*

Although only the IMQ was validated in a CFS population, all the scales would seem to have reasonable reliability and validity according to a subsequent study (Clark, Bormann, Cropanzano, & James, 1995). The coping strategies measured by the scales were shown to be related to outcome measures such as *hassles and uplifts, physical symptoms, satisfaction with life, positive affectivity,* and *negative affectivity.*

Studies investigating the relationships between variables measured by these scales and illness outcome have demonstrated several trends. For example, there are significant associations between coping and psychological or physical health. Ray et al. (Ray, Weir, et al., 1993; Ray et al., 1995a), using the IMQ, found that maintaining activity was negatively associated with impairment; whereas accommodating to the illness, in the form of restricting activity, predictably had the opposite effect. Behavioral disengagement, or giving up and withdrawing effort from the illness, was associated with increased impairment and emotional disturbance. Similarly, Heijmans (1998), using the Utrecht Coping Scale, found that problem-focused coping and seeking social support were positively correlated with mental health (Heijmans, 1998). Further studies have found that cognitive and behavioral disengagement are associated with greater perceived illness burden, disruptions in social relationships, disability, and mental health; whereas increased positive reinterpretation and seeking social support are associated with improved psychological health (Antoni et al., 1994; Moss-Morris, Petrie, & Weinman, 1996).

Cognitions

Illness Attributions   Beliefs about the illness will influence both mood and how the patient copes with the illness. It is important to understand and to assess causal attributions as they are related to illness behavior and hence outcome (Sensky, 1990). The Symptoms Interpretation Questionnaire (Robbins & Kirmayer, 1991) assesses the tendency to ascribe symptoms to one of three causes—somatic, emotional, or normalizing. Butler, Chalder, and Wessely (2001) found that CFS patients tend to make more somatic attributions for their illness compared with controls from a fracture clinic. This tendency may be a predisposing as well as a perpetuating factor in CFS. Beliefs about the condition can affect beliefs about the course of the illness and the degree to which the patient can control it. Illness attributions can be assessed simply using a single-item, 5-point verbal rating that asks patients to what extent they believe their fatigue is psychological or physical (Wessely & Powell, 1989). A similar measure is the disease conviction subscale of the Illness Behaviour Questionnaire (Pilowsky & Katsikitis, 1994). Several studies have found an association between attributing the CFS to a physical cause and poor outcome (Chalder, Power, & Wessely, 1996; Sharpe, Hawton, Seagroatt, & Pasvol, 1992; Vercoulen et al., 1996).

Negative Automatic Thoughts   Also important are beliefs about the meaning of the fatigue and the consequences of activity. Catastrophic beliefs about the consequences of activity, have been associated with increased disability and fatigue (Petrie, Moss-Morris, & Weinman, 1995). Unexpected fatigue during or after exercise or as a result of trying to "do too much too soon" may also reinforce fear and avoidance of activity and other illness beliefs (Wessely, Butler, Chalder, & David, 1991). Deale et al. found that beliefs about avoidance of exercise and activity were associated with change in avoidance behavior and in turn good outcome (Deale, Chalder, & Wessely, 1998).

ILLNESS PERCEPTIONS

Leventhal and colleagues defined illness representations as patients' implicit commonsense beliefs about their illness. The schema or cognitive representation that a person has about his or her illness can influence coping behavior and, as a result, adaptive outcomes such as disability and quality of life (Lau & Hartman, 1983; Leventhal, Meyer, & Nerenz, 1980). Each patient will have ideas about the symptoms of the illness and will label (*identity*), the etiology (*cause*), how long the illness will last (*time line*), possibilities for cure (*cure*), and implications of the illness for the future (*consequences*).

Several studies have been carried out using Leventhal's model. This is just one theoretical perspective on psychological mechanisms in CFS and encompasses many of the elements already discussed. (Much of the confusion surrounding psychological mechanisms in CFS arises because different terms are often used to describe similar concepts.)

Weinman et al. have developed the Illness Perception Questionnaire, which assesses each of the dimensions outlined by Leventhal's model. The identity scale consists of 12 core symptoms that the patient rates on a 4-point scale ranging from *all the time* to *never*. The other four scales are presented in mixed order and are scored on a 5-point Likert scale ranging from *strongly disagree* to *strongly agree* (cause, 10 items; time line, 3 items; consequences, 7 items; control/cure, 6 items). The questionnaire has been shown to be reliable and valid in varied patient groups (Weinman, Petrie, Moss-Morris, & Horne, 1996).

The questionnaire has been used to assess illness perceptions and their relation to illness outcome in CFS. It has been found that illness perceptions predict disability and psychological well-being. In addition, illness perceptions influence coping strategies—patients who believe they have some control over their CFS report significantly more positive coping responses. Most significantly, the score on the identity subscale has been found to have the most significant association with measures of dysfunction, fatigue, and psychological adjustment (Moss-Morris et al., 1996). Similarly, Heijmans et al. found that scores on the IPQ were predictive of illness characteristics such as physical functioning and fatigue levels. In some studies, illness perceptions have been found to be more predictive of outcome than coping strategies.

PSYCHIATRIC STATUS AND WELL-BEING

Fatigue is highly associated with emotional disorder. As has already been discussed, the number of somatic symptoms experienced is related to psychiatric diagnosis. This may be because many CFS symptoms overlap with those of psychiatric disorders such as depression; it may be that they share a cause or that one gives rise to the other. What is important is that mood can mediate the course of CFS. Depression and anxiety are associated with increased fatigue at rest and perceived sense of effort when performing tasks. These effects can exacerbate the symptoms of CFS by amplifying the patient's illness experience. Depression is associated with poor outcome in many studies (Sharpe et al., 1992; Wilson et al., 1994). It also reduces motivation to engage in activity, and so reinforces avoidance behavior. Given the interrelation of CFS and psychiatric disorders, mood should be an important component of any assessment—presence of disorders such as anxiety or depression will doubtless affect outcome and, if severe, may require treatment in their own right.

The GHQ (Goldberg, 1972) is perhaps the most widely used measure of psychiatric disorder. This self-administered scale consists of four subscales—*somatic symptoms, anxiety and insomnia, social dysfunction,* and *severe depression.* There are four versions ranging from 12 to 60 items, all well validated in many clinical populations. However, the GHQ has been found less effective than a structured psychiatric interview in CFS (Farmer et al., 1996), perhaps because some items may confound with CFS.

The Symptoms Checklist-90-revised (SCL-90-R; Derogatis, 1983) and a shorter 53-item version, the Brief Symptom Inventory (BSI; Derogatis, 1975), measure psychological and psychiatric dimensions. They consist of nine subscales—somatization, obsessive-compulsive, interpersonal sensitivity, depression, anxiety, hostility, phobic anxiety, paranoid ideation, and psychoticism. Both have good psychometric properties although 15% to 20% of their items overlap with symptoms of CFS. However, the BSI was shown to be sensitive to change in depression level after cognitive-behavioral treatment (Friedberg & Krupp, 1994).

The Clinical Interview Schedule—revised (CIS-R; Lewis et al., 1992) is a semistructured interview that has also been adapted as a computerized self-report measure, so removing the risk of observer bias. There is a range of structured and semistructured interviews, such as the Diagnostic Interview Schedule (Robins, Helzer, Croughan, & Ratcliff, 1991) and the Schedules for Clinical Assessment in Neuropsychiatry (Wing et al., 1990). Just as with self-report measures, however, these interviews should be interpreted with caution as results from different interview schedules do not always agree (Brugha, Jenkins, Taub, Meltzer, & Bebbington, 2001; Eaton, Neufeld, Chen, & Cai, 2000).

Brief instruments used specifically for the detection of depression include the Beck Depression Inventory (Beck et al., 1961), the Centre for Epidemiological Studies—Depression (CES-D; Radloff, 1977), and the Zung Self-Rating

Depression Scale (SDS; Zung et al., 1965). All have been well validated in clinical populations, but their validity in fatiguing illnesses has not been confirmed. In all scales, there is a significant degree of overlap between symptoms of depression and symptoms of CFS. In the Zung Depression Scale this proportion is as high as 30% to 40% (Jason & Friedberg, 1998). Adjustments may possibly be made for this by increasing the cutoff score when using the scale in CFS populations.

The Hospital Anxiety and Depression Scale (Zigmond & Snaith, 1983) has been widely used in CFS (Ray, Jefferies, & Weir, 1995b) and has been shown to be sensitive to change after cognitive behavior therapy (Sharpe et al., 1996). Symptoms relating to somatization of mood or to physical illness have been intentionally excluded. However, it has been suggested that the scale might *underestimate* cases of depression.

MEASURING FATIGUE IN CONTEXT

As discussed in the previous section, interacting variables within an individual may serve to perpetuate CFS. These will be unique in each case and their assessment can assist in understanding the particular factors that are pertinent for a specific individual. However, persons with CFS do not exist in a vacuum, and it is also important to assess the context in which they live and how this might affect their condition. Significant contributing factors to any condition include social support and demands placed on the individual.

Although the support people with CFS receive from others will affect outcome, this relationship is not straightforward. First, there may be a discrepancy between the *perceived* amount of support and the *actual* level of support that people with CFS receive. In addition, it is important to assess the sort of support that is given and the effects that it might have. *Too little* support is clearly unhelpful; however, *too much* support can also be damaging.

Patients' views as to the amount of support they receive can be assessed using the Perceived Social Support Inventory, a 20-item questionnaire, scored on a 5-point scale, that measures support received from family and friends. The questionnaire has been shown to be reliable and valid in a variety of patient and nonpatient samples (Procidano & Heller, 1983). Other issues may be at work such as the degree to which they feel others view their condition as legitimate and the degree of pressure they feel from others for being physically less able (e.g., not being able to go to work or to help with household duties). How patients perceive others' view of them certainly *has an effect* on social support. Many people with CFS report a change in social relationships because "no one understood what my illness was" (Schweitzer, Kelly, Foran, Terry, & Whiting, 1995).

In addition, even relationships that the patient sees as *positive* may be detrimental. In some studies, membership in a self-help group has been found to be independently associated with either poor prognosis or poor compliance with treatment (Sharpe et al., 1992; Wearden et al., 1998). It is also of value to assess the coping strategies of people close to the patient. It has been found that relatives of patients as well as patients themselves make significantly more somatic attributions for symptoms (compared with people who have bone fractures; Butler et al., 2001). We have already suggested that beliefs about the condition affect the course of CFS, and it seems likely that relatives and close friends can confirm these beliefs. Similarly, relatives or a partner can affect the outcome of the illness if their responses inadvertently provide positive reinforcement of illness behavior. Although there are few, if any, formally validated scales for assessing these variables, it may be possible to adapt questionnaires designed for patients with CFS or to simply ask relatives or partners direct questions about their beliefs and responses to illness behavior.

Demands or stress may also be important precipitating or perpetuating factors in the condition. They can be assessed by measures of life stresses and events such as the Life Events and Difficulties Schedule (Bruce-Jones, White, Thomas, & Clare, 1994) and the PERI list of life events (Dohrenwend, Krasnoff, Askenasy, & Dohrenwend, 1978). The concepts of demands and stress are, however, vague and subjective; there are large individual differences about what is stressful and what are acceptable achievements at work, home, or school.

AN INTEGRATIVE APPROACH

Fatigue and its related symptoms have been discussed in terms of behavior, subjective feeling states, different kinds of underlying mechanisms, and the context of the individual's life and circumstances. There are complex relationships between fatigue, other CFS symptoms, cognitions, behavior, and environment. Objective measures yield little information either about the experience of fatigue and other symptoms, or about the factors that perpetuate them.

In conditions such as CFS, a traditional dualistic approach is not helpful. Although the etiology of the condition remains obscure, a complex interaction of physiological, cognitive, behavioral, affective, and social factors seems to be responsible for the development and maintenance of fatigue and disability.

The cognitive-behavioral model is an approach that draws on all these elements and that takes account of the subjective element. In the cognitive-behavioral model of CFS, a distinction is drawn between the predisposing, precipitating, and perpetuating factors of CFS. What triggers CFS may not be the same as what maintains it. Although the causes of CFS are unknown, the factors that perpetuate it, such as maladaptive beliefs and behaviors, are potentially treatable (Chalder, Butler, & Wessely, 1996; Wessely et al., 1991). Beliefs, behaviors, emotions, and physiology interact and feed into each other in a self-perpetuating way. According to the theory, the perception of symptoms may lead to rest and avoidance of exercise and consequent deconditioning, which will exacerbate the symptoms. This behavior is often symptom-driven (and can be mediated by anxiety that increases symptom focusing) and is influenced by idiosyncratic illness beliefs (such as "activity makes it worse" and "I have an incurable disease"). Often people with CFS develop a pattern of intense bursts of activity followed by worsening of symptoms of pain and exhaustion. This pattern confirms illness beliefs and can lead to periods of rest and inactivity.

Cognitive-behavioral therapy (CBT) aims to increase activity levels gradually by providing education about the detrimental effects of inactivity and symptom focusing, by gradually increasing goals for daily activity to disprove fears about worsening of symptoms, and by addressing emotional problems that might result from and/or perpetuate the condition. CBT can also be carried out in the context of family therapy to engage others around the person with CFS in changing illness beliefs and behavior. The approach is collaborative; patient and therapist work together to identify goals for treatment and to agree on a program of consistent, planned activity and rest.

CBT has been demonstrated to be effective in randomized controlled trials. It has been shown to reduce functional impairment (Sharpe et al., 1996), to be as effective as counseling (Ridsdale et al., 2001), more effective than relaxation techniques (Deale, Chalder, Marks, & Wessely, 1997), including a 5-year follow-up (Deale, Husain, Chalder, & Wessely, 2001), and to be more effective than guided support groups (Prins et al., 2001).

Also found to be effective in CFS is graded exercise therapy (GET). Like CBT, this treatment has also been shown to be successful in randomized controlled trials (Fulcher & White, 1997; Powell, Bentall, Nye, & Edwards, 2001; Whiting et al., 2001). This is a behavioral treatment; however, it may involve implicit challenging of maladaptive cognitions (as to the potential danger of exercise), and change during GET and CBT may well be mediated by a common mechanism. Research is currently being carried out into possible factors mediating change over the course of therapy.

CONCLUSION

It is impractical to consider CFS as a condition that can be objectively quantified. So far, objective measures of CFS symptoms have offered no answers as to etiology and have served only to raise doubts about the legitimacy of the condition. Subjective symptoms characterize CFS, and as such, it is best to assess it with subjective tools. Clinicians should keep in mind that *a subjective symptom remains a real symptom*; any symptom that causes distress should be taken seriously.

Finally, it is futile to assess either fatigue or the person experiencing it in isolation. Symptoms should be assessed in the context of each other and of the individual. This approach will shed light on how symptoms interact to perpetuate the condition, allowing advances in understanding and treatment.

REFERENCES

Antoni, M., Brickman, A., Lutgendorf, S., Klimas, N., Imia-Fins, A., Ironson, G., et al. (1994). Psychosocial correlates of illness burden in chronic fatigue syndrome. *Clinical Infectious Diseases, 18*(Suppl. 1), 73–78.

Barsky, A. J., Goodson, J. D., Lane, R. S., & Cleary, P. D. (1988). The amplification of somatic symptoms. *Psychosomatic Medicine, 50*, 510–519.

Beck, A., Ward, C., Mendelson, M., Mock, J., & Erbaugh, J. (1961). A scale for measuring depression. *Archives General Psychiatry, 4*, 561–571.

Bergner, M., Bobbitt, R. A., Carter, W. B., & Gilson, B. S. (1981). The Sickness Impact Profile: Development and final revision of a health status measure. *Medical Care, 19*, 787–805.

Blakely, A. A., Howard, R. C., Sosich, R. M., Murdoch, J. C., Menkes, D. B., & Spears, G. F. (1991). Psychiatric symptoms, personality and ways of coping in chronic fatigue syndrome. *Psychological Medicine, 12*, 347–362.

Broadbent, D. E., Cooper, P. F., Fitzgerald, P., & Parkes, K. R. (1982). The Cognitive Failures Questionnaire (CFQ) and its correlates. *British Journal of Clinical Psychology, 21*(Pt. 1), 1–16.

Bruce-Jones, W. D., White, P. D., Thomas, J. M., & Clare, A. W. (1994). The effect of social adversity on the fatigue syndrome, psychiatric disorders and physical recovery, following glandular fever. *Psychological Medicine, 24,* 651–659.

Brugha, T. S., Jenkins, R., Taub, N., Meltzer, H., & Bebbington, P. E. (2001). A general population comparison of the Composite International Diagnostic Interview (CIDI) and the Schedules for Clinical Assessment in Neuropsychiatry (SCAN). *Psychological Medicine, 31,* 1001–1013.

Buchwald, D., Pearlman, T., Umali, J., Schmaling, K., & Katon, W. (1996). Functional status in patients with chronic fatigue syndrome, other fatiguing illnesses, and healthy controls. *American Journal of Medicine, 171,* 364–370.

Buchwald, D., Sullivan, J., & Komaroff, A. (1987). Frequency of chronic active Epstein-Barr virus infection in a general medical practice. *Journal of the American Medical Association, 257,* 2303–2307.

Butler, J. A., Chalder, T., & Wessely, S. (2001). Causal attributions for somatic sensations in patients with chronic fatigue syndrome and their partners. *Psychological Medicine, 31,* 97–105.

Carver, C. S., Scheier, M. F., & Weintraub, J. K. (1989). Assessing coping strategies: A theoretically based approach. *Journal of Personality and Social Psychology, 56,* 267–283.

Chalder, T., Butler, S., & Wessely, S. (1996). Inpatient treatment of chronic fatigue syndrome. *Behavioral Psychotherapy, 24,* 351–365.

Chalder, T., Power, M., & Wessely, S. (1996). Chronic fatigue in the community: A question of attribution. *Psychological Medicine, 26,* 791–800.

Checkley, S. (1996). The neuroendocrinology of depression and chronic stress. *British Medical Bulletin, 52,* 597–617.

Clark, K. K., Bormann, C. A., Cropanzano, R. S., & James K. (1995). Validation evidence for three coping measures. *Journal of Personality Assessment, 65,* 434–455.

Clements, A., Sharpe, M., Simkin, S., Borrill, J., & Hawton, K. (1997). Chronic fatigue syndrome: A qualitative investigation of patients' beliefs about the illness. *Journal of Psychosomatic Research, 42,* 615–624.

David, A., Pelosi, A., McDonald, E., Stephens, D., Ledger, D., Rathbone, R., et al. (1990). Tired, weak, or in need of rest: Fatigue among general practice attenders. *British Medical Journal, 301,* 1199–1202.

Deale, A., Chalder, T., Marks, I., & Wessely, S. (1997). A randomised controlled trial of cognitive behaviour versus relaxation therapy for chronic fatigue syndrome. *American Journal of Psychiatry, 154,* 408–414.

Deale, A., Chalder, T., & Wessely, S. (1998). Illness beliefs and treatment outcome in chronic fatigue syndrome. *Journal of Psychosomatic Research, 45,* 77–83.

Deale, A., Husain, K., Chalder, T., & Wessely, S. (2001). Long-term outcome of cognitive behavior therapy versus relaxation therapy for chronic fatigue syndrome: A 5-year follow-up study. *American Journal of Psychiatry, 158,* 2038–2042.

Derogatis, L. R. (1975). *Brief symptom inventory.* Towson, MD: Clinical Psychometric Research.

Derogatis, L. R. (1983). *SCL-90-R administration, scoring and procedure manual—II.* Towson, MD: Clinical Psychometric Research.

Dohrenwend, B. S., Krasnoff, L., Askenasy, A. R., & Dohrenwend, B. P. (1978). Exemplification of a method for scaling life events: The Peri Life Events Scale. *Journal of Health and Social Behavior, 19,* 205–229.

Eaton, W., Neufeld, K., Chen, L., & Cai, G. A. (2000). Comparison of self-report and clinical diagnostic interviews for depression: Diagnostic interview schedule and schedules for clinical assessment in neuropsychiatry in the Baltimore Epidemiologic Catchment Area follow-up. *Archives of General Psychiatry, 57,* 217–222.

Farmer, A., Chubb, H., Jones, I., Hillier, J., Smith, A., & Borysiewicz, L. (1996). Screening for psychiatric morbidity in subjects presenting with chronic fatigue syndrome. *British Journal of Psychiatry, 168,* 354–358.

Ferrans, C. E., & Powers, M. J. (1985). Quality of Life Index: Development and psychometric properties. *Advances in Nursing Science, 8,* 15–24.

Ferrans, C. E., & Powers, M. J. (1992). Psychometric assessment of the Quality of Life Index. *Research in Nursing and Health, 15,* 29–38.

Fischler, B., Dendale, P., Michiels, V., Cluydts, R., Kaufman, L., & De Meirleir, K. (1997). Physical fatigability and exercise capacity in chronic fatigue syndrome: Association with disability, somatization and psychopathology. *Journal of Psychosomatic Research, 42,* 369–378.

Fisk, J., Pontefract, A., Ritvo, P. G., Archibald, C. J., & Murray, T. J. (1994). The impact of fatigue on patients with multiple sclerosis. *Canadian Journal of Neurological Sciences, 21,* 9–14.

Fisk, J., Ritvo, P., Ross, L., Haase, D., & Marrie, T. (1994). Measuring the functional impact of fatigue: Initial validation of the Fatigue Impact Scale. *Clinical Infectious Diseases, 18*(Suppl. 1), 579–583.

Friedberg, F., & Krupp, L. B. (1994). A comparison of cognitive behavioral treatment for chronic fatigue syndrome and primary depression. *Clinical Infectious Diseases, 18,* S105–S110.

Fukuda, K., Straus, S., Hickie, I., Sharpe, M., Dobbins, J., & Komaroff, A. (1994). The chronic fatigue syndrome: A comprehensive approach to its definition and study. *Annals of Internal Medicine, 121,* 953–959.

Fulcher, K., & White, P. (1997). Randomised controlled trial of graded exercise in patients with chronic fatigue syndrome. *British Medical Journal, 314,* 1647–1652.

Goldberg, D. (1972). *The detection of psychiatric illness by questionnaire.* Oxford, England: Oxford University Press.

Harwood, R. H., Jitapunkul, S., Dickinson, E., & Ebrahim, S. (1994). Measuring handicap: Motives, methods, and a model. *Quality in Health Care, 3,* 53–57.

Harwood, R. H., Rogers, A., Dickinson, E., & Ebrahim, S. (1994). Measuring handicap: The London Handicap Scale, a new outcome measure for chronic disease. *Quality in Health Care, 3,* 11–16.

Heijmans, M. (1998). Coping and adaptive outcome in chronic fatigue syndrome: Importance of illness cognitions. *Journal of Psychosomatic Research, 45,* 39–51.

Hickie, I., Koojer, A., Hadzi-Pavlovic, D., Bennett, B., Wilson, A., & Lloyd, A. (1996). Fatigue in selected primary care settings: Socio-demographic and psychiatric correlates. *Medical Journal of Australia, 164,* 585–588.

Hickie, I., Lloyd, A., Hadzi-Pavlovic, D., Parker, G., Bird, K., & Wakefield, D. (1995). Can the chronic fatigue syndrome be defined by distinct clinical features? *Psychological Medicine, 25,* 925–935.

Hotopf, M., Noah, N., & Wessely, S. (1996). Chronic fatigue and minor psychiatric morbidity after viral meningitis: A controlled study. *Journal of Neurology Neurosurgery and Psychiatry, 60,* 504–509.

Jason, L., & Friedberg, F. (1998). *Understanding chronic fatigue syndrome: An empirical guide to assessment and treatment.* Washington, DC: American Psychological Association.

Jones, M., & Mellersh, V. (1946). Comparison of exercise response in anxiety states and normal controls. *Psychosomatic Medicine, 8,* 180–187.

Karnofsky, D. A., Abelmann, W. H., Craver, L. F., & Burchenal, J. H. (1948). The use of the nitrogen mustards in the palliative treatment of carcinoma. *Cancer, 1,* 634–656.

Kerns, R. D., Turk, D. C., & Rudy, T. E. (1985). The West Haven-Yale Multidimensional Pain Inventory (WHYMPI). *Pain, 23,* 345–356.

Krupp, L. B., LaRocca, N. G., Muir-Nash, J., & Steinberg, A. D. (1989). The fatigue severity scale: Application to patients with multiple sclerosis and systemic lupus erythematosus. *Archives of Neurology, 46,* 1121–1123.

Lamb, L., Stevens, P., & Johnson, R. (1965). Hypokinesia secondary to chair rest from 4 to 10 days. *Aerospace Medicine, 36,* 755–763.

Lau, R. R., & Hartman, K. A. (1983). Commonsense representations of common illnesses. *Health Psychology, 2,* 167–185.

Leventhal, H., Meyer, D., & Nerenz, D. R. (1980). The commonsense representation of illness danger. In S. Rachman (Ed.), *Medical psychology* (Vol. 2, pp. 7–30). New York: Pergamon Press.

Lewis, G., Pelosi, A., Araya, R., & Dunn, G. (1992). Measuring psychiatric disorder in the community: A standardised assessment for lay interviewer. *Psychological Medicine, 22,* 465–486.

Loge, J. H., Ekeberg, O., & Kaasa, S. (1998). Fatigue in the general Norwegian population: Normative data and associations. *Journal of Psychosomatic Research, 45,* 53–65.

Marks, I. (1986). *Behavioural psychotherapy: Maudsley pocket book of clinical management.* Bristol, England: Wright.

Martin, M., & Jones, G. V. (1986). Ageing and patterns of change in everyday memory and cognition. *Human Learning, 5,* 63–74.

Melzack R. (1983). The McGill Pain Questionnaire. In R. Melzack (Ed.), *Pain management and assessment* (pp. 41–48). New York: Raven Press.

Michelson, D., Licinio, J., & Gold, P. (1995). Mediation of the stress response by the hypothalamic-pituitary-adrenal axis. In M. Friedman, D. Charney, & A. Deutsch (Eds.), *Neurobiological and clinical consequences of stress: From normal adaption to PTSD* (pp. 225–238). Philadelphia: Lippincott-Raven.

Monk, T. H., Buysse, D. J., Welsh, D. K., Kennedy, K. S., & Rose, L. R. (2001). A sleep diary and questionnaire study of naturally short sleepers. *Journal of Sleep Research, 10,* 173–179.

Monk, T. H., Reynolds, C. F., Kupfer, D. J., Buysse, D. J., Coble, P. A., Hayes, A. J., et al. (1994). The Pittsburgh sleep diary. *Journal of Sleep Research, 3,* 111–120.

Morriss, R., Wearden, A., & Mullis, R. (1998). Exploring the validity of the Chalder Fatigue Scale in chronic fatigue syndrome. *Journal of Psychosomatic Research, 45,* 411–417.

Moss-Morris, R., Petrie, K., & Weinman, J. (1996). Functioning in chronic fatigue syndrome: Do illness perceptions play a role? *British Journal of Health Psychology, 1,* 15–25.

Mosso, A. (1904). *Fatigue.* London: Swan Sonnenschein.

Muscio, B. (1921). Is a fatigue test possible? *British Journal of Psychology, 12,* 31–46.

Parker, A. J., Wessely, S. C., & Cleare, A. J. (2001). The neuroendocrinology of chronic fatigue syndrome and fibromyalgia. *Psychological Medicine, 31,* 1331–1345.

Pawlikowska, T., Chalder, T., Hirsch, S., Wallace, P., Wright, D., & Wessely, S. (1994). A population based study of fatigue and psychological distress. *British Medical Journal, 308,* 743–746.

Pepper, C., Krupp, L., Friedberg, F., Doscher, C., & Coyle, P. (1993). A comparison of neuropsychiatric characteristics in chronic fatigue syndrome, multiple sclerosis and major depression. *Journal of Neuropsychiatry and Clinical Neurosciences, 5,* 200–205.

Petrie, K., Moss-Morris, R., & Weinman, J. (1995). The impact of catastrophic beliefs on functioning in chronic fatigue syndrome. *Journal of Psychosomatic Research, 39,* 31–37.

Pilowsky, I., & Katsikitis M. (1994). A classification of illness behaviour in pain clinic patients. *Pain, 57,* 91–94.

Powell, P., Bentall, R., Nye, F., & Edwards, R. (2001). Randomised controlled trial of patient education to encourage graded exercise in chronic fatigue syndrome. *British Medical Journal, 322*(7283), 387–390.

Prins, J. B., Bleijenberg, G., Bazelmans, E., Elving, L. D., de Boo, T. M., Severens, J. L., et al. (2001). Cognitive behaviour therapy for chronic fatigue syndrome: A multicentre randomised controlled trial. *Lancet, 357,* 841–847.

Procidano, M. E., & Heller, K. (1983). Measures of perceived social support from friends and from family: Three validation studies. *American Journal of Community Psychology, 11,* 1–24.

Radloff, L. S. (1977). The CES-D scale: A self-report depression scale for research in the general population. *Applied Psychological Measurement, 1,* 385–401.

Ray, C., Jefferies, S., & Weir, W. R. (1995a). Coping with chronic fatigue syndrome: Illness responses and their relationship with fatigue, functional impairment and emotional status. *Psychological Medicine, 25,* 937–945.

Ray, C., Jefferies, S., & Weir, W. R. (1995b). Life-events and the course of chronic fatigue syndrome. *British Journal of Medical Psychology, 68*(Pt. 4), 323–331.

Ray, C., Phillips, L., & Weir, W. R. (1993). Quality of attention in chronic fatigue syndrome: Subjective reports of everyday attention and cognitive difficulty, and performance on tasks of focused attention. *British Journal of Clinical Psychology, 32*(Pt. 3), 357–364.

Ray, C., Weir W., Phillips, S., & Cullen, S. (1992). Development of a measure of symptoms in chronic fatigue syndrome: The profile of fatigue-related symptoms (PFRS). *Psychology and Health, 7,* 27–43.

Ray, C., Weir, W., Stewart, D., Miller, P., & Hyde, G. (1993). Ways of coping with chronic fatigue syndrome: Development of an illness management questionnaire. *Social Science and Medicine, 37,* 385–391.

Rhoten, D. (1982). Fatigue and the postsurgical patient. In C. Norris (Ed.), *Concept clarification in nursing* (pp. 277–300). Rockville, MD: Aspen Press.

Ridsdale, L., Godfrey, E., Chalder, T., Seed, P., King, M., Wallace, P., et al. (2001). Chronic fatigue in general practice: Is counselling as good as cognitive behaviour therapy? A U.K. randomised trial. *British Journal of General Practice, 51,* 19–24.

Riley, J., Ahern, D., & Follick, M. (1988). Chronic pain and functional impairment: Assessing beliefs about their relationship. *Archives of Physical Medicine and Rehabilitation, 69,* 579–582.

Robbins, J. M., & Kirmayer, L. J. (1991). Attributions of common somatic symptoms. *Psychological Medicine, 21,* 1029–1045.

Robins, L. N., Helzer, J. E., Croughan, J., & Ratcliff, K. S. (1991). National Institute of Health Diagnostic Interview Schedule: Its history, characteristics and validity. *Archives General Psychiatry, 38,* 381–389.

Sahakian, B. J., & Owen, A. M. (1992). Computerized assessment in neuropsychiatry using CANTAB: Discussion paper. *Journal of the Royal Society of Medicine, 85,* 399–402.

Salkovskis, P. M. (1992). Psychological treatment of noncardiac chest pain: The cognitive approach. *American Journal of Medicine, 27,* 114S–121S.

Schmaling, K. B., DiClementi, J. D., Cullum, C. M., & Jones, J. F. (1994). Cognitive functioning in chronic fatigue syndrome and depression: A preliminary comparison. *Psychosomatic Medicine, 56,* 383–388.

Schweitzer, R., Kelly, B., Foran, A., Terry, D., & Whiting, J. (1995). Quality of life in chronic fatigue syndrome. *Social Science and Medicine, 41,* 1367–1372.

Sensky, T. (1990). Patients' reaction to illness. *British Medical Journal, 300,* 622–623.

Servaes, P., van der Werf, S., Prins, J., Verhagen, S., & Bleijenberg, G. (2001). Fatigue in disease-free cancer patients compared with fatigue in patients with chronic fatigue syndrome. *Supportive Care in Cancer, 9,* 11–17.

Sharpe, M., Archard, L. C., Banatvala, J. E., Borysiewicz, L. K., Clare, A. W., David, A., et al. (1991). Chronic fatigue syndrome: Guidelines for research. *Journal of the Royal Society of Medicine, 84,* 118–121.

Sharpe, M., Hawton, K., Seagroatt, V., & Pasvol, G. (1992). Follow up of patients presenting with fatigue to an infectious diseases clinic. *British Medical Journal, 305,* 147–152.

Sharpe, M., Hawton, K., Simkin, S., Suraway, C., Hackmann, A., Klimes, I., et al. (1996). Cognitive behaviour therapy for chronic fatigue syndrome: A randomized controlled trial. *British Medical Journal, 312,* 22–26.

Shreurs, P. J., van der Willige, G., Tellegen, B., & Brosschot, J. F. (1993). *The Utrecht coping list manual.* Lisse, The Netherlands: Swets & Zeitlinger.

Shulman, L. M., Taback, R. L., Bean, J., & Weiner, W. J. (2001). Comorbidity of the nonmotor symptoms of Parkinson's disease. *Movement Disorders, 16,* 507–510.

Smets, E. M., Visser, M. R., Garssen, B., Frijda, N. H., Oosterveld, P., & de Haes, J. C. (1998). Understanding the level of fatigue in cancer patients undergoing radiotherapy. *Journal of Psychosomatic Research, 45,* 277–293.

Smith, A. (1991). Cognitive changes in myalgic encephalomyelitis. In R. Jenkins & J. Mowbray (Eds.), *Post-viral fatigue syndrome* (pp. 179–194). Chichester, England: Wiley.

Stewart, A., Hays, R., & Ware, J. (1988). The MOS short-form general health survey: Reliability and validity in a patient population. *Medical Care, 26,* 724–732.

Thomas, P. K. (1987). Postviral fatigue syndrome. *Lancet, 1,* 218–219.

Tollison, C. D., & Hinnant, D. W. (1996). Psychological testing in the evaluation of the patient in pain. In N. S. Waldman & A. P. Winnie (Eds.), *Interventional pain management* (pp. 119–128). Philadelphia: Saunders.

Vercoulen, J. H., Swanink, C. M., Fennis, J. F., Galama, J. M., van der Meer, J. W., & Bleijenberg, G. (1994). Dimensional assessment of chronic fatigue syndrome. *Journal of Psychosomatic Research, 38,* 383–392.

Vercoulen, J. H., Swanink, C. M., Fennis, J. F., Galama, J. M., van der Meer, J. W., & Bleijenberg, G. (1996). Prognosis in chronic fatigue syndrome: A prospective study on the natural course. *Journal of Neurology Neurosurgery and Psychiatry, 60,* 489–494.

Ware, J. E., Jr., & Sherbourne, C. D. (1992). The MOS 36-item short-form health survey (SF-36). I: Conceptual framework and item selection. *Medical Care, 30,* 473–483.

Wearden, A., Morriss, R., Mullis, R., Strickland, P., Pearson, D., Appleby, L., et al. (1998). A double-blind, placebo controlled treatment trial of fluoxetine and a graded exercise programme for chronic fatigue syndrome. *British Journal of Psychiatry, 172,* 485–490.

Weinman, J., Petrie, K., Moss-Morris, R., & Horne, R. (1996). The illness perception questionnaire: A new method for assessing the cognitive representation of illness. *Psychology and Health, 11,* 431–445.

Wessely, S. (1996). Chronic fatigue syndrome: Summary of a report of a joint committee of the Royal Colleges of Physicians, Psychiatrists and General Practitioners. *Journal of the Royal College of Physicians of London, 30,* 497–504.

Wessely, S. (2001). Chronic fatigue: Symptom and syndrome. *Annals of Internal Medicine, 134,* 838–843.

Wessely, S., Butler, S., Chalder, T., & David, A. (1991). The cognitive behavioural management of the postviral fatigue syndrome. In R. Jenkins & J. Mowbray (Eds.), *Postviral fatigue syndrome* (pp. 305–334). Chichester, England: Wiley.

Wessely, S., Chalder, T., Hirsch, S., Pawlikowska, T., Wallace, P., & Wright, D. J. (1995). Postinfectious fatigue: Prospective cohort study in primary care. *Lancet, 345,* 1333–1338.

Wessely, S., Hotopf, M., & Sharpe, M. (1998). *Chronic fatigue and its syndromes.* Oxford, England: Oxford University Press.

Wessely, S., & Powell, R. (1989). Fatigue syndromes: A comparison of chronic postviral fatigue with neuromuscular and affective disorder. *Journal of Neurology Neurosurgery and Psychiatry, 52,* 940–948.

White, P., Thomas, J., Amess, J., Crawford, D., Grover, S., Kangro, H., et al. (1998). Incidence, risk and prognosis of acute and chronic fatigue syndromes and psychiatric disorders after glandular fever. *British Journal of Psychiatry, 173,* 475–481.

White, P. (2000). The role of physical inactivity in the chronic fatigue syndrome. *Journal of Psychosomatic Research, 49,* 283–284.

Whiting, P., Bagnall, A. M., Sowden, A. J., Cornell, J. E., Mulrow, C. D., & Ramirez, G. (2001). Interventions for the treatment and management of chronic fatigue syndrome: A systematic review. *Journal of the American Medical Association, 286,* 1360–1368.

Wilson, A., Hickie, I., Lloyd, A., Hadzi-Pavlovic, D., Boughton, C., Dwyer, J., et al. (1994). Longitudinal study of the outcome of chronic fatigue syndrome. *British Medical Journal, 308,* 756–760.

Wing, J. K., Babor, T., Brugha, T., Burke, J., Cooper, J. E., Giel, R., et al. (1990). SCAN: Schedules for clinical assessment in neuropsychiatry. *Archives General Psychiatry, 47,* 589–593.

Winningham, M. L., Nail, L. M., Burke, M. B., Brophy, L., Cimprich, B., Jones, L. S., et al. (1994). Fatigue and the cancer experience: The state of the knowledge. *Oncology Nursing Forum, 21,* 23–36.

Wittenborn, J., & Buhler, R. (1979). Somatic discomforts among depressed women. *Archives of General Psychiatry, 36,* 465–471.

World Health Organization. (1980). *International classification of impairments, disabilities and handicaps: A manual of classification relating to the consequences of disease.* Geneva, Switzerland: Author.

World Health Organization. (1997). *Measuring Quality of Life: The World Health Organisation Quality of Life Instruments* (The WHO-QOL-100 and the WHO-QOL-BREF). Geneva, Switzerland: Author.

Zigmond, A., & Snaith, R. (1983). The Hospital Anxiety and Depression Scale. *Acta Psychiatrica Scandinavica, 67,* 361–370.

Zuber, J., & Wilgosh, L. (1963). Prolonged immobilization of the body: Changes in performance and the electroencephalogram. *Science, 140,* 306–308.

Zung, W. W., Richards, C. B., & Short, M. J. (1965). Self-rating depression scale in an outpatient clinic: Further validation of the SDS. *Archives General Psychiatry, 13,* 508–515.

CHAPTER 18

Functional Capacity Evaluation

KEVIN McCULLY

SELF-REPORTED EXCESSIVE weakness and fatigue is an integral part of the definition of chronic fatigue syndrome (Holmes et al., 1988). In addition, CFS patients report postexertional fatigue as a dominant symptom in their response to exercise (Komaroff, 1993). The results of studies to examine strength and endurance capacity of CFS patients have varied, from findings of large impairments (De Becker, Roeykens, Reynders, McGregor, & De Meirleir, 2000; Paul, Wood, Behan, & MacLaren, 1999) to findings of no impairment (Kent-Braun, Sharma, Weiner, 1993; Stokes, Cooper, & Edwards, 1988). The key issue is why patients who report major deficits in muscle function do not always have measurable deficits. In addition, does the magnitude of the measured deficits seen with CFS explain the symptoms? Although this review cannot offer definitive answers to these questions, it provides a background on how exercise capacity is measured and summarizes previous studies of exercise capacity in CFS.

MEASURING EXERCISE CAPACITY

Exercise capacity can be divided into three main areas: cardiorespiratory fitness, musculoskeletal function, and motor skill (Tritschler, 2000a). This review focuses on cardiorespiratory and musculoskeletal function. In general, functional tests can be divided into laboratory tests, field tests, and questionnaires. Laboratory tests use specialized equipment and can provide better control over experimental conditions as well as address mechanistic questions. Field tests are simpler and thus easier to administer. They have the advantage of being able to more closely match real-life activities and situations but are less controlled than laboratory tests and provide less information. Questionnaires are simple to administer, and they can address complex issues such as interactions between environmental issues (spouse support, socioeconomic status) and physical capacity. But questionnaires are sensitive to subject perceptions, such as subjects' memories of previous

The comments of Lee Stoner are appreciated. Supported by NIH HL65179.

capacity. Subjects may also underreport or overreport physical activity depending on how they perceive the test will be used. The limitations in self-report measures of physical activity and exercise capacity make it necessary to use direct measurement methods.

MEASURING CARDIORESPIRATORY FITNESS

Because of the prevalence of cardiovascular disease, cardiorespiratory fitness is considered to be the most important measure of fitness in determining overall health (Tritschler, 2000a). For patients with CFS, the issue is not cardiovascular disease, but the functional impact of reduced cardiovascular capacity. The gold standard for measuring cardiorespiratory fitness is to measure maximum aerobic power (Sutton, 1992). This is done by using incremental exercise to obtain a maximum or peak value for oxygen consumption (Taylor, Buskirk, & Henschel, 1955). This provides a theoretical upper limit for aerobic exercise. It also has been correlated with exercise performance. Interpretation of this measure is that it represents a mixture (~40%) of genetic capacity and (~60%) environmental issues (training/activity level) (Katzmarzyk, Gledhill, Lerusse, & Bouchard, 2001). This means that while activity level or illness can alter $\dot{V}O_2$max, the variations in genetic contributions make this difficult to interpret. Many CFS patients were physically active prior to getting CFS, and this complicates the selection of appropriate control subjects for research studies. For example, would the best control subject for a CFS patient who was a competitive gymnast prior to having CFS be a person who has never shown any aptitude in sports and has never been physically active (typical sedentary control)? Or a control subject who has shown great aptitude for endurance sports (marathon runner), but who has not done any exercise over the same time period as the CFS patient? Typically, both types of control subjects are used (just as long as they are not currently active), but this is rarely if ever discussed in research papers (Bazelmans, Bleijenberg, van der Meer, & Folgering, 2001). When comparing exercise capacity between patients with CFS and control subjects, it is also important to make sure that they have the same amount of muscle mass (controlling for size and percentage of body fat).

The $\dot{V}O_2$max test has methodological issues that influence the interpretation of the results (Noakes, 1988). It is usually an incremental test that is sensitive to the rate of work increment as well as the duration of the test. Large work increments do not allow time for oxidative metabolism to keep up with energy demand and result in early increases in glycolytic metabolism. The increases in lactic acid and the breakdown in phosphocreatine produce metabolites that have been implicated in causing muscle fatigue (Allen, 2002; Wilson, McCully, Mancin, Boden, & Chance, 1988). Once the test reaches work levels that are above the glycolytic threshold (lactate threshold, anaerobic threshold, ventilatory threshold), the buildup of fatigue-causing metabolites makes the exercise nonsustainable. Tests that are too long (small work increments) can fatigue subjects at lower relative work levels. This is particularly true of less fit subjects (such as those with CFS). The duration of $\dot{V}O_2$max tests recommended by the American College of Sports Medicine is 8 to 12 minutes (ACSM, 2000). A number of different standardized protocols (rate and magnitude of work increments) have been used (ACSM, 2000). These may or may not be appropriate for CFS patients. Another issue with $\dot{V}O_2$max tests is the exercise equipment used. The most common forms of equipment are cycle ergometers and motorized treadmills. Treadmill walking/running uses more muscle mass and usually results in higher oxygen consumption values than cycle exercise. Treadmill exercise is somewhat trickier to execute, as the end-of-test condition requires stopping the treadmill or having the subject step off the treadmill. This can be difficult to coordinate when the subject is moving rapidly and is tired, and the investigator wants to make sure the subject exercises to the absolute maximum. Cycle ergometry exercise is safer in that regard. The subject is sitting, and the test stops when the subject stops pedaling.

A final issue with $\dot{V}O_2$max tests is that they are dependent on subjects exercising to their limit, or until they fatigue. Although in theory, the incremental test continues until measured oxygen consumption levels off, this is often not the case. Commonly, the last work levels obtained have linearly increasing oxygen consumption values. Even if oxygen consumption is reported to level off, the definition of leveling off is often not a true plateau, but a significant decrease in the rate of increase. The lack of a plateau in oxygen consumption makes the test very sensitive to subject motivation. As reduced motivation may be a component of CFS, this is a major concern. Several end-of-test criteria have been used to document a maximal effort in tests where oxygen consumption does not level off (ACSM, 2000). These have included a combination of end-exercise blood lactate levels (> 4 or 8 mM), RER values (> 1.1 or 1.15), heart rate values (> 90% predicted max), and exertion levels (>17 on Borg scale). These values are based on the logic that the test results in significant glycolysis, and if significant glycolysis occurred, then the test must be maximal. Or if the subject achieved maximal effort and/or heart rate, then the test was maximal. These values help in interpreting the test, and allow exclusion of submaximal tests. But the concern with CFS patients is that glycolytic capacity may be altered (Arnold, Bore, Radda, Styles, & Taylor, 1984), perceived exertion with exercise is enhanced, and autonomic control of heart rate may be altered. And studies with CFS patients have used relaxed criteria. To acknowledge the lack of a plateau in the maximum exercise tests, the term $\dot{V}O_2$peak is sometimes used instead of $\dot{V}O_2$max. Nonetheless, $\dot{V}O_2$max tests remain the best measure of whole body aerobic capacity.

The glycolytic threshold (sometimes referred to as the anaerobic threshold) is often used as an index of cardiorespiratory function. This is the work level associated with significant increases in anaerobic glycolysis, which can be characterized by increases in blood lactate levels and the compensatory changes associated with increased lactate. This includes increased respiration due to increased CO_2 levels, and increased heart rate due to increased activation of respiratory muscles (Inbar, Dlin, Rotstein, & Whipp, 2001). Glycolytic thresholds maybe more sensitive to changes in endurance capacity and activity level than $\dot{V}O_2$max. But the glycolytic threshold can be difficult to measure precisely.

Alternative measures of maximum aerobic capacity are to use submaximal exercise and predict maximal efforts. This includes incremental exercise to a submaximal level, and using measured heart rate to extrapolate to the oxygen consumption at maximal heart rate (Tritschler, 2000a). This approach avoids the need to obtain a maximal effort from CFS patients, but depends heavily on the ability to estimate maximal heart rate. To estimate maximum heart rate, the formula of maximum heart rate = 220–age is often used, even though this is inaccurate on an individual basis. Other approaches to estimate cardiorespiratory capacity are to use a submaximal effort test such as the 1-mile run/walk or the 6-minute walk (Kline et al., 1987). These are relatively simple tests and may test a critical domain of function in

CFS, which is the ability to sustain activity. The key to these tests is maintaining consistent motivation throughout the test, and between subjects. Especially in CFS, performance on submaximal exercise tests may reflect motivation and perception of effort, rather than being an index of maximal exercise capacity.

ASSESSING MUSCULOSKELETAL FITNESS

Three aspects of muscle function are important in CFS, muscle strength, muscle endurance, and susceptibility to injury. Strength measurements are a common and useful method of assessing muscle function (Skinner, Baldini, & Gardner, 1990; Tritschler, 2000b). However, muscle strength can be difficult to measure accurately in human subjects. While minimizing contributions from synergistic and antagonistic muscles, the examiner must take care to assure maximal muscle fiber recruitment and accurate measurement of the forces produced by the muscle of interest and, finally, accurate normalization of the strength to the size of the muscle. Muscle strength is usually thought to be directly related to muscle mass. The term *muscle quality* has been used to indicate the amount of force a muscle can produce per unit cross-sectional area. If the patient has impaired central neural activation or neuromuscular transmission, however, muscle weakness can occur even in the presence of normal muscle strength. Because maximal muscle activation is difficult to obtain with voluntary effort, especially with large muscle groups, muscle strength measurements sometimes use electrical stimulation to assess muscle activation.

Measuring strength is usually done with a maximum single effort (Skinner et al., 1990; Tritschler, 2000b). This can be done using free weights or weight machines by measuring the ability to successfully lift a weight (1RM max). This requires performing several lifts at increasing levels until the subject can no longer execute the lift. In practice, it is critical to guess close to the person's maximum to reduce the number of lifts the subject must do (ideally 3–6), and to carefully define what is meant by good form. Novice subjects often learn how to lift the weight with repeated trials, so suboptimal technique can make it easy to underestimate the maximal effort. The advent of isokinetic machines has meant that muscle strength can be measured in a single effort where the speed of the contraction is held constant and the resistance needed to control the speed against the subject's effort is recorded. This reduces the need for the expert guess and can provide detailed information on the effects of speed of movement on muscle strength. In general, it is harder to fully activate a muscle when it is moving rapidly. This is a better approach than lifting weights, but it can result in a dizzying array of numbers for each subject, which leads to statistical issues of how to interpret them.

A concern with testing strength with a single maximum effort is that the high force levels might result in injury to muscles, ligaments, or joints. Using several submaximal efforts avoids the risk of injury associated with maximal strength testing. The subject is told to lift the weight as many times as possible; the number of repetitions and the weight are used to extrapolate to the single maximal effort. This does not work well for predicting a maximal effort (ACSM, 2000) and still requires the subject to put in a maximal effort (even if on submaximal weights).

To overcome the effect of differences in motivation on strength measurements, electrical stimulation can be used (Kent-Braun et al., 1993). Electrodes can be placed over the motor nerve or the endplate regions of the muscle. Transcranial magnetic stimulation has been used on CFS subjects to examine the role of central motor processing on the development of muscle force (Sacco, Hope, Thickbroom, Byrnes, & Mastaglia, 1999; Zaman, Puri, Main, Nowicky, & Davey, 2001). Electrical stimulation can be used to eliminate potential differences in central drive (motivation and central nervous system impairment). Electrical stimulation varies from feeling "strange" to painful depending on the method of stimulation and its intensity. In general, to obtain high levels of stimulation, the highest tolerable stimulation levels are needed. If patients with CFS have enhanced pain sensitivity (and some do), this might be a problem. Small muscle groups like the adductor pollis in the hand can be maximally activated, but larger muscle groups like the tibialis anterior and the quadriceps muscles are usually activated at much lower levels (as low as 15% of a maximal voluntary effort). This means that much of the muscle is not activated with electrical stimulation, and potential differences in the degree of activation are possible between test subjects. Voluntary exercise shows an orderly recruitment pattern of muscle fibers (same units activate first, same units activate late) with increasing exercise intensity. Electrical stimulation results in a different recruitment pattern that alters the type of muscle activated as well as the circulation patterns to the active muscle. In addition, electrical stimulation does not recruit synergistic muscles as does voluntary activation. This can be good or bad; for example, one would like to activate only the muscle of interest, but some muscles such as the biceps attach at a very loose joint (shoulder) that requires activation of synergistic muscles to stabilize the joint and thus reduces compliance. All of these issues make direct comparisons difficult between electrically stimulated force and voluntary force. To get around this and address whether a patient population group such as people with CFS might have an altered central drive, electrical stimulation has been used to enhance voluntary force development. Two approaches have been used. One is a twitch interpolation method and the other uses bursts of stimuli, but both look at the amount of extra force that electrical stimulation adds to a voluntary effort (Kent-Braun et al., 1993; Stackhouse et al., 2001). If the person is maximally activating the muscle, then electrically stimulating it should not result in an increase in force level. A difficulty with this approach is that the initial phase of training studies, especially with older subjects, demonstrates rapid increases in strength that have been attributed to increases in muscle activation (Pyka, Linderberger, Charette, & Marcus, 1994). Other studies, however, have shown that with the superimposed electrical stimulation protocols even the older subjects are activating 97% of their muscle on the initial test period (Stackhouse et al., 2001). These two observations do not agree and may indicate that the electrical stimulation protocol might overestimate the amount of muscle mass that is being recruited. Even so, these approaches have merit in detecting differences in activation between individuals with CFS and controls.

Musculoskeletal endurance is measured as the ability of a subject to sustain a given force level, or the amount of decline in force with a given force protocol. This is usually done with exercise protocols lasting 2 to 20 minutes. Rarely do investigators mention the underlying mechanisms associated with the fatigue protocol (Allen, 2002; Edwards, 1983), and these will vary with the type of protocol chosen. Short, high-intensity protocols produce large changes in metabolite levels (such as phosphate and H^+) and result in metabolic inhibition of force development. Longer protocols produce less dramatic metabolic changes and will increasingly depend on the balance between energy demand and energy supply, with glycolysis becoming less important as the protocols lengthen out to 5 minutes or more. Long protocols will also result in greater sequestration of calcium and more calcium-related fatigue. Short protocols have the advantage of being more reproducible and are less susceptible to differences in motivation than long protocols. Even slight changes in motivation can have a large effect on a protocol that lasts 20 minutes (think of the effect of a favorable crowd on athletic performance, and athletes are highly motivated!). Electrical stimulation can be used to account for differences in motivation. The area of muscle recruited with electrical stimulation is thought to be different from that for voluntary activities, and this can influence the rate and amount of fatigue seen. Voluntary stimulation recruits motor units starting with smaller, more endurance-type fibers. Electrical stimulation recruits a mixture of larger more fatigable fibers first, along with fibers directly under the stimulation electrodes.

Another approach is to avoid performance altogether and to measure metabolic pathways using oxidative and glycolytic enzymatic concentrations and rates. Muscle biopsies can be used, where a small piece of muscle (size of one-half a pea) is taken from the muscle with a specialized biopsy needle through an opening made in the skin (Edwards, Gibson, Clague, & Helliwell, 1993). This method is invasive and thus somewhat limited in application. A noninvasive approach is to measure the balance of use and production of high-energy phosphates using magnetic resonance spectroscopy (Kent-Braun et al., 1993; McCully, Natelson, Iotti, Sisto, & Leigh, 1996). Oxidative muscle metabolism is thought to be regulated in part by levels of ADP (Chance et al., 1986). Measures of phosphocreatine and muscle pH can be used as markers of ADP levels (Kent-Braun et al., 1993; McCully et al., 1996; Wong, Lopachuk, & Zhu, 1992) or to measure changes in muscle oxygen saturation using near infrared spectroscopy (NIRS; McCully & Natelson, 1999). Oxygen concentrations also influence oxidative metabolism (Richardson, Leigh, Wagner, & Noyszewski, 1999), and reduced muscle oxygen saturation may reflect limitations in oxidative metabolism (McCully, Halber, & Posner, 1994). Magnetic resonance spectroscopy and NIRS require specialized equipment (magnetic resonance spectroscopy is expensive; NIRS is relatively cheap), but can work well. The metabolic measurements only examine one aspect of muscle endurance, and it can be hard to interpret the functional significance of impaired metabolic measurements. For example, is the detection of impaired oxidative metabolism adequate to explain symptoms of fatigue in CFS, or is it just a marker for underlying abnormalities?

Muscle injury and the susceptibility to exercise-induced muscle injury is also a component of musculoskeletal function (Armstrong, 1984). It is possible that CFS is associated with enhanced exercise-induced muscle injury. As exercise-induced muscle injury has a delayed component related to the involvement of inflammatory pathways, abnormal immune/inflammatory processes in patients with CFS might increase muscle injury. Numerous markers of muscle injury have been used, including reduced strength, increased inflammation, increased muscle edema, increases in muscle proteins in serum, and indexes of muscle soreness (Cannon et al., 1998; Shellock, Fukunaga, Mink, & Edgerton, 1991). Baseline levels of injury/soreness can be measured as in fibromyalgia, but it may be better to evaluate the response to a test bout of exercise. This can be a standard exercise test for evaluating cardiorespiratory function or musculoskeletal function (Sisto et al., 1996), but it can also be designed to enhance the muscle damage that occurs by including high-force contractions such as "eccentric" actions (McCully et al., 1988). The amount of damage is hard to standardize and potentially threatening to the subject. There also seems to be rapid adaptation to exercise that reduces the amount of exercise-induced muscle damage that must be taken into account when administering such a test (Hough, 1902).

EXERCISE CAPACITY AND CFS

Cardiorespiratory function in CFS has been assessed by using both maximal exercise tests and estimation of maximum with submaximal tests. Several studies have reported patients with CFS to have near-normal $\dot{V}O_2$max values (Kent-Braun et al., 1993; Riley, O'Brien, McCulskey, Bell, & Nicholls, 1990). Kent-Braun and colleagues tested six subjects with CFS using a cycle ergometer and found that those with CFS had slightly lower peak $\dot{V}O_2$peak values, but these values were within the normal range for sedentary controls. Sisto and colleagues (1996) found slightly lower $\dot{V}O_2$max values in patients with CFS compared with controls (28.1 ± 5.1 compared with 32.1 ± 4.3 mL/kg/min). Interestingly, they found a higher percentage of patients with CFS do not reach their criteria for obtaining $\dot{V}O_2$max. Stokes and colleagues (1988) did not attempt to obtain $\dot{V}O_2$peak values, but did find patients with CFS to have slightly, but not significantly, lower heart rates at the highest obtained work levels compared with normal controls. Montague and colleagues (1988) also tested CFS patients with submaximal exercise tests. Compared with normal subjects, CFS patients had reduced exercise capacity associated with slow acceleration of heart rate and increased fatigue of skeletal muscles during the test. Bazelmans and colleagues (2001) reported patients with CFS to have maximum work levels and $\dot{V}O_2$max values that were 85% to 88% of controls, respectively. These differences were not statistically different ($n = 20$ per group). This study had several interesting aspects. First is that although $\dot{V}O_2$max was not statistically different between patients with CFS and controls, a higher percentage of those with CFS did not reach the authors' criteria for a maximal test. Second, the authors used height, age, and sex to predict $\dot{V}O_2$max and found that CFS and controls had the same fitness levels (difference between measured and predicted $\dot{V}O_2$max). In contrast to the relatively small changes reported in the preceding papers, a study by De Becker and colleagues (2000) found patients with CFS to demonstrate considerably lower $\dot{V}O_2$max values and glycolytic threshold values compared with controls (Figure 18.1). This article has several interesting aspects. First, they were able to test an extremely large number of subjects, including 427 patients with CFS and 204 age-matched controls (De Becker et al., 2000). This makes the study far more comprehensive than any previous CFS study on this topic. The second aspect concerns some of the methods used in the study. Control subjects performed standard work levels and reached $\dot{V}O_2$max values similar to other studies (Bazelmans et al., 2001; Sisto et al., 1996). But the patients with CFS did a different exercise protocol with much lower exercise intensities to keep the duration of exercise the same. Both groups reached the same criteria for a maximum test (RER > 1.0 and heart rate > 85% of predicted max). But these criteria are lenient compared with what is typically used (see discussion of $\dot{V}O_2$max measurements), and the CFS group had significantly lower RER and heart-rate values compared with controls. Reduced motivation and increased pain are both common problems when testing individuals with CFS, as they report higher perceived effort and pain at any given work level than do healthy controls (Bazelmans et al., 2001; Gibson, Carroll, Clague, & Edwards, 1993; Riley et al., 1990). In addition, the investigators used an unorthodox method to obtain the glycolytic threshold. Glycolytic threshold was

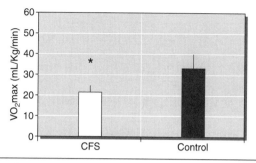

Figure 18.1   Maximal Oxygen Consumption Values for CFS and Control Subjects. Tests were done on a cycle ergometer and are means + *SD*. The key to this study was that 427 CFS and 204 control subjects were tested. *Source:* "Exercise Capacity in Chronic Fatigue Syndrome," by P. De Becker, J. Roeykens, M. Reynders, N. McGregor, and K. De Meirleir, 2000. *Archives of Internal Medicine, 160,* pp. 3270–3277.

reported as the exercise level at which the respiratory quotient reaches 1.0. This is not the usual method of making this measurement (ACSM, 2000; Inbar et al., 2001), making it difficult to compare it with other studies. Another recent study found intermediate results; patients with CFS had 85% of the $\dot{V}O_2$max (mlO_2/min) of the values of controls (Inbar et al., 2001). This study is interesting because the authors are very experienced in exercise testing. But the patients with CFS were heavier, having a body mass index of 29.5 compared with 25.4 in the controls (body mass index is height in meters divided by the square of the weight in kilograms). This suggests the CFS subjects may have had less muscle mass than the controls, and there was some evidence based on bioimpedance measurements that this was the case (Inbar et al., 2001). It is unclear whether differences in $\dot{V}O_2$max between groups would have been more or less if accurate measures of muscle mass were used to normalize the $\dot{V}O_2$max measurements (this comment is appropriate for all the $\dot{V}O_2$max studies). In summary, several studies have found reduced $\dot{V}O_2$max values compared with controls. But other studies do not find clearly lower $\dot{V}O_2$max values in patients with CFS. It is not certain whether the method of testing or normalizing for muscle mass alone can explain the results. It would be interesting to have the same subjects tested in different laboratories.

Muscle strength has been measured in CFS using different muscle groups and measurement methods. Lloyd and colleagues (Lloyd, Phales, & Gandevia, 1988) found that patients with CFS ($n = 20$) were not weaker than control subjects ($n = 20$). Their strength measurements consisted of isometric tension measured during a maximum voluntary effort of the elbow flexors. Stokes and colleagues (1988) found maximal strength of the quadriceps muscles of patients with CFS ($n = 22$) to be within the range for normal subjects (Figure 18.2). However, some of the subjects appeared to be below the range for normal subjects. Whether this might indicate a subpopulation of impaired CFS subjects is not clear. In contrast to these studies, a study of quadriceps muscle strength found large differences between subjects with CFS and controls, with CFS subjects having only 61% of the strength of controls (Paul et al., 1999). As with whole body exercise capacity, it is not known why some studies find large impairments in muscles of patients with CFS, while other studies do not.

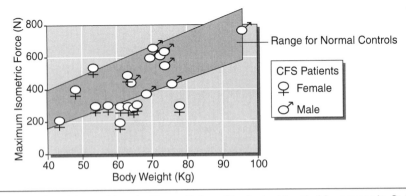

Figure 18.2 Quadriceps Muscle Strength in a Single Isokinetic Movement in Subjects with CFS. The range for control subjects is shown by the darker shaded area. Note that some subjects with CFS appear outside the normal range, but on average subjects with CFS did not differ from controls. *Source:* "Normal Muscle Strength and Fatigability in Patients with Effort Syndromes," by M. Stokes, R. Cooper, and R. H. T. Edwards, 1988, *British Medical Journal, 297*, pp. 1014–1017.

MEASUREMENT OF MUSCLE ENDURANCE IN PATIENTS WITH CFS

Lloyd and colleagues (1988) found that muscle endurance was not different between patients with CFS and controls using an endurance test consisting of a series of 18 maximal contractions of the elbow flexor muscles. However, they did find some indication of impaired recovery of muscle strength during recovery in those with CFS. Similarly, Paul and colleagues (1999) found no difference in the rate of fatigue (despite large differences in strength) between patients with CFS and controls, but did find a slower rate of recovery. Stokes and colleagues (1988) found no difference in the rate of fatigue in the adductor pollicis muscle under blood flow intact as well as under ischemic conditions. Wong and colleagues (1992) found CFS patients ($n = 22$) fatigued sooner than control subjects ($n = 21$) during a ramp exercise protocol using the calf muscles. However, Wong and colleagues did not normalize the exercise levels to subject strength, and the CFS and control groups contained different proportions of male and female subjects. Kent-Braun and colleagues (1992) found that patients with CFS reached lower work levels in an incremental exercise protocol, although it was not strictly an endurance protocol. This study used superimposed electrical twitches to test for changes in central drive. They found that the increased fatigue seen in the CFS patients could be primarily explained as a drop in neural activation of the muscle, not as changes in muscle function. The reduced neural activation correlated well with increased perceptions of pain and discomfort in the patients with CFS at the end of the exercise. A study by Sacco and colleagues (1999) found reduced muscle endurance in patients with CFS. The protocol consisted of a much longer duration of exercise than most fatigue studies (Figure 18.3). The longer duration protocol may have resulted in a greater influence of central fatigue, and the CFS subjects did have increased perceived exertion compared with control subjects (Sacco et al., 1999). In summary, muscle endurance does not seem to be impaired in individuals with CFS if the exercise protocol involves relatively contractions, even

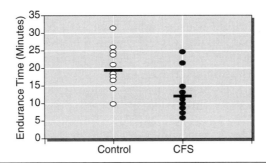

Figure 18.3 Endurance Time for Sustaining a 20% MVC Isometric Contraction with the Biceps Muscles. Note the relatively long duration of the test (5–33 minutes) emphasizes the role of central drive in determining the endurance time. *Source:* "Corticomotor Excitability and Perception of Effort during Sustained Exercise in Chronic Fatigue Syndrome," by P. Sacco, P. Hope, G. Thickbroom, M. Byrnes, and F. Mastaglia, 1999, *Clinical Neurophysiology, 110,* pp. 1883–1891.

if the contractions are maximal. But CFS patients appear to have reduced central drive compared with control subjects and reduced performance in long-duration activities that emphasize central drive.

Measurements of muscle metabolism using both invasive and noninvasive methods have been made in individuals with CFS. Behan and colleagues (Behan, More, & Behan, 1991) reported type II (fast twitch) fiber atrophy ($n = 39$), mitochondrial abnormalities ($n = 25$), and mildly excessive lipid levels ($n = 24$) in muscle biopsies from 50 patients with CFS (a total of 40 subjects had abnormal biopsies). In separate studies, Byrne and colleagues (Byrne & Trounce, 1987; Byrne, Trounce, & Dennett, 1985) initially found type II fiber atrophy and reduced oxidative capacity in two CFS patients, but later found no abnormalities in fiber size or oxidative enzymes in a larger sample ($n = 20$) of CFS patients. Edwards and associates (1993) reported some evidence of abnormalities in patients with CFS, but concluded that the number and extent of the abnormalities were in the range of that expected in control subjects.

Some studies have used MRS to evaluate patients with CFS. The first study was a case report, which found a single patient with CFS to be abnormal (Arnold et al., 1984). This abnormality consisted of early acidosis during exercise, which was thought to reflect abnormal regulation of muscle metabolism. A follow-up study found greater depletion of phosphocreatine, increases in inorganic phosphate, and increased acidosis at any given work level for CFS patients compared with controls (Wong et al., 1992). But the Wong et al. study used the same absolute workloads for all subjects, and compared patients with CFS consisting of 6 men and 16 women, to controls consisting of 11 men and 10 women. Thus, the differences seen between individuals with CFS and controls in this study were likely a result of the differences in muscle mass between men and women. A study by Kent-Braun et al. (1993) that used electrical and voluntary stimulation of skeletal muscle found no differences in muscle metabolism in CFS patients compared with controls. A study by Barnes, Taylor, Kemp, and Radda (1993) using forearm exercise found 12 of 46 patients with CFS to have abnormally high or low ADP levels during steady level exercise. ADP levels represent the degree of mitochondrial activation and reflect changes in phosphocreatine and pH. A study of phosphocreatine recovery rates after exercise in the calf muscles found CFS patients to have slightly slower rates of recovery (~25%) than control subjects, with 6 of the 20 CFS subjects showing decreased muscle pH (McCully et al., 1996). In a follow-up study, the rate of recovery of oxygen saturation after exercise was slower in CFS subjects compared with controls (McCully & Natelson, 1999) (Figure 18.4). It was suggested that slower recovery of oxygen saturation indicated abnormal oxygen delivery and might explain the slower recovery in muscle metabolism (slower phosphocreatine recovery).

The finding of impaired oxygen delivery in CFS appears attractive because several studies have reported abnormal vascular control in CFS. Orthostatic

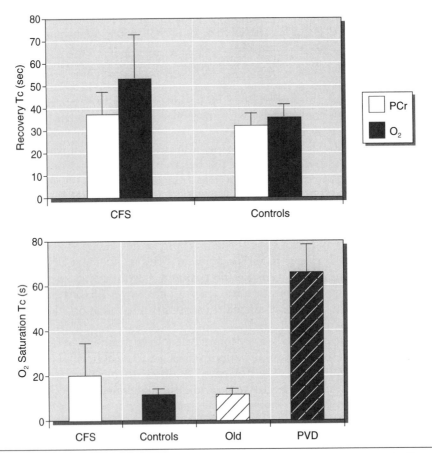

Figure 18.4 The Left Panel Shows Recovery of Phosphocreatine and Muscle Oxygen Saturation after Exercise in CFS and Control Subjects. Note that the subjects with CFS had slower (longer) recovery times (Tc is time constant of recovery). The slower oxygen recovery Tc values might help to explain the longer phosphocreatine recovery values. The figure on the right shows the rate of recovery of oxygen saturation after 4 minutes of cuff ischemia (no change in phosphocreatine with this duration of ischemia). Subjects with CFS show large variations in response, but were slower than age-matched controls. Old healthy subjects (76 years on average) and older subjects with peripheral arterial vascular disease (PVD) are shown for comparison. Values are mean + *SD*.

hypotension during a tilt table test has been used as a method of evaluating sympathetic function (DeLorenzo, Hargreaves, & Kakkar, 1997; Freeman & Komaroff, 1997). DeLorenzo et al. found that 22 of 78 subjects with CFS had orthostatic hypotension. Freeman and Komaroff found that 25% of subjects with CFS had orthostatic hypotension. This and decreased systolic pressure in Phase II of the Valsalva maneuver was used as evidence of abnormal sympathetic tone. They also found evidence of parasympathetic abnormalities based on abnormal expiration/ inspiration ratios during breathing and greater maximal minus minimal heart rates during breathing (Freeman & Komaroff, 1997). However, Sendrowski, Buker, and Gee (1977) did not find evidence of sympathetic abnormalities in CFS patients. They used pupillary dilation to measure sympathetic dennervation hypersensitivity. In addition to the sympathetic and parasympathetic nervous systems, other neurohumoral pathways have been implicated in CFS (Crofford & Demitrack, 1996). One thing is clear from these studies. There is a great need to determine if these potential abnormalities have an impact on the symptomatology of CFS. A possible effect of dysregulation in autonomic and neurohormonal systems is impairment of muscle blood flow and production of an abnormal response to exercise (Montague et al., 1988). This could occur as either reduced blood flow during exercise or a slowed increase in flow during the onset of exercise. In either case, inadequate blood flow could impair oxidative metabolism and increase glycolytic metabolism, leading to earlier fatigue. While not studied in CFS, studies have reported abnormal muscle blood flow in fibromyalgia (Bennett, 1989; Lindh, Johansson, Hedberg, Henning, & Grimby, 1995). Reduced oxidative metabolism due to reduced blood flow may occur in patients with CFS. But additional studies are needed to correlate these findings and show that the magnitude of the effects is in the expected range.

Skeletal muscle pathology has been examined in patients with CFS. This is important because exercise-induced muscle injury is a mechanism for postexertional muscle soreness and pain in normal subjects (Armstrong, 1984). As mentioned, Behan et al. (1991) found that a large percentage of CFS subjects had abnormal muscle pathology. Edwards et al. (1993) also found evidence for muscle abnormalities by histological ($n = 108$) and electron microscopic ($n = 22$) examination of iopsies from CFS patients. However, the occurrence of abnormalities was rare in any given sample and Edwards et al. concluded that CFS samples were not different from control samples. The disagreement between these studies is not easily resolved. Elevated inorganic phosphate relative to phosphocreatine (Pi/PCr) measured with MRS has been used as an indirect measure of muscle injury (McCully et al., 1988). Resting muscle Pi/PCr ratios were not found to be elevated in either fibromyalgia patients (Jubrias, Bennett, & Klug, 1994) or in patients with CFS (McCully et al., 1996). In a study that examined the delayed effects of strenuous exercise, no delayed alterations were reported in ratings of vigor and fatigue (Sisto et al., 1996) and muscle metabolism (McCully et al., 1996) in CFS subjects compared with controls. Individuals with CFS may have abnormal immune/inflammation responses as indicated by cytokine response to injury (Cannon et al., 1998), but the implication of this is not clear. A study has found evidence of increased oxidative damage in muscles of patients with CFS (Fulle et al., 2000). But it is not clear how this finding fits with previous studies suggesting that muscle injury does not play a significant role in CFS.

Deconditioning is a potential confounding variable when assessing exercise capacity in CFS. Individuals with CFS report very reduced activity levels, and this complaint is a part of the diagnosis of CFS (Schluederberg et al., 1992). Several studies using pedometers and accelometers have found CFS subjects to have activity levels that are ~75% of that of controls (van der Werf, Prins, Vercoulen, van der Meer, & Bleijenberg, 2000; Vercoulen et al., 1996). Bazelmans et al. (2001) examined accelometer data from the ankle collected over two weeks in CFS and control subjects. Their CFS patients had activity levels that were 58% of that of controls. Reduced activity levels are associated with reduced $\dot{V}O_2$max, muscle metabolism, and muscle blood flow (Convertino, 1997; Kroese, 1977). Deconditioning in normal subjects has been associated with slower phosphocreatine recovery rates (McCully, Kahihira, & Vandenborne, 1991). Because of this, many of the changes in muscle function reported in patients with CFS could be a result of the reduced activity levels (Wagemaker, 1999). Bazelmans et al. (2001) concluded that factors other than physical fitness cause the lower activity levels, fatigue, and impairment in CFS. They found no difference in fitness level between individuals with CFS and controls, despite the greatly reduced activity levels. In any case, it can be difficult to find control subjects who are normal but as inactive as individuals with CFS. Patients with other diseases who have similar activity levels will most likely have other medical problems that will complicate the comparisons (Kent-Braun, Sharma, Miller, & Weiner, 1994).

Relatively few studies have objectively examined the impact of exercise training on symptoms of CFS (Whiting et al., 2001). The few training studies that have been done have used low intensity interventions (Coutts, Weatherby, & Davie, 2001), in part to avoid the postexertional crises that most patients with CFS report having. A study by Powell and colleagues (Powell, Bental, Nye, & Edwards, 2001) used an education program to encourage exercise in patients with CFS. The investigators did not record how much exercise the patients actually performed. These studies (Coutts et al., 2001; Powell et al., 2001) report improvement in symptoms compared with standard medical care, although few of the patients could be called cured. The success of the programs was attributed more to reducing stress levels and to coping better with symptoms than to actually improving exercise capacity.

CONCLUSION

Sophisticated studies have been performed to evaluate physical capacity in subjects with CFS. These studies have examined cardiovascular function, muscle strength, muscle endurance/metabolism, and muscle injury. The studies do not lend themselves to a simple summary. Many of the studies find little or no abnormality in CFS subjects despite self-reports of significant functional impairment. Other studies report large reductions in exercise capacity in CFS patients, similar to findings for patients with major medical diseases (i.e., heart failure). The discrepancies may be due to methodological differences between studies in performing the tests, or in diagnosing and defining CFS. There seems to be a consistent finding of increased perceived exertion during exercise and reduced central drive in patients with CFS. There is also some evidence that patients with CFS have abnormal autonomic nervous system function that might contribute to reduced oxygen delivery. An important question when interpreting these findings is whether they are a primary alteration that results in CFS symptoms, or the result of deconditioning due to CFS. This is a difficult question to answer, as deconditioning is a contributing factor to all major medical illnesses (Levine, Johnson, & McCully, 1999).

The key to CFS may be to go back to one of the major complaints of CFS patients. Despite having normal or near normal exercise capacity measurements, almost all patients with CFS report an inability to sustain "normal" activity levels. If they try to do this, they report a gradual deterioration of health that forces them to reduce their activity levels. Exercise programs have been successfully implemented with CFS patients, but the programs were very mild in intensity, and individuals with CFS can report "resting up for the training sessions." To understand exercise capacity in CFS, it seems better to focus on the sustainable level of activity that a patient can tolerate and to measure what happens when a CFS patient fails to tolerate a given activity level. This is a difficult proposition, but may be required to understand physical capacity in CFS.

REFERENCES

ACSM. (2000). *ACSM's (American College of Sports Medicine's) guidelines for exercise testing and prescription* (6th ed.). Philadelphia: Lippincott, Williams, & Wilkins.

Allen, D. (2002). Role of calcium in muscle fatigue. *Canadian Journal of Applied Physiology, 27,* 83-96.

Armstrong, R. (1984). Mechanisms of exercise-induced delayed onset muscular soreness: A brief review. *Medicine and Science in Sports and Exercise, 16,* 529–538.

Arnold, D., Bore, P., Radda, G., Styles, P., & Taylor, D. (1984). Excessive intracellular acidosis of skeletal muscle on exercise in a patient with a postviral exhaustion/fatigue syndrome. *Lancet, 1,* 1367–1369.

Barnes, P., Taylor, D., Kemp, G., & Radda, G. (1993). Skeletal muscle bioenergetics in the chronic fatigue syndrome. *Journal of Neurology, Neurosurgery, and Psychiatry, 56,* 679–683.

Bazelmans, E., Bleijenberg, G., van der Meer, J. W., & Folgering, H. (2001). Is physical deconditioning a perpetuating factor in chronic fatigue syndrome? A controlled study on maximal exercise performance and relations with fatigue, impairment, and physical activity. *Psychological Medicine, 31,* 107–114.

Behan, W., More, I., & Behan, P. (1991). Mitochondrial abnormalites in the postviral fatigue syndrome. *Acta Neuropathologica, 83,* 61–65.

Bennett, R. (1989). Muscle physiology and cold reactivity in the fibromyalgia syndrome. *Rheumatic Disease Clinics of North America, 15,* 135–147.

Byrne, E., & Trounce, I. (1987). Chronic fatigue and myalgia syndrome: Mitochondrial and glycolytic studies in skeletal muscle. *Journal of Neurology, Neurosurgery, and Psychiatry, 50,* 743–746.

Byrne, E., Trounce, I., & Dennett, X. (1985). Chronic relapsing myalgia (postviral): Clinical histological and biochemical studies. *Australian and New Zealand Journal of Medicine, 15,* 305–308.

Cannon, J., Angel, J., Abad, L., O'Grady, J., Lundgren, N., Fagioli, L., et al. (1998). Hormonal influences on stress-induced neutrophil mobilization in health and chronic fatigue syndrome. *Journal of Clinical Immunology, 4,* 291–298.

Chance, B., Leigh, J., Kent, J., McCully, K., Nioka, S., Clark, B., et al. (1986). Multiple controls of oxidative metabolism of living tissues as studied by 31-P MRS. *Proceedings of the National Academy of Sciences, USA, 83,* 9458–9462.

Convertino, V. (1997). Exercise and adaptation to microgravity environments. In J. Fregly & C. Blatteis (Eds.), *Handbook of physiology: Adaptation to the environment*. Bethesda, MD: American Physiological Society.

Coutts, R., Weatherby, R., & Davie, A. (2001). The use of a symptom "self-report" inventory to evaluate the acceptability and efficacy of a walking program for patients suffering with chronic fatigue syndrome. *Journal of Psychosomatic Research, 51*, 425–429.

Crofford, L., & Demitrack, M. (1996). Evidence that abnormalities of central neurohormonal systems are key to understanding fibromyalgia and chronic fatigue syndrome. *Rheumatic Disease Clinics of North America, 22*, 267–284.

De Becker, P., Roeykens, J., Reynders, M., McGregor, N., & De Meirleir, K. (2000). Exercise capacity in chronic fatigue syndrome. *Archives of Internal Medicine, 160*, 3270–3277.

DeLorenzo, F., Hargreaves, J., & Kakkar, V. (1997). Pathogenesis and management of delayed orthostatic hypotension in patients with chronic fatigue syndrome. *Clinical Autonomic Research, 7*, 185–190.

Edwards, R., Gibson, H., Clague, J., & Helliwell, T. (1993). Muscle histopathology and physiology in chronic fatigue syndrome. *CIBA Foundation Symposium, 173*, 102–117.

Edwards, R. H. (1983). Biochemical bases of fatigue in exercise performance: Catastrophe theory of muscular fatigue. In H. G. Knuttgen, J. H. Vogel, & J. H. Poortmaas (Eds.), *Biochemistry of Fatigue* (Vol. 13, pp. 3–28). Champagne, IL: Human Kinetics.

Freeman, R., & Komaroff, A. (1997). Does the chronic fatigue syndrome involve the autonomic nervous system? *American Journal of Medicine, 102*, 357–364.

Fulle, S., Mecocci, P., Fano, G., Vecchiet, I., Vecchiet, A., Racciotti, D., et al. (2000). Specific oxidative alterations in vastus lateralis muscle of patients with the diagnosis of chronic fatigue syndrome. *Free Radical Biology and Medicine, 29*, 1252–1259.

Gibson, H., Carroll, N., Clague, J.E., & Edwards, R. H. (1993). Exercise performance and fatigability in patients with chronic fatigue syndrome. *Journal of Neurology, Neurosurgery, and Psychiatry, 56*, 993–998.

Holmes, G., Kaplan, J., Gantz, N. M., Komaroff, A. L., Schonberger, L., Straus, S. E., et al. (1988). Definition of the chronic fatigue syndrome [Letter to the editor]. *Annals of Internal Medicine, 109*, 512.

Hough, T. (1902). Ergographic studies in muscular soreness. *American Journal of Physiology, 7*, 76–92.

Inbar, O., Dlin, R., Rotstein, A., & Whipp, B. (2001). Physiological responses to incremental exercise in patients with chronic fatigue syndrome. *Medicine and Science in Sports and Exercise, 33*, 1463–1470.

Jubrias, S., Bennett, R., & Klug, G. (1994). Increased incidence of a resonance in the phosphodiester region of 31P nuclear magnetic resonance spectra in the skeletal muscle of fibromyalgia patient. *Arthritis and Rheumatology, 37*, 801–807.

Katzmarzyk, P., Gledhill, N., Lerusse, L., & Bouchard, C. (2001). Familial aggregation of 7-year changes in musculoskeletal fitness. *Journal of Gerontology: Biological Sciences*(56A), B497–B502.

Kent-Braun, J., Sharma, K., Miller, R., & Weiner, M. (1994). Postexercise phosphocreatine resynthesis is slowed in multiple sclerosis. *Muscle and Nerve, 17*, 835–841.

Kent-Braun, J., Sharma, K., & Weiner, M. (1993). Central basis of muscle fatigue in chronic fatigue syndrome. *Neurology, 43*, 125–131.

Komaroff, A. (1993). *Clinic presentation of chronic fatigue syndrome*. Paper presented at the Ciba Foundation Symposium (No. 173), Chichester, England.

Kroese, A. (1977). The effect of inactivity on reactive hyperemia in the human calf: A study with strain gauge plethysmography. *Scandanavian Journal of Clinical Laboratory Investigation, 37,* 53–58.

Lindh, M., Johansson, G., Hedberg, M., Henning, G., & Grimby, G. (1995). Muscle fiber characteristics, capillaries, and enzymes in patients with fibromyalgia and controls. *Scandanavian Journal of Rheumatology, 24,* 34–37.

Lloyd, A., Phales, J., & Gandevia, S. (1988). Muscle strength, endurance, and recovery in the postinfection fatigue syndrome. *Journal of Neurology, Neurosurgery, and Psychiatry, 51,* 1316–1322.

McCully, K., Argov, Z., Boden, B. P., Brown, R. L., Bank, W. J., & Chance, B. (1988). Detection of muscle injury in humans with 31-P magnetic resonance spectroscopy. *Muscle and Nerve, 11,* 212–216.

McCully, K., Halber, C., & Posner, J. (1994). Exercise-induced changes in oxygen saturation in the calf muscles of elderly subjects with peripheral vascular disease. *Journal of Gerontology: Biological Sciences, 49,* B128–B134.

McCully, K., Kahihira, H., & Vandenborne, K. (1991). Noninvasive measurements of activity-induced changes in muscle metabolism. *Journal of Biomechanics, 24*(Suppl.1), 153–162.

McCully, K., & Natelson, B. (1999). Impaired oxygen delivery in chronic fatigue syndrome. *Clinical Science, 97,* 603–608.

McCully, K., Natelson, B., Iotti, S., Sisto, S., & Leigh, J. (1996). Reduced oxidative muscle metabolism in chronic fatigue syndrome. *Muscle and Nerve, 19,* 621–625.

Montague, T., Marrie, T., Bewick, D., Spencer, C. A., Kornreich, F., & Horacek, B. N. (1988). Cardiac effect of common viral illnesses. *Chest, 94,* 919–925.

Noakes, T. (1988). Implications of exercise testing for prediction of athletic performance: A contemporary perspective. *Medicine and Science in Sports and Exercise, 20,* 319–330.

Paul, L., Wood, L., Behan, W., & MacLaren, W. (1999). Demonstration of delayed recovery from fatiguing exercise in chronic fatigue syndrome. *European Journal of Neurology, 6,* 1–7.

Powell, P., Bental, R., Nye, F., & Edwards, R. (2001). Randomized control trial of patient education to encourage graded exercise in chronic fatigue syndrome. *British Medical Journal, 322,* 1–5.

Pyka, G., Linderberger, E., Charette, S., & Marcus, R. (1994). Muscle strength and fiber adaptations to a year-long resistance training program in elderly men and women. *Journal Gerontology, 49,* M22–M27.

Richardson, R. S., Leigh, J. S., Wagner, P. D., & Noyszewski, E. A. (1999). Cellular PO2 as a determinate of maximal mitochondrial O_2 consumption in trained skeletal muscle. *Journal of Applied Physiology, 87,* 325–331.

Riley, M., O'Brien, C., McCulskey, D., Bell, N. P., & Nicholls, D. P. (1990). Aerobic work capacity in patients with chronic fatigue syndrome. *British Medicine Journal, 301,* 953–956.

Sacco, P., Hope, P., Thickbroom, G., Byrnes, M., & Mastaglia, F. (1999). Corticomotor excitability and perception of effort during sustained exercise in chronic fatigue syndrome. *Clinical Neurophysiology, 110,* 1883–1891.

Schluederberg, A., Straus, S., Peterson, P., Blumenthal, S., Komaroff, A. L., Spring, S. B., et al. (1992). Chronic fatigue syndrome research: Definition and medical outcome assessment. *Annals of Internal Medicine, 117,* 325–331.

Sendrowski, D., Buker, E., & Gee, S. (1977). An investigation of sympathetic hypersensitivity in chronic fatigue syndrome. *Optical Vision Science, 74,* 660–663.

Shellock, F. G., Fukunaga, T., Mink, J. H., & Edgerton, V. R. (1991). Acute effects of exercise on MR imaging of skeletal muscle: Concentric and eccentric actions. *American Journal of Radiology, 179,* 765–768.

Sisto, S. A., LaManca, J., Cordero, D. L., Bergen, M. T., Ellis, S. P., Drastal, S., et al. (1996). Metabolic and cardiovascular effects of a progressive exercise test in patients with chronic fatigue syndrome. *American Journal Medicine, 100,* 634–640.

Skinner, J., Baldini, F., & Gardner, A. (1990). Assessment of fitness. In C. Bouchard, R. Shepard, & T. Stephens (Eds.), *Exercise, fitness, and health* (pp. 109–120). Champaign, IL: Human Kinetics.

Stackhouse, S., Stevens, J., Lee, S., Pearce, K., Snyder-Mackler, L., & Binder-Macleod, S. (2001). Maximum voluntary activation in nonfatigued and fatigued muscle of young and old individuals. *Physical Therapy, 81,* 1102–1109.

Stokes, M., Cooper, R., & Edwards, R. H. T. (1988). Normal muscle strength and fatigability in patients with effort syndromes. *British Medical Journal, 297,* 1014–1017.

Sutton, J. R. (1992). $\dot{V}O_2$max-new concepts on an old theme. *Medicine and Science in Sports and Exercise, 24,* 30–37.

Taylor, H., Buskirk, E., & Henschel, A. (1955). Maximal oxygen uptake as an objective measure of cardio-respiratory performance. *Journal of Applied Physiology, 8,* 73–80.

Tritschler, K. (2000a). Assessing cardiorespiratory fitness. In K. Tritschler (Ed.), *Practical measurement and assessment* (5th ed., pp. 243–276). Baltimore: Lippincott, Williams, & Wilkins.

Tritschler, K. (2000b). Assessing musculoskeletal and motor fitness. In K. Tritschler (Ed.), *Practical measurement and assessment* (5th ed., pp. 277–315). Baltimore: Lippincott, Williams, & Wilkins.

van der Werf, S., Prins, J., Vercoulen, J. H., van der Meer, J. W., & Bleijenberg, G. (2000). Identifying physical activity patterns in chronic fatigue syndrome using actigraphic assessment. *Journal of Psychosomatic Research, 49,* 373–379.

Vercoulen, J. H., Swanink, C. M., Zitman, F. G., Vreden, S. G., Hoofs, M. P., Fennis, J. F., et al. (1996). Randomized, double-blind, placebo-controlled study of fluoxetine in chronic fatigue syndrome. *Lancet, 347,* 858–861.

Wagemaker, H. (1999). Chronic fatigue syndrome: The physiology of people on the low end of the spectrum of physical activity. *Clinical Science, 97,* 611–613.

Whiting, J., Bagnall, A., Sowden, A., Cornell, J., Mulrow, C., & Ramirez, G. (2001). Interventions for the treatment and management of chronic fatigue syndrome: A systematic review. *Journal of the American Medical Association, 286,* 1360–1367.

Wong, R., Lopachuk, G., & Zhu, G. (1992). Skeletal muscle metabolism in the chronic fatigue syndrome. In vivo assessment by ^{31}P nuclear magnetic resonance spectroscopy. *Chest, 102,* 1716–1722.

Zaman, R., Puri, B., Main, J., Nowicky, A., & Davey, N. (2001). Corticospinal inhibition appears normal in patients with chronic fatigue syndrome. *Experimental Physiology, 86*(5), 547–550.

CHAPTER 19

Structured Diagnostic Interviews and Self-Rating Scales

FRED FRIEDBERG

IN 1992, THE National Institute of Mental Health and the National Institute of Allergy and Infectious Diseases sponsored a conference on guidelines for CFS research (Schluederberg et al., 1992) that recommended the evaluation of six behavioral and psychosocial domains: fatigue, mood disturbance, functional status, sleep disturbance, global well-being (i.e., psychiatric status), and pain. In the absence of markers of disease progression in CFS, validated psychometric measures of physical, psychological, and social functioning may be better predictors of patient status than physiological and function indexes alone (Barr & Schumacher, 1995). In addition, these timesaving, mostly self-administered pen-and-paper tests allow clinicians to obtain informative behavioral profiles of their patients.

This chapter provides an overview of both formal psychodiagnostic interviews and psychometric instruments as applied to CFS populations. In addition to psychiatric status, measures of functional status, coping, social support, locus of control, pain, and illness attribution are briefly reviewed. The advantages and disadvantages of each of these measures are summarized, and recommendations for clinical and research settings are offered.

ASSESSMENT DILEMMAS

Psychiatric assessment has received considerable attention in CFS because of the apparently high levels of comorbidity reported in psychodiagnostic studies (Friedberg & Jason, 2001). Because CFS is defined by symptomatic and behavioral criteria, rather than a specific biomedical test, how to distinguish CFS from psychiatric disorder is an important clinical and research concern. Perhaps most problematic, the CFS symptoms of fatigue, cognitive difficulty, and sleep disturbance overlap with several psychiatric disorders. Furthermore, the chronic pain and flulike symptoms often reported by CFS patients are sometimes experienced by patients with primary psychiatric disorder (Friedberg & Jason, 1998). Although research-based structured psychiatric interviews have devised rules for classification of psychiatric and medical symptoms, these rules vary considerably as a function of the specific interview instrument and the particular modifications used by investigators for CFS populations. In addition, the interviews may be administered by clinicians or nonclinicians with little training or experience in these procedures.

On the other hand, many psychometric measures of psychiatric status are designed for use with psychiatric populations. Thus, endorsed items, including somatic symptoms, are generally classified as psychiatric phenomena. This may lead to erroneous psychodiagnoses in CFS samples. This chapter addresses these assessment difficulties as they apply to specific evaluative instruments used in CFS samples.

PSYCHODIAGNOSTIC INTERVIEWING IN CFS

It is generally accepted that the gold standard in determining psychiatric diagnoses is the formally structured or semistructured interview that queries patients about the presence or absence of specific symptoms. The Structured Clinical Interview for *DSM-IV* (SCID; First, Spitzer, Gibbon, & Williams, 1996) is a comprehensive psychodiagnostic interview that is designed to determine *DSM-IV* diagnoses. It is intended to be administered by a mental health clinician who can exercise independent judgment on how ambiguous or vague symptoms are to be categorized, that is, as psychiatric or organic. The Diagnostic Interview Schedule (DIS; Robins, Helzer, Cottler, & Goldring, 1989; Robins & Regier, 1991) is also a comprehensive diagnostic instrument for the *DSM-III-R*; however, it is designed for administration by trained technicians rather than mental health professionals. Therefore, the rules of categorization of organic versus psychiatric symptoms are predetermined and much less influenced by interviewer judgment.

Given the overlap of the symptoms of fatigue, sleep disturbance, concentration difficulty, and psychomotor retardation in both CFS and specific psychiatric disorders (e.g., major depression, dysthymia, generalized anxiety disorder), some studies of CFS have excluded fatigue as a criterion for psychiatric diagnoses (e.g., Wessely & Powell, 1989). However, other less frequent overlap symptoms have been presumably left to clinical judgment or simply counted as symptoms of psychiatric disorders. The following two studies illustrate the psychodiagnostic difficulties in CFS.

In one study (Johnson, DeLuca, & Natelson, 1996a) that assessed somatization disorder in CFS, the *DSM-III-R* symptoms of somatization disorder were categorized as "psychiatric" or "physical" using different criteria sets to diagnose somatization disorder. The study found that changing the attribution of somatization disorder symptoms from psychiatric to physical dramatically affected the rates of somatization disorder diagnoses in CFS. The authors concluded that the classification of CFS symptoms as psychiatric or physical strongly influences which category CFS falls into. Thus, the diagnosis of somatization disorder may be of limited use in populations in which the etiology of the illness has not been established.

In a similar vein, Taylor and Jason (1998) investigated whether overall psychiatric comorbidity rates in individuals with CFS changed as a function of the type and scoring of psychiatric interview instruments used. The number of *DSM-III-R*, Axis I, psychiatric diagnoses were assessed two times for each of the 18 participants with CFS, once using the DIS and once using the SCID. Fifty percent of participants received at least one current psychiatric diagnosis on the DIS, whereas only 22% received a current psychiatric diagnosis on the SCID. Because the DIS was neither developed nor intended for use with CFS populations, scoring the DIS according to its original guidelines was not sensitive to symptom overlap between CFS and psychiatric illnesses such as somatization disorder and depression. The rigidity of DIS scoring compared with that of the SCID, which allows for clinical judgment, appeared to account for the much greater frequency of psychiatric disorders. These findings were consistent with prior studies that found higher rates of psychiatric diagnoses from use of the DIS (Katon, Buchwald, Simon, Russo, & Mease, 1991; Kruesi, Dale, & Straus, 1989; Manu, Lane, & Matthews, 1993) than from the SCID (Hickie, Lloyd, Wakefield, & Parker, 1990; Lloyd, Hickie, Boughton, Spencer, & Wakefield, 1990; Pepper, Krupp, Friedberg, Doscher, & Coyle, 1993).

Given these diagnostic difficulties in the research applications of structured psychiatric interviews, it is not surprising that general practice physicians also make errors of psychiatric attribution in CFS patients. Deale and Wessely (2000) compared a standardized interview schedule for psychiatric diagnoses with diagnoses previously given to patients with CFS by general practice and hospital physicians. The comparison revealed that physicians misdiagnosed 68% of the patient sample. In most cases, a psychiatric diagnosis was erroneously made by the physicians because no evidence was found in the formal psychodiagostic interview of any past or current psychiatric disorder. Of the patients who had not previously received a psychiatric diagnosis by the physicians, about 35% had a treatable psychiatric disorder in addition to CFS. The authors of the study advised doctors to focus on the subtle features that differentiate CFS from psychiatric disorders and to use a brief screening measure for psychiatric comorbidity (see next section).

CLASSIFICATION GUIDELINES FOR CFS AND PSYCHIATRIC DISORDER

For the researcher, psychiatric diagnoses in CFS are most reliably made with a structured interview schedule that incorporates clinical judgment and relevant research data. The following guidelines are useful in psychodiagnostic assessment for both the researcher and the clinician (Friedberg & Jason, 1998, 2001).

DEPRESSION

Depression and CFS share the symptoms of fatigue, concentration difficulty, and sleep disturbance. Fatigue should be categorized as a CFS symptom if it is the most prominent and disabling symptom in the clinical presentation. The patient experiences this type of fatigue as being distinctly different from normal fatigue and tiredness. In contrast, fatigue in primary depression is rated as much less debilitating (Johnson, DeLuca, & Natelson, 1996b). Similarly, concentration difficulty is often much more subjectively profound in patients with CFS than in patients with primary depression. Distinguishing the overlap symptom of sleep disturbance may be more difficult. Clinically, CFS patients will report a keyed-up mentally active feeling when they are trying to go to sleep, whereas this feature does not seem to be so pronounced in primary depression.

Several symptoms that distinguish CFS and depression can also be identified in the clinical setting. CFS patients often complain of postexertional malaise and prolonged fatigue after exercise—symptoms that are atypical in primary depression (Komaroff et al., 1996). Patients with primary depression often respond to activity and exercise regimes with substantial mood elevation, instead of symptom flare-ups (e.g., Brosse, Sheets, Lett, & Blumenthal, 2002). This is a key distinction between CFS and depression. In addition, painful lymph nodes, flulike symptoms, pressure headaches, and alcohol intolerance all tend to be much more common in CFS and are much less likely to be reported in primary depression (Komaroff et al., 1996).

If a diagnosis of CFS has been established prior to the psychodiagnostic interview, concurrent symptoms of depression may present somewhat differently from primary depression. Comparative studies of CFS and depression (Johnson et al., 1996b) have found that clinical depression symptoms in CFS tend to manifest as depressed mood rather than anhedonia, as would be the case in primary depression. CFS patients are also more likely to attribute their lack of activity to low energy than to loss of interest. In addition to anhedonia, primary depression patients are more likely to express hopelessness and low self-esteem (Powell, Dolan, & Wessely, 1990).

ANXIETY

Anxiety symptoms are a frequent concomitant in CFS (e.g., Fischler, Cluydts, De Gucht, Kaufman, & De Meirleir, 1997). Although the symptoms of fatigue, concentration difficulty, sleep disturbance, and perhaps other symptoms (e.g., palpitations) may superficially overlap between CFS and generalized anxiety disorder, the relatively sudden onset of CFS (several days to several weeks) contrasts with the usually long-standing nature of generalized anxiety disorder. The onset of CFS may increase the severity of premorbid anxiety symptoms, although it is not clear whether this change is a reaction to CFS or an inherent feature of the illness.

SOMATIZATION DISORDER

Although CFS and somatization disorder share many characteristics, including pain, gastrointestinal, pseudoneurological, and sexual symptoms, there are important differences as well. CFS is characterized by sudden onset, usually in the late 20s to early 30s, while the initial symptoms of somatization disorder begin in adolescence and progress gradually to full-blown somatization by age 25 (American Psychiatric Association [APA], 1994). Furthermore, severe disabling fatigue is the primary symptom in CFS, whereas fatigue is not a listed criterion for somatization disorder.

Clinicians can assess comorbid somatization disorder in CFS by inquiring about somatization symptoms prior to CFS onset. A history of multiple somatization symptoms that predate CFS onset may suggest comorbid somatization disorder. If somatization-like complaints are associated with the onset of CFS, these complaints may be symptoms of CFS or somatization, or they may represent a new stress symptom secondary to CFS. A patient-completed stress/symptom diary will help the patient and the clinician identify how stress can increase CFS symptoms. Because both CFS and somatization are medically unexplained, it may not be possible to delineate all of the symptoms of these disorders (Johnson, DeLuca, & Natelson, 1996a).

RATING SCALES

Both clinicians and researchers may find a screening instrument useful to detect psychiatric disorders in patients with CFS. As with psychological interviews, pen-and-paper psychometric measures are subject to difficulties in interpreting and classifying symptoms. In addition, the original construction of most of these measures is based on standardization samples that usually do not include medical patients in general or CFS patients in particular. Thus, psychometric instruments are likely to classify many CFS symptoms (e.g., fatigue, sleep disturbance) as psychiatric features, which may result in the overestimation of psychiatric comorbidity.

This section briefly reviews psychometric devices that may be useful in a CFS assessment of depressive features, functional status, global well-being, coping, social support, pain, locus of control, illness behavior, and illness attribution.

DEPRESSION RATING SCALES

Because depression is the most commonly diagnosed psychiatric disorder in CFS (Friedberg, 1996), a psychometric tool for depression screening is advisable. Several depression rating scales have long track records as clinical instruments in studies of primary depressive disorders, such as the Beck Depression Inventory (BDI; Beck, 1967) and the Center for Epidemiologic Studies Depression Scale (CES-D; Radloff, 1977). In medical conditions, these scales tend to overestimate the co-occurrence of clinical depression because they incorporate items related to somatic illness. For example, BDI assessment of CFS patients (Johnson et al., 1996b) revealed that 53% of nondepressed CFS patients exceeded the depression cutoff score of 10. Raising the cutoff score on the BDI to 14 or 20 still resulted in misdiagnoses in more than a third of the sample. If clinicians query their patients about any endorsed item on a depression scale being CFS- or depression-related or both, diagnostic errors will be less likely.

A rating scale that addresses the problem of overlapping symptoms between psychiatric and medical illness is the Hospital and Anxiety Depression Scale (HADS; Zigmond & Snaith, 1983). The HADS consists of two 8-item subscales, one relating to depression and the other to anxiety. The HADS excludes items related to physical illness symptoms or somatic depression. An initial study of the HADS in 136 CFS patients found it to be a valid and efficient screening instrument for depression and anxiety disorders in comparison with gold standard structured diagnostic interviews (Morriss & Wearden, 1998). The HADS has been used in several psychological studies of CFS (e.g., Ray, Jefferies, & Weir, 1995) and has shown sensitivity to treatment effects in CFS (Sharpe et al., 1996).

FUNCTIONAL STATUS MEASURES

Physical and role function in CFS has been evaluated with standardized instruments that vary widely in their focus and suitability to CFS patients. The often used Karnofsky Performance Scale (KPS; Karnofsky, Abelmann, Craver, &

Burchenal, 1948) is a clinician-administered test of physical performance and dependency rated on a scale of 0 to 100, with 10 fixed rating points. The KPS discriminates moderate to severe physical disability, but it is relatively insensitive to milder impairments, such as part-time and full-time employment. Despite its 50-year history, the KPS has not been subject to validation studies (Bowling, 1991), although it has shown sensitivity to treatment change in CFS (Sharpe et al., 1996).

The comprehensive Sickness Impact Profile (SIP; Deyo, Inui, Leininger, & Overman, 1982) contains 136 items that assess the effect of illness on activities, behaviors, emotional well-being, and social function. Both test-retest reliability and internal consistency are high on the SIP, and convergent and discriminant validity as well as sensitivity to treatment change have been demonstrated (Bowling, 1991). Its principal disadvantage in CFS is that patients who experience concentration difficulty and rapid mental fatigue may have trouble completing the SIP.

The 36-item Medical Outcome Study Short-Form-36 (SF-36; Stewart, Hays, & Ware, 1988; J. E. Ware & Sherbourne, 1992) evaluates functioning on the dimensions of physical activities, mental health, social functioning, bodily pain, energy and fatigue, and perceptions of health. In CFS samples, the SF-36 has been validated as a measure of functional status (Buchwald, Pearlman, Umali, Schmaling, & Katon, 1996). The measure has also distinguished CFS from other fatiguing illnesses (Buchwald et al., 1996) and has demonstrated sensitivity to treatment change in CFS (Deale, Chalder, Marks, & Wessely, 1997). Perhaps the disadvantage of the SF-36 is that gradations of severe disability may be obscured because very few items address low functioning, such as self-care activity. In such cases the KPS or the SIP would be more suitable.

GLOBAL MEASURES OF PSYCHIATRIC STATUS OR WELL-BEING

Multiscale instruments of psychiatric status detect psychiatric disorders by using cutoff scores. In medical populations, endorsed somatic symptoms on these tests may result in overdiagnosis of psychiatric disorder, although these instruments may be useful in detecting high levels of generalized psychological distress.

The General Health Questionnaire (GHQ; Goldberg, 1972) is a well-established measure of psychiatric status that has been evaluated in CFS (Buchwald, Pearlman, Keith, Katon, & Schmaling, 1997; Farmer et al., 1996) with mixed results. One study (Buchwald et al., 1997) reported that an adjusted cutoff score yielded adequate sensitivity and specificity for co-occurring psychiatric disorder in CFS. On the other hand, a second study (Farmer et al., 1996) indicated that the GHQ was a poor screener for psychiatric morbidity in CFS compared with a structured psychiatric interview. Given these contradictory results, it is not clear whether the GHQ should be recommended.

The Minnesota Multiphasic Personality Inventory (MMPI; MMPI-2; Halfaway & McKinley, 1940, 1989) is an extensive questionnaire (566 items) requiring one to three hours administration time. The test contains 10 clinical scales and 3 validity scales. The MMPI shows a 49% to 50% correct classification rate for psychiatric disorder in psychiatric populations (Morrison, Edwards, & Weissman, 1994). However, a study that compared MMPI profiles for patients with neurological, psychiatric, or chronic pain disorders (Cripe, Maxwell, & Hill, 1995) found that these groups could not be differentiated with clinical inspection or discriminant function analysis.

Despite many research attempts to distinguish functional and organic illness using the MMPI, no successful classification strategy has been established (Fiedler, Kipen, DeLuca, Kelly, & Natelson, 1996; Willcockson, 1985). Most commonly, clinically significant elevations on Scale 1 (Hypochondriasis) and Scale 3 (Hysteria) have been found in CFS patients (Blakely et al., 1991; Fiedler et al., 1996; Schmaling & Jones, 1996). These scales contain physical symptoms including several CFS symptoms.

Rather than using the MMPI to generate psychiatric diagnoses, a brief structured psychiatric interview for depressive and anxiety disorders (e.g., the Schedule for Affective Disorders and Schizophrenia) may be a preferred alternative for the CFS patient. Such an interview will be less taxing for the patient and will yield more definitive diagnostic data.

The 90-item Symptom Checklist (SCL-90-R; Derogatis, 1983) and its abbreviated version, the 53-item Brief Symptom Inventory (BSI; Derogatis, 1975), were initially developed to identify nine psychiatric dimensions, although factor-analytic studies have revealed moderate-to-high correlations between the dimensions. Perhaps these measures more accurately reflect generalized distress than the presence of a psychiatric diagnosis (Bonynge, 1993). For CFS evaluation, it should be noted that CFS symptoms are contained on the somatization and obsessive-compulsive subscales. It may be more useful to calculate separate scores for these two subscales to assess CFS symptoms versus psychiatric phenomena (Bernstein, Jaremko, & Hinkley, 1994).

PERSONALITY DISORDER DIAGNOSIS

Behavioral studies in CFS suggest that characterological factors may be associated with CFS. Personality data in CFS studies have revealed tendencies to overwork that are manifested by compulsive traits (Pepper et al., 1993), "action proneness" (Van Hondenhouve, Onghena, Neerinchx, & Hellin, 1995), "hard-driving" tendencies (Lewis, Cooper, & Bennett, 1994), and overcommitted lifestyles (N. C. Ware, 1993). (Excessive perfectionism, a trait that is perhaps related to an achievement-oriented lifestyle, has not been found in CFS [Blenkiron, Edwards, & Lynch, 1999; Wood & Wessely, 1999].) It has been argued that such tendencies toward hyperactive lifestyles may be a contributing factor to the development and persistence of CFS (Friedberg & Jason, 2001). Thus, the measurement of Axis II traits and disorders may have both etiologic and treatment implications.

One of the more frequently used measures of Axis II traits is the Millon Clinical Multiaxial Inventory (MCMI, MCMI-II, and MCMI-III; Millon, 1987; Millon, Millon, & Davis, 1994), a 175-item measure of 10 personality disorders. The MCMI has been used in psychiatric studies of CFS (e.g., Pepper et al., 1993) to determine personality disorder diagnoses. The MCMI-II has shown a high rate of false positives in a psychiatric outpatient population when compared with the Structured Clinical Interview for *DSM-III-R,* Axis II (Guthrie & Mobley, 1994). On the other hand, a negative test result in this study was usually an accurate indication that the participant did not have a personality disorder. The authors suggested that the MCMI-II should be considered a screening instrument for Axis II disorder, with positive results indicating the need for a more extensive evaluation.

ANGER SCALES

A neglected area of psychometric evaluation in CFS is the affective dimension of anger. Anger is often a reaction to the frustration of unpredictable disabling symptoms, uninformative feedback on etiology, repeated treatment failures, and the medical rejection and stigmatization that these patients often experience (Friedberg & Jason, 1998). Empirical studies in chronic pain populations have found relationships between unexpressed anger and pain intensity in chronic pain patients (Kerns, Rosenberg, & Jacob, 1994), lower awareness of anger in chronic pain patients compared with other medical patients (Braha & Catchlove, 1986), and greater anger suppression in chronic pain patients compared with healthy controls (Hatch et al., 1991). In a comparative study of CFS, multiple sclerosis, and healthy controls (Natelson et al., 1995), the controls rated themselves as feeling significantly less anger/hostility on the profile of mood states anger subscale than did patients in the illness groups.

Two well-researched anger measures may be useful in a CFS evaluation. The Spielberger State-Trait Anger Expression Inventory (STAXI; Spielberger, 1988) comprises 44 items, from which are derived six scales. The State Anger Scale measures the magnitude of angry feelings at the time the test is taken. The Trait Anger Scale measures how an individual is disposed characterologically to react with anger. The Anger In Scale measures the frequency of angry feelings that are contained or held in. The Anger Out Scale measures how frequently an individual will express aggressive behavior toward other persons or objects in the environment. The Anger Control scale measures the frequency that an individual attempts to contain the expression of anger. Finally, the Anger Expression Scale is a composite scale that provides a general index of the frequency that anger is expressed regardless of whether the anger is expressed inward or outward.

Because the previously cited studies of anger in chronic pain populations indicate that the anger experience may be suppressed, the STAXI may be useful in identifying the nonobvious dimensions of anger experienced by people with CFS. The STAXI offers the advantage of distinguishing important dimensions of anger that are consistent with the limited research literature on anger and chronic illness.

The Cook and Medley (1954) Hostility Scale (Ho) is a 50-item measure that describes many aspects of hostility. High scores on the Ho have shown enhanced risk of cardiovascular disease and maladaptive psychosocial features including marital conflict, ineffective coping styles, and proneness to negative affect (Miller, Smith, Turner, Guijarro, & Hallet, 1996). The Ho has been criticized as containing numerous dimensions, some of which may not be correlated with health outcomes (Steinberg & Jorgensen, 1996).

COPING

Maladaptive coping in CFS has been associated with greater impairments in several studies. These studies have revealed the following maladaptive strategies in varying proportions of participants: denial of CFS diagnosis (Antoni et al., 1994), a tendency to catastrophize (Petrie, Moss-Morris, & Weinman, 1995), behavioral disengagement (Antoni et al., 1994), and cognitive and behavioral avoidance (Heiman, 1994). The measures of coping summarized here all have adequate psychometric properties.

The empirically derived Ways of Coping Scale (Folkman & Lazarus, 1980) separates coping into two factorially distinct categories: Problem-focused coping is intended to solve a problem, whereas emotion-focused coping is designed to regulate distress (e.g., relaxation) when a problem cannot be resolved. The theoretically based COPE scales (Carver, Scheier, & Weintraub, 1989) incorporate problem- and emotion-focused coping as well as three additional scales (e.g., venting of emotions). In contrast to the WOC and the COPE, which are based on a test construction sample of healthy people, the Illness Management Questionnaire (IMQ; Ray, Weir, Stewart, Miller, & Hyde, 1993) was validated on a sample of CFS patients. The IMQ identifies four types of problem solving: maintaining activity, accommodation to the illness, focusing on symptoms, and information seeking. These coping measures can assist the clinician in identifying helpful versus unhelpful forms of coping in their patients and thus play a role in treatment planning.

SOCIAL SUPPORT

Some studies suggest that social support may have implications for psychosocial interventions and clinical outcome. In CFS patients, perceived social support was positively correlated with impairment (Schmaling & DiClemente, 1995) and fatigue severity (Schmaling, Smith, & Buchwald, 2000) in descriptive studies; was negatively associated with fatigue in a community-based intervention (Schlaes & Jason, 1996); and was negatively associated with relapse after exposure to a hurricane in a prospective study (Lutgendorf et al., 1995). Using a sample of CFS patients, a 28-item social support inventory developed by Ray (1992) identified two factor dimensions, positive and negative social support. Positive support was inversely related to anxiety, whereas negative support was directly related to both anxiety and depression. Apart from these important associations, the clinician may want to review specific items that reflect low, positive support or high, negative support in order to address the possibility that low levels of beneficial support may be contributing to distress and impairment.

LOCUS OF CONTROL AND PERCEIVED CONTROL

Locus of control has shown important relationships to health outcomes. Form C of the Multidimensional Health Locus of Control Scale was developed to measure the illness-specific locus of control beliefs of people with an existing health problem (Wallston, 1989). An internal locus of control signifies the individual's level of responsibility for illness outcomes; others' locus of control indicates reliance on others to control the illness; and a chance locus of control reflects beliefs that illness outcome is dependent on chance, luck, or fate. These three loci of control have been replicated in a CFS patient sample (Ray et al., 1995). An internal locus of control has been associated with favorable outcomes such as more active behavioral coping in low back patients (Harkapaa, Jarvikoski, Mellin, Hurri, & Luoma, 1991), improved self-care and knowledge of their disease in MS patients (Wassem, 1991), and long-range clinical improvements in psychophysiological disorders (McLean & Pietroni, 1990).

An internal health locus of control may be similar to a subjective sense of control over symptoms that has been studied in CFS. A naturalistic outcome study in CFS (Vercoulen et al., 1996) found that the strongest predictor of improvement over an 18-month period was a sense of control over symptoms. The statistical analyses suggested that this sense of control over symptoms preceded fatigue reductions. Using the same measure of control over symptoms in a controlled clinical trial of cognitive-behavioral therapy, Prins et al. (2001) also found that a higher sense of control predicted more improvement. Furthermore, a one-year prospective study of CFS patients (Ray, Jefferies, & Weir, 1997) found an interesting relationship between a sense of illness control and impairments. Patients who believed that their own actions influenced their illness had less impairment one year later, and this was unrelated to the severity or length of their illness.

PAIN MEASURES

Muscle and multijoint pain are common symptomatic features in CFS. In addition, fibromyalgia, a syndrome characterized by widespread pain, is frequently reported among CFS patients (e.g., Friedberg, Dechene, McKenzie, & Fontanetta, 2000). Two comprehensive validated measures of the subjective pain experience are the West Haven-Yale Multidimensional Pain Inventory (Kerns, Turk, & Rudy, 1985) and the McGill Pain Questionnaire (Melzack, 1983). Alternatively, if a brief measure of the pain experience is desired, focused pain ratings using numerical rating scales are useful to assess the severity of pain in CFS patients. Numerical rating scales for pain have adequate psychometric properties as pain intensity measures (Karoly & Jensen, 1987).

ILLNESS BEHAVIOR AND ATTRIBUTION

Although illness behavior is a normal manifestation of clinical syndromes, it becomes a cause for clinical concern if impairments are more severe than expected by health professionals. Assessment devices for illness behavior seek to determine if illness behavior is abnormal. The Illness Behavior Questionnaire (IBQ; Pilowsky, Spence, Cobb, & Katsikitis, 1984) is a 62-item instrument that measures illness behavior on seven subscales such as general hypochondriasis and disease conviction. Despite the potential usefulness of the IBQ, methodological problems were associated with the procedures employed to develop the instrument. Most significantly, too few individuals participated in the original scale development for adequate item analysis or the development of specific subscales (Karoly & Jensen, 1987). As a result, subsequent studies have found some, but not all, of the seven original dimensions (e.g., Main & Waddell, 1987; Pilowsky, 1993). The IBQ in its present form lacks the construct validity required to recommend it as a useful instrument in the assessment of CFS (Karoly & Jensen, 1987).

Illness attribution is based on the patients' view of their illness as "physical," "psychological," or some combination of the two. Physical attributions have been predictive of poor outcomes in some studies (Butler, Chalder, Ron, & Wessely, 1991; Sharpe et al., 1996; Wilson et al., 1994), but not in others (Deale & Chalder, 1998). Studies in CFS patients suggest that beliefs about activity avoidance (Deale & Chalder, 1998) and lack of control of the illness (Heiman, 1994) are better outcome predictors than illness attribution.

Finally, maladaptive beliefs about fatigue symptomatology may reflect a specific category of illness behavior that is amenable to psychosocial intervention. The Fatigue-Related Cognition Scale (FRCS) is a validated 14-item instrument (Friedberg & Jason, 1998; Friedberg & Krupp, 1994) that identifies dysfunctional beliefs related to abnormal persistent fatigue (e.g., "I have no control over my fatigue."). The FRCS is a rapid assessment tool of fatigue beliefs suitable for clinical assessment.

GLOBAL ASSESSMENT OF CHANGE (GAC)

The GAC is a single generalized rating of the patient's or the investigator's perception of change in the patient's well-being between two time points. Global well-being is a subjective term that may reflect both physical and psychological changes. A 7-point global assessment of change rating ranging from very much worse to very much improved has shown sensitivity to treatment in a cognitive-behavioral treatment study in CFS (Sharpe et al., 1996) and in an EMDR study in fibromyalgia (Friedberg, 2001). On the other hand, a clinical study of 45 CFS patients (Schwartz & Jones, 2000) that incorporated a 5-point GAC showed questionable validity. When the GAC rating obtained after one year of treatment was compared with the results of the SF-36, no significant correlation was found between the Physical Component Summary of the SF-36 and the GAC ($r = -.04$) or the Mental Component Summary and the GAC ($r = .12$). The authors concluded that their specific GAC did not accurately or adequately reflect changes in physical and mental functioning as measured by a validated outcome instrument, that is, the SF-36. Thus, the 5-point GAC alone may have obscured more fine-grained, but important changes in functional status. Based on these disparate findings, it would seem advisable to use the more sensitive 7-point GAC.

Despite the absence of extensive validation data for the GAC, it is important to patients as a reflection of their general sense of well-being and health. It may be desirable to query patients about the reasons for their GAC rating during an outcome assessment. This information may help clarify any discrepancies between the GAC and standard psychometric instruments.

SELECTION OF MEASURES

The selection of measures for each assessment domain depends on the questions being asked and the instruments that appear most relevant and appropriate to those questions. The researcher's choice of specific measures may be somewhat arbitrary although it is advisable to select devices with established psychometric properties and prior use with CFS patients.

For the busy clinician, brief psychometric measures that are targeted to likely psychological and physical impairments would appear to be most useful. A standard depression scale such the BDI or the HADS, in combination with a physical function measure such as the SF-36, will provide the clinician with a broadly based overview of the patient. These measures are also sensitive to clinical intervention and can verify psychological and behavioral change as well as target persistent problems for focused clinical efforts. For psychodiagnosis, the clinician is best advised to use a semistructured clinical interview designed to categorize CFS and psychiatric symptoms (Friedberg & Jason, 1998).

REFERENCES

Antoni, M. H., Brickman, A., Lutgendorf, S., Klimas, N., Imia-Fins A., Ironson, G., et al. (1994). Psychosocial correlates of illness burden in chronic fatigue syndrome. *Clinical Infectious Diseases, 18*(Suppl. 1), S73–S78.

Barr, J. T., & Schumacher, G. E. (1995). A teaching strategy to incorporate patient-centered outcomes assessment in health professional curricula: The class-generated patient profile. *Journal of Allied Health, 24,* 65–78.

Beck, A. J. (1967). *Depression: Clinical, experimental and theoretical aspects.* New York: Harper & Row.

Bernstein, I. H., Jaremko, M. E., & Hinkley, B. S. (1994). On the utility of the SCL-90-R with low back pain patients. *Spine, 19,* 42–48.

Blakely, A. A., Howard, R. C., Sosich, R. M., Murdoch, J. C., Menkes, D. B., & Spears, G. F. (1991). Psychiatric symptoms, personality and ways of coping in chronic fatigue syndrome. *Psychological Medicine, 21,* 347–362.

Blenkiron, P., Edwards, P. R., & Lynch, S. (1999). Association between perfectionism, mood, and fatigue in chronic fatigue syndrome: A pilot study. *Journal of Nervous and Mental Disorders, 187,* 566–570.

Bonynge, R. R. (1993). Unidimensionality of SCL-90-R scales in adult and adolescent crisis samples. *Journal of Clinical Psychology, 49,* 212–215.

Bowling, A. (1991). *Measuring health: A review of quality of life measurement scales.* Philadelphia: Open University.

Braha, R. E., & Catchlove, R. F. (1986). Pain and anger: Inadequate expression in chronic pain patients. *Pain Clinics, 1,* 125–129.

Brosse, A. L., Sheets, E. S., Lett, H. S., & Blumenthal, J. A. (2002). Exercise and the treatment of clinical depression in adults: recent findings and future directions. *Sports Medicine, 32,* 741–760.

Buchwald, D., Pearlman, T., Kith, P., Katon, W., & Schmaling, K. (1997). Screening for psychiatric disorders in chronic fatigue and chronic fatigue syndrome. *Journal of Psychosomatic Research, 42,* 78–94.

Buchwald, D., Pearlman, T., Umali, J., Schmaling, K., & Katon, W. (1996). Functional status in patients with chronic fatigue syndrome, other fatiguing illnesses, and healthy individuals. *American Journal of Medicine, 101,* 364–370.

Butler, S., Chalder, T., Ron, M., & Wessely, S. (1991). Cognitive behavior therapy in chronic fatigue syndrome. *Journal of Neurology, Neurosurgery, and Psychiatry, 54,* 153–158.

Carver, C. S., Scheier, M. F., & Weintraub, J. K. (1989). Assessing coping strategies: Atheoretically based approach. *Journal of Personality and Social Psychology, 56,* 267–283.

Cook, W. W., & Medley, D. M. (1954). Proposed hostility and pharisaic-virtue scales for the MMPI. *Journal of Applied Psychology, 18,* 414–418.

Cripe, L. I., Maxwell, J. K., & Hill, E. (1995). Multivariate discriminant function analysis of neurologic, pain and psychiatric patients with the MMPI. *Journal of Clinical Psychology, 51,* 258–268.

Deale, A., & Chalder, T. (1998). Illness beliefs and treatment outcome in chronic fatigue syndrome. *Journal of Psychosomatic Research, 45,* 77–83.

Deale, A., Chalder, T., Marks, I., & Wessely, S. (1997). Cognitive behaviour therapy for chronic fatigue syndrome: A randomized controlled trial. *American Journal of Psychiatry, 154,* 408–414.

Deale, A., & Wessely, S. (2000). Diagnosis of psychiatric disorder in clinical evaluation of chronic fatigue syndrome. *Journal of the Royal Society of Medicine, 93,* 310–312.

Derogatis, L. R. (1975). *Brief Symptom Inventory.* Towson, MD: Clinical Psychometric Research.

Derogatis, L. R. (1983). *SCL-90-R administration, scoring and procedure manual—II.* Towson, MD: Clinical Psychometric Research.

Deyo, I. E., Inui, T. S., Leininger, J. D., & Overman, S. (1982). Physical and psychological functions in rheumatoid arthritis: Clinical use of a self-administered instrument. *Archives of Internal Medicine, 142,* 879–882.

Farmer, A., Chubb, H., Jones, I., Hillier, J., Smith, A., & Borysiewicz, L. (1996). Screening for psychiatric morbidity in subjects presenting with chronic fatigue syndrome. *British Journal of Psychiatry, 168,* 354–358.

Fiedler, N., Kipen, H. M., DeLuca, J., Kelly, M., & Natelson, B. (1996). A controlled campaign of multiple chemical sensitivities and chronic fatigue syndrome. *Psychosomatic Medicine, 58,* 38–49.

First, M. B., Spitzer, R. L., Gibbon, M., & Williams, J. B. (1996). *Structured clinical interview for DSM-IV axis I disorders—patient edition* (SCID—I/P version 2.0). New York: New York State Psychiatric Institute, Biometrics Research Department.

Fischler, B., Cluydts, R., De Gucht, Y., Kaufman, L., & De Meirleir K. (1997). Generalized anxiety disorder in chronic fatigue syndrome. *Acta Psychiatrica Scandinavica, 95,* 405–413.

Folkman, S., & Lazarus, R. (1980). An analysis of coping in a middle aged community sample. *Journal of Health and Social Behaviour, 21,* 219–239.

Friedberg, F. (1996). Chronic fatigue syndrome: A new clinical application. *Professional Psychology: Research and Practice, 27,* 487–494.

Friedberg, F. (2001). *EMDR in fibromyalgia: A pilot study.* Manuscript submitted for publication.

Friedberg, F., Dechene, L., McKenzie, M., & Fontanetta, R. (2000). Symptom patterns in long-duration chronic fatigue syndrome. *Journal of Psychosomatic Research, 48,* 59–68.

Friedberg, F., & Jason, L. A. (1998). *Understanding chronic fatigue syndrome: An empirical guide to assessment and treatment.* Washington, DC: American Psychological Association.

Friedberg, F., & Jason, L. A. (2001). Chronic fatigue syndrome and fibromyalgia. Clinical assessment and treatment. *Journal of Clinical Psychology, 57,* 433–455.

Friedberg, F., & Krupp, L. B. (1994). A comparison of cognitive behavioral treatment for chronic fatigue syndrome and primary depression. *Clinical Infectious Diseases, 18*(Suppl. 1), S105–S110.

Goldberg, D. (1972). *The detection of psychiatric illness by questionnaire.* London: Oxford University Press.

Guthrie, P. C., & Mobley, B. D. (1994). A comparison of the differential diagnostic efficiency of three personality disorder inventories. *Journal of Clinical Psychology, 50,* 656–665.

Halfaway, S. R., & McKinley, J. C. (1940). A multiphasic personality schedule: Construction of the schedule, *Journal of Psychology, 10,* 249–254.

Halfaway, S. R., & McKinley, J. C. (1989). *MMPI-II,* Minneapolis: University of Minnesota Press.

Harkapaa, K., Jarvikoski, A., Mellin, G., Hurri, H., & Luoma, J. (1991). Health locus of control beliefs and psychological distress as predictors for treatment outcome in low-back pain patients: Results of a 3-month follow-up of a controlled intervention study. *Pain, 46,* 35–41.

Hatch, J. P., Schoenfeld, L. S., Boutros, N. N., Seleshi, E., Moore, P. J., & Cyr-Provost, M. (1991). Anger and hostility in tension-type headache. *Headache, 31,* 302–304.

Heiman, T. (1994, October) *Chronic fatigue syndrome and vocational rehabilitation: Unserved and unmet needs.* Paper presented at the American Association for Chronic Fatigue Syndrome Research Conference, Ft. Lauderdale, FL.

Hickie, I., Lloyd, A., Wakefield, D., & Parker, G. (1990). The psychiatric status of patients with chronic fatigue syndrome. *British Journal of Psychiatry, 156,* 534–540.

Johnson, S. K., DeLuca, J., & Natelson, B. H. (1996a). Assessing somatization disorder in the chronic fatigue syndrome. *Psychosomatic Medicine, 58,* 50–57.

Johnson, S. K., DeLuca, J., & Natelson, B. H. (1996b). Depression in fatiguing illness: Comparing patients with chronic fatigue syndrome, multiple sclerosis and depression. *Journal of Affective Disorders, 39,* 21–30.

Karnofsky, D. A., Abelmann, W. H., Craver, L. F., & Burchenal, J. H. (1948). The use of nitrogen mustards in the palliative treatment of carcinoma. *Cancer, 1,* 634–656.

Karoly, P., & Jensen, M. P. (1987). *Multimethod assessment of chronic pain.* Oxford, England: Pergamon Press.

Katon, W. J., Buchwald, D. S., Simon, G. E., Russo, J. E., & Mease, P. J. (1991). Psychiatric illness in patients with chronic fatigue and rheumatoid arthritis. *Journal of General Internal Medicine, 6,* 277–285.

Kerns, R. D., Rosenberg, R., & Jacob, M C. (1994). Anger expression and chronic pain. *Journal of Behavioral Medicine, 17,* 57–67.

Kerns, R. D., Turk, D. C., & Rudy, T. E. (1985). The West Haven-Yale Multidimensional Pain Inventory (WHYMPI). *Pain, 23,* 345–356.

Komaroff, A. L., Fagioli, L. R., Geiger, A. M., Doolittle, T. H., Lee, J., Kornish, R. J., et al. (1996). An examination of the working case definition of chronic fatigue syndrome. *American Journal of Medicine, 100,* 56–64.

Kruesi, M. J., Dale, J., & Straus, S. E. (1989). Psychiatric diagnosis in patients who have chronic fatigue syndrome. *Journal of Clinical Psychiatry, 50,* 53–56.

Lewis, S., Cooper, C. L., & Bennett, D. (1994). Psychosocial factors and chronic fatigue syndrome. *Psychological Medicine, 24,* 661–671.

Lloyd, A. R., Hickie, I., Boughton, C. R., Spencer, O., & Wakefield, D. (1990). Prevalence of chronic fatigue syndrome in an Australian population. *Medical Journal of Australia, 153,* 522–528.

Lutgendorf, S. K., Antoni, M. H., Ironson, Klimas, N., Patarca, R., & Fletcher, M. A. (1995). Physical symptoms of chronic fatigue syndrome are exacerbated by the stress of Hurricane Andrew. *Psychosomatic Medicine, 57,* 310–323.

Main, C. J., & Waddell, G. (1987). Psychometric construction and validity of the Pilowsky Illness Behavior Questionnaire in British patients with chronic low back pain. *Pain, 28,* 13–25.

Manu, P., Lane, T. J., & Matthews, D. A. (1993). Chronic fatigue and chronic fatigue syndrome: Clinical epidemiology and aetiological classification. In B. R. Bock & J. Whelan (Eds.), *Chronic fatigue syndrome* (pp. 23–42). New York: Wiley.

McLean, J., & Pietroni, P. (1990). Self-care, who does best? *Social Science and Medicine, 30,* 591–596.

Melzack, R. (1983). The McGill Pain Questionnaire. In R. Melzack (Ed.), *Pain management and assessment.* New York: Raven Press.

Miller, T. Q., Smith, T. W., Turner, C. W., Guijarro, M. L., & Hallet, A. J. (1996). A meta-analytic review of research on hostility and physical health. *Psychological Bulletin, 119*(2), 322–348.

Millon, T. (1987). *Millon Clinical Multiaxial Inventory-II, manual* (2nd ed.). Minneapolis, MN: National Computer Systems.

Millon, T., Millon, C., & Davis, R. D. (1994). *Millon Clinical Multiaxial Inventory-III, manual* (2nd ed.). Minneapolis, MN: National Computer Systems

Morrison, T. L., Edwards, D. W., & Weissman, H. N. (1994). The MMPI and MMPI-II as predictors of psychiatric diagnosis in an outpatient sample. *Journal of Personality Assessment, 62,* 17–30.

Morriss, R. K., & Wearden, A. J. (1998). Screening instruments for psychiatric morbidity in chronic fatigue syndrome. *Journal of the Royal Society of Medicine, 91,* 365–368.

Natelson, B. H., Johnson, S. K., DeLuca, J., Sisto, S., Ellis, S. P., Hill, N., et al. (1995). Reducing heterogeneity in chronic fatigue syndrome: A comparison with depression and multiple sclerosis. *Clinical Infectious Diseases, 21,* 1204–1210.

Pepper, C. M., Krupp, L. B., Friedberg, F., Doscher, C., & Coyle, P. K. (1993). A comparison of neuropsychiatric characteristics in chronic fatigue syndrome, multiple sclerosis, and major depression. *Journal of Neuropsychiatry and Clinical Neurosciences, 5,* 200–205.

Petrie, K., Moss-Morris, R., & Weinman, J. (1995). The impact of catastrophic beliefs on functioning in chronic fatigue syndrome. *Journal of Psychosomatic Research, 39,* 31–38.

Pilowsky, I. (1993). Dimensions of illness behavior as measured by the Illness Behavior Questionnaire: A replication study. *Journal of Psychosomatic Research, 37,* 53–62.

Pilowsky, I., Spence, N., Cobb, J., & Katsikitis, M. (1984). The Illness Behavior Questionnaire as an aid to clinical assessment. *General Hospital Psychiatry, 6,* 123–130.

Powell, R., Dolan, R., & Wessely, S. (1990). Attribution and self-esteem in depression and chronic fatigue syndromes. *Journal of Psychosomatic Research, 34,* 65–67.

Prins, J. B., Bleijenberg, G., Bazelmans, E., Elving, L. D., de Boo, T. M., Severens, J. L., et al. (2001). Cognitive behaviour therapy for chronic fatigue syndrome: A multicenter randomized controlled trial. *Lancet, 357,* 841–847.

Radloff, L. S. (1977). The CES-D scale: A self-report depression scale for research in the general population. *Applied Psychological Measurement, 1,* 385–401.

Ray, C. (1992). Positive and negative social support in a chronic illness. *Psychological Reports, 71,* 977–978.

Ray, C., Jefferies, S., & Weir, W. R. (1995). Coping with chronic fatigue syndrome: Illness responses and their relationship with fatigue, functional impairment and emotional status. *Psychological Medicine, 25,* 937–945.

Ray, C., Jefferies, S., & Weir, W. R. (1997). Coping and other predictors of outcome in chronic fatigue syndrome. *Journal of Psychosomatic Research, 43,* 405–415.

Ray, C., Weir, W., Stewart, D., Miller, P., & Hyde, G. (1993). Ways of coping with chronic fatigue syndrome: Development of an illness management questionnaire. *Social Science and Medicine, 37,* 385–391.

Robins, L. N., Helzer, J., Cottler, L., & Goldring, E. (1989). *National Institute of Mental Health Diagnostic Interview Schedule, version three revised, DIS-III-R.* St. Louis, MO: Washington University School of Medicine, Department of Psychiatry.

Robins, L. N., & Regier, D. A. (1991). *Psychiatric disorders in America: The ECA study.* New York: Free Press.

Schlaes, J. L., & Jason, L. A. (1996). A buddy/mentor program for people with chronic fatigue syndrome. *CFIDS Chronicle, 9,* 21–25.

Schluederberg, A., Straus, S. E., Peterson, P., Blumenthal, S., Komaroff, A. L., Spring, S. B., et al. (1992). Chronic fatigue syndrome research: Definition and medical outcome assessment. *Annals of Internal Medicine, 117,* 325–331.

Schmaling, K. B., & DiClementi, J. D. (1995). Interpersonal stressors in chronic fatigue syndrome: A pilot study. *Journal of Chronic Fatigue Syndrome, 3/4,* 153–158.

Schmaling, K. B., & Jones, J. F. (1996). MMPI profiles of patients with chronic fatigue syndrome. *Journal of Psychosomatic Research, 40,* 67–74.

Schmaling, K. B., Smith, W. R., & Buchwald, D. S. (2000). Significant other responses are associated with fatigue and functional status among patients with chronic fatigue syndrome. *Psychosomatic Medicine, 6,* 444–450.

Schwartz, S. N., & Jones, R. (2000). Measuring outcomes of treatment in chronic fatigue syndrome: A comparison of simple questioning vs. use of a validated outcome instrument (short form 36). *Journal of Chronic Fatigue Syndrome, 6,* 3–10.

Sharpe, M., Hawton, K., Simkin, S., Suraway, C., Hackmann, A., Klimes, I., et al. (1996). Cognitive behaviour therapy for the chronic fatigue syndrome: A randomised controlled trial. *British Medical Journal, 312,* 22–26.

Spielberger, C. D. (1988). *Manual for the State-Trait Anger Expression Inventory* (STAXI). Odessa, FL: Psychological Assessment Resources.

Steinberg, L., & Jorgensen, R. S. (1996). Assessing the MMPI-based Cook-Medley Hostility Scale: The implications of dimensionality. *Journal of Personality and Social Psychology, 70*(6), 1281–1287.

Stewart, A. L., Hays, R. D., & Ware, J. E. (1988). The MOS Short-Form General Health Survey: Reliability and validity in a patient population. *Medical Care, 26,* 724–735.

Taylor, R. R., & Jason, L. A. (1998). Comparing the DIS with the SCID: Chronic fatigue syndrome and psychiatric comorbidity. *Psychology and Health, 13,* 1087–1104.

Van Houdenhove, B., Onghena, P., Neerinckx, E., & Hellin, J. (1995). Does high action-proneness make people more vulnerable to chronic fatigue syndrome? A controlled psychometric study. *Journal of Psychosomatic Research, 39,* 633–640.

Vercoulen, J. H., Swanink, C. M., Fennis, J. F., Galama, J. M., van der Meer, J. W., & Bleijenberg, G. (1996). Prognosis in chronic fatigue syndrome: A prospective study on the natural course. *Journal of Neurology, Neurosurgery, and Psychiatry, 60,* 489–494.

Wallston, K. A. (1989). Assessment of control in health care settings. In A. Steptoe & A. Appels (Eds.), *Stress, personal control and health* (pp. 85–106). Chichester, England: Wiley.

Ware, J. E., & Sherbourne, C. D. (1992). The MOS 36-item Short-Form Health Survey (SF-36). I: Conceptual framework and item selection. *Medical Care, 30,* 473–483.

Ware, N. C. (1993). Society, mind and body in chronic fatigue syndrome: An anthropological view. In G. R. Boch & J. Whelan (Eds.), *Chronic fatigue syndrome* (pp. 62–81). New York: Wiley.

Wassem, R. (1991). A test of the relationship between health locus of control and the course of multiple sclerosis. *Rehabilitation Nursing, 16,* 189–193.

Wessely, S., & Powell, R. (1989). Fatigue syndromes: A comparison of chronic postviral fatigue with neuromuscular and affective disorders. *Journal of Neurology, Neurosurgery, and Psychiatry, 52,* 940–948.

Willcockson, N. K. (1985). Discrimination of brain-damaged from functional psychiatric and medical patients with the MMPI. *Proceedings of the 1985 Clinical Psychology Short Course.* Presidio of San Francisco: Letterman Army Medical Center.

Wilson, A., Hickie, I., Lloyd, A., Hadzi-Pavlovic, D., Boughton, C., Dwyer, J., et al. (1994). Longitudinal study of outcome of chronic fatigue syndrome. *British Medical Journal, 308,* 756–759.

Wood, B., & Wessely, S. (1999). Personality and social attitudes in chronic fatigue syndrome. *Journal of Psychosomatic Research, 47,* 385–397.

Zigmond, A. S., & Snaith, R. P. (1983). The Hospital Anxiety and Depression Scale. *Acta Psychiatrica Scandinavia, 67,* 361–370.

CHAPTER 20

Neurocognitive Assessment

JOHN DeLUCA and LANA TIERSKY

OBJECTIVE NEUROPSYCHOLOGICAL IMPAIRMENT is well documented in chronic fatigue syndrome (CFS; Tiersky, Johnson, Lange, Natelson, & DeLuca, 1997). There is preliminary evidence that such cognitive problems are related to functional decline (Christodoulou et al., 1998) and severity of brain abnormalities on magnetic resonance imaging (MRI) (Lange et al., 1999). Additionally, cognitive complaints are one of the most frequent and debilitating symptoms of CFS (Abbey & Garfinkle, 1991; Christodoulou et al., 1998; Komaroff, 1994), with complaints of impaired cognitive function reported in up to 85% to 95% of patients (Grafman, 1994; Komaroff & Buchwald, 1991). Because both objective and subjective neuropsychological deficits are hallmarks of the illness, their accurate evaluation is essential to the care of the individual with CFS. This chapter provides a broad understanding of the components and concerns related to the neuropsychological assessment process in persons with CFS.

The chapter begins with a brief overview of CFS that highlights some of the main controversies pertaining to its etiology. This is followed by a presentation of the evaluation approach. Each component of the comprehensive evaluation, including the psychological evaluation, the neuropsychological evaluation, and the assessment of functional status, is discussed in turn. Finally, differential diagnostic concerns are discussed.

CONCEPTUALIZING CFS

BACKGROUND

CFS is a heterogeneous illness that is characterized by extreme fatigue and rheumatologic, infectious, and cognitive symptoms (Fukuda et al., 1994). To aid in diagnosis and treatment, a case definition for the illness was published in 1988 (Holmes et al., 1988), was revised in 1991 (Schluederberg et al., 1992), and revised again in 1994 (Fukuda et al., 1994). Prevalence estimates for the disorder vary based on the case definition used as well as on the characteristics of the study sample. A study comprising individuals involved in a health maintenance organization (HMO) in the United States found that the point prevalence varies from 0.08 percent to 0.3 percent when the 1988 case definition is used (Buchwald, Umali, Kith, Pearlman, & Komaroff, 1995). A community-based study completed in the United States found prevalence rates of 0.4 percent when the 1994 criteria were used (Jason et al., 1999). However, another study completed in the United Kingdom, which used the less restrictive 1994 case definition, found the prevalence to be as high as 2.6% among primary care attendees (Wessely, Chalder, Hirsch, Wallace, & Wright, 1997). Although the exact prevalence is unclear, CFS has been found to predominantly affect women in middle age (Komaroff, 1994). In addition, individuals from a variety of socioeconomic and ethnic backgrounds develop CFS (Jason et al., 2000).

Based on the diversity inherent in the population suffering from the illness, the most recent modification to the CFS case definition (Fukuda et al., 1994) emphasized stratification techniques to identify homogeneous subgroups for research purposes. A technique that has proven useful is dividing subjects based on their psychiatric history. For example, compared with CFS patients without lifetime or concurrent psychopathology, individuals with CFS who develop a psychiatric disorder after their illness onset suffer from less severe cognitive impairment, have fewer brain lesions on MRI, demonstrate less disability over time, and are more likely to be employed when examined longitudinally (DeLuca, Johnson, Ellis, & Natelson, 1997; Lange et al., 1999; Tiersky et al., 2001). Thus, psychiatric history is an important factor when attempting to complete the neuropsychological evaluation.

ETIOLOGY

The etiology of CFS remains unknown, and, as a result, two divergent positions regarding its cause have emerged. One position is that CFS is a manifestation of a psychiatric disorder, whereas the other position maintains that CFS is organic or a form of physical illness (Jones, Ray, Minnich, Hicks, Kibler, & Lucas, 1985; Manu, Matthews, & Lane, 1988). This dualistic view has led to confusion in diagnostic classification and, thus, in treatment. In the International Classification of Diseases-10 (ICD-10) diagnostic system, CFS-like syndromes with nearly identical descriptions are placed in both psychiatric and neuralgic categories (David & Wessely, 1993). These divergent classifications may lead to different treatment strategies that can range from the use of medications to behavioral and exercise therapies (Wessely, Hotopf, & Sharpe, 1998).

Several lines of research have been used to support the psychiatric hypothesis of CFS. One line of support is that there is a high degree of psychiatric comorbidity in CFS (Wessely, Chalder, Hirsch, Wallace, & Wright, 1996) with incidence rates of concurrent psychiatric diagnoses ranging from 23% (Pepper, Krupp, Friedberg, Doscher, & Coyle, 1993) to 75% (Wessely et al., 1997), depending on the sample characteristics. Common comorbid psychiatric conditions in CFS include major depression, dysthymia, generalized anxiety disorder, and panic disorder (Wessely et al., 1998). A second line of support for the psychiatric hypothesis is that many CFS symptoms overlap with those of psychiatric disorders. Partly because of symptom similarity, it is often argued that CFS or another fatigue-related condition, chronic fatigue (CF), is a manifestation of affective disorders such as major depression (D. B. Greenberg, 1990; Manu et al., 1988) or "atypical depression" (Abbey & Garfinkle, 1991). CFS is also often considered a variant of the somatoform disorders such as hypochondriasis (Manu, Affleck, Tennen, Morse, & Escobar, 1996) or somatization disorder (Shorter, 1992).

It is true that the symptoms of CFS overlap with those of several psychiatric disorders, and that there is a high degree of psychiatric comorbidity in the illness. These facts, however, do not fully support a hypothesis of psychiatric etiology for several reasons. First, having a psychiatric condition does not preclude someone from having a comorbid physical illness. Anxiety and affective disorders often accompany common medical conditions, such as coronary artery disease, hypertension, and diabetes (Sherbourne, Wells, Meredith, Jackson, & Camp, 1996; Wells et al., 1989). Second, many CFS patients do not meet the criteria for any form of psychopathology (e.g., DeLuca et al., 1997; Johnson, DeLuca, & Natelson, 1999). Finally, as noted, there is significant overlap between the symptoms of CFS and those of many psychiatric disorders, such as fatigue, cognitive problems, and sleep difficulties. Yet, several CFS symptoms (e.g., postexertional malaise, tender lymph nodes, sore throat) are not characteristic of psychiatric illness (American Psychiatric Association [APA], 1994; Fukuda et al., 1994). The mere presence of comorbid psychopathology does not prove its causation in CFS.

The second of the dualistic hypotheses pertaining to the etiology of CFS suggests that CFS is a medical illness. Some researchers believe that viral or other infectious agents cause the illness (Natelson, Cohen, Brassloff, & Lee, 1993; Schwartz et al., 1994). An often-noted sudden illness onset and the infectious nature of some of the symptoms are used to support this causal explanation (Hay & Jenkins, 1994; Komaroff, 1994). Other authors suggest, however, that the cause is not infectious, but is due to brain abnormalities. Data from neuroimaging studies (e.g., Lange et al., 1999; Natelson et al., 1993; Schwartz et al., 1994), as well as studies that have investigated neuroendocrine abnormalities (Demitrack, 1994) and autonomic nervous system dysfunction (Sisto et al., 1995) lend support for this hypothesis.

Similar to the psychiatric etiologic hypotheses for CFS, the medical hypotheses also fail to explain the origin of this heterogeneous disorder. Although studies have examined the role of numerous infectious agents in the etiology of CFS, there is no consistent evidence for an infectious cause (for a review, see Mawle, Reyes, & Schmid, 1993; Mawle et al., 1995). There is also no clear evidence of immune dysregulation (for review, see Buchwald & Komaroff, 1991; Lloyd, Wakefield, & Hickie, 1993; Strober, 1994). Finally, brain abnormalities are not observed in all CFS patients. It remains unclear whether brain abnormalities are a cause of the illness or a consequence of another pathological process.

Neither the medical nor the psychiatric hypothesis, by itself, is sufficient to explain the etiology of all CFS patients. Thus, some authors suggest an integration of these two hypotheses. The biopsychosocial model takes into account both medical and psychiatric factors in the initiation and maintenance of CFS (for review, see Sharpe, 1996). Understanding this model is useful to the diagnostician because it emphasizes behavioral, psychological, and emotional factors that might maintain the illness. Identifying these factors and offering ways to treat them are important aspects of any evaluation.

THE FUNDAMENTALS OF THE
NEUROPSYCHOLOGICAL EVALUATION PROCESS

The neuropsychological evaluation can be divided into at least two components: the psychological assessment and the cognitive assessment. A third area of evaluation is the functional assessment. Each is discussed in turn in this section. The neuropsychological approach that we present addresses the following referral questions commonly encountered by the neuropsychologist evaluating the CFS patient:

1. What is the differential diagnosis?
2. What impairments (if any) does the individual suffer from?
3. What is the best approach to treatment of these impairments?
4. Are the symptoms organic versus psychiatric in origin?
5. Is this person disabled by these impairments?

The general approach to psychological assessment is presented first, followed by the cognitive assessment of the CFS patient.

THE PSYCHOLOGICAL ASSESSMENT

As noted, psychiatric status has been found to affect neuropsychological functioning, and, therefore, a focused psychological evaluation needs to be conducted. Complaints of objective cognitive impairment are greater in CFS patients with concurrent psychiatric illness than those with no psychiatric disturbance (see Tiersky et al., 1997, for a review). As such, determining a patient's psychiatric status will aid the clinician in the differential diagnostic process and provide some information on which to generate cognitive performance expectations. Moreover, assessing neuropsychological functioning in isolation tells little about the patient's adaptability and potential functional capacities. Thus, without the psychological evaluation, there is inadequate information to generate treatment recommendations.

The psychological portion of the comprehensive neuropsychological evaluation should include assessment of the following three areas: (1) background and current functional history; (2) psychiatric illness, including presence and severity; and (3) personality functioning.

Background and Current Functional History   This part of the evaluation focuses on standard information gathered in the typical neuropsychological assessment. For organizational purposes, it is useful to categorize the needed information into the following chronological stages of development: prenatal, infancy, adolescence, early adulthood, middle adulthood, and late adulthood (Maxmen & Ward, 1995). For each time frame, a medical and psychosocial history should be obtained. When gathering the medical history, emphasis should be on discovering any history of neurological disease or involvement, including head injury. Moreover, when evaluating the medical history in infancy, it should be determined whether the patient met major developmental milestones at the target ages. The psychosocial history should include a thorough assessment of academic achievement, including any learning difficulties. Occupational history and current living situation, social involvement, and financial stability should also be evaluated when gathering the psychosocial information. Finally, family medical and psychiatric history should also be obtained.

Another area that should be thoroughly evaluated during this portion of the evaluation is the history of the presenting problem. In addition to documenting the development of CFS symptoms in general, a detailed account of the patient's subjective cognitive disturbances should be gathered. The onset, course, and severity of each symptom should be noted. Finally, the effects of these symptoms on functional ability should be determined. (This issue is discussed in more detail later in the chapter.)

Generally, a standard clinical interview is performed to obtain the necessary background and current functional information. However, there are structured instruments that are useful in gathering this information. Such instruments include the Adult Neuropsychological History (G. Greenberg, 1994), the Medical Profile Questionnaire (Mueller, 1996), and the Personal History Checklist for Adults (Schinka, 1989).

Psychiatric Symptoms On completion of this portion of the evaluation, the clinician should be able to provide a Five-Axis Diagnostic and Statistical Manual of Mental Disorders-*DSM-IV* (APA, 1994) diagnosis. It is important to determine if the individual suffers from any Axis I and/or II conditions. However, Axis III, IV, and V are also crucial to the neuropsychological assessment process. Beyond their general use, emphasis is recommended in the following areas. On Axis III, attention should be given to any medical condition that might affect cognitive functioning, and Axis IV should emphasize environmental problems that may exacerbate cognitive difficulties. Finally, Axis V will be used to direct the functional evaluation, which is the final stage in the neuropsychological evaluation process. The following texts provide a useful framework for completing the Five-Axis diagnosis: The Clinical Interview using the *DSM-IV*, volumes 1 and 2 (Othmer & Othmer, 1994a, 1994b) and The First Interview: Revised for the *DSM-IV* (Morrison, 1994).

Inquiring as to the presence of psychiatric symptoms to complete an Axis I or II diagnosis in CFS can be challenging. Although the best measure to use remains a subject of debate, many studies have used structured interviews to identify psychopathology in CFS (Taylor & Jason, 1998). Two commonly used structured instruments include the Structured Clinical Interview for the *DSM-IV* (SCID-I and SCID II) (First, Spitzer, Williams, & Gibbon, 1997; First, Gibbon, Spitzer, Williams, & Benjamin, 1997) and the Diagnostic Interview Schedule for the *DSM-IV* (DIS; Robins, Cottler, Bucholz, & Compton, 1995). For several reasons, Taylor and Jason (1998) advocate the use of the SCID rather than the DIS when assessing psychopathology in CFS. First, the SCID, unlike the DIS, is a semistructured clinical interview that allows for the collection of comprehensive data about the individual's symptoms and functioning. When determining whether specific clinical symptoms are present, the interviewer should take into account all available sources of information. Moreover, it is recommended that to administer the SCID, the interviewer have knowledge of psychopathology and clinical experience. Thus, the trained clinician can use the data obtained by the SCID to make a more accurate differential diagnosis, which is often difficult because of symptom overlap. A limitation of the DIS is that there is no method by which the interviewer can account for overlapping symptoms, which may lead to inaccurate diagnosis. In general, the DIS does not leave room for clinical judgment on the part of the interviewer. In contrast, for research purposes, trained nonclinicians can administer the DIS and follow strict criteria, which can be an advantage when individual differences from clinical judgment are not desirable.

The SCID can be used to evaluate both Axis I and II pathology, whereas the DIS only assesses Antisocial Personality Disorder on Axis II. Both the SCID and the DIS provide information about the presence or absence of psychopathology. However, the DIS, unlike the SCID, cannot provide any information about the severity of the symptoms. If the DIS is used, ancillary measures can determine symptom severity and provide additional information to accompany the findings of the SCID.

With caution, instruments such as the Beck Depression Inventory (BDI) (Beck, Ward, Mendelson, Mock, & Erbaugh, 1961), Center for Epidemiologic Studies Depression Scale (CES-D; Radloff, 1977), Beck Anxiety Inventory (Beck, Epstein, Brown, & Steer, 1988), and the Symptom Checklist-90 Revised (Derogatis, 1994) can all be used to assess the severity of an Axis I psychiatric disorder in CFS, if done cautiously. Authors have found that due to the symptom overlap, severity of a psychiatric disorder can be over-estimated when using these measures in CFS (see Friedberg & Jason, 1998, for a discussion). To eliminate this problem, authors have found it valuable to only examine subsets of the items on these scales in determining the severity of a psychiatric disorder. For example, Johnson, DeLuca, and Natelson (1996) divided the BDI into the following subscales: mood, self-reproach, somatic, and vegetative symptoms. Using this strategy, these authors were then able to document specific changes in mood and cognitions characteristic of depression.

Personality Functioning   As noted, the assessment of psychiatric disturbance in CFS should also include the evaluation of Axis II pathology, as the presence of a personality disorder will affect treatment recommendations. The SCID-II is recommended for assessing Axis II pathology. This instrument is comprehensive and includes all of the Axis II conditions noted in the *DSM-IV*. If time does not permit administering the SCID, the Personality Diagnostic Questionnaire-4 (PDQ-4) (Hyler, 1994) is a brief screening tool that can be used. However, because the PDQ-4 is only a screening tool, it provides limited information for the evaluation process.

Other Information   Finally, during this part of the psychological evaluation, information should also be gathered as to any prior psychotherapeutic interventions, including the type, duration, and frequency. Attention should also be given to the prior and current history of medication. It is important to determine whether the patient is taking any medication, psychotropic or otherwise, that might affect cognitive functioning.

Instruments, such as the Minnesota Multiphasic Personality Inventory II (MMPI-II; Butcher et al., 1989), can be used to assess other facets of personality functioning. The MMPI-II pattern often observed in persons with CFS may include elevations on scales 1, 2, 3, 7, and 8 (Schmaling & Jones, 1996). Although this pattern is frequently associated with somatoform tendencies, this interpretation must be made with extreme caution since it is also observed in persons with brain damage such as TBI, epilepsy, multiple sclerosis (MS), and spinal cord injury (Bornstein & Kozora, 1990; Derry, Harnadek, McLachlan, & Sonotrop, 1997; Gass, 1991; Meyerink, Reitan, & Selz, 1988).

THE COGNITIVE ASSESSMENT

Subjective Complaints   Subjective cognitive complaints are very common in CFS. Several studies have found that these complaints are more frequent and more severe in CFS than in persons with MS or clinical depression (Cope, Pernet, Kendall, & Davis, 1995; DeLuca, Johnson, Beldowicz, & Natelson, 1995; McDonald, Cope, & David, 1993). Despite the frequency and severity, there is little evidence of a relationship between these subjective complaints and objective neuropsychological findings in CFS (Cope et al., 1995; Grafman et al., 1993; Ray, Phillips, & Weir, 1993; Vercoulen et al., 1998). Cope et al. (1995) reported that fatigue and anxiety measures were most predictive of cognitive complaints in CFS. Smith (1991) found that CFS patients with the highest complaints of cognitive problems also demonstrated higher levels of psychopathology. Ray et al. (1993) reported that the degree of subjective cognitive complaints correlated with emotional distress, fatigue, and reports of physical malaise.

Assessment of subjective cognitive complaints is usually done with standard instruments such as the Cognitive Failures Questionnaire (Broadbent, Cooper, Fitzgerald, & Parkes, 1982).

The Discrepancy between Subjective Complaints and Objective Impairment   Often the neuropsychologist completing an evaluation for the individual with CFS is faced with inconsistencies. For instance, individuals with CFS often complain of cognitive difficulties exceeding those that are evident from objective assessment. Although there are myriad possible explanations for this discrepancy, at least three should be considered in any evaluation. The first is that the neuropsychological measures used may not be "ecologically valid." That is, the test instruments do not tap functions that have obvious realistic value in the patient's everyday life. A second possible reason is that the cognitive tests used may not be sensitive to subtle cognitive impairment. The third possible explanation is that the patient may, indeed, be malingering.

The lack of ecological validity of many neuropsychological assessment instruments is a common problem for the neuropsychologist (Heinrichs, 1990; Wilson, 1993). One solution is to include instruments in the evaluation that more directly tap functional skills as opposed to specific cognitive processes or impairments. The neuropsychological evaluation may yield subtle deficits in cognitive functioning that are genuine. However, the effects of these deficits on functional status is the greater issue. The ability to perform an everyday task that is cognitively challenging may interact with noncognitive factors such as fatigue, pain, personality, or emotional reactivity. Such variables must be factored into the evaluation to explain the discrepancies between the subjective complaints and objective performance. The magnitude of subjective complaints can be associated with the degree of emotional distress that the patient has in dealing with the cognitive impairment and its effects on daily life. As such, an adequate assessment of noncognitive factors, including functional status, is very important in the assessment of the patient with CFS (see later in this chapter).

Although few clinicians like to consider the possibility that their patients are less than fully motivated to perform optimally, or may even be malingering, it is nonetheless important to empirically investigate effort in CFS. The few studies that have investigated effort or malingering in CFS have produced mixed findings.

One study found that some CFS patients perform suboptimally on a measure of effort (van der Werf, Prins, Jongen, van der Meer, & Bleijenberg, 2000). However, another found that only 6 subjects out of 103 (i.e., 5.8%) demonstrated performances suggestive of feigned impairment (Tiersky et al., 2000). Nonetheless, tests of effort and malingering need to be part of the neuropsychological evaluation in persons with CFS, especially when the evaluation is being completed for disability determination or other situations involving monetary reward.

Objective Cognitive Assessment   When performing the neuropsychological evaluation in CFS, careful assessment of the following cognitive domains is necessary as these areas are those most often found to be impaired: attention/concentration, speed of information processing, and verbal memory. Still, as the neuropsychological evaluation is performed for differential purposes, the evaluation should be comprehensive and include assessment of other areas of cognitive ability such as general intellectual ability, language, motor functioning, nonverbal memory, visuospatial skills, and executive functioning. As deficits are not necessarily observed in these areas, low scores may suggest an alternative diagnosis. For an extensive review of the studies examining impaired cognitive functioning, the reader is referred to Tiersky et al. (1997).

Table 20.1 presents a sample neuropsychological evaluation test battery.

A review of the literature demonstrates that CFS sufferers most often perform in the average to above-average range of general intellectual abilities (IQ), and that these skills do not decline over time (Tiersky et al., 1997), although studies comparing actual premorbid data to post-CFS data have not been conducted. With this in mind, performances on tests of other cognitive domains are often compared with overall IQ scores as an estimate of premorbid functioning. It should be kept in mind that these IQ scores are indeed an estimate of premorbid intellectual functioning, and other factors (age, education, occupation, etc.) should also influence the estimated premorbid ability. Importantly, subtle changes in performance in other cognitive domains, while remaining within normal limits, may represent a substantial decline relative to intellectual ability. Patients may perceive such declines as significant as they are not able to perform as well as they once could, despite scoring within normal limits.

Intellectual skills are most often assessed using the Wechsler Adult Intelligence Scales (WAIS-R) now in its third edition (Wechsler, 1997). Some tests on the WAIS-R (e.g., Digits Symbol, Arithmetic) may be somewhat sensitive to the reduced processing speed and/or efficiency often observed in persons with CFS, but may not substantially alter the overall IQ indexes.

The literature on motor assessment has been inconsistent, with some studies finding no differences from healthy controls (Riccio, Thompson, Wilson, Morgan, & Lant, 1992) and others finding slowed motor performance (Marshall, Forstot, Callies, Peterson, & Schenck, 1997; Michiels et al., 1996). The finger-tapping test and grooved pegboard from the Halstead-Reitan Neuropsychological Battery are two instruments that have been used for the assessment of fine manual movement.

The literature suggests that CFS patients are able to perform within normal limits on tests of simple attention, such as digit span. However, with increased complexity, CFS patients perform significantly below that of healthy controls, particularly on tests requiring processing speeds that are sufficiently challenging to tax the central executive component of working memory. The Paced Auditory Serial

Table 20.1

Suggested Battery for the Comprehensive Neuropsychological Evaluation

Psychological Measures	Neuropsychological Measures	Functional Measures
Background Clinical Interview and Neurobehavioral history questionnaire	*Subjective cognitive* CFQ	*Clinical interview* Sf-36 or SIP
Psychological symptoms SCID or DIS and SCL-90R	*IQ* WAIS III (Specific subsets and indexes are also used in other domains)	
Personality MMPI-2	*Fine motor* Grooved Pegboard & FTT	
	Attention/concentration/Speed of information processing PASAT, Stroop, and Connor's CPT II	
	Learning and memory CVLT, & ROCF	
	Executive Category Test	
	Visuospatial ROCF	
	Language FAS	
	Malingering TOMM	

Note: Category Test = Category Test, computer version; CFQ = Cognitive Failures Questionniare (BroadBent, 1982); Connor's CPT = Connor's Continual Performance Task; CVLT = California Verbal Learning Test, 2nd ed.; DIS = Diagnostic Interview Schedule for the *DSM-IV*; FAS = Controlled Oral Word Association Task; FTT = Finger Tapping Test; MMPI-2 = Minnisota Multiphasic Personality Inventory-2; PASAT = Paced Auditory Serial Addition Task, ROCF = Rey Osterreith Complex Figure Task; SCID = Structured Clinical Interview for the *DSM-IV*; SCL-90R = Symptom Checklist 90-Revised; SF-36 = Medical Outcomes Study Health Questionnaire Short Form; SIP = Sickness Impact Profile; Stroop = Stroop Color and Word Test; TOMM = Test of Memory and Malingering; WAIS-III = Weschsler Adult Intellegence Scale, 3rd ed.

Addition Test (PASAT) has been consistently shown to differentiate CFS from healthy controls over several studies from a variety of laboratories (e.g., DeLuca, Johnson, & Natelson, 1993; DeLuca et al., 1995, 1997; Marshall et al., 1997; but see Kane, Gantz, & DiPino, 1997). The PASAT is a complex cognitive task that measures divided attention as well as speed of information processing. The PASAT requires that the subject listen to an audiotape that presents a string of randomized single digits. The subject must listen to the string of numbers, add each digit to the one that immediately preceded it, and say the answer aloud. The digits are presented in four sets of 50 digits (the number of digits in a set depends on the version of the test administered), and the rate of presentation of the digits increases across sets. For a more detailed discussion of the PASAT, the reader is referred to Lezak (1995).

Simple and complex reaction time measures may prove useful in the evaluation. Susceptibility to interference has been evaluated using the Stroop tests in patients with CFS. Also, the Digit Symbol subtest of the WAIS-R has demonstrated sensitivity between CFS and healthy controls. Interestingly, the Trail Making Test of the Halstead-Reitan Neuropsychological Battery has generally been shown to lack sensitivity in CFS despite its excellent sensitivity in many neurological populations.

Regarding learning and memory, the research studies have been inconsistent. However, recent work suggests that CFS patients have difficulty in the learning or acquisition of information (Johnson, DeLuca, Diamond, & Natelson, 1998; Joyce, Blumenthal, & Wessely, 1996; Marshall et al., 1997; Michiels, Cluydts, & Fischler, 1998; Smith, Behan, Bell, Millar, & Bakheit, 1993) and not in the retrieval of learned material from long-term storage. Further, recent research suggests that the learning difficulties observed in CFS patients are related to their difficulties in complex concentration and information-processing speed and/or efficiency. Once CFS patients adequately learn the information, performance on recall and recognition is not impaired. This differential between learning versus recall and recognition is important for two reasons. First, knowing that difficulties are in the acquisition of information focuses intervention strategies on improving learning instead of on methods to aid retrieval. Second, CFS patients can be comforted that once they learn information adequately, the loss of information over time is the same as that observed in healthy individuals.

For assessment, measures that assess learning are recommended. Instruments that do not contain a learning assessment (e.g., paragraph recall such as Logical Memory from the Wechsler Memory Scales, now in its third edition) are not recommended. Verbal memory is perhaps best assessed using the California Verbal Learning Test-Second Edition (CVLT-II), which contains significant assessment measures of learning. On the CVLT, the influence of these learning measures (e.g., serial vs. semantic processing, learning slope) should play a key role in the traditional interpretation of recall versus recognition. Traditionally, impaired recall relative to recognition has been interpreted as retrieval failure. In the presence of impaired learning indexes, however, this simple interpretation must be made with extreme caution.

For visual memory, there really is not a good test of learning. The Rey-Osterreith Complex Figure Test (ROCFT) provides a measure whereby the initial copy of the figure can be scored, followed by immediate and delayed recall (Lezak, 1995). Although factors that influence the encoding of the ROCFT can be scored (e.g., Lange, Waked, Kirshblum, & DeLuca, 2000), this may be too cumbersome for the traditional clinical evaluation. The best that the clinician can do is compare delayed recall relative to immediate recall. If there is little loss of information from immediate to delay, then it can be assumed that what was encoded was adequately maintained. However, if there is significant loss from immediate to delay, this may suggest compromised consolidation or retrieval.

In general, the literature suggests that higher cognitive functions such as language, executive processes (e.g., set-shifting, fluency, abstract reasoning, planning), and perceptual skills are not impaired in persons with CFS. This is not to say that individual CFS patients should be intact on all of these measures. There is much individual variability, and patients must be examined individually for their own particular strengths and weaknesses. However, when significant differences are found on tests of higher cognitive functions, other potential reasons for such findings need to be entertained.

The Functional Assessment

The functional evaluation is an essential part of the process. Its overall purpose is to determine to what extent patients' psychological and neuropsychological impairments impact their ability to function in their daily environment. It is best completed using a clinical interview augmented by standardized questionnaires. Moreover, interviewing a family member or other person close to the patient is often useful to most accurately determine the level of functioning.

The clinical interview provides the patient's perspective on the extent to which psychological and neuropsychological impairments affect everyday tasks. A good reference point for beginning the discussion of neuropsychological difficulties is using the Cognitive Failures Questionnaire (CFQ). Likewise, evaluation of the extent to which psychological problems impact everyday abilities can be ascertained by reviewing the information gathered during the psychological portion of the evaluation. It is often helpful to review with patients the Global Assessment of Functioning (*DSM-IV*, Axis V) diagnosis as well as the symptom history.

Clinical information is often augmented by the use of structured instruments. Two useful questionnaires are the SF-36 Health Survey (Ware, Snow, Kosinski, & Gandek, 1997) and the Sickness Impact Profile (SIP; Deyo & Inui, 1983). The SF-36 and the SIP have been used in CFS research to evaluate functional limitations and health-related quality of life (for a discussion, see Tiersky et al., 2000). These instruments can be modified so that they are used with a family member to collect information about the individual with CFS. By integrating clinical data with the data generated by the questionnaires, the clinician can obtain the most comprehensive picture of an individual's functioning.

Finally, the emotional state of patients at the time of the evaluation may influence their report of functional ability. Where there is a high degree of emotional distress, it is useful to interview a family member to determine to what extent the patient is disabled by cognitive and psychiatric symptoms. This does not preclude a family interview for CFS patients without psychiatric history to obtain the most comprehensive picture of a person's difficulties. A family member might point out additional areas of strength and weaknesses that the patient with CFS does not acknowledge.

Differential Diagnostic Concerns in the Neuropsychological Evaluation Process

As noted, the high degree of psychiatric comorbidity in individuals with CFS complicates the differential diagnostic process (Wessely et al., 1998). The two major psychiatric conditions that must be considered in the differential diagnosis are depression and somatization disorder. This chapter concentrates on depression and how this can be differentiated from CFS. Other medical conditions such as MS or Lyme disease must also be considered in the differential diagnosis. See Tiersky et al. (1997) for issues regarding differential diagnosis between CFS and MS.

It is important to keep in mind that depression, like CFS, is a heterogeneous disorder (Ray, 1991; Wessely et al., 1998). Depressed subjects from different referral sources often differ in their specific depressive symptomotology (Wessely et al., 1998). Symptoms of affective disturbance and cognitive distortions (e.g., excessive guilt, feelings of worthlessness and hopelessness) are common in patients presenting to tertiary care facilities. Somatic complaints, however, are often predominant in patients presenting to primary care facilities (Abbey & Garfinkle, 1991). As such, the heterogeneity in symptomotology in persons with clinical depression must be considered when performing a differential diagnosis in CFS.

Differentiating between CFS and Depression: Symptomatic Issues   Several factors complicate the differentiation of CFS from depression. Major depression and CFS share many common symptoms such as fatigue, cognitive complaints, and somatic and vegetative symptoms. Also, depression is the most common concurrent psychiatric disorder in CFS (Friedberg & Jason, 1998). As such, patients with CFS can also be significantly depressed, further complicating the diagnostic process. The following section emphasizes similarities and differences between CFS and depressed patients, which may aid in differential diagnoses.

Phenomenological Features

FATIGUE   The symptom of fatigue is common to both CFS and depression. Unexplained persistent fatigue is the major diagnostic feature of CFS. "Fatigue or loss of energy" (APA, p. 327) is also one of the diagnostic features of a major depressive episode. Despite being a prominent feature of both disorders, fatigue appears to be more prevalent and severe in CFS (Friedberg & Krupp, 1994; Komaroff et al., 1996; Natelson et al., 1993; Pepper et al., 1993), although the literature is not consistent (Wessely & Powell, 1989). As such, self-reported fatigue is not likely to be a sensitive factor in the differential diagnosis.

SOMATIC SYMPTOMS   It is not surprising that CFS and depression have many somatic symptoms in common, in addition to fatigue. Prominent somatic features that are common to both CFS and depression include sleep disturbance and cognitive difficulties (APA, 1994; Fukuda et al., 1994). Other somatic symptoms, such as abdominal pain, chest pain, nausea, excessive gas, blurred vision, shortness of breath, dizziness, and lump in throat, can also be common to CFS and depression (Johnson et al., 1996).

Despite the similarities, numerous symptoms distinguish the two disorders. Of those symptoms that are part of the symptom criteria for defining CFS, infectious symptoms (i.e., fever/chills, sore throat, swollen glands) are reported to be more common in CFS than in major depression (Komaroff et al., 1996). Also, a sudden onset of symptoms is reported in the vast majority of CFS patients, but not in depression (Friedberg & Jason, 1998). Moreover, muscle weakness (a criterion for 1988 CFS case definition), myalgia, postexertional malaise, headaches, and arthralgia have also been found to be more common in CFS than in depression (Friedberg & Jason, 1998; Komaroff et al., 1996). A patient presenting with sudden onset of flu-like symptoms accompanied by aches, pains, and postexertional fatigue may be more likely to be suffering from CFS than depression. Other symptoms, which are not part of the CDC case definition, such as poor appetite, alcohol intolerance, and tingling sensations have also been found to be more common in persons who complain of chronic fatigue than in depression (Komaroff et al., 1996).

SLEEP DISTURBANCE   While common in both CFS and depression, some features of the sleep impairment appear to differ in the two disorders (Friedberg &

Jason, 1998). One of the primary features of the sleep difficulties in depression appears to be early morning wakening (APA, 1994). This is not a primary difficulty in CFS. Moreover, Morriss, Wearden, and Battersby (1997) found that compared with depressed subjects, CFS patients more commonly reported being awakened by pain and took naps during the day.

AFFECTIVE AND COGNITIVE/PSYCHOLOGICAL FUNCTIONING Despite similarities in the somatic presentation of CFS and depression, significant differences in the affective and cognitive features of the illnesses exist. For instance, anhedonia and/or diminished mood are the primary features of major depression and are observed less often in CFS. Patients with CFS more often express frustration about not being able to participate in activities than they show a lack of interest in so doing (Wessely et al., 1998). Moreover, Johnson et al. (1996a) found that CFS patients reported less severe mood symptoms on the BDI than subjects with major depression. In contrast, affective symptoms such as irritability (Komaroff et al., 1996) and loss of libido (Friedberg & Jason, 1998) are found to be common in both disorders.

Cognitive features of depression can also distinguish CFS from major depression. Johnson et al. (1996a) found that depressed patients endorsed more "self-reproach" symptoms (i.e., believing that one is a failure and/or deserving punishment) on the BDI than MS or CFS patients. In contrast, CFS subjects endorsed more somatic items than the depressed subjects. Persons with CFS are less likely to demonstrate feelings of guilt (Johnson et al., 1996; Powell, Dolan, & Wessely, 1990; Shanks & Ho-Yen, 1995) and lowered self-esteem (Johnson et al., 1996; Powell et al., 1990) than individuals with major depression.

ILLNESS ATTRIBUTION Illness attribution represents one of the main cognitive features distinguishing persons with CFS and depression. Powell, Dolan, and Wessely (1990) reported that the single factor of believing that the illness had a physical cause separated a group of CFS patients from a group of affective controls. Powell et al. (1990) also found that CFS subjects attributed their illness to a physical cause, whereas subjects with depression attributed their illness to a psychological cause. This external attributional style is thought to protect the CFS sufferers' self-esteem at the cost of reducing a sense of self-efficacy (Wessely et al., 1998). In contrast, depressed individuals are noted to most often have an internal attributional style that diminishes self-esteem (Powell et al., 1990).

PERSONALITY CHARACTERISTICS Individuals with depression are more likely to suffer comorbid personality disorders than individuals with CFS. Johnson, DeLuca, and Natelson (1996b) and Pepper et al. (1993) both found Axis II disorders to be more common among patients with major depression than those with CFS. Also, the degree of personality pathology is similar to that observed in persons with MS (Johnson et al., 1996b). As such, the presence of long-standing personality dysfunction may suggest the presence of a major depressive disorder instead of CFS.

MELANCHOLIC DEPRESSION By definition, the presence of either a melancholic or psychotic depression precludes a diagnosis of CFS (Fukuda et al., 1994). Melancholic depression is characterized by distinctive diagnostic features not common to CFS such as loss of pleasure in all (or most) activities or lack of emotional reactivity; distinct quality of depressed mood, which is often not elevated even in CFS patients with high BDI Scores (Johnson et al., 1996a); excessive guilt; and early morning awakening (APA, 1994). Unlike other depressive subtypes, melancholic depression is not easily confused with CFS.

Differentiating CFS from Major Depression: Neuropsychological Features Complaints of cognitive impairment are common in CFS and depression. Subjective cognitive complaints between the two are similar, with complaints of deficits in attention/ concentration being prominent in both (APA, 1994; Tiersky et al., 1997; Wessely et al., 1998). One study found that subjects with major depression were more likely to report difficulty thinking, while CFS subjects were more likely to report forgetfulness (Komaroff et al., 1996). However, as noted, CFS subjects demonstrate more severe and frequent cognitive complaints than subjects with depression (Cope et al., 1995; DeLuca et al., 1995; McDonald et al., 1993; Ray et al., 1993; Smith, 1991; Smith et al., 1993).

WHEN DEPRESSION AND CFS CO-OCCUR The question often arises as to whether the neuropsychological deficits observed can be explained by depression. It is important to determine this differential because depression can be more readily treated than CFS. Studies examining the relationship between neuropsychological functioning and affective disorders in CFS have reported variable findings. Whereas several studies report that neuropsychological performance in CFS correlates with symptoms of depression, anxiety, emotional distress, and/or somatic symptoms (Krupp, Sliwinski, Masur, Friedberg, & Coyle, 1994; Marshall et al., 1997; McDonald et al., 1993; Ray et al., 1993; Schmaling, DiClementi, Cullum, & Jones, 1994; Wearden & Appleby, 1996), others find no relationship (Cope et al., 1995; DeLuca et al., 1993, 1995; Grafman et al., 1993; Joyce et al., 1996; Smith, 1991; Smith et al., 1993). Yet, others have reported that CFS patients perform more poorly on the PASAT than an affective disorders group (Marshall et al., 1997) or demonstrate greater memory impairment than depressed subjects (Sandman, Barton, Nackoul, Goldstein, & Fidler, 1993).

The question of whether psychopathology (primarily depression) can explain the neuropsychological deficits observed in CFS was directly addressed by DeLuca et al. (1997). These authors compared neuropsychological performance between 21 CFS subjects without psychopathology (either historically or concurrent with their illness) and 15 CFS subjects with psychopathology concurrent with their illness (but no psychopathology prior to illness). This study found that it was the CFS subjects *without* psychopathology who showed the neuropsychological impairments. These data are clearly incompatible with a model of depression-induced cognitive impairment in CFS.

In all, the neurocognitive deficits observed in CFS cannot simply be explained by the presence of depression alone (DeLuca et al., 1997; Marcel, Komaroff, Fagioli, Kornish, & Albert, 1996). However, depression may influence performance and certainly increases the probability of subjective cognitive complaints.

Differentiating CFS from Depression: Other Distinguishing Features
RESPONSE TO MEDICATION Vercoulen et al. (1996) randomly assigned CFS and major depressive subjects to either fluoxetine (Prozac) or a placebo condition for 8 weeks. There was no effect of fluoxetine in improving any CFS symptoms, or in subjective ratings of fatigue, severity of depression, neuropsychological complaints, sleep disturbances, or physical activity. The authors concluded that the processes underlying depressive symptoms in CFS subjects (even with comorbid depression) are different from those observed in patients with major depression (where fluoxetine has been shown to be effective). A more recent study (Wearden et al., 1998) found that fluoxetine did improve mood but no other symptoms of CFS.

NEUROENDOCRINE   Several studies have shown significant differences between persons with CFS and those with major depression in the responsivity of the hypothalamic-pituitary-adrenal (HPA) axis. Specifically, CFS subjects produce hypocortisolism, which is in marked contrast to the hypercortisolism found among individuals with depression (Cleare et al., 1995; Demitrack et al., 1991; Scott & Dinan, 1998; Scott, Medbak, & Dinan, 1998). These data strongly suggest a mild, centrally induced adrenal insufficiency in CFS (see Chapter 16 for more details).

NEUROIMAGING   Several studies have used brain imaging technology to examine whether there are structural and functional abnormalities in CFS patients. Lange et al. (1999) reported no differences in cerebral abnormalities between the CFS (46.2%) and healthy (31.6%) groups. However, when the CFS group was partitioned into subjects with or without psychopathology concurrent with their illness, significantly more abnormalities were observed in the CFS group *without* psychopathology (66.7%) compared to the CFS group with psychopathology (primarily depression: 22.2%) and controls (31.6%). Greco, Tannock, Brostoff, and Costa (1997) reported similar findings when stratifying the CFS group by the presence or absence of psychopathology.

Regarding functional neuroimaging, whereas some SPECT studies have reported significant differences between CFS subjects and depressed subjects (Costa, Tannock, & Brostoff, 1995; Schwartz et al., 1994), some have not (Goldstein, Mena, Jouanne, & Lesser, 1995). The only SPECT study to stratify CFS subjects into those with and without psychopathology reported similar findings to those previously described using MRI (Costa et al., 1995). Namely, significantly reduced brainstem hypoperfusion was greatest in CFS subjects without psychopathology.

CONCLUSION

Cognitive dysfunction is a key symptom in persons with CFS. The comprehensive neuropsychological evaluation is geared toward understanding actual cognitive problems, the person's subjective impressions of these problems, the psychological and psychiatric comorbidities that may affect the actual or perceived cognitive problems, and the effect of these problems on everyday life. Only a trained psychologist, preferably one experienced in working with CFS patients, should perform such a comprehensive examination. From this evaluation, treatment recommendations can be tailored to the patient's individual needs. For example, specific cognitive interventions may help CFS patients who do not have psychiatric comorbidity. CFS patients with concurrent and/or a history of psychiatric problems may require more intensive psychotherapy and/or psycho-educational approaches. Several well-designed clinical trials have shown Cognitive Behavioral Therapy to be effective in improving symptoms, psychological well-being, and quality of life in persons with CFS (Prins et al., 2001). Such therapeutic approaches may significantly improve the CFS individual's ability to function cognitively and better cope with these problems in their everyday life.

REFERENCES

Abbey, S. E., & Garfinkle, P. E. (1991). Chronic fatigue syndrome and depression: Cause, effect, or covariate. *Review of Infectious Diseases, 13* (Suppl. 1), S73–S83.

American Psychiatric Association. (1994). *Diagnostic and statistical manual of mental disorders* (4th ed.). Washington, DC: Author.

Beck, A. T., Epstein, N., Brown, G., & Steer, R. A. (1988). Beck Anxiety Inventory. *Journal of Consulting and Clinical Psychology, 56*(6), 893–897.

Beck, A. T., Ward, C. H., Mendelson, M., Mock, J., & Erbaugh, J. (1961). An inventory for measuring depression. *Archives of General Psychiatry, 4,* 561–571.

Bornstein, R. A., & Kozora, E. (1990). Content bias of the MMPI scale in neurological patients. *Neuropsychiatry, Neuropsychology and Behavioral Neurlogy, 3,* 200–205.

Broadbent, D. E., Cooper, P. F., Fitzgerald, P., & Parkes, K. R. (1982). The Cognitive Failures Questionnaire (CFQ) and its correlates. *British Journal of Clinical Psychology, 21*(1), 1–16.

Buchwald, D., & Komaroff, A. L. (1991). Review of laboratory findings for patients with chronic fatigue syndrome. *Rev Infect Disorder, 3* (Suppl. 1), S12–S18.

Buchwald, D., Umali, P., Kith, P., Pearlman, T., & Komaroff, A. (1995). Chronic fatigue and the chronic fatigue syndrome: Prevalence in a Pacific Northwest Health Care System. *Annals of Internal Medicine, 123,* 81–88.

Butcher, J. N., Dahlstrom, W. G., Graham, J. R., Tellegen, A., & Kaemmer, B. (1989). *Manual for the Restandardized Minnesota Multiphasic Personality Inventory: MMPI-2.* Minneapolis: University of Minnesota Press.

Christodoulou, C., DeLuca, J., Lange, G., Johnson, S. K., Sisto, S. A., Korn, L., et al. (1998). Relation between neuropsychological impairment and functional disability in patients with chronic fatigue syndrome. *Journal of Neurology, Neurosurgery, and Psychiatry, 64,* 431–434.

Cleare, A. J., Bearn, J., McGregor, A., Allain, T., Wessely, S., Murray, R. M., et al. (1995). Contrasting neuroendocrine responses in depression and chronic fatigue syndrome. *Journal of Affective Disorders, 35,* 283–289.

Cope, H., Pernet, A., Kendall, B., & Davis, A. (1995). Cognitive functioning and magnetic resonance imaging in chronic fatigue syndrome. *British Journal of Psychiatry, 167,* 86–94.

Costa, D. C., Tannock, C., & Brostoff, J. (1995). Brainstem profusion is impaired in chronic fatigue syndrome. *Quarterly Journal of Medicine, 88,* 767–773.

David, A., & Wessely, S. (1993). Chronic fatigue, ME and the ICD-10. *Lancet, 342,* 1247–1248.

DeLuca, J., Johnson, S. K., Beldowicz, D., & Natelson, B. H. (1995). Neuropsychological impairments in chronic fatigue syndrome, multiple sclerosis, and depression. *Journal of Neurology, Neurosurgery, and Psychiatry, 58,* 38–43.

DeLuca, J., Johnson, S. K., Ellis, S. P., & Natelson, B. H. (1997). Cognitive functioning is impaired in patients with chronic fatigue syndrome devoid of psychiatric disease. *Journal of Neurology, Neurosurgery, and Psychiatry, 62,* 151–155.

DeLuca, J., Johnson, S. K., & Natelson, B. H. (1993). Information processing in chronic fatigue syndrome and multiple sclerosis. *Archives of Neurology, 50,* 301–304.

Demitrack, M. A. (1994). Neuroendocrine aspects of chronic fatigue syndrome: Implications for diagnosis and research. In S. E. Straus (Ed.), *Chronic fatigue syndrome* (pp. 285–308). New York: Marcel Dekker.

Demitrack, M. A., Dale, J. K., Straus, S. E., Laue, L., Listwak, S. J., Kruesi, M. J., et al. (1991). Evidence for the impaired activation of the hypothalamic-pituitary-adrenal axis in patients with chronic fatigue syndrome. *Journal of Clinical Endocrinology and Metabolism, 73,* 1–11.

Derogatis, L. (1994). *The SCL-90-R. Symptoms Checklist-90-R. Administration, Scoring, and Procedures Manual* (3rd ed.). Minneapolis, MN: National Computer Systems.

Derry, P., Harnadek, M. C., McLachlan, R. S., & Sonotrop, J. (1997). Influence of seizure content on interpreting psychopathology on the MMPI-2 in patients with epilepsy. *Journal of Clinical and Experimental Neuropsychology, 19,* 396–404.

Deyo, R. A., & Inui, T. S. (1983). Measuring functional outcomes in chronic disease: A comparison of traditional scales and a self-administered health status questionnaire in patients with rheumatoid arthritis. *Medical Care, 21,* 180–192.

First, M. B., Gibbon, M., Spitzer, R. L., Williams, J. B., & Benjamin, L. (1997). *Structured clinical interview for DSM-IV Axis II Personality Disorders* (SCID-II). Washington, DC: American Psychiatric Press.

First, M. B., Spitzer, R. L., Williams, J. B., & Gibbon, M. (1997). *Structured clinical interview for DSM-IV Axis I Disorders* (SCID-I), clinician version. Washington, DC: American Psychiatric Press.

Friedberg, F., & Jason, L. A. (1998). *Understanding chronic fatigue syndrome: An empirical guide to assessment and treatment.* Washington, DC: American Psychological Association.

Friedberg, F., & Krupp, L. B. (1994). A comparison of cognitive behavioral treatment for chronic fatigue syndrome and primary depression. *Clinical Infectious Diseases, 18*(1), 105–110.

Fukuda, K., Straus, S. E., Hickie, I., Sharpe, M. C., Dobbins, J. G., & Komaroff, A. (1994). The chronic fatigue syndrome: A comprehensive approach to its definition and study. *Annals of Internal Medicine, 121,* 953–959.

Gass, C. S. (1991). MMPI-2 interpretation and closed head injury: A correction factor. *Psychological Assessment, 3,* 27–31.

Goldstein, J. A., Mena, I., Jouanne, E., & Lesser, I. (1995). The assessment of vascular abnormalities in late life chronic fatigue syndrome by brain SPECT: Comparison with late life major depressive disorder. *Journal of Chronic Fatigue Syndrome, 1,* 55–79.

Grafman, J. (1994). Neuropsychological features of chronic fatigue syndrome. In E. Straus (Ed.), *Chronic fatigue syndrome,* (pp. 263–284). New York: Marcel Dekker.

Grafman, J., Schwartz, V., Dale, J. K., Scheffers, M., Houser, C., & Straus, S. E. (1993). Analysis of neuropsychological functioning in patients with chronic fatigue syndrome. *Journal of Neurology, Neurosurgery, and Psychiatry, 56,* 684–689.

Greco, A., Tannock, C., Brostoff, J., & Costa, D. (1997). Brain MR in chronic fatigue syndrome. *American Journal of Neuroradiology, 18,* 1265–1269.

Greenberg, D. B. (1990). Neurasthenia in the 1980's: Chronic mononucleosis, chronic fatigue syndrome, and anxiety and depressive disorders. *Psychosomatics, 31,* 129–137.

Greenberg, G. (1994). *Adult neuropsychological history.* Worthington, OH: IDS Publishing.

Hay, J., & Jenkins, F. J. (1994). Human herpes virus and chronic fatigue syndrome. In S. E. Straus (Ed.), *Chronic fatigue syndrome* (pp. 181–197). New York: Marcel Dekker.

Heinrichs, W. R. (1990). Current and emergent applications of neuropsychological assessment problems of validity and utility. *Professional Psychology: Research and Practice, 21*(3), 171–176.

Holmes, G. P., Kaplan, J. R., Gantz, N. M., Komaroff, A. L., Schonberger, L. B., Straus, S. E., et al. (1988). Chronic fatigue syndrome: A working case definition. *Annals of Internal Medicine, 108,* 387–389.

Hyler, S. E. (1994). *Personality Diagnostic Questionnaire (PDQ-4)* (4th ed.). New York: New York State Psychiatric Institute.

Jason, L. A., Richman, J. A., Rademaker, A. W., Jordan, K. M., Plioplys, A. V., Taylor, R. R., et al. (1999). A community based study of chronic fatigue syndrome. *Archives of Internal Medicine, 159*(18), 2129–2137.

Jason, L. A., Taylor, R. R., Kennedy, C. L., Jordan, K., Song, S., Johnson, D. E., et al. (2000). Chronic fatigue syndrome: Sociodemographic subtypes in a community-based sample. *Evaluation and the Health Professions, 23*(3), 243–263.

Johnson, S. K., DeLuca, J., Diamond, B. J., & Natelson, B. H. (1998). Memory dysfunction in fatiguing illness: Examining interference and distraction in working memory. *Cognitive Neuropsychiatry, 3,* 269–285.

Johnson, S. K., DeLuca, J., & Natelson, B. H. (1996). Depression in fatiguing illness: Comparing patients with chronic fatigue syndrome, multiple sclerosis and depression. *Journal of Affective Disorders, 39,* 21–30.

Johnson, S. K., DeLuca, J., & Natelson, B. H. (1999). Chronic fatigue syndrome: Reviewing the research findings. *Annals of Behavioral Medicine, 21,* 258–271.

Jones, J., Ray, G., Minnich, L., Hicks, M., Kibler, R., & Lucas, D. (1985). Evidence for active Epstein-Barr virus infection in patients with persistent, unexplained illnesses: Elevated anti-early antigen antibodies. *Annals of Internal Medicine, 102,* 1–7.

Joyce, E., Blumenthal, S., & Wessely, S. (1996). Memory, attention, and executive function in chronic fatigue syndrome. *Journal of Neurology, Neurosurgery, and Psychiatry, 60,* 495–503.

Kane, R. L., Gantz, N. M., & DiPino, R. K. (1997). Neuropsychological and psychological functioning in chronic fatigue syndrome. *Neuropsychiatry, Neuropsychology, and Behavioral Neurology, 10*(1), 25–31.

Komaroff, A. L. (1994). Clinical presentation and evaluation of fatigue and chronic fatigue syndrome. In S. E. Straus (Ed.), *Chronic fatigue syndrome* (pp. 61–84). New York: Marcel Dekker.

Komaroff, A. L., & Buchwald, D. (1991). Symptoms and signs of chronic fatigue syndrome. *Review of Infectious Diseases, 13,* S8–S11.

Komaroff, A. L., Fagioli, L. R., Geiger, A. M., Doolittle, T. H., Lee, J., Kornish, J., et al. (1996). An examination of the working case definition of chronic fatigue syndrome. *American Journal of Medicine, 100,* 56–64.

Krupp, L. B., Sliwinski, M., Masur, D. M., Friedberg, F., & Coyle, P. K. (1994). Cognitive functioning and depression in patients with chronic fatigue syndrome and multiple sclerosis. *Archives of Neurology, 51,* 705–710.

Lange, G., DeLuca, J., Maldjian, J. A., Lee, H. J., Tiersky, L. A., & Natelson, B. H. (1999). Brain MRI abnormalities exist in a subset of patients with chronic fatigue syndrome. *Journal of the Neurological Sciences, 171,* 3–7.

Lange, G., Waked, W., Kirshblum, S., & DeLuca, J. (2000). Influence of organizational strategy on visual memory performance following stroke: Cortical/subcortical and left/right hemisphere contrasts. *Archives of Physical Medicine and Rehabilitation, 81,* 89–94.

Lezak, M. D. (1995). *Neuropsychological assessment* (3rd ed.). New York: Oxford University Press.

Lloyd, A. R., Wakefield, D., & Hickie, I. (1993). Immunity and the pathophysiology of chronic fatigue syndrome. *Ciba Found Symp., 173,* 176–187.

Manu, P., Affleck, G., Tennen, H., Morse, P. A., & Escobar, J. I. (1996). Hypochondriasis influences quality-of-life outcomes in patients with chronic fatigue. *Psychotherapy and Psychosomatics, 65*(2), 76–81.

Manu, P., Matthews, D. A., & Lane, T. J. (1988). The mental health of patients with a chief complaint of chronic fatigue: A prospective evaluation and follow-up. *Archives of Internal Medicine, 148,* 2213–2217.

Marcel, B., Komaroff, A. L., Fagioli, L. R., Kornish, R. J., II, Albert, M. S. (1996). Cognitive deficits in patients with chronic fatigue syndrome. *Biological Psychiatry, 40,* 535–541.

Marshall, P. S., Forstot, M., Callies, A., Peterson, P. K., & Schenck, C. H. (1997). Cognitive slowing and working memory difficulties in chronic fatigue syndrome. *Psychosomatic Medicine, 59*(1), 58–66.

Mawle, A. C., Reyes, M., & Schmid, D. S. (1993). Is chronic fatigue syndrome an infectious disease? *Infect Agents Dis., 2*, 333–341.

Mawle, A. C., Nisenbaum, R., Dobbins, J. G., Gary, H. E., Jr, Stewart, J. A., Reyes, M., et al. (1995). Seroepidemiology of chronic fatigue syndrome: a case-control study. *Clin Infect Dis., 21*, 1386–1389.

Maxmen, J. S., & Ward, N. G. (1995). *Essential psychopathology and its treatment* (2nd ed.). New York: Norton.

McDonald, E., Cope, H., & David, A. (1993). Cognitive impairment in patients with chronic fatigue: A preliminary study. *Journal of Neurology, Neurosurgery, and Psychiatry, 56*, 812–815.

Meyerink, L. H., Reitan, R. M., & Selz, M. (1988). The validity of the MMPI with multiple sclerosis patients. *Journal of Clinical Psychology, 44*, 763–769.

Michiels, V., Cluydts, R., & Fischler, B. (1998). Attention and verbal learning in patients with chronic fatigue syndrome. *Journal of the International Neuropsychological Society, 4*, 456–466.

Michiels, V., Cluydts, R., Fischler, B., Hoffmann, G., Le Bon, O., & De Meirleir, K. (1996). Cognitive functioning in patients with chronic fatigue syndrome. *Journal of Clinical and Experimental Neuropsychology, 18*, 666–677.

Morrison, J. (1994). *The first interview: Revised for the DSM-IV*. New York: Guilford Press.

Morriss, R. K., Wearden, A. J., & Battersby, L. (1997). The relation of sleep difficulties to fatigue, mood and disability in chronic fatigue syndrome. *Journal of Psychosomatic Research, 42*(6), 597–605.

Mueller, J. (1996). *The Medical Profile Questionnaire* (Synopsis). Odessa, FL: Psychological Assessment Resources.

Natelson, B. H., Cohen, J. M., Brassloff, I., & Lee, H. J. (1993). A controlled study of brain magnetic resonance imaging in patients with fatiguing illnesses. *Journal of the Neurological Sciences, 120*, 213–217.

Othmer, E., & Othmer, S. (1994a). *The clinical interview using DSM-IV, Vol. 1: Fundamentals*. Washington, DC: American Psychiatric Press.

Othmer, E., & Othmer, S. (1994b). *The clinical interview using DSM-IV, Vol. 2: The Difficult Patient*. Washington, DC: American Psychiatric Press.

Pepper, C. M., Krupp, L. B., Friedberg, F., Doscher, C., & Coyle, P. K. (1993). A comparison of neuropsychiatric characteristics in chronic fatigue syndrome, multiple sclerosis, and major depression. *Journal of Neuropsychiatry and Clinical Neurosciences, 5*, 200–205.

Powell, R., Dolan, R., & Wessely, S. (1990). Attributions and self-esteem in depression and chronic fatigue syndrome. *Journal of Psychosomatic Research, 21*, 665–673.

Prins, J. B., Bleijenberg, G., Bazelmans, E., Elving, L. D., de Boo, T. M., Severens, J. L., et al. (2001). Cognitive behavior therapy for chronic fatigue syndrome: A multicentre randomized control trial. *Lancet, 357*, 841–847.

Radloff, L. S. (1977). The CES-D Scale: A self-report depression scale for research in the general population. *Applied Psychological Measurement, 1*, 385–401.

Ray, C. (1991). Chronic fatigue syndrome and depression: Conceptual and methodological ambiguities. *Psychological Medicine, 21*, 1–9.

Ray, C., Phillips, L., & Weir, W. R. (1993). Quality of attention in chronic fatigue syndrome: Subjective reports of everyday attention and cognitive difficulty, and performance on tasks of focused attention. *British Journal of Clinical Psychology, 32*, 357–364.

Riccio, M., Thompson, C., Wilson, B., Morgan, R. D., & Lant, A. F. (1992). Neuropsychological and psychiatric abnormalities in myalgic encephalomyelitis: A preliminary report. *British Journal of Clinical Psychology, 31,* 111–120.

Robins, L. N., Cottler, L., Bucholz, K., & Compton, W. (1995). *Diagnostic Interview Schedule, Version IV.* St Louis, MO: Department of Psychiatry, Washington School of Medicine.

Sandman, C. A., Barton, J. L., Nackoul, K., Goldstein, J., & Fidler, F. (1993). Memory deficits associated with chronic fatigue immune dysfunction syndrome. *Biological Psychiatry, 33,* 618–623.

Schinka, J. (1989). *Personal History Checklist for Adults.* Odessa, FL: Psychological Assessment Resources.

Schluederberg, A., Straus, S. E., Peterson, P., Blumenthal, S., Komaroff, A., Spring, S., et al. (1992). Chronic fatigue syndrome: Definition and medical outcome assessment. *Annals of Internal Medicine, 117,* 325–331.

Schmaling, K. B., DiClementi, J. D., Cullum, M., & Jones, J. F. (1994). Cognitive functioning in chronic fatigue syndrome and depression: A preliminary comparison. *Psychosomatic Medicine, 56,* 383–388.

Schmaling, K. B., & Jones, J. F. (1996). MMPI profiles of patients with chronic fatigue syndrome. *Journal of Psychosomatic Research, 40,* 67–74.

Schwartz, R. B., Garada, B. M., Komaroff, A. L., Tice, H. M., Gleit, M., Jolesz, F. A., et al. (1994). Detection of intracranial abnormalities in patients with chronic fatigue syndrome: Comparison of MRI imaging and SPECT. *American Journal of Radiology, 162,* 935–941.

Scott, L. V., & Dinan, T. G. (1998). Urinary free cortisol excretion in chronic fatigue syndrome, major depression and in healthy volunteers. *Journal of Affective Disorders, 47,* 49–54.

Scott, L. V., Medbak, S., & Dinan, T. G. (1998). The low dose ACTH test in chronic fatigue syndrome and in health. *Clinical Endocrinology, 48,* 733–737.

Shanks, M. F., & Ho-Yen, D. O. (1995). A clinical study of chronic fatigue syndrome. *British Journal of Psychiatry, 166,* 798–801.

Sharpe, M. (1996). Chronic fatigue syndrome. *Psychiatric Clinics of North America, 19*(3), 549–573.

Sherbourne, C. D., Wells, K. B., Meredith, L. S., Jackson, C. A., & Camp, P. (1996). Comorbid anxiety disorder and the functioning and well-being of chronically ill patients of general medical providers. *Archives of General Psychiatry, 53,* 889–895.

Shorter, E. (1992). *From paralysis to fatigue: A history of psychosomatic illness in the modern era.* New York: Free Press.

Sisto, S. A., Tapp, W., Drastal, S., Bergen, M., DeMasi, I., Cordero, D., et al. (1995). Vagal tone is reduced during paced breathing in patients with the chronic fatigue syndrome. *Clin Auton Res. 5,* 139–143.

Smith, A. P. (1991). Cognitive changes in myalgic encephalomyelitis. In R. Jenkins & J. F. Mowbray (Eds.), *Postviral fatigue syndrome* (pp. 179–194). New York: Wiley.

Smith, A. P., Behan, P. O., Bell, W., Millar, K., & Bakheit, M. (1993). Behavioral problems associated with the chronic fatigue syndrome. *British Journal of Psychology, 84,* 411–423.

Strober, W. (1994). Immunological function in chronic fatigue syndrome. In S. E. Straus (Ed.), *Chronic fatigue syndrome* (pp. 207–237). New York: Marcel Dekker.

Taylor, R. R., & Jason, L. A. (1998). Comparing the DIS and the SCID: Chronic fatigue syndrome and psychiatric comorbidity. *Psychology and Health, 13,* 1087–1104.

Tiersky, L. A., Johnson, S. K., Lange, G., Natelson, B. H., & DeLuca, J. (1997). Neuropsychology of chronic fatigue syndrome: A critical review. *Journal of Clinical and Experimental Neuropsychology, 19*(4), 560–586.

Tiersky, L. A., Natelson, B. H., Ottenweller, J., Lange, G., Fiedler, N., & DeLuca, J. (2000). Functional status and mood in Persian Gulf registry veterans with fatiguing illness. *Military Psychology, 12*(4), 233–248.

van der Werf, S. P., Prins, J. D., Jongen, P. J., van der Meer, J. W., & Bleijenberg, G. (2000). Abnormal neuropsychological findings are not necessarily a sign of cerebral impairment: A matched comparison between chronic fatigue syndrome and multiple sclerosis. *Neuropsychiatry, Neuropsychology, and Behavioral Neurology, 13,* 199–203.

Vercoulen, J. H., Bazelmans, C. M., Swanink, C. M., Galama, J. F., Fennis, J. W., van der Meer, J. W., et al. (1998). Evaluating neuropsychological impairment in chronic fatigue syndrome. *Journal of Clinical and Experimental Neuropsychology, 20,* 144–156.

Vercoulen, J. H., Swanink, C. M., Zitman, F. G., Vreden, S. G., Hoofs, M. P., Fennis, J. F., et al. (1996). Randomized, double-blind, placebo-controlled study of fluoxetine in chronic fatigue syndrome. *Lancet, 347,* 858–861.

Ware, J. E., Snow, K. K., Kosinski, M., & Gandek, B. (1997). *The SF-36 Health Survey,* manual and interpretation guide. Boston: Medical Outcomes Trust.

Wearden, A. J., & Appleby, L. (1996). Research on cognitive complaints and cognitive functioning in patients with chronic fatigue syndrome: What conclusions can we draw? *Journal of Psychosomatic Research, 41*(3), 197–211.

Wearden, A. J., Morriss, R. K., Mullis, R., Strickland, P. L., Pearson, D. J., Appleby, L., et al. (1998). Randomized, double-blind, placebo-controlled treatment trial of fluoxetine and graded exercise for chronic fatigue syndrome. *British Journal of Psychiatry, 172,* 485–490.

Wechsler, D. (1997). *Wechsler Adult Intelligence Scale* (3rd ed.). San Antonio, TX: Psychological Corporation.

Wells, K. B., Stewart, A., Hays, R. D., Buram, A., Rogers, W., Daniels, M., et al. (1989). The functioning and well-being of depressed patients. *Journal of the American Medical Association, 262,* 914–919.

Wessely, S., Chalder, T., Hirsch, S., Wallace, P., & Wright, D. (1996). Psychological symptoms, somatic symptoms and psychiatric disorder in chronic fatigue and chronic fatigue syndrome: A prospective study in primary care. *American Journal of Psychiatry, 153*(8), 1050–1059.

Wessely, S., Chalder, T., Hirsch, S., Wallace, P., & Wright, D. (1997). The prevalence and morbidity of chronic fatigue and chronic fatigue syndrome: A prospective primary care study. *American Journal of Public Health, 87,* 1449–1455.

Wessely, S., Hotopf, M., & Sharpe, M. (1998). *Chronic fatigue and its syndromes.* Oxford, England: Oxford University Press.

Wessely, S., & Powell, R. (1989). Fatigue syndromes: A comparison of chronic postviral fatigue with neuromuscular and affective disorder. *Journal of Neurology, Neurosurgery, and Psychiatry, 52,* 940–948.

Wilson, B. A. (1993). Ecological validity of neuropsychological assessment: Do neuropsychological indexes predict performance on everyday activities? *Applied and Preventive Psychology, 2*(4), 209–215.

PART V

TREATMENT AND INTERVENTION

CHAPTER 21

Medical Intervention and Management

PAUL LEVINE, STANLEY SCHWARTZ, and GLORIA FURST

T HE CAREGIVER RESPONSIBLE for working with patients with chronic fatigue syndrome (CFS) is often confronted with severely disabled and debilitated patients who have a number of well-justified concerns. This chapter highlights some of the important advances made in the management of CFS in the past decade.

Two important considerations went into the development of this chapter. The first is the realization that while CFS is now a widely recognized disorder (Levine, 1998), it is clearly a heterogeneous one with multiple case definitions, including four that were reviewed in a detailed literature analysis conducted by the Agency for Health Care Research and Quality (2001). In the United States, most attention has been given to the two research definitions developed under the auspices of the U.S. Centers for Disease Control and Prevention (CDC; Fukuda et al., 1994; Holmes et al., 1988), the latter apparently having less specificity (increased heterogeneity) while also having greater sensitivity (Jason et al., 1999). Factor analysis has revealed a number of different subgroups (Young, Simmens, Kang, Mahan, & Levine, 2001), with some patients presenting with an acute onset dominated by symptoms suggestive of infection, some having a very gradual onset and few infectious-type symptoms, some with a fibromyalgia-like component predominating, and many with other predominating symptoms or a mixture of the different symptom complexes. In addition to fatigue, cognitive disorders and sleep disturbances are among the most common (Komaroff, 1994), but not every CFS patient has both. Meanwhile, because the currently accepted research definition (Fukuda et al., 1994) is under consideration and likely to be revised, it is important for clinicians to realize that this definition is a research definition; and they need to carefully evaluate patients with fatigue, cognitive symptoms, sleep disturbances, and pain, considering their management according to the principles described in the next section. Eventually, as laboratory tests and the biological markers are better understood, distinct subgroups of CFS may allow some stratification similar to the substratification of mixed connective tissue disease, which often can declare itself as sclerodema, systemic lupus erythematosus, or other related disorders with different clinical and laboratory manifestations.

The second important consideration for this chapter is the desire to concentrate on the evaluation and management of those manifestations of CFS that have been generally accepted by the scientific community. This is a difficult and controversial area, but we have taken the findings of recent meetings that have extensive discussions of CFS management:

1. A consensus conference by the Pioneer Foundation held in Reno, Nevada, in July 2000 focusing on rehabilitation, postural hypotension, sleep disorders, and infectious manifestations (Levine et al., 2001).
2. A consensus conference held in October 2000 by the National Institutes of Health (U.S. Department of Health and Human Services, Chronic Fatigue Syndrome Coordinating Committee, 2000).
3. The biannual meeting of the American Association for Chronic Fatigue Syndrome, a professional organization devoted to research on the etiology, pathogenesis, and management of CFS, which was held in January 2001 in Seattle, Washington (Patarca, 2001).
4. A meeting organized in March 2001 by the Chronic Fatigue and Immune Dysfunction Syndrome (CFIDS) Association of America and the CDC in Washington, DC, on neuroendocrine disorders (Papanicolou, 2001).

Observations contained in this chapter were presented at the Seattle meeting, and pertinent comments have been incorporated.

EVALUATION OF CHRONIC FATIGUE SYNDROME

There are a number of phases in the course of CFS as described by Fennell (1995), and evaluation must be an ongoing process (Levine, 1998). In part, this is because a number of treatable disorders can mimic CFS, and continued evaluation is necessary to be certain an alternative diagnosis is not missed. In addition, CFS patients develop disorders independent of their CFS; therefore, new symptomatology requires reevaluation, and the onset of new symptoms should not automatically be attributed to the CFS. Finally, physically and psychologically, the patient may go through significant changes over the course of the illness, and ongoing evaluation and support are critical to maximizing improvement if a procedure is working and to minimizing detrimental effects if the patient is having an adverse response.

Evaluation of chronic fatigue in clinical practice should include a careful history, a thorough physical examination, and laboratory tests. The clinicians should pay particular attention to the sleep history, any history of psychological or psychiatric disease, and any history of prescribed and recreational drug use. A standard physical examination should also include an estimation of nutritional status, muscle strength, and mood.

A standard battery of laboratory tests should suffice for the evaluation of most patients (Fukuda et al., 1994). Additional laboratory tests may be required based on unusual symptoms, physical findings, geographic residence, or travel history.

When the diagnosis of CFS is under consideration, even before the six-month target of unexplained debilitating fatigue is reached, several important approaches should be undertaken while the exclusion of alternative diagnoses is in progress.

First, the patient should be told that attention to the basics of management is important and the patient has a major role in determining the outcome of the illness. Symptomatic treatment is essential, and attention to the sleep disorder, if present (see details in next section), is critical because prolonged sleep disturbance has been documented as one etiology for fibromyalgia syndrome (Goldenberg, 1999). A careful regulation of the activity pattern is also critical, particularly in adolescents, because the new patient is unfamiliar with the illness and may actually use "good days" to "catch up" and thereby overexert beyond capacity, causing a significant "crash" or relapse, which delays recovery. Therefore, budgeting energy expenditure may minimize this effect and help the patient to maintain a more consistent and reliable level of activity, a practice that is useful in a variety of fatiguing illnesses.

CLINICAL MANAGEMENT OF CHRONIC
FATIGUE SYNDROME

The management of CFS can be divided into two broad categories: (a) general techniques that are applicable to most CFS patients and (b) specific forms of treatment that are applicable to patients with particular manifestations.

Clinicians often recognize that patients with CFS demonstrate an increased sensitivity to medication side effects. People who feel poorly in general may be less tolerant of minimal adverse reactions and, consequently, may abandon medication trials prematurely. Applying treatment principles from geriatric medicine, such as initially using only fractions of customary doses and giving medications less frequently in the beginning, may allow patients with CFS to use medications that might otherwise not be tolerated.

GENERAL APPROACHES

Management of Sleep Disorders   Treatment of disordered sleep is a cornerstone in the overall management of CFS. Sleep is fundamental to energy, cognitive function, and management of pain. Indeed, it may be difficult to distinguish some of the symptomatology of CFS from that of sleep deprivation in patients who sleep very poorly.

As recently reviewed (Levine et al., 2001), a careful sleep history is essential. Simply noting that the patient sleeps poorly is an inadequate substitute for the sleep history. The clinician should inquire as to whether the patient has difficulty initiating sleep (sleep onset insomnia), difficulty maintaining sleep due to multiple awakenings (sleep fragmentation), and/or is experiencing early morning awakening. The characteristic disturbance of sleep in patients with CFS, especially those with fibromyalgia-like somatic pain, is fragmentation of sleep with frequent awakenings. Such patients may not achieve satisfactory periods of deep sleep and may have sleep patterns characterized by alpha intrusion or alpha delta sleep when studied by polysomnography (Moldofsky, 1993).

A drug history is also critically important in evaluating and treating sleep. Patients with CFS may have sleep problems exacerbated by medications given to correct other symptoms. For example, serotonin reuptake inhibitor antidepressants may cause or worsen sleep onset insomnia even when they help mood symptoms. Opioid analgesics, especially those used near bedtime, may result in sleep fragmentation. Certain benzodiazepines such as clonazepam may eventually lead to sleep fragmentation and early morning awakening. An awareness that medications may cause deterioration in sleep patterns will help the clinician avoid polypharmacy and the usual futility of treating the side effects of one medication with another medication.

Improvement of sleep hygiene may assist patients in obtaining better sleep without the use of pharmaceuticals. Sleep phase shift problems may be more common in patients with CFS (Hickie & Davenport, 1999). Clockwise shift of sleep phase (the tendency for natural sleepiness to occur later in the evening with a corresponding tendency to sleep later into the morning) may lead to difficulties with early morning awakening, poor physical and cognitive performance in the morning, and difficulty maintaining attendance and punctuality on the job.

Sleep onset insomnia may be temporarily benefited by the use of very short-acting hypnotics such as zolpidem. The benefit of long-term use of this or other hypnotic medication is unclear and may lead to dependence.

The presence of a primary comorbid sleep disorder such as periodic leg movement syndrome may exacerbate symptoms of CFS. Obtaining historical observations from a sleep partner may be valuable. Patients who have persistent sleep disturbances despite adequate management efforts should be considered for referral to a sleep specialist.

Tricyclic antidepressants or tricyclic analogs such as cyclobenzaprine, when used in very low doses, may reduce sleep fragmentation and improve sleep quality without causing undue sedation during waking hours. Such medications should be introduced very slowly with gradual upward adjustments in doses. Intolerance to one tricyclic agent should not preclude trials of other agents selected based on their side effect profiles.

Management of Cognitive Difficulties Cognitive impairment, one of the most consistent findings in CFS, is also one of the most difficult to manage. Several manifestations of cognitive disturbance may be found, including depression, forgetfulness, word-finding difficulties, and so on. Specific techniques have been found to be helpful for each of these symptoms.

Although the disturbances in cognitive function are well described in CFS, they may be more perceptual than real for some patients (Michiels & Cluydts, 2001; van der Werf, Prins, Jongen, Van der Meer, & Bleijenberg, 2000). Nonetheless, it is an extremely distressing symptom for patients, especially those whose livelihoods depend on the ability to remember, focus, and concentrate. Standard neuropsychological testing may help to distinguish the cognitive disturbance of CFS from that of other structural brain disorders and help to reassure patients. In addition, the neuropsychologist may be able to provide patients with guidance to help overcome some of the impairment. For example, patients with CFS have been shown to have more difficulty recalling information acquired verbally than acquired visually (Michiels, Cluydts, & Fischler, 1998; Michiels, de Gucht, Cluydts, & Fischler, 1999). The use of memo pads or electronic digital assistants can help patients cope with this impairment.

Central nervous system stimulants such as methylphenidate, amphetamines, and the new novel antinarcolepsy drug modafinil have been used to treat cognitive impairment although good placebo-controlled studies are not available to validate their effectiveness. One small unpublished study showed no statistical benefit from methylphenidate when compared to placebo (S. N. Schwartz, personal communication, 1995). The use of central nervous system stimulants does carry the risk of dependence, exacerbation of sleep disturbance, and other drug-specific complications such as hepatic dysfunction from pemoline or hypertension from methylphenidate.

Other treatments that have been studied include intravenous gammaglobulin (Lloyd, Hickie, Wakefield, Boughton, & Dwyer, 1990; Peterson et al., 1990; Rowe, 1997), selegiline (Natelson et al., 1998), growth hormone (Moorkens, Wynants, & Abs, 1998), galantamine (Snorrason, Geirsson, & Stefansson, 1996), hydrocortisone (Cleare et al., 1999; McKenzie et al., 1998), acyclovir (Straus et al., 1988), and moclobemide (Hickie et al., 2000). At present, none of these treatments has shown a clear benefit in clinical use, and none is widely used for treatment.

Other Important General Management Problems   A variety of common symptoms, including depression, are often also seen in CFS, and some medications, including antidepressants, are often effective at much lower doses than those used in clinical depression. Some of these medications may also be effective in improving sleep for patients who do not suffer from depression. Existing studies have compared the benefit of antidepressants to placebo in the overall management of CFS (Goodnick & Jorge, 1999; Hickie, 1999; Natelson et al., 1996, 1998; Shatzberg, 2000; Vercoulen et al., 1996). Whether antidepressants help a more selective subgroup of patients with depressed mood has not been as well studied. Chronic pain, poor sleep, severe contraction of social activities, and loss of job—problems experienced by many patients with CFS—may produce situational depressive reactions. The use of standard depression-measuring instruments, discussed elsewhere in this book, may guide the clinician in determining whether antidepressant therapy may be helpful. Unreasonable expectations from the use of antidepressant therapy may create disappointment. Antidepressants may help mood and outlook, although not globally improve energy levels.

One important tool that has proven useful in controlled studies is cognitive behavioral therapy (Bagnall, Whiting, Wright, & Sowden, 2001; Deale, Chalder, Marks, & Wessely, 1997; Sharpe et al., 1996), but the successful application of this technique depends on having skilled therapists available.

Regardless of the etiology and manifestations of CFS, there are general rehabilitation techniques that any patient with CFS or fatiguing illness can use. A detailed description will soon be available, but some general guidelines follow.

Rehabilitation Management   Referral to rehabilitation services should occur as soon as symptoms begin to affect the daily functioning of the patient even if this precedes the diagnosis. Early intervention may help reduce the effects of deconditioning and provide the patient with tools to manage symptoms initially and during fluctuations over time. It is important to give patients a sense that they have some control when they receive a diagnosis of a long-term, debilitating, uncertain, and little-understood disease. Although pharmaceutical management is still inconsistent, rehabilitation evaluation and treatment are independent of diagnosis and are directed at improving and/or maintaining participation in life activities. It is important to consider timing before initiating rehabilitation services. In the early stages of the diagnostic process, the patient may not be prepared to accept long-term lifestyle changes. It is best to introduce only essential management strategies such as self-care, immediate cognitive issues, and activities to prevent major physical deconditioning.

Initially, as well as after CFS has entered a more chronic stage, persons with CFS are at risk for overdoing activities, which often results in exacerbation of fatigue and other symptoms, possibly for a prolonged period of time. It is difficult for individuals to recognize that they have done too much because the response to the overactivity is often delayed for from a day or two up to a week afterwards (Sisto, 1992). In the early stages, patients often try to maintain premorbid activity levels, which are inconsistent with their current abilities. In the more chronic phase, when patients experience "good" days, they are likely to inappropriately increase their activity level (Cox, 1999; Swan & Furst, 1996).

The ideal rehabilitation team should include the referring physician and/or on-site physiatrist, occupational and physical therapists, speech therapist/pathologist, social worker, psychologist, and vocational and/or rehabilitation counselor. Each member of the team has both unique and complementary evaluations and treatment services to provide; this varies according to the patient's level of acceptance and length of time living with CFS. Following is a general description of rehabilitation services that may be provided. In each case, initial evaluations consider the patient's goals and provide information about previous and current levels of psychosocial and physical function.

The occupational therapist (OT) works with patients to set priorities consistent with their current level of function (Furst, 1987, 1995). Treatment includes techniques for fatigue management including evaluation of work heights, sitting instead of standing to do certain activities, body position, and use of adaptive equipment (Furst, 1987, 1999; Furst, Gerber, & Smith, 1987; Furst, Gerber, Smith, Fisher, & Shulman, 1987; Gerber et al., 1987; Packer, Brink, & Sauriol, 1995). For example, using a shower chair rather than standing in the shower and showering at night instead of the morning can reduce the energy needed for morning self-care. As difficulties related to cognition, such as inability to focus and loss of short-term memory problems, cause significant inability to perform role activities, the OT helps the patient develop environmental cues and various techniques to reduce the effect of these cognitive problems. The long-term fatigue often results in considerable aerobic and musculoskeletal deconditioning. In conjunction with patient priorities, a program of graded daily activities can improve aerobic capacity and reduce deconditioning. This may include as little as sitting up 10 minutes twice a day for very disabled individuals, to walking one-half block twice daily for others. The activity should be continued for a week or more before increasing time and/or frequency of the activity.

The physical therapist (PT) may begin with proper breathing techniques aimed at lower rib expansion in lying, sitting, and then standing positions. Muscle stretching, massage, and myofacial release may all be part of early PT intervention. In addition, an exercise program may begin very gradually with exercises without gravity, progressing to working against gravity and eventually with resistance from weights and/or exercise equipment such as treadmills or a stationary bike. All of these programs are done very gradually, changing activities no more frequently than weekly and possibly even less frequently until the activity can be done with no delayed fatigue or exacerbation of symptoms. The patient is often given a home program (Bazelmans, Bleijenberg, Van der Meer, & Folgering, 2001; Sisto, 1992, 1995; Vercoulen et al., 1997). Psychologists are often called on to evaluate cognitive problems; however, many of these evaluations do not demonstrate the problems identified by the patient. Because cognitive complaints often include word finding and inability to attend to reading, the speech pathologist has evaluations that identify specific areas of language dysfunction, focus on difficulties, and reading problems and provide methods to compensate (Moss, 1995).

Family, coworkers, and friends of the patient are all affected by CFS and need to be considered in treatment recommendations by all members of the rehabilitation team. Although social workers, psychologists, and vocational counselors can provide emotional support for the patient and family, they each have additional unique services. The social worker can often assist in securing needed home health services and provide a liaison to community services such as Meals on Wheels and financial assistance. In addition to testing and emotional support services, specially trained psychologists can provide cognitive behavioral therapy (CBT) designed to help the patient recognize and modify disease-related behaviors (Bienkiron, 1999; Friedberg & Jason, 1998).

The vocational and/or rehabilitation counselor can provide short-term vocational solution-based, as well as long-term, counseling and liaison with employers and/or schools. They often provide guidance concerning work-related community resources such as Social Security disability and the Americans with Disabilities Act (ADA). The vocational counselor provides evaluation and testing of job-related skills, which helps to determine ability to return to the current job or identify skills and recommendations if vocational change is indicated.

Whether before, at initial diagnosis, or after years of illness, CFS patients should be referred to rehabilitation services. Appropriate rehabilitation evaluation and treatment can provide the patient with both assistance and skills to reduce the effects of the symptoms of CFS and allow for maximal levels of productive, meaningful activity.

Management of Pain   Pain management in CFS presents challenges to the clinician. Pain may be minimal and confined to periodic headaches and sore throats in some patients. In other patients, moderate-to-severe musculoskeletal pain, similar to that seen in fibromyalgia, may be a dominant symptom and often the patient's primary source of distress (Bennett, 1995; Goldenberg, 1999; Turk & Okifuji, 2000; Winfield, 1999).

Treatment of sleep may improve or ameliorate pain in some patients. Other patients require the regular use of nonopioid analgesics such as acetaminophen. Treatment of depressed mood has been reported to benefit pain management in some studies (Goodnick & Sandoval, 1993) but not in others (Morriss et al., 1999).

The clinician must weigh the potential benefits of opioid use with several potential risks. The regular use of opioids may by itself produce increased fatigue, sleep disturbance, and cognitive impairment, symptoms that can be indistinguishable from the underlying CFS. No clinical studies are available that specifically address the use of opioids in the treatment of CFS. The use of opioid analgesics in the management of fibromyalgia remains controversial, and some authorities do not recommend their use (Barkhuizen, 2001; Leventhal, 1999; Sorenson et al., 1997).

SPECIFIC APPROACHES

CFS is clearly a heterogeneous disorder (Levine, 1998); among the subtypes suggested are acute versus gradual onset, infectious versus noninfectious, presence versus absence of psychiatric comorbidity, and symptom subtypes (Fukuda et al., 1994; Young et al., 2001). We have recently performed factor analysis studies on Gulf War veterans, a group well documented to have a large proportion of CFS and Gulf War Syndrome cases (Fukuda et al., 1998). We have shown very little overlap between deployed veterans with apparent CFS and symptoms that fit under categories such as *infectious* and those with *musculoskeletal* (Young et al., 2001).

The approach to management in patients who present with fibromyalgia-like symptoms appears to be no different from that recommended for fibromyalgia (see previous discussion). Particular scrutiny, however, is being given to the subgroup with manifestations suggestive of an infectious process. As in the management of infections in the non-CFS patient, treatment should specifically target clinically significant bacterial or fungal infections, and prophylactic treatment is likely to be both ineffective and dangerous. Viral infections often are associated with CFS, and, indeed, infectious mononucleosis or glandular fever caused most often by Epstein-Barr virus has been reported to progress to CFS in approximately 25% of mononucleosis cases (White et al., 1998). Other infectious agents including Cytomegalovirus (CMV) and human herpesvirus-6 (HHV-6) have been reported to precipitate CFS (Ablashi et al., 1996; Salit, 1997); HHV-6 has been of particular concern in some patients because activation can enhance symptoms (N. Klimas, personal communication, 2001).

Other studies have looked at an association between CFS and HHV-6 infection but have not found a relationship (Wallace, Natelson, Gause, & Hay, 1999) or have not been able to establish HHV-6 as the cause of CFS (Ablashi et al., 2000; Di Luca et al., 1995). One report showed successful treatment of HHV-6 infection in a CFS patient whose illness followed acute HHV-6 infection but showed no clinical improvement in the CFS, although the blood was cleared of large HHV-6-infected cells and plasma HHV-6 antigen while antibody levels fell from 1:640 to normal (levels 1:160; Ablashi et al., 1996). Treatment of viral infections in CFS patients in general has not been successful, including a trial of acyclovir (Straus et al., 1988).

Despite these many studies, an infectious etiology for the persistence of symptoms in people with CFS has never been proven. Clinicians treating patients with CFS should be very wary of basing antiviral treatment on the results of antibody tests, especially in the case of Epstein-Barr virus and HHV-6.

Along with the previously mentioned viruses, other microorganisms touted as causes of chronic fatigue include mycoplasmas and chlamydias. The evidence for these microorganisms causing CFS is largely anecdotal although a small number of studies have shown mycoplasma nucleic acids are found more commonly in the serum of patients with CFS than in normal controls (Nasralla, Haier, & Nicolson, 1999; Vojdani et al., 1998). The significance of this finding has not been adequately evaluated.

In a small study evaluating a synthetic double-stranded RNA drug with putative antiviral and immunomodulatory effects, poly(I).poly(C12U) (Ampligen®) showed possibly beneficial results (Strayer et al., 1994). A multicenter, randomized controlled trial of this agent is currently being conducted.

An interesting approach to the issue of infectious disease has been suggested by Suhadolnik and coworkers, who noted an increase in several components of the innate antiviral defense pathway, the interferon-inducible 2–5A synthetase/RNase L antiviral pathway, in blood from a heterogeneous population of CFS patients (Suhadolnik et al., 1994, 1997). Termed the *37-kDa RNase L*, this new form of RNase L is more active than the native enzyme (Shetzline & Suhadolnik, 2001). The level of expression of the 37-kDa RNase L correlates positively with the level of disability experienced by individuals with CFS (Suhadolnik et al., 1999). A small independent study by De Meirleir and coworkers confirmed the presence of the 37-kDa RNase L in CFS and demonstrated its absence in healthy controls and individuals diagnosed with depression or fibromyalgia (De Meirleir et al., 2000).

It is of interest that these workers found the abnormality in a much higher percentage of those patients meeting the 1988 case definition as compared to those meeting the 1994 case definition (K. De Meirleir, personal communication, 2000). The identification of a subset of patients with a specific laboratory marker has led some workers to attempt putative antiviral therapy monitoring changes in RNase L levels as demonstration of efficacy.

CONCLUSION

As noted previously, the armamentarium of the caregiver has many tools that can be applied to assist patients in dealing with CFS. Any clinician hoping to use evidence-based medicine as the foundation for treating CFS may be sorely disappointed. Important recent reviews of evidence-based medicine have, however, documented the importance of cognitive behavior therapy and graded exercise therapy as big elements of management if skilled therapists are available (Bagnall et al., 2001; Whiting et al., 2001). Although cognitive behavioral therapy and rehabilitation therapies have demonstrated some success in limited studies, these modalities may not be readily available in some communities. Because of the heterogeneity of CFS as currently defined and the likelihood that a number of different disorders are grouped under the same definition, it will take considerable time before we best understand what specific treatment would be most likely to benefit a given patient.

The lack of good studies should not impede the good practice of medicine, however. The relief of distress, even when a cure is unavailable, has long been the foundation of medical treatment. Treating sleep disturbance, pain, mood disorders, and cognitive disturbance, as well as helping the patient adjust to an illness that may be chronically disabling, socially impairing, and financially draining, are all within the scope of dedicated and caring physicians and caregivers.

REFERENCES

Ablashi, D. V., Eastman, H. B., Owen, C. B., Roman, M. M., Friedman, J., Zabriskie, J. B., et al. (2000). Frequent HHV-6 reactivation in multiple sclerosis (MS) and chronic fatigue syndrome (CFS) patients. *Journal of Clinical Virology, 16*(3), 179–191.

Ablashi, D. V., Levine, P. H., De Vinci, C., Whitman, J. E., Jr., Pizza, G., & Viza, D. (1996). Use of anti HHV-6 transfer factor for the treatment of two patients with chronic fatigue syndrome (CFS): Two case reports. *Biotherapy, 9,* 81–86.

Agency for Health Care Research and Quality. (2001). *Defining and managing chronic fatigue syndrome*. Retrieved October 30, 2001, from http://www.ahrq.gov/clinic /cfssum.htm.

Bagnall, A. P., Whiting, P., Wright, K., & Sowden, A. J. (2001). *The effectiveness of interventions used in the treatment/management of chronic fatigue syndrome and/or myalgic encephalomyelitis in adults and children*. Retrieved October 30, 2001, from http://www .york.ac.uk/inst/crd/cfsrep.pdf.

Barkhuizen, A. (2001). Pharmacologic treatment of fibromyalgia. *Current Pain and Headache Reports, 5*(4), 351–358.

Bazelmans, E., Bleijenberg, G., Van der Meer, J. W., & Folgering, H. (2001). Is physical deconditioning a perpetuating factor in chronic fatigue syndrome? A controlled study on maximal exercise performance and relations with fatigue, impairment and physical activity. *Psychological Medicine, 31*(1), 107–114.

Bennett, R. M. (1995). Fibromyalgia: The commonest cause of widespread pain. *Comprehensive Therapy, 21*(6), 269–275.

Bienkiron, P. (1999). Who is suitable for cognitive behavioral therapy? *Journal of the Royal Society of Medicine, 92*, 222–229.

Cleare, A. J., Heap, E., Malhi, G. S., Wessely, S., O'Keane, V., & Miell, J. (1999). Low-dose hydrocortisone in chronic fatigue syndrome: A randomized crossover trial. *Lancet, 353*, 455–458.

Cox, D. L. (1999). *Occupational therapy and chronic fatigue syndrome*. London: Whurr.

Deale, A., Chalder, T., Marks, I., & Wessely, S. (1997). Cognitive behavior therapy for chronic fatigue syndrome: A randomized controlled trial. *American Journal of Psychiatry, 154*, 408–414.

De Meirleir, K., Bisbal, C., Campine, I., De Becker, P., Salehzada, T., De Mettre, E., et al. (2000). A 37 kDa 2–5A binding protein as a potential biochemical marker for chronic fatigue syndrome. *American Journal of Medicine, 108*, 99–105.

Di Luca, D., Zorzenon, M., Mirandola, P., Colle, R., Botta, G. A., & Cassai, E. (1995). Human herpesvirus 6 and human herpesvirus 7 in chronic fatigue syndrome. *Journal of Clinical Microbiology, 33*(6), 1660–1661.

Fennell, P. A. (1995). The four progressive stages of the CFS experience: A coping tool for patients. *Journal of Chronic Fatigue Syndrome, 1*, 69–79.

Friedberg, F., & Jason, L. A. (1998). *Cognitive behavioral intervention in understanding chronic fatigue syndrome: An empirical guide to assessment and treatment*. Washington, DC: American Psychological Association.

Fukuda, K., Nisenbaum, R., Stewart, G., Thompson, W. W., Robin, L., Washko, R. M., et al. (1998). Chronic multisymptom illness affecting air force veterans of the gulf war. *Journal of the American Medical Association, 280*(11), 981–988.

Fukuda, K., Straus, S. E., Hickie, I., Sharpe, M. C., Dobbins, J. G., & Komaroff, A. (1994). The chronic fatigue syndrome, a comprehensive approach to its definition and study. *Annals of Internal Medicine, 121*, 953–959.

Furst, G. (1987). *Instructors guide for use with rehabilitation through learning: Energy conservation and joint protection: A workbook for persons with rheumatoid arthritis*. Bethesda, MD: National Institutes of Health, Department of Rehabilitation Medicine.

Furst, G. (1995). Occupational therapy in multidisciplinary innovations in research, theory and clinical practice. *Journal of Chronic Fatigue Syndrome, 1*(3/4), 91–93.

Furst, G. (1999). Measuring fatigue in chronic fatigue syndrome: Why and how. *Journal of Chronic Fatigue Syndrome, 5*, 55–59.

Furst, G. P., Gerber, L. H., & Smith, C. C. (1987). *Rehabilitation through learning: Energy conservation and joint protection: A workbook for persons with rheumatoid arthritis.* Bethesda, MD: National Institutes of Health, Department of Rehabilitation Medicine.

Furst, G. P., Gerber, L. H., Smith, C., Fisher, S., & Shulman, B. (1987). A program for improving energy conservation behaviors in adults with rheumatoid arthritis. *American Journal of Occupational Therapy, 41,* 102–111.

Gerber, L. H., Furst, G. P., Smith, C., Shulman, B., Smith, C., Thornton, B., et al. (1987). Patient education program to teach energy conservation behaviors to patients with rheumatoid arthritis: A pilot study. *Archives of Physical Medicine and Rehabilitation, 68,* 422–445.

Goldenberg, D. L. (1999). Fibromyalgia syndrome a decade later: What have we learned? *Archives of Internal Medicine, 159*(8), 777–785.

Goodnick, P. J., & Jorge, C. M. (1999). Treatment of chronic fatigue syndrome with nefazodone. *American Journal of Psychiatry, 156*(5), 797–798.

Goodnick, P. J., & Sandoval, R. (1993). Psychotropic treatment of chronic fatigue syndrome and related disorders. *Journal of Clinical Psychiatry, 54*(1), 13–20.

Hickie, I. (1999). Nefazodone for patients with chronic fatigue syndrome. *Australia and New Zealand Journal of Psychiatry, 33*(2), 278–280.

Hickie, I., & Davenport, T. (1999). A behavioral approach based on reconstructing the sleep-wake cycle. *Cognitive and Behavioral Practice, 6,* 442–450.

Hickie, I. B., Wilson, A. J., Wright, J. M., Bennett, B. K., Wakefield, D., & Lloyd, A. R. (2000). A randomized, double-blind placebo-controlled trial of moclobemide in patients with chronic fatigue syndrome. *Journal of Clinical Psychiatry, 61,* 643–648.

Holmes, G. P., Kaplan, J. E., Gantz, N. M., Komaroff, A. L., Schonberger, L. B., Straus, S. E., et al. (1988). Chronic fatigue syndrome: A working case definition. *Annals of Internal Medicine, 108,* 387–389.

Jason, L. A., King, C. P., Richman, J. A., Taylor, R. R., Torres, S. R., & Song, S. (1999). U.S. case definition of chronic fatigue syndrome: Diagnostic and theoretical issues. *Journal of Chronic Fatigue Syndrome, 5*(3/4), 3–33.

Komaroff, A. L. (1994). Clinical presentation and evaluation of fatigue and chronic fatigue syndrome. In S. E. Straus (Ed.), *Chronic fatigue syndrome* (pp. 61–84). New York: Marcel Dekker.

Leventhal, L. J. (1999). Management of fibromyalgia. *Annals of Internal Medicine, 131*(11), 850–858.

Levine, P. H. (1998). Chronic fatigue syndrome comes of age. *American Journal of Medicine, 105*(3A), 2S–6S.

Levine, P. H., Klimas, N., Armitage, R., Fredericks, R., Stewart, J., Torch, W., et al. (2001). Nevada chronic fatigue syndrome consensus conference. *Journal of Chronic Fatigue Syndrome, 9,* 53–62.

Lloyd, A., Hickie, I., Wakefield, D., Boughton, C., & Dwyer, J. (1990). A double-blind, placebo-controlled trial of intravenous immunoglobulin therapy in patients with chronic fatigue syndrome. *American Journal of Medicine, 89,* 561–568.

McKenzie, R., O'Fallon, A., Dale, J., Demitrack, M., Sharma, G., Deloria, M., et al. (1998). Low-dose hydrocortisone for treatment of chronic fatigue syndrome: A randomized controlled trial. *Journal of the American Medical Association, 280*(12), 1061–1066.

Michiels, V., & Cluydts, R. (2001). Neuropsychological functioning in chronic fatigue syndrome: A review. *Acta Psychiatrica Scandinavica, 103*(2), 84–93.

Michiels, V., Cluydts, R., & Fischler, B. (1998). Attention and verbal learning in patients with chronic fatigue syndrome. *Journal of the International Neuropsychology Society, 4*(5), 456–466.

Michiels, V., de Gucht, V., Cluydts, R., & Fischler, B. (1999). Attention and information processing efficiency in patients with chronic fatigue syndrome. *Journal of Clinical and Experimental Neuropsychology, 21*(5), 709–729.

Moldofsky, H. (1993). Fibromyalgia, sleep disorder and chronic fatigue syndrome. *Ciba Foundation Symposium, 173*, 262–271.

Moorkens, G., Wynants, H., & Abs, R. (1998). Effect of growth hormone treatment in patients with chronic fatigue syndrome: A preliminary study. *Growth Hormone and IGF Research, 8*, 131–133.

Morriss, R. K., Ahmed, M., Wearden, A. J., Mullis, R., Strickland, P., Appleby, L., et al. (1999). The role of depression in pain, psychophysiological syndromes and medically unexplained symptoms associated with chronic fatigue syndrome. *Journal of Affective Disorders, 55*(2/3), 143–148.

Moss, S. E. (1995). Cognitive/linguistic deficits associated with chronic fatigue syndrome in multidisciplinary innovations in research, theory and clinical practice. *Journal of Chronic Fatigue Syndrome, 1*(3/4), 95–100.

Nasralla, M., Haier, J., & Nicolson, G. L. (1999). Multiple mycoplasmal infections detected in blood of patients with chronic fatigue syndrome and/or fibromyalgia syndrome. *European Journal of Clinical Microbiology and Infectious Diseases, 18*(12), 859–865.

Natelson, B. H., Cheu, J., Hill, N., Bergen, M., Korn, L., Denny, T., et al. (1998). Single-blind, placebo phase-in trial of two escalating doses of selegiline in the chronic fatigue syndrome. *Neuropsychobiology, 37*(3), 150–154.

Natelson, B. H., Cheu, J., Pareja, J., Ellis, S. P., Policastro, T., & Findley, T. W. (1996). Randomized, double-blind, controlled placebo-phase in trial of low dose phenelzine in the chronic fatigue syndrome. *Psychopharmacology, 124*, 226–230.

Packer, T. L., Brink, N., & Sauriol, A. (1995). *Managing fatigue: A six week course for energy conservation.* San Antonio, TX: Therapy Skill Builders.

Papanicolou, D. (2001). Symposium addresses neuroendocrine aspects of CFS. *CFS Research Review, 2*, 9.

Patarca, R. (2001). Innovations in chronic fatigue syndrome research and clinical practice. *Journal of Chronic Fatigue Syndrome, 8*(3/4), 1–121.

Peterson, P. K., Shepard, J., Macres, M., Schenck, C., Crosson, J., Rechtman, D., et al. (1990). A controlled trial of intravenous immunoglobulin G in chronic fatigue syndrome. *American Journal of Medicine, 89*, 554–560.

Rowe, K. S. (1997). Double-blind randomized controlled trial to assess the efficacy of intravenous gammaglobulin for the management of chronic fatigue syndrome in adolescents. *Journal of Psychiatric Research, 31*(1), 133–147.

Salit, I. E. (1997). Precipitating factors for the chronic fatigue syndrome. *Journal of Psychiatric Research, 31*(1), 59–65.

Schatzberg, A. F. (2000). New indications for antidepressants. *Journal of Clinical Psychiatry, 61*(Suppl. 11), 9–17.

Sharpe, M., Hawton, K., Simkin, S., Suraway, C., Hackmann, A., Klimas, I., et al. (1996). Cognitive behavior therapy for the chronic fatigue syndrome: A randomized controlled trial. *British Medical Journal, 312*(7022), 22–26.

Shetzline, S. E., & Suhadolnik, R. J. (2001). Characterization of a 2', 5'-oligoadenylate (2–5A)-dependent 37-kDa RNase L. Azido photoaffinity labeling and 2–5A-dependent activation. *Journal of Biological Chemistry, 276*, 23707–23711.

Sisto, S. A. (1992). Rehabilitation of the patient with chronic fatigue syndrome. *New Jersey Rehabilitation,* pp. 4–6.

Sisto, S. A. (1995). Rehabilitation of the patient with chronic fatigue syndrome in multidisciplinary innovations in research, theory and clinical practice. *Journal of Chronic Fatigue Syndrome, 1*(3/4), 101–103.

Snorrason, E., Geirsson, A., & Stefansson, K. (1996). Trial of a selective acetylcholinesterase inhibitor, galanthamine hydrobromide, in the treatment of chronic fatigue syndrome. *Journal of Chronic Fatigue Syndrome, 2,* 35–54.

Sorenson, J., Bengtsson, A., Ahlner, J., Henriksson, K. G., Ekselius, L., & Bengtsson, M. (1997). Fibromyalgia—are there different mechanisms in the processing of pain? A double blind crossover comparison of analgesic drugs. *Journal of Rheumatology, 24*(8), 1615–1621.

Straus, S. E., Dale, J. K., Tobi, M., Lawley, T., Preble, O., Blaese, R. M., et al. (1988). Acyclovir treatment of the chronic fatigue syndrome. Lack of efficacy in a placebo-controlled trial. *New England Journal of Medicine, 319*(26), 1692–1698.

Strayer, D. R., Carter, W. A., Brodsky, I., Cheney, P. R., Peterson, D. L., Salvato, P., et al. (1994). A controlled clinical trial with a specifically configured RNA drug, poly(I).poly(C12U), in chronic fatigue syndrome. *Clinical Infectious Diseases, 18*(Suppl. 1), 88–95.

Suhadolnik, R. J., Peterson, D. L., Cheney, P. R., Horvath, S. E., Reichenbach, N. L., O'Brien, K., et al. (1999). Biochemical dysregulation of the 2–5A synthetase/RNase L antiviral defense pathway in chronic fatigue syndrome. *Journal of Chronic Fatigue Syndrome, 5,* 223–242.

Suhadolnik, R. J., Peterson, D. L., O'Brien, K., Cheney, P. R., Herst, C. V., Reichenbach, N. L., et al. (1997). Biochemical evidence for a novel low molecular weight 2–5A-dependent RNase L in chronic fatigue syndrome. *Journal of Interferon and Cytokine Research, 17,* 377–385.

Suhadolnik, R. J., Reichenbach, N. L., Hitzges, P., Sobol, R. W., Peterson, D. L., Henry, B., et al. (1994). Upregulation of the 2–5A synthetase/RNase L antiviral pathway associated with chronic fatigue syndrome. *Clinical Infectious Diseases, 18,* S96–S104.

Swan, L., & Furst, G. (1996, Spring). Occupational therapy: A new approach for persons with CFS. *CFIDS Chronicle 9,* 48–49.

Turk, D. C., & Okifuji, A. (2000). Pain in patients with fibromyalgia syndrome. *Current Rheumatology Reports, 2*(2), 109–115.

U.S. Department of Health and Human Services Chronic Fatigue Syndrome Coordinating Committee. (2000). *Chronic fatigue syndrome: State of the science conference.* Arlington, VA, October 23–24, 2000. Retrieved October 30, 2001, from http://www4.od.nih.gov/cfs/reports.html.

van der Werf, S. P., Prins, J. B., Jongen, P. J., Van der Meer, J. W., & Bleijenberg, G. (2000). Abnormal neuropsychological findings are not necessarily a sign of cerebral impairment: A matched comparison between chronic fatigue syndrome and multiple sclerosis. *Neuropsychiatry, Neuropsychology, and Behavioral Neurology, 13*(3), 199–203.

Vercoulen, J. H., Bazelmans, E., Swanink, C. M., Fennis, J. F., Galama, J. M., Jongen, P. J., et al. (1997). Physical activity in chronic fatigue syndrome: Assessment and its role in fatigue. *Journal of Psychiatric Research, 31*(6), 661–673.

Vercoulen, J. H., Swanink, C. M., Zitman, F. G., Vreden, S. G., Hoofs, M. P., Fennis, J. F., et al. (1996). Randomized, double-blind-placebo controlled study of fluoxetine in chronic fatigue syndrome. *Lancet, 347,* 858–861.

Vojdani, A., Choppa, P. C., Tagle, C., Andrin, R., Samimi, B., & Lapp, C. W. (1998). Detection of mycoplasma genus and mycoplasma fermentans by PCR in patients with chronic fatigue syndrome. *FEMS Immunology and Medical Microbiology, 22*(4), 355–365.

Wallace, H. L., II, Natelson, B., Gause, W., & Hay, J. (1999). Human herpesviruses in chronic fatigue syndrome. *Clinical and Diagnostic Laboratory Immunology, 6*(2), 216–223.

White, P. D., Thomas, J. M., Amess, J., Crawford, D. H., Grover, S. A., Kangro, H. O., et al. (1998). Incidence, risk and prognosis of acute and chronic fatigue syndromes and psychiatric disorders after glandular fever. *British Journal of Psychiatry, 173,* 475–481.

Whiting, P., Bangall, A., Sowden, A. J., Cornell, J. E., Mulrow, C. D., & Ramirez, G. (2001). Interventions for the treatment and management of chronic fatigue syndrome. *Journal of the American Medical Association, 286*(12), 1360–1368.

Winfield, J. B. (1999). Pain in fibromyalgia. *Rheumatic Diseases Clinics of North America, 25*(1), 55–79.

Young, H., Simmens, S. J., Kang, H. K., Mahan, C. M., & Levine, P. H. (2001, January). *Factor analysis of fatiguing syndrome in Gulf War era veterans: Implications for etiology and pathogenesis.* Paper presented at the meeting of the American Association of Chronic Fatigue Syndrome, Seattle, WA.

CHAPTER 22

Phase-Based Interventions

PATRICIA A. FENNELL

T HE FOUR-PHASE Model (Fennell, 1993, 1995, 1998, 2001, 2004) is a method for assessing and treating chronic fatigue syndrome (CFS) that addresses the characteristic heterogeneity of the illness. The model asks clinicians to assess and treat patients in three domains—the physical-behavioral, the psychological, and the social-interactive—in each of the four phases. The phases help to capture the changing experience of CFS patients over time. The model is both a holistic approach that deals with the complex interactions of body-mind and a systems approach that addresses the social and work worlds of CFS patients. It borrows from the biopsychosocial paradigm for managing chronic illness (Engel, 1997) and stresses the importance of the interactions among the biological, psychological, and social domains of patients' lives (Nicassio & Smith, 1995). This chapter provides an overview of the assessments and treatments recommended for CFS patients as they progress through the phases.

Readers may find it helpful to refer periodically to Chapter 8 in this volume (Jason, Fennell, Taylor, 2003) as they read the following discussion of assessment and treatment in the Four-Phase Model. That chapter delineates the typical experience of individuals with CFS in three domains—the physical-behavioral, the psychological, and the social-interactive—in each of the four phases. It also discusses how the Four-Phase Model relates to stage or phase theory in general and why it seems a particularly useful way to look at chronic illnesses such as CFS.

PHASE PLACEMENT

Phase placement is key to using the Four-Phase Model. While clinicians are taking histories and carrying out their other examinations, they should remain alert to the characteristic presentations of each phase. In addition to their own assessment methods, clinicians may find it helpful to use the 20-item Fennell Phase Inventory, an empirically tested phase placement instrument developed for CFS patients (Fennell, 1998). This model has been applied to a CFS population for empirical validation (Jason et al., 1999, 2000a, 2000b; Van Hoof, Coomins, Cluydts, de Meirleir,

2003a, 2003b). Once clinicians have established the phase patients are in, further assessments and subsequent treatments are selected to fit the patients' current status. Phase placement is evaluated at the initial visit, but it is regularly revisited as time passes to see how patients are progressing.

PLACEMENT IN PHASE 1 (CRISIS)

Patients in Phase 1 can exhibit significant diagnostic and treatment urgency. The locus of treatment and cure lies totally outside themselves. The locus of the disease also seems totally external, yet at the same time these individuals may engage in self-pathologizing and hold themselves responsible for their illness experience. Many have intrusive negative ideations that can alternate with denial that anything is seriously wrong. They have little tolerance for the ambiguity of their symptoms. They want a clear diagnosis, they want treatment, they want a cure, and they want it immediately.

PLACEMENT IN PHASE 2 (STABILIZATION)

Patients in Phase 2 feel the locus of control beginning to return to themselves. They enter into a seeking mode where they search for alternative sources of treatment, social support, and social identification. They are less likely to hold themselves responsible for their illness, or do so less often. They suffer fewer ideations and engage less in denial. These individuals still have little tolerance for chronicity. Instead, as they anxiously await a definitive cure, they frequently try to pass for normal, sometimes to their own detriment because such activity can exacerbate symptoms.

PLACEMENT IN PHASE 3 (RESOLUTION)

Patients in Phase 3 have come to a true awareness that their illness is chronic, and their former life has changed forever. This recognition often produces existential questioning or despair. Patients in Phase 3 show much greater self-compassion for their suffering and grief for their losses. They have greater tolerance for the ambiguity of their illness and have developed many practical coping skills. They have increasingly internalized the locus of control in their lives and are more aware of societal effects. These individuals begin constructing their own illness experience and start establishing a new self to live their altered lives. This takes place within a context of searching for philosophical or spiritual meaning.

PLACEMENT IN PHASE 4 (INTEGRATION)

Patients in Phase 4 deeply understand their illness to the point of regarding serious relapse simply as another manifestation of its cyclic character. They have integrated their pre and post illness selves into a new self that is completely congruent with what they authentically think and feel they are. They have little tolerance for negative attitudes in others or in society, and they try to internalize only what they believe to be true. These individuals have reconstructed their societal roles and relationships and have forged a new life in which illness, while an aspect of their existence, is not the whole of it. They continue to engage in meaningful development as their lives and experiences evolve.

RECYCLING

Patients ordinarily proceed through the phases in sequence, but as in other stage models, they can slip back into a prior phase, or recycle, sometimes several times (Prochaska, Norcross, & DiClemente, 1994; Sutton, 1997). At times, they may exhibit some symptoms characteristic of two different phases. Attainment of Phase 4 (Integration) is not a permanent condition; other illnesses, accidents, or personal tragedies can produce crises that return patients to the chaos of Phase 1. When patients have progressed through the phase process once, however, they have gained knowledge that makes it possible for them to move forward more swiftly and efficiently (DiClemente, 1991). They understand what is happening to them more quickly, and they know the techniques to improve their situation. They also have the skills to seek and use necessary clinical help.

TYPICAL PHASES WHEN PATIENTS PRESENT

Clinicians typically first see CFS patients while they are in Phase 1 or Phase 2. Although it is necessary to establish which phase the patient is in, clinicians should carry out most of the recommended assessments and treatments for Phase 1 patients, even if they first appear in Phase 2. It is particularly important to take a complete medical history and conduct a psychosocial evaluation to assess trauma, all in the context of establishing a warm, egalitarian relationship. Clinicians also should ask patients to start writing a personal narrative and educate them in the phase sequence (see later).

IMPORTANCE OF TRAUMA

It is hard to overestimate the importance of assessing for trauma, whether it arises from the illness itself, from pre- or comorbid conditions, from reactions of the patient's social or work contacts, or from the health care experience. This is especially pertinent in light of research that has drawn attention to the effects of cumulative trauma or adversity. Cumulative trauma or adversity can result in a spectrum of trauma-related disorders ranging from the more benign, such as anxiety, to the severe, such as posttraumatic stress disorder (PTSD; Alonzo, 2000; Fullilove, Lown, & Fullilove, 1992; Turner & Lloyd, 1995). Individuals who repeatedly suffer traumas that may not meet the diagnostic criteria of PTSD in the strict clinical sense (Scott & Stradling, 1994) may nonetheless experience symptoms that manifest at any point on a continuum of symptomology from severe PTSD to what has been called subclinical PTSD (Blank, 1993; Vrana & Lauterbach, 1994). Cumulative adversity and the possible resulting continuum of trauma disorders can affect the patient's ability to cope with the illness experience, the health care system, and other life domains (Alonzo, 2000). Patients may develop impeded responses to their own symptoms and the use of health care as a result of an accumulated burden of adversity. This has been investigated in trauma induced by treatment for certain specific medical conditions such as heart disease and cancer (Alonzo, 2000; Alonzo &

Reynolds, 1996). Clinically, however, it can also be a response to many chronic conditions that expose patients to various and repeated traumas.

GOALS OF ASSESSMENT AND TREATMENT

All the following goals and activities of assessment and treatment are not expected to occur with every CFS patient, nor are the goals or activities pursued all at one time. The process takes place throughout the phase sequence. The goals and activities are recommendations from which clinicians choose those that fit into the clinical situation and within practical limitations. Some of these recommendations are familiar practices for experienced clinicians, but they may prove helpful to clinicians who are newly engaged with CFS patients.

ASSESSMENT

Throughout the course of the phases, during assessment, the clinicians' goals are to establish the patient's phase placement, review the medical record, conduct psychological or psychiatric interviews, evaluate for trauma, including cultural and iatrogenic traumatization, conduct ancillary assessments as needed, and ask the patient to write or revise a personal narrative. Clinicians attempt to work with patients as traditional patients, but also as partners and as consumers. Assessment should consider pre- and coexisting conditions and take into account disruption of normal developmental stages. If possible, assessment should include the patient's significant others.

TREATMENT

During treatment, the clinician should remain informed of test results and interviews conducted by other members of the patient's health care team. Clinicians should be aware of all treatment protocols and medications, especially any potentially harmful interactions among medications.

MATCHING INTERVENTIONS TO PHASE

Like other stage theories that have argued matching intervention to stage provides the best outcomes (DiClemente, 1991; Prochaska, DiClemente, & Norcross, 1992; Prochaska, Norcross, & DiClemente, 1994; Prochaska & Velicer, 1997), the Four-Phase Model can inform clinicians about what they may expect over time and can help identify the best times and ways to intervene to improve the patient's quality of life. Conversely, attempting interventions at the wrong time may prove less effective and may undermine the possibility of the same interventions being effective at a later phase when the patient would ordinarily be responsive to them. The Four-Phase Model may also suggest more comprehensive interventions that take into account interaction among the multiple domains in which patients experience CFS.

GOALS OF TREATMENT BY PHASE

The goal of treatment in the first or crisis phase is to contain the crisis and reduce trauma. In practice, this means that clinicians should establish a bond with patients, affirm the patients' illness and suffering experience, begin to teach them to take note of their immediate situation, and create physical and/or psychological safety plans, if necessary. The goal in Phase 2 is stabilization and restructuring of the patients' daily life. To achieve this, clinicians teach patients to collect data, differentiate among their experiences, develop insight, and to set new norms and goals in their lives. The goal in Phase 3—resolution—is the development of meaning. Patients decide on their own what is meaningful to them, but clinicians facilitate the process by helping them to grieve their losses, maintain insight, and reframe their experiences. The goal in Phase 4 is to help patients achieve integration.

The Chronic Illness Workbook (Fennell, 2001), a practical manual for patients with chronic illness and for their families, contains many specific exercises that clinicians may find useful when treating their CFS patients, especially those in Phases 1 and 2.

PHASE 1: CRISIS

ASSESSMENT

Physical-Behavioral Domain

MEDICAL HISTORY AND PHYSICAL ASSESSMENT   It is necessary to review the patient's medical history and perform a complete examination. Clinicians may wish to order a neuro/psych review, and it is almost always advisable to conduct a sleep evaluation, although it may not be necessary to see a sleep specialist. Although many chronic illness patients are in a deconditioned state and suffer from other disorders that affect them physically, Phase 1 focuses on containment—that is, helping patients reduce their fears, their anxieties, and their overwhelming urgency. Once they have achieved sustainable and operational activities of daily living and have thereby regained a small sense of control over their lives, it is then usually a better time to investigate the efficacy of physical or occupational therapy.

ACTIVITY LEVEL ASSESSMENT   Clinicians need to thoroughly assess the patient's activity levels and activity threshold. During the crisis, and usually the chaos, of Phase 1, it is frequently desirable for clinicians to try to simplify patient activities as much as possible in order to make the patient's life functional. In Phase 2, many patients will be physically and psychologically capable of expanding this activity level significantly, but in the containment effort of Phase 1, it is best to simplify the patient's life as much as possible (Fennell, 2001, 2004).

Clinicians can employ scaled activity measurements such as the Medical Outcome Survey (MOS-SF-36; Friedberg & Jason, 1998; McHorney, Ware, Lu, & Sherbourne, 1994; McHorney, Ware, & Raczek, 1993); and fatigue scales such as the Fatigue Severity Scale (Krupp, 1989) and the Multidimensional Assessment of Fatigue (Belza, Henke, Yelin, Epstein, & Gilliss, 1993). If using measurements of this sort, it is best to employ at least two with each patient to overcome deficiencies in any individual measurement. Other clinicians may prefer to rely on their own extensive individualized questioning (Fennell, 2001, 2004). This kind of questioning first tries to establish what the patient's physical constitution was before and has now become, since CFS onset. It then seeks information on the amount and nature of the patient's activities, hour by hour, during the day.

Psychological Domain

GENERAL PSYCHOLOGICAL INTERVIEW   After obtaining a phase placement of the patient, clinicians should conduct a general psychosocial interview to obtain an up-to-date profile of the patient's cognitive, emotional, and social symptoms. Elements found in Phase 1 patients may include a loss of psychological control, ego loss, intrusive shame, self-hatred, and despair, shock, and disorientation; disassociation; fear of others; isolation; and mood swings. It is important to assemble as much personal and health information as is reasonable from patients, families, and social networks, including information relating to preexisting psychological conditions such as substance abuse, depression, trauma, and so on.

TRAUMA ASSESSMENT   It is important for clinicians to carry out a trauma assessment. By the time CFS patients reach a clinician, they may have been suffering both the trauma of their illness and the trauma caused by its onset for some time. Clinicians also need to investigate for pre- and coexisting traumas and for traumas caused by social stigmatization and disbelief from the patient's social and work network. It is equally important to probe for possible iatrogenic trauma. It is not uncommon for CFS patients to have experienced disbelief from medical personnel. Besides being hurtful to the patient, it usually discourages candid and accurate reporting by the patient. As mentioned, cumulative trauma or adversity appears to have additional negative effects of which clinicians should be aware.

DEVELOPMENTAL ISSUES   Clinicians need to assess for developmental issues and also concurrent life crises, such as a teenage daughter's pregnancy, marital difficulty, and so forth. Patients with chronic illnesses or disabilities continue to experience ordinary developmental and life processes simultaneously with the phases of their illness. In addition, patients' changing patterns of activity at home or at work affect their experience of CFS, as does their changing level of personal energy. All these non-illness processes, cycles, or arcs are affected by matters other than health, and at the same time have a profound effect on health (Carter & McGoldrick, 1988; Henderson, 1997; Mercer, 1989; Newby, 1996; Rankin & Weekes, 1989; Register, 1987; Rolland, 1987; Rosman, 1988; Woodgate, 1998). The dips and surges of adolescent adjustment, for example, may synchronize with phases of CFS in a way that exaggerate both the developmental and the illness effects. The sequence of physical and psychological reactions attendant on the death of a loved one or a decision to return to work can have profound interactions with the experience of CFS. The issues related to the event and to CFS have to be teased apart from each other for patients to develop and refine successful illness-coping skills.

PSYCHIATRIC EVALUATION   Depending on the information gathered during the psychosocial interview, clinicians may want to order full psychiatric evaluations of their patients.

PATIENT PERSONAL NARRATIVE   Clinicians should ask their CFS patients to create a personal narrative of their lives. This "document" can take many forms, since writing discourages or presents difficulties for some patients. They may make audiotapes, they may bring in photos and tell the clinician about the people and events portrayed, or the clinician may simply need to elicit the information in conversation. Patients should be encouraged to break their lives into 7-year segments. Each segment should include all the physical, emotional, social, and environmental issues, that is, information from the physical-behavioral, psychological, and social-interactive domains as described in Chapter 8 of this volume, that were important to them at that time. Clinicians can indicate areas for patients to consider, such as family, friends, school or work, sex and partners, health, hopes and plans, troubles and fears. Clinicians need to take a respectful and egalitarian stance toward the personal narrative. It will reflect the patient's own hierarchies, evaluations, and understandings, not those of a standard medical history or the typical psychological and social categories. The personal narrative is an enormously rich source of information about the patient. In later phases, it can become part of the treatment when the patient revises and reframes past experience.

Social-Interactive Domain

FAMILY, COUPLES, AND WORK EVALUATIONS   In Phase 1, the participants in the patients' social systems have some of the same reactions that the patients have. They can experience shock, disbelief, and even aversion to the illness. They can suffer vicarious traumatization. What happens to patients imposes an unwanted change on the people in the patients' social worlds as well. The physiological and psychological symptoms that patients experience have a direct impact on their families, and the family response has a direct impact on patients (Beardslee, Versage, & Gladstone, 1998; Bull & Jervis, 1997; Doherty, McDaniel, & Hepworth, 1994; Henderson, 1997; Nicassio & Smith, 1995; Yeheskel, Biderman, Borkan, & Herman, 2000). Coworkers, employers, and others in the community may respond in ways that increase negative social, psychological, and physiological symptoms (Roessler & Sumner, 1997; Satcher, 1992; Satcher & Hendren, 1991; Scambler & Hopkins, 1990; Ware, 1998). And how the health care system defines the patient's condition, both for the patient and for the community at large, will affect the patient's self-image and the world's response to the patient (Anderton, Elfert, & Lai, 1989; Doherty, McDaniel, & Hepworth, 1994; Scambler & Hopkins, 1990; Tait, Chibnall, & Richardson, 1990).

Unlike the patient, however, the social system does not suffer directly the symptoms that constantly force the patient to recognize that something is wrong. As a consequence, social system actors can more easily deny that there is a problem. On the other hand, some families attempt to shield patients from anything that might remind them of their condition, creating what one researcher refers to as the "trauma membrane" (Lindy, Grace, & Greene, 1981). Families may discourage patients from seeking treatment or from carrying out treatment protocols because these would remind the patient of the condition.

When a patient's friends and family are forced to acknowledge the patient's illness, they usually respond as if the patient were suffering an acute illness. How they behave usually depends on their response to illness in general. Their attitudes will strongly affect patient responses, coping, and compliance. Attitudes in the workplace not only will affect how well a patient progresses and copes, but may have powerful financial implications for the patient.

Depending on how mature a family, social, or work network patients have, the others in their lives begin to line up on a continuum that ranges from support through suspicion to outright condemnation. Clinicians need to carry out, if possible, a couples evaluation and a family evaluation. If the patient is still working, it may also be desirable to carry out a work evaluation.

TREATMENT

Physical-Behavioral Domain

OVERARCHING STRATEGY   It is important for clinicians to understand that the following treatment interventions and those for the subsequent phases are suggestive rather than exclusive. Many activities are ones that clinicians are already carrying out. While providing some new treatment approaches, the Four-Phase Model functions largely as a new organizing and strategizing paradigm. Under its umbrella, clinicians employ the interventions that they feel work most effectively in their practice. It is a question of strategy and tactics. The strategy involves comprehending CFS in a new way that includes all the systems in the patients' lives. It allows clinicians to understand what general kinds of interventions are necessary and effective at each phase and what kinds will be ineffective until later. Some readers may find the author's particular assessments and interventions (the tactics) helpful, but the essential objective is for clinicians to embrace the new clinical and empirical strategy that this paradigm presents.

BUILDING A TEAM   It is very rare for only one clinician to be involved in the assessment and treatment of CFS patients. By the time a clinician sees CFS patients, they have usually seen several other health care professionals. The clinician needs to include those clinicians who fit the particular ongoing needs of each patient into a multidisciplinary team. If a potential team does not yet exist, then the clinician should develop one. Members of the team will probably change over time, but it is essential that they all work together and keep one another informed of findings and treatment protocols. It is highly desirable for one clinician to act as team leader. This person's job is to make sure that all information flows among the parties, to call attention when medications and protocols appear to conflict, and to spend the necessary time with the patient to establish a warm and supportive relationship. Because of the constraints on the time of primary physicians, the team leader may well be a psychologist, clinical social worker, or nurse practitioner (Carbone, 1999; van Eijk & de Haan, 1998; Wagner et al., 2001). In fact, the clinician functioning as the psychotherapist may well be the team member most suited to address the individual and interactive aspects of the patient's culture, personal history, personality, and relationships. They are most likely to recognize the individual differences of patients rather than the communality within the disease (Nicassio & Smith, 1995).

MEDICAL PROTOCOLS   The goal of treatment in Phase 1 is trauma and crisis management. To this end, clinicians may recommend pain or sleep management protocols to address a particularly acute presenting problem, but by and large physical treatments for CFS will be lifestyle management ones. However, clinical social workers or psychologists working with CFS patients need to know what medical findings have been made and what protocols ordered. They also need to understand the patient's prior medical history.

ESTABLISH PHYSICAL-BEHAVIORAL GOALS   Clinicians have to establish physical-behavioral goals for patients. They need to set up systems to ensure that patients take their medications, understand recommended changes in diet, understand sleep hygiene techniques, and so forth.

RESTRUCTURING ACTIVITIES   On the basis of the activities assessment, clinicians work with patients to restructure their activities of daily living (ADLs). Later, after the crisis of Phase 1 is contained, clinicians will work on the entire range of patient activity. It is essential for patients to begin to recognize the relationship between energy expenditure and experience of symptoms. Different measures can help them understand the connection between particular actions or activities and exacerbated symptoms, but essentially they need to track all their daily activities and symptoms for an extended period, usually one to two weeks (Fennell, 2001, 2004). Clinicians teach patients to recognize connections and then learn ways to use the energy they have more effectively. They can teach patients to simplify and trade off activities. If clinicians can begin to make patients aware that they have a new set of physiological, cognitive, and psychological boundaries, they will have made marked progress.

Using the activity threshold levels reported during assessment, clinicians work with patients to establish realistic activity patterns. Reassuring the patients that these new activity routines are not permanent changes, but temporary ones to protect and increase their functioning in their present situation, clinicians teach patients to stretch out jobs, reorganize them, or eliminate them (Fennell, 2001, 2004; Furst, Gerber, & Smith, 1985, 1997). Activity restructuring in Phase 1 focuses on the activities of daily living.

PHYSICAL SAFETY PLAN   It may be very important to set up a physical safety plan so that patients do not harm themselves or exacerbate the symptoms of the crisis phase. If patients become cognitively confused when tired or at certain times of day, then they must understand that they should not drive at those times. Patients who have always gone jogging may have to be discouraged from this level of exercise. Patients' response to heat or humidity may make it imperative for them to get air conditioning. Some patients may require a psychiatric safety plan if they are severely depressed.

Psychological Domain

ESTABLISHING A WARM RELATIONSHIP   Many CFS patients have experienced disbelief and even mistreatment by the time they come to the clinician. They are often highly sensitive to anything that might be construed as chilly or critical behavior. Therefore, the most essential intervention in the psychological domain is the establishment of a warm, candid, egalitarian relationship (Baumann, 1997; Rood, 1996). By statements and actions, clinicians need to continually convey to patients that the two are comrades in their activities together—equally human, made of the same flesh and subject to the same ills and suffering. While acknowledging that they are experts in matters that patients may not understand, clinicians must clearly indicate that expertise does not make them better or otherwise superior human beings. They should convey the sense that they have chosen their work and that they honor their work and the patients they work with. Clinicians also need to acknowledge their ongoing countertransferential responses, assess them, and when possible, utilize them to benefit the relationship with the patient. Many psychological techniques can prove effective in the treatment of CFS patients if they are carried out by clinicians who genuinely regard their patients as equal, suffering humans.

AFFIRMING THE ILLNESS AND TRAUMAS   Establishing a good relationship with patients begins with an affirmation of the patients' description of their illness and their traumas, if present (Baumann, 1997; Rood, 1996). This affirmation should be apparent through the clinicians' words, eye contact, body language, and general affect. They should actively listen to what patients are saying and react with empathy. Among many other benefits, this affirmation helps to overcome the prior experiences that patients have had with disbelief and stigmatization. It is essential that clinicians help patients to identify and then affirm the trauma that has occurred in their lives (Saigh & Bremner, 1999; van der Kolk, McFarlane, & Weisaeth, 1996). In Phase 1, trauma of illness onset is particularly important. By teaching patients to recognize and grieve for the ways that CFS has disrupted their old lives, clinicians can help patients begin to take control of their new reality.

EDUCATING PATIENTS ABOUT THE PHASES   Clinicians need to introduce patients to the phase experience. In addition to speaking about the phases, they may want to have patients read descriptive materials, such as *The Chronic Illness Workbook* (Fennell, 2001). Learning about the phases is both educational and gives patients a significant coping tool because the phase sequence allows patients to begin to understand and map their experience. It helps them to begin rewriting their illness narrative and encourages them to see that they can have a meaningful future. Patients need to become conscious of the many elements that come into play in their illness, from its physical and psychological aspects to its effects on their lives with others. They need to begin to understand that all these elements will change over time.

DEVELOPING INSIGHT   To change behavior, CFS patients must develop insight, and integral to this activity is the development of the observing self (Kornfield, 1993; Levine, 1979; Morse, 1997; Stein, 1996). As patients collect the data for their daily activities and symptoms charts, clinicians encourage patients to treat their information gathering "scientifically." The patients begin to recognize that they can look dispassionately at themselves and what is happening to them. They can then be guided to separate content—all the different things that happen to them over time—from process—the repeated ways in which they tend to do things or react to situations. While observation skills are developing, patients can begin learning to identify and specifically differentiate chaotic experiences. They can learn to affirm their fears, losses, and suffering as well as their functional and dysfunctional adaptations (Jung, 1990; Mattoon, 1985; Stein, 1996).

EDUCATION IN EGO LOSS   Patients usually need to be educated about the ego loss that most CFS patients experience during Phase 1 (Bose, 1995; Drench, 1994). While patients are being overcome by their illness and possible trauma experience, their private basic ego emerges as a way of coping. Some patients report being unable to maintain their public persona. They tell of bursting into tears uncontrollably or becoming angry at wholly inappropriate moments. They may find themselves regressing. They may begin behaving or talking in a diffident, awkward, childlike manner quite unlike their old self. Such behavior will occur in most CFS patients to one degree or another, even in previously well-integrated personalities. This is a normal response to traumatic change. When patients struggle most of the time to pass as emotionally normal—just as they often attempt to pass for physically normal—they will usually experience even more unwanted intrusions of the child ego. Emotional passing is a coping technique and as new understanding and coping skills are developed through the phases, patients cease to pass except for consciously chosen reasons.

HELPFULNESS OF CHILD EGO   Clinicians can point out that although patients may feel great shame and embarrassment, the child ego has actually helped them

(Bose, 1995; Klein & Schermer, 2000; Morse, 1997; Perrig & Grob, 2000). It communicates information that patients will not otherwise articulate, even to themselves, and it has gained them attention, help, or other benefits. Eventually the patients progress out of this state as they move through the phases, but only when they have processed what has happened to them, grieved for their losses, established new methods of living, and begun constructing a sustainable, authentic new self.

LOSS AND GRIEVING   The losses that CFS patients experience can be overwhelming if clinicians do not help them acknowledge and grieve those losses. Clinicians can begin to teach patients that loss produces grief, and that they need to engage, feel, and understand their grief in an ongoing fashion before they can move toward a more meaningful, positive life (Bose, 1995; Cutcliffe, 1998; Prigerson et al., 1997). Clinicians need to permit structured grieving during sessions together, but they also need to help patients structure daily times when patients can grieve as necessary. This may be encouraged by having the patients set aside time to listen quietly to music, to meditate, or to write in a journal. During Phase 1, such structured times for reflection and allowing the inflow of feelings should be considered as part of the patient's basic ADLs.

CONTAINMENT OF FEAR AND CHAOS   Clinicians help to contain the chaos of Phase 1 by addressing patients' fear of the future (Baumann, 1997; Henderson, 1997; Morse, 1997) and by asserting positive values—the worth of the patient as a human, the value of the patient's experience, the ongoing willingness of the clinician to work with the patient (Nouwen, 1972). Clinicians also perform the important function of acting as witnesses of the patient's experience (Baumann, 1997; Bose, 1995).

Social-Interactive Domain   Social systems issues are essential in treating chronically ill patients, yet they are often ignored (Agnetti, 1997; Axtell, 1999; Rolland, 1984). Clinicians need to keep cognizant of the practical issues relating to family and work systems and the traumas these systems may be suffering, as well as the traumas they may be inflicting on patients. How social system actors behave usually depends on their response to illness in general. In Phase 1, many will attempt either to control the situation or to flee. Their reactions resemble those they would have toward acute illness. It is in Phase 2 that truly distinctive changes occur in the social-interactive work of CFS patients.

FAMILY TRAUMA AFFIRMATION AND EDUCATION   It is desirable for clinicians to try to build a relationship with the family members. If they have experienced traumas of their own related to the patient's illness—loss, changed roles and responsibilities, or sometimes simply exposure to the patient's own suffering—clinicians affirm that suffering. They also educate the family members about CFS. Clinicians may want to discuss cultural attitudes about being strong and not acknowledging suffering and evaluate with family members the utility of these attitudes. They can guide family members in methods of listening and supporting one another.

PRACTICAL FAMILY MANAGEMENT ISSUES   In addition to working with the emotional issues, clinicians should help the patient and partner or family members deal with practical matters. These relate to coordinating care, carrying out household activities, handling financial problems, providing long-term care, and so on. Children in a family suffer when a parent is ill, and other family members may be affected as well. Illness changes everyone's roles and responsibilities, but these are not always acknowledged and they are often resented. Clinicians need to help patients identify hostile or judgmental attitudes coming from family members and teach them appropriate methods of responding.

In chronic illnesses like CFS, a family member or the partner often becomes very controlling (Agnetti, 1997; Doherty & Colangelo, 1984; Doherty, Colangelo, & Hovander, 1991). Clinicians may be able to initiate self-observing processes that will help the family or couple work on this. Clinicians can also model for family members both what the patient needs and what the family members need.

COUPLES ISSUES   Clinicians need to deal with the relations between partners, including their changing roles and responsibilities, their finances, their social lives, and their companionability. In addition, CFS almost always raises issues of sexuality (Agnetti, 1997; Doherty & Colangelo, 1984; Doherty, Colangelo, & Hovander, 1991; Reiss, Gonzalez, & Kramer, 1986). Both partners need to learn that although the illness may severely restrict the sexual activities they have known in the past, there are many ways to express closeness and physical engagement. In Phase 1, the patient's urgency and pain can more or less preclude ordinary sexual life. It is also possible for the reduced ego state of some patients to bring about inappropriate parental relations with a partner that exclude sexuality. Although the patient may not yet be able to return to life as a sexual partner, the couple can be encouraged to establish a more fraternal relationship until the patient has built up more ego strength.

WORKPLACE INTERVENTIONS   When chronic illness patients such as those with CFS are still functioning well enough to continue working, they often face difficulties similar to those at home (Gulick, 1991; Houser & Chace, 1993; Roessler & Rumrill, 1998). They may not have been able to work at their usual pace and may have frequently taken sick leave. Their coworkers may have become judgmental and stigmatizing. And patients may also face practical problems in a workplace not geared to their level of disability. Hence, clinicians may want to arrange a workplace or employer intervention to inform an employer, for example, about CFS or to discuss CFS with coworkers who have become judgmental or stigmatizing. Clinicians may also be able to help patients reorganize their workplace schedule or workstation arrangements. If patients apply for disability, they need to be helped to find informed assistance—the process is fraught with difficulties.

PATIENT ADVOCACY   Clinicians are often in the role of patient advocates vis-à-vis other health care providers, the patients' HMOs, the disability companies, and the federal and state governments (Boyer, 1999; Stephens, 1989). Clinicians should remember that they can be both objective and dispassionate and still remain the patient's advocate (Boyer, 1999; Stephens, 1989). As patients become less urgent and more capable, clinicians begin teaching them how to be their own advocates and how to act as consumers in the health care system (Anderton et al., 1989; Baumann, 1997).

COUNTERTRANSFERENCE IN PHASE 1

It is a given of the Four-Phase Model that throughout the therapeutic process clinicians react emotionally to patients ongoingly. Countertransferential reactions are not inappropriate, but simply a human response (Pearlman & Saakvitne, 1995; Rood, 1996; Wilson & Lindy, 1994). What is important about countertransference is that clinicians recognize their feelings, acknowledge them, process them, and use them if possible.

It is not unusual for clinicians facing patients with the emotions typical of Phase 1 to feel some degree of aversion, fear, or anger (Figley, 1995; Schwartz-Salant & Stein, 1995). Patient neediness and impatience can distance some practitioners. Clinicians can feel disbelief (Pearlman & Saakvitne, 1995; Rood, 1996; Wilson & Lindy, 1994). The patient's story may trigger past or present trauma in the clinician's own life (Figley, 1995; Nouwen, 1972). Clinicians may want to reject the patient. On the other hand, clinicians may be filled with admiration for the patient, overidentifying with the patient's bravery, stoicism, or persistence (Figley, 1995; Pearlman & Saakvitne, 1995; Wilson & Lindy, 1994). All these feelings are normal and reasonable, but distract the clinician from the patient (Alexandris & Vaslamatzis, 1993; Olkin, 1999; Pearlman & Saakvitne, 1995; Wilson & Lindy, 1994), and all require analysis and understanding. Clinicians need to know how their own feelings may be altering their relations with their patients.

Clinical Stance in Phase 1   In Phase 1 particularly, clinicians need to strive for equal exchange. They need to exhibit compassion and affirmation. They need to model toleration for the emotions of the patient and for the ambiguity of the patient's situation. They need to help normalize the patient's situation. In Phase 1, they try to encourage patients to *allow* their suffering—not to endorse it, but to acknowledge its existence and the reasons for its existence.

PHASE 2: STABILIZATION

ASSESSMENT

Physical-Behavioral Domain

PLATEAU   Patients in Phase 2 have usually reached a plateau. Their symptoms do not necessarily improve or get worse, but move through what have become familiar manifestations.

FIRST-TIME PATIENTS   Patients who first come to clinicians when they are in Phase 2 should receive the same full workup that is given to a Phase 1 patient. If, however, the patient has been with the clinician during Phase 1, then Phase 2 is a time for a medical review.

PHYSICAL REVIEW FOR PHASE 2 PATIENTS   Clinicians check the patient's physiological status and review protocols and medications to see whether they need to be changed or eliminated. Certain medications for pain, depression, or sleep may no longer be needed, or not in the same dosages. Clinicians and patients should review the patients' activities again, using the same measures carried out during Phase 1. By Phase 2, it may be feasible to introduce physical therapy or a mild exercise program that might have been impossible for many patients in Phase 1. Clinicians often find that patients are more capable and compliant when they reach this phase. Even when patients have perhaps been fully capable of physical programs in Phase 1, they are usually so overwhelmed by their chaotic situation that they need to achieve a degree of containment first, which is often best achieved by cutting back on activities. In Phase 2, a degree of control has returned to patients, and their physical symptoms usually stabilize as well. This makes it possible for them to handle more activities both physically and psychologically.

ACTIVITY THRESHOLD   Clinicians may find it useful to have patients fill out activity sheets and body charts as they did in Phase 1. Since Phase 2 patients have usually attained a degree of stability and their symptoms exhibit a certain predictability, the body and activity assessments will offer clinicians several intervention options, from potential rehabilitation programs to psychological self-awareness activities.

Psychological Domain
   PHASE PLACEMENT   The first aspect of the psychological evaluation of CFS patients is always phase placement, since the phase dictates many of the subsequent treatment interventions. Phase 2 patients have usually become less urgent, feel more in control, and are less self-pathologizing. But they often exhibit increased caution because of the secondary wounding they experience. They can withdraw socially from many of their former connections, but at the same time they begin searching for new supporters, usually others with CFS. Stabilization and order return in part because Phase 2 patients find others who will not discriminate against them (Gilden, Hendryx, Clar, Casia, & Singh, 1992; Hinrichsen, Revenson, & Shinn, 1985; Humphreys, 1997; Nash & Kramer, 1993). Their lowered sense of urgency allows them to make better use of support organizations because Phase 2 patients do not have the same insistent need or expectation of immediate remedial help from such groups.

   Phase 2 patients typically have not yet accepted that CFS is chronic and so feel dissatisfaction that they have not been cured. They often begin looking for treatments that appear to promise swifter positive outcome. Their inability to acknowledge the chronicity of their illness can lead to boundary confusion. They do not understand that they cannot do what they used to do in the way that they used to accomplish it. The failure to normalize and the ambiguity of their condition generate a new kind of suffering (Agnetti, 1997; Axtell, 1999; Rolland, 1984).

   Again, the Fennell Phase Inventory may be helpful for some clinicians in making phase placement.
   REVISION OF PERSONAL NARRATIVE   Clinicians should ask patients in Phase 2 to create, revise, or extend their personal narrative. This activity helps patients become more self-aware and encourages reflection on what has happened to them since they became sick. They begin teasing out issues that may hinder integration of CFS into their lives, and if they are beginning to gain insight, they usually start to reinterpret some of their narrative in light of their new understanding.
   TRAUMA ASSESSMENT   Clinicians should continue with trauma assessment, in particular investigating the possible presence of pre- or coexisting traumas, iatrogenic trauma, and societal stigmatization. Patients in Phase 1 can identify only the most salient aspects of trauma, given their chaos, and it is easy for them to confuse the kinds of trauma they experience. But with the relative stability of Phase 2, the new or revised personal narrative helps them explore trauma in detail. They can also begin reviewing cultural responses to disease in general and CFS in particular. Here it can help to discuss how attitudes in the health care profession and in society at large change as a disease becomes enculturated. Some patients will recognize that society is evolving in its reaction to CFS and that societal conditions continue to change. This kind of discussion relates directly to the exploration of the disease that many Phase 2 patients are carrying

out on their own and with the contacts they may be establishing with CFS support groups.

When patients reach the relative stability of Phase 2, it is a good idea to reassess their protective psychological defenses. Characterological traits and disorders can prevent patients from developing sufficient insight to achieve appropriate adaptation to CFS. If it becomes apparent that the patient suffers from a personality disorder or pronounced characterological traits, these issues have to be addressed in the treatment concurrently with the illness coping concerns.

Social-Interactive Domain

COUPLES/FAMILY REVIEW   If possible, clinicians should conduct a more extensive couples/family review in Phase 2 because this is usually a very difficult time for families. They have expected the patient to normalize, to resume pre-illness life patterns, and that has not happened. Family members can become angry, disappointed, or resentful. It is hard to overestimate the level of impact that CFS can have on a family. True recognition of chronicity does not usually occur in families until Phase 3, when it occurs with the patient, but in Phase 2, the sheer persistence of the changed family situation brings changes in the family response. It is not uncommon for families or partners to become tired and discouraged during Phase 2. They can give up on the patient and either divorce or cease to offer any meaningful support, aid, or assistance.

ROLES AND RESPONSIBILITIES   The review should focus on current roles and responsibilities in the family and what family attitudes are toward the current arrangement. It is essential to determine everyone's assumptions and expectations prior to attempting any interventions that take the new realities into consideration. Clinicians should try to elicit a family or partner narrative of the illness. The very creation of this story often helps family members by bringing contradictory understandings and unarticulated assumptions to light. In any case, clinicians should evaluate the family's potential vicarious traumas.

SPECIFIC COUPLES ISSUES   Clinicians should also conduct an in-depth couples evaluation. As in Phase 1, this should address issues of sexuality, socialization, roles and relationships, friendship, and companionability. Phase 2 is often a slow trial by fire for couples as both members gradually realize that the illness is permanent and their life together must change completely. Both partners come to comprehend that the sick partner's condition is going to persist indefinitely and the couple's life will never return to its pre-illness state. It is not only patients who need eventually to integrate their illness into their lives, but their partners need to integrate their spouse's condition into their lives as well. Many partners cannot deal with the new situation and leave.

WORKPLACE ASSESSMENTS   In the workplace as well, the patient's failure to normalize can create resentment, sometimes anger, and often fear. While employers and coworkers may have accepted what they believed was a temporary disruption in a worker's productivity, they often dislike the prospect of a worker performing at a lower capacity long term. The clinician is often the person best suited to conducting a workplace intervention to teach the employer or immediate superior about CFS, how it may impact the sick person's work performance, and what general modifications in work arrangements will produce the best results. A physical or occupational therapist can often best assess what adjustments need to be made in the patient's actual workspace or work process to minimize physical stress.

TREATMENT

Physical-Behavioral Domain

MEDICAL AND MEDICATIONS REVIEW   Assessment may indicate that medical protocols need to be changed or medications altered. It is likely that physical or occupational therapy will be sustainable and helpful at this point. It is important for clinicians to keep all health care team members informed about the changes.

ACTIVITIES REVIEW   Here, and in the psychological and social-interactive interventions as well, clinicians may find the exercises in *The Chronic Illness Workbook* (Fennell, 2001) are useful or suggest other activities they may wish to carry out with patients. Not only are many patients in Phase 2 physically more capable of action, but, more importantly, they are also psychologically capable of engaging in intentional change. By waiting until Phase 2 to carry out more extensive interventions, clinicians can achieve greater success. The activities review for Phase 2 patients usually indicates that their activity threshold has risen because they have reached a plateau of symptoms. Patients can, with care, do more than they could before. This frequently leads them to overdo because they continually think that their greater energy means they have "gotten better." Overexertion may lead to worsening symptoms and sometimes even relapse. This cycle can repeat itself many times unless clinicians teach patients how to observe, analyze, and monitor their activities. If a person works to exhaustion, completion of the task does not bring the physical and psychological benefit necessary for a sense of well-being (Bedell, 2000; Hinojosa & Kramer, 1997; Polatajko, 2000; Primeau, 1996; Reberio & Polgar, 1999).

MULTIPLE ACTIVITIES   In addition to needing appropriate satisfaction after completing tasks, people need to perform many actions or tasks over the course of each day to experience a high quality of life.

FOUR CATEGORIES OF ACTIVITIES   All individuals need a well-balanced mixture of life activities. Activities fall, roughly, into four categories. There are the activities of daily living (ADLs) and self-care, activities of personal development and enrichment (anything from rock climbing to reading, or fly-fishing to meditation), activities that relate to an individual's social and family world, and finally activities that relate to work or employment. This last category includes not only paid employment but, for example, the ADL activities that a mother carries out for her children or the volunteer work of a reading aide in a school. To enjoy a balanced and meaningful life, people usually need to engage in activities from all four categories regularly (Bedell, 2000; Hinojosa & Kramer, 1997; Primeau, 1996).

HOW PEOPLE CUT BACK ACTIVITIES   When people overextend or when they become ill, they are forced to eliminate activities. Usually they first cut out activities having to do with personal enrichment. They then cut back on social activities and begin neglecting or stretching out ADLs. Because people need the income, paid employment activities are usually the last to go.

EDUCATION AND DATA COLLECTION   Clinicians need to teach their patients the very difficult concept that sheer doggedness and hard work will not, despite cultural assurances, necessarily produce desirable results. If individuals, even healthy individuals, persist in tasks beyond their current capabilities, they will repeatedly fail. Patients need to comprehend deeply that the same is true for them. If they persist in attempting what is beyond their capacity, they will very likely fail and possibly precipitate a relapse in their illness.

A great deal of education occurs when patients collect daily activity data. In Phase 2, they have attained sufficient containment to keep detailed activity sheets in which they record how much time they spend carrying out the activities they attempt throughout the day. In addition to recording what they do and for how long they do it, they also record how they feel and what their symptoms are during each activity. They report on time spent eating, resting, and sleeping, with comments on the effects of the food and the quality of the rest or sleep. Throughout the data collection process, clinicians emphasize the scientific, emotionally neutral nature of the task, and this neutrality has a normalizing effect. Not only does objective examination of their lives allow patients to see what is actually happening to them and how, to a degree, they can manage it, but it also helps relieve unreasoning fear and terror. The patients' condition may not be what they would wish for themselves, but they can still examine it matter-of-factly and perhaps even alter it to their benefit.

SELECTING ACTIVITIES FROM EACH CATEGORY   Clinicians can help their patients to differentiate and organize their activities by category. They then work with them to achieve a more balanced and meaningful activity reduction. People, even very sick people, should engage in some activities in each of the four areas, if possible, although activity in the work area is sometimes very limited. Even patients who are severely disabled need more activities than a few simple ADLs. They should engage in some personal development and enrichment, and they need some regular social activities. They also find satisfaction in volunteering to do nondemanding tasks.

LISTING DESIRES, REQUIREMENTS, AND RESPONSIBILITIES   Clinicians should ask patients to list the things that they want to do, the things they believe they should do, and what their actual responsibilities are. When patients compare these lists to their activities, normalization failure usually becomes dramatically apparent (Fennell, 2001, 2004). Still, it can take considerable time for patients to comprehend, first, how their activities relate to their symptoms, and second, how drastically they must adjust their expectations and responsibilities. Usually the sheer act of data collection causes some patients to begin activity modification without any direction from health care professionals, but making global changes usually requires active help from clinicians.

SELECTING AN ACTIVITIES MONITOR   Clinicians should recommend that patients identify a good friend to be an activities monitor. This should be a person in regular contact with the patient—someone whom the patient trusts, likes, and will listen to. The monitor can see when the patient is getting overtired and overextended and advise the patient to slow down before precipitating a collapse. Patients can also talk with their activities monitor prior to a special occasion or taking a trip.

Psychological Domain

ESTABLISHING A WARM RELATIONSHIP   If the Phase 2 patient is new to the clinician, then the clinician must first establish a warm, equal relationship and affirm the patient's illness and trauma. All the issues discussed in Phase 1 on this topic are relevant here. It will then be necessary for the clinician to teach the patient about the phase process and to begin introducing the patient to the observing self and to the distinction between content and process. Given the diminished chaos of Phase 2 patients, this work sometimes proceeds more quickly than similar work in Phase 1.

BOUNDARY SETTING   The principal problem Phase 2 patients face is their inability to recognize appropriate boundaries for themselves, whether in physical activity, psychological stamina, cognitive ability, or social activities. The slightly increased energy levels of Phase 2 encourage patients to engage in all sorts of activities that they have missed, and initially they often feel wonderful. For aggressive, achieving personalities, this is a particularly attractive lure, but the same reaction happens with patients who were generally easygoing and laid back prior to their illness. Their old internal governors are no longer appropriate, and they have not yet developed new ones to keep them from overdoing. Moreover, nearly everything and everyone in their environment, including themselves, is urging them to return to their former life.

DEVELOPING ANALYTICAL SKILLS   It is therefore essential for clinicians to work with these patients to refine their self-observation skills and to deepen their analytic ability. The collection of activity and symptom data, plus reflection about desires and expectations, gives patients and clinicians the actual individual substance of the patients' lives to work with. Patients can learn to see that they habitually spend more energy than they have, and that when they do, they suffer disproportionately. They start to compare how much energy different activities require and over time learn to choose lower-energy-consuming activities that they also enjoy. They need to develop insight, almost always with the help of the clinician, and then they must struggle to maintain these insights over time. Throughout this lengthy process, they must endure, because that is much of what they are learning, the daily experience of what they cannot do, of what they have lost (Bedell, 2000; Gignac & Cott, 1998; Gignac et al., 2000; Small & Lamb, 1999).

MAINTAINING INSIGHT   Learning to maintain insight is one of the most difficult tasks for patients. Often they leave the clinician's office with a clear vision of what they can and cannot do and good intentions to make healthy choices, only to lose that insight and those good intentions during the following days because they feel diminished by limitations that run so counter to their former roles. Perception developed for years prior to their illness about who and what they are make it hard for patients to maintain insight. They keep reverting to their old ways of thinking and behaving. Monitoring activities, altering activities, overcoming psychological defenses to acknowledging limitations—all these processes take time and patience. Insight usually has painful components. It forces the patients to look at what they are now as opposed to what they were. It causes grief as patients keep being forced to look at their losses. Living with CFS requires daily surrenders that exacerbate the sense of worthlessness (Hatcher, 1973; Horowitz, 1987; Pulver, 1992; Silbermann, 1967).

ENCOURAGING GRIEVING   Clinicians can inform patients—can predict for them—that they may very well feel an overwhelming sense of loss and grief, but can assure them that such feelings are completely normal. Clinicians encourage patients to express what they feel, whether to sympathetic others, in prayer, in writing, or whatever works for them. Clinicians particularly encourage patients to seek out others, which accomplishes two things at once. It allows patients to grieve as they must, and it introduces them to a new social life in which they are accepted.

NEW VALUES AND NORMS   With the maintenance of insight, however, comes the growing ability to examine their values and develop a new set of norms. Patients gradually come to realize that they cannot fulfill their life values in the same way that they used to. In some cases, they may have to reinterpret what is important to them in life. That is, they may have to change their values. But in some cases they may come to understand that they can fulfill their old values in different ways (Fennell, 2001).

PHASE 1-PHASE 2 LOOP   The work of Phase 2 is very difficult for patients to accomplish and even harder to maintain. Building insight is never easy, especially when it involves recognizing the permanent loss of the person's former life. It is equally difficult for patients to change their values and norms, especially when they did not choose to do so, but were forced to by their illness. The internal personal pressures to reject what has happened is enough to make patients ignore what they have learned and attempt a return to the old life. This may cause relapse, or relapses may happen totally apart from patient behavior, in either case throwing the patient back into Phase 1. Sometimes patients are able to move again into Phase 2 on their own because they learned how to reduce their activities and contain the crisis the first time around. But some patients simply seek solace in easily accessible anodynes such as alcohol. Some move from crisis to crisis in a perpetual experience of Phase 1. Social pressures tend to encourage the Phase 1-Phase 2 loop. The social actors in a patient's world usually want a return to the old life. Since this pressure conforms so completely with the patient's own wish to return to the precrisis life, it is hard to maintain insight or a commitment to new values and norms.

Social-Interactive Domain

REACTING TO THE PATIENT'S FAILURE TO NORMALIZE   The greatest difficulty facing partners and families in Phase 2 is the failure of patients to normalize. Family members have not usually accepted the concept of chronicity any more than the patients have. They have hoped, but also expected, that the patients would improve and then resume their former life activities. When patients do not, family members can be disappointed, angry, resentful, and confused. Patients' families must be made aware that patients will not return to their pre-illness state, and that it can be harmful to encourage patients to perform more activities than their activity thresholds permit. To the greatest extent possible, clinicians need to work with partners and families to help them revise family roles and responsibilities and to deal with any traumas.

FAMILY THERAPY   If the patient's medical team does not already include a clinician who is familiar with family therapy techniques, it is usually desirable to seek a consultation at this time or to add such a person to the team. This clinician needs to investigate the family's issues and educate the family to the illness phases and the permanent reality of the patient's CFS. The family therapist works with the family to identify the roles and responsibilities that each family member had prior to the illness and then turns the discussion to clarification of the family's basic values. The goal is to develop new norms and to reassign roles and responsibilities in a way that does not harm the patient or overburden the other family members (Fennell, 2001, 2004).

FINANCIAL ISSUES   Financial issues are extremely important. It may be desirable for the family to consult a financial planner to assess their situation and to make the best decisions possible. Some families have sufficient resources, even without the patient working, to buy household or child-care assistance. But when families cannot afford these services, they need to learn to do things differently. Sometimes this means "reducing keystrokes"—learning how to accomplish basic maintenance tasks with a minimum of effort. Other situations may require families to modify former standards. Clinicians can point out that by doing so, they will be better able to hold firm on matters where they do not want to make compromises.

COUPLES INTERVENTIONS   Couples interventions can be particularly important in Phase 2. It is not uncommon for the relationship to have been intensely strained by the patient's failure to normalize. Many of the interventions resemble (or are part of) family interventions (e.g., adapting roles, responsibilities, finances). But clinicians also need to address the issues of sex—how couples can continue to have a sexual life by learning new practices, perhaps developing sensuality as well as sexuality, and choosing the best times. They need to resolve issues of socializing so that the healthy partner can have independent contacts as well as the more limited contacts the couple share jointly. They need to develop new ways to be companionable together—to be friends—that do not immediately exhaust the patient.

NEGOTIATIONS WITH EMPLOYERS   Work interventions in Phase 2 depend on whether the patient can work at all and if so, how much. The clinician and patient need to determine whether the patient can, in fact, continue full-time work or whether the patient needs to try to arrange for part-time or flextime hours. Clinicians can often usefully intervene to educate an employer about the nature of CFS and give a reliable account of the patient's actual capacities, describing what the patient will be able to do if facilitating arrangements are put in place.

ERGONOMIC AND INFORMATIONAL INTERVENTIONS   When patients continue to work, it is often advisable to carry out interventions in the workplace such as those mentioned in Phase 1. These are either examinations of the work environment to make it more ergonomically suitable to the patient, or they are discussions with superiors or coworkers about the nature of the patient's illness.

DISABILITY   If employment is no longer possible, clinicians help patients obtain disability benefits or refer them to specialists who can help them.

COUNTERTRANSFERENTIAL ISSUES IN PHASE 2

Failure to Normalize   In Phase 2, clinicians may suffer any of the reactions typical of Phase 1. In addition, they frequently have reactions similar to those of patients and family members when the patient fails to normalize. Even though clinicians know that CFS is chronic, everyone feels social pressure to move toward cure (Figley, 1995; Marbach, 1999; Schlesinger, Druss, & Thomas, 1999; Schwartz-Salant & Stein, 1995).

Conflict   Clinicians also may find themselves in conflict with Phase 2 patients who have become dissatisfied with their own progress. The seeking behavior of patients hoping to find new doctors or new treatments can be irritating, frustrating, or cause a rupture in the relationship (Alexandris & Vaslamatzis, 1993; Olkin, 1999; Pearlman & Saakvitne, 1995; Wilson & Lindy, 1994).

Clinicians frequently experience conflict with patients' families, whose behavior may reward patients for unhealthy behaviors and punish them for healthy ones. Laziness and selfishness may appear to motivate some families when they insist that the patient must return to incapacitating former roles and responsibilities. To make matters worse, clinicians with Phase 2 patients often find themselves in conflict with HMOs, hospitals, or social agencies. These organizations tend to want patients moved out of the system, whereas the clinicians know that their patients still need support and education.

Vicarious Traumatization   With Phase 2 patients, clinicians often suffer the vicarious traumatization of practicing with marginalized or disregarded patient populations. Compared with other chronic illnesses, CFS continues to be the object of professional and cultural stigma, although this situation is improving.

Clinical Stance in Phase 2   Clinicians should coach their patients in ways to manage different life scenarios. They need to help them structure a new life with new norms and values, using a phase template. And, like a parent protecting a newly mobile child, the clinician provides trustworthy boundaries so that patients can learn about their new world in safety. Clinicians need to assure patients that although they may not believe it at this point, but must take it on faith, what they learn now and how they come to live can be meaningful and fulfilling.

Clinicians should also model the tolerance for chronicity that patients so desperately need in Phase 2. They should encourage patients to engage the grief reaction so that they can react to their suffering consciously, instead of ignoring it, which frequently produces neurotic suffering and reactions.

In Phase 2, clinicians encourage patients to meet their suffering with compassion, for when they begin to extend compassion to themselves, they are moving toward self-acceptance and the possibility of making a new life.

PHASE 3: RESOLUTION

ASSESSMENT

Physical-Behavioral Domain

FIRST-TIME PATIENTS   It is rare, but not unheard of, for a new patient to be in Phase 3. If clinicians have new patients who are in Phase 3, they should conduct a complete physical examination as they would with any new patient.

PLATEAU, RELAPSE, IMPROVEMENT   Phase 3 patients have often reached a long-term plateau, although their symptoms may be more intense than they were in Phase 2. The patients' greater coping skills tend to make them less bothered by the symptoms, and by their changing nature, than they were in Phase 2. Patients may improve, but they may also suffer relapse.

REVIEW TREATMENT PROTOCOLS AND MEDICATIONS   It is important to review treatment protocols and medications regularly, to eliminate those that are no longer needed, and to adjust those that the patient continues; but regular medical reviews probably do not have to be as frequent as they were at first. The patient's activity threshold also should be regularly reviewed.

PATIENTS AS HEALTH CARE MANAGERS   Clinicians should begin assessing the readiness of their patients to become their own health care managers.

Psychological Domain

PHASE PLACEMENT   Phase placement is the first evaluation. When patients arrive at Phase 3, more and more their sense of control firmly resides inside themselves. They are now able to differentiate between those things over which they can exert real control and those they cannot. They have also learned how to do some of the emotional heavy lifting required to tolerate both chronicity and ambiguity. Phase 3 patients have often developed significant skills for coping with their symptoms and managing their day-to-day lives. As a consequence, their anxieties and despair focus less on pain, exhaustion, or other manifestations of their illness. Phase 3 patients have also finally recognized that they are not going to return to the way they were and that their life has changed forever. Accompanying this recognition is usually a serious, sometimes profound, feeling of existential despair.

REVISING THE PERSONAL NARRATIVE   Clinicians encourage patients to continue revising their personal narrative. Indeed, it is sometimes the narrative that reveals to clinicians that patients have entered Phase 3. The narrative may also draw attention to the patient's existential questioning although that is likely to appear in conversations with the clinician, who by now should be a trusted figure in the patient's life.

Social-Interactive Domain

FAMILY/COUPLES REVIEWS   Clinicians need to conduct a family case management review and a couples case management review. Part of the existential despair that Phase 3 patients feel emerges from their feeling that they are a burden to their partner and family (Canam & Acorn, 1999; Faison, Faria, & Frank, 1999; Hall, Stein, Roter, & Rieser, 1999; Helseth, 1999). Clinicians need to evaluate how the patient's significant others are coping and how well they and the patient have developed methods for monitoring and changing situations that arise in the family context.

BROADENING THE SOCIAL WORLD   Clinicians also observe and encourage Phase 3 patients as they go beyond their immediate family sphere into a wider social world. Their association with other CFS patients may be their way into the world again, but they often find other avenues through creative activity and other interests (to be discussed later).

WORK ASSESSMENTS   Again clinicians carry out a work evaluation if the patient is still employed.

TREATMENT

Physical-Behavioral Domain

MEDICAL REVIEW AND EDUCATION OF PATIENT   Besides carrying out the regular medical/medications review, clinicians begin teaching those patients who are capable of doing so how to become their own care coordinators and health care advocates. They actively encourage patients to take charge, to learn what they should monitor and how often, what symptoms they should report immediately, what health care professionals they should see regularly, and how often they should see them. Clinicians train patients how to be conscious partners in assessing their treatment protocols and their medications.

ACTIVITIES MONITOR   Clinicians also teach Phase 3 patients how to become their own activity threshold monitors. Patients may be encouraged to continue a relationship with the activities monitor they selected earlier, but increasingly patients should be able to recognize on their own when they are overdoing and how to pull back. Patients need to be prepared to adjust and shift with the changes that life and their illness bring. As they absorb and process the interventions of Phases 2 and 3, they gain reasonable effective methods for doing this (Bezard, Imbert, & Gross, 1998).

Dynamic and Static Disability   Phase 3 is a good time to introduce patients to the contrast between static and dynamic disability. Almost all CFS patients suffer dynamic disability, that is, disability that fluctuates over time. Sometimes they are so exhausted that they are mobile only with the aid of a wheelchair. Sometimes they are cognitively impaired so constantly that they cannot perform many ordinary daily tasks like cooking or balancing the checkbook. But other times, the same person may be able to walk about completely unaided or think with great clarity. Clinicians need to make patients aware that society conceives disability as static, unchanging. Society also tends to recognize only visible disabilities. Patients need to learn that when they are disabled, they have the same rights under the Americans with Disabilities Act as do those with static disabilities. They also have these rights whether their disabilities are visible or not.

Psychological Domain
Engaging Grief Reaction   To deal with the issues of Phase 3, clinicians need to engage the patients' grief reaction. In Phase 1 and Phase 2, patients learned to allow their suffering and then to address it with compassion. In Phase 3, they learn to respect themselves for enduring their suffering. There may or may not be positive lessons they can learn from their suffering, but simply by virtue of enduring it, they deserve respect. This respect finds expression in articulated self-compassion, which is one of the identifying characteristics for clinicians of Phase 3 patients. Clinicians actively model compassion for the patient's suffering and also the respect for it that patients need to develop. This is an essential antithetical intervention. Clinicians also need to emphatically affirm the patient's mourning. They have to actively explore the life-illness dilemma that patients find themselves facing. All the while they must also help patients maintain their hard-won insight and engage in issue reframing.

Development of Meaning   The single most important intervention activity with Phase 3 patients concerns the development of meaning. In Phase 2, patients expanded and refined their insight into their illness and activities that they began in Phase 1. This essential insight is both difficult to achieve and hard to maintain. But even this kind of insight is not enough to sustain them for the long haul (Prochaska, DiClemente, & Norcross, 1992; Prochaska, Norcross, & DiClemente, 1994). Patients also need to place their lives in a wider context of meaning, first about the illness experience that has been imposed on them, but more importantly about what makes a life, even one as constrained as theirs, worth living. Patients' success in achieving the resolution that allows them to integrate their illness into their lives depends largely on the exploration of meaning (Frankl, 1983; Hellstrom et al., 1999; Jobst et al., 1999; Kissane, 2000; Magid, 2000).

Some people never contemplate issues of meaning either because their lives are sufficiently stress-free or because their lives are subject to such dislocation and threat that they never have any opportunity to reflect on issues of meaning. But most people require and make the effort to find some sense of meaning in life. They do this to avoid existential despair and survive emotionally the difficulties that disrupt the lives of most individuals, healthy or sick. Illness, whether acute or chronic, often stimulates the desire to find meaning, since it threatens the individual with pain, suffering, and sometimes even death. Individuals can pass through episodes of acute illness and, once the crisis has passed, forget the questions that arose while they were sick. But for those with chronic illness, the previous state of well-being never returns, even when they achieve a plateau of symptoms.

If patients find themselves in a dark tunnel of despair, they must be encouraged to work through it, even without any promise of a light at its end. Patients usually must begin by using the clinician's faith that they can come through this experience to lead a full and rewarding life. Patients know their old life has burned to the ground. Part of the clinician's persuasive power at this juncture comes from knowing and articulating to patients that working with them is worthwhile because the clinician knows this renewal, like the phoenix rising from the ashes, can and does happen.

CREATIVE ACTIVITY   Creation of meaning and a new identity occurs most smoothly when patients deeply engage their creative processes in a personally rewarding way. Some patients will write, but others will paint, carve, compose, dance, sing, or build. The activity may not even be something traditionally considered creative. It may consist of tying fishing flies or training dogs, designing a new fall wardrobe, or becoming involved in political activities. There are nonverbal activities that can help patients build a sense of meaning. Music, or the experience of simply being in nature, can directly affect a patient's spirit and generate a profound sense of inhabiting a meaningful place in the cosmos. What matters is that the activity is personally significant to the patient and engages the patient's imaginative and creative energies. Ultimately, patients will use their awakened creativity to construct their illness narrative as a proud story of heroism, but getting to this point may be a long, circuitous process (Aberbach, 1989; Edwards, 1993; Holm-Hadulla, 1996).

ANTITHETICAL EXPERIMENTATION   As a way to explore possibilities for the new self that Phase 3 patients begin to construct, clinicians can encourage them to engage in antithetical experimentation. They urge patients to "try on" totally antithetical roles, identities, or emotions. Sometimes illness has forced patients, quite unwillingly, into roles or situations totally unlike their old selves. Clinicians can help patients see or imagine benefits from new personality characteristics and understand the purposes and satisfactions that can arise out of different roles. Eventually clinicians help patients to see that even their suffering can be productive and worthy of their respect.

STRIVING FOR AUTHENTICITY   To create a new self and to locate true meaning in their lives, patients must build solidly by striving for complete authenticity. They often do not know how to "do" this. Clinicians tell them to observe and note how they truly think and feel about current experiences and their prospects for the future, not how they believe they are supposed to feel. Patients should accept as true of themselves only those feelings and thoughts that feel completely genuine and real. They must try to reject the pretenses that they have maintained until now in order to meet societal or family or even their own inner expectations. Clinicians must assert that all the patient's authentic feelings are acceptable expressions as long as they do not actually hurt themselves or other people. Obviously, it is very important that patients carry out this process in a safe place with a safe person or people.

Value of Rage and Grief   At first, the authentic Phase 3 feelings may be a miasma of rage, pain, grief, and misery. But clinicians should assure patients that even these emotions have real value because they are genuine. Gradually as patients strip themselves bare of pretense, they slowly find and collect some positive values that they genuinely assent to.

Relief of Authenticity   Phase 3 patients are usually relieved to stop pretending. And as they begin creating a new, authentic identity, they also begin making a new set of choices about their mix of activities from the four groups. They often radically revise their priorities about how they will expend their limited practical energy.

Old and New Self   Building a new self requires identifying the characteristics of the precrisis self and analyzing just how much of that old self has actually been lost. In many cases, what is lost is a method of expression, not the characteristic itself. Clinicians can often help patients identify aspects of themselves that they can and want to include in their new self.

Exploring Different Philosophies and Traditions   Clinicians can also encourage patients to explore unfamiliar philosophical, spiritual, and cultural understandings of life, suffering, and meaning because these traditions can give patients new insights. Most patients will be somewhat acquainted with some Western traditions, usually either Christianity or Judaism. But they may be completely unaware of how Buddhists conceive the purpose of suffering or how secular philosophers from the ancient Greeks and Chinese to present-day ethicists and psychologists regard the meaning of human existence. A Christian may benefit from reading the ways Sufi philosophers frame the purpose of existence, and a Jew may benefit from considering the insights of certain Hindu mystics. For those who are uncomfortable with traditional religious framing of purpose, psychologists like Carl Jung or philosophers like Martin Buber may offer evocative conceptions. Some humanists propose that people themselves develop definable humanity as they assert meaningfulness to their short stay in existence by behaving in ways that make life better for themselves and those around them in the world. Nonverbal experiences of music or nature may reach directly into a person's visceral perception of the universe and transform it in much the same way that mystics are said to be transformed by momentary perceptions of Oneness or God.

Clinician Neutrality   The role of clinicians is not to select or evaluate the beliefs of patients, but to guide them into a significant, truly authentic examination of the larger order and their place in it. Clinicians do this while continuing to help patients observe and analyze the practical issues of their daily lives.

Spiritual/Philosophical Reactions in Phase 1   Patients have distinct spiritual and philosophical reactions in the different phases. In Phase 1, patients fear that their condition is some sort of specific or nebulous damnation, and any philosophical or spiritual response they have is at worst primitive or magical and at best placatory. This response occurs regardless of patients' level of education or prior intellectual sophistication. Even persons who had little or no religious life prior to their illness may secretly believe or openly assert that God has abandoned them, that there is no God at all, or that God is punishing them with this illness (Dyson, Cobb, & Forman, 1997; Kuipers, 1991; Sugarek, Dyo, & Holmes, 1988; Sumner, 1998). Many people in Western cultures carry deep fears that an angry avenging deity may exist and that bad fortune, particularly illness, is a sign of deserved punishment. The clinician's role in Phase 1 is to provide some generalized sense of philosophical and spiritual comfort. They need to receive the patient's statements compassionately and with understanding, but then suggest that there are other ways to view the situation and affirm that the patient is not going to hell.

SPIRITUAL/PHILOSOPHICAL REACTIONS IN PHASE 2   In Phase 2, patients are capable of greater attention and reflection, but initially they are still preoccupied with the practical. As a sense of control begins to return to them, however, and as they find others who support and empathize with them, the search for emotional and spiritual containment draws many of them into fairly hierarchical, authoritative religious structures. They do not usually attempt to develop individual or specific meaning for themselves, but use traditional formulations that already exist, often the religion of their childhood or that of a sympathetic person of like kind. Phase 2 patients often believe that if they practice their religion assiduously and scrupulously, God will eventually reward them for their compliant behavior. Many take their physical plateau state as a sign of this. This is a positive response and the clinician should support it for the containment that it provides in Phase 2, but it is not a sufficient response later in the phase process. Because Phase 2 is also a time of seeking, some patients become angry with the God of their past for allowing their illness to occur, and they seek a more satisfactory spiritual connection. If they meet others with CFS who have found spiritual or philosophical solace in a particular practice, they may gravitate toward the same practice. Again, where a Phase 2 patient's spiritual life does not hurt the patient or others, it is best for the clinician to passively support whatever course the patient chooses.

SPIRITUAL/PHILOSOPHICAL REACTIONS IN PHASE 3   In Phase 3, however, clinicians want to encourage patients to seek authenticity above all. Patients have to establish the new integrated self, based on beliefs and feelings that they affirm wholeheartedly. Their lives have to be suffused with meaning that they embrace with sincere conviction and that they periodically reexamine for its authenticity to them. During Phase 3, patients arrive at a personal selection of philosophical and spiritual beliefs that, although constantly shifting and changing, are deeply meaningful to them. Their felt cosmology becomes internalized and reflects their internalized locus of control. It also matches the psychological mastery that patients acquire in Phase 3. At the same time, they may find it comforting or aesthetically and socially pleasing to continue formal religious practice in a faith that they do not altogether agree with, but whose forms link them to their past, their family, and their friends.

Social-Interactive Domain

FAMILIES AND DESPAIR   In Phase 3, partners and families who have continued to support the patient often suffer their own "dark night of the soul" when they acknowledge that the patient is not going to get better and that life must change permanently. Clinicians may need to support them through this time or refer them to specialists who can.

DEVELOPING MAINTENANCE PROCESSES   The time is also coming when maintenance and review of family issues devolves on the patients and their partners and families. Clinicians need to help both families and couples establish self-management reviews and procedures so that they can adapt with the least stress to changing circumstances.

EXPANDING THE SOCIAL WORLD   Phase 3 patients often begin to move out into the world more actively. They are much more aware of societal attitudes and stigmatization, and patients are now far more likely to confront people about negative reactions. They sometimes engage in social or political action for CFS or for other causes that they think are important. Often illness has raised their consciousness about many social issues that did not seriously concern them when they were healthy. Phase 3 patients also work more actively on their social network. They seek to integrate new supporters to replace those they have lost, but increasingly they are also willing to give former friends a chance. Friends who were avoidant out of ignorance or embarrassment sometimes welcome the opportunity to reconnect. But Phase 3 patients typically do not struggle to reengage former friends or family members who continue to stigmatize or condemn them.

WORK ISSUES   In Phase 3, patients relate to their work life much as they do to the outside world in general. Where before they often tried to continue in their job even though its conditions made this very difficult, they now take a more assertive stance. Some request the necessary adaptations to their environment or work schedule. Others find that they cannot continue to work, and they seek disability. Yet others look for completely different work in a field that is more meaningful to them. Clinicians support patients in whatever way possible. They may assist patients in renegotiating current job arrangements, improving the job environment, accomplishing job separation, or filing for disability.

COUNTERTRANSFERENTIAL ISSUES IN PHASE 3

Inadequacy   Clinicians can suffer a sense of inadequacy when faced with the existential despair of Phase 3 patients. Many people, including clinicians, have not examined their basic beliefs any more deeply than CFS patients have prior to their illness. Clinicians are now confronted with vast and terrifying questions that they worry about for themselves, not just for their patients. They may feel depressed at the endless trials their patients face. They may experience a great sense of professional uselessness. These feelings can consciously or unconsciously make them want to withdraw from their patients. They may find themselves canceling appointments or ceasing to pay attention to the patients when they are in the office. Clinicians may reject patients altogether. They may assert that the patients need to seek aid from others, that what they need is beyond the scope of the clinician's competence. But clinicians who choose to process their feelings and who understand that in Phase 3 they are dealing with the deepest issues of the human condition can achieve a kind of resolution of their own.

Clinical Stance in Phase 3   Clinicians carry out an all-important witnessing function. The patient's journey may not be the clinician's personal struggle or agony, but clinicians are the ones who see it and who reflect it back to the patient. They validate the patient's experiences, they acknowledge the patient's mourning, they witness the patient's painstaking construction of a new self, and they honor the patient's bravery and persistence. The act of witnessing is powerful and can be transforming in and of itself.

Clinicians also help patients engage in antithetical experimentation, they guide them into creative work, and they teach them and model for them the process of standing with one's self. Clinicians carry out a parallel process with the patients, moving toward authenticity with them and seeking meaning with them, even though clinicians may not arrive at the same or even similar meanings as the patient has found. Clinicians are also selective about what they will share of their personal explorations. In Phase 3, clinicians teach their patients to meet their suffering with respect.

PHASE 4

Phase 4 patients integrate their illness into a whole and meaningful life. They no longer live merely as an illness writ large, but as individuals with varied interests and engagements, despite how limited they may be physiologically. And by reengaging in many areas in their lives, Phase 4 patients persuade family, friends, and coworkers to regard them as individuals for whom illness is no longer their only defining characteristic (Baker & Stern, 1993; Michael, 1996; Willems, 2000).

This is not to say that Phase 4 patients arrive at a perfect life, without pain, suffering, frustration, or stigmatization. What it means is that much of the time they manage to live graciously despite the rigors of both life and their chronic illness. They have developed an understanding that doing this—living graciously in the effort—is worthwhile. Even when the effort is difficult, they attribute high value to the sheer process, which in turn nurtures a renewed sense of self-esteem.

Very few individuals are so fortunate as to live in Phase 4 constantly. Most experience it transiently, at best for extended periods. Pain, exhaustion, or multiplying problems related to their original illness can wear them down, making them reexperience some of the confusion and distress of earlier phases. Despite their awareness, patients will have occasions when they call into question the understandings and positions they thought they had reached at the end of Phase 3. Life often brings events or other illnesses that knock patients back into prior phases, even though the new crisis does not pertain directly to the original illness.

Living with chronic illness is a dynamic process, not a static one, even when patients have successfully moved through the phase process. Unlike what is posited for some stage models of behavioral change (Prochaska, DiClemente, & Norcross, 1992; Prochaska, Norcross, & DiClemente, 1994), even those who navigate the four phases successfully do not exit the process. Rather, they maintain themselves in Phase 4 as much of the time as they can. During these periods, however, Phase 4 patients can experience true transcendence of their CFS.

ASSESSMENT

Phase 4 patients understand the phases and recognize that integrating their illness into a complete life is a dynamic process. They know how to use the techniques they have learned, but they also know when they should seek professional help and how to do so. They have developed a new self that integrates aspects of their precrisis self with a new, authentic self that they have developed gradually during the phases of their illness experience. They have reconstructed their self-definition and hence their relationships with others. They have engaged in an ongoing search for meaning. They focus outward, seeking to lead as full a life as possible. But Phase 4 patients also know that their experiences of integration and even transcendence will come under assault from life crises or different illnesses.

Like other people, these prospects scare them. But they know how to live daily in the present and to work with their fears and their grief. On good days, they are able to do just that. On bad days, they hang onto their new faith that they can work toward better days (Fennell, 1995, 2001, 2004; Jason, Fennell, Taylor, Fricano, & Halpert, 2000).

Physical-Behavioral Domain

PATIENTS AS THEIR OWN CARE COORDINATORS   Phase 4 patients may continue in a plateau state, they may improve, or they may relapse. Before releasing them to become their own care coordinators, clinicians may want to carry out an overall medical review. If it appears that it may be necessary for disability claims, they may also order a neuro/psych review or other auxiliary assessments.

Psychological Domain

ROLE AND IDENTITY INTEGRATION   Clinicians witness the patients' clarification of their new identities and roles.

REVIEW OF MAINTENANCE PROCESSES   Clinicians urge patients to periodically review and revise their personal narrative as a way to keep in touch with themselves and with their evolving understanding of their lives. Clinicians also evaluate patients' ability to maintain insight and continue the reframing experience.

ONGOING CREATIVE ACTIVITY AND MEANING DEVELOPMENT   Clinicians observe and recommend that Phase 4 patients continue to engage in creative activities and to broaden their quest for meaning.

INTEGRATION ASSESSMENT   In preparation for ending regular sessions with patients, clinicians observe how well patients have integrated their illness into their lives, and whether they are able to live meaningfully despite chronicity and ambiguity.

Social-Interactive Domain

REVIEW OF MAINTENANCE PROCESSES   Clinicians review the couples and family maintenance protocols and establish or review work maintenance protocols.

NEW AND REINTEGRATED FRIENDS   Patients have usually created new networks of friends, but many also find they can reintegrate some old friends temporarily lost during earlier phases. Social life has once again become important to patients because they want to live in and of the world. Since they are open about their condition and do not permit discrimination, they choose supportive friends.

ALTERNATIVE JOBS OR VOCATIONS   Phase 4 patients who are able to work often change the kind of work they do altogether. In the restructuring of self, they discover what is important to them, including working in an area that has meaning for them. Even those on disability, within the limits of their health, may discover that they want to volunteer their services to support activities that they value (Howard & Howard, 1997).

TREATMENT

The overarching clinical goal of Phase 4 is the integration of the patient's suffering as part of a meaningful, sustaining, and even rewarding life. The major treatment issue is to assure the amalgamation of desired elements of the patient's precrisis self with the newly constructed self. Clinicians need to ensure that patients have a firm grasp of the insight and intervention techniques they have learned throughout the phase process. Given the crises that life can bring, patients will need to return to these techniques when events require.

Physical-Behavioral Domain

TRAINING IN SELF-MAINTENANCE   Since Phase 4 is when clinicians separate from patients, interventions are largely those intended to assure that the patient can manage without the clinician's regular help. Clinicians make sure that patients understand how to act as their own care coordinators. They alert patients to those things that should make them seek professional help again.

RELAPSE/STABILIZATION/INTEGRATION CYCLE   Clinicians work with patients to make sure they comprehend the recovery-stabilization-resolution-integration cycle as it relates to relapses or serious worsening of symptoms.

TRANSIENCE OF PHASE 4   Clinicians remind patients that most people attain integration for periods of time at best. The issues that bothered patients during Phase 2 and 3 may reemerge, and life or illness crises can throw them back into Phase 1. Nonetheless, patients have learned how to respond and where to find useful and supportive resources.

Psychological Domain

MAINTENANCE OF NEW SELF   Patients need to have a firm grasp on their new self before they go unaided into the world. Clinicians can help them establish ways to maintain this new amalgam of old and new self and review its viability under stress.

FREE WILL   Clinicians emphasize that patients daily exercise their free will in committing to the phase processes they have learned. Their choice involves largely unrecognized hard work, but it is worth the effort because of the better life it makes possible.

CONTINUED CREATIVE WORK AND NARRATIVE   Clinicians encourage patients to continue their creative activities or initiate new ones. They predict for patients that the creative impulse will follow a cyclic period of its own, with times of great imaginative richness, but other times when the impulse slacks off. Clinicians also recommend that patients continue to compose and revise their private illness narrative even after they leave formal therapy (Axtell, 1999; Longmore, 1995; Pastio, 1995; Wade, 1994a, 1994b).

CONTINUED MEANING DEVELOPMENT   Clinicians also support patients in their ongoing spiritual or emotional growth. They remind patients that periodically they will need to review and renew the conclusions they have reached so that meaning in their lives does not become flat or stale. In Phase 4, the search for meaning spreads over patients' entire lives and into all four areas of activity. They no longer concentrate solely on their personal place in the universe. They seek to locate the meaning of everyday activities. They explore what they contribute in family and social relationships. They examine their work to see whether that is meaningful. They also look at how their sense of meaning applies to others in the universe. They become seekers in every sense of the word, especially seekers of meaning (Axtell, 1999; Longmore, 1995; Pastio, 1995; Wade, 1994a, 1994b).

LIVING WITH PARADOX   Phase 4 patients take on the difficult task of living with paradox. They find worth in endurance and exhibit faith in themselves and their future despite the chronicity and ambiguity of their situation (Albrecht & Devlieger, 1999; Larson, 1998; Schaefer, 1995).

Social-Interactive Domain

EXPANDING SOCIAL ACTIVITY AND RECRUITING "INTEGRATED SUPPORTS" Clinicians urge patients to continue their creative and social action. They support and encourage patients in their recruitment, development, and maintenance of supporters for their new integrated selves. Phase 4 patients not only reject society's rejection, but may actively work to change social attitudes and to protect and inform those who have only recently begun to suffer from CFS. Phase 4 patients further show their integration of suffering through their creative work, which points to their belief that even people in unpromising situations can add richness and substance to life (Axtell, 1999; Longmore, 1995; Pastio, 1995; Wade, 1994a, 1994b).

NEW JOBS, NEW VOCATIONS If called on, clinicians may carry out workplace interventions, but Phase 4 patients often find themselves engaging in totally new and different work or vocational activities. As they have come to value their authenticity, Phase 4 patients increasingly want to expend their energy only in meaningful ways, so if their physical condition permits, they seek jobs or volunteer work that supports causes they care about.

COUNTERTRANSFERENTIAL ISSUES IN PHASE 4

Attachment, Loss, and Pride It is not unusual for clinicians to feel attachment to their Phase 4 patients. They can feel grief and loss that the patients are leaving the practice, but at the same time great pride in all that the patients have accomplished. In the darkest times, their patients have courageously continued. They have believed in the clinicians' faith that the process would work for them, even when they may have had little personal faith that it would do so (Nouwen, 1972).

CLINICAL STANCE IN PHASE 4

Integrating the Illness into a Full Life Clinicians support the free-will commitment of patients to engage in the "daily acts of bravery" that living with illness requires. They support their patients' social and creative action and encourage them in their efforts to live with the paradox or mystery of life. Clinicians carry out their parallel process of integration. They affirm the desirability and necessity for patients to integrate their suffering into their lives. And then they release them to act for themselves independently in the world.

SPIRITUAL/PHILOSOPHICAL PERSPECTIVE IN PHASE 4

Increased Awareness on All Levels Phase 4 patients have increasingly heightened awareness of meaning on all levels of their existence. This makes them demand more from everything they do, even if they must live with pain and limitations.

Meaning—A Never-Ending Search Phase 4 patients have become seekers for the rest of their lives. Time and events in life are constantly shaking up perceptions that once seemed clear and eternal. They know that they may never answer all the questions, but they find satisfaction in pursuing the process and experiencing brief moments of illumination.

Bottom-Line Truth   Truth or authenticity is the bottom line for Phase 4 patients. When they are in that true place that has meaning, they can live in the mystery of a universe where very bad things can happen to good people, or just ordinary people. The rest of the time, like most people, patients struggle with the paradoxes of life and fight to fend off doubts, fears, and pains. Yet even here, in the battle itself, meaning and transcendence may be found.

REFERENCES

Aberbach, D. (1989). Creativity and the survivor: The struggle for mastery. *International Review of Psycho-Analysis, 16*(3), 273–286.

Agnetti, G. (1997). Facing chronic illness within the family: A systems approach. *New Trends in Experimental and Clinical Psychiatry, 13*(2), 133–139.

Albrecht, G. L., & Devlieger, P. J. (1999). The disability paradox: High quality of life against all odds. *Social Science and Medicine, 48*(8), 977–988.

Alexandris, A., & Vaslamatzis, G. (Eds.). (1993). *Counter-transference: Theory, technique, teaching*. London: Karanc Books.

Alonzo, A. A. (2000). The experience of chronic illness and posttraumatic stress disorder: The consequences of cumulative adversity. *Social Science and Medicine, 50*, 1475–1484.

Alonzo, A. A., & Reynolds, V. R. (1996). Emotions and care-seeking during acute myocardial infarction: A model for intervention. *International Journal of Sociology and Social Policy, 16*(9/10), 97–122.

Anderton, J. M., Elfert, H., & Lai, M. (1989). Ideology in the clinical context: Chronic illness, ethnicity, and the discourse on normalization. *Sociology of Health and Illness, 11*(3), 253–278.

Axtell, S. (1999). Disabilities and chronic illness identity: Interviews with lesbians and bisexual women and their partners. *Journal of Gay, Lesbian, and Bisexual Identity, 4*(1), 53–72.

Baker, C., & Stern, P. N. (1993). Finding meaning in chronic illness as the key to self care. *Canadian Journal of Nursing Research, 25*(2), 23–36.

Baumann, S. L. (1997). Contrasting two approaches in a community-based nursing practice with older adults: The medical model and Parse's nursing theory. *Nursing Science Quarterly, 10*(3), 124–130.

Beardslee, W. R., Versage, E. M., & Gladstone T. G. (1998). Children of affectively ill parents: A review of the past 10 years. *Journal of the American Academy of Child and Adolescent Psychiatry, 37*(11), 1134–1141.

Bedell, G. (2000). Daily life for eight urban gay men with HIV/AIDS. *American Journal of Occupational Therapy, 54*(2), 197–206.

Belza, B., Henke, C. J., Yelin, E. H., Epstein, W. V., & Gilliss, C. L. (1993). Correlates of fatigue in older adults with rheumatoid arthritis. *Nursing Research, 42*, 93–99.

Bezard, E., Impert, C., & Gross, C. E. (1998). Experimental models of Parkinson's disease: From the static to the dynamic. *Review of Neuroscience, 9*(2), 71–90.

Blank, A. S. (1993). The longitudinal course of posttraumatic stress disorders. In J. R. Davidson & E. B. Foa (Eds.), *Posttraumatic stress disorder: DSM-IV and beyond* (pp. 3–22). Washington, DC: American Psychiatric Press.

Bose, J. (1995). Trauma, depression, and mourning. *Contemporary Psychoanalysis, 31*(3), 399–407.

Boyer, K. M. (1999). Disability benefits: What is the social security administration thinking? *Journal of Medical Practice Management, 14*(6), 297–300.

Bull, M., & Jervis, L. (1997). Strategies used by chronically ill older women and their caregiving daughters in managing posthospital care. *Journal of Advanced Nursing, 25,* 541–547.

Canam, C., & Acorn, S. (1999). Quality of life for family care givers with people with chronic health problems. *Rehabilitative Nursing, 24*(5), 192–196, 200.

Carbone, L. (1999). An interdisciplinary approach to the rehabilitation of open-heart surgical patients. *Rehabilitation Nursing, 24*(2), 55–61.

Carter, B., & McGoldrick, M. (Eds.). (1988). *The changing family life cycle: A framework for family therapy* (2nd ed.). New York: Gardner Press.

Cutcliffe, J. R. (1998). Hope, counseling and complicated bereavement reactions. *Journal of Advanced Nursing, 28*(4), 754–761.

DiClemente, C. C. (1991). Motivational interviewing and the stages of change. In W. R. Miller & S. Rollnick (Eds.), *Motivational interviewing: Preparing people for change* (pp. 191–202). New York: Guilford Press.

Doherty, W. J., & Colangelo, N. (1984). The family FIRO model: A modest proposal for organizing family treatment. *Journal of Marital and Family Therapy, 10*(1), 19–29.

Doherty, W. J., Colangelo, N., & Hovander, D. (1991). Priority setting in family change and clinical practice: The family FIRO model. *Family Practice, 30,* 227–240.

Doherty, W. J., McDaniel, W. J., & Hepworth, J. (1994). Medical family therapy: An emerging arena for family therapy. *Association for Family Therapy, 16,* 31–46.

Drench, M. E. (1994). Changes in body image secondary to disease and injury. *Rehabilitation Nursing, 19*(1), 31–36.

Dyson, J., Cobb, M., & Forman, D. (1997). The meaning of spirituality: A literature review. *Journal of Advanced Nursing, 26*(6), 1183–1188.

Edwards, G. M. (1993). Art therapy with HIV-positive patients: Hardiness, creativity and meaning. *Arts in Psychotherapy, 20*(4), 325–333.

Engel, G. L. (1997, April 8). The need for a new medical model: A challenge for biomedicine. *Science, 196,* 129–136.

Faison, K. J., Faria, S. H., & Frank, D. (1999). Caregivers of chronically ill elderly: Perceived burden. *Journal of Community Health Nursing, 16*(4), 243–253.

Fennell, P. A. (1993). A systematic, four-stage progressive model for mapping the CFIDS experience. *CFIDS Chronicle,* Summer, 40–46.

Fennell, P. A. (1995). The four progressive stages of the CFS experience: A coping tool for patients. *Journal of Chronic Fatigue Syndrome, 1*(3/4), 69–79.

Fennell, P. A. (1998). Capturing the different phases of the CFS illness. *CFIDS Chronicle, 11*(3), 3–16.

Fennell, P. A. (2001). *The chronic illness workbook: Strategies and solutions for taking back your life.* San Francisco: New Harbinger.

Fennell, P. A. (2004). *Managing chronic illness using the Four-Phase treatment approach: A mental health professional's guide to helping chronically ill people.* Hoboken, NJ: Wiley.

Figley, C. R. (1995). *Compassion fatigue.* New York: Brunner/Mazel.

Frankl, V. E. (1983). Meaninglessness: A challenge of psychologists. In T. Millon (Ed.), *Theories of personalities and psychopathology* (3rd ed., pp. 256–263). New York: Holt, Rinehart and Winston.

Friedberg, F., & Jason, L. A. (1998). *Understanding chronic fatigue syndrome: An empirical guide to assessment and treatment.* Washington, DC: American Psychological Association.

Fullilove, M. T., Lown, A., & Fullilove, R. E. (1992). Crack 'hos and skeezers: Traumatic experiences of women crack users. *Journal of Sex Research, 29*(2), 275–287.

Furst, G., Gerber, L. H., & Smith, C. (1985). *Rehabilitation through learning: Energy conversation and joint protection—A workbook for persons with rheumatoid arthritis.* Washington, DC: U.S. Department of Health and Human Services, NIH.

Furst, G., Gerber, L. H., & Smith, C. (1997). *Energy conservation: A workbook for persons with fatigue.* Washington, DC: U.S. Department of Health and Human Services, NIH.

Gignac, M. A., & Cott, C. (1998). A conceptual model of independence and dependence for adults with chronic physical illness and disability. *Social Science and Medicine, 47*(6), 739–753.

Gignac, M. A., Cott, C., & Badley, E. M. (2000). Adaptation to chronic illness and disability and its relationship to perceptions of independence and dependence. *Journals of Gerontology: Series B, Psychological Sciences and Social Sciences, 55,* 362–372.

Gilden, J. L., Hendryx, M. S., Clar, S., Casia, C., & Singh, S. P. (1992). Diabetes support groups improve health care of older diabetic patients. *Journal of the American Geriatrics Society, 40,* 147–150.

Gulick, E. (1991). Reliability and validity of the Work Assessment Scale for persons with multiple sclerosis. *Nursing Research, 40,* 107–112.

Hall, J. A., Stein, T. S., Roter, D. L., & Rieser, N. (1999). Inaccuracies in physicians' perceptions of their patients. *Medical Care, 37*(11), 1164–1168.

Hatcher, R. L. (1973). Insight and self-observation. *Journal of American Psychoanalytical Association, 21*(2), 377–398.

Hellstrom, O., Bullington, J., Karlsson, G., Lindqvist, P., & Mattson, B. (1999). A phenomenological study of fibromyalgia: Patient perspectives. *Scandinavian Journal of Primary Health Care, 17*(1), 11–16.

Helseth, L. D. (1999). Primary care physicians' perceptions of diabetes management: A balancing act. *Journal of Family Practice, 48*(1), 37–42.

Henderson, P. A. (1997). Psychosocial adjustment of adult cancer survivors: Their needs and counselors' interventions. *Journal of Counseling and Development, 75,* 188–194.

Hinojosa, J., & Kramer, P. (1997). Statement—fundamental concepts of occupational therapy: Occupation, purposeful activity, and function. *American Journal of Occupational Therapy, 51*(10), 864–866.

Hinrichsen, G. A., Revenson, T. A., & Shinn, M. (1985). Does self-help help? An empirical investigation of scoliosis peer support groups. *Journal of Social Issues, 41*(1), 65–87.

Holm-Hadulla, R. (1996). The creative aspect of dynamic psychotherapy: Parallels between the construction of experienced reality in the literary and the psychotherapeutic process. *American Journal of Psychotherapy, 50*(3), 360–369.

Horowitz, M. H. (1987). Some notes on insight and its failures. *Psychoanalytic Quarterly, 56*(1), 177–196.

Houser, R., & Chace, A. (1993). Job satisfaction of people with disabilities placed through a project with industry. *Journal of Rehabilitation, 59,* 45–48.

Howard, B. S., & Howard, J. R. (1997). Occupation as spiritual activity. *American Journal of Occupational Therapy, 51*(3), 181–185.

Humphreys, K. (1997, Spring). Individual and social benefits of mutual aid self-help groups. *Social Policy,* 12–19.

Jason, L. A., Fennell, P. A., Klein, S., Fricano, G., Halpert, J., & Taylor, R. R. (1999). An investigation of the different phases of the CFS illness. *Journal of Chronic Fatigue Syndrome, 5*(3/4), 35–54.

Jason, L. A., Fennell, P. A., & Taylor, R. R. (Eds.) (2003). *Handbook of chronic fatigue syndrome.* Hoboken, NJ: Wiley.

Jason, L. A., Fennell, P. A., Taylor, R. R., Fircano, G., & Halpert, J. A. (2000). An empirical verification of the Fennell Phases of the CFS illness. *Journal of Chronic Fatigue Syndrome, 6*(1), 47–56.

Jason, L. A., Fricano, G., Taylor, R. R., Halpert, J., Fennell, P. A., Klein, et al. (2000). Chronic fatigue syndrome: An examination of the phases. *Journal of Clinical Psychology,* December, 1497–1508.

Jobst, K. A., Shostak, D., & Whitehouse, P. J. (1999). Diseases of meaning, manifestations of health, and metaphor. *Journal of Alternative Complementary Medicine, 5*(6), 495–502.

Jung, C. (1990). *Collected works of Carl Jung* (Vols. 6, 7, 13, 16). Princeton, NJ: Princeton University Press.

Kissane, D. W. (2000). Psychospiritual and existential distress: The challenge for palliative care. *Australian Family Physician, 29*(11), 1022–1025.

Klein, R., & Schermer, V. (2000). *Group psychotherapy for psychological trauma.* New York: Guilford Press.

Kornfield, J. (1993). *A path-with-heart.* New York: Bantam Books.

Krupp, L. B. (1989). The Fatigue Severity Scale: Application to patients with multiple sclerosis and systemic lupus erythematosis. *Archives of Neurology, 46,* 1121–1123.

Kuipers, J. (1991). Mexican-Americans. In J. N. Giger & R. E. Davidhizar (Eds.), *Transcultural nursing: Assessment and intervention.* St. Louis, MO: Mosby Year Book.

Larson, E. (1998). Reframing the meaning of disability of families: The embrace of paradox. *Social Science and Medicine, 47*(7), 865–875.

Levine, S. (1979). *A gradual awakening.* New York: Doubleday.

Lindy, J. D., Grace, M. C., & Green, B. L. (1981). Survivors: Outreach to a reluctant population. *American Journal of Orthopsychiatry, 51*(3), 468–478.

Longmore, P. K. (1995, September/October). The second phase: From disability rights to disability culture. *Disability Rag and Resource,* 4–11.

Magid, C. S. (2000). Pain, suffering, and meaning. *Journal of the American Medical Association, 283*(1), 114.

Marbach, J. J. (1999). Medically unexplained chronic orofacial pain. *Medical Clinics of North America, 83*(3), 691–710.

Mattoon, M. A. (1985). *Jungian psychology in perspective.* New York: Free Press.

McHorney, C. A., Ware, J. E., Jr., Lu, J. F., & Sherbourne, C. D. (1994). The MOS 36-item short-form health survey (SF-36): III. Tests of data quality, scaling assumptions, and reliability across diverse patient groups. *Medical Care, 32,* 40–66.

McHorney, C. A., Ware, J. E., & Raczek, A. E. (1993). The MOS 36-item short form health survey (SF-36): II. Psychometric and clinical test of validity in measuring physical and mental health constructs. *Medical Care, 31,* 247–263.

Mercer, R. J. (1989). Response to life-span development: A review of theory and practice for families with chronically ill members. *Scholarly Inquiry for Nursing Practice, 3*(1), 23–27.

Michael, S. R. (1996). Integrating chronic illness into one's life: A phenomenological inquiry. *Journal of Holistic Nursing, 14*(3), 251–267.

Morse, J. M. (1997). Responding to threats to integrity of self. *Advances in Nursing Science, 19*(4), 21–36.

Nash, K., & Kramer, K. D. (1993). Self-help for sickle cell disease in African American communities. *Journal of Applied Behavioral Science, 29,* 202–215.

Newby, N. M. (1996). Chronic illness and the family life-cycle. *Journal of Advanced Nursing, 23,* 786–791.

Nicassio, P. M., & Smith, T. W. (Eds.). (1995). *Managing chronic illness: A biopsychosocial perspective.* Washington, DC: American Psychological Association.

Nouwen, H. J. (1972). *The wounded healer.* New York: Doubleday.

Olkin, R. (1999). *What psychotherapists should know about disability.* New York: Guilford Press.

Pastio, D. (1995, September/October). Identifying with our culture-ourselves. *Disability Rag and Resource,* p. 11.

Pearlman, L. A., & Saakvitne, K. W. (1995). *Trauma and the therapist.* New York: Norton.

Perrig, W. J., & Grob, A. (Eds.). (2000). *The control of unwanted states and psychological health.* Mahwah, NJ: Erlbaum.

Polatajko, H. J. (2000). Dynamic performance analysis: A framework for understanding occupational performance. *American Journal of Occupational Therapy, 54*(1), 65–72.

Prigerson, H. G., Shear, M. K., Frank, E., Beery, L. C., Silberman, R., Prigerson, J., et al. (1997). Traumatic grief: A case of loss-induced trauma. *American Journal of Psychiatry, 154*(7), 1003–1009.

Primeau, L. A. (1996). Work and leisure: Transcending the dichotomy. *American Journal of Occupational Therapy, 50*(7), 569–577.

Prochaska, J. O., DiClemente, C. C., & Norcross, J. C. (1992). In search of how people change: Applications to addictive behavior. *American Psychologist, 47*(9), 1102–1114.

Prochaska, J. O., Norcross, J. C., & DiClemente, C. C. (1994). The Transtheoretical Model of Change and HIV prevention: A review. *Health Education Quarterly, 21*(4), 471–486.

Prochaska, J. O., & Velicer, W. F. (1997). The Transtheoretical Model of Health Behavior Change. *American Journal of Health Promotion, 12*(1), 38–48.

Pulver, S. E. (1992). Psychic change: Insight or relationship? *International Journal of Psychoanalysis, 73*(Pt. 2), 199–208.

Rankin, S., & Weekes, D. P. (1989). Life-span development: A review of theory and practice for families with chronically ill members. *Scholarly Inquiry for Nursing Practice, 3*(1), 3–22.

Reberio, K. L., & Polgar, J. M. (1999). Enabling occupational performance optimal experiences in theory. *Canadian Journal of Occupational Therapy, 66*(1), 14–22.

Register, C. (1987). *The chronic illness experience.* Center City, MN: Hazelton.

Reiss, D., Gonzalez, S., & Kramer, N. (1986). Family process, chronic illness, and death: On the weakness of strong bonds. *Archives of General Psychiatry, 43,* 795–804.

Roessler, R. T., & Rumrill, P., Jr. (1998). Reducing workplace barriers to enhance job satisfaction: An important postemployment service for employees with chronic illness. *Journal of Vocational Rehabilitation, 10,* 219–229.

Roessler, R. T., & Sumner, G. (1997). Employer opinions about accommodating employees with chronic illness. *Journal of Applied Rehabilitation Counseling, 28*(3), 29–34.

Rolland, J. S. (1984). Toward a psychosocial typology of chronic and life-threatening illness. *Family Systems Medicine, 2*(3), 245–261.

Rolland, J. S. (1987). Chronic illness and the life cycle: A conceptual framework. *Family Process, 26,* 203–221.

Rood, R. P. (1996). Patient and physician responsibility in the treatment of chronic illness. *American Behavioral Scientist, 39*(6), 729–751.

Rosman, B. L. (1988). Family development and the impact of a child's chronic illness. In C. J. Falicov (Ed.), *Family transitions: Continuity and change over the life cycle* (pp. 293–309). New York: Guilford Press.

Saigh, P. A. & Bremner, J. E. (Eds.). (1999). *Posttraumatic stress disorder: A comprehensive text.* Needham Heights, MA: Allyn & Bacon.

Satcher, J. (1992). Responding to employer concerns about the ADA and job applicants with disabilities. *Journal of Applied Rehabilitation Counseling, 23*(3), 37–40.

Satcher, J., & Hendren, G. R. (1991). Acceptance of the Americans with Disabilities Act of 1990 by persons preparing to enter the business field. *Journal of Applied Rehabilitation Counseling, 22*(2), 15–18.

Scambler, G., & Hopkins, A. (1990). Generating a model of epileptic stigma: The role of qualitative analysis. *Social Science and Medicine, 30*(11), 1187–1194.

Schaefer, K. M. (1995). Women living in paradox: Loss and discovery in chronic illness. *Holistic Nursing Practice, 9*(3), 63–74.

Schlesinger, M., Druss, B., & Thomas, T. (1999). No exit? The effect of health status on dissatisfaction and disenrollment from health plans. *Health Services Research, 34*(2), 547–579.

Schwartz-Salant, N., & Stein, M. (Eds.). (1995). *Transference countertransference.* Wilmette, IL: Chiron.

Scott, M. J., & Stradling, S. G. (1994). Posttraumatic stress disorder without the trauma. *British Journal of Clinical Psychology, 33,* 71–74.

Silbermann, L. (1967). Reflections on working through and insight. *Israeli Annals of Psychiatry and Related Disciplines, 5*(1), 53–60.

Small, S., & Lamb, M. (1999). Fatigue in chronic illness: The experience of individuals with chronic obstructive pulmonary disease and with asthma. *Journal of Advanced Nursing, 30*(2), 469–478.

Stein, M. (1996). *Practicing wholeness.* New York: Continuum International.

Stephens, W. M. (1989). Six ways to guarantee denial of your patient's social security disability benefits. *Journal of the Tennessee Medical Association, 2*(5), 273.

Sugarek, N. J., Dyo, R., & Holmes, B. (1988). Locus of control and beliefs about cancer in a multiethnic clinic population. *Oncology Nursing Forum, 15*(4), 481–486.

Sumner, C. H. (1998). Recognizing and responding to spiritual distress. *American Journal of Nursing, 98*(1), 26–30.

Sutton, S. R. (1997). Transtheoretical model of behavior change. In A. Baum, S. Newman, J. Weinman, R. West, & C. McManus (Eds.), *Cambridge handbook of psychology, health and medicine* (pp. 180–183). Cambridge, MA: Cambridge University Press.

Tait, R. C., Chibnall, J. T., & Richardson, W. D. (1990). Litigation and employment status: Effects on patients with chronic pain. *Pain, 43,* 37–46.

Turner, R. J., & Lloyd, D. A. (1995, December). Lifetime traumas and mental health: The significance of cumulative adversity. *Journal of Health and Social Behavior, 36,* 360–376.

van der Kolk, B. A., McFarlane, A. E., & Weisaeth, L. (Eds.). (1996). *Traumatic stress: The effects of overwhelming stress on mind, body and society.* New York: Guilford Press.

van Eijk, J. T., & de Haan, M. (1998). Care for the chronically ill: The future role of health care professionals and their patients. *Patient Education and Counseling, 35,* 233–240.

Van Hoof, E., Coomins, D., Cluydts, R., de Meirleir, K. (2003a). *Fennell phases: Toward a management program for patients with chronic fatigue syndrome.* Manuscript in preparation.

Van Hoof, E., Coomins, D., Cluydts, R., de Meirleir, K. (2003b). *Psychological management of CFRS by the Fennell Phases.* Manuscript in preparation.

Vrana, S., & Lauterbach, D. (1994). Prevalence of traumatic events and posttraumatic psychological symptoms in a nonclinical sample of college students. *Journal of Traumatic Stress, 7*, 289–302.

Wade, C. M. (1994a, November/December). Creating a disability aesthetic in the arts. *Disability Rag and Resource*, 29–31.

Wade, C. M. (1994b, September/October). Identity. *Disability Rag and Resource*, 32–36.

Wagner, E. H., Glasgow, R. E., Davis, C., Bonomi, A. E., Provost, L., McCulloch, D., et al. (2001). Quality improvement in chronic illness care: A collaborative approach. *Joint Commission Journal on Quality Improvement, 27*(2), 63–80.

Ware, N. C. (1998). Sociosomatics and illness course in chronic fatigue syndrome. *Psychosomatic Medicine, 60*, 394–401.

Willems, D. (2000). Managing one's body using self-management techniques: Practicing autonomy. *Theoretical Medicine and Bioethics, 21*(1), 23–38.

Wilson, J. P., & Lindy, J. D. (Eds.). (1994). *Countertransference in the treatment of PTSD.* New York: Guilford Press.

Woodgate, R. L. (1998). Adolescents' perspective of chronic illness: It's hard. *Journal of Pediatric Nursing, 13*(4), 210–223.

Yeheskel, A., Biderman, A., Borkan, J. M., & Herman, J. (2000). A course for teaching patient-centered medicine to family medicine residents. *Academic Medicine, 75*(5), 494–497.

CHAPTER 23

Cognitive-Behavioral Therapies

GIJS BLEIJENBERG, JUDITH PRINS, and ELLEN BAZELMANS

IN TWO SYSTEMATIC reviews (Reid, Chalder, Cleare, Hotopf, & Wessely, 2000; Whiting et al., 2001), cognitive-behavioral therapy (CBT) and graded exercise therapy proved to be consistently effective treatments for chronic fatigue syndrome (CFS). In this chapter, we first define cognitive-behavioral therapy and explain what is known about the indications and contraindications for its use in chronic fatigue syndrome. The practice of CBT as an outpatient treatment is then discussed in detail and is illustrated with two case studies. Pitfalls for therapists and other ways of applying CBT are also discussed.

WHAT IS COGNITIVE-BEHAVIORAL THERAPY FOR CHRONIC FATIGUE SYNDROME?

Cognitive-behavioral therapy is a general psychotherapeutic method directed at changing condition-related cognitions and behaviors. In controlled studies, CBT has appeared to be effective in conditions such as panic disorder, depression, obsessive-compulsive disorder (OCD), and irritable bowel syndrome (IBS) (see, e.g., Greene & Blanchard, 1994; Hawton, Salkovskis, Kirk, & Clark, 1989; Payne & Blanchard, 1995; Van Dulmen, Fennis, & Bleijenberg, 1996; Vollmer & Blanchard, 1998). Therapy is directed at specific cognitions and behaviors relevant for each disorder, which implies that a clinician would not use the same CBT for depression as for IBS or OCD. Thus, CBT for CFS has to be directed at the cognitions and behaviors related to that syndrome.

The absence of a somatic explanation for CFS does not exclude the possibility that a somatic event may have triggered the symptoms. Therefore, it is necessary to distinguish the factors initiating the complaints, or symptoms, from the factors that perpetuate them. Facilitating factors can also be differentiated. These factors make people more vulnerable to the development of CFS. Little conclusive knowledge is available about the facilitating and initiating factors. In contrast, considerable data can be found about the perpetuating factors in CFS. CBT is aimed at changing these latter factors.

DEVELOPMENT OF A MODEL FOR
PERPETUATING FACTORS IN CFS

Vercoulen et al. (1998) have developed a model of perpetuating factors in CFS. In this model (Figure 23.1), investigators tested to what extent chronic fatigue could be explained by somatic attributions, sense of control over symptoms (self-efficacy), physical activity level, functional impairment, focussing on bodily symptoms and depression. It was found that depression could not be fitted into the model. Depression does not seem to play an important role in perpetuating the complaints. This is in agreement with findings in follow-up studies on CFS (e.g., Clark et al., 1995). The other factors could be included in the model on the basis of structural equation modeling. The model appeared to explain fatigue in CFS patients but did not explain fatigue in MS patients (Vercoulen et al., 1998). A strong focus on bodily symptoms, low levels of physical activity, and a poor sense of control contribute to increased severity of the fatigue and functional impairment. Strong somatic attributions have only an indirect influence on fatigue, via lower levels of physical activity.

Most factors in the model of perpetuating factors in CFS have been found in other studies as well (e.g., by Heijmans 1998; Wessely, Hotopf, & Sharpe, 1998). Recently, the model was tested on new longitudinal data, and again it appeared to fit. Because the model shows causal relations between perpetuating factors and complaints, it is an appropriate basis for treatment. However, the model also has limitations. First, it does not include factors like social support and fear of symptoms of fatigue. Second, the model mainly applies to patients with a long duration of complaints. As yet, not all aspects of the model have been shown to be valid for CFS patients of relatively short duration. It is conceivable that patients do not start focusing on bodily symptoms until the complaints have existed for a longer period. The development of these perpetuating factors over time is not clear.

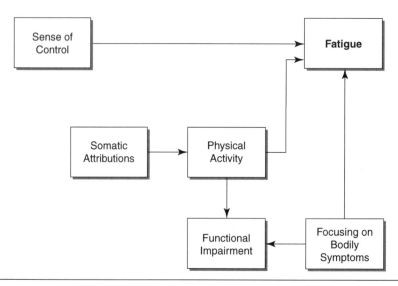

Figure 23.1   Model of CFS, Developed and Tested with LISREL. *Source:* "The persistence of fatigue in chronic fatigue syndrome and multiple sclerosis: Development of a model," by J. H. Vercoulen, O. R. Hommes, C. M. Swanink, P. J. Jongen, J. F. Fennis, J. M. Galama, et al., 1998, *Journal of Psychosomatic Research, 45,* pp. 507–517.

The model of perpetuating factors in CFS has been the basis for the development of the cognitive-behavioral treatment (Prins & Bleijenberg, 1999; Prins et al., 2001). Because of the central role of cognitions, also in relation to activity, the treatment starts with changing cognitions. Complaint-enhancing cognitions that patients manifest include a strong focus on bodily symptoms, a decided tendency to attribute their symptoms to physical causes, and a belief that they are powerless and cannot do anything about the symptoms. The CBT protocol for CFS is directed at decreasing somatic attributions and the patients' focus on bodily symptoms, increasing their sense of control over their symptoms, and restoring the balance in activity patterns.

CONTROLLED STUDIES INTO CBT FOR CFS

In the early 1990s, clinical trials with CFS patients revealed that cognitive and behavioral interventions had a favorable effect on CFS symptoms. The first uncontrolled study was published about the effect of CBT in 27 CFS patients (Butler, Chalder, Ron, & Wessely, 1991). The treatment was aimed at enhancing self-efficacy and encouraging activities that patients had been avoiding because of the complaints. The treatment proved effective in 22 of the participating patients. A 4-year follow-up revealed that the effect was still present in 80% of the patients (Bonner, Ron, Chalder, Butler, & Wessely, 1994).

Another open study conducted during the same period found that CBT was effective in reducing depressive complaints, but not the fatigue-related symptoms. In this particular CBT, however, the focus was on acceptance of the CFS-related limitations and not on activity enhancement (Friedberg & Krupp, 1994). Subsequently, investigators carried out randomized controlled studies into the effects of CBT, and these were evaluated in several review studies (Price & Couper, 2000; Reid et al., 2000; Whiting et al., 2001).

In the first controlled study (Lloyd et al., 1993), both CBT and medical treatment were combined with immunotherapy or placebo. Thus, treatment was never stand-alone CBT. The therapy consisted of a mere 6 sessions of 30 to 60 minutes during which the patients were encouraged to be more active in the home and an attempt was made to reduce feelings of helplessness. As was to be expected, results were disappointing. None of the groups treated had a larger effect than those receiving the standard medical treatment. The CBT was too short, and the combination with immunotherapy or placebo aggravated the somatic attributions instead of reducing them.

Sharpe et al. (1996) compared CBT with a control condition without treatment. The treatment consisted of 16 weekly sessions and was aimed at cognition changes and a gradual increase in activity. The controls only received standard medical care, mainly consisting of reassurance that no organic disease had been diagnosed. Compared with the controls, a significantly greater number of patients who had received CBT improved as far as their physical functioning was concerned at 12-month follow-up. Improvement mostly occurred during the follow-up period, which can be best explained from the relatively short treatment duration. However, since the control group did not receive any treatment, it remained unclear whether the treatment effect was to be attributed to elements of the CBT or to nonspecific factors such as attention by the therapist.

This aspect was controlled for in the study by Deale, Chalder, Marks, and Wessely (1997) in which they compared CBT and relaxation therapy. Both treatments consisted of an average of 13 sessions spread over 6 months. The CBT was educational with an emphasis on behavioral changes. Not until the patient had made certain advances in activity levels was cognitive restructuring started. The relaxation therapy entailed progressive muscle relaxation, visualization, and exercises inducing rapid relaxation. Sixty CFS patients were randomly assigned to CBT or relaxation therapy. A drawback of this study was that the same therapist treated all the patients. The CBT proved to have a significantly greater effect than the relaxation therapy and was still present at a 6-month follow-up. After conclusion of the CBT, the somatic attributions were unchanged, and they were not found to predict a poorer outcome. Attitudes toward the avoidance of activity had changed in the CBT group, but not in the control group. This change coincided with a positive treatment outcome (Deale, Chalder, & Wessely, 1998). The condition of the immune system did not change during the treatment, nor was it predictive of improvement following CBT (Peakman, Deale, Field, Mahalingam, & Wessely, 1997). At five years follow-up, lasting benefits of CBT were found in the patients of this study (Deale, Husain, Chalder, & Wessely, 2001).

Wearden et al. (1998) studied the effects of the antidepressive drug fluoxetine or a placebo both with and without graded exercise therapy. No placebo was offered for the graded exercise therapy, as was provided in the study that follows. Of the 136 patients, 96 completed the 6-month program and could be included in the assessment. There were more dropouts among those who had been prescribed graded exercise therapy. Merely one-third of the patients completed this 6-month program. Nevertheless, graded exercise therapy showed significant improvement in fatigue symptoms and functional impairments, whereas the effect of fluoxetine was not significant.

To investigate whether gradually increasing the levels of physical activity alone suffices in treatment of CFS patients, Fulcher and White (1997) compared graded exercise therapy with a treatment combining flexibility and relaxation sessions. Whereas the rationale for most types of CBT for CFS is fear and avoidance of activity, the treatment proposed by Fulcher and White is based on a physiological model of deconditioning. For 3 months, their patients worked on their physical condition on a weekly basis. The gradual increase of physical activity resulted in a significantly greater number of self-reports claiming improvement than the combination of relaxation and flexibility exercises. Whether this was a sustained effect could not be established because, following the study, over half of the controls also received graded exercise therapy.

The first treatment protocol developed by our own research group has much in common and can best be compared with the programs by Sharpe and Deale (Prins & Bleijenberg, 1999). The treatment consists of 16 sessions. The initial sessions deal with impeding cognitions. Subsequently, patients practice recognizing and respecting limits, and finally, increasing the activity levels becomes the central component. The main goal of the treatment is full recovery, the supplementary objective being return to the workplace. This treatment protocol was tested in a randomized controlled trial in 270 CFS patients (Prins et al., 2001). CBT was compared with two conditions: guided support groups and natural course. CBT proved to yield significantly greater effects on fatigue symptoms and functional impairments than the other two conditions. One of the most noteworthy aspects of this study was that therapists who had no prior experience with CBT for CFS administered the therapy, which implies that this type of CBT is transferable.

Seen in a 4-year perspective, CBT as applied in this study proved to be cost-effective (when productivity costs were taken into account) compared with natural course. However, the treatment protocol was not effective for all patients. In contrast to the relatively active CFS patients, who specifically benefited from the treatment, the patients with a low or passive activity pattern hardly did. The nature of the first protocol may explain this finding. Learning to cope with limitations is of little relevance to a group of patients who already are extremely low in activity. This method strongly reinforces passive CFS patients in their inactivity. In addition, the protocol paid too little attention to those cognitions that maintain the low levels of activity in passive CFS patients. The cognition that activity negatively affects the symptoms leads to a fear of activity and a fear of aggravated complaints, which both become debilitating factors in the activity-enhancing stage of the program.

Based on these findings, and in addition to the treatment protocol evaluated in the preceding study (Prins et al., 2001), a second treatment program was developed specifically targeting CFS patients with a low activity pattern. This second protocol has since been amply applied in clinical practice and is presently being tested. Both treatment programs are described later in this chapter.

Powell, Bentall, Nye, and Edwards (2001) examined the effectiveness of shorter treatments. In their program, all CFS patients were given the following explanation for their complaints. Prolonged decrease in activity has led to a deterioration of the physical condition, both at the cardiovascular and muscle level. This gives rise to complaints, even at a low level of activity, that are aggravated by desynchronization of the circadian rhythm. A gradual increase in activity may turn this negative, downward spiral into an upward one. In this way, the patients were encouraged and motivated to gradually expand their activities. The patients, who had all received the same explanation, were randomized over a control group receiving standardized medical treatment and three treatment conditions ranging from minimal to maximal intervention: 7 sessions; 12 sessions, of which 9 were by telephone; and 15 sessions, of which 5 were by telephone. At a 12-month follow-up, the patients in the 3 treatment conditions were found to have improved significantly more in their physical functioning and fatigue symptoms than the controls. There were no differences between these 3 groups. It was concluded that CFS can be successfully treated in fewer sessions. The treatment in this study was administered by a single experienced therapist, which does not lend weight to the conclusions drawn and does not indicate whether a similar result could have been achieved had several therapists participated. Notwithstanding this drawback, the findings from this study are in line with our clinical experience that, compared with less experienced counselors, skilled therapists need fewer sessions to achieve positive results with patients suffering from CFS.

ASPECTS TO CONSIDER BEFORE STARTING CBT

ANALYSIS OF THE COMPLAINTS

Table 23.1 lists questions that can be helpful in the analysis of chronic fatigue. Symptoms are addressed in a very concrete way. It is always helpful to ask patients to describe a normal day (e.g., the day before), and to describe what they do and do not do between the moment they get up until the moment they go to bed.

Table 23.1

Analysis of Complaints

Questions to Help Analyze Chronic Fatigue

Dimension: Somatic

- What are the patient's complaints (symptoms)? What are the associated functional impairments?
- How does the patient spend the day and how do the complaints manifest themselves in the course of the day (description of a normal day)?
- Is this description exemplary of other days? Are there any fluctuations in the occurrence of the complaints?
- When did the complaints mentioned first manifest themselves? In what way?
- Has the patient tried to find (professional) help?

Dimension: Cognitions

- Is the patient satisfied with any physical examinations that have been given?
- What are the patient's views on the causes of the complaints?
- Does the patient see other ways of influencing the complaints?
- Does the patient have a tendency to catastrophize the complaints?
- What views does the patient have on CFS?
- What is the patient's attitude regarding his or her complaints?
- What is the patient's attitude toward a psychological intervention?

Dimension: Emotions

- Does the patient have any feelings of anxiety that the complaints will get worse?
- Is the patient afraid to undertake activities?

Dimension: Behavior

- What medication or diets is the patient on, and what other treatments is the patient undergoing at this moment?
- What does the patient do to prevent complaints from getting worse?
- What activity pattern is typical for this patient (predominantly passive; both active and passive at times, and subsequently passive; still relatively active)?
- What activities does the patient no longer undertake due to the complaints?
- What about the patient's sleep pattern?
- Do the complaints affect the patient's concentration, memory, or other mental activities?
- Do the complaints influence the patient's social activities?
- What were the patient's occupational activities? Since when has the patient stopped working?
- What type of benefit does the patient receive (social, unemployment, or disability)?
- Is the patient involved in any legal procedures in relation to benefits?

Dimension: Social Environment

- What effects do the patient's complaints have on his or her social environment (work, family, or social circle)?
- How do the patient's family members (spouse) react to his or her complaints?
- What are their ideas about the complaints?
- How do they react when the patient is affected by the complaints?

Table 23.1 *Continued*

Questions to Help Analyze the Patient's Work Situation

Does the patient still hold a job? If so, what kind of work does it involve and for how many hours?

Has the patient's work situation changed as a result of the fatigue?

When was the last time the patient worked? When did the patient stop working?

Does the patient still see (former) colleagues from work?

Is there any chance for the patient to return to the (former) job?

Does the patient think his or her employer will be willing to cooperate in this matter?

Are there any problems involving medical examination authorities?

What is the patient's financial status or prospect in this respect?

Has the patient lodged any legal claims or started occupational procedures in relation to the CFS?

In doing so, the therapist can get an idea of the patient's physical, mental, and social activities and impairments. Job histories can also provide insights. Is returning to the same job a possibility? Are Social Security or disability benefits being received, or are legal procedures underway to get financial benefits?

Furthermore, patients' expectations are important. What is their attitude toward CBT? Are patients convinced that they have been sufficiently examined somatically? How strong are the somatic attributions? Are patients prepared to consider their complaints in a nonsomatic way? What about their self-efficacy? It is useful to invite a patient's spouse for the first interview. The partner not only can give hetero-anamnestic information but also can learn about the rationale of the treatment.

At this stage, instruments to assess the degree of fatigue are useful (see, e.g., Chalder Fatigue Scale, Chalder, Berelowitz, Pawlikowska, Watts, & Wessely, 1993; Checklist Individual Strength, Vercoulen et al., 1994; Beurskens et al., 2000; Bültmann et al., 2000; Shortened Fatigue Scale, Alberts, Vercoulen, & Bleijenberg, 2001). Other instruments can assess the extent of the functional impairment (see, e.g., Sickness Impact Profile, Bergner, Bobbit, Carter, & Gilson, 1981; SF-36, Ware & Sherbourne, 1992). Additionally, clinicians can assess patients' sense of control over symptoms (self-efficacy; Prins et al., 2001), causal attributions (Prins et al., 2001), and their focus on bodily symptoms (van der Werf, de Vree, van der Meer, & Bleijenberg, 2002; Vercoulen et al., 1998).

ASSESSMENT OF THE ACTIVITY PATTERN

The activity pattern of the patient determines the type of CBT that should be used. A diagnostic assessment is necessary to establish this pattern. An actometer or accelerometer is best suited for this purpose and allows the easy and accurate measurement of activity levels (Tyron, 1991). An actometer is a motion-sensing device that can record and quantify human physical activity. It is small and light and can be worn around the ankle or the wrist. Its small size makes the actometer suitable for long-term and continuous motion recording. A typically passive patient has an average daily activity score, recorded by an actometer around the ankle, below the norm score for CFS patients (= 66) on 11 or 12 of a total of 12 days (van der Werf, Prins, Vercoulen, van der Meer, & Bleijenberg, 2000). However, since many therapists do not have access to an actometer, they must determine the activity pattern by means of an anamnesis, which is a less accurate and more complicated method. Although nearly all CFS patients claim that they hardly do anything anymore, when the therapist seriously questions them about their activities, the distinction between relatively active patients and those with a low activity pattern usually becomes much clearer. Talking through a normal day with the patient allows the therapist to derive the degree and extent of the patient's activity. The following questions can help determine whether the patient is passive or relatively active: "How much time do you spend lying down on your bed or couch each day? How often (per day/per week) do you leave the house? For how long? What is the maximum time you spend walking at a stretch?" The patient with a low activity pattern spends a great deal of time lying down, does not walk for long periods, and goes out infrequently. The answers to the last two queries also depend on the support the patient receives. Thus, a CFS patient who lives alone and does not get any help is compelled to be active enough to go out for food and other necessities.

As stated, the patient's activity pattern determines which protocol to use for treatment. The daily records that the patient keeps later on during the treatment can be useful for testing this initial pattern as well as for determining the definitive pattern.

Psychiatric Disorders

Another diagnostic task is to establish whether the patient has any serious psychosocial or psychiatric problems. On average, such problems are found in only half of the patients at most (Prins, Bazelmans, van der Werf, van der Meer, & Bleijenberg, 2002). A discussion of the psychosocial aspects of the fatigue symptoms may suggest possible psychosocial or psychiatric problems. If the patient has seen a psychologist, psychiatrist, or social worker in the past, it may make it easier to discuss any such problems in more detail. If psychosocial or psychiatric problems are found to be present, their relationship with the chronic fatigue needs to be determined; that is, whether the problems result from the fatigue syndrome (consequences) or are facilitating or initiating factors (antecedents). Sometimes the therapist finds no direct link with the development or onset of the CFS.

If the psychosocial or psychiatric problems are mainly consequential to the syndrome, CBT can be initiated without delay. These consequential problems—for example, awkward family interactions that stem from having a sick patient in the home—are resolved in the course of the treatment.

If the problems are antecedent to the CFS, they usually become a constituent part of the CFS-specific CBT. Since the problems have been proven to be directly associated with the fatigue, as is the case with high achievers or patients with a premorbid subassertiveness, they obviously also need to be dealt with to guarantee a successful treatment outcome. In certain cases, the established psychosocial or psychiatric problems may not be associated with the CFS.

In most cases, the treatment opted for will entail a CFS-specific CBT in which the therapist pays explicit attention to the indicated problems. Proven mental problems are seldom a reason to refrain from prescribing CBT for CFS. In isolated cases, it will be decided to treat the indicated psychosocial or psychiatric problems separately at a later stage. By contrast, the severity of the comorbidity may sometimes make it necessary to treat the comorbid symptoms prior to the CBT.

CLAIMS FOR DISEASE-RELATED BENEFITS

Studies into CBT for CFS have shown that patients who are involved in legal procedures in connection with their illness (e.g., insurance issues and/or invalidity benefit claims) should not be offered CBT (Prins, Bazelmans, et al., 2002) since it has been established that such patients have a significantly poorer treatment outcome than patients to whom this does not apply. During such procedures, patients need to convince the other party of the severity of their complaints and impairments, and this does not accord with a treatment aimed at improvement or recovery from the symptoms involved. Based on these findings, CFS patients still actively pursuing such legal procedures are no longer prescribed CBT in the clinical practice.

Another important and perhaps obvious contraindication for CBT is the patient's motivation. If a patient does not want CBT and also cannot be motivated by the referring party or therapist, prescribing the therapy is useless. This holds for both CFS-related and other complaints. It is out of the question to try to make CFS patients comply with CBT treatment by threatening to cancel their disability benefit; instances of such threats have been reported.

PRACTICE OF CBT FOR CFS

In this section, we first discuss the differences between the two types of CBT protocols (for low-active or passive and relatively active CFS patients) in general terms. Techniques to motivate the patient for the treatment are then described including how to create the right conditions for treatment and how to describe and explain the modus operandi. In addition, suggestions for planning other concurrent treatments and for formulating the aims of the treatment are discussed. Following this general explanation of the model, the roles of cognitions and behaviors in relation to the fatigue are outlined in the context of the different complaint analyses for low-active and relatively active CFS patients. And finally, the treatment objectives are further specified: return to work and/or other personal goals. The preceding steps apply for the treatment of both passive and relatively active CFS patients. Table 23.2 provides an outline of this program.

DISTINCTION BETWEEN RELATIVELY ACTIVE AND PASSIVE CFS PATIENTS

If the patient's activity pattern has earlier been assessed on the basis of an anamnesis and not with an actometer, the patient's daily records may help the therapist identify the definitive activity type. Relatively active patients still are able to do some paid work for several hours per day, do some domestic chores, and are socially active to some extent or engage in certain leisure activities or hobbies. By contrast, passive patients mainly spend a lot of time in bed, seldom leave the house, and undertake few or no household tasks. Relatively active CFS patients

Table 23.2
Outline of the Treatment

Introduction and Intake

Motivating the Patient for the Treatment

- Explanation of modus operandi and rationale of the treatment to patient and spouse.
- Precondition:
  –No other concurrent treatments.
- Aim:
  –Full recovery.
- Explanation of the treatment model:
  –Distinguishing initiating and perpetuating factors.
  –Role of cognitions and behaviors (thoughts and actions).

Defining Perpetuating Factors

- Determining and defining the activity level.
- Determining and defining fatigue-related cognitions.
- Defining the treatment goal (work, other personal targets).

Treatment

Relatively Active CFS Patients

- Explanation of perpetuating factors:
  –Nonaccepting cognitions.
  –Activity peaks.

Challenging Complaint-Enhancing Cognitions

- Nonacceptance, high demands, not respecting limits.

Balance between Rest and Activity

- Peak-stop exercises:
  –Physical, mental, social.
- Setting a base level.
- Changing the attitude toward the environment:
  –Learning to communicate limits.

Systematic Increase of Activities

- Physical activity program:
  –Graded and systematic raise in duration of frequent activities (walking or cycling)
- Action plan for work-resumption or for achieving personal goals, specification and realization.

Passive CFS Patients

- Explanation of perpetuating factors:
  –Anxious cognitions.
  –Inactivity.

Challenging Activity-Impeding Cognitions

- Fear of increase in complaints.

Systematic Increase of Activities

- Physical activity program:
  –Raising frequency and duration of activities gradually and systematically (walking or cycling).
- Mental activity program:
  –Systematically raising the duration of reading, time at the computer, and so on.
- Social activity program:
  –Graded expansion of daily, social activities (visits, phone calls).
- Action plan for work-resumption or for achieving personal goals, specification, and realization.
- Changing the attitude toward the environment:
  –Learning to expand limits.

mostly have cognitions that entail making high demands on themselves, wanting to do (too) much, and refusing to accept the current situation. Low-active CFS patients primarily exhibit anxious cognitions about the negative effect that activity may have on their symptoms.

In the initial stage of the treatment of the relatively active patient, first learning to recognize and accept the current state of fatigue and functional impairment is central. The sessions that follow are aimed at reducing the level of activity and learning to respect the limitations. After achieving this balance, the clinician and patient start to build up the level of activity. Passive or low-active patients, constituting about 25% of all CFS patients, on the other hand, already have such a low activity level that reducing it any further and reinforcing their need to respect their limitations can only be counterproductive. Because these patients are afraid of aggravating their symptoms, they tend to cut down on as many activities as possible almost every day. In their case, the essence of the treatment is to commence with a systematic activity-building program as soon as possible.

EXPECTATIONS OF THE TREATMENT AND THE ROLE OF SELF-ACTIVITY

To increase the chance of a successful outcome, a key aspect of the CBT is creating the right treatment conditions. In this context, the patient's attitude toward the treatment first needs to be established. Frequently, patients adopt a passive, wait-and-see pose: "Okay, show me your [the psychologist's] tricks first." This attitude may originate from the referral process. When patients feel that they have not received a thorough physical examination, they may not be receptive to a cognitive-behavioral approach. To resolve this issue, the therapist might ask these patients what additional diagnostic tests should have been conducted and whether they broached their concerns during the consultations with their physician. Patients who remain dubious should have the option to discuss the matter once more with their physician. Our experience has been that patients who have such a consultation come back to us with much stronger motivation.

CFS patients often have low expectations about a psychological intervention. Skepticism is the norm: "There's nothing wrong with me, mentally, so what am I doing here with this psychologist?" Changing an opinion like this can be difficult. After getting this attitude on the table for discussion, the therapist can explain to the patient how psychological factors—thoughts, feelings, and behaviors—may contribute to physical symptoms in general and CFS in particular.

At this stage, it is also worthwhile to explain the role of self-activation in the treatment. It helps clarify patients' expectations and encourages their participation during the treatment.

NO OTHER TREATMENTS DURING CBT FOR CFS

Patients afflicted by physical symptoms and strong physical attributions tend to place the solution to their problems outside themselves. They search vigorously for counselors who will cure them of their complaints. Frequently, for a lengthy period and in vain, they have been on medications or special diets in an effort to alleviate their symptoms.

The therapist must first ask the patient to report all current treatments, of whatever nature. The therapist then explains that it is understandable that the patient has tried each and every means available to get rid of the complaints. However, to ensure success, it is now essential to give full attention to the CBT and to refrain from any concurrent treatments. It is best for the patient to complete one treatment before trying any alternative treatments. Pivotal to treating CFS with cognitive-behavioral therapy is that patients be able to attribute all of their progress to changes in their cognitions and behaviors. When patients undergo two treatments simultaneously, it is difficult to prove which of the two interventions is responsible for the improvements. Therefore, the therapist should ask patients in clear terms whether they are prepared to terminate other ongoing treatments, and if so, when. Only after patients have complied with this requirement can they begin treatment with CBT.

However, a patient who has been on a particular diet for a long period, without the involvement of a professional, does not need to stop that diet before CBT. Since the diet apparently has no effect on the symptoms, it can be seen as a stable factor that is unlikely to interfere with the therapeutic process.

GOAL SETTING AND EXPLANATION OF THE TREATMENT

Objective: Recovery   The aim of the treatment is to modulate the fatigue, thereby reducing the symptoms and enabling patients to return to work or resume other normal, daily activities. Recovery is the therapist's goal (Prins, Bleijenberg, & van der Meer, 2002). Recovery, or cure, should be interpreted as meaning that the patient's self-view is no longer that of a patient suffering from CFS but is that of a healthy individual. After all, healthy people at times also feel tired or experience pain. Recovery, however, does not imply a return to one's old self. Before the onset of CFS, the extremely active lives that some patients led may even have contributed to the development of their symptoms. Helping patients to look on and treat their body in a different way automatically entails that they will never feel the way they did before the illness. Recovery in this context means adopting a new lifestyle, in which patients are aware of their body's normal limitations.

The therapist describes the intended recovery in such a way that it becomes a real and feasible target for the patient. Together, they inventory the activities that the patient needs to be able to do again in order to feel like a healthy person. Try to prevent the patient from becoming discouraged or debilitated by anxiety or the notion that the set targets are no longer obtainable or that recovery is still a long way off. Recovery may be formulated in terms of the number of hours spent working at one's job, doing the shopping, preparing meals, taking the kids to school, playing sports, reading, visiting friends, and so on. This way, recovery no longer is a general and abstract goal that the therapist has established but becomes a realistic target that the patient, with the help of the therapist, can work toward achieving. These goals as well as the steps (subtargets) to achieve these objectives are formulated during the initial CBT sessions. Here, relatively active CFS patients tend to set themselves targets that are too high, whereas low-active patients aim too low.

Objective: Return to Work   Before a return to work is possible, the therapist and the patient need to fully clarify and discuss the (former) work situation and financial status in relation to medical evaluations and benefit claims. Recovery from CFS may have considerable impact on any future work and/or benefits. It is important for patients to be aware that they will eventually lose (the right to) any disability payments in case of recovery. Furthermore, if they do not succeed in finding a new job, their financial situation may become even worse. This is why it is necessary to discuss patients' work expectations at an early stage. When finding a job is likely to pose serious problems and a patient has become dependent on benefits, the chances of recovery or improvement are slim. It is therefore important to ask patients whether they anticipate that recovery will have negative financial consequences. Financial consequences or the wish not to go back to work or to cut down on hours to have more time for housework or leisure activities almost certainly will stand in the way of recovery. It is necessary to formulate alternative personal objectives for the final goals if return to work is not an option, or if the patient only wants to work part-time on recovery despite the possible financial consequences. These may involve being able to fulfill domestic or caregiver duties, attending training courses, finding work as a volunteer, or performing other daily tasks. The goals are formulated in such a way that patients who have actually achieved them can perceive themselves as healthy individuals.

HOMEWORK ASSIGNMENTS

By doing homework assignments effectively, patients learn new cognitions and behaviors. At the start of each session, the patient and therapist together can select specific cognitions and behaviors from the assignments to discuss during that session. Prior to the session, the therapist should try to assess—based on the patient's perpetuating cognitions and behaviors—what these assignments can accomplish and which aspects should receive the most attention.

When a patient finds a certain assignment too taxing, try to determine the specific problem. How does the patient perform the task? If possible, have the patient formulate a feasible alternative. It is the patient who sets the priorities. Emphasize that it is important to complete the homework assignments in ways that can be sustained over time.

EXPLANATION OF THE MODEL OF PERPETUATING

The patient learns, in broad terms, the distinction between initiating and perpetuating factors. The therapist explains that, instead of looking for causes for the complaints, which is no longer useful at this stage, it makes far more sense to focus on ways to resolve them. ("How do I get rid of them?")

The following issues may be raised: What has caused the complaints is not known. What has become clear is that at present the symptoms cannot be explained by a persistent virus, nor by a dysfunction of the immune system, digestive disorders, or other physical causes. The key question therefore should not be "What causes the complaints?" but instead, "What can I do to get rid of them?" The onset of the fatigue may have been somatic, but this is no longer relevant. Explain that it is far more useful for the patient to look for ways to reduce the symptoms.

To better relate to the patient's perceptions when discussing cognitions and behaviors, it is helpful to employ the terms and expressions the patient uses. The fatigue-related cognitions and behaviors the patient has mentioned earlier may be used to explain their relation to the patient's symptoms. Following this explanation, the therapist assigns a self-observation task designed to increase the patient's understanding of those cognitions and behaviors that affect the fatigue.

TREATMENT OF THE RELATIVELY
ACTIVE CFS PATIENT

CHALLENGING COMPLAINT-ENHANCING COGNITIONS

When treating perpetuating cognitions, it is important not to simply challenge any single cognition but to find the leitmotiv for all of them. Certain cognitions and particular behaviors will recur regularly. The patient's self-observations form the basis for an inventory of those beliefs. These self-observations also allow the therapist to detect any unexpressed cognitions in various situations.

The therapist explains how the patient's cognitions and behaviors may influence the fatigue symptoms. Without expressing any judgment as to whether these are right or wrong, the therapist asks whether the patient recognizes the effects of cognitions and behaviors on the fatigue. This helps the therapist to relate to the patient. The patient may see things differently and should express those views. Again, explore whether the cognitions and behaviors the patient mentions contribute to or alleviate the fatigue.

The therapist challenges the most significant and most frequently recurring cognitions. The easiest way to do this is by asking the patient whether a particular belief helps reduce the complaints. Beneficial or helpful cognitions lead to a reduction of the fatigue; impeding cognitions enhance the symptoms. If the therapist does not agree with the patient about whether a particular cognition is helpful, they should try to determine the exact effect this cognition has on the fatigue.

Examples of impeding cognitions are "Will this never end?" "I simply can't go on like this," "I should be able to do this, for Pete's sake," and "It's not right that I have others do everything for me all the time."

The patient can practice helpful cognitions at home; for example, "So, okay, I feel tired right now. Well, it can't be helped. It's no use worrying about it because this will only make me feel even more tired." The patient can write down beneficial cognitions in the self-observation list. This *acceptance exercise* may help the patient think of other helpful cognitions: "I don't have to be able to do everything," "Everyone has their limits, so this also holds for me," or "Even 'healthy people' have their limits as to what they can do and these are different for everyone; and when these limits are lower than you'd like, it doesn't mean you're sick."

RECOGNIZING AND RESPECTING LIMITATIONS

The therapist explains to the patient that not respecting personal limits may negatively affect the complaints. It is wiser to stick to one's limits initially and from there to work toward a gradual and systematic expansion. Many patients exceed their limits to such a degree that they cause or aggravate symptoms. In such cases, the *peak-stop exercise* is recommended for a limited period. The exercise is a short-term aid to bring down the patient's activity level and prevent peaks in activity and the resultant fatigue. It helps set an appropriate base level. It will make itself redundant because eventually CFS patients, like healthy individuals, become able to have activity peaks without negative consequences.

Some CFS patients tend to exceed their limits so frequently and to such an extent that the negative effects do not manifest themselves until after they have stopped their activities or even the day after. Patients and therapists here need to try to find an activity level that does not aggravate complaints. This allows patients to determine the duration of their activities in advance. They are taught to cease the activity in time to prevent any complaints from manifesting themselves. At this stage of the treatment, the positive cognitions of CFS patients often are not conducive to prevent aggravating the fatigue: "I know that when I do too much today, I will have to pay for it tomorrow, but at least I will have enjoyed myself today." When discussing a timely cessation of activities, it is important to make such cognitions explicit and to have the patient use them during the peak-stop exercise. The therapist also needs to closely monitor that patients who apply the peak-stop exercise do not lapse into total inactivity and spend the entire day lying in bed or on the couch. The exercise is about finding the right balance between periods of rest and periods of activity. Figure 23.2 depicts the optimal changes in activity level and limits aimed at during the treatment that do not cause extreme fatigue.

A proper application of the peak-stop exercise will allow the patient to determine a *base level.* By base level, we mean the total activities a person can do—spread over the day—without these causing extreme fatigue. In determining this base level, both the therapist and patient will get a clearer picture of what the patient's typical activities are on a normal day. Base-level activities include actions like getting up, taking a shower, getting dressed, preparing meals, doing the shopping, tidying, doing the dishes, taking the kids to and picking them up from school, spending time on domestic work or doing paid work. Which activities to include in the base level depends on the patient's personal circumstances, which differ from patient to patient. Some may still be able to go out to work a few hours per day, whereas others will have reached the base level after taking a shower, getting dressed, and eating breakfast. The essence of a good base level is that there are no activity peaks, nor activities that cause extreme fatigue. Determining the base level is about finding out which activities to include and how to spread them over the day. Activities that result in extreme fatigue should be omitted unless they can be divided and spread out. Furthermore, the base level should leave some room for maneuver. A base level is inflexible if it means the patient

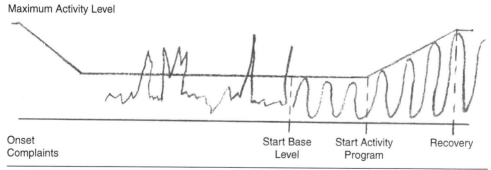

Figure 23.2 Time Course of the Level of Activity before and during the Treatment of CFS. Representation of the time course of the activity level and the maximum activity level below which there are no complaints. The figure shows the period before the start of the treatment and the subsequent intented changes in these levels during the course of the treatment of a relatively active CFS patient.

must function at maximum ability all the time and any extra activity will lead to extreme fatigue. Unexpected events or unforeseen activities—so much a part of life—need to fit within the set level. In addition, the base level needs to allow room for the activity program, to be described later.

If, after several sessions, a relatively active CFS patient is still seriously fatigued and has improved little since the start of treatment, an evaluation of the base level may reveal that the patient still does too much or for too long a period. The way the patient goes about things (e.g., in a hurried, tense, or perfectionist manner) also may explain the fatigue. Both instances warrant special attention and need to be resolved.

THE BASE LEVEL AND THE SLEEP PATTERN

Many CFS patients are troubled by a disease-related desynchronization of the sleep pattern. They tend to sleep long hours, sleep or lie down frequently during the day, or cannot get to sleep at night even though they are feeling extremely tired. Patients may believe that, since they are so tired, they need a lot of sleep. However, sleeping often or for many hours does not solve the problem and can even be counterproductive. Some patients may feel the need to sleep late but consequently will not be able to get to sleep at night, which disrupts their sleep pattern. It is essential to try to normalize the sleep pattern of these patients as quickly as possible. This implies going to bed and getting up at fixed times and not taking naps during the day. Establishing a regular sleep pattern also is an important element of a patient's base level.

THE BASE LEVEL AND WORK

There are patients who still work, usually part-time. It is necessary to establish the extent to which the job can be fitted into the base level. Patients who are financially dependent on their job may be anxious about temporarily working fewer hours for fear of losing the job. Together with the patient, try to determine whether the job is compatible with the agreed-on base level and look again at how the patient fulfills tasks. If the job does not exceed the established limits, continuing at work may be useful because it is a way to evaluate how the person deals with work. Is the patient always pressed for time, always busy? Is there hardly any time for a break? Decide, together with the patient, whether the work approach is adequate or needs adjustment.

After explaining and talking through the base level, the therapist asks the patient to try to determine a base level and to make notes of daily activities, the results of which they will evaluate during the next session. Usually, patients are asked to put their base level down on paper. In the course of the treatment, patients try to reduce their daily activities and learn to put the base level into practice.

THE BASE LEVEL AND THE ENVIRONMENT

During the sessions involving the base level, it may be useful to talk about the possible consequences this base level can have on the patient's environment. Since CFS patients, in the context of the base-level program, will try to reduce their activities, this may elicit negative reactions from the patient's environment. The patient no longer meets (presupposed) requirements and no longer lives up to perceived expectations. Generally, the best way to resolve this matter is to involve those in the patient's environment in the treatment and to jointly seek temporary solutions for any emerging problems. Involving the spouse or significant others may help the patient comply with the base level.

GRADED ACTIVITY PROGRAM

Activities can be divided into three categories: physical, mental, and social. In nearly all cases, treatment starts with a physical activity program. The patient selects a simple physical activity to perform every day and records its duration. The aim is to have the patient gradually and systematically increase the frequency or duration of this particular activity.

Walking and cycling are typical examples of such an activity. Swimming is less suitable since it is difficult to perform on a daily basis and involves many additional actions, such as going to the swimming pool, finding a cubicle, getting changed, and so on. The activity program needs to start at a realistic, manageable level. In general, a relatively active CFS patient starts with an activity that can be carried out twice a day and whose duration can be increased every day.

The raise in the duration of the activity is usually expressed in minutes. Starting with a 5-minute walk twice a day, the second day this is raised to 6, and the third day to 7 minutes twice daily, and so on. If necessary, the therapist may assure the patient that an increase by 1 minute will not constitute any danger. There is no strain, and there will be no negative consequences. An increase of 5 minutes per week is a common target. This gives the patient the opportunity to skip the activity once or twice or to refrain from raising the walking time. The initial level will be realistic and feasible, as has been agreed on by both patient and therapist. For patients who think they can start with at least a 25-minute walk (which is common assumption by relatively active patients), the starting period should be set for half this estimated time at most. In practice, patients are best advised to begin with a 10-minute walk twice a day and should be asked to indicate the actual duration of each activity on a chart.

In general, the activity program will involve a maximum of 60 minutes of walking or cycling. By that time, most patients will have become aware that they are capable of doing more without experiencing extreme fatigue and that they recover faster than before. The original base level has by then already been automatically enhanced. Gradually, patients are now replacing walking or cycling with other activities. These often involve going back to work or resuming activities that are part of personal targets.

The activity program of relatively active patients is not about improving their physiological condition since, as far as is known at present, these patients are not deconditioned in a physiological sense (Bazelmans, Bleijenberg, van der Meer, & Folgering, 2001). If this were the aim, the program would have to take a different form. Rather, the focus of the activity program is a gradual and systematic increase in activity. Patients who experience being able to achieve this—if approached in the right way—enhance their sense of control and this helps bring about a positive self-efficacy.

By analyzing stagnations in the activity program, it is possible to trace impeding cognitions or difficulties that patients might have with respecting limitations.

It will also help patients feel (more) confident that they actually are capable of these activities if they use positive cognitions and learn how to carry out and distribute these activities. In addition, mental and social activities may be systematically expanded to prepare the patient for a return to work.

The activity program is likely to be fraught with difficulties. Patients may not stick to the program consistently and may make insufficient progress. A closer examination may reveal that they are undertaking additional activities that do not form part of the base level. That they have not complied with the agreed terms may imply that the base level was set too high and, consequently, was not flexible enough. In such cases, it is recommended to lower the base level so that it once again leaves patients room for maneuver, after which they can resume the program. Alternatively or additionally, activity-related cognitions may be evaluated more closely. Usually, this involves helping patients to get their priorities right. At this moment, these should be with the treatment.

Another problem that may arise is that patients step up their activities faster than has been agreed. The kick in the teeth usually comes later: The patient can no longer sustain the program and either stops altogether ("The program is no use") or does very little ("I am at the end of my tether"). Once the setback has occurred, the only way forward is to have the patient start from scratch, at the agreed level, but this time with a safe daily buildup. If the problem is detected before any real damage has been done, the motto is to get the patient to slow down.

MAKING A WORK-RESUMPTION PLAN

From the very start of the treatment, the therapist makes clear that full recovery, and a consequent return to work, is the ultimate goal. Patients estimate how many hours they will be able to work after recovery and which tasks they must be able to perform. Patients then draw up a plan, detailing the necessary steps, which is presented to the patient's employer, company doctor, and/or medical adviser of the insurance company. When the activity program has reached the appropriate stage, a start can be made toward accomplishing the proposed steps. This plan of action also applies to those patients for whom a return to work is not possible and who have set other, more personal targets.

The guidelines for a work-resumption plan are similar to those used for the graded activity program. Patients are to start from a realistic and feasible base level, need to increase the activity level gradually, and must stick to the program. Have patients work out the plan in detail; have them indicate clearly, for each day that they include in the scheme, whether they will go to work, how many hours they will work, and which activities will be involved.

MAKING A PLAN FOR ACHIEVING PERSONAL GOALS

When a return to work is not an option, the action plan that is drawn up stipulates how to achieve personal targets. The three steps are comparable to those described for the plan aimed at a return to work:

1. *Final goal.* Which activities that will promote a self-perception of being healthy does the patient want to be able to perform again?

2. *Base level.* What is the patient capable of at this moment without resultant complaint-enhancing effects?
3. *Graded activity plan.* How can the patient build up the activity level without negatively affecting the symptoms?

Also with this action plan, the patient is asked to commit the steps to paper, taking into account any problems that may arise, and compliance with the activity plan is evaluated. When a particular step involves minor or one-off personal targets (e.g., a vacation), it may suffice to try to anticipate likely problems.

TREATMENT OF THE PASSIVE CFS PATIENT

CHALLENGING ACTIVITY-IMPEDING COGNITIONS

In contrast to the relatively active CFS patients, the low-active CFS patients have cognitions of fear based on their perception that activity will enhance their symptoms. As a result, these patients engage in little or no activity during the day and instead spend a lot of time lying in bed or resting on the couch. Restructuring these anxious cognitions is central in the treatment of the passive patient. Furthermore, since the patient's environment is also often overly concerned, it is essential to involve the patient's spouse, relatives, or friends in the treatment. Patients may verbalize activity-impeding cognitions such as "I can't do anything on my own anymore, and others have to help me all the time" or "As soon as I start feeling tired or start having pain I have to stop everything I'm doing." Compared with relatively active patients, it is generally more complicated to challenge the cognitions of passive patients without also involving behavior. This is why it is beneficial to start the graded exercise program as soon as possible. Positive cognitions such as the following examples should be encouraged: "I will stop looking back to try to find an explanation for my complaints; from now on I'm going to do something about them." "By raising the level of my activities step by step, I will be able to push my physical capabilities even further." "If I get complaints by being active, it doesn't necessarily mean that I should stop doing what I'm doing; it's just a sign that it has been some time since I've been active, and my body simply needs to get used to it again." Again, at this stage, the therapist should ask patients to keep a record of their cognitions.

THE USE OF HANDICAP AIDS

Both passive and, to a lesser extent, relatively active CFS patients use aids, such as a walking stick or wheelchair. Like medication for pain relief, such aids tend to obscure the symptoms and impairments of patients. In addition, they may undermine the confidence-building process that allows patients to believe in their own ability to recover. Therefore, one of the first goals will be to gradually eliminate the use of any such aids. (After all, a wheelchair does not allow the patient to independently perform the steps of the activity program.) Usually, the therapist can accomplish this by simply explaining the situation and having the patient agree not to use the aids. The patient may want to gradually reduce the use of the walking stick or wheelchair. This requires a concrete plan of action, indicating the time frame, for example, a maximum of 2 to 3 weeks. Even though not using the aid is likely to result in an even further decrease in activities, starting the activity program at this lowered base level offers the better prospect.

PHYSICAL ACTIVITY PROGRAM FOR LOW-ACTIVE CFS PATIENTS

Contrary to relatively active CFS patients, low-active CFS patients are likely to need a physical program to improve their condition. The program also must convince patients that physical complaints are not a sign to stop the activities. Because of their low level of activities and their belief that they are hardly capable of anything, the base level for these patients will be far lower than that for relatively active patients. The initial daily frequency of the activity, however, is higher and preferably set at 6 times a day (i.e., twice in the morning, twice at noon, and twice in the evening). A 1-minute walk is commonly chosen as a first activity. Low-active patients seldom opt for cycling. A minute is added each day, with a total of 5 minutes per week. This leaves 2 minutes to spare, allowing the patient to skip a day or to refrain from raising the duration of the exercise.

It is important to point out to patients that a 1-minute increase is absolutely safe and that there is no danger, whatsoever, of overtaxation. Emphasize that with these small but consistent increments, a great deal of progress can be made in only a few weeks, barring exceptional circumstances (see Figure 23.3). It is common to cut back the frequency of the walks from 6 times a day to 2 or 3 times a day after several weeks. Even before reaching a certain level such as a twice-a-day 60-minute walk, patients will find that they are now able to undertake other activities. By then, patients will also have noticed that recovery from an activity is much faster.

As with the more active CFS patients, passive patients may experience stagnations during the graded activity program. Regularly, the program will be interrupted or stopped because of illness. It is important to define what being ill means. A comparison with work and reporting sick may be helpful: "There is no clear line between being sick and not being sick. Someone may have been feeling a little under the weather for several days but has still continued to go to work, until the moment that this person really knows he is 'sick' and decides to stay home. At some point, he decides not to label himself as sick any more, even though he may still feel far from fit, and he goes back to the office. At work, things will not run

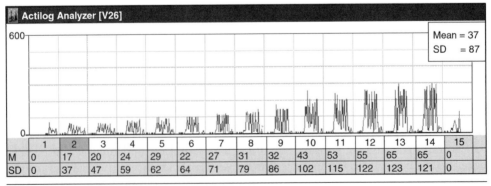

Figure 23.3 Example of Progress in a Low-Activity Patient's Activity Level Six Times a Day, as Recorded by Means of an Actometer during 14 Days.

smoothly the first couple of days, and he will wear out quickly." This is the approach patients should take for the activity program. When patients have decided that they are sick, walking should cease because exercising less will not help. Not until patients have resolved to go back to work ("I'm not sick enough to stay home from work anymore") and no longer label themselves as sick, should they return to the program. Patients can then pick up from where they left off and continue the steps as agreed.

Another problem may be that although progress was made earlier, this has come to a standstill. Initially, the program seemed to produce the intended results, but at some point ("I simply can't manage more than 12 minutes"), progression halted. First the phasing prior to the delay is evaluated. If this is found to have been too fast, the patient is best advised to return to the last manageable level and to work back up from there. The delay may also be due to activity-related cognitions, as illustrated by views such as "If I go on walking, I will probably start getting complaints" or "Just as I thought, I am already starting to feel tired, I'd best go back." After discussing these impeding thoughts, the therapist may encourage more helpful cognitions: "It's all right to feel tired" or "There's no harm in feeling tired."

MENTAL ACTIVITY PROGRAM FOR PASSIVE CFS PATIENTS

Once an activity program is under way, the patient and therapist concomitantly agree on and start a mental activity program. Many passive CFS patients experience difficulties performing activities that require concentration, such as reading, doing crossword puzzles, or working at a computer. At first, the activity should be carried out 2 or 3 times a day for perhaps 5 minutes. This is gradually increased so that at the end of the week the patient has doubled the time spent on the task. Although the more active CFS patients may have similar concentration problems at times, with these patients the deficiency manifests itself predominantly while planning the steps for a return to work (or personal targets).

The type of mental activity also plays a role. Certain patients may want to start with a textbook. This should be allowed, but patients are usually better off to choose less complex material. It may even be advisable to start with a children's book. The patient should make the final decision, however, because the program is about promoting a positive self-efficacy. Patients may also tend to spend more time on the activity (e.g., at the computer) than initially agreed on. By pointing out that the consequences are usually not felt until (much) later, it generally is easy to convince patients to stick to the program.

SOCIAL ACTIVITY PROGRAM FOR PASSIVE CFS PATIENTS

The social activity program for passive patients does not commence until they have made progress in the preceding areas. Activities such as making telephone calls, chatting with friends, or making social calls are added gradually according to the same principles as the other programs. It needs to be noted that some passive patients engage in lengthy telephone conversations regularly since this is their only opportunity to make contact with the outside world. They are not always aware how fatiguing these calls can be. It is recommended to make an early start in helping the patient adjust to having shorter calls several times a day. Since the social activity program also affects the patient's environment, the patient needs to inform others of the program. The patient decides on the content of the information.

LEARNING TO RELY LESS ON SUPPORT FROM OTHERS

Frequently, passive CFS patients have rallied the support of a considerable number of people. It is also common for the patient's environment to be just as concerned and anxious as the patient. This may contribute to maintaining the complaints. If this seems to be the case, the spouse or another key player from the patient's environment should be invited to attend a session to discuss how to cut back on this support.

PLANNING A RETURN TO WORK AND ACHIEVING PERSONAL GOALS

As with the more active CFS patient, when return to work is the low-active patient's ultimate goal, an action plan is drawn up. For these patients, a return to work may seem like a far less feasible, perhaps even unobtainable, target than it is for the more active patients. Adapting the activity programs to the patient's ultimate goal from the very start of the treatment will help create the right conditions to achieve a return to work.

The action plan for more personal goals closely follows the steps of the activity programs. The discrepancy between the patient's current situation and the aim of the treatment (to be able to take on normal, daily activities again) is usually considerable in passive CFS patients. Initially, they may think that they will never be able to reach this target. Based on these feelings, they may give up on the idea of a return to work sooner than the more active patients and opt for personal targets as their ultimate goal.

When discussing the steps toward achieving one or more personal targets, patients are asked to make an inventory of the activities belonging to that particular target. Usually under the guidance of the therapist, patients then identify the anticipated problems and formulate solutions using whatever techniques they have already applied successfully. These resolutions may be structured along the principles of a gradual, step-by-step, activity-building scheme and can involve making special preparations, practicing helpful cognitions, and informing the environment.

RELAPSE PREVENTION FOR LOW-ACTIVE AND RELATIVELY ACTIVE PATIENTS

To prevent a relapse, it is paramount to enhance patients' self-activity in each phase of the treatment. Whereas the therapist initially challenges the patients' cognitions, introduces helpful cognitions, and moderates behavior or teaches necessary skills, this guidance becomes steadily less over time and the therapist takes more of a back seat. After 6 to 10 sessions, the therapist's role should mainly be supportive in analyzing recovery-impeding factors and reinforcing goal-directed steps. Increasingly making it the patient's own responsibility to detect and anticipate difficulties and to find solutions will enhance the patient's self-efficacy and reduce somatic attributions. The patient by this time is no longer a patient and has learned how to influence his or her occasional symptoms.

Treatment usually consists of 10 to a maximum of 20 sessions, The number will depend on the therapist's experience with the treatment as well as on the patient's condition. After completion of the actual treatment, follow-up sessions are conducted with the single purpose of monitoring whether the patient has sustained the treatment effect.

LIFESTYLE CHANGES

Every patient has a specific lifestyle. Some will have difficulties with communicating their limits to others; others may be perfectionists. There are also patients who have such an intense fear of failure that they will be extremely apprehensive about achieving the treatment goals and consequently will drop out of treatment at an early stage. To prevent relapse, patients are advised to pay specific attention to their own known weaknesses. Different lifestyles may either induce patients to do too much or too little. Both behaviors can send a patient once more into a downward spiral. Patients who become aware of these innate weak spots may prevent a relapse or learn how to resolve the situation in time.

GETTING RID OF THE "PATIENT LABEL"

Many patients find it hard to stop seeing themselves as patients. The term chronic fatigue syndrome seems to suggest a permanent condition. The fact that many CFS patients have been suffering from symptoms for some time before they are referred for CBT does not encourage them to have an optimistic outlook for a full recovery. In addition, patients who are referred to a psychotherapist for CFS generally assume that they will learn to cope with their complaints, not that they will learn to perceive themselves as healthy individuals again. This is why this goal should be one of the first points on the treatment agenda. In the final phase of the treatment, the therapist raises this point again by asking patients what they think still needs to happen before they can replace the marker reading "patient" with a label indicating "healthy." The response of healthy individuals who are suffering from all kinds of flulike symptoms will be quite different from the reactions of CFS patients, who usually interpret such incidental complaints by saying, "I told you, didn't I? I still have CFS."

FOLLOW-UP AND TREATMENT EVALUATION

The purpose of the follow-up sessions is to discuss with ex-patients how they have been dealing with the fatigue. Have they learned enough to tackle any recurring symptoms? Here, the follow-up sessions mainly take the shape of revision lessons or a refresher course. The therapist reinforces patients' positive approaches toward the fatigue or their behaviors that help prevent extreme symptoms. Far better still, the therapist should have ex-patients reinforce themselves and thus help to establish a positive self-efficacy. It is also recommended to go through all the positive effects of the treatment once more. Most patients who have been successfully treated will still report feeling tired frequently, although this no longer takes extreme forms and recovery occurs more quickly. In other words, the fatigue has been normalized. Concomitant complaints like muscle pain or joint ache will usually have disappeared gradually in the course of the treatment.

TWO CASE STUDIES

Susan, a Relatively Active Patient

Susan, a mother of two children aged 1 and 3, is 38 years old when she is referred for CBT by her internist. Her husband has accompanied her on her first visit to the clinic. Apart from severe symptoms of fatigue, Susan also mentions headache, muscle pains, and joint ache as serious concomitant complaints. The fatigue symptoms first started manifesting themselves after a tonsillectomy 8 years ago.

Four years ago, after a dramatic worsening of her fatigue symptoms, Susan no longer felt able to continue working as a home health aide. At the time of referral, Susan has been on full disability benefit for 3 years. Several medical reassessments all confirmed that, due to her chronic fatigue, she was no longer able to fulfill the heavy physical demands her work as a home health aide placed on her, resulting in a 65% disability.

Every weekday, at 6:30 in the morning, Susan takes on her caregiver duties and starts bathing, diapering, dressing, and feeding the children. She follows this with some simple domestic chores. Frequently, she starts feeling shaky or nauseous while performing these tasks, but she keeps egging herself on and tries to ignore the complaints. If she has really reached the end of her tether, she goes and sits on the couch and tries to relax. Still, she keeps being troubled by thoughts that she is leaving her kids to fend for themselves and is a lazy mother. Sunday is the only day she can sleep in and leave the children's care to her spouse, which does not mean that she feels any less tired. She barely undertakes any physical activities that day.

Susan's self-formulated goal is a recovery from the chronic fatigue complaints, thus creating more opportunities for spare-time activities. Her concrete objective is to learn to react differently to her feelings of fatigue. Susan will have to learn to postpone tasks or just leave them be and to be less demanding of herself (and others). Further, a subtarget will be learning to have others do certain tasks or to ask others for help. Susan tends to claim most of the tasks for herself and hardly ever asks her husband or others to help her. After her recovery, Susan also wants to be able to do some paid work outside the home again. Consequently, a return to work becomes one of the primary objectives. The idea of doing a few hours of paid work every week after her recovery really appeals to Susan. This idea is further specified and 16 hours per week becomes the (initial) target, but it will not involve working as a home health aide. Prior to her most recent position, she had several years of experience with administrative work, which she now prefers to take up again.

Next, the functional analysis is discussed with Susan. At the first signs of fatigue, she tends to respond with impeding, irrational thoughts: "I just have to keep on going and finish my work," "It isn't normal and can't be right that I tire so easily," "If I take some rest, I am leaving my kids to fend for themselves and then I am a lazy mother." These cognitions keep her physically active, which soon aggravates the complaints. When Susan has completed the housework she made herself do, she is exhausted. She feels powerless and guilty for not being able to change this pattern.

With the acceptance exercises, Susan learns to adopt the following helpful cognitions when the fatigue kicks in: "Okay, so I'm feeling tired right now. Simply accept it. Things will only get worse if I try to fight it." She has kept a record of her cognitions earlier in the treatment, which has made her more aware of any fatigue-perpetuating cognitions. Concurrently, she begins with the peak-stop exercise. As soon as these exercises have helped her set the right base level, she starts with the activity program.

Susan opts for cycling to build up her activity level. She starts with a 10-minute bike ride twice a day, and it is agreed that she will increase each ride by 1 minute, with a minimum of 5 minutes per week. During the activity program Susan keeps a record of her progress by filling out an activity chart. In the second week, however, she starts complaining of enhanced feelings of tiredness and pain. A look at her chart reveals that her program lacks consistency. Together, Susan and the therapist explore what factors may be playing a role here. It turns out that Susan frequently does not give priority to the program because she feels that certain other things that may present themselves really need to be resolved first. This analysis also reveals that the issue of asking others for help keeps warranting special attention. During the following weeks, Susan manages to gradually build up the bike rides to 1 hour twice a day. She feels better all the time and has noticed that she can now cope with far more than before. She starts expressing her doubts about the bike rides because they take up so much of her time. It is agreed that she will stick to a 1-hour ride per day but will spend the other hour on one of her hobbies.

In the course of the treatment, Susan is required to apply for a part-time post (as a desk clerk for four mornings a week) at a local job center. Susan had not really reckoned with such an early return to work, but the job did match her wish for a 16-hour-a-week office job perfectly. Because she had made such good progress with the activity program, it was decided, by mutual consent, that she would indeed go for an interview and the steps for a return to work were drawn up. In addition, Susan made an inventory of the problems she was likely to encounter in this new job. Learning to leave tasks until later and easing the demands on herself and others remained the prime focal points.

Ann, the Low-Active Patient

Ann, a young woman of 20, has been referred for CBT. Her parents are also present during the first session. Ann proves quite capable of describing her complaints. She constantly feels tired and often has pains in her muscles and joints. Even after a minor exertion, these complaints become worse. This means she can do very little. She also has difficulties concentrating. Recently, she picked up a few of her textbooks again, but she did not even manage to finish a single page. According to her parents, Ann used to be a lively, cheerful, and active girl. She did well in school, engaged in sports, and played the piano. Her complaints first began in her fourth year of high school, when she contracted mononucleosis, from which she never fully recovered. Both Ann and her parents feel that there is something physically wrong with her because what else could explain her persistent complaints? Yet, all the doctors that have examined Ann have not been able to find any physical explanation for her symptoms. Besides, all this has not done her any good.

When Ann is describing what her normal day is like, she starts crying. Her misery overwhelms her when she realizes the lousy state she is in. She feels completely powerless because there is absolutely nothing she can do to change things. Every day takes on more or less the same pattern; there is practically no variation.

When Ann wakes up, usually around 9 A.M., she already feels tired. Her mother has prepared breakfast for her downstairs, after which Ann goes and lies down on the couch for a while until she has gathered enough strength to climb back up the stairs to her room, where she goes back to bed. She hardly ever gets dressed. Most times she falls asleep, but sometimes she just leafs through some magazines. At about 1 o'clock, her mother brings her lunch, which she eats lying in bed, after which she usually stays in bed until about 3 or 4 P.M., resting and looking at the pictures in her magazines. Listening to the radio is too tiring for her: Any sound or noise makes her feel even more tired. In the late afternoon Ann goes back downstairs. Occasionally, she invites a friend to visit her, but listening to her friends' chatter also tires her easily. At times, when she starts feeling too tired, she even asks her visitors to leave. She watches television once in a while, but usually only children's programs. Most days she goes back up to her room around 8 P.M., where she usually falls asleep pretty fast.

The therapist discusses with Ann whether she thinks she may be able to go back to school. After listening to an explanation of the step-by-step approach, Ann offers to think about adult education. Going back to school ("But that is still a long way off") is chosen as her final target. Ann also wants to pick up one of her sports again.

Ann is mainly anxious about her complaints getting worse, which is why she tries to take it easy, as much as she can. She also tends to continuously focus on her body. The therapist challenges thoughts like "When I feel tired, there must be something physically wrong with me" and explains that Ann's fatigue no longer has a warning function since she feels tired all the time anyway. Moreover, getting tired is not bad; there's no harm. Getting tired is okay. Better still, like most people her age, she should try not to pay any attention to feeling tired. Thus, Ann is not asked to keep a record of how tired she feels. It is also agreed that she will stay up all day, will not go to bed in the afternoon, and will spend most of the day downstairs in the living room. Armed with the cognition "there's no harm in getting tired," Ann starts her activity program.

Ann has chosen walking, starting with a 1-minute walk 4 times a day. She records her walks scrupulously and makes steady progress. Soon she has reached 20 minutes per walk. But then she falls ill and cancels her sessions. She does not return until 6 weeks later. She has had a bad flu. It is decided that the best thing to do is to pick up from where she left off and restart the program with four 20-minute walks a day and build up from there.

For her mental activity program, Ann chooses reading and starts with a simple but captivating children's novel. The three daily reading sessions soon become longer. She is enjoying them and after a few weeks reports that reading gets easier all the time. She can also manage reading the newspaper better now. In preparation for her return to school, Ann decides, after consultation, to look up her old schoolbooks again and see which topics she might like to read up on. She would also like to do some computer games again. She succeeds in drawing up a plan for these activities according to the principles applied earlier.

During the subsequent stage of the treatment, after it has become clear that Ann wants to take adult classes, she and the therapist discuss what would be the best approach. Ann needs to go to a different town for these classes, and she is afraid that this will be too tiring. This problem is also tackled with the step-by-step method. She will start by taking a daily bus ride to a location of her own choice, for example, the shopping mall, and will spend some time there before taking the bus back. Every week, the traveling distance is increased gradually until it equals the time it will take her to travel to school.

The plan to go back to school is taking shape and gets more concrete. Ann has inquired about which courses she can take. As laid down in the action plan, Ann wants to reach her final target, being able to attend all the scheduled classes and do her home assignments, in 8 weeks' time. She wants to begin by attending at least one class per subject once a week, if possible, and build from there. With this approach, Ann finds herself able to do more all the time without developing any (new) complaints. When she is attending all of her classes and is managing her homework, she decides to pick up one of her sports again. She goes running and also systematically builds up this activity, little by little. Ann still feels tired at times, but she now knows this is a healthy way to feel. She no longer considers herself to be a CFS patient.

OTHER WAYS OF APPLYING CBT FOR CFS

CFS in Adolescents

The CBT for the treatment of CFS as described in this chapter has initially been developed for and tested with adults. Although controlled studies into the effects of CBT in adolescents are still lacking, CBT is also considered suitable for the treatment of young CFS patients, provided that the therapist takes their individual circumstances into account. Participation of the parents in their child's treatment is a precondition.

Not only the adolescent's own reactions toward the fatigue but also the attributions and reactions of the parents will determine how their child deals with the complaints. In addition, the specific developmental tasks the adolescent is facing (e.g., efforts toward autonomy, identity, and separation), need to be reckoned with. These efforts, in fact, are in conflict with the adolescent's present dependence imposed by the affliction (Pipe & Wait, 1995). With children under the age of 15, the parents will frequently act as a kind of cotherapist. With adolescents over this age, the parents will often have to learn to step back and encourage their child to take responsibility for the treatment.

Group Therapy

CBT for CFS can also take the form of group therapy. Although as yet no studies are available in the literature on the subject, several CFS patients in our center were treated in a group setting. Group therapy is most suitable for patients whose functional impairment is moderate.

Successful treatment is most likely if the group is relatively homogeneous and the participants are in a comparable stage of life. Groups of 8 patients may consist of both passive and relatively active CFS patients, provided that the latter are in the majority. It is far more difficult "to get patients moving" in a group that consists largely or exclusively of patients with a predominantly passive activity pattern. The progress of some members of the group can set an encouraging example for other patients. Comparing and discussing the participants' individual actometer patterns may help the patients visualize which direction their activity program should take.

Our current group therapy program comprises 14 two-hour sessions over approximately 6 months. All sessions are conducted under the guidance of two therapists. The three key ingredients are provision of information, the actual group interactions, and homework assignments. The therapists explain the elements of the program in an interactive fashion using the approach discussed in the earlier sections. During the remainder of the sessions, the patients discuss this information and compare it with their own experiences. For the clinical practice, the advantage of group therapy mainly lies in being able to treat several patients simultaneously.

CBT ADMINISTERED BY FAMILY DOCTORS

Some CFS patients may also be treated by their family physician. However, several important criteria need to be met. The GP needs to be adequately informed of CFS, but also, and perhaps more importantly, needs to be prepared and able to allot sufficient amounts of time to the treatment. Furthermore, the physician needs to be able to select those CFS patients who are most likely to benefit from the treatment. This usually implies CFS patients who are still relatively active and for whom the majority of prognostic factors are favorable. No comorbidity should be present, and there should be a predominantly positive self-efficacy about the symptoms, moderate somatic attributions, no repetitive use of medication, and a social environment with a positive attitude toward the patient's recovery. Only when these conditions exist will therapy by the GP offer any prospects of success. As yet, no data are available on the possibilities and effectiveness of CBT for the treatment of CFS as administered by the family doctor.

TREATMENT OF INPATIENTS

In the studies described earlier in this chapter, the therapies provided were always on an outpatient basis. Chalder, Butler, and Wessely (1996) reported an uncontrolled study involving six inpatients of a clinic that specialized in the treatment of CFS. They provide a comprehensive description of the treatment they developed for their patients, most of whom were all but completely inactive and bedridden. The treatment starts with a low-level activity program and is directed at separating the symptoms a patient experiences from the tendency to immediately cease the activities. Next, the program focuses on reestablishing a normal sleep pattern and limiting periods of rest to fixed times. Although an uncontrolled study, the effects reported are encouraging. Five of the six patients showed considerable improvement, and this effect was still present 3 months after their release from the clinic.

Cox and Findley (1998) also described CBT and graded activity of CFS patients in an inpatient setting. They claimed at 6 months postdischarge, a perceived increase in level of ability in 82% compared with activity prior to their admission to hospital.

PITFALLS FOR THERAPISTS

The cognitive-behavioral treatment of CFS patients frequently poses specific problems, which may involve the treatment itself but also, and particularly, may concern the therapist-patient interaction and the patient's motivation. First, some recommendations are given for therapists intending to practice CBT for CFS. Next, some of the pitfalls a therapist is likely to encounter in the course of the treatment are discussed.

WHO SHOULD PRACTICE CBT?

The study by Prins et al. (2001), in which the effect of CBT in CFS patients was investigated, involved 13 therapists. They reported that treating CFS patients had been more difficult than the treatment of patients with a different somatic symptomatology or patients with psychosocial or psychiatric problems (Prins et al., 2001). This seems to be the general impression of most therapists. It turned out that therapists with little experience in the treatment of patients suffering from somatic complaints have difficulty preventing patients from dropping out. This illustrates the importance of adequate training and preparation. Knowledge of and experience in applying cognitive-behavioral therapy with patients who have a somatic illness is a prerequisite. In addition, therapists must keep themselves informed of the current scientific research into CFS. This also enables therapists to explain and clarify the rationale of their actions and may facilitate the patient's treatment. As a matter of course, any therapist working with this category of patients, needs to secure adequate supervision, preferably conducted by therapists experienced in CBT treatment.

RECOVERY OR MANAGING THE FATIGUE?

Some therapists believe that full recovery as the final goal of CBT for CFS is too ambitious. They prefer to restrict the treatment to helping patients learn to manage the fatigue. However, this implies that, though patients may perhaps learn to control or deal with their complaints, they will still think of themselves as patients, with all that this entails. Thus, normal feelings of tiredness will be considered in the light of the syndrome. Like an athlete who will never jump higher if he does not put the bar higher, the patient will, generally speaking, never be able to achieve more than the goal the therapist and patient have set for themselves. This is true for CFS patients in particular because they often hold on to the idea that CFS is a permanent condition that will never be cured. Therapists who put the bar at "being able to manage the fatigue" will accomplish less for and with their patients.

Sometimes a therapist may agree hastily to targets that are too low or vague. When a patient who formerly worked full time defines a target as a partial return to work, the therapist will feel relieved because at least the patient has set a concrete target and will leave it at that. But does reaching this goal mean the patient really has recovered or is technically still a patient? The latter is indeed the case when the individual still receives a partial disability allowance, which, in turn, implies that both the patient and his or her social environment will keep on thinking in terms of "CFS patient." A target that states "I want to be able to take up work as a volunteer" is an example of a goal that is far too vague. The chances of success are limited unless the patient and therapist clearly define the kind of work, job opportunities, location, and the number of hours. Moreover, there are no criteria for checking progress or testing whether the goal has been achieved. Thus, therapists may find themselves in deep water if they go along with low-level or vaguely defined treatment goals.

FROM PROTOCOL TOWARD PERSONALIZED TREATMENT

When a particular treatment has been comprehensively described in a protocol, therapists may be tempted to simply start treating patients with this protocol in hand. They may even inform their patients that treatment will be based on such a protocol. However, to ensure a successful outcome, the actual treatment must be tailored to each individual patient and be directed at the patient's particular cognitions and behaviors. The danger of working with a protocol lies in the risk that accountability is placed with the protocol and not with the therapist and patient. The therapist may say (or think): "This protocol simply doesn't work," or the patient may tell the therapist, "I have done everything you asked me to do, but it has not worked at all." Perhaps the therapist will subsequently start looking for new or alternative solutions. Either way, both parties fail to take personal responsibility for the problems. The therapist has not translated the protocol into an individualized approach to fit the patient, and the patient has taken the therapist's suggestions as the prescribed and only approach without adapting the instructions to his or her own personal situation. To prevent this from happening, the treatment must be fine-tuned to the patient's individual cognitions. At the behavioral level, the therapist needs to encourage patients to find their own solutions to change impeding behaviors. An additional risk is that, when patients, in their personal lives, do not successfully apply the techniques discussed during the sessions, the therapist may start trying too hard to find alternative solutions. Instead, it is essential to help patients build up their self-confidence by holding them more accountable for the program. This is all the more important because self-confidence and personal responsibility are prerequisites for the later sessions when patients have become familiar with the treatment's underlying principles.

NONCOMPLIANCE WITH HOMEWORK ASSIGNMENTS

If patients fail to carry out homework assignments or do not bring records or charts along to the sessions, this is often taken as a sign that they are resisting treatment. However, it may well indicate that the therapist's instructions have been too complicated or vague. This is often the case with assignments related to drawing up action plans. The therapist then needs to probe for possible obstacles and encourage patients to find alternative ways to complete the assignment appropriately.

FOCUSING ON BODILY SYMPTOMS

A strong focus on bodily symptoms has proven to be a major determinant of fatigue. One of the mediating factors of CBT is aimed at reducing patients' focus on bodily symptoms. In practice, changing this tendency often proves difficult. One of the pitfalls is that the therapist's approach to the subject can intensify the focus on bodily symptoms. Asking patients at each and every session whether the complaints of fatigue have diminished is not productive. Nor is it wise to have patients continue reporting the degree of the fatigue after the third or fourth session. In fact, these constant queries are likely to enhance the perceived fatigue. Although patients are supposed to direct their attention to other things, they are being prompted to pay even more attention to the way they feel.

THE SUITABILITY OF THE TREATMENT FOR CHRONIC FATIGUE ASSOCIATED WITH OTHER ILLNESSES

Chronic fatigue is a common, often reported complaint and is not restricted to chronic fatigue syndrome. It is also prevalent in patients suffering from multiple sclerosis (MS), neuromuscular diseases, or chronic pancreatitis, and in patients who have suffered a stroke (van der Werf, van den Broek, Anten, & Bleijenberg, 2001) or who have been successfully treated for cancer (Servaes, Verhagen, & Bleijenberg, 2002; Vercoulen et al., 1996).

The model that lies at the base of the CBT for CFS as described in this chapter was found not to fit MS patients suffering from chronic fatigue. This suggests that the present model needs to be adapted to this group. Current clinical experience with the treatment of chronic fatigue in MS patients is limited, however, and to date no empirical research has been conducted. This also applies to most of the other conditions mentioned. The only exception is that research into chronic fatigue after successful cancer treatment has been stepped up in recent years. The fatigue-related symptoms following cancer treatment have been found to be quite distinct from those observed in CFS in several aspects. Thus, former cancer patients reported far fewer instances of muscle pains, joint ache, and headache, and mentioned low activity patterns only rarely (Servaes, Prins, Verhagen, & Bleijenberg, 2002). Also, with former cancer patients, a distinction needs to be made between patients in whom the fatigue symptoms are recent (occurring within 12 months following treatment) and patients who have been suffering from fatigue for a longer period. There are indications that in the first group of patients, the patient needs to come to terms with having (had) cancer and having undergone invasive medical treatment before being able to overcome the fatigue. The treatment for the latter group possibly resembles the treatment of the more active CFS patients most. The findings of clinical trials with this group of patients, in which an individualized treatment protocol was used, look promising. However, before drawing any firm conclusions, investigators need to conduct controlled studies to provide empirical evidence for the effects found.

REFERENCES

Alberts, M., Vercoulen, J. H., & Bleijenberg, G. (2001). Assessment of fatigue: The practical utility of the subjective feeling of fatigue in research and clinical practice. In A. Vingerhoets (Ed.), *Assessment in behavioral medicine* (pp. 301–327). East-Sussex: Brunner/Routledge.

Bazelmans, E., Bleijenberg, G., van der Meer, J. W., & Folgering, H. (2001). Is physical deconditioning a perpetuating factor in chronic fatigue syndrome? A controlled study on maximal exercise performance and relations with fatigue, impairment and physical activity. *Psychological Medicine, 31,* 107–114.

Bergner, M., Bobbit, R. A., Carter, W. B., & Gilson, B. S. (1981). The Sickness Impact Profile: Development and final revision of a health status measure. *Medical Care, 19,* 787–805.

Beurskens, A. J., Bültmann, U., Kant, I. J., Vercoulen, J. H., Bleijenberg, G., & Swaen, G. M. (2000). Fatigue amongst working people: Validity of a questionnaire measure. *Occupational and Environmental Medicine, 57,* 353–357.

Bonner, D., Ron, M., Chalder, T., Butler, S., & Wessely, S. (1994). Chronic fatigue syndrome: A follow-up study. *Journal of Neurology, Neurosurgery, and Psychiatry, 57*, 617–621.

Bültmann, U., de Vries, M., Beurskens, A. J., Bleijenberg, G., Vercoulen, J. H., & Kant, I. J. (2000). Measurement of prolonged fatigue in the working population: Determination of a cut-off point for the Checklist Individual Strength. *Journal of Occupational Health Psychology, 5*, 411–416.

Butler, S., Chalder, T., Ron, M., & Wessely, S. (1991). Cognitive behavior therapy in chronic fatigue syndrome. *Journal of Neurology, Neurosurgery, and Psychiatry, 54*, 153–158.

Chalder, T., Berelowitz, G., Pawlikowska, J., Watts, K., & Wessely, S. (1993). Development of a fatigue scale. *Journal of Psychosomatic Research, 37*, 147–153.

Chalder, T., Butler, S., & Wessely, S. (1996). In-patient treatment of chronic fatigue syndrome. *Behavioral and Cognitive Psychotherapy, 24*, 351–365.

Clark, M. R., Katon, W., Russo, J., Kith, P., Sintay, M., & Buchwald, D. (1995). Chronic fatigue: Risk factors for symptom persistence in a 2.5 year follow-up study. *American Journal of Medicine, 98*, 187–195.

Cox, D. L., & Findley, L. J. (1998). The management of chronic fatigue syndrome in an inpatient setting: Presentation of an approach and perceived outcome. *British Journal of Occupational Therapy, 61*, 405–409.

Deale, A., Chalder, T., Marks, I., & Wessely, S. (1997). Cognitive behavior therapy for chronic fatigue syndrome: A randomized controlled trial. *American Journal Psychiatry, 154*(3), 408–414.

Deale, A., Chalder, T., & Wessely, S. (1998). Illness beliefs and treatment outcome in chronic fatigue syndrome. *Journal of Psychosomatic Research, 45*, 77–83.

Deale, A., Husain, K., Chalder, T., & Wessely, S. (2001). Long-term outcome of cognitive behavior therapy versus relaxation therapy for chronic fatigue syndrome: A 5-year follow-up study. *American Journal of Psychiatry, 158*, 2038–2042.

Friedberg, F., & Krupp, L. B. (1994). A comparison of cognitive behavioral therapy in chronic fatigue syndrome. *Clinical Infectious Diseases, 18*(Suppl. 1), 105–109.

Fulcher, K. Y., & White, P. D. (1997). Randomized controlled trial of graded exercise in patients with the chronic fatigue syndrome. *British Medical Journal, 314*, 1647–1652.

Greene, B., & Blanchard, E. B. (1994). Cognitive therapy for irritable bowel syndrome. *Journal of Consulting and Clinical Psychology, 62*, 576–582.

Hawton, K., Salkovskis, P. M., Kirk, J., & Clark, D. M. (1989). *Cognitive behavior therapy for psychiatric problems, a practical guide.* New York: Oxford University Press.

Heijmans, J. W. (1998). Coping and adaptive outcome in chronic fatigue syndrome: Importance of illness cognitions. *Journal of Psychosomatic Research, 45*, 39–51.

Lloyd, A. R., Hickie, I., Brockman, A., Hickie, C., Wilson, A., Dwyer, J., et al. (1993). Immunologic and psychologic therapy for patients with chronic fatigue syndrome: A double-blind, placebo-controlled trial. *American Journal of Medicine, 94*, 197–203.

Payne, A., & Blanchard, E. B. (1995). A controlled comparison of cognitive therapy and self-help groups in the treatment of irritable bowel syndrome. *Journal of Consulting and Clinical Psychology, 63*(5), 779–786.

Peakman, M., Deale, A., Field, R., Mahalingam, M., & Wessely, S. (1997). Clinical improvement in chronic fatigue syndrome is not associated with lymphocyte sunsets of function or activation. *Clinical Immunology and Immunopathology, 82*, 83–91.

Pipe, R., & Wait, M. (1995). Family therapy in the treatment of chronic fatigue syndrome in adolescence. *ACCP Review News, 17*, 916.

Powell, P., Bentall, R. P., Nye, F. J., & Edwards, R. H. (2001). Randomized controlled trial of patient education to encourage graded exercise in chronic fatigue syndrome. *British Medical Journal, 322*, 1–5.

Price, J. R., & Couper, J. (2000). *Cognitive behavior therapy for adults with chronic fatigue syndrome* (Cochrane Review). In The Cochrane Library (issue 2). Oxford, England: Update Software.

Prins, J. B., Bazelmans, E., van der Werf, S., van der Meer, J. W., & Bleijenberg, G. (2002). Cognitive behavior therapy for chronic fatigue syndrome: Predictors of treatment outcome. *Excerpta Medica International Congress Series, 1241,* 131–135.

Prins, J. B., & Bleijenberg, G. (1999). Cognitive behavior therapy for chronic fatigue syndrome: A case study. *Journal of Behavior Therapy and Experimental Psychiatry, 30*(4), 325–339.

Prins, J. B., Bleijenberg, G., Bazelmans, E., Elving, L., de Boo, T., Severens, J. L., et al. (2001). Cognitive behavior therapy for chronic fatigue syndrome: A multicenter randomized controlled trial. *Lancet, 357,* 841–847.

Prins, J. B., Bleijenberg, G., & van der Meer, J. W. (2002). Chronic fatigue syndrome and myalgic encephalomyelitis: Correspondence. *Lancet, 359,* 1699.

Reid, S., Chalder, T., Cleare, A., Hotopf, M., & Wessely, S. (2000). Extracts from clinical Evidence: Chronic fatigue syndrome. *British Medical Journal, 320,* 292–296.

Servaes, P., Prins, J., Verhagen, C., & Bleijenberg, G. (2002). Fatigue after breast cancer and in chronic fatigue syndrome, similarities and differences. *Journal of Psychosomatic Research, 52,* 453–459.

Servaes, P., Verhagen, C., & Bleijenberg, G. (2002). Determinants of chronic fatigue in disease-free breast cancer patients, a cross-sectional study. *Annals of Oncology, 13,* 589–598.

Sharpe, M., Hawton, K., Simkin, S., Suraway, C., Hackman, A., Klimes, I., et al. (1996). Cognitive therapy for chronic fatigue syndrome: A randomized controlled trial. *British Medical Journal, 312*(7022), 22–26.

Tyron, W. (1991). *Activity measurement in psychology and medicine.* New York: Plenum Press.

van der Werf, S., de Vree, B., van der Meer, J. W., & Bleijenberg, G. (2002). The relations among body consciousness, somatic symptom report, and information processing speed in chronic fatigue syndrome. *Neuropsychiatry, Neuropsychology, and Behavioral Neurology, 15,* 2–9.

van der Werf, S., Prins, J. B., Vercoulen, J. H., van der Meer, J. W., & Bleijenberg, G. (2000). Identifying physical activity patterns in chronic fatigue syndrome using actigraphic assessment. *Journal of Psychosomatic Research, 49*(5), 372–379.

van der Werf, S., van den Broek, H. L., Anten, H. W., & Bleijenberg, G. (2001). Experience of severe fatigue long after stroke and its relation to depressive symptoms and disease characteristics. *European Neurology, 45,* 28–33.

Van Dulmen, S., Fennis, J. F., & Bleijenberg, G. (1996). Cognitive-behavioral group therapy for irritable bowel syndrome: Effects and long-term follow-up. *Psychosomatic Medicine, 58,* 508–514.

Vercoulen, J. H., Hommes, O. R., Swanink, C. M., Jongen, P. J., Fennis, J. F., Galama, J. M., et al. (1996). The measurement of fatigue in multiple sclerosis: A comparison with patients with chronic fatigue syndrome and healthy subjects. *Archives of Neurology, 53,* 642–649.

Vercoulen, J. H., Hommes, O. R., Swanink, C. M., Jongen, P. J., Fennis, J. F., Galama, J. M., et al. (1998). The persistence of fatigue in chronic fatigue syndrome and multiple sclerosis: Development of a model. *Journal of Psychosomatic Research, 45,* 507–517.

Vercoulen, J. H., Swanink, C. M., Fennis, J. F., Galama, J. M., van der Meer, J. W., & Bleijenberg, G. (1994). Dimensional assessment of chronic fatigue syndrome. *Journal of Psychosomatic Research, 38*(5), 383–392.

Vollmer, A., & Blanchard, E. B. (1998). Controlled comparison of individual versus group cognitive therapy for irritable bowel syndrome. *Behavior Therapy, 29*, 19–33.

Ware, J. E., & Sherbourne, C. D. (1992). The MOS 36-item short-form health survey (SF-36). I: Conceptual framework and item selection. *Medical Care, 30*, 173–183.

Wearden, A. J., Morriss, R. K., Mullis, R., Strickland, P. L., Pearson, D. J., Appleby, L., et al. (1998). Randomized, double-blind, placebo-controlled treatment trial of fluoxetine and graded exercise for chronic fatigue syndrome. *British Journal of Psychiatry, 172*, 485–490.

Wessely, S., Hotopf, M., & Sharpe, M. (1998). *Chronic Fatigue and its Syndromes.* Oxford/New York/Tokyo: Oxford University Press.

Whiting, P., Bagnall, A., Sowden, A. J., Cornell, J. E., Mulrow, C. D., & Ramirez, G. (2001). Interventions for the treatment and management of chronic fatigue syndrome. *Journal of American Medical Association, 286*, 1360–1366.

CHAPTER 24

Stress and Immunity

MICHAEL H. ANTONI and DONNA E. WEISS

T HE CHRONIC FATIGUE syndrome (CFS) is characterized by physical symptoms that bring about severe limitations in the lifestyle and vocational
activities of previously vital, productive, and successful individuals (Komaroff & Buchwald, 1991, 1998). Symptoms associated with CFS include debilitating fatigue, low-grade fever, lymph node pain and tenderness, pharyngitis,
myalgias, arthralgias, cognitive difficulties, and mood changes (Buchwald, Sullivan, & Komaroff, 1987). A malaise-like fatigue appears to dominate the clinical
picture in patients with CFS, though depressive features are also commonly observed (Jones & Straus, 1987; Taerk, Toner, Salit, Garfinkel, & Ozersky, 1987).
Whether depression is a cause, cofactor, effect, or correlate of CFS is, however, unknown (Abbey & Garfinkel, 1991). Along with the physical and affective
symptoms, there is a growing evidence that patients with CFS may also show
abnormalities on several indexes of immune functioning (e.g., elevated IgG,
impaired natural killer cell cytotoxicity (NKCC; Klimas, Salvato, Morgan, &
Fletcher, 1990). They may also show elevated levels of circulating cytokine
peptides and/or mRNA, and abnormalities in the numbers and activation
states of certain lymphocyte subpopulations (Buchwald, Cheney, & Peterson,
1992; Caligiuri et al., 1987; Klimas, Patarca, & Fletcher, 1992; Klimas et al., 1990;
Landay, Jessop, Lennette, & Levy, 1991; Lutgendorf, Antoni, et al., 1995; Patarca,
Klimas, Lutgendorf, Antoni, & Fletcher, 1994; Salvato, Klimas, Ashman, &
Fletcher, 1988). This pattern, along with the physical symptom picture, is not inconsistent with a chronic activation of the immune system.

Disturbances in mood, however, may be reactive to the physical limitations
that fatigue and related symptoms impose on the CFS patient. If so, these psychological symptoms may be best viewed as *distress reactions* that are secondary to the
cytokine-induced flulike symptoms and cognitive deficits (shortened attention
span, concentration difficulties, memory problems, impaired problem solving,
dyslogia; Brickman & Fins, 1993) that are common symptoms of CFS. As an example of the *role of distress responses in exacerbating or maintaining CFS symptoms*,
Kennedy (1988) suggested that as CFS patients' ability to concentrate and attend
decreases, anxiety and irritability may increase (1) in an attempt to achieve

arousal levels that can meet task demands, or (2) because of simple frustration. The anxiety and distress may further deplete energy resulting in additional decrements in attention and vigilance that worsen the fatigue symptoms. Others have suggested that a depressive syndrome may develop in response to these physical symptoms (Taerk et al., 1987).

Separating out CFS-induced cognitive difficulties from depressive responses is difficult in this population. However, we have related the severity of cognitive deficits in CFS patients to two factors. The first one is greater physical impairments (Karnovsky scores) and illness burden (Sickness Impact Profile, SIP scores). The second one is greater impairments in lymphocyte responses to phytohemagglutinin (PHA) and elevated serum neopterin levels in CFS patients, a finding that held after controlling for major depressive disorder diagnosis (MDD) and severity of depression (Beck Depression Inventory, BDI scores; Beck, Ward, Mendelson, Mock, & Erbaugh, 1961; Lutgendorf, Klimas, Antoni, Brickman, & Fletcher, 1995). This finding suggested that (1) these cognitive deficits may be caused by the same "third variable(s)" that brings about the immunologic abnormalities in CFS, and (2) the cognitive and immunologic abnormalities are not merely a by-product of a clinical depressive syndrome. Complicating the picture further and possibly further dysregulating the immune system is that distress responses (as well as depressive states) are known to relate to several of the immunologic indexes (e.g., lymphocyte proliferative responsivity to PHA) just noted for CFS patients. Because distress reactions may be a common denominator contributing to multiple abnormalities (fatigue, immune dysfunction) that characterize this syndrome, effective treatment needs to focus on reducing the patients' distress reactions in a way that recognizes the interdependency among CFS symptom severity, psychological response processes, and the immune system. No treatments have used such a systems orientation to address CFS.

Cognitive-behavioral stress management (CBSM) interventions reduce distress and reactive depressive states by modifying patients' outlook, cognitive appraisals, and coping strategies (Turk, Holzman, & Kerns, 1986) and—when presented in a group format—may also improve their perceptions of social support. These group interventions have also been shown to modulate immunologic indexes such as NKCC (Fawzy, Kemeny, Cousins, Fawzy, & Fahey, 1990) among populations suffering from other immune-related illnesses. Although generalizing these benefits to CFS patients has risks, some work has begun to explore the degree to which similar interventions affect CFS symptoms. An initial mechanistic research question concerns whether the cognitive-behavioral processes modulated by CBSM predict the severity of physical symptoms and lifestyle disturbances (e.g., fatigue-associated compromise in activities of daily living) that CFS patients experience. Addressing this question is the primary aim of this chapter. Our conceptual model specifies the ways in which psychological distress and immunologic abnormalities may act as *mediator variables* contributing to the exacerbation and/or maintenance of CFS physical symptoms.

MODEL FOR MULTIPLE INFLUENCES ON CFS MAINTENANCE

We propose a framework describing multiple biological and psychological factors that may relate to the maintenance of the physical symptoms and illness burden associated with CFS (see Figure 24.1). Previously, other investigators have outlined a multifactorial model for possible *etiologic factors* involved in CFS including Epstein-Barr virus (EBV) infection, other viruses, and mental stress and depression-associated reactivation of EBV as risk factors (e.g., Evans, 1991). In contrast, we present a *model for maintenance and exacerbation of CFS.* We have integrated findings from our lab with the extant literature concerning the immunologic, physical, and affective correlates of CFS. Our model proposes an immunologic dysregulation (due to unknown causes) characterized by chronic lymphocyte activation with elevated expression of lymphocyte activation markers, episodic increased expression of interleukin-1 (IL-1) and tumor necrosis factor (TNF)-α and β peptide and soluble receptor in serum, and mRNA in circulating lymphocytes, and other soluble activation markers such as neopterin. This immune activation is accompanied by decrements in NKCC and lymphocyte proliferation that may compromise an individual's ability to control latent virus reactivation and new viral infections. Cytokine-mediated physical symptoms such as fatigue and assorted inflammatory symptoms may cause increased distress and depressed mood in patients with CFS. These psychological reactions may sensitize patients to attend more to their symptoms, possibly triggering catastrophic appraisals and hopelessness. These psychological phenomena may also contribute to latent virus reactivation (Jenkins & Baum, 1995) as well as decrements in NKCC and lymphocyte proliferative responses (Byrnes et al., 1998). We propose that CFS patients present with immune system dysregulation and a symptom picture that they may exacerbate and possibly maintain by their reactions to their symptoms. Other external stressors also may contribute to immune system parameters that are important for efficient resolution of reactivated latent viruses or new viral infections. Efficient resolution of viral or other types of infections must strike a balance between a sufficiently potent response and one that is time limited. The tendency toward insufficient front-line responses such as NKCC in

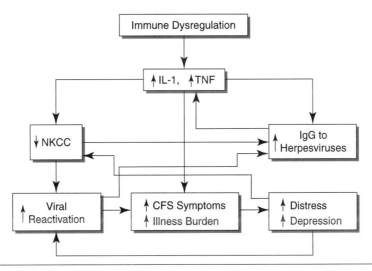

Figure 24.1 Conceptual Model for the Interaction of Immune Dysregulation, Psychological States, and Chronic Fatigue Syndrome (CFS) Symptoms. IL-1 = Interleukin-1; TNF = Tumor necrosis factor; NKCC = Natural killer cell cytotoxicity; IgG = Immunoglobulin-G.

combination with prolonged states of cellular activation and proinflammatory cytokine secretion characterize the inefficient immune profile of many patients with CFS.

Cytokine Dysregulation Associated with CFS Clinical Symptoms

TNF-α and β are primary modifiers of the inflammatory and immune activation that animals produce in response to injury or infection. TNF-α or cathexin and TNF-β (lymphotoxin) share 30% sequence homology and react with the same receptors on cell surfaces (Tartaglia & Goeddel, 1992). We know that IL-1, a cytokine that plays a key role in antigen presentation, is also associated with pyrogenic changes (e.g., fever) that accompany inflammatory reactions. These cytokines are primarily produced by macrophages. Overproduction, inappropriate expression of IL-1 and/or TNF, and TNF injections have been associated with fever, slow-wave sleep induction, and appetite suppression (Dinarello, Cannon, & Wolff, 1986; Shoham, Davenne, & Cady, 1987). TNF is a known pyrogen and also appears to provoke slow-wave sleep (Shoham et al., 1987), which may underlie the fatigue, lassitude, and excessive sleepiness associated with this syndrome (Moldofsky, 1989). We found that CFS patients show significantly elevated TNF-α and β levels compared with controls (Patarca et al., 1994).

Cytokine Effects on the Immune System

TNF proinflammatory effects may be mediated by induction of gene expression for neutrophil activating protein-1 and macrophage inflammatory proteins resulting in neutrophil migration and degranulation (Dinarello, 1992). Thus, TNF elevations may be associated with markers of macrophage activation such as serum neopterin elevations. Our work also suggests that TNF mRNAs in CFS patients are produced by activated lymphocytes: (1) TNF-β proteins correlate significantly (p), which is in line with the parallel increased relative levels of HLA-DR expressing CD8 cells in CFS patients. Thus, immune system dysregulation/overactivation in CFS patients might be best reflected in a combination of measures that would include cytokine protein and mRNA levels, and serum neopterin to index macrophage activation, and enumeration of activated lymphocyte subsets (e.g., CD8-HLA-DR and CD26+CD2+ percentages). Chronic T-cell activation can lead to decreased lymphocyte proliferative responsiveness to specific and nonspecific stimuli and to decreased NKCC (Klimas et al., 1990). Thus, chronic lymphocyte activation with elevated expression of lymphocyte activation markers may relate to impairments in cell-mediated immune functions—proliferative and cytotoxic responses of lymphocytes—that have been observed in CFS (Lloyd, Hickie, Hickie, Dwyer, & Wakefield, 1992; Lloyd, Wakefield, Dwyer, & Boughton, 1989; Lloyd, Wakefield, & Hickie, 1993).

Cytokine Effects on Cognitive Functioning

Knowledge is accumulating on cytokine-nervous system interactions that may be mediated by endocrine mechanisms including interactions between IL-1 and several hypothalamic pituitary adrenal (HPA) axis peptides and glucocorticoids (Berkenbosch, VanOers, del Rey, Tilders, & Besedovsky, 1987; Besedovsky, del Ray,

Sorkin, & Dinarello, 1986; Demitrack, & Crofford, 1998; Moldofsky, 1995; Scott, & Dinan, 1998; Scott, Medbak, & Dinan, 1998; Sternberg, 1993; Visser et al., 1998). An extensive discussion of these interactions is beyond the scope of this chapter. Other work suggests that both IL-1 and TNF when injected into the brain can augment the release of growth hormone, which is also known to be elevated during self-limiting viral infections (Kelley, 1989). Moreover, elevations in IL-1α and TNF-α have been shown to affect brain function in isolated reports. These cytokine abnormalities may result from a reactive depression in which memory symptoms are secondary. Few or no studies relating cytokine elevations to cognitive dysfunction have systematically controlled for comorbid depression. We found that other indexes of immune system dysregulation—greater serum neopterin levels and reduced lymphocyte proliferative responses to mitogens—are related to the severity of cognitive difficulties that CFS patients suffer, independent of depression (Lutgendorf, Klimas, et al., 1995). These abnormalities were associated with increased cognitive difficulties and greater physical illness burden, and these findings held after statistically controlling for a *DSM-III* diagnosis of Major Depressive Disorder (MDD) and after controlling for severity of depressed affect as measured on psychiatric interview (Lutgendorf, Klimas, et al., 1995).

STRESSORS, CYTOKINES, AND SYMPTOMS

Our model holds that the interaction of *psychological factors* (distress associated with either CFS-related symptoms or external stressful life events) and *immunologic dysfunction* (indicated in signs of chronic overactivation) contribute to (1) CFS-related physical symptoms (e.g., fatigue, joint pain, cognitive difficulties, fever) and increases in illness burden; and (2) dysfunction in the immune system's ability to survey viruses (indicated in impaired NKCC and lymphocyte proliferative responses to PHA). One study found an association between psychosocial stressors, immunomodulation, and the incidence and progression of rhinovirus infections in healthy normals (Cohen, Tyrrell, & Smith, 1991). Here, the rates of respiratory infections and clinical colds increased in a dose-response fashion with increases in psychological stress across all five of the cold viruses studied. If viruses related to upper respiratory infections (URIs) are not well controlled by immune surveillance mechanisms (e.g., NKCC) in CFS patients who are exposed to stressors, then patients may suffer more frequent and protracted URIs that are accompanied by prolonged elevations in proinflammatory cytokines. Alternatively, distress increases may modulate the immune system possibly exacerbating cytokine dysregulation, which then intensifies physical (e.g., inflammatory) symptoms. Such a recursive system may act as a positive feedback loop thereby accounting for the chronicity of CFS and its refraction to interventions focusing solely on symptom reduction. This model is in line with recent theory suggesting that stress effects on viral infections may have relevance for chronic fatigue syndrome patients (Glaser & Kiecolt-Glaser, 1999).

Our *distress-based model* is empirically supported in data from our lab showing apparent distress effects in parallel with symptom exacerbation in South Florida CFS patients who were monitored in the months preceding and following the landfall of Hurricane Andrew. Patients living in a hurricane exposure area (Dade County) had significantly greater severity of CFS symptom relapses (using clinician-rated fatigue levels and ability to engage in work-related activities). They also showed significantly greater pre-poststorm increases in illness burden compared with age- and gender-matched CFS patients from the same clinical practice living in an adjacent geographic region, Broward/Palm Beach County, that was not in the storm's path (Lutgendorf, Antoni, et al., 1995). The influence of the storm's impact on the severity of symptom relapses and illness burden appeared to be mediated by the patients' distress reaction to the storm (e.g., perceived death threat, feeling emotionally affected in the weeks following the storm). Social support provisions and an optimistic outlook moderated the contribution of distress reactions to relapse severity (Lutgendorf, Antoni, et al., 1995). Greater optimism and social support provisions were also associated with lower elevations in peripheral cytokines such as TNF among storm victims (Antoni, 1994). Importantly, greater pre-poststorm increases in TNF concentrations in the circulation were associated with greater increases in the severity and frequency of CFS symptoms in the Dade County sample (Antoni, 1994).

IMMUNOLOGIC DISTURBANCES OF CFS PATIENTS

A major premise of the proposed model, drawn from a growing literature and our observations in extensive work with CFS samples, is that persons diagnosed with CFS evidence multiple immunologic disturbances measurable with cell-mediated and humoral immune functions, lymphocyte activation markers, and cytokine indexes. A second major premise is that several of these immunologic disturbances are correlated with the physical symptoms and behavioral/lifestyle compromise reported by these patients.

CELLULAR AND NATURAL IMMUNE FUNCTION DISTURBANCES

Among CFS patients, the following immunologic abnormalities have been noted: depressed responses to PHA and pokeweed mitogen (PWM; Kibler, Lucas, Hicks, Poulos, & Jones, 1985); impaired NKCC and a decreased number of CD56+CD3− lymphocytes—an NK phenotype (Caligiuri et al., 1987); and diminished in vitro production of gamma interferon (IFN-γ) and IL-2 by cultured lymphocytes (Kibler et al., 1985). In a more recent study of CFS patients by this latter group, NKCC was not found to be reduced (Jones, 1991). We have reported low levels of NKCC, but an elevated number of NK cells, indexed as CD56+ lymphocytes (Klimas, Salvato, Morgan, & Fletcher, 1990; Tarsis, Klimas, & Baron, 1988; Salvato et al., 1988). Thus, a qualitative defect may be present in these patients' NK cells. Our observation of a low value of kinetic lytic units per NK cell suggests a profound impairment of NK cell cytotoxic activity. Our work suggests that these decrements in NKCC may be due to a defect in the production of perforin, an important soluble factor produced by cytotoxic (NK and CD8 T-lymphocytes) cells during their interaction with targets (Maher, 2000). Low NKCC has been reported in other studies of CFS (Behan, Behan, & Bell, 1985; Buchwald & Komaroff, 1991; Caliguri et al., 1987) as well as another condition resembling CFS—low NK syndrome (LNKS; Aoki, Usuda, & Miyakoshi, 1985, 1987). Poor NK cell function may be related to the impaired ability of lymphocytes from CFS patients to produce IFN-γ in response to mitogenic stimulation (Klimas et al., 1990). Inability of lymphocytes to produce IFN-γ might represent a cellular immune exhaustion as a consequence of persistent viral stimulus, a theory that is supported by the elevation of leukocyte 2'5' oligoadenylate synthetase (Straus, Tosato, & Armstrong, 1985), an IFN-induced enzyme in lymphocytes of CFS patients. Although no primary NK deficiency diseases have been identified, abnormalities in NK cells may be important in conferring protection against viruses associated with respiratory infections. The lack of IFN-γ production may impair activation of immunoregulatory circuits and NKCC (Knop, Stremer, & Neuman, 1982; Targan & Stebbing, 1982; Zlotnick, Shimonkewitz, & Gefter, 1983).

Pursuing the hypothesis that interventions that normalize NK functioning might abrogate the low-grade fever and fatigue in LNKS, a condition resembling CFS in many but not all ways, one group has tested the effects of immunopotentiators among patients diagnosed with LNKS. They found in single-blind trials (contents of medication were not revealed to patients) that the administration of antipyretics, nonsteroidal anti-inflammatory drugs, or antibiotics had no detectable effects on fever. However, lentinan, a glucon extracted from Japanese mushrooms, improved clinical symptoms and increased NKCC and antibody-dependent cellular cytotoxicity (ADCC) in patients with LNKS (Miyakoshi, Aoki, & Mizukoshi, 1984). Although preliminary, this is one of the only studies to document parallel improvement in CFS-like clinical symptoms and NKCC following an experimental manipulation. However, this study did not focus specifically on Centers for Disease Control (CDC)-diagnosed CFS patients.

LYMPHOCYTE PHENOTYPE ALTERATIONS

There have been reports, including ones from our laboratory (Cruess, Klimas, Helder, Antoni, & Fletcher, 2000; Klimas et al., 1990; Salvato et al., 1988; Tarsis et al., 1988), of alterations in the distribution of T and B cell subsets among samples of CFS patients. In reference to T-helper/inducer (CD4) and T-suppressor/cytotoxic (CD8) cell counts, discrepant results have been reported. Straus et al. (1985) reported a statistically higher percentage of CD4 lymphocytes with a normal number of CD8 cells and CD4/CD8 ratio.

Our work has focused on identifying more specific subsets of these lymphocytes that underlie specific regulatory functions. Among CFS patients, we found elevated numbers of T cells expressing the activation marker, CD26 (also reported elevated in multiple sclerosis [Hafler, Fox, & Manning, 1985]), CD8 cells expressing the class II marker, (I2), and B cells co-expressing the NK cell marker, CD56. The research teams of both Levy and Landay also noted elevated HLA/DR antigens expressing CD8 cells, identified as cytotoxic T cells in 150 CFS patients (Landay, 1991; Levy, 1991). We also observed *lower* values for a subset of CD4 cells associated with suppressor/cytotoxic cell induction (Morimoto, Letvin, Distato, Aldrich, & Schlossman, 1985) (CD4+CD45RA+), with the majority of CFS patients having absolute counts > 1 *SD* below the normal mean. Franco et al. (Franco, Kawa, & Doi, 1987) have also described a decreased number of CD4+CD45RA+ lymphocytes in 2 patients with severe chronic active EBV infection. Depletion of the CD4+ CD45RA+ lymphocyte subset in our patients may favor B cell dysregulation. A similar mechanism of impaired immunoregulation may play a central role in the pathogenesis as well as in the perpetuation of some chronic viral infections and perhaps, CFS.

An Italian study of immunologic phenotypes in 30 CFS patients and 30 sex- and age-matched controls found the following pattern for the CFS patients: reduced CD56+ cells and CD16+CD3– cells but increases in cytotoxic T cells with NK activity, and in circulating B-lymphocytes (Tirelli, Pinto, & Marotta, 1993). This group also found significant elevations in T-cells expressing several activation markers and in the total number of T-cells expressing HLA-DR antigens. The authors concluded that a subset-specific decrease in NK cells along with evidence of T-lymphocytes that appear to be chronically activated might represent a consistent finding in CDC-defined cases of CFS. This sample displayed many of the clinical and immunologic features that we have observed in CFS patients in Miami as well as those observed in other labs in the United States and abroad (Borysiewicz, Haworth, & Cohen, 1986; Landay et al., 1991; Morimoto, Reinherz, Schlossman, Schur, Mills, & Steinberg, 1980; Rose, Ginsberg, Rothstein, Ledbetter, & Clark, 1985, 1988).

Summary of Immune Findings

CFS patients appear to show a wide variety of immune system abnormalities—impaired NKCC and proliferation to PHA, elevated cytokine levels, and increased numbers of activated lymphocyte subsets. However, little previous research has systematically investigated the association between these immunologic abnormalities and physical health status in this population and this, in part, may account for the lack of an effective treatment for this chronic syndrome. The conceptual model guiding our research proposes that the psychological and immunologic status of the individual interact with one another as well as with physical symptoms of CFS. In doing so, they perpetuate a positive feedback loop that maintains the CFS physical symptoms.

PSYCHOIMMUNOLOGIC ASSOCIATIONS IN CFS

The coexistence of psychological and immunologic abnormalities in CFS patients suggests that these features may be related to one another. Additionally, because psychosocial stressors and individuals' coping responses to stressors may affect the immune system, it is important to consider their role in the maintenance of CFS-associated physical symptoms. Depressed affect, which is commonly observed in CFS, is also known to relate to the immune system.

Depression and Immunity

There is considerable evidence that depression itself may modulate immune status (Calabrese, Kling, & Gold, 1987), and this may account, in part, for the immunologic abnormalities associated with CFS. Although several studies have related clinical depression and depressed affect to poorer lymphocyte responses to mitogens such as PHA, Stein, Miller, and Trestman (1991) note that consistent or reproducible evidence seems to be lacking for lymphocyte proliferative responses, as well as NKCC and lymphocyte phenotype impairments in patients with MDD. Irwin et al. (1990) found significant decreases in NKCC associated with depressive disorders. However, Schleifer et al. (Schleifer, Keller, Bond, Cohen, & Stein, 1989), using appropriate interassay controls, found no direct association between depression and lymphocyte phenotypes, lymphocyte responses to PHA, Con-A or PWM, nor with NKCC. Specific features of depressive syndromes (e.g., sleep abnormalities, changes in diet, mood) may be responsible for alterations in immune function seen in some depressed patients.

STRESSORS AND CHANGES IN IMMUNE FUNCTION

A sizable literature relating stressors to immune system modulation has evolved in the past two decades. Many groups have reviewed this literature, the most comprehensive being that of Ader, Felten, and Cohen (2000). Among the most common, though not necessarily consistent, immune measures related to the experience of stressors are NKCC, proliferative responses of lymphocytes to mitogens such as PHA, and IgG antibody titers against (and T-cytotoxic killing of) herpesviruses (Herbert & Cohen, 1993; Kiecolt-Glaser & Glaser, 1992). Less commonly, stressors were associated with abnormalities in lymphocyte distributions, lymphocytes expressing IL-2 receptors (Glaser, Kennedy, Lafuse, & Kiecolt-Glaser, 1990). One study found stressor-associated abnormalities in phorbol-ester inhibition of radiation-induced apoptosis in peripheral blood leukocytes—an important process related to immune system self-monitoring of pathogen (virus)-infected immunocompetent cells (Tomei, Kiecolt-Glaser, Kennedy, & Glaser, 1990). Several of these stress-induced immune changes may have significance for the pathophysiology of CFS given that this syndrome is associated with (1) reduced NKCC, (2) elevations in herpesvirus antibody titers, and (3) abnormalities in lymphocyte distributions and activation states.

PSYCHOSOCIAL MODERATORS OF STRESS-INDUCED IMMUNOMODULATION

Previous work has related lower social support provisions to impaired NKCC in spouses of cancer patients, a finding that appeared to be at least partially independent of depression (Baron, Cutrona, & Hicklin, 1990). Another study of spousal caregivers found that those who reported lower social support and greater distress about their spouse's dementia-related behaviors at intake showed the greatest and most consistent negative changes in immune function at 1-year follow-up (Kiecolt-Glaser, Dura, & Speicher, 1991). These findings suggest a role for social support as a moderator of stress-induced impairments in the immune system. Another set of putative moderators of stressor effects on the immune system includes the individual's psychological responses (e.g., cognitive appraisals, coping strategies) to stressors. We found that a cognitive-behavioral stress management (CBSM) intervention (including progressive muscle relaxation and cognitive restructuring) significantly lowered distress levels. It also increased or buffered decrements in NK cell counts and NKCC, and blastogenic responses to PHA in asymptomatic gay men measured at several time points over the 5 weeks preceding and following notification of their human immunodeficiency virus—type 1 (HIV-1) serostatus (Antoni et al., 1991). Follow-up analyses of these effects showed that increases in NKCC over the 10-week CBSM intervention period were associated with increases in coping strategies related to acceptance and social support seeking, and to increases in perceptions of social support provisions in these individuals (Antoni, Lutgendorf,

Ironson, Fletcher, & Schneiderman, 1996). Increases in NKCC were also correlated with greater frequency of home practice of the CBSM techniques (progressive muscle relaxation) being taught, suggesting that feelings of greater treatment efficacy were related to NKCC increases.

We also observed that CBSM lowered HIV+ men's IgG antibody titers to herpesviruses such as EBV, human herpesvirus-type 6 (HHV-6) and herpes simplex virus-type 2 (HSV-2), indicating better cellular control over these latent viruses (Cruess, Antoni, et al., 2000; Esterling et al., 1992; Lutgendorf et al., 1997). Again, greater increases in social support and relaxation skills learned were associated with the largest decreases in antibody titers (Antoni et al., 1996; Cruess, Antoni, et al., 2000). These studies suggest that coping responses, social support, and behavioral stress management interventions may modulate abnormal distress states and immune system indicators in stressed CFS patients. Intervention-induced alterations in psychological and immune status may be relevant for the maintenance of CFS physical symptoms.

MODEL FOR COGNITIVE-BEHAVIORAL INTERVENTION IN CFS

A positive feedback mechanism may maintain the physical and affective presentation of chronic fatigue syndrome. There is also a lack of knowledge concerning an etiologic agent responsible for the onset of CFS. Thus, interventions to reduce psychological distress and alter cognitive appraisal aspects (e.g., CBSM) may be effective in interrupting the mechanism maintaining or exacerbating some of the health complaints associated with the syndrome. In line with the recursive CFS maintenance model presented previously, we designed a cognitive behavioral intervention to interrupt certain components of this feedback system, focusing especially on those components that may impact both mental and physical health. In a second model, we now outline how such intervention may impact physical (and affective) status by *tension reduction, altered cognitive appraisals and coping strategies*, and *modulation of immune functioning* (see Figure 24.2). CBSM may affect CFS physical symptoms by first modulating a set of intervention targets. Changes in these intervention targets are hypothesized to improve physical symptoms by reducing distress and modulating immune function, or alternatively, by altering symptom appraisals.

COGNITIVE-BEHAVIORAL THERAPY WITH CFS PATIENTS

Sharpe et al. (1996) notes that cognitive-behavioral therapy (CBT) is well suited to address both behavioral and cognitive therapeutic goals for CFS patients. *Behavioral goals* such as achieving realistic patterns of physical activity and energy expenditures interspersed with regular rest periods and enjoyable (non-task-related) activities can be accomplished with time and activity management schedules. Patients can learn to relax, reduce tension, and control breathing patterns with regular relaxation exercises and related imagery techniques. These latter goals may improve the quality of rest and sleep as well as lowering basal distress or tension levels. *Cognitive goals* include correcting distorted appraisals about illness, reducing feelings of helplessness, and discouraging the avoidance of most activities, pleasant and unpleasant. Cognitive therapy techniques such as cognitive restructuring, problem

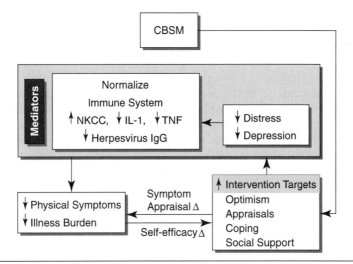

Figure 24.2 Conceptual Model for the Effects of Cognitive Behavioral Stress Management (CBSM) Intervention on Proximal Intervention Targets and Their Effects on Distal Outcomes of Distress and Depression, Immune System Status, and Physical Symptoms in Patients with Chronic Fatigue Syndrome. NKCC = Natural killer cell cytotoxicity; IL-1 = Interleukin-1; TNF = Tumor necrosis factor; IgG = Immunoglobulin-G.

solving, and coping skills training are especially effective in addressing these goals in certain populations. Sharpe et al. note that CBT may be effective in breaking the vicious cycle of fatigue, negative cognitions, increased attention to symptoms, distress reactions, physiologic arousal and other changes, and exacerbation of CFS symptoms, including fatigue. Moreover, CBT may be preferred over medications by CFS patients who are reluctant to take drugs or endure their side effects (Sharpe et al., 1996).

Several studies have demonstrated the effectiveness of cognitive-behavioral treatment in the reduction of concomitant emotional factors of CFS (i.e., anxiety, depression), negative cognitions, physical symptoms (particularly fatigue), physiological arousal, and distress reactions in CFS patients (Butler, Chalder, & Ron, 1991; Deale, Chalder, Marks, & Wessely, 1997; Friedberg & Krupp, 1994; Lloyd, Hickie, & Brockman, in press; Prins et al., 2001; Sharpe et al., 1996). In one study, Butler et al. (1991) used a CBT intervention designed to correct dysfunctional thinking and encourage the abandonment of avoidant coping strategies with 32 CFS patients and found reductions in depressive symptoms, functional disabilities (illness burden), and CFS-related physical symptoms, independent of medication status. However, this study had no control condition. Lloyd et al. compared immunologic therapy (transfer factor injections) versus CBT in 90 CFS patients using a double-blind randomized, placebo-controlled trial and found no differences between CBT, immunologic therapy, and placebo injections. All three groups showed significant improvements in fatigue, depression, and functional abilities. Friedberg and Krupp (1994) compared CBT versus a no-treatment condition in 44 CFS patients and found that the CBT group showed significant reductions in fatigue-related cognitions and marginally significant reductions in depression symptom scores but no reductions in stress-related symptoms (using the Global Severity Index) or fatigue severity. Reductions in fatigue-related cognitions were correlated with reductions in depression scores suggesting a possible cognitive appraisal change mediating the depression symptom reductions. This study failed to randomize patients to groups, thus precluding causal interpretations. Prins et al. (2001), in a sample of 278 CFS patients, found that those randomized to a 16-week (1 hour per week) individual CBT intervention showed clinically significant improvement in fatigue severity and functional impairment over a 14-month period compared with patients assigned to either the contact-time matched support group or the natural course condition. Interestingly, within the CBT condition greater improvements were associated with a higher sense of control, less passive activity patterns, and less focusing on bodily symptoms. This suggests that both cognitive and behavioral changes during the intervention were important in producing its benefits.

SUMMARY OF CBT EFFECTS IN CFS

Two of the three CBT intervention studies that showed significant effects with CFS patients failed to randomize patients to conditions. The fourth, a double-blind, randomized placebo control design did not produce significant changes in Profile of Mood States (POMS) scores—the only psychological measure assessed. We have found the fatigue subscale of the POMS—designed to tap the transient, affective qualities of fatigue—to be an insensitive measure of the fatigue reported by CFS patients, which is experienced and described by them along much more cognitive and somatic dimensions. Studies using other measures of fatigue severity, however, did reveal beneficial effects. Three of the CBT studies failed to assess effects beyond the acute treatment period (e.g., 6–9 weeks for the Friedberg & Krupp, 1994, study) while a fourth followed patients for 14 months (Prins et al., 2001). On the other hand, all four protocols stressed the importance of altering cognitive appraisals. In particular, the Friedberg and Krupp (1994) CBT protocol was a group therapy format that used the following intervention strategies/techniques: shared coping and consensual validation of symptoms and disabilities by group members; relaxation training and guided imagery; instruction in cognitive coping skills to challenge and replace catastrophic appraisals of the illness; cognitive restructuring of guilt-evoking performance expectations; and individualized behavioral prescriptions to make lifestyle changes consonant with the physical and energy limitations brought about by CFS. These techniques are entirely compatible with those that we have developed in our CBSM protocol for CFS patients and that we have evaluated extensively with other populations dealing with a chronic medical condition—HIV-1 infection.

CBSM EFFECTS ON AFFECT AND IMMUNE STATUS

We have demonstrated that CBSM may (1) modulate immunologic status as reflected in increased lymphocyte responses to PHA and NKCC (Antoni et al., 1991), and (2) reduce psychological distress reactions (Antoni et al., 1991) in individuals exposed to a potent psychosocial stressor (HIV-1 seropositivity notification). Other labs have noted similar stress-buffering effects for intervention packages that include progressive muscle relaxation (PMR), across a wide age range (Kiecolt-Glaser et al., 1985; Kiecolt-Glaser, Glaser, & Strain, 1986) as well as in some moderately immunocompromised populations (Fawzy, Kemeny, et al., 1990; Gruber, Hall, Hersh, & Dubois, 1988). According to our intervention model, interventions such as PMR may normalize immunologic status and reduce distress.

PMR has been shown to reduce affective distress in anxious community volunteers (Hoelscher, Lichstein, & Rosenthal, 1984) and psychiatric inpatients with marked anxiety problems (Townsend, House, & Addario, 1975). Geriatric residents of independent living facilities assigned to group relaxation demonstrated a significant increase in NKCC at the end of a 4-week intervention; changes in NKCC did not occur for either a social contact group or a no-contact control group (Kiecolt-Glaser et al., 1985). A 6-week group intervention program that combined coping skills training with relaxation increased NK cell counts and NKCC in early-stage melanoma patients (Fawzy, Kemeny, et al., 1990). They also found that immunologic changes appeared to parallel a shift toward the use of more active coping strategies for dealing with the illness (Fawzy, Cousins, et al., 1990). Our CBSM intervention package is designed to reduce anxiety using relaxation and imagery techniques, and to decrease depressed affect through cognitive restructuring. This intervention may also modify stressor appraisals and active coping skills and enhance social support through the group format. Ultimately, it may increase self-efficacy, personal control, and mastery among CFS subjects who are undergoing the pervasive burden of this debilitating syndrome. Such changes are hypothesized to enhance behavioral lifestyle activities, decrease affective disturbances, and reduce the severity of CFS-associated symptoms such as fatigue. These changes, in turn, might lead to normalization of some components of the immune system.

CONCLUSION

Psychosocial factors may influence the mood, immunologic, and physical abnormalities that characterize CFS. Based on the empirical evidence gathered to date, interventions to alter psychological responses to CFS-related burdens and external stressors may modify some of these mood, immunologic, and physical abnormalities. CBSM intervention may modulate the presenting physical symptoms of CFS by several pathways. First, enhanced psychological status (increased feelings of self-efficacy and sense of control and decreased rumination) may reduce the perceived severity of CFS physical symptoms (e.g., chronic pain perceptions are markedly affected by cognitive appraisal factors, Turk et al., 1986). Second, improved psychological status, if accompanied by reductions in distress and depression may also help to normalize immunologic functioning (Antoni et al., 1991). Third, modulation of immunologic status may also impact physical status by way of increased surveillance of ubiquitous viruses (e.g., rhinoviruses, herpesviruses). Finally, enhancing immune surveillance against virally associated infections (e.g., upper respiratory infections) may have clinical effects on CFS physical symptoms and cytokine effects due to lowered virally induced elevations in immunologic activation and production of pro-inflammatory cytokines such as TNF. Thus, CBSM intervention may modulate several psychological and physical problems of CFS patients.

REFERENCES

Abbey, S., & Garfinkel, P. (1991). Chronic fatigue syndrome and depression: Cause, effect or covariate. *Reviews of Infectious Diseases, 13*(1), S73–S83.

Ader, R., Felten, D., & Cohen, N. (Eds.). (2000). *Psychoneuroimmunology.* New York: Academic Press.

Antoni, M. H. (1994, August) *A psychoneuroimmunologic model for chronic fatigue syndrome.* Paper presented at the annual meeting of the American Psychological Association, Los Angeles.

Antoni, M. H., Baggett, L., Ironson, G., LaPerriere, S., August, S., Klimas, N., et al. (1991). Cognitive behavioral stress management intervention buffers distress responses and immunologic changes following notification of HIV-1 seropositivity. *Journal Consulting and Clinical Psychology, 59*(6), 906–915.

Antoni, M. H., Lutgendorf, S., Ironson, G., Fletcher, M. A., & Schneiderman, N. (1996). CBSM intervention effects on social support, coping, depression and immune function in symptomatic HIV-infected men. *Psychosomatic Medicine, 58,* 86.

Aoki, T., Usuda, Y., & Miyakoshi, H. (1985). A novel immunodeficiency: Low NK syndrome (LNKS) *Japanese Journal of Medicine, 3212,* 14–17.

Aoki, T., Usuda, Y., & Miyakoshi, H. (1987). Low natural killer syndrome: Clinical and immunologic features. *Natural Immunity and Growth Regulation, 6,* 116–118.

Baron, R., Cutrona, C., & Hicklin, D. (1990). Social support and immune function among spouses of cancer patients. *Journal of Personality and Social Psychology, 59,* 344–352.

Beck, A., Ward, C., Mendelson, M., Mock, J., & Erbaugh, E. (1961). An inventory for measuring depression. *Archives of General Psychiatry, 4,* 561–571.

Behan, P., Behan, W., & Bell, E. (1985). The postviral fatigue syndrome, an analysis of the findings of 50 cases. *Journal of Infection, 10,* 211–222.

Berkenbosch, F., VanOers, J., del Rey, A., Tilders, F., & Besedovsky, H. (1987). Corticotropin-releasing factor-producing neurons in the rat activated by interleukin-1. *Science, 238,* 524–526.

Besedovsky, H., del Ray, A., Sorkin, E., & Dinarello, C. A. (1986). Immunoregulatory feedback between interleukin-1 and glucocorticoid hormones. *Science, 233,* 652–654.

Borysiewicz, L., Haworth, S. J., & Cohen, J. (1986). Epstein-Barr virus-specific immune defects in patients with persistent systems following infectious mononeucleosis. *Quarterly Journal of Medicine, 58,* 111–121.

Brickman, A., & Fins, A. (1993). Psychological and cognitive aspects of chronic fatigue syndrome. In P. Goodnik & N. Klimas (Eds.), *Chronic fatigue and related immunodeficiency syndrome* (pp. 67–94). Washington, DC: American Psychiatric Press.

Buchwald, D., Cheney, P., & Peterson, J. (1992). A chronic illness characterized by fatigue, neurologic and immunologic disorders, and active human herpesvirus-type 6 infection. *Annals of Internal Medicine, 116,* 103–113.

Buchwald, D., & Komaroff, A. (1991). Review of laboratory findings for patients with chronic fatigue syndrome. *Reviews of Infectious Diseases, 13,* S12–S18.

Buchwald, D., Sullivan, J., & Komaroff, A. (1987). Frequency of chronic active Epstein-Barr virus infection in a general medical practice. *Journal of the American Medical Association, 257,* 2303–2307.

Butler, S., Chalder, T., & Ron, M. (1991). Cognitive behavior therapy in chronic fatigue syndrome. *Journal of Neurology, Neurosurgery, and Psychiatry, 54,* 153–158.

Byrnes, D., Antoni, M. H., Goodkin, K., Efantis-Potter, J., Simon, T., Munajj, J., et al. (1998). Stressful events, pessimism, natural killer cell cytotoxicity, and cytotoxic/

suppressor T-cells in HIV+ Black women at risk for cervical cancer. *Psychosomatic Medicine, 60,* 714–722.

Calabrese, J., Kling, M., & Gold, P. (1987). Alteration in immunocompetence during stress, bereavement, and depression: Focus on neuroendocrine regulation. *American Journal of Psychiatry, 144,* 1123–1124.

Caligiuri, M., Murray, C., Buchwald, C., Levine, H., Cheney, P., Peterson, D., et al. (1987). Phenotypic and functional deficiency of natural killer cells in patients with chronic fatigue syndrome. *Journal of Immunology, 139,* 3306–3313.

Cohen, S., Tyrrell, D. A., & Smith, A. P. (1991). Psychological stress and susceptibility to the common cold. *New England Journal of Medicine, 325*(9), 606–612.

Cruess, S., Antoni, M. H., Cruess, D., Fletcher, M. A., Ironson, G., Kumar, M., et al. (2000). Reductions in HSV-2 antibody titers after cognitive behavioral stress management and relationships with neuroendocrine function, relaxation skills, and social support in HIV+ gay men. *Psychosomatic Medicine, 62,* 828–837.

Cruess, S., Klimas, N., Helder, L., Antoni, M. H., & Fletcher, M. A. (2000). Immunologic status correlates with severity of physical symptoms and perceived illness burden in chronic fatigue syndrome patients. *Journal of Chronic Fatigue Syndrome, 7*(1), 39–52.

Deale, A., Chalder, T., Marks, I., & Wessely, S. (1997). Cognitive behavioral therapy for chronic fatigue syndrome: A randomized controlled trial. *American Journal of Psychiatry, 154,* 408–414.

Demitrack, M., & Crofford, L. (1998). Evidence for and pathophysiologic implications of hypothalamic-pituitary-adrenal axis dysregulation in fibromyalgia and chronic fatigue syndrome. *Annals of the New York Academy of Sciences, 840,* 684–697.

Dinarello, C. (1992). Interleukin-1 and tumor necrosis factor: Effector cytokines in autoimmune diseases. *Seminars in Immunology, 4*(3), 133–145.

Dinarello, C., Cannon, J., & Wolff, S. (1986). Tumor necrosis factor (cachectin) is an endogenous pyrogen and induces production of interleukin-1. *Journal of Experimental Medicine, 163,* 1433–1450.

Esterling, B., Antoni, M. H., Schneiderman, N., Carver, S., LaPerriere, A., Ironson, G., et al. (1992). Psychosocial modulation of antibody to Epstein-Barr viral capsid antigen and human herpesvirus type-6 in HIV-1 infected and at risk gay men. *Psychosomatic Medicine, 54,* 296–317.

Evans, A. (1991). Chronic fatigue syndrome: Thoughts on pathogenesis. *Reviews of Infectious Diseases, 13*(1), S56–S59.

Fawzy, F., Cousins, N., Fawzy, N., Kemeny, M., Glashoff, R., & Morton, D. (1990). A structured psychiatric intervention for cancer patients: Effects on coping and affect. *Archives of General Psychiatry, 47,* 720–725.

Fawzy, F., Kemeny, M., Cousins, N. M., Fawzy, N., & Fahey, J. (1990). A structured psychiatric intervention for cancer patients: Changes over time in immunologic measures. *Archives of General Psychiatry, 47,* 729–735.

Franco, K., Kawa, H. A., & Doi, K. (1987). Remarkable depression of CD4+2H4+ T cells in severe chronic active Epstein-Barr virus infection. *Scandinavian Journal of Immunology, 26,* 769–773.

Friedberg, F., & Krupp, L. (1994). A comparison of cognitive behavioral treatment for chronic fatigue syndrome and primary depression. *Clinical Infectious Diseases, 18,* 5105–5110.

Glaser, R., Kennedy, S., Lafuse, W., & Kiecolt-Glaser, J. (1990). Psychological stress-induced modulation of IL-2 receptor gene expression and IL-2 production in peripheral blood leukocytes. *Archives of General Psychiatry, 47,* 729–735.

Glaser, R., & Kiecolt-Glaser, J. (1999) Stress-associated immune modulation: Relevance to viral infections and chronic fatigue syndrome. *American Journal of Medicine, 105,* 355–425.

Gruber, B., Hall, N., Hersh, S., & Dubois, P. (1988). Immune system and psychologic changes in metastatic cancer patients using ritualized relaxation and guided imagery. *Scandanavian Journal of Behavioral Therapy, 17,* 25–86.

Hafler, D. H., Fox, D. A., & Manning, M. E. (1985). In vivo activated T lymphocytes in the peripheral blood and cerebrospinal fluid of patients with multiple sclerosis. *New England Journal of Medicine, 312,* 1405–1411.

Herbert, T., & Cohen, S. (1993). Depression and immunity: A meta-analytic review. *Psychological Bulletin, 113*(3), 472–486.

Hoelscher, T., Lichstein, K., & Rosenthal, T. (1984). Objective vs. subjective assessment of relaxation compliance among anxious individuals. *Behavioural Research and Therapy, 22,* 187–193.

Irwin, M., Caldwell, G., Smith, T., Brown, S., Schuckit, M. A., & Gillin, J. C. (1990). Major depressive disorder, alcoholism, and reduced natural killer cell cytotoxicity: Fole of severity of depressive symptoms and alcohol consumption. *Archives of General Psychiatry, 47,* 713–718.

Jenkins, F., & Baum, A. (1995). Stress and reactivation of latent herpes simplex virus: A fusion of behavioral medicine and molecular biology. *Annals of Behavioral Medicine, 17,* 116–123.

Jones, J. (1991). Serologic and immunologic responses in chronic fatigue syndrome with emphasis on the Epstein-Barr virus. *Reviews of Infectious Diseases, 13*(1), S26–S31.

Jones, J., & Straus, S. (1987). Chronic Epstein-Barr virus infection. *Annual Review of Medicine, 38,* 195–209.

Kelley, K. (1989). Growth hormone, lymphocytes and macrophages. *Biochemistry and Phamacology, 38,* 705.

Kennedy, S. (1988). Fatigue and fatigability. *British Journal of Psychiatry, 153,* 1–5.

Kibler, R., Lucas, D., Hicks, M., Poulos, B. T., & Jones, J. F. (1985). Immune function in chronic active Epstein-Barr virus infection. *Journal of Clinical Immunology, 5,* 46–54.

Kiecolt-Glaser, J., Dura, J., & Speicher, C. (1991). Spousal caregivers of dementia victims: Longitudinal changes in immunity and health. *Psychosomatic Medicine, 53,* 345–362.

Kiecolt-Glaser, J., & Glaser, R. (1992). Psychoneuroimmunology: Can psychological interventions modulate immunity? *Journal of Consulting and Clinical Psychology, 60*(4), 569–575.

Kiecolt-Glaser, J., Glaser, R., & Strain, E. (1986). Modulation of cellular immunity in medical students. *Journal of Behavioral Medicine, 9,* 5–21.

Kiecolt-Glaser, J., Glaser, R., Williger, D., Stout, J., Messick, G., Sheppard, S., et al. (1985). Psychosocial enhancement of immunocompetence in a geriatric population. *Health Psychology, 4,* 25–41.

Klimas, N., Patarca, R., & Fletcher, M. A. (1992). Psychoneuroimmunology and chronic fatigue syndrome. In N. Schneiderman & A. Baum (Eds.), *Perspective in behavioral medicine.* Hillsdale, NJ: Erlbaum.

Klimas, N., Salvato, F., Morgan, R., & Fletcher, M. A. (1990). Immunologic abnormalities in chronic fatigue syndrome. *Journal of Clinical Microbiology, 28*(6) 1403–1410.

Knop, J., Stremer, R., & Neuman, C. (1982). Inerferon inhibits the suppressor T cell response of delayed hyersensitivity. *Nature, 296,* 757–758.

Komaroff, A., & Buchwald, D. (1991). Symptoms and signs of chronic fatigue syndrome. *Reviews of Infectious Diseases, 13*(Suppl.), S8–S11.

Komaroff, A., & Buchwald, D. (1998). Chronic fatigue syndrome: An update. *Annual Review of Medicine, 49,* 1–13.

Landay, A. L. (1991, November 18) Paper presented at CIFDS Conference on CFS, Charlotte, NC.

Landay, A. L., Jessop, C., Lennette, E. T., & Levy, J. A. (1991). Chronic fatigue syndrome: Clinical condition associated with immune activation. *Lancet, 338*(8769), 707–712.

Levy, J. (1991, November 18). Paper presented at CIFDS conference on CFS, Charlotte, NC.

Lloyd, A., Hickie, I., Hickie, C., Dwyer, J., & Wakefield, D. (1992). Cell-mediated immunity in patients with chronic fatigue syndrome, healthy controls and patients with major depression. *Clinical and Experimental Immunology, 87,* 76–79.

Lloyd, A., Wakefield, D., Dwyer, J., & Boughton, C. (1989). Immunological abnormalities in the chronic fatigue syndrome. *Medical Journal of Australia, 151,* 122–124.

Lloyd, A., Wakefield, D., & Hickie, I. (1993). Immunity and the pathophysiology of chronic fatigue syndrome. *CIBA symposium.* Chichester, England.

Lloyd, A. R., Hickie, M. D., & Brockman, A. (in press). Immunological and psychological therapy for patients with chronic fatigue syndrome: Double-blind, placebo-controlled trial. *American Journal of Medicine.*

Lutgendorf, S., Antoni, M. H., Ironson, G., Klimas, N., Patarca, R., & Fletcher, M. A. (1995). Physical symptoms of chronic fatigue syndrome are exacerbated by the stress of Hurricane Andrew. *Psychosomatic Medicine, 57,* 310–323.

Lutgendorf, S., Antoni, M. H., Ironson, G., Klimas, N., Starr, K., McCabe, P., et al. (1997) Cognitive behavioral stress management decreases dysphoric mood and herpes simplex virus-type 2 antibody titers in symptomatic HIV-seropositive gay men. *Journal of Consulting and Clinical Psychology, 65,* 31–43.

Lutgendorf, S., Klimas, N., Antoni, M. H., Brickman, A., & Fletcher, M. A. (1995). Relationships of cognitive difficulties to immune measures, depression and illness burden in chronic fatigue syndrome. *Journal of Chronic Fatigue Syndrome, 1*(2), 23–41.

Maher, K. (2000). Studies of natural killer cell function in chronic fatigue syndrome. *International Journal of Behavioral Medicine, 7*(Suppl. 1), 99.

Miyakoshi, H., Aoki, T., & Mizukoshi, M. (1984). Acting mechanisms of Lentinan in human. II: Enhancement of nonspecific cell-mediated cytotoxicity and an interferon induced response. *International Journal of Immunopharmacol, 6,* 373–379.

Moldofsky, H. (1989). Nonrestorative sleep and symptoms after a febrile illness in patients with fibrosis and chronic fatigue syndrome. *Journal of Rheumatology, 16*(19), 150–153.

Moldofsky, H. (1995). Sleep, neuroimmune and neuroendocrine functions in fibromyalgia and chronic fatigue syndrome. *Advances in Neuroimmunology, 5,* 39–56.

Morimoto, C., Letvin, N. L., Distato, J. A., Aldrich, W. R., & Schlossman, S. F. (1985). Characterization of the human suppressor/inducer T cell subset. *Journal of Immunology, 134,* 1508.

Morimoto, C., Reinherz, E. L., Schlossman, S. F., Schur, P. H., Mills, J., & Steinberg, A. D. (1980). Alternatives in immunoregulatory T cell subsets in active systemic lupus erythmatosus. *Journal of Clinical Investigation, 66,* 1171.

Patarca, R., Klimas, N., Lutgendorf, S., Antoni, M. H., & Fletcher, M. A. (1994). Dysregulated expression of tumor necrosis factor (TNF) in the chronic fatigue immune dysfunction syndrome: Interrelationships with cellular sources and soluble immune mediator expression patterns. *Clinical Infectious Diseases, 18,* S147–S153.

Prins, J., Bleijenberg, G., Bazelmans, E., Elving, L., deBoo, T., Severens, J., et al. (2001). Cognitive behaviour therapy for chronic fatigue syndrome: A multicentre randomised controlled trial. *Lancet, 357*(9259), 841–847.

Rose, L., Ginsberg, A., Rothstein, J., Ledbetter, J., & Clark, E. (1985). Fluctuation of CD4+ T-cell subsets in remitting-relapsing multiple sclerosis. *Proceedings of the National Academy of Sciences, USA, 82,* 7389–7393.

Rose, L., Ginsberg, A., Rothstein, T., Ledbetter, J., & Clark, E. (1988). Selective loss of a subset of T helper cells in active multiple sclerosis. *Annals of Neurology, 24,* 192–199.

Salvato, F., Klimas, N., Ashman, M., & Fletcher, M. (1988). Immune dysfunction among chronic fatigue syndrome patients with evidence of Epstein-Barr virus reactivation. *Journal of Clinical Cancer Research, 7,* 89.

Schleifer, S., Keller, S., Bond, R., Cohen, J., & Stein, M. (1989). Major depressive disorder and immunity: Role of age, sex, severity and hospitalization. *Archives of General Psychiatry, 46,* 81–87.

Scott, L., & Dinan, T. (1998). Urinary free cortisol excretion in chronic fatigue syndrome, major depression and in healthy volunteers. *Journal of Affective Disorders, 47,* 49–54.

Scott, L. V., Medbak, S., & Dinan, T. G. (1998). Blunted adrenocorticotropin and cortisol responses to corticotropin-releasing hormone stimulation in chronic fatigue syndrome. *Acta Psychiatrica Scandinavica, 97,* 450–457.

Sharpe, M., Hawton, K., Simkin, S., Suraway, C., Hackman, A., Klimes, I., et al. (1996). Cognitive behavior therapy for chronic fatigue syndrome: A randomized controlled trial. *British Medical Journal, 312,* 21–26.

Shoham, S., Davenne, D., & Cady, A. (1987). Recombinant tumor necrosis factor and interleukin 1 enhance slow-wave sleep. *American Journal of Physiology, 253,* R142.

Stein, M., Miller, A. H., & Trestman, R. L. (1991). Depression, the immune system, and health and illness. *Archives of General Psychiatry, 481,* 71–176.

Sternberg, E. (1993). Hypoimmune fatigue syndromes: Disease of the stress response? *Journal of Rheumatology, 20,* 418–421.

Straus, S. E., Tosato, G., & Armstrong, G. (1985). Persisting illness and fatigue in adult with evidence of Epstein-Barr. *Annals of Internal Medicine, 102,* 7–16.

Taerk, G., Toner, B. B., Salit, I. E., Garfinkel, P. E., & Ozersky, S. (1987). Depression in patients with neuromyasthenia (benign myalgic encephalomyelitis). *International Journal of Psychiatry in Medicine, 41,* 49–56.

Targan, S., & Stebbing, N. (1982). In vitro interactions of purified cloned human interferons on NK cells enhanced activation. *Journal of Immunology, 129,* 934–935.

Tarsis, S., Klimas, N., & Baron, G. (1988, October). Immunological considerations in chronic Epstein-Barr. *Immune abnormalities in chronic fatigue syndrome.* Third International Symposium on Epstein Barr Virus and Associated Diseases, Rome.

Tartaglia, L., & Goeddel, D. (1992). Two TNF receptors. *Immunology Today, 13,* 151–153.

Tirelli, U., Pinto, A., & Marotta, G. (1993). Clinical and immunologic study of 205 patients with chronic fatigue syndrome: A case series from Italy. *Annals of Internal Medicine, 153,* 116–120.

Tomei, L., Kiecolt-Glaser, J., Kennedy, S., & Glaser, R. (1990). Psychological stress and phorbol ester inhibition of radiation-induced apoptosis in human PBLs. *Psychiatry Research, 33,* 59–71.

Townsend, R., House, J., & Addario, D. (1975). A comparison of biofeedback-mediated relaxation and group therapy in the treatment of chronic anxiety. *American Journal of Psychiatry, 132,* 598–601.

Turk, D., Holzman, A., & Kernas, R. (1986) Chronic pain. In K. Holroyd & I. Creer (Eds.), *Self-management of chronic disease: Handbook of clinical interventions and research.* Orlando, FL: Academic Press.

Visser, J., Blauw, B., Hinloopen, B., Broomer, E., de Kloet, R., Kluft, C., et al. (1998). CD4 T lymphocytes from patients with chronic fatigue syndrome have decreased interferon-γ production and increased sensitivity to dexamathasone. *Journal of Infectious Diseases, 177,* 451–454.

Zlotnick, A., Shimonkewitz, P., & Gefter, M. L. (1983). Characterization of the gamma interferon-mediated induction of antigen-presenting ability in P388D cells. *Journal of Immunology, 131,* 2814.

CHAPTER 25

Development of the SMART-ENERGY Program

DONNA E. WEISS, LYNN M. HELDER, and MICHAEL H. ANTONI

DEVELOPMENT OF THE SMART-ENERGY PROGRAM

SMART-ENERGY IS an intervention program that we developed for men and women with chronic fatigue syndrome (CFS). SMART stands for Stress Management And Relaxation Training. This intervention was created and is currently being tested as part of an NIH-funded clinical trial conducted by the Departments of Psychology and Medicine at the University of Miami. CFS is a chronic illness characterized by *physical symptoms*. These include debilitating fatigue, low-grade fever, lymph node pain and tenderness, pharyngitis, myalgias, and arthralgias; *cognitive deficits* such as shortened attention span, concentration difficulties, memory problems, impaired complex problem-solving speed, and dyslogia; and *mood changes*, predominantly depressive symptoms (Buchwald, Sullivan, & Komaroff, 1987; Jones & Strauss, 1987; Taerk, Toner, Salit, Garfinkel, & Ozersky, 1987). The severity of this symptom picture likely results in decreased overall quality of life, further declines in mood, lifestyle limitations, and decreased vocational functioning in previously highly functional individuals (Komaroff & Buchwald, 1991; Taerk et al., 1987).

Our general model holds that the interaction of psychological factors (i.e., distress and depression) with immunologic dysfunction can exacerbate physical symptoms, increase the illness burden (e.g., disrupt daily activities), and cause a further decline in immune system functioning. Thus, we hypothesize that effective treatment must address the interaction of CFS symptom severity, psychological factors, and immune system functioning. The initial impetus for this work was to determine whether a group-based cognitive-behavioral intervention could improve the psychological, cognitive, immunologic, and physical health status in CFS patients. A cognitive-behavioral treatment approach was selected because many of the reported symptoms of CFS patients are cognitive (memory problems, inattention, and difficulty focusing) and behavioral (forced inactivity). In addition, several studies have demonstrated the effectiveness of cognitive-behavioral treatment in the reduction of concomitant emotional factors of CFS (anxiety and depression), negative cognitions, physical symptoms (particularly fatigue), physiological arousal, and distress reactions in CFS patients (Butler, Chalder, & Ron, 1991; Deale, Chalder, Marks, & Wessely, 1997; Friedberg & Krupp, 1994; Sharpe et al., 1996).

The structure and content of each component of the intervention was partially adopted from a similar protocol implemented with HIV-infected patients at the University of Miami (Antoni, 1997). Our research has demonstrated the efficacy of these cognitive-behavioral stress management (CBSM) techniques with HIV patients, another chronic illness associated with decrements in functioning and quality of life. In one study, a group of 47 asymptomatic, healthy gay men participated in a CBSM group that met twice weekly in groups of 4 to 6 patients for 10 weeks prior to being notified of their HIV-1 antibody status (Antoni et al., 1991). The CBSM participants who tested HIV+ showed significant increases in active coping, planning, and seeking emotional support, as well as decreases in passive coping strategies (denial and disengagement). The intervention also served as a buffer against loneliness and decrements in perceived social support among these group members. Furthermore, compared with control subjects, the HIV+ CBSM participants showed no significant pre-post changes in depression (whereas control subjects showed significant increases in depression) and had significant positive changes on immunologic measures.

In a second cohort of HIV+ gay men who had been dealing with their diagnosis for some time, participation in the CBSM intervention resulted in significant decreases in mental disengagement, denial, and behavioral disengagement (helplessness). These men showed significant increases in active coping, planning, and acceptance coping across the 10-week intervention period. An additional set of findings was that among HIV+ symptomatic persons, CBSM decreased depressed mood and general distress levels. It also improved cell-mediated immunologic control of herpes viruses such as Epstein-Barr virus (EBV), human herpes virus-Type 6 (HHV-6), and herpes simplex virus-Type 2 (HSV-2; Cruess et al., 2000; Esterling et al., 1992; Lutgendorf et al., 1997). Our findings from evaluation of this intervention conducted over the past 10 years suggest that CBSM reduced psychological distress reactions in individuals exposed to a psychosocial stressor (notification of HIV-1 seropositivity). Further, intervention-related changes in coping strategies (i.e., denial) and increased perceived social provisions were associated with a buffering of specific immune system reactions to stressors (Antoni et al., 1991). Some of the content of the SMART-ENERGY program is based on the 10-week program that was designed for HIV+ gay men, but it has been enhanced with an emphasis on particular symptom exacerbations and associated losses (job, social activities, and self-image) that accompany CFS (Helder, 1996).

GOALS OF THE SMART-ENERGY PROGRAM

Our primary goals are to assist patients with the psychological adjustment to their illness, to improve daily functioning, and to enhance their ability to cope with daily life stressors by providing them with the following seven cognitive-based skills and techniques:

1. Teach participants anxiety-reduction skills including deep muscle relaxation, relaxing imagery, and autogenics.
2. Reduce mood changes associated with CFS such as depression and hopelessness.
3. Modify maladaptive beliefs and cognitive appraisals of general stressful situations by using cognitive restructuring and specifically designed guided imagery.
4. Modify maladaptive cognitive appraisals of somatic and affective symptoms by using cognitive restructuring.
5. Enhance interpersonal conflict resolution skills and anger expression through assertiveness training and anger management.
6. Enhance factors contributing to quality of life and self-esteem by cognitive restructuring and goal setting.
7. Facilitate connectedness by providing a supportive group environment and increasing use of social support networks (Helder, 1996).

Ultimately, we seek to enhance self-efficacy, personal control, and mastery among CFS patients who are undergoing the pervasive burden of this debilitating syndrome.

WHY USE A GROUP FORMAT?

A group-based CBSM model is the general treatment strategy underlying the SMART-ENERGY program. A group format was chosen for several reasons. First, this format provides patients with social support from professionals who understand the difficulties associated with CFS. This is a particularly important component of treatment with CFS patients. Before receiving their diagnosis, many CFS patients have seen numerous treatment professionals in various disciplines. Diagnosis is complicated, and some professionals do not acknowledge the syndrome's existence. Unlike most other illnesses, no single test or procedure can diagnose CFS, and patients must persist in trying to discover what is causing their symptoms. Many CFS patients relate that they were told their symptoms were "all in [their] head" and that they received referrals to mental health professionals. Thus, our CBSM group is commonly the first experience of CFS patients in having their illness acknowledged and validated. The social support of the group format may serve to buffer stress.

Second, the group format allows patients to interact with others who experience similar problems with their chronic illness, giving them a sense that they are not alone in their struggle. Third, the supportive environment of the group format facilitates the learning of valuable coping strategies from both the group leader and other patients. This knowledge enhances feelings of self-efficacy and mastery while reducing feelings of powerlessness. Here, both group members and group leaders serve as coping role models and providers of social support. This modeling discourages avoidance and encourages active coping strategies, as well as adaptive emotional expression, in dealing with CFS symptoms. Fourth, the social comparison available in the group can facilitate adherence to the cognitive and behavioral techniques taught in that group. Fifth, the group format provides a unique opportunity for presentation of individual problems and collaborative problem solving.

Finally, a group format is both time-efficient and cost-effective compared with individual-based counseling.

FORMAT OF THE SMART-ENERGY PROGRAM

The SMART-ENERGY program is a closed, structured group intervention, meeting once weekly for 2 hours over 12 weeks in groups of 5 to 8 members, facilitated by a group leader. During the first session, participants receive a workbook that summarizes the goals for each session and includes handouts, homework assignments, and self-monitoring sheets. Each session begins with a didactic portion because participants' energy levels and ability to concentrate tend to be better at the beginning of the group and decrease with time in the group session. The previous week's homework assignment is also reviewed at the beginning of each session.

INTERVENTION STRATEGIES

The goals, content, and homework assignments for each of the 12 sessions are delineated in Table 25.1.

The first 90 minutes of each session are devoted to the didactic presentation of psychoeducational information and stress management techniques. The early group sessions focus on psychoeducational materials: Patients are provided with general information about CFS, medical treatments of CFS, and health behaviors. Participants are introduced to the biopsychosocial model of chronic illness and the course of CFS. It stresses an integrated systems approach to illness in which biological, psychological, and social systems interact with and affect one another (Engel, 1980). Participants then learn specific stress management skills and appropriate coping strategies for dealing with their individual responses to stress and precipitants of symptom exacerbation. Adaptive coping skills training teaches participants to break stressors down into manageable parts (controllable versus uncontrollable aspects), to appropriately match problem-focused and emotion-focused coping strategies to the stressful situation, and to use active instead of passive coping strategies. These techniques increase participants' ability to manage stressful situations, as well as show them the importance of perception and appraisal in the stress response and in symptom occurrence. Participants begin to self-monitor daily stressors and stress responses to sharpen their awareness of the ways in which they may be systematically distorting their stressor appraisals. We encourage participants to describe recent psychosocial stressors and their coping responses, which we then use for in-session behavioral role-playing. This early discussion of stress and coping lays the groundwork for the CBSM techniques that are taught next.

SPECIFIC CBSM TECHNIQUES

The CBSM techniques used in our intervention provide participants with an increased sense of personal control and self-efficacy. They have also been shown to provide physiological (immunologic modulation) and psychological (decreased depressive symptomatology) benefits (Antoni et al., 2001; Cruess et al., 2000; Lutgendorf et al., 1997).

Table 25.1

Session Goals, Content, and Homework Assignments for the SMART-ENERGY Program

Session	Goal(s) of Session	Content of Session	Homework Assignment
1	Get to know participants. Introduce cognitive therapy. Teach various aspects of the stress response.	Group guidelines and goal setting. Relationship between thoughts, feelings, and physiological responses. Introduction to relaxation as a coping strategy. Effects of stress (cognitive, emotional, behavioral, physical, and social).	Relaxation Frequency Monitoring Daily Stress Level and Sleep Record Activity Schedule
2	Describe the biopsychosocial perspective of illness. Describe the mind-body relationship. Introduce the rationale for cognitive-behavioral therapy in the treatment of CFS.	Explanation of the biopsychosocial model of illness. Cognitive-affective-physiological stress response processes. The appraisal process. Explanation of fight-or-flight response.	Relaxation Frequency Monitoring
3	Illustrate the effect of perception on mood. Teach participants how to identify cognitive distortions.	Thought-affect relationship. Review of cognitive distortions.	Relaxation Frequency Monitoring Daily Record of Dysfunctional Thoughts
4	Teach participants to dispute cognitive distortions. Review problem-focused and emotion-focused coping skills.	Process of change in restructuring negative automatic thoughts (from unconscious distorted thoughts to unconscious rational thoughts). Categories of self-talk. Disputation of irrational/automatic thoughts. Discussion of problem-focused versus emotion-focused coping.	Relaxation Frequency Monitoring Daily Record of Dysfunctional Thoughts
5	Teach participants to refute irrational beliefs. Introduction to coping.	The formation of beliefs. Specific irrational beliefs. Definition of coping.	Relaxation Frequency Monitoring Daily Record of Dysfunctional Thoughts Monitoring Coping Responses to Stressful Situations

Table 25.1 *Continued*

Session	Goal(s) of Session	Content of Session	Homework Assignment
6	Teach participants adaptive coping skills. Describe the components and process of communication.	Uncontrollable versus controllable stressors. Problem-focused versus emotion-focused coping. Active versus passing coping strategies. The four components of communication (sender, receiver, message, and context). Listening skills (attending, invitational, reflective).	Relaxation Frequency Monitoring Daily Record of Dysfunctional Thoughts Listening Skills Monitoring Sheet
7	Describe four communication styles. Teach assertiveness skills.	Review of the four styles of communication (passive, aggressive, passive-aggressive, and assertive). Barriers to assertive communication. Sending an assertive message.	Relaxation Frequency Monitoring Daily Record of Dysfunctional Thoughts Assertive Communication Monitoring Sheet
8	Describe ways we solve problems. Teach conflict management skills.	Steps to conflict resolution. Anger management.	Relaxation Frequency Monitoring Daily Record of Dysfunctional Thoughts
9	Describe internal conflicts and the role of anxiety and fear in the development of self-esteem. Teach self-esteem enhancement skills.	Introduction to self-esteem. Determinants of self-esteem. Self-esteem as a function of increasing successes and decreasing expectations.	Relaxation Frequency Monitoring Daily Record of Dysfunctional Thoughts
10	Differentiate between self-esteem and self-concept. Describe how self-esteem is established and the role of societal attitudes in self-esteem development. Teach how to enhance self-esteem within relationships.	Definition of self-concept. Formation of self-concept. Components of self-esteem. Social influences on self-concept. Shifting expectations. Development of new reference groups.	Relaxation Frequency Monitoring Daily Record of Dysfunctional Thoughts

(continued)

Table 25.1 *Continued*

Session	Goal(s) of Session	Content of Session	Homework Assignment
11	Explain the concept of quality of life. Establish an understanding of the various components that contribute to one's perception of life satisfaction. Provide an understanding of each participant's personal standards and goals. Provide ideas for adjusting goals to be more realistic, attainable, and fulfilling for the CFS patient.	Introduction to quality of life. Personal fulfillment. Strategies for enhancing quality of life.	Relaxation Frequency Monitoring Daily Record of Dysfunctional Thoughts Daily Stress Level and Sleep Record
12	Provide an understanding of how health contributes to the quality of life. Promote and encourage the development of positive self-evaluation by each participant.	Continued quality of life discussion. Summary of group highlights. Participant and leader discussion of each participant's progress.	

Raising Awareness of Cognitive Appraisals　The cognitive intervention begins by presenting the idea that cognitions precede behavioral (e.g., health behaviors), affective (e.g., depressed mood), social (e.g., withdrawal), physical (e.g., muscle tension), and physiological (e.g., hormonal) responses to stressors. These sessions then address the monologue participants carry on within themselves, and they learn how to restructure distorted "self-talk." Participants first gain an understanding of automatic thoughts and cognitive distortions. They are then asked to identify and monitor their perceptions, automatic thoughts, and cognitive distortions in stressful situations. Monitoring automatic thoughts associated with negative emotions increases their awareness of cognitive appraisals that precede changes in emotion and enables participants to learn how automatic thoughts and cognitive distortions may magnify symptoms and contribute to loss of perceived control. Participants then learn how to use rational thought replacement to substitute cognitive reappraisals, as well as other strategies for disputing and restructuring cognitive distortions, thereby reducing distress responses. Through in-session behavioral role-playing, participants receive feedback in a supportive group environment and can practice their newly learned skills.

Interpersonal Skills, Self-Esteem, and Quality of Life　The middle sessions shift in focus to participants' transactions with others. We continue to use cognitive-behavioral coping strategies to improve interpersonal communication, self-esteem, and quality of life, and to encourage appropriate emotional expression and assertiveness skills. We teach participants about the four communication styles (i.e., passive, aggressive, passive-aggressive, and assertive), as well as assertiveness skills, anger management, and conflict resolution. By presenting effective ways to engage in interpersonal exchanges and relationships, we hope to help participants improve their social support networks, decrease conflict, express their needs to others more precisely, and improve overall communication with health care professionals and with significant others. This latter phase of the program integrates aspects of the earlier program modules, particularly cognitive appraisals of stressors, within the context of interpersonal stressors and resources.

Accessing Social Resources   The final four sessions focus on self-image, self-esteem, and identification of ways to increase quality of life, including accessing appropriate sources of social support. Throughout the group sessions, participants receive feedback from group members and the group leader on their acquisition of skills when individual problems are addressed and homework is reviewed. The combination of social support and self-reinforcement seems to increase participants' use of these strategies while fostering self-efficacy, self-esteem, and a sense of personal control.

Relaxation   The last 30 to 45 minutes of each session are devoted to a relaxation and guided imagery exercise. We have incorporated relaxation because these techniques have been associated with improvements in anxiety, immunologic status, and numerous somatic complaints (e.g., headaches, arthralgia; Antoni et al., 1991; Cruess et al., 2000; Helder, 1996). In contrast to the sequence in our CBSM interventions for individuals with HIV infection (Antoni, 1997) and breast cancer (Antoni et al., 2001), we conduct the relaxation exercises at the end of each SMART-ENERGY session. This arrangement allows for a rest period, reduces anxiety, and provides a sense of well-being as participants leave the group experience. The relaxation exercises contain two components. The first is muscle relaxation, which teaches participants to systematically reduce tension throughout all of their major muscle groups. Participants use imagery of muscle groups rather than progressive muscle relaxation (tensing and relaxing muscle groups) because tensing of muscle groups may increase the fibromyalgia symptoms that many CFS patients experience. In addition to reducing anxiety, relaxation training may help participants overcome the sleep problems associated with CFS.

The second component of relaxation is guided imagery, which teaches participants ways to use mental imagery to bring about a total state of relaxation. We use images as metaphors for optimal functioning and encourage participants to apply them in an individualized way to their daily experience. The guided imagery techniques have been developed to reinforce the principles taught in the didactic portion of the session, such as changing beliefs (Helder, 1996). Some members tend to learn and acquire skills better when presented with information in a didactic manner, whereas others tend to assimilate information better through images and metaphors. The CBSM intervention provides both styles of skill acquisition, each component reinforcing the other. Participants are provided with several tapes that contain the in-session relaxation exercises. We encourage each therapist to record these tapes in his or her own voice. Participants are instructed to practice the relaxation exercises at home daily. They use a weekly self-report monitoring sheet to record the frequency of their relaxation practice and rate its effectiveness on a Likert scale.

SPECIAL CLINICAL ISSUES WHEN USING THE SMART-ENERGY PROGRAM

GENDER IMBALANCE

Because the sex ratio for CFS is nine women to every one man (Ravicz, 2000), it is impossible to attain gender balance in CFS groups. Typically, our therapy groups either consist of all women or include a lone man. Thus, the therapist must consider how gender affects the psychological adjustment and lifestyle changes that result from CFS. In one of our groups consisting of four women and one man, the women began to discuss their struggles in completing household chores, which were formerly simple, effortless tasks. They shared stories about how their spouses automatically expect these chores to be done and do not accept the limitations that have resulted from their illness. The sole male participant related:

> Let me say one thing to all you ladies. I'm in the same situation as you. I do the laundry. I do the cooking. My wife works. Actually, I'm in the reverse role of what a man normally is. So, about doing the laundry, I have the same problem. Over the past few years, my wife and I, we got it worked out pretty good where she can come home and expect that I was supposed to do something and it's not done because I just got sidetracked.

This illustrates how important it is for the group leader to avoid isolating the typical lone male patient and instead to foster an environment that permits and accepts discussion of gender. Furthermore, special issues may take precedence for the male CFS patient such as the stigma and secretiveness surrounding the illness and the inability to fulfill traditionally masculine roles (e.g., being the breadwinner, lifting heavy objects, engaging in mechanical tasks around the house). Societal factors may play a role in the gender imbalance seen with CFS.

In another group session, the female participants discussed the lack of support and acceptance they received from their spouses related to their illness. The following dialogue transpired between the male participant and one of the female participants. The male patient related:

> I'm in the opposite situation of where you guys are. My wife, when I got sick, she got all kinds of books, read about it, and she stayed home for three weeks and took care of me 'til I could get out of bed and do some stuff and she's always been there to help me.

The female participant then replied:

> Because she's a woman. I'm sorry to say it because women are more nurturing . . . men are not trained to be nurturing. Some men are nurturing, some others are not.

This dialogue illustrates how male significant others may respond in a less supportive manner toward female CFS patients than the reverse—a common source of frustration for many of our female participants. In yet another session, the female participants related the difficulties they encountered in getting disability compensation payments for their illness. The male participant stated:

With the sickness at the beginning, I didn't go through all the pain and suffering that a lot of the people have gone through. I was very fortunate. My doctor picked up on it immediately. Within 6 months, they said I was disabled. I had chronic fatigue and that was it. All these horror stories and stresses with people going to doctors and they can't find out what's wrong. That's a very stressful point with chronic fatigue. Thinking of all the horror stories that I've heard, and knock on wood, I've been very lucky at this stuff. Somebody has been there up in the sky helping me along because all the things that everybody has had a hard time with, I haven't.

In response, a female participant stated:

It makes me very angry, not at you, I'm happy for you, but I just see how tilted our society is. Guys get support, they get everything done. It's really messed up, but I'm happy for you guys, at least it's somebody.

These examples illustrate the gender challenges that men and women may face in the CFS experience.

CHILDHOOD TRAUMA EXPERIENCES AND CFS

An additional issue concerns the reported histories of childhood trauma experiences, particularly sexual abuse, among many of our female CFS patients. Most female sexual abuse survivors prefer female therapists because they are terrified of men, have concerns about revictimization, or believe a woman will show greater empathy (Courtois, 1988). Thus, the gender of the therapist needs to be considered in delivering such an intervention. Will a group of female CFS patients be as likely to express themselves freely and openly with a male group leader, particularly about childhood trauma experiences?

Therapist gender is also a consideration in conducting the relaxation exercises. Will a female CFS patient, who is also a trauma survivor, be able to relax to the voice of a male group leader? Since many of our CFS patients are sexual abuse survivors, we have taken special care in our muscle relaxation exercises to exclude references to the pelvis or other sexual regions of the body. In fact, one participant asked the therapist privately if these parts of the body were omitted from the relaxation tapes because many CFS patients have histories of sexual abuse. She related that although she was a rape survivor, she still felt the need to heal those parts of her body. She stated:

The belly button down region of the body is ignored on the relaxation tapes and the relaxation tapes don't feel complete.

Thus, in conducting relaxation exercises and creating relaxation tapes, the group leader should consider whether to include sexual regions of the body. When we initially devised our intervention, we included these body parts in the exercises. However, it resulted in increased and visible emotional distress in some of our female abuse survivors who had never processed their abuse issues in psychotherapy. Thus we have since excluded these body parts because the visible distress of group members during the relaxation exercises can be disruptive to the group process. The exercises should omit these body parts unless the group is directed by skilled cotherapists, one of whom who could address such issues individually with any participant who showed distress in session as a result of the relaxation exercises.

CLARIFYING WHETHER THE SMART-ENERGY PROGRAM IS A SUPPORT GROUP, STRESS MANAGEMENT TRAINING, OR GROUP PSYCHOTHERAPY

As mentioned, many CFS patients have been referred to various mental health professionals and told that their symptoms are "all in their head" prior to finally receiving their CFS diagnosis. In delivering our intervention, we take special care to inform patients that we are not conducting the intervention because we believe that their symptoms are *caused by* stress or psychological factors. Instead, we emphasize that by learning stress management skills, patients can expect to get a better grasp on their physical symptoms, improve their mood, and enhance their quality of life. We present our program as a total wellness program for overall health, not as a psychotherapy group. Instead of referring to our intervention as a therapy group, we call it a *stress management course/training*. Using this language is important because it does not communicate or reinforce the belief that CFS is a psychiatric illness.

CHARACTERISTICS OF THE GROUP SETTING

Another issue that has arisen in delivery of the SMART-ENERGY intervention is whether participants should sit in chairs around a table or simply in a circle without a table. Consistent with our presentation of the intervention as a training experience, we have opted to conduct the intervention with the group leader and participants sitting around a table; the leader makes use of a whiteboard to present material. Although some group therapists may believe that this arrangement interferes with the group process, our patients have responded well to the format as it minimizes the group psychotherapy feel.

In addition to gender composition and the practical issues of running the group (e.g., table vs. no table), there is a limited window of opportunity during the day when CFS patients are at their optimal level of functioning. It is too fatiguing for most CFS patients to travel during rush hour. Most patients also report that they are not able to function at their best in the early morning hours. Therefore, we recommend conducting CBSM groups between the hours of 11:00 A.M. and 3:00 P.M.

Many of our patients have reported attending various patient-led support groups prior to participating in our program. We have repeatedly heard stories from our patients describing support groups with patients who whine excessively about their illness. Based on their negative experiences with support groups, patients are sometimes reluctant to participate in our program. Again, this is why it is important to communicate the difference between this intervention and a support group to patients from the outset, emphasizing the intervention as a place where patients will learn new skills to help them cope with their illness within a supportive environment. Two participants who were asked how they distinguished a support group from the CBSM intervention revealed the following:

The support groups I attended were "bitch-and-moan" sessions. I wasn't interested at all. In this [SMART-ENERGY] group, we were supportive of one another. We focused on getting skills individually to make changes. We were able to get the perspective from others and were able to speak it out in a constructive way.

I attended a support group in the past. This was different. There was a real agenda that fit the group.

SPECIFIC CHALLENGES FOR SMART-ENERGY GROUP LEADERS

MAINTAINING THE GROUP FOCUS

Many CFS patients have seen multiple treatment providers before finally receiving their CFS diagnosis. When they come to the CBSM group, they are relieved to have found a place where their illness is accepted. They are also thrilled to bond with other patients who share the same illness. The danger is that patients can spend too much time relating CFS stories to one another, which can cut into the time available for the intervention. A further complication is that these patients tend to have attention and concentration impairments that can make it difficult to stay on task. Thus, the group leader must empathize with the patients' difficulties and foster a supportive group environment while providing frequent redirection to ensure that all the group members participate and that they cover the necessary components of the intervention.

BALANCING THE FOCUS BETWEEN VENTING FRUSTRATIONS AND BUILDING PRODUCTIVE SKILLS

A frequent theme in CFS support groups in the community is, "No one understands what I am going through because of this illness." This is likely related to the lack of support within the medical community surrounding CFS, as well as the frustration CFS patients experience from others' nonacceptance of their illness. For example, one participant obtained a handicapped sticker for her car but only used it on days when her CFS symptoms were incapacitating and severely impaired her mobility. She related a subsequent distressing interaction with a male stranger, who demanded to know why she was entitled to park in a handicapped space when she appeared perfectly healthy and "normal." Many of our patients tell us that they often encounter similar reactions. They feel that others treat their illness differently, no matter how disabling, than they do visible symptoms (e.g., a broken leg or arm). The invisibility of symptoms and such reactions are sources of stress for CFS patients. These experiences may lead some CFS patients to externalize blame for their illness, which can translate into adopting a victim or martyr role. The CBSM group is one of the few places where patients feel safe exchanging horror stories about how others misunderstand their illness. However, the group leader must maintain a balance between allowing for adequate venting and making sure that the intervention does not take on the atmosphere of a support group, where patients excessively relate such stories in the context of a bitch-and-moan session. One strategy is to simply ask participants how they view the CBSM group as different from a support group, and then address any beliefs that may be interfering with their ability to benefit from the intervention.

SETTING LIMITS

One of the most rewarding facets of conducting stress management groups with CFS patients is that they are advocates and are truly motivated. They possess all of the qualities that are necessary to benefit from a CBSM intervention—they are educated, intelligent, have excellent group attendance, actively participate, complete most homework assignments, and are invested in improving their health (Ironson, Antoni, & Lutgendorf, 2001). This can at times be time consuming for the group leader, who must set clear and firm limits to prevent therapist burnout. This may be particularly difficult for therapists who have worked with other patient populations who are not as motivated or invested in their healing. It is rewarding for group leaders to work with patients who are compliant with treatment; therefore, they may be more apt to provide these patients with extra attention. It is important to discuss the parameters of the therapeutic relationship during the first group session. We inform participants that they will have 2 hours of the group leader's undivided attention during the group. However, contact with the group leader outside the group will take place only in an emergency or when a participant needs to inform the leader of a missed session. If a participant is unable to attend a group, we usually provide an opportunity for the group leader to review the missed material briefly during session breaks or during a brief (5 minutes or less) phone call. The participant workbook that we provide to group members highlights the information covered in the group sessions and minimizes the time spent reviewing missed material. The group leader must take care not to become each participant's individual therapist. When group members are in crisis or need adjunctive individual psychotherapy, they should be referred to another professional. Allowing CFS patients to have unlimited therapeutic contact could result in burnout for group leaders and may foster the patients' emotional dependency.

CONTINUED ADHERENCE AFTER GROUP INTERVENTION

In delivering the CBSM intervention, it is important to identify factors that will contribute to participants' continued adherence after termination. Here is what one participant said in response to another participant who was discussing the gains she made in the group:

> I have a word of warning. I agree with you wholeheartedly about the benefits. Don't be surprised if you slip back some and remember that you can also come back from that. As we get away from it, it kind of fades a bit. For me, it's been like doing it all over again, like I've never done it. I wish there were booster classes or something like that. I think it should be like you do it [the program] and then every 4 months or something, you have a one-hour session. I find that, even though intellectually, I can work through a lot of the processes, actually taking it to heart and believing it and having it really set it in as a way of life is another thing.

Many of our participants have suggested that "booster sessions" after group termination would be helpful in maintaining their learned skills. Beck, Rush, Shaw, and Emery (1979) suggest, "... ultimately, regularly scheduled booster sessions once or twice a year enable the patient to continue to consolidate the gains made in therapy." We do not actively encourage or discourage continuing participant contact after the group ends, although many participants find it helpful to continue this contact, which indicates the beneficial effects of the group's social support.

CONCLUSION

Driven by a theoretical model for the role of stressors and psychobiological processes in the maintenance of CFS symptoms (Antoni & Weiss, in press), we designed a CBSM intervention targeting several facets that characterize CFS patients' stress responses. The goals of this CBSM program include improving participants' psychological adjustment to CFS, enhancing their ability to cope with daily life stressors, and increasing their sense of self-efficacy and mastery. CFS patients are particularly good candidates for this CBSM intervention because of their high motivation and intelligence. They also welcome the acknowledgment and acceptance of their illness from the scientific community. It is unclear whether the group's social support, or the tools that participants acquire to gain mastery over life stressors, or a combination of these factors, may effect the treatment outcomes observed. It is our hope that such intervention strategies will ultimately be useful in both clinical and research settings to help CFS patients enhance their overall quality of life and possibly the course of illness.

REFERENCES

Antoni, M. H. (1997). Cognitive behavioral stress management for gay men learning of their HIV-1 antibody test results. In J. Spira (Ed.), *Group therapy for patients with chronic medical diseases* (pp. 55–91). New York: Guilford Press.

Antoni, M. H., Baggett, L., Ironson, G., LaPerriere, S., August, S., Klimas, N., et al. (1991). Cognitive behavioral stress management intervention buffers distress responses and immunologic changes following notification of HIV-1 seropositivity. *Journal of Consulting and Clinical Psychology, 59*(6), 906–915.

Antoni, M. H., Lehman, J., Kilbourn, K., Boyers, A., Yount, S., Culver, J., et al. (2001). Cognitive-behavioral stress management intervention decreases the prevalence of depression and enhances benefit finding among women under treatment for early-stage breast cancer. *Health Psychology, 20,* 20–32.

Antoni, M. H., & Weiss, D. (in press). Stress, immunity, and chronic fatigue syndrome: A conceptual model to guide the development of treatment and research. In L. Jason, P. Fennell, & R. Taylor (Eds.), *Handbook of chronic fatigue syndrome and other fatiguing illnesses.* New York: Wiley.

Beck, A. T., Rush, J. A., Shaw, B. F., & Emery, G. (1979). *Cognitive therapy of depression.* New York: Guilford Press.

Buchwald, D., Sullivan, J., & Komaroff A. (1987). Frequency of chronic active Epstein-Barr virus infection in a general medical practice. *Journal of the American Medical Association, 257,* 2303–2307.

Butler, S., Chalder, T., & Ron, M. (1991). Cognitive behavior therapy in chronic fatigue syndrome. *Journal of Neurology, Neurosurgery, and Psychiatry, 54,* 153–158.

Courtois, C. A. (1988). *Healing the incest wound: Adult survivors in therapy.* New York: Norton.

Cruess, S., Antoni, M. H., Cruess, D., Fletcher, M. A., Ironson, G., Kumar, M., et al. (2000). Reductions in HSV-2 antibody titers after cognitive behavioral stress management and relationships with neuroendocrine function, relaxation skills, and social support in HIV+ gay men. *Psychosomatic Medicine, 62,* 828–837.

Deale, A., Chalder, T., Marks, I., & Wessely, S. (1997). Cognitive behavioral therapy for chronic fatigue syndrome: A randomized control trial. *American Journal of Psychiatry, 154,* 408–414.

Engel, G. L. (1980). The clinical application of the biopsychosocial model. *American Journal of Psychiatry, 137,* 535.

Esterling, B., Antoni, M. H., Schneiderman, N., LaPerriere, A., Ironson, G., Carver, C., et al. (1992). Psychosocial modulation of antibody to Epstein-Barr viral capsid antigen and human herpes virus-type 6 in HIV-1 infected and at-risk gay men. *Psychosomatic Medicine, 54,* 354–371.

Friedberg, F., & Krupp, L. (1994). A comparison of cognitive behavioral treatment for chronic fatigue syndrome and primary depression. *Clinical Infectious Diseases, 18,* 105–109.

Helder, L. (1996). *A cognitive behavioral group intervention for chronic fatigue patients.* Unpublished manuscript, University of Miami, Coral Gables, FL.

Ironson, G., Antoni, M. H., & Lutgendorf, S. (2001). Psychosocial interventions for HIV-infected persons. In M. Chesney & M. H. Antoni (Eds.), *Health psychology and HIV disease: From transmission to treatment.* Washington, DC: American Psychological Association.

Jones, J., & Strauss, S. (1987). Chronic Epstein-Barr virus infection. *Annual Review of Medicine, 38,* 195–209.

Komaroff, A., & Buchwald, D. (1991). Symptoms and signs of chronic fatigue syndrome. *Reviews of Infectious Diseases, 13*(Suppl.), S8–S11.

Lutgendorf, S., Antoni, M. H., Ironson, G., Klimas, N., Starr, K., McCabe, P., et al. (1997). Cognitive behavioral stress management decreases dysphoric mood and herpes simplex virus-type 2 antibody titers in symptomatic HIV-seropositive gay men. *Journal of Consulting and Clinical Psychology, 65,* 31–43.

Ravicz, S. (2000). *Thriving with your autoimmune disorder: A woman's mind-body guide.* Oakland, CA: New Harbinger.

Sharpe, M., Hawton, K., Simkin, S., Suraway, C., Hackman, A., Klimes, I., et al. (1996). Cognitive behavior therapy for chronic fatigue syndrome: A randomized controlled trial. *British Medical Journal, 312,* 21–26.

Taerk, G., Toner, B. B., Salit, I. E., Garfinkel, P. E., & Ozersky, S. (1987). Depression in patients with neuromyasthenia (benign myalgic encephoalomyelitis). *International Journal of Psychiatry in Medicine, 17,* 49–56.

CHAPTER 26

Exercise Therapy

CHRISTOPHER R. SNELL, J. MARK VANNESS, STACI R. STEVENS,
SHAWN G. PHIPPEN, and W. LINE DEMPSEY IV

EXACERBATION OF SYMPTOMS following even minimal physical exertion is common among chronic fatigue syndrome (CFS) patients (Komaroff & Buchwald, 1991). It follows then that many persons with CFS have either learned to avoid all types of bodily exertion or continue to engage in physical activity and suffer the consequences. Ironically, this activity avoidance behavior can precipitate a cycle of deconditioning wherein hypokinetic effects further compound the problems manifest in CFS (De Lorenzo et al., 1998; Rowbottom, Keast, Pervan, & Morton, 1998; Vercoulen et al., 1997). Indeed, many CFS symptoms are easily confused with those resulting from low fitness levels (McCully & Natelson, 1999). Not surprisingly, physicians frequently prescribe exercise as remediation for these symptoms, and persons with CFS often attempt to recondition themselves. However, given the nature of CFS, these attempts to get fit are invariably doomed to failure, which is reflected in the conflicting reports on conditioning and CFS found in the literature (Sisto, 1993). The logic of using exercise to treat CFS may seem inescapable (McCully, Sisto, & Natelson, 1996; Shephard, 2001). However, controlled studies evaluating exercise therapy as a treatment for CFS are limited in number and variously beset by methodological inadequacies, problems of subject selection, and high dropout rates (Whiting et al., 2001). Additionally, the exercise-induced pain experienced by many CFS patients can encourage a belief that physical activity is dangerous and possibly associated with organ damage (Goshorn, 1998). Despite the equivocal findings, there is sufficient positive evidence to suggest that exercise can be efficacious in the treatment of CFS (Whiting et al., 2001). With insight to the pathophysiology of CFS and an understanding of energy metabolism, it is possible to design therapeutic exercise interventions that can ameliorate the debilitating effects of CFS while avoiding postexertional malaise and other ancillary symptoms.

OXIDATIVE IMPAIRMENT AS A SOURCE OF
REDUCED WORK CAPACITY IN CFS

CFS patients commonly complain about muscle pain and weakness. Patients often report a reduction in physical activity and experience the return of severe symptoms following even moderate levels of exertion (McCully, Sisto, et al., 1996). The widespread incidence of these symptoms among patients has prompted researchers to investigate muscle function and structure in CFS.

Oxidative, or aerobic, energy pathways provide most of the energy that is needed for muscle contraction during physical activity. These pathways rely on the delivery of oxygen from the blood to the mitochondria to provide substrate for the production of energy. In some CFS patients, these aerobic pathways appear unable to provide adequate energy (McCully, Natelson, Iotti, & Leigh, 1996). The source of oxidative limitation observed in CFS is unclear, but the result is an inability to perform sustained aerobic work (Fischler et al., 1997; Fulcher & White, 2000; Riley, O'Brian, McCluskey, Bell, & Nicholls, 1990; Sisto et al., 1996).

Several studies involving CFS patients have found defects in oxidative metabolism (Make & Jones, 1997; McCully & Natelson, 1999; McCully, Natelson, et al., 1996; Riley et al., 1990; Wong et al., 1992). Atrophy of fast twitch muscle fibers has also been reported along with mitochondrial abnormalities (P. O. Behan, Behan, & Bell, 1985; W. H. Behan, Holt, Kay, & Moonie, 1999; Byrne & Trounce, 1987; Gow et al., 1994).

Some CFS patients show evidence of an abnormally early intracellular acidosis during exercise (Arnold, Bore, Radda, Styles, & Taylor, 1984, 1985), and it is believed that this may represent excessive lactic acid formation (Jamal & Hansen, 1989). While this hypothesis is supported by some researchers (Lane, Woodrow, & Archard, 1994), others have found no consistent abnormalities of glycolysis, mitochondrial metabolism, or pH regulation among CFS patients (Barnes, Taylor, Kemp, & Radda, 1993).

Fulle et al. (2000) examined specific alterations in vastus lateralis muscle in patients diagnosed with CFS. Their results revealed significant differences in oxidative damage to DNA and lipids as well as increased activity of several antioxidant enzyme systems when they compared the CFS patients to normal, age-matched controls. The authors suggest that the possibility of muscle tissue degeneration in patients with CFS might partially explain this diminished functioning.

The poor performance of some CFS patients in response to cardiopulmonary exercise testing may result from a physiological limitation that inhibits their use of oxygen, despite no problems introducing inspired oxygen to the lungs and bloodstream. Even though the volume of air exchanged (V_E) during exercise is normal, the volume of oxygen from the air that the patients are actually able to use (VO_2) is diminished (VanNess, Snell, Fredrickson, Strayer, & Stevens, 2001). It is possible that damage to the organelles (mitochondria) inside muscles could reduce their ability to fully use available oxygen during aerobic activity. This could explain the early acidosis and high lactate levels seen in some CFS patients in response to exercise (VanNess et al., 2001).

McCully and Natelson (1999) postulate that the diminished oxidative capacity of CFS patients may be associated with reduced blood flow resulting from autonomic dysregulation. They note that their own findings in this area parallel earlier research linking fibromyalgia, which often overlaps with CFS, and abnormal autonomic tone (Vaeory, Qiao, Morkrid, & Forre, 1989). As a point of caution, they are unwilling to conclude that the reduced oxygen delivery associated with CFS results from anything other than inactivity.

The hypothesized link between CFS and abnormalities in cardiovascular autonomic control goes some way toward explaining the presence of somatic symptoms such as fatigue and pain without clear evidence of organic corollaries (Pagani & Lucini, 1999). McCully, Natelson, et al. (1996) observe that most research has found CFS patients to possess normal muscle strength and muscular endurance, which is either normal or slightly diminished. Similarly, histological evidence of mitocondrial impairment or defects in oxidative metabolism is inconclusive. However, during exercise, CFS patients perceive themselves to be working harder and in greater pain at any given workload when compared to healthy controls (Farquhar, Hunt, Taylor, Darling, & Freeman, 2002; Rowbottom et al., 1998). In the absence of any obvious deficits in muscle function, the apparent diminished aerobic capacity of CFS patients may be predicated on various regulatory abnormalities including cardiac autonomic imbalance (Pagani, Lucini, Mela, Langewit, & Malliani, 1994), neuroendocrine disturbances (Demitrack, 1977), dysfunction of the hypothalamic-pituitary-adrenal axis (HPA; Demitrack & Crofford, 1998), and immune dysregulation (Klimas, Salvato, Morgan, & Fletcher, 1990).

The abnormal HPA axis physiology found in some patients suggests that CFS may be a stress-related disorder (Demitrack & Crofford, 1998). In a normal stress response, the release of corticotropin-releasing hormone (CRH) stimulates the release of cortisol, which in turn promotes mobilization of the body's energy systems. Low cortisol levels observed in some CFS patients have been linked to reduced adrenal capacity (Bou-Holaigah, Rowe, Kan, & Calkins, 1996; Scott, Medbak, & Dinan, 1998; Scott et al., 1999), which may explain the blunted cardiovascular response to aerobic exercise noted in several studies (De Becker, Roeykens, Reynders, McGregor, & De Meirleir, 2000; VanNess et al., 2001). In addition to depressing physical performance, this abnormal cardiovascular response to stress may result in failure to adequately perfuse active muscles during exercise. The resulting tissue hypoxia and buildup of metabolites would inhibit continuous muscular exertion and promote earlier onset of fatigue. In the postexercise condition, impaired tissue blood flow prevents adequate clearance of metabolites, resulting in sustained muscular pain and fatigue.

A normal neural and humoral response to exercise results in the redistribution of blood flow and mobilization of fuel substrates to provide energy for sustained muscle contraction. Activation of the sympathoadrenal system (via descending sympathetic neurons from the hypothalamus and stimulation of the adrenal medulla to release epinephrine) results in elevated heart rate and blood pressure during exercise and increased glucose production by the liver. Production of CRH in the hypothalamus causes release of adrenal corticotrophic hormone (ACTH) from the pituitary, which in turn stimulates release of cortisol from the adrenal cortex to increase production of glucose from proteins (gluconeogenesis). The sympathoadrenal system also inhibits visceral functions, such as digestion, and inflammatory and immune responses. It is possible that dysregulation at one or more sites along the HPA axis is responsible for alterations to this response in CFS, contributing to early onset of fatigue during exercise and prolonged recovery after exercise (Freeman & Komaroff, 1997; Pagani et al., 1994). Impaired sympathetic activation (originating from hypothalamic and medullary neurons) and/or blunted release of cortisol from the adrenal glands prompts inefficient homeostatic adjustments to physical exertion (see Figure 26.1). An understanding of the constraints imposed by the pathology associated with CFS is essential if exercise prescriptions are to avoid unrealistic expectations for increases in physical working capacity and functionality.

ROLE OF THE IMMUNE SYSTEM

The neuroendocrine and immune systems are highly interactive. Even subtle immunological changes can induce dramatic disturbances in neuroendocrine

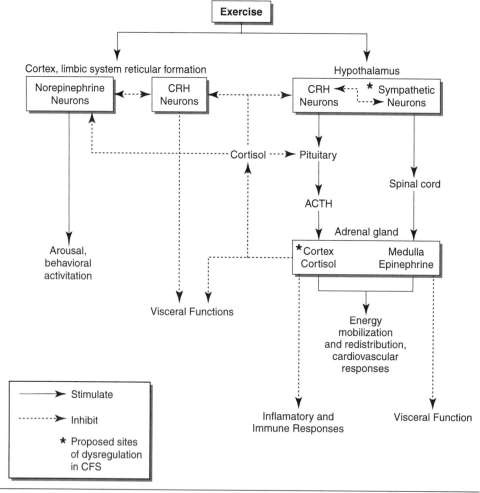

Figure 26.1 Integrated Response to Physical Exertion. Neurohumoral responses during exercise that result in cardiovascular activation (increase in heart rate, blood pressure, and redistribution of blood to muscles) and energy mobilization (hepatic glucose production and gluconeogenesis) to provide oxygen and substrates to the working muscles. Highlighted on the figure are possible sites on the hypothalamo-pituitary-adrenal axis where abnormal responses have been observed in patients with CFS.

function (Grossman & Costa, 1993). Shephard (2001) suggests that these disturbances may create a condition similar to overtraining in athletes, where the stress of heavy training can provoke immunosuppression. Repeated activation of the HPA axis associated with training stress results in a shift from cell mediated to humoral immunity, thus increasing susceptibility to infection (Clow & Hucklebridge, 2001). When the affected athletes attempt to exercise, they frequently regress in common with the many CFS patients who also experience exacerbation of symptoms following physical activity.

Immunological findings in CFS research tend to be inconsistent. However, this inconsistency may be an artifact of inadequate research design and inappropriate statistical analyses (Hanson, Gause, & Natelson, 2001). A significant body of research supports the hypothesis that CFS symptoms result from immune system dysregulation (e.g., Buchwald, Wener, Pearlman, & Kith, 1997; Klimas, 1998; Klimas et al., 1990; Komaroff, Geiger, & Wormsley, 1988; Lloyd, Hickie, Hickie, Dwyer, & Wakefield, 1992; Lloyd, Wakefield, Boughton, & Dwyer, 1989; Suhadolnik et al., 1994, 1997; Tirelli et al., 1993; Tirelli, Marotta, Improta, & Pinto, 1994). It has been suggested that many of these symptoms, including reduced aerobic work capacity, can be linked specifically to dysregulation of the 2-5A antiviral pathway, which is characterized by an upregulation of the enzyme Ribonuclease L (RNase L; Englebienne, Herst, De Smet, D'Haese, & De Meirleir, 2001).

In a healthy individual, the size of the RNase L protein is 80 kilodaltons (kDa). In many of the patients with CFS, the presence of the 80 kDa RNase L protein is diminished or not seen at all. However, a unique lower molecular weight form of RNase L (37 kDa) is present. The presence of this 37 kDa RNase L can differentiate between CFS and illnesses with similar clinical presentations (Suhadolnik et al., 1994) and predict severity of symptoms in patients with CFS (De Meirleir et al., 2000).

A study involving 73 CFS patients reported that those patients exhibiting upregulated RNase L enzyme activity performed significantly lower on an exercise test than those with normal levels (Snell, VanNess, Strayer, & Stevens, 2002). In addition to this study, independent research by Suhadolnik and associates reported that increased RNase L activity correlated with decreases in activities of daily living in patients diagnosed with CFS. It was also suggested that elevated RNase L activity is a good predictor of the development of muscle pain, fatigue, and decreased mental condition in patients with CFS (McGregor, 1999).

It has been hypothesized that dysregulation in the 2-5A-dependent RNase L antiviral pathway suggests the presence of chronic viral infection and that the various cytokines produced by the body to fight this infection may be implicated in the general fatigue and muscle weakness found in CFS (Suhadolnik et al., 1997). The 2-5A antiviral mechanisms are regulated by the cytokine interferon (Roelens et al., 2001). It has been proposed that dysregulation of the 2-5A pathway results in the release of certain protein fragments, which disrupt normal ion and amino acid transport. Ion channel dysfunction can be linked to various CFS-related symptoms such as transient hypoglycemia, night sweats, chemical hypersensitivity, immunodeficiency, depression, monoamine neurotransmitter dysfunction, reduced pain threshold, loss of muscle potassium, anemia, CNS abnormalities, and visual problems (Englebienne et al., 2001).

Further support for the notion of cytokine-mediated symptoms in CFS comes from research involving medicinal use of interferon-alpha. When used to treat patients with malignant melanoma, this cytokine induced symptoms of depression, anxiety, fatigue, pain, and cognitive dysfunction similar to CFS. While most symptoms were reduced by administration of an antidepressant, the symptoms of fatigue were less responsive to treatment (Musselman et al., 2001). A symptom complex similar to that found in CFS has also been observed when interferon-alpha is used to treat hepatitis B (McDonald et al., 1987).

REHABILITATION IN CHRONIC FATIGUE SYNDROME

As previously noted, conditioning programs often form a central role in the treatment of CFS. Although published research in the area of exercise and rehabilitation for CFS is limited, exercise therapy has received a great deal of support as a treatment for fibromyalgia (Sim & Adams, 1999). There is an overlap between CFS and fibromyalgia, with some patients exhibiting symptoms that warrant concurrent diagnosis of both conditions (Shephard, 2001).

Fibromyalgia affects about 2% to 4% of the population (Bailey, Starr, Alderson, & Moreland, 1999; Littlejohn, 2001). The American College of Rheumatology criteria for diagnosis of fibromyalgia require a history of widespread pain (at least three months) and pain at 11 of 18 tender points on digital palpation with an approximate force of 4 kg (Wolfe et al., 1990). When treating patients with fibromyalgia and other chronic pain syndromes, exercise has been used to counter the effects of decreased activity such as atrophy, weakness, and contracted joints, with pain being only indirectly addressed (Offenbächer & Stucki, 2000).

A review of exercise studies in fibromyalgia could not find a consensus that exercise is beneficial for the treatment of fibromyalgia symptoms although it appears helpful for improving patients' fitness levels and increasing capacity to carry out normal everyday tasks (Clark, Jones, Burckhardt, & Bennett, 2001). For many fibromyalgia patients, exercise-induced pain can prove an impediment to adherence. This could explain the problem of attrition noted in a number of studies. Patients may have ceased participation when the intensity of the exercise exceeded their tolerance levels. Individual differences among fibromyalgia patients with respect to severity of both primary and secondary symptoms point to the need for individualized exercise prescriptions (Clark et al., 2001). Matching exercise type and intensity to the needs and capabilities of individual patients could be vital to enhancing adherence and maximizing benefits, but further research is necessary before definitive conclusions can be drawn.

Some success in the treatment of CFS has been achieved using graded exercise therapy (Whiting et al., 2001). This approach prescribes a gradual progression in exercise intensity above current levels with the goal of improving patients' overall fitness levels, including cardiovascular endurance. While the principle of progressive conditioning appears well founded, optimal patterns of reconditioning remain undefined (Shephard, 2001).

In a comparison of graded exercise and treatment with the antidepressant fluoxetine, it was found that patients' health perceptions and feelings of fatigue were significantly improved following the exercise program while fluoxetine improved only depression (Wearden et al., 1998). Fulcher and White (1997) compared the effects of graded aerobic exercise to relaxation and flexibility exercises in the treatment of CFS. Sixteen of the 29 exercise treatment patients rated themselves "much" or "very much" better following the intervention compared with 8 of 30 patients in the relaxation and flexibility group who reported improvement. Only the graded exercise group showed a significant increase in aerobic capacity, while both groups saw significant increases in strength.

Despite the apparent positive results, generalization from these two studies to the broader CFS population remains limited. As observed by Shephard (2001), the patients on whom these findings are based were high-functioning CFS patients, able to regularly attend outpatient workout sessions, who likely represent less than 10% of CFS cases.

If exercise therapy is to be made available to a broader spectrum of CFS patients, implementation of home-based programs designed specifically to accommodate lower functioning individuals will be necessary. Such programs should start at levels consistent with a patient's functional status and gradually increase in duration and intensity as the patient accommodates to the exercise regimen. A primary consideration is that the patient should recover completely from each exercise bout before again engaging in physical activity. As a general rule, any activity that results in a resting heart rate increase of more than 20 beats per minute should not be repeated (Young, 1999).

Given their status, many low-functioning CFS patients will likely have developed patterns of activity avoidance. These maladaptive patterns must be overcome if exercise therapy is to be successful. According to Powell, Bentall, Nye, and Edwards (2001), activity avoidance behaviors result in part from inaccurate illness beliefs. In a study using patient education to counter such beliefs, they found that describing the role of disrupted physiological regulation in fatigue symptoms and encouraging home-based exercise resulted in a significant number of patients achieving satisfactory outcomes in physical functioning along with improvements in fatigue, sleep, disability, and mood. However, they did report that a number of patients dropped out of the intervention groups.

It would appear that even if the initial reluctance to engage in an exercise program can be overcome, there still remains a high probability of patient dropout. Possible reasons for this, as previously noted as to exercise and fibromyalgia, could center on exercise intensity, particularly as it interacts with a patient's energy reserves. When the physical demands of the exercise program exceed patients' capabilities, they stop exercising. As a potential solution to this problem, it might prove useful to include energy conservation education as well as therapeutic exercise as parts of a comprehensive treatment program. A key role of energy conservation in this context is to enable an environment in which exercising is possible. Energy conservation education can help patients more effectively manage their fatigue and lessen the limiting effects of this health problem. By learning to conserve energy during activities of daily living, patients can then benefit by using their energy reserves for exercise.

Saving energy is an important strategy for managing a number of conditions other than CFS. Historically, energy conservation interventions have been used in the treatment of rheumatoid arthritis, multiple sclerosis, and chronic obstructive pulmonary disease (COPD). The National Institutes of Health (NIH) developed an energy conservation program for rheumatoid arthritis patients that effectively improved the quality of life for participants (Gerber et al., 1987). The NIH has revised this program specifically for patients experiencing fatigue, but it has yet to be evaluated in a controlled study.

Careful activity management was included by Marlin, Anchel, Gibson, Goldberg, and Swinton (1998) as part of a comprehensive, multidisciplinary intervention for CFS. The program also included medical care for any ongoing disease or pathology and pharmacological management of psychiatric disorders where appropriate. The energy conservation component was part of an individualized cognitive-behavioral therapy program implemented by a behavioral therapist working with patients in their own homes. This therapy combined cognitive interventions dealing with patients' beliefs about CFS, vocational and avocational goal-setting, sleep management strategies, dietary modifications, social support, and physical exercise included as part of a structured approach to the gradual increase in daily activity. Of the 51 patients treated, 45 either returned to gainful employment or were functioning at a work-equivalent level. While these results are encouraging, the authors note that their study does not permit selective evaluation of the intervention's individual elements. It is also the case that one-on-one therapy expenses preclude the adoption of such approaches for many CFS patients. However, a telling aspect of this study is the importance given to individualized treatment and the need to incorporate adequate rest along with gradual but consistent increases in daily activity. This begins by establishing baseline levels for exercise and physical activity that are well within each patient's capacity to comply with program requirements.

When designing therapeutic exercise programs for the treatment of CFS, it is of paramount importance that initial exercise intensities are consistent with current disability levels. The American College of Sports Medicine (ACSM) has specific rehabilitation guidelines for special populations such as cardiac and pulmonary patients. Recommended strategies include aerobic exercise in addition to flexibility, interval, and resistance strength training. Exercise intensity is based on measures obtained from cardiopulmonary exercise testing. Currently, these strategies have not been applied to the treatment of CFS.

IMPORTANCE OF CARDIOPULMONARY
EXERCISE TESTING

Cardiopulmonary exercise testing (CPX) is a functional assessment that allows for the simultaneous evaluation of the responses of the cardiovascular, respiratory, and muscular systems to exercise (Higginbotham, 1994; Mahler & Franco, 1996). Electrocardiography during the test monitors heart function at rest and under exercise conditions. The vascular response to exercise is monitored through blood pressure readings. Measurement of gas exchange via breath by breath analysis accurately quantifies aerobic capacity. CPX noninvasively measures oxygen consumption, carbon dioxide production, minute ventilation, respiratory exchange, and ventilatory threshold. These measurements are accomplished by analyzing the air expired while an individual performs physical work, such as bicycle ergometry or walking on a treadmill. The results from CPX can determine the factors causing exertional intolerance, the severity of functional impairment, and the parameters for therapeutic exercise intervention (J. Meyers & Gullestad, 1998).

Cardiologists, pulmonologists, and exercise physiologists have been using cardiopulmonary exercise testing for years in disease management. The interpretation of gas exchange measurements during exercise has particular prognostic and diagnostic value. Physiologic abnormalities detected through CPX can implicate the functional limitation resulting from disease. This type of testing is commonly used for the diagnosis and assessment of coronary heart disease, peripheral vascular disease, cardiomyopathy, chronic obstructive lung disease, metabolic disorders of skeletal muscle, and several others (K. Meyers et al., 1996; Wasserman, Hansen, Sue, Casaburi, & Whipp, 1999). By using a diagnostic algorithm (Sue & Wasserman, 1991), the results of a CPX study can delineate the cause of dyspnea (shortness of breath) as either a cardiac or pulmonary limitation. These types of algorithms can be used to identify the exact mechanism of exercise limitation in patients with cardiac and pulmonary disease or to determine the basis for fatigue and other forms of exercise intolerance (Neuberg, Friedman, Weiss, & Herman, 1988; Wasserman et al., 1999). CPX testing has been used for both diagnosis and follow-up evaluation of patients with a variety of metabolic myopathies including McArdles' syndrome, carnitine palmitoyl transferase deficiency, pyruvate dehydrogenase deficiency, and mitochondrial electron transport chain disorders (Elliot et al., 1989). Evidence of impaired oxygen delivery to active muscles during CPX testing has also been found in HIV-seropositive subjects (Johnson et al., 1990).

Frequently, exercise testing has also been employed to assess disability by examining functional capacity and oxygen uptake. Disability levels can be categorized based on peak oxygen consumption levels (VO_2) derived from gas exchange measurements (Weber & Janicki, 1986). The American Medical Association (AMA) specifies four classes of functional impairment ranging from "no impairment of the whole person" to "severe impairment of the whole person." Classification is based solely on objective measurement of maximal oxygen consumption during an exercise test (AMA, 1990). Several studies have used cardiopulmonary exercise testing to evaluate CFS patients (De Becker et al., 2000; Fulcher & White, 1997, 2000; Riley et al., 1990; Stevens, 1995), but only two (Make & Jones, 1997; VanNess et al., 2001) have stratified CFS patients in terms of physical capacity using AMA guidelines (AMA, 1990). A number of studies have found CFS patients to possess normal or near normal values for maximal oxygen consumption (Kent-Braun, Sharma, & Weiner, 1993; Riley et al., 1990; Sargent, Scroop, Nemeth, Burnet, & Buckley, 2002). Using AMA guidelines, such CFS patients would not be classified as functionally impaired.

In addition to quantifying disability in CFS, CPX testing has important implications for developing individualized exercise prescriptions and evaluating therapeutic exercise interventions. Personalized programs can be designed to maximize rehabilitation by using the appropriate heart rate and workload derived from the exercise test (Franklin, Whaley, & Howley, 2000). Anaerobic threshold, determined noninvasively through examination of the ventilatory response to exercise and measurement of lactic acid levels in the bloodstream, provides for greater specificity when developing an exercise prescription. These objective measures can be assessed before and after an exercise intervention to determine program efficacy (K. Meyers et al., 1996; Wasserman et al., 1999).

Because many symptoms of CFS appear to involve the mechanisms of exercise intolerance, CPX testing can add to the understanding of CFS pathology. The test data parallel the functional performance of those bodily systems involved during successful exercise. This allows for both joint and separate evaluation of those systems to identify particular patterns in the data that indicate the source of dysfunction (Sue, 1994).

EXERCISE THERAPY FOR CFS

While some success has been achieved employing graded aerobic exercise in the treatment of CFS (Fulcher & White, 1997; Wearden et al., 1998), this appears limited to a subset of higher functioning patients able to undertake regular aerobic exercise. For a vast majority of CFS patients, the graded aerobic exercise approach may not be feasible because of limitations in their capacity to fully use oxygen during physical activity.

The research findings suggest that oxidative (aerobic) metabolism may be compromised in some CFS patients, resulting in an overreliance on nonoxidative (anaerobic) metabolism. Therefore, when these patients attempt to exercise, or merely complete activities of daily living employing a dysfunctional energy system (aerobic energy pathways), the symptoms and disability in CFS are frequently intensified. This results in an exacerbation of the symptom complex and perpetuates fatigue.

Because these nonoxidative systems appear sensitive to training in CFS patients, targeted programs for increasing the capacity of these systems provide potentially efficacious treatment options (Snell & Stevens, 1998). Nonoxidative pathways include the phosphagen system and glycolysis. The phosphagen system supplies energy for muscle contraction for a matter of seconds, and its duration is dependent on the amount of Adenosine triphosphate (ATP) and phosphocreatine stored in the muscle. With repeated depletion and repletion during exercise training, ATP and phosphocreatine stores in the muscle increase to supply energy for longer periods of time. The activity of the glycolytic system is dependent only on energy needs and, in the absence of adequate oxygen delivery, the ability to remove and metabolize lactic acid. This energy system is capable of supplying energy for up to several minutes. Regular exercise for at least four to six weeks increases glycolytic enzyme density and enhances the muscle and liver pathways that remove and metabolize lactate.

AN INCLUSIVE THERAPEUTIC MODEL FOR REHABILITATION IN CFS

This therapeutic model is concerned with addressing the physical basis for CFS and the role of exercise therapy in controlling the symptoms and disability that accompany CFS. Developing sensitivity to the symptoms associated with CFS is an essential element of this model. Successful education and participation in exercise that uses and strengthens the nonoxidative, or anaerobic energy systems, will improve function and enhance performance of daily activities.

The key factors in treatment comprise positive engagement with the therapist, patient education, implementation of appropriate anaerobic exercise (AE), and follow-up. Behavioral goals include helping patients understand the relationship of fatigue to the mechanisms of energy production in the body, redefining exercise, prescribing appropriate exercise, increasing daily physical activity, and improving quality of life. The aim of this therapy is to engage CFS patients in AE to improve function and enhance performance of current and future activities. Patients should also be able to transfer these principles to the physical activities employed in daily living. The principle of specificity is an integral part of the exercise prescription. Exercises are specifically designed to mirror activities of daily living so that patients can achieve functional gains. This is similar to the training of specific energy systems for athletic performance. As a result of the intervention, patients should leave the AE treatment empowered, possessing the means to manage CFS instead of feeling victimized and controlled by the illness.

PHASE 1: ENGAGEMENT AND EDUCATION

The engagement and education phase introduces patients to the therapist and the treatment schedule. This component of the model is extremely important in creating an understanding and acceptance of the treatment. During this phase, the program rationale and goals for the three phases of treatment are introduced. This program introduction is helpful in guiding the education process. The patients are then provided an overview of each phase of treatment and acquainted with the potential benefits of this therapeutic approach.

During Phase 1, the reconceptualization of traditional exercise is facilitated through education. The patient must be taught that conventional wisdom and theories on how to exercise are not appropriate for the CFS population. The therapist should assist patients in redefining successful outcomes for exercise and physical activity by emphasizing the importance of metabolic energy systems and the benefits of using anaerobic exercise over traditional, aerobic exercise.

In this education phase, it is important to emphasize the need for restraint. Typically, patients with CFS have a history of trying to do too much when starting *any* exercise treatment, even "appropriate" AE therapy. The prevailing outcome experienced by CFS patients following an exercise intervention is one of failure and fatigue. The lack of success in this area may be attributed directly to the dysfunctional long-term, aerobic energy system found in CFS.

When this phase has been discussed, the AE model should be explained. Detailed information concerning the rationale for this treatment is presented to each patient. The rationale for the intervention will establish a foundation enabling the patient to proceed confidently to the next phase of treatment. The potential benefits for this form of therapy should be reviewed. Patients should be told to expect possible changes in the following areas: improved strength, improved flexibility, reduced pain, greater mental clarity, sense of accomplishment and enhanced function, improved quality of life, the ability to complete activities of daily living with greater ease, and learning to use exercise as a positive coping tool in CFS. Education about the AE model encompasses the following areas:

- Physical basis for CFS
- Role of fatigue in CFS
- Recovery response
- Symptom sensitivity

When the patient is able to comprehend and is willing to accept this new model for exercise, the Phase 1 goals have been achieved. This is an indication that the patient is prepared for the Phase 2 AE prescription.

PHASE 2: EXERCISE PRESCRIPTION AND MONITORING

The therapist should review the flexibility and exercise guidelines with the patient before the AE program. For the patients to be successful and follow the focus of Phase 2, further explanation of the AE program is warranted.

The therapist should monitor the patient's response to exercise, not only during and immediately after the session, but also the day after the AE treatment. When discussing likely outcomes, the therapist should tell patients not to expect AE to overcome or cure CFS. However, the program should give them a measure of control over the illness and empower them to function at a potentially higher level.

CFS patients with cognitive dysfunction have difficulty with learning and processing new information. Therefore, it is desirable to use multiple instructional and reinforcement strategies for each exercise prescription. For example, tell the patients what is required of them (auditory). Demonstrate each exercise for the patient (visual). Have the patient model the exercise that was demonstrated (kinesthetic). Provide feedback and reinforce proper exercise technique with verbal affirmation.

The AE program for Phase 2 consists of Stage 1: *Stretching and Strengthening* and Stage 2: *Stretching and Resistance Training*. The first stage is primarily focused on developing functional strength and flexibility. These strengthening exercises should use body weight as the only form of resistance, and the stretching exercises comprise nonballistic, active stretching. Exercises should be functional and focus on movements used in everyday life employing the principle of specificity for exercise training, which states that the body adapts to exercise challenges in ways that are very specific to the demands placed on it. The AE program is, therefore, designed to promote increases in strength and range of motion that assist patients to more easily perform activities of daily living.

Sample exercises during Stage 1 include stretching the hands, which is an excellent way to improve circulation and increase mobility of the fingers. Holding, grasping, and picking up objects are tasks that are used repeatedly during daily activity. Likewise, getting up out of a chair is a functional movement that CFS patients must employ several times a day. It is a very specific activity requiring adequate leg strength. In addition to using muscles of the lower legs, the core stabilizing muscles of the abdominals and lower back are also involved. Patients may use their arms for assistance if they lack the strength to stand without upper body support. For an exercise called the *sit and stand,* patients are required to sit on the edge of a chair and then stand up. From the standing position, the patient is instructed to slowly sit back down and then repeat the exercise. It is recommended to start with one set of two to four repetitions and build slowly to a maximum of eight repetitions. This multijoint exercise strengthens the quadriceps, hamstrings, gluteal, and gastrocnemious muscles. Static contraction of the abdominal and lower back muscles helps to maintain proper posture during the exercise. The *sit and stand* is an efficient way to strengthen many muscle groups using only one exercise. As a desired outcome, patients should find it easier to climb a flight of stairs or get up from the couch.

The second stage of AE treatment is primarily focused on increasing strength and flexibility beyond the levels attained during Stage 1. This stage should incorporate additional resistance exercises for strength training above the body weight exercises performed during Stage 1. Latex resistance bands provide a cost-effective method to incorporate added resistance training at home or at the office. They are easily portable and take up little space, so patients may also travel with them.

The *chest press* is typical of exercises in Stage 2. It is another multijoint exercise involving the shoulder, elbow, wrists, and fingers. A resistance band is placed around the back just below the shoulder blades. From a seated position, the patient is instructed to grasp each end of the band close to the chest and then press the band forward until both arms are fully extended. The band is then returned in a controlled manner to the starting position. Changing hand position to create greater resistance from the band increases the challenge of this exercise. A useful way to integrate stretching in the program is to follow each strength exercise with a stretch targeting muscles that have just been worked. In the case of the *chest press,* a stretch that focuses on the chest and triceps complements the strengthening exercises. Such exercises also provide for neuromuscular adaptation and motor learning. Although patients may accept deconditioning and the corresponding muscle atrophy as part of their illness, this need not be the case. Not only can stretching and strengthening programs reverse muscle deconditioning, but also patients may benefit from the increased facilitation of motor neurons during exercise.

Improvement rates during this stage vary across patients. A higher functioning patient improves faster than a lower functioning patient. Additionally, as with many exercise programs, performance may plateau and improvement cease. This is usual, and patients should be encouraged to maintain their current levels of fitness even in the absence of further measurable functional gains.

After reaching the midpoint of treatment, patients should begin to work toward developing independence from therapist contact. Reliance on the therapist for exercise progression and functional goal setting will decrease as patients start to set their own goals.

PHASE 3: MAINTAINING FUNCTIONAL GAINS

Phase 3 involves maintaining the function gained as a result of the treatment and includes assessing these gains through follow-up sessions after the AE therapy sessions are completed. The focus of Phase 3 is to promote independence and assist patients in setting their own goals to maintain the functional gains achieved during the AE treatment. Assessment of the AE intervention for each patient is also an important element of Phase 3. The therapist should evaluate whether patients have achieved the goals set for Phases 1 and 2. What specific goals have the patients achieved, and why were they successful in achieving these goals? Conversely, if a patient was not successful, changes can be made for future sessions. It is important to provide feedback on the intervention; the ultimate goal is to enable patients to establish their own goals and achieve them without therapist contact. Patients should leave the session feeling confident they possess coping skills that will help them control their illness.

WHEN EXERCISE DOES WORK OUT

It is hardly surprising that the role of exercise in the treatment of CFS is poorly understood. A review of interventions employed to treat and manage CFS could find only three exercise studies that met minimum standards for validity, that is, randomized controlled or controlled trials with patient diagnosis of CFS according to any established criteria. All three studies employed a graded exercise approach. While these studies did show promising results, they were conducted with only those CFS patients able to attend the study centers for treatment. Two of the studies also reported patient withdrawals possibly related to the intervention (Whiting et al., 2001). It is apparent that while some CFS patients are able to tolerate traditional reconditioning approaches, many others find such regimens both painful and unproductive.

The failure of many patients to benefit from traditional approaches to exercise may result from an inability to sustain a normal stress response (Demitrack & Crofford, 1998). There is evidence to suggest that this may stem from alterations in autonomic nervous system activity (McCully & Natelson, 1999; Pagani & Lucini, 1999) linked to immune dysfunction (Englebienne et al., 2001). This hypothesis is consistent with the diminished cardiac response seen in some CFS patients during cardiopulmonary exercise testing (De Becker et al., 2000; VanNess et al., 2001).

For such patients, a revised approach to rehabilitation might be warranted. Rather than attempts at reconditioning through sustained bouts of aerobic exercise, for example, running on a treadmill or pedaling a stationary bike, exercise that employs and strengthens the anaerobic energy systems may be more productive. Anaerobic exercise therapy uses short duration activities designed to increase strength and flexibility. The goal is to help patients perform activities of daily living with enhanced vigor and less pain while avoiding risk of sudden relapse. With success managing CFS through anaerobic exercise therapy, patients can be *empowered* and feel less *victimized* by their illness (Snell, Stevens, & VanNess, 2001, p. 119).

REFERENCES

American Medical Association. (1990). *Guide to the evaluation of permanent impairment* (3rd ed.). Chicago: American Medical Association.

Arnold, D. L., Bore, P. J., Radda, G. K., Styles, P., & Taylor, D. J. (1984). Excessive intracellular acidosis of skeletal muscle on exercise in a patient with postviral exhaustion/fatigue syndrome, a ^{31}P magnetic resonance study. *Lancet, 1,* 1367–1369.

Arnold, D. L., Bore, P. J., Radda, G. K., Styles, P., & Taylor, D. J. (1985). Enhanced intramuscular acidosis during exercise by patients with postviral exhaustion syndrome [Abstract]. *Neurology, 35*(Suppl. 1), 165.

Bailey, A., Starr, L., Alderson, M., & Moreland, J. (1999). A comparative evaluation of a fibromyalgia rehabilitation program. *Arthritis Care and Research, 12,* 336–340.

Barnes, P. R., Taylor, D. J., Kemp, G. J., & Radda, G. K. (1993). Skeletal muscle bioenergetics in the chronic fatigue syndrome. *Journal of Neurology, Neurosurgery, and Psychiatry, 56,* 679–683.

Behan, P. O., Behan, W. M., & Bell, E. J. (1985). The postviral fatigue syndrome: Analysis of the findings in 50 cases. *Journal of Infection, 10,* 211–222.

Behan, W. M., Holt, I. J., Kay, D. H., & Moonie, P. (1999). In vitro study of muscle aerobic metabolism in chronic fatigue syndrome. *Journal of Chronic Fatigue Syndrome, 5,* 3–16.

Bou-Holaigah, I., Rowe, P. C., Kan, J., & Calkins, H. (1996). The relationship between neurally mediated hypotension and the chronic fatigue syndrome. *Journal of the American Medical Association, 274*(12), 961–967.

Buchwald, D., Wener, M. H., Pearlman, T., & Kith, P. (1997). Markers of inflammation and immune activation in chronic fatigue and chronic fatigue syndrome. *Journal of Rheumatology, 24*(2), 372–376.

Byrne, E., & Trounce, I. (1987). Chronic fatigue and myalgia syndrome, mitochondrial and glycolytic studies in skeletal muscles. *Journal of Neurology, Neurosurgery, and Psychiatry, 50,* 746.

Clark, S. R., Jones, K. D., Burckhardt, C. S., & Bennett, R. (2001). Exercise for patients with fibromyalgia: Risks versus benefits. *Current Rheumatology Reports, 3*(2), 135–146.

Clow, A., & Hucklebridge, F. (2001). The impact of psychological stress on immune function in the athletic population. *Exercise Immunology Review, 7*, 5–17.

De Becker, P., Roeykens, J., Reynders, M., McGregor, N., & De Meirleir, K. (2000). Exercise capacity in chronic fatigue syndrome. *Archives of Internal Medicine, 160*(21), 3270–3277.

De Lorenzo, F., Xiao, H., Mukherjee, M., Harcup, J., Suleiman, S., Kandziola, Z., et al. (1998). Chronic fatigue syndrome: Physical and cardiovascular deconditioning. *Quarterly Journal of Medicine, 91*(7), 475–481.

De Meirleir, K. D., Bisbal, C., Campine, K., De Becker, P., Salehzada, T., Demettre, E., et al. (2000). A 37kDa 2-5A binding protein as a potential biochemical marker for chronic fatigue syndrome. *American Journal of Medicine, 108*, 99–105.

Demitrack, M. A. (1977). Neuroendocrine correlates of chronic fatigue syndrome: A brief review. *Journal of Psychiatry Research, 31*, 69–82.

Demitrack, M. A., & Crofford, L. J. (1998). Evidence for and pathophysiologic implications of hypothalamic-pituitary-adrenal axis dysregulation in fibromyalgia and chronic fatigue syndrome. *Annals New York Academy of Science, 840*, 684–697.

Elliot, D. L., Buist, N. R., Goldberg, L., Kennaway, N. G., Powell, B. R., & Luehl, K. S. (1989). Metabolic myopathies: Evaluation by graded exercise testing. *Medicine, 68*, 163–172.

Englebienne, P., Herst, C. V., De Smet, K., D'Haese, A., & De Meirleir, K. (2001). Interactions between RNase L ankyrin-like domain and ABC transporters as a possible origin for pain, ion transport, CNS and immune disorders of chronic fatigue immune dysfunction syndrome. *Journal of Chronic Fatigue Syndrome, 8*(3/4), 83–102.

Farquhar, W. B., Hunt, B. E., Taylor, J. A., Darling, S. E., & Freeman, R. (2002). Blood volume and its relation to peak O_2 consumption and physical activity in patients with chronic fatigue. *American Journal of Physiology Heart Circulation Physiology, 282*, H66–H71.

Fischler, B., Dendale, P., Michiels, V., Cluydts, R., Kaufman, L., & De Meirleir, K. (1997). Physical fatigability and exercise capacity in chronic fatigue syndrome: Association with disability, somatization and psychopathology. *Journal of Psychosomatic Research, 42*, 369–378.

Franklin, B. A., Whaley, M. H., & Howley, E. T. (Eds.). (2000). *ACSM's guidelines to exercise testing and prescription* (6th ed.). Philadelphia: Lippincott, Williams, & Wilkins.

Freeman, R., & Komaroff, A. L. (1997). Does the chronic fatigue syndrome involve the autonomic nervous system? *American Journal of Medicine, 102*, 357–364.

Fulcher, K. Y., & White, P. D. (1997). Randomized controlled trial of graded exercise in patients with the chronic fatigue syndrome. *British Journal of Medicine, 314*, 1647–1652.

Fulcher, K. Y., & White, P. D. (2000). Strength and physiological response to exercise in patients with chronic fatigue syndrome. *Journal of Neurology, Neurosurgery, and Psychiatry, 69*(3), 302–307.

Fulle, S., Mecocci, P., Fano, G., Vecchiet, I., Vecchini, A., Racciotti, D., et al. (2000). Specific oxidative alterations in vastus lateralis muscle of patients with the diagnosis of chronic fatigue syndrome. *Free Radical Biology in Medicine, 29*(12), 1252–1259.

Gerber, L., Furst, G., Shulman, B., Smith, C., Thornton, B., Liang, M., et al. (1987). Patient education program to teach energy conservation behaviors to patients with rheumatoid arthritis: A pilot study. *Archives of Physical Medicine and Rehabilitation, 68*, 442–445.

Goshorn, R. K. (1998). Chronic fatigue syndrome: A review for clinicians. *Seminars in Neurology, 18*(2), 237–242.

Gow, J. W., Behan, W. M., Simpson, K., McGarry, F., Keir, S., & Behan, P. O. (1994). Studies on enterorvirus in patients with chronic fatigue syndrome. *Clinical Infectious Disease, 18*(Suppl. 1), S126–S129.

Grossman, A., & Costa, A. (1993). The regulation of hypothalamic CRH: Impact of in vitro studies on the central control of the stress response. *Functional Neurology, 8,* 325–334.

Hanson, S. J., Gause, W., & Natelson, B. (2001). Detection of immunologically significant factors for chronic fatigue syndrome using neural-network classifiers. *Clinical and Diagnostic Laboratory Immunology, 8*(3), 658–662.

Higginbotham, M. (1994). The role of gas analysis in stress testing. *Primary Care, 21,* 557–567.

Jamal, G. A., & Hansen, S. (1989). Postviral fatigue syndrome, evidence for underlying organic disturbance in the muscle fiber. *European Neurology, 29*(5), 273–276.

Johnson, J. E., Anders, G. T., Blanton, H. M., Hawkes, C. E., Bush, B. A., McAllister, C. K., et al. (1990). Exercise dysfunction in patients seropositive for the human immunodeficiency virus. *American Review of Respiratory Disorders, 141,* 618–622.

Kent-Braun, J., Sharma, K., & Weiner, M. (1993). Central basis of muscle fatigue in chronic fatigue syndrome. *Neurology, 43,* 125–131.

Klimas, N. G. (1998). Pathogenesis of chronic fatigue syndrome and fibromyalgia. *Growth Hormone IGF Research, 8*(Suppl. B), 123–126.

Klimas, N. G., Salvato, F. R., Morgan, R., & Fletcher, M.A. (1990). Immunologic abnormalities in chronic fatigue syndrome. *Journal of Clinical Microbiology, 28,* 1403–1410.

Komaroff, A. L., & Buchwald, D. (1991). Symptoms and signs of chronic fatigue syndrome. *Reviews of Infectious Diseases, 13*(Suppl. 1), S8–S11.

Komaroff, A. L., Geiger, A. M., & Wormsley, S. (1988). IgG subclass deficiencies in chronic fatigue syndrome. *Lancet, 1*(8597), 1288–1289.

Lane, R. J., Woodrow, D., & Archard, L. C. (1994). Lactate responses to exercise in chronic fatigue syndrome. *Journal of Neurology, Neurosurgery, and Psychiatry, 57,* 662–663.

Littlejohn, G. (2001). Fibromyalgia: What is it and how do we treat it? *Australian Family Physician, 30*(4), 327–333.

Lloyd, A., Hickie, I., Hickie, C., Dwyer, J., & Wakefield, D. (1992). Cell-mediated immunity in patients with chronic fatigue syndrome, healthy control subjects and patients with major depression. *Clinical Experimental Immunology, 87*(1), 76–79.

Lloyd, A., Wakefield, D., Boughton, C. R., & Dwyer, J. M. (1989). Immunological abnormalities in the chronic fatigue syndrome. *Medical Journal of Australia, 151*(3), 122–124.

Mahler, D., & Franco, M. (1996). Clinical applications of cardiopulmonary exercise testing. *Journal of Cardiopulmonary Rehabilitation, 16,* 357–365.

Make, B., & Jones, J. F. (1997). Impairment of patients with chronic fatigue syndrome. *Journal of Chronic Fatigue Syndrome, 3*(4), 43–55.

Marlin, R. G., Anchel, H., Gibson, J. C., Goldberg, W. M., & Swinton, M. (1998). An evaluation of multidisciplinary intervention for chronic fatigue syndrome with long-term follow-up, and a comparison with untreated controls. *American Journal of Medicine, 105*(3A), 110S–114S.

McCully, K. K., & Natelson, B. H. (1999). Impaired oxygen delivery in chronic fatigue syndrome. *Clinical Science, 97,* 603–608.

McCully, K. K., Natelson, B. H., Iotti, S., & Leigh, J. S. (1996). Reduced oxidative muscle metabolism in chronic fatigue syndrome. *Muscle Nerve, 19,* 621–625.

McCully, K. K., Sisto, S. A., & Natelson, B. H. (1996). Use of exercise for treatment of chronic fatigue syndrome. *Sports Medicine, 21,* 35–48.

McDonald, J. A., Caruso, J., Karaviannis, P., Scully, L. J., Harris, J. R., Forster, G. E., et al. (1987). Diminished responsiveness of male homosexual chronic hepatitis B virus carriers with HTLV-III antibodies to recombinant alpha-interferon. *Hepatology, 7*(4), 719–723.

McGregor, N. R. (1999, September 9–12). *The biochemistry of chronic pain and fatigue.* Second World Congress on Chronic Fatigue Syndrome and Related Disorders, Brussels, Belgium.

Meyers, J., & Gullestad, L. (1998). The role of exercise testing and gas-exchange measurement in the prognostic assessment of patients with heart failure. *Current Opinions in Cardiology, 13,* 145–155.

Meyers, K., Westbrook, S., Schiwaibold, M., Hajiric, R., Lehmann, M., & Roskamm, H. (1996). Cardiopulmonary determinants of functional capacity in patients with chronic heart failure compared with normals. *Clinical Cardiology, 19,* 944–948.

Musselman, D. L., Lawson, D. H., Gumnick, J. R., Manatunga, A. K., Penna, S., Goodkin, R. S., et al. (2001). Paroxetine for the prevention of depression induced by high-dose interferon alpha. *New England Journal of Medicine, 344,* 961–966.

Neuberg, G., Friedman, S., Weiss, M., & Herman, M. (1988). Cardiopulmonary exercise testing: the clinical value of gas exchange. *Archives of Internal Medicine, 148,* 2221–2226.

Offenbächer, M., & Stucki, G. (2000). Physical therapy in the treatment of fibromyalgia. *Scandinavian Journal of Rheumatology, 113,* 78–85.

Pagani, M., & Lucini, D. (1999). Chronic fatigue syndrome: A hypothesis focusing on the autonomic nervous system. *Clinical Science, 96,* 117–125.

Pagani, M., Lucini, D., Mela, G. S., Langewit, W., & Malliani, A. (1994). Sympathetic overactivity in subjects complaining of unexplained fatigue. *Clinical Science, 87,* 655–661.

Powell, P., Bentall, R. P., Nye, F. J., & Edwards, R. H. T. (2001). Randomized controlled trial of patient education to encourage graded exercise in chronic fatigue syndrome. *British Medical Journal, 322,* 387–390.

Riley, M. S., O'Brian, C. J., McCluskey, D. R., Bell, N. P., & Nicholls, D. P. (1990). Aerobic work capacity in patients with chronic fatigue syndrome. *British Medical Journal, 301,* 953–956.

Roelens, S., Herst, C. V., D'Haese, A., De Smet, K., Fremont, M., De Meirleir, K., et al. (2001). G-actin cleavage parallels 2-5A-dependent RNase L cleavage in peripheral blood mononuclear cells—relevance to a possible serum-based screening test for dysregulations in the 2-5A pathway. In R. Patarca-Montero (Ed.), *Innovations in chronic fatigue syndrome research and clinical practice* (pp. 63–82). New York: Haworth Medical Press.

Rowbottom, D., Keast, D., Pervan, Z., & Morton, A. (1998). The physiological response to exercise in chronic fatigue syndrome. *Journal of Chronic Fatigue Syndrome, 4*(2), 33–49.

Sargent, C., Scroop, G. C., Nemeth, P. M., Burnet, R. B., & Buckley, J. D. (2002). Maximal oxygen uptake and lactate metabolism are normal in chronic fatigue syndrome. *Medicine and Science in Sports and Exercise, 34*(1), 51–56.

Scott, L. V., Medbak, S., & Dinan, T. G. (1998). Blunted adrenocorticotropin and cortisol responses to corticotropin-releasing hormone stimulation in chronic fatigue syndrome. *Acta Psychiatrica Scandinavica, 97,* 450–457.

Scott, L. V., Teh, J., Reznek, R., Martin, A., Sohaib, A., & Dinan, T. G. (1999). Small adrenal glands in chronic fatigue syndrome, a preliminary computer tomography study, *Psychoneuroendocrinology, 24,* 759–768.

Shephard, R. J. (2001). Chronic fatigue syndrome, an update. *Sports Medicine, 31*(3), 167–194.

Sim, J., & Adams, N. (1999). Physical and other nonpharmacological interventions for fibromyalgia. *Baillière's Best Practice and Research, 3,* 507–523.

Sisto, S. A. (1993). Chronic fatigue syndrome: An overview and intervention guidelines. *Neurology Reports, 17,* 30–34.

Sisto, S. A., La Manca, J., Cordero, D. L., Bergen, M. T., Ellis, S. P., Drastal, S., et al. (1996). Metabolic and cardiovascular effects of a progressive exercise test in patients with chronic fatigue syndrome. *American Journal of Medicine, 100,* 634–640.

Snell, C. R., & Stevens, S. R. (1998). Opening the envelope. *CFIDS Chronicle, 11*(2), 12–13.

Snell, C. R., Stevens, S. R., & VanNess, J. M. (2001). Chronic fatigue syndrome, ampligen, and quality of life: A phenomenological perspective. *Journal of Chronic Fatigue Syndrome, 8*(3/4), 117–121.

Snell, C. R., VanNess, J. M., Strayer, D. R., & Stevens, S. R. (2002). Physical performance and prediction of 2-5A Synthetase/RNase L antiviral pathway activity in patients with chronic fatigue syndrome. *International Journal of In Vivo Research, 16*(3).

Stevens, S. R. (1995). Using exercise testing to document functional disability in CFS. *Journal of Chronic Fatigue Syndrome, 1*(3/4), 127–129.

Sue, D. Y. (1994). Integrative cardiopulmonary exercise testing: Basis and application. *Medicine, Exercise, Nutrition and Health, 3,* 32–55.

Sue, D. Y., & Wasserman, K. (1991). Impact of integrative cardiopulmonary exercise testing on clinical decision making. *Chest, 99,* 931–938.

Suhadolnik, R. J., Peterson, D. L., O'Brien, K., Cheney, P. R., Herst, C. V., Reichenbach, N. L., et al. (1997). Biochemical evidence for a novel low molecular weight 2-5A-dependent RNase L in chronic fatigue syndrome. *Journal Interferon Cytokine Research, 17*(7), 377–385.

Suhadolnik, R. J., Reichenbach, N. L., Hitzges, P., Sobol, R. W., Peterson, D. L., Henry, B., et al. (1994). Upregulation of the 2-5A synthetase/RNase L antiviral pathway associated with chronic fatigue syndrome. *Clinical Infectious Diseases, 18*(Suppl. 1), S96–S104.

Tirelli, U., Marotta, G., Improta, S., & Pinto, A. (1994). Immunological abnormalities in patients with chronic fatigue syndrome. *Scandinavian Journal of Immunology, 40*(6), 601–608.

Tirelli, U., Pinto, A., Marotta, G., Crovato, M., Quaia, M., De Paoli, P., et al. (1993). Clinical and immunologic study of 205 patients with chronic fatigue syndrome. *Archives of Internal Medicine, 153*(1), 116–117, 120.

Vaeory, H., Qiao, Z., Morkrid, L., & Forre, O. (1989). Altered sympathetic nervous system response in patients with fibromyalgia (fibrositis syndrome). *Journal of Rheumatology, 16,* 1460–1465.

VanNess, J. M., Snell, C. R., Fredrickson, D. M., Strayer, D. R., & Stevens, S. R. (2001). Assessment of functional impairment by cardiopulmonary exercise testing in patients with chronic fatigue syndrome. In R. Patarca-Montero (Ed.), *Innovations in chronic fatigue syndrome research and clinical practice* (pp. 103–110). New York: Haworth Medical Press.

Vercoulen, J. H., Bazelmans, E., Swanink, C. M., Fennis, J. F., Galama, J. M., Jongen, P. J., et al. (1997). Physical activity in chronic fatigue syndrome: assessment and its role in fatigue. *Journal of Psychiatric Research, 31*(6), 661–673.

Wasserman, K., Hansen, J. E., Sue, D. Y., Casaburi, R., & Whipp, B. J. (1999). *Principles of exercise testing and interpretation.* Philadelphia: Lippincott, Williams, & Wilkins.

Wearden, A. J., Morris, R. K., Mullis, R., Strickland, P. L., Pearson, D. J., Appleby, L., et al. (1998). Randomised, double-blind, placebo-controlled treatment trial of fluoxetine and graded exercise for chronic fatigue syndrome. *British Journal of Psychiatry, 172,* 485–490.

Weber, K. T., & Janicki, J. S. (1986). *Cardiopulmonary exercise testing: Physiologic principles and clinical applications.* Philadelphia: Saunders.

Whiting, P., Bagnall, A., Sowden, A., Cornell, J., Mulrow, C., & Ramirez, G. (2001). Interventions for the treatment and management of chronic fatigue syndrome. *Journal of the American Medical Association, 286,* 1360–1368.

Wolfe, F., Smythe, H. A., Yunus, M. B., Bennett, R. M., Bombardier, C., Goldenberg, D. L., et al. (1990). The American College of Rheumatology 1990 criteria for the classification of fibromyalgia: Report of the multicenter criteria committee. *Arthritis Rheumatology, 33,* 160–172.

Wong, R., Lopachuk, G., Zhu, G., Walker, D., Catellier, D., Burton, D., et al. (1992). Skeletal muscle metabolism in the chronic fatigue syndrome, in vivo assessment by ^{31}P nuclear magnetic resonance spectroscopy. *Chest, 102,* 1716–1722.

Young, M. (1999). How I treat return to sport after postviral fatigue. *British Journal of Sports Medicine, 33,* 173.

CHAPTER 27

Nutritional Approaches

RICHARD A. VAN KONYNENBURG

A DEQUATE NUTRITION IS a fundamental requirement for both the maintenance of health and the treatment of disease. The human body needs at
least minimum amounts of about 40 essential nutrients to sustain life. Optimum health implies larger amounts. The essential nutrients include the water-
soluble and fat-soluble vitamins, minerals, essential amino acids, and essential
fatty acids. Also needed are some additional nitrogen for protein synthesis, a sufficient amount of some combination of the substrates that supply energy (carbohydrates, fats, and protein), a small amount of metabolizable carbohydrate to
prevent ketosis, indigestible carbohydrate (fiber) to aid the gastrointestinal tract,
and water (Baron, 2001).

Nutritional surveys such as the Third National Health and Nutrition Examination Survey (NHANES III; Alaimo et al., 1994) and the Continuing Survey of
Food Intake of Individuals (CSFII; Cleveland, Goldman, & Borrud, 1996) have
shown that the intakes of several essential nutrients by substantial fractions of
the U.S. population are less than the minimum requirements judged to be needed
just to prevent deficiency diseases (Institute of Medicine 1997, 1998, 2000, 2001;
National Research Council [NRC], 1989). While questions can always be raised
about the validity of the individual RDA levels, which are, after all, revised periodically, it is nevertheless reasonable to suspect from this that nutritional deficiencies might be contributing factors in the etiologies of some chronic diseases
and syndromes.

As shown later in this chapter, there are at least three reasons that nutritional
approaches can be expected to be productive in treating chronic fatigue syndrome (CFS). First, although the etiology or etiologies of CFS are currently unknown, review of the literature suggests that inadequate nutrition is a possible
contributing factor. Second, many persons with CFS (PWCs) exhibit gastrointestinal abnormalities that can affect the absorption of nutrients, and nutritional
approaches can be helpful in their treatment. Third, there is evidence that some
nutrients can act pharmacologically to produce beneficial effects in CFS when
given at dosages above those that satisfy normal physiological requirements. For

these reasons, nutritional approaches should be given an important place in the treatment of CFS.

A smaller but significant body of literature supports the use of nutritional approaches in fibromyalgia (FM).

In the opinion of this contributor, these are strong reasons why clinicians treating CFS and FM patients need to become knowledgeable about nutritional approaches to these disorders. An additional reason is the reality that many PWCs and PWFs are currently self-treating with a variety of nutritional supplements. In 1994, the U.S. government passed the Dietary Supplement and Health Education Act, under which many naturally occurring substances, some having pharmacological activity, can be sold without prescription. In a Canadian study (Logan & Bested, 2003a) of 134 CFS patients (meeting the Fukuda et al. 1994 criteria) who visited a clinic using "evidenced-based medicine," 92.5% of the 79% who responded to a survey reported that they take nonprescription dietary supplements. The average intake was 6.0 different supplements per day, and a total of 109 different types of dietary supplements and herbal remedies were used by this group. It would seem to be in the best interests of both the patient and the clinician if all the therapeutic modalities in use on the patient could be taken into account and coordinated by the clinician to maximize the benefit and avoid deleterious interactions. To do this effectively, a clinician must have a knowledge of the evidence-based use of nutritional approaches in CFS and FM.

There are, however, several difficulties involved in applying nutritional approaches to CFS and FM. The first is the limited number of nutritional studies in these disorders completed to date, due in part to the challenge of obtaining funding for nutritional studies. Because nutrients are generally not patentable, the commercial incentive to do definitive nutritional studies is often inadequate to supply the motivation for the investment required.

A second difficulty is that these disorders are currently not well defined. There is mounting evidence that the population composed of all patients who satisfy the criteria in the current case definition for CFS (Fukuda et al., 1994) is a heterogeneous population, composed of a number of subsets (as was acknowledged by the authors of the definition). This has been found to be true from several standpoints: clinical (Racciatti, Barberio, Vecchiet, & Pizzigallo, 1999), biochemical (McGregor et al., 2000), immunological (Patarca-Montero, Mark, Fletcher, & Klimas, 2001), and epidemiological (Jason, Taylor, Kennedy, & Torres, 2001). Researchers in each discipline have been studying different sample populations of PWCs and have been using their own sets of criteria to distinguish subsets. So far, there has been no combined effort to establish a common set of subsets, which is sorely needed. This will require a cooperative effort, with representatives of several disciplines studying the same group of PWCs.

When a sample population of PWCs is selected for a nutritional study using only the case definition criteria of Fukuda et al. (1994) or one of the earlier sets of criteria for CFS that has been published, it is likely that the sample population will also be heterogeneous. Therefore, it will be difficult to observe sharp distinctions between a PWC group and a normal control group in a study looking for nutritional deficiencies. It will also likely be difficult to see clear differences between the outcomes for a treatment group and a placebo group in a nutritional treatment trial, particularly if the results for all members of each group are averaged together, as has often been the case in the past.

A third difficulty in applying nutritional approaches in these disorders is that in CFS and FM, as is true for many other conditions, we are faced with the reality that we do not yet understand the etiology, the pathogenesis, or the pathophysiology. Because it is recognized that nutritional requirements in disease states can differ substantially from those in health and that appropriate nutrition is specific to particular disorders (Zeman, 1991), this lack of understanding has important consequences for our ability to apply nutritional approaches in the most therapeutic way.

A fourth difficulty is that these disorders are syndromes without agreed-on biochemical markers. As a result, in nutritional studies, as well as in other types of treatment studies, it is a challenge to find objective measures of outcome. In many cases, the only information available concerning the effects of a particular nutrient in treating CFS comes from clinical experience. In clinical work on CFS, the outcomes are frequently evaluated based on subjective patient reports of symptom improvement. Thus, clinical experience usually does not meet the standard of peer-reviewed, randomized, double-blind, placebo-controlled trials with objective measures of outcome and high statistical significance. Nevertheless, in many cases, clinical experience provides the best information that is currently available, as well as clues to promising areas for future controlled trials.

The result of all these factors, as Werbach (2000) has summed it up, is: "The scientific literature is fairly sparse, and promising nutritional treatments usually lack adequate scientific proof."

In spite of these challenges and difficulties, nutritional strategies have been developed for CFS and FM, and some have proven to be beneficial. They are described in this chapter. Because of the significant overlap in symptoms between CFS and FM, nutritional data pertinent to FM are reviewed together with the CFS literature. In view of the early state of maturity of this field, clinical experience is included in this review, with appropriate cautions about its scientific limitations.

CLINICAL CONSIDERATIONS IN APPLYING NUTRITIONAL APPROACHES TO PATIENTS WITH CHRONIC FATIGUE SYNDROME AND FIBROMYALGIA

Some important factors should be considered in the clinical application of diet and nutrition in these disorders, including gastrointestinal problems, food allergies and intolerances, interactions, nutritional balance, toxicity limits, cost, convenience, simplicity, and variety. These are discussed briefly.

GASTROINTESTINAL PROBLEMS

If a nutritional approach is to have any chance of success, it is obvious that digestion and absorption of nutrients must take place. Because many PWCs have gastrointestinal problems that may interfere with digestion or absorption, these problems should receive attention as a prerequisite to a nutritional approach. Possible causes of malabsorption in CFS include gastric mobility problems, abnormal bacterial or yeast proliferation in the small intestine (dysbiosis), and food allergies, sensitivities, or intolerances.

Burnet and Chatterton (2001) studied 121 CFS patients satisfying the Fukuda et al. (1994) criteria and 56 healthy controls. They found by questionnaires that 86%

of the CFS patients and 56% of the controls had one or more upper gastrointestinal symptoms. The authors reported: "The controls had increased esophageal symptoms of heartburn and acid reflux, whereas the CFS group had increased gastric symptoms, especially bloating after a small meal and abdominal discomfort. Vomiting was not common. The CFS group all had increased large bowel symptoms of fecal urgency, nocturnal diarrhea, loose consistency of the stools, and increased frequency." Gastric emptying studies were performed on 29 CFS patients who had symptoms of fullness and bloating and 8 controls with idiopathic fatigue, and it was found that 91% of the CFS patients had delayed gastric emptying, predominantly of the liquid phase, compared to the controls.

YEAST INFECTIONS

Intestinal yeast proliferation by *Candida albicans* continues to be a controversial topic because this yeast is present in the gut of normal, healthy individuals, and it is difficult to diagnose an overgrowth. Nevertheless, clinical experience (Jessop, 1989 as cited in Crook, 2001; Teitelbaum et al., 2001) suggests that intestinal yeast proliferation is a factor in many cases of CFS. A new test that detects the tartaric acid produced by the yeast promises to be more definitive than previous tests in distinguishing normal yeast population from overgrowth (Shaw, 2001).

Cozon, Perret-Liaudet, Fatoohi, and Brunet (2003) studied Type IV cell-mediated delayed immunity to *C. albicans* in 100 patients who had had fatigue for more than 6 months and who also had four or more minor criteria for CFS. They measured T-cell activation in vitro using flow cytometry after 24-hour whole blood culture with *C. albicans* antigen. They also performed intradermal injection with *C. albicans* antigen and measured neopterin in the urine of 67 patients before and after the skin test. They found an abnormal delayed reactivity to *C. albicans* in 59 of the 100 patients. They also found an abnormal systemic reaction to the skin test in 57 of 98 patients, and it was significantly correlated to the delayed reactivity ($p <$ .0001). Neopterin excretion was found to be increased after the skin test only in patients who showed systemic reaction. This work shows that *C. albicans* is a significant factor in a major subset of PWCs.

IRRITABLE BOWEL SYNDROME

Irritable bowel syndrome (IBS) is also commonly diagnosed in CFS and FM (Aaron & Buchwald, 2001; Gomborone, Gorard, Dewsnap, Libby, & Farthing, 1996; Hudson, Goldenberg, Pope, Keck, & Schlesinger, 1992; Lubrano et al., 2001; Wessely, Nimnuan, & Sharpe, 1999; Whitehead, Palsson, & Jones, 2003). Although the cause of a particular case of IBS is often not understood, in many cases IBS appears to result from small intestinal bacterial overgrowth (Pimentel, Chow, & Lin, 2002, 2003). According to Teitelbaum et al. (2001), "Treating the various bowel infections frequently resolved severe gastrointestinal symptoms, often previously diagnosed as irritable bowel syndrome, that had been present for years."

Pimentel, Chow, Hallegua, Wallace, and Lin (2001) found that of 815 subjects undergoing lactulose hydrogen breath testing for assessment of small intestinal bacterial overgrowth (SIBO), 123 patients had FM. Those with SIBO were treated with antibiotics. At the initial and follow-up visits, subjects were asked to rate their symptoms. Symptoms scores before and after treatment were compared. Of the 123 subjects with FM, 96 (78%) were found to have SIBO. Returning subjects reported a 57 ±29% overall improvement in symptoms with significant improvement in bloating, gas, abdominal pain, diarrhea, constipation, joint pains, and fatigue ($p < .05$).

Butt, Dunstan, McGregor, and Roberts (2001) reported on the observation of bacterial colonosis in patients with persistent fatigue. According to these authors, "Patients with this condition usually present with multiple disorders including gastrointestinal symptoms, characterized by an absence of gastrointestinal inflammation and a marked alteration of intestinal microbial flora. This condition of unknown etiology is manifested in patients with CFS, FM, irritable bowel syndrome and autism." They reported significantly lower counts of Escherichia coli and Bifidobacterium spp. and significantly higher counts of Enterococcus spp. in patients with fatigue as compared to healthy controls. They also found strong positive correlations between the Enterococcus spp. count and neurological and cognitive symptoms in CFS (nervousness, memory loss, forgetfulness, confusion, and mind going blank).

Corsello (1999) has published a treatment program for bowel healing that includes bowel scrubbing, bowel soothing, and bowel repopulation. According to Corsello, this program has been effective in thousands of patients. It uses only nutritional supplements, which is an important feature in view of evidence that use of antibiotics to treat irritable bowel syndrome increases the likelihood of more bowel symptoms four months later by a factor of three (Maxwell, Rink, Kumar, & Mendall, 2002). Corsello has emphasized the importance of treating the bowel early in the treatment program, before toxins or pathogens in the rest of the body are dealt with, so that there will be a clear pathway out of the body for toxins before they are mobilized.

FOOD ALLERGIES, SENSITIVITIES, AND INTOLERANCES

There are several different types of food allergies, sensitivities, and intolerances. Type I allergy (immediate, IgE-mediated, and also called *atopy*) was initially reported (Straus, Dale, Wright, & Metcalfe, 1998) to be highly prevalent in CFS. However, later studies (Ferre et al., 2003; Kowal, Schacterele, Schur, Komaroff, & Dubuske, 2002; Repka-Ramirez et al., 2001) have not found IgE-mediated allergies to be more prevalent in PWCs than in normal controls.

Food sensitivities and intolerances, on the other hand, have been found to be important factors in both CFS (Emms et al., 2001a, 2001b; Logan & Bested, 2003a) and in FM (Haugen, Kjeldsen-Kragh, Nordvag, & Forre, 1991). In the survey performed by Logan and Bested (2003b) the most commonly reported offending food was wheat, followed by dairy, corn, tomato, and caffeinated beverages. Verrillo and Gellman (1997) list the following as foods to which PWCs most commonly report intolerances: stimulants (such as caffeine), alcohol, sweeteners, animal fats, artificial colors, flavors, preservatives, and monosodium glutamate (MSG). Smith, Terpening, Schmidt, and Gums (2001) described four cases of FM diagnosed by the American College of Rheumatology (ACR) criteria in which the symptoms were markedly improved or completely resolved by eliminating MSG and aspartame from the diet. Rechallenge with foods containing these substances caused return of the symptoms. Separate rechallenge with MSG and aspartame were not reported. The evidence presented for MSG being the causative agent in these cases appears to this contributor to be stronger than that for aspartame.

The mechanism for the development of many food sensitivities appears to be that partially digested dietary protein can cross the intestinal barrier and be absorbed into the blood stream (Hemmings & Williams, 1978), causing a response by the immune system (Husby, 1988). This is more likely in the case of abnormally high intestinal permeability (leaky gut), which can be evaluated by an intestinal permeability test (Fleming, Kapembwa, Laker, Levin, & Griffin, 1990; Hollander, 1999).

A sensitivity to gluten (found in wheat, rye, barley, and oats), also known as celiac disease or nontropical sprue, was found in 2 of 100 PWCs and none of 100 controls (Skowera et al., 2001). These cases were found by endomysial antibody (EMA) testing and were confirmed by enzyme-linked immunosorbent assay (ELISA) and jejunal biopsy. A smaller study (Petri et al., 2001) of 56 patients and 56 controls did not find any cases of celiac disease in either group by EMA testing. However, this study is not incompatible with the Skowera et al. study because of its smaller size. The statistical power calculation showed that this study could not reliably detect positive EMA in the population of CFS patients at levels below 5% to 6%.

It is interesting to note that the association of food sensitivities with disorders apparently identical to those now defined as CFS and FM has a long history. Randolph (1945, 1976) reviewed these topics and described cases in which food sensitivities were not only associated but also were found to be the causes of these disorders.

In view of the evidence for the importance of food allergies, sensitivities, and intolerances in CFS and FM, it seems clear that the diagnosis and treatment of such problems must be given attention if nutritional approaches to CFS and FM are to be successfully applied. It appears also to be true that some cases of these disorders will actually resolve completely if the objectionable foods are avoided. The "gold standard" for diagnosis of food allergies, sensitivities, and intolerances is the use of a double-blind, placebo-controlled food elimination and rechallenge. Because this is very time consuming, alternative methods of testing have been developed. King and King (1998) have reviewed these alternative methods.

INTERACTIONS BETWEEN NUTRIENTS AND BETWEEN NUTRIENTS AND MEDICATIONS

Some nutrients interact deleteriously with each other in the digestive tract. Others compete with each other for absorption by the gut or for transport across the blood-brain barrier. An example of deleterious interaction is proteolytic enzymes (such as bromelain) intended for absorption into the blood to break down fibrin in cases of hypercoagulation, taken together with nondenatured whey protein, intended for promoting the synthesis of glutathione. This combination decreases the availability of the enzymes for absorption and results in the breakdown of the protein, which appears to be most effective when intact.

An example of the blood-brain barrier transport competition is the amino acid L-tryptophan taken together with the branched chain amino acids. These amino acids all use the same transporters; therefore, large amounts of one suppress the absorption of the others.

As a result of such effects, some supplements are best ingested at separate times on an empty stomach to avoid breaking them down or suppressing their absorption.

Taking care to prevent undesirable interactions between nutrients and medications can be important in the treatment of CFS when these two treatment modalities are used simultaneously. Such interactions have been tabulated by Hendler and Rorvik (2001).

BALANCE BETWEEN NUTRIENTS

The body operates as an integrated biochemical system. As such, it has simultaneous requirements for all the essential nutrients, as discussed previously. It is, therefore, important in nutritional treatment to make sure that all these nutrients are being supplied at levels at least comparable to the RDA levels, either from the diet or from supplements. Particular nutrients can then be supplied at elevated levels, using this as a foundation, if larger amounts of those nutrients have been found to be beneficial.

For example, if individual free-form amino acids are used as part of a nutritional approach, it is important to take them with a mix of amino acids, peptides, or dietary protein to avoid serious imbalances in the total amino acids intake. The body has limited ability to make up for such imbalances and must have sufficient amounts of the full range of amino acids in the blood stream to support the synthesis of protein.

In general, the work of biochemistry is carried out by means of biochemical pathways, which consist of sequences of individual reactions. Various nutrients may be needed to support certain individual reactions within a pathway. If all the needed nutrients for a particular pathway are available in adequate supply except one, the particular reaction that needs the missing nutrient acts as the rate-limiting reaction for the entire pathway and blocks its function. Therefore, it is wise to make sure that all the nutrients needed for the complete pathway are supplied. For the entire organism, this can be ensured by supplying all the known essential nutrients, at least in amounts comparable to the RDA.

TOXICITY

The statement that all substances are toxic at sufficiently high dosages is attributed to Paracelsus (1493–1541; Klaassen, 1996). This has been found to be true even with essential nutrients. The Institute of Medicine (1997, 1998, 2000, 2001) has established safe upper limits for the dosages of nutrients in the general population for cases in which sufficient data were available. While these limits are intended to apply to healthy people and cannot automatically be assumed to be precisely appropriate for PWCs, they nevertheless provide some guidance for avoiding overdosage. The Institute made it clear that their intent in setting these limits was not to preclude use of higher dosages in supervised therapeutic situations. This is an important point in the nutritional treatment of CFS because for some nutrients, particular beneficial effects are achieved only with pharmacological dosages, as is discussed later in connection with vitamin B12.

COST, CONVENIENCE, SIMPLICITY, AND VARIETY

Patient compliance is required if a nutritional approach is to succeed. Two realities of CFS are that many PWCs are too disabled to continue in gainful employment (Komaroff et al., 1996), and many have difficulty in obtaining disability status. Because nutritional approaches are often not covered by insurance, cost is, therefore, a particularly important consideration affecting compliance. Convenience is a significant factor because many PWCs do not have enough energy to perform significant shopping or food preparation activities (Komaroff et al., 1996). Keeping the regimen simple is also important because of the impairment in short-term memory and concentration that frequently accompanies CFS (Fukuda et al., 1994). Particular foods in the diet should be eaten at intervals rather than every day to decrease the probability of developing intolerances or allergies to particular foods (Murray & Pizzorno, 1998).

NUTRITIONAL APPROACHES

The types of approaches used in the past have had a range of rationales and sophistication, depending on the information used in developing them. They have involved both the overall diet and particular nutritional supplements. These approaches are described briefly.

THE BALANCED DIET AND RDA APPROACH

In the absence of specific information about the etiology, pathogenesis, and pathophysiology of this disorder, some authors have offered diet and nutrition recommendations for CFS based on current guidelines of what constitutes an appropriate diet for normal, healthy individuals. I call this the *balanced diet and RDA approach.* This advice often reflects that given by government or government-related agencies, such as the U.S. Department of Agriculture (1992) and the Food and Nutrition Board of the National Research Council (NRC, 1989), more recently part of the Institute of Medicine (1997, 1998, 2000, 2001). An example is the paper by Morris and Stare (1993): "In the absence of published studies describing specific nutrition interventions that benefit patients with CFS, the dietary pattern recommended for these individuals should be based on sound nutritional principles and common sense. A prudent approach is to advise patients with CFS to consume a variety of foods daily from among and within the basic food groups, with an emphasis on eating low-fat foods, such as fruit, vegetables, high-fiber breads and cereals; low-fat milk and its products; and small or modest portions of lean meat, chicken, or fish." These authors emphasize the importance of maintaining a reasonable weight using such a diet. In cases where marginal nutrient intakes are known or suspected, they recommend "a general multivitamin/mineral supplement that provides no more than the RDA for each nutrient."

While this approach provided a starting point when few specific data were available, there are some difficulties with it both in principle and from treatment experience. In principle, inherent in such an approach is the assumption that nutritional guidelines developed for normal, healthy people (as are the RDAs and the basic food groups or food guide pyramid) are appropriate for PWCs. However, the experience in clinical nutrition as applied to other disease states would reasonably call to question this assumption, and, in fact, the National Research Council specifically pointed out in the tenth edition of the RDA report (NRC, 1989) that the RDAs were not intended to be applied to those with chronic diseases. Furthermore, it is not appropriate to use RDA levels as guidelines when attempting to determine optimal nutrition even for normal, healthy people, because they are actually set at levels just sufficient to prevent deficiency diseases in 97% to 98% of all healthy persons (Institute of Medicine, 1997).

In practice, many PWCs have been found to be intolerant of diets high in carbohydrate foods (St. Amand & Marek, 1999), especially those having high glycemic indexes (Jenkins et al., 1981), while the largest section of the USDA food guide pyramid is dominated by such foods (e.g., bread, rice, and pasta; U.S. Department of Agriculture, 1992). In addition, as already noted, some essential nutrients used in treating CFS, such as vitamin B12, are found to have the desired therapeutic benefits only when dosages considerably larger than the RDA levels are used. Accordingly, the balanced diet and RDA approach does not appear to be the best strategy for diet and nutrition in CFS at our present state of understanding of this disorder.

OTHER APPROACHES INVOLVING THE DIET IN GENERAL

In the case of FM, four papers have been published concerning diet. The first was a small study by Hostmark, Lystad, Vellar, Hori, and Berg (1993) in Norway. Eight women and two men with FM were placed on a three-week vegetarian diet. There was no control group. Three women and one man underwent fasting for 8 to 10 days as part of the therapy. Some physical activity (mostly walking) was part of the daily routine for the two men and five of the women. At the end of the treatment period, the two men and five of the women reported increased subjective well-being. In addition, the levels of serum peroxide, atherogenic lipid, apolipoproteins, and fibrinogen were observed to be significantly decreased. In view of its limitations (e.g., small group size, short duration, no control group, the complications of fasting and exercise, and the subjective measure of improvement), it is not possible to draw firm conclusions from this study.

Two Finnish papers (Hanninen et al., 2000; Kaartinen et al., 2000) describe a study of the use of a "living food" vegan diet in FM. The living food diet consists entirely of noncooked, plant-based foods. Included are berries, fruits, vegetables and roots, nuts, germinated seeds, and sprouts. The diet contains no coffee, tea, alcohol, or table salt; thus, it is low in sodium. It contains no cholesterol, and its lipids are rich in unsaturated fatty acids. Several items in the diet are fermented and are rich in lactobacilli.

In this study, Finnish female FM patients were divided into two groups, according to their choice—18 in the intervention group and 15 in the control group. The intervention group ate the living food diet for three months, while the control group continued their usual omnivorous diet, which was not described. Relative to the control group, the intervention group had a significant decrease in pain, improved quality of sleep, reduced morning stiffness, and improvements in their scores on the General Health and Health Assessment questionnaires, as well as a rheumatologist's questionnaire. The number of tender points showed a tendency toward improvement ($p = .07$). There was no change in the handgrip pressure power or the results of an exercise test. Laboratory tests showed significant decreases in serum cholesterol, urinary sodium, and the body mass index. When those in the intervention group returned to their previous omnivorous diet after three months on the live foods diet, their symptoms became worse once again. The authors concluded that the live foods diet alleviated the symptoms of FM, at least in the short run. Hanninen et al. recommended supplementing this diet with vitamin B12, vitamin D, and calcium, because sufficient amounts of these nutrients are not supplied by this diet.

This trial exhibited improvements over the earlier study, in terms of group size, test duration, and the use of a control group. However, the duration of three months is not long enough for the effects of some deficiencies to be manifested.

The fourth paper described a seven-month trial in FM of a mostly raw, vegan diet called the *Hallelujah diet* (Donaldson, Speight, & Loomis, 2001). The subjects initially consisted of 30 people with a previous diagnosis of FM by a rheumatologist, using the ACR criteria (Wolfe et al., 1990), 28 females and 2 males, but not all subjects had 11 or more tender points at the time of the study. There was no control group. Twenty-six subjects returned dietary surveys at two months; 20 subjects returned surveys at the beginning, end, and at either two or four months of intervention; three subjects were lost to follow-up. Nutrient intake was calculated from the dietary surveys. All 26 of the subjects who returned dietary surveys at two months were found to be taking in less than RDA levels of vitamin B12, vitamin D, and calcium. Of the essential nutrients reported, some of the subjects were also taking in less than RDA levels of protein, niacin, vitamin E, folate, iron, or zinc. Nevertheless, over the seven-month period of study, significant improvements in symptoms were found, with 19 of the initial 30 subjects classified as responders. Significant improvements were found in physical performance measures except for hand grip strength, which decreased, and isometric shoulder endurance, which showed no change. There was significant improvement in all the subscales of the Fibromyalgia Impact Questionnaire (FIQ) at seven months. This survey is specifically designed to measure the impact of FM on a person's life (Burckhardt, Dark, & Bennett, 1991). Significant improvement was also found in the quality of life as measured by the QOL survey (Flanagan, 1982) and in seven subheadings of the health status as measured by the short form health survey (SF-36; Ware & Sherbourne, 1992). Significant improvement was not found in the subheading of bodily pain, although there was a trend toward improvement, while significant improvement in this area was found in the FIQ and the physical performance measurements. The authors suggested that the improvements resulted from a synergy of physiological and psychological factors. They noted that the limitations of the study included the fact that all the subjects did not currently meet the diagnostic criteria of FM, the unblinded nature of the study, the lack of a control group, and the small size of the treatment group.

These studies suggest that vegan diets may improve the symptoms of FM over periods of a few months. However, serious reservations about prospects for the longer term must be maintained because of the significant deficiencies in several essential nutrients that these diets appear to have. Indeed, a study by the lead author of the fourth paper discussed previously (Donaldson, 2000) found that the Hallelujah diet was deficient in vitamin B12 and recommended measures to compensate for this. If vegan diets are to be tested in FM for longer durations, it would appear that they should be augmented with supplements to supply the deficient nutrients. Hence, the benefits of vegan diets (such as high levels of antioxidants, fiber, and Lactobacilli) could be obtained, while lessening the possibility of deficiencies in essential nutrients.

In the case of CFS, no controlled studies of diet have been published. However, I have received reports from PWCs indicating that high protein, low carbohydrate, low-fat diets have decreased symptom severity. In addition, St. Amand and Marek (1999), who do not distinguish between CFS and FM, have found a particular low carbohydrate diet beneficial for the subset of patients who have hypoglycemia or who experience carbohydrate cravings. In view of these reports and treatment results, such diets appear to be worthy of controlled study for CFS, bearing in mind that a single diet probably is not optimal for all subsets.

PWC-Directed Trial and Error Testing of Particular Nutrients

Many PWCs who self-treat with nutrients have tried supplementing one nutrient at a time for a trial period, noting whether there is any improvement in symptoms. By means of support groups, CFS periodicals, and the Internet, PWCs are able to exchange information, sometimes finding that a particular nutrient seems to be beneficial for a number of PWCs, thus leading to something of a straw poll consensus. The shortcomings of this hit-or-miss approach include low statistical significance; subjective measures of outcome; lack of placebo control; nonblinded conduct of experiments; no basis in known etiology, pathogenesis, or pathophysiology; lack of consideration of complete biochemical pathways or synergistic effects between nutrients; and no allowance for the heterogeneous nature of the total population of PWCs. Nevertheless, this approach may provide clues that can be followed up by controlled testing.

Trials Using Combinations of Nutrients

A few trials have used nutritional approaches incorporating several nutrients simultaneously. Such approaches comply with the knowledge that biochemical systems are complex and require sufficient amounts of many separate nutrients to function properly. However, they have the disadvantage that several variables are changed at the same time; therefore, it is impossible to understand which one or ones are responsible for any changes observed. Nevertheless, the results are indicative of whether nutrition can have an impact on CFS.

Stewart (1991) analyzed the nutritional status of 16 postviral fatigue syndrome patients and found that 4 of 9 patients had serum vitamin A values at or just below the limits of normal. Vitamin B1 and B6 states were borderline or deficient in more than half the patients in which they were measured (7 and 11 patients, respectively). Serum vitamin C was below or at the lower end of normal in the two subjects for which this estimate was made. Serum zinc was below normal in 8 of 16. Serum copper was below normal in 2 of 16. Erythrocyte magnesium values were subnormal in 9 of the 15 assessed. According to Stewart, all subjects were given a variety of vitamin and mineral preparations providing nutrients that had been found lacking in laboratory tests. The daily dosage of most vitamins was between 5 and 20 times the RDA and that for minerals was between 1 and 2 times the RDA. Comprehensive multivitamin, multimineral supplements were often used, in addition. Of the 16 subjects presented, 8 had either full or good improvement as defined by complete or substantial clearance of fatigue and other symptoms to a point that allowed them to return to premorbid levels of work and social activity. Because of the lack of a control group, the small sample size, and the several variables, this study should be considered only as suggestive of benefits of multiple nutrients in CFS. Nevertheless, two of the nutrients found to be deficient in this study (zinc and magnesium) were also found to be lower in PWCs than in controls in the later study by Grant, Veldee, and Buchwald (1996), which is discussed later (see section on the Myers cocktail).

Martin, Ogston, and Evans (1994) selected a group of CFS patients using criteria based on clinical experience, which included fulfilling at least two of three of the following: muscle pain for at least three months, mental or physical fatigue at rest or on minimal exercise for at least three months, and persistent or relapsing course of illness for at least three months. In addition, they required that the patients had been well before their illness and that other obvious organic causes for the symptoms had been excluded. For this study, they also required that the patients have Cocksackie B IgG-neutralizing antibody levels equal to or greater than 1:512. They gave the treatment group a vitamin, mineral, and amino acid supplement. The amounts of some of the minerals were about three times the RDAs, and the amounts of some of the vitamins were considerably larger. A second group of these patients received a placebo. After three months, there was a crossover of the groups. Fifteen patients in each group completed the first three months of the trial, and 10 in one group and 9 in the other completed the full six months, including the crossover. A general health questionnaire and a physical questionnaire were used to assess severity of symptoms, and the sum of scores from these two was evaluated. According to the authors, "The pattern of results showed a larger change in physical, general health, and total scores (indicating better recovery) for the patients taking the vitamin and mineral mixture, but the analyses of variance could not find a statistically significant effect due to treatment. A study of the individual responses showed a fair range in the small groups studied." Again, this study should be viewed as suggestive, rather than conclusive. Perhaps a larger number of subjects would have revealed statistical significance, because the trends in all the measures showed uniform improvement for the treated group.

Brouwers, van der Werf, Bleijenberg, van der Zee, and van der Meer (2002) performed a prospective randomized placebo-controlled, double-blind, 10-week trial of a polynutrient supplement on 53 patients (16 males, 37 females) fulfilling the Fukuda et al. (1994) criteria for CFS. According to the authors, the composition of the polynutrient supplement "resembled the multivitamin use reported by CFS patients and was compatible with the advice regarding supplement use in CFS found on CFS informational pages on the internet." No particular internet pages were cited in the paper. The outcome measures were scores on the fatigue severity subscale of the Checklist Individual Strength, a symptoms occurrence checklist, eight subscales of the Sickness Impact Scale, physical activity measured by actometer, patient rating of daily fatigue, and self-reported improvement at follow-up. The results were that no significant differences were found between the placebo and the treated group on any of the outcome measures.

An examination of the dosages used in this study for several of the nutrients shown in the peer-reviewed literature to be most beneficial in CFS reveals them to be much lower than dosages usually found to be therapeutic in this disorder. For example: magnesium—20 milligrams per day, vitamin B-6—6 milligrams per day, vitamin B12—3 micrograms per day, vitamin C—250 milligrams per day, selenium—50 milligrams per day, calcium—315 milligrams per day. The suggested dosage ranges shown in Table 27.1 can be seen to be considerably larger

Table 27.1
Approximate Dosage Ranges* for Supplements for Chronic
Fatigue Syndrome and Fibromyalgia Based on the Literature

Nutrient	Chronic Fatigue Syndrome	Fibromyalgia
Vitamin A	700 to 3,000 mcg/day (2,300 to 10,000 IU/day)	700 to 3,000 mcg/day (2,300 to 10,000 IU/day)
Vitamin B1	10 to 200 mg/day	10 to 200 mg/day
Vitamin B2	10 to 50 mg/day	1.1 to 10 mg/day
Vitamin B3	14 to 35 mg/day	14 to 35 mg/day
Pantothenic acid	5 to 50 mg/day	5 to 50 mg/day
Vitamin B6	50 to 100 mg/day	50 to 100 mg/day
Biotin	30 to100 mcg/day	30 to 100 mcg/day
Choline	425 to 3,500 mg/day	425 to 3,500 mg/day
Folic Acid	400 to 1,000 mcg/day	400 to 1,000 mcg/day
Vitamin B12	6,000 to 70,000 mcg IM/week, (3 week trial)	6,000 to 70,000 mcg IM/week (3-week trial)
Vitamin C	2,000 mg/day	2,000 mg/day
Vitamin D	5 to 50 mcg/day (200 to 2,000 IU/day)	5 to 50 mcg/day (200 to 2,000 IU/day)
Vitamin E	100 to 400 mg/day (150 to 600 IU/day)	100 to 400 mg/day (150 to 600 IU/day)
Vitamin K	100 mcg/day	100 mcg/day
Calcium	1,000 mg/day	1,000 mg/day
Chromium	25 to 400 mcg/day	25 to 400 mcg/day
Copper	900 to 3,000 mcg/day	900 to 3,000 mcg/day
Iodine	150 mcg/day	150 mcg/day
Iron	8 (men) 18 (women) mg/day	8 (men) 18 (women) mg/day
Magnesium	100 mg IM/week, 600 mg orally/day (as glycinate or malate) (8-week trial)	100 mg IM/week, 600 mg orally /day (as glycinate or malate) (8-week trial)
Manganese	2 to 5 mg/day	2 to 5 mg/day
Molybdenum	45 to 250 mcg/day	45 to 250 mcg/day
Potassium	500 to 2,000 mg/day	500 to 2,000 mg/day
Selenium	55 to 400 mcg/day	55 to 400 mcg/day
Sodium (as chloride)	If diagnosis of neurally mediated hypotension, increase intake moderately.	Diet supplies adequate amount.
Zinc	8 to 40 mg/day	8 to 40 mg/day
Nondenatured whey protein (test for mercury first—see text)	Dosage depends on particular product used. Low dosage is best at beginning. Serum cysteine should be monitored. Best taken with alpha lipoic acid and essential nutrients. (3-month trial)	Dosage depends on particular product used. Low dosage is best at beginning. Serum cysteine should be monitored. Best taken with alpha lipoic acid and essential nutrients. (3-month trial)

Table 27.1 *Continued*

Nutrient	Chronic Fatigue Syndrome	Fibromyalgia
L-glutamine	Best started low and worked up to 20 g/day. Use together with mixed amino acids or high-quality dietary protein. (3-week trial)	Not shown to be needed.
L-lysine	For herpes simplex, 500 to 3,000 mg/day, with meals. Use together with mixed amino acids or high-quality dietary protein. (1-week trial)	Diet supplies adequate amount.
5-HTP (with carbidopa)	Not recommended unless serotonergic activity is low.	100 mg 3 times/day (3-month trial)
Essential fatty acids	If deficient, 280 mg GLA and 135 mg EPA daily. (3-month trial)	4.5 g fish oil/day (3-month trial)
Alpha lipoic acid (test for mercury first—see text)	100 to 600 mg/day (3-month trial with nondenatured whey protein)	100 to 600 mg/day (3-month trial with nondenatured whey protein)
Bioflavonoids	OPCs: 50 to 200 mg/day; Quercetin: 200 to 1,200 mg/day; citrus bioflavonoids: 2 to 6 g/day (3-week trial)	OPCs: 50 to 200 mg/day; Quercetin: 200 to 1,200 mg/day; citrus bioflavonoids: 2 to 6 g/day (3-week trial)
Coenzyme Q-10	100 to 300 mg/day (3-month trial)	100 to 300 mg/day (3-month trial)
L-Carnitine	1 to 2 g 3 times/day (3-month trial)	Not shown to be needed.
Malic acid	2,400 mg/day (8-week trial)	2,400 mg/day (8-week trial)
SAMe	200 mg IM/day; 400 mg orally, 2 times/day (6-week trial)	200 mg IM/day; 400 mg orally, 2 times/day (6-week trial)

Note: These ranges apply to nonpregnant, nonlactating adults. g = grams; mg = milligrams; mcg = micrograms. For contraindications, see *PDR for Nutritional Supplements,* by S. Hendler and D. Rorvik, eds., 2001, Montvale, NJ: Medical Economics. Many of the nutrients at the levels shown can be supplied using a general, high-potency nutritional supplement. Those nutrients without a trial time shown are suggested to be taken regularly. If magnesium or vitamin B12 are not found to be particularly beneficial at the elevated dosages shown (after the trial periods shown), it is suggested that they be continued at 350 mg per day and 2.4 mcg per day, respectively, because they are essential nutrients.

than these. This study had a larger number of subjects and was better controlled than the earlier studies cited previously. However, the dosages of nutrients that were used appear to have been too small to effect significant changes in the patients. One wonders what the results would have been if the supplement had had a potency comparable to those used in the earlier studies by Stewart (1991) or Martin et al. (1994). In addition, the fact that three patients in the treatment group of this study dropped out because of nausea suggests that there may have been gastrointestinal problems in the patients that were not treated prior to the nutritional trial. As noted earlier, this reviewer believes that dealing with such problems as part of the treatment program is a prerequisite to the success of nutritional approaches in CFS.

Another approach using a combination of nutrients is represented by chlorella. *Chlorella pyrenoidosa* is a unicellular green alga that grows in fresh water. Dietary supplements derived from chlorella are rich in protein, vitamins, minerals, and other bioactive substances. Their use in FM has been the subject of studies by R. E. Merchant and coworkers, who have performed an open-label pilot study as well as a randomized, double-blind, placebo-controlled, crossover study.

In the pilot study (Merchant, Carmack, & Wise, 2000), 18 PWFs (persons with fibromyalgia) supplemented their diets with 10 grams of chlorella and 100 mL of liquid chlorella extract per day for two months. The tender point index was found to decrease from 32 to a mean of 25, representing a statistically significant ($p = .01$) decrease in pain intensity. Patient interviews and self-assessment questionnaires showed that seven patients felt that the supplements had improved their FM symptoms. Six felt that they had experienced no change, and five believed that their symptoms had worsened.

In the double-blind study (Merchant, Andre, & Wise, 2001), 37 PWFs completed the treatment arm of the study, and 34 also completed the placebo arm. The treatment consisted of 50 Sun Chlorella™ tablets and 100 mL of liquid chlorella extract (Wakasa Gold™) each day for three months. The placebo consisted of 50 placebo tablets and 100 mL of placebo liquid each day for the same period. These treatments were supplemental to the regular diets of the PWFs. There was a one-month washout period before the crossover. The response parameters followed were sleep, pain, global well-being, and fatigue as reported by the patients, as well as tender point index and global well-being as assessed by a physician. A 50% or more improvement in at least four parameters was considered a positive response. Nineteen percent of those who completed the treatment arm had a positive response, compared to 9% of those completing the placebo arm. Considering the self-assessment parameters alone, the comparison of those who noted a 50% or greater improvement in at least two of the parameters showed 57% for the treatment versus 29% for the placebo. The Fibromyalgia Impact Questionnaire showed a steady, statistically significant drop in the score while chlorella was used, compared to varying levels of improvement and a nonstatistically significant change at the end of three months for the placebo. A questionnaire dealing with pain, anxiety, sleep, and gastrointestinal problems showed steady, statistically significant improvements when chlorella was used, and the observed improvements were statistically significant compared to placebo ($p = .004$). This work suggests that chlorella is helpful for relieving symptoms in some PWFs and that it should receive more study for use in FM.

Another nutritional approach that involves a combination of several nutrients used simultaneously is commonly referred to as the *Myers cocktail*. This cocktail, attributed to the late John Myers, has been modified and popularized by Alan Gaby (Gaby, 2002). The cocktail is administered intravenously, and this differs from the other combined nutritional approaches discussed in this review in that it bypasses the normal processes of ingestion, digestion, and absorption, delivering significant amounts of several nutrients directly to the blood stream in a relatively short period of time. The basic formulation is comprised of magnesium chloride hexahydrate 20%—2 to 5 mL, calcium gluconate 10%—1 to 3 mL, hydroxocobalamin (vitamin B12) 1,000 micrograms per mL—1 mL, pyridoxine hydrochloride (vitamin B6) 100 micrograms per mL, dexpanthenol (vitamin B5) 250 milligrams per mL—1 mL, B complex 100—1 mL, and vitamin C 222 milligrams per mL—4 to 20 mL. Sometimes modifications of the basic formulation are used. Gaby (2002) reports having administered approximately 15,000 of these injections over an 11-year period to 800 to 1,000 different patients, and he estimated that over 1,000 doctors in the U.S. were using the Myers cocktail at the time of writing. It is used for a wide variety of clinical conditions, including CFS and FM. Gaby suggests that the efficacy of this cocktail results from its ability to achieve higher serum concentrations of nutrients than oral or intramuscular administration and that its inclusion of magnesium is particularly important.

According to Gaby (2002), "Approximately ten patients with chronic fatigue syndrome (CFS) received a minimum of four treatments (usually once weekly for four weeks), with more than half showing clear improvement. One patient experienced dramatic benefit after the first injection, whereas in other cases three or four injections were given before improvement was evident. A few patients became progressively healthier with continued injections and were eventually able to stop treatment. Several others did not overcome their illness, but periodic injections helped them to function better."

Gaby (2002) also reports, "The author has given the Myers' to approximately 30 patients with fibromyalgia; half have experienced significant improvement, in a few cases after the first injection, but more often after three or four treatments."

The reported benefits of the Myers cocktail in CFS (Gaby, 2002; Goldberg, 1998) suggest problems in digestion or absorption in many cases of CFS. This proposition is also consistent with results of the study by Grant et al. (1996). That study showed that while the dietary intakes of nutrients by a group of PWCs were actually higher in many cases than those of a healthy control group, and more were taking vitamin and mineral supplements, the measured levels in the blood were lower for magnesium and zinc and, in a few cases, some of whom were smokers, vitamin C. Grant et al. found nutrient deficiencies in 36% of the patients, compared to 20% of the control subjects. Several of the nutrients included in the Myers cocktail are the same ones that were found to below normal in CFS patients in the study by Grant et al. and deficient in the study by Stewart (1991). In view of this and the many anecdotal reports of its clinical benefits, the Myers cocktail should receive more controlled testing.

TESTING FOR NUTRITIONAL DEFICIENCIES

In this approach, a small population of PWCs is tested for nutritional deficiencies; it is then recommended that the particular nutrients at levels below normal be supplemented in PWCs in general, without actually testing the response to such supplementation. Although this is a step forward in trying to match nutrition to actual, observed needs of PWCs, this approach has shortcomings in principle. First, inherent in this approach is the assumption of a homogeneous population, whereas considerable evidence indicates that the PWC population is actually composed of a number of subsets. Second, the assumption behind this approach, that correcting deficiencies in nutrients is the appropriate purpose for their use in treating CFS, ignores the possibility that nutrients might be used for their pharmacological effects. Third, in our current ignorance of the etiology, pathogenesis, and pathophysiology of CFS, this approach must necessarily be entirely empirical. Therefore, if a deficiency is found in a particular nutrient, it is not clear whether the cause is too low an intake, too low an absorption, too high an excretion, or in cases of nutrients that can be broken down biochemically, accelerated utilization or accelerated breakdown by some aspect of the disease process. Consequently, without performing repletion testing, it is not clear that increasing the intake of a particular nutrient found to be deficient would actually be beneficial.

DEFICIENCY AND REPLETION TESTING OF INDIVIDUAL NUTRIENTS

The next approach takes the previous one a step further, by observing the outcomes of supplementing the nutrients found by testing to be at levels below normal in PWCs. This is again an important step forward—it overcomes the uncertainty about whether increasing the intake of deficient nutrients will actually bring about improvement. However, problems still remain with this approach. One, because of a lack of objective diagnostic measures for the severity of the illness, the outcome measures are still often based on subjective reporting of symptoms by the PWCs.

The assumption behind this approach, that the goal is simply to correct a deficiency, is a second problem. The possibility of benefits from pharmacological doses is still ignored.

A third issue is whether near-term symptom improvement is a valid measure of the effectiveness of a particular supplement in view of the widespread anecdotal reports of an initial worsening of symptoms in the case of some treatments claimed to be effective. In various contexts, this initial worsening has been called a *healing crisis,* or has been attributed to a Herxheimer reaction, or, in the case of the guaifenesin treatment, it has been called *cycling* (St. Amand & Marek, 1999). It is not always a simple matter to choose the length of time over which symptom response should be observed before conclusions are reached. Supplements of some nutrients, for example, the essential fatty acids, are diluted by the body's much larger inventory of lipids; therefore, an impact from supplementing may not be seen for a considerable length of time.

In addition, this approach still suffers from the problem of not accounting for the heterogeneous population. Finally, while this approach may result in a lessening of symptoms and hence an improvement in the quality of life, in the absence of an understanding of the etiology, pathogenesis, and pathophysiology of CFS, there is still no basis to expect that it will bring about a cure. While such a goal may seem unrealistic in view of the history of lack of success in finding cures for many other chronic diseases, the present contributor's position is that the research and clinical communities should settle for nothing less.

Notwithstanding these difficulties, the deficiency and repletion testing approach represents a major part of the current application of nutrition to the treatment of CFS. Data based on this approach are discussed further in the sections on individual nutrients later in this chapter.

NUTRITIONAL TREATMENT OF PARTICULAR ASPECTS OR SYMPTOMS OF CHRONIC FATIGUE SYNDROME

Another nutritional approach has been to treat particular aspects or symptoms of CFS using nutrients found helpful for lessening the severity of these aspects or symptoms in other conditions. For example, the gastrointestinal manifestations of irritable bowel syndrome (IBS) have been treated with a variety of dietary and nutritional substances (such as Lactobacillus acidophilus bacteria), and these have also been used when IBS occurs in CFS (Teitelbaum, 2001). Orthostatic hypotension is another aspect that has been treated nutritionally, for example, by increased salt and water intake (Engstrom & Martin, 2001). Immune system dysfunction has been treated with nutrients known to be particularly needed by the immune system, such as protein; vitamins A, C, and E; carotenes; vitamin B12 and folic acid; other B vitamins; iron; zinc; and selenium (Murray & Pizzorno, 1998).

Oxidative Stress   An aspect of CFS that has been receiving more attention recently (Logan & Wong, 2001) and that may occupy a fundamental position in the pathogenesis is oxidative stress. The healthy cell operates at a more reducing oxidation-reduction potential than is found in the environment. This relatively reducing state is maintained by a "network" of antioxidant enzymes and other antioxidants that work together (Packer & Colman, 1999) and have as their basis the tripeptide glutathione. The other four network antioxidants are vitamins C and E, coenzyme Q-10, and alpha lipoic acid. Vitamin E is regenerated by vitamin C, coenzyme Q-10, and alpha lipoic acid. Vitamin C is regenerated by glutathione and alpha lipoic acid. Glutathione and coenzyme Q-10 are built up by alpha lipoic acid. Alpha lipoic acid and glutathione are regenerated metabolically. Bioflavonoids, which are not part of the network, regenerate vitamin C and boost production of vitamin E and glutathione.

Ali (1990) found by high-resolution, phase-contrast microscopy that there were morphologic abnormalities in the erythrocyte cell membranes in 50% to 80% of patients with persistent chronic fatigue. These abnormalities included crenation, sharp angulation, spike formation, and rigidity. (Abnormal red blood cell shapes in patients with myalgic encephalomyelitis had previously been observed by Mukherjee, Smith, & Maros, 1987, and by Simpson, 1989, using scanning electron microscopy.) Fifteen minutes after infusing patients with 15 grams of the water-soluble antioxidant ascorbic acid (vitamin C), Ali examined samples of blood cells again and found that more than 80% of these abnormalities had been reversed. In 1993, he proposed the hypothesis that chronic fatigue is a state of accelerated oxidative molecular injury (Ali, 1993).

Cheney (1999a) found that PWCs are almost universally low in whole blood glutathione and that indicators of the function of the chemically reduced form of glutathione, including the concentrations of urinary lipid peroxides, citric acid, and alpha ketoglutarate are especially affected. The concentrations of urinary lipid peroxides and citric acid are found to rise, and the concentration of alpha ketoglutarate is found to decrease, relative to normal values. Because glutathione is the basis of the antioxidant network, this is evidence of a serious state of oxidative stress in CFS.

Three studies have provided additional support for the proposition that oxidative stress is an important factor in CFS. Richards, Roberts, Mathers, et al. (2000) and Richards, Roberts, McGregor, Dunstan, and Butt (2000) reported significantly elevated malondialdehyde (an indicator of lipid peroxidation) and methemoglobin (the oxidized-iron state of hemoglobin) in the red blood cells of 33 PWCs relative to 27 age- and sex-matched controls, and these elevations were strongly associated with symptom expression. They also found that the PWCs divided statistically into two groups, one having significantly elevated erythrocyte reduced glutathione levels relative to the control group and the other having significantly lower erythrocyte reduced glutathione levels. This suggests serious derangements in the redox control in the red blood cells of PWCs.

Fulle et al. (2000) analyzed biopsy specimens from the vastus lateralis muscle of six CFS patients and healthy age-matched controls. They found significantly higher levels of 8-hydroxy-2-deoxyguanosine (an indicator of oxidative damage to DNA) and malondialdehyde. Protein carbonyl (an indicator of oxidative damage to protein) was not significantly elevated. They also found significantly elevated levels of the selenium-dependent peroxidase, soluble catalase, glutathione mu and pi transferase, and total (reduced plus oxidized) glutathione, all indicators of oxidative stress.

Manuel y Keenoy, Moorkens, Vertommen, and De Leeuw (2001) compared the antioxidant status and lipoprotein peroxidation of a group of 33 patients who satisfied the Holmes et al. (1988) definition of CFS and a group of 28 patients with unexplained chronic fatigue lasting more than one month but not meeting the definition of CFS (thus, not a normal, healthy control group). They found a similar antioxidant status for the two groups, except that the CFS group had significantly lower serum transferrin concentrations and higher susceptibility of lipoproteins to peroxidation in vitro. (Transferrin binds iron in a nonredox-sensitive state, thus preventing it from catalyzing the formation of oxidizing free radicals.) They also found that the CFS group showed a more intense influence of LDL cholesterol and of transferrin on peroxidation in vitro, suggesting additional pro-oxidant effects. In men, but not in women, vitamin E tended to be lower in CFS patients.

Vecchiet et al. (2003) studied the relationship between musculoskeletal symptoms and blood markers of oxidative stress in CFS. They compared 21 PWCs who satisfied the Fukuda et al. (1994) criteria with 20 normal subjects. Among the PWCs, there were 14 females and 7 males, aged 46 +/-10 years. They found in patients versus controls that there was a shorter lag phase. (The lag phase is the time found to be necessary to initiate peroxidation of the low-density lipoproteins [LDLs] in a standard test. It is a measure of the degree of antioxidant protection in the LDLs.) There were also lower vitamin E concentrations in plasma and in the LDLs, higher LDL thiobarbituric acid reactive substances (TBARs), higher fatigue, and lower muscle pain thresholds to electrical stimulation. They found significant linear correlations between fatigue and TBARs, pain thresholds and lag phase, and pain thresholds and vitamin E levels in both plasma and LDLs. A significant inverse linear correlation was found between fatigue and lag phase, fatigue and vitamin E, and between pain thresholds and TBARs. This study shows that increased oxidative stress and decreased antioxidant defenses are directly related to the severity of the symptoms in CFS.

Kennedy, Spence, McLaren, Hill, and Belch (2003) measured markers of oxidative stress in 47 patients (18 male, 29 female) with a mean age of 47.5 years and age range of 19 to 63 years who fulfilled the Fukuda et al. (1994) criteria for CFS. They also measured these markers in 34 sex- and age-matched (13 males, 21 females, mean age of 45.9 years, age range of 19 to 63 years) healthy volunteers. They found that the CFS patients had significantly increased levels of isoprostanes ($p = .005$) and oxidized LDLs ($p = .02$), and that they had significantly lower levels of the reduced form of glutathione ($p = .05$) and of high-density lipoproteins ($p = .001$). This study further supports the prior evidence for oxidative stress in CFS. The authors of this study suggested that the elevated isoprostanes, which are formed by catalyzed oxidation of arachidonic acid, may be particularly important in the pathogenesis of CFS because they are potent vasoconstrictors.

Eisinger, Gandolfo, Zakarian, and Ayavou (1997) studied 25 female FM patients who met the ACR criteria for FM (Wolfe et al., 1990) and 20 female age-matched controls. Comparing the patients to the controls, they found significantly increased blood plasma protein carbonyls ($p < .01$), which is evidence for protein peroxidation. This was correlated with significantly decreased plasma thiols ($p < .01$), which is evidence for oxidative stress. They also found markedly decreased plasma glutathione ($p < .05$) and significantly decreased plasma nitric oxide ($p < .01$), which are additional indicators of oxidative stress. Vitamin E and antioxidant enzymes were found to be normal, as was malondialdehyde.

Hein and Franke (2002) measured serum levels of pentosidine in FM patients and healthy subjects. Pentosidine is an advanced glycation end-product (AGE) formed as a result of nonenzymatic reactions between sugar-derived aldehyde groups and protein amino groups, known as the *Maillard reaction.* It is a cross-linked structure of lysine and arginine, requiring both glycation and oxidation, and is closely related to oxidative processes. It is thus a marker of oxidative stress. There were 41 FM patients who satisfied the ACR criteria, of ages between 15 and 65 years (5 males, 36 females), and 56 healthy subjects whose ages ranged between 21 and 75 years (26 males, 30 females). The FM patients were found to have significantly elevated serum pentosidine compared to the healthy subjects. This is evidence for the presence of oxidative stress in FM.

It appears from these results that oxidative stress is also present in FM, but that it is of a somewhat different character from that in CFS. In CFS, the lipids appear to be affected, while the proteins are not. In FM, the opposite appears to be true.

Taken together, these studies indicate that oxidative stress and the depletion of reduced glutathione are significant features of at least a major subset of PWCs and also of PWFs. Various nutritional measures can be applied in response and are discussed later in the sections on individual nutrients.

While approaches that involve treating particular aspects or symptoms of CFS appear to be ad hoc in nature, they have often been found to bring about an improvement in the quality of life, especially when several aspects of the symptomatology are treated simultaneously. Some clinicians specializing in CFS have combined multiple types of pharmaceutical therapy with nutritional therapy in an integrated approach. Teitelbaum et al. (2001) describe a clinical trial of such an approach. The treatment of particular aspects or symptoms of CFS using nutritional therapies complements the deficiency and repletion testing approach described. Further discussion of this is found in the sections on individual nutrients. Together, these two approaches represent most of the current state of the art in applying nutrition to the treatment of CFS.

REVIEW OF THE LITERATURE ON USE OF INDIVIDUAL NUTRIENTS IN CHRONIC FATIGUE SYNDROME AND FIBROMYALGIA

VITAMINS

Vitamin A   Among its many biological actions, vitamin A has been found to be essential for proper function of the immune system and to have antioxidant activity; and because clear immune dysfunction and oxidative stress are present in CFS, vitamin A should be considered part of a nutritional approach.

As noted earlier, Stewart (1991) found that four of nine postviral fatigue patients had serum vitamin A values at or below the lower limits of normal. Grant et al. (1996) did not find a vitamin A deficiency in CFS patients, but they noted that 89% were taking vitamin and mineral supplements at 100% to 200% of the RDA levels.

Retinoic acid, a derivative of vitamin A, has been found to be important in maintaining an adequate level of circulating natural killer (NK) cells in rats (Zhao & Ross, 1995). Natural killer cells are one of the first lines of defense against viral infections, which are common in CFS. Retinoic acid has also been found to increase the activity of macrophages in mice (Katz et al., 1987). Macrophages form an important part of the cell-mediated immune response to viral and intracellular bacterial infections, which are common in CFS. Deficiency of vitamin A causes oxidative damage to liver mitochondria in rats, involving an increase in oxidized glutathione, malondialdehyde, and 8-oxo-deoxyguanosine and an 80% decrease in the ratio of reduced glutathione to oxidized glutathione (Hendler & Rorvik, 2001). When administered to surgical patients in large doses (90 to 135 milligrams per day) for seven days, vitamin A significantly increased lymphocyte proliferation (Hendler & Rorvik, 2001). The effects of vitamin A on the immune system are not due simply to reversal of vitamin A deficiency, because many of its effects are further enhanced by larger doses. Pinnock, Douglas, and Badcock (1986) supplemented vitamin A at 450 micrograms per day in a group of 59 Australian children of preschool age, who had normal serum vitamin A levels and a history of frequent respiratory illness. The treatment resulted in 19% fewer episodes suggestive of respiratory infection, when compared with 48 receiving placebos ($p < .05$). Because of its observed antioxidant and immune-enhancing actions, vitamin A should receive further testing in CFS.

Thiamin (Vitamin B1)   Thiamin plays important roles in the metabolism of carbohydrates and branched-chain amino acids and is a cofactor in the transketolase reactions in the pentose phosphate pathway (Hendler & Rorvik, 2001). This pathway regenerates nicotinamide adenine dinucleotide phosphate (reduced; NADPH). One of the important functions of NADPH is to assist the enzyme glutathione reductase in regenerating reduced glutathione, which appears to be depleted in many PWCs, hence, the importance of examining thiamin status. Thiamin status is usually evaluated by measuring the activity of the enzyme transketolase, from red blood cells, before and after thiamin pyrophosphate is added in vitro.

As noted earlier, Stewart (1991) found the thiamin status to be borderline or deficient in more than half of postviral fatigue syndrome patients tested, as measured by transketolase activity. Howard, Davies, and Hunnisett (1992) reported thiamin deficiencies in PWCs to be common in their experience. Grant et al. (1996) found normal thiamin activity in the PWCs they studied. However, it must be recalled that 89% of their PWC group reported use of 100% to 200% of the RDA for vitamin/mineral supplements, as compared to 40% of their control group. Heap, Peters, and Wessely (1999) studied 12 PWCs who met the Oxford criteria (Sharpe et al., 1991) and who had abstained from any vitamin preparation during their illness, compared to 18 healthy sex- and age-matched controls. They found a functional deficiency of thiamin in the PWCs, as evaluated by transketolase activity.

Eisinger and Ayavou (1990) found a significantly larger effect of thiamin pyrophosphate on the transketolase activity in red blood cells of 13 FM patients than in those of 12 controls ($p < .01$). Combining this with their prior finding that thiamin pyrophosphate was a more effective treatment than thiamin hydrochloride, they inferred an abnormality in thiamin metabolism in FM rather than a dietary deficiency. That is, the problem is not the availability of thiamin but its conversion into thiamin pyrophosphate, which is the form needed by transketolase. Eisinger, Zakarian, Plantamura, Clairet, and Ayavou (1992) studied 53 FM patients compared to 36 controls and again found a significantly larger transketolase activity coefficient in the FM patients ($p < .01$), indicating impaired thiamin status. Eighteen FM patients compared to six healthy controls were found to have a significantly lower affinity of transketolase to thiamin pyrophosphate, and four FM patients showed a higher affinity after treatment with phosphocreatine. This combination of results suggests that the abnormalities are related to deficits in magnesium or ATP, which are necessary for phosphorylation of thiamin-dependent enzymes. In later work, Eisinger, Bagneres, Arroyo, Plantamura, and Ayavou (1994) found benefits of a triple treatment (thiamin; a phosphorylation stimulator such as phosphocreatine, ATP, or the drug piracetam; and magnesium) on transketolase activity in FM patients.

There is evidence for thiamin functional deficiency in both CFS and FM. Although treatment trials specifically for thiamin alone have not been reported for CFS, thiamin supplementation should be considered as a part of nutritional treatment of CFS because it is an essential nutrient. The triple treatment of Eisinger, Bagneres, et al. (1994) may be beneficial in CFS as well as in FM.

Riboflavin (Vitamin B2)   Riboflavin is essential in the production of energy by the cells and serves as a cofactor for a family of proteins called flavoenzymes (Hendler & Rorvik, 2001). Riboflavin status is commonly measured by evaluating the activity of one of these enzymes, glutathione reductase, from red blood cells, before and after adding flavin-adenine dinucleotide (FAD). This test is very relevant to CFS, given the depletion of reduced glutathione in many PWCs. Heap et al. (1999) found evidence for significant functional deficiency of riboflavin in CFS using this method. Eisinger, Clairet, Brue, and Ayavou (1993) found normal riboflavin status in 20 FM patients as compared to 13 normal controls. It appears that riboflavin supplementation is advisable in CFS but perhaps is not as important in FM.

Niacin (Vitamin B3)   Niacin has two forms, namely nicotinic acid and nicotinamide. Niacin's biochemical effects are mediated principally by its metabolite nicotinamide adenine dinucleotide (NAD+), which, together with its reduced form NADH, among other functions, transfers the potential free energy from the oxidation of carbohydrates, fats, and proteins to the production of ATP. Niacin is also the basis for the phosphorylated version of this coenzyme, NADP+, and for its reduced form, NADPH, which is needed to reduce glutathione (Hendler & Rorvik, 2001).

No reports have been published concerning niacin measurements in CFS or FM. Because of its important functions in ATP production and glutathione reduction, both of which appear to be deficient in CFS, niacin should receive study for use in CFS and, in the meantime, should probably be supplemented at least at a basic minimum level.

One clinical trial was reported (Forsyth et al., 1999) on the use of NADH in CFS. The trial was a randomized, double-blind, placebo-controlled, crossover study. Twenty-six PWCs who met the Fukuda et al. (1994) criteria were given 10 mg of NADH or placebo for a four-week period each, with a four-week washout period between. It was found that 8 of the 26 responded favorably to NADH in contrast to 2 of 26 to placebo. A favorable response was defined as at least a 10% improvement in a scoring system that measured the severity of patient-reported symptoms. An interesting (and unexplained) finding in this study was that the urinary concentration of the serotonin metabolite, 5-hydroxyindole acetic acid (5-HIAA), which was initially elevated in 50% of the patients, was normal after the treatment.

Questions were raised (Colquhoun & Senn, 2000) about the presentation and analysis of the data in the Forsyth et al. (1999) paper, which were not addressed in detail in a response from one of the authors (Bellanti, 2000). However, the latter did report that a larger, more definitive study was being planned.

Questions have also been raised about this treatment from an absorption standpoint. According to Hendler and Rorvik (2001), there is little pharmacokinetic data on supplemental NADH. According to these authors, it is not clear how much of an administered dose is absorbed and what the metabolic course is of any absorbed NADH. If NADH is transported into cells, it is highly unlikely that any would enter mitochondria.

A study was performed in rats (Gross & Henderson, 1983) using NAD that was labeled with carbon-14 in either the adenine or the pyridine part of the molecule. This study showed that the molecule was broken down in the intestinal juice and in the mucosal cells and that nicotinamide (a form of niacin) was the major compound absorbed and possibly the only labeled compound absorbed.

On the other hand, this contributor has received anecdotal reports from some PWCs who experienced rapid improvements in symptoms from NADH that were not obtained by taking niacinamide (nicotinamide).

In view of these unresolved questions, it is not currently possible to reach a conclusion about the efficacy in CFS of supplementing NADH (as distinguished from supplementing niacin). As Hendler and Rorvik (2001) note, larger trials are recommended.

Pyridoxine (Vitamin B6)   Vitamin B6 is involved in a wide range of biochemical reactions, including the metabolism of amino acids and glycogen; the synthesis of nucleic acids, hemoglobin, sphingomyelin, and other sphingolipids; and the synthesis of the neurotransmitters serotonin, dopamine, norepinephrine, and gamma-aminobutyric acid (GABA; Hendler & Rorvik, 2001). It is also important to note that vitamin B6 is needed in particular for the conversion of methionine to cysteine, which is usually the limiting amino acid in the synthesis of glutathione. As mentioned earlier, glutathione has been found to be depleted in many PWCs. In addition, vitamin B6 is important in transamination reactions of amino acids. These reactions are used, among other functions, to feed amino acids into the Krebs cycle for energy production. Because of the evidence for a catabolic state of muscle protein in CFS (Dunstan et al., 2000), it appears that amino acids are being consumed for fuel at higher than normal rates. Transamination reactions are thus likely to be taking place at elevated rates in PWCs.

As also noted earlier, Stewart (1991) found the vitamin B6 status to be borderline or deficient in more than half the postviral fatigue syndrome patients in which it was evaluated, using the red cell glutamic-oxalacetic transaminase activity. Heap et al. (1999) found a significant ($p < .001$) functional deficiency of vitamin B6 in CFS patients, as evaluated from the red cell aspartate aminotransferase activity.

In FM, Eisinger, Zakarian, Mathieu, and Ayavou (1989) reported evidence of normal vitamin B6 status.

Treatment trials of vitamin B6 in CFS have not been reported. However, supplementation with B6 is likely to produce benefit because it is an essential nutrient, there is some evidence for deficiency in CFS, and it plays an important role in the burning of proteins for fuel, which seem to be elevated in CFS. Vitamin B6 should be accompanied by riboflavin and magnesium, which are necessary to convert pyridoxine to its bioactive state, pyridoxal-5-phosphate. While perhaps not as important in FM, vitamin B6 should, nevertheless, be used if magnesium is supplemented because the two have extensive biochemical interactions (Murray, 1996).

Folic Acid   Folic acid participates in the synthesis of DNA, RNA, and proteins. It is involved in DNA replication and repair, maintenance of the integrity of the genome, and regulation of gene expression. Folate deficiency produces megaloblastic anemia. Other symptoms and signs of folate deficiency are weakness, fatigue, irritability, headache, difficulty concentrating, cramps, palpitations, shortness of breath, and atrophic glossitis. The similarity of this list with the list of symptoms found in CFS prompted a search for folate deficiency in this disorder.

Jacobson et al. (1993) and Jacobson (1994) measured serum folate in 60 patients who met a set of criteria based on the criteria for CFS of Holmes et al. (1988) and Sharpe et al. (1991). These measurements were initiated on the basis that earlier work by Jacobson et al. in viral and mycoplasmal infections had shown low serum folate. They reported that 50% of the patients were found to be deficient in serum folate, and an additional 13% had low borderline values. A review of their diets did not reveal low folic acid intakes. On the other hand, Regland et al. (1997) found normal levels of serum folate in 24 women who satisfied both the Holmes et al. (1988) criteria for CFS and the ACR criteria (Wolfe et al., 1990) for FM. It is not clear why the results of these two studies differed.

Bengtsson et al. (1986) tested the serum folate levels in 36 primary FM patients who met the Yunus, Masi, Calabro, Miller, and Feigenbaum (1981) FM criteria and found normal levels in all.

Kaslow, Rucker, and Onishi (1989) evaluated the effect on patients who met the Holmes et al. (1988) criteria for CFS of intramuscular self-injections of an extract of bovine liver together with added folic acid and cyanocobalamin. The daily dosage was 800 micrograms of folic acid and 220 micrograms of cyanocobalamin equivalent. Fourteen patients participated in a crossover study in which all received one week of the treatment and one week of placebo. In addition, 11 patients completed a follow-on open-label treatment that lasted two more weeks. Although significant improvements in functional status and symptoms were found with both the treatment and the placebo, the former was not found to be more effective than the latter.

As Werbach (2000) has pointed out, the dosage and duration in this trial were much smaller than those successfully used to treat depression and fatigue in cases of folate deficiency (Botez, Botez, Leveille, Bielmann, & Cadotte, 1979; Godfrey et al., 1990). In the first of these, the dosage and duration were 10,000 micrograms per day (orally) and two to three months to relieve fatigue and depression. In the second, 15,000 micrograms per day were given orally for six months.

In view of the conflicting results of measurements of serum folate and the small dosage and duration of the only reported trial of folic acid in CFS, it is not clear whether a folate deficiency is present in CFS or whether supplementation with folic acid will produce benefits. More research is needed.

Vitamin B12 (Cyanocobalamin, Methylcobalamin, Hydroxocobalamin) Vitamin B12 is involved in DNA and RNA synthesis and protection of the genome, maintenance of the nervous system, and synthesis of molecules involved in fatty acid biosynthesis and the production of energy. It works together with folate to convert homocysteine to methionine, and it serves as a cofactor in the conversion of methylmalonyl-CoA to succinyl-CoA, which is important in the catabolism of several amino acids and fatty acids. Deficiencies produce hematological, neurological, and gastrointestinal effects. Cyanocobalamin is the principal form of vitamin B12 used in nutritional supplements. Methylcobalamin, one of the two coenzyme forms of B12 in the body, is also available for nutritional supplementation. Hydroxocobalamin is available for parenteral use. The term *cobalamin* encompasses all the forms of vitamin B12 (Hendler & Rorvik, 2001).

In urinary organic acids tests of more than 100 CFS patients, Lapp and Cheney found that 33% had elevated homocysteine, 38% had elevated methylmalonate, and 13% had both (Lapp, 1999; Lapp & Cheney, 1993). Methylmalonate is a sensitive and specific indicator for vitamin B12 deficiency. Elevated homocysteine can be caused by vitamin B12 deficiency, among other possible causes.

Evengard et al. (1996) reported that vitamin B12 levels were below their detection limit of 3.7 pmol/L in the cerebrospinal fluid of 10 of 16 CFS patients. (The normal range of values of vitamin B12 for their laboratory was not given in the abstract of their talk.)

Regland et al. (1997) measured vitamin B12 in the blood serum of 24 female patients and in the cerebrospinal fluid of 12 of them, all of whom met the criteria for both FM (Wolfe et al., 1990) and CFS (Holmes et al., 1988). They found the serum vitamin B12 level to be normal in all patients in which it was measured. However, the vitamin B12 levels in the cerebrospinal fluid were "suspiciously low" (between 5 and 10 pmol/L) in 9 of 12, and "pathologically low" (2.9 pmol/L) in one of 12. Normal values were considered 10 to 20 pmol/L. The low values in the patients were significantly correlated with failing memory, fatigability, and a set of factors that describe neurasthenia. These researchers also observed elevated levels of homocysteine in the cerebrospinal fluid in all 12 patients investigated, but the homocysteine levels in the blood serum were above the reference limit in only 2 of 24. Because vitamin B12 is a cofactor (together with folate) in the conversion of homocysteine to methionine, the authors suggested that a cerebral vitamin B12 deficiency might be an important contributor to the increased homocysteine concentrations observed in the cerebrospinal fluid.

Bengtsson et al. (1986) found normal serum cobalamin levels in all 34 primary FM patients tested, who met the Yunus et al. (1981) criteria.

As to treatment, no evidence has been presented that vitamin B12 is effective in CFS as a dietary supplement. The efficacy of high-dose injections of vitamin B12 in CFS, on the other hand, has considerable support from clinical experience. The major proponents of this treatment have been Lapp and Cheney (Lapp, 1999; Lapp & Cheney, 1993), who reported that patients feel an increase in energy, stamina, or well-being within 12 to 24 hours of receiving an injection and that the effects last for two to three days. They also found a threshold of response at a dosage of 2,000 to 2,500 micrograms per injection. They initially used vitamin B12 in the form of cyanocobalamin (Lapp, 1999) at a dosage of 3,000 micrograms intramuscularly every two to three days. Lapp and Cheney reported that an informal poll of their patients, who numbered more than 2,000 at the time, indicated that 50% to 80% improved to some extent with high-dose vitamin B12 injections (Lapp, 1999).

High-dose vitamin B12 injections have also been used in other disorders. Dettori and Ponari (1973) reported successfully using intramuscular doses of 10,000 micrograms per day to relieve pain of peripheral neuropathy. Hieber (1974) described the beneficial use of 5,000 micrograms of hydroxocobalamin either intramuscularly or intravenously to treat various vertebral pain syndromes. Newbold (1989) reported finding optimum doses for different patients with a variety of diagnoses that ranged from 3,000 micrograms four times per week to 9,000 micrograms daily, using the Minnesota Multiphasic Personality Inventory to evaluate the effects.

The folate study in CFS by Kaslow et al. (1989) described in the folic acid section also incorporated vitamin B12 and found no benefit greater than that of the placebo. However, the dosage used (220 micrograms per day of cyanocobalamin equivalent) was well below the threshold reported by Lapp and Cheney and, therefore, may have been too low to produce observable benefit.

Regland et al. (1998) reported an open trial of 1,000 microgram weekly injections of hydroxocobalamin for at least three months in 10 women who met criteria for both CFS and FM. All the patients initially had elevated homocysteine in their cerebrospinal fluid, and there was a significant positive correlation between this and fatigability. In addition, the initial levels of vitamin B12 in the cerebrospinal fluid correlated both with fatigability and 15 selected items on the Comprehensive Psychopathological Rating Scale (CPRS-15) that correspond to neurasthenia. They found that the treatment was significantly more beneficial if the patient did not carry the thermolabile allele of the polymorphic gene methylenetetrahydrofolate reductase (MTHFR). They concluded that the vitamin B12 deficiency was probably contributing to the increased homocysteine levels and that the effect of vitamin B12 supplementation is dependent on whether the available methyl groups are further deprived by the existence of themolabile MTHFR.

Other mechanisms by which high-dose vitamin B12 brings benefits to PWCs have been suggested. Simpson (1991) studied the effect of vitamin B12 on the distribution of shapes of the red blood cells in myalgic encephalomyelitis patients who initially had a greater than normal fraction of nondiscocyte cells. He reported that half the patients experienced an improved sense of well-being within one day, which was correlated with a decrease in the fraction of nondiscocytes. Patients who did not experience greater well-being showed no change in the shape distribution of their red blood cells. Simpson has proposed that the symptomatic improvement in the patients under B12 treatment resulted from improved oxygenation of tissues that was made possible by correcting the red blood cell shape abnormalities, thus promoting better transport of the cells through the capillaries.

Cheney has suggested that high-dose vitamin B12 acts to detoxify the brain (Cheney, 1999b). According to Houeto, Hoffman, Imbert, Levillain, and Baud (1995), clinical studies have shown that hydroxocobalamin may be a safe, rapid, and effective cyanide antidote. Vitamin B12 can also catalyze the oxidation of sulfite, and there is some evidence that it is effective in treating sulfite-induced hypersensitivity (D. W. Jacobsen, Simon, & Singh, 1984). Pall (2001) has suggested that vitamin B12's therapeutic action in CFS results from its demonstrated ability to scavenge nitric oxide. Vitamin B12 derivatives are also capable of methylating heavy metals, thus rendering them more mobile in biological systems. In fact, it is interesting to note that the only known methylating agents capable of methyl transfer to the mercuric ion in biological systems are derivatives of vitamin B12 (Ridley, Dizikes, & Wood, 1977). It seems conceivable that high-dose vitamin B12 may be acting to methylate heavy metals in the brain, thus rendering them able to cross the blood-brain barrier and be removed from the brain, the reverse of the process by which they can be transported into the brain. Although there is not complete agreement on the species involved, there thus appears to be considerable support for the general hypothesis that vitamin B12 may act as a detoxifier in CFS.

Whatever the mechanism or mechanisms may be, it seems clear that high-dose vitamin B12 injections bring considerable clinical benefit to PWCs. This treatment merits controlled study.

Vitamin C　Vitamin C is one of the five antioxidants of the fundamental "network" of antioxidants in the body (Packer & Colman, 1999). It has important roles in the immune system and is involved in the synthesis of collagen and other connective tissue components, L-carnitine, corticosteroids, and other substances (Hendler & Rorvik, 2001).

As noted earlier, Stewart (1991) found deficient blood serum vitamin C in the two postviral syndrome patients in which it was measured. Ali (1990) observed improvement in red blood cell membrane shapes after injecting vitamin C in patients with chronic fatigue, and Grant et al. (1996) found that 2 of 28 PWCs had low serum vitamin C. However, again it should be noted that 89% of the PWCs in the Grant et al. study were supplementing vitamins and minerals at 100% to 200% of the RDA levels and that some were smokers. Smoking is known to deplete vitamin C. Thus, very little direct data bears on the question of whether PWCs are deficient in vitamin C.

Indirect arguments in favor of including vitamin C in nutritional treatment of PWCs and PWFs are that vitamin C is the main water-soluble antioxidant in the body and that it is essential for proper function of the immune system. As discussed earlier, there is considerable evidence for oxidative stress in CFS, and immune dysfunction is very much part of the disease process (Patarca-Montero et al., 2001). There is also evidence for oxidative stress in FM. In the absence of statistically significant data on vitamin C levels in PWCs or PWFs or results of controlled trials, vitamin C should, nevertheless, be included for these reasons.

Cheney (1999b) has argued that because reduced glutathione is normally used to regenerate vitamin C, the amount of vitamin C supplementation in CFS should be limited to about 2,000 mg per day. This value is still much higher than the current RDAs (75 and 90 mg for women and men, respectively) and is, in fact, equal to the tolerable upper intake level for normal, healthy people currently recommended by the Institute of Medicine (2000). Cheney further recommends that other antioxidants such as bioflavonoids and alpha lipoic acid be included to assist in the regeneration of vitamin C. In this way, the reduced glutathione will be spared and can more easily be built up to normal concentrations.

Vitamin D   Vitamin D is the principal regulator of calcium homeostasis in the body. It is an essential nutrient when there is insufficient exposure to the ultraviolet radiation in sunlight to generate the D_3 form of the vitamin (cholecalciferol) within the body (Hendler & Rorvik, 2001). Vitamin D_3 is sequentially converted by enzymes in the liver and the kidneys to more potent forms of the vitamin, 25-OH D_3 and 1,25-$(OH)_2D_3$.

Hock (1997) found that nine CFS patients had low serum levels of 25-OH D_3. They were treated with 10,000 I.U. per day of cholecalciferol, but their symptoms did not noticeably improve.

Hoskin, Clifton-Bligh, Hansen, Fulcher, and Gates (2000) measured serum levels of 25-OH D_3 in 37 women who met the Oxford criteria for CFS (Sharpe et al., 1991) and 20 healthy controls. They did not find a significant difference between the groups ($p < .19$).

Wynants and Moorkens (2003) measured serum 25-OH D_3 in 49 female patients diagnosed with CFS, 60 with FM, and 82 with autonomic dysfunction. The age range was 17 to 68 years. The study was done in Antwerp, Belgium. They found that 17% of the CFS patients, 14% of the FM patients, and 21% of those with autonomic dysfunction had subnormal levels of 25-OH D_3.

Huisman et al. (2001) measured serum levels of 25-OH D_3, 1,25-OH D_3, and parathyroid hormone in 25 female FM patients. The patients were Caucasian, aged 18 to 65 years with a mean age of 44.5 years, and satisfied the ACR criteria. They were recruited in January through March of 2000 in London, Ontario, Canada. The researchers found that 48% of the patients had 25-OH D_3 levels less than 50 nmol/L. They confirmed this to be the level at which parathyroid hormone is stimulated, and expressed the view that it should thus be considered as the threshold for deficiency. This may be a higher deficiency threshold than was used in the other studies described in this chapter.

Based on these studies, it appears that it would be advisable to measure serum levels of 25-OH D_3 in both PWCs and PWFs and to supplement with vitamin D when it is found to be deficient. Supplementation would probably be particularly important for PWCs who are forced to remain in their homes and are, therefore, unable to receive much sunlight, especially if they also do not consume vitamin-D-fortified foods, such as milk, which many PWCs do not, because of allergies.

Vitamin E (Tocopherols and Tocotrienols)   Vitamin E provides the primary antioxidant protection for the lipids in the body and is one of the five antioxidants termed *network antioxidants* by Packer and Colman (1999) because of their ability to work together to greatly enhance their antioxidant effect. Vitamin E also plays an important role in the maintenance of the immune system. Supplementation with higher than recommended dietary levels of vitamin E enhances humoral and cell-mediated immunity (Hendler & Rorvik, 2001). As noted earlier, vitamin E was found to be deficient in male PWCs by Manuel y Keenoy et al. (2001). In addition, Vecchiet et al. (2003), in the study described earlier, found low vitamin E levels in both plasma and low-density lipoproteins in PWCs. Because of its roles as an antioxidant and supporter of the immune system and because of these measured results, vitamin E should receive further study as part of nutritional treatment in CFS. Both the tocopherols and the tocotrienols should be studied because of their different roles.

MINERALS

Calcium Calcium is an essential mineral with a wide range of biological roles. A major constituent of bones and teeth, calcium is essential for functions such as muscle contraction, nerve conduction, the beating of the heart, blood coagulation, glandular secretion, the production of energy, and the maintenance of immune function (Hendler & Rorvik, 2001). Blood serum calcium level is not a good indicator of calcium status because it is tightly controlled by the parathyroid glands. The best indicators are measures of the calcium in bone, such as bone mineral density (BMD). Hoskin et al. (2000) measured the BMD using dual energy x-ray absorptiometry (DEXA) in 37 nulliparous women of mean age 25 who met the Oxford criteria for CFS (Sharpe et al., 1991) and 20 age-matched controls. They found that the BMD was significantly lower at the trochanteric region of the hip ($p < .002$) in the CFS group. No significant differences were found at the other sites measured. A calcium intake questionnaire showed that the calcium intake of the CFS group was significantly lower ($p < .006$), but as noted previously in the section on vitamin D, serum levels of 25-OH vitamin D were not significantly different.

Appelboom and Schoutens (1990) studied 28 premenopausal women with FM and 16 controls with femoropatellar osteoarthritis, periarthritis of the shoulder, or low back pain. They found that the 24-hour retention of radioactively labeled pyrophosphate and the Fogelman index were significantly higher in the FM group, which suggest an accelerated rate of bone turnover in this group. Although most clinical conditions with high bone turnover result in the long run in demineralization, these researchers did not detect this using dual-photon absorptiometry.

S. Jacobsen et al. (1993) studied 12 premenopausal women with FM and 12 controls matched by age, height, weight, and body mass index. They found that the urinary excretion of both hydroxyproline and calcium relative to urinary creatinine excretion was significantly higher in the FM group ($p = .01$), indicating increased bone resorption. However, this result was linked to significantly lower urinary creatinine excretion ($p = .02$), placing this conclusion in doubt. It is not clear whether the decreased creatinine excretion resulted from decreased physical activity or reduced muscle mass. The relation between markers of bone formation and resorption in the FM group was found to be low, indicating an imbalance between bone formation and resorption in some of the patients. Two of the CFS patients were found to have potentially increased bone turnover. Measurement of the BMD by dual photon absorptiometry did not show a significant difference between the FM group and the controls. However, the ability to discriminate differences with this technique was only about 20% with 80% power.

Swezey and Adams (1999) studied 24 women (ages 33 to 60 years) who met the ACR criteria for FM (Wolfe et al., 1990) and 48 age-matched and ethnically matched controls. They measured the BMD using DEXA, which is a more sensitive technique than dual photon absorptiometry, and found a significantly lower BMD of the spine ($p < .05$) in the FM patients of all age groups. The femoral neck BMD was also lower, but it reached significance ($p < .05$) only in the 51 to 60 age group.

It appears that there is evidence for decreased BMD in both CFS and FM and evidence for accelerated bone turnover in at least some FM patients. The decreased BMD could have been caused by a lower calcium intake in the case of the Hoskin et al. (2000) CFS study (where it was evaluated) or by either lower calcium or vitamin D intake in the Swezey and Adams (1999) study (where they were not evaluated). Lower physical activity, which is common in PWCs and PFCs, could also account for the lower BMDs.

Nijs, De Meirleir, Englebienne, and McGregor (2002) have suggested that the deregulation of the 2,5A synthetase RNase-L antiviral pathway and the associated channelopathy that is observed in many PWCs may lead to a higher demand for calcium on the part of the cells. Although there is considerable uncertainty, it also seems possible that these results, taken together, could be explained by excessive calcium loss in the urine. As discussed in the section on magnesium, there is evidence that PWCs suffer from a partial diabetes insipidus, caused by abnormally low secretion of arginine vasopressin. It has been shown in rats that low arginine vasopressin leads to increased loss of calcium in the urine (Bouby, Trinh-Trang-Tan, & Bankir, 1984; de Rouffignac, Corman, & Roinel, 1983). As also described in the magnesium section, citric acid excretion is elevated in patients suffering from fatigue and pain. Citric acid is an effective chelator for calcium, and there is a correlation between increased citric acid excretion and increased excretion of positive ions such as calcium (Bioscreen, 2000). It will require further study to determine if excess urinary loss of calcium or increased cellular absorption of calcium occur in CFS and FM, but, in the meantime, it would seem wise to supplement calcium in both.

Iron Iron is an essential component of hemoglobin, myoglobin, aconitase, and the cytochromes. These molecules are involved, respectively, in the transport of oxygen, in the Krebs cycle, and in the transfer of electrons in the process of oxidative phosphorylation that is involved in producing ATP, the energy currency of the cell (Hendler & Rorvik, 2001).

van Rensburg et al. (2001) measured serum iron in 10 women and 5 men who met the Fukuda et al. (1994) criteria for CFS and age- and sex-matched controls. They found that the PWCs had significantly decreased serum iron compared to controls ($p < .02$). When the female patients were considered separately, this decrease was even more significant ($p < .0003$). The mean transferrin saturation of the female patients was also significantly lower than that of the controls ($p < .005$). In the female PWCs, both the serum iron and the dehydroepiandrosterone sulfate (DHEA-S) were significantly decreased and correlated.

The use of iron in CFS should receive more study. In the meantime, iron should probably be supplemented at minimum levels. It is important to avoid excessive iron supplementation because of the catalytic effect of free iron on the generation of hydroxyl free radicals and, hence, exacerbation of the state of oxidative stress.

Magnesium Magnesium also has a wide range of functions in the body; it is involved in more than 300 reactions. Magnesium is necessary for every major metabolic process, including the production of cellular energy and the synthesis of nucleic acids and proteins. Among other functions, it is important for the electrical stability of cells, the maintenance of membrane integrity, muscle contraction, nerve conduction, and the regulation of vascular tone (Hendler & Rorvik, 2001).

The basis for suspecting that magnesium might be useful in the treatment of CFS has been presented in detail by Seelig (1996, 1998). She described the many similarities in symptomatology between CFS and latent tetany syndrome, which is caused by magnesium deficiency.

The search for magnesium deficiency in CFS has employed a variety of methods and has produced mixed results. The methods used have included analysis of whole blood, plasma, serum, red blood cells, and white blood cells. Magnesium loading (also called magnesium tolerance, magnesium challenge, or magnesium retention) testing has also been used. Most recently, ion-specific electrode analysis of serum and energy dispersive x-ray analysis of sublingual epithelial cells have been used. The challenge in magnesium studies in general has been to find a method that will serve as a reliable indicator of the body's overall magnesium status (Seelig, 1998). The intracellular concentrations in major tissues such as skeletal muscle and nerve are of most interest in CFS. Although muscle biopsies can be performed, in general, less invasive measures are preferred. Blood serum magnesium level has not been found to be a reliable indicator of body magnesium status (Institute of Medicine, 1997), and no significant correlation has been found among magnesium concentrations in mononuclear cells, plasma, or red blood cells (Elin & Hosseini, 1985). In normal subjects, lymphocyte and skeletal muscle magnesium were found to correlate well but not in patients with congestive heart failure (Dyckner & Wester, 1985). Evidence supporting correlation between red blood cell magnesium and skeletal muscle magnesium has not been presented, and this correlation has been questioned (Coghlan & Natello, 1992).

Among the several past studies that have been reported on CFS using various approaches, some have found magnesium deficiency (Cox, Campbell, & Dowson, 1991; Grant et al., 1996; Howard et al., 1992; Jessop, 1992, as cited in Werbach, 2000), while others have not (Altura et al., 1994; Clague, Edwards, & Jackson, 1992; Deulofeu, Gascon, Gimenez, & Corachan, 1991; Gantz, 1991; Hinds, Bell, McMaster, & McCluskey, 1994).

More recently, Moorkens et al. (1997) and Manuel y Keenoy et al. (2000) measured the magnesium status of 93 patients with unexplained chronic fatigue (median age 38 years; 25% male; 16% smokers; 54% with CFS, according to the Holmes et al. [1988] criteria; and 52% with FM, according to the ACR criteria). Thirty-seven percent were taking nutritional supplements "once in a while." Magnesium deficiency (deficiency in body stores) was evaluated with an intravenous magnesium retention (or loading) test. Patients with more than 20% magnesium retention in this test were judged to be moderately deficient, and they numbered 44, or 47% of the total. Very few were found to be severely deficient (defined as those having more than 50% retention on this test). Serum and red blood cell magnesium levels were also measured and for all except three patients were found to be in the normal ranges. Dietary intakes of magnesium were evaluated, and magnesium stores and blood concentrations were found not to be related to them. No association was found between the presence of magnesium deficiency and the satisfaction of the criteria for CFS or FM in this group of patients with unexplained chronic fatigue. Note that comparison was not made to healthy controls.

Wynants and Moorkens (2003), in the study described above in the section on vitamin D, also measured magnesium in the serum and red blood cells and in 24-hour urine specimens of patients with CFS, FM, and autonomic dysfunction, respectively. They found that the serum magnesium was normal in all patients except for two with autonomic dysfunction. Twenty-four percent of the CFS patients, 27% of those with FM, and 53% of those with autonomic dysfunction had low magnesium levels in their red blood cells. Twenty-eight percent of the patients with CFS, 35% of those with FM, and 34% of those with autonomic dysfunction showed low magnesium in their 24-hour urine samples.

Although the magnesium loading test has been found to be a reliable index of total body magnesium in most cases (Seelig, 1998), its validity depends on normal handling of magnesium by the kidneys. It has been observed that patients with postviral fatigue syndrome and CFS have significantly low baseline arginine-vasopressin levels when compared with healthy subjects and thus suffer from a partial diabetes insipidus (Bakheit, Behan, Watson, & Morton, 1993; Bell, 1998). This is consistent with the observation of a mild defect in urine concentrating ability in PWCs (De Lorenzo & Kakkar, 1996). It has been observed in rats that low arginine-vasopressin produces excessive urinary magnesium excretion (Bouby et al., 1984; de Rouffignac et al., 1983). Arginine vasopressin has been found to enhance magnesium absorption in the distal tubule of the kidneys in mice (Dai et al., 2001). High magnesium loss observed in children suffering from nocturnal enuresis was corrected by treatment with desmopressin, an antidiuretic analog to arginine-vasopressin (Natochin & Kuznetsova, 2000). Taking all this into account, it would seem that the magnesium loading test may not accurately reflect the magnesium status of PWCs.

Sublingual epithelial cell magnesium was found to correlate well with cardiac tissue magnesium (Haigney et al., 1995), which in turn has been found to correlate well with skeletal muscle tissue magnesium (Moller Jensen et al., 1991). This method may, therefore, be one of the most accurate available for evaluating the magnesium status of the tissues in a relatively noninvasive manner. This method is now commercially available, but a formal study of its application to CFS has not yet been published. However, Seelig (1998) noted, "In a personal communication, C. N. Shealy has informed me that of 25 consecutive CFS patients, 72% exhibited Mg deficiency by the sublingual test." This method should be used in a controlled study, combined with magnesium supplementation and symptom evaluation, to evaluate its effectiveness as a method of measuring the magnesium status of CFS patients.

Based on the previously cited evidence, it is my opinion that there is a magnesium deficiency in CFS. This deficiency may result from excessive magnesium wasting in the urine because of a deficiency in the secretion of arginine-vasopressin or because of excessive urinary excretion of citrate, which is an effective chelator of magnesium. Bioscreen Pty, Ltd. (2000) has reported that increased excretion of citric acid is the most common change they see in the analysis of the urine of pain/fatigue patients and that increased citric acid excretion is associated with increased excretion of positively charged ions such as magnesium. Magnesium deficiency in CFS may also result in part from poor absorption of magnesium by the intestine because of the gastrointestinal problems commonly found in CFS, which were described earlier.

In FM studies, magnesium deficiency was found by Romano and Stiller (1993) and by Magaldi, Moltoni, Biasi, and Marcolongo (2000). Eisinger, Plantamura, Marie, and Ayavou (1994) found normal or below-normal magnesium levels in red blood cells and above-normal levels in white blood cells. Prescott, Norregaard, Rotbol, Pedersen, Danneskiold-Samsoe, and Bulow (1992) and Prescott, Norregaard,

Rotbol, Pedersen, and Danneskiold-Samsoe (1992) did not find magnesium deficiency in FMS.

A few magnesium treatment studies have been reported. In CFS, Cox et al. (1991) performed a randomized double-blind, placebo-controlled trial on patients who exhibited low red blood cell magnesium. Fifteen patients were given 200 mg of IM magnesium (50% magnesium sulfate, 1 g in 2 ml) weekly for six weeks, and 17 were given placebo. Twelve of the 15 who received magnesium reported that they had benefited from the treatment in terms of higher energy level, better emotional state, and less pain, while only three in the placebo group reported benefit. Significant increases in whole blood and red blood cell magnesium were observed in the treatment group but not in the placebo group. After treatment, red cell magnesium was within the normal range in all of the treatment group but in only one of the placebo group.

Clague et al. (1992) performed an open trial in which 12 CFS patients who did not exhibit low blood levels of magnesium were given a 580 mg IV infusion of magnesium. Twenty-four hour urine collection showed that the patients did not retain significantly more magnesium than six controls. The patients did not experience an improvement in symptoms. Because these patients did not have low blood magnesium initially, these results do not contradict those of Cox et al. (1991).

Moorkens et al. (1997) and Manuel y Keenoy et al. (2000), in the study described previously, went on to do a treatment trial. Patients found to be magnesium deficient with the intravenous retention test were asked to participate in a magnesium supplementation trial aiming at dietary intakes of 10 mg of magnesium per kg body weight for at least three months. Of the first 34 who agreed to participate, 24 returned for retesting. In these 24 patients, the magnesium retention on the test decreased from a median of 46% (range of 21% to 88%) to 17% (range of −79% to +95%). Of these 24 patients, however, 11 patients were found to be "nonresponders" in that they maintained a magnesium retention of 20% or more despite supplementation. These nonresponders were found to have persistently lower glutathione levels. Correlations were sought between magnesium status and several parameters related to the oxidant-antioxidant balance. Most of these, including lipid susceptibility to in vitro peroxidation, did not correlate. However, magnesium-deficient patients were found to have lower total antioxidant capacity in plasma, which was related to serum albumin, and serum levels of vitamin E and its interrelated stage of lipid peroxidation were found to be improved by magnesium supplementation.

Two other FM magnesium treatment studies have been reported. Both studies used a combination of magnesium and malic acid (discussed in a later section). Because both studies used this combination, it is not possible to separate the effects of the two supplements.

The first study (Abraham & Flechas, 1992) was an open trial in which 15 FMS patients received a daily oral dosage of 300 to 600 mg of magnesium and 1,200 to 2,400 mg of malate for eight weeks. The mean tender point index was reduced from 19.6 to 6.5, and all patients reported significant improvement of pain within 48 hours of starting the treatment. Six of the patients were then placed on placebo. Within 48 hours, their pain had increased, and by two weeks, their mean tender point index had risen to 21.5.

The second (follow-up) study (Russell, Michalek, Flechas, & Abraham, 1995) was a double-blind crossover study. They used a daily oral dosage of 300 mg of magnesium and 1,200 mg of malic acid as the treatment, alternated with a placebo in random order for four weeks per course, with a two-week washout period before each treatment or placebo course. No clear improvement was found in terms of pain, tenderness, or functional or psychological measures. The double-blind trial was followed by a six-month open-label trial at dosages up to 600 mg of magnesium and 2,400 mg of malic acid. Eighteen patients experienced benefits in pain and tenderness at two months, and 16 continued for the full six months, again reporting benefits in pain and tenderness.

Magnesium has been widely prescribed by clinicians who treat CFS or FM patients. Some use the oral form, with or without malic acid, some use the IM magnesium sulfate form, and some use both (Ali, 1995; Carpman, 1995; Cheney & Lapp, 1993; Conley, 1998; Murray, 1994; Natelson, 1998; Pellegrino, 2001; Stoff & Pellegrino, 1992; Teitelbaum, 1996; Teitelbaum et al., 2001). The fact that the IM-injected form of magnesium continues to be used for treatment of CFS and FM is testimony to belief in its efficacy on the part of many PWCs, because this form of treatment is painful.

Considering all the available evidence, it is this contributor's opinion that magnesium treatment, including oral supplementation and IM and IV injection as part of the Myers' cocktail discussed earlier, is beneficial for many PWCs and PWFs. As discussed by Gaby (2002), certain precautions should be taken with IV injections of magnesium to avoid producing hypotension or hypokalemia.

Potassium   Potassium is the main positive ion inside the cells of the body. Among other functions, potassium is important in the transmission of nerve impulses; the contraction of cardiac, skeletal, and smooth muscle; the production of energy; the synthesis of nucleic acids; the maintenance of intracellular tonicity; and the maintenance of normal blood pressure (Hendler & Rorvik, 2001).

Normally, about 98% of the body's potassium is inside the cells. For this reason, a measurement of total body potassium (TBK) is essentially a measurement of total intracellular potassium. The higher potassium concentration inside cells is maintained by the sodium-potassium ATP-ase ion pumps, which transport potassium into the cells and transport sodium out against the concentration gradients. During exercise, there is a net movement of potassium out of skeletal muscle cells because the ion pumps are unable to keep up with the release of potassium caused by action potentials (Clausen & Everts, 1989).

De Lorenzo and Kakkar (1996) measured the urinary excretion of potassium in 19 CFS patients who met the Holmes et al. (1988) criteria and who also had neurally mediated hypotension and 19 age- and sex-matched healthy controls. They did not find a significant difference in the 24-hour potassium excretion, although they did find a significantly lower urinary concentration of potassium and a significantly higher daily urine volume in the PWCs.

Preedy, Smith, Salisbury, and Peters (1993) measured TBK amounts in five patients who met the Smith (1989) criteria for acute onset postviral fatigue syndrome and found them to be in the normal range, compared to age-, sex-, and height-matched controls.

Burnet, Yeap, Chatterton, and Gaffney (1996) measured the TBK in 20 patients with CFS who met the Oxford (Sharpe et al., 1991), Australian (Lloyd, Hickie, Boughton, Spencer, & Wakefield, 1990), and Fukuda et al. (1994) criteria and 20 healthy age-, sex-, and weight-matched controls. They found significantly lower

TBK in the PWCs (p = .011). To determine whether this measured difference was actually due to differences in intracellular potassium concentrations or only to differences in average total mass of the cells that contain potassium, it was necessary to compare the total lean body mass and bone mass of the patients and controls. A second study (Burnet, Chatterton, Gaffney, & Scroop, 1998) found that eight pairs of the subjects in the Burnet et al. (1996) study who were given whole body DEXA scans showed no significant difference in the amount of lean body mass or total bone mass. These findings, combined with the earlier measurements, indicate that the intracellular potassium concentrations were lower in the PWCs than in the normal controls.

In the second study (Burnet et al., 1998), 51 PWCs were divided into two groups, namely, those with fatigue symptoms only (29 patients) and those who had both fatigue and myalgia (22 patients), based on their own assessments. It was found that only the group with fatigue showed a significant reduction in TBK, and in half, the reduction was more than 10% of normal values estimated for age, weight, and sex. In the group with both fatigue and myalgia, there was no reduction in TBK. They also measured serum potassium levels, which were found to be normal in all subjects.

In a third study (Burnet, Scroop, Chatterton, & Yeap, 1999), PWCs and controls exercised for 10 minutes on a cycle ergometer at a work load of 75% of maximum oxygen consumption. Serial measurements of blood plasma potassium were taken during and after the exercise. It was found that the maximum increase in plasma potassium with exercise in the PWCs was significantly lower than in the controls (p = .013). This lower increase was attributed to the lower TBK found in the earlier studies.

No studies of potassium supplementation in CFS have been reported. However, the symptoms observed in potassium deficiency (muscle weakness, fatigue, mental confusion, irritability, heart disturbances, and problems in nerve conduction and muscle contraction, according to Murray, 1996) exhibit considerable overlap with those seen in CFS. It appears, therefore, that potassium supplementation studies in CFS would be advisable.

Selenium   Selenium is used in four glutathione peroxidase enzymes, three enzymes involved in converting thyroid hormones (T4 to T3), three thioredoxin reductases, and three others. Thus, selenium is very important to the antioxidant system as well as to thyroid hormone function. Selenium deficiency appears to depress the effectiveness of various components of the immune system. Because selenium is not an essential nutrient for plants, the amount in food is a function of the selenium content in the soil on which the food is grown; thus, it varies geographically (Hendler & Rorvik, 2001).

Eisinger, Plantamura, et al. (1994) reported no significant difference between the serum selenium levels measured in 18 French female FM patients and those measured in 20 healthy controls. In a later study involving 25 female patients and 20 controls, Eisinger et al. (1997) found slightly but not significantly decreased plasma selenium.

Reinhard, Schweinsberg, Wernet, and Kotter (1998) measured serum selenium in 68 FM patients (59 females, 9 males) who met the ACR criteria (Wolfe et al., 1990) and in 97 healthy female controls from the Tubingen region of Germany.

They found that the FM patients had significantly lower serum selenium levels than the controls ($p < .05$). This was true when the females were considered separately and when they were considered together with the males. They also found a wider range of serum selenium concentrations in patients than in controls. They did not ascertain whether the participants in the study took mineral supplements.

Although no data have been reported on selenium in CFS, nevertheless, because of its important roles in the antioxidant enzyme system, the conversion of thyroid hormones, and the immune system, all of which have variously been found to be dysfunctional in PWCs, it deserves to receive study. It appears that selenium supplementation is advisable in those PWCs who exhibit oxidative stress, low conversion of the thyroid hormone T4 to T3, or immune dysfunction, which may include essentially all of them. In FM, it appears that selenium should be supplemented because of the observed lower values than in normal controls.

Sodium Sodium is the principal extracellular positively charged ionic species in the body. It is important for regulating the volume of the blood plasma, for acid-base balance, for nerve and muscle function, and for its use by the sodium-potassium ATP-ase ion pump, which is essential for maintaining osmotic balance and cell membrane potentials, among other things.

Many PWCs are unable to be upright for a few minutes without experiencing orthostatic hypotension, accompanied by syncope in some, or orthostatic tachycardia, or both (Bou-Holaigah, Rowe, Kan, & Calkins, 1995; Rowe & Calkins, 1998). Orthostatic hypotension has also been found to be associated with FM (Bou-Holaigah et al., 1997). Orthostatic hypotension and tachycardia have been found to be produced by venous pooling of blood in the lower body, apparently because of impairment of the normal orthostatic increase in norepinephrine release at the terminals of the sympathetic nerves innervating leg veins (Streeten, 2001; Streeten, Thomas, & Bell, 2000). These orthostatic problems may also be aggravated by a partial diabetes insipidus that appears to be present in CFS (see previous magnesium section). A treatment found beneficial is increased consumption of sodium chloride (Rowe & Calkins, 1998). Sodium ions are the most osmotically active component of the blood plasma, and increased plasma osmolality normally provokes intense thirst via the osmoreceptors in the hypothalamus (Ganong, 2001). The ensuing higher intake and retention of water increases the blood volume. Although the kidneys increase their excretion of sodium, a higher steady-state blood volume can be achieved by continued elevated consumption of salt and water. To maintain proper balance between sodium and potassium (Murray, 1996), particularly in view of the findings described in the section on potassium, augmenting the potassium intake should be considered when this treatment is used in CFS.

Zinc Zinc plays catalytic, structural, or regulatory roles in more than 200 metalloenzymes in biological systems. Zinc is required for proper function of the immune system, including T-lymphocyte activity. According to Hendler and Rorvik (2001), zinc deficiency results in a number of abnormalities including the following: thymic involution, depressed delayed hypersensitivity, decreased peripheral T-lymphocyte count, decreased proliferative T-lymphocyte response to phytohemagglutinin (PHA), decreased cytotoxic T-lymphocyte activity, depressed

T helper lymphocyte function, depressed natural killer cell activity, depressed macrophage function (phagocytosis), depressed neutrophil functions (respiratory burst, chemotaxis), and depressed antibody production.

As mentioned earlier, Stewart (1991) found deficient blood serum zinc in 8 of 16 postviral fatigue syndrome patients analyzed. It should be noted that serum zinc measurements are not a sensitive index of zinc status (Institute of Medicine, 2001), so individuals with low serum zinc levels are probably depleted. Jessop (1992, as cited in Werbach, 2000) reported that almost one-third of 1,300 patients in an informal, clinical study were low in zinc as seen in blood tests or as judged by the presence of white spots on nails (leukonychia). Also, as noted earlier, Grant et al. (1996) found the serum zinc levels lower in their CFS patients than in their controls, even though a larger percentage of the former reported using vitamin and mineral supplements at 100% to 200% of the RDA levels. van Rensburg et al. (2001) measured serum zinc in 10 women and 5 men who met the Fukuda et al. (1994) criteria for CFS and age- and sex-matched controls. They found no significant difference. Eisinger, Plantamura, et al. (1994) reported measuring similar levels of serum zinc in 13 FM patients, as compared to 20 age-matched, healthy controls with similar male-female ratios. Rogers (1990) reported that red blood cell zinc levels were abnormally low in 54% of 250 randomly selected patients claiming sensitivity to chemicals.

No studies of zinc supplementation in CFS have been reported; however, because of its observed deficiency in some studies and its importance for the immune system, which is dysfunctional in CFS, as well as for many other biochemical systems in the body, it should receive controlled testing.

PROTEINS AND AMINO ACIDS

Proteins are long chain molecules that are fundamental to the structure and functions of all cells. The collagen framework of the bone, the collagen and elastin of the skin, and the fibers of the muscle cells are all proteins, as are the antibodies of the immune system (Matthews, van Holde, & Ahern, 2000).

Proteins are composed of various proportions of 20 amino acids linked in particular sequences characteristic of the different proteins. These chains assume various shapes, depending on their makeup. Amino acids are smaller molecules that have a central carbon atom (the alpha carbon), a carboxyl group on one end, an amino group (containing a nitrogen atom) on the other end, and a side chain that is characteristic of the particular amino acid. Of the 20 different amino acids that comprise proteins, eight are known to be essential in healthy adults, because they cannot be synthesized in the human body from other nutrients: isoleucine, leucine, lysine, methionine, phenylalanine, threonine, tryptophan, and valine. Two additional amino acids are essential in juveniles: alanine and histidine. Histidine may also be essential in adults, but this has not been proven. The nonessential amino acids used to make proteins are arginine, asparagine, aspartic acid, cysteine, glutamine, glutamic acid, glycine, proline, serine, and tyrosine. Each of the essential amino acids has a different daily requirement, depending on the proportions used in the body's proteins and for other purposes apart from forming proteins. Cysteine can be converted in the body to provide about 30% of the methionine requirement, and tyrosine can be converted to provide about 50% of the phenylalanine requirement.

In addition to contributing to the makeup of proteins, individual amino acids have other special functions in the body. A biologically important amino acid that is not found in protein is taurine. The amino acids found naturally in the body have left-handed chirality. *Chirality* refers to the relative orientation of the chemical groups making up the amino acid molecule. It is possible to construct amino acid molecules with the same set of atoms but oriented differently relative to each other in the molecule. These different configurations are designated as left-handed and right-handed. Because those that occur naturally in biological systems are the left-handed type, their names are often preceded by an *L*, as, for example, L-lysine.

For a normal, healthy, nonpregnant, nonlactating adult, the recommended dietary allowance of U.S. dietary protein is 0.8 grams per kilogram of body weight per day (NRC, 1989), which amounts to about 55 grams per day for a person weighing 150 pounds. In setting this requirement, it was assumed that the intake of the other energy-producing nutrients (carbohydrates and fats) was adequate.

There is evidence that many PWCs are not able to use carbohydrates (St. Amand & Marek, 1999) or fats (Dunstan et al., 2001) properly for the production of energy and that the protein in their bodies is broken down more rapidly than normal. There is also evidence that the concentrations of many of the amino acids are below normal in the blood of PWCs (Bralley & Lord, 1994). Under these conditions, it can be expected that their protein requirements are higher than those of normal, healthy adults. As noted earlier, many PWCs report benefits from diets that are high in protein and low in carbohydrates and fats. Such diets have not yet received controlled study in CFS, but this should be done.

Nondenatured Whey Protein   Until recently, the only important characteristics of a dietary amino acid from a nutritional standpoint were thought to be its amino acid composition and its digestibility (NRC, 1989). This belief was based on the theory that proteins are completely broken down in the digestive tract and are absorbed into the bloodstream as individual amino acids. Later research has shown that this is not true. It is now known that dipeptides, tripeptides, and even some large fragments of proteins and whole proteins are absorbed into the blood (Hemmings & Williams, 1978; Husby, 1988). The absorption of whole immunoglobulins by the gut of young mammals is one example. While there is still much that is not understood about this process, it appears that the process facilitates the development of the still-immature immune system in newborn mammals by admitting substances useful for this purpose.

Bounous, Kongshavn, and Gold (1988) found in experiments with mice that their humoral immune response was significantly higher if they were fed a diet including whey protein concentrate (from cow's milk) than if they were fed a diet of any other type of commercially available food protein. In addition, Bounous and Gold (1991) found that the humoral immune response was highest in mice fed a diet containing nondenatured whey protein. (The pasteurization and processing temperatures currently used in the production of conventional whey protein products change the physical conformation of the protein molecules, i.e., denature them. Avoidance of high temperatures in processing is necessary to produce nondenatured whey protein.) The experiments also showed that this type of whey protein produced higher levels of tissue glutathione. It is known that whey proteins are particularly rich in cysteine and glutamic acid-cysteine neighboring residue pairs (Eigel et al., 1984). Cysteine and glutamic acid are two of the three amino acids needed for the synthesis of glutathione; the third is glycine. It is also known that glutathione is important in the function of the immune system (Packer & Colman, 1999). Bounous and coworkers found that it is not only the amounts of the cysteine or the glutamic acid-cysteine pairs in the protein that matter but also something associated with their physical conformation. The biochemical mechanisms involved in producing this interesting result are not yet understood, but this contributor suspects that low-temperature processing preserves the cysteine in its reduced state, while pasteurization oxidizes it to cystine, which is not as readily useable for the synthesis of glutathione.

Lands, Grey, and Smountas (1999) supplemented nine healthy young adult humans and nine healthy sex- and age-matched controls with a nondenatured whey protein product and casein placebo, respectively, in a randomized, double-blind trial. The dosage was 20 grams per day, and the duration was three months. They found that the lymphocyte glutathione levels increased significantly in the treatment group, but not in the placebo group. Furthermore, both the peak muscle power and the 30-second work capacity increased significantly in the treatment group, but not in the control group.

Cheney tested a nondenatured whey protein product on a small number of PWCs in his practice (Cheney, 1999a, 1999b). He reported success in rebuilding glutathione and in suppressing both viral and intracellular bacterial infections.

No controlled trials of nondenatured whey protein in CFS or FM have yet been reported, but this treatment warrants controlled testing. It appears advisable in such trials to test first for mercury. If elevated mercury levels are found, either a careful detoxification of mercury should be performed before attempting to build glutathione using nondenatured whey protein, or this process should be approached slowly. During supplementation with nondenatured whey protein, indicators of glutathione function, such as urinary lipid peroxides, citric acid and alpha ketoglutarate, or blood cell glutathione should be monitored to assess the growth of the glutathione inventory. Blood serum cysteine levels should also be monitored to guard against cysteine toxicity (Janaky, Varga, Hermann, Saransaari, & Oja, 2000), since some PWCs have inefficient conversion of cysteine to sulfate. These precautions are recommended because it has been found that mercury inhibits the rate limiting enzyme for glutathione synthesis (gamma glutamylcysteine synthetase; Chung, Maines, & Reynolds, 1982) and the enzyme that reduces the oxidized form of glutathione (glutathione reductase; Chung et al., 1982; Zabinski, Dabrowski, Moszczynski, & Rutowski, 2000). Because glutathione normally binds and removes mercury from the body, the possibility should be considered that long-term glutathione depletion in a PWC may have allowed the buildup of mercury in the body. Such a buildup may inhibit the synthesis and chemical reduction of glutathione, resulting in a vicious cycle. In this case, the elevated mercury must be dealt with first by detoxification, or the glutathione must be rebuilt slowly. This detoxification must be performed carefully to avoid transferring mercury into the brain from other tissues.

Because of the observed glutathione depletion in both CFS and FM, and because of the observed efficacy of nondenatured whey protein in building glutathione, this type of supplement appears beneficial in both CFS and FM. The possibility of allergy to whey proteins should be considered when using nondenatured whey protein supplements, but it should not be assumed that an allergy to milk necessarily implies an allergy to the proteins in the whey fraction because the allergen may actually be in the casein, which passes into the curd fraction during the curdling of the milk.

Branched-Chain Amino Acids   The branched-chain amino acids (BCAA) consist of leucine, isoleucine, and valine. These amino acids are oxidized primarily by skeletal muscle. They compete with tryptophan to cross the blood-brain barrier. Castell, Yamamoto, Phoenix, and Newsholme (1999) proposed supplementing BCAAs in CFS. No trials have been reported, but there does appear to be merit to this proposal. As noted earlier, elevated muscle catabolism has been observed in CFS (Dunstan et al., 2000), and abnormally low serum concentrations of the BCAAs have also been reported (Bralley & Lord, 1994). In addition, Logan (2001) and Werbach (2001) have reviewed evidence that serotonergic activity is elevated in CFS. Serotonin is biosynthesized from tryptophan, and elevating BCAA concentrations in the serum by supplementation would tend to reduce the transport of tryptophan into the brain. The suggestion to supplement BCAAs in CFS awaits testing.

Maes et al. (2000) measured the plasma branched-chain amino acids in 21 FM patients who met the ACR criteria (Wolfe et al., 1990) and 33 normal controls. They found the plasma BCAAs to be significantly lower in the PWFs and suggested that a supplementation trial of BCAAs be conducted in FM. Earlier measurements in FM by Russell, Michalek, Vipraio, Fletcher, and Wall (1989) and Yunus, Dailey, Aldag, Masi, and Jobe (1992) had not shown significantly lower BCAA levels. The discrepancy between these findings needs to be resolved. Perhaps the different selection criteria used for the subjects, as listed for the earlier studies in the section on L-tryptophan, explain the different results. However, with our current understanding of these results, the use of branched-chain amino acids in FM does not appear to be warranted.

L-Glutamine   Glutamine is the most abundant amino acid in the body as a whole as well as in the blood and in the skeletal muscles. The primary fuel for the enterocytes, the colonocytes, and the lymphocytes, glutamine is also important for the function of the kidneys. Normally, the main supply of glutamine to the blood comes from the skeletal muscles (Hendler & Rorvik, 2001).

Rowbottom et al. (1998) measured the plasma and muscle glutamine concentrations in 16 PWCs who met the Holmes et al. (1988) criteria and 16 age- and sex-matched healthy controls. They found that the PWCs had significantly lower plasma and muscle glutamine levels ($p < .001$ and $p = .027$, respectively). However, only four of the PWCs had muscle glutamine concentrations that fell below the range of values for the controls. They then performed a 26-week, double-blind, placebo-controlled trial in which PWCs were given either 2 g per day of tablets of glutamine or placebo. No side effects were observed. They found that the glutamine levels in the plasma and muscle increased significantly ($p = .020$ and $p = .037$) in the treatment group but not in the placebo group. However, improvements in symptomatic status were not observed in the treatment group. There was also no difference in the incidence of upper respiratory tract infections. A higher dose of glutamine might have had an observable impact, because the plasma glutamine levels were raised only to the low end of the range found in the controls at the dosage of 2 g per day. According to Hendler and Rorvik (2001), the recommended doses for those with cancer, AIDS, trauma, burns, infections, and other stress-related conditions range from 4 to 21 grams daily.

Because the functions of both the intestines and the immune system are compromised in many PWCs, and because the muscles are in a catabolic state, supplementation with glutamine at higher doses should receive study.

L-Lysine   Lysine has been used to suppress the herpes simplex viruses 1 and 2 (responsible for cold sores and genital lesions, respectively), which require a high arginine to lysine ratio (Hendler & Rorvik, 2001). It is also reported to be effective against the virus *Varicella zoster*, which is responsible for shingles (Balch & Balch, 2000). The most effective dosage schedule appears to be 1,000 milligrams, 3 times per day (Murray & Pizzorno, 1998). Because viral infections abound in CFS, this may provide relief to some PWCs. No tests have been reported in CFS.

L-Serine   Serine is needed for conversion of methionine to cysteine (Matthews et al., 2000). Serine is also in reversible chemical equilibrium with glycine, which means that low serine implies low glycine. Both cysteine and glycine are needed to synthesize glutathione, found to be low in CFS and implicated in the observed state of oxidative stress, as discussed earlier.

The University of Newcastle group in Australia observed significantly lower than normal levels of serine in the urine of PWCs and found that urinary serine excretion was negatively correlated with neurological symptoms and total symptoms (McGregor et al., 1996). Before identified as serine, it was referred to by this group as CFSUM-2. Subsequent work by the group (Butt et al., 1998) found that the low urinary excretion of serine in CFS was associated with a disturbed gastrointestinal microbial flora. Seventeen of 27 PWCs had a significantly lower percentage of E. coli bacteria in their feces than did four controls ($p < .03$). Additional experiments by Butt et al. showed that E. coli bacteria produce serine. It was suggested that an important part of the body's serine supply is normally produced by bacteria in the intestine and that the reason for lower urinary excretion in CFS is that the bacteria that normally provide serine are diminished in number.

Emms, Thrift, et al. (2001) reported an unblinded, nonplacebo-controlled study in which 28 CFS patients satisfying the Fukuda et al. (1994) criteria and having low urinary serine excretion were supplemented with 1 to 3 g L-serine daily ($n = 17$) or in combination with other mineral, protein, or probiotic supplements ($n = 11$). The mean treatment time was 14.6 weeks, with a range up to 74 weeks. The patients completed 86-question symptom severity checklists before and after the treatment. Significant reductions in symptom expression were seen in core CFS diagnostic symptoms—cognitive, neurological, and musculoskeletal symptoms.

Russell et al. (1989) studied 20 FM patients who met the Russell, Vipraio, Morgan, and Bowden (1986) criteria for FM and compared them to 20 normal, pain-free controls matched by age, sex, and race. They found that the FM patients had significantly lower serum serine than did matched normal controls ($p = .028$).

Yunus et al. (1992) found that 29 FM patients who met the Yunus, Masi, and Aldag (1989) criteria had significantly lower serum serine than did 30 healthy controls ($p < .01$). No trials of serine supplementation have been reported in FM.

Because of the promising results of the preliminary studies, serine supplementation should receive double-blind, placebo-controlled study in CFS.

Taurine   Taurine is a nonprotein amino acid synthesized in the body from L-cysteine and the principal free amino acid in many tissues. It is present in high amounts in the brain, retina, myocardium, skeletal and smooth muscle, platelets, and neutrophils. Taurine is involved in formation of bile acid conjugates in the liver, which are essential for fat absorption in the intestine. Taurine serves as an antioxidant, protecting against hypochlorite. Its use has shown some benefit in congestive heart failure, hypertension, and seizures. A great deal is not yet understood about the roles of taurine in human physiology (Hendler & Rorvik, 2001).

Bralley and Lord (1994) found that 64% of the 25 PWCs they studied were low in plasma taurine. No clinical trials have been reported on the use of taurine separately in CFS or FM. However, taurine has received some clinical use, and there are positive reports of its benefits in treating chronic fatigue (Ali, 1995). It should receive controlled testing in CFS.

L-Tryptophan and 5-Hydroxytryptophan (5-HTP)   Tryptophan, one of the essential amino acids, is the precursor for the biosynthesis of serotonin and melatonin. The fact that serotonin has important functions related to pain, mood, and sleep suggests that L-tryptophan may be implicated in CFS and FM. 5-Hydroxytryptophan (5-HTP), a metabolite of tryptophan, is the immediate substrate for biosynthesis of serotonin. While tryptophan can also be used by the body for protein synthesis and the production of niacin and must compete with other amino acids for entry into the brain, 5-HTP is not used for these other purposes and readily crosses the blood-brain barrier without competition (Birdsall, 1998). L-tryptophan is currently not available in the United States as a nutritional supplement, while 5-HTP is. L-tryptophan is available by prescription from compounding pharmacies.

Several measurements of tryptophan in PWCs have been reported. Eaton and Hunnisett (1991) reported that two of 21 patients had abnormally low urinary excretion of tryptophan (less than 30 micromoles per 24 hours), while none of 20 controls did. The patients had severe fatigue of definite onset, lasting more than six months and present more than 50% of the time.

Bralley and Lord (1994) found that 80% of 25 subjects who met the Holmes et al. (1988) criteria were low in plasma tryptophan. Although other amino acids were also found to be low in many subjects, abnormally low tryptophan was observed most frequently.

Rigden (1995) reported that 19 of 24 subjects had abnormal tryptophan levels, but no other details were given.

Castell et al. (1999) found that the pre-exercise concentration of plasma-free tryptophan in PWCs was higher than in controls ($p < .05$) and that it did not change during or after exercise. In contrast, in the control group, the plasma-free tryptophan concentration increased at maximum exercise, peaking at five minutes post-exercise and returning to baseline levels at 60 minutes. During and after exercise, the plasma-free tryptophan levels in the PWCs were thus lower than in the controls.

Vassallo et al. (2001) measured the plasma-free tryptophan concentration and the transport ratio in 20 PWCs. (The *transport ratio* is defined as the ratio of the molar concentration of tryptophan to the sum of the molar concentrations of the other plasma large neutral amino acids. This ratio reflects how readily tryptophan can enter the brain, because it shares a transport mechanism with these other amino acids at the blood/brain barrier.) These PWCs met the ICD-10 (International Classification of Diseases by the World Health Organization) criteria for neurasthenia, and all but one met both the Oxford criteria (Sharpe et al., 1991) and the Fukuda et al. (1994) criteria for CFS. Vassallo et al. found that the values of these parameters were significantly decreased compared to the values in 21 healthy controls. The plasma total tryptophan levels were not significantly different in PWCs and controls. They were not able to explain why the plasma-free tryptophan results differed from those in the Castell et al. (1999) study, though Castell was an author on both. They speculated that the exercise challenge test used in the first study may have been a stressful prospect for the CFS subjects and may thus have affected their free tryptophan levels.

Moldovsky and Warsh (1978) found in studying eight FM patients who met the Moldovsky, Scarisbrick, England, and Smythe (1975) criteria that the plasma-free tryptophan was inversely related to the severity of subjective pain.

Russell et al. (1989) studied 20 female FM patients who met the Russell et al. (1986) criteria and 20 age-, sex-, and race-matched normal controls and found that the FM patients exhibited significantly lower levels of total serum tryptophan ($p = .002$) as well as six other amino acids: alanine, histidine, lysine, proline, serine, and threonine.

Yunus et al. (1992) studied 29 patients who met the Yunus et al. (1989) criteria for FM, compared with 30 healthy controls. They found that the plasma tryptophan level was lower in the FM patients, showing a trend toward significance ($p < .09$). Histidine and serine were found to be significantly lower in the FM patients. They also found that the transport ratio of tryptophan was significantly decreased in the FM patients. In addition, they found that when considering the patients and controls together, the number of reported pain sites as well as poor sleep showed a significant inverse correlation with the tryptophan transport ratio.

Schwarz et al. (1999) studied 51 serum samples from 20 patients who met the ACR criteria (Wolfe et al., 1990). They found a strong negative correlation between Substance P and tryptophan. Substance P is associated with pain, a correlation trending toward significance in this particular study ($p = .075$). High levels of tryptophan were significantly related to low pain scores.

Maes et al. (2000) measured the plasma tryptophan in 21 FM patients who met the ACR criteria (Wolfe et al., 1990) and 33 normal controls. They found no significant difference in plasma tryptophan between the patients and the controls, but there was a trend toward lower values in the FM patients ($p = .051$).

While CFS and FM appear to be similar in the finding of low plasma-free tryptophan in both, Logan (2001) has cited a considerable body of evidence that supports the proposition that they are very different, even opposite, in terms of serotonergic activity. FM has been shown to involve lower than normal serotonergic activity, while in CFS there are several indications that it is higher than normal. Werbach (2001) has also discussed this difference. Thus, supplementing with either L-tryptophan or 5-HTP would probably not be beneficial in CFS. No treatment trials of either used alone have been reported for CFS. However, Bralley and Lord (1994) supplemented the subjects in the study described with a mixture of free-form amino acids, including tryptophan, tailored to the deficiencies found in each subject. The dosage of the amino acid mixture was 15 g per day for three months. Five subjects dropped out, two because of diarrhea and cramping, one because of a complete relapse after two months of improvement, and two for reasons unrelated to the treatment. Of the 20 who completed the trial, 75% experienced 50% to 100% improvement in symptoms, 15% had a 25% to 50% improvement, and 10% had no improvement. Retesting of the plasma amino acids after the treatment showed improvements in the levels, and the number of improved levels was correlated with the degree of symptom improvement. It should be noted that the amino acid mixture they used contained high concentrations of the other plasma large neutral amino acids, which may have limited the effect of the supplemental tryptophan on the transport ratio.

In FM, three treatment trials of 5-HTP have been reported, two by the same group. The first study (Caruso, Sarzi Puttini, Cazzola, & Azzolini, 1990) was a 30-day, double-blind, placebo-controlled study with 50 FM patients who met the Yunus et al. (1981) criteria. Twenty-five of the patients received 100 mg of 5-HTP orally three times per day. The other 25 received placebo. Seven of the treatment group reported side effects, including headache, diarrhea, somnolence, gastric pain, and abdominal pain. Two patients in each group dropped out of the study. In the 5-HTP group, one dropped out for reasons unrelated to the treatment and the other because of diarrhea. In the treatment group, improvement was observed in the number of tender points; the intensity of pain; and the amount of sleep, anxiety, fatigue, and morning stiffness, with both the patients and the physicians concluding that 5-HTP was significantly more effective than placebo.

The second study (Sarzi Puttini & Caruso, 1992) was a 90-day open-label study, again with 50 FM patients meeting the Yunus et al. (1981) criteria and with a treatment of 100 mg of 5-HTP taken orally three times per day. There was significant improvement in all the clinical variables monitored: number of tender points, subjective pain score, morning stiffness, sleep quality, anxiety, and fatigue. Overall evaluation by both the patients and the investigator indicated a "good" or "fair" clinical improvement in about half of the patients at intervals during 15 to 90 days of treatment. Thirty percent of the patients taking 5-HTP reported side effects, including gastric pain, somnolence, diarrhea, headache, paresthesias, myalgias, and abdominal pain, but only one was withdrawn from the study (because of gastric pain).

The third study (Nicolodi & Sicuteri, 1996) was a randomized, 12-month study with sex- and age-matched controls that compared the effects of four treatments: 5-HTP alone, amitriptyline, pargyline or phenelzine, and pargyline or phenelzine together with 5-HTP. When 5-HTP was given alone, the dose was 400 mg per day orally. When given with pargyline or phenelzine, the 5-HTP dose was 200 mg per day orally. A total of 200 subjects met the ACR criteria for FM (Wolfe et al., 1990) and the criteria for migraine. Eight percent of those on 5-HTP alone experienced nonsevere stomachache as a side effect, but none withdrew from the study. All four treatment groups showed significant improvements in pain scores compared to the pain level after the one-month placebo period that was conducted before the treatment trial. The combined treatment of pargyline or phenelzine with 5-HTP produced significantly greater benefit than the other treatments, including 5-HTP alone.

A concern raised about 5-HTP is that some commercially available preparations contain contaminants of the type found in the 5-HTP associated with cases of eosinophilia myalgia syndrome (Klarskov, Johnson, Benson, Gleich, & Naylor, 1999; Michelson et al., 1994; Williamson, Klarskov, Tomlinson, Gleich, & Naylor, 1998). Another concern is that large doses of 5-HTP may theoretically produce a condition known as serotonin syndrome, although not reported to have been produced by 5-HTP in humans. Hendler and Rorvik (2001) do not recommend supplemental 5-HTP. According to these authors, a combination of 5-HTP with carbidopa is available in Europe, and this combination appears to have a safer profile. However, those who wish to use this combination product must do so only under medical supervision and prescription. Doses of 100 mg to 2 g daily are required to observe any desired effect (Hendler & Rorvik, 2001). Without concomitant carbidopa, these doses can be dangerous for some individuals, and lower doses, which are available as dietary supplements, are not likely to have the desired effect (Hendler & Rorvik, 2001).

In addition to these precautions, it would appear to be wise to assess the serotonergic activity in a particular patient as part of the process of deciding whether to use 5-HTP. It appears to be beneficial in FM, which has been shown to involve decreased serotonergic activity, but it may not be beneficial in CFS because of the increased serotonergic activity that appears to be present (Logan, 2001; Werbach, 2001). Because there is considerable comorbidity of these disorders, the use of 5-HTP is probably best decided on a case-by-case basis, and effort should be made to ensure that the preparation used does not contain significant amounts of the contaminants implicated in cases of eosinophilia myalgia syndrome.

L-Tyrosine   Tyrosine is the substrate for the synthesis of dopamine, norepinephrine, and epinephrine, as well as melanin and the thyroid hormones (Matthews et al., 2000).

McGregor et al. (1996) analyzed urine by gas chromatography—mass spectrometry of 20 PWCs who met the Sharpe et al. (1991) criteria and 45 age- and sex-matched controls. They reported that the PWCs had significantly elevated urinary excretion of tyrosine ($p = .02$). This finding was supported by later work by this group in collaboration with the Royal North Shore Hospital, reported by Bligh et al. (1999). They analyzed urine from 100 CFS patients and 83 age- and sex-matched normal controls and found significantly increased urinary tyrosine excretion in the PWCs ($p < .04$). The tyrosine excretion was correlated with symptoms of fatigue, muscle pain, lymph node pain, and cognitive disturbance. Blood serum levels of tyrosine in CFS have not been reported. Russell et al. (1989) and Yunus et al. (1992) reported no significant differences between the blood serum tyrosine levels in PWFs and normal controls. These studies were described in the L-tryptophan section.

In view of the observations of elevated urinary tyrosine in PWCs and normal serum tyrosine levels in PWFs, it does not appear that tyrosine should be specifically supplemented without a finding of low blood serum level in a particular patient.

ESSENTIAL FATTY ACIDS

The essential fatty acids (EFAs) are composed of the omega-3 series based on alpha linolenic acid and the omega-6 series based on linoleic acid. They have two important functions in the body. The first is to become part of the phospholipid structure of all membranes and to confer fluidity and flexibility to them. This affects the function of the various proteins in the membranes and the passage of red blood cells through the capillaries. The second important function of the EFAs is to serve as precursors for synthesis of the eicosonoids, which include the prostaglandins. These play roles in a variety of systems, including the female reproductive cycle, the cardiovascular system, inflammatory responses, and the causation of pain.

Behan, Behan, and Horrobin (1990) measured the concentrations of fatty acids in the phospholipid fraction of the red blood cell membranes of 63 postviral fatigue syndrome patients and 32 normal controls. They found that the patients had significantly reduced levels of total EFAs, especially the omega-6 series, and particularly arachidonic acid and adrenic acid, as compared to the controls.

Howard et al. (1992) reported that deficiencies of EFAs in their CFS patients are common.

Behan et al. (1990) went on to carry out a three-month, randomized, double-blind, placebo-controlled trial of EFA therapy on patients diagnosed with postviral fatigue syndrome. There were 39 patients in the treatment group and 24 in the placebo group. The treatment consisted of a mixture of evening primrose oil and fish oil. The daily dosage included 288 mg gamma-linolenic acid (GLA), 136 mg eicosapentaenoic acid (EPA), 88 mg docosahexaenoic acid (DHA), and 2,040 mg linoleic acid. The placebo included 400 mg of linoleic acid in liquid paraffin. They found that at one month, 74% of the treatment group and 23% of the placebo group assessed themselves as improved over the baseline, with the degree of improvement (in terms of fatigue, myalgia, dizziness, poor concentration, and depression) being much greater in the treatment group. At three months, the corresponding figures were 85% and 17% ($p < .0001$), because the placebo group had reverted toward their baseline state, while those in the treatment group showed continued improvement. The EFA levels in the red blood cell membranes of the placebo group rose, but only the increases in adrenic acid and oleic acid were significant. The EFA levels in the treatment group showed substantially greater increases and were corrected to normal by the end of the trial.

Simpson (1992, 1997) suggested that the beneficial effects of EFAs in postviral fatigue syndrome are due to improvement in blood rheology. He presented evidence of misshapen red blood cells in patients with myalgic encephalomyelitis and recalled earlier work (Simpson, Olds, & Hunter, 1984) in which it had been shown that the filterability of the blood of smokers had been improved by taking evening primrose oil.

Gray and Martinovic (1994) briefly described treatment of a case series in a private general practice setting involving 29 CFS patients and using a combination of dietary EFAs, graded mental/physical activity/exercise, and psychotherapy. Twenty-seven of the 29 showed significant improvement in three months or less, when only 2 of the 29 had shown any improvement over the previous year. Twenty who had been unfit for full-time duties for more than three years before treatment became fit for full-time duties in an average of 111 days after beginning treatment. Twenty-seven of 28 who were followed out to 16 months were still improved compared to pretreatment, and 20 had experienced more improvement beyond that from the initial three months of treatment.

Warren, McKendrick, and Peet (1999) attempted to replicate the Behan et al. (1990) trial. They studied 50 patients who met the Oxford criteria (Sharpe et al., 1991) and 25 age- and sex-matched controls for the first 25 of the patients. The treatment was the same as in the Behan et al. trial, but the placebo was sunflower oil, containing linoleic acid, saturated fatty acids, monounsaturated fatty acids, and a small amount of alpha linolenic acid. It is not clear from the wording in their paper what the daily dose of these was in the placebo group. Before the treatment, they did not see any significant differences in the red blood cell fatty acids composition between the patients and the controls. They also did not see significant differences in posttreatment symptoms between the treatment and control groups, nor did they see significant differences in the fatty acids composition of the red blood cells posttreatment. This lack of significant improvement may not be inconsistent with the Behan et al. study because Warren et al. appear to have sampled a different subset of patients, based on the different criteria and the different findings in initial red blood cell EFA levels. Warren et al. noted that the Oxford criteria (Sharpe et al., 1991), which they used, do not require the patient to have suffered from a demonstrable viral illness, which was a criterion in the Behan et al. (1990) study. Warren et al. also pointed out that it is not clear whether the placebo they used had a therapeutic benefit of its own, because the patients on the sunflower oil placebo showed a trend toward greater improvement than those in the treatment group.

Ozgocmen, Catal, Ardicoglu, and Kamanli (2000) conducted an open-label, noncontrolled, single-blind study of omega-3 EFA treatment in FM. They studied 12 female patients who met the ACR criteria (Wolfe et al., 1990). The treatment consisted of four weeks of 4.5 g of fish oil per day. The daily dose included 1,600 mg of total omega-3 EFAs, of which 810 mg was EPA and 540 mg was DHA. Nine mg of vitamin E were also included. They found significant decreases in total cholesterol, tender point counts, pain, fatigue, and depression and a significant increase in chest expansion.

Taken together, these studies suggest that EFA supplementation can be beneficial in both CFS and FM but that it is important to ascertain whether a deficiency is present before deciding on this treatment, because it did not appear to be helpful when deficiencies were known to be absent. It can be expected that there will be a greater depletion of essential fatty acids in PWCs who have a high state of oxidative stress because the essential fatty acids are polyunsaturated and, as such, are the most vulnerable fatty acids to lipid peroxidation (Levine & Kidd, 1986). This vulnerability is consistent with the fact that a rise in isoprostanes is a sensitive indicator of oxidative stress. This sensitivity can be seen in the work of Kennedy et al. (2003), cited previously in the section on oxidative stress. Isoprostanes result from peroxidation of arachidonic acid, which is an omega-6 fatty acid, one of the two classes of essential fatty acids.

OTHER NUTRIENTS

Alpha Lipoic Acid   Alpha lipoic acid is a cofactor in energy-producing reactions in the body as well as one of the network antioxidants (Packer & Colman, 1999). It is soluble in both water and lipids, readily crosses the blood-brain barrier, and is able to regenerate other antioxidants, including vitamins E and C, coenzyme Q-10, and glutathione. It has been used for the treatment of polyneuropathies and liver disease (Hendler & Rorvik, 2001).

No reports have been published concerning the use of alpha lipoic acid in CFS or FM. However, in view of its important functions in energy production and its great versatility in the antioxidant system, it should be tested but with the following precaution. As with nondenatured whey protein, the mercury level in the body should be tested before using alpha lipoic acid in CFS. If mercury is elevated, it should be carefully detoxified from the body before using alpha lipoic acid. The rationale for this is: If glutathione has been depleted for an extended period in a PWC, it can be expected that mercury might have been allowed to build up, because mercury is normally detoxified from the body by glutathione. I have received anecdotal reports from some PWCs who experienced a worsening of symptoms involving the central nervous system when taking alpha lipoic acid, which they associated with having prior high mercury levels. Although no studies in humans that are directly pertinent to this issue have been published, alpha lipoic acid was found to decrease the biliary excretion of methylmercury in rats (Gregus, Stein, Varga, & Klaassen, 1992). The authors suggested that this resulted from the temporary formation of dihydrolipoic acid-glutathione mixed disulfide and its transport into the bile. Because the glutathione thus transported could not bind methylmercury as it normally does, it was unable to transport methylmercury into the bile. Because methylmercury readily enters the brain and acts as a neurotoxin (Klaassen, 1996), this action of alpha lipoic acid is a plausible basis for the reports from PWCs of worsening of central nervous system symptoms. This issue should receive careful study.

Bioflavonoids   Bioflavonoids are a group of plant pigments that are largely responsible for the colors of many fruits and flowers. They include the oligomeric proanthocyanidins (OPCs) found in grape seeds and the bark of pine trees, quercetin, citrus bioflavonoids, and green tea polyphenols (Murray, 1996). One important property of the bioflavonoids is that they are powerful antioxidants, and they are able to regenerate vitamin C. Because reduced glutathione is depleted in many PWCs and because the reduction of dehydroascorbate (oxidized vitamin C) places an oxidation load on reduced glutathione, Cheney (1999b) has recommended use of bioflavonoids in the treatment of CFS. This suggestion appears to have merit for both CFS and FM. Packer and Colman (1999) noted that Anthony W. Martin has found a particular brand of oligomeric proanthocyanidins helpful in many PWCs. Bioflavonoids should receive controlled study for both CFS and FM.

Bromelain   Bromelain is the collective term for enzymes (principally proteolytic enzymes) derived from the stem, leaves, and fruit of the pineapple plant (Hendler & Rorvik, 2001). Among other properties, bromelain enhances the activity of one of the fibrinolytic enzymes in the body (Ako, Cheung, & Matsuura, 1981). It has been used for the treatment of varicose veins (Murray & Pizzorno, 1998).

Berg, Berg, Couveras, and Harrison (1999) have presented evidence that the blood of many PWCs is hypercoagulated because of immune system activation of coagulation, which deposits fibrin in their capillaries, impeding the flow of blood. Because of the fibrinolysis-enhancing property of bromelain, it may be useful in such cases and should be tested.

Coenzyme Q-10   Coenzyme Q-10 (Co Q-10) is important both for its role of transferring reducing equivalents from glycolysis and the Krebs cycle into the respiratory chain to power the production of ATP and for its role as a member of the basic antioxidant network in the cells. Co Q-10 has been used successfully to treat various types of heart disease (Murray & Pizzorno, 1998).

Langsjoen, Langsjoen, and Folkers (1993) measured blood levels of Co Q-10 in 28 CFS patients as part of a total group of 115 patients who had symptoms of fatigue and activity impairment, atypical precordial pain, and cardiac arrhythmia.

Other patients in the group had diagnoses of hypertensive cardiovascular disease and mitral valve prolapse. The mean Co Q10 level in the patient group as a whole was 0.855 micrograms per ml, compared to 1.07 micrograms per ml for a control group of 54 patients without cardiac disease. The researchers went on to treat this group with Co Q-10 at doses from 180 to 240 milligrams daily, orally, with and without peanut butter, and to examine them at six-month intervals. They found significant increases in the blood level of Co Q-10, correlated with dose and with use of peanut butter, which improved absorption of the Co Q-10. They also found significant improvements in New York Heart Association class, diastolic function measured electrocardiographically, myocardial thickness, and fractional shortening. The blood pressure was restored to normal in the few PWCs who had high blood pressure.

Lister (2002) performed an open, uncontrolled study of the use of Co Q-10 combined with Ginkgo biloba extract in 25 volunteer subjects of either sex who had been clinically diagnosed with FM. The subjects were permitted to continue with prescribed medication but were discouraged from taking additional nutritional supplements. The dosages were 200 mg of Co Q-10 and 200 mg of Ginkgo biloba, standardized to contain 24 mg of flavone glycosides and 6 mg of terpene lactones. These were taken at the same time daily.

Evaluation was performed using the Dartmouth Primary Care Cooperative Information Project/World Organization of Family Doctors (COOP/WONCA) Quality of Life Questionnaire initially and at 4-week intervals for a total of 16 weeks. The subjects also completed a self-rated evaluation of how they felt at the end compared to the beginning and were asked if they wished to continue with the supplements.

Two subjects withdrew for personal reasons, unrelated to the treatments. For the remaining subjects, the quality-of-life scores continued to show improvement after each 4-week interval, with a significant overall improvement at day 84 compared to day zero ($p < .02$). Sixty-four percent felt that the treatment was of some benefit. Nine percent reported feeling worse, and 27% reported no change. Adverse effects were reported by 42% of the subjects, but all were considered to be related to FM and to be of little or no clinical significance. Sixty-eight percent expressed the view that they would like to continue with the treatments. Because this was a combined treatment with both Co Q-10 and Ginkgo biloba, it is not possible to separate the contribution of the Co Q-10 in this study. Nevertheless, the beneficial results are interesting.

Co Q-10 has been found beneficial by CFS clinicians and has been widely used for several years (Holzschlag, 1993; Lapp, 1992). This is understandable in view of the state of oxidative stress and the deficiency in energy production in CFS and the important roles played by Co Q-10 in both the antioxidant system and in mitochondrial energy production. In view of the observed state of oxidative stress in FM, as well as the suggestive results of the small combined study previously cited, it appears that Co Q-10 would also be beneficial in FM. Larger controlled studies would, however, be desirable.

L-Carnitine   Carnitine is synthesized mainly in the liver and the kidneys, and body stores are found mostly in skeletal and cardiac muscle. It has at least two major functions. The first is to transport long-chain fatty acids into the mitochondria where they can be oxidized to produce bioenergy in the form of ATP. The second is to remove short-chain and medium-chain fatty acids from the mitochondria to maintain proper levels of coenzyme A there (Hendler & Rorvik, 2001). Carnitine is present in the blood serum as free carnitine and as acylcarnitine, which is carnitine bound to one of the fatty acids.

Kuratsune et al. (1994) reported measurements of total and free carnitine in the blood serum of 38 Japanese PWCs (19 males and 19 females) who met the Holmes et al. (1988) criteria and a database of 308 normal controls (177 males and 131 females). They calculated the serum acylcarnitine by subtracting the free from the total carnitine. They found that the acylcarnitine was significantly lower in both the male and female PWCs than in the corresponding controls ($p < .001$). They also found that the level of serum acylcarnitine was correlated with the severity of the symptoms.

Grant et al. (1996), in the study described earlier, found a significantly increased ratio of acylcarnitine to free carnitine in the serum of 28 PWCs as compared to 10 normal controls; they also found that serum levels of both free carnitine and acylcarnitine tended to be higher. A high ratio of acylcarnitine to free carnitine has been termed *carnitine insufficiency* and is characteristic of impaired mitochondrial function (Campos et al., 1993).

In a second study, Kuratsune et al. (1998) measured the same parameters as in their first study, but in 57 Swedish female PWCs who met either the Holmes et al. (1988) criteria or the Fukuda et al. (1994) criteria. They found significantly lower levels of both free carnitine and acylcarnitine in 46 normal Swedish females than in the normal Japanese females. In the Swedish female PWCs, the levels of serum acylcarnitine were significantly lower than in the normal Swedish females ($p < .001$), and the levels of free carnitine were also lower ($p < .05$). They also studied more Japanese PWCs (146 patients, of which 64 were males and 82 were females) and compared them to the 308 controls from their first study. They again found significantly lower acylcarnitine in both male and female PWCs.

Plioplys and Plioplys (1995) measured serum carnitine in 35 American patients (27 females and 8 males) who met the Holmes et al. (1988) criteria. They found significantly lower total carnitine, free carnitine, and acylcarnitine in both the female and the male PWCs when compared to Mayo Clinic normative data for total and free carnitine and to the Kuratsune et al. (1994) controls for acylcarnitine. The acylcarnitine levels in the Plioplys PWCs did not differ significantly from those in the Kuratsune PWCs. Plioplys and Plioplys (1995) also found an inverse correlation between fatigue severity and both free and total carnitine.

Majeed, De Simone, Famularo, Marcelline, and Behan (1995) evaluated the serum free and acylcarnitine in 14 male and 13 female Scottish patients who met the Holmes et al. (1988) and Sharpe et al. (1991) criteria, as well as in 80 age- and sex-matched controls. They also evaluated the same parameters in the peripheral blood lymphocytes (PBLs) of 13 male patients. They found that the levels of total, free, and acylcarnitine in the blood serum of the PWCs were not significantly different from those in the controls, although there was a trend ($p < .094$) toward lower levels of serum-free carnitine in the male patients compared to the healthy male controls. They also found that the total, free, and acylcarnitine levels were significantly lower in the PBLs of the PWCs than in those of the controls.

Soetekouw et al. (2000) measured serum carnitine in 25 Dutch female PWCs who met the Fukuda et al. (1994) criteria and 25 matched controls, in a blinded fashion. They did not find significant differences in levels of total carnitine, free carnitine, or 20 carnitine esters between CFS patients and controls. They also did not find a significant correlation between the levels of total carnitine, free carnitine, and acylcarnitine and the score of the Checklist Individual Strength fatigue and Sickness Impact Profile total subscales.

Byrne and Trounce (1987) evaluated total carnitine in muscle biopsies of 11 patients with "chronic disabling asthenia and myalgia of obscure etiology." They found no significant difference compared to a control group of six.

Bengtsson, Cederblad, and Larsson (1990) evaluated total, free, and acylcarnitine from muscle biopsies of 22 Swedish female FM patients who met the Yunus (1981) criteria. They found normal levels. Matsumoto (1999) noted that evidence for a lower than normal level of serum acylcarnitine is lacking in the majority of patients with FM.

Grau et al. (1992) treated 20 Spanish Caucasian patients who met the Holmes et al. (1988) CFS criteria with 4 grams of L-carnitine per day, taken orally, for three months. No significant improvement was reported for any patient at one and three months after treatment began.

Plioplys and Plioplys (1997) treated 28 American patients in an unblinded crossover trial comparing L-carnitine and amantadine (a drug that has been used to treat multiple sclerosis, influenza, and Parkinson's disease). There were 16 females and 12 males, all of whom met the Holmes et al. (1988) criteria, the Australian criteria (Lloyd et al., 1990), the Oxford criteria (Sharpe et al., 1991), and the Fukuda et al. (1994) criteria. The L-carnitine dose was 1 g, three times per day, given orally for two months, with a two-week washout period between the two treatment periods. They found statistically significant clinical improvement in 12 of the studied parameters after eight weeks of treatment. None of the parameters showed deterioration. The greatest improvement took place between four and eight weeks of L-carnitine treatment. They also found that the patients who had higher acylcarnitine levels improved more in the obsessive-compulsive index of the Symptom Checklist 90-R, which consists of multiple psychologic test categories and general summary scales (Derogatis, 1977), and in the CFS Impairment Index total scores. One patient was unable to complete the treatment because of the side effect of diarrhea.

Vermeulen, Kurk, and Scholte (2001) reported on three studies of carnitine-containing substances in CFS, conducted in the Netherlands. The first was an open-label study of 150 patients who satisfied the Fukuda et al. (1994) criteria, using 1 g of L-carnitine twice per day. After six months, 104 of the patients (69%) reported improvement of symptoms of fatigue, cognition, and/or pain.

The second study was a randomized double-blind study with 18 CFS patients. Six were treated with oral acetyl-L-carnitine at 1 g per day plus L-carnitine at 1 g per day. Six received twice the dosage, and the other six received a placebo. After six months, major improvement was reported by four patients in the low dosage group, none in the high dosage group, and one in the placebo group.

The third study was an open-label study involving 90 CFS patients treated with three separate treatments: acetyl-L-carnitine at 1 g twice per day, propionyl-L-carnitine at 1 g twice per day, or both. The patients were evaluated using the following: Clinical Global Impression (CGI), fatigue score (MFI-20), cognition (Stroop test), and pain (MPQ-DLV). At the initial screening, the patients' complaints and cognitive performance were assessed. This was repeated after a two-month no-treatment period, and then the patients were randomly distributed into the three treatment groups and were treated for six months. Two weeks after the last visit in the treatment period, the patients were seen for follow-up.

The results of the third study were that in the no-treatment period, 15% of the patients improved, as evaluated by the CGI. After treatment for six months, 61% improved in the single, low-dosage groups and 36% improved in the double, high dosage group ($p = .05$). The improvement after six months was significant in all groups for the CGI, the fatigue score, and the Stroop test ($p < .05$). At the follow-up, two weeks after the treatment was stopped, 52% of the patients in the low-dose group and 41% in the high-dose group had had a relapse of CFS.

The wide variation in the results of these studies probably results from the heterogeneity of the population defined by the existing criteria for CFS. It does appear, however, that a subset of PWCs has irregularities in levels of free and/or acylcarnitine and that at least some PWCs benefit from supplementation with L-carnitine. There also appear to be racial or perhaps dietary factors that cause differences in the levels of carnitine in the blood serum in normal, healthy people from different countries.

Malic Acid Malic acid is found in both the cytosol and the mitochondria of cells. It serves both as a Krebs cycle intermediate and as part of the malate-aspartate shuttle for transporting reducing equivalents from the cytosol to the mitochondrial matrix. It is thus important in aerobic glycolysis of carbohydrates as well as in complete oxidation of carbohydrates, fats, and proteins to produce bioenergy in the form of ATP.

No tests have been reported concerning the use of malic acid in CFS, but it appears to merit testing, in view of the roles it plays in biochemical processes relevant to CFS.

Two trials have been reported concerning the use of malic acid in conjunction with magnesium to treat FM, as discussed in the earlier section on magnesium (Abraham & Flechas, 1992; Russell et al., 1995). Because malic acid has not been tested independently of magnesium, it is not possible to reach a conclusion about its efficacy alone in FM. However, as discussed in the magnesium section, there is some evidence that larger doses of the combination than were used in the double-blind trial may be beneficial in FM. It may be that larger doses of malic acid alone would be found to produce benefit, but more research is needed to determine this.

MELATONIN

Melatonin is a hormone secreted by the pineal gland. It is involved in setting the timing of circadian rhythms. Recently, melatonin supplementation has become popular in the general population as a possible aid for sleep disorders (Hendler & Rorvik, 2001). A few studies have sought to determine the natural levels and possible benefits of supplementary melatonin in CFS and FM. Other studies have examined the diurnal variation of the melatonin level in relation to other circadian rhythms. Only the studies of melatonin levels and trial treatments are discussed here. Melatonin is included in this chapter because it is sold in the United States as a nutritional supplement.

Korszun et al. (1999) studied the 24-hour melatonin and cortisol levels in nine premenopausal women with FM with or without comorbid CFS (Wolfe et al., 1990, criteria) and eight premenopausal women with CFS (Holmes et al., 1988, criteria), as well as 17 age- and menstrual cycle phase-matched controls. They found that the nighttime (2300 to 0650) plasma melatonin levels were significantly higher in the FM patients than in the controls ($p < .05$), but there was no significant difference in melatonin levels between the CFS patients and the controls.

Knook, Kavelaars, Sinnema, Kuis, and Heijnen (2000) measured the nighttime levels of melatonin in the saliva of 13 adolescent CFS patients (Fukuda et al., 1994, criteria) and 15 healthy age- and sex-matched controls. They found that the melatonin levels were significantly higher in the CFS patients, compared with controls, at midnight, 0100 hours, and 0200 hours ($p < .001$). No differences were observed in timing of melatonin increase in saliva between patients and controls. Time of sleep onset and duration of sleep did not differ significantly between the patients and the controls. However, all the CFS patients and only one of the controls reported unrefreshing sleep.

van de Luit, van der Meulen, Cleophas, and Zwinderman (1998) studied the 24-hour ambulatory blood pressure and heart rate of 17 CFS patients who met the Holmes at al. (1988) criteria and of 12 age- and sex-matched controls with similar body mass indexes. They found that the amplitudes of the variations in systolic and diastolic blood pressure and in heart rate were 2.9 to 9.0 times as large in the CFS patients as in the controls. In particular, the systolic blood pressures of CFS patients consistently fell below 100 mm Hg during the nighttime. In a subsequent open-label pilot study, four of the patients were given 4 mg of melatonin daily for four weeks. This treatment was found to significantly reduce the nighttime systolic blood pressure to even lower values, rather than improving them ($p < .02$). This was accompanied by worsening of symptoms of fatigue.

Williams, Waterhouse, Mugarza, Minors, and Hayden (2002) studied the effects of melatonin and phototherapy separately on PWCs. They began with 62 patients who had been diagnosed using the Oxford criteria (Sharp et al., 1991). Twenty were eliminated for various reasons, including diagnostic uncertainty and reluctance or inability to meet the practical demands of the protocol. Of the 42 patients who entered the study, 12 dropped out variously because of time, social demands, and change of employment. Of the 30 who completed the study, 13 were males, 17 were females, the mean age was 44.5 years, and the mean duration of illness was 3.6 years.

The complete study lasted 60 weeks, including 12-week periods each of melatonin treatment, phototherapy, two placebo periods, and a washout period. The melatonin treatment consisted of 5 mg capsules taken orally each evening for 12 weeks, 2.5 hours before the median time of going to bed for the previous 4 weeks. The phototherapy used a 2,500-lux lightbox. Each morning for 12 weeks the patients sat within 30 cm of the lightbox screen for 1 hour, starting 30 minutes after the median time of rising during the previous 4 weeks. The severity of symptoms and general quality of life were evaluated using visual analog scales, Shortform SF-36 health survey, mental fatigue inventory, and Hospital Anxiety and Depression Scale. The researchers also monitored the body temperature for 48 hours, followed by monitoring blood levels of naturally secreted melatonin under dark conditions.

The results were that neither melatonin treatment nor phototherapy showed any significant effect on any of the principal symptoms or on general measures of physical or mental health. Compared with placebo, neither body temperature rhythm nor onset of melatonin secretion was significantly altered by either treatment, except for a slight advance of temperature phase (0.8 hours, $p = .04$) with phototherapy.

Summarizing the results in CFS, the melatonin levels in one study were not significantly different from normal, and in another study, they were significantly above normal. Thus, no evidence has been presented of a melatonin deficiency in CFS. Furthermore, in the two treatment studies in CFS, melatonin was found to make the symptoms worse in one and to have no effect in the other. Thus, there does not appear to be a basis in the current research literature for the use of supplementary melatonin in CFS. However, I have received anecdotal reports from some PWCs indicating that supplementary melatonin has improved their quality of sleep. Furthermore, clinicians experienced in treating CFS (Lapp, 2003; Teitelbaum, 2002) continue to recommend a trial with melatonin to correct sleep problems in individual PWCs before stronger remedies are tried and report that it is effective in some patients. Because the level of melatonin changes significantly with age, and because it is a hormone, there may be considerable variation in its effects among different subsets of PWCs, as well as between men and women and between adolescents and older adults. Furthermore, the effects may depend strongly on the dosage. A dosage as low as 300 micrograms has been found to be more effective than dosages of several milligrams in some studies of melatonin use (Life Extension Foundation, 2001).

Taking all of this into consideration, it appears that it would be advisable to continue to maintain melatonin as an option to try in treating sleep problems in individual PWCs and that dosages lower than those used in the previously cited studies should be tried. Melatonin appears not to help most PWCs but may be useful in the isolated case.

Concerning studies of melatonin in FM, Wikner, Hirsch, Wetterberg, and Rojdmark (1998) studied the nighttime serum melatonin levels and the nighttime urinary melatonin excretion in eight FM patients (Wolfe et al., 1990 criteria) and eight healthy age-, sex-, and body mass index-matched controls. They found that the FM patients had 31% lower melatonin secretion (as determined from serum melatonin levels) during the hours of darkness (2300 to 0700 hours) than the controls ($p < .05$) and that the peak value of serum melatonin was significantly lower in the patient group ($p < .05$). The timing of the peak serum melatonin value did not differ significantly between the two groups. When the total melatonin secretion was determined for the longer time interval between 1800 and 0800 hours, it was found that the total melatonin secretion over this period did not differ significantly between the two groups. Furthermore, the difference in the amount of melatonin excreted in the urine for the two groups was also not statistically significant.

Press et al. (1998) measured the nocturnal levels of 6-sulphatoxymelatonin, a metabolite of melatonin, in the urine (collected from 2200 to 0700 hours) of 39 female FM patients (Wolfe et al., 1990, criteria) and 39 age-matched healthy female controls. They found that the levels were not significantly different for the two groups. Furthermore, among individual patients, they did not find any correlation between the level of this metabolite and disease duration, reproductive status, sleep, and mood disturbances. These researchers also conducted a survey on the Internet of FM patients who were using melatonin, specifically asking to what degree melatonin helped to relieve their pain. Forty-four patients responded. Their average dosage was 3 mg per day. Almost half reported that melatonin had no effect on their pain. Thirty percent reported a slight effect, and 20% reported moderate to major effect. The authors viewed these results as interesting, though not scientific.

Klerman, Goldenberg, Brown, Maliszewski, and Adler (2001) monitored the melatonin levels in the blood of 10 premenopausal women with FM (Wolfe et al., 1990, criteria) and 12 healthy premenopausal control women during constant routine, low-light conditions. They found no significant differences between the two groups in the peak and trough values of melatonin or in the average values over 24 hours of the constant routine. In comparing their results to the contrasting results of Wikner et al. (1998) and Korszun et al. (1999), Klerman et al. suggested that these earlier studies may have used light levels that were high enough to partially suppress melatonin levels. While this may explain why there were different results between Klerman et al. and the earlier studies, it does not explain why differences were seen between the FM patients and the control groups in these earlier studies.

Citera et al. (2000) treated 21 consecutive clinical FM patients (19 of whom completed the study) with 3 mg of melatonin at bedtime in a four-week, open-label pilot study. Symptom severities were monitored, and urinary 6-sulphatoxymelatonin levels were measured in the 21 patients and in 20 age- and sex-matched healthy controls. There was no placebo control. At day 30, several parameters were found to be significantly improved with melatonin treatment: the median values for the tender point count and severity of pain at selected points, patient and physician global assessments, and visual analogue scale assessment of pain and sleep. Other variables also improved but did not reach clinical significance. Lower levels of the melatonin metabolite were found in the FM patients as compared with the controls ($p = .06$).

The reports of the measurement of melatonin levels in FM patients appear to be contradictory, with one showing them to be higher than normal, one lower than normal, and two suggesting that they are not significantly different from normal. The only treatment study that has been reported did suggest benefits, but it lacked placebo control. Under these circumstances, it is not possible to reach a firm conclusion about the efficacy of melatonin supplementation in FM. A larger, randomized placebo-controlled double-blind study is needed.

Methylsulfonylmethane (MSM)   MSM is an organic sulfur-containing compound that occurs naturally in a variety of fruits, vegetables, grains, and in animals, including humans, in at least trace amounts. The biological role of MSM is not known (Hendler & Rorvik, 2001). Sulfur from MSM was found to be incorporated into protein methionine and cysteine when fed to guinea pigs (Richmond, 1986). MSM has also been found to be absorbed by humans and to cross the blood-brain barrier (Rose, Chalk, Galloway, & Doddrell, 2000).

While no controlled clinical trials have been reported, MSM has been used to relieve pain in FM at typical dosages of 2 to 10 grams per day. Anecdotal reports are positive (Jacob, Lawrence, & Zucker, 1999). MSM should receive controlled testing in FM.

S-adenosylmethionine (SAMe)   The function of SAMe in the body is to donate a one-carbon methyl group in the process called *methylation*. SAMe is formed in the body by a reaction between methionine and ATP. It serves as the methyl group donor in the biosynthesis of DNA and RNA nucleic acids, phospholipids, proteins, epinephrine, melatonin, creatine, and other molecules (Hendler & Rorvik, 2001). SAMe is important in the synthesis of several sulfur-containing compounds in the body, including glutathione, taurine, and various sulfur-containing cartilage components. It has been used for the treatment of depression, osteoarthritis, liver disorders, migraine, and FM (Murray, 1996).

No reports have been published on the use of SAMe in CFS, but there have been several studies in FM (Di Benedetto, Iona, & Zidarich, 1993; Grassetto & Varotto, 1994; Jacobsen, Danneskiold-Samsoe, & Andersen, 1991; Tavoni, Vitali, Bombardieri, & Pasero, 1987).

The first study (Tavoni et al., 1987) was a randomized, double-blind, placebo-controlled crossover study of 17 PWFs using a daily dose of 200 mg of SAMe intramuscularly and placebo for 21 days, with a two-week washout period. This study found that the number of trigger points and painful anatomic sites decreased significantly with the treatment ($p < .02$) but not with the placebo. In addition, scores on both the Hamilton and the Scala di Autovalutazione per la Depressione (SAD) rating scales improved after SAMe treatment ($p < .05$ and $p < .005$, respectively), but there were no significant changes after placebo. No major side effects were observed.

The second study (B. Jacobsen et al., 1991) was a randomized, double-blind, placebo-controlled study with 22 PWFs in the treatment group and 22 PWFs in the placebo group. The two groups received a daily dose of 800 mg SAMe and placebo, respectively. The treatment period was six weeks. Improvements were seen in clinical disease activity ($p = .04$), pain experienced during the last week ($p = .002$), fatigue ($p = .02$), morning stiffness ($p = .03$), and mood evaluated by Face Scale ($p = .006$) in the treatment group compared to placebo. The tender point score, isokinetic muscle strength, mood evaluated by the Beck Depression Inventory, and side effects did not differ between the two groups.

The third study (Di Benedetto et al., 1993) was a randomized, open comparison between treatment with SAMe and with TENS (transcutaneous electrical nerve stimulation), with 15 PWFs in each group. The treatments lasted six weeks, and the SAMe dose was 200 mg intramuscularly and 400 mg orally per day. It was found that the SAMe treatment significantly decreased the total number of tender points ($p < .01$), had a significant beneficial effect on the subjective symptoms of pain and fatigue ($p < .05$), and significantly reduced the scores on the Hamilton Depression and Anxiety Rating Scales and Zung's Self-Rating Scale for Depression. SAMe was found to be devoid of adverse effects.

The fourth study (Grassetto & Varotto, 1994) was an open, nonplacebo-controlled study involving 47 PWFs for a period of six weeks, using a daily SAMe dose of 200 mg intramuscularly plus 800 mg orally. In this study, SAMe was found to significantly decrease the tenderness of painful sites ($p < .01$), significantly improve the general well-being evaluated by the Visual Analog Scale ($p < .01$), and significantly reduce the mean scores for the Hamilton Rating Scale for Depression, the Zung Self-Rating Scale, the Hamilton Rating Scale for Anxiety, and Lorish and Maisiak's Face Scale (all $p < .01$). SAMe was well-tolerated and no adverse side effects were reported.

Additional studies in FM and precautions to be taken in the use of SAMe are discussed by Fetrow and Avila (2001).

There appears to be good evidence that SAMe is useful in the treatment of FM. It should also be tested for CFS. No significant side effects have been reported. However, individuals with bipolar disorder should not take SAMe unless under strict medical supervision because it may lead to the manic phase in these people (Murray, 1996). It is advisable to supplement with vitamins B6, B12, and folic acid when supplementing with SAMe to prevent the buildup of homocysteine, which increases the risk of heart disease (Hendler & Rorvik, 2001).

CONCLUSIONS ABOUT THE USE OF DIET AND NUTRITIONAL SUPPLEMENTS IN CHRONIC FATIGUE SYNDROME AND FIBROMYALGIA BASED ON REVIEW OF THE LITERATURE

Data on the use of diet and nutritional supplements in chronic fatigue syndrome and fibromyalgia are far from complete, and many of the relevant studies have not yet been replicated. The population currently diagnosed with CFS in particular appears to be heterogeneous, being composed of a number of subsets. Nevertheless, it is possible, based on the literature, to provide some suggestions that may be of help in these disorders. The application of these nutritional approaches to

Table 27.2
Nutritional Supplementation for CFS*

Nutrient	Tentative Protocol	Possible Benefits
Folic Acid	1–10 mg/day (3-month trial)	↓Fatigue and depression; improved immune function
Vitamin B12	Total of 6,000–70,000 μg IM/week (3-week trial)	↓Fatigue, depression, and pain; improved microcirculation
Vitamin C	10–15 g daily	Improved immune function, ↓pain; improved microcirculation
Magnesium	If ↓ RBC Mg: 100 mg IM/week × 6 weeks —And malic acid Mg: 600 mg/day; malic acid 2,400 mg/day (8-week trial)	Subjective improvement ↓Muscle pain
Sodium	If diagnosis of neurally mediated hypotension: ↑Sodium intake moderately	Subjective improvement
Zinc	135 mg/day × 15 days	↑Muscle strength and endurance; ↓pain and fatigue; improved immune function
L-Tryptophan	In fibromyalgia: 5-hydroxytryptophan 100 mg 3 times daily (3-month trial)	↓Pain and fatigue
L-Carnitine	1–2 g 3 times daily (3-month trial)	Improvement that can be dramatic
Coenzyme Q-10	100 mg daily (3-month trial)	Marked improvement with ↑muscle endurance
Essential fatty acids	280 mg GLA and 135 mg EPA daily (3-month trial)	General improvement

*Note: Werbach recommended that "a general high-potency vitamin/mineral supplement" be used together with the supplements listed in this table. Reprinted with permission from "Nutritional Strategies for Treating Chronic Fatigue Syndrome," by M. R. Werbach, 2000, *Alternative Medicine Review, 5*, pp. 93–108.

individual cases should be medically supervised and will require considerable reliance on individual testing and clinical experience. It should be taken into account that individual nutrients may be more likely to be beneficial in subsets of individuals who exhibit particular deficiencies for them or symptomatology that has been found to benefit specifically from them.

A previous review of the use of individual nutrients in these disorders was made by Werbach (2000), and his recommendations are reproduced by permission in Table 27.2. Although I am largely in agreement with these recommendations, differences and additions are noted in Table 27.1 (see pp. 592–593).

In terms of diet for CFS, I suggest that high-protein, low-carbohydrate, low-fat diets be explored, augmented by the supplements listed in Table 27.1.

It appears that vegan diets, augmented by the supplements listed in Table 27.1 to reduce the likelihood of deficiencies, should be tested in FM for longer times than a few months.

Table 27.1 presents a compilation of dosage ranges for individual nutrients for both CFS and FM, based on review of the literature. Table 27.1 includes not only those nutrients found to be particularly beneficial to tested groups of people with these disorders, but also nutrients currently held to be essential by the Institute of Medicine of the National Academy of Sciences. The latter have been included to ensure that nutritional treatment of these disorders is complete and balanced. Because a state of oxidative stress has been shown to be present in many people with CFS and FM, Table 27.1 includes significant dosages of several antioxidants. Where possible, the dosage ranges for nutrients found to be particularly beneficial are based on the review of CFS and FM literature. In other cases, the dosages have been determined based on guidance not only from the Institute of Medicine (1997, 1998, 2000, 2001), but also from Hendler and Rorvik (2001) and from Murray (1996).

THE FUTURE: DIFFERENTIATION OF SUBSETS AND HYPOTHESIS-DRIVEN NUTRITIONAL APPROACHES

Further significant advances in the application of nutrition to the treatment of CFS and FM, as well as further significant advances in treatment in general, will require two main thrusts:

1. Interdisciplinary efforts to separate the current heterogeneous population into a commonly agreed-on set of well-defined subsets.
2. More emphasis on hypothesis-driven research.

Division into subsets is necessary to more effectively target nutritional approaches to this heterogeneous population, as well as to provide more well-defined groups for more precise study of etiology and pathogenesis.

Comprehensive hypotheses are needed for the various subsets that cover etiology, pathogenesis, and pathophysiology and have their basis at the biochemical and physiological levels. These hypotheses should span several different medical specialties, in view of the wide range of symptomatology observed.

Useful information for constructing such hypotheses will be supplied by patient responses to nutritional approaches that have been used in the past, together with a wide variety of other pertinent types of data. These data are available from epidemiology; genetic studies; patient histories, including circumstances of onset, courses of illness, and symptomatology; immunology; neuroendocrinology; microbiology; biochemical parameter measurements; brain scanning results; response to pharmaceutical treatments; physiological measurements; and others.

Because of the indispensable nature of nutrition in health and disease, as well as its close and detailed interaction with metabolism, nutrition will continue to play an important role both in these hypotheses themselves and in treatments that result from them.

REFERENCES

Aaron, L. A., & Buchwald, D. (2001) A review of the evidence for overlap among unexplained clinical conditions. *Annals of Internal Medicine, 134,* 868–881.

Abraham, G. E., & Flechas, J. D. (1992). Management of fibromyalgia: Rationale for the use of magnesium and malic acid. *Journal of Nutritional Medicine, 3,* 49–59.

Ako, H., Cheung, A. H., & Matsuura, P. K. (1981). Isolation of a fibrinolysis enzyme activator from commercial bromelain. *Archives Internationales de Pharmacodynamie et de therapie [International Archives of Pharmacodynamics and Therapy], 254*(1), 157–167.

Alaimo, K., McDowell, M. A., Briefel, R. R., Bischof, A. M., Caughman, C. R., Loria, C. M., et al. (1994). *Dietary intake of vitamins, minerals, and fiber of persons aged 2 months and over in the United States: Third national health and nutrition examination survey* (Phase I, 1988–91. Advance data from vital and health statistics; no. 258). Hyattsville, MD: U.S. Department of Health and Human Services, National Center for Health Statistics.

Ali, M. (1990). Ascorbic acid reverses abnormal erythrocyte morphology in chronic fatigue syndrome [Abstract]. *American Journal of Clinical Pathology, 94,* 515.

Ali, M. (1993). Hypothesis: Chronic fatigue is a state of accelerated oxidative molecular injury. *Journal of Advancement in Medicine, 6*(2), 83–96.

Ali, M. (1995). *The canary and chronic fatigue.* Denville, NJ: Life Span Press.

Altura, B. T., Burack, J. L., Cracco, R. Q., Galland, L., Handwerker, S. M., Markell, M. S., et al. (1994). *Scandinavian Journal of Clinical Laboratory Investigation, 54*(Suppl. 217), 53–67.

Appelboom, T., & Schoutens, A. (1990). High bone turnover in fibromyalgia. *Calciferous Tissue International, 46,* 314–317.

Bakheit, A. M., Behan, P. O., Watson, W. S., & Morton, J. J. (1993). Abnormal arginine-vasopressin secretion and water metabolism in patients with postviral fatigue syndrome. *Acta Neurologica Scandinavica, 87*(3), 234–238.

Balch, P. A., & Balch, J. F. (2000). *Prescription for nutritional healing* (3rd ed.). New York: Avery/Penguin Putnam.

Baron, R. B. (2001). Nutrition. In L. M. Tierney, Jr., S. J. McPhee, & M. A. Papadakis (Eds.), *Current medical diagnosis and treatment* (40th ed., p. 1222). New York: McGraw-Hill.

Behan, P. O., Behan, W. M., & Horrobin, D. (1990). Effect of high doses of essential fatty acids on the postviral fatigue syndrome. *Acta Neurologica Scandinavica, 82,* 209–216.

Bell, D. S. (1998). Vasopressin, circulating blood volume and CFS [Abstract]. *Proceedings of the 1998 Sydney Conference on Chronic Fatigue Syndrome,* Alison Hunter Memorial Foundation, P.O. Box 2093, BOWRAL NSW 2576, Australia.

Bellanti, J. A. (2000). Response to letters to the editor. *Annals of Allergy, Asthma, and Immunology, 84,* 639–640.

Bengtsson, A., Cederblad, G., & Larsson, J. (1990). Carnitine levels in painful muscles of patients with FM. *Clinical and Experimental Rheumatology, 8,* 197–200.

Bengtsson, A., Henriksson, K. G., Jorfeldt, L., Kagedal, B., Lennmarken, C., & Lindstrom, F. (1986). Primary fibromyalgia, a clinical and laboratory study of 55 patients. *Scandinavian Journal of Rheumatology, 15*, 340–347.

Berg, D., Berg, L. H., Couveras, J., & Harrison, H. (1999). Chronic fatigue syndrome and/or FM as a variation of antiphospholipid antibody syndrome: An explanatory model and approach to laboratory diagnosis. *Blood Coagulation and Fibrinolysis, 10*(7), 435–438.

Bioscreen Pty, Ltd. (2000). Bioscreen Information Service. Available from http://www .bioscreen.com.au.

Birdsall, T. C. (1998). 5-Hydroxytryptophan: A clinically-effective serotonin precursor. *Alternative Medicine Review, 3*(4), 271–280.

Bligh, P. C., Niblett, S., Hoskin, L., Dunstan, R. H., Fulcher, G., McGregor, N., et al. (1999). Biochemical abnormalities in chronic fatigue syndrome [Abstract]. *Proceedings of the 1999 Sydney Conference on Chronic Fatigue Syndrome,* Alison Hunter Memorial Foundation, P.O. Box 2093, BOWRAL NSW 2576, Australia.

Botez, M. I., Botez, T., Leveille, J., Bielmann, P., & Cadotte, M. (1979). Neuropsychological correlates of folic acid deficiency: Facts and hypotheses. In M. I. Botez & E. H. Reynolds (Eds.), *Folic acid in neurology, psychiatry, and internal medicine* (pp. 435–461). New York: Raven Press.

Bouby, N., Trinh-Trang-Tan, M. M., & Bankir, L. (1984). Stimulation of tubular reabsorption of magnesium and calcium by antidiuretic hormone in conscious rats. Study in Brattleboro rats with hereditary hypothalamic diabetes insipidus. *Pflugers Archiv: European Journal of Physiology, 402*(4), 458–464.

Bou-Holaigah, I., Calkins, H., Flynn, J. A., Tunin, C., Chang, H. C., Kan, J. S., et al. (1997). Provocation of hypotension and pain during upright tilt table testing in adults with FM. *Clinical and Experimental Rheumatology, 15*, 239–246.

Bou-Holaigah, I., Rowe, P. C., Kan, J., & Calkins, H. (1995). The relationship between neurally mediated hypotension and the chronic fatigue syndrome. *Journal of the American Medical Association, 274*(12), 961–967.

Bounous, G., & Gold, P. (1991). The biological activity of undenatured dietary whey proteins: Role of glutathione. *Clinical and Investigative Medicine, 14*, 296–309.

Bounous, G., Kongshavn, P., & Gold, P. (1988). The immunoenhancing property of dietary whey protein concentrate. *Clinical and Investigative Medicine, 11*, 271–278.

Bralley, J. A., & Lord, R. S. (1994). Treatment of chronic fatigue syndrome with specific amino acid supplementation. *Journal of Applied Nutrition, 46*(3), 74–78.

Brouwers, F. M., van der Werf, S., Bleijenberg, G., van der See, L., & van der Meer, J. W. M. (2002). The effect of a polynutrient supplement on fatigue and physical activity of patients with chronic fatigue syndrome: A double-blind randomized controlled trial. *Quarterly Journal of Medicine, 95* 677–683.

Burckhardt, C. S., Dark, S. R., & Bennett, R. M. (1991). The Fibromyalgia Impact Questionnaire: Development and validation. *Journal of Rheumatology, 18*, 728–733.

Burnet, R. B., & Chatterton, B. E. (2001). Gastro-intestinal symptoms and gastric emptying studies in chronic fatigue syndrome [Abstract]. *Proceedings of the Third International Clinical and Scientific Meeting on Myalgic Encephalopathy/Chronic Fatigue Syndrome,* Alison Hunter Memorial Foundation, P.O. Box 2093, BOWRAL NSW 2576, Australia.

Burnet, R. B., Chatterton, B. E., Gaffney, R. D., & Scroop, G. C. (1998). Total body potassium in the chronic fatigue syndrome [Abstract]. *Proceedings of the 1998 Sydney Chronic Fatigue Syndrome Conference,* Alison Hunter Memorial Foundation, P.O. Box 2093, BOWRAL NSW 2576, Australia.

Burnet, R. B., Scroop, G. C., Chatterton, B. E., & Yeap, B. B. (1999). Serum potassium and hormone responses to exercise in chronic fatigue syndrome [Abstract]. *Proceedings of the 1999 Sydney Chronic Fatigue Syndrome Conference,* Alison Hunter Memorial Foundation, P.O. Box 2093, BOWRAL NSW 2576, Australia.

Burnet, R. B., Yeap, B. B., Chatterton, B. E., & Gaffney, R. D. (1996). Chronic fatigue syndrome: Is total body potassium important? [Letter]. *Medical Journal of Australia, 164,* 384.

Butt, H. L., Dunstan, R. H., McGregor, N. R., & Roberts, T. K. (2001). Bacterial colonosis in patients with persistent fatigue [Abstract]. *Proceedings of the Third International Clinical and Scientific Meeting on Myalgic Encephalopathy/Chronic Fatigue Syndrome,* Alison Hunter Memorial Foundation, P.O. Box 2093, BOWRAL NSW 2576, Australia.

Butt, H. L., Dunstan, R. H., McGregor, N. R., Roberts, T. K., Harrison, T. L., & Grainger, J. R. (1998). Low urinary serine output is associated with an altered faecal microbial flora in chronic fatigue/pain patients [Abstract]. *Proceedings of the 1998 Sydney Chronic Fatigue Syndrome Conference,* Alison Hunter Memorial Foundation, P.O. Box 2093, BOWRAL NSW 2576, Australia.

Byrne, E., & Trounce, I. (1987). Chronic fatigue and myalgia syndrome: Mitochondrial and glycolytic studies in skeletal muscle. *Journal of Neurology, Neurosurgery, and Psychiatry, 50,* 743–746.

Campos, Y., Huertas, R., Lorenzo, G., Bautista, J., Gutierrez, E., Aparicio, M., et al. (1993). Plasma carnitine insufficiency and effectiveness of L-carnitine therapy in patients with mitochondrial myopathy. *Muscle and Nerve, 16,* 150–153.

Carpman, V. (1995). CFIDS treatment: The Cheney Clinic's strategic approach. *CFIDS Chronicle, 8*(2), 38–45.

Caruso, I., Sarzi Puttini, P., Cazzola, M., & Azzolini, V. (1990). Double-blind study of 5-hydroxytryptophan versus placebo in the treatment of primary FM syndrome. *Journal of International Medical Research, 18,* 201–209.

Castell, L. M., Yamamoto, T., Phoenix, J., & Newsholme, E. A. (1999). The role of tryptophan in fatigue in different conditions of stress. In G. Huether, W. Kochen, T. J. Simat, & H. Steinhart (Eds.), *Tryptophan, serotonin, and melatonin—basic aspects and applications* (pp. 697–704). New York: Kluwer Academic/Plenum Press.

Cheney, P. R. (1999a). *Evidence of glutathione deficiency in chronic fatigue syndrome.* American Biologics 11th International Symposium, Vienna, Austria. Tape No. 07–199 available from Professional Audio Recording, P.O. Box 7455, La Verne, CA 91750 (1-800-227-4473).

Cheney, P. R. (1999b). Chronic fatigue syndrome: A perspective on pathophysiology, diagnosis, and treatment. Lecture presented to the CFIDS Support Group of Dallas-Fort Worth, Euless, Texas, on May 15, 1999. Video tape available from Carol Sieverling, 513 Janann St., Euless, TX 76039.

Cheney, P. R., & Lapp, C. W. (1993, Fall). Entero-hepatic resuscitation in patients with chronic fatigue syndrome: A pyramid of nutritional therapy. *CFIDS Chronicle,* 1–3.

Chung, A. S., Maines, M. D., & Reynolds, W. A. (1982). Inhibition of the enzymes of glutathione metabolism by mercuric chloride in the rat kidney: Reversal by selenium. *Biochemical Pharmacology, 31*(19), 3093–3100.

Citera, G., Arias, M. A., Maldonado-Cocco, J. A., Lazaro, M. A., Rosemffet, M. G., Brusco, L. I., et al. (2000). The effect of melatonin in patients with fibromyalgia: A pilot study. *Clinical Rheumatology, 19*(1), 9–13.

Clague, J. E., Edwards, R. H., & Jackson, M. J. (1992). Intravenous magnesium loading in chronic fatigue syndrome. *Lancet, 340,* 124–125.

Clausen, T., & Everts, M. E. (1989). Regulation of the Na, K-pump in skeletal muscle. *Kidney International, 35,* 1–13.

Cleveland, L. E., Goldman, J. D., & Borrud, L. G. (1996). *Data tables: Results from USDA's 1994 continuing survey of food intakes by individuals and 1994 diet and health knowledge survey.* Beltsville, MD: U.S. Department of Agriculture, Agricultural Research Service.

Coghlan, H. C., & Natello, G. (1992). Erythrocyte magnesium in symptomatic patients with primary mitral valve prolapse: Relationship to symptoms, mitral leaflet thickness, joint hypermobility and autonomic regulation. *Magnesium and Trace Elements, 10*(2/4), 205–214.

Colquhoun, D., & Senn, S. (2000). Letter to the editor. *Annals of Allergy, Asthma, and Immunology, 84,* 639.

Conley, E. J. (1998). *America exhausted—breakthrough treatments of fatigue and fibromyalgia.* Flint, MI: Vitality Press.

Corsello, S. (1999). *The ageless woman.* New York: Corsello Communications. Available from http://www.corsello.com.

Cox, I. M., Campbell, M. J., & Dowson, D. (1991). Red blood cell magnesium and chronic fatigue syndrome. *Lancet, 337,* 757–760.

Cozon, G. J. N., Perret-Liaudet, A., Fatoohi, A. F., & Brunet, J.-L. (2003). In vivo and in vitro abnormal cellular reactivity to Candida albicans in patients with CFS [Abstract]. *Conference syllabus, sixth international conference on chronic fatigue syndrome, fibromyalgia and related illnesses.* Chantilly, VA: American Association for Chronic Fatigue Syndrome.

Crook, W. G. (2001). *Tired, So Tired and the Yeast Connection* (p. 39). Jackson, TN: Professional Books.

Dai, L. J., Ritchie, G., Kerstan, D., Kang, H. S., Cole, D. E., & Quamme, G. A. (2001). Magnesium transport in the renal distal convoluted tubule. *Physiological Review, 81*(1), 51–84.

De Lorenzo, F., & Kakkar, V. V. (1996). Twenty-four-hour urine analysis in patients with orthostatic hypotension and chronic fatigue syndrome. *Australia and New Zealand Journal of Medicine, 26,* 849–850.

Derogatis, L. R. (1977). *SCL-R-90 scoring manual. I: Scoring, administration and procedures.* Baltimore: Johns Hopkins University School of Medicine, Clinical Psychometrics Unit.

de Rouffignac, C., Corman, B., & Roinel, N. (1983). Stimulation by antidiuretic hormone of electrolyte tubular reabsorption in rat kidney. *American Journal of Physiology, 244*(2), F156–F164.

Dettori, A. G., & Ponari, O. (1973). Antalgic effect of cobamide in the course of peripheral neuropathies of different etiopathogenesis. *Minerva Medica, 64*(21), 1077–1082.

Deulofeu, R., Gascon, J., Gimenez, N., & Corachan, M. (1991). Magnesium and chronic fatigue syndrome [Letter]. *Lancet, 338,* 641.

Di Benedetto, P., Iona, L. G., & Zidarich, V. (1993). Clinical evaluation of S-adenosyl-L-methionine versus transcutaneous electrical nerve stimulation in primary FM. *Current Therapeutic Research, 53*(2), 222–229.

Donaldson, M. S. (2000). Metabolic vitamin B12 status on a mostly raw vegan diet with follow-up using tablets, nutritional yeast, or probiotic supplements. *Annals of Nutrition and Metabolism, 44,* 229–234.

Donaldson, M. S., Speight, N., & Loomis, S. (2001). Fibromyalgia syndrome improved using a mostly raw vegetarian diet: An observational study. *BMC Complementary and Alternative Medicine, 1,* 7.

Dunstan, R. H., McGregor, N. R., De Becker, P., Roberts, T. K., De Meirleir, K., & Butt, H. L. (2001, January 26–29). Analysis of serum lipid changes associated with self-reported fatigue, muscle pain and the different chronic fatigue syndrome factor analysis symptom clusters [Abstract No. 059]. *Proceedings of the Fifth International Research,*

Clinical and Patient Conference. Seattle, WA: American Association for Chronic Fatigue Syndrome.

Dunstan, R. H., McGregor, N. R., Roberts, T. K., Butt, H., Niblett, S. H., & Rothkirch, T. (2000). The development of laboratory-based tests in chronic pain and fatigue: Muscle catabolism and coagulase negative staphylococci which produce membrane damaging toxins. *Journal of Chronic Fatigue Syndrome, 7*(1), 23–27.

Dyckner, T., & Wester, P. O. (1985). Skeletal muscle magnesium and potassium determinations: Correlation with lymphocyte contents of magnesium and potassium. *Journal of the American College of Nutrition, 4,* 619–625.

Eaton, K. K., & Hunnisett, A. (1991). Abnormalities in essential amino acids in patients with chronic fatigue syndrome. *Journal of Nutritional Medicine, 2,* 369–375.

Eigel, W. N., Butler, J. E., Ernstrom, C. A., Farrel, H. M., Harwalkar, V. R., Jennes, R., et al. (1984). *Journal of Dairy Science, 67,* 1599–1631.

Eisinger, J., & Ayavou, T. (1990). Transketolase stimulation in fibromyalgia. *Journal of the American College of Nutrition, 9*(1), 56–57.

Eisinger, J., Bagneres, D., Arroyo, P., Plantamura, A., & Ayavou, T. (1994). Effects of magnesium, high energy phosphates, piracetam and thiamin on erythrocyte transketolase. *Magnesium Research, 7*(1), 59–61.

Eisinger, J., Clairet, D., Brue, F., & Ayavou, T. (1993). Absence of correlation between magnesium and riboflavin status. *Magnesium Research, 6*(2), 165–166.

Eisinger, J., Gandolfo, C., Zakarian, H., & Ayavou, T. (1997). Reactive oxygen species, antioxidant status and fibromyalgia. *Journal of Musculoskeletal Pain, 5*(4), 5–15.

Eisinger, J., Plantamura, A., Marie, P. A., & Ayavou, T. (1994). Selenium and magnesium status in FM. *Magnesium Research, 7*(3/4), 285–288.

Eisinger, J., Zakarian, H., Mathieu, F., & Ayavou, T. (1989). Statut B1–B6 et pathologie fonctionnelle. *Lyon Mediterranee Medical, 25,* 12365–12368.

Eisinger, J., Zakarian, H., Plantamura, A., Clairet, D., & Ayavou, T. (1992). Studies of transketolase in chronic pain. *Journal of Advancement in Medicine, 5*(2), 105–113.

Elin, R. J., & Hosseini, J. M. (1985). Magnesium content of mononuclear blood cells. *Clinical Chemistry, 31*(3), 377–380.

Emms, T. M., Roberts, T. K., Butt, H. L., Buttfield, I., McGregor, N. R., & Dunstan, R. H. (2001a). Food intolerance in chronic fatigue syndrome [Abstract No. 15]. *Proceedings of the Fifth International Research, Clinical and Patient Conference.* Seattle, WA: American Association for Chronic Fatigue Syndrome.

Emms, T. M., Roberts, T. K., Butt, H. L., Buttfield, I., McGregor, N. R., & Dunstan, R. H. (2001b). Food intolerance as a co-morbidity in chronic fatigue syndrome [Abstract]. *Proceedings of the Third International Clinical and Scientific Meeting on Myalgic Encephalopathy/Chronic Fatigue Syndrome,* Alison Hunter Memorial Foundation, P.O. Box 2093, BOWRAL NSW 2576, Australia.

Emms, T. M., Thrift, M., Buttfield, I., Roberts, T. K., Butt, H. L., Dunstan, R. H., et al. (2001). Supplementation with L-serine shows potential for symptom management in chronic fatigue syndrome (ME/CFS) [Abstract]. *Proceedings of the Third International Clinical and Scientific Meeting on Myalgic Encephalopathy/Chronic Fatigue Syndrome,* Alison Hunter Memorial Foundation, P.O. Box 2093, BOWRAL NSW 2576, Australia.

Engstrom, J. W., & Martin, J. B. (2001). Disorders of the autonomic nervous system. In E. Braunwald, A. S. Fauci, D. L. Kasper, S. L. Hauser, D. L. Longo, & J. L. Jameson (Eds.), *Harrison's principles of internal medicine* (15th ed., pp. 2416–2421). New York: McGraw-Hill.

Evengard, B., Nilsson, C. G., Astrom, G., Lindh, G., Lindqvist, L., Olin, R., et al. (1996, October 13–14). Cerebral spinal fluid vitamin B12 deficiency in chronic fatigue syndrome [Abstract]. *Proceedings of the American Association for Chronic Fatigue Syndrome Research Conference,* San Francisco.

Ferre, L., Alegre, J., Ruiz, E., Cervera, C., Vazquez, A., Garcia Quintana, A. M., et al. (2003). Atopy prevalence in chronic fatigue syndrome [Abstract]. *Conference syllabus, sixth international conference on chronic fatigue syndrome, fibromyalgia, and related illness.* Chantilly, VA: American Association for Chronic Fatigue Syndrome.

Fetrow, C. W., & Avila, J. R. (2001). Efficiency of the dietary supplement S-adenosyl-L-methionine. *Annals of Pharmacotherapy, 35,* 1414–1425.

Flanagan, J. C. (1982). Measurement of quality of life: Current state of the art. *Archives of Physical and Medical Rehabilitation, 63,* 56–59.

Fleming, S. C., Kapembwa, M. S., Laker, M. F., Levin, G. E., & Griffin, G. E. (1990). Rapid and simultaneous determination of lactulose and mannitol in urine, by HPLC with pulsed amperometric detection, for use in studies of intestinal permeability. *Clinical Chemistry, 36*(5), 797–799.

Forsyth, L. M., Preuss, H. G., MacDowell, A. L., Chiazze, L., Jr., Birkmayer, G. D., & Bellanti, J. A. (1999). Therapeutic effects of oral NADH on the symptoms of patients with chronic fatigue syndrome. *Annals of Allergy, Asthma, and Immunology, 82,* 185–191.

Fukuda, K., Straus, S. E., Hickie, I., Sharpe, M. C., Dobbins, J. G., & Komaroff, A. (1994). The chronic fatigue syndrome: A comprehensive approach to its definition and study. *Annals of Internal Medicine, 121,* 953–959.

Fulle, S., Mecocci, P., Fano, G., Vecchiet, I., Vecchini, A., Racciotti, D., et al. (2000). Specific oxidative alterations in vastus lateralis muscle of patients with the diagnosis of chronic fatigue syndrome. *Free Radical Biology and Medicine, 29,* 1252–1259.

Gaby, A. R. (2002). Intravenous nutrient therapy: The "Myers' Cocktail." *Alternative Medicine Review, 7,* 389–403.

Ganong, W. F. (2001). *Review of medical physiology* (20th ed.). New York: McGraw-Hill.

Gantz, N. M. (1991). Magnesium and chronic fatigue [Letter]. *Lancet, 338,* 66.

Godfrey, P. S., Toone, B. K., Carney, M. W., Flynn, T. G., Bottiglieri, T., Laundy, M., et al. (1990). Enhancement of recovery from psychiatric illness by methylfolate. *Lancet, 336,* 392–395.

Goldberg, B. (Ed.). (1998). *Alternative medicine guide to chronic fatigue, fibromyalgia, and environmental illness.* Tiburon, CA: Future Medicine.

Gomborone, J. E., Gorard, D. A., Dewsnap, P. A., Libby, G. W., & Farthing, M. J. (1996). Prevalence of irritable bowel syndrome in chronic fatigue. *Journal of the Royal College of Physicians of London, 30,* 512–513.

Grant, J. E., Veldee, M. S., & Buchwald, D. (1996). Analysis of dietary intake and selected nutrient concentrations in patients with chronic fatigue syndrome. *Journal of the American Dietetic Association, 96,* 383–386.

Grassetto, M., & Varotto, A. (1994). Primary FM is responsive to S-adenosyl-L-methionine. *Current Therapeutic Research, 55*(7), 797–806.

Grau, J. M., Casademont, J., Pedrol, E., Fernandez-Sola, J., Cardellach, F., Barros, N., et al. (1992). Chronic fatigue syndrome: Studies on skeletal muscle. *Clinical Neuropathology, 11*(6), 329–332.

Gray, J. B., & Martinovic, A. M. (1994). Eicosanoids and essential fatty acid modulation in chronic disease and the chronic fatigue syndrome. *Medical Hypotheses, 43,* 31–42.

Gregus, Z., Stein, A. F., Varga, F., & Klaassen, C. D. (1992). Effect of lipoic acid on biliary excretion of glutathione and metals. *Toxicology and Applied Pharmacology, 114,* 88–96.

Gross, C. J., & Henderson, L. M. (1983). Digestion and absorption of NAD by the small intestine of the rat. *Journal of Nutrition, 113*(2), 412–420.

Haigney, M. C., Silver, B., Tanglao, E., Silverman, H. S., Hill, J. D., Shapiro, E., et al. (1995). Noninvasive measurement of tissue magnesium and correlation with cardiac levels. *Circulation, 92*(8), 2190–2197.

Hanninen, O., Kaartinen, K., Rauma, A.-L., Nenonen, M., Torronen, R., Hakkinen, S., et al. (2000). Antioxidants in vegan diet and rheumatic disorders. *Toxicology, 155,* 45–53.

Haugen, M., Kjeldsen-Kragh, J., Nordvag, B. Y., & Forre, O. (1991). Diet and disease symptoms in rheumatic diseases—results of a questionnaire based survey. *Clinical Rheumatology, 10,* 401–407.

Heap, L. C., Peters, T. J., & Wessely, S. (1999). Vitamin B status in patients with chronic fatigue syndrome. *Journal of the Royal Society of Medicine, 92,* 183–185.

Hein, G., & Franke, S. (2002). Are advanced glycation end-product-modified proteins of pathogenetic importance in fibromyalgia? *Rheumatology, 41,* 1163–1167.

Hemmings, W. A., & Williams, E. W. (1978). Transport of large breakdown products of dietary protein through the gut wall. *Gut, 19,* 715–723.

Hendler, S., & Rorvik, D. (Eds.). (2001). *PDR for nutritional supplements.* Montvale, NJ: Medical Economics.

Hieber, H. (1974). Treatment of vertebragenous pain and sensitivity disorders using high doses of hydroxocobalamin. *Medizinische Monatsschrift [Medical Monthly Magazine], 28,* 545–548.

Hinds, G., Bell, N. P., McMaster, D., & McCluskey, D. R. (1994). Normal red cell magnesium concentrations and magnesium loading tests in patients with chronic fatigue syndrome. *Annals of Clinical Biochemistry, 31,* 459–461.

Hock, A. D. (1997). Fatigue and 25-hydroxyvitamin D levels. *Journal of Chronic Fatigue Syndrome, 3*(3), 117–127.

Holmes, G. P., Kaplan, J. E., Gantz, N. M., Komaroff, A. L., Schonberger, L. B., Straus, S. E., et al. (1988). Chronic fatigue syndrome: A working case definition. *Annals of Internal Medicine, 108,* 387–389.

Holzschlag, M. (1993, Summer). CoQ10, malic acid and magnesium may improve CFIDS/FM symptoms. *CFIDS Chronicle,* 93–94.

Hoskin, L., Clifton-Bligh, P., Hansen, R., Fulcher, G., & Gates, F. (2000). Bone density and body composition in young women with chronic fatigue syndrome. *Annals of the New York Academy of Sciences, 904,* 625–627.

Hostmark, A. T., Lystad, E., Vellar, O. D., Hori, K., & Berg, J. E. (1993). Reduced plasma fibrinogen, serum peroxides, lipids, and apolipoproteins after a 3-week vegetarian diet. *Plant Foods for Human Nutrition, 43,* 55–61.

Houeto, P., Hoffman, J. R., Imbert, M., Levillain, P., & Baud, F. J. (1995). Relation of blood cyanide to plasma cyanocobalamin concentration after a fixed dose of hydroxocobalamin in cyanide poisoning. *Lancet, 346,* 605–608.

Howard, J. M., Davies, S., & Hunnisett, A. (1992). Magnesium and chronic fatigue syndrome [Letter]. *Lancet, 340,* 426.

Hudson, J. I., Goldenberg, D. L., Pope, H. G., Jr., Keck, P. E., Jr., & Schlesinger, L. (1992). Comorbidity of FM with medical and psychiatric disorders. *American Journal of Medicine, 92,* 363–367.

Huisman, A. M., White, K. P., Algra, A., Harth, M., Vieth, R., Jacobs, J. W. G., et al. (2001). Vitamin D levels in women with systemic lupus erythmatosus and fibromyalgia. *Journal of Rheumatology, 28*(11), 2535–2539.

Husby, S. (1988). Dietary antigens: Uptake and humoral immunity in man. *Acta Pathologica, Microbiologica, et Immunologica Scandinavica (APMIS), 96*(Suppl. 1), 1–40.

Institute of Medicine. (1997). *Dietary reference intakes for calcium, phosphorus, magnesium, vitamin D and fluoride.* Washington, DC: National Academy of Sciences.

Institute of Medicine. (1998). *Dietary reference intakes for thiamin, riboflavin, niacin, vitamin B6, folate, vitamin B12, pantothenic acid, biotin, and choline.* Washington, DC: National Academy of Sciences.

Institute of Medicine. (2000). *Dietary reference intakes for vitamin C, vitamin E, selenium, and carotenoids.* Washington, DC: National Academy of Sciences.

Institute of Medicine. (2001). *Dietary reference intakes for vitamin A, vitamin K, arsenic, boron, chromium, copper, iodine, iron, manganese, molybdenum, nickel, silicon, vanadium, and zinc.* Washington, DC: National Academy of Sciences.

Jacob, S. W., Lawrence, R. M., & Zucker, M. (1999). *The miracle of MSM.* New York: Berkley Books.

Jacobsen, B., Danneskiold-Samsoe, B., & Andersen, R. B. (1991). Oral S-adenosylmethionine in primary fibromyalgia: Double-blind clinical evaluation. *Scandinavian Journal of Rheumatology, 20,* 294–302.

Jacobsen, D. W., Simon, R. A., & Singh, M. (1984). Sulfite oxidase deficiency and cobalamin protection in sulfite sensitive asthmatics. *Journal of Allergy and Clinical Immunology, 73*(Suppl.), 135.

Jacobsen, S., Gam, A., Egsmose, C., Olsen, M., Danneskiold-Samsoe, B., & Jensen, G. F. (1993). Bone mass and turnover in fibromyalgia. *Journal of Rheumatology, 20,* 856–859.

Jacobson, W. (1994). Folate and chronic fatigue syndrome [Letter]. *Neurology, 44,* 2214–2215.

Jacobson, W., Saich, T., Borysiewicz, L. K., Behan, W. M., Behan, P. O., & Wreghitt, T. G. (1993). Serum folate and chronic fatigue syndrome. *Neurology, 43,* 2645–2647.

Janaky, R., Varga, V., Hermann, A., Saransaari, P., & Oja, S. S. (2000). Mechanisms of L-cysteine neurotoxicity. *Neurochemical Research, 25,* 1397–1405.

Jason, L. A., Taylor, R. R., Kennedy, C. L., & Torres, S. R. (2001). Subtyping patients with chronic fatigue syndrome in a community-based sample [Abstract No. 11]. *Proceedings of the Fifth International Research, Clinical and Patient Conference.* Seattle, WA: American Association for Chronic Fatigue Syndrome.

Jenkins, D. J., Wolever, T. M., Taylor, R. H., Barker, H., Fielden, H., Baldwin, J. M., et al. (1981). Glycemic index of foods: A physiological basis for carbohydrate exchange. *American Journal of Clinical Nutrition, 34,* 362–366.

Kaartinen, K., Lammi, K., Hypen, M., Nenonen, M., Hanninen, O., & Rauma, A.-L. (2000). Vegan diet alleviates fibromyalgia symptoms. *Scandinavian Journal of Rheumatology, 29,* 308–313.

Kaslow, J. E., Rucker, L., & Onishi, R. (1989). Liver extract-folic acid-cyanocobalamin vs. placebo for chronic fatigue syndrome. *Archives of Internal Medicine, 149,* 2501–2503.

Katz, D. R., Drzymala, M., Turton, J. A., Hicks, R. M., Hunt, R., Palmer, L., et al. (1987). Regulation of accessory cell function by retinoids in murine immune responses. *British Journal of Experimental Pathology, 68,* 343–350.

Kennedy, G., Spence, V., McLaren, M., Hill, S., & Belch, J. (2003). Increased plasma isoprostanes and other markers of oxidative stress in chronic fatigue syndrome [Abstract]. *Conference syllabus, sixth international conference on chronic fatigue syndrome, fibromyalgia, and related illnesses.* Chantilly, VA: American Association for Chronic Fatigue Syndrome.

King, H. C., & King, W. P. (1998). Alternatives in the diagnosis and treatment of food allergies. *Otolaryngologic Clinics of North America, 31*(1), 141–156.

Klaassen, C. D. (1996). *Casarett and Doull's toxicology, the basic science of poisons* (5th ed.). New York: McGraw-Hill.

Klarskov, K., Johnson, K. L., Benson, L. M., Gleich, G. J., & Naylor, S. (1999). Eosinophilia-myalgia syndrome case-associated contaminants in commercially available 5-hydroxytryptophan. *Advances in Experimental Medicine and Biology, 467*, 461–468.

Klerman, E. B., Goldenberg, D. L., Brown, E. N., Maliszewski, A. M., & Adler, G. K. (2001). Circadian rhythms of women with fibromyalgia. *Journal of Clinical Endocrinology and Metabolism, 86*(3), 1034–1039.

Knook, L., Kavelaars, A., Sinnema, G., Kuis, W., & Heijnen, C. J. (2000). High nocturnal melatonin in adolescents with chronic fatigue syndrome. *Journal of Clinical Endocrinology and Metabolism, 85*(10), 3690–3692.

Komaroff, A., Fagiolo, L., Doolittle, T., Gandek, B., Gleit, M. A., Guerriero, R. T., et al. (1996). Health status in patients with chronic fatigue syndrome and in general population and disease comparison groups. *American Journal of Medicine, 101*, 281–290.

Korszun, A., Sackett-Lundeen, L., Papadopoulos, E., Brucksch, C., Masterson, L., Engelberg, N. C., et al. (1999). Melatonin levels in women with fibromyalgia and chronic fatigue syndrome. *Journal of Rheumatology, 26*(12), 2675–2680.

Kowal, K., Schacterele, R. S., Schur, P. H., Komaroff, A. L., & DuBuske, L. M. (2002). Prevalence of allergen-specific IgE among patients with chronic fatigue syndrome. *Allergy and Asthma Proceedings, 23*, 35–39.

Kuratsune, H., Yamaguti, K., Lindh, G., Evengard, B., Takahashi, M., Machii, T., et al. (1998). Low levels of serum acylcarnitine in chronic fatigue syndrome and chronic hepatitis type C, but not seen in other diseases. *International Journal of Molecular Medicine, 2*, 51–56.

Kuratsune, H., Yamaguti, K., Takahashi, M., Misaki, H., Tagawa, S., & Kitani, T. (1994). Acylcarnitine deficiency in chronic fatigue syndrome. *Clinical Infectious Diseases, 18*(Suppl.), S62–S67.

Lands, L. C., Grey, V. L., & Smountas, A. A. (1999). Effect of supplementation with a cysteine donor on muscular performance. *Journal of Applied Physiology, 87*(4), 1381–1385.

Langsjoen, P. H., Langsjoen, P. H., & Folkers, K. (1993). Isolated diastolic dysfunction of the myocardium and its response to CoQ10 treatment. *Clinical Investigator, 71*, 5140–5144.

Lapp, C. W. (1992). Chronic fatigue syndrome is a real disease. *North Carolina Family Physician, 43*(1), 6–11.

Lapp, C. W. (1999). Using vitamin B-12 for the management of CFS. *CFIDS Chronicle, 12*(6), 14–16.

Lapp, C. W. (2003). Chronic fatigue syndrome: A diagnostic and management challenge [Slides]. *Conference syllabus, sixth international conference on chronic fatigue syndrome, fibromyalgia and related illnesses.* Chantilly, VA: American Association for Chronic Fatigue Syndrome.

Lapp, C. W., & Cheney, P. R. (1993, Fall). The rationale for using high-dose cobalamin (vitamin B-12). *CFIDS Chronicle Physicians Forum*, 19–20.

Levine, S. A., & Kidd, P. M. (1986). *Antioxidant adaptation: Its role in free radical pathology.* San Leandro, CA: Allergy Research Group.

Life Extension Foundation. (2001). What is the proper dose of melatonin? *Life Extension Magazine, 7*(5), 65–68.

Lister, R. E. (2002). An open pilot study to evaluate the potential benefits of coenzyme Q-10 combined with Ginkgo biloba extract in fibromyalgia syndrome. *Journal of International Medical Research, 30,* 195–199.

Lloyd, A. R., Hickie, I., Boughton, C. R., Spencer, O., & Wakefield, D. (1990). Prevalence of chronic fatigue syndrome in an Australian population. *Medical Journal of Australia, 153,* 522–528.

Logan, A. C. (2001). Letter to the editor. *Alternative Medicine Review, 6*(1), 4–5.

Logan, A. C., & Bested, A. C. (2003a). Chronic fatigue syndrome: An assessment of dietary/herbal supplement intake by patients in a clinical setting [Abstract]. *Conference syllabus, sixth international conference on chronic fatigue syndrome, fibromyalgia and related illnesses.* Chantilly, VA: American Association for Chronic Fatigue Syndrome.

Logan, A. C., & Bested, A. C. (2003b). Dietary modifications, food sensitivities, and migraine headaches reported by CFS patients [Abstract]. *Conference syllabus, sixth international conference on chronic fatigue syndrome, fibromyalgia and related illnesses.* Chantilly, VA: American Association for Chronic Fatigue Syndrome.

Logan, A. C., & Wong, C. (2001). Chronic fatigue syndrome: Oxidative stress and dietary modifications. *Alternative Medicine Review, 6*(5), 450–459.

Lubrano, E., Iovino, P., Tremolaterra, F., Parsons, W. J., Ciacci, C., & Mazzacca, G. (2001). Fibromyalgia in patients with irritable bowel syndrome: An association with the severity of the intestinal disorder. *International Journal of Colorectal Disease, 16,* 211–215.

Maes, M., Verkerk, R., Delmeire, L., van Gastel, A., van Hunsel, F., & Sharpe, S. (2000). Serotonergic markers and lowered plasma branched-chain-amino acid concentrations in fibromyalgia. *Psychiatry Research, 97,* 11–20.

Magaldi, M., Moltoni, L., Biasi, G., & Marcolongo, R. (2000). Modifications of intracellular calcium and magnesium in the pathophysiology of FM. *Minerva Medica, 91*(7/8), 137–140.

Majeed, T., De Simone, C., Famularo, G., Marcelline, S., & Behan, P. O. (1995). Abnormalities of carnitine metabolism in chronic fatigue syndrome. *European Journal of Neurology, 2,* 425–428.

Manuel y Keenoy, B., Moorkens, G., Vertommen, J., & De Leeuw, I. (2001). Antioxidant status and lipoprotein peroxidation in chronic fatigue syndrome. *Life Sciences, 68,* 2037–2049.

Martin, R. W., Ogston, S. A., & Evans, J. R. (1994). Effects of vitamin and mineral supplementation on symptoms associated with chronic fatigue syndrome with Cocksackie B antibodies. *Journal of Nutritional Medicine, 4,* 11–23.

Matsumoto, Y. (1999). Fibromyalgia syndrome. *Nippon Rinsho, 57*(2), 364–369.

Matthews, C. K., van Holde, K. E., & Ahern, K. G. (2000). *Biochemistry* (3rd ed.). San Francisco: Addison Wesley Longman.

Maxwell, P. R., Rink, E., Kumar, D., & Mendall, M. A. (2002). Antibiotics increase functional abdominal symptoms. *American Journal of Gastroenterology, 97,* 104–108.

McGregor, N. R., Dunstan, R. H., Zerbes, M., Butt, H. L., Roberts, T. K., & Klineberg, I. J. (1996). Preliminary determination of a molecular basis to chronic fatigue syndrome. *Biochemical and Molecular Medicine, 57,* 73–80.

McGregor, N. R., Niblett, S., Bligh, P. C., Dunstan, R. H., Fulcher, G., Hoskin, L., et al. (2000). The biochemistry of chronic pain and fatigue. *Journal of Chronic Fatigue Syndrome, 7*(1), 3–21.

Merchant, R. E., Andre, C. A., & Wise, C. M. (2001). Nutritional supplementation with Chlorella pyrenoidosa for fibromyalgia syndrome: A double-blind, placebo controlled, crossover study. *Journal of Musculoskeletal Pain, 9*(4), 37–54.

Merchant, R. E., Carmack, C. A., & Wise, C. M. (2000). Nutritional supplementation with Chlorella pyrenoidosa for patients with fibromyalgia syndrome: A pilot study. *Phytotherapy Research, 14*(3), 167–173.

Michelson, D., Page, S. W., Casey, R., Trucksess, M. W., Love, L. A., Milstien, S., et al. (1994). An eosinophilia-myalgia syndrome related disorder associated with exposure to L-5-hydroxytryptophan. *Journal of Rheumatology, 21,* 2261–2265.

Moldovsky, H., Scarisbrick, P., England, R., & Smythe, H. (1975). Musculoskeletal symptoms and non-REM sleep disturbance in patients with "fibrositis syndrome" and healthy subjects. *Psychosomatic Medicine, 37,* 341–351.

Moldovsky, H., & Warsh, J. J. (1978). Plasma tryptophan and musculoskeletal pain in nonarticular rheumatism ("fibrositis syndrome"). *Pain, 5,* 65–71.

Moller Jensen, B., Klaaborg, K. E., Alstrup, P., Arendrup, H., Klitgard, N. A., & Pedersen, K. E. (1991). Magnesium content of the human heart. *Scandinavian Journal of Cardiovascular Surgery, 25*(2), 155–158.

Moorkens, G., Manuel y Keenoy, B., Vertommen, J., Meludu, S., Noe, M., & De Leeuw, I. (1997). Magnesium deficit in a sample of the Belgian population presenting with chronic fatigue. *Magnesium Research, 10,* 329–337.

Morris, D. H., & Stare, F. J. (1993). Unproven diet therapies in the treatment of the chronic fatigue syndrome. *Archives of Family Medicine, 2,* 181–186.

Mukherjee, T. M., Smith, K., & Maros, K. (1987). Abnormal red-blood-cell morphology in myalgic encephalomyelitis. *Lancet, 2*(8554), 328–329.

Murray, M. T. (1994). *Chronic fatigue syndrome: How you can benefit from diet, vitamins, minerals, herbs, exercise, and other natural methods.* Rocklin, CA: Prima.

Murray, M. T. (1996). *Encyclopedia of nutritional supplements.* Rocklin, CA: Prima.

Murray, M. T., & Pizzorno, J. (1998). *Encyclopedia of natural medicine* (2nd ed., rev.) Rocklin, CA: Prima.

Natelson, B. H. (1998). *Facing and fighting fatigue.* New Haven, CT: Yale University Press.

National Research Council. (1989). *Recommended dietary allowances* (10th ed.). Washington, DC: National Academy of Sciences.

Natochin, Y. V., & Kuznetsova, A. A. (2000). Nocturnal enuresis: Correction of renal function by desmopressin and diclofenac. *Pediatric Nephrology, 14*(1), 42–47.

Newbold, H. L. (1989). Vitamin B-12: Placebo or neglected therapeutic tool? *Medical Hypotheses, 28,* 155–164.

Nicolodi, M., & Sicuteri, F. (1996). Fibromyalgia and migraine, two faces of the same mechanism. In G. A. Filippini, C. V. Costa, & A. Bertazzo (Eds.), *Recent advances in tryptophan research* (pp. 373–379). New York: Plenum Press.

Nijs, J., De Meirleir, K., Englebienne, P., & McGregor, N. (2002). Chronic fatigue syndrome: A risk factor for osteopenia? *Medical Hypotheses, 60*(1), 65–68.

Ozgocmen, S., Catal, S. A., Ardicoglu, O., & Kamanli, A. (2000). Effect of omega-3 fatty acids in the management of fibromyalgia syndrome [Letter]. *International Journal of Clinical Pharmacology and Therapeutics, 38*(7), 362–363.

Packer, L., & Colman, C. (1999). *The antioxidant miracle.* New York: Wiley.

Pall, M. L. (2001). Cobalamin used in chronic fatigue syndrome therapy is a nitric oxide scavenger. *Journal of Chronic Fatigue Syndrome, 8*(2), 39–44.

Patarca-Montero, R., Mark, T., Fletcher, M. A., & Klimas, N. G. (2001). Immunology of chronic fatigue syndrome. *Journal of Chronic Fatigue Syndrome, 6*(3/4), 69–107.

Pellegrino, M. J. (2001). *Inside fibromyalgia*. Columbus, OH: Anadem.

Petri, H., Graffelman, A. W., Springer, M. P., Mearin, L., von Blomberg, B. M., & Visser, J. T. (2001). Coeliac disease and chronic fatigue syndrome. *International Journal of Clinical Practice, 55*, 71.

Pimentel, M., Chow, E. J., & Lin, H. C. (2002). Eradication of small intestinal bacteria overgrowth reduces symptoms of irritable bowel syndrome. *American Journal of Gastroenterology, 95*, 3503–3506.

Pinnock, C. B., Douglas, R. M., & Badcock, N. R. (1986). Vitamin A status in children who are prone to respiratory tract infections. *Australian Paediatric Journal, 22*, 95–97.

Plioplys, A. V., & Plioplys, S. (1995). Serum levels of carnitine in chronic fatigue syndrome: Clinical correlates. *Neuropsychobiology, 32*, 132–138.

Plioplys, A. V., & Plioplys, S. (1997). Amantadine and L-carnitine treatment of chronic fatigue syndrome. *Neuropsychobiology, 35*, 16–23.

Preedy, V. R., Smith, D. G., Salisbury, J. R., & Peters, T. J. (1993). Biochemical and muscle studies in patients with acute onset postviral fatigue syndrome. *Journal of Clinical Pathology, 46*(8), 722–726.

Prescott, E., Norregaard, J., Rotbol, P., Pedersen, L., & Danneskiold-Samsoe, B. (1992). Fibromyalgia and magnesia [Letter]. *Scandinavian Journal of Rheumatology, 4*, 206.

Prescott, E., Norregaard, J., Rotbol, P., Pedersen, L., Danneskiold-Samsoe, B., & Bulow, P. (1992). Red blood cell magnesium and fibromyalgia [Abstract No. 154]. *Scandinavian Journal of Rheumatology*, (Suppl. 94), 31.

Press, J., Phillip, M., Neumann, L., Barak, R., Segev, Y., Abu-Shakra, M., et al. (1998). Normal melatonin levels in patients with fibromyalgia syndrome. *Journal of Rheumatology, 25*(3), 551–555.

Racciatti, D., Barberio, A., Vecchiet, J., & Pizzigallo, E. (1999). Clinical and pathological characterization of 238 patients of a chronic fatigue syndrome Italian center. *Journal of Chronic Fatigue Syndrome, 5*(3/4), 61–70.

Randolph, T. G. (1945). Fatigue and weakness of allergic origin (allergic toxemia) to be differentiated from "nervous fatigue" or neurasthenia. *Annals of Allergy, 3*, 418–430.

Randolph, T. G. (1976). Ecologically oriented myalgia and related musculoskeletal painful syndromes. In L. D. Dickey (Ed.), *Clinical ecology* (pp. 213–223). Springfield, IL: Charles C Thomas.

Regland, B., Andersson, M., Abrahamsson, L., Bagby, J., Dyrehag, L. E., & Germgard, T. (1998). One-carbon metabolism and CFS [Abstract]. *Proceedings of the 1998 Sydney Chronic Fatigue Syndrome Conference*, Alison Hunter Memorial Foundation, P.O. Box 2093, BOWRAL NSW 2576, Australia.

Regland, B., Andersson, M., Abrahamsson, L., Bagby, J., Dyrehag, L. E., & Gottfries, C. G. (1997). Increased concentrations of homocysteine in the cerebrospinal fluid in patients with fibromyalgia and chronic fatigue syndrome. *Scandinavian Journal of Rheumatology, 26*, 301–307.

Reinhard, P., Schweinsberg, F., Wernet, D., & Kotter, I. (1998). Selenium status in fibromyalgia. *Toxicology Letters, 96/97*, 177–180.

Repka-Ramirez, M. S., Naranch, K., Park, Y. J., Velarde, A., Clauw, D., & Baraniuk, J. N. (2001). IgE levels are the same in chronic fatigue syndrome (CFS) and control subjects when stratified by allergy skin test results and rhinitis types. *Annals of Allergy, Asthma and Immunology, 87*(3), 218–221.

Richards, R. S., Roberts, T. K., Mathers, D., Dunstan, R. H., McGregor, N. R., & Butt, H. L. (2000). Investigation of erythrocyte oxidative damage in rheumatoid arthritis and chronic fatigue syndrome. *Journal of Chronic Fatigue Syndrome, 6*(1), 37–46.

Richards, R. S., Roberts, T. K., McGregor, N. R., Dunstan, R. H., & Butt, H. L. (2000). Blood parameters indicative of oxidative stress are associated with symptom expression in chronic fatigue syndrome. *Redox Report, 5*, 35–41.

Richmond, V. L. (1986). Incorporation of methylsulfonylmethane sulfur into guinea pig serum proteins. *Life Sciences, 39*, 263–268.

Ridley, W. P., Dizikes, L. J., & Wood, J. M. (1977). Biomethylation of toxic elements in the environment. *Science, 197*, 329–332.

Rigden, S. (1995). Entero-hepatic resuscitation program for CFIDS. *CFIDS Chronicle, 8*(2), 46–49.

Rogers, S. A. (1990). Zinc deficiency as model for developing chemical sensitivity. *International Clinical Nutrition Review, 10*(1), 253–259.

Romano, T. J., & Stiller, J. W. (1993, August 22–27). Magnesium deficiency in fibromyalgia patients [Abstract No. 494]. *Abstracts book for the Seventh World Congress on Pain,* Paris, France. Available from IASP Publications, International Association for the Study of Pain, 909 NE 43rd St., Suite 306, Seattle, WA 98105.

Rose, S. E., Chalk, J. B., Galloway, G. J., & Doddrell, D. M. (2000). Detection of dimethyl sulfone in the human brain by in vivo proton magnetic resonance spectroscopy. *Magnetic Resonance Imaging, 18*, 95–98.

Rowbottom, D., Keast, D., Pervan, Z., Goodman, C., Bhagat, C., Kakulas, B., et al. (1998). The role of glutamine in the aetiology of the chronic fatigue syndrome: A prospective study. *Journal of Chronic Fatigue Syndrome, 4*(2), 3–22.

Rowe, P. C., & Calkins, H. (1998). Neurally mediated hypotension and chronic fatigue syndrome. *American Journal of Medicine, 105*(3A), 15S–21S.

Russell, I. J., Michalek, J. E., Flechas, J. D., & Abraham, G. E. (1995). Treatment of fibromyalgia syndrome with super malic: A randomized, double-blind, placebo controlled, crossover pilot study. *Journal of Rheumatology, 22*, 953–958.

Russell, I. J., Michalek, J. E., Vipraio, G. A., Fletcher, E. M., & Wall, K. (1989). Serum amino acids in fibrositis/fibromyalgia syndrome. *Journal of Rheumatology, 16*(Suppl. 19), 158–163.

Russell, I. J., Vipraio, G. A., Morgan, W. W., & Bowden, C. L. (1986). Is there a metabolic basis for the fibrositis syndrome? *American Journal of Medicine, 81*(3A), 50–54.

Sarzi Puttini, P., & Caruso, I. (1992). Primary fibromyalgia syndrome and 5-hydroxy-L-tryptophan: A 90-day open study. *Journal of International Medical Research, 20*, 182–189.

Schwarz, M. J., Spath, M., Muller-Bardorff, H., Pongratz, D. E., Bondy, B., & Ackenheil, M. (1999). Relationship of substance P, 5-hydroxyindole acetic acid and tryptophan in serum of fibromyalgia patients. *Neuroscience Letters, 259*, 196–198.

Seelig, M. S. (1996). Might magnesium deficiency play a role in the chronic fatigue syndrome? [Abstract No. 93]. *Journal of the American College of Nutrition, 15*(Suppl.), 538–539.

Seelig, M. S. (1998). Review and hypothesis: Might patients with the chronic fatigue syndrome have latent tetany of magnesium deficiency? *Journal of Chronic Fatigue Syndrome, 4*(2), 77–108.

Sharpe, M. C., Archard, L. C., Banatvala, J. E., Borysiewicz, L. K., Clare, A. W., David, A., et al. (1991). A report—chronic fatigue syndrome: Guidelines for research. *Journal of the Royal Society of Medicine, 84*, 118–121.

Shaw, W. (2001). *Test for yeast described on Web site for Great Plains Laboratory.* Available from www.greatplainslaboratory.com.

Simpson, L. O. (1989). Nondiscocytic erythrocytes in myalgic encephalomyelitis. *New Zealand Medical Journal, 102*, 126–127.

Simpson, L. O. (1991). Myalgic encephalomyelitis [Letter]. *Journal of the Royal Society of Medicine, 84*, 663.

Simpson, L. O. (1992). Chronic tiredness and idiopathic chronic fatigue: A connection? *New Jersey Medicine, 89,* 211–216.

Simpson, L. O. (1997). Myalgic encephalomyelitis (ME): A haemorheological disorder manifested as impaired capillary blood flow. *Journal of Orthomolecular Medicine, 12*(2), 69–76.

Simpson, L. O., Olds, R. J., & Hunter, J. A. (1984). Changes in rheological properties of blood in cigarette smokers taking Efamol: A pilot study. *Proceedings of the University of Otago Medical School, 62,* 122–123.

Skowera, A., Peakman, M., Cleare, A., Davies, E., Deale, A., & Wessely, S. (2001). High prevalence of serum markers of coeliac disease in patients with chronic fatigue syndrome [Letter]. *Journal of Clinical Pathology, 54,* 335–336.

Smith, D. G. (1989). Myalgic encephalomyelitis. *The Royal College of General Practitioner's members' reference book.* London: Sabercrow.

Smith, J. D., Terpening, C. M., Schmidt, S. O. F., & Gums, J. G. (2001). Relief of fibromyalgia symptoms following discontinuation of dietary excitotoxins. *Annals of Pharmacology, 35,* 702–706.

Soetekouw, P. M., Wevers, R. A., Vreken, P., Elving, L. D., Janssen, A. J., van der Veen, Y., et al. (2000). Normal carnitine levels in patients with chronic fatigue syndrome. *Netherlands Journal of Medicine, 57,* 20–24.

St. Amand, R. P., & Marek, C. C. (1999). *What your doctor may not tell you about fibromyalgia.* New York: Warner Books.

Stewart, A. (1991). Nutrition and the postviral fatigue syndrome. In R. Jenkins & J. F. Mowbray (Eds.), *Postviral fatigue syndrome.* New York: Wiley.

Stoff, J. A., & Pellegrino, C. R. (1992). *Chronic fatigue syndrome* (Rev. ed.). New York: HarperCollins.

Straus, S. E., Dale, J. K., Wright, R., & Metcalfe, D. D. (1988). Allergy in the chronic fatigue syndrome. *Journal of Allergy and Clinical Immunology, 81,* 791–795.

Streeten, D. H. (2001). Role of impaired lower-limb venous innervation in the pathogenesis of the chronic fatigue syndrome. *American Journal of the Medical Sciences, 321*(3), 163–167.

Streeten, D. H., Thomas, D., & Bell, D. S. (2000). The roles of orthostatic hypotension, orthostatic tachycardia, and subnormal erythrocyte volume in the pathogenesis of the chronic fatigue syndrome. *American Journal of the Medical Sciences, 320*(1), 1–8.

Swezey, R. L., & Adams, J. (1999). Fibromyalgia: A risk factor for osteoporosis. *Journal of Rheumatology, 26,* 2642–2644.

Tavoni, A., Vitali, C., Bombardieri, S., & Pasero, G. (1987). Evaluation of S-adenosylmethionine in primary fibromyalgia. *American Journal of Medicine, 83*(Suppl. 5A), 107–110.

Teitelbaum, J. (1996). *From fatigued to fantastic!* New York: Penguin Putnam.

Teitelbaum, J. (2001). *From fatigued to fantastic!—completely revised and updated.* New York: Penguin Putnam.

Teitelbaum, J. (2002). Effective treatment of chronic fatigue syndrome and fibromyalgia: A double-blind study. *Conference syllabus, latest 21st century medical advances in the diagnosis and treatment of fibromyalgia, chronic fatigue syndrome and related illnesses.* Los Angeles, CA: Advanced Medical Conferences International.

Teitelbaum, J. E., Bird, B., Greenfield, R. M., Weiss, A., Muenz, L., & Gould, L. (2001). Effective treatment of chronic fatigue syndrome and fibromyalgia: A randomized, double-blind, placebo-controlled, intent-to-treat study. *Journal of Chronic Fatigue Syndrome, 8*(2), 3–28.

U.S. Department of Agriculture. (1992). *The food guide pyramid* [*Home and Garden* Bulletin No. 252]. Washington, DC: U.S. Department of Agriculture, Human Nutrition Information Service.

van de Luit, L., van der Meulen, J., Cleophas, T. J., & Zwinderman, A. H. (1998). Amplified amplitudes of circadian rhythms and nighttime hypotension in patients with chronic fatigue syndrome: Improvement by inopamil but not by melatonin. *Angiology, 49*(11), 903–908.

van Rensburg, S. J., Potocnik, F. C., Kiss, T., Hugo, F., van Zijl, P., Mansvelt, E., et al. (2001). Serum concentrations of some metals and steroids in patients with chronic fatigue syndrome with reference to neurological and cognitive abnormalities. *Brain Research Bulletin, 55*(2), 319–325.

Vassallo, C. M., Feldman, E., Peto, T., Castell, L., Sharpley, A. L., & Cowan, P. J. (2001). Decreased tryptophan availability but normal postsynaptic 5-HT2c receptor sensitivity in chronic fatigue syndrome. *Psychological Medicine, 31*(4), 585–591.

Vecchiet, J., Cipollone, F., Falasca, K., Mezzetti, A., Pizzigallo, E., Bucciarelli, T., et al. (2003). Relationship between musculoskeletal symptoms and blood markers of oxidative stress in patients with chronic fatigue syndrome. *Neuroscience Letters, 335,* 151–154.

Vermeulen, R. C., Kurk, R. M., & Scholte, H. R. (2001). Carnitine, acetylcarnitine and propionylcarnitine in the treatment of chronic fatigue syndrome [Abstract]. *Proceedings of the Third International Clinical and Scientific Meeting on Myalgic Encephalopathy/Chronic Fatigue Syndrome,* Alison Hunter Memorial Foundation, P.O. Box 2093, BOWRAL NSW 2576, Australia.

Verrillo, E. F., & Gellman, L. M. (1997). *Chronic fatigue syndrome: A treatment guide.* New York: St. Martin's Griffin.

Ware, J. E., Jr., & Sherbourne, C. D. (1992). The MOS 36-item short-form health survey (SF-36). I: Conceptual framework and item selection. *Medical Care, 30,* 473–483.

Warren, G., McKendrick, M., & Peet, M. (1999). The role of essential fatty acids in chronic fatigue syndrome: A case-controlled study of red-cell membrane essential fatty acids (EFA) and a placebo-controlled treatment study with high doses of EFA. *Acta Neurologica Scandinavica, 99*(2), 112–116.

Werbach, M. R. (2000). Nutritional strategies for treating chronic fatigue syndrome. *Alternative Medicine Review, 5*(2), 93–108.

Werbach, M. R. (2001, November). Serotonin in chronic fatigue syndrome and fibromyalgia. *Townsend Letter for Doctors and Patients, 220,* 140.

Wessely, S., Nimnuan, C., & Sharpe, M. (1999). Functional somatic syndromes: One or many? *Lancet, 354,* 936–939.

Whitehead, W. E., Palsson, O., & Jones, K. R. (2002). Systematic review of the comorbidity of irritable bowel syndrome with other disorders: What are the causes and implications? *Gastroenterology, 122,* 1140–1156.

Wikner, J., Hirsch, U., Wetterberg, L., & Rojdmark, S. (1998). Fibromyalgia: A syndrome associated with decreased nocturnal melatonin secretion. *Clinical Endocrinology, 49,* 179–183.

Williams, G., Waterhouse, J., Mugarza, J., Minors, D., & Hayden, K. (2002). Therapy of circadian rhythm disorders in chronic fatigue syndrome: No symptomatic improvement with melatonin or phototherapy. *European Journal of Clinical Investigation, 32,* 831–837.

Williamson, B. L., Klarskov, K., Tomlinson, A. J., Gleich, G. J., & Naylor, S. (1998). Problems with over-the-counter 5-hydroxyl-L-tryptophan [Letter]. *Nature Medicine, 4*(9), 983.

Wolfe, F., Smythe, H. A., Yunus, M. B., Bennett, R. M., Bombardier, C., Goldenberg, D. L., et al. (1990). The American College of Rheumatology 1990 criteria for the classification of FM: Report of the multicenter criteria committee. *Arthritis and Rheumatism, 33,* 160–172.

Wynants, H., & Moorkens, G. (2003). Magnesium and vitamin D status in female patients with CFS, fibromyalgia or autonomic dysfunction [Abstract]. *Conference syllabus, sixth international conference on chronic fatigue syndrome, fibromyalgia and related illnesses.* Chantilly, VA: American Association for Chronic Fatigue Syndrome.

Yunus, M. B., Dailey, J. W., Aldag, J. C., Masi, A. T., & Jobe, P. C. (1992). Plasma tryptophan and other amino acids in primary fibromyalgia: A controlled study. *Journal of Rheumatology, 19,* 90–94.

Yunus, M. B., Masi, A. T., & Aldag, J. C. (1989). Preliminary criteria for primary fibromyalgia syndrome (PFS): Multivariate analysis of a consecutive series of PFS, other pain patients, and normal controls. *Clinical and Experimental Rheumatology, 7,* 63–69.

Yunus, M. B., Masi, A. T., Calabro, J. J., Miller, K. A., & Feigenbaum, S. L. (1981). Primary fibromyalgia (fibrositis): Clinical study of 50 patients with matched normal controls. *Seminars in Arthritis and Rheumatism, 11,* 151–171.

Zabinski, Z., Dabrowski, Z., Moszczynski, P., & Rutowski, J. (2000). The activity of erythrocyte enzymes and basic indices of peripheral blood erythrocytes from workers chronically exposed to mercury vapors. *Toxicology and Industrial Health, 16*(2), 58–64.

Zeman, F. J. (1991). Clinical nutrition and dietetics (2nd ed.). New York: Macmillan.

Zhao, Z., & Ross, A. C. (1995). Retinoic acid repletion restores the number of leukocytes and their subsets and stimulates natural cytotoxicity in vitamin-A deficient rats. *Journal of Nutrition, 125,* 2064–2073.

CHAPTER 28

Rehabilitation Counseling

DONALD USLAN WITH CONTRIBUTIONS BY GRAHAM J. PATRICK,
PAUL B. BROWN, NEIL CONATY, PATRICIA YOUNGMAN,
KIM BENNETT, GLORIA FURST, LUCY SWAN AND JAMES R. BLAIR

HISTORICAL BACKGROUND

THE PROBLEMS OF physically disabled people led to the founding of the Cleveland (Ohio) Rehabilitation Center in 1899. During World War I, the Red Cross Institute for Crippled and Disabled Men (now the Institute for the Crippled and Disabled) was organized in New York City. The laws for workers' compensation enacted in many states between 1911 and 1920 created an awareness of the need for rehabilitating those injured in industrial accidents; 12 states established rehabilitation laws toward the end of this period. To aid the multitude of disabled World War I veterans, Congress passed the Smith-Sears Soldier Rehabilitation Act in June 1918. It was the first of many measures for people disabled in military service.

Federal aid to the states for the rehabilitation of civilians began with the Vocational Rehabilitation Act of 1920, amended in 1943 by the Barden-La Follette Act. That legislation established the Office of Vocational Rehabilitation (now the Office of Special Education and Rehabilitative Services, a unit of the Department of Education since 1980). More recent federal legislation has focused on severely disabled individuals, promoted public involvement in the rehabilitation process, and funded the National Institute of Disability and Rehabilitation Research.

WHAT IS REHABILITATION COUNSELING?

Vocational rehabilitation helps chronically ill or physically injured people maximize their work potential. The rehabilitation activity, or "plan," depends on the patients' condition, how they manage their life requirements while fulfilling their work requirements, and what changes can be made to fit their work into the whole treatment picture. Vocational rehabilitation also includes working with clients and their attorneys to allow the patient to work part-time, take a leave of absence, go back to work, or change their work entirely if necessary.

Rehabilitation counseling may also mean directly assisting employers, insurers, or physicians as well as providing information on other possible care interventions. The counselor may recommend reasonable modifications to a job or workstation, or discuss legal issues such as disability benefits. Vocational rehabilitation involves implementing plans that keep work part of the picture and make receiving disability benefits a temporary part of the treatment plan instead of a long-term goal.

Rehabilitation counseling serves individuals with disabilities and limitations by helping them learn how to manage physical restrictions that limit their activities or functioning. Because of the counselors' close association with the medical model of care, they must understand medical terminology, diagnosis, medications, prognosis, vocational evaluation of disability-related limitations, and the world of work. These professionals must also be familiar with a wide range of health care disciplines (e.g., physical therapy, occupational therapy, massage, chiropractic, acupuncture, naturopathy, speech and communication therapy, and psychology). Finally, counselors must be cognizant of the community resources that are available to help patients improve their level of functioning.

Rehabilitation counselors use a pragmatic, or goal-oriented, approach with short, midrange, and long-term goals and time frames for increasing work or lifestyle options. In assisting patients, counselors incorporate disability evaluation, patient education, health care systems, and care coordination. The concept of patients going through levels or phases in coping with their condition is important. During the therapy sessions, counselors encourage clients to increase their options by pursuing their own research, completing the homework assignments, identifying specific problems, and developing possible solutions.

Vocational evaluation is a comprehensive process that systematically uses work, real or simulated, for assessment and vocational exploration. The purpose is to assist individuals in vocational development (Weiss, 1980). The evaluation incorporates medical, psychological, social, vocational, academic, cultural, and economic data.

PAIN MANAGEMENT AND STRESS MANAGEMENT

Pain management and stress management are applications of clinical counseling techniques for the reduction of pain, stress, and suffering. Pain management is used with chronic and non-life-threatening illness or injury conditions lasting at least 6 months. Tools, techniques, and principles from the discrete healing arts are blended and reformulated as a holistic application to reduce pain and suffering (Horowitz, 1998). Stress management is used for a variety of personal responses to life, occupational and family stressors (McGuigan, 2000).

For individuals in chronic pain and stress, proven pain management coping skills and strategies can enhance healthy daily functioning and improve pain responses. Focusing on strategies to manage pain helps patients reduce or cope with it more effectively. Although doctors and adjunctive health care professionals are vital for successful chronic pain and stress management, the client plays an important role through lifestyle, beliefs, and emotions that can heighten or lessen pain sensitivity.

Useful techniques include individual biofeedback relaxation (autogenics, guided imagery, progressive relaxation), hypnosis, meditation, treatment sessions to facilitate coping skills, cognitive rehabilitation, pain management coping strategies, and homework to incorporate these strategies into a participant's life.

DISABILITY MANAGEMENT

For physical or medical conditions that last longer than 6 months, disability management is the skill of coping with a long-term impairment that affects psychological adjustment, family, financial, spiritual, and social domains of life. By assisting clients with strategies and working with interdisciplinary services as well as the clients' extended support system, counselors can help persons with a disability learn to live well with their condition.

Traditional counseling approaches and rehabilitation techniques are used. These include goal identification and review, time frames, monitoring of change, workplace performance, conflict resolution, assertiveness, problem solving, choices and options, restrictions and boundaries, pacing and limit setting, transitional models of improvement, case management, advocacy, community services, team meeting, risk analysis, contingency planning, and the phases of illness.

Rehabilitation Strategies

The lifestyle limitations and challenges imposed by a chronic health condition require serious consideration of the role of "work." Work means many things to people: money, survival, dignity, self-esteem, entertainment, socialization, empowerment, career, and structure. Work is also the effort involved in managing, living with, and even improving a serious, long-term health problem. So, when thinking about how to work with CFS or FMS, the counselor must look at the patient's condition in a long-term context. Preventing the condition from getting worse is essential, especially after working at significant improvement. Creative thinking in this (as well as other) areas of the patient's health care will pay dividends.

Health and Improvement Considerations

Reduced Work Activity   The most difficult health period is usually at the onset of the illness. The needs vary for each individual, but most people benefit from a period of part-time work or a leave of absence. They use this time to rest, focus on treatment approaches, and reduce stress. Restricted work activity for 30 to 90 days as soon as possible maximizes the likelihood of returning more readily to normal work activity.

Recognition of Emotional and Lifestyle Adjustment   The diagnosis of a chronic health problem is traumatic for patients. The changes in physical stamina, mental abilities, financial condition, and family relationships may represent significant losses. Although the tendency to deny the changes is understandable, emotional reactions to these changes are part of a natural healing process. Allowing the natural grieving processes to occur, which can include powerful emotions such as anger and sadness, can improve patients' health. Counselors can provide guidance to patients who are having difficulty adjusting to changes in their health.

Return-to-Work Planning

Transitional Work   A graduated return-to-work plan, after medical leave, offers an excellent opportunity for assessing the patient's response to the demands and stress of work. A typical plan considers "spacing and pacing." "Spacing" means allowing a day of rest between each day of work activity. "Pacing" means starting out at a reasonable minimum of hours, and gradually adding more over the course of weeks and months. Example: After 60 days of medical leave, a person with chronic fatigue syndrome (CFS) or fibromyalgia syndrome (FMS) might go back to work for 3 hours per day, Mondays, Wednesdays, and Fridays, adding an hour per workday every other week. The hours would be increased up to a reasonable limit (or decreased if the patient did not respond well).

Light-Duty Work or Part-Time Work   Working for a brief period in a less demanding position also reduces stress. For example, a department supervisor with significant responsibilities could take a position as a planner in a different department for 90 days. This position has no supervisory responsibilities, less noise and activity, fewer deadline demands, and a slower pace. Changing from full-time work to part-time work on a permanent basis can also reduce stress and assist pacing.

Self-Employment   If feasible, this option offers the maximum flexibility, especially if some or all of the work can be performed at home. Extensive free information is available through the Small Business Administration.

EMPLOYER STRATEGIES

The Direct Approach   Asking the employer to help figure out how to adapt the job to your patient's limitations is the best first step. Because conditions like CFS and FMS may not be apparent to others, formally alerting the supervisor or superiors about the condition and trying to work with them can go a long way.

Using a Health Care Professional   Some employers respond more constructively to altering a job if a member of the patient's health care team, such as a rehabilitation counselor, occupational therapist, or physician, outlines the restrictions with suggestions, including proposed time frames.

Americans with Disabilities Act (ADA)   Employers need to make "reasonable accommodation" for a wide variety of apparent and nonapparent disabilities, specifically including chronic fatigue syndrome. These accommodations can involve restructuring the job, modifying equipment and policies, and altering work schedules. Many of these changes can be made at no cost.

Using a Legal Professional   Some employers may need to be educated or reminded that there are severe state and federal penalties for discrimination against the handicapped. An attorney who has the patient's best work interests in mind, is familiar with state and federal labor laws, and is willing to work with the health care treatment team can provide enormous assistance.

COPING STRATEGIES

CARING FOR THE CAREGIVERS

Caregivers do not get enough care, acknowledgment, or attention . . . from the patient, from medical practitioners, from themselves. The friends, families, and loved ones of people with chronic diseases, the caregivers, have special needs that are often unrecognized or unacknowledged by patients or professional health care practitioners. Yet, patients do not live in a vacuum. They are part of a family, however it may be defined, and the whole family in some way suffers with the patient.

As a psychotherapist and rehabilitation counselor, I see mostly patients with long-term chronic medical conditions such as fibromyalgia and chronic fatigue syndrome. These patients can only progress and gain maximum improvement to the extent that their caregiving system is healthy. Patients often make the following remarks about their conditions and their support system:

- "I want the freedom to talk. I don't want to minimize my stuff."
- "I don't want to be a burden to my family."
- "It's depressing to have someone keep listening about how sick I am."
- "I hate the disease."
- "It's not fair."
- "I function on brain power, but, I can't use it anymore."
- "I hate it when they tell me I don't look sick."
- "I hate it when they tell me I look sick."
- "I want someone to validate what I am experiencing."

Recently, a patient said to me, "The hardest thing for me was, and is, being misunderstood, such as not being able to do some engagement or go on a date because I feel sick. You're damned if you do, you're damned if you don't . . . if you do make an appearance at a family gathering, but if you're less than enthusiastic or tired, then people think you are inconsiderate or a flake. If you call ahead and try to be considerate and just say you can't do it, you get the same response. This leads to perpetual defensiveness, which requires too much energy and is a hard pattern to change."

This is all enough to drive a family member crazy.

The art of becoming a patient and learning to handle many complex new things takes time and energy. The anxiety of waiting for test results, the emotional adjustment to a diagnosis (or lack of one), the possibility of needing to see many medical consultants, make appointments, and share concerns with friends and family are just a few of the changes that may happen in a short time. Then, patients must expend additional effort to change their lifestyle and learn how to take care of themselves.

All the while, the patients' loved ones are struggling to cope with the medical condition and the dramatic changes in lifestyle, work, and finances this can cause. Yet, no one gives them a "prescription" for their changes. Seldom do they receive sympathy or attention. There is no "prognosis" for their change in condition. Yet, their lifestyle will change right along with the patients.

Patients often describe caregivers as being "thoughtful," "sensitive," "considerate," "the best husband in the world." They may say, "She does everything for me," or "I don't know where I'd be without my friend." However, patients sometimes fail to realize that as they are making important life changes in activities, schedules, work, and housekeeping, their caregivers are making similar changes (Ferrari & Jason, 1997).

Spouse and "Significant Other" Roles   Intimate relationships fall into three types: (1) patients with no love relationship, or one that is fragile; (2) a nonmarital love relationship; and (3) marriages. Each of these three situations presents unique challenges. Men often have a different style of coping with these relationship problems.

Patients with No "Love" Relationship   For those men and women who either had no well-developed support network, or whose illness contributed to the loss of their friends, the challenges seem insurmountable. They often feel as if they are doomed to a life of loneliness. These people reason, "Who would want someone with a chronic disease?"

Isolation and low self-esteem can be toxic forms of stress, a dangerous enemy to chronic illness. Strategies for patients in these situations include not only using support groups for general socializing, but seeking out people who can understand and accept the limitations of the illness. This is usually more difficult in the early stage of the condition and may require many months of effort. Persons suffering from fatigue and pain can still listen, give, take an interest in, call on the phone, write letters, and use humor to cultivate caring friends. The logistics may be harder, and it can become a lesson in learning about other people and their ability to handle a disability in someone, but it is possible for patients to develop lifelong caring friends. They must be careful, however, not to substitute health care professionals for social or intimate caregivers.

Nonmarital Love Relationships   The lack of a marriage contract makes a love relationship more fragile because it lacks the legal and moral commitment to "love and to cherish, in sickness and in health."

Patients should be careful not to burden their significant other with needs and demands that could be spread out among other supporters. Sometimes significant others do not deliberately complain or make negative comments, but they still send such messages with nonverbal facial expressions of frustration, "short fuse," coming home late, and volunteering to do work around the house but "forgetting" to do it. Counselors can suggest ways to meet and anticipate caregivers' needs. One patient encouraged her boyfriend (without conveying guilt) to go camping and hiking with his friends, so he could socialize in activities that were beyond her strength at that time.

Marriages   The challenge to a marriage differs from that of a "boyfriend/girlfriend" relationship. Both parties often believe that they "can work it out." Such statements as "We've been together for a long time," "We've been through many rough things together," "We understand each other so well we can read each other's minds," or "We're tied at the hip forever" can be danger signals. There are some truths in these statements, but a long-term, prolonged chronic illness that probably has a depressive component requires new coping strategies.

Many spouses express doubts about the medical credibility of unusual health conditions. Patients then either try to convince their spouse of their illness or exhibit some other problem behavior such as minimizing (or maximizing) symptoms. It can be helpful for the spouse to accompany the patient to appointments with health care providers whenever possible. There are also many excellent self-help reading and workbooks available on coping with chronic conditions and keeping marriages healthy.

The couple might consider joining or starting a couple support group to share issues and solutions in marriages that must deal with the stress of having a chronic medical condition. A practitioner skilled and knowledgeable about chronic physical or medical conditions can offer other useful suggestions.

Above all, remind couples to attempt to keep a sense of play, enjoyment, fun, and humor in their relationship. This is an essential ingredient for a well-balanced marriage.

Minor Children   A parent's chronic condition can easily confuse and frighten young children, especially if they are preverbal or have limited verbal skills. Parents often express guilt at the effect their condition has on their young children. Maintaining physical and emotional security is extremely important. Demonstrating a "parent team" in handling problems related to the medical condition relieves children's fears about harm coming to them. The lessons children learn from watching their parents handle a serious life crisis can help prepare them for some of the roadblocks they will surely meet in adult life.

COPING WITH GRIEF

The Patient   In coming to an acceptance of their condition, patients usually need to make emotional adjustments through a process called *grieving*. They grieve for what they have lost, such as their health, hobbies, or perhaps dreams or goals. Patients need to learn that these aspects of self are not necessarily lost, but instead, must be adapted to meet the new circumstances.

People go through five steps in grieving: denial, bargaining, anger, sadness, then, finally, acceptance. It is often difficult to go through these steps, and friends or professionals can help the patient.

The Family   Loved ones need to allow themselves to take a vacation from the stress of their position. Structuring responsibilities and allowing for breaks and task sharing with others can break the tension and make caregiving more manageable. Caregivers have to go through the same steps of grieving because they have lost and must change many important parts of their life, including their former relationship with the patient. Taking care of someone can be stressful and tiring. Expressing this to the patient can seem threatening, inconsiderate, or inappropriate. But, unless the family members can express negative as well as positive feelings and thoughts, they may become more distant from the person who is ill, or suffer themselves.

To cope with the changes, family members can ask questions, read, and learn about the condition; go to support group meetings; and talk to other caregivers. Creativity always seems to help people cope with life. Counselors can suggest that caregivers use creative approaches in preparing foods, developing tools to assist the patient around the house, and getting the job done in novel ways.

Encourage a positive attitude that incorporates humor, lightheartedness, goal setting, and optimistic plans for the future.

Professional guidance through a mental health practitioner or similar professional can assist the family in coming to terms with the sometimes-profound changes a chronic illness can bring. Problems often arise for caregivers, and the medical team's and the patient's planning should include the support system.

PAIN AND MEDICATIONS

The quest to manage pain and fatigue, as well as the many other symptoms of fibromyalgia and chronic fatigue syndrome, can be long and frustrating. Patients may have difficulty finding a doctor or doctors with whom they can communicate and receive good care and proper diagnosis. Because the need for treatment and the response to treatment may change over the years, a long-term relationship with the same doctor is beneficial. Patients and their relationship with their primary medical practitioner form the core of the treatment plan. A long and trusting relationship is essential to assure the continuing accuracy of the diagnosis. Many times, the secondary and variable symptoms of fibromyalgia or chronic fatigue syndrome can be confused with other conditions such as an ear infection or the flu. A doctor who knows the patient's history, life stressors, and response to treatment and medications can more readily determine whether a new course of action is required.

Medications need periodic reevaluation. Old medications sometimes lose or change their effectiveness. New medications or new uses for old medications become available. Fine-tuning or creative thinking can work seeming miracles. The best doctors are true artists in their use of medications. They may try a change of a sleeping medication here, a slightly lower dosage of antidepressant, a bit of a mood stabilizer, or possibly an over-the-counter product—and voilà! What emerges is the portrait of a well-managed patient who can benefit from other treatments and handle life better.

However, the question of pain medications can threaten even the best doctor-patient relationship. The words *pain medication* mean different things to different doctors, and the term *pain management* can further confuse the issue. Pain management represents the combined effort of physicians, patients, and the many allied health care practitioners to alter the experience of pain. Pain medication is specifically the realm of a doctor.

For some, Prozac is a pain medication. Neurontin, a medication used for many different purposes, was originally a seizure medication. It is also used to treat mood disorders as well as some cognitive problems, and now it is being used in pain control. Anti-inflammatory medications can be used as a pain medication.

Most patients and doctors, however, identify pain medications with narcotics and opioids. This class of medications is highly regulated by the Food and Drug Administration. Although experiences vary from state to state, the prescribing of opioids is a sensitive issue for physicians. Scholarly documentation is lacking on their effectiveness for many medical conditions. There are few guidelines for the use of narcotics and many examples of patient and prescription misuse. Doctors have had their licenses threatened, or at least their reputations stained, even by the legitimate and conservative use of opioids.

In many regions of the country, there has been a "McCarthy" era of witch hunting for doctors who prescribe opioids. A couple of years ago, a doctor friend of mine, who was highly experienced in pain medication use, was hauled before the state medical review board based on a complaint by his patient's insurance claims manager. The claims manager saw frequent renewed prescriptions for narcotics and assumed the doctor was engaging in criminal behavior. Many doctors in the medical community heard about this nightmarish experience, which confirmed their worst fears about prescribing such pain medications.

My friend was able to reason with the medical review board and demonstrated to them that he knew more about the proper prescriptive use of opioids than they did. They agreed and realized that it was a statewide problem because there were no established standards. Monthly meetings of doctors who used opioids in pain management were then established, and gradually their conservative application has been accepted for many conditions, including fibromyalgia and chronic fatigue syndrome.

Pain medications can be an understandably sensitive issue to doctors because many of them have been the victims of prescriptive drug abuse by patients. It may be unfair for a doctor to generalize a bad experience with one patient to all patients, but a patient's narcotic abuse can jeopardize a physician's livelihood and reputation.

Before prescribing opioids, here are a few things for physicians to consider:

- Doctors should have expertise in the area of CFS or FMS and should have treated many patients, attended workshops, or read reputable articles.
- Doctors without extensive experience should have a consultation with such an expert before prescribing opioids to a patient.
- It is essential to review all the medications and therapies the patient has tried and to discuss the patient's current level of pain. Perhaps a different or stronger type of pain medication would help.
- Openly discuss with the patient any substance-dependent or addictive history.
- If there is a history of addiction, alcohol abuse, or other substance abuse, the prescribing of opioids is rarely advisable.
- If the patient is insistent, consider a consultation referral to a board-certified pain management physician or board-certified addictionologist. These are both physician specialties with expertise in the assessment, treatment, and monitoring of medical conditions with the use of opioids. They can either prescribe or advise patients about these types of medication. This approach may resolve the problem without damaging the primary doctor-patient relationship.

Most physicians take a long-term view of their patients, and one controversial issue does not destroy a relationship. As in all relationships, trust and communication can offset occasional rough moments.

HELPING PATIENTS LEARN TO LIVE WITH CHRONIC FATIGUE SYNDROME

Problems with physicians aside, CFS or FMS patients need to learn how to consider the source of negative, ignorant, or hostile statements. Counseling can help them develop a variety of responses in their repertoire. Some people are simply not worth responding to or expending energy on. Others warrant a thoughtful educative response. And others may deserve a firm rejection of their comments.

When persons are fatigued and in pain, all critical comments may seem hurtful and accusatory. To help patients deal with these matters, counselors can offer them the following guidelines.

Patient Guidelines

DEALING WITH HOSTILITY   Some family members who seem to be hostile may not realize the price you pay in fatigue and pain if you fail to set limits to activities. With greater understanding, they may become your greatest supporters.

Try to give anyone that you care about a brief explanation of the condition on a one-to-one basis, without trying to justify the medical illness; just describe the facts of your experience. You may want to give your relative one of the many thoughtful brochures about CFS or FMS from the *Fibromyalgia Network* or other sources. Most likely, you learned long ago to avoid sensitive arguments about religion or politics; now you should add medical conditions to this list of sensitive subjects. If conflicts continue, try to stay away from persons who remain hostile. As a last measure, you may need to confront them to point out that their comments are destructive and that you cannot have contact with them if they persist in giving you their opinions and judgments.

GAINING YOUR PHYSICIAN'S SUPPORT   As a patient, it can be difficult for you to handle a doctor who shoots down your therapeutic suggestions, especially when this doctor is your HMO gatekeeper. If you are frustrated with the lack of support from your primary care physician, carefully consider whether you should find another doctor or try to influence the physician's opinions. Some physicians object to therapies that are unrelated to their own philosophy or that cannot be billed to the HMO. Other physicians may simply lack experience in treating CFS or FMS.

Consider, first, whether your request is fair and legitimate. Asking for a referral to a therapy that most physicians—even those with experience with CFS or FMS—would consider "out there," "on the edge," or "marginal" is unfair to the physician. However, if a treatment procedure or modality has demonstrated benefits in general or to CFS and FMS in particular, it is justifiable to request the physician's support. Providing information from a legitimate source, such as the Fibromyalgia Network and discussing the benefits of the therapy with your doctor may be helpful. Or, you may request the physician's support for the referral, with the proviso that later the two of you can judge the therapy's effectiveness and jointly raise your learning curve about this condition. I have many patients who liked and respected their physicians, but found them too conservative about referrals to other services. Give your doctor the opportunity to team up with you, but remember that you are the manager of your treatment team and thus must take final responsibility for your choice of treatment.

TIPS ON CONTROLLING YOUR ANGER   The frustrations of having a chronic medical problem such as fibromyalgia, chronic fatigue syndrome, or similar conditions like arthritis can sometimes spill over onto the people we love and care about. The fatigue or pain can seem to take over your personality. The monster in you comes out. Lack of restorative sleep and cognitive confusion can cause you to misunderstand or misinterpret what someone else has said or done. Your medical problems and special needs can also wear out your family and loved ones, and they can become short-tempered and cranky. Sometimes the causes speak to an underlying problem, such as depression, which needs the focus of a professional counselor. However, using common sense can solve many problems of anger.

It is important to distinguish between words related to anger that describe how you feel. Anger is a basic and common emotion that we all experience and need to express for healthy adjustment. Sometimes, anger is a fleeting feeling that helps us understand our emotional state. It can also be a strong reaction to someone's expectations or something going on in our social setting. Addressing the problem in a reasonable manner can usually resolve such matters.

Anger can also reflect stress and a buildup of pressure. You can often reduce it with some form of release such as stress management or, if possible, physical activity. Try to know your own emotional makeup so you can tell whether you are "on-target" with your anger or are directing anger "off-target." If the emotion you are labeling "anger" continues for an extended period, it may require your management and extra effort, even the help of family and friends.

The words in the following list are associated with anger. Try to identify the words you use, and whether they speak to your true emotions or may be a function of your illness:

Aggressive	Hostile	Provoked
Annoyed	Incensed	Resentful
Bitter	Indignant	Sore
Boiling	Inflamed	Unpleasant
Cross	Infuriated	Upset
Enraged	Insulting	Worked up
Fuming	Irritated	
Hateful	Offensive	

The most basic, sensible way to deal with anger is simply to be aware of your own emotional state and take responsibility. To say to your partner, perhaps with a little humor, "I'm really irritable today, let's talk about this another time, or I might bite your head off" can be, ironically, very reassuring. Or, "I'm in a very bad mood, I'm going to take a time-out" can tell your loved one that you want to protect your relationship by not saying something you don't mean or acting in a way you will regret.

Try to recognize and verbalize anger when you are experiencing it. State how you feel with a specific "I" statement using a courteous, respectful, assertive manner (e.g., "I am angry with you because you didn't do what I asked and you said you would do it" versus "You make me so angry when you say you will do things and never do them").

The following are some other tips for managing anger:

- Develop an awareness of your feelings and behaviors.
- Minimize or avoid stressful situations.
- Exercise (according to your doctor or physical therapist's recommendations).
- Do not take responsibility for people and other things that you cannot control.
- Use visualization and other stress management techniques such as progressive relaxation, meditation, biofeedback, guided imagery.
- Be aware of your self-talk. What you say to yourself will determine how you think and feel.
- Communicate with your partner and family or friends.

- Develop resources and a support system that will encourage positive changes in you and in your life.
- Implement self-care behaviors. People who take care of themselves feel better about who they are, have more energy, and are more likely to be happy.
- Lower your expectations and set realistic goals.
- Treat yourself to something pleasurable. Give yourself a reward.
- Take responsibility for your own emotions and responses.
- Attitude will greatly influence your success or failure. If you have a negative attitude, do not expect good things to happen.
- Analyze past reactions to important events that tend to be stressful, such as holidays or family gatherings, and recall your reactions. Try to change a situation or your behavior so you can change your reactions.

Reducing, controlling, and directing anger in a healthy way can help you manage your illness and may help to manage some symptoms. It certainly will make it easier for your support system to give you the help you need (Capuano Sgambati, 1998).

Survival Techniques for Loved Ones

Although fibromyalgia and chronic fatigue syndrome are still poorly understood medical conditions, sufferers and professionals are developing a large body of information about coping with these conditions. There are newsletters, support groups, Internet sites, books, lectures, television broadcasts, journals, conferences, and professionals of all types willing to offer help and advice, some of it good, some not so good. Special products for sufferers include aids for just about every need—their sleep, diet, health, feet, eyes, and heads! Excellent researchers struggle to understand the social, psychological, biochemical, and physical dimensions of these and related conditions. Legal and disability professionals and institutions struggle with the social and occupational impact of these conditions.

But, what about the loved ones?

What about husbands and wives, mothers and fathers, sons and daughters. What about grandparents and grandchildren? How about friends and neighbors?

Knowing someone with FM or CFS can be a challenging experience. Living with one can be even more difficult. The loved ones need compassion and understanding from FM and CFS patients as well as from the professional community. They need education, help, and special tools that can enable them to support and assist the patient. They also need to preserve their own quality of life. They need to keep their spirits high and their health intact. The tools and techniques patients learn to regain their health are also important for loved ones to keep their health.

Do these complaints sound familiar?

- Sleep problems that keep the FM sufferer from getting a good night's sleep by waking frequently during the night also keep their bedmate from awakening refreshed.
- The fatigue experienced by the CFS patient requires loved ones to maintain almost all the housecleaning functions, causing resentment and possibly a dirty house.
- Young children of sufferers whine or misbehave because they lack attention.

- The sufferer must miss work or stop work because of the CFS, which causes financial stress for the whole family. The spouse begins to experience serious anxiety and worry over money. Children sense something is wrong or troubling their parents.
- The patient's irritability, moodiness, and occasional lashing because of pain and discomfort trigger self-doubt, loneliness, and depression in the spouse.
- The spouse's efforts to care and provide for the person with the chronic medical condition never seem to be enough. Deep compassion and loyalty as well as efforts to anticipate needs do not seem to help, resulting in a feeling of inadequacy or despair about the future.

Some of the problems loved ones must deal with, such as the patient's forgetfulness, can seem relatively simple and occasionally even humorous. Patients may turn circles a few times before accomplishing a simple task, or stare blankly for a minute as they try to recall what they were talking about. Such behavior usually does not seriously upset caregivers. However, providing long-term care can still cause severe problems for loved ones. Lack of exercise and poor diet can lead to a general health decline. Withdrawal from social support can cause a feeling of isolation. Prolonged stress can increase the likelihood of hypertension and heart attack. Denial of needs can fuel anger and irritability. Work performance and attendance can suffer because of the patient's relapses or medical appointments. Anxiety or depression requiring medications or counseling can result from having too much to do and too many things to take care of. Loved ones may have a deep-seated fear that the situation will never change for the better. These caregivers require their own care plan and treatment approach. Here are some suggestions:

- Health care professionals must consider the effect of the medical condition on the whole family and be willing to take an interest in them.
- Encourage loved ones to protect their own physical health with regular medical checkups.
- Caregivers need relief from a job that continues 24 hours a day. Developing or pursuing their own hobbies, interests, and activities by themselves or with friends can give them renewed energy in assisting the patient.
- Exercise helps mental and physical health. Health care professionals should encourage caregivers to engage in regular physical activity.
- Communicating to loved ones that it is beneficial for them to *not* take care of the patient occasionally can be very freeing for them.
- Consider supportive counseling for loved ones to help them adjust to and cope with the sometimes-profound changes in the patient. They have their own grief at losing the healthy person they knew.
- Most loved ones avoid making negative comments that could discourage the recovery of the FM or CFS patient. They may need a safe place to vent their frustration, confusion, disappointment, and fear.

Having a chronic medical condition can be all-consuming. Persons who are otherwise giving can become obsessed with their illness. Counselors should urge them to carve out time to care for and nurture their loved ones in the best way they are able. It takes little physical strength for patients to express concern for the well-being of their loved ones and to support their efforts at taking care of themselves.

The sufferer of FM or CFS cannot improve or recover unless their loved ones stay healthy. Their survival requires good communication with the patient and with health care professionals, a balance of demands in life, and thoughtful assistance.

DAILY COPING WITH FATIGUE AND PAIN

As a medical psychotherapist and rehabilitation counselor for over 20 years, by far the problem I have heard patients and their families voice most often is the difficulty of pacing to avoid running out of energy. Even as patients apply themselves to the medications, treatments, and lifestyle changes needed to get the most out of their improvement, the relapses and setbacks become a roller-coaster ride of hope and disappointment. The rehabilitation process of developing a healthier body requires a patient to be determined, hopeful, and optimistic. Yet, the frequent frustrations undermine healthy thinking, part of developing a healthier body, and they challenge and confuse family and support systems.

Last summer, I was invited to participate in the Nevada Think Tank on the Rehabilitation of Chronic Fatigue Syndrome. This was an opportunity for researchers and rehabilitation professionals from around the country to compare notes about which treatment approaches were constructive and helpful. My division was composed of allied health care clinicians from the fields of physical therapy, psychology, exercise physiology, occupational therapy, speech therapy, and vocational rehabilitation. After acknowledging that physicians do not use rehabilitation professionals nearly often enough to benefit patients, the participants agreed that the greatest challenge in caring for patients was assisting them in the art of pacing and setting limits and boundaries.

The CFS and FMS patients who show improvement are those who master pacing themselves and managing their expenditure of energy. This is an art form, a skill that requires the attention to detail of an accountant. It combines assertiveness and determination in staying on the task of recognizing the limitations of energy and using this precious resource frugally.

A patient of mine parked her car at the airport. Later, when she went to find it, her cognitive problems plagued her, as the car was not where she thought it should be. She had one of those hand-held devices with her key which, when pressed, turned on the lights and beeped the horn. She was forced to walk up and down every aisle and parking level for over an hour with her family trailing along, aiming the key as she went until finally the lights of her car flashed and the horn honked at her! But, she was so exhausted that she had to sit in the car to rest. Her family was tired, too, and frustrated and angry at her forgetfulness.

Because of this experience, she became a devoted user of a Day-Timer to track her appointments, important events, and things to do; to list phone numbers—and to jot down where she parked her car.

Together, we developed an approach for using the Day-Timer to follow her daily activities, tasks, and responsibilities; and we carefully estimated the energy each one consumed. We assumed that she had to budget her salary (energy) like a paycheck so that it covered her daily bills (tasks). We used dried lima beans to represent payment: She was paid 24 lima beans a day—one for each hour. Getting out of bed, getting dressed, eating breakfast, and getting her children off to school took 6 beans, leaving her 18. Doing some basic straightening of the house took another five beans, leaving 13. She then took a brief rest, replenishing three beans, with 16 now in the savings account. Going shopping, visiting the doctor, calling a friend, preparing dinner, receiving her family used 12 more beans, leaving 4 for the rest of the evening. She could choose to save these for the next day, and have 28 beans, or she could spend some time with her husband and children, or perhaps, take time for herself and use up the remaining four beans. This was a trial-and-error process, and her family thought she was a flaming nut at first as she walked around with a plastic bag full of lima beans (gives a whole new meaning to the term "bean counter").

After a while, though, she became expert in pacing herself and seldom went into debt for overspending lima beans. Her family graphically understood the fragility and precision of energy management. Her mastery of pacing and setting limits for her own energy, as well as for the demands and expectations of her family and friends, facilitated her slow, gradual improvement to where she began to feel she was living close to a "normal" life.

She does not have to use lima beans anymore. And by the way, her family hates lima bean soup.

PATIENT ADVOCACY AND SELF-ADVOCACY

Why the Need for Advocacy?   When I see patients with chronic illnesses, their lives have been turned upside down. Their partners and loved ones may think they are crazy, lazy, depressed, or have lost their enjoyment of life. Their bosses may think that this once marvelous worker has simply decided to kick back and become a slacker. Their children are usually scared to death at the change in their parent. The truth is that these patients are exhausted, lost, frightened, and have very little in the way of direction. Advocacy by health care professionals encompasses these people who are chronically ill. They need help navigating the waters. They have not received any training; they have no expertise in the business of being sick. Advocacy is not just education; it empowers the patient. In developing the process and mind-set of advocacy, the counselor teaches patients that they have a right and responsibility in their own getting better or living with illness. And it means they are entitled to help in their health and coping. They are entitled to an intervention. Once patients acknowledge stress, strain, and the difficult impact on themselves and family, then advocacy validates the experiences.

What Is Advocacy?   Advocacy means assisting patients in working their way to their highest level of functioning. It involves teaching patients how to be consumers of health care and how to hire and fire practitioners. It includes assertiveness training by example, with the use of every possible community resource. It also may mean teaching patients to be articulate about what they need and urging them to take advantage of support groups and organizations.

As an advocate, I educate patients about various systems, their functions, limitations, means of access, and the pros and cons of becoming involved in that system. I challenge the belief that patients cannot have rich and satisfying lives even if sick. It may mean helping them develop a treatment plan or a return-to-work plan. I might need to walk them over to physical therapy or some other treatment provider. Sometimes it is appropriate to give their physician feedback about medications and suggest changes.

Vocational advocacy means assisting patients in altering their work life to fit the current and future needs of their illness. I may teach them about state and federal laws concerning disability accommodation or help them draft a letter to their supervisor explaining the disability. It may require consulting a physician about how to draft a response to an insurance company, or actually drafting the response for the physician. It may involve filling out a disability form for a nurse. For lonely and isolated patients, advocacy can consist of hooking them up with a CFS support group, social group, church, or synagogue to give them a sense of belonging. It means giving them published guides to self-help books, or lending a book and taking the risk of not seeing it again. If the need for legal assistance is apparent, I teach and share by example what good legal care means and supply recommendations.

How to Use Advocacy with Patients in a Clinical Setting   On an integrated team, everyone has the responsibility for patient advocacy. No one practitioner is enough. The skills of a particular discipline—be it physician, nurse, occupational therapist, or care coordinator—are not necessarily the skills a patient needs to learn to live with illness. We have the responsibility to support patients in finding the right solution for their particular needs. In a clinical setting, health care professionals sometimes need to think outside their own disciplines and be willing to discuss approaches and perceptions of patients with colleagues. One provider may think the patient is a troublemaker or is overly dependent or manipulative; whereas another practitioner may believe the same patient is capable of change or is simply scared to death. The richness of a diverse clinical team, then, can serve patients in many dimensions. The education of family and the support of caregivers are essential elements in advocacy, for if the support system does not grow and change, the patient cannot improve and cope. In our therapy groups, we teach the value of self-management and self-advocacy as well as the skills for using various resources. We bring in family members to experience all treatment modalities and expose them to the latest research, theories, practicalities, and issues of the patient's medical condition. Group members are encouraged to use each other outside the group for resources and support. Within the group, the members share their experiences and resources to develop self-management and self-advocacy skills. This approach reinforces the belief that although professionals have much to offer, the patients themselves have vastly superior resources.

Examples of Advocacy and Resources   Patients' needs for which community resources may be available include AIDS, adoption, anger management, chemical dependency, child abuse, consumer affairs, day care, dental care, disability, divorce, emergency assistance, employment, English language classes, ethnic services, financial assistance, human rights, legal assistance, landlord/tenant problems, veterans' benefits, vocational rehabilitation, youth services.

Resources include the Division of Vocational Rehabilitation; family services with religious affiliations including Jewish, Catholic, and Presbyterian Family Services; employment resources such as Joblines; domestic violence resources; consumer affairs such as the Better Business Bureau and Consumer Credit Counseling Services; Department of Labor; ethnic resources; and referral services.

The Elements of Advocacy   The elements in advocacy challenge the notion that patients are passive recipients of care. Counselors confront self-defeating behaviors and lack of compliance; they teach patients to help themselves and to assume control over their illness by learning how to manage it and their providers.

DISABILITY

DEFINITIONS

Americans with Disabilities Act (ADA) and State Laws.   As of July 1, 1992, employers need to make "reasonable accommodation" for a wide variety of apparent and nonapparent disabilities, specifically conditions such as chronic fatigue syndrome. The ADA protects a disabled individual from job or hiring discrimination if the employee has a *physical or mental impairment that substantially limits a major life activity* or a history of the same. The impairment must be *substantial*, defined as significantly limiting or restricting a major life activity such as hearing, seeing, speaking, walking, breathing, performing manual tasks, caring for oneself, learning, or working. Accommodations may include restructuring the job, modifying equipment and policies, and altering work schedules. Many of these can be made at little or no cost.

"COBRA" (Consolidated Omnibus Budget Reconciliation Act).   If employment is terminated, extensions to health insurance are available for up to 18 months based on an individual payment rate, with extensions of up to 11 additional months for those with disabilities if approved by the Social Security Administration.

Department of Social and Health Services.   "Welfare," "Food Stamps," and "General Assistance" coupons for payment of medical care are available through this state agency.

Dictionary of Occupational Titles, 4th ed.   This is the standard reference text, published by the Department of Labor, listing all identified jobs (about 14,000) in the U.S. economy, as well as some basic characteristics of each job, such as Specific Vocational Preparation (SVP). This is the time required by a typical worker to learn the techniques, acquire the information, and develop the facility needed for average performance in a specific job-worker situation.

This training may be acquired in a school, work, military, institutional, or vocational environment. It does not include the orientation time required of a fully qualified worker to become accustomed to the special conditions of any new job. Specific vocational training includes vocational education, apprenticeship training, in-plant training, on-the-job training, and essential experience in other jobs.

Specific vocational training includes training given in any of the following circumstances:

1. Vocational education (high school, commercial, or shop training; technical school; art school; and that part of college training which is organized around a specific vocational objective).
2. Apprenticeship training (for apprenticeable jobs only).
3. In-plant training (organized classroom study provided by an employer).
4. On-the-job training (serving as learner or trainee on the job under the instruction of a qualified worker).

5. Essential experience in other jobs (serving in less responsible jobs, which lead to the higher-grade job, or serving in other jobs that qualify).

The following is an explanation of the levels of specific vocational preparation:

Level Time

1. Short demonstration only.
2. Anything beyond short demonstration up to and including 1 month.
3. Over 1 month up to and including 3 months.
4. Over 3 months up to and including 6 months.
5. Over 6 months up to and including 1 year.
6. Over 1 year up to and including 2 years.
7. Over 2 years up to and including 4 years.
8. Over 4 years up to and including 10 years.
9. Over 10 years.

Note: The levels of this scale are mutually exclusive and do not overlap. Specific vocational preparation—years of formal or informal preparation time—includes educational requirements, physical requirements, and other demands and qualifying factors.

New Occupational Titles. A newly revised 1998 Standard Occupational Codes with the companion O*NET-SOC system, lists the occupations under O*NET. O*NET Online: www.online.onetcenter.org.

Disability Forms. These have become an art form. Most insurers have difficulty providing physicians with forms to report health and physical factors for CFS because it has "nonobjective" evidence. Cardiac, psychiatric conditions, and back injury can be categorized into "function" or "limitations." Conditions that have "flares" or cycles and inconsistently reported subjective information, with primary symptoms of fatigue and/or pain and cognition present a challenge to physician, insurer, and patient.

Division of Vocational Rehabilitation. Typically, the Division of Vocational Rehabilitation (DVR) focuses on habilitation, not rehabilitation, which is the focus of workers' compensation. The definition of habilitation implies that the person has never functioned at an adequate or optimal level. Habilitation involves services to improve the skills and abilities of people with disabilities so that they can function at a maximal level in society. Usually, these are people without skills, such as the chronically mentally ill. Conversely, rehabilitation consists of services to restore as much as possible the functioning that has been lost through disease or injury.

When a referral from a health care practitioner for a client with CFS or FMS goes to a DVR counselor who understands the condition and its limitations, it represents a potentially successful case because of the usually excellent work history and long-term positive prognosis for return to work.

Labor and Industries Attorney. These attorneys specialize in the field of workers' compensation.

Medicaid Different from Medicare. A state-run program designed primarily to help those with low income and little or no resources. Although the federal government helps pay for Medicaid, each state has its own rules about who is eligible and what is covered under Medicaid. Medicare provides basic protection against the cost of health care, but does not cover all medical expenses. There are two parts: Hospital Insurance (Part A) and Medical Insurance (Part B).

Personal Injury Protection. In those situations where an automobile accident has contributed to a health condition, the Personal Injury Protection (PIP) portion of automobile insurance may cover traditional and nontraditional treatment needs and loss of income. PIP is a no-fault component of auto liability insurance that protects the insured regardless of fault. PIP benefits usually include income replacement, medical benefits, and loss of essential service coverage. The latter provides a maximum daily amount that can be paid to a nonfamily member to do chores or other activities that the injured person customarily performed.

Reasonable Accommodation. The logical adjustment made to a job and/or the environment that enables an otherwise qualified person with a disability to perform the duties of that position.

Short- and Long-Term Disability (STD and LTD). These two types of coverage provide partial replacement income when an individual is temporarily or permanently unable to work due to disability. Usually LTD and STD replace about two-thirds of regular income, but are offset by Social Security Disability Insurance (SSDI) or workers' compensation benefits. STD typically covers disabilities of 6 months or less. LTD benefits depend on each policy and what the purchaser bought. Typically, the first 2 years of the policy consider disability to be the inability to do the insured's same occupation. After 2 years, the standard loosens to consider whether someone can do "any" occupation, a lower standard of disability.

Most employers provide plans to cover illness. Sick time, medical leave, and short- and long-term disability plans may be available. Each plan is unique, so a copy of the entire policy is necessary. Issues to consider in the policy include part- or full-time disability, ability to work at the same job or any job while disabled, duration of the plan, and financial incentives to return to work.

Social Security Administration "SSD" (Supplemental Security Disability) and "SSDI" (Social Security Disability Insurance) are plans for the *temporarily, transitionally,* or *permanently* disabled. They are available based on financial need or amount of time worked. The steps to receive benefits include initial application, initial Disability Determination Services (DDS; a state function) decision, First Appeal: Reconsideration, Second Appeal: Administrative Law Judge, Third Appeal: Appeals Counsel, Subsequent Appeal: federal court.

Claimants are considered disabled if they are unable to do any kind of work for which they are suited and the disability is expected to last for at least a year or to result in death. The criteria for disability become less stringent as the applicant becomes older: under 50, 50 to 54, 55 to 60, over 60. To be considered disabled, a person cannot earn over $500.

Social Security Attorney. This is an attorney who specializes in the federal laws of the Social Security Administration and the Administrative Law Judge appeals. Typically, an attorney is not needed until after the first two rejection levels. Then, the attorney does not charge a fee unless the case is won, and then only with the approval of the administrative law judge. The fee is based on a portion of the retroactive payment only, not current benefits.

Workers' Compensation, aka Department of Labor and Industries Types of Workers' Compensation, include *state* public and private, "self-insured" workers' compensation systems, and *federal* workers' compensation systems (Longshore and Harborworkers Act, Jones Act, Federal Employees Liability Act). Some "self-insured" may be "self-administered" or hire an administration firm.

Workers' Compensation is an insurance system with each insurer serving as an insurance carrier. Consider the model of automobile insurance with its players: claims agent, estimator, body and fender worker, engineer, and the car itself. Correlate each of these to claims manager, independent medical examiner, physical therapist, doctor, and "injured worker."

The insurance carrier's obligation to the injured worker is to restore the loss. In most cases, the ideal way to accomplish this is to return the worker to the job-at-injury. Consequently, retraining for a new occupation is not considered except when there are no other options for a return to work. The emphasis is on light duty or graduated return to work, job modifications based on transferable skills, and short-term, on-the-job training. When formal retraining is considered, it is usually very short term (less than one year) and vocationally oriented.

Essentially, all work-related physical injures or occupational diseases are covered. Some examples of covered occupational diseases are black or brown lung, asbestosis, hearing loss from noise exposure, toxic exposures, and exposure to the AIDS virus. Typically not covered are injuries or diseases that are related to occupational stress (e.g., heart attacks, ulcers, psychiatric conditions, and substance abuse). Psychiatric conditions that impede progress in rehabilitation may be covered for the short term to aid recovery.

It is usually difficult to correlate CFS and FMS with an on-the-job injury, unless there was a precipitating event such as repetitive trauma to the arms leading to fibromyalgia or a motor vehicle accident (MVA) that occurred during the job and can be demonstrated to have led to FMS. Some attorneys specializing in this area of the law believe that if workplace stress is clearly exacerbating CFS or FMS symptoms, a case can be made for workers' compensation time loss, medical benefits, and possibly vocational benefits.

Vocational Rehabilitation Concepts: Reduced Work Activity

The most difficult health period is usually at the onset of the illness. Many people benefit from a period of reduced work or a leave of absence to rest, focus on treatment approaches, and reduce stress.

Transitional Work. A graduated return-to-work plan, after medical leave, offers an opportunity to assess response to the demands and stress of work. This approach was described in an earlier section of this chapter.

Light-Duty Work or Part-Time Work. As discussed earlier in this chapter, working for a period of time in a less demanding position also serves to reduce stress.

Self-Employment. This option offers maximum flexibility, especially if some or all of the work can be performed at home.

Vocational Rehabilitation Evaluation/Disability Evaluation.   A comprehensive evaluation incorporates patient interviews and reviews the medical and other health care practitioner opinions used to form and justify diagnoses, restrictions, and limitations (usually the primary care provider's opinion). The evaluation also includes relevant health variables such as health history and current symptomology to form a basis for assumptions about ability to work and provide recommendations for returning to work, staying at work, or outlining periods off work and interventions. It may include vocational testing if relevant.

Vocational Testing.   This is a standardized and normed type of psychometric testing. There are three kinds: aptitude, achievement, and interest. They are used for vocational evaluation and planning. Examples: Achievement: Wide Range Achievement Test, Peabody Individual Achievement Test; Aptitude: General Aptitude Test Battery, Crawford Small Parts Dexterity Test; Interest: Career Assessment Inventory, Wide Range Interest-Opinion Test.

STRATEGIES FOR DEALING WITH DISABILITY AND VOCATIONAL REHABILITATION

Dealing with Employers   Asking the employer to help figure out how to make the job work for the employee/patient and acknowledging reasonable limitations is the optimal first step—especially with conditions like CFS and FMS, which may not be apparent to others. Formally alerting a supervisor or superiors of the condition, what it means, and trying to work with them can go a long way.

Using a Health Care Professional   Some employers respond more constructively to altering a job if some member of the health care team, such as a physician, rehabilitation counselor, occupational therapist, or treating nurse outlines the restrictions with suggestions, including proposed time frames.

Using a Legal Professional   Some employers may need to be educated or formally reminded that there are severe state and federal penalties for discrimination against the handicapped. It is helpful to use an attorney who is familiar with state and federal labor laws and is willing to work with a health care treatment team.

REHABILITATION AND DISABILITY DETERMINATION

Disability can be a major issue in chronic fatigue syndrome. In the medical condition of fibromyalgia syndrome (FMS), with many clinical similarities to CFS, an estimated 25 percent of the patients seen in rheumatology practices receive disability benefits. The Social Security Administration has had difficulty determining how to approach (CFS) as a disabling condition. Similarly, the private disability insurance field does not have the tools to evaluate or understand CFS.

Other medical conditions have markers and standards for understanding impairment. Breast cancer patients have ratings and recovery percentages. Cardiac patients are compared to a disability scale with severity levels of impairment. The field of workers' compensation physical injuries has impairment ratings. Measurements of range of motion and strength are used to determine degree of impairment as outlined by the American Medical Association Guide to the Evaluation of

Permanent Impairment. However, when applied to CFS, these standards indicate little or no impairment.

Current Determinants of Disability   Because of the as yet undetermined cause or causes of CFS, no objective markers exist to document a mutually acceptable definition. The possible multiple causes of CFS indicate it may be a heterogeneous syndrome, making objective markers difficult to identify. The tools often used to assist in determining disability are few and not necessarily reliable or consistently applied to CFS. If, in the future, objective measures using biological markers (e.g., immune abnormalities), standardized testing impairment ratings, or other quantitative measurements become available, insurers will more readily accept the medical, physical, or biological origins of CFS for determination of disability.

The Social Security Administration (SSA), which has attempted to come to terms with CFS as a disabling medical condition, often uses its "mental impairments" standards, such as depression, to determine disability. The mental impairment model allows the SSA to consider *functional impairments* in activities of daily living and occupational functioning more readily than the medical disease model. If a person does not meet the strict Centers for Disease Control criteria for CFS due to exclusionary conditions, this model of functional impairment does not preclude acceptance of *chronic fatigue* (CF) as a disabling condition. Psychological and medical disabilities have no discrepancy in benefits for Social Security Administration programs. However, this paradigm involves using a *DSM-IV* (American Psychiatric Association's *Diagnostic and Statistic Manual IV*) diagnosis. Unless the psychological condition is based on the accepted presence of CFS as a medical condition, this diagnosis is offensive to many persons with CFS because it implies psychological origins instead of the physical source of symptoms. Also, the private long-term disability insurance industry typically has a limitation on any psychological condition versus lifetime benefits for medical impairments. Many patients fear a Social Security determination of benefits based on psychological impairment because of its potential limitations for a coexisting long-term disability claim, despite reassurance by the SSA that SSA files are sealed and unavailable to outside parties.

Independent medical examinations (IMEs) typically do not function merely as a second opinion to the primary care physician or as a consultation to the insurer, but, rather, as an adversary under the guise of a medical evaluator. An IME may have two or three specialty physicians (typically orthopedics or neurology) with little or no applicability to chronic fatigue syndrome. A psychiatric assessment can be problematic if it is based on nonobjective symptoms representing somatic complaints, instead of on the medical validity of CFS. The Minnesota Multiphasic Inventory (MMPI) can be problematic in the assessment of persons with chronic medical problems. Neuropsychological testing may not be effective in determining cognitive impairment.

Forms that physicians receive to document disability are frequently inadequate and/or unsuitable to CFS since such forms typically have been designed for musculoskeletal injuries. These forms do not address the flares or cycles of fatigue and/or pain, variations in cognitive functioning, and the need for physical accommodation. These forms may provide limited check-boxes indicating specific weight categories the patient is able to lift and carry during the workday. Furthermore, physicians are asked to judge work ability or impairment, an area in which they typically do not have training.

Standards   A reasonable consensus of *standards of care, standards of rehabilitation,* or *standards of disability* in CFS represents the best interests of all parties. Effective medical treatment, rehabilitation, and determinations of disability minimize the management effort of providers, the time and waiting with consequential growing impairment by patients, administrative waste by payors, and the financial costs to insurers, providers, and patients alike. It will benefit the CFS patient and professional community to fashion reasonable guidelines and work with payors to determine what patient profile, symptom constellation, criteria, or responses to intervention fall inside as well as outside the guidelines.

Proposal   The discussion of disability in CFS should focus on two areas: (1) *rehabilitation,* or the effort to prevent or treat the impairments of a person with CFS so that he or she will not need or minimally need to be considered unable to work and (2) *disability,* or the condition of a significantly impaired person who is no longer able to maintain gainful employment on a short-term or long-term basis. *Disability,* then, can only be considered after *rehabilitation* efforts have failed to maintain the patient on the job or failed to return a CFS sufferer to the job. These rehabilitation interventions serve to document and act as objective standards for determining disability.

REHABILITATION   A legitimate effort to raise the practical lifestyle and occupational functional level of persons with CFS may need to incorporate, in addition to medical workups, elements from the following therapies: physical therapy, stress management techniques, occupational therapy, acupuncture, nutrition and dietary counseling, vocational rehabilitation, and psychotherapy. Health care professionals, through debate and dialogue, should attempt to prioritize and clarify which of these or other interventions are most efficacious.

DISABILITY   Impairment and disability cannot be determined in CFS by physical or chemical testing. Impairment or disability relative to work and personal activities of daily living (ADL) functioning may be determined by subjective report, professional assessment, and/or objective performance in workplace testing and evaluation. Thus, key criteria for determination of impairment or disability are the credibility of the patient based on the individual's accuracy and validity as a historian; determination of psychological sequela; objective performance such as work history and performance based on physical capacity evaluation; efforts to remain at work and return to work after onset; coworker and employer assessment; and professional health care provider judgment based on experience with a patient over time and compared with other patients presenting with similar features.

DISABILITY EVALUATION COMPONENTS   Evaluations should be performed by licensed and/or certified providers working within the domain and scope of their professional practice and licensure. They should have received training in the criteria, etiology, history, and treatment alternatives for conditions such as CFS using standardized protocols from the fields of medicine, psychiatry, or psychology, occupational therapy, performance-based physical capacity evaluation, and vocational evaluation.

In recent years, treatment models of care and functional assessment of CFS have received more attention, but disability determination for patient applicants with CFS remains inadequate, sluggish, and sometimes even unfair and inhumane. It is essential to develop standardized reporting forms and to establish minimal expertise requirements for evaluators of disability. Critical issues in treatment and rehabilitation preliminary to assessment of impairment, as well as disability standards and protocols, must be reviewed, reevaluated, and resolved. Objective measures such as functional evaluations, neuropsychological testing, and exercise endurance testing need to be incorporated into a vocational assessment of ability to work. Only through such measures can professionals achieve a standard of evaluation endorsed by the CFS community and acceptable to the disability insurance industry.

OTHER REHABILITATION APPROACHES: REHABILITATION INTERVENTIONS

Health care professionals who work with CFS patients need to consider incorporating the following elements into the long-term rehabilitation plan, in addition to medical workups and medications (this list is by no means exhaustive):

- *Preventive health.* Ergonomics, safety assessment, employer training and consultation, provider training and education, health education.
- *Care management.* Community resources (access/referral/advocacy), patient training and education.
- *Natural health intervention.* Acupuncture, naturopathy, chiropractic, biofeedback, massage, and nutrition/dietary treatment and intervention.
- *Psycho/social intervention.* Medical conditions counseling, cognitive and functional therapies, vocational counseling, group/individual/ family therapy, general psychotherapy, pain management, stress management, lifestyle adjustment counseling, addictions and chemical dependency treatment and counseling, career counseling, bibliotherapy, cognitive rehabilitation, and support groups.
- *Physical intervention.* Physical therapy, postural alignment, spinal assessment and treatment, muscular conditioning, injury prevention, and education.
- *Occupational intervention.* Occupational therapy, job site assessment and modification, daily living skills, adaptive therapies, work hardening/conditioning, vocational counseling, return-to-work interventions, home access and safety assessment, environmental assessment and planning.

The following sections present suggestions contributed by other health care professionals. Notes cited at the end of each section identify these contributors.

USING BIOFEEDBACK TO LISTEN TO YOUR BODY

The notion that human beings are in continuous interaction with their internal and external environments is widely recognized and accepted. In fact, such interactions largely shape our behavior. Several successful biofeedback protocols take advantage of the innate ability of humans to learn to regulate their internal environments. The protocols work by using biofeedback instrumentation to introduce information concerning the relationship between clients' physiological events and key aspects of their internal environment such as beliefs, thoughts, and feelings.

Biofeedback thus involves helping clients tune in to and listen to their bodies. This body awareness has many beneficial implications. Clients can learn to change their internal responses, and bioinstrumentation reinforces success.

The biofeedback process uses noninvasive sensors designed to detect a biophysical signal such as electromyographic muscle activity (EMG), electrodermal skin resistance (EDR), peripheral skin temperature, pulse rate, breath volume, sphincter muscle tone, or electroencephalographic (EEG) brain wave activity. The sensors generally act as transducers that change the biophysical activity into an electrical signal. Digital instruments are used to interpret the electrical signal and separate a true signal from artifact using amplifiers and filters. The resulting digital signal is then usually sent to a personal computer (PC) that presents the information as graphs, audio tones or, in some cases, video games controlled by the biophysical signal.

Biofeedback practice is holistic, with a focus on the needs and functions of the body, mind, and spirit as an integrated whole. The actual therapeutic process in biofeedback is called self-management. Self-management involves helping clients identify their own goals in terms of a particular problem. Through therapeutic contracts, biofeedback instrumentation, and cognitive behavioral techniques, clients are helped to change behaviors, feelings, and thought patterns associated with the identified problem. The biofeedback instrumentation helps the client listen to the body and make the connection between arousal and stressful events, interpretation of events, and any associated physiological problems the client has developed. The client learns to identify and use innate strengths instead of weaknesses or pathology. Clients work toward goals they have chosen and experience rewards they have earned, thus reinforcing behavior change and success.

Biofeedback treatments (James & Folen, 1996) have over 30 years of proven clinical efficacy in treating many problems such as tension headaches, insomnia, anxiety, hypertension, muscle fatigue, incontinence, and chronic pain. More recent applications have included certain cognitive or behavioral problems such as learning disability, posttraumatic stress, and addictions.[1]

SLEEP

To sleep, perchance to dream.

—William Shakespeare, *Hamlet*

In treating sleep disorders, the fundamental problem for clinicians is recognizing their existence. Insomnia afflicts 10 percent of the population, but few of these individuals receive treatment. Physicians do not know the correct questions to ask, and patients are reluctant to bring up seemingly trivial complaints. Many physicians focus on what appears to be more serious illness, thus overlooking underlying and treatable sleep disorders. And, even when they ask the correct questions, the answers may contain myriad confusing, nonspecific complaints that do not point to a sleep disorder. Adding one simple question to the history is likely to result in maximum yield: "How are you sleeping?"

---

[1] Contributed by Graham J. Patrick, PhD, ARNP.

This section provides a brief look at some of the symptoms associated with sleep disorders to help clinicians arrive at the appropriate diagnosis. Complaints that may reflect an underlying sleep disorder are fatigue, daytime somnolence, pain, restless legs, cognitive problems, and psychiatric problems including depression.

Many people with a presenting complaint of pain have an underlying sleep disorder. The chronic pain disorder fibromyalgia is associated with a sleep disorder and includes all of the previously mentioned symptoms. By definition, fibromyalgia requires a history of diffuse pain accompanied by at least 11 of 18 tender points. These patients also commonly complain of fatigue, cognitive problems, daytime somnolence, depression, restless legs, headaches, and irritable bowel syndrome. They are not refreshed on awakening and many awaken feeling worse than when they went to sleep. Electroencephalographic abnormalities have been reported in the majority of these patients who have an alpha intrusion during Stage 4 sleep. Furthermore, rapid eye movement is reduced in about 50 percent of patients with fibromyalgia. Since it is difficult to successfully treat the symptomatic fibromyalgia patient without attempting to normalize sleep, it is imperative to inquire about a sleep disturbance in any patient who presents with chronic pain. Often, restoration of normal sleep will result in reduced pain, increased energy, greater cognitive abilities, and improved mood. Sleep apnea is common for the male patient with fibromyalgia: It may be appropriate to refer all male fibromyalgia patients for a sleep study.

Daytime somnolence may be the presenting complaint for patients with obstructive sleep apnea or narcolepsy. Distinguishing between these two sleep disorders is not difficult. For individuals with sleep apnea, other symptoms include fatigue, snoring, early morning and nocturnal headache, enuresis, depression, cognitive problems, and sexual impotence. Most of these complaints are nonspecific, but when a bed partner observes apnea, then the diagnosis is almost certain. Some or all of the following physical findings may be helpful in making the correct diagnosis: obesity, increased neck circumference, enlarged tonsils, nasal obstruction, hypertension, and lower extremity edema. Thus, the obese, hypotensive male patient who snores is quickly referred for a sleep study to rule out sleep apnea.

What about making this diagnosis in a female? Typically, women with this disorder have an underslung jaw, a small oropharyngeal space, and are underweight. Sleep apnea is often overlooked in women. Yet, even many male patients remain undiagnosed since assessment of sleep is often not a routine part of the medical history. This is unfortunate since treatment is often successful in reducing or even eliminating symptoms.

Daytime somnolence is also the most frequent complaint of patients with narcolepsy. Distinguishing this disorder from obstructive sleep apnea is straightforward if the patient complains of cataplexy as well. But this complaint may not surface unless the patient is asked a specific question. Less often, these patients have sleep paralysis and hallucinations. Since patients with narcolepsy are prone to automobile and home injuries, these individuals must be diagnosed and referred to a sleep center promptly. Treatment helps the majority of these patients.

Restless legs are another clinical presentation often associated with a sleep disorder. The severity of sensations increases in these patients during rest, and they have a compelling need to move their limbs. Chronic conditions associated with this syndrome include diabetes, peripheral neuropathy, and Parkinson's disease. Since these diseases commonly aggravate restless legs, every attempt should be made to identify and control these disorders when present. Patients with restless legs syndrome often benefit from avoiding alcohol and caffeine. Although the mechanism of this syndrome is unknown, anti-Parkinson or antiseizure medications often help these patients.

Depression is so commonly associated with sleep disorders that clinicians can assume a person with depression suffers from one or more of the following problems: difficulty in initiating and maintaining sleep, abnormalities in REM and non-REM sleep stages, and altered patterns of nocturnal hormone secretion. Since sleep disturbance is associated with a significant risk of relapse and recurrence of depression, clinicians understand and treat sleep abnormalities in depressed patients.

Severe fatigue or cognitive problems may also be manifestations of a sleep disorder. However, these complaints are nonspecific and warrant a careful evaluation to exclude physical or emotional problems as their etiology. A full history should be undertaken along with a complete physical exam. Routine and exotic laboratory tests may be ordered to find an organic basis for these complaints. Some patients may require more extensive tests such as a chest X ray, MRI scan of the brain, lumbar puncture, and psychiatric consultation. If these studies are all normal, then a trial of a medication such as an antidepressant or hypnotic may be warranted. Some patients may benefit from sleep hygiene techniques, if not a frank referral to a sleep center.

Restful sleep is essential to the functioning individual. Yet insomnia, which may affect 10 percent of the population, is often not diagnosed. This has tremendous consequences for the individual and society. Many sleep-deprived patients are tired, cognitively impaired, depressed, and accident-prone. These problems beg for a remedy. Better understanding of the symptoms associated with a sleep disorder will enable us to successfully recognize and treat them.[2]

ACUPUNCTURE FOR CHRONIC FATIGUE SYNDROME AND FIBROMYALGIA

FM and CFS are marked by global symptoms: pain in many areas of the body at once, fatigue, poor sleep, and digestive disturbances to name a few. Acupuncture, with its homeostatic effect, can be a powerful tool in combating these symptoms (Sandberg, Lundeberg, & Gerdle, 1999).

Acupuncture, the insertion of thin, sterilized needles at precise points of the body, has been practiced in Asia for over two thousand years. In that time, a vast clinical knowledge base has evolved based on careful observation of the progression of symptoms and signs. The acupuncturist takes a detailed history, checks the pulse, observes the tongue, and gently palpates specific areas of the body to diagnose a pattern of disharmony. Some examples of these disharmonies are an excessive amount of heat in the body, a deficiency of restorative powers (Yin) or kinetic energy (Yang), or an inability of the blood to nourish the muscles and other tissues.

After forming a diagnosis, the acupuncturist devises a treatment for the imbalance and quickly inserts needles with a virtually painless technique. Within several minutes, the body begins to react to the needles: The tissues below the skin lightly grab onto them, and there can be a slight redness around the insertion sites. These are the outward signs of the bodily processes the treatment

---

[2] Contributed by Paul B. Brown, MD, PhD.

stimulates. During this time, patients often report feeling very relaxed and sometimes fall asleep. Once treatment is complete, usually after about 20 to 40 minutes depending on the body's reaction, the needles are removed and disposed of. Acupuncture needles are not reused.

Immediate effects of acupuncture include increased relaxation and pain relief. People often notice improved sleep and digestion as well. With continuing treatment, FM and CFS flares can become milder and less frequent.

Acupuncture works well with other therapies including medication, physical therapy, counseling, and massage. Western medical treatment often consists of drug therapies to address each symptom. These drugs can assist in managing pain, restoring sleep, and normalizing digestion. However, many people with FM and CFS are sensitive to medications and require careful monitoring and adjustment of doses. Sometimes a drug that alleviates one symptom may exacerbate another. With acupuncture treatment, patients are often able to work with their physicians to reduce dosages or even eliminate difficult medications. Since acupuncture is virtually without side effects, these gains are not offset by other unwanted symptoms.

When considering acupuncture treatment, it is important for patients to find a practitioner with whom they feel comfortable. The acupuncturist should have experience dealing with chronic conditions and be willing to communicate with physicians and the other practitioners on the health care team.[3]

COGNITIVE REHABILITATION IN CHRONIC FATIGUE SYNDROME AND FIBROMYALGIA

Failure to remember appointments or how to drive to a place that they have visited a thousand times are the kinds of difficulties patients frequently report after a traumatic brain injury (TBI). But, they can also be manifestations of CFS or FM patients, who report similar losses in attention, memory, organization, ability to plan, and cognitive fatigue. In fact, there seem to be more similarities than differences in the symptoms reported. Because of these similarities, the research-driven treatment techniques from TBI have recently begun to be applied to CFS and FM individuals (Dobkin, 2002).

The initial step in planning cognitive rehabilitation is to test the brain process areas (thinking skills). In-depth testing can be completed with a neuropsychologist who is trained in diagnosing causation as well as in determining specific deficit areas and strengths. A speech/language pathologist is able to assess overall cognitive/communication skills and provide the treatment. Once a plan is developed, a person needs to commit to 1 to 2 sessions a week, if possible, for the best results.

Although gains in foundational brain processes such as attention/concentration and speed of information processing have now been demonstrated, the areas of memory, organization, and planning seem to have the strongest impact on the lives of individuals with CFS and FM. Problems in these areas are particularly responsive to treatment techniques such as compensatory memory systems and the habitual use of checklists. This is not the kind of Day-Timer system typically used but a highly structured, organized way of approaching everyday tasks. It involves close one-on-one work with a therapist trained in

---

[3] Contributed by Neil Conaty, LAc.

compensatory problem-solving strategies. A speech/language pathologist with such training can provide additional information to support groups who request it. The possibilities for improving cognitive function may be broader than health care practitioners realize at this time. Application of these remedial techniques is just beginning.[4]

PHYSICAL THERAPY FOR CHRONIC FATIGUE SYNDROME AND FIBROMYALGIA

Physical therapy (PT) is often prescribed for people with FMS or CFS. Treatment approaches including exercise, hands-on work to decrease joint or muscle pain, help with relaxation, and information about pacing, sleep, self-treatment, and self-care activities. Because research studies have shown that aerobic exercise can be helpful in decreasing tender point pain and increasing a sense of well-being, it is a frequent component of PT treatment. For persons with CFS or FMS who have experienced the effects of overdoing an activity, this approach may seem somewhat counterintuitive. However, physical therapists help guide people into a healthy exercise routine without flaring their symptoms. This can include guidance on the exercise prescription dosage, including type of exercise (e.g., jarring vs. nonjarring) and its intensity, duration, and frequency. Record keeping is also important to help patients modify their exercise program to avoid symptom flares.

Many persons with FMS and CFS have pain that is associated with a biomechanical problem (e.g., plantar fasciitis, patellar pain, low back or neck pain). Sometimes the increased "efficiency" of the pain transmission system in these patients contributes to their discomfort. Pain may interfere with sleep, as well as contribute to the difficulty of coping with CFS and FMS. Orthopedic physical therapists assess and treat biomechanical problems with joint mobilization, massage, and exercises designed to balance muscle alignment around problem joints. Once pain in the affected areas is decreased and movement patterns are more efficient, less energy is required for activities of daily living.

Research indicates that the autonomic nervous system may be involved in FMS or CFS symptoms. The autonomic nervous system is involved in the fight-or-flight response to stress. To affect this system, patients can learn techniques that will increase activity in the part of the autonomic nervous system conducive to relaxation. These techniques might include deep breathing, progressive relaxation, or methods to increase peripheral blood flow. In addition, sleep is frequently disrupted in at least 70 percent of FMS patients, so adjusting the sleep environment, relaxing, and exercising at an optimal time before sleep might be a subject covered in PT treatment.

Physical therapy is one of several treatment approaches routinely used in the treatment of FMS and CFS. It is easy to integrate PT in a treatment plan as long as providers communicate effectively, carefully plan appointments, and prudently allocate financial and insurance resources. When choosing a physical therapist, it is important to find someone who has experience working with FMS or CFS, who is willing to let the patient be part of the team (will listen to the patient's suggestions and concerns), and who is responsive to the reaction to treatment. In areas where there are no physical therapists experienced in FMS or CFS, a good choice

---

[4] Contributed by Patricia Youngman, MS, CCC-Sp.

would be a therapist who works with chronic illnesses (e.g., rheumatic diseases) and is willing to use diverse resources and treatment suggestions. Although many physical therapists who work with sports injuries are comfortable treating FMS or CFS, some may expect a level of exertion or progress that is unrealistic for these conditions.

Finally, not everyone is ready for the stresses of PT. If it takes all the energy a patient can muster to get dressed to keep an appointment, it may not be the time to start PT. Or the patient may need just a few visits to learn some exercises and self-treatment techniques. Patients need to be straightforward with their physical therapist about what they need—the therapist will appreciate it.[5]

OCCUPATIONAL THERAPY FOR PERSONS WITH CHRONIC FATIGUE SYNDROME

Although fatigue is a frequent complaint in today's society and common in many medical conditions, the functional and emotional consequences of fatigue often receive little attention. Occupational therapists, historically, have focused on helping people to continue everyday pursuits despite illness. As clinicians experienced in the evaluation and management of symptoms of fatigue, pain, and cognitive disturbance, occupational therapists can offer help for those who must cope with the impact of CFS on daily activities (Cox & Findley, 1998).

Occupational therapists have a variety of evaluations to assess CFS symptoms. In a structured interview, the therapist typically asks for descriptions of work, home, and leisure activities. Information is also gathered about previous and current daily routines in the context of social and family considerations, priorities, and problems or concerns. The difficulties that the individual considers to be most important are identified and addressed first in treatment goals.

The Role Checklist gathers information on the individual's perceived participation in various roles (parent, worker, homemaker, etc.) in the past, present, and future, and the degree to which these roles are valued over time. The NIH Activity Record (ACTRE) is a self-report log completed for a 2-day period. The ACTRE provides quantified information on the frequency and/or percentage of time the patient spends being physically active, resting, and participating in self-care, role, and leisure activities. Severity of fatigue and pain; balance of activity and rest; quantity and quality of fatigue, pain, and difficulty associated with activities; and participation in meaningful or enjoyable activities can also be documented with the ACTRE. Additional individual assessments of fatigue, pain, hand function, and cognition are often included based on individual need. The combined results of these assessments identify treatment goals and suggest patterns that may need to be changed or altered.

When treating the patient with CFS, the occupational therapist may provide adaptive equipment and/or techniques to facilitate self-care. Therapeutic activities may improve strength and coordination, endurance, and cognitive and process skills (e.g., attention, organization). In collaboration with the patient, the OT may recommend changes in the home or work environment, activity patterns, or balance of productive and leisure activities to conserve energy. Doing too much at one time is a common problem for persons with CFS. This often results in several days when even minimal activity is impossible.

---

[5] Contributed by Kim Bennett, PhD, RPT.

Teaching energy conservation has been a part of OT treatment for individuals with major medical conditions such as stroke, multiple sclerosis, and arthritis. The term *energy conservation* is used in occupational therapy to address how to budget personal energy and set priorities. Just as in financial management, CFS patients need to determine how they are "spending" their energy. An OT is trained to facilitate setting priorities for energy use and matching the individual's values and goals to develop an optimal plan for using available resources. Making changes in personal habits and changing the actual manner of execution of daily tasks require repetition and practice. The therapist can help plan goals to build strength and coordination, endurance, and cognitive functioning through activities that are part of the patient's daily routine.

Energy conservation techniques include an analysis of how patients undertake the specific activities that make up their daily routine. Do work heights support optimal posture or drain energy and contribute to chronic pain? Is the individual standing to do an activity that could be done sitting instead? Can the patient reduce the number of times stairs are climbed? Are workspaces organized for convenience? Many adaptations are simple to implement: adding small wood blocks to raise a table or desk height, adjusting a computer monitor to eye level, using a rolling chair to reduce standing time, having a headset phone instead of a handheld phone. Shower chairs, railings, mobile arm supports, and storage systems for closets and kitchens also can provide significant energy savings. For hand or wrist pain, the therapist may recommend and construct splints or orthotics to improve function and reduce if not eliminate pain.

The therapist can more effectively identify problems while observing the individual perform typical activities. Observing the activity gives the individual and the therapist an ideal opportunity to collaborate in finding the most energy-efficient approach to the activity and any adaptive devices that might be helpful. An occupational therapy clinic can be a surprising environment. There may be a kitchen, laundry facilities, a bedroom, a computer workstation, even simulated work sites.

Frequently, when struggling to cope with fatigue, an individual may give up meaningful activities to accomplish those that are most essential. Reducing social contacts and outside activities often results in isolation and depression. Friends and family members often misunderstand the limitations of fatigue and interpret the patient's behavior as disinterest. The role of education is critical. As the individual learns new energy-saving strategies, it is necessary to explain to others why they are necessary. The OT often acts as an advocate in the workplace (home or school) to facilitate accommodations to the needs of the person with CFS.

Because making any changes in behavior is difficult, no matter how beneficial, the OT is also a part of the rehabilitation team. This team may include a physiatrist (doctor of physical medicine), physical therapist, speech therapist, recreational therapist, and vocational rehabilitation specialist in addition to the occupational therapist. The advantage of a team approach is the contribution of each discipline's expertise in creating a comprehensive program. It may take from 4 to 6 weeks to establish effective behavior changes and see improvement. Such a combined approach is essential for the complexity of CFS management.[6]

---

[6] Contributed by Gloria Furst, MPH, OTR/L; and Lucy Swan, MOT, OTR/L.

BEYOND THE TRADITIONAL MODEL

LIVING WELL WITH A CHRONIC ILLNESS: A SHORT-TERM COUNSELING AND MEDITATION GROUP

Based on a grant to pay for eight patients of a rheumatologist to participate in a program without cost to them, a hybrid group model was developed for eight 2-hour sessions called "Living with a Chronic Illness." The purpose of these sessions was to explore the life issues that had arisen as a consequence of chronic rheumatic illnesses, including chronic fatigue syndrome. A rehabilitation counselor experienced in psychotherapy and coping skills facilitated the group, along with a rehabilitation physician trained in psychotherapy and meditation. The aim of these sessions was to enhance the quality of life through promoting personal understanding of illness. Meditation and relaxation skills were taught and practiced.

Patients reported that daily "mindful" meditation (awareness of the present through breathing and focus) practiced 10 minutes per day was very helpful in reducing stress, and allowed them to consider the changes they were experiencing in a more positive light. Patient feedback was extremely supportive of the model's benefits in integrating meditation, practical coping skills, and limited counseling interventions.[7]

MULTIDISCIPLINARY "MANAGED" CARE: A COMPREHENSIVE GROUP TREATMENT MODEL

BACKGROUND

In the late 1980s, with health care dollars soaring and a public that did not seem to be using fewer services or getting any healthier, we formed the Center for Comprehensive Care. We are independent health care practitioners. These programs and services typically include acupuncture (including traditional Chinese herbal medicine) and mental health (including vocational rehabilitation), in addition to physical therapy, occupational therapy, tai chi, and health education. Health education includes pain management and stress management techniques, diet and nutrition, meditation, sleep hygiene, and self-management skills. The practices are located in a large, multispecialty outpatient urban medical center amid numerous hospitals, medical clinics, and independent physician practices. Physician consultants include researchers from the University of Washington and rheumatologists or internists with expertise in the disease entities programmatically defined, such as upper extremities, persistent pain, unremitting fatigue, and rheumatic conditions.

PROBLEMS AND ISSUES

In the outpatient setting, the internist or primary care physician is the gatekeeper and guide of the system. In complicated case scenarios, the physician often refers for and is sequencing four or five modalities. In these cases, physicians need help in appropriate triaging of their patient. This sensitive position requires someone with a vision from or into allopathy and complementary medicine. The conventional model of medical care assumes a patient receives "aid," "help," or "solace"

---

[7] Contributed by James R. Blair, LAc; and Donald Uslan, MA, MBA.

from the physician or health care provider. One-to-one physician care, with specialist consultation scheduled at some point in the future, heightens patients' anxiety in response to the specialty or technical expertise, placing them in a passive role. This is often a setup for the patients' anger or disillusionment. Although many physicians try to help their patients assume responsibility and self-care, this is simply not practical in the world of brief office visits and harried professional support staff.

PHILOSOPHY OF CARE

The fundamental philosophy of the model is an integrated care plan. It allows medical care to access allied health as well as alternative modalities and is a more cost-effective means of health care delivery.

The principles on which these ideas are based are simple. "Linear" or "stacked" therapeutic interventions, where the patient goes from one type of intervention to another, were not cost-effective. Integrated service delivery where modalities were timed and sequenced seemed to be the answer. The question was how to provide a high-quality service within the marketplace.

In any triage/treatment system within the health care profession, communication is the key to providing good care. In many case scenarios, the communication occurs after the fact, leaving strong clinical potentials untouched.

In 1988, we began conceptualizing and designing a model of health care delivery based on a multidisciplinary care treatment model that would allow for physician interface and input when appropriate. In Phase 1 of this project, we determined this community had an unmet need in the treatment of chronic autoimmune disorders. These conditions tend to be long-term, do not present objective medical findings, and cost substantial sums of money for consultations and diagnostic procedures. Patients often seek nontraditional medical services due to a perceived dissatisfaction with conventional medical treatments. These alternative forms of therapy tend to be expensive and ineffective. Phase 2 consisted of two demonstration groups and the inclusion of health education and patient assessment and compliance efforts. The present Phase 3 consists of the broader use of the model by the medical community and its application to other chronic care conditions including the work injury conditions of cumulative trauma disorder (upper extremity), general musculoskeletal injuries, and multiple chemical sensitivities.

MULTIDISCIPLINARY CARE VERSUS MANAGED CARE

The term *multidisciplinary care* implies concepts such as coordination of care, communication among providers, communication with patients, patient empowerment, self-management, nonduplication of care, provider acceptance of their discipline's limitations and strengths, provider knowledge and appreciation of other disciplines' contribution to care, the ability to avoid jargon and to have a working knowledge of the jargon from other disciplines. Multidisciplinary care is an important part of the treatment regime for complex medical problems that do not respond satisfactorily to conventional medical care. There are two views of multidisciplinary care: coordinated linear services and the programmatic model.

The term *managed care* suggests exactly the model the multidisciplinary care supports. Managing, implies logical movement along a continuum, coordination among providers, and compassionate insurer or institutional concern. All that is missing from this model is a form of patient self-empowerment. However, managed care actually implies "managed costs." Multidisciplinary care is friendly to this.

CHRONIC MEDICAL CONDITIONS

Chronic medical conditions present a special anathema to the medical community. Most medical treatment systems are designed to quickly handle ("cure") acute, short-lived problems. Problems that resist conventional care diagnosis and intervention through pharmaceutical or surgical means frustrate medical practitioners. Allied health care providers then become the second tier of treatment choice. However, these providers typically see themselves as augmenting medical care, and they seek short-term solutions. Health care providers who handle enigmatic, long-term, potentially expensive care are few and far between. These disciplines include oncology, rheumatology, mental health, and alternative care. Chronic care drives the health care budget (and drives the financial and emotional anxieties of patients, providers, and financiers, alike).

A process-oriented form of treatment empowers the patient and the medical system and decreases health care utilization *and its cost*. Process-oriented treatment means helping patients take responsibility for their own health care. Providers must give and share the tools of the patients' own health care improvement. There are no immediate cures, solutions, or answers for chronic illness. The answers lie in the process itself and in fundamental changes in lifestyle. Many medical modalities are used inappropriately; they are, therefore, ineffective and drive up costs. To solve these problems, we honor the patients' part in the process and integrate, under the primary care physicians' span of control, effective, coordinated treatment approaches.

CONCLUSION

We propose a model of creative integration of alternative and allied health care to assist primary care physicians and their designated specialists in the delivery of high-quality health care. By using groups of patients who actively participate in acquiring information, understanding, and healing—in conjunction with standard pharmaceutical and diagnostic practices—we can achieve lower costs and greater patient satisfaction.

CASE EXAMPLES

Americans with Disabilities Act and Fibromyalgia: A Case Study in Modification and Accommodation

Background

A 38-year-old female claims examiner for a major insurance company in Bellevue, Washington, is married and the mother of two. She has recently been promoted. She has had a difficult 18 months with a Labor and Industries claim for an on-the-job injury for right shoulder strain, right lateral epicondylitis, cervical dislocation, and right wrist sprain. She has also struggled with chronic fatigue syndrome and fibromyalgia syndrome for more than 5 years, but felt that she had it under control until her on-the-job injuries. Labor and Industries would not accept FMS as part of her industrial insurance claim. She sought the help of a rehabilitation counselor after her industrial insurance claim had been closed.

Problem

After discussions with her and her physician, it was noted that her growing fatigue, difficulty concentrating, and forgetfulness were adversely affecting her performance on the job. She was shortly to undergo a performance evaluation for a 6-month review of her recent promotion. The patient felt that she needed to tell her employer about her illness, but feared losing her job as a result.

Intervention

A reduction in her daily work schedule was an obvious starting point to improve her performance. However, this accommodation would require disclosure of her illness to her employer. After much discussion about the protection offered under the provisions of the Americans with Disabilities Act (ADA), she agreed to allow her rehabilitation counselor to meet with her employer. The purpose of the meeting was to explain both her illness and request accommodation of her daily work schedule. The ADA Law and the employer's responsibilities under this law would also be reviewed.

Outcome

The meeting with the employer and immediate supervisor opened discussion of her and FMS. They readily agreed to modify her schedule. More importantly, this set a process for future discussions of her condition and the need for changing accommodations as her condition changes. The employer expressed acknowledgment to the rehabilitation counselor for approaching him in a nonthreatening and nonadversarial manner (without attorneys). The client now feels more in control of the situation and has shown definite improvement in her functioning, although her situation requires close monitoring by her attending physician and rehabilitation counselor.

Private Employer and Fibromyalgia Syndrome: A Case Study in Accommodation and Disability Benefits

Background

A 44-year-old married woman with no children has been working for a large retail jewelry business as a payroll administrator for many years. She has been attempting to maintain her workload despite the diagnosis and treatment for her medical condition of fibromyalgia. She has attempted to schedule medical and other treatment appointments around her work schedule. The employer has been supportive of her condition and appointments, but does not realize the level of effort the employee must put forth to maintain her high quality of performance.

Problem

It has become clear to her rheumatologist and rehabilitation counselor that the patient is beginning to suffer under her workload. Her need for rest is increasing, her normally positive mood and outlook have been increasingly negative, with irritability, agitation, anxiety, and depression becoming obvious to her husband and treatment team. She is beginning to experience anxiety around financial issues as her providers suggest she take Family Medical Leave Act (FMLA) time off of up to 12 weeks to rest and focus on treatment. The employer, although concerned about how to cover her job duties, was supportive of the time off.

Intervention

This client had sufficient financial coverage in the form of sick time, vacation time, and short-term disability benefits to cover the 12 weeks off. During that time, she focused on practical matters in rehabilitation counseling such as pacing herself, setting limits and boundaries, and coming to terms with the long-term implications of her condition on her work and personal life, as well as her identity as a hard-working, achieving worker. She realized that she would not be able to return to work for more than three days per week for the foreseeable future and began to cope with this loss.

Meetings with the employer revealed that her long-term insurance policy would supplement her loss of wages for the first year to 100 percent and 95 percent for the succeeding years. Working three days a week would allow her to rest and continue to focus on her therapies the other two days per week, with weekends for additional recovery and family time. However, her employer was not able to put her back into her position as payroll manager on a part-time basis and was not willing to set up a job-sharing arrangement. She had to take a lower paying, less responsible position in a different department.

Outcome

The employer was understanding and accommodating to the best of his ability as a business owner, and the client, while struggling with the loss of her career, gained the opportunity to focus on recovery while maintaining financial security.

REFERENCES

Capuano Sgambati, J. R. (1998). The relationship among anger expression, coping, impact of sickness, in chronic fatigue syndrome. *Dissertation Abstracts International: Section B: The Sciences and Engineering, 59*(2-B), 0902. (UMI).

Cox, D. L., & Findley, L. J. (1998). The management of chronic fatigue syndrome in an inpatient setting: Presentation of an approach and perceived outcome. *British Journal of Occupational Therapy, 61*(9), 405–409.

Dobkin, B. H. (2002). Cognitive rehabilitation: An integrative nueropsychological approach. *Neurology, 58*(10), 1578.

Ferrari, J. R., & Jason, L. A. (1997). Caring for people with chronic fatigue syndrome: Perceived stress versus satisfaction. *Rehabilitation Counseling Bulletin, 40*(4), 240–250.

Honig, H. A. (1999). Reasonable employment accomodations for persons with disabilities: A policy capturing approach. *Dissertation Abstracts International: Section B: The Sciences and Engineering, 60*(3-B), 1336. (UMI).

Horowitz, S. (1998). Chronic pain management: Integrative approaches to a whole-life challenge. *Alternative and Complementary Therapist, 4*(4), 231–235.

James, L. C., & Folen, R. A. (1996). EEG biofeedback as a treatment for chronic fatigue syndrome: A controlled case report. *Behavioral Medicine, 22*(2), 77–81.

McGuigan, J. F. (2000). Why might stress management methods be effective? In D. T. Kenny & J. G. Carlson (Eds.), *Stress and health: Research and clinical applications* (pp. 151–161). Amsterdam: Harwood Academic.

Rubin, S. E., & Roessler, R. T. (2001). *Foundations of the vocational rehabilitation process.* Austin, TX: ProEd.

Sandberg, M., Lundeberg, T., & Gerdle, B. (1999). Manual acupuncture in fibromyalgia: A long-term pilot study. *Journal of Musculoskeletal Pain, 7*(3), 39–58.

Weiss, L. (1980). Vocational evaluation: An individualized program. *Archives of Physical Medicine and Rehabilitation, 61*(10), 453–454.

PART VI

PEDIATRIC AND COMMUNITY ISSUES

CHAPTER 29

Chronic Fatigue
Syndrome in Adolescence

MARK SCOTT SMITH and BRYAN D. CARTER

Case Study

At 15, Jason was enjoying his middle adolescent years. He was a very good student, had a number of close friends, and was active in sports. While he had experimented with sex and alcohol, he was not actively involved in risk-taking behaviors. He came from a stable, supportive family with no history of mood disorders. Following a short flu-like febrile illness, Jason's expected recovery became prolonged. Nine months later, he continued to complain of severe fatigue, inability to sustain normal physical activity without exhaustion, frequent headaches, muscle aches, intermittent sore throat, lack of refreshing sleep, and difficulty concentrating. Although his physician initially suspected infectious mononucleosis, repeated physical examinations and laboratory tests were normal. A consulting psychologist found no evidence supporting a mental health problem and urged his physician to pursue organic causes further. Subsequent consultations and diagnostic studies performed by specialists in infectious disease, endocrinology, rheumatology, neurology, and child psychiatry shed no further light on the cause of Jason's symptoms. Therapeutic trials with several antidepressants, attention to proper sleep hygiene, and limited efforts to gradually increase physical activity produced no obvious improvement.

Two years after onset of his symptoms, Jason was missing many days of school and had dropped out of all sports and extracurricular activities. With a partial school attendance program and home tutoring, he maintained above-average grades. Over time, his physicians, friends, and teachers became skeptical of the validity of his physical complaints although his parents continued to vigorously pursue a medical diagnosis. Jason acknowledged feeling depressed about his inability to pursue normal activities, but he denied feelings of anxiety or guilt, self-deprecating thoughts, inability to experience pleasurable activities, or suicidal ideas. Two and a half years after onset, his symptoms began to improve, and he slowly began resuming normal activities. By three years, feeling almost back to normal, Jason resumed vigorous activities, graduated from high school, and went to college.

DEFINITION

For more than a century, clinicians have described a puzzling syndrome with the predominant symptom of severe disabling fatigue that has been given various names, including neuromyasthenia, myalgic encephalomyelitis, postviral fatigue syndrome, and the chronic fatigue and immune dysfunction syndrome. Because the cause is unknown and many other names connote specific unproven etiologies, the term *chronic fatigue syndrome* (CFS) currently seems most appropriate.

To qualify for the diagnosis of CFS, persistent or intermittent fatigue must cause significant functional disability for at least six months and be unexplained after a comprehensive medical and psychological evaluation. There has been considerable professional debate as to the need to identify other physical symptoms in addition to profound fatigue to specify the diagnosis of CFS. A symposium of clinical researchers in Great Britain proposed the Oxford criteria that require only the presence of chronic disabling fatigue without medical explanation regardless of the presence of additional symptoms (Sharpe, Archard, & Banatvala, 1991). The Centers for Disease Control (CDC) criteria, developed in 1988 by an international working group of expert clinicians, required the presence of eight additional symptoms to meet CFS criteria (Holmes et al., 1988). Patients who met criteria for psychiatric disorders were excluded from this CFS case definition. Some argued that requiring more symptoms increased the likelihood of specifying a discrete medical condition, while others pointed out that the presence of multiple physical symptoms frequently was associated with somatoform (psychosomatic) disorders. Additionally, many experts noted that some psychiatric conditions (particularly anxiety and depression) might arise as a consequence of persistent disabling fatigue, and the exclusion of these individuals from CFS case definition was problematic.

In response, the 1994 revised CDC case definition of CFS (see Table 29.1) reduced the number of required physical symptoms (in addition to fatigue) to four and allowed the coexistence of nonmelancholic depression, anxiety, and psychosomatic disorders (Fukuda et al., 1994). Most current researchers use these 1994 CDC CFS criteria and attempt to subclassify those patients that have coexisting psychological conditions that are not exclusionary. While there has been some debate as to the applicability of these criteria for adolescents, they are useful in the comparison of study populations. It must be recalled, however, that these symptoms simply reflect a general consensus of expert opinion based on clinical experience. There is no scientific rationale for claiming that one individual has "real" CFS because he or she meets CDC CFS criteria while another with only a few symptoms does not have the disorder.

EPIDEMIOLOGY

While the complaint of chronic fatigue is very common among adults in primary care practice, it is relatively uncommon in adolescents and rare in children. Adult community-based studies estimate the point prevalence of CFS to be from 75 to

Table 29.1
Revised Case Definition for Chronic Fatigue Syndrome

I. Clinically evaluated, unexplained, persistent or relapsing fatigue that meets the following criteria:
   A. Of new or definite onset.
   B. Associated with substantial reduction in previous levels of occupational, educational, social or personal activities.
   C. Not the result of ongoing exertion.
   D. Not substantially reduced by bed rest.

II. Concurrent occurrence of ≥ four of the following symptoms, all of which must have persisted or recurred for at least six months and must not have pre-dated the fatigue:
   A. Substantially impaired short-term memory or concentration.
   B. Sore throat.
   C. Tender cervical or axillary adenopathy.
   D. Myalgias.
   E. Polyarthralgias.
   F. Headache of a new type, pattern or severity.
   G. Unrefreshing sleep.
   H. Post-exertional malaise lasting ≥ 24 hours.

III. The following conditions exclude an individual from the diagnosis:
   A. Any active medical condition that may explain symptoms.
   B. Any past or current diagnosis of a major depressive disorder with psychotic or melancholic features, bipolar affective disorders, schizophrenia, delusional disorders, dementias, anorexia nervosa and bulimia nervosa.
   C. Alcohol or substance abuse within 2 years before onset or anything afterward.
   D. Severe obesity.

IV. The following conditions do not exclude the diagnosis:
   A. Any condition defined primarily by symptoms that cannot be confirmed by laboratory tests, including fibromyalgia, anxiety disorders, somatoform disorders, nonpsychotic or non-melancholic depression, neurasthenia, and multiple chemical sensitivity disorder.

Adapted from "The Chronic Fatigue Syndrome: a Comprehensive Approach to Its Definition and Study," by K. Fukuda, S. Straus, I. Hickie, M. C. Sharpe, J. G. Dobbins, and A. Komaroff, 1994, *Annals of Internal Medicine, 121,* pp. 953–959.

2,600 per 100,000 with an increased female to male ratio and variable differences in social class (Buchwald, Umali, Kith, Pearlman, & Kamaroff, 1995; Jason et al., 1999; Wessely, Chalder, Hirsch, Wallace, & Wright, 1997). Scant pediatric data exist, but CFS appears to be more common with advancing age, and estimates of adolescent prevalence range from 23 to 116 per 100,000 with an approximate 2.5:1 female:male ratio (Marshall, 1999). Experience in the University of Washington Adolescent Clinic suggests that CFS is relatively increased in the Caucasian population with no consistent trend in socioeconomic status (see later discussion). However, because most such data are from referred populations that may promote selection bias, it is difficult to ascertain whether ethnic, racial, or socioeconomic factors are of importance. Dismissive terms such as *yuppie flu* are not based on strong epidemiological evidence.

ETIOLOGY

While numerous theories have been proposed (see Table 29.2), the etiology of CFS is unknown. It is not established that all patients meeting CFS diagnostic criteria have the same condition nor that adolescent and adult cases represent the same disorder. Additionally, it is important to note that, although small numbers of adolescents are often included, most populations evaluated for possible etiologic factors are composed of adult CFS patients. A review of the current evidence suggests that adolescent CFS may not be a homogenous disorder and that a single causative factor is unlikely to be found (Jordan et al., 1998; Marshall, 1999; Richards, 2000). It is probable that the etiology of CFS involves multiple factors with variable expression in any individual case. Although unproven, factors of importance may include a genetic predisposition to fatiguing illness (Hickie, Kirk, & Martin, 1999); physiological vulnerability (Mawle et al., 1997; Neeck & Crofford, 2000; Stewart et al., 1999); precipitating factors such as infectious agents, antigens, or stress (Johnson, DeLuca, & Natelson, 1999); and sustaining factors such as illness attributions that reject the contribution of psychological factors (Butler, Chalder, & Wessely, 2001), maladaptive coping styles (Ax, Greg, & Jones, 2001), and reinforcement of illness behavior (Brace, Smith, McCauley, & Sherry, 2000).

VIRAL INFECTION

Because of the frequent presence of clinical features that are compatible with the precipitation of illness by acute infection and subtle immunological findings compatible with immune activation such as activated CD8 cells and reduced natural killer cell activity (Patarca-Montero, Mark, Fletcher, & Klimas, 2000), there has been major interest in the possible role of latent or persistent viral infection in CFS. The current wave of interest in this perplexing condition was revived in the 1980s with the use of sophisticated laboratory techniques that suggested a role for the Epstein-Barr virus (chronic EBV infection) to researchers in the United States (Jones, 1986) and enteroviruses (e.g., Coxsackie virus-induced myalgic encephalomyelitis) to those in Great Britain (Yousef et al., 1988).

Although some cultural belief in the relationship between certain viruses and CFS persists (e.g., chronic mono), subsequent well-designed studies have not supported the purported relationship between these viruses and CFS. Multiple RNA and DNA viruses have been considered as causative agents in CFS, but to date, none have been confirmed in this role (Levy, 1994). Recently, interest has centered

Table. 29.2
Etiology of the Chronic Fatigue Syndrome

- Unknown
- Prominent theories include:
  - Persistent latent viral infection
  - Subtle immune system activation
  - Impaired hypothalamic-pituitary-adrenal axis
  - Atypical depression, anxiety, or somatoform disorder
  - Sleep disorder
  - Abnormal neuromuscular function
  - Orthostatic intolerance

on the potential role of reactivated latent herpesviruses in CFS. The potential role of infectious agents in CFS, while representing an important area of ongoing investigation, remains undefined.

IMMUNE DYSFUNCTION

Altered immunological responses are known to occur in many medical and psychological disorders in response to allergic, infectious, and stressful stimuli (Ader, Cohen, & Felten, 1995). Immune system activation involving cytokine release may produce many of the symptoms commonly noted in CFS (Baron et al., 1991). Multiple immunological studies of CFS patients, using diverse populations and methodologies, have produced inconsistent results in T-cell function, mitogen responses, natural killer cell activity, and cytokine response (Marshall, 1999; Patarca-Montero et al., 2000). While minor immunologic abnormalities do appear to occur frequently in CFS and a subset of patients seems to have immune system activation (Buchwald, Wener, Pearlman, & Kith, 1997), it is difficult to ascertain whether these responses are primary, secondary, or epiphenomena. In view of the current evidence, ascribing the disorder to *immune dysfunction* seems to be a premature conclusion.

HYPOTHALAMIC-PITUITARY-ADRENAL AXIS

Some evidence suggests that the hypothalamic-pituitary-adrenal (HPA) endocrine axis might be impaired in CFS, resulting in mild hypocortisolism (Demitrack et al., 1991; Cleare, Blair, Chambers, & Wessely, 2001). This is of interest because low cortisol secretion is found in Addison's disease of the adrenal gland and is associated with chronic fatigue. Attenuated response to exogenous corticotropin releasing hormone (CRH) is also seen in anorexia nervosa and major depressive disorder, but these conditions are associated with increased cortisol secretion. A study using a rigorous design and an intravenous synacthen protocol did not support previous results indicating low adrenal reserve in CFS (Hudson & Cleare, 1999). Additionally, a double-blind, controlled trial of low-dose hydrocortisone therapy in CFS showed minimal improvement of symptoms and suppressed adrenal glucocorticoid responsiveness (McKenzie et al., 1998). HPA axis perturbations may occur with many conditions including stress, sleep disturbance, chronic illness, medication use, and psychological disorders. Currently, there is no definitive evidence that a disturbance in the HPA axis plays a major role in the etiology of CFS.

SLEEP DISORDER

While sleep abnormalities have been demonstrated in several small studies of CFS patients (Fischler et al., 1997; Krupp, Jandorf, Coyle, & Mendelson, 1993; Morriss et al., 1993; Sharpley, Clements, Hawton, & Sharpe, 1997), no definitive pattern has emerged. CFS patients have been found to have difficulty initiating sleep, spend more time in bed, sleep less efficiently, and have more frequent nocturnal awakenings than healthy controls. One study found that adolescents with CFS showed significantly higher levels of sleep disruption than healthy controls (Stores, Fry, & Crawford, 1998). The importance of primary sleep disorders in the etiology of CFS remains undefined, but it appears unlikely that this is the primary cause.

NEUROMUSCULAR DYSFUNCTION

Several early studies suggested metabolic and physiological abnormalities of neuromuscular function in CFS (Arnold, Radda, Bore, Styles, & Taylor, 1983; Jamal & Hansen, 1985). More recent studies in CFS patients have shown normal intracellular muscle metabolism (Barnes, Taylor, Kemp, & Radda, 1993), normal muscle biopsies (Plioplys & Plioplys, 1995), unrevealing single fiber electromyographic responses (Roberts & Byrne, 1994), and normal muscle physiology (Gibson, Carroll, Clague, & Edwards, 1993). Current research, therefore, suggests normal peripheral neuromuscular function and places emphasis on a central component of muscle fatigue in CFS (Kent-Braun, Sharma, Weiner, Massie, & Miller, 1993). Several studies have shown that CFS patients performing exercise perceive a much greater sense of effort than normal subjects despite normal muscular strength (Kent-Braun et al., 1993; Lloyd, Gandevia, & Hales, 1991). It has been suggested that a disturbed sense of effort may cause CFS patients to devote more attention to both motor output and sensory feedback during exercise and thereby reduce tolerance for physical activity (Lawrie, MacHale, Power, & Goodwin, 1997).

ORTHOSTATIC INTOLERANCE

Orthostatic intolerance refers to symptoms of dizziness or fainting on assuming an upright posture. In the elderly or patients with autonomic nervous system disorders, additional symptoms such as palpitations, weakness, anxiety, impaired reasoning, and blurred vision are often reported (Low et al., 1995). Many of the symptoms of CFS are compatible with those of orthostatic intolerance. Recently, there has been considerable research interest in the concept that subclinical, persistent, or intermittent orthostatic intolerance might be the cause of symptoms in many CFS patients. Adult CFS studies using tilt-table and other autonomic nervous system tests have produced conflicting results (Bou-Holaigah, Rowe, Kan, & Calkins, 1995; LaManca et al., 1999; Poole, Herrell, Ashton, Goldberg, & Buchwald, 2000).

However, positive tilt-table studies have been more consistent in adolescents, indicating an increased incidence of orthostatic hypotension, postural orthostatic tachycardia syndrome (POTS, a variant of orthostatic hypotension), and disturbances of consciousness or actual fainting in those with CFS when compared with normal adolescents (Rowe, Bou-Holaigah, Kan, & Calkins, 1995; Stewart et al., 1999). It has been hypothesized that subacute or chronic dysregulation of autonomic control of orthostatic blood pressure and heart rate precipitated by an event such as a viral infection may be important in CFS. Additionally, vascular abnormalities have been demonstrated in adolescent POTS that may be related to either autonomic dysfunction or abnormalities in local circulatory regulation (Stewart & Weldon, 2001).

It is important to note that inactivity with consistent bed rest (or decreased gravity) in otherwise healthy adults has been shown to produce orthostatic blood pressure responses. To date, the possible role of deconditioning has not been assessed adequately in adolescents with CFS.

ATYPICAL ANXIETY, DEPRESSION, AND SOMATIZATION

Because there is a well-established relationship among anxiety, depression, and fatigue (Chen, 1986), it is reasonable to consider psychological factors as contributing to either the etiology or maintenance of CFS. Several adult studies comparing CFS patients with normal controls have shown a higher incidence of premorbid and current psychiatric disorder in CFS patients (Lane, Manu, & Matthews, 1991; Wessely, Chalder, Hirsch, Wallace, & Wright, 1996). It is important to note that in both adults and adolescents who meet current CDC criteria for CFS, more than one-third have concurrent psychiatric diagnoses—predominantly depression and, less often, anxiety disorders (Smith et al., 1991). Several studies have found adolescent CFS patients have more internalizing symptoms, somatic complaints, or functional disability than comparison groups of adolescents with chronic disorders such as arthritis, cancer, or cystic fibrosis (Carter, Kronenberger, et al., 1999; Peclovitz, Septimus, & Friedman, 1995; Walford, McNelson, & McCluskey, 1993). Although adolescents with CFS who do *not* have concurrent psychiatric diagnoses often endorse symptoms such as decreased energy, difficulty with concentration and memory, and sleep problems, they do not often endorse depressed or anxious mood, self-deprecating thoughts, anhedonia, or suicidal ideation (Carter, Edwards, Kronenberger, Michalczyk, & Marshall, 1995; Carter, Kronenberger, Edwards, Michalczyk, & Marshall, 1996).

Adolescents with CFS have been shown to report a high incidence of premorbid physical, psychological, and familial problems, though adjustment tends to be normal for social abilities and self-esteem (van Middendorp, Geenen, Kuis, Heijnen, & Sinnema, 2001). They may also be more prone to problems with anxiety even when symptoms of CFS remit (Garralda, Rangel, Levin, Roberts, & Ukoummune, 1999). Furthermore, adolescents with CFS often report experiencing diminished competence in domains such as athletics, recreational activities, and romantic involvement. These functional impairments may have significant implications for transitioning into young adulthood (Walker, 1999). Indeed, the deleterious impact of CFS on adolescents' social adjustment and school attendance/adjustment during such a critical time in their development may be the most significant clinical issue for this patient population (Gray et al., 2001).

While psychological factors appear to be of major importance in at least one-third of adolescents with CFS, their etiological role remains largely undetermined. Mainstream clinical thinking tends to conceptualize CFS as being either secondary to depression or anxiety or a somatic presentation of a primary affective disorder. Some have suggested that CFS be recognized primarily as a functional somatization disorder, much like recurrent abdominal pain, somatoform pain disorder, or irritable bowel syndrome (Wessely, Nimnuan, & Sharp, 1999). Two investigations suggest that psychological distress in adolescents with CFS is not solely attributable to the limitation of physical and social activity caused by a chronic illness (Carter, Kronenberger, et al., 1999), nor to the stress of having a chronic disorder without clear-cut organic manifestation (Smith, Marsigan, Martin-Herz, & Womack, 2001).

Undeniably, there is considerable overlap of clinical symptoms between CFS and these somatoform conditions that begs for explanation. Because adolescents with CFS report multiple symptoms involving many bodily systems with no clear etiology or effective treatment, it is tempting to engage in reductionistic thinking and ascribe patients' persistent, debilitating symptoms to psychological or emotional factors. A more sophisticated model is needed to understand and effectively manage CFS symptoms. For example, the depressive symptoms in CFS have been found to follow a pattern that is more like that seen in multiple sclerosis than in clinically depressed patients (Johnson, DeLuca, Diamond, & Natelson, 1996). Thus, the subjective report of depression and anxiety in adolescent CFS may be the result of overlapping symptomatology, reaction to the functional disability imposed by fatigue, and/or neurocognitive deficits in attention, concentration, and memory that result in a frustrating loss of mental efficiency.

Similarly, certain premorbid indexes of adjustment seem to be associated with the longitudinal outcome of adolescent CFS (Carter, Noojin, et al., 1999). Thus, a complex interaction of premorbid individual and family characteristics with physiological events is likely to determine illness manifestation as well as functional and psychological outcome. Additionally, one observed psychological characteristic that seems to differentiate adolescents with chronic fatigue from those with other chronic disorders is a tendency to minimize the role of psychological factors in illness manifestation and recovery (Carter et al., 1996; Smith et al., 2001). In fact, a style of illness attribution that fails to endorse the role of psychological factors seems to be associated with poorer symptomatic and functional outcome in adolescents with chronic fatigue (Carter, Kronenberger, et al., 1999).

PRESENTATION

In most systematic reports, onset of CFS in adolescents follows an acute febrile illness in approximately two-thirds of cases while one-third may develop symptoms insidiously (Carter et al., 1995; Krilov, Fisher, Friedman, Reitman, & Mandel, 1998; Smith et al., 1991). One report suggests that the clinical course is persistent in approximately two-thirds of adolescent cases and intermittent with remissions and relapses of several months' duration in the other third.

Figure 29.1 displays the symptoms reported by 100 adolescents with medically unexplained chronic fatigue of longer than six months' duration (mean duration 18.7 ±12.9 months), who were evaluated in the University of Washington Adolescent Clinic. This sample consists of 70 girls and 30 boys ranging from 9 to 18 years old with a mean age of 14.8 ±1.9 years. The sample is 97% Caucasian with a 4-Factor Hollingshead Index of Social Status mean score of 44.7 ±12.7 in a normal distribution. In addition to profound, disabling fatigue, common symptoms in descending order included headache, nonrefreshing sleep, exercise intolerance, weakness, insomnia, decreased concentration, excessive sleeping, sore throat, muscle aches, joint aches, irritability, impaired reasoning, swollen glands, light sensitivity, depressed mood, fever, and memory loss.

All patients had debilitating fatigue that significantly interfered with daily activities, particularly school attendance. Physical examinations and laboratory tests were generally nonrevealing. No adolescent patient had more than four fibromyalgia tender points and neurological examinations were all normal. At intake, in addition to symptomatology, adolescents were asked to complete questionnaires as to anxiety (Spielberger, Gorsuch, & Lushene, 1970), depression (Kovacs, 1992), somatization (Walker, Garber, & Green, 1991), and functional disability (school days missed in the past six months).

Not surprisingly, because of the demand characteristics of the definition, adolescents who met the CDC CFS criteria (CDC⁺ adolescents) endorsed more

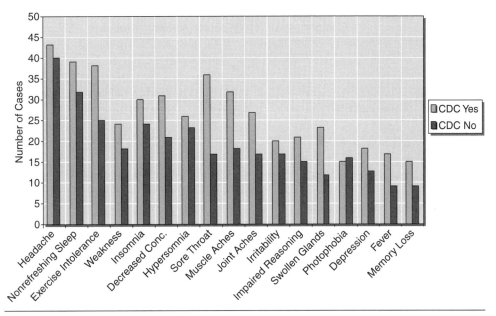

Figure 29.1 Symptoms of 100 Adolescents Evaluated at the University of Washington Adolescent Clinic with Medically Unexplained, Profound Chronic Fatigue of Greater than 6 Months Duration Compared by 1994 CDC CFS Criteria.

symptoms than those who did not (CDC$^-$). A few other interesting differences emerged when patients were characterized by CDC criteria. CDC$^+$ adolescents were predominantly female (40 girls, 7 boys) whereas CDC$^-$ adolescents had a fairly normal sex distribution (30 girls, 23 boys). CDC$^+$ adolescents reported a statistically significant increased presence of headache, exercise intolerance, insomnia, sore throat, impaired reasoning, muscle aches, joint aches, swollen glands, fever, and nonrefreshing sleep in comparison with CDC$^-$ adolescents. Although anxiety and depression scores did not differ between groups, the CDC$^+$ adolescents had statistically higher somatization scores and missed school days (see Table 29.3).

EVALUATION

The physical examination in adolescents with CFS is generally unremarkable. Despite frequent report of the sensation of swollen glands and sore throat, examination of the head and neck usually is normal. Although some authors have suggested that poor peripheral circulation and postural blood pressure changes are common in adolescent CFS, we have not noted this association. Routine supine to standing blood pressure measurements usually do not reveal orthostatic changes, although a special test with a tilt table may demonstrate orthostatic intolerance. Growth and development and pubertal progression are unaffected by CFS. Weight loss or growth delay suggests an occult underlying organic disorder, major depression, or an occult eating disorder. Although common in adults with CFS, more than a few positive fibromyalgia tender points are uncommon in adolescent patients. Complaints of concentration and memory difficulties are common, but neurological and mental status examination usually is normal.

Table 29.3

Comparison of Adolescents (Anxiety,
Depression, Somatization, and Functional Disability)

	CDC CFS Criteria	
	Yes	No
Anxiety (STAI-T)	43.1 ±13.5 (*n* = 28)	37.8 ±10.5 (*n* = 35)
Depression (CDI)	10.9 ±7.9 (*n* = 44)	8.9 ±7.5 (*n* = 44)
Somatization (CSI)*	35 ±13.1 (*n* = 27)	24.4 ±14.8 (*n* = 34)
School days missed in past 6 months*	57.9 ±37.4 (*n* = 43)	32.6 ±34.6 (*n* = 47)

*$p < .01$

A selected laboratory evaluation—including a complete blood count, markers for inflammation, thyroid studies, electrolytes, kidney function tests, liver function tests, and a urinalysis—is indicated in the evaluation of unexplained chronic fatigue in adolescents. Unless specifically suggested by history and physical exam, other laboratory studies such as special immunological tests, viral titers, or cortisol levels rarely are useful in establishing the diagnosis of adolescent CFS. Neuroimaging studies of adult CFS patients have produced ambiguous results and are not routinely recommended. Cardiovascular tilt-table testing may be useful in patients with symptoms suggestive of orthostatic intolerance.

Because careful psychosocial evaluation demonstrates anxiety and/or depressive disorders in many adolescents with CFS, mental health consultation is appropriate in most cases. While fatigue is a common complaint in anxiety and depression, many adolescents with CFS do not meet criteria for psychiatric disorders. It may be difficult to ascertain whether anxiety and depression are primary or secondary conditions when present with CFS. A few studies have suggested that certain personality traits such as perfectionism and maintaining unrealistic performance standards are common in adolescents with CFS (Hoogveld, van Aken, Prins, De Jong, & Bleijenberg, 2001; Rangel, Garralda, Levin, & Roberts, 2000). Although malingering appears to be rare in children and adolescents with CFS, the level of school absenteeism is very high in comparison with other common adolescent disorders (Newacheck, McManus, & Fox, 1991). The role of school avoidance has not been systematically evaluated but seems an unlikely primary explanation in the majority of cases. Nevertheless, continued school absenteeism further isolates the patient and promotes the sick role. Many adolescents with CFS and their parents feel that others often do not validate the disorder as a true medical condition. Consequently, they may be defensive and resistant to discussion concerning the role of psychosocial factors and stress. While the nature of the relationship is still unclear, it is nonetheless important to note that psychological factors are common in adolescent CFS and may play an important role in precipitation or maintenance of the disorder.

Unfortunately, it is often more difficult getting adolescents with CFS and their parents to submit to routine standard psychological or psychiatric evaluation. Indeed, patients with CFS and their families are often reluctant to perceive psychological factors as playing a role in illness presentation or recovery. In addition, most extensive evaluations are typically associated with health care centers affiliated with major medical schools or clinics, typically in conjunction with an organized research project with a standardized protocol. Measures employed are often those developed or adopted by investigators to answer specific research questions. In contrast, this chapter focuses primarily on accessible standardized clinical measures of utility in assessing psychological variables relevant to identifying the needs of adolescents who present with CFS.

It is recommended that, whenever possible, the psychological or psychiatric evaluation be conducted within the structure of the treating physician's facilities to minimize reluctance to follow through on the referral. Patients and parents need reassurance that the referral does not mean that the physician believes the symptoms are "all in your head" or that the physician will abandon the patient and no longer provide medical monitoring. However, this collaborative arrangement is more likely to be available only in medical center and teaching hospital settings where there are more extensive professional resources.

With adolescents, particularly in the 12- to 16-year age range, it is important to obtain parent report of behaviors and symptoms, along with self-report. Adolescents are particularly prone to minimizing symptom reporting on objective measures, although at least one study has shown fairly high correspondence between parent report and adolescent patient report with youth with CFS (Carter et al., 1995).

AFFECTIVE SYMPTOMS AND SOMATIZATION

Because as many as one-third of adolescents with CFS may have clinical levels of depression and/or anxiety, it is important to assess adequately for these psychological conditions. Standardized self-report questionnaires for adolescents include the 27-item Children's Depression Inventory (CDI; Kovacs, 1992), the Revised Children's Manifest Anxiety Scale (R-CMAS; Reynolds & Richmond, 1985), the 20-item Spielberger State-Trait Anxiety Inventory for Children (Spielberger, 1973), the Behavioral Assessment System for Children (BASC-Self Report; Reynolds & Kamphaus, 1992), the Youth Self Report (Achenbach & Edelbrock, 1987), and the Minnesota Multiphasic Personality Inventory—Adolescent (MMPI-A; Butcher et al., 1992). These inventories provide valid and reliable indexes of clinical depression and anxiety. In addition, the BASC and MMPI-A provide more extensive assessment of internalizing and externalizing behavioral problems, although these are infrequently seen in CFS patients. Somatic complaints may be assessed with the Children's Somatization Inventory (CSI; Walker et al., 1991), which consists of 35 symptoms that are rated on whether they have been experienced over the previous two-week period.

Parent report measures include the Behavioral Assessment System for Children (BASC-Parent-Report; Reynolds & Kamphaus, 1992) and the Child Behavior Checklist (CBCL; Achenbach & Edelbrock, 1983).

Both instruments are reliable and valid and assess for both internalizing and externalizing difficulties.

Familial and Attributional Factors

Like so many variables observed in youth with CFS, it is difficult to tell the chicken from the egg. Studies have documented changes in the family when a member has CFS (Jackson, 1999), but the data are primarily correlational and cannot determine whether these are causal or secondary to making accommodations demanded in caring for an adolescent with CFS. Two frequently used measures of family functioning are the 90-item Family Environment Scale (FES; Moos & Moos, 1983), which can be completed by all family members, and the Family Adaptability and Cohesion Scale (Faces-II; Olson & Porter, 1983). These measures assess factors such as cohesiveness, expressiveness in communication, and conflict.

Though still under development, the 43-item Health Experiences Inventory (HEI; Carter & Kronenberger, unpublished manual) is designed to assess patient and parent beliefs and attitudes about a number of relevant psychological, attitudinal, and attributional factors. Preliminary factor analysis of the HEI was generally supportive of the rationally derived scales, including reluctance to change, overprotectiveness, confidence in treating health care providers, psychological-mindedness (i.e., belief that psychological factors play a role in illness and recovery), and acceptance of nontraditional treatments.

Measures of Functional Disability

The 1988 CDC CFS criteria specified that patients must experience a 50% reduction in activity to qualify for case status. However, this was dropped in the 1994 revision because it was almost impossible to quantify, particularly in pediatric cases. The Functional Disability Inventory (FDI; Walker & Greene, 1991) is a 15-item scale that adequately surveys everyday activities and settings where illness may affect the functional ability of the adolescent. Functional impact of illness is important to assess periodically throughout the course of CFS.

Structured Diagnostic Interviews

The Schedule for Affective Disorders and Schizophrenia for School-Aged Children (K-SADS; Ambrosini, Metz, Prabucki, & Lee, 1989) is representative of the structured interview instruments for assessing emotional and behavioral disorders in children and adolescents. However, these instruments require a level of training and a duration of time to administer that make them primarily useful in a research setting only.

Neurocognitive Functioning

Primary neurocognitive deficits, which may be experienced in as many as one-third of adolescents with CFS, most often involve deficits in attention, concentration, verbal memory, visual memory, reaction time, and complex auditory information processing (Tiersky, Johnson, Lange, Natelson, & DeLuca, 1997), while global intellectual functioning remains intact. More specifically, difficulties with complex information processing tasks and reduced speed of processing have been documented (DeLuca, Johnson, Beldowicz, & Natelson, 1995). Thus, patients with CFS may experience difficulties in learning (i.e., encoding) rather than recall. Interestingly, comorbidity of depression and/or anxiety is associated with more impairment in these abilities.

While formal cognitive and neuropsychological testing may be of some value for those patients experiencing severe difficulties in these functions, testing abnormalities are often subtle when compared to the patient's description of day-to-day problems with concentration and memory (Dobbs, Allen, & Kiss, 2001). Both the Continuous Performance Test (CPT; Conners, 1994) and the Test of Variables of Attention (TOVA; Greenberg & Waldman, 1993) are valid and useful instruments to assess sustained attention and vigilance. Both have visual and auditory versions, and some aspects are assessed via computer administration. Though used primarily in a research context, the Paced Auditory Serial-Addition Test (PASAT; Gronwall, 1977; Kane, Ganta, & DiPino, 1997) and the Stroop Test (Golden, 1978) have proven useful in assessing these deficits. However, the subtlety of the deficits seen in patients with CFS may not justify the routine clinical use of more extensive neuropsychological batteries at the present time. The most important clinical concern is to ascertain the impact of these cognitive difficulties on the adolescent's functioning and to devise appropriate coping strategies and interventions (e.g., educational accommodations).

After a careful review of the history, physical and psychological examination, and selected laboratory data, the differential diagnosis of CFS in adolescents should include the disorders shown in Table 29.4.

MANAGEMENT

Although the prognosis for the vast majority of children and adolescents with CFS is good, a prolonged course is common, and functional disability is often marked (Bell, Jordan, & Robinson, 2001; Carter, Kronenberger, et al., 1999).

As with most disabling chronic disorders of unknown etiology, myriad claims as to the therapeutic efficacy of various agents have been promulgated. A recent review found relatively few adult studies with appropriate methodology and sufficient data to draw conclusions concerning efficacy for most treatments except cognitive behavioral therapy and graduated exercise therapy (Whiting et al., 2001).

These behavioral interventions were found to decrease symptoms of fatigue and improve physical functioning.

Table 29.4
Differential Diagnosis of Adolescent Chronic Fatigue Syndrome

---

Subacute infectious disease (e.g., mononucleosis, hepatitis, tuberculosis).

Occult systemic disease (e.g., cardiopulmonary disorder, hypothyroidism, Addison's disease, connective tissue disease, neoplasm, renal failure, inflammatory bowel disease).

Marked psychosocial stress in family, peer, school, or community relationships.

Depression, anxiety, somatoform disorder, occult eating disorder.

Drug and alcohol abuse.

Sleep disorder.

It is often useful, however, to target individual symptoms with specific therapy. Headache and arthralgia may respond to nonsteroidal agents. Symptoms of orthostatic intolerance may respond to treatment with salt, mineralocorticoids, peripheral vasoconstrictors, serotonin reuptake inhibitors, and resistance exercise training. Regardless of whether anxiety and depressed mood are primary or secondary to CFS, their recognition and treatment is imperative in the management of adolescent CFS. Most anxious and depressed adolescents benefit from psychotherapy, and the addition of a serotonin reuptake inhibitor is often useful.

After a careful medical and psychological/psychiatric evaluation, the use of an adaptive, rehabilitative model similar to that used in the management of chronic pain syndromes seems appropriate for adolescent CFS. The identification of maladaptive illness attributions and cognitions (e.g., learned helplessness, catastrophizing) should lead to attempts to validate the present disability yet promote healthy coping mechanisms. Unintentional parental reinforcement of illness behavior should be tactfully pointed out, and suggestions for reinforcement of wellness behavior should be made. For some, avoidance of potentially stress-producing situations (e.g., peer interactions and school demands) may become a source of secondary gain associated with CFS; therefore, school attendance and regular peer contacts are to be encouraged. Indeed, a number of studies have shown that adolescents with more severe academic and social dysfunction at the onset of illness fare more poorly in longitudinal follow-up (Bell et al., 2001; Carter, Noojin, et al., 1999).

Contrary to some CFS patient advocacy group recommendations, prolonged bed rest and marked physical inactivity actually promote further deconditioning and persistence of CFS. Accordingly, the clinician should take time to address patient and parental illness beliefs and attributions and attempt to provide a hypothetical model of CFS as a basis of a rational treatment program. A brief explanation of circadian rhythms may enhance acceptance of sleep hygiene suggestions for avoidance of prolonged daytime napping and sleep phase shifts that advance the hours of going to sleep and subsequent morning awakening. A review of the effects of deconditioning may provide an appropriate introduction to a gentle incremental exercise program with emphasis on strength, flexibility, and graduated aerobic conditioning. Emphasis on the importance of acquiring normal coping skills and social competence may promote acceptance of recommendations for regular school attendance, which could begin with a partial-day attendance plan. Although often administratively expedient, total home schooling may further isolate the patient and serve to promote the sick role. Perhaps most important is the provision of well-integrated multidisciplinary services among a group of professionals who have a good understanding of CFS in adolescents and access to appropriate referral sources to meet the myriad needs of patients with this chronic, debilitating illness.

OUTCOME

Few longitudinal data exist for adolescent CFS, and most reports result from the evaluation of referred patients in academic centers (Bell et al., 2001; Carter et al., 1995; Krilov et al., 1998). These reports indicate that, although symptoms may persist for months to several years, patients and their parents describe a satisfactory outcome in the majority of cases. Roughly half report complete recovery, a third report marked improvement with some residual symptoms, and the remainder report persistent CFS symptoms that are unchanged or worse.

FOLLOW-UP

The proper management of adolescent CFS requires close follow-up to reevaluate symptoms and monitor and reinforce the treatment plan. At each visit, specific symptom control should be addressed and a careful medical assessment (including weight) made to detect any change or new findings. Review and reinforcement of the therapeutic plan as to sleep normalization, gradual increase in physical activity, and return to normal activities should be made at regular intervals. Mood, coping efforts, and psychosocial status should be monitored and supportive counseling provided. Brief visits with patient and parents separately allow confidential, frank discussion and may impart a sense of mastery and control to the adolescent patient. Parental interviews should assess parents' perception of their child's physical and emotional status, treatment adherence, and difficulties implementing techniques designed to promote wellness behavior. Adherence to recommendations for increased physical activity and school attendance may be particularly problematic and require periodic reevaluation and program modification.

Opportunity should be provided to discuss current theories and proposed treatments that may have come to the attention of the family through the media. Recognizing that frustrated families may seek unproven alternative treatments, the compassionate primary care provider can provide information as to rationale and safety and assurance that ongoing primary care will not be compromised. Given the data indicating an ultimate favorable prognosis for most cases of adolescent CFS, an optimistic stance by the provider seems appropriate, and patients and parents should be advised that the majority of adolescent CFS patients improve with time.

REFERENCES

Achenbach, T. M., & Edelbrock, C. (1983). *Manual for the Child Behavior Checklist and Revised Behavior Profile.* Burlington: University of Vermont, Department of Psychiatry.

Achenbach, T. M., & Edelbrock, C. (1987). *Manual for the Youth Self-Report and Profile.* Burlington: University of Vermont, Department of Psychiatry.

Ader, R., Cohen, N., & Felten, D. (1995). Psychoneuroimmunology: Interactions between the nervous system and the immune system. *Lancet, 345,* 99–103.

Ambrosini, P. J., Metz, G., Prabucki, K., & Lee, J. (1989). Videotaped reliability of the 3rd ed. of the K-SADS. *Journal of the American Academy of Child and Adolescent Psychiatry, 28,* 723–728.

Arnold, D. L., Radda, G. K., Bore, P. J., Styles, P., & Taylor, D. J. (1983). Excessive intracellular acidosis of skeletal muscle on exercise in a patient with a postviral exhaustion/fatigue syndrome. *Lancet, 2,* 1367–1369.

Ax, S., Greg, V. H., & Jones, D. (2001). Coping and illness cognitions: Chronic fatigue syndrome. *Clinical Psychology Review, 21*(2), 161–182.

Barnes, P. R., Taylor, D. J., Kemp, G. J., & Radda, G. K. (1993). Skeletal muscle bioenergetics in the chronic fatigue syndrome. *Journal of Neurology, Neurosurgery, and Psychiatry, 56,* 679–683.

Baron, S., Tyring, S. K., Fleischmann, W. R., Coppenhaver, D. H., Niesel, D. W., Klimpel, G. R., et al. (1991). The interferons: Mechanism of action and clinical applications. *Journal of the American Medical Association, 266,* 1375–1383.

Bell, D. S., Jordan, K., & Robinson, M. (2001). Thirteen year follow-up of children and adolescents with chronic fatigue syndrome. *Pediatrics, 107,* 994–998.

Bou-Holaigah, I., Rowe, P. C., Kan, J., & Calkins, H. (1995). The relationship between neurally mediated hypotension and the chronic fatigue syndrome. *Journal of the American Medical Association, 274,* 961–967.

Brace, M., Smith, M. S., McCauley, E., & Sherry, D. D. (2000). Family reinforcement of illness behavior: A comparison of adolescents with chronic fatigue syndrome, juvenile arthritis, and healthy controls. *Developmental and Behavioral Pediatrics, 21,* 332–339.

Buchwald, D., Umali, P., Kith, P. A., Pearlman, T., & Kamaroff, A. L. (1995). Chronic fatigue and the chronic fatigue syndrome: Prevalence in the Pacific Northwest health care system. *Annals of Internal Medicine, 123,* 81–88.

Buchwald, D., Wener, M., Pearlman, T., & Kith, P. A. (1997). Markers of inflammation and immune activation in chronic fatigue and chronic fatigue syndrome. *Journal of Rheumatology, 24,* 372–376.

Butcher, J. N., Williams, C. L., Graham, J. R., Archer, R., Tellegen, A., Ben-Porath, Y. S., et al. (1992). *Minnesota Multiphasic Personality Inventory—Adolescent version* (MMPI-A). Minneapolis: University of Minnesota Press.

Butler, J. A., Chalder, T., & Wessely, S. (2001). Causal attributions for somatic sensations in patients with chronic fatigue syndrome and their partners. *Psychological Medicine, 31,* 97–105.

Carter, B. D., Edwards, J. F., Kronenberger, W. G., Michalczyk, L., & Marshall, G. S. (1995). Case control study of chronic fatigue in pediatric patients. *Pediatrics, 95,* 179–186.

Carter, B. D., & Kronenberger, W. G. (2001). *Health Experiences Inventory.* Unpublished manual.

Carter, B. D., Kronenberger, W. G., Edwards, J. F., Marshall, G. S., Schikler, K. N., & Causey, D. L. (1999). Psychological symptoms in chronic fatigue and juvenile rheumatoid arthritis. *Pediatrics, 103,* 975–979.

Carter, B. D., Kronenberger, W. G., Edwards, J. F., Michalczyk, L., & Marshall, G. S. (1996). Differential diagnosis of chronic fatigue in children: Behavioral and emotional dimensions. *Journal of Developmental and Behavioral Pediatrics, 17,* 16–21.

Carter, B. D., Noojin, A. B., Kronenberger, W. G., Edwards, J. F., Roehrig, H., Robinson, S., et al. (1999, April 22). *Longitudinal outcome of chronic fatigue in children and adolescents: Predictors of functioning and adjustment.* Paper presented at the Seventh Florida Conference on Child Health Psychology, University of Florida Health Sciences Center, Gainesville, FL.

Chen, M. (1986). The epidemiology of self-perceived fatigue among adults. *Preventive Medicine, 15,* 74–81.

Cleare, A. J., Blair, D., Chambers, S., & Wessely, S. (2001). Urinary free cortisol in chronic fatigue syndrome. *American Journal of Psychiatry, 158,* 641–643.

Conners, C. K. (1994). *The Continuous Performance Test (CPT): Use as a diagnostic tool and measure of treatment outcome.* Paper presented at the annual meeting of the American Psychological Association, Los Angeles.

DeLuca, J., Johnson, S. K., Beldowicz, D., & Natelson, B. H. (1995). Neuropsychological impairments in chronic fatigue syndrome, multiple sclerosis, and depression. *Journal of Neurology, Neurosurgery, and Psychiatry, 58,* 38–43.

Demitrack, M. A., Dale, S. K., Straus, S. E., Laue, L., Listwak, S. J., & Kruesi, M. J. (1991). Evidence for impaired activation of the hypothalamic-pituitary-adrenal axis in patients with chronic fatigue syndrome. *Endocrinology, 73,* 1224–1234.

Dobbs, B. M., Allen, R., & Kiss, I. (2001). Working memory deficits associated with chronic fatigue syndrome. *Journal of the International Neuropsychological Society, 7*, 285–293.

Fischler, B., Le Bon, O., Hoffmann, G., Cluydts, R., Kaufman, L., & De Meirleir, K. (1997). Sleep anomalies in the chronic fatigue syndrome: A comorbidity study. *Neuropsychobiology, 35*, 115–122.

Fukuda, K., Straus, S., Hickie, I., Sharpe, M. C., Dobbins, J. G., & Komaroff, A. (1994). The chronic fatigue syndrome: A comprehensive approach to its definition and study. *Annals of Internal Medicine, 121*, 953–959.

Garralda, E., Rangel, L., Levin, M., Roberts, H., & Ukoummune, O. (1999). Psychiatric adjustment in adolescents with a history of chronic fatigue syndrome. *Journal of the American Academy of Child and Adolescent Psychiatry, 38*, 1515–1521.

Gibson, H., Carroll, N., Clague, J. E., & Edwards, R. H. (1993). Exercise performance and fatigability in patients with chronic fatigue syndrome. *Journal of Neurology, Neurosurgery, and Psychiatry, 56*, 993–998.

Golden, C. J. (1978). *The Stroop Color Word Test.* Chicago: Stoelting.

Gray, D., Parker-Cohen, N. Y., Seiner, S. H., Achilles, J., & McMahon, W. M. (2001). A comparison of individual and family psychology of adolescents with chronic fatigue syndrome, rheumatoid arthritis, and mood disorders. *Journal of Developmental and Behavioral Pediatrics, 22*, 234–242.

Greenberg, L. M., & Waldman, I. D. (1993). Developmental normative data on the Test of Variables of Attention (TOVA). *Journal of Child Psychology and Psychiatry and Allied Disciplines, 34*, 1019–1030.

Gronwall, D. (1977). Paced Auditory Serial Addition Task: A measure of recovery from concussion. *Perceptual and Motor Skills, 44*, 367–373.

Hickie, I., Kirk, K., & Martin, N. (1999). Unique genetic and environmental determinants of prolonged fatigue: A twin study. *Psychological Medicine, 29*, 259–268.

Holmes, G. P., Kaplan, J. E., Gantz, N. M., Komaroff, A. L., Schonberger, L. B., Straus, S. E., et al. (1988). Chronic fatigue syndrome: A working case definition. *Annals of Internal Medicine, 108*, 387–389.

Hoogveld, S., van Aken, M., Prins, J., De Jong, L., & Bleijenberg, G. (2001, January). *Personality characteristics of adolescents with chronic fatigue syndrome.* Paper presented at the 5th International Conference of the American Association of Chronic Fatigue Syndrome, Seattle, WA.

Hudson, M., & Cleare, A. J. (1999). The 1 microgram short synacthen test in chronic fatigue syndrome. *Clinical Endocrinology, 51*, 625–630.

Jackson, E. L. (1999). The effects on siblings in families with a child with chronic fatigue syndrome. *Journal of Child Health Care, 3*, 27–32.

Jamal, G. A., & Hansen, S. (1985). Electrophysiological studies in the postviral fatigue syndrome. *Journal of Neurology, Neurosurgery, and Psychiatry, 48*, 691–694.

Jason, L. A., Richman, J. A., Rademaker, A. W., Jordan, K. M., Plioplys, A. V., Taylor, R. R., et al. (1999). A community-based study of chronic fatigue syndrome. *Archives of Internal Medicine, 159*(18), 2129–2137.

Johnson, S. K., DeLuca, J., Diamond, B. J., & Natelson, B. H. (1996). Selective impairment of auditory processing in chronic fatigue syndrome: A comparison with multiple sclerosis and healthy controls. *Perceptual Motor Skills, 83*, 51–62.

Johnson, S. K., DeLuca, J., & Natelson, B. H. (1999). Chronic fatigue syndrome: Reviewing the research findings. *Annals of Behavioral Medicine, 21*, 258–271.

Jones, J. F. (1986). Chronic Epstein-Barr virus infection in children. *Journal of Infectious Diseases, 5*, 503–504.

Jordan, K. M., Landis, D. A., Downey, M. C., Osterman, S. L., Thurm, A. E., & Jason, L. A. (1998). Chronic fatigue syndrome in children and adolescents. *Journal of Adolescent Health Care, 22,* 4–18.

Kane, R. L., Ganta, N. M., & DiPino, R. K. (1997). Neuropsychological and psychological functioning in chronic fatigue syndrome. *Neuropsychiatry, Neuropsychology, and Behavioral Neurology, 10,* 25–31.

Kent-Braun, J. A., Sharma, K. R., Weiner, M. W., Massie, B., & Miller, R. G. (1993). Central basis of muscle fatigue in chronic fatigue syndrome. *Neurology, 43,* 125–131.

Kovacs, M. (1992). *The Children's Depression Inventory manual.* North Tonawanda, NY: Multi-Health Systems.

Krilov, L. R., Fisher, M. F., Friedman, S. B., Reitman, D., & Mandel, F. S. (1998). Course and outcome of chronic fatigue in children and adolescents. *Pediatrics, 102,* 360–366.

Krupp, L. B., Jandorf, L., Coyle, P. K., & Mendelson, W. B. (1993). Sleep disturbance in chronic fatigue syndrome. *Journal of Psychosomatic Research, 37,* 325–331.

LaManca, J. J., Peckerman, A., Walker, J., Kesil, W., Cook, S., Taylor, A., et al. (1999). Cardiovascular response during head-up tilt in chronic fatigue syndrome. *Clinical Physiology, 19,* 111–120.

Lane, T. J., Manu, P., & Matthews, D. A. (1991). Depression and somatization in the chronic fatigue syndrome. *American Journal of Medicine, 91,* 335–344.

Lawrie, S. M., MacHale, S. M., Power, M. J., & Goodwin, G. M. (1997). Is the chronic fatigue syndrome best understood as a primary disturbance of the sense of effort? *Psychological Medicine, 27,* 995–999.

Levy, J. A. (1994). Viral studies of chronic fatigue syndrome. *Clinical Infectious Diseases* (Suppl. 1), S117–S120.

Lloyd, A. R., Gandevia, S. C., & Hales, J. P. (1991). Muscle performance, voluntary activation, twitch properties and perceived effort in normal subjects and patients with chronic fatigue syndrome. *Brain, 114,* 85–98.

Low, P. A., Opfer-Gehrking, T. L., McPhee, B. R., Fealy, R. D., Benarroch, E. E., Willner, C. L., et al. (1995). Prospective evaluation of clinical characteristics of orthostatic hypotension. *Mayo Clinic Proceedings, 70,* 617–622.

Marshall, G. S. (1999). Report of a workshop on the epidemiology, natural history, and pathogenesis of chronic fatigue syndrome in adolescents. *Journal of Pediatrics, 134,* 395–405.

Mawle, A. C., Nisenbaum, R., Dobbins, J. G., Gary, H. E., Jr., Stewart, J. A., Reyes, M., et al. (1997). Immune responses associated with chronic fatigue syndrome: A case control study. *Journal of Infectious Diseases, 175,* 136–141.

McKenzie, R., Dale, J., Demitrack, M., O'Fallon, A., Sharma, G., Deloria, M., et al. (1998). Low-dose hydrocortisone for treatment of chronic fatigue syndrome: A randomized controlled trial. *Journal of the American Medical Association, 280,* 1061–1066.

Moos, R. H., & Moos, B. S. (1983). Clinical applications of the family environment scale. In E. E. Filsinger (Ed.), *Marriage and family assessment: A sourcebook for family therapy* (pp. 253–273). Beverly Hills, CA: Sage.

Morriss, R., Sharpe, M., Sharpley, A. L., Cowen, P. J., Hawton, K., & Morris, J. (1993). Abnormalities of sleep in patients with the chronic fatigue syndrome. *British Medical Journal, 306,* 1161–1164.

Neeck, G., & Crofford, L. J. (2000). Neuroendocrine perturbations in fibromyalgia and chronic fatigue syndrome. *Rheumatic Disease Clinics of North America, 26,* 989–1002.

Newacheck, P. W., McManus, M. A., & Fox, H. D. (1991). Prevalence and impact of chronic illness among adolescents. *American Journal of Diseases in Children, 145,* 1367–1373.

Olson, D. H., & Porter, J. (1983). Family Adaptability and Cohesion Evaluation Scales. In E. E. Filsinger (Ed.), *Marriage and family assessment: A sourcebook for family therapy* (pp. 299–315). Beverly Hills, CA: Sage.

Patarca-Montero, R., Mark, T., Fletcher, M. A., & Klimas, N. G. (2000). Immunology of chronic fatigue syndrome. *Journal of Chronic Fatigue Syndrome, 6,* 69–107.

Peclovitz, D., Septimus, A., & Friedman, S. B. (1995). Psychological correlates of chronic fatigue syndrome in adolescent girls. *Developmental and Behavioral Pediatrics, 16,* 333–338.

Plioplys, A. V., & Plioplys, S. (1995). Electron-microscopic investigation of muscle mitochondria in chronic fatigue syndrome. *Neuropsychobiology, 32,* 175–181.

Poole, J., Herrell, R., Ashton, S., Goldberg, J., & Buchwald, D. (2000). Results of isoproterenol tilt table testing in monozygotic twins discordant for chronic fatigue syndrome. *Archives of Internal Medicine, 160,* 3461–3468.

Rangel, L., Garralda, E., Levin, M., & Roberts, H. (2000). Personality in adolescents with chronic fatigue syndrome. *European Child and Adolescent Psychiatry, 9,* 39–45.

Reynolds, C. R., & Kamphaus, R. W. (1992). *BASC: Behavioral Assessment System for Children manual.* Circle Pines, MN: American Guidance Service.

Reynolds, C. R., & Richmond, B. O. (1985). *Revised Children's Manifest Anxiety Scale (R-CMAS) manual.* Los Angeles: Western Psychological Services.

Richards, J. (2000). Chronic fatigue syndrome in children and adolescents: A review article. *Clinical Child Psychology and Psychiatry, 5,* 31–51.

Roberts, L., & Byrne, E. (1994). Single fibre EMG studies in chronic fatigue syndrome: A reappraisal. *Journal of Neurology, Neurosurgery, and Psychiatry, 57,* 375–376.

Rowe, P. C., Bou-Holaigah, I., Kan, J. S., & Calkins, H. (1995). Is neurally mediated hypotension an unrecognised cause of chronic fatigue? *Lancet, 345,* 623–624.

Sharpe, M., Archard, L. C., & Banatvala, J. E. (1991). A report—chronic fatigue syndrome: Guidelines for research. *Journal of the Royal Society of Medicine, 84,* 118–121.

Sharpley, A., Clements, A., Hawton, K., & Sharpe, M. (1997). Do patients with "pure" chronic fatigue syndrome (neurasthenia) have abnormal sleep? *Psychosomatic Medicine, 59,* 592–596.

Smith, M. S., Marsigan, J. L., Martin-Herz, S. P., & Womack, W. M. (2001, January). *A comparison of adolescents with chronic fatigue and migraine.* Paper presented at the 5th International Conference of the American Association of Chronic Fatigue Syndrome, Seattle, WA.

Smith, M. S., Mitchell, J., Corey, L., Gold, E., McCauley, E. A., & Glover, D. (1991). Chronic fatigue in adolescents. *Pediatrics, 88,* 195–202.

Spielberger, C. D. (1973). *STAIC Preliminary Manual for the State-Trait Anxiety Inventory for Children.* Palo Alto, CA: Consulting Psychologists Press.

Spielberger, C. D., Gorsuch, R. L., & Lushene, R. E. (1970). *STAI manual for the State-Trait Anxiety Inventory.* Palo Alto, CA: Consulting Psychologists Press.

Stewart, J. M., & Weldon, A. (2001). Reflex vascular defects in the orthostatic tachycardia syndrome of adolescents. *Journal of Applied Physiology, 90*(6), 2025–2032.

Stewart, J. M., Weldon, A., Arlievsky, N., Gewitz, M. H., Li, K., & Munoz, J. (1999). Orthostatic intolerance in adolescent chronic fatigue syndrome. *Pediatrics, 103,* 116–121.

Stores, G., Fry, A., & Crawford, C. (1998). Sleep abnormalities demonstrated by home polysomnography in teenagers with chronic fatigue syndrome. *Journal of Psychosomatic Research, 45,* 85–91.

Tiersky, L., Johnson, S. K., Lange, G., Natelson, B. H., & DeLuca, J. (1997). Neuropsychology of chronic fatigue syndrome: A critical review. *Journal of Clinical and Experimental Neuropsychology, 19,* 560–586.

Walford, G. A., McNelson, W., & McCluskey, D. R. (1993). Fatigue, depression and social adjustment in chronic fatigue syndrome. *Archives of Diseases in Childhood, 68,* 384–388.

Walker, L. S. (1999). The evolution of research on recurrent abdominal pain: History, assumptions, and a conceptual model. In P. McGrath & G. Finley (Eds.), *Chronic and recurrent pain in children and adolescents.* Seattle, WA: IASP Press.

Walker, L. S., Garber, J., & Green, J. W. (1991). Somatization symptoms in pediatric abdominal patients: Relation to chronicity of abdominal pain and parent somatization. *Journal of Abnormal Child Psychology, 19,* 379–394.

Walker, L. S., & Greene, J. W. (1991). The Functional Disability Inventory: Measuring a neglected dimension of child health status. *Journal of Pediatric Psychology, 16,* 39–58.

Wessely, S., Chalder, T., Hirsch, S., Wallace, P., & Wright, D. (1996). Psychological symptoms, somatic symptoms, and psychiatric disorder in chronic fatigue and chronic fatigue syndrome: A prospective study in primary care. *American Journal of Psychiatry, 153,* 1050–1059.

Wessely, S., Chalder, T., Hirsch, S., Wallace, P., & Wright, D. (1997). The prevalence and morbidity of chronic fatigue and chronic fatigue syndrome: A prospective primary care study. *American Journal of Public Health, 87,* 1449–1455.

Wessely, S., Nimnuan, C., & Sharp, M. (1999). Functional somatic syndromes: One or many? *Lancet, 354,* 936–940.

Whiting, P., Bagnall, A. M., Sowden, A. J., Cornell, J. E., Mulrow, C. D., Ramirez, G., et al. (2001). Interventions for the treatment and management of chronic fatigue syndrome. A systematic review. *Journal of the American Medical Association, 286,* 1360–1368.

Yousef, G. E., Bell, E. J., Mann, G. F., Murugesan, V., Smith, D. G., McCartney, R. A., et al. (1988). Chronic enterovirus infection in patients with postviral fatigue syndrome. *Lancet, 1,* 146–150.

CHAPTER 30

Psychological and Educational Issues for Children and Adolescents

BRYAN D. CARTER and TANYA STOCKHAMMER

OTHER AUTHORS IN this volume have provided detailed descriptions of chronic fatigue syndrome (CFS) in pediatric populations, including diagnostic, epidemiological, endocrinologic, cardiac, and infectious/immunological perspectives. Because the presence of affective, neurocognitive, and physical symptoms without clear organic pathology is frequently found in CFS, we attempt to address the role that psychological factors may play in the etiology, differential diagnosis, and management of CFS in children and adolescents. Admittedly, the data on these factors are highly preliminary, and causal connections between psychological factors and CFS are far from validation.

DILEMMAS IN PSYCHOLOGICAL RESEARCH WITH CFS IN CHILDREN AND ADOLESCENTS: THE "PSYCHE OR SOMA?" AND "THE CHICKEN OR EGG?" QUESTIONS

Perhaps one of the most controversial and debated issues in adolescents with CFS, as well as adults, is whether the psychological symptoms that frequently co-occur suggest an underlying, distinct psychiatric disorder. Indeed, the multitude of somatic symptoms manifested by some patients raises the question of whether CFS is actually a psychiatric somatization syndrome. Table 30.1 lists the features of somatization in youth, and the temptation to categorize CFS as a somatoform disorder can be seen (e.g., Wessely, Nimnuan, & Sharpe, 1999). Unfortunately, this is often expressed distressingly by patients and parents, in recounting the numerous invalidating encounters they have had with physicians, health care professionals, educators, and peers.

Therefore, from a causal perspective, what makes it so tempting to lump CFS with the somatization conditions, such as recurrent abdominal pain, chronic tension headaches, irritable bowel syndrome, and so on? The answer entails developing some understanding of the somatization process. Somatization is believed to

Table 30.1
Appearance and Features of Somatiform Disorder

---

1. Physical symptoms without physical basis
2. Not intentional
3. Recent stressor
4. Defensiveness about psychological explanation of symptom
5. Age 6 and older
6. Failure of lab tests and exams to support physical complaints
7. Presence of an illness model
8. Secondary gain
9. Past history of somatic complaints
10. Focus on somatic sensations ("body scanning")
11. Family dysfunction
12. Family focus on illness issues

---

involve a defensive mechanism whereby psychological and interpersonal conflicts are manifested in the form of physical complaints and symptoms, rather than expressed more directly in terms of affective or behavioral problems. This renders sufferers often incapable of confronting the conflict directly but able to avoid it because of their physical incapacitation. Thus, the symptoms serve a functional role via the mechanisms of denial and avoidance and may be reinforced via secondary gain, for example, reduced anxiety and stress and increased attention from others. Despite extensive organic work-ups, a clear underlying physiological condition is typically not identified that can be clearly linked to the patient's symptom pattern. For the treating physician, such a clinical presentation is frustrating because the professional has little to offer in terms of a clear-cut etiological explanation, validated treatments/interventions, and short-term prognostic optimism. Thus, a primarily psychological explanation may be attractive in light of such diagnostic and treatment frustration.

To further encourage a primarily psychological explanation of CFS, a number of studies have shown youth with CFS and CFS-like syndromes to have levels of depression and anxiety—particularly frequent somatic complaints—at levels well above their peers with well-delineated illnesses (Carter, Kronenberger, et al., 1999; Gray et al., 2001; Pelcovitz, Septimus, & Friedman, 1995), though typically lower than peers with diagnosed depressive disorders (Carter, Edwards, Kronenberger, Michalczyk, & Marshall, 1995; Gray et al., 2001; Smith et al., 1991), with the exception of somatic symptoms. Though likely a measurement artifact of behavioral scales that measure somatic complaints, youth with CFS repeatedly demonstrate numbers of somatic symptoms well above their peers with established medical conditions.

An alternate explanation is that affective disturbance in youth with CFS results primarily from a number of stressors associated with having a difficult to diagnose and, to some extent, untreatable physical condition that has significant functional impact on the individual. Most of the data on affective functioning in youth with CFS is cross-sectional. In a number of studies, only a minority of patients report clinical levels of depression and/or anxiety (Carter et al., 1995; Smith et al., 1991).

Thus, affective symptoms may represent a reaction to the functional changes and losses experienced by the child or adolescent, as well as increased dependency and loss of autonomy. However, in one study, youth with CFS were found to have levels of affective disturbance greater than their peers with juvenile rheumatoid arthritis (JRA), even when the functional impact on social and physical activities was similar (Carter, Kronenberger, et al., 1999). One distinct difference between youth with CFS and JRA that may account for the observed disparity in affective symptoms is that CFS is still diagnosed primarily by exclusion of other explanatory conditions and may not have attained the level of legitimacy/validity in the medical and lay community as conditions such as JRA.

To date, there is no confirmatory body of scientific evidence to resolve this debate. Therefore, perhaps the most utilitarian model is a dynamic-interactive one in which an adolescent with a premorbid vulnerability experiences an insult, for example, viral illness or significant psychosocial stressor. The resulting symptom picture may include profound fatigue and multiple somatic complaints, that is, neuroendocrineimmune dysfunction. In some individuals, a pattern of systemic disregulation is established that impairs their ability to function normally in physical and social arenas. The prolonged frustration of seeking a clear diagnosis and treatment approach may contribute to symptom exacerbation and feelings of hopelessness. Interdependency on parents/caretakers and reduced demands on the patient may establish a level of adaptation below their premorbid baseline level and, at times, produce secondary gain associated with the ill role. Reduced physical activity can lead to deconditioning, which increases the likelihood of further postexertional malaise. Thus, a closed system may result with periods of slight waxing and waning of symptoms but with overall functional decline. Taylor and colleagues (Taylor, Friedberg, & Jason, 2001) have proposed a symptom-stress model that attempts to explain the mechanism in stress creation in CFS, as well as support the use of cognitive and behavioral interventions with CFS patients. Richards (2000) has described the vicious circle experienced by youth with CFS that may contribute to chronic disability.

This dynamic-interactive model may be explanatory for only a subset of CFS patients, but particularly applicable to those with premorbid anxiety problems and family dynamics that may overemphasize restriction from activity to avoid symptom exacerbation. Obviously, this model is in need of empirical validation because studies to date can neither confirm nor deny this nor other competing hypothetical perspectives. Therefore, we propose this dynamic-interactional model as a more utilitarian perspective at the present state-of-the-art of CFS psychological research. While clinical experience would suggest that this model is valuable in conceptualizing at least one significant subset of CFS patients, others have posited that CFS and affective disorder are actually different end points with a similar etiological route (Blakely et al., 1991).

Finally, the need to assess the impact of patients' and families' typically lengthy and inconclusive efforts to have CFS diagnosed cannot be overemphasized, as well as the indefinite course, limited treatment options, and highly variable outcomes. Perhaps no other syndrome has as much stigma and skepticism leveled at it, which undoubtedly contributes to the psychological impact of having CFS (Taylor et al., 2001).

PSYCHOLOGICAL SYMPTOMS IN CHILDREN AND ADOLESCENTS WITH CFS

The lack of evidence for a single infectious agent, absence of laboratory markers for CFS, conflicting immunologic data, and conspicuous discrepancies between the intensity of symptoms and the rare occurrence of objective physical findings has led many to conclude that CFS is primarily a psychiatric disorder. Few studies address psychological issues in children with chronic fatigue. Studies in adults with CFS have found that they fail to exhibit the degree of affective disturbance seen in psychiatrically depressed adult patients (Pepper, Doscher, & Hirsch, 1994). Young people with chronic fatigue demonstrate higher levels of depressive symptoms and premorbid personality problems than children and adolescents who have routine medical problems (Smith et al., 1991), who have validated medical illness such as JRA (Carter, Kronenberger, et al., 1999; Rangel, Garralda, & Hall, in press), cystic fibrosis (Walford, McNelson, & McCluskey, 1993), cancer (Pelcovitz et al., 1995), or who are healthy (Carter et al., 1995; Smith et al., 1991). In some studies, up to three-fourths of pediatric patients with chronic fatigue meet diagnostic criteria for affective disorder.

Garralda and colleagues (Garralda, Rangel, Levin, Roberts, & Ukoumunne, 1999), using the Oxford criteria for CFS, retrospectively diagnosed CFS in adolescents by reviewing their medical charts, going back as far as five years. They then conducted structured diagnostic interviews (K-SADS) that reviewed psychiatric symptoms experienced by the adolescents over the previous 12 months. At least half of adolescents whose chart reviews met criteria for CFS also met criteria for the diagnosis of both anxiety and depressive disorder on the semistructured diagnostic interview, which was significantly higher than in a healthy comparison group.

In a study by Smith, Martin-Herz, Womack, and Marsigan (in press), youth with CFS had elevated self-reported anxiety scores similar to that found in a comparison group of adolescents with chronic migraine headache. Both groups were significantly higher in anxiety than a healthy comparison group, but a larger combined group of adolescents with unexplained chronic fatigue (some meeting and others failing to meet CFS case criteria) had anxiety scores lower than the migraine subjects. Compared to youth suffering from migraine headaches and healthy controls, fatigued (combined group) adolescents had higher depressive symptom scores. Somatization for CFS and the combined chronic fatigue group was significantly higher than for those experiencing migraine headaches and healthy controls.

Compared to children with affective disorders, such as major depression and dysthymia, children with chronic fatigue are less likely to report primary symptoms of depression, such as negative affect with suicidal ideation and severe dysphoria (Carter et al., 1995; Carter, Kronenberger, Edwards, Michalczyk, & Marshall, 1996). Symptoms and profiles on depressive measures are typified by multiple somatic complaints (Baetz-Greenwalt, Jensen, Lee, & Brouhard, 1994), reduced physical and social activity (Walford et al., 1993), and difficulty experiencing pleasure in activities they formerly enjoyed (Blakely et al., 1991; Carter et al., 1995).

Recent studies of CFS in adolescents have focused on self-image, personality factors, and the strengths and coping styles adopted by patients (e.g., Garralda et al., 1999; Rangel, Garralda, Levin, & Roberts, 2000; van Middendorp, Geenen, Kuis, Heijnen, & Sinnema, 2001) rather than merely characterizing psychopathology. While many adolescents with CFS perceive themselves as less competent than their nonaffected peers in athletics, dating, and participation in recreational activities, they generally report normal self-esteem and social abilities, high internal locus of control, denial of fear of failure, and normal achievement motivation; and they tend to use palliative and optimism-based coping strategies (van Middendorp et al., 2001). By contrast, adolescent subjects in the studies conducted by Garralda et al. (1999) and Rangel and colleagues (2000) were more likely than their healthy peers to have higher levels of the following personality features: conscientiousness, vulnerability, lowered self-esteem, feelings of worthlessness, lowered social competence, and emotional liability.

In summary, studies of psychological symptoms and personality characteristics of youth with CFS suggest that they have more affective disturbance, primarily depression and anxiety, than most other medically ill peers and even more so than their healthy age mates. They tend to have less affective disturbance than peers with diagnosed affective disorders. Clinically, their level of diagnosable affective disturbance ranges from about one-third up to three-fourths of subjects coming to specialty clinics for fatigue-related complaints. Not surprisingly, report of somatic complaints is higher than most illness comparison groups, perhaps due in part to methodological limitations of scales that measure this construct. Conflicting data exist on self-esteem, social competence, and personality factors, suggesting the need for much more research in this area.

Methodologically, findings as to psychiatric symptoms and diagnosis appear to be highly dependent on the method of assessment, for example, patient self-report versus structured diagnostic interview or parent report and study design characteristics. Structured diagnostic interview schedules can lead to overdiagnosis of psychiatric syndromes in these patients, in part, because somatization and affective syndromes include many of the physical complaints shared with CFS. Therefore, a multimethod assessment approach—with data obtained from the child, parents, siblings, and teachers—is advisable for both research and practice applications.

FUNCTIONAL IMPACT OF CFS IN CHILDREN AND ADOLESCENTS

ACADEMIC FUNCTIONING

The impact of CFS on the academic, social, and extracurricular activities of school-age children can be considerable (Carter & Marshall, 1995). In many cases, school attendance is severely disrupted, with a substantial number of school-age patients reporting frequent absenteeism and receiving lengthy homebound instruction even when compared to other illness groups (Baetz-Greenwalt et al., 1994; Bell, Jordan, & Robinson, 2001; Brace, Scott Smith, McCauley, & Sherry, 2000; Carter & Marshall, 1995; Feder, Dworkin, & Orkin, 1994; Gray et al., 2001; Marshall, Gesser, Yamanishi, & Starr, 1991; Smith et al., 1991, in press; Walford et al., 1993). Krilov and colleagues (Krilov, Fisher, Friedman, Reitman, & Mandel, 1998) reported that most adolescents with CFS had a dramatic increase in school absenteeism, worsening of school performance, and a decrease in social activities associated with their condition. Feder and colleagues (1994) studied 31 new adolescents seen over a two-year period, almost two-thirds of whom were honor students before the onset of their fatigue. After onset, 48% became homebound with only 13% able to attend school regularly. Smith and colleagues (in press) found patients with fatigue and CFS to have more days of absence (mean of 44 days missed) than adolescents with migraine headaches (mean of seven days missed) or healthy controls (mean of less than one day absence) over a six-month period. In their longitudinal follow-up of 35 youth with CFS, Bell and colleagues (2001) found that almost two-thirds missed at least one month of school, with almost one-fourth missing two years or more. School absenteeism correlated highly with long-term functional outcome; that is, none in the higher school absenteeism group reported complete recovery from CFS an average of 13 years after diagnosis.

Neurocognitive difficulties—for example, attention, concentration, short-term memory difficulties, and so on—are frequent accompaniments of CFS and have been found to be more severe than seen in patients with depression (Friedberg & Jason, 1998). While likely to have a deleterious impact on academic efficiency and functioning, no studies to date have directly investigated the impact of these deficits on specific learning and academic tasks in children and adolescents. Rather, it is generally assumed that these subjectively reported difficulties impair academic performance based on academic decline reported in some studies (Feder et al., 1994). Obviously, this is an area in need of much more extensive investigation, particularly if we are to make meaningful recommendations for academic assistance and accommodation for the adolescent with CFS.

SYMPTOM PERSISTENCE

While longitudinal outcome data on functioning in adolescents with CFS is relatively scant, a growing body of data suggests that a significant percent continue to have symptoms and functional impairment years after illness onset (Bell et al., 2001; Carter, Noojin, et al., 1999; Krilov et al., 1998). In the longitudinal follow-up by Bell and colleagues (2001), 80% of the affected children and adolescents reported "satisfactory outcome" of their CFS, although a majority of these patients still reported mild to moderate symptoms on occasion an average of 13 years after diagnosis. Twenty percent of their patients reported that they "remained ill" with considerable activity limitations and symptoms.

Carter and colleagues (Carter, Noojin, et al., 1999), in a follow-up of 25 participants with CFS from their original study (Carter et al., 1995), found that almost half of the 19 respondents still had ongoing symptoms of fatigue an average of five years from diagnosis, with the majority reporting moderate to good improvement since diagnosis. A third of the subjects reported that their activity level was still "below average." When asked to evaluate their present condition relative to when they were first diagnosed, only 7% rated themselves as "worse," with no subjects feeling "the same," and the rest of the sample feeling "mildly better" (13%), "moderately better" (27%), or "much better" (53%). Krilov and colleagues (1998) followed youth up to four years after evaluation for CFS and found 95% of the families considered their child "cured" or "improved," whereas only 5% considered their child to be "the same."

As Marshall (1999) has indicated, these findings suggest that CFS in adolescents presents a symptom picture similar to that found in adults. However, the impact of persistent symptoms and functional impairment on youth during a time of such critical developmental and social changes is much less well understood.

FAMILY IMPACT AND ROLE IN ILLNESS

As in almost any chronic illness, family members often play a strong mediational role when there is a child with CFS. Persistence in seeking a diagnosis for their child's symptoms, interpreting medical and psychological information to the patient, decision-making concerning school attendance and social/physical activity, and so on are just a few of the roles that parents play in helping their son or daughter with CFS.

Garralda and Rangel (2001) found that parental failure to subscribe to the possibility that psychological factors could be contributing to the maintenance of CFS symptoms was associated with poor outcome. Seventy-five percent of the "poor outcome" group rejected the belief that psychological factors played a role in illness maintenance, versus 35% of the "good outcome" group. Parental restriction of the child with CFS from physical and social activity has been associated with poorer outcome (Carter, Noojin, et al., 1999). Brace and colleagues (2000) found that both parent- and child-reported parental encouragement of illness behaviors were significantly higher in CFS patients than in JRA patients. Interestingly, families of JRA and CFS patients were not significantly different on measures of family adaptability and cohesion, suggesting that there is no specific family "type" that would differentiate these two illness groups. Similar results have been obtained comparing family characteristics of adolescents with CFS and pediatric oncology controls in remission (Pelcovitz et al., 1995).

SOCIAL AND RECREATIONAL IMPACT

As reported previously, many young persons with CFS report decreased social involvement with peers secondary to the debilitating functional impact of their illness (Krilov et al., 1998; van Middendorp et al., 2001), despite their perception that they generally have good social adjustment. More than half of the parents of adolescents with CFS reported that their children's social activities were decreased over their premorbid level, compared to only 22% of the CFS patients themselves, an average of five years postdiagnosis (Carter, Noojin, et al., 1999). Bell and colleagues (2001), noting that the long-term social impact of CFS on adolescents seemed to parallel their overall perceived illness outcome, found that almost 47% felt that CFS affected their social adjustment at least to a mild degree, with 8.6% reporting a moderate social effect and 11.4% reporting a severe effect on social adjustment. Krilov and colleagues (1998) studied 42 children with chronic fatigue and found that almost 50% reported rarely or never getting together with friends for activities, with 75% participating in minimal to no sports activities.

These data do little to describe the impact of CFS on the social development of adolescents, where increased independence from family and immersion into the world of peers is the norm. What is needed is more in-depth follow-up interviews, assessment of social functioning and adjustment, and perhaps even peer perceptual measures to give a more complete understanding of the impact of CFS in adolescents on adult social adjustment.

ATTRIBUTION AND
PSYCHOLOGICAL MINDEDNESS

A number of studies have shown that adolescents with CFS and their parents are more likely to attribute their illness to environmental and constitutional factors, for example, viral or immune dysfunction, while minimizing the role of psychological or stress-related factors in illness onset, maintenance, exacerbation, and outcome (Carter et al., 1996; Carter, Noojin, et al., 1999; Garralda & Rangel, 2001; Smith et al., in press). This finding is often stable even when comparing other illness groups, such as youth with JRA (Carter, Kronenberger, et al., 1999) and migraine headaches (Smith et al., in press). Carter and colleagues (Carter, Kronenberger, et al., 1999) suggest that the psychological distress found in youth with CFS is not solely attributable to the stress of having a chronic illness that limits physical and social activity. There are indications that pediatric CFS patients with more favorable outcome are those who see a relationship between psychological/attitudinal factors and illness/recovery and whose parents encourage participation in activities and have higher expectations for the performance of chores (Carter, Kronenberger, et al., 1999). However, these findings require additional empirical support in light of other contradictory findings among adults with CFS (Smith et al., in press).

Illness attributions may also be subject to change. Krilov and colleagues (1998), in a CFS treatment study, found that at a four-year follow-up after receiving services, 71% of the families of youth with CFS believed that the cause involved a combination of medical and psychological factors, compared to 27% believing it was purely medical. This is in contrast to the belief model of a sample of 25 pediatric CFS patients at the time of diagnosis: 90% of the adolescents endorsed biological factors, with 72% of parents in agreement (Garralda & Rangel, 2001). This would suggest that patient/family member attitudes toward the psychological-physical interplay might be modified via both experience and intervention.

It has been suggested that youth with CFS and their parents may have unrealistic views of normal fatigue levels; that is, fatigued adolescents and their parents estimate normal levels of fatigue in healthy teens at significantly lower levels than that of their healthy peers and their parents (Garralda & Rangel, 2001). Distorted health perceptions may play a mediating role in patient/parent likelihood of overemphasizing undue restrictions that may contribute to duration and functional illness outcome.

PSYCHOLOGICAL APPROACHES TO INTERVENTION

COGNITIVE THERAPY

Because psychological and social morbidity can contribute to disability and dysfunction in CFS, psychotherapeutic interventions have been proposed. Cognitive behavioral therapy (CBT) attempts to modify maladaptive thinking and attributional patterns to enhance feelings of self-efficacy and decrease activity avoidance. Improvement in a majority of patients was reported in an uncontrolled study of 32 adults using CBT (Butler, Chalder, Ron, & Wessely, 1991). Benefits included reduced functional disability and lessened anxiety, depressive symptoms, and somatic complaints. A double-blind placebo-controlled study comparing CBT alone, or in combination with immunotherapy, showed no benefits from any treatment method (Lloyd et al., 1993), while another controlled study of CBT resulted in reduced depressive symptoms but no reduction in severity of stress or fatigue (Friedberg & Krupp, 1994). However, in the subgroup of patients with high levels of depressive symptoms, global improvement was noted. Price and Couper's (2000) review of 13 randomized controlled trials of CBT in adults with CFS concluded that CBT improved functioning and reduced symptoms of fatigue.

Combined CBT and family therapy were found to be effective in restoring a 14-year-old girl to premorbid functioning, while supportive therapy, combined with behavioral techniques and increased physical activity, resulted in improvement in five children (Vereker, 1992). A behavioral program of graduated mobilization facilitated by negotiated rewards enabled a 15-year-old boy to make a complete recovery that was sustained at nine-month follow-up. A similar program for a 14-year-old boy was successful while he was in the hospital. However, without full parental support, the progress was not sustained when he went home. CBT may be most useful in patients with significant depression. Promising preliminary results have also been reported using CBT in the overlapping syndrome of fibromyalgia in adults (Nielson, Walker, & McCain, 1992) and children (Walco & Ilowite, 1992).

Unfortunately, there have been no randomized controlled studies of CBT in the treatment of children and adolescents with CFS. This treatment modality would seem to hold some promise, particularly in light of the observation that attributional and attitudinal factors may play a role in the course and outcome of CFS. By design, CBT targets patient/parent belief systems that may impact on health behaviors associated with long-term outcome, for example, setting realistic expectations for physical activities and social/academic participation.

FAMILY INTERVENTION

Because of the often-forced dependency of adolescents with CFS on family for support and assistance, parental involvement is often critical to successful management and treatment. Parental encouragement of emotional expression (not just focusing on somatic symptoms and disability), problem solving, and active coping (Brace et al., 2000) have been shown to be important components to successful treatment efforts. Indeed, the employment of active coping strategies, as opposed to avoidant approaches, has been associated with better long-term functioning in CFS as well as other chronic illnesses. While most of the data are correlational, parental emphasis on reduced physical and social activity has been associated with poorer outcomes in adolescent CFS (Carter, Noojin, et al., 1999). Depression, which has been shown to at least co-occur with CFS to a significant degree, can be worsened by withdrawal from activities, increased time spent in bed, and decreased activity. Family and cognitive interventions targeted at depressive symptoms and corresponding beliefs/attitudes that contribute to discouragement and demoralization may be helpful in limiting the morbidity and progression of symptoms in CFS. A better understanding of the nature of parental worry and reinforcement in CFS in youth is also much needed to inform intervention efforts.

EDUCATIONAL IMPLICATIONS AND ACCOMMODATION

Because of the significant impact of adolescent CFS on school attendance, considerable attention must be given to academic arrangements to accommodate the functional, neurocognitive, and psychological impact of this debilitating illness

(Richards, 2000). Studies of clinical populations of youth seen for chronic fatigue and CFS often reveal premorbid academic functioning that was above average, with many patients being described as high achievers. Maintaining superior academic performance in the midst of the waxing and waning pattern of illness exacerbations is most challenging for the adolescent, the family, and the patient's educators.

It is most important for the patient, parents, treating physician/health care professionals, and the school to establish a working relationship early in the course of the illness. Early intervention should be aimed at minimizing the impact of the adolescent's illness on academic attendance and performance. Initial efforts may focus on educating the school as to the diagnosis and natural history of CFS in youth and anticipating the possible course for the patient.

Perhaps the most controversial issue concerning the education of the adolescent with CFS is that of school attendance versus what has been variously called homebound school, home hospital (United States), and home tuition (United Kingdom). Some professionals express concern about unduly reinforcing the "ill" role and stress approximating normal school attendance and involvement in extracurricular activities as much as possible. One study (Arzomand, 1998) indicated that while 57% of parents of adolescents with CFS favored homebound schooling, only 26% of educators and 7% of physicians were in agreement. Many professionals fear that frequent and lengthy absence will increase the likelihood that the patient will adopt avoidance coping strategies and perhaps even develop school refusal or school phobia, that is, separation anxiety disorder.

Others advocate that the adolescent with CFS is often too ill to tolerate even partial attendance at school and that special accommodations are often needed for lengthy periods of time. In the United States, adolescents with severe CFS documented by their physician are often eligible for educational accommodations under two federal laws: the Individuals with Disabilities Education Act (IDEA) and Section 504 of the Rehabilitation Act of 1973. Students identified with a medically diagnosed condition such as CFS can have their educational programs individualized to address their special needs, to include weekly home instruction provided by the public school system, part-time attendance, independent study arrangements, correspondence courses, modification of physical education requirements, and classroom modifications to address neurocognitive difficulties associated with CFS (e.g., tutoring, placement to minimize distractions, being given more time to complete tests and assignments, rest periods during the school day).

Referral of adolescents with CFS for comprehensive psychological assessment should be a strong consideration, particularly in youth who experience significant decline in academic performance. Assessment of cognitive and academic achievement should be standard, with supplemental testing to further assess attention and concentration, short-term memory, and other relevant neurocognitive skills. Personality assessment and evaluation of adjustment and coping difficulties—for example, depression/anxiety, self-esteem, and coping styles—should be included along with assessment of family interaction and functioning.

The standard for meeting the educational needs of youth with CFS should emphasize a balanced approach. On one hand, it is important to avoid overly reinforcing the patient for behaviors associated with the "sick" role, potentially setting up a pattern of avoidance and social isolation. On the other hand, there often are periods of illness exacerbation where regular full-time attendance is difficult, if not impossible. Flexibility is important on the part of the school, patient, family, and health care providers to adjust their approach accordingly while continuing to emphasize optimism and promote optimal functioning in the academic and social arena.

THE MULTIDISCIPLINARY MANAGEMENT TEAM: A REHABILITATION PERSPECTIVE

As Richards (2000) has pointed out, many patients and families are very reluctant to accept even a partial psychological explanation for their CFS symptoms and/or adjustment to and management of their illness. This makes the ongoing involvement and coordination of the adolescent's primary and specialty care physicians and health care professionals all the more important. Most professionals develop an internal working model of CFS, and these beliefs and attitudes, just as in the CFS patient and family, may lead to conflicts with different professionals over the approach to take in management and treatment. Close communication and agreement is paramount for efficacious care. From this perspective, psychological care that is integrated into the primary medical team is least likely to evoke resistance to psychological interventions. While guidelines for responsible care of adolescents with CFS have been provided (Marshall & Carter, 1997, 2002), including both medical and psychological aspects of this perplexing illness, more empirically validated treatment approaches, especially from a multidisciplinary perspective, need to be developed. Until such evidence is available, all members of the treatment process need to focus on efforts to foster optimism in patients and parents with the aim of returning the adolescent to normal functioning as soon as possible. Judicious referral to medical specialists—for example, cardiology, psychiatry, and so on—should be done with care, while keeping the long-term management and treatment responsibility coordinated within the core CFS treatment team.

WHERE DO WE GO FROM HERE?

As with so many disorders in youth, the research on CFS in adolescents needs to be accelerated to catch up with that in adults. The fact that the incidence of CFS in adolescents is lower than that in adults adds to this difficulty. There is virtually no area of research into CFS in adolescents that does not need investigation. Studies of the psychological factors associated with CFS in youth, both etiologically and from a management and treatment perspective, will undoubtedly play an important future role in our efforts to understand CFS and care for adolescents with this perplexing illness.

REFERENCES

Arzomand, M. L. (1998). Chronic fatigue syndrome among school children and their educational needs. *Journal of Chronic Fatigue Syndrome, 4,* 59–69.

Baetz-Greenwalt, B., Jensen, V., Lee, A., & Brouhard, B. H. (1994). Chronic fatigue syndrome (CFS) in children and adolescents: A somatoform disorder often complicated by treatable organic illness. *Pediatric Research, 35,* 173.

Bell, D. S., Jordan, K., & Robinson, M. (2001). Thirteen year follow-up of children and adolescents with chronic fatigue syndrome. *Pediatrics, 107,* 994–998.

Blakely, A. A., Howard, R. C., Sosich, R. M., Murdoch, J. C., Menkes, D. B., & Spears, G. F. (1991). Psychiatric symptoms, personality, and ways of coping in chronic fatigue syndrome. *Psychological Medicine, 21*(2), 347–362.

Brace, M. J., Scott Smith, M., McCauley, E., & Sherry, D. D. (2000). Family reinforcement of illness behavior: A comparison of adolescents with chronic fatigue syndrome, juvenile arthritis, and healthy controls. *Journal of Developmental and Behavioral Pediatrics, 21*(5), 332–339.

Butler, S., Chalder, T., Ron, M., & Wessely, S. (1991). Cognitive behavior therapy in chronic fatigue syndrome. *Journal of Neurology, Neurosurgery, and Psychiatry, 54*(2), 153.

Carter, B. D., Edwards, J. F., Kronenberger, W. G., Michalczyk, L., & Marshall, G. S. (1995). Case control study of chronic fatigue in pediatric patients. *Pediatrics, 95*(2), 179–186.

Carter, B. D., Kronenberger, W. G., Edwards, J. F., Marshall, G. S., Schikler, K. N., & Causey, D. L. (1999). Psychological symptoms in chronic fatigue and juvenile rheumatoid arthritis. *Pediatrics, 103*(5, Pt. 1), 975–979.

Carter, B. D., Kronenberger, W. G., Edwards, J. F., Michalczyk, L., & Marshall, G. S. (1996). Differential diagnosis of chronic fatigue in children: Behavioral and emotional dimensions. *Journal of Behavioral and Developmental Pediatrics, 17*(1), 16–21.

Carter, B. D., & Marshall, G. S. (1995). Diagnosis and management of chronic fatigue in children and adolescents. *Current Problems in Pediatrics, 25*, 281–293.

Carter, B. D., Noojin, A. B., Kronenberger, W. G., Edwards, J. F., Roehrig, H., Robinson, S., et al. (1999, April 22). *Longitudinal outcome of chronic fatigue in children and adolescents: Predictors of functioning and adjustment.* Paper presented at the Seventh Florida Conference on Child Health Psychology, University of Florida Health Sciences Center, Gainesville, FL.

Feder, H., Dworkin, P. H., & Orkin, C. (1994). Outcome of 48 patients with chronic fatigue: A clinical experience. *Archives of Family Medicine, 3*(12), 1049–1055.

Friedberg, F., & Jason, L. A. (1998). *Understanding chronic fatigue syndrome: An empirical guide to assessment and treatment.* Washington, DC: American Psychological Association.

Friedberg, F., & Krupp, L. B. (1994). A comparison of cognitive behavioral treatment for chronic fatigue syndrome and primary depression. *Clinical Infectious Diseases, 18*(Suppl. 1), S105–S110.

Garralda, E., & Rangel, L. (2001). Childhood chronic fatigue syndrome. *American Journal of Psychiatry, 158*(7), 1161.

Garralda, E., Rangel, L., Levin, M., Roberts, H., & Ukoumunne, O. (1999). Psychiatric adjustment in adolescents with a history of chronic fatigue syndrome. *Journal of the American Academy of Child and Adolescent Psychiatry, 38*(12), 1515–1521.

Gray, D., Parker-Cohen, N. Y., White, T., Clark, S. T., Seiner, S. H., Achilles, J., et al. (2001). A comparison of individual and family psychology of adolescents with chronic fatigue syndrome, rheumatoid arthritis, and mood disorders. *Journal of Developmental and Behavioral Pediatrics, 22*(4), 234–242.

Krilov, L. R., Fisher, M., Friedman, S. B., Reitman, D., & Mandel, F. S. (1998). Course and outcome of chronic fatigue syndrome in children and adolescents. *Pediatrics, 102*(2, Pt. 1), 360–366.

Lloyd, A. R., Hickie, I., Brockman, A., Hickie, C., Wilson, A., Dwyer, J., et al. (1993). Immunologic and psychologic therapy for patients with chronic fatigue syndrome: A double-blind placebo-controlled trial. *American Journal of Medicine, 94*(2), 197–203.

Marshall, G. S. (1999). Report of a workshop on the epidemiology, natural history, and pathogenesis of chronic fatigue syndrome in adolescents. *Journal of Pediatrics, 134*, 395–405.

Marshall, G. S., & Carter, B. D. (1997). Chronic fatigue syndrome. In S. Long, C. Prober, & L. Pickering (Eds.), *Principles and practice of pediatric infectious diseases.* Philadelphia: Churchill Livingstone.

Marshall, G. S., & Carter, B. D. (2002). Chronic fatigue syndrome. In S. Long, C. Prober, & L. Pickering (Eds.), *Principles and practice of pediatric infectious diseases* (2nd ed., pp. 1118–1128). Philadelphia: Churchill Livingstone.

Marshall, G. S., Gesser, R. M., Yamanishi, K., & Starr, S. E. (1991). Chronic fatigue in children: Clinical features, Epstein-Barr virus and human herpesvirus 6 serology and long-term follow-up. *Pediatric Infectious Diseases Journal, 10*(4), 287–290.

Nielson, W. R., Walker, C., & McCain, G. A. (1992). Cognitive-behavioral treatment of fibromyalgia syndrome. *Journal of Rheumatology, 19,* 98–103.

Pelcovitz, D., Septimus, A., & Friedman, S. B. (1995). Psychological correlates of chronic fatigue syndrome in adolescent girls. *Journal of Developmental and Behavioral Pediatrics, 16,* 333–338.

Pepper, C. M., Doscher, C., Hirsch, M. (1994). Comparison of the psychiatric and psychological profiles of patients with chronic fatigue syndrome, multiple sclerosis, and major depression. *Clinical Infectious Diseases* (Suppl. 1), S86.

Price, J. R., & Couper, J. (2000). Cognitive behavior therapy with chronic fatigue syndrome. *Cochrane Database of Systematic Reviews, 2,* 41.

Rangel, L., Garralda, M. E., & Hall, A. (in press). Psychiatric adjustment in chronic fatigue syndrome of childhood and in juvenile idiopathic arthritis. *Psychological Medicine.*

Rangel, L., Garralda, E., Levin, M., & Roberts, H. (2000). Personality in adolescents with chronic fatigue syndrome. *European Child and Adolescent Psychiatry, 9*(1), 39–45.

Richards, J. (2000). Chronic fatigue syndrome in children and adolescents: A review article. *Clinical Child Psychology and Psychiatry, 5,* 31–51.

Smith, M. S., Martin-Herz, S. P., Womack, W. M., & Marsigan, J. L. (in press). Anxiety, depression, somatization, functional disability, and illness attribution in adolescent chronic fatigue syndrome and migraine. *Pediatrics.*

Smith, M. S., Mitchell, J., Corey, L., Gold, D., McCauley, E. A., Glover, D., et al. (1991). Chronic fatigue in adolescents. *Pediatrics, 88*(2), 195–202.

Taylor, R., Friedberg, F., & Jason, L. (2001). *A clinician's guide to controversial illnesses: Chronic fatigue syndrome, fibromyalgia, and multiple chemical sensitivities.* Sarasota, FL: Professional Resource Exchange.

van Middendorp, H., Geenen, R., Kuis, W., Heijnen, C. J., & Sinnema, G. (2001). Psychological adjustment of adolescent girls with chronic fatigue syndrome. *Pediatrics, 107*(3), E35.

Vereker, M. (1992). Chronic fatigue syndrome: A joint pediatric-psychiatric approach. *Archives of Diseases in Childhood, 67,* 550–555.

Walco, G. A., & Ilowite, N. T. (1992). Cognitive-behavioral intervention for juvenile primary fibromyalgia syndrome. *Journal of Rheumatology, 19*(10), 1617–1619.

Walford, G. A., McNelson, W., & McCluskey, D. R. (1993). Fatigue, depression, and social adjustment in chronic fatigue syndrome. *Archives of Diseases in Children, 68,* 384–388.

Wessely, S., Nimnuan, C., & Sharpe, M. (1999). Functional somatic syndromes: One or many? *Lancet, 354,* 936–939.

CHAPTER 31

Community-Based Interventions

LEONARD A. JASON and RENÉE R. TAYLOR

Illness is a world of its own, another place of reality, that is quite apart from the one we normally inhabit in the ordinary dailiness of health. It has its own geography beneath depths of darkness, its own gravity at the farthest bottom of life, its own laws and commandments that strip us of all notions of the mind . . . and the desires of the heart. And it offers an extraordinary—if at times frightening—vantage point from which to view the terrain of one's life.

Kat Duff (1993, p. 4)

A KEY QUESTION FOR practitioners and researchers who work with individuals with chronic fatigue syndrome (CFS) is how to conduct research in an accurate, sensitive, and comprehensive way without inadvertently stigmatizing those with this syndrome. Despite evidence against the hypothesis that depression is responsible for CFS (Antoni et al., 1994; Friedberg & Krupp, 1994; Ray, 1991), many medical practitioners, as well as friends and families of people with CFS, continue to believe that the illness is related to psychological dysfunction and that the symptoms can be relieved if so desired by the individual (Jason, Richman, et al., 1997). It is often mistakenly believed that if people continue to be sick for years without improvement, that they must be sabotaging their own recovery or seeking some form of secondary gain.

Financial support for this study was provided by NIAID grant number AI49720. Portions of this chapter were printed in the following article: Jason, L. A., Kolak, A. M., Purnell, T., Cantillon, D., Camacho, J. M., Klein, S., and Lerman, A. (2001). Collaborative ecological community interventions for people with chronic fatigue syndrome. *Journal of Prevention and Intervention in the Community, 21,* 35–51.

726

AN ECOLOGICAL APPROACH

An ecological approach to research and service delivery in CFS offers one means of understanding the fundamental intrapersonal, social, and larger systemic issues involved in this syndrome. According to Kingry-Westergaard and Kelly (1990), a central principle of an ecological approach involves using multiple methods to understand complex qualities of relationships and systems. One of these methods for helping to understand what we claim to know is the collaborative relationship between the researcher and the participants. This means that concepts and hypotheses are developed and tested by both the researcher and the participants. In a sense, the ecological endeavor is a discovery process wherein different parties share different constructions of a context, learn of the events and processes that help define their understanding of the contexts, and work together to define the research activity. Ecological validity results from the integration of the perspectives of multiple stakeholders into the planning and process of research. This mutually empowering, egalitarian, and respectful relationship is a key aspect of community interventions (Serrano-Garcia, 1990).

Kelly (1986) has posited that ecological principles should be used by professionals who join in long-term collaborative relationships with persons and settings. By involving participants actively in the planning of interventions, the recipients of the programs receive support, learn to identify resources, and become better problem solvers who are more likely to manage future problems and issues. Interventions that have been generated from collaboratively defined, produced, and implemented change efforts are more apt to endure. By involving participants in the design of the research, investigators might gain a greater appreciation of the culture and unique needs of the community and heighten the possibilities that research findings are used to benefit the community. An ecological approach would involve examining a community's basic values, analyzing community traditions for responding to community problems, creating citizen advisory groups to gather community support and interpret the goals of an intervention, and assessing positive and negative second-order ripple effects of an intervention.

This chapter uses this ecological model as a conceptual framework that orients a series of descriptive examples (many of these examples are also contained in Jason et al., 2001). We target in this article those aspects of Kelly's (1986) ecological model that are most relevant to understanding the distinctive contributions of community psychology to a joint university-advocacy group effect and an interdisciplinary research collaboration. We argue that the initiation of social change from an ecological perspective best involves interdisciplinary and community collaboration. Two questions are addressed in this chapter:

1. How can an ecologically based response be initiated to deal with multilayered problems caused by CFS that severely interfere with quality of life?
2. What contributions can an ecological model offer to those interested in CFS research?

EVALUATING ATTITUDES

A starting point for understanding the many perspectives that can influence treatment decisions and resource availability for individuals with CFS involves assessing attitudes toward individuals with the syndrome. Although research on the theory and assessment of attitudes toward people with CFS is limited, there is extensive research on attitudes toward people with other disabilities, including those with other chronic illnesses (Shlaes, Jason, & Ferrari, 1999). Several theories in the disability literature explain negative attitudes toward people with disabilities. Wright (1988) believes that three main factors affect attitudes toward people with disabilities: saliency of the disability, value attributed to the disability, and context in which the disabled person is experienced. *Saliency* refers to how clearly the disability stands out. This variable includes concealability of the disability and the aesthetic qualities of the disability (Schmelkin, 1988). *Value* refers to whether the salient characteristic is regarded as being negative, either by the observer or society at large. *Context* takes into account both external and intrapsychic context. External context is composed of the conditions present when the observer has contact with the disabled individual.

The theory of saliency, value, and context can be applied to negative attitudes toward people with CFS. According to this theory, the visible manifestations of the illness have an effect on attitudes. For instance, someone with CFS who is using a wheelchair may be judged differently than someone who can walk. It is also possible that the individual in the chair is judged more negatively, based on the value American society places on individualism and functioning without assistance (Westbrook, Legge, & Pennay, 1993). Finally, attitudes toward an individual with CFS are affected by situational variables. Perceptions of a sick colleague whose inability to do work has a negative effect on the observer may lead to more negative attitudes than an observer who has a close friend with CFS. Attitudes toward CFS are also affected by the personality and values of the observer. Someone who holds a culturally ingrained belief that illness is a punishment from God has different attitudes toward an individual with CFS than someone who believes that illness is a random occurrence.

Another model used in the disability literature to explain negative attitudes toward people with disabilities is the minority-group model. Supporters of this model believe that negative attitudes toward individuals with disabilities are a result of discrimination and prejudices that are similar to those directed toward other minority groups. According to this model, physical surroundings and society are responsible for the disability, as opposed to the medical condition itself (Hahn, 1990; Soder, 1990). People with disabilities can be exploited and oppressed by both the environment and people in society, because they have often been labeled as deviant and disadvantaged (Fine & Asch, 1990; Katz, Hass, & Bailey, 1988; Meyerson, 1990).

The minority model can be applied to people with CFS on several levels. People with CFS are often viewed as being disabled because of an inability to perform, or continue to perform, according to the standards set by physically healthy people. Generally, taking time out for self-care and healing is not supported by bosses, doctors, friends, and family, who may assume that individuals with CFS need to increase their levels of stimulation and activity. As a result, many with CFS are forced to abandon their old lifestyle for one that allows for such important health-related activities. Typically, people with CFS are given a relatively short time to fight their illness and are abandoned and isolated when they are unable to get well. According to this model, the majority groups' lack of acceptance for the minority group (people with CFS) often results in people with CFS experiencing losses in social and occupational connections. People with CFS also may experience hostility and resentment from doctors when they are unable to conform to expectations for physical health by fully recovering.

Shlaes et al. (1999) developed the CFS Attitude Test (CAT), a reliable measure contained in Appendix A at the end of the chapter. The CAT has three factors:

1. *Responsibility for CFS* includes five items that assess the extent to which a person believes that individuals with CFS are responsible for getting sick.
2. *Relevance of CFS* includes four items that assess the extent to which a person believes that CFS is a valid illness that should receive serious consideration by society.
3. *Traits of People with CFS* includes four items that assess the extent to which a person believes that individuals with CFS possess personality characteristics that are responsible for the illness.

Test-retest reliability analysis showed that the CAT subscale scores, as well as the CAT composite score, were consistent over a six-week period.

Results of CAT administration demonstrated that beliefs about the responsibility of people with CFS for their illness, the relevance of CFS, and the personality traits of people with CFS are related. If an individual holds the belief that people with CFS are responsible for their illness, it is likely that they also believe that people with CFS have negative personality characteristics, such as being compulsive or overly driven. The finding that many people believe that individuals with CFS are responsible for their illness and have psychological traits that contribute to the development of the illness is consistent with Susan Sontag's statement that illness is often blamed on psychological inadequacy, particularly when there is limited scientific knowledge about the illness (Sontag, 1978). It is possible that physicians and society at large feel uncomfortable not knowing the cause of CFS and attribute psychological causes to the development of CFS as a means of reducing this discomfort. When illness is blamed on psychological aspects of the ill individual, it becomes his or her responsibility for the development and cure of the illness, which gives a certain amount of relief from responsibility to both physicians and society for helping the ill and developing effective treatments for CFS.

An additional finding that people with CFS are considered different and deserve to be treated differently is consistent with the minority-group model. In this model, negative attitudes toward individuals with disabilities result from discrimination and prejudices similar to those experienced by other minority groups (Soder, 1990). It is possible that people perceive individuals with CFS as deviant, dependent, and disadvantaged, thus deserving of differential treatment by people who are not physically ill.

Findings from CAT assessment did not support the idea that people have negative attitudes toward individuals with CFS as a result of discomfort from interacting with them or a belief in a just world. It is possible that the negative attitudes toward people with CFS that have been documented are a function of past government and media portrayals of CFS as either nonexistent, trivial, or a function of a neurotic, overworked, stressed way of life, as was depicted in the labeling of CFS as the *yuppie flu*. Media may have helped to shape attitudes about CFS without altering people's attitudes about their interpersonal interactions with people with CFS or about the fairness of society in general (as reflected in the belief in a just world). The way the media and the government portrayed CFS also may have played a role in attributions made concerning the psychological health of people with CFS. People may choose not to support or interact with people with CFS more as a function of blaming them for their illness or believing them to be psychologically unstable than as a function of experiencing discomfort at the thought of this type of interaction. Instead, beliefs and prejudices about individuals with CFS may manifest in less obvious ways, through avoidance, discrimination in the workplace, or through unsolicited advice about how to get well from a friend or family member. Again, these findings strengthen the concepts supported by the minority model concerning discrimination and prejudice experienced by people with CFS.

In addition to testing theories about attitudes toward people with CFS, the CAT can be used to screen and train volunteers who work with individuals with CFS. The debilitating nature of the syndrome means that many people with CFS depend on others to assist with daily living tasks, such as cleaning, cooking, and laundry. Programs designed to provide social support for people with CFS may need to train providers who have little information about the illness. It is important to have a method of measuring the effectiveness of the training program in promoting the acquisition of factual information about the illness and changing negative attitudes toward, or incorrect beliefs about, CFS. The CAT can be used as a pretest/posttest measure to assess attitudes about CFS before and after training to evaluate the effects of training on volunteers.

Physicians who encounter patients with CFS in their practices play a significant role in communicating knowledge and perpetuating certain attitudes about this syndrome among other health care professionals and among the public. A recent study (Taylor, Jason, Kennedy, & Friedberg, 2001) evaluated whether differing treatment recommendations for CFS by physicians influenced attributions about CFS among mental health practitioners. Participants prompted by a case study describing one of three forms of recommended treatment (pharmacology using Ampligen, cognitive behavioral therapy with graded activity, or cognitive coping skills) answered a series of questions assessing their attributions about the illness, including impressions about its etiology, diagnostic accuracy, severity, prognosis, and the expected outcome of the proposed treatment. Participants who read the case study proposing treatment with Ampligen were more likely to report that the patient was correctly diagnosed and more likely to perceive the patient as disabled than those whose case study described cognitive-behavioral therapy with graded activity as the treatment. Results of this investigation supported the hypothesis that physician recommendation for CFS treatment can influence subsequent attributions about a patient's illness among mental health practitioners.

A clearer understanding of how this illness is conceptualized by physicians and policymakers can lead to a more sophisticated understanding of the process by which stigmatizing attitudes are formed, ultimately leading to better methods of educating both the public and health care professionals about scientific findings as to the actual nature and etiology of CFS and the treatment options available to patients. This type of education is particularly important because an increased awareness of the true nature of the illness will most likely result in increases in research regarding etiology and treatment of CFS, services, treatment options, and social support. All of these variables have the potential to dramatically improve the quality of life for people living with this illness and speak to the importance of continuing to develop our understanding of attitudes toward chronically ill individuals.

EPIDEMIOLOGY FROM AN ECOLOGICAL STANDPOINT

When a new disease syndrome such as CFS is recognized, studies on etiology and prevalence can shape public policy. For example, the number of individuals identified with the syndrome may influence the federal and state resources allocated for research, prevention, and intervention (Friedberg & Jason, 1998). Community psychologists have key roles to play in epidemiological research with new disease syndromes. The first generation of CFS epidemiological studies was flawed because of its reliance on physician referrals, resulting in findings that underestimated the prevalence of CFS, thus minimizing the seriousness of this illness. In such a situation, community psychologists could participate in assembling multidisciplinary teams to conduct more rigorously designed research that better estimates prevalence of the syndrome. As a consequence, we could help set the agenda for how the epidemiological research is conceptualized, which could influence the development of public policy.

Developing a Research Team

Beginning in 1991, Leonard Jason and Judy Richman began assembling a research team to work with individuals diagnosed with CFS. At the time, few services were available for people with this illness, and many medical personnel were skeptical of its existence. Rather than attempting first to develop social or community interventions, we felt the most important objective was to conduct basic research into the prevalence of this syndrome. In the early 1990s, this disorder was considered a relatively rare condition, affecting fewer than 20,000 people in the United States (Gunn, Connell, & Randall, 1993).

Our research team in Chicago included professionals from diverse areas, including epidemiology, psychiatry, medicine, immunology, sociology, biostatistics, and community psychology. The team included more than 15 individuals from different training perspectives. Members of the Chicago Chronic Fatigue Syndrome (CFS) Association, a local self-help and advocacy organization, also actively participated in meetings where the methods of our studies were discussed. The group was united in gathering pilot CFS epidemiological data from a random community sample, validating measurement approaches and instruments, and developing and securing a grant proposal to study the epidemiology of CFS in a large-scale community sample (Jason, Wagner, et al., 1995). Our initial findings indicated that more than 400,000 had CFS in the United States, a figure more than 20 times higher than the official rates from the Centers for Disease Control (Jason, Taylor, et al., 1995). This pilot work was used to secure a National Institutes of Health (NIH) grant involving a large community-based epidemiology study of CFS, which has found rates of CFS among minorities that are higher than among Caucasians (Jason, Richman, Rademaker, et al., 1999). Our work using random community samples is now being used by other investigators, including those from the CDC. In an earlier research project, we assessed the prevalence of CFS among nurses (Jason et al., 1993), and data from this study encouraged a nurse with CFS to form the organization called *Medical Professionals/Persons with CFS* (Gail Dahlen, personal communication, March 31, 1998). Bringing together scientists from different disciplines is a critical step in seeking a better understanding and more thorough investigation of complex disease entities and conditions.

When community psychologists address population issues that are not easily explained, such as CFS, we can advocate for research that avoids stigmatization potentially caused by biases and unexamined assumptions. Key decisions were made within a sociopolitical context in which CFS was assumed a psychologically based problem (Friedberg & Jason, 1998). Many physicians continue to believe that most individuals with CFS have a psychiatric illness. Because of the controversy surrounding the CFS diagnoses, people with the syndrome face frequently disbelieving attitudes from their doctors, family, and/or friends, and many experience profound losses in their support systems. One major consequence is that many people with CFS feel dissatisfied with their medical care and go outside traditional medicine to be treated for their illness (Jason, Ferrari, Taylor, Slavich, & Stenzel, 1996).

NEEDS ASSESSMENT

Another means by which ecological validity can be achieved involves direct solicitation of patients' perspectives concerning service and resource needs. Vercoulen et al. (1996) provided an 18-month follow-up of 246 patients with CFS, finding that only 3% reported complete recovery and 17% reported improvement. It is possible that these discouraging follow-up statistics result in part from lack of effective supports available in the community to help recover (Ware & Kleinman, 1992). The key question concerns types of changes that might be most important. We next review several large-scale surveys that have assessed patients' perspectives.

To more effectively assess the needs of people with CFS, Jason et al. (1996) analyzed a brief survey of open- and closed-ended items designed to assess participants' use of and preference for a variety of services. The questionnaire consisted of 14 five-point (1 = undesirable; 5 = extremely desirable) rating scales. These items were developed with consultation from members of the Chicago CFS Association. Respondents with CFS ($n = 984$) were instructed to indicate their preference for each of the 14 hypothetical rehabilitation services that might assist their recovery. This was the first survey of its kind distributed to a national sample of people with CFS. Advocacy services were the highest rated factor—not surprisingly—given the discrimination and negative attitudes that people with this disorder endure. Preferred advocacy efforts included a telephone hotline service providing immediate advice and assistance on recovery, an advocacy worker to secure financial resources and legitimize the service needs of individuals with CFS, and a volunteer caregiver system to provide assistance with daily chores and errands. Respondents with CFS also made a strong plea for needed education in the medical field, government, and public. Educational efforts would aim to increase knowledge as to the legitimacy and existence of CFS as a disease entity. In turn, increased knowledge would increase the quality of medical care, financial resources, and services offered for individuals with CFS. The second-highest priority items were self-help groups providing emotional support and current treatment information. This result is consistent with other studies indicating that individuals with CFS need continued social and emotional support to cope effectively with their illness.

These data helped set priorities for the subsequent development of service programs because areas were identified as having significant need (e.g., housing, jobs, volunteer buddies, etc.), but no services or programs were currently available to meet these needs. We did not need to create self-help groups or telephone hotlines because these were already established in the Chicago metropolitan area.

A COLLABORATIVE RELATIONSHIP

In addition to learning about the needs from people, nationally, with CFS, our research team began building a collaboration with the local Chicago CFS Association. We followed an ecological model in developing this relationship. Thus, the university personnel and self-help group members were equal parties in both the design and implementation of the interventions. We next report on a series of intervention pilot programs that address issues such as daily assistance, employment, and housing.

DAILY ASSISTANCE

One way community psychologists can intervene to empower persons with CFS, as well as individuals with other disabilities, is by developing volunteer caregiving programs. For people with CFS, helping with daily chores on a regular basis was perceived as one of the higher priority needs by the national sample (Jason et al., 1996).

In our first collaborative effort with the Chicago CFS Association, Shlaes and Jason (1996) developed a buddy-mentor program where people with CFS received a volunteer buddy and a mentor who had CFS. The buddy was an individual in the community who agreed to spend one hour a week conducting home visits with an individual with CFS. Buddy-participant matches were made based on needs/interests assessments completed by the participants and buddies. Mentors were individuals with CFS who were willing and able to engage in two hours of phone contact each month with the participants. The role of mentor was designed to include informational support and emotional support. After the end of the program, the Chicago CFS Association took over the mentorship portion of the program and currently provides mentors to its members.

Our research team continues to work on developing and evaluating pilot volunteer programs for people with CFS. We are currently developing feedback systems to help people with CFS track their fatigue levels, energy, and chosen activities (King, Jason, Frankenberry, Jordan, & Tryon, 1997). One of our research forms was devised by a member of the Chicago CFS Association. Our research team had developed a global measure of expended energy on a daily basis. A member of the self-help group felt that a more precise instrument would better capture activities, so she developed this form and collected pilot data on the new instrument.

Much of the controversy surrounding illness management for CFS centers on the uncertainty about an appropriate balance between rest and activity. What has been slowly emerging from this debate is the prescription of energy conservation and the use of moderation (King et al., 1997). In our work with the volunteer program, we have learned that by avoiding overexertion, persons with CFS can avoid setbacks and relapses, while increasing their tolerance to activity. We believe suggestions for treatment plans and illness management should be based on individualized assessments and tailored to the patient's situation. For example, patients with CFS identified as continually overexerting themselves are advised to cut back and conserve their energy resources so that long-term gains in their tolerance to activity can be made. Our work suggests that not all persons with CFS need to either increase or decrease their activity levels; instead, they should use moderation and energy conservation. This strategy, which we call the *envelope theory*, was suggested by a member of the self-help program who had been provided a buddy.

Evidence supporting the energy conservation model exists. For example, in the Shlaes and Jason (1996) intervention study, participants who received the buddy-mentor intervention were able to conserve energy and experienced significant decreases in fatigue severity, while the control group experienced significant increases in fatigue severity. In addition, a time series study by Jason, Tryon, Frankenberry, and King (1997) found that energy expended, physical exertion, and mental exertion were positively related to fatigue.

Pesek, Jason, and Taylor (2000) worked with three participants using this envelope approach. A buddy program that had been previously developed (Shlaes & Jason, 1996) was combined with an intervention involving the envelope theory. The participants were visited once a week for approximately two hours. The buddy worked with each of the participants, helping them see how discrepancies in perceived and expended energy levels could be reduced as dictated by the envelope theory. The buddy also visited the participants weekly and assisted them with tasks to help reduce activities that might be too exhausting for them to complete (e.g., moving heavy objects).

The study's principal finding was that an intervention combining the buddy program and principles from the envelope theory assisted the three participants in reducing fatigue severity over time. All three participants reported a decrease in fatigue severity (from an overall mean rating of 64.2% to 36.7%) and five of the eight major CFS symptoms as measured by the symptom rating form, indicating that the intervention was associated with improvements in fatigue and somatic symptoms. It appears that once the participants learned to function within their energy envelopes and received some help with housework or overwhelming tasks, they experienced some symptom relief. This assistance allowed participants to reduce their level of overexertion, which may be associated with worsening of symptoms. In addition, spending more time relaxing and conserving energy probably helped them feel better.

These findings support the research of King and associates (1997) and Jason, Melrose, and colleagues (1999), who contend that customized treatment plans should be developed so that interventionists can work within the range of available energy resources for each individual with CFS. When the participants in the studies by King and associates (1997) and Jason, Melrose, and colleagues (1999) kept their perceived and expended energy levels within a similar range, they also experienced reductions in fatigue severity.

Deale and associates (Deale, Chalder, Marks, & Wessely, 1997) and Sharpe and colleagues (1996) endorse cognitive-behavioral treatments with graded activity. Their programs encourage participants with CFS to increase their activity levels. In contrast, Friedberg (1999) argues that many patients with CFS may already be overexerting themselves, and they may need to reduce their overall activity levels. The envelope theory would not endorse recommendations to either unilaterally increase or decrease activity. Some people with CFS need to be encouraged to increase their activity because they have the appropriate amount of perceived energy to do so. However, some people with CFS need to be encouraged to do less so as to decrease the discrepancy between perceived and expended energy. Once this has been accomplished, it would be possible to slowly increase the amount of activity they might engage in. The key is to not overexpend their energy supplies or consistently go outside their envelope of available energy.

Recently, a grant funded by the National Institute of Allergy and Infectious Diseases was awarded to Leonard Jason to compare cognitive-behavioral therapy with graded activity (Deale et al., 1997; Sharpe et al., 1996), cognitive coping skills therapy with the envelope model (Friedberg, 1999), graded activity alone, and a relaxation control. This project provides the first opportunity to evaluate effectiveness of these interventions in improving functioning in CFS.

Not only do people with CFS benefit from having helpers, but also volunteers benefit from their experience. Ferrari and Jason (1997) found that caregivers to people with CFS consistently reported more satisfaction than stress from caregiving. This finding suggests that caregiving, in and of itself, can be a fulfilling experience that satisfies personal and emotional needs for the caregiver. By working directly with people with CFS, volunteers can learn a great deal about the lives of people with disabilities and the obstacles they need to overcome.

The program developed by Shlaes and Jason (1996) was our first mentor/buddy program, and we have continued to refine and develop our programming with close input from the Chicago CFS Association. Again, an ecological model has guided our work on this project. In the near future, we will develop a joint committee of university researchers and self-help group members from the Chicago CFS Association. The university personnel will recruit volunteers for an expanded buddy program, and the members of the joint committee will be involved in establishing a training program for volunteers and a system for jointly supervising the volunteers. Therefore, both parties will be involved in all decision-making processes, and we expect both groups to be highly committed to these interventions.

EMPLOYMENT

For many people with CFS, fatigue seriously interferes with work (Friedberg & Jason, 1998). Typically, only 13% to 15% of people with CFS are able to continue full-time employment after becoming ill, and 77% report significant financial hardship, with many reporting that they have exhausted their savings and have been forced into debt (Anderson & Ferrans, 1997). Loss of work can be a devastating and demoralizing experience. Many people with CFS believe there is little hope of finding employment, particularly employment with a flexible schedule. People with CFS may have more energy on some days than on others and no way of predicting their energy levels. Flexibility at the work site is a key need for people with CFS in search of part-time employment. Furthermore, many people with CFS are chemically sensitive and require jobs that are relatively chemical free. For example, a freshly painted office or newly installed carpet might trigger a severe allergic reaction in a person with CFS. One survey found that as many as 40% of people with multiple chemical sensitivities might have CFS (LeRoy, Davis, & Jason, 1996).

Most agencies are still not sure how to develop supportive programs for people with severe energy deficits. Because people with this syndrome often appear healthy when they come into service agencies seeking job counseling or other services, the service providers often do not understand that these individuals might have only a few hours each week to give to an employer. Full-time employment is not possible for most people with this syndrome. What is needed is job assessment, part-time job opportunities, support, and encouragement, followed by a gradual increase in the number of hours devoted to work each day.

To address these employment issues more effectively, a member of the DePaul University research team and a group of people with CFS formed a part-time job committee to develop a job bank. A collaborative DePaul University-Chicago CFS

Association effort, this group was different from more traditional self-help groups because the primary focus was on helping members discover job opportunities. The participants of the part-time job committee also attended the monthly self-help support meetings sponsored by the Chicago CFS Association.

A well-known disability lawyer was invited to attend one of the meetings to share his knowledge in this area. He discussed eligibility requirements for obtaining Social Security benefits and ways to transition into part-time job opportunities without losing medical and financial benefits of the Social Security disability program. The committee decided to create a job bank to provide listings of part-time jobs that might be appropriate for people with CFS. Some home-based employment opportunities, such as multilevel marketing, proofreading, and home office computing, might allow people with CFS to set their own work schedules. The researcher and six people with CFS met monthly to locate and review part-time jobs and place them in the job bank.

The job committee gave members a chance to gain emotional support and encouragement when thinking about ways of rejoining the workforce on a part-time basis. The support group allowed participants to reduce their sense of isolation, to develop confidence, and to have a forum to discuss common problems (Maton, 1989). Several people were able to begin part-time house sitting, pet sitting, and telemarketing jobs. The job directory continues to be updated and is available to all members of the Chicago CFS Association. A key feature of this program is that it was developed with input and structure from both university students and members of the self-help group, and this collaborative relationship helped each party stay committed to the project.

We experienced many advantages in employing this type of ecological approach. By working cooperatively with members of the self-help community in planning the functions and activities of the job committee, our research team gained a better appreciation of the needs and talents of those in the self-help group, and the students appreciated the fact that our work was valued by the community members. In addition, these collaborative experiences helped the leadership of the CFS organization to develop high levels of trust with the DePaul University investigators because they came to see them as allies who were interested in working cooperatively with them on the planning of new services.

HOUSING

Because people with CFS are often unable to work, many find themselves in danger of losing their housing. Davis, Jason, and Banghart (1998) examined people with multiple chemical sensitivities (MCS) who reported living in safe housing versus those who reported living in unsafe housing. They found that those who had safe housing in comparison to unsafe housing were significantly less disabled. Many people with CFS could profit from a setting or community to protect them so that their health can improve. At present, these types of treatment settings are not available for people with CFS.

We first sought input on housing initiatives through a survey distributed by a national newsletter for people with CFS (based on the survey described earlier, Jason et al., 1996). We collaborated with members of the Chicago CFS Association in developing the items for this survey. Respondents indicated housing services were a moderately desirable need among people with CFS. Using five-point

(1 = undesirable; 3 = moderately desirable; 5 = extremely desirable) rating scales, our respondents gave average ratings of 3.5 to the statement: "Allowing a carefully screened person to live in the home of someone with chronic fatigue syndrome. The healthy person would help with errands, chores and provide support, and in return would have a place to live and a small stipend." On average, respondents rated 3.4 for the item: "A referral service where people with chronic fatigue syndrome can find roommates to share housing." They rated 3.3 for the item: "An integrated home with people with chronic fatigue syndrome living on the bottom floor, college students on the second floor, and a couple or family as the house manager. The student helpers would be assigned to help the people with chronic fatigue syndrome with errands, chores, and cooking, and so on."

A shared housing program has the potential of providing an inexpensive place to live without dependence on outside agencies or governmental programs. A shared housing program might involve others sharing their homes with people with CFS. During this time of state and federal funding cutbacks, developing programs that are financially independent and self-supporting is a high-priority goal. Sharing monthly expenditures for rent, utilities, and food is the obvious benefit. In addition, people with CFS might save energy by sharing some household duties such as cleaning and shopping, activities that can be overwhelming for people with CFS who live alone. Further, emotional well-being can be increased by living with a sympathetic housemate who understands the illness and can provide support.

We have contacted various organizations and agencies that successfully implemented shared housing programs for elderly populations. We have accomplished this work in close association with members of the CFS self-help group because many of the agencies we interviewed were suggested to us by contacts in the self-help community. As a result, many individuals with CFS from across the country have contacted our research team about setting up a housing program, and they have discussed their own difficulties in obtaining housing. A woman in California was forced to live in her van until she found housing. A man from Pennsylvania is beginning to set up congregate housing for people with CFS who might benefit from living in a toxic-free environment. We have shared this information with others across the country who are interested in establishing housing programs.

We also shared our findings on possible housing initiatives with members of the Chicago CFS Association. Many thought that the programs described previously could provide an important service to the CFS community. For the past two years, the university group has been collaborating with members of the Chicago CFS Association in developing a grant proposal to support these types of housing initiatives.

When individuals have a condition this debilitating and lack affordable housing, their condition often deteriorates further. We have talked to a number of people who have CFS and have been homeless, and we have listened to people that are so desperate that they have considered, attempted, or committed suicide. Some of these unfortunate outcomes might have been prevented had affordable housing been available in a safe and protected environment.

Yet, what might a psychologist offer in this arena? This type of community development—the construction of affordable housing—seemed off limits and beyond our technical expertise. However, a Housing and Urban Development (HUD) program offers Section 811 housing. In brief, this HUD grant allows an organization to request funds to purchase land and renovate or construct new housing. Once the housing is constructed, all at the government's expense, the rent for those in the building is subsidized by HUD so that a person never has to pay more than 30% of his or her adjusted gross income for rent. In addition, services could be provided to residents, again funded by HUD, for transportation to a supermarket or medical appointments or for meal services. The Chicago CFS Association was very interested in working with us on this grant application.

We initially decided to get as much information as possible about this 811 initiative. We called the U.S. Department of Housing and Urban Development's Midwest office in Chicago and spoke with a representative whose title was "Community Builder." We learned that individuals with CFS would qualify for this initiative as long as they received Social Security disability or SSI disability.

In December, the HUD Community Builder spoke to our coalition for several hours. The president, Carol Howard, and the vice president of the Chicago CFS Association, Connie Van der Eb, as well as other members of our group, learned that the federal government has had these types of HUD programs for many years. The Section 811 programs are for small group homes for individuals with developmental delays, physical disabilities, or mental illness. The grant would allow construction of a building of up to 20 independent apartments. Only seven HUD housing applications in this category were submitted in Illinois the previous year, and five were funded, which suggested an excellent chance for funding.

To submit an 811 application, a group must have site control over the land; that is, the owner of the land would sell our group an option that reserved the land for our use until we received the HUD funding. We would also need to hire a consultant to work on the grant application. To submit a competitive application, our group would need funds to pay for an environmental site assessment (about $2,000), $10,000 for upfront costs to pay a housing and grant consultant, and $10,000 for what is called a *minimal capital investment* to cover issues such as site control over the land. The Community Builder gave us the name of a probable donor for this worthy cause.

We then contacted a consultant, who agreed to work with our group after we had secured a site for the building. Because the Chicago CFS Association had only a few thousand dollars in its account, our group realized that the HUD funders might question our ability to actually manage an expensive housing project. Lutheran Social Services of Illinois agreed to be the agency submitting the grant. They would establish a not-for-profit board to manage the building, and members of the Chicago CFS Association would be appointed as members of this board.

We now had a consultant with experience in writing these grants, an agency with experience in managing these types of projects, and a possible funding source to cover the costs of land and other grant-related expenses. At this point, we had talked to about 30 to 35 different organizations in Chicago that had experience with housing issues, and our group felt that we were on the right course of action.

We spent the next two months looking for available land, and while we did locate several buildings that could have been renovated, it appeared that HUD preferred to have vacant land because it costs more to renovate buildings to be compliant with Americans with Disabilities Act (ADA) housing standards than to build a new building. In addition, we learned that the funds from HUD would generally not cover demolition costs or the costs of purchasing a building that was to be demolished, so it was imperative to find vacant land. We soon realized that the city of Chicago had very few vacant plots of land in safe areas that were not already purchased for commercial purposes. Although we had been advised to find the land before scheduling the meeting with the commissioner of housing, we scheduled the meeting because we felt that the commissioner might be able to find vacant land and the funds needed to submit the application.

In February, we arranged a meeting with the commissioner of housing for Chicago. Twelve people were invited to this meeting, representing a variety of different organizations including the president, vice president, and board members of the Chicago CFS Association; a representative from Lutheran Social Services; our grant consultant; our realtor; and several representatives from DePaul University. After we made a brief presentation on the need for affordable housing for people with CFS and other types of fatiguing illnesses, the commissioner said he could help us secure land in empowerment zones, but such land would be in high crime areas. Our consultant, however, indicated that HUD would probably not approve grants in these areas, particularly because the residents would have disabilities and safety issues would be involved. The commissioner then mentioned that we could apply for a capacity building grant, but for only $5,000. If we wanted a predevelopment loan, which could be for a larger amount, it would have to go before the city council, and we would not get the loan before May, when our grant was due. In addition, if we were to get these funds, the site for the building would have to be in Chicago, and in our prior efforts, we had been unsuccessful in locating an available three to five plots of land in Chicago that met the specifications for our proposed building.

Our group had hoped to leave the meeting with land identified and funds; however, we left with neither. Although very disappointing, several other possibilities had been brought up at this meeting. For example, on Lincoln Avenue, there were several tax increment financing (TIF) districts, and an alderman and a representative from the city planning department scheduled a meeting with our group to discuss the building of our HUD project on land in this TIF district. (TIF is problematic land or buildings that need to be redeveloped.) In this TIF site, motels were being used for illegal activities, and the alderman wanted to get rid of these motels in his district. The alderman offered to write a letter indicating that we could have site control over the land in his district where a motel was located, but the motel owner would probably sue us for loss of the business. The alderman was confident that we would win the legal battle, but the judge would probably make us pay a higher than market value for the building because the owner would not only be losing the motel but also his means of making a living. The alderman said that if our building was income generating, he could possibly get the cost of the motel and land donated to us by the city, but because we were a nonprofit and would not be generating income, he could not get the city council to get us this property for free. The alderman hoped that the HUD funding would pay for this motel and legal costs, but we informed the alderman that the HUD funds would not pay for either the building or demolition costs.

We now had only two and a half months before the grant needed to be submitted, and we were in a race with time to find vacant land and funding. We then learned about available land in the suburbs that had been zoned for commercial purposes on the first floor but that could be residential on higher floors. The developer indicated that he would construct the building and then sell our group 10 to 15 units for our HUD project. This would solve many problems, for we would not have to pay about $10,000 for site control and pay for an environmental assessment on the land. Our only costs to submit the grant would involve paying for our grant consultant. We then checked with our Community Builder at HUD, who liked the idea of working with a realtor in developing a project that would house individuals from our group as well as others from the general community and have commercial space in the building. However, HUD's legal department required that we have site control over the land and entire building that was to be built. We could not just purchase apartments from a building not yet built because the building had to be built to ADA standards. However, if the building was already constructed and met ADA standards, we could establish an arrangement with the owners to have certain units purchased by our group. If however, people were currently living in the units, we would have to pay relocation fees to the current occupants, and the HUD grant would not pay these expenses. Therefore, if the building had been built by a developer and met ADA standards but was not occupied, we could negotiate with the owners to take possession of certain units. The only problem with this scenario was that if the building was built, the owners would not be able to get funds from the HUD grant in more than a year, so they would lose income for that period. Of course, no owner would enter into such an arrangement.

What had seemed relatively straightforward and simple—to write a HUD grant application—turned out to be complex and difficult. Every time we pursued a particular course of action (the previous discussion represents about 20% of the efforts that we have made to date), we would repeatedly confront problems of identifying land that would fit our needs for the HUD grant. Our group continues to explore new ideas, and we will continue our work with our coalition to get affordable housing for individuals with CFS.

We believe that the best way to start and maintain a viable housing program is to work collaboratively with those in need of housing. We began our work in this area by learning from organizations that already provided housing, even if the interventions had been developed for different populations. In this manner, we could provide people with CFS examples of successful programs and empower them to create and maintain similar programs. Collaboration between community psychologists and people with CFS allows both groups to work from a strengths perspective, with each group gaining insights and knowledge from the other. By listening to the needs of each group and respectively involving each party in decision making, each of the parties begins to trust the other, communications are facilitated, and both parties can become more invested in, and committed to, the research process.

CAPACITY-BUILDING IN A CENTER FOR INDEPENDENT LIVING

Centers for independent living can offer a unique contextual base from which individuals with CFS can self-advocate and navigate a variety of service delivery systems. Nationwide centers for independent living, in existence since the late 1960s, serve people with a wide range of physical and cognitive disabilities. These centers were developed to empower individuals with disabilities to advocate for themselves socially, economically, and politically, allowing them to take control over their own lives and direct their service utilization in an informed and independent manner. The core services offered by centers for independent living can include information and referral, peer counseling, civil rights and advocacy, housing renter assistance and homeownership counseling, technical and transportation assistance, public education, and independent living skills training. These services are shaped by the independent living philosophy, which encourages people with disabilities to gain both physical and psychological independence by acknowledging their power as consumers, educating themselves about their disability, self-advocating for political and economic rights, and decreasing dependence on others (including medical professionals). The philosophy rejects any situation or entity that places individuals with disabilities in a position of inferiority.

The CFS Empowerment Project is a collaborative research and demonstration project that we recently initiated in collaboration with Chicago's largest center for independent living, Access Living, and the Chicago CFS Association. The research project follows a repeated-measures, control group design, and it is the first of its kind to be funded by the National Institute on Disability and Rehabilitation Research. The intervention under evaluation involves a 12-month capacity-building program for individuals with CFS. It uses goal setting, peer-facilitated education, financial support for resource acquisition, and principles of the independent living philosophy to improve quality of life, access to community-based resources, and functioning.

The first phase (group phase) of the program is composed of peer-facilitated illness management groups; the second phase (case coordination phase) is dedicated to one-on-one peer-based self-advocacy coaching and case coordination activities. The group phase consists of an eight-session peer counseling group that takes place biweekly over a 16-week period in the center for independent living. The sessions are co-led by a trained peer counselor with CFS and Renée Taylor, a licensed clinical psychologist with expertise in this area. During the first group meeting, participants are engaged in a focus group process in which they are asked to select 7 of 12 available topics of educational relevance to them that they would like to cover in the seven subsequent group meetings. In addition, they are asked to provide detailed information about their specific needs and about the nature of the information they are seeking within each topic area. These 12 topics are:

1. The envelope theory (use of activity pacing to manage CFS symptoms; Jason, Melrose, et al., 1999).
2. Fennell's (1993) Four-Phase Model of CFS (psychosocial stages of development).
3. Cognitive coping skills (Friedberg & Jason, 1998).
4. Economic self-sufficiency (focusing on availability of community-based resources, including food service, transportation, and housing).
5. Employment issues (issues related to vocational rehabilitation, modifying employment, accommodations under the ADA, and issues involved in obtaining Social Security and disability income).
6. Personal relationships (partner, family, friends, coworkers, employers, etc.).
7. Relating to medical providers.
8. Current medical treatments (those that carry some research evidence).
9. Alternative medical approaches (those that carry some research evidence).
10. Nutritional approaches.
11. Self-relaxation and meditation.

12. Journal-writing as a therapeutic tool. Empowering participants to take control over the nature and direction of the intervention within a structured format facilitates ecological validity regarding issues of importance and relevance to consumers and exemplifies a collaborative research relationship in action.

An ongoing aspect of the program designed to increase collaboration between researchers and participants and enhance relevance of the intervention for each individual involves collaborative goal setting between participants and peer counselors and continuing collaborative monitoring of participants' progress related to those goals. In the group phase, this is accomplished during the first hour of each group before the interactive educational lecture component. Each participant is given between 5 and 10 minutes to update the other group members regarding his or her progress on behaviorally focused, attainable goals. During the case coordination phase of the program, peer counselors conduct weekly 30-minute phone sessions with participants during which continual goal monitoring occurs and participants receive social support, encouragement, self-advocacy training, and assistance with resource acquisition. This program is currently underway, and results regarding the efficacy of this approach will be released following program implementation.

The ecological-collaborative model was used as the underlying theoretical model for working on these projects. By bringing together self-help group members, community-agency representatives, and students from university-based settings, we believe that better social and community interventions, such as housing initiatives, can be developed to allow us to more sensitively extend services to patients with CFS. The dearth of similar programs developed to date might result from an enduring belief by many physicians that CFS is a psychiatric rather than a medical disorder. In such a situation, community psychologists can participate in assembling collaborative teams to develop service programs that are requested, but currently not available, to most people with this syndrome. These types of actions can allow community psychologists to help set the agenda for how service delivery programs are developed for people with CFS, and such activities could have influential roles in helping shape public policy.

OTHER COLLABORATIVE PROJECTS WITH THE CHICAGO CHRONIC FATIGUE SYNDROME ASSOCIATION

Our university volunteers have also assisted the Chicago CFS Association in other capacities. For example, one research assistant helped the CFS group leader create a directory of resources for people with CFS in the Chicago metropolitan area. This resource directory has now become an important asset to the organization, and its sales generate income for the self-help organization. The directory is now revised and updated each year by members of the self-help group. Members of our research teams have also assisted the CFS group leader with the assembling and mailing of the organization's newsletter, as well as the reorganization of its filing system. The help of healthy volunteers in these types of activities has been well received by the members of the CFS self-help group; it increases their commitment to our collaborative relationship. We have also been working with the CFS support group to develop a proposal for a comprehensive multidimensional center for helping people with CFS (see Appendix B).

Members from the CFS research team have also collaborated with the Chicago CFS Association in an effort to assist children and parents of children who are suffering from CFS. To assess the needs of these children and their parents, our research team developed, in collaboration with members of the Chicago CFS Association, a short survey of open- and closed-ended questions designed to evaluate the need for possible services. All of the mothers enthusiastically responded to the suggestion of organizing a support group so that their children could meet other children with CFS. This information was passed to the executive director of the Chicago CFS Association, who is currently working to serve the needs of these people.

DISCUSSION

In 1991, we began assembling a research team to work with individuals with CFS. At the time, few social services were available for people with this illness. Our first priority was to collect data on the epidemiology of this syndrome. We felt that the most important need was to provide accurate estimates of the prevalence of this syndrome. We next began a collaborative relationship with the Chicago CFS Association, based on an ecological model. A series of social and community interventions have been mounted to address issues such as employment, shared housing, and daily assistance. Through the process of developing and implementing these intervention models, both our research team and members of committees from the local CFS support group have benefited.

Much of the focus of this chapter has been on collaboration between a self-help organization and university collaborators. In some cases, the intervention led to research, as with the buddy/mentor study and our subsequent development of a model of energy conservation. The Chicago CFS Association benefited from a series of innovative demonstration projects provided to their members. Some of the pilot projects were incorporated into regular programming, such as the Chicago CFS self-help group subsequently using the resource directory and the mentor system. An excellent working relationship with the self-help group organization means undergraduate and graduate students have no difficulty recruiting participants from members of the self-help group when they need to interview participants with CFS for honors projects or theses. Members of the self-help group also have been instrumental in identifying areas for us to investigate; for example, the idea for the buddy/mentor system came from one of the self-help group members.

Our university-based community psychology resources supported and strengthened the directions determined by the self-help group. For example, using the youthful energy of university students to help persons with CFS achieve their independent living goals without formal agency involvement is a great resource-need match. This kind of multiintervention has much potential for formulating an integrative perspective for community psychologists working with CFS, persons with other disabilities, and other people in crisis.

Some readers may wonder whether CFS is a potentially reversible disability, such as a medical disorder that will eventually be addressed by pharmacological intervention. If so, some might then argue that the involvement of the community psychologist may be phased out as medical progress is made. The prospect for identifying a single etiological agent is uncertain, but even if it were to be identified, as with HIV/AIDS, there still would be a need for the development of service programs for those with this illness. Alternatively, if CFS does not have a clear-cut etiology but is a complex disorder involving genetic, constitutional, environmental, and psychological factors, medication might be palliative but not curative, and the role of the community psychologist will probably be larger and more enduring, involving both advocacy and health promotion.

Approaches to treatment must be comprehensive, addressing a variety of care needs. For example, advocacy focused on securing appropriate medical treatment and on the allocation of government resources for treatment has been cited as a high-priority need for individuals with CFS. People with CFS may desire (and need) an advocacy program in which the public and the medical community become better educated about the problems and difficulties associated with the syndrome. Some patients may need assistance from others, be it personal or professional forms of support, to complete daily living tasks. Living arrangements that include "healthy" individuals may be needed by people with CFS because weakness from this illness might prevent them from accomplishing necessary chores. Finally, a sense of community in which mutual social support is promoted may prevent isolation, depression, and preoccupation with the illness among patients with CFS. A key question concerns the highest priority needs, especially from the perspective of the patient with CFS. Collaborative research, as described throughout this chapter, can be a key tool for helping set this agenda, and it can work in mutually rewarding ways with self-help organizations so that the needs of both parties are met and so that they learn from each other and become invested in the relationship and interventions.

Our conclusions concerning the benefits of collaboration, using an ecological model, also apply to working with people with other types of disabilities (e.g., people with osteoporosis who are homebound, people with energy management issues such as cerebral palsy, and people facing public and professional skepticism and antipathy such as people with AIDS). An increasing knowledge of the different psychological, social, community, and medical factors that account for chronic illnesses might help the field of community psychology develop more sophisticated models and more effective interventions. In addition, we become a more caring and humane society when we work collaboratively with community groups in investing resources in the establishment of decent living conditions for all our citizens.

Dr. Lollar, director of the CDC Office on Disability and Health, was recently asked to head up the chapter on disabilities for the Healthy People 2010 document. Seventy people worked on this important chapter, which has as its mission to improve the health of people with disabilities. According to Dr. Lollar, 16% to 18%, or about 50 million Americans, experience an activity limitation due to an impairment or health condition (Lollar, 2000). The federal government and the CDC are most interested in developing policies to help states improve public health programs related to health promotion and prevention of secondary conditions among people with disabilities. These types of federal agencies have important partnership roles to play with the CFS community to improve services to those with this condition.

APPENDIX A

CHRONIC FATIGUE SYNDROME ATTITUDES TEST QUESTIONS

For each item below, place a number on a scale from 1 to 7 (1 indicates strong disagreement and 7 indicates strong agreement with the statement):

_____ 1. Employers should be permitted to fire those with CFS.

_____ 2. People with CFS are just depressed.

_____ 3. More federal funds should be allocated for research on CFS.

_____ 4. People with CFS are lazy.

_____ 5. CFS is not a real medical illness.

_____ 6. The majority of people with CFS were competitive, driven to achieve, and compulsive before they got sick.

_____ 7. I would not sit on a toilet that a person with CFS had just used.

_____ 8. CFS is not as big a problem as the media suggests.

_____ 9. People with CFS would get better if they really wanted to be healthy.

_____ 10. CFS is primarily a psychological disorder.

_____ 11. If people with CFS rest, they will get better.

_____ 12. People with CFS are to blame for getting sick.

_____ 13. CFS is a form of punishment from God.

Scoring Directions

Scale 1 (Responsibility for CFS): Add items 2, 4, 7, 12, and 13.

Scale 2 (Relevance of CFS): Add items 1, 5, 8, and reverse of score item 3.

Scale 3 (Traits of People with CFS): Add items 6, 9, 10, and 11.

APPENDIX B

PROPOSED MULTIDISCIPLINARY AND MULTIDIMENSIONAL CHRONIC FATIGUE SYNDROME ASSESSMENT AND TREATMENT CENTER

To respond to the preferences and needs expressed by people with CFS, a demonstration program needs to be established that provides a place of central access for advocacy, support, and services as part of an overall CFS assessment and treatment center. A center of this type would organize treatment services and daily living tasks and act as an advocacy organization to provide needed comprehensive treatment to assist with management of symptoms of this illness. A variety of services could be offered at such a center by medical and social service personnel. A primary care physician, a nurse, and a psychologist would be available at the center to see patients. Two full-time office managers would be available to coordinate the following areas: finance/marketing, legal issues, general assessment policies, triage and referral, housing services, advocacy, and program evaluation. One social worker, one rehabilitation counselor, one advocate, and one physical therapist would be hired to develop social service programs. One full-time secretary would be available for record keeping and appointments.

Space for a physician's office, therapist's office, advocacy worker, rehabilitation worker, and physical therapist and phones for Hotline and meeting rooms would be provided at the center.

ADVOCACY SERVICES TO COUNTER THE DISCRIMINATION AND NEGATIVE ATTITUDES

An advocacy worker would be hired to help legitimize the service needs of individuals with CFS. Education in the medical field, government, and public would aim to increase knowledge as to the legitimacy and existence of CFS as a disease entity. The advocacy worker would provide education for individuals with CFS and their families and friends, community practitioners, and the public. Education would focus on increasing understanding of the illness and reducing stigmatization. Physician education would be a high-priority activity. The center staff would maintain regular contacts with and encourage participation in the CFIDS Association of America, Inc., and continuously provide information to the *CFIDS Chronicle* as to center activities.

One of the first steps in dealing with a disability is to be fully informed about the nature of disability, services and benefits available and how to access them, laws that protect the rights of persons with disabilities, and community resources for obtaining needed services. The center would maintain a comprehensive resource and reference library and stay updated on rules and regulations and services of federal, state, and local agencies that serve persons with disabilities. This information would be provided to patients, families, friends, professionals, and the public. The center would also conduct workshops and seminars and distribute various flyers and brochures.

Through involvement in committees and advisory boards; meetings with agencies and service providers; and working closely with federal, state, and local officials and representatives, the center would advocate for the appropriate changes needed to create a community that allows for the acknowledgment and provision of resources for individuals with CFS.

ASSESSMENT

Patients would be provided a comprehensive assessment to aid in the selection of an appropriate intervention program. Continuous multidimensional assessment would be an essential element of the program because the disability experience does not always conform to the methods and requirements of preexisting assessment practices that *medical* professionals have been trained to apply. The medical assessment would consist of a variety of laboratory tests as well as a complete physical examination to determine what might be the cause of the fatigue. If necessary, specialized tests (e.g., sleep studies) would be ordered to determine possible causes of the symptoms. Neurological and psychological assessments would be administered by a clinical psychologist to measure the degree of cognitive, neurological, and psychological impairment resulting from CFS. Furthermore, the assessment would measure general emotional functioning and adjustment to CFS and determine the appropriateness of individual psychotherapy, couple and/or family counseling, group therapy, psychotropic medications, or a combination of these treatments.

MEDICAL AND PHARMACOLOGICAL TREATMENT

A physician who specializes in CFS would hold regular office hours to treat various CFS-related physical illnesses and symptoms. The physician would also be available to write needed prescriptions during office hours. A psychiatrist who specializes in treating individuals with CFS would be available for appointments on a weekly basis to provide individual eclectic psychotherapy, to write prescriptions for psychotropic medications, and to monitor medication intake. A list of physicians who have particular expertise on topics such as CFS and chronic pain would be available, and the center physician would make referrals to these specialists if disorders or symptoms were encountered that need these types of services.

INDIVIDUAL, COUPLES, AND FAMILY PSYCHOTHERAPY

A psychologist and social worker would be available for appointments on a weekly basis to administer various forms of psychotherapy.

PHYSICAL THERAPIST

Physicians often tell patients with CFS to be as active as they can, but frequently they provide little specific help on what that might be and no experience on exactly which exercises will help. The physical therapist would be available to patients to assess activities that might be engaged in and to develop individualized programs of activity.

CASE MANAGEMENT

A social worker would be available for full case management of patients with CFS. Sometimes people with CFS need specific help in locating services and completing paper work for services such as public aid or Social Security disability. The social worker would be available so that patients would have an advocate to ensure that needed and appropriate social services were provided.

STRUCTURED SELF-HELP EDUCATIONAL GROUPS

An ongoing series of six weekly one-and-one-half-hour self-help educational groups would be offered at the center for helping individuals who have been newly diagnosed. The sessions would include etiological, diagnostic, and theoretical information about CFS; immune system functioning and enhancement strategies; pain and stress management strategies (including mental imagery, abdominal breathing, meditation, yoga, biofeedback, progressive muscle relaxation, and other relaxation techniques); behavioral coping strategies; information about environmental and structural modification; communication skills and relationship building; and legal, financial, and political issues surrounding disability. If enough children and adolescents with CFS were identified, specific informational groups would be developed for these youngsters and their parents.

UNSTRUCTURED SELF-HELP GROUPS

Unstructured self-help groups would also meet on a weekly basis to provide consumers with a place to express feelings and obtain social and emotional support from those who share a common illness experience.

CFS MENTORSHIP PROGRAM

Individuals who have recovered or significantly adjusted to CFS would be solicited as volunteer mentors for individuals with more severe levels of disability. Some of the mentors would be assigned to program participants in independent living situations and would be available for emotional and informational support concerning CFS.

VOLUNTEER SUPPORT PROGRAM

A volunteer caregiver system would provide assistance with daily chores and errands. The youthful energy of university students would help persons with CFS achieve their independent living goals. Volunteers would help with errands, housekeeping, and cooking if necessary.

HOTLINE REFERRAL SERVICE

A telephone hotline service would be developed to provide immediate advice and assistance on recovery. Hotline counselors would be provided a referral booklet containing a listing of all possible referral needs, including alternative medical specialists, physical therapists, nutritionists, and other mental health workers.

JOB ASSESSMENT, PART-TIME JOB OPPORTUNITIES, AND ADVOCACY TO RESTRUCTURE CURRENT JOB RESPONSIBILITIES TO MAINTAIN EMPLOYMENT

First, there would be an assessment of whether the person's present job could be kept at present health level, considering all benefits available (sick leave and ADA accommodations) and type of profession. Second, if the person with CFS had stabilized and was searching for employment, an assessment would occur (see next paragraph). Third, a program would be established to develop job skills and readiness for a job. The Social Security Administration does allow people with disabilities to attempt to return to work, without a reduction in benefits until the person is capable of functioning independently.

A counselor would be responsible to coordinate and conduct an assessment for determining vocational rehabilitation needs, as appropriate in each individual case. A comprehensive assessment of the unique strengths, resources, priorities, interests, and needs, including the need for supported employment, would be performed. A determination of the goals, objectives, nature, and scope of vocational rehabilitation services to be included in the individualized written rehabilitation program of an individual would be conducted. The purpose of this comprehensive assessment would be to obtain information necessary to identify the rehabilitation needs of the individual and to develop a personalized rehabilitation program for that individual.

The assessment could include, to the degree needed to make such a determination, an assessment of the personality, interests, interpersonal skills, intelligence and related functional capacities, educational achievements, work experience, vocational aptitudes, personal and social adjustments, and employment opportunities of the individual, and the medical, psychiatric, psychological, and other pertinent vocational, educational, cultural, social, recreational, and environmental factors that affect the employment and rehabilitation needs of the individual. Dependent on the individual, the assessment could include an appraisal of the patterns of work behavior of the individual and services needed for the individual to acquire occupational skills and to develop work attitudes, work habits, work tolerance, and social and behavior patterns necessary for successful job performance, including the utilization of work in real job situations to assess and develop the capacities of the individual to perform adequately in a work environment. The complete and thorough assessment would require between 30 days and 90 days, dependent on each individual case, to allow the counselor to coordinate and obtain necessary information for each client.

Objectives include developing individually written rehabilitation plans by reviewing medical, psychological, social, vocational, aptitudes, abilities, and interests evaluations. Programs would be developed to improve the lifestyle management of participants. Counseling on the impact of CFS on personal relationships, stress and relaxation procedures, coping with problems involving memory and concentration difficulties, job readiness skill attainment, and job placement counseling would be offered to each participant. A counselor would discuss eligibility requirements for obtaining Social Security benefits and ways to transition into part-time job opportunities without losing medical and financial benefits of the Social Security disability program.

A counselor would be available to conduct disability awareness training with the employers of the patients. Specific information about the disability itself and subsequent impairments and impediments to the work environment would be addressed. The counselor would provide the employer with specific job modification and restructuring plans relative to the individual needs that could be implemented on the job and help facilitate the individual's return, or entry, to work. In addition, rehabilitation legislation training (i.e., The Rehabilitation Act, Section 504, and The Americans with Disability Act) would be given to employers to inform them of the regulations that govern these laws and their subsequent responsibilities. The counselor would serve as an advocate concerning legal rights, use of legal and medical resources available through community rehabilitation programs (i.e., Access Living and other advocacy groups), and financial issues (i.e., health insurance, crisis funding).

Housing Resources

The social worker would establish housing options for people with CFS. In addition, the university self-help group collaborative team would continue to work toward securing funds from the Section 811 program to construct housing. A shared housing program has the potential of providing an inexpensive place to live for those undergoing a crisis. The social worker would also develop a shared housing program that would involve others sharing their homes with people with CFS.

OTHER SERVICES TO BE DEVELOPED

To bring support groups to people who are homebound and/or bedridden, a social worker would provide these individuals with computers so that they can participate with online support chat rooms.

The center staff would develop and update a directory of resources for people with CFS.

CONCLUSION

A multidisciplinary and multidimensional CFS assessment and treatment center is needed now to help persons who are very ill, unable to work, and socially isolated by the debate on specific medical pathology. The proposed center would bring together appropriate medical professionals to service patients with the best available methods and provide a place to improve those methods. The center would also provide a place from which to conduct physician and therapist education focused on rehabilitation, a need stated by those professionals in a recent survey.

Approaches to treatment must be comprehensive, addressing a variety of care needs. For example, advocacy focused on securing appropriate medical treatment and on the allocation of government resources for treatment has been cited as a high-priority need for individuals with CFS. People with CFS desire an advocacy program in which the public and the medical community become better educated about the problems and difficulties associated with the syndrome. Some patients with CFS may need assistance from others to complete daily living tasks. Living arrangements that include "healthy" individuals to provide for daily, mundane activities, may be needed by people with CFS, because weakness from this illness might prevent them from accomplishing necessary chores. Finally, a sense of community in which mutual social support is promoted may prevent isolation, depression, and preoccupation with the illness among patients with CFS.

The dearth of service programs developed to date for patients with CFS might result from the fact that many physicians continue to believe that the syndrome is predominantly a psychiatric rather than a medical disorder. Frequently, physicians treating patients with CFS do not know what to do for their rehabilitation needs, and they are influenced by the idea that it is a psychiatric disease; consequently, they often make inappropriate referrals. This center would be a clear demonstration that there are constructive, therapeutic actions that can be taken beyond diagnosis. Such a center could ultimately become a training site where open-minded physicians can learn to better deal with this disease. We believe that a demonstration program could help the public and medical personnel better understand how comprehensive services can be designed and provided to people with CFS. Besides the immediate help delivered by the proposed center, it could become a model for centers elsewhere on the value of a comprehensive approach in the diagnosis and treatment of CFS.

REFERENCES

Anderson, J. S., & Ferrans, C. E. (1997). The quality of life of persons with chronic fatigue syndrome. *Journal of Nervous and Mental Diseases, 185,* 359–367.

Antoni, M. H., Brickman, A., Lutgendorf, S., Klimas, N., Imia-Fins, A., Ironson, G., et al. (1994). Psychosocial correlates of illness burden in chronic fatigue syndrome. *Clinical Infectious Diseases, 18*(Suppl. 1), S73–S78.

Davis, T. H., Jason, L. A., & Banghart, M. A. (1998). The effect of housing on individuals with multiple chemical sensitivities. *Journal of Primary Prevention, 19,* 31–42.

Deale, A., Chalder, T., Marks, I., & Wessely, S. (1997). Cognitive behaviour therapy for chronic fatigue syndrome: A randomized controlled trial. *American Journal of Psychiatry, 154,* 408–414.

Duff, K. (1993). *The alchemy of illness.* New York: Pantheon Books.

Fennell, P. A. (1993, Summer). A systematic, four-stage progressive model for mapping the CFIDS experience. *CFIDS Chronicle,* 40–46.

Ferrari, J. R., & Jason, L. A. (1997). A study of long-term volunteer caregiving to persons with CFS: Perceived stress vs. satisfaction. *Rehabilitation Counseling Bulletin, 40,* 240–250.

Fine, M., & Asch, A. (1990). Disability beyond stigma: Social interaction, discrimination, and activism. In M. Nagler (Ed.), *Perspectives on disability* (pp. 61–74). Palo Alto, CA: Health Markets Research.

Friedberg, F., (1999). A subgroup analysis of cognitive-behavioral treatment studies. *Journal of Chronic Fatigue Syndrome, 5,* 149–159.

Friedberg, F., & Jason, L. A. (1998). *Understanding chronic fatigue syndrome: An empirical guide to assessment and treatment.* Washington, DC: American Psychological Association.

Friedberg, F., & Krupp, L. B. (1994). A comparison of cognitive behavioral treatment for chronic fatigue syndrome and primary depression. *Clinical Infectious Diseases, 18*(Suppl. 1), S105–S110.

Gunn, W. J., Connell, D. B., & Randall, B. (1993). Epidemiology of chronic fatigue syndrome: The Centers-for-Disease-Control study. In B. R. Bock & J. Whelan (Eds.), *Chronic fatigue syndrome* (pp. 83–101). New York: Wiley.

Hahn, H. (1990). The politics of physical difference: Disability and discrimination. In M. Nagler (Ed.), *Perspectives on disability* (pp. 118–123). Palo Alto, CA: Health Markets Research.

Jason, L. A., Ferrari, J. R., Taylor, R. R., Slavich, S. P., & Stenzel, C. L. (1996). A national assessment of the service, support, and housing preferences by persons with chronic fatigue syndrome: Toward a comprehensive rehabilitation program. *Evaluation and the Health Professions, 19,* 194–207.

Jason, L. A., Kolak, A. M., Purnell, T., Cantillon, D., Camacho, J. M., Klein, S., et al. (2001). Collaborative ecological community interventions for people with chronic fatigue syndrome. *Journal of Prevention and Intervention in the Community, 21,* 35–51.

Jason, L. A., Melrose, H., Lerman, A., Burroughs, V., Lewis, K., King, C. P., et al. (1999). Managing chronic fatigue syndrome: Overview and case study. *AAOHN Journal, 47,* 17–21.

Jason, L. A., Richman, J. A., Friedberg, F., Wagner, L., Taylor, R., & Jordan, K. M. (1997). Politics, science, and the emergence of a new disease: The case of Chronic fatigue syndrome. *American Psychologist, 52,* 973–983.

Jason, L. A., Richman, J. A., Rademaker, A. W., Jordan, K. M., Plioplys, A. V., Taylor, R. R., et al. (1999). *A community-based study of chronic fatigue syndrome. Archives of Internal Medicine, 159,* 2129–2137.

Jason, L. A., Taylor, R., Wagner, L., Holden, J., Ferrari, J. R., Plioplys, A. V., et al. (1995). Estimating rates of chronic fatigue syndrome from a community based sample: A pilot study. *American Journal of Community Psychology, 23,* 557–568.

Jason, L. A., Taylor, S. L., Johnson, S., Goldston, S., Salina, D., Bishop, P., et al. (1993). Prevalence of chronic fatigue syndrome-related symptoms among nurses. *Evaluation and the Health Professions, 16*(14), 385–399.

Jason, L. A., Tryon, W. W., Frankenberry, E. L., & King, C. P. (1997). Chronic fatigue syndrome: Relationships of self-ratings and actigraphy. *Psychological Reports, 81,* 1223–1226.

Jason, L. A., Wagner, L., Taylor, R., Ropacki, M. T., Shlaes, J., Ferrari, J., et al. (1995). Chronic fatigue syndrome: A new challenge for health care professionals. *Journal of Community Psychology, 23,* 143–164.

Katz, I., Hass, G., & Bailey, J. (1988). Attributional ambivalence and behavior toward people with disabilities. In H. Yuker (Ed.), *Attitudes toward persons with disabilities* (pp. 47–57). New York: Springer.

Kelly, J. G. (1986). Context and process: An ecological view of the interdependence of practice and research. *American Journal of Community Psychology, 14,* 581–594.

King, C. P., Jason, L. A., Frankenberry, E. L., Jordan, K. M., & Tryon, W. (1997). Managing chronic fatigue syndrome through behavioral monitoring of energy levels and fatigue: A case study demonstration of the envelope theory. *CFIDS Chronicle, 10,* 10–14.

Kingry-Westergaard, C., & Kelly, J. G. (1990). A contextualist epistemology for ecological research. In P. Tolan, C. Keys, F. Chertok, & L. Jason (Eds.), *Researching community psychology: Issues of theory and methods* (pp. 23–31). Washington, DC: American Psychological Association.

LeRoy, J., Davis, T. H., & Jason, L. A. (1996). Treatment efficacy: A survey of 305 MCS patients. *CFIDS Chronicle, 9,* 52–53.

Lollar, D. (2000). Healthy People 2010: Introduction and report. In G. W. White, A. D. Branstetter, & T. Seekins (Eds.), *Secondary conditions among people with disabilities from minority cultures: Proceedings and recommendations of a working conference* (pp. 59–89). Lawrence: University of Kansas, Research and Training Center on Independent Living.

Maton, K. I. (1989). Toward an ecological understanding of mutual-help groups: The social ecology of "fit." *American Journal of Community Psychology, 17,* 729–753.

Meyerson, L. (1990). The social psychology of physical disability: 1948–1988. In M. Nagler (Ed.), *Perspectives on disability* (pp. 13–23). Palo Alto, CA: Health Markets Research.

Pesek, J. R., Jason, L. A., & Taylor, R. R. (2000). An empirical investigation of the envelope theory. *Journal of Human Behavior in the Social Environment, 3,* 59–77.

Ray, C. (1991). Chronic fatigue syndrome: Conceptual and methodological ambiguities. *Psychological Medicine, 21,* 1–9.

Schmelkin, L. (1988). Multidimensional perspectives in the perception of disabilities. In H. Yuker (Ed.), *Attitudes toward persons with disabilities* (pp. 127–137). New York: Springer.

Serrano-Garcia, I. (1990). Implementing research: Putting our values to work. In P. Tolan, C. Keys, F. Chertok, & L. Jason (Eds.), *Researching community psychology: Issues of theory and methods* (pp. 171–182). Washington, DC: American Psychological Association.

Sharpe, M., Hawton, K., Simkin, S., Suraway, C., Hackmann, A., Klimes, I., et al. (1996). Cognitive behaviour therapy for the chronic fatigue syndrome: A randomized controlled trial. *British Medical Journal, 312,* 22–26.

Shlaes, J. L., & Jason, L. A. (1996). A buddy/mentor program for people with chronic fatigue syndromes. *CFIDS Chronicle, 9,* 21–25.

Shlaes, J. L., Jason, L. A., & Ferrari, J. R. (1999). The development of the Chronic Fatigue Syndrome Attitudes Test: A psychometric analysis. *Evaluation and the Health Professions, 22,* 442–465.

Soder, M. (1990). Prejudice or ambivalence? Attitudes toward persons with disabilities. *Disability, Handicapped, and Society, 5,* 227–241.

Sontag, S. (1978). *Illness as metaphor.* New York: Farrar, Straus and Giroux.

Taylor, R. R., Jason, L. A., Kennedy, C. L., & Friedberg, F. (2001). Effect of physician-recommended treatment on mental health practitioners' attribution for chronic fatigue syndrome. *Rehabilitation Psychology, 46,* 165–177.

Vercoulen, J. H., Swanink, C. M., Fennis, J. F., Galama, J. M., van der Meer, J. W., & Bleijenberg, G. (1996). Prognosis in chronic fatigue syndrome: A prospective study on the natural course. *Journal of Neurology, Neurosurgery, and Psychiatry, 60,* 489–494.

Ware, N. C., & Kleinman, A. (1992). Culture and somatic experience: The social course of illness in neurasthenia and chronic fatigue syndrome. *Psychosomatic Medicine, 54,* 546–560.

Westbrook, M., Legge, V., & Pennay, M. (1993). Attitudes toward disabilities in a multicultural society. *Social Science Medicine, 36,* 615–623.

Wright, B. (1988). Attitudes and the fundamental negative bias: Conditions and corrections. In H. Yuker (Ed.), *Attitudes toward persons with disabilities* (pp. 3–21). New York: Springer.

Author Index

Subject Index